To Becky,

With warm memories of
good sharings at Deena's
workshop.

Dan Benor
July 18, 2004

Healing Research - Volume II

Consciousness, Bioenergy and Healing

Self-Healing and Energy Medicine for the 21st Century

by

Daniel J. Benor, M.D.

ISBN: 0-9754248-0-7

Parts of this book appeared in a previous European version as *Healing Research: Holistic Energy Medicine and Spirituality*, Copyright © 1992 Daniel J. Benor, M.D.

Benor, Daniel J.
  Consciousness, bioenergy, and healing / by Daniel J. Benor.

Includes bibliographical references and index.

1. Mental healing. 2. Consciousness. 3. Spiritual healing. 4. Mind
and body therapies. I. Title. II. Series: Benor, Daniel J. Healing
research ; v. 2.
  [DNLM: 1. Spiritual Therapies. 2. Bioelectric Energy Sources. 3.
Consciousness. 4. Mind-Body Relations (Metaphysics) 5. Psychotherapy.

Wholistic Healing Publications
P.O. Box 502
Medford, NJ 08055
(877) 432-5777 Fax (609) 714-3553
Orders at http://www.wholistichealingresearch.com/Store/Booknew.asp#v2

ACKNOWLEDGMENT OF PERMISSIONS TO REPRODUCE MATERIALS

I thank the many authors and publishers who have generously granted their permission to reproduce quotes in this book, in the spirit of healing.

I specifically acknowledge permissions for:
Benor, R. A holistic view to managing stress, In: Ronald A. Fisher & Pearl McDaid, *Palliative Day Care,* London: Arnold/ Hodder Headline Group 1996, figure no. 12.1.

Besant, A and Leadbeater, CW, *Thought-Forms*, Wheaton, IL: Quest/ Theosophical 1971, Orig. 1925. Used by permission of The Theosophical Publishing House, The Theosophical Society, Adyar, Madras 600 020, India

Reprinted from *J of Psychosomatic Research,* Volume 43, Miller, M. & Rahe, R H. Life changes scaling for the 1990s, 279-292, © 1997 with permission of Elsevier Science

For paid permissions, I acknowledge:

The Atman Project by Ken Wilber. Quest Books, Wheaton, IL.

From: UNCOMMON THERAPY: The Psychiatric Techniques of Milton H. Erickson MD. By Jay Haley. Copyright © 1986, 1973 by Jay Haley. Used by permission of W. W. Norton & Company, Inc.

Swift, G. A contextual model for holistic nursing practice, from J. Holistic Nursing 1994, 12(3), 265-281, figures1 & 2, © 1994 by Sage Publications, Inc. Preprinted by Permission of Sage Publications, Inc.

CONTENTS

CONTENTS (Continued)

TABLES

FIGURES

DEDICATION

This book is dedicated to the many healers who have been my teachers – through the years of university, medical school, psychiatric training, and then through the countless workshops and classes with healers of a rainbow spectrum of wholistic approaches. This book is also dedicated to the careseekers who have been wonderful teachers themselves, helping me understand the wonders of the human condition.

This "baby" has been more than twenty years in gestation. I know it will continue to grow and mature, as my various teachers continue to bring me into ever deeper awarenesses of the spiritual truths that inform and quicken the adventure we call life.

I hope that a deeper wholistic awareness of our interconnection with each other and with the world around us will promote healings of societies and nations – not only of individuals - because our planet is in dire need of healing.

This book is also dedicated to the seekers who want to find deeper ways for helping themselves, as well as for helping others.

I wish you good healings!

FOREWORD

I have been exploring the realms of healing and parapsychology for more than forty-five years, and my interests have led me to perform extensive evaluations of clairvoyant diagnosis. The research I have conducted in this field has thoroughly convinced me of its validity and usefulness.

Dr. Benor's book goes well beyond anything that I have seen, in documenting the abundance of work that has been done in the psychic-healing field. It would take several years to accumulate all of the information Dr. Benor provides, assuming one could locate all of the sources.

As in every such work, this outstanding presentation by Dr. Benor is not likely to sway or appeal to the mentally inflexible or to those with traditionally closed minds. But for the individual who is truly interested in exploring the information available, and who has a concept of that which is not "known" or is "uncontrolled," *Healing Research* provides an encyclopedic compilation of the material that has been made available up to this point in time. I am personally delighted to have had the opportunity to review the manuscript prior to its publication. Work such as this deserves wide dissemination.

– C. Norman Shealy, MD, PhD[1]

Introduction

In our scientific zeal to isolate specifics, it also is important to recognize that, in healing, we may not, as so long assumed, be dealing with a linear activity alone – that is of "what is done to whom" – but rather with a larger, more encompassing gestalt of physical, emotional, mental and spiritual relationships which can be activated in many ways, of which the hands of the healer may be one.

   Unless the individual, as center of his own gestalt, is inspired to take ultimate responsibility for his own well-being – on all levels – any healing which takes place may be short lived.

   Real healing, therefore, must be "wholing," hence holy, if it is to be long lasting – and worthy of mankind's unfolding potentials.
                                               – Jeanne Pontius Rindge

Consciousness, Bioenergy and Healing examines ways in which people can heal themselves and ways in which they can be helped to heal through Complementary/ Alternative Medicine (CAM).

CAM includes many self-healing approaches, such as relaxation, meditation, imagery, journaling, fitness and proper diet. Self-healing can be boosted further by using caregiver/ therapist modalities such as acupuncture, homeopathy and other methods that conventional medicine has largely ignored, but which the public have embraced in a big way. (The glossary at the end of the book explains terms that may be unfamiliar.)

This is the second in a series of books exploring *wholistic spiritual healing,* which involves treatment by the laying-on of hands and by mental intent/ meditation/ prayer. In Volume I of *Healing Research,* I reviewed a substantial body of published research on spiritual healing – which involves treatment by the laying-on of hands and by mental intent/ meditation/ prayer. Two thirds of these studies demonstrate significant effects of healing.

Many healers suggest that it is a biological energy (*bioenergy*) interaction between the healer and healee[2] which produces the healing effects. Healers report that they harmonize healees' bioenergies that have become disorganized through trauma, toxins, disease or degenerative processes.

While skeptics theorize that healing is no more than a placebo ("sugar pill") effect, produced by healers' suggestions and healees' expectations, this theory is clearly contradicted by the research evidence of healing effects on animals, plants and other living things. The fact that healers can improve the health of animals and plants supports the healers' claims that healing is definitely more than a placebo.

The skeptics may not be entirely wrong, however. The placebo effect is actually a manifestation of the enormous self-healing capacities of people to alter their own states of health and illness. Self-healing can be activated intentionally or unconsciously by caregivers or by people working to heal themselves, with far-reaching consequences that are beyond anything that is commonly taught in medical schools. Wise physicians who prescribe medicine know well that if they present to the patient, an enthusiastic description of anticipated benefits can enhance the effect of the pill. Self-healing can similarly contribute to treatments of any sort, including spiritual healing.

> *Are we so afraid to be wrong that we hide from the truth?*
> John MacEnulty (9/ 13/ 03)

We are therefore left with a serious question when we explore spiritual healing in humans. What part of the apparent effects of healer interventions might be due to suggestion on the part of healers, or expectations on the part of healees?

This second volume of *Healing Research* therefore explores the following issues:

1. How is it that many people can heal themselves of serious physical diseases and psychological dis-eases?

Two broad answers to this question are apparent. The first is that everyone has vast psychological resources which they can activate for effective self-healing. It is estimated that only five percent of our brain capacity is within our conscious awareness or under our conscious control. Major portions of our brains are constantly monitoring and regulating body functions that we take completely for granted. Our minds and bodies are intimately linked – so much so that many therapists are beginning to acknowledge this fact with the terms *mind-body* and *bodymind*. Varieties of CAM therapies teach how to use our minds to diagnose and treat our own psychological and physical conditions – to a far greater extent than was previously believed possible. A broad range of self-healing capacities is explored in this volume of *Healing Research*.

The second answer to this question about self-healing is that the body consists of energy as well as matter.CAM therapists suggest that we can harmonize the biological energy patterns of the body, and that this, in turn, harmonizes and heals the physical body itself.

Coming from the opposite direction, these same bodymind mechanisms may contribute to the original development of a variety of illnesses. Out psychological stresses and traumas can express themselves as physical disease though mechanisms discussed below. Prevention of illness through these same self-healing techniques is therefore another aspect of CAM treatment.

2. How do biological energy therapies contribute to healing?

While Western medicine has focused primarily on the physical body, CAM thera-pists have long been aware that living creatures also possess *biological energy bodies* – which are composed of emotional, mental, relational, and spiritual levels of subtle energies. Each of these biofield levels is intimately interlinked with the others. Each level contributes to our states of health and illness, and each energy field may be addressed, individually or in concert with the others, to improve physical, psychological, relational and spiritual health.

We will consider numerous complementary/ alternative therapies,[3] each of which addresses biological energies in the body. Each therapy has its own traditions and understandings of how these bioenergies function, and how we can utilize them to promote health and treat illness: from the ancient Chinese study of *qi* to the mod-ern practices of acupressure; from Biblical healings by Christ and the apostles through touch, handkerchiefs and prayer, to modern varieties of the laying-on of hands in Therapeutic Touch and Reiki; from herbalism of traditional societies to modern naturopathy.

It is not yet clear whether the various CAM therapies are addressing different energies, or whether there is a single energy field that responds differently to dif-ferent interventions. For instance, acupuncture treats symptoms and disorders by stimulating *meridians* (biological energy lines in the body) and *chakras* (major energy centers on the midline of the body). In spiritual healing[4] (Reiki, Healing Touch), therapists use their hands to address the energy field that surrounds the entire body, as well as to assess states of health and intervene through the chakras. Homeopathy and flower essences offer vibrational remedies that are taken orally, to interact with the entire organism. We can begin to clarify how these energies function by studying all of these therapies with their various biological energies approaches.

Extensive experience in various traditions suggests ways that energy fields in and around the body affect our physical health:

Western medicine has been slow to explore these therapies, and slower yet to accept and integrate them within its fold. Volume II of *Healing Research* describes mind-body medicine and spiritual healing as common denominators among all therapies – in conventional medicine and CAM therapies.

Building on our clinical picture of bioenergies, we will then seek explanations for the mechanisms of action of biological energies.

Western (Newtonian) Medicine Meets Bioenergy Medicine

Modern research in quantum physics studies the behavior of particles and energies at the subatomic level. Quantum physics has proven two theories that challenge many of our conventional scientific concepts:

One theory is that matter and energy are interconvertible. While physical objects are addressed as gross matter in Newtonian physics, in quantum physics we can consider atomic and subatomic units of matter as either particles or as energies.

The other theory is that the precise nature of some of the smallest units of matter remains indeterminate until they are actually observed. Only when an observer perceives their state do they take on the characteristics by which we define and identify them.

This indeterminacy suggests that objective reality as we know it is an illusion. In fact, at any given moment, we are surrounded by and composed of possibilities and probabilities rather than facts. The very act of scientific observation and measurement actually influences the outcome of the phenomenon being observed.

While these principles have been accepted as relating to inanimate matter, they have not been applied to living organisms by conventional science. These two principles fundamentally call into question our long-held Western belief in progressive, irreversible states of disease processes. People's physical conditions may vary according to the manners in which they perceive their own states, and may be altered as well by how caregivers perceive them. If the smallest units of subatomic matter can be seen as either particles or as waves of energy, then the function of *bioenergy* within the physiological processes of the body takes on a new significance. Bioenergy of a disease process can be altered by outside energies. The can offer caregivers and healees ways in which to heal that have not been used in Western medicine.

Intuitives and mystics have been making observations similar to those of quantum physicists over several millennia.[5] The ancient knowledge of our ancestors is now being reconsidered in the light of a substantial body of research that is reviewed in this book. After centuries of independent development, these two seemingly separate paths are converging.

As we progress toward the fullest understanding of our bodies and how they function in the world, we will benefit from both of these healing traditions. Quantum physics has not supplanted Newtonian physics. Each still has its place. It is the same with Newtonian medicine and wholistic, bioenergy medicine. This book considers the best of both, to offer a unified theory to guide and inspire the future of healing practice.

Healing in practice

CASE: "Linda," a pretty but frail woman who looked ten years older than her age of 36, consulted me for a series of disabling chronic problems. She had been suffering for eight years from fatigue, headaches, stomachaches, muscle aches, weakness, fitful sleep and sometimes even sleepless nights, extreme tiredness, mental "fuzziness" and multiple food allergies.

Her family doctor had initially treated her headaches and stomachaches with a variety of medications. While these partially alleviated her pains, they worsened her mental "fog" and seriously diminished the quality of her life that was already limited by her multiple symptoms.

Prior to her illness, she had worked long hours as a broker in an investment company. As she began having difficulties maintaining the wearing pace of work that her job demanded, her employer was less than sympathetic. This added stress was the straw that forced her to seek leave on medical disability – a difficult challenge when her doctor could not find a specific medical diagnosis to explain her multiple symptoms. Her boyfriend of three years left her, not finding the emotional resources to support her through her ordeal. He, like her employer, accused her of being lazy and of making up her symptoms to avoid her demanding job.

With the help of a wholistic physician, we established that Linda was suffering from chronic fatigue syndrome, fibromyalgia and candidiasis – all diagnoses that conventional medicine often does not even acknowledge, much less treat. Over a period of two years, her multiple symptoms required a series of dietary changes, nutritional supplements, lifestyle adjustments and counseling. Spiritual healing, acupuncture and self-healing techniques helped her to deal with her pain and to regain her normal sleep patterns. Gradually, she was able to return to work and to resume a normal life – after coming to appreciate that her body demanded appropriate attention and coddling, which was actually an expression of her inner emotional needs for the same.[6]

Linda's case is not unusual. There are many problems for which conventional medicine can offer only limited, symptomatic relief. CAM therapies often are much more helpful with these symptoms and illnesses.

The content and style of this volume
In the domains of energy medicine that are explored in this volume, the portal of logic and linear analysis represents only one of several doorways to understanding and interacting with our world. There are additional approaches

The content and style of this book will help you appreciate that Complementary/ Alternative Medicine has its own ways of perceiving, understanding and addressing health and illness. While different in many ways from conventional, Western ways of adressing health issues, CAM is a valid scientific system in and of itself.

In conventional science and medical care, logic and linear reasoning are seen as the only valid methods for analyzing and comprehending the world of matter – which is the sphere of our presumed "objective" reality (including the human body). Even if this view is valid, it clearly is not comprehensive enough to explain or to guide us in effectively navigating the complex realms of our subjective experiences, which include the emotions of love, anger, anxiety, and hate, and the personal contexts of relationships, collective culture, and spiritual awareness. All of these impact our experiences of both health and illness in numerous ways – yet they are beyond the realm of direct examination or objective measurement. They are ignored and neglected in most of conventional Western medical care.to these explorations that are equally valid – through emotion, intuition, imagery, metaphor, bioenergies and spiritual awareness.

Conventional science dismisses these approaches as inaccurate, subjective, imaginary or mystical – in short, as a lot of nonsense. This bias of linear belief and thinking is illustrated in the very word "non-*sense*." Many aspects of CAM approaches are not directly accessible to our outer senses, and not measurable by "objective" instruments. The assumption in Western medicine is, therefore, that these cannot be valid or effective factors for treatment, which in fact they are not – within those frames of reference of a conventional medical system that is restricted to linear approaches for assessments and physical interventions for treatments.

Many aspects of the approaches used in CAM therapies are not cut from the fabric of the physical, quantifiable world of our outer senses. They are woven instead of the inner sense of intuition, often including spiritual awarenesses, which are just as valid as our outer senses. To dismiss these aspects of our whole selves is to ignore the greater portion of the information that is available to us.

> *The reasonable man adapts himself to the world. The unreasonable one persists in trying to adapt the world to himself. Therefore, all progress depend on the unreasonable man.*
> – George Bernard Shaw

The worlds of inner knowing are inclusive rather than exclusive. They are better understood with *both/ and* approach rather than through *either/ or* dichotomies. They allow us to see the outer, physical world as one part of the structure of reality, which is connected and interwoven with the inner worlds. We are given a left brain hemisphere that specializes in linear awareness and processes, as well as a right brain that specializes in intuitive, patterned awarenesses. If we disregard the potential of the intuitive, we are ignoring at least half of the images that our brain is capable of projecting on the screen of our consciousness, not to mention the vast and incredibly rich variety of information that is available through much of our unconscious mind.

Extensive research in parapsychology[7] shows that our minds can reach outside the limits of our physical body, and can also connect with events from the past and the future. These awarenesses may extend beyond space and time, into spiritual dimensions.

Because such concepts are at variance with Western scientific ways of thinking, many conventional caregivers still reject wholistic concepts. Others, more open to the both/ and approach, are able to see these contradictions as reasons to re-examine the basic assumptions of conventional science and medicine. This book makes a strong case for the proposition that it is time to bring Western medical science into the world of a broader reality – or, more accurately, of broader realit*ies*.

Wholistic integrative care

Modern Western (Newtonian) medicine is excellent for dealing with infections and physical trauma, and it is currently being used to explore the field of genetic engineering – which holds both wonderful promises and potential disasters of unknown magnitude.

Wholistic medicine is much more useful in many cases than Newtonian medicine for dealing with chronic illnesses and psychological problems, as we see in countless clinical examples – like in Linda's story.

Wholistic care is also a challenge to CAM therapists. Many CAM practitioners make the opposite error of not applying linear analyses to their therapies. CAM therapists may rely entirely on their inner awarenesses to guide their assessments and treatments. They may neglect linear evaluations of their clinical assessments, formal analyses of the results of their therapies, and experimental validations of theories to explain their "unusual" results. This can lead to the error of accepting approaches that are no more than placebos, born of theories that have no substantiation beyond the imaginations of those who propose them. We know that suggestion is an aspect of every healthcare intervention. There may be remedies used in homeopathy, flower essence therapy and aromatherapy, or manipulations practiced in chiropractic and craniosacral therapy, or rituals recommended in spiritual healing which are of no more value than a sugar pill. Linear analyses that explore whether therapies actually accomplish what they purport to do are ethically necessary, in order to assure that we are not charging for services that are, in effect, variations on the theme of suggestion.

Many CAM practitioners are now acknowledging the need for objective linear studies to confirm that their approaches are potent and effective. Chapter 2 of this volume reviews extensive research that does precisely that, with growing numbers of studies of CAM therapies published by conventional caregivers in medical journals. There is a considerable body of evidence confirming that acupuncture, massage, biofeedback, spiritual healing, creative arts therapies, and other CAM approaches offer significant benefits.

Despite their differences, there is every reason to suggest that CAM and conventional therapies can and should be used in combination with each other. Integrative systems of care provide the best of all possible therapeutic worlds.

It is important to note that using conventional linear language to describe non-linear treatments will distort the analysis of these interventions to some extent. To provide a truer taste of the essence of wholistic and bioenergy interventions, this volume includes counterpoint quotations that are matched to the discursive text. Through metaphor, imagery, poetry, humor and linear contrasts, we can open ourselves toward the wider nature of these interventions, which draw upon and resonate with the gestaltic, intuitive and spiritual aspects of our consciousness for healing on multiple levels.

> *Knowing with the heart is a complement to knowing with the head;*
> *knowing with the head is a balance to knowing with the heart.*
> *– D.B.*

The complexities of relationships between body, emotions, mind, relationships and spirit make it difficult to analyze these elements and their interconnections separately. There will therefore be overlaps and interdigitations in various sections of the analysis of wholistic healing in this book. It is somewhat like exploring the patterns of threads in a multi-colored carpet, where some hues will be more visible because they are on the surface and more densely threaded in some places, while other colors may still be present but more subtly contributing their hue in that section, and yet other tints may be present but only visible beneath the surface after some probing.

The Four Volumes of *Healing Research*

Though Volume II of this series is complete in itself, it also serves as an extension of the material covered in Volume I, and creates a basis for understanding materials presented in Volumes III and IV. Taken as a whole, the four volume series presents a thorough exploration of the theories and processes of spiritual healing and bioenergy medicine, as well as a broad examination of the related scientific research.

Volume I: Scientific Validation of a Healing Revolution
The first volume in the series summarizes an extensive body of research confirming claims by spiritual healers that they can effect improvements in the health of the healees who flock to them, suffering from all the ailments known to humankind.

Volume I defines *spiritual healing* (abbreviated to *healing*) as any purposeful intervention by one or more persons wishing to help another living being to change for the better, using processes of focused intention, or light manual contact or hand movements near the subject of the healing. Healers may also invoke outside agents such as God, Christ, or other individual "higher powers," as well as spirits and universal or cosmic forces or energies. They may call upon special healing energies or forces residing within themselves, apply various techniques of psychokinesis (mind over matter), or activate self-healing powers or energies that are latently present in the healees.

Volume I also reviews anecdotal reports, and an impressive body of research which demonstrates significant healing effects on people, animals, plants, bacteria, yeasts, cells in laboratory culture, enzymes, and DNA.Out of 191 controlled studies of healing, 124 demonstrate significant effects. If we select from these the 37 most rigorous studies, 25 show effects that could occur only one time in 100 and another 12 at a level of 2 to 5 times in 100.

This volume further discusses how spiritual healing may be seen as part of the spectrum of parapsychological, or *psi* phenomena.[8] The term *psi* is derived from the Greek letter Ψ (pronounced *sigh*), and is used in parapsychology to denote the phenomena of telepathy, clairsentience, psychokinesis (PK), and pre- or retro-cognition.[9]

Based on the evidence from the controlled studies presented in Volume I, supported further by many less rigorous studies and anecdotal reports, I take it as a given that spiritual healing does exist, beyond any reasonable doubt.

Volume I addresses the question, "Is there adequate research to confirm the hypothesis that spiritual healing is effective?" or more simply, "Does spiritual healing work?" and answers with a resounding "Yes!" Volume I also supplies a wealth of clues to the mystery of *how* healing works.

Volume II: Consciousness, Bioenergy and Healing

Volume II continues where Volume I left off, to further address the question: "How does healing work?" This volume deals with therapies involving subtle energies that healers can sense with their hands, and that some can visually perceive as auras of color around living beings. Many variations on the theme of bioenergy medicine are explored in this volume. These energies have been reported for thousands of years, yet mainstream modern science has been slow to acknowledge, much less examine them.

Biological energies appear to interact in turn with environmental energies. Research is explored on the effects of earth energies, sunspots, and other influences of heavenly bodies as suggested by astrology, and their relevance to spiritual healing is considered.

Environmental energies interact with the bodymind and with the bioenergy body. We commonly acknowledge this by noting that some places have positive energies or "vibes" – such as a church or a special place in nature. Similarly, we may feel negative vibrations in other places, without apparent reason. These can be so distinctly unpleasant that we avoid being in that space.

We are beginning to appreciate that these perceptions may actually relate to healing energies and harmful energies, as they impact our own biofield and bodymind.

In conclusion, I summarize the observations and research discussed in each of the chapters of volume II, and point toward several pathways into a future of integrated care. The separate themes of each chapter are interwoven throughout the fabric of this volume, and the threads are so intricately intertwined and the patterns so complex that it is impossible to separate them entirely from one another. Together they form an over-arching pattern that is as yet beyond our full understanding. The entire tapestry of existence is contained in the concatenation of the design.

The popular version of Volume II, *How Can I Heal What Hurts,* reviews and discusses the studies of self-healing, CAM and bioenergy therapies in less detail, with explanations appropriate for lay readers. It is not referenced as extensively as the Professional editon. It contain an additional chapter with a collection of self-healing exercises.

Volume III: Science, Spirit, and the Eternal Soul

After centuries of ignoring spiritual aspects of healing, Western science is now applying its own methodology to explore and confirm an inner nature of Nature that does not conform to common, linear logic.

Volume III explores studies of consciousness extending outside the body, as in out-of-body and near-death experiences.

Volume III also reviews research from quantum physics that observers actually shape what they perceive, and therefore that there is no way to define an *objective* reality, as Western science has presumed. The processes and phenomena observed by scientists may be altered by their axiomatic assumptions, through the methods and instruments used for their observations, and the interpretations they impose on their data. Ever so subtly, the so-called "impartial" scientific observers influence that which they observe, in the very process of observing it.

What appears to be an objective statement is actually *a statement of collective agreement* among observers concerning the commonality of their subjective experience. Thus, the so-called 'objective' stance, championed so enthusiastically by traditional scientific medicine, is really just a cover-up for a "subjective" stance, a stance which attempts to separate and dissect things which cannot ultimately be separated or dissected. Furthermore, in spite of the fact that the subject-object division is an untenable proposition, modern medicine persists in choosing to invalidate subjective experience in favour of what it conceives as an objective – with disastrous results.
– Michael Greenwood and Peter Nunn (p.29)

Volume III further explores extensive research on the mystical and spiritual aspects of healing, including fascinating evidence for the survival of the spirit after death. Though this kind of spirituality was the exclusive reserve of religion in Western society during recent centuries, other societies have traditionally used it in practical ways for healing illness.

Amazingly, the findings from research in spiritual dimensions that has been published from laboratories on six continents is largely coherent and for the most part interdigitates and presents a coherent picture of spiritual dimensions of reality.

In Volume III, I invite you to explore with me these realms of healing that are paradoxically distant yet very near at hand. They are far from the *material* universe that conventional Western society has proposed as the only real and valid one. Yet they are as near as they can possibly be, for they reside within each of us and can be explored quite readily if we are willing to examine our inner awarenesses and to explore our relationships to our surroundings with open minds and hearts.

Volume IV: Compendium of Theories and Practices in Spiritual Healing

Volume IV synthesizes the materials from the three preceding volumes, and presents a range of theories to explain the processes of spiritual healing. It also includes my personal experiences with healing as a medical doctor, psychotherapist, healer and researcher.

Does all of this stretch your credulity to the point of discomfort? Have I exceeded your *boggle threshold*? Your skepticism is clearly warranted, because until recently many of the claims referred to above were made without the benefit of validation through modern scientific investigation. Today we are beginning to comprehend these subjects through more systematic research, and through better understanding of the underlying assumptions – both on the side of conventional medicine and CAM therapies. We are also beginning to legitimize our own individual, personal explorations of these realms through our inner senses.

The length of these volumes is a reflection of the complex structure of the house of our human existence. Our linear methods of examining and analyzing this edifice lead us to shine a spotlight into each of its windows one at a time. But we must not forget that while we are examining any one room, myriads of vital activities are proceeding in all of the other rooms simultaneously. In fact, the "windows" and "walls" we perceive are largely of our own creation, produced by the very process of investigation through our physical rather than our intuitive senses. The metaphor of the house better suits the study of physical aspects of health. For CAM and bioenergy medicine, the image of a complex web of interpenetrating energy fields is more appropriate.

The *Healing Research* series considers the healing powers of our body, mind, emotions, relationships (with each other and with our environment) and spirit as an inextricably interwoven and unified system. The benefits of the wholistic approach is well illustrated in a story related by a woman patient to Bernie Siegel, a wholistic surgeon. This patient complained to him that during exploratory surgery her previous surgeon had discovered that she was suffering from inoperable cancer. As she awoke from the anesthesia, her surgeon had told her that all that she could do was to hope and pray. "How do I do that?" she asked. He replied, "That's not my department." She therefore sought out Dr. Siegel, a surgeon who is comfortable helping people deal with spiritual as well as physical issues.

This series is intended to help us respond to such pleas with our hearts and our spirits, and not only with our minds. I suggest that you skim the chapters in each book before reading them, or read each volume with the expectation that you will re-read it in the future. The complexity, integrity and beauty of the web of our existence cannot be appreciated fully by examining its infinite strands individually. This study, in all its complexity, is not simply an intellectual exercise. Understanding our intimate relationships with each other and with the world around us is essential to our healing of this planet and of our relationships with it.

> *Man did not weave the web of life,*
> *He is merely a strand in it.*
> *Whatever he does to the web,*
> *He does to himself.*
> — Chief Seattle

Chapter 1

Self-Healing

This need to dissect and examine each separate component of life may have originally led to specialization. The specialization... has become increasingly specific, so that today we find the absurd situation of a specialty mechanic polishing his small part to a high degree of efficiency without caring whether the whole functions...
                                                        – Paul Solomon

Health professionals are increasingly aware that people receiving treatment play major roles in maintaining their own health or illness. This chapter examines mind-body connections and wholistic approaches to physical and psychological problems.

Poor health is not a thing that exists separately from a sick person – a thing to hand over to a specialist whose manipulations will make *it* better. The first step in a wholistic approach is to understand the meaning of the illness. "What is going wrong?" should be the initial question, and this should be asked not only with respect to the *physical* aspects of the illness, but also with consideration for the larger context of the person's life. There are certainly mechanical factors to consider – for example, people who suffer from backaches may be straining their backs by lifting incorrectly or by sitting for long periods in a chair that is not well matched to the height of their work. But we should look beyond these physical mechanics and ask, "Why are they allowing themselves to lift things incorrectly? Does the pain in their back partially result from tensions originating in emotional factors? Could this person be holding back anger, for instance, which is putting tension into muscles that end up in spasm?" Is there a part of them that might welcome the secondary gain of attention and sympathy that is associated with having the pain?

More subtle and complex still are the connections between emotional factors and ailments of known external and internal physical origin. For example, although everyone is exposed to viruses and bacteria, only some get sick. In addition to physical factors, such as poor diet or impaired immune functions, psychological issues may also contribute to our vulnerability to infection. For instance, research shows that we are much more vulnerable to all sorts of illnesses during times of bereavement or other emotional stresses. Pains from known physical causes, such as trauma or neurological disorders, may be markedly worsened if we are emotionally upset. To access these levels of complexity in illness we must ask, "What do you think your body might be telling you through this symptom?"

This link between emotion and illness has even been schematized in a *Life-Events Inventory*. (See Table II-1.) Such factors as death of a spouse, loss of a job, or retirement are obvious sources of stress in people's lives. More surprising inclusions on the stress list are positive events, such as marriage and relocation. However, any factor that involves change or increases tension can apparently predispose us to illness. A score of more than 200 life change units (LCU) on this *Inventory* indicates that we are in serious risk of becoming ill, and scores of 300 or higher are commonly found in patients with major illnesses (Miller/ Rahe).

Emotional stresses can predispose people not only to infections, but also to metabolic, cardiovascular and degenerative diseases, and even to cancer. Strong emotions can make the body susceptible to illness due to sheer exhaustion, or through alterations in the level of muscle tension, hormones, antibodies, or white blood cells, and probably also through variations in several levels of biological energies that are as yet poorly defined[10]

One well-studied aspect of the mind-body relationship is the link between Type A personality and heart disease. People with this personality type are extremely driven to achieve personal goals that often are poorly defined. They are intensely competitive; hotly pursue advancement and recognition; tend to push themselves to complete tasks rapidly; and over-schedule activities that have strict deadlines. Research (Friedman/ Rosenman) showed a correlation of Type A personality with elevated cholesterol, early development of heart disease, risk of angina (heart pains) and heart attacks, and death from heart disease.[11] Hostility seemed to be the primary factor in predicting Type A susceptibility to risk from heart disease (J. Williams).

A common denominator in Type A behaviors is the poor management of aggression. In an excellent review of this (and related mind-body) research, Harris Dienstfrey (1991) points out that aggression is not a uniform characteristic in all people:

> ...Some people are aggressively competitive because it is a sport-like activity that gives them pleasure. Some people are aggressively competitive because they are filled with envy. Some people are aggressively competitive because they want to prove their superiority over other people. (p. 23)

People with type B personality are not driven by ambition or competitiveness, or worried by deadlines. In subsequent research, while it was found that people with Type B personality were more prone to die from recurrent heart attacks (Ragland/ Brand). However, Type A people were seven times more prone to have heart disease (Friedman/ Rosenman).

Table II-1.   Life Events Questionnaire

Life change event	LCU
Health	
An Injury or illness which kept you in bed a week or more or sent you to the hospital	74
An injury or illness which was less serious than above	44
Major dental work	26
Major change in eating habits	27
Major change in sleeping habits	26
Major change in your usual type and/ or amount of recreation	28
Work	
Change to a new type of work	51
Change in your work hours or conditions	35
Change in your responsibility at work	
More responsibility	29
Fewer responsibility	21
Promotion	31
Demotion	42
Transfer	32
Troubles at work	
With your boss	29
With coworkers	35
With person under your supervision	35
Other work troubles	28
Major Business adjustment	60
Retirement	52
Loss of job	
Laid off from work	68
Fired from work	79
Correspondence course to help you in your work	18
Home and Family	
Major change in living conditions	42
Change in residence	
Move within the same town	25
Move to a different town, city, or state	47
Change in family get-togethers	25
Major change in health or behavior of family member	55
Marriage	50
Pregnancy	67
Miscarriage or abortion	65
Gain of a new family member	
Birth of a child	66
Adoption of a child	65
A relative moving in with you	59
Spouse beginning or ending work	46
Child leaving home	

To attend college	41
Due to marriage	41
For other reasons	45
Change in arguments with spouse	50
In-law problems	38
Change in the marital status of your parents	
Divorce	59
Remarriage	50
Separation from spouse	
Due to marital problems	76
Due to work	53
Divorce	96
Birth of a grandchild	43
Death of spouse	119
Death of other family member	
Child	123
Brother or sister	102
Parent	100
Personal or social	
Change in personal habits	26
Beginning of ending of school or college	38
Change of school of college	35
Change in political beliefs	24
Change in religious beliefs	29
Change in social activities	27
Vacation	24
New, close, personal relationships	37
Engagement to marry	45
Girlfriend or boyfriend problems	39
Sexual difficulties	44
"Falling out" of a close personal relationship	47
An accident	48
Minor violation of the law	20
Being held on jail	75
Major decision regarding your immediate future	51
Death of a close friend	70
Major personal achievement	36
Financial	
Major change in finances	
Increased income	38
Decreased income	60
Investment and/ or credit difficulties	56
Loss or damage of personal property	43
Moderate purchase	20
Major purchase	37
Foreclosure on a mortgage or loan	58

*From Miller/ Rahe

These psychological variables have not been taken into account by most investigators of conventional or wholistic medicine. They tend to lump all aggression under the same generic label. In my clinical practice I find that the concept of the Type A personality is readily appreciated and helpful to people who have difficulty relaxing, and who are constantly on the go.[12] In addition, cardiac counseling regarding healthy diet and other life habits, combined with focused counseling to address Type A behaviors, can reduce the risk of recurrent heart attacks by half (Ornish).

Reduction of tensions can decrease the incidence and severity of many other illnesses as well. This is one of the most important ways in which doctors, therapists and healers can be effective. The mere presence of a caregiver, inviting careseekers to share their anxieties, may alleviate their distress and initiate self-healing.

It is sad that our society has focused so much on addressing caregiving through cognitive approaches, looking primarily at physical reasons for illness and treating the problems people have rather than the people who have the problems.[13]

Addressing careseekers from the heart rather than from the head can offer a spectrum of more healing approaches. Making people who are ill comforatable and listening to their anxieties and complaints, simple and indirect as this is, can bring about dramatic reductions in tensions. When they are more relaxed, their self-healing capacities are dramatically enhanced. This will be explored and explained in greater detail, below

Spontaneous remissions of serious illnesses have been acknowledged by conventional medicine, though rarely studied. These can occur without the intervention of professional therapists or healers.[14] We all have enormous innate potentials for self-healing that are largely unexplained, unexplored, and even unacknowledged by conventional medicine. Many of these will be detailed in this chapter.

The growing wholistic health movement takes these factors into account in its various forms of clinical practice. It suggests that the role of healthcare providers should shift from assuming responsibility for curing patients to advising careseekers on ways in which they can care for themselves through their own choices, such as with proper diet, exercise, attention to self-nurturance, making healthy choices in relationships, and changing those factors which are stressful and draining of energies.

Wholistic or *whole person care* acknowledges the intimate connection between mind, emotions, and body. In both obvious and subtle ways, people may predispose themselves toward illness. But with proper attitudes and practices people can prevent illness, and even cure it when it does develop. Chapter I explores many of the ways in which this can be done.

Wholistic health practitioners also encourage integration of less-accepted treatments, such as homeopathy and acupuncture, into conventional Western medical practices. Their focus is on maintaining health and helping people to deal with the roots of illnesses when they appear, rather than simply treating the *symptoms* of ill health.

Let me invite you now to look through some of the many windows in the house of wholistic healing, to see how people can make themselves ill or make themselves better.

I start with basic explanations of how your bodymind develops, evolves and functions.

PSYCHODYNAMICS AND PSYCHOPATHOLOGY

The neurotic builds dream castles in the air.
The psychotic lives in them.
The psychiatrist collects the rent.

– Anonymous

Personality development

We have each built up the person we are today from a lifetime of experiences, starting in the womb. Our biological regulators – including our genetic programs, nervous system, hormones, immune system and biological energy fields – are like a computer that is infinitely more complex than any hardware or software program that has yet been developed by modern technology. We are endowed with physical and psychological characteristics that are uniquely ours, and our bodies will have a range of capabilities to perceive and respond to our environment. We will have strengths and weaknesses that may help us to resist environmental stresses, or leave us vulnerable to challenges such as physical and emotional fatigue, substances in foods and airborne particles that may cause allergies, assaults on our immune system from bacteria and viruses, severe changes in temperature, and the like.

The psychological characteristics that make up our personality can be analyzed and described according to many psychological perspectives. I share a few here that I have found particularly helpful.

Stella Chess and Alexander Thomas identified a series of traits that are evident when we are a month old, and will persist with minimal changes throughout our lives. These include:

1. activity levels – high or low;
2. rhythmicities in eating, sleeping and other activities – preferences for regular or irregular schedules;
3. adaptability – flexible and going with the flow, or rigid and easily rattled by changes;
4. approach/ withdrawal – extroverted and reaching out spontaneously, or quiet, withdrawn, and passive;
5. threshold for response – sensitive and quick to respond, or unbothered and slow to respond to noise, intrusive touch, and other environmental stimuli;
6. intensity – preferring gentle, quiet exchanges, or rough and tumble interactions;
7. moods – even, with a narrow range, or punctuated with wideranging ups and downs;
8. distractibility – shifting gears easily or with difficulty from one awareness or activity to another;
9. persistence – remaining focused on tasks with greater or lesser intensity.[15]

Another typology of human characteristics was devised by Carl Jung. Jung pointed out that everyone has a personality type that is dominant in the area of one or two of four parameters, which are paired in polar opposites. These are the polarities of *thinking* ←→ *feeling*, and *intuition* (inner senses) ←→ *sensation* (outer senses). He also noted that there are introverted and extraverted styles of relating to the world. (See Figure II-1.)

Figure II-1. Jungian polarities

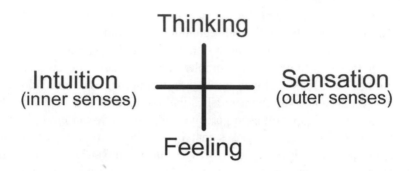

Thinking

Intuition
(inner senses)

Sensation
(outer senses)

Feeling

Thinking type people organize their perceptions of the world and their responses to it through logical analysis and planning. They usually do not pay much attention to their feelings, and may even denigrate feelings as *illogical, unreasonable,* and *unreliable*. A scheduled, predictable world is most comfortable for the thinking types.

Feeling types types are defined by Jung in terms of *values*, but my own view is that these types may also be described in terms of *emotionality*. The feeling types experience life as a montage of emotions and values. Experiences that are emotionally charged feel real and alive, interesting and exciting, and are highly valued. Thoughts alone are colorless, plans are acted upon if one is in the right mood, and communication is engaged through the tones and nuances of interaction more than through their content. The feeling types respond most to activities and experiences that excite and stimulate, be it with attraction or withdrawal.

> *The heart has reasons that reason knows nothing of.*
> – Blaise Pascal

Intuitive types grasp information in patterns and gestalts. They intuit their way through situations, often without even thinking or verbalizing to themselves the process by which they make their decisions. Perceptions come in wholes – and any individual part that they might analyze represents less than the truth. They instinctively know the right thing to do in familiar situations. Faced with new challenges, the intuitive may guess rather than deduce solutions, using specific details and logical reasoning. Many intuitives suffer in school, as they come up with correct answers but are unable to explain how they arrived at them.

The intuitive mind is a sacred gift and the rational mind is a faithful servant. We have created a society that honors the servant and has forgotten the gift.
        – Albert Einstein (*attributed*)

Sensation types notice every detail in the world around them – form, color, and sound are the threads with which they weave the fabric of their reality. Everything has its place. Shaping, organizing and moving bodies and objects around is important and satisfying. Every incident has its cause and effect, and if these are not apparent in the present, it is merely because insufficient efforts have been applied to fitting things into their proper order.[16]

Nothing is more indisputable than the existence of our senses.
        – Jean Le Rond d'Alembert

While thinking is often viewed as a limiting approach to transcendent aware-ness, it can also be a stepladder into the spiritual. The goal is to achieve inner balance.

Discipline and letting go, the two paths as one, guide me always.
Work and trust, another way of saying it.
Knowing takes us to its limit, its edge. We go beyond.
We learn, come to understanding, let go of our understanding and pass into the unknowable, the highest knowledge.
Without discipline we increase our ignorance.
Without letting go we build a prison of information.
The two paths merge as one, breathing in, breathing out.
        – John MacEnulty (8/ 29/ 2003)

Each of these polarities may be expressed through an *introverted* (inner directed) or *extroverted* (outer directed) style of relating to the world.

Introverted people are guided by inner awareness, heeding their feelings and intentions to direct their actions and responses to the world around them. The expectations and demands of the outer environment will not influence them as strongly as their inner worlds of thought and emotions. Such people will appear thoughtful, introspective and quiet, if they are of a moderately introverted disposition. They are their own worst critics, setting their inner barometers for behavior and response according to their own opinion of themselves, and not readily influenced by external pressures. Extremes of introversion are seen as deviant from psychological and social norms, and may include excessive shyness, social isolation, disregard for expectations of friends and family, and the like.

In contrast, *extroverts* are outgoing and highly responsive to social situations. They seek interactions with others, care about others' expectations, and want to conform in order to be accepted. At the extremes of the scale, extroverts are unhappy unless others join them in their exuberance. Some may seem to have no opinions of their own, structuring their world around others' views and norms.

Another pattern of extroversion may be seen in hypomanic or manic personalities, who force their views upon others and experience their emotions through the reactions of others, having great difficulty in perceiving their own roles in creating the responses set up by their own behaviors.

Within each of these polarities there are degrees of insightfulness and wide ranges of behavior, so the basic polarities explain some but not all aspects of people's various ways of being in the world.

Extroverts focus on objects/ people external to themselves, and experience the world as a series of interactions with these *outside* objects. *Introverts* are focused on their inner awarenesses, living their conscious lives under the influence of whichever of the four polarities are dominant in them, without becoming too tightly bound to the outer world.

While each person may readily acknowledge their own primary traits, they may not be aware that their polar opposites are also alive and active in the *shadow* aspects of their being – those parts of themselves that exist outside of their conscious awareness.[17] Until recently we have been encouraged to maintain cultural stereotypes of men as thinking/ sensation primaries, and women as feeling/ intuitive primaries. Women's liberation has been a transforming force in helping us to acknowledge our neglected polar opposites, giving women permission and encouragement to develop their *thinking* and *sensation* aspects, and encouraging men to acknowledge their *feeling* and *intuitive* sides.

> *Some of my instincts tell me not to follow some of my other instincts.*
> – Ashleigh Brilliant (no. 1992)

The shadow aspects of our personalities seek expression just as much as our conscious polarities do. For instance, a *thinking* primary person will also have feelings that want and need to be expressed. If the feelings are held in, they tend to build up until they find some outlet, often under conditions of pressure or stress, when the dominant polarity loses some of its control. When these repressed feelings finally do come to expression, it is often through interactions with other people that stir the *shadow* to strong responses, and many times the eruption into consciousness and expression in words or actions occurs in ways that are counter-productive. Explosions of emotion, in turn, often generate negative reactions. Such experiences discourage people from giving vent to their shadow sides.

Unconsciously, people commonly choose a friend or mate with opposite polar preferences to find stimulation and balance, but also because they can let the other express the aspects of themselves that they would rather not acknowledge or deal with. For example, a husband (with primary introverted, thinking/ sensation functions) may be happy to see his wife (with primary extroverted, intuitive/ feeling functions) handle the decorating and social affairs at home. The wife may likewise leave the finances, automobile maintenance and home repairs to her husband – thus each avoids engagement with their shadow or *inferior* polarities. This kind of arrangement can work in the opposite direction as well. The feeling partner can help the thinking partner to be more aware of their own feelings, and vice-versa.

If my heart could do my thinking would my brain begin to feel?
– Van Morrison

The *shadow* aspect of our unconscious mind also shuts away those parts of our being that make us uncomfortable, and that we would rather not acknowledge to ourselves and to others. This shadow carries all of our unacknowledged, deeply buried old hurts with their accompanying angers and resentments; all the little and great envies and desires that parents and religious institutions teach us we ought not to have, though we invariably do – and more besides.[18]

These *shadow* aspects of our psychological makeup are every bit as much a part of ourselves as the other aspects that are within our conscious awareness. As such, they influence our beliefs, perceptions, feelings and actions – often completely without our conscious awareness. These are our irrational desires and fears, our un*reason*able reactions – precisely because they abide and function deep below the level of our reasoning mind. They operate outside of our *persona* – the part of our selves that we construct and groom in order to present the best possible face to ourselves and to those around us. We may become aware of our *shadow* parts when we catch ourselves in excessively strong outbursts of hurt or angry feelings, when we examine our dreams, or when others point out that they feel our behaviors are inappropriate.

In addition to managing *shadow* aspects of our emotions and personalities, our unconscious mind also serves as a vast storehouse for memories, feelings, and intuitive awarenesses. But while the unconscious is very much a part of us, it is difficult to perceive and comprehend.

> It is difficult to become consciously aware of the unconscious! This way of thinking is, for most of us, a vast unknown that we visit each night in our dreams, but usually find irrelevant to daily life. Since it is unfamiliar, some people think of it as strange, even frightening, and therefore necessary to keep under control.
>
> If you think of the stars in the night sky as separate points of light, the circling mind connects them to the constellations. It joins apparently disparate things with bonds of analogy, metaphor, and possibility. It spins an infinity of choices. It is where your words exist before you speak them. It is the "you" that has no face. It is the source of ritual, mystery, and magic, the sacred space within you, where prayer originates.
>
> – Dawna Markova (p.26)

These basic functional structures of our personalities are the skeleton programs upon which the flesh of our lives is sculpted – both systematically, by family, school, religion, and other societal institutions, and coincidentally, through our life experiences.

Few people stop to realize that the basic programs running in their personal bio-computers were written by a child. As children, we learn from experience how to respond to the world around us. If we were raised in nurturing and trustworthy environments, we learned to trust. If our family was loving, we learned to form emotionally satisfying intimate relationships with others. If our early environment was one of misunderstanding or abuse, we had to learn to protect ourselves.

As infants, we have a restricted comprehension of our environment, and limited abilities to cope with it. Much of our learning occurs before we've even had the chance to develop language or reasoning capacities. The coping programs children develop are mostly unconscious, and are stored in parts of the mind that exist below conscious awareness. They are so basic to our overall personality structure that they become second nature, and their influence seems self-evident – "That's just the way I am."

These personality factors are certainly relevant to how people respond to health challenges, and may explain some of the differences between those who respond and those who remain indifferent to healing interventions.

Personality disorders and psychoses

Consider the agony of an infant who yearns for warmth and closeness but receives only harshness and indifference from its parent(s). Unable to conceive of time in the future (because its unprogrammed computer has yet to learn that concept), the infant is aware only that it is miserable, and likely to remain so forever.

Rather than allowing us to suffer, our unconscious mind may intervene to help in several ways. It may bury some of our hurts in forgetfulness, keeping them isolated from our conscious mind so that we suffer less. It may, for instance, shut away the hurt of being unloved, and allow a facade of indifference to develop, to hide this fundamental insecurity from ourselves. Unfortunately, this also leads to the shutting off (*repression*) of portions of our being from our own conscious awareness. It reduces the immediate pain of rejection, but it does so by sweeping the hurt feelings under the carpet of our unconscious mind, where they remain stored in all their intensity. Thus neglected, they can fester like a boil, subtly influencing or sometimes grossly poisoning our future relationships through our unresolved hurts from the buried past.

Our unconscious mind may redefine reality for us, so that horrendous, unbearable truths are softened to tolerable miseries. Rather than accepting that your parents do not want *you,* your child mind may create fantasies that *you have done something for which you are being punished.* As a result, you may develop a negative self-image, anticipating hurt and rejection from anyone close to you.

Much of our understanding of psychology comes from analytic dissection of observable behaviors. However, much of our behavior is based on our underlying feelings, both conscious and unconscious. Daniel Goleman, in his best-selling book, *Emotional Intelligence,* shows that emotional awarenesses and interactions are not simply second-rate experiences that are somehow inferior to our thinking ways of engaging with the world. Emotions are not logical, in the sense that they are not built upon consciously reasoned patterns and plans. In our Western culture, we are conditioned to believe that anything that is not *logical* is not *reasonable.* But our emotions have reasons for existing, even though we may not be consciously aware of them. Furthermore, our emotional reactions may guide us with greater accuracy and deeper truth – since they are not as easily misled by superficial appearances, or prejudiced by logical expectations.

As children, many of us convince ourselves that showing our feelings is the wrong thing to do, as this can upset our parents. Therefore, beginning in earliest childhood, our behavior may be programmed by our unconscious mind to avoid showing feelings.

> *The subconscious, like the earth, knows only to reproduce what is planted in it.*
>
> – Alice Steadman

These unconscious programs are self-validating. Mistrustful people see their interactions with others through mistrusting eyes, and therefore respond to others with defensive behaviors. They will generally steer clear of close relationships in order to avoid what they see as inevitable disappointment. Other people will tend to react in a complementary manner, not seeking relationships with those who send out signals that they do not want others close to them. This in turn confirms what the mistrustful people already believed – that they are unwanted. They may even view any trusting approaches by others with suspicion (Laing 1960; 1970).

This process may be influenced by factors such as the age and developmental stage at which traumas or lack of adequate emotional support are experienced, by the availability or absence of emotionally nourishing alternatives for the suffering person or by inherited genetic predispositions. The complex interplay of multiple factors produces a great diversity of symptomatology, and sometimes leads to disagreements even among experienced clinicians about causes and diagnoses of emotional disorders.

Problems of a moderate nature in this category may lead to what we term *personality disorders*, an example of which can be seen in the person who is excessively shy. More serious imbalances may lead to inward withdrawal and social isolation. The opposite, of extremely volatile and stormy relationships, may occur in a borderline personality disorder. The borderline craves closeness but strongly fears rejection, and is constantly struggling with those who are close to them – over issues of trust, mutual responsibilities for problems in the relationship and major fears of rejection.

The most severe disturbances of this kind may precipitate (or contribute to) psychoses, particularly in those who are genetically susceptible. Psychotics are individuals who have retreated so far from interaction with others that they have difficulty differentiating between their inner and outer worlds. Their emotional responses may be inappropriate and out of place in the outer world. Anyone may become psychotic if they are exposed to sufficiently severe stress. Those who are chronically psychotic are labeled *schizophrenic*.

> *Removing symptoms is like taking the lid off the pot, so it is no longer boiling over. Finding the emotional causes is like taking the pot off the stove.*
>
> – James Gordon

Problematic personality disorders may require prolonged psychotherapy for change to occur. On the other hand, the most reliable treatment for psychoses is with tranquilizers. Properly prescribed, they can greatly reduce psychotic symptomatology, and allow people to live a reasonably normal life. However, if the major tranquilizers are used alone, without accompanying therapeutic treatment, they are very often unsatisfactory as a long-term solution. For one thing, they can produce unpleasant and debilitating side effects. Furthermore, they do not alter patterns of behavior deriving from complex, psychological processes and family interactions that maintain and perpetuate severely malfunctioning modes of relating. These require psychotherapy for effective treatment.

Neuroses

Discrete traumatic experiences, milder cases of unsatisfied emotional needs, and successful defense in a person of stronger genetic constitution may result in less severe protective responses on the part of the unconscious mind.

The trauma precipitating a neurotic crystallization into a lifelong crippling habit need not be a major one. It may simply be an insult that is poorly tolerated by the immature programming in the computer of a child's unconscious mind, which may then convince the child to suppress certain aspects of their being. Typically, children will have an encounter with a parent in which they feel that they cannot be themselves and still be loved.

Case: Two-year-old Tommy presents his mother with a picture that he drew. Previously she may have praised him for his drawings, but this time she furiously scolds him, "You bad child! How could you do something like that? Go to your room!"

If the child is not told that his mother is only upset this time because he drew the picture on the wall, and if he is overwhelmed by the intensity of her anger and the words "You bad child" (which he has heard many times before, expressed with strong feeling), he may internalize a negative image of himself. Thereafter, he may hold off from sharing similar aspects of himself, believing that he is being bad.

Minor but painful experiences of this sort can be emotionally crippling in little ways. More serious emotional injuries naturally lead to more serious emotionally debilitating consequences.

Processes of this kind can be repressed from the child's conscious mind by that part of him which protects him from emotional distress – his unconscious mind.

However, in order to censor emotional material effectively, the unconscious has to be aware of what it is protecting the child from. It must plant a prominent sign on the spot in the carpet under which it has swept the discomforts, identifying what is hidden there. Then it has to stand vigilant guard by that spot, to keep the dirt from being stirred up into conscious awareness by future life events. All of these efforts demand considerable emotional energies, and create tensions in the unconscious mind, which constantly maneuvers to screen out potentially distressing facts and feelings in order to prevent emotional pains from reaching the conscious mind.

If it is particularly vigilant, the unconscious may go a step further. It may continue to distance Tom from situations that threaten to stir up the repressed emotions that he felt as a child. In later life, a person like Tom may find himself avoiding women, for instance, as a result of the accumulated minor and major painful experiences he had with his mother.

Anxiety is the warning signal from the unconscious to the conscious mind that some external or internal threat is perceived or anticipated, or that the habitual rules for safe and acceptable behavior are being transgressed. If we can become aware of the factors that are causing the anxiety, we can deal with the cause, whereupon the anxiety will dissipate. It is when the unconscious succeeds in masking from our awareness the origin of our anxiety that we run into difficulty. It is when Tom becomes uncomfortable with his pattern of avoiding women for no logical reason that he may become aware of the workings of his unconscious mind.[19]

Mental defense mechanisms

We all hold mental constructs of our selves in our minds. These are complex edifices that we build as we grow, drawing on our experiences of personhood – as individuals and as members of family and society. The frame for the house we build is provided in our genetic makeup. The bricks and mortar are given to us by our family and culture. The ways in which we lay them down, and the appearance of the facade that we design to protect ourselves and present ourselves to the world, will be determined by our personal reactions to the world of our experience.

However, our defenses are not constructed only to protect us against the outer world. We also build dark closets and cellars where we can dump unpleasant experiences and feelings that we do not wish to deal with, or which we feel are beyond our capacities to master through less drastic measures. If these experiences were sufficiently traumatic, we may need massive doors behind which to barricade them from our conscious awareness.

In general, we tend to feel that the walls we have constructed around ourselves *are* our selves. We defend them valiantly against confrontations with others, whose outer fortifications are inevitably different from our own. We become uncomfortable when questioned about our choices of materials, or the shape we give to our walls. It is easier to maintain the fantasy that these walls are genetic inheritances, or the products of our childhood training, rather than admitting that they are the result of our own choices. We actually have many options for introducing new colors, or undertaking extensive remodeling. Whether we choose to add defenses or reconstruct our boundary defenses may influence our openness or resistance to healing or dis-ease or disease.

We have many ways of defending the boundaries of what we experience as our selves. If we are very firm in our defenses and our walls are thick, we may simply ignore the differences between ourselves and others.

We may rationalize that others have constructed their walls based on mistaken beliefs, from plans that were given to them by ignorant designers. We may elevate ourselves by denigrating others, claiming that our architects descended from traditions that are closer to God. We may also excuse others for their ignorance in misinterpreting the Master's designs.

> *Painful events need not sink us into depression. They become debilitating because of how we interpret and react to them.*
> — Kenneth Cohen (2003, p. 194)

If our defenses are not as massive, our unconscious mind may eventually hint to us that we might be needlessly hiding behind our ramparts, or going about in suits of armor that might in reality be unnecessary burdens. These inner voices are most likely to emerge as we mature, and when we are not operating under over-whelming stresses. If we are uncomfortable with such inner hints, we may repress them, sometimes without ever letting them reach our consciousness. If we do allow them to surface to awareness, or if circumstances confront us with our dis-proportionate responses to what others handle better, we may deny that such questions have arisen within us. We may project our doubts onto others, blaming *them* for making us uncomfortable.

For instance, we may commonly remark, "He made me angry when he said that…" But in reality, no one can *make* us feel something that is alien to our-selves. More often we resonate with something the other person does or says, and we don't wish to acknowledge that the feelings aroused in us are related to the *shadows* in our dark closets. Such encounters challenge our beliefs, and often we are more comfortable hiding behind our carefully constructed defenses. Rather than acknowledge our inner sensitivities, we project blame for them upon others (Benor 2003).

CASE: If Gerry calls me a jerk, my response could be anger if I feel insecure and she rattled the door on the closet behind which I hid my past hurts that led me to be insecure and angry. Gerry offers me the lovely opportunity to dump some of my anger on her. It is easier for me to be angry than to examine what lies behind that door which makes me vulnerable to be upset by such a taunt. If I'm not inse-cure, I don't have to bite on the bait. I might ask myself questions such as, "What did I say or do to offend Gerry?" or "Why is Gerry in a bad mood today?"

Our fears keep us locked into our defenses – fears of being hurt by attackers, and fears of failing or otherwise disappointing ourselves and others. Our defenses in turn hold our earliest fears locked inside of us, and the fear of being re-traumatized keeps us from releasing these earlier fears. We are often tied into knots of fears, as Ronald Laing has so brilliantly pointed out:

Among healers and wholistic therapists, involvement in spiritual development may actually be a form of defense against awareness of their own emotional ten-sions. Blaming our misfortunes on bad *karma* or getting deeply involved in spiritual practices may in fact be *spiritual bypasses* around psychological prob-lems.

I don't respect myself
I can't respect anyone who respects me.
I can only respect someone who does not respect me
I respect Jack
Because he does not respect me.

I despise Tom
Because he does not despise me.

Only a despicable person
can respect someone as despicable as me.

I cannot love someone I despise.

Since I love Jack
I cannot believe he loves me.

What proof can he give?

— Ronald Laing 1970 (p.18)

There are numerous other ways in which we may defend ourselves from uncomfortable awarenesses (A. Freud), and it is beyond the scope of this book to explore all of these here. The examples above should suffice to explain the principles behind our habits and methods of hiding our own feelings from ourselves. However, let us now consider the special area of defenses in which the body may participate.

Understanding defense mechanisms is also important for an appreciation of collective angers that can lead to war. Dealing with such angers and hatreds is another level of healing.

NORMALITY

Mental health doesn't mean always being happy - if it did, nobody would qualify.

— Ashleigh Brilliant (no. 3929)

Now that we have reviewed some types of psychological problems, you may well ask, "So, how do you get to be a normal person?"

The answer is that there is no general agreement on a definition of psychological normality. Everyone has some measure of defensiveness, some unresolved hurts, and various quirks of personality that make her or him uniquely different from everyone else. On the positive side, most would agree that normal people have a flexibility to behave and respond adaptively to various challenges and stresses in their lives. On the negative side, a lack of individuality or a blandness that blends totally into the acceptable norms of behavior may be perceived as being abnormal because this lacks individuality.

> Anybody who behaved normally all of the time would not be completely normal.
>
> – Ashleigh Brilliant

The concept of psychological normality encompasses a general range of individuality that is acceptable within a given community and culture. The acceptability of differing beliefs and behaviors varies between countries and cultures, and even in different communities within the same culture.

Everyone also has their own emotional breaking points – situations and stresses that will prove intolerable, and will result in psychological decompensation. At what point, then, can we say that a person is psychologically abnormal? While we all have general concepts of normality, and can readily agree when presented with an example of a person whose behaviors or beliefs deviate in major ways from our accepted norms, we may still have difficulty judging for ourselves and agreeing with others when confronted with individuals who do not deviate so extremely from our shared idea of normality.

A second factor in determining the line between normality and abnormality depends entirely upon the individual in question. While others may not feel that a certain person is abnormal, this person may herself believe that she is not normal. In other cases, the subjects may lack awareness that they are abnormal – as perceived by others.

So in the end, we must simply live with complex general standards for distinguishing between psychological normality and abnormality, between sanity and insanity. And there will always be broad gray areas in which a person's normality may be disputed.

> *Who I really am is one of those difficult questions I prefer to leave to the experts.*
>
> – Ashleigh Brilliant (no. 5151)

Some of the above may appear to be rather nit-picking, and the reader may be wondering why this is relevant. The assessment of psychological disorders and of their severity is of major importance in assessing whether various treatments are helpful to people in dealing with those disorders. The inherent variability in human nature challenges the researcher to develop valid and reliable ways of assessing deviations from normality.

Standardized psychological questionnaires are often used for such purposes. When these are given to thousands of subjects, norms for responses can be tabulated. These then becomes a helpful tool for clinicians and researchers in assessing psychological abnormalities and changes that may be the brought about by a given treatment (Jacobson/ Truax). They are culture-specific, however, so they must be recalibrated for various ethnic groups.

> *Without deviation from the norm, progress is not possible."*
>
> - Frank Zappa

PSYCHOSOMATIC DISORDERS

What a man thinks of himself, that is which determines, or rather, indicates, his fate.

— Henry David Thoreau (1854)

The body can become a series of battlegrounds in the unconscious mind's maneuvers to protect us from unpleasant experiences.

When danger is perceived, either consciously or unconsciously, the body becomes tense. This is an automatic reflex reaction involving the nervous system and hormones. The body is preparing to respond to the perceived threat by fleeing or fighting. When we fight or flee the tension is discharged, and our bodies can again relax.

When either circumstances or the unconscious mind prevent us from dealing with the sources of our tension, there can be a chronic buildup of stress without appropriate release. Our bodies then suffer the consequences of prolonged tension. Blood pressure rises, muscles remain taut and may spasm, and stress hormones continue to circulate. People frequently are unaware that emotional tensions lie behind their symptoms, because these processes are managed by the unconscious mind.

Tense muscles will ultimately start to complain by hurting. Backaches and headaches are common results of stress, but other muscles can also spasm and ache. Once we feel the pain, a vicious circle is initiated: pain → anxiety → more muscle tension → spasm → increased pain, → increased anxiety and so on.

Similar muscle spasms produce a narrowing of the airways in the bronchioles, bringing on asthmatic attacks; tension in arteries throughout our body resulting in elevated blood pressure; spasms in cardiac arteries causing angina (heart pain from insufficient blood supply) and in muscles along the skull producing migraines; excessive gastric acid secretion leading to heartburn and ulcers; spasm in the gut, and other such disorders.

More subtle and insidious changes in the immune system may also occur due to chronic tensions. White cells and antibodies are less effective in protecting the health of people who are under stress. This may contribute to their developing infections, and may increase their susceptibility to serious illnesses such as AIDS and cancer.

Secondary gain is another psychological mechanism which can initiate cycles that maintain and perpetuate pain and other symptoms. Pain may be useful in some situations, despite the fact that it causes us discomfort and we consciously wish to be rid of it. For example, pain can provide an acceptable excuse for not attending a social event that might be stressful, for avoiding unwanted sexual relations, for not going to work, or for side-stepping other unpleasant obligations or demands. Conversely, a symptom may bring us caring responses from family and friends, and greater closeness – in relationships where we hesitate to ask for such attention, or where others hesitate to offer it.

The unconscious mind, searching for the most immediate way to relieve our anxieties, might thus help us avoid facing stressful situations by aggravating pains that are present due to any cause. A chronic headache may flare up "conveniently" (though unconsciously) when my mother-in-law phones to invite me to dinner. Secondary gain may then reinforce the pain-tension-spasm cycle when this pattern recurs in other situations as well.[20]

> *The sick man is more than half a rascal. He may only be sick because he hasn't the courage to clean house.*
> — Sherwood Anderson

Subtle energy blocks and imbalances that occur as a result of tension and stress may also produce a variety of symptoms. I will discuss this further in subsequent sections.

THE BODY'S REGULATING SYSTEMS

The deeper levels of the brain concern themselves with monitoring and regulating the vital, routine functions of the body, such as breathing, temperature control, heartbeat, and blood pressure. They also maintain a suitable chemical balance in the bloodstream to provide an optimal environment for the various tissues and organs.

These functions are controlled via a diffuse network of nerves that run from the brain, along the spinal cord and out through various nerves to reach every part of the body. This network is called the *autonomic nervous system (ANS)*. The ANS tenses skeletal muscles via the *sympathetic nervous system (SNS),* and relaxing them via the *parasympathetic nervous system (PNS)*.

The SNS is activated to prepare for fight or flight. It increases the heart rate and blood pressure, and stimulates the adrenal glands to produce adrenaline and steroids. It constricts arteries in the extremities in order to increase the blood available to larger muscles and internal organs. It heightens anxiety and alertness to potential dangers. All of these factors serve us well in emergencies, as they increase our awareness of what is going on around us, and enhance our strength and stamina for immediate physical response to danger. However, when the SNS is chronically activated, as in conditions of long-term, low-grade stress, it can be harmful to our health, as discussed in the section above, on vicious circles.

The PNS also activates the digestive tract and other organs of the body. Again, these functions are beneficial as long as the organ functions remain within a normal range. But when chronically over-activated, various problems, such as ulcers, can result.

Hormones are chemical regulators in the body. They act as catalysts in chemical reactions, facilitating and regulating the biochemical activity of the body to make it more efficient. Hormones prepare us for action, assist in initiating digestive processes, regulate blood sugar levels, respond when allergens intrude in the body, prepare the uterus for pregnancy, bring on lactation, and more.

The *pituitary* and *pineal glands*, located at the base of the brain, are centers for regulating hormone production in endocrine glands around the body. These crucial regulating organs are also influenced by our states of mind and emotions. Stress can therefore produce over-activity of the endocrine glands , as in the condition of hyperthyroidism.

The *immune system,* consisting of white cells and antibodies, protects the body against invading organisms that cause disease. Over-activity of this system can cause problems such as allergies, and may also contribute to chronic illnesses such as arthritis, asthma, and other disorders.

With chronic stress producing chronic over-activity of the nervous, endocrine and immune systems, these systems can become exhausted and depleted. They will then be unable to provide us with optimal protection, and we may develop chronic fatigue syndrome, fibromyalgia or other stress-related illnesses.

While the correlation between chronic stress and immune system disorders was known for many years, no mechanism was known to explain how stress causes these changes. Recently it has been discovered that there are several dozens of *neuropeptides* (chemical messengers) that are produced by nerve cells in the brain to communicate with each other. These same neuropeptides are also found in white cells. We are just beginning to appreciate that the immune system is so closely knit together with the nervous system that they may in fact function together as a single system.[21] Receptors for neuropeptides are also found in the spinal cord, intestines, kidneys, gonads and other organs. This suggests yet another mechanism whereby the brain/ mind and body may act in concert.

Since our states of mind can influence the levels of activity in all of these systems, they also offer us access to self-corrective measures for alleviating our own physical problems. Direct access to our unconscious control mechanisms can be achieved through hypnosis, biofeedback, imagery, focused relaxation therapy and other techniques, while indirect access is available through any of the various stress reduction techniques.[22]

While direct interventions to alter our maladaptive body functions are available, we often find that the unconscious mind resists changes in its habitual patterns of response to stress. Psychotherapy may be needed along with these techniques in order to deal with psychological defenses.

TALKING/ RELATIONAL PSYCHOTHERAPY[23]

A person who diagnoses and prescribes for his own afflictions has a fool for a physician and often a corpse for a patient.
— Anonymous

How can we find our way out of maladaptive patterns? While it is possible to learn from life experiences and to reprogram our own unconscious mind, the process of doing this is usually quite challenging and difficult. It can be extremely difficult to identify the ruts we have worn through the habitual tracks we tread. We may dig such deep ruts for ourselves that we cannot even see out of them to find other paths by which to travel. It is often extremely hard for people in the thick of emotional difficulties to see alternatives to their unhelpful or maladaptive behaviors, much less get to the roots of their own problems and deal with them. We tend to try harder in the ways we already know rather than seeking new ways to cope, even if the old approaches have not succeeded, and may actually have contributed to our problems. In effect, we are only digging our ruts ever deeper. For instance, if we habitually withdraw from stressful situations, we may completely isolate ourselves when we are under severe stress. This can lead to a state of depression that leaves us with less energy to cope – and thus a type of vicious circle is established.

> *But he that hides a dark soul, and foul thoughts*
> *Benighted walks under the midday sun,*
> *Himself is his own dungeon.*
> — John Milton (1637)

Another common problem is that the unconscious mind, programmed in childhood to protect us against emotional dangers and distresses, is quite resistant to change. We may be far removed from the original hurts that initiated our defensive habits, but we still tend to avoid similar psychological discomforts as though the original dangers were still present. Without any conscious awareness that we are doing so, we resist all logical arguments for change. Jessica Macbeth observed that "Resistance is about standing on yourself and saying you can't move…"

Tom's father shouted at him a lot when he was young, and would spank him severely if he talked back. Tom learned to protect himself by clamming up and doing his best to not stir his father's wrath. In later life, Tom was unable to assert himself with his boss at work, even when he knew he was in the right. He would cringe if his boss raised his voice, and was constantly afraid of criticism – even though he was very knowledgeable and skilled in his job. He sought counseling when his co-workers repeatedly challenged him over why he didn't stand up to his boss.

The very act of consulting a health care professional may in itself reduce tension, since it gives us someone who can provide support, and we can then hope for some relief. Many methods of psychotherapy are available, involving an enormous variety of therapist-client interactions. These range from simple, supportive relationships to introspective, reflective processes (such as psychoanalysis and psychodynamic therapy), to more action-oriented therapies (such as cognitive behavior modification, gestalt therapy and psychodrama). They may include techniques such as hypnosis, relaxation, meditation and bodywork, as well as therapeutic family and group interactions, and they may also involve attention to mind-body relationships.

CASE: Tom chose a gestalt therapist, whose way of working with people is to have them hold a dialogue between various aspects of their problem. Tom held a discussion between the part of himself that wanted to have it out with his boss and the part that was afraid to do so. Over a series of therapy session, this led to explorations of other times when tom had had conflicts like this, particularly in his childhood.

How does psychotherapy work? Jean Shinoda Bolen (1979, p. 69 - 70) discusses how psychoanalysis, one of the many forms of psychotherapy, can help.

> [D]oing analysis is analogous to gardening. The relationship between analyst and patient, with its rules of confidentiality and its quality of sanctuary where it is safe to bring up anything, serves as a container for the process of growth. Removing weeds and rocks, and tilling and watering the soil are preliminary tasks in gardening and are like the psychotherapy phase of analysis. The hindrances to growth, the weeds and rocks – whether in one's early family life or in one's current situation – need to be eliminated. Whatever has crowded out the individual's growth needs to be recognized and removed. Water, that is like feeling, must be brought to the situation in order to allow the defenses to soften and be penetrated. In this way, feelings from others can get through to provide nourishment, like water gets through to the roots of a plant that have been in parched, thick, clayey soil. In analysis, growth occurs underground or deep in the unconscious; later,
> it manifests itself in what shows above ground.
> What comes into being depends on the nature of the seed. A good gardener helps each plant to grow fully and produce whatever it was meant to: whether fruit or vegetable or flower, to be fully whatever it was meant to be – oak, redwood, geranium or cactus.
> Often an analyst is a supporting pole for a period of time in another person's life. Most growing things become sturdy enough to eventually continue on their own, absorbing the water and sunshine of the environment, taking nourishment from the soil in which they are now deeply rooted, in a life of significant soil.

The therapist provides a safe environment in which to explore what is hurting or emotionally unsettled. She helps to sharpen the focus on where problems lie, and how they developed. As we develop greater trust, the therapist gives support so that we don't have to be afraid that releasing our feelings will overwhelm us. She can point out ways in which we might over- or under-estimate our participation, responsibilities, or guilt in creating, maintaining, or deepening our own problems. Our feelings toward the therapist and our beliefs about what she feels toward us will be similar to feelings and beliefs we have with regard to other people, but in therapy we can discuss them openly. The therapist can provide feedback as to where we may be distorting or exaggerating our reactions to her, and can thereby help us to correct our erroneous beliefs and maladaptive responses.

Being in the presence of a person who is unconditionally accepting and who gives us reliably objective feedback provides a corrective emotional experience. We may learn to trust that another person can really be there for us – in ways that our parents and mentors may not have been able to be. At first, this awareness may be accompanied by anger or hurt. Eventually, therapy may help us to reach understanding and forgiveness.

Analysis of our dreams and fantasies can be enormously productive in revealing our unconscious patterns of belief and responses to challenges in our lives. Dreams may also be keys to some of the doors behind which we locked our feelings when they were too painful for us to deal with.

CASE: Tom released intense feelings in several of the hypnotherapy sessions. These stimulated dreams, which opened into earlier and earlier memories of traumatic experiences. The turning point in the therapy came when he recalled a minor, but to four year old Tom a very traumatic experience. Tom was all dressed up for Easter services. He loved going to church because this was a time his family was together in a relaxed atmosphere – in contrast to the frequent tensions at home. His mother was often exhausted from being both a homemaker and working as a saleswoman in a department store, and his father was often short-tempered after working long hours as a taxi driver. In the middle of the Easter service, Tom needed to go to the bathroom. His father shushed him several times when he tried to ask to be taken to the restroom. Unable to hold it in any longer, he wet himself. His father, obviously embarrassed (and probably feeling some guilt for having ignored Tom's needs) shamed Tom publicly when he saw he had wet his pants.

Tom felt doubly betrayed by his father, first for not having responded to his needs, and second, for shaming him in front of several other children in the church.

We may learn as much from the *hows* of our interactions as we do from the *whats*. Analyzing our thought processes and our interpersonal interactions may more quickly reveal how our unconscious mind works than attacking the content of our thoughts and beliefs.

CASE: Tom's healing in therapy came as much from the acceptance extended by his therapist as it did from the release of the buried memories and feelings. This corrective experience was a balm for the wounds he had carried from this and other painful interactions with his father.

All of these aspects of psychotherapy can help us let go of the childhood programming that may be exerting a negative influence in our adult lives.

CASE: Coming to trust his therapist, Tom began to shed his distrust and fear of authority figures – a distrust generalized by his unconscious mind in its attempts to protect him from further anticipated betrayals and traumas, as he had experienced with his father. Gradually, Tom became more assertive at work and was eventually able to stand up for himself with his boss – not in a confronting or angry way, but in a manner that invited understanding and constructive changes. The processes of positive change that are involved in psychotherapy also have great bearing on our understanding of how self-healing and healer-healing work. The unconditionally accepting relationship of caregiver with careseeker is a major element in every therapeutic interaction.

There is also a caution here, however, in interpreting reports of positive effects of healing interventions. Because people may respond to the therapeutic relationship alone, any treatment – whether it be through bioenergies, physical manipulation of the body or administration of medications, herbal remedies or flower essences – must take into account the possibility that the presence of the caregiver may have been an essential element in the treatment.

Beyond the caring attention of the therapist, there are many theories and clinical approaches to helping through psychotherapy. Several of these are discussed below, others are detailed in the next chapter. Appendix A provides a brief description of a range of psychotherapies.

PHYSICAL SYMPTOMS ADDRESSED BY PSYCHOTHERAPY

We often experience various physical sensations when repressed feelings are activated unconsciously under stress. As discussed above, these may range from muscle tension and tightness to spasms and pain. Such reactions may simply be conditioned responses of tension in our bodies, which became associated with early traumas or with the expression of particular unpleasant emotions. Alternatively, the actual memory of the emotion may have been stored in some way within the complaining muscles and tendons,[24] or in another aspect of our body functions. Let us look, for illustration, at a person with a psychosomatic problem.

CASE: Susan, a 23-year-old university student, came for psychotherapy because she was lonely and depressed. Susan's father had been killed in an auto accident when she was eight years old. She felt deeply hurt, and also furious with him for "abandoning" her. The unconscious does not differentiate between loss through abandonment, divorce, death or illness. The unavailability of a parent to meet the child's needs creates a justifiable rage.

Eight-year-old Susan told her mother she was angry, but her mother was grieving the loss of her husband and became upset by her daughter's words. Susan then felt guilty for adding to her mother's burden of pain. In the course of this drama, Susan learned not to express her emotions. Her unconscious mind then stepped in to protect her from feeling her unpleasant emotions, which were also partially unacceptable to her own conscience. Her unconscious helped her by keeping these feelings buried so that they were no longer consciously experienced as a source of anguish. This worked well as a temporary solution, but it eventually had unfortunate consequences. Susan's unconscious mind, in its attempts to protect her from feeling hurt, began to work overtime. Any experience that might potentially remind Susan of the unpleasant memories locked away in her dark mental closets had to be prevented from disturbing her. This constant awareness of *what to keep away from* was manifested in Susan's conscious mind as a sense of uneasiness and irritability in any related situations that she encountered later in life. Although she had a pleasant personality and was good-looking, she had no real friends. Whenever she started to get close to someone, she would get into silly arguments with them, and soon ended the relationship. Susan's unconscious was trying to protect her, first from the unresolved childhood grief over her father's death with the pain and anger of being abandoned, and second, from the possibility of suffering the same feelings of rejection and hurt if she allowed anyone else to get close to her emotionally.

Susan's psychotherapist helped her to search her unconscious memories and feelings in order to understand her current irrational behavior. Once the roots of the problem were identified, Susan experienced many of the repressed emotions with considerable intensity. There were several therapy sessions during which she raged and cried as though her father had just recently died. These emotions were released from her unconscious at this point in her life because she could now cope with them more competently. Furthermore, she trusted in her therapist's support to help her to deal with these emotions and to find more constructive ways of handling rejections – both real and feared. Although the feelings of anger and hurt were still painful, Susan had many more alternatives for coping with them as an adult.

After working through the pent-up anger she felt toward her father, Susan found she no longer needed to distance herself from her friends.

The intensity of such releases of emotions (*abreactions*) testifies to how well the unconscious represses these feelings. They remain in their dark closets, carefully guarded from scrutiny but intact in all their raw power. This is especially common with grief, which is one of the most painful experiences in life.

Cues that can alert us to seek psychotherapy often take the form of somatic complaints. We may have headaches or other symptoms for which our doctor cannot identify a physical cause. Sometimes it is enough for the doctor simply to ask us what might be making us feel tense, and we realize what is making us up tight. In other instances we might need to speak with a counselor or therapist to discover the sources of the tension underlying our physical problems. The psychotherapist can help us work out what is triggering the symptoms and why. Often the symptom turns out to be a learned (*conditioned*) response, which became associated with tension in the context of an original emotional trauma. Thereafter, we may experience the same response in similarly tense situations.[25] A case of this kind was presented to me when a young man sought my help with a personal problem.

CASE: Peter, aged 22, would become nauseous whenever he faced the prospect of dating a girl. If he forced himself to take the girl out, he sometimes even vomited. He had avoided dealing with the problem for several years by burying himself in his studies. Now that he was out of school and working, he was becoming increasingly frustrated and angry with himself.

Peter was successful in his work as a teacher, seemed otherwise free of emotional problems, and could not see any logical reason for his difficulties. I decided that behavioral therapy promised to provide the most direct relief, and I taught Peter some relaxation techniques. I then asked him to fantasize, while in a relaxed state, that he was approaching women to talk with them, or that they were approaching him. This taught him to remain relaxed when getting close to women. After three weeks of practice, Peter reported that his feeling of nausea in the presence of women was much reduced.

During the following session, Peter spontaneously recalled an important event from his senior year in high school. He had been in the school cafeteria where his best friend's girlfriend worked. As she dished a portion of peas onto his plate, she hinted that she would like him to ask her out. He was very upset, feeling attracted to her, but also reluctant to betray his best friend. He declined politely, but felt nauseous and could not finish his meal. *That was when it had all started.*

Once Peter's unconscious mind released these memories with their attached emotions, he no longer felt any nausea in the presence of women. Peter's unconscious had kept him away from women in his adult life because of conflicts that had been buried deep in his psyche some years earlier. His headaches and nausea cleared up when his emotional conflict was sorted out.

While insights into the origins of a problem may surface during behavioral therapies, this is not a requirement for cures of chronic symptoms. People may relinquish their physical problems without any awareness of the possible origins or ongoing causes behind them.

Psychotherapy, which helps to uncover the processes by which the unconscious protects the conscious mind, has contributed significantly to our understanding of healing. The unconscious mind behaves in a very literal, mechanistic, computer-like fashion. Its reactions are involuntary, reflexive, and frequently simplistic to the point of childish irrationality. Situations that make us uncomfortable are dealt with for the *immediate* resolution of the problem and the reduction of the associated anxieties. The unconscious mind, in its childish way, does not consider the long-range implications of such protectiveness over the whole person. Psychological conflicts are rapidly repressed and unpleasant tensions are reduced. However, muscle tensions and other symptoms that frequently accompany emotional stress may then accumulate, with no apparent cause to explain their presence.

This is most clearly and dramatically seen in *conversion* reactions (sometimes called *hysterical* reactions). In these cases, drastic changes such as paralyses or sensory deficits may appear quite suddenly, with no apparent physical cause. Here is a clinical example of how this might occur.

CASE: John was a church-going, well-mannered, 32-year-old clerk, and a good husband and father to two lovely children. Under stress from company problems that threatened his job, combined with some unexpected financial burdens at home, he exploded one day in anger at his wife. He even raised his fist, but did not strike her. This was very uncharacteristic of him, and he was immediately apologetic and remorseful. The next morning he awoke with a feeling of weakness in his right arm. This developed over the next two days into total paralysis of the arm and hand.

Neurological evaluation showed no disease, but it revealed a pattern of paralysis typical of a conversion reaction. In psychotherapy John proved to be a good hypnotic subject. Under trance he revealed that he had been so angry at his wife that he was ready to strike her. This was clearly very much out of character, and contrary to the dictates of his conscience. It was apparent that John's unconscious mind had punished him through this paralysis for feeling the extreme anger, and at the same time had prevented him from expressing this dangerous emotion. John made a very rapid recovery as his anger was uncovered during hypnotic trance. This process of repressing his feelings and hiding them from his own awareness was explained to him, and with the help of further the psychotherapy he no longer had to repress his anger or punish himself for it.

Since all of these processes occur in the unconscious mind, people are initially unaware of the causes of their conversion symptoms. When a subject reveals the roots of his symptoms under hypnosis, the strong emotions that were repressed may be released. Upon coming out of the hypnotic trance, he can be instructed to recall the information he had repressed. In many cases this process will relieve his symptoms permanently. Hypnosis[26] is particularly effective in treating conversion reactions, and with appropriate therapy they may be cleared up very quickly.

The process is the same, whether it leads to conversion reactions or simply to feelings that are buried in the unconscious without external symptoms. The pain of sexual, physical, or emotional abuse, for instance, may be repressed in this way, when the trauma is still fresh and overwhelming. However, the buried hurts may later produce disabling psychological symptoms. With the support of a therapist, the pain can be released, and the symptoms will then resolve.

> *Though this be madness, yet there is method in it.*
> – William Shakespeare (*Hamlet*)

Arthur Janov vividly describes how headaches, ulcers, constipation, asthma, hypertension, muscle tensions, epilepsy and many other problems have been alleviated as a result of his method of therapy, which prescribes screaming to enable the release of pent-up emotions. Janov's descriptions are amongst the clearest I have found on releasing tensions, as well as other symptoms associated with emotional blocks, through psychotherapy.[27]

Other avenues for uncovering the meanings in the various ways the body speaks – through gestures, sensations and symptoms - and for releasing symptoms have been developed in several mind-body psychotherapies.

Gestalt therapy calls for people in treatment to imagine themselves as the part of their body that has made an idiosyncratic unconscious movement, as in a nervous tic (Perls).

CASE: In the example of Peter mentioned above, I noticed that his hands were clenched into fists. When I asked him about this gesture, he had no clue what his body might be saying. I instructed him to speak for his fists – that is, to put words to the gesture. In this way he was able to get in touch with and verbalize anger, which he then realized had been provoked by his best friend's girlfriend. His unconscious mind had been expressing this anger in nonverbal communication through his muscles, as well as through his stomach.

Physical symptoms such as pain may also clear up when their meaning is perceived through gestalt therapy, as a person puts words to the tensions behind the symptom and emotions locked within the body are released.

Relaxation techniques such as muscle relaxation, meditation, and breathing exercises can help to relieve many aspects of emotional and physical stresses.[28] Most of these techniques are easily learned and profoundly effective.

You might wish to take a brief break from reading to explore one of these right now. (Do not tighten any muscles during the following exercise if they are injured, strained or in pain.) Using your dominant hand, clench your fist and bring it up tightly towards your shoulder. Hold the tension for about half a minute, connecting with your hand and arm muscles through their tightness. Take a deep breath and *slowly* begin to release the tension in these muscles. Pay attention to how they let go of their tightness. *Slowly* let your arm relax so that your hand, which is also relaxing, gradually lowers itself until it comes to rest on your lap or at your side. Tell the muscles to continue releasing their tension while your hand and arm remain still. Don't force your fingers to open. Let them stay curled in a relaxed position. When you feel they are about as relaxed as they can get, take another deep breath and blow out any further tension that might remain, in preparation for moving your hand. Notice any differences you can feel between your two hands.

Now do the same with your other hand. Your hands respond readily to such exercises because they are used to taking orders to grasp and release, to gesture and serve you in so many ways.

Were the rest of your muscles listening in when you relaxed your hands? As we relax any part of the body, the remaining muscles tend to relax as well.

If you have the time, you might wish to give yourself the pleasure of a deliberate, total-body relaxation, starting with your toes and extending upward, one step at a time, through your calves, thighs, buttocks, lower back, belly, chest and upper back, hands, arms, shoulders and neck, and face. This is an excellent way to let go of a day's tensions and worries, or to ease yourself to sleep.

Another bodymind therapist, Wilhelm Reich, was a psychiatrist who was one of Freud's disciples He believed that a life force, which he called *orgone energy,* permeates all things in the universe. . Reich felt that health depends on maintaining an adequate flow of this energy throughout the body. He postulated that for various defensive reasons, people with mental disturbances develop muscular rigidity (*armoring*), which is often associated with sexual inhibitions. This tension could block the natural flow of body energy. Reich developed a variety of breathing and muscular exercises to help release these energy blocks. His disciples subsequently branched out and developed variations on his methods.

Bioenergetics uses exercises and stress postures to achieve similar results.[29] *Core-energetics therapy* is another related approach.[30] *Rolfing* is a form of therapy in which very deep massage and pressure are applied to the body in order to heighten sensations, sometimes to the point of inducing pain. Unconscious memories and feelings locked within the muscles, tendons and fascia may be released through this method (Hunt; Reid).

The *Feldenkrais, Alexander, and Hellerwork methods* are gentler forms of body-based psychotherapy. They aim to build posture and correct habits of movement so that people feel better within their bodies. They focus on improving positive behaviors, in addition to addressing pathological patterns

Rubenfeld Synergy Therapy extends this type of body work to focus on the emotions underlying body tensions and other symptoms, helping to release habitual defensive patterns along with whatever energy has been locked into the body in a maladaptive way.

Massage, in its many variations[31] may release muscle tensions.

Working with the body through any of these or other approaches may help to release such defensive patterns much more quickly than talking therapy alone.

Initially, however, this kind of work may raise anxieties and confused feelings because the unconscious mind believes that the defensive patterns it has employed for many years, usually programmed in childhood, are needed for protection. On the positive side, Ilana Rubenfeld (p.20) explains how such confusion could actually facilitate change.

> "Fusion" means "union." "Con" can mean either "with" or "opposed to." Thus the word "confusing" means both a pulling apart *and* a joining, both of which are vital to the process of change. I encourage clients to feel confused, because you have to be willing to be disorganized in order to get reorganized. If you are in a dysfunctional habit pattern, it cannot be changed unless it is interrupted, and interruption means confusion. We get anxious and hate it; it's often bewildering. But we cannot experiment with new, *non*habitual behavior unless we experience the discomfort of our old ways breaking apart. We cannot change without first falling into what I have called "the fertile void."

These therapies all aim to release tensions and their associated memories from the mind and body. They demonstrate that the unconscious mind will frequently lock up conflicting emotions, complex problems, and uncomfortable memories inside the muscles and tissues of our bodies. In the practice of these and related therapies, chronic pains and other symptoms are often relieved when physical and emotional tensions, with associated memories and emotions, are finally released.[32]

Spiritual healing is another therapy that can relieve many symptoms in similar ways. Aspects of psychotherapy are always involved in healing – through therapists' suggestions and through expectations of healees. This does not mean that healing is merely a form of suggestion. The controlled studies reviewed in Volume 1 show that healing is significantly more than just a placebo effect.

Meditation may bring about spontaneous emotional releases, sometimes with marked improvements in physical symptoms. It appears that when we calm ourselves through meditation, the unconscious mind realizes it does not have to protect us any more from feeling the hurts of old traumas that it buried at the time we experienced them. Meditators who are unprepared for such releases may be surprised, distressed or even dismayed – feeling that these are negative effects of meditation. They are usually only negative if the meditator responds with fear.

These therapies provide many avenues for addressing psychological and physical problems. Pain is particularly responsive, even when it is caused by known physical causes such as trauma, arthritis or other disease processes that clearly have physical causes.

PHYSICAL SYMPTOMS ADDRESSED BY BODYWORK AND BIOENERGY THERAPIES

Massage in its numerous variations[33] can alleviate many symptoms, including pain and anxiety. By manually kneading the muscles, massage releases chronic physical tensions. Emotional tensions, stored in the muscles, tendons and ligaments, may be released at the same time. As happens with meditation, such releases may be unexpected.

Skeptics might suspect that spiritual healing is no more than a mechanical manipulation, a kind of massage that uses simple physical methods of tissue-kneading to relieve tension through muscular relaxation. In practice, the laying-on of hands actually involves only light touch at the most, and frequently includes hand-movements that are made around the healee's body without actually touching. The application of pressure for the release of symptoms, as would be applied in massage, is not used in spiritual healing.

Healing is really much more than a form of body therapy. It reduces anxieties and seems to directly relax the muscles, or to activate mechanisms within the healee's body to release tensions in the muscles, without physical pressure.

Healing may in fact be a helpful adjunct to enhance massage and other body therapies. My own clinical experience is that healing facilitates these releases considerably more than the physical interventions alone. Several therapy approaches have been developed that include healing, such as Network Spinal Analysis and the Bowen technique.[34]

Many CAM therapists may even be healers without knowing it – especially those involved in manual therapies. Growing numbers of these therapists are consciously including healing in their ministrations, finding that the combination of the two is more potent than either of the practices used alone.

Spiritual healing also has a broad range of overlaps with various forms of psychotherapy and body therapies. Another of the common suspicions of skeptics (and it certainly was one of my own initial impressions) is that reports of spiritual healings must involve hysterical symptoms that are cured through suggestion, or through the healer's soothing presence or counseling. While this may be true in a few cases, there are many more instances of confirmed problems of physical origins that have responded to spiritual healing.

In my personal explorations of bodymind therapies and healing, I have come through a series of steps of increasing awareness and comprehension. Even though I started out with an interest in psychosomatic medicine, my initial understanding was that simple relaxation of voluntary muscles was all that a person could achieve in therapy. I then learned about relaxation of the so-called involuntary muscles (gut, bronchioles, arterioles); next about hormonal balances achieved with relaxation; then about bioenergies; and last about interactions of the mind with the immune system. At each step, I thought I had arrived at the ultimate appreciation of mind-body interactions. I wonder what will come next!

PSYCHOLOGICAL CONDITIONING (REINFORCEMENT) AND BEHAVIOR THERAPY

Ivan Pavlov's study is a classic in the area of psychological conditioning (also called *reinforcement*). He demonstrated that if a bell is rung whenever food is presented to a dog, the dog will learn to associate the sound of the bell with the food. He will start to salivate whenever he hears the bell, even if he does not receive food at that time. In other words, the dog has become conditioned to the bell as a stimulus producing salivation.

Such conditioning can occur in humans without our conscious awareness. If psychologists smile (or in any other manner provide *reinforcements*) whenever their clients behave in a particular way, such as reporting dreams or discussing their feelings, the clients will be conditioned by such reinforcements to repeat the behaviors with a greater frequency. This is one of the reasons why Freudian clients come to have Freudian dreams, while Jungian clients have Jungian dreams. They are simply fulfilling their therapists' expectations, responding to reinforcements provided by their respective therapists. This may occur without the conscious awareness of either therapists or clients.

The examples presented above are from the controlled context of the psychologist's office. However, the same principles apply in the less structured settings of everyday life. Anyone may have a sudden sensation of physical tension (such as tightness in muscles or stomach cramps) when they experience an emotional event. This may subsequently lead to inadvertent conditioning of the body to become tense (or to cramp up) whenever that emotion is felt or the event is recalled or repeated. Such randomly reinforced connections between bodily conditions and environmental stimuli or emotional reactions may be totally unconscious. We may suffer a number of physical symptoms, believing them to be purely related to malfunctions of our body. We may have no awareness of any connection with the original chain of events that reinforces and maintains those symptoms. Remember that Peter, who felt nausea associated with dating women, at first had no idea how this symptom had developed.

Psychotherapists have learned to relieve symptoms using these same processes of reinforcement, in what is called *behavior therapy*. Therapists repattern their clients' responses to stimuli, so that the clients will no longer suffer from physical discomfort (Wolpe). The natural conditioning or reinforcing circumstances are first identified, and the clients are then taught to relax or to respond in some other, more adaptive manner to the same stimuli. The case of Peter, described earlier, again illustrates this process.

A popular version of this technique is *cognitive behavioral therapy*, in which the therapist confronts the client with the illogical nature of their fears.

CASE: Harry was terrified of dogs. He readily admitted that although he had been bitten by a dog as a child, this was no reason to cringe every time he passed a little dog on a leash while walking down the street – as much as twenty or thirty years later. The avoidance of dogs may have been a good survival technique in childhood but it was totally unnecessary, inconvenient, and sometimes embarrassing to him a quarter of a century later, at age 32.

Prior to therapeutic interventions, clients tend to hold onto such symptoms quite tenaciously.

CASE: Harry's cognitive behavior therapist suggested a pattern of exercises that paired positive images with the fearful feelings which arose whenever Harry even thought of a dog. Every time he mentally pictured a dog and felt he wanted to cringe, the therapist directed him to imagine himself on a beach on a warm, relaxing holiday. Harry would then relax, basking in the sun of his mental beach imagery. By repeatedly alternating this process of imagining a dog, then imagining a relaxing scene, Harry was able to reprogram his unconscious, automatic dog alarm so that it no longer went off whenever he saw a harmless dog.

It may not be necessary to achieve *conscious awareness* of the original causes of tensions in order to be rid of them. We may let go of old patterns of behavior when new and better ones serve us better – but too often our habit patterns are firmly engrained, and do not change, even if they are maladaptive. A fear of heights or of flying, which might have developed from negative experiences that we may not even recall, can keep us from hiking up a lovely mountain or from flying off on a refreshing holiday, or even from emptying leaves out of the drain spout, if this simple task requires us to climb a ladder.

Sometimes our unconscious habits can be quite complex in their origin and their expression.

CASE: Gina's fear of her verbally abusive father had generalized over her 25 years of life into a fear of any authority figure, a hesitant manner of relating to anyone with a loud voice, and anxieties about dating men. Since there was no single image that she could use for conditioning herself to let go of all of these fears and defensive habits, her therapist helped her to *partialize* her problems. Gina made a list of all of her fears, then chose which one she wanted to work on first. She was able to *shape her behaviors# one at a time, to overcome the entire complex of her fears, and to eliminate the residues of real pain that she had experienced in childhood because of her abusive father.

Richard Bandler and John Grinder have taken the concept of conditioning several steps further. They use related techniques to establish more adaptive responses, or even chains of responses, of an emotional and cognitive nature. They touch the client at a randomly chosen part of his body, as a means of *anchoring* (conditioning) the response that they are teaching. For example,

CASE: George was so nervous about speaking in public that he would forget his materials, fumble helplessly with notes he had prepared and stuttered – despite the fact that he was an excellent teacher in a one-to-one situation. The therapist told him to picture himself in a lecture situation where he would be highly anxious. The therapist then touched George on one of his knuckles while he was imaging himself in that situation. Next, the therapist instructed George to picture himself feeling competent, relaxed and comfortable in giving a lecture to a large audience – while the therapist touched him on the next knuckle, near the first "an-chor." On touching each spot again, the feeling that had been anchored there was elicited. (*This is an important observation, in and of itself – as discussed below.*) The therapist then touched the two spots simultaneously, and the positive anchor neutralized the negative one. This conditioned George to relinquish his chronic, distressing patterns and to feel confident and comfortable when lecturing in pub-lic.

You might wish to explore this technique for yourself. Sit comfortably in a chair, and keep your hands in one position on your thighs throughout the exercise. Re-turn to a memory of something that made you sad. When you feel the sadness, press your right thigh with one finger of your right hand, and hold the pressure for a few moments. Then release the pressure without moving your hand from where it is resting. Now release the sad memory, taking a few deep breaths to blow away all traces of the feelings it evoked in your mind and body. Next, turn to a happy memory. When you feel the joy of it, press on your left thigh with one finger of your left hand, and hold the pressure for a few moments. Then release the pres-sure without moving your hand from where it is resting. Now release the happy memory, taking a few deep breaths to blow away all traces of the feelings it evoked in your body. Do not move your hands or fingers from the position they are in.

Now, simultaneously press both of the fingers that you used previously, holding the pressure for a few moments. Then return to the sad memory and observe the feelings that you experience. The following footnote will describe what many people find when performing this exercise. (The information is provided in a footnote so that you can be sure you did not read it subliminally and conform to a suggestion, rather than allowing yourself to have your own, unbiased experi-ence.)[35]

Anchoring can also be achieved through pairing of auditory, visual and visual-ized (imagined) stimuli. These techniques are practiced under the title of *Neurolinguistic Programming (NLP)*. They are potent methods for changing long-standing maladaptive responses.

NLP clearly demonstrates how easily and quickly the body may become linked through conditioning to respond to various stimuli – spontaneously in the creation of problems and therapeutically in resolving them. We saw in the case of George that once an image and its related feelings were anchored in a body location by a touch, the same image and feelings would be elicited on repeatedly touching the same spot. If a person happens to have a body sensation at a time when she has a negative experience, the memory of that experience may become linked to the sensation. At any time in the future that the same body sensation occurs, the memory of the negative experience may be invoked again. This may explain how traumatic experiences produce some physical symptoms, as discussed below.

Behavioral techniques can be highly effective in treating discrete problems such as phobias and focused anxieties, as in fear of heights or fear of speaking in pub-lic. Recent research also confirms that these techniques can be potently effective in treating depression, particularly when combined with antidepressant medica-tion. (Blackburn/ Moore).

RESEARCH IN PSYCHOTHERAPY

The efficacy of interventions in psychodynamic psychotherapy has been difficult to assess because of the subjective nature of the complaints that bring people to treatment. Various psychological tests (standardized, validated questionnaires) are the instruments that facilitate replicable research on psychological problems. There are well-validated tests for diagnosing anxiety, depression, attention deficit disorders, schizophrenia, and so on.

Research in psychotherapy is also hampered and open to criticism because of the difficulty of establishing long-term control groups that have received no interventions. People with problems usually speak with friends, family, clergy, and casual advisors such as hairdressers and bartenders, all of whom may be helpful (though unacknowledged) therapists.

Nevertheless, research that has been replicated in various settings by varieties of therapists and researchers confirms that psychotherapy is beneficial. The benefits of behavioral interventions have been particularly well documented, sometimes demonstrating a rate of efficacy that is comparable to or better than that of psychoactive medications for problems such as anxiety and depression.[36]

Cost-effectiveness is a very clear measure of psychotherapeutic interventions, and psychotherapy performs well by this criterion. For example, in one study, frequent users of medical clinics who received psychotherapy reduced their numbers of visits to doctors, and required fewer diagnostic procedures, fewer days in the hospital, fewer emergency room visits, and fewer prescriptions for medication (Cummings/ Bragman). Savings of ten to twenty percent in medical expenses were achieved. People with chronic pain who received ten group sessions for psychotherapy and relaxation methods reduced their clinic visits by thirty-six percent, compared with those who did not participate in these sessions. Annual savings were $100 per person (Caudill et al.). In another study, elderly people with hip fractures required fewer days of rehabilitation, and fewer rehospitalizations (Strain).

CONDITIONING THE IMMUNE SYSTEM

Research has revealed that conditioning (psychological reinforcement) can influence biochemical processes within the body. The most startling discovery in this area has been that our immune responses can also be conditioned through focused intent.

Experiments by Robert Ader and Nicholas Cohen have demonstrated that the immune systems of mice can be conditioned to respond to chemical stimuli. When experimenters gave mice saccharine mixed with cyclophosphamide (a chemical that produces severe abdominal pains), they found that the mice could be conditioned to respond to the saccharine alone as though they were receiving both chemicals. Some of the mice that received only saccharine after undergoing the conditioning process even died. In their search to understand why this happened, Ader and Cohen found that cyclophosphamide suppresses the immune system. They then deduced that the saccharine alone was having the same effect on the conditioned mice, to the point that they were succumbing to infections (Ader et al. 1979). Subsequent experiments confirmed this conjecture. .

This breakthrough has generated an enormous number and variety of studies and has led to further insight into how the mind and the immune system interact.[37]

Until recently, science had no explanation for how the immune system could *remember* an antigen, even many years after an initial exposure to it. People who have had measles or other diseases, or who have been immunized against these diseases in childhood, will be able to fight off similar viruses for many years, sometimes throughout the rest of their lives.

One possible explanation involves the white blood cells, which form a major component of the immune system. In the past few years it has been discovered that white cells contain many of the same chemicals that nerve cells produce at their junctures (neuropeptides). This suggests that the white cells may pass information on to the brain for storage. It also suggests that the mind may influence the immune system through these same neuropeptides. In effect, the white blood cells appear to act as an extension of the *central nervous system.*[38]

In many of the same ways that the mind can influence the immune system, it appears that it can also affect the cardiovascular system. Dean Ornish has shown that a combination of relaxation, meditation, and imagery therapy, together with regular exercise and a healthy diet, can bring about dramatic improvements in the condition of people with cardiac disease, even if they are very seriously ill and in need of cardiac surgery.[39] The Ornish approach is finding increasing acceptance as a technique for dealing with cardiovascular disease.

The interactions of the mind with the immune system have been called *psycho-neuroimmunology* (*PNI*). More on this below.

BODY-MIND THERAPIES AND SPIRITUAL HEALING

Many of the levels on which spiritual healing may occur overlap with the fields of practice of both conventional and unconventional psychotherapies.

Therapists who treat body tensions are directly addressing the broader interactions of people with their own bodies. Conceptualizations of mind-body unity help them to formulate physical exercises that can facilitate the therapy. Reich, Lowen, Pierrakos, Feldenkrais and others who have explored body-focused therapies have developed astonishing shortcuts to reaching, releasing, analyzing and clearing repressed emotional traumas. They have demonstrated that if the therapist is comfortable with touch and with intense emotional expressions, then clients will be more likely to benefit from the therapy. Healers may apply many of these same methods intuitively, without deliberately planning these interventions.

Conventional Freudian and psychodynamic psychotherapies have emphasized the analysis of thoughts and the cautious verbal exploration of repressed emotions. In this approach, the mind-body connection has often been ignored, or worse – avoided. Thirty years ago I was warned by several of my psychiatry instructors about the dangers of touching clients – a convention that not only persists today, but has actually been written into law in some states in America. Unfortunately, this blanket caveat becomes a feedback loop that can be initiated by the therapist, leading to unfortunate self-fulfilling prophecies. If, for whatever reason, therapists are not comfortable with touching, then they will surely convey their anxieties to their clients, by their verbal tone and non-verbal communications. These can then cue clients to believe that it might be dangerous if they are touched by their therapists (or by extension, if they are touched by anyone else). This can lead either to repression of feelings and avoidance of touch, or to anxieties if they do allow themselves such interactions. At the same time, therapists will feel that their caution is validated by their clients' anxious responses. This type of negative feedback loop is comparable to to the apocryphal story of the mental patient who snapped his fingers loudly and frequently "to scare away the tigers." When someone pointed out that there were no tigers around, he replied, "See! It works!" In the same way, a client's fears and a therapist's anxieties can be woven into a vicious circle that will benefit neither of the participants.

The issue of the avoidance of touch during psychotherapy has been complicated by cases of therapists who have sexually abused their clients. This has increased the professional pressure on therapists to avoid touching, lest their caring touch be misinterpreted as a sexual advance.

In contrast, most spiritual healers are comfortable with touching healees, and this may actually facilitate self-healing in all of the many ways that touch is comforting, enhances bonding and promotes relaxation.

Reinforcement theories and practices demonstrate how tensions can become linked to certain environmental or internal cues. In the example of Neurolinguistic Programming discussed above, we observed that through focused touch one can weaken old perceptions and negative emotional responses and anchor new, positive ones. Not only does this demonstrate ways in which initial tensions may get caught within the body, but it also provides a means for the therapist to introduce new emotional responses to old anxiety-triggering cues. Including the bodymind in therapy represents a major advance beyond basic conditioning techniques.

As we saw in the example of the laboratory mice, more recent research indicates that immune responses can also become conditioned. It is therefore highly probable that behavior therapy and other psychotherapies can also contribute to the treatment of illness through enhancement of immune functions.

These observations suggest bases for understanding the ways in which the body internalizes stresses, and then develops the disease patterns of malfunction. Similarly, these mechanisms point to ways in which healers may evoke more constructive and healthy patterns of behavior and bodily function without needing to activate psi powers.

A healer can provide relief from emotional problems in several other ways as well. For instance, healers usually take time to listen to their clients' problems. This is something that conventional doctors and nurses are doing less and less, as pressures from limited budgets and "efficient" medical management limit the time they spend with patients.

Healers may also be helpful when people become stuck in vicious circles of anxiety and tension associated with pain and illness. Simply offering hope may be enough to reduce anxiety, and may thus relieve tensions and reduce the discomforts of the entire vicious circle. The very suggestion that people may be getting help from spiritual healing may produce relief through placebo effects.[40] Healers may also discuss ways for healees to relax and avoid stressors, and this can have a similar result.

Some healers are adept at psychological counseling. They might be able to help people deal with secondary gains by confronting healees about their needs for attention which their symptoms and illnesses may generate, and by suggesting ways to approach difficult situations that they are avoiding.. Healers may provide emotional support, and also introduce hope, acceptance and comforting spiritual awarenesses.

Healers may thus be able to help their clients through a variety of clinical interventions, even if they have no special spiritual healing abilities.

Conversely, there may often be elements of psi and healing that appear in conventional psychotherapy – unbidden and perhaps even without the conscious awareness of the therapists or clients.[41] Some therapists can intuit their clients' tensions, inner conflicts and needs; some have a healing *presence* that clients warm to. Such assertions may seem speculative, but they are supported in research. A wealth of studies confirm that most people have psi abilities.[42] Similarly, several healing studies demonstrate that many people who make no claim to healing abilities can produce healing effects. It does not require a great leap of faith to believe that therapists of all varieties may introduce aspects of psi and healing in their therapy

PSYCHOLOGICAL CONDITIONING, FEEDBACK LOOPS, AND SPIRITUAL HEALING

There are many possible connections between conditioning and spiritual healing, especially touch-healing. During a laying-on of hands, a healer may reprogram a healee's responses to a stressful situation without even being aware of doing so, as in Neurolinguistic Programming (NLP).

My experience with NLP and my observations of spiritual healings lead me to believe that in most cases, far more occurs in healing sessions than a mere reconditioning of responses to given stimuli. Conditioning is a part but not all of what may occur in spiritual healing, the whole.

Psychoneuroimmunology introduces a new understanding of the potential control that the mind can exercise over the body. The mind's influence over the immune system is another clue to mechanisms whereby the body might "spontaneously" rid itself of diseases, including cancer (Everson/ Cole; O'Regan), with the help of visualization techniques (such as those described by Achterberg and Simonton), suggestion, or spiritual healing. The mechanisms involved may reside

within the healee (Roud), who can activate them when encouraged by the therapist
. There can be both positive and negative effects of the circular connections between the body and the unconscious mind. On the positive side, body functions such as blood pressure and temperature are kept within limits that are optimal for survival. If our heart rate slows down, our nervous system sends signals to accelerate it. If the ambient temperature rises, we sweat. These automatic reactions help to keep body processes functioning within physical and chemical ranges that are conducive to life.[43]

On the negative side, such feedback loops may become stuck in *vicious circles.* For instance, we have already considered how anxiety can produce muscle tension. If this becomes a chronic condition, it may eventually lead to muscular spasms → pain → anxiety → tension, → worse spasms → etc., in a cycle that can become difficult to interrupt.

Feedback loops function on psychological and social levels as well. In relating to other people, we all tend to adopt certain patterns. These are determined partly by the personality we develop starting at birth (Thomas/ Chess/ Birch), but to an even greater extent they are influenced by feedback that we receive in the course of our social interactions. Having adopted a particular set of patterns, we usually continue to follow them without much thought. If three-year-old Sally knows she can get a good response from her parents by whining, she will be likely to whine automatically when she asks for something. In turn, her parents will get used to her behaving as a whiner, although they may still complain about it. It is easier for them to respond automatically to her whining behavior than to encourage her to act in new ways, which would require them to think before reacting to her new approach. The rebellious teenager invites stricter controls, which stimulate further rebellion. The nagging wife sets off the drinking husband, who goes out and drinks because she nags, which only brings more nagging… and so on.

> *My, how you've changed since I've changed.*
> – Ashleigh Brilliant (no. 285)

Such relational patterns may be experienced as positive rather than negative, but they may still be maladaptive. A husband may be better at math than his wife, and may therefore take on the responsibilities of handling all of the bills and other finances in a marriage, while his wife may take on all the responsibilities for social arrangements. While such tacit, complementary partnerships may be convenient, they also leave each partner without the challenges that could develop their skills in the reciprocal areas of responsibility. In a more problematic variation on this theme, a child may be helped (in homework, tasks of daily living or making decisions) by parents to the extent that the child never develops the skills or confidence to care for herself. The parents feel needed in being helpful, the child feels nurtured in being cared for. We call these relationships *co-dependent.*

An understanding of these types of feedback loops is important to the practice of psychotherapy and healing in several ways. First of all, persons who are ill relate to the world as *people-with-symptoms.* Even though these symptoms may be troublesome or even devastating in their effects, people caught up in vicious circles may have difficulty in relinquishing the maladaptive behaviors that perpetuate their own suffering (Greenwood/ Nunn).

CASE: Morris, a young man in his early twenties had scarred corneas from infancy. When corneal transplants were first developed he was a prime candidate for this procedure, which promised to restore full *vision. Upon the removal of his bandages, his family and the doctors were all tremendously excited to see his response to his newly acquired ability to see.

After adapting to his new perceptions, Morris was absolutely delighted. Over a period of a few months, however, he became seriously depressed and finally committed suicide.

A psychological post-mortem revealed that it had been too difficult for him to adjust to life as a seeing person. He had been used to receiving extra help because of his blindness, and when he could see, he was expected to cope more independently. Unfortunately, he could not adapt to the new expectations.

This is an extreme example, but it illustrates the difficulty of adjusting to life after the symptoms to which a person may have become completely accustomed are finally eliminated.

In many instances people *consciously* wish to be cured of their symptoms, but *unconsciously* have numerous reasons for retaining them (secondary gains), and may therefore unconsciously resist improving.

Relatives of people who experience this kind of dramatic healing may similarly find it difficult to adjust to their recovery. The sick person may have been satisfying many needs of other family members through their illness, such as permitting or encouraging more open displays of affection or caring; providing an excuse for avoiding uncomfortable situations, such as traveling or work; or keeping a spouse or other relative from leaving the relationship. Their symptoms may also have become entangled in various power struggles for dominance or competition.

Relatives often subtly encourage family members to remain ill, or at least not to improve too rapidly or too completely.[44] In the illustration presented above of the drinking husband and the nagging wife, even if the husband were to stop drinking, he might encounter responses such as: "Well! So you forgot to stop at the bar on the way home today, did you?" or "I wonder how long this bout of sobriety can last!" Once we get ourselves into chronic vicious circles, it is difficult to extricate ourselves, and to differentiate between cause and effect.

> *The chicken is the egg's way of getting more eggs.*
>   –   Alan Watts

Psychotherapy may be able to break vicious circles of negative interactions, partly through elements of suggestion and gradual symptom relief. In addition, a positive seed may be planted in the minds of the participants, and the opposite of a vicious circle may be established. For lack of a commonly accepted phrase, I have coined the term, *sweetening spiral*. With healing we may feel better → be less tense → have less pain → feel better → etc. Similar sweetening spirals can develop in our social interactions as we progress through the healing process. Helping and pleasing others, they are more likely to help and please us.

Figure II-2 Positive transformation

Image courtesy of Keith Chopping

There are other subtle therapist-client feedback loops that can develop in the course of treatment. In conventional psychotherapies, and especially in psychoanalysis, the therapist is frequently cautioned against delving into psychologically conflictual areas too quickly, lest the client be overwhelmed by anxiety and possibly even decompensate into psychosis.

My personal experience as a therapist for people with a variety of emotional problems in America, England and Israel contradicts these caveats. If a therapist is comfortable with (and not afraid of) their clients' expressions of intense emotions, and if the clients have confidence in the therapist, then there is very little danger that clients will be frightened unduly by their own feelings, even when these are quite intense.

Similar observations about handling intense emotions have been made by therapists practicing *Gestalt Therapy* (Perls), *Transactional Analysis* (Schiff) and *Primal Scream Therapy* (Janov).

Doctors, patients and researchers frequently get stuck in self-validating feedback loops. For instance, conventional doctors may enjoy feeling competent and needed. They may relate to their patients in authoritarian manners, heightening their sense of superiority. Many patients are pleased to come to a specialist who can identify, explain and treat their problems, and are often comforted by being given a diagnosis and a prescription. By keeping the focus at the level of symptoms and physical illnesses, these doctors and patients avoid dealing with underlying emotional issues that may be causing and perpetuating the problems.

Similarly, healers and healees may also develop feedback loops of beliefs and practices.

A healer's reputation for bringing about rapid improvements in people's health might predispose healees to relinquish their illnesses more readily. Part of the success reported by healers may also be due to self-selection of healees who are emotionally ready to get better. Healees' high expectations when they come for spiritual healing may facilitate more rapid change, as compared with the expectations they might bring to other health care professionals whose methods are more familiar and predictable. Healees may need only the "permission" of the healer to abandon old habit patterns and adopt new ones.

In a complementary manner, healers who are not afraid of their healees' emotional intensity may facilitate releases of long-repressed conflicts and feelings, merely through their own acceptance that this is safe for the client to do.

Not all such feedback loops are positive. Healers' egos may become inflated when they are successful in helping people. They may push healees to improve when healees are not yet emotionally ready – because the healers want the aggrandizement of dramatic results and adulation from healees and other observers, not to mention the fees they may charge. Healees may choose healers of this sort when they are not ready to explore their psychological issues that lie behind their symptoms.

Feedback loops can act to slow the acceptance of healing within conventional medicine. Many in the scientific community have tended toward skepticism and disbelief in psi and spiritual healing, as they find the related phenomena too alien to their customary belief systems. (To put it more colloquially, healing exceeds their *boggle threshold*.) People who are uncomfortable with information that contradicts their world view are more likely to turn to others who share their disbelief for confirmation of the views they already hold, rather than re-examining (much less relinquishing) their perspectives.

Let me share a response I received in my search for surgeons to participate in a research project on healing:

> *Benor:* Here are some experiments on animals, plants, enzymes and humans, which show that healing works.
> *Surgeon.* Why are you giving me references from such weird sources? Aren't there articles in reputable journals?
> *Benor:* Reputable journals have been prejudiced against publishing such articles.
> *Surgeon.* How can I believe, then, that these are reputable studies? Why wouldn't better journals publish these results?
> *Benor:* It seems they aren't comfortable with this sort of thing.
> *Surgeon.* Well, what you tell me looks promising, but what will my colleagues think? What about my patients? They'll probably say I'm some sort of nut case!
> *Benor:* We can explain that we're doing this study to explore whether such forms of healing are effective. It may be that it's all due to the effects of suggestion. If that's true, the study will also be useful.
> *Surgeon:* I'll have to think it over…

Surgeon (at a later date): You know, if this stuff about healing were actually true, I'd have to change my whole belief system. It can't be true!

Such attitudes have nourished the prejudice against research into spiritual healing, and against the publication of related studies. There is a clear social resistance to change, and this is reinforced by feedback loops of social disapproval of any deviation from the norm.[45]

> *[I]gnorance of ignorance... is the fundamental limit of our knowledge.*
> – Francis Jeffrey

To examine spiritual healing we must be willing to rise above these defensive feedback loops, and change our established patterns of belief.

Healers who work in research settings anecdotally confirm many of the speculations voiced above. They tell me that people who are referred to them by doctors differ significantly in their expectations from people who are self-referred for healing. They find that there is often less readiness to change in the doctor-referred patients, who may have various emotional reasons for holding onto their illnesses. The referring doctor may actually want these patients to get well more than the patients do themselves.

Returning to positive feedback loops in spiritual healing, we often find that healing seems to require a strong belief on the part of healers in their own ability to heal successfully. To some degree, the greater their confidence, the greater the healers' effectiveness may be.

The healees' confidence in the healer is likewise an important factor in the relative success or failure of healing. Healers may function best when they can successfully establish an atmosphere of confidence in and enthusiasm for spiritual healing. The belief and encouragement of those around them may strengthen their own belief and confidence, and thus enhance their healing effectiveness.[46]

Conversely, disbelief on the part of observers or participants may inject a hint of uncertainty into healers' minds, which may then interfere with their healing effectiveness. This situation has been frequently observed by those involved in psi and healing research. Gifted subjects almost uniformly report that they feel inhibited by skeptical observers. Disbelievers and skeptics have viewed this as a *hedge* on the part of healers. They regard it as an excuse for evasion of scrutiny by investigators who might expose the healers (or psi subjects) as fakes or charlatans. While this may be so in some instances, it is unlikely to apply to the practices of many gifted, sincerely dedicated, and highly successful healers.

We will consider some of these issues further at the end of this chapter, under the headings of *transpersonal psychotherapy* and *psi and psychotherapy*.

Theoretical consideration of feedback loops

Cognitive feedback loops function on many levels. Gary Schwartz (1984) is a biofeedback specialist and researcher in bioenergy interactions. He hypothesizes that there are nine principal levels of processes. They link imagery and physiol-

ogy in a hierarchical system that ranges from cellular homeostasis to social interaction:

9. Social interactions
8. Motivation and belief
7. Education and insight
6. Cognitive-emotional-behavioral, and environmental self-control
5. Discrimination training
4. Motor skills learning
3. Operant conditioning
2. Classical conditioning
1. Homeostatic-cybernetic self-regulation

> [T]hese levels of processes are organized hierarchically, from the
> more micro to the more macro, from the physical and biological,
> through the psychological, to the social. We can therefore posit the
> existence of biological imagery, psychological imagery, and social
> imagery. Then we can consider the levels of psychoneurophysiologi-
> cal processes involved with each of these levels of imagery... (p. 36)

Through links of imagery connecting various levels of feedback loops,
Schwartz suggests that the mind may influence homeostatic mechanisms at
many levels. Therapists may intervene at any of these levels to help their
clients alter maladaptive patterns of body, mind, emotion and relational dysfunctions.

Schwartz's list is actually simplified. For instance, further levels are readily apparent in the physical system. We might subdivide regulative functions of level
(1) into atomic, molecular, cellular, tissue, organ, neurohumoral, energy field and
organismic levels. His observations are also relevant to visualizations used in
therapy. [47] At the opposite end of the spectrum, we may add various dimensions
of spirit. [48]

Schwartz further observes that systems tend to assume autonomous purposes
and to persist in the course set by their original purpose until new imagery initiates new connections within and between levels – in effect, "replacing the worn
or outmoded gears," "resetting the thermostat," or redefining the programming. [49]

More relevant to our discussion of therapies, there is the hierarchy of conventional medicine:

5. Spirit
4. Relationships
3. Mind
2. Emotions
1. Body

Each level has elements that influence the levels above and below it, and each is
influenced by those levels in return. Conventional medicine views the body as the

base of the pyramid, upon which all the others stand. Emotions, mind and spirit are seen as the products of the brain's electrochemical and hormonal processes.

Wholistic healing may reverse this hierarchy, viewing spirit as the base of the pyramid. Other models may equally apply, as discussed in the next chapter.[50]

SUGGESTION

> *Notoriously, throughout the ages, warts are likely to respond to any method other than the orthodox treatment of the time. Orthodox suggestion with or without hypnosis in the hospital or consulting room is less likely to result in the disappearance of a wart than, for example, the burying of half a potato in the light of a full moon. It may be of significance that many forms of treatment which are successful while the rationale is accepted by the therapist begin to fail when new information casts doubt on this acceptance. The sword of logic pierces the shield of conviction, and treatment technique is no longer successful, one of the main factors in the 'suggestion' situation having been eliminated. Too much, but still not enough, knowledge may thus be a handicap in therapeutics.[51]*
>
> – Louis Rose

Suggestion is a most effective way of bringing about changes in numerous physical and psychological conditions. Most people will respond favorably to verbal and non-verbal suggestions that their condition will improve – when these are given by a therapist or other authority figure. Pains will decrease, anxieties will melt away, blood pressure will go down, and the potency of other therapies may be markedly enhanced.

For instance, post-surgical pain can be reduced by telling people that after surgery they may feel some pain, but that the anesthetic will last for a number of hours, and they can then receive pain medicine if they need it. They are thus mentally prepared to deal with pain, so they don't get anxious when they experience it. Because they are not nervously anticipating the pain, their stress hormones and muscle tensions will be lower, they will not be as tense, and will deal more calmly with the pain when it comes. The experience of the pain will therefore not be as intense or distressing. This can markedly reduce the severity of the pain that they experience and significantly reduce the need for pain medicine.

Suggestions may be given directly, as described above, or they may subtly accompany other therapeutic interventions. A pill handed to you by a nurse with the comment, "Here, this will take your headache away," will have a more potent effect than a pill left at your bedside with the comment, "Take this if you need something for pain."

Suggestions can be profoundly effective when given by a strong authority figure and when applied deliberately, as will be discussed below.

Scope for the skeptics who doubt that spiritual healing is real

Sadly, suggestion is often viewed in Western medicine as a less legitimate intervention or a treatment of lesser value than other forms of therapy, rather than
being seen as beneficial in and of itself, or as a form of self-healing that can and
should be actively promoted.

For a variety of reasons, our society has come to denigrate the self-healing aspect of getting well. Doctors emphasize the contributions that they can offer
toward healing illnesses, such as prescribing medications and surgical interventions, but they largely ignore the contribution that healees bring to their own
healing.

Doctors label self-healing as a *sugar-pill* or *placebo reaction,*[52] with a pejorative
connotation. To a doctor seeking scientific evidence for the efficacy of a new
treatment, the placebo effect is a nuisance because it makes it difficult to judge
whether patients are responding to the treatment itself or simply to the suggestion
that they are receiving something that will help them.[53]

Let me illustrate this with a rather extreme example of components of suggestion in spiritual healing,. The following excerpt is a typical specimen of the
skeptic's point of view. With a clearly disparaging attitude, journalist George
Bishop describes first-hand encounters with several healers, including Dr. Harold
Plume and his mediumistic guide Hoo Fang,[54] *Kathryn Kuhlman,*[55] *Oral Roberts,*
and others.[56]

Bishop draws parallels between patients going to healers and patients being
treated with placebos by physicians. He feels that both healers and physicians can
alleviate symptoms, but that there is an added danger with spiritual healing. The
healer does not have the education to know when medical treatment is required,
in addition to or in place of suggestion or emotional release. Bishop believes that
because healing treatments are not derived from logical, linear mentation, they are
simply not to be trusted. He discounts the value of healing intuition, and clearly
has no familiarity with medical clairsentience.

Bishop is especially thorough in his portrayal of the intense emotional atmosphere of a revival meeting (often termed *faith healing*, or *spiritual healing* in the
US), and in his discussion of how this might contribute to the healings by heightening suggestibility. He himself attended such a gathering with specific
instructions from the program director of his radio station to expose the healer's
(presumedly) fraudulent operation. His personal experience as a skeptic struggling with effects of suggestion illustrates well the challenges generated by
unconventional healings. It is often difficult to move beyond the boundaries of
the perceived limits of our world!

> ...I stationed myself in the healing line and was soon in the glare of
> the floodlit stage shuffling toward an evangelist who appeared to be
> healing all comers.
> ...I felt myself caught up in the general excitement. The lights glar-
> ing down from the tent poles, the crowd chanting prayers and
> punctuating them with great shouts of thanks to the Lord when a heal-
> ing was announced, the organ hitting inspirational chords... I found
> myself getting anxious to do my part, to do what was expected of me.

I craned my neck to one side to see what the procedure was so that, when my turn came, I wouldn't foul the whole thing up... By the time I was two people away from the evangelist I regretted being there most heartily – I was not afraid of what would happen to me as much as I feared disappointing the crowd...

The healer merely gave Bishop a quick blessing and passed him along the line. Bishop was relieved that he had not given a poor performance.

...The feeling of participation, even though one... may be, as in the writer's case, specifically opposed to it, is fairly common to anyone not used to the glare of a public spotlight before a large, enthusiastic crowd... This eagerness to go along, tacked onto a basic emotional instability and honed by a team of shrewd, experienced selection assistants, makes for a successful, inspiring healing revival that has the audience reaching appreciatively for purse and wallet.

Bishop's views are typical of people who have only a superficial understanding of healing. The unfortunate consequence of such preconceived biases is that valuable observations, especially when they are still in their infancy, may be thrown out along with the bath water of rejected beliefs. We tend to automatically discredit whatever is unfamiliar, if it is not consistent with our conventional belief systems. [57] It is far easier to declare that such observations are foolishness than it is to re-examine our belief systems and perhaps be confronted with facts that don't fit and require revisions of the ways we understand and relate to the world.

The value of suggestion
Spiritual healing can teach us much about the power of suggestion.

A healer's greatest magic lies in a patient's willingness to believe. Imagine a miracle and you're half way there.
                    – Dana Scully (Gillian Anderson, *The X-Files*)

Many researchers consider suggestion to be a worthwhile, legitimate and important part of various forms of healing. For example, Jerome Frank (1961), a psychiatrist at Johns Hopkins University, presents a classic discussions on the value of suggestion in many contexts. Though this material was written 25 years ago, much of Frank's wisdom remains valid today.

  Frank begins by considering the complex skein of interactions between patients and their environments. Illness, especially when chronic, reduces patients' self-esteem, restricts their interactions with their environment, and eventually can lead to despair. In turn, this can cause family and friends to withdraw, since they feel that the patients' illnesses threaten their own security. The result is a vicious circle of increasing frustration and withdrawal on the part of all participants.

  Frank feels that modern medicine focuses mainly on the illness itself and its social ramifications, rather than on the whole patient and the greater context in which he lives. Non-medical healers regard illness "as a disorder of the total person, involving not only his body but his image of himself and his relations to his group; instead of emphasizing conquest of the disease, they focus on stimulating or strengthening the careseeker's natural healing powers" (p. 47). Frank adds that people's relationship with their world, including their spiritual world, is included in the scope of the healer's ministrations. Illness is viewed as a manifestation of the dysfunction of a person within their total environment. Although purely physical causes are recognized as contributing to disease, the healer does not concentrate on these exclusively. The function of the healer is usually far broader than that of the Western doctor.

The patient's background provides the healer with a wider range of *handles* for intervention than are usually appreciated or employed in Western medicine. Frank points out that patients come to a healer with a set of expectations about how the healer will conduct the treatment. The patient feels that the healer is endowed with either powerful personal abilities or the skill to channel potent forces from higher sources such as spirits, cosmic energies, Christ or God. With this mind-set, the patient is primed to respond to the healer's suggestions.

Healers act in ways that enhance these pre-existing expectations. They will usually first invoke the aid of potent outside sources of healing power – through prayers, channeling of spirit guides, or explanations of the cosmic energies that they feel they are transmitting. This also will allow them to disavow personal responsibility for any potential failures. If the healing either occurs slowly or does not materialize at all, the fault can be attributed to the external agencies, whose ways are inscrutable to human beings. Healers may also refer those patients whom they suspect they cannot help to other practitioners. These attitudes and maneuvers maintain the image of the healer's power, and thus preserve a high expectation of success in the patients.

The healer may act to concentrate the power of expectation even further. A group of patients whose hopes have been collectively raised through prayers, hymns, sermons or other invocations of higher powers will encourage the individual patient's anticipation of success. Such is the atmosphere of waiting rooms, prayer-halls and American faith healers' mass rallies. Expectations are further strengthened when patients see the healer appear to, or actually succeed in healing other patients.[58]

Frank also reviews the literature on persuasion from vantage of experimental psychology. He cites the work of Robert Rosenthal (1969) on experimenters in psychological laboratories who give a myriad of unconscious, subtle cues to experimental subjects, thereby inducing them to conform to the investigators' expectations. Experimenters may often be utterly unaware that they are subtly guiding their subjects in these sorts of ways to respond in particular manners.

The following is a classic example of unwitting effects of suggestion that were caused by experimenters' own expectations.

CASE: An experimenter gave several assistants a series of photographs to show to the experimental subjects, who were asked to rate the photographs according to the degree of success or failure demonstrated in the faces of the people in the photographs. Half of the assistants were told that previous experience had shown that the photos were rated successful, while the other half were advised the opposite – while the photographs were actually selected because they actually were rated independently as being neutral regarding a successful appearance. The assistants repeatedly obtained results that confirmed their expectations! They were not told that they themselves were the subjects of the investigation and were totally unaware that they had biased the results of the photograph evaluations.

Analysis of tapes of these interviews revealed multiple, subtle verbal cues given by the assistants to the subjects. Many of these cues were transmitted very rapidly, and thus were able to influence the subjects' first response (Rosenthal 1969).

This phenomenon of experimenter bias has since been labeled the *experimenter effect* or the *Rosenthal effect*. Similar results have been noted in numerous learning experiments. For instance, when laboratory assistants were told that a particular group of rats were more intelligent than average, they found that those rats performed better on maze tests, and the reverse occurred when they were told that the rats were less intelligent than average. When teachers were told that certain students were bright (though actually they were no brighter than average), these students improved on their intelligence test scores, while others in the same class did not (Rosenthal 1963).[59]

Frank also discusses the effects of suggestion in medical settings, where it is usually called the placebo effect. Doctors cue their patients to expect particular results from their treatments. Patients can even be led to expect physiological effects that are opposite to the known pharmacological properties of a drug. For instance, a woman with nausea and vomiting was given ipecac, which causes vomiting, but she was told that this medicine would calm her stomach. In this case, the drug had the suggested effect rather than its known pharmacological result of stimulating vomiting (Wolf 1950).

Frank considers numerous other factors in therapist-patient interactions that lead to psychotherapeutic change, and his book provides an excellent review of suggestion as an essential part of all forms of healing.

Lessons from medical anthropology

Emilio Servadio (1963) studied folk healers in the Italian countryside, focusing on unconscious and paranormal factors. He noted that patients' concepts of what disease means may vary enormously according to their cultural background. He found that "There is a whole range of pathological or psychopathological phenomena that are evidently, though quite unconsciously, lived from inside as an 'ill' more in a moral than in a universal medical sense."

Such ills may be blamed on numerous factors, including the *evil eye*, witchcraft, evil spirits or punishment for evil thoughts or deeds. Within these cultural beliefs, patients may appropriately anticipate that the required healing will come from a magician or healer with magical powers, rather than from a modern doctor. The magician interacts with the patient in a manner that is consonant with the patient's beliefs and expectations, and in this way provides a form of basic psychotherapy that is culture-specific. The magician addresses factors that are of vital importance to the patient under the patient's own belief system. Such factors would not even be considered by the modern doctor. Therefore, in these cases the doctor often has less success than the magician or healer.

A large number of studies have been published on culture-specific illnesses and their treatments.[60] David Landy presents a thorough review of such cultural factors as they interact with medical problems. None of these studies, however, seriously addresses the spiritual healing aspect of medical anthropology.[61] Even among experts in the area of healing practices in other cultures, many are unaware of the spiritual healing components in shamanistic healings.

Placebo effects

Placebo effects are responses by patients to inactive medication or treatment, and as such, they clearly represent reactions to suggestion. Approximately one-third of all patients with almost any ailment who receive any form of treatment will report some improvement. This is true even if the treatment is only a chemically ineffective sugar pill. The placebo effect, sometimes termed the *sugar-pill reaction*, has been thoroughly researched, and has obvious relevance to healing research.[62]

> *Belief is a potent medicine.*
> – Steven E. Locke and Douglas Colligan

The term *placebo* derives from the Latin, "I shall please" and "placate."

Placebo effects were recognized as early as the Sixteenth Century. In 1572, Michel de Montaigne observed that "There are men on whom the mere sight of medicine is operative." He gave the following example:

> [There was] a man who was sickly and subject to [kidney] stone, who often resorted to enemas, which he had made up for him by physicians, and none of the usual formalities was omitted... Imagine him then, lying on his stomach, with all the motions gone through except that no application has been made! This ceremonial over, the apothecary would retire, and the patient would be treated just as if he had taken the enema; the effect was the same as if he actually had... When, to save the expense, the patient's wife tried sometimes to make do with warm water, the result betrayed the fraud; this method was found useless and they had to return to the first. (Cogprints)

There are many variations on the theme of placebo reactions. For instance, people may have a stronger reaction to an experimental drug when they know that the comparison drug they may be given is also an active medication, rather than an inert substance (Rochon et al.). Experimental subjects have a stronger response to either placebos or aspirins when these are identified by a well-known brand name than when they are given blank tablets (Branthwaite/ Cooper). When subjects were given either chloral hydrate (a strong sedative) or amphetamine (a stimulant) without receiving any clues as to which they were getting, they were unable to tell the differences between the effects of the two medications (Lyerly et al.).

Figure II-3.

Cartoon by Bill Sykes, from *Caduceus,* 1988,
Issue No. 3, with permission of the publishers

The placebo reaction is not restricted to medicinal therapies, and may occur with any form of treatment. This forces ethical therapists to examine what proportion of their ministrations may stimulate placebo reactions. The seriousness of the problem in evaluating medical treatment is demonstrated by Beecher's (1961) research on a type of cardiac surgery called *internal mammary artery ligation.* The consists of tying off minor arteries that appear to divert blood unnecessarily away from the heart. Patients with angina (heart pains experienced upon exertion) who underwent this surgery reported definite improvement as a result of their treatment. Objective positive changes were even noted on their electrocardio-grams and on tests of physical exertion. The ligation involved major surgery, with all the attendant risks of hospitalization, exposure to anesthesia and invasion of the body. However, the benefits appeared to outweigh the risks and costs.

> *Our body is a machine for living. It is organized for that. It is its na-ture. Let life go on in it unhindered and let it defend itself, it will do more than if you paralyze it by encumbering it with remedies.*
> – Leo Tolstoy (1865-9)

Beecher conducted a study in which patients in one group were told that they would receive the cardiac surgery, but in fact were given only a superficial surgi-cal skin wound, while another group actually underwent the full operation. The findings of the study showed that those who had the sham surgery improved just as much as those who had the actual procedure. This was true even in regard to the objective measures by cardiograms and tests of physical stress.

Modern medicine has generally viewed suggestion and placebo effects with disdain and disparagement, complaining that susceptible patients waste doctors' valuable time with imagined problems that clear up without real treatment. What these doctors are actually saying is that people don't always bring them the medical problems that they were trained to treat. Many complementary therapists and spiritual healers know the wisdom of providing emotional support, so that people can gather the energies they need to heal themselves.

Placebo reactions are forms of self-healing. Though neglected and even denigrated by our mechanistic Western society, they are well recognized and widely used by shamans and other effective healers to help people deal with their diseases and dis-eases.

The mechanism by which placebos work is still a matter of conjecture. The unconscious mind is clearly prone to being imprinted with messages given by authority figures, as well as by oneself. Emphatic or authoritative statements or even simple repetitions of words may impact people deeply, programming their unconscious minds to respond to particular stimuli.

There is ample evidence that we ourselves program our own bodies to develop symptoms and illnesses through negative suggestion. Metaphors relating to body parts and functions abound. See Table II-2 for a sampling of these (Benor 2002).

If a person repeatedly says, "What a pain in the neck this is!" or "My blood pressure is rising!" it is not a surprise that their body may develop neck pain or hypertension. While this is not a researched observation, I have seen this occur many times in my practice of psychotherapy.[63]

Negative placebo effects (*nocebo effects*) may also occur. A common way for grim negative suggestions to be implanted is when a doctor tells patients they have only so many months to live. In effect, this is as bad as placing a curse on a person, whose unconscious mind may respond literally – conforming to the expectations of this authority figure by bringing an end to life at the predicted time.[64]

In traditional cultures, shamans may deliberately curse or put a hex on a person, sometimes causing illness and even death. While this may appear medically unethical, the shaman in many cultures serves the multiple functions of doctor, counselor, arbitrator of interpersonal and inter-tribal conflicts, and mediator between man and nature and between man and the spirit worlds. In these cultures, there are no police, no courts, and no jails. The shaman therefore uses nocebo hexes to enforce social justice – placing a curse on a person who is accused of a transgression and removing it when restitution has been made.

It is not surprising to learn that in different cultures there may be different distributions of common psychosomatic problems. For instance, placebos have been enormously helpful to German people suffering from stomach ulcers (up to 60 percent rates of healing), while far fewer respond in Brazil (7 percent). On the other hand, placebos administered in the treatment of hypertension are relatively ineffective in Germany, compared to the responses in other countries (Moerman). While this has yet to be confirmed in research, I would speculate that some of these differences relate to body metaphors that may be more common in one language than another, leading to more nocebo effects for those particular organs in one culture than in another.

Table II-2. Body terms and metaphors
BODY: disembodied; em--
HEAD: ache, big, brainy; bursting, cool, dense; fat; foggy; fuzzy; good; have -- examined; like a hole in the --; hot; -- in a good space; into your --; light; migraine; numbskull; pig; poor -- for; reaching a --; shit--; splitting; stuffed; swelled/ swollen; thick (head; skull)
MIND: blew; brainless; closed; deep; dreaming; drifting; --ful; fuzzy; --less; losing one's-; muzzy; nervous (wreck); of two --; open; out of one's --; shallow; sleeping on decision; sticks in my --; thinker; thinking straight; thoughtful; thoughtless
NERVES: found; high strung; lost; nerveless; -- of steel; nervous; nervy; rattled; raw; shaken; shattered; shot; some --; taut; tense; up tight; unnerving; wound up; wracked
EYES: black; blank; bleary; blinded; bright; burning with desire; clouded; cried my -- out; crinkled; cross-eyed (with tiredness or overwork); don't want to see; empty; clear; cross-eyed; scathing glance (look); keen; nobody home; red-eyed; sad; can't see straight; sharp; shot lightning from --; shut--; sight for sore --; tearful; tearjerker; twinkling; weeping -- out
NOSE: bent out of shape; big; blocked; bloody; brown --; cut off to spite face; gets up my -; nosy; Pinocchio; sniffs out; snooty; snotty; sticking -- into someone's business
EARS: cloth; deaf; don't want to hear that; --ful; keen; musical; sensitive; sharp
MOUTH: big; bigger than stomach; bite (has a -- to it; lip; -- off more than can chew; tongue); biting remark; chew (lip; on; up); fat lip; foot in --; chew on that; get chops around a situation; keep your -- shut; lip(s) (giving a bunch of --); loose tongue; sharp tongue; well, shut my --; shut up; slip of the tongue; smile; sour taste; speak (clearly; up); speechless; spit it out; stiff upper lip; tastes (bad, bitter, good, sharp, sour, sweet); teeth on edge; tight lipped; tongue in cheek; tongue tied; toothless; voice (cool; crooning; grating; piercing; warm)
NECK: full up to my --; pain in the --; sticking -- out; stiff
THROAT: can't swallow down; choking on--; choked up; cough up; craw full; full up to--; sticks in my --; (can't; hard to) swallow that; swallow down (feelings; insults; pride; sorrow)
CHEST: get it off --; puffed out
BREASTS: generous; giving; milk of human kindness; nurturing; weaning
LUNGS: breathe easy; blow (cool; gasket; hot and cold; it; off steam; stack; temper); blown away; can't breathe; catch one's breath; cough up; froze; holding one's breath; puffing; take a breather; take a deep breath; wheezing along
HEART: ache; attack; big; bleeding; blood boiling; blood pressure up; break; cold; cross your -- and hope to die; cruel; eating my -- out; empty; -- felt; frozen; full; --less; good; lonely; open; palpitated; pierced; pressured; --rending; sticks in my --; shaken to the core of my --; shut down; skipped a beat; sticks in my --; stopped; swelled; warm; warmed; weighing on --; -- went out to
BLOOD: bad; bloody; -- brother/ sister; cold --; -- froze; hot --; in my --; thin --; warm --
STOMACH: bellyaching; belly full; belly laugh; burns; can't --; digest; eaten up with (anger; jealousy); eating (away at; heart out; words); full (of it; up to); gut feeling; hungry for…; indigestion; in knots; lies heavy in gut; like a rock; rumbling; sick to --; sensitive; soured; spill guts; hard to stomach; stuffed; swollen; tears one's guts apart; want to (could) vomit
SPLEEN: --ful; splenetic; venting --
LIVER: bilious; jaundiced; liverish
KIDNEYS/ BLADDER: holding back; big/ little pisher/ pisser; pissed drunk; pissed/ peed off; wet knickers/ pants;
WOMB/ OVARIES: birthing (idea; project); broody; good flow; knocked up; menstrual (pre-, post); pregnant (expectation, pause)
PENIS/ TESTES: balls (has, no); balled/ balls-up; big balls; cock- (around; half; up); dick (around; face: head); jerk-off; prick; schmuck; wanker

VAGINA: cunt; loose; pussy, putz
SEX: coming on; fuck (--er; --ed up; off); loose; orgasmic; oversexed; pimp; sexy; sleazy; sowing (and reaping) wild oats; turned on; undersexed; whore
ANUS/ BUTTOCKS: ass; asshole; bum; butt (in, out); constipated; fart; fat; holding (back; in, tight); pain in--; shit (head, hot, face; in pants); soft as a baby's bottom; tight ass
BACK: -- against the wall; --breaking; --up; backed into it; bent (over backwards, all out of shape); get one's -- up; --off; pat on --; pain in --; sit up and pay attention; stiff
ARMS/ HANDS: black/ brown thumb; cold hands/ warm heart; pain in the elbow; even handed; fighting tooth and nail; fumbling; giving the finger; green thumb; ham fisted; heavy handed; lend/ lift a hand; light fingered; limp wrist; nimble fingers; raise a fist/ hand; rule of thumb; sharp elbows; sticky fingers; stiff arm; strong arm; all thumbs; thumbs up; tight fisted; two left hands
LEGS/ FEET: Achilles' heel; best foot forward; cold feet; dipping a toe in the water; down at the heels; earthed; flat footed; footing bills; foot in (grave, it; mouth); foot loose; grounded; kicking (the bucket; habit; myself; up a fuss); knees (turned to jelly; weak); on the ground; shot self in foot; stand (can't--; last--; make a--; -- firm; --tall); stepping out; sticking a foot out; stood up; stumblefoot; stand (alone; firm; proud; take a --; tall; to-gether; --up; --up and be counted); two left feet; walking a (narrow; straight) line; well heeled
MUSCLES: aching; bearing up; can't bear; burdened; carrying a burden/ load/ weight; flexible; frozen; hang loose; overburdened; pull self together; rigid (with fear); rooted to the spot; (having) shakes; stiff; in stitches; up tight; (sick and) tired; weighed down; wob-blies; wound up
SPINE/ SKELETON: being straight; burdened; can't bear it; carrying (a load; too much); chill went up my --; crooked; feel it in my bones; rigid; pointing the bone; shivers up --; shoulder up; spine chilling; --less; can't stand --; stand tall; stand up and be counted; stooped over; stooping to; stretched (too far; to breaking point); all twisted up; unsup-ported
SKIN: allergic to…; blanched; blushed; breaking out; burning up; made my -- creep; flaky; flushed; itching to; pale; picking (at; on); pimply; red faced; thick; thin; ticklish; tore my -- out
HAIR: bad hair day; bristled; hackles rose; hair turned grey; pulling my hair out; stood on end
TOUCH: aching to--; easy touch; smooth touch; tickled; touched; touching; touchy; un-touchable
FEEL: bad; calm; emotional (overcome); feelings (bury, frenzied, good, hide, hurts to…; uplifting), smooth; like square peg in round hole; tied up;
BALANCE: balanced; on an even keel; flipped out; im--; lost --; pushover; set me back; un--; upset
DEATH: cry oneself to --; dead (end; heat; on my feet; on target; roll over and play); --of me; (nearly) died of (embarrassment; fright; shame); doing me in; dying to; end of me; ending up; finished me off; killing me; nearly died; scared to --; sick to --; slays me; wish I was dead

It is clear that placebos can be potent activators for self-healing. Recent rsearch shows that placebo reactions produce changes in the brains of people who are suffering from depression (Leuchter AF et al.) and of people anticipating that they will receive nicotine (S. Gonzalez). One would expect similar findings with other placebo responses. It will be interesting to see whether there are any limits to self-healing responses as reflected in activity in the brain and the rest of the body.

Suggestion, placebo effects and the need for formal research in healing
Most skeptics, like George Bishop, regard spiritual healing as nothing more than a placebo. They tend to take an element of the whole to be the whole.

While placebo effects are invariably a part of healing and of every other therapy, as we noted above, this is no indication that they provide a full explantion for healing effects. Many other factors contribute to healings as well. The metaphor I find most useful to illustrate this is a set of weighing balances (like those for fruit and vegetables in country markets). We may put a big weight of stress in one pan, and in the other we put the efforts and therapies used to deal with the stress, adding measures of relaxation, proper diet, hope, will, love and healing to cope with stress. Finally, when we add suggestion to the pan, the balance tips, and healing occurs. A casual observer might thus assume that suggestion is the one factor that tipped the balance. But we should also be aware of the hope, will, love, healing, and other measures that have also contributed to the healing.[65] (See Figure II-4.)

Figure II-4. A variety of factors counter stress

It is probably more challenging to identify and weigh the causal factors that contribute to spiritual healing than to many other therapies. We have no reliable measures as yet to tell us whether various healers' contributions have the effect of adding a grape, a watermelon, or nothing at all to the balance of health and illness. No clear and consistent physiological responses of healing have been found that could provide such feedback. With effects of healing on the physical world we are no better off. While various effects of healing on water have been observed, these have not been correlated with effects of healing in humans or other organisms.[66]

The skeptics who focus only on suggestion effects may in fact be entirely right in the case of some healers. I have observed healers whose efforts seem to involve little more than a good bedside manner. But I have met many other healers who have brought about striking improvements in severe medical problems, when medicine had nothing more to offer. Were these due to consummate skill in suggestion? The controlled studies, especially with non-human subjects, would say otherwise.

The difficulty is that in any particular case it is impossible to identify which problems are responding to suggestion and which, if any, are responding to something else. It is for this reason that careful, double-blinded, controlled studies of healing (and all other forms of treatment) are needed.

Acceptance

Acceptance is one contributor to healing that is vastly under-rated clinically and sorely neglected in research. Randall Mason et al. noted that the rates of recovery for patients undergoing retinal detachment surgery varied widely. They studied psychological elements and the speed of wound-healing following this surgery, identifying a critical factor they called *acceptance*. This is the ability to take in stride the stress of having to undergo surgery. (See Table II-3, on the next pages.)

Patients with a high degree of acceptance appreciate the difficulties involved in their illness, but do not overreact or excessively fear the effects of surgery on their future. Although they may fear the procedures involved and may feel pain, they are able to remember that their discomforts will be temporary – which significantly alters their relationship with their illness. A high degree of optimism is maintained, even if these patients are warned that possible negative effects such as blindness may result from the surgery. By contrast, patients with low acceptance seem to lose perspective. They become overly concerned about the possible negative results of surgery, to the point that this may become emotionally overwhelming.

> *Acceptance of reality is the beginning of taking responsibility for your life. Often you can control events, but just as often you must adapt to circumstances beyond your control. How you adapt – the thoughts you think, the words you speak, and the attitude you take – determines your state of health and your chance for recovery...*
> – Barbara Hoberman Levine (p.40)

In this study, the authors found that the rate of physical healing correlated very significantly with the presence of high (contrasted with low) acceptance. When the study was repeated by the same authors, their initial findings were confirmed.

This factor has not been studied by others, but it seems likely that this contributes to the variability of responses to healing and other therapies. It may also be related to meta-anxiety, discussed later.

> *The Lord gave, and the Lord took away.*
> *Blessed be the name of the Lord.*
> – Job

The will to live

Curt Richter of Johns Hopkins University experimented on this important factor in healing – the will to live (Watson 1975). He arranged for rats to swim in a container of water that was roiled constantly so that the rats could not rest. He kept them in the water until they died of exhaustion. In this experiment, Richter found that wild rats died more quickly than domesticated ones. However, if the wild rats were removed from the water just prior to death, they quickly recovered. When subsequently returned to the tank, they continued swimming much longer than previously. The experience of being removed once from the tank had apparently given them hope. Thereafter they were willing to exert themselves for much longer periods than they had been before, prior to the hope-instilling experience.[67]

Lyall Watson, commenting on Richter's experiment, speculates that the rats' initial behavior may be similar to that of humans who have been *hexed* or cursed with a death-sentence. Such people can become ill, though they suffer from no recognizable medical problems. They may languish and die within a few weeks or days, despite all medical efforts to help them. Watson surmises that they die from loss of hope.[68]

The potentially fatal nature of the feeling of hopelessness was demonstrated in German concentration camps in the *musselman phenomenon*. Some prisoners survived for months under grueling conditions, but then gave up the struggle to live, perhaps because of despair that they would ever be free. They simply gave up and died, even though no additional stress was applied. No physical explanations for their deaths were apparent. They appeared to have lost the will to live.

Others have shown the opposite: the ability put off death. It is not rare to find people with terminal illnesses lingering past the medically predicted date of their death – when they have a specific reason to stay alive. They may wait for the arrival of a relative from afar, for the celebration of a date of particular importance (such as a family birthday, graduation or holiday).

Conversely, there are those who are ready to let go of their anchors to physical life but linger and linger – until a member of the family or significant other comes to a point where they can let go of the relationship. The decision to let go may occur without any direct communication between the relative who is holding on and the person who is waiting to die. The release to break the link to life appears to be communicated telepathically or in some other, spiritual dimension.

Suggestion, in summary

A major portion of the change that transpires following any treatment may be the product of suggestion or placebo effects. This is commonly taken to indicate that the complaints of patients who improve due to suggestion are imaginary or are caused by emotional or physical tensions, and are therefore susceptible to self-healing by suggestion that helps them to relax emotionally and physically. In fact, the opposite appears more likely: suggestion can alter many body processes, for illness or health.

Spiritual healing, combined with an element of suggestion, may inject a will to live and to fight for health, and/ or may encourage an attitude of acceptance. Few healers have considered these factors. Any of the organ systems that respond to suggestion could conceivably be responding to healers' interventions through the healers' suggestions, rather than through spiritual healing. The same is true for every other CAM intervention.

Table II-3. Acceptance scales

REACTION SCALES	Accepts totally	Accepts cautiously	Accepts with reservations	Accepts w/ resignation	Rejects
1. Reaction to Detachment	Confronts directly	Shaken but goes on	Advances fearfully	Bogged down	Trapped, back-to - wall
2. Reaction to Surgeon	Trusts	Praises hopefully	Seeks reassurance	Submits	Suspects
3. Reaction to Surgery	Optimistic about results	Hopefully certain about success	Vacillates in expectation	Unwilling to hope	Pessimistic
4. Reaction to Chaplain	Companionship in interpreting life	Seeks agreement for positive philosophy	Seeks consolation avoids discussion of inner conflict	Seeks respect for virtue and wisdom of compliance	Perceives as alien force or expects him to mourn
5. Reaction to Others	Meets on equal terms	Acts as host	Is not sure how to react	Expects sympathy and concern	Gives sense that no response to him is adequate

6. Coping Ability	Confident he can cope	Hopefully he can cope	Ambivalent about coping ability	Doubtful he can cope	Convinced he cannot cope
7. Self Care Ability	Able to do things for self and be helpful	Tries to do things for self and cooperate	Torn between desire to do and inability to do	Helpless and makes obvious displays of it	Acts as if entitled to services
8. Self-Image	Accepts self and situation (without special concern)	Displays positive image (embarrassed by dependence)	Keeps things in check (ambivalent about dependence)	Self-pitying (recognizes dependence with pity)	Sulking or detachment (angry over dependence)
9. Conversation	Willing to converse in depth	Pursues pleasant conversation	Caught between response and preoccupation	Talks mostly about affliction of self	Avoids open contacts with others
10. Philosophy of evil	Accepts bad with good	Wonders how the bad fits	Seeks assurance 'this is not all bad'	What can you 'do'? (It's Gods will)	'It's a dirty trick'

* From Mason, et al.

Alternatively, it is possible that some healers have a psychic gift of eliciting or stimulating self-healing, which is similar to the processes elucidated in studies of suggestion, but more powerful than suggestion alone (perhaps operating through telepathy, as reported by C. M. Barrows – in the section on hypnotic suggestion below). Well-structured, double-blind studies could probably tease out the more likely among these alternatives. With this hypothesis I do not mean to indicate that all placebo reactions are examples of spiritual healing. Clearly, many placebo effects are caused by socially induced suggestion, relaxation, or other self-healing processes that are familiar to Western medicine.

Let us now continue our exploration of the mechanisms of suggestion in greater depth.

HYPNOSIS

> *From a psychobiological perspective… so-called resistance is a prob-*
> *lem in accessing state bound information and transducing it into a*
> *form in which it can be utilized for problem-solving.*
>   – Ernest Rossi (1986a, p. 87)

Historical Notes
In the middle of the nineteenth century, Franz Anton Mesmer developed and popularized a treatment he called *animal magnetism,* which was the forerunner of hypnosis. In his induction technique he performed what he called *magnetic passes* around the body of the subject. Initially he did this with iron magnets, but later he used only his hands. Part of the process appears to have involved elements common to laying-on of hands healing. Today, hypnosis is a widely practiced form of psychotherapy, practiced without passes of the hypnotists' hands around the body.

Hypnosis is a special, extremely powerful method of harnessing the power of suggestion. In some instances it seems to involve direct activation of unconscious portions of the mind.[69]

Profound awareness of an amazing spectrum of bodily functions and alterations in these functions may be brought about through hypnosis. Pains resulting from many different causes can be markedly reduced or eliminated using this technique (McGlashan et al.). This discovery has led to a better understanding of pain, by demonstrating that it is more than a series of messages transmitted from a part of the body that is experiencing stress or damage. The subjective experience of pain is much more complex than the stimulation of nerve endings that transmit impulses to the brain, which in turn interprets them as physical pain.

Under hypnosis, people may be told that they have no pain, and their pain can simply stop. This may be pain from an injury to the skin such as a burn, from a deeper injury like surgery, from cancer or from other causes. In some cases, people will report that their pain has completely disappeared. At other times they report that it is still there, but they don't have to attend to it or worry about it, and it no longer bothers them. People under hypnosis can also be induced to alter their memory of chronic *intermittent* pain, so that they are not left with the hopeless feeling that they have nothing to anticipate but more pain throughout the rest of their lives. This is a true blessing, because the anticipation of more pain may produce as much misery as the experience of pain itself.

From the mid-nineteenth century, hypnotic suggestion has even enabled surgeons to operate without anesthesia. The effectiveness of hypnotic anesthesia for major surgical procedures has been confirmed in the scientific literature in recent decades, in cases of cardiac surgery, hemorrhoidectomy, ligation and stripping of veins, and caesarian section (M. Murphy 1992c).

When patients' limbs are placed in plaster casts and their joints are immobilized for a considerable length of time, the joints typically "freeze" and are very stiff and painful upon removal of the casts. If the limbs are immobilized under hypnosis, even for weeks at a time, they may not freeze up or hurt when movement is resumed.

The skin is especially responsive to hypnotic suggestion. If a deeply hypnotized subject is told that she is being touched with a hot iron, she may develop redness and even blistering on her skin – although in actuality she has only been prodded by the finger of the hypnotist. Herpetic blisters (shingles) may also be brought out under hypnosis (Ullman 1947). Several cases of *fish-skin disease* (congenital ichthyosiform erythrodermia of Brocq, abbreviated as ichthyosis), which is normally unresponsive to medical treatment, showed dramatic improvement under hypnosis (Barber 1984). Burns heal more rapidly with hypnosis (Ewin 1979), and warts may be eliminated, even under a very light trance. The hypnotist simply suggests that after several days (commonly two weeks) the warts will fall off – and in a high percentage of cases they actually do. It should be noted that numerous forms of suggestion other than hypnosis may be just as effective in removing warts (e.g. painting the wart with food coloring).[70]

Hypertension (high blood pressure) responds well to hypnosis (Benson 1977; Deabler, et al.), as does asthma.[71] Bone fractures can also heal more quickly under hypnotic suggestion (Ginandes/ Rosenthal). In isolated cases, it has even been shown that traumatic bleeding may be halted through hypnosis. Patients who are prepared for surgery with hypnotic suggestions bleed very little during their operations.[72]

Another form of bleeding that hypnosis has been helpful in controlling is hemophilia. Persons suffering from this condition lack particular biochemical clotting factors, due to genetic defects. This causes them to bleed profusely from even the slightest cut, often for days. They may even die from a minor cut if they are not treated. Yet with hypnosis hemophiliacs can undergo dental extractions, a procedure that normally could be fatal to them (Dubin/ Shapiro; Fredericks). In one investigation, the need for blood transfusions in a group of child hemophiliacs was decreased by a factor of 10 over the period of a year, through the application of self-hypnosis (LaBaw).

Hormonal changes can also be induced under hypnosis. Favorable responses have been recorded with diabetes (McCord 1968b), menstrual problems (Erickson 1977), and breast development (Staib/ Logan; R. Willard).

There are four styles of hypnotic induction that are commonly employed. The first utilizes monotonous, rhythmic stimulation such as focusing on a swinging

pendulum or other object, while the hypnotist suggests that the subject will relinquish control over their own behavior to the hypnotist. The second method
solicits the active cooperation of the subject, and uses more direct suggestions
without elaborate inductions (Bandler/ Grinder). The third is a more coercive
technique, in which hypnotists forcefully assert their authority, and subjects instantly relinquish their will to the hypnotist (Haley 1973). And last, there is self-
hypnosis, in which subjects give themselves instructions to enter a hypnotic state.

Most people are able to enter some levels of the hypnotic state, ranging from
slight relaxation to very deep trance. Estimates vary, but a commonly accepted
standard for conventional approaches is that one in five can enter a clinically useful trance state for deep work, while two out of three can do light suggestive work
under hypnosis. Practitioners of NLP estimate that the percentages are actually
much higher. Herbert Spiegel and David Spiegel developed a screening test for
hypnotic susceptibility. They instruct the prospective subject to roll their eyes
upward as far as they can. The less the iris is visible below the margin of the upper eyelid, the greater the susceptibility to hypnotic induction. Close to three-
quarters of those who are rated susceptible using this test are able to enter a clinically productive trance state.

In deeper hypnotic states, a person's unconscious mind appears to be open to
interventions by the hypnotist. Vast stores of memory that are normally inaccessible to the subject's conscious mind may thus be explored. For example,
hypnotic subjects may connect with long-forgotten memories from very early
childhood. This is called *hypnotic regression.* Some even claim to recall memories from their own birth, and from within their mother's womb (Chamberlain;
Verny).

Taking this a big step further, there are practitioners who report successes in
resolving clients' current-life problems by accessing memories of past-life traumas that have persisted into the present, and are causing current difficulties.[73]

When subjects relinquish control of their conscious mind, the hypnotist is able
to suggest alternative behaviors that the subjects' unconscious mind may accept.
To some extent, the hypnotist is able to reprogram perceptions and conceptualizations held by the subject.

Dabney Ewin, a burn specialist and hypnotist, suggests that people experiencing
severe trauma may commonly enter a state that is equivalent to a trance. This
makes them particularly open to helpful suggestions from those who are caring
for them – for example, to minimize their acute suffering from pain.

With deeper trance, the subject may also have no memory of what occurs under
hypnosis.

Hallucinations suggested by the hypnotist may be fully experienced by subjects
in all sensory modalities, as though they are real experiences. For example, if a
person in hypnotic trance is told that there is a cute animal or a dangerous one
present in the room, they will behave exactly as if they can perceive that animal
in the room. Conversely, sensory blocks may also be inserted under hypnosis.
Subjects may report negative hallucinations, meaning that they are unable see
something that is actually present, because the hypnotist has told them that it is
not there. When commanded by the hypnotist, subjects may develop "amnesia"
for particular events or thoughts.

The response of the unconscious mind under hypnosis is extremely concrete and literal, so hypnotherapists learn to state suggestions very precisely and sequence them with care. An apocryphal story tells of a hypnotherapist who lost contact with his subject when he gave the instruction: "You will hear nothing but the sound of my voice." The subject stopped responding entirely, and it was only hours later that she wakened on her own. She had apparently taken the first four words of his instruction literally, and had simply tuned out all sounds, so that she could not accept any further suggestions.

Lessons from hypnosis have been helpful in other areas of therapy. The unconscious mind can respond quite literally to suggestions that are given without hypnosis, in a concrete manner which is similar to that observed under hypnosis. Psychotherapists often find that their patients have absorbed parental injunctions or scoldings during their childhood, which have remained imprinted in their unconscious minds. Words said forcefully in anger, such as "You stupid fool!" or "You clumsy oaf!" can have devastating consequences for the rest of a person's life, if the unconscious mind is deeply imprinted with that negative self-image.

Subjects may also be induced to do strange and ludicrous things by stage hypnotists for the amusement of an audience. For example, when told that they are chickens, they may cluck, flap their arms, and make other bird-like motions. Such casual and frivolous use of hypnosis is deplorable, and sometimes dangerous. People may accept hypnotic suggestions in such a setting that can open up serious conflicts that were previously repressed. In one such case, the subject did not come out of a stage trance for several days.

Usually, subjects will not cooperate with suggestions that go against their moral or ethical beliefs. If told to do something that would compromise their normal standards, subjects are likely to simply refuse, or even to waken from the trance. However, a crafty hypnotist may trick subjects into believing that they are acting under circumstances which accord with their morals, when in fact they do not.

Research on hypnosis

Despite centuries of study, experts do not agree on what actually occurs during hypnosis, much less on the mechanisms that could explain it.

Leslie LeCron, an expert hypnotist, suggests that the trance state achieved by mesmerists of the last century may have been different from the hypnotic states commonly invoked today. For one thing, the mesmerists' inductions lasted four or five hours. The passes of hands around the body performed during these inductions may also have produced effects not often observed today, and this may account for some variations between early and modern reports. For example, the mesmerists refer to a very deep stage of hypnosis called *plenary trance*, which was achieved through inductions that lasted several hours, and which is rarely seen today. In this state, physiological processes such as heartbeat and breathing were markedly reduced. Subjects were reportedly able to remain in plenary trance for up to two weeks, not requiring food or drink. These deep trances may also account for some of the early reports of successful induction of psi abilities under hypnosis.

Theodore X. Barber, who researched hypnotic phenomena for many years, reviewed many studies on the physiological effects of hypnosis (1961, 1984). He found that many of the results achieved with hypnosis can be equaled by subjects who apply their own willpower, enhanced with suggestion, to physical tasks – *without hypnotic induction* (Barber 1984; Barber/ Wilson 1978). Barber maintains that what is commonly assumed to be a special mental state that is induced under hypnosis does not actually represent an altered state of consciousness or trance. Critics of his views propose that all subjects who follow suggestions are, in effect, in a state of hypnosis. Barber counters with the criticism that studies of hypnotic phenomena rarely include a control group that is given suggestion without hypnotic induction (Dienstfrey 1991). When Barber studied both modalities, he actually found that suggestion without induction was superior in producing many effects (Barber/ Wilson 1978).

Sheryl Wilson and Theodore Barber identify a personality type that they find in about four percent of the population. This is an individual who has the ability to visualize mental images extremely vividly, is able to enter trance states quite easily, and is prone to experiencing psi phenomena. (Psi abilities were found in 92 percent of the specially gifted individuals studied). The authors suggest that psi does not correlate with hypnosis per se, but rather with people who have this special personality type, who are excellent candidates for hypnosis.[74]

Other reports mention the expression of unusual abilities under hypnosis. A. Shaposhnikov describes hypnotic techniques that he claims can develop the subject's ability to stimulate tissue regeneration, and can also produce *skin vision,*[75] telepathy and psychokinesis.[76]

At the turn of the century, C. M. Barrows reported numerous cases in which he telepathically suggested away the pains of toothaches, facial spasms and other disorders. He was able to achieve excellent results even when his subjects were completely unaware that he was attempting telepathic hypnotic anesthesia. He carefully experimented with the states of mind that he experienced during the treatments, and found that focusing on the desired outcome state in the patient was successful, but that intentionally attempting to transmit the instructions was not.

In the mid-nineteenth century, a number of scientists explored the use of remote hypnotic inductions in treating selected subjects (Dossey 2000; Inglis 1992). Under carefully controlled conditions, they were repeatedly able to induce trance from a distance, and in some cases even to transmit orders that were executed by the subjects.

Leonid Vasiliev, a (then) Soviet researcher, also found that he could induce hypnotic trances telepathically with selected subjects, and he was able to demonstrate this repeatedly in controlled laboratory conditions.[77] Under hypnosis, some of his subjects' muscles could be made to contract when the hypnotist pointed his finger at the muscle or at its innervating nerve. Benson Herbert[78] (1973) noted that under hypnosis, some of Vasiliev's subjects could locate the position of the hypnotist's hand when their eyes were closed and the hypnotist's hand was not touching their body.

Vladimir L. Raikov another (then) Soviet researcher, claimed that he could suggest to hypnotized subjects that they were reincarnated artists, thereby enhancing their artistic talents (Ostrander/ Schroeder 1970; Raikov 1971). This technique was effective only in subjects who were able to achieve deep trance states

Another case that may have some relevance to the subject of hypnosis regards the legendary Indian rope trick, performed by fakirs in the East. Typically a performer gathers an audience around him and introduces his young assistant. The fakir throws a rope into the air, where it hangs – apparently suspended without visible support. The fakir then sends his assistant (usually a young boy) up the rope, and the boy disappears at the top. When the fakir orders him down, there is no response. The fakir, seemingly enraged, grabs a sword and climbs the rope, also disappearing at its nether end. Sounds of a struggle are heard, and the dismembered body of the boy comes tumbling piecemeal down to the ground. The fakir then climbs down the rope with his bloody sword, and covers the bodily remains of the boy with a cloth. A moment later he removes the cloth and the boy rises, unharmed.

A lawyer named Mordecai Merker presents a case for *mass telepathic hypnosis* as an explanation of the Indian rope trick. His evidence, which he feels would stand up in any court, consists of eyewitness accounts from a variety of apparently reliable people who claim that they have photographed performances of the rope trick, but found that the photographs did not correspond with their recollections of the events. The pictures showed that the fakir and his assistant were throwing the rope up into the air, but that the rope merely fell to the ground and the fakir and his helper simply remained motionless for the duration of the performance, as did the audience.

Eric Dingwall (1974) has reviewed much of the same rope trick evidence, but he discounts it as unreliable, though he does not clearly state his reasons for rejecting it. Marc Cramer, while avowing that this sort of phenomenon is merely a stage magician's trick, presents photographs that seem to support Merker's descriptions.

On the basis of the evidence, my impression is that mass hypnosis seems a possible explanation for the Indian rope trick.

Skeptics propose that some cases of apparent healings, especially *psychic surgery,* could likewise be the result of mass hypnosis. In psychic surgery, developed separately in the Philippines and South America, healers perform surgical operations without anesthesia or sterile technique. Healees experience no pain, no bleeding and no infections. Their wounds heal very rapidly, sometimes instantly. Some psychic surgeons use knives, others insert their bare hands into the body. Here, the mass of evidence reviewed in *Healing Research, Volume III* appears to contradict the hypnosis hypothesis and support the legitimacy of the psychic surgery.[79]

Possible mechanisms for physical effects experienced under hypnosis
One hypothesis commonly adduced to explain many of the above-mentioned physical phenomena is that people have a natural ability to control the muscles surrounding their blood vessels. This is normally a function of the autonomic nervous system, and as such it usually is not under conscious control. However, biofeedback clearly demonstrates that it is possible to bring such processes under volitional control.

Reddening of the skin under hypnosis is caused by dilation of blood vessels, and sophisticated laboratory instruments have been used to confirm capillary vaso-lation and accelerated capillary blood flow in the skin under hypnotic suggestion (Grabowska 1971). Bleeding can be halted by the reverse process, i.e. by a constriction of blood vessels. Warts may disappear because they are deprived of nutrition due to constriction of blood vessels, which can lead to their "starvation," so that they dry out and slough off. It is hypothesized that cancers might similarly be deprived of sustenance (Clawson/ Swade 1975) by restriction of blood flow. Blistering under hypnosis is harder to explain. By extending known mechanisms, one could imagine blood vessels dilating sufficiently to allow exudation of serum into the tissues.

In treatment of asthma, the primary effect of hypnosis is probably a relaxation of muscle spasm in the bronchioles (tubes leading to the lungs). There may also be allergen-specific antibodies or other blood components that respond to hypnosis.

Many hypnotic effects may derive in part from psychological relaxation, for example in cases of hypertension, asthma, hormonal disorders and other conditions. Emotional relaxation could interrupt the vicious circle of stress → anxiety → tension → physical symptoms → more anxiety → more tension, etc.

No one has yet proposed adequate hypotheses to explain cases in which ichthyosis and hemophilia improve under hypnosis. Though we cannot as yet completely explain cases like this and many others, it is evident from studies of hypnosis that a vast potential resides within each of us for self-healing, which can be released through the power of suggestion.

Hypnosis and psychotherapy
Hypnosis has been used in psychotherapy (hypnotherapy) to explore the unconscious foundations of patients' symptoms and conflicts. With hypnotic treatment, memory may be remarkably improved, and patients may achieve extremely accurate recall of minute details from earlier years. During this form of therapy, psychological defenses are often bypassed. Even memories that were repressed following severe traumatic experiences may be retrieved. Details that otherwise might require many weeks or months to extract from the patient's memory can be recovered rapidly - in a few sessions or sometimes even in a few minutes. Emotional blocks can also be lifted under hypnosis, either temporarily or permanently. Unconscious causes underlying neurotic conflicts may be more rapidly revealed in a hypnotic trance, while they might not otherwise be recognized by patients in their conscious state. [80]
The following is another composite example.

CASE: Fourteen-year-old Linda was raped by a boyfriend. She felt utterly betrayed and devastated. She dared not tell her parents or friends, because she knew they would blame her rather than offer understanding or support. Within days, she "forgot" about the incident – that is, she pushed it out of her conscious mind.

Being a bright student, Linda buried herself in her studies. She went on to a successful career in nursing, which provided much satisfaction. It also gave her the excuse to avoid romantic involvement with men, because when she was not working evening shifts she was sleeping off her exhaustion from overwork.

But when the initial bloom of satisfactions in her professional advancements faded, Linda became depressed. A hypnotherapist suggested that she go back to the past under trance to discover the reasons for her unhappiness, and the rape came to light in the first session. Working through the emotional trauma associated with this experience took many months. Linda had to get in touch with and resolve her buried feelings of fear, outrage, anger, betrayal, guilt, sadness, and deep hurt. Eventually she was able to do all of this, and she came to a healing place of forgiveness for herself and for the rapist. Linda then stopped running away from relationships, and was happily married several years later.

Posthypnotic suggestions are another potential benefit of hypnotherapy. These are instructions given by hypnotherapists to subjects who are in hypnotic trance, with the injunction that they should be acted upon at some point after the subjects come out of the trance, and without memory of the hypnotic instructions. Subjects will usually carry out these suggestions very literally, as though their unconscious mind has been specifically programmed for the task. This can be helpful in strengthening patients' resolve, and in reminding them to change unhealthy habits such as overeating and smoking. For instance, suggestions may be implanted to make people recall the consequences of smoking every time they reach for a cigarette.

One classical use of hypnosis, developed by Charcot and Freud, is to explore the repressed conflicts that can lead to *hysterical* (today called *conversion*) symptoms. These are symptoms of psychogenic origin, typically a paralysis or sensory malfunction, which derive from unconscious psychological conflicts. Sufferers may experience intense anger, inappropriate sexual arousal or other unacceptable feelings. In order to protect them, their unconscious mind can completely isolate these emotions from their conscious awareness. In some cases it might even go further – causing the body to develop physical symptoms – in order to prevent them from taking any action based on the forbidden emotions, and simultaneously to punish them for harboring these feelings. Such physical symptoms can influence a very wide range of sensory and motor systems throughout the body. They may include muteness, deafness, blindness, various paralyses, and many types of altered sensations, ranging from lack of dermal sensitivity to severe pains.

Multiple personality disorder (MPD) is another syndrome for which hypnosis can be an effective therapy.[81] People with MPD have unconsciously split off and isolated the aspects of themselves that they find difficult to integrate within their primary personality. Sexual feelings are commonly isolated in this way, when the superego (conscience) cannot tolerate them. This rather extreme method of coping with uncomfortable feelings is usually found only in cases of very severe abuse in childhood. The helpless child may use this drastic form of psychological self-defense to isolate intensely painful experiences and feelings that would otherwise be overwhelming. Once the pattern of personality splitting under stress is established, it may be repeated in later life in reaction to further traumas.

Under hypnosis, the various personality "multiples" can be contacted and addressed by the hypnotist. With long-term hypnotherapy it is possible to help people reintegrate the divided aspects of their personality.[82]

While multiple personality is an extreme and rather rare disorder, all of us have functional personality splits in varying degrees. You may behave differently toward your wife than you behave toward your children, and in yet another manner with your neighbor, your doctor, and so on. There are facets of yourself that come forward and other facets that are reticent to express themselves to each person with whom you interact. At various times you may be more or less open to the characteristics in yourself that you consider to be faults or shortcomings. In effect, you may appear to be a different person under different circumstances, in different moods, or surroundings and in the context of different relationships.[83]

A caution is in order here. It must be stressed that only competent therapists should use these hypnotherapy techniques. Injudicious probing of unconscious conflict by untrained hypnotists can produce anxiety, and can even worsen existing psychiatric conditions. Furthermore, posing leading questions during hypnosis can produce false responses and false memories if subjects compliantly respond to direct or implied suggestions.

Hypnosis does not necessarily require the repeated intervention of a therapist. Some people can learn to hypnotize themselves. The actual mechanisms of self-hypnosis remain unclear, inasmuch as subjects are giving the instructions to themselves, while simultaneously receiving and responding to them. It has been hypothesized that people may be able to "split" their consciousness in order to achieve this.[84] Self-hypnosis can aid relaxation and reinforce posthypnotic suggestions.

Hypnosis and spiritual healing

Hysterical symptoms (conversion reactions) usually develop in people with a type of personality that responds well to hypnosis and other sorts of suggestions. This means that almost any authoritative figure can initiate healing if they suggest a behavioral improvement while the patient is in a supportive setting, or conversely, if they command the hysteric to change in the context of a highly charged, emotional environment. Such atmospheres are deliberately created by some American faith healers. Although no studies have been conducted in this area, it seems entirely within the realm of probability that interventions by religious leaders, appropriate prayers, visits to shrines such as Lourdes, and other suggestive curative agents could produce relief of conversion symptoms. This is especially likely in the case of revival meetings, where the contagious enthusiasm and emotionality of audience participation could further heighten the effects of suggestion. Because of this possibility, medical professionals have suspected that many reports of the more dramatic spiritual healings are considerably less miraculous than naive lay people might take them to be. Such cures are presumed by many knowledgeable health practitioners to be no more than remission of conversion symptoms.

Psychiatrist William Sargant illustrates this assumption. He studied a variety of healers in many countries and concluded that their ministrations were successful almost exclusively when they were dealing with hysterical symptoms.

My own impression is that this conclusion is too exclusive. Some alleged healings undoubtedly are due to such processes, but I seriously doubt that all of them are. The clearest evidence showing that healings in revival meeting settings are far more than conversion reactions comes from a remarkable book by Richard Casdorph. Investigating a series of healings by the late Kathryn Kuhlman, who gave healings in these sorts of settings, Casdorph provides detailed case presentations, including confirmation of organic disease by examining physicians, with laboratory and X-ray reports (reproduced in the book) prior to and following healing treatments, and personal reports by the healed and their families. Casdorph describes cured cases that include bone cancer, malignant brain tumor[85], disabling arthritis, and multiple sclerosis. When supported by laboratory studies, none of these could be due to conversion reactions.

Explorations of Multiple Personality Disorder point to some possible explanations for healing. Remarkable studies show that when one "member" of a multiple personality is allergic, diabetic, cross-eyed, exhausted, or in other ways physically debilitated, other personalities in that same individual may not exhibit these physical conditions at all, or not to the same degree.[86] Furthermore, EEGs and brain blood flow patterns may differ when different personalities are present.[87] These findings seem to indicate that the body is an extension of the mind, and that with a change of mind the body can be dramatically transformed. From this we can speculate that spiritual healing may in some cases entail the relinquishing of unhealthy templates for mental/ emotional personality or self-image, and/ or conversely, the acceptance of healthy ones.

In cases of MPD, a fragment of the self may be identified that has access to knowledge about all of the separate personalities. This "individual" may become an ally of the therapist in integrating all of the parts into a coherent whole.

Within the cast of MPD characters there may be yet another personality that is so much more aware and emotionally centered as to be an enormous resource to the therapist in helping the client sort out the other, emotionally troubled personalities. Ralph Allison and Gretchen Sliker, each writing about MPD and related phenomena, call this the *Inner Self-Helper*. At times this fragment of the MPD patient's self appears to possess wisdom and knowledge far exceeding what would be expected in a person suffering from this syndrome, and this may indicate access to something in the realms of transpersonal dimensions, such as a collective consciousness or *higher* consciousness.

Healers often suggest that healees call upon their *higher selves* to find the causes and cures for their illnesses. Such suggestions may allow us to access aspects of our unconscious minds that we otherwise would not exercise. In my own practice I have found that some people indeed possess this hidden ability. We have only to call upon our inner self-helper to discover the reasons for our woes and problems, and to learn the steps we may take to alleviate and correct them.

A more conventional explanation of this phenomenon is also possible. It may be that we clothe our unconscious mind or spirit in the raiment of a wise advisor, who can interpret the messages we receive from our deeper selves or from transpersonal awareness. Each of us could endow our inner helper with the personality and garments we imagine she or he merits, much as each of us molds our picture of the Deity worshipped in our culture to resonate with our own expectations.[88]

> *God created man in His image and man returned the compliment.*
> – Jerome Lawrence/ Robert E. Lee

Suggestive and hypnotic influences without formal induction
Helpful responses to suggestion may also occur in cases other than psychosomatic illness. People suffering from emotional problems or physical ailments of organic

origin may benefit from suggestion as well. Here I have deliberately used the word "suggestion" rather than "hypnosis," although this distinction is in itself a gray area.

The late Milton Erickson was one of the world's greatest hypnotists (Rossi 1986a). He was especially skillful in using methods of suggestion in clinical situations without invoking the classical hypnotic trance (Haley 1973), as in the following incident involving his son.

> Three-year-old Robert fell down the back stairs, split his lip, and knocked an upper tooth back into the maxilla. He was bleeding profusely and screaming loudly with pain and fright. His mother and I went to his aid. A single glance at him lying on the ground screaming, his mouth bleeding profusely and blood spattered on the pavement, revealed this was an emergency requiring prompt and adequate measures.
>
> No effort was made to pick him up. Instead, as he paused for breath for fresh screaming, I told him quickly, simply, sympathetically and emphatically, "That hurts awful, Robert. That hurts terrible."
>
> Right then, without any doubt, my son knew that I knew what I was talking about. He could agree with me and he knew that I was agreeing completely with him. Therefore he could listen respectfully to me, because I had demonstrated that I understood the situation fully. In pediatric hypnotherapy, there is no more important problem than so speaking to the patient that he can agree with you and respect your intelligent grasp of the situation as he judges it in terms of his own understanding.
>
> Then I told Robert, "And it will keep right on hurting." In this simple statement, I named his own fear, confirmed his own judgment of the situation, demonstrated my good intelligent grasp of the entire matter and my entire agreement with him, since right then he could foresee only a lifetime of anguish and pain for himself.
>
> The next step for him and for me was to declare, as he took another breath, "And you really wish it would stop hurting." Again, we were in full agreement and he was ratified and even encouraged in this wish. And it was his wish, deriving entirely from within him and constituting his own urgent need. With the situation so defined, I could then offer a suggestion with some certainty of acceptance. This suggestion was, "Maybe it will stop hurting in a little while, in just a minute or two." This was a suggestion in full accord with his own needs and wishes, and, because it was qualified by a "maybe it will," it was not a contradiction to his own understanding of the situation. Thus he could accept the idea and initiate his responses to it.
>
> As he did this, a shift was made to another important matter, important to him as a suffering person, and important in the total psychological significance of the entire occurrence - a shift that in itself was important as a primary measure in changing and altering the situation.

The next procedure… was a recognition of the meaning of the injury to Robert himself – pain, loss of blood, body damage, a loss of the wholeness of his normal narcissistic self-esteem, of his sense of physical goodness so vital in human living.

Robert knew that he hurt, that he was a damaged person; he could see his blood upon the pavement, taste it in his mouth, and see it on his hands. And yet, like all other human beings, he too could desire narcissistic distinction in his misfortune, along with the desire even more for narcissistic comfort. Nobody wants a picayune headache; if a headache must be endured, let it be so colossal that only the sufferer could endure it. Human pride is so curiously good and comforting! Therefore Robert's attention was doubly directed to two vital issues of comprehensible importance to him by the simple statements, "That's an awful lot of blood on the pavement. Is it good, red, strong blood? Look carefully, Mother, and see. I think it is, but I want you to be sure."

Thus there was an open and unafraid recognition in another way of values important to Robert. He needed to know that his misfortune was catastrophic in the eyes of others as well as his own, and he needed tangible proof that he himself could appreciate. By my declaring it to be "an awful lot of blood," Robert could again recognize the intelligent and competent appraisal of the situation in accord with his own actually unformulated, but nevertheless real, needs.

By this time Robert had ceased crying, and his pain and fright were no longer dominant factors. Instead, he was interested and absorbed in the important problem of the quality of his blood.

His mother picked him up and carried him to the bathroom, where water was poured over his face to see if the blood "mixed properly with water" and gave it a "proper pink color." Then the redness was carefully checked and reconfirmed, following which the "pinkness" was reconfirmed by washing him adequately, to Robert's intense satisfaction, since his blood was good, red, and strong and made water rightly pink.

Then came the question of whether or not his mouth was "bleeding right" and "swelling right." Close inspection, to Robert's complete satisfaction and relief, again disclosed that, all developments were good and right and indicative of his essential and pleasing soundness in every way.

Next came the question of suturing the lip. Since this could easily evoke a negative response, it was broached in a negative fashion to him, *thereby precluding an initial negation by him,* and at the same time raising a new and important issue. This was done by stating regretfully that, while he would have to have stitches taken in his lip, it was most doubtful if he could have as many stitches as he could count. In fact, it looked as if he could not even have ten stitches, and he could count to twenty. Regret was expressed that he could not have seventeen stitches, like his sister, Betty Alice, or twelve, like his brother, Allan; but comfort was offered in the statement that he would have more stitches than his siblings, Bert, Lance, or Carol. Thus the entire situation became transformed into one in which he could share with his older siblings a common experience with a comforting sense of equality and even superiority. In this way he was enabled to face the question of surgery without fear or anxiety, but with hope of high accomplishment in cooperation with the surgeon and imbued with the desire to do well the task assigned him, namely, to "be sure to count the stitches." In this manner, no reassurances were needed, nor was there any need to offer further suggestions regarding freedom from pain.

Only seven stitches were required to Robert's disappointment, but the surgeon pointed out that the suture material was of a newer and better kind than any that his siblings had ever had, and that the scar would be an unusual "W" shape, like the letter of his Daddy's college. Thus the fewness of the stitches was well compensated.

The question may well be asked at what point hypnosis was employed. Actually, hypnosis began with the first statement to him and became apparent when he gave his full and undivided, interested and pleased attention to each of the succeeding events that constituted the medical handling of his problem.

At no time was he given a false statement, nor was he forcibly reassured in a manner contradictory to his understandings. A community of understanding was first established with him and then, one by one, items of vital interest to him in his situation were thoughtfully considered and decided, either to his satisfaction or sufficiently agreeable to merit his acceptance. His role in the entire situation was that of an interested participant, and adequate response was made to each idea suggested.

This vignette illustrates how dramatic changes can be brought about in the experiences and attitudes of people with severe physical problems, using the principles of hypnosis. Erickson's suggestions to his son were effective on numerous levels. First the child's *meta-anxiety* (anxiety about being anxious, with the distinct potential for leading a child to panic in a frightening situation) was eliminated. His attention was then redirected to aspects of the situation that his parents showed to him in a new light, demonstrating not only their understanding of the situation, but also their control over it. The child's pain was either reduced via his altered perception, or forgotten when his attention was redirected.

Another example shows how hypnotists may also be able to dramatically influence people's *self-perceptions* and *self-image*. Erickson was asked to help a 14 year-old girl who had developed the idea that her feet were much too large. Over a period of three months she became increasingly withdrawn, not wanting to go to school or church, or even to be seen in the street. She would not allow the subject of her feet to be discussed, and would not go to a doctor. In the role of a physician, Erickson visited the girl's mother, who happened to be sick at the time.

Studying the girl, I wondered what I could do to get her over this problem. Finally I hit upon a plan. As I finished my examination of the mother, I maneuvered the girl into a position directly behind me. I was sitting on the bed talking to the mother, and I got up slowly and carefully and then stepped back awkwardly. I put my heel down squarely on the girl's toes. The girl, of course, squawked with pain. I turned on her and in a tone of absolute fury said, "If you would grow those things large enough for a man to see, I wouldn't be in this sort of a situation!" The girl looked at me, puzzled, while I wrote out a prescription and called the drugstore. That day the girl asked her mother if she could go out to a show, which she hadn't done in months. She went to school and church, and that was the end of a pattern of three months' seclusiveness. I checked later on how things were going, and the girl was friendly and agreeable.

This interaction demonstrates how extensive changes in a person's attitudes and behaviors may be introduced through subtle clinical suggestions. My training and experience as a psychiatrist would suggest that the girl was suffering a severe phobic or obsessive disorder, or even a psychotic decompensation. She seemed to be withdrawing from reality into an inner, autistic world created out of her own fears. I would have predicted that prolonged psychotherapy, possibly involving the prescription of tranquilizers, would be required. Yet Erickson brought about dramatic improvements in this girl's perceptions of herself and in her behavior through a single meeting with her.

It is impossible to know, from the meager details provided, whether this girl had a very limited, focal phobia, or whether other psychopathology was present. While it is difficult to generalize from a single case report, such a dramatic improvement in a teenager with such severe symptoms suggests that others with similar problems might benefit from these sorts of interventions. In other cases, however, more generalized or more severe pathology in the child or in the family might prevent such brief interventions from having as dramatic results as reported in this case.

Explaining hypnosis

Authorities on the subject disagree about the nature and even the substance of hypnosis. Furthermore, numerous experiments demonstrate that merely through an exertion of their own willpower, people can accomplish much that is currently thought to be possible only under hypnotic trance. Bandler and Grinder, following in the footsteps of Erickson and other gifted therapists, have developed hypnotic techniques that do not require elaborate trance induction processes (such as monotonous repetition of instructions or focusing the eyes on a pendulum). In their systems of therapy,[89] hypnotic induction is achieved very rapidly by the therapist simply giving instructions to the subject. This supports Barber's contention that hypnosis may be no more than a mutual agreement between hypnotist and subject that each will behave in particular ways, since people can perform most of the feats ascribed to hypnotic trance when they are not hypnotized, merely by exerting maximum effort.

Although opinions differ on what hypnosis is, several common denominators appear in the classical descriptions of this type of phenomenon:

1. focusing of attention on limited sensory cues and thought processes;
2. exclusion of extraneous sensory cues and thought processes;
3. instructions given in a repetitive, even monotonous manner by oneself or another person, usually in a rhythmic pattern, or instructions given in an authoritative manner by another person, as in NLP;
4. a particular mind-set, with a series of culturally determined expectations for behavior conducive to hypnotic trance;
5. enhanced access to unconscious memories and repressed emotions;
6. improved abilities to imprint new information in memory;
7. increased control over bodily functions;
8. enhanced ability or even an internal compulsion to apply oneself to specific goals, once these goals have been impressed upon the mind under hypnosis;
9. behavior throughout the hypnotic and posthypnotic states resembling everyday conduct as governed by the unconscious mind, e.g. using literal, concrete, simplistic logic and thought processes (such as taking the hypnotist's suggestions literally, and repressing awareness of parts or all of the hypnotic experience after waking from the trance state);
10. ability to suspend belief and judgment in accordance with suggestions given, even when they contradict everyday reality;
11. ability to isolate and compartmentalize mental and emotional aspects of the self.

Experts disagree about the psychological mechanisms involved in hypnotic trance. Hypnotists also differ in the criteria for depth of trance. Moreover, no commonly accepted method of objectively identifying the presence or depth of a trance state has yet been developed.[90] Some feel that suggestions given to subjects in light trance may ultimately (although perhaps not immediately) be as effective as those given in deep trance. Others feel that hypnosis is merely a socially determined agreement between hypnotist and subject that each will behave in particular ways, since people can perform most of the feats ascribed to hypnotic trance when they are not hypnotized, merely by exerting maximum effort.

The mechanisms by which people are able to greatly enhance their control over mind and body while they are in the hypnotic trance state is not clear. One hypothesis is that under hypnosis, greater concentration allows them to apply their mental energies more effectively. This can be compared to learning disciplines that allow maximal use of physical force, such as karate. Merely by concentrating, without apparent hypnotic induction, practitioners can achieve feats of unusual strength, such as stretching the body rigidly between two chairs with only head and heels supported. The question remains whether they may be practicing the equivalent of self-hypnosis (whatever that is).

Another theory is that unconscious portions of the brain and/ or mind are accessed under hypnosis, which would explain the greater range of stored information available and the enhanced control over physiological functions.

If we take this a step further, we encounter the further possibility that vast potentials for self-healing exist within us, but they are blocked by cultural disbeliefs that hypnosis is able to bypass. Given permission, encouragement and support, we are able to activate our self-healing capacities.

Underlying the effectiveness of suggestion and hypnosis is the ability to alter our perceptions and beliefs about ourselves. Our emotional and physical pains may not change in their intensity, but our beliefs about them may shift, so that they do not make us as anxious, afraid, depressed or bitter.

> [T]he belief system that possesses perception is not just abstract in nature. It is fuelled by imaginative, creative power. It is an active, dynamic shaping of the meaning and impact of the world by the mind. And so to rethink the world in the act of seeing it means putting out a deep re-appraisal of what we see. Then we start to experience the world as being different...
>
> – John Heron (p. 55)

Metaphors and imagery in suggestion and hypnosis

Metaphors and imagery may form another basis for suggestion. For example, Milton Erickson might talk at length with a patient about planting and growing tomatoes. Embedded within his discussion would be imagery that could be translated metaphorically to apply to the patient's life and problems. "*Planting tomato seeds*" could suggest planting seeds of inspiration or change in the person's life. "*Preparing the soil, watering plants, and applying fertilizer*" could suggest giving the proper attention to details that might help to bring the patient's projects to fruition.

In our everyday use of language, body-related words are frequently used metaphorically to describe our relationships, and body parts are used in metaphors that describe our emotional reactions. For example, a particular weakness may be called someone's *Achilles' heel*. An annoying person or situation may become *a pain in the butt* or *a headache*. I might *have a hard time swallowing* something that *I don't want to hear*. Someone who complains may be *bellyaching*, or speaking in other metaphoric body language, as summarized earlier in Table II-2.

If we say such phrases emphatically or repeat them often to ourselves, or if others say them to us, we may begin to tense up the part of our body that is addressed in the metaphor. Chronically tense muscles can eventually go into spasm and cause serious pain. This can in fact often be a mechanism by which we develop an enormous range of somatic symptoms, such as tension headaches and bellyaches.[91]

More serious illnesses can develop when chronic tensions activate the autonomic nervous system and neurohormonal mechanisms. Psychosomatic theory recognizes that there are particular illnesses that can be strongly correlated with chronic stress, including asthma, hypertension, thyroid dysfunction, peptic ulcers, irritable bowel syndromes, migraines, and more.[92]

Chronic stress can also affect the immune system, leading to the development of other illnesses and syndromes. These include allergies (particularly those that are manifested in the skin – our boundary with the world around us), chronic fatigue syndrome, fibromyalgia, and cancer.[93]

When we delve even further into the physiological mechanisms of disease and healing, we find that there is an energetic aspect to the body that can play a crucial role in these regards. As discussed in greater depth in Chapter 3, the mind can shape our *biological energy fields*, which in turn will influence the physical body.[94] The contributions of biofields to health and illness add another dimension to *mind-body* (or *bodymind*) medicine.

Many doctors, nurses and other conventional caregivers focus exclusively on the physical body and are completely unaware of any of these additional mechanisms for developing symptoms and illnesses. They will therefore treat the symptoms of these illnesses, but ignore underlying stresses that may be contributing to, or actually causing and maintaining the problems. This is like tightening the lid on a pot of soup that is boiling over, rather than turning down the heat or removing the pot from the stove.

By exploring the meanings of symptoms and helping patients to vocalize what their bodies are saying, we can decipher the physiological metaphors for dis-ease in people's lives that often manifest as disease. This is one of the main contributions of wholistic medicine.

Yet another benefit of healing metaphor can be found in the generalization of imagery that can be internalized in very personal ways, thus influencing many related problems that may be present in numerous nuances and variations. Conflicts that grew and generalized from a single original trauma may be cleared, completely outside of conscious awareness, through the imagery and metaphors.

CASE: Jeremy came to therapy for help to overcome a fear of speaking in public. Though he was a successful bank manager, he found himself panicking when he had to speak to any group of people and therefore made a poor impression at public and corporate meetings. Understandably, this was seriously hindering his career. As he began work in psychotherapy, he found that this was actually only one of many anxieties – all relating back to early lessons he had learned in growing up with very strict and critical parents. He was afraid to explore new situations, anxious when faced with several choices, browbeaten by his wife, and still unable to contradict his parents when they made unreasonable suggestions and demands.

By working with imagery of a monster that was always critical, Jeremy was able through this single root of his problems to reach many of the branches on the tree of anxieties that grew out of his childhood experiences. Just as anxieties may generalize from a single traumatic experience,

Such generalizations of an initial problem may escape notice, and may not be dealt with through more direct approaches that focus on cognitive awareness and that may miss some of the emotional and other branches of problems. Metaphors and imagery reach into a person's unconscious and help to heal whatever problems resonate with them.[95]

It seems very likely that Erickson's stepping on the girl's foot dealt metaphorically with many more branches and roots of problems than were apparent in the chief complaint of her feet being too big.

More on suggestion and spiritual healing

Reports reviewed above have demonstrated that good hypnotic subjects are also likely to have psi abilities. The nature and reasons for this correlation are as yet unclear.

Vasiliev's observation that under hypnosis subjects' muscles contracted when the hypnotist pointed at them or their innervating nerve may be explained in several ways. Telepathic control may be involved, although this seems unlikely, since Vasiliev arranged for anatomically naive experimenters to point to nerves, and the appropriate muscles still contracted. One could theorize that the subjects were able to read the minds of the experimenters. The existence of this sort of *super-ESP* would be stretching accepted psi explanations a little, but it is not beyond the realm of the psychologically conceivable.[96] Another possibility is that the hypnotic state produces greater receptivity in the subject to a field or emanation originating in the experimenter. This might or might not be related to healing energies.

The receptors for psi impressions in the brain have yet to be identified. The correlation of hypnosis with psi suggests that identical or overlapping sections of the brain might be involved in both phenomena. This would appear a fertile subject for research with brain imaging.[97]

Wilson's and Barber's observations on the power of simple suggestion and maximal investment of efforts may be relevant to healing in several ways. Some healings may partially or totally owe their success to suggestions of the hypnotic type.[98] Subtle but potent suggestions, perhaps even given without conscious intent by healers, may produce some of the improvements attributed to healings. A few healers use hypnotic suggestions deliberately for relaxation and hypnotherapy, in addition to giving spiritual healing., They report that each of these approaches enhances the effects of the other.

Healers may also release blocks to innate self-healing abilities, either through spiritual healing or through suggestion. Many healers claim that they do no more than catalyze or activate healees' own healing powers. Healees may then heal their own body/ mind.

Some studies have demonstrated that hypnotic trance and other alternative states of consciousness enhance abilities to use psi faculties (Honorton/ Krippner 1969). I do not know of any study on the effects of hypnosis per se on healers' abilities. But since healing gifts often appear in persons who are gifted with other psi faculties, there is every reason to believe that hypnosis might be a helpful adjunct in teaching student healers, or enhancing already developed healing abilities.

Further observations have supported this theory:

1. Meditation has been recommended as a path to developing healing abilities.[99] Meditational and hypnotic states of mind appear to overlap in many ways.

2. Most healers report that they enter a meditative state when they are performing healings.

3. Healers who invoke the aid of spirits often use variants of hypnosis to enter the mediumistic (channeling)[100] state, in which they diagnose and heal.

The compartmentalizing of aspects of the self under self-hypnosis resembles in a loose way what occurs in Multiple Personality Disorder. One portion of the self gives hypnotic instructions and another portion accepts them. Such splittings of the self indicate that the mind can isolate modules of consciousness or of the personality, which then appear to function independently of each other. Consciousness of the *self* as an entity may alternate between the modules, or may coexist within separate modules.

When a split in consciousness occurs, it may appear to the self and to others that an alien personality is *possessing* the individual. Some healers claim they can help by eliminating "possessing entities," and it may be that in some such cases they are actually healing unconscious mental splits.[101]

The complexities of these issues can only lead one to agree with William James: "Our science is a drop, our ignorance a sea."

BIOFEEDBACK

O Lord, there are tubes in the body which should be opened and tubes in the body which should be closed. If it be thy will, let those which should be open remain open and those which should be closed remain closed.

– Jewish prayer

Biofeedback is something we all use without being aware of it. A child learns to aim the spoon into her mouth through visual biofeedback. She sees her hand moving and learns to adjust the movements of her hand and arm muscles so that the food lands where she wants it to.

Electronic and mechanical devices may provide people with information about their internal physiological states, of which they are otherwise unaware. Many of these states are highly correlated with emotional tensions, and this is why they form the basis for lie detector tests, for example. These technologies can also be helpful learning tools to help people control their own internal reactions to stress. An electrode may be placed on the body to measure the surface *electrical skin resistance* (ESR) or underlying muscle tension. The measurements are displayed on a dial or translated into a tone that varies with the amount of tension. People can use this feedback to alter their internal states, because they can immediately tell when they are doing something that either increases or decreases their tension. Biofeedback can thus enable people to gain control over many body processes.[102]

Through biofeedback we can learn to influence many other physical functions on a conscious basis, even those that are normally controlled by our body's unconscious, automatic regulating mechanisms. This control is not achieved spontaneously because under normal conditions there is no sensory feedback available. For example, you are usually unaware of your heart rate or blood pressure and therefore have no way of either increasing or decreasing them. With biofeedback you can learn to alter these and many other of your body's functions voluntarily.

In biofeedback therapy, subjects are told to alter the level shown on the dial or to change the tone that represents a given physiological measurement. Instructions are not provided on how to do this, since no effective descriptions for this process have yet been found. In fact, subjects will usually do best if they do not force themselves to relax. Elmer Green (1972) observes:

> In active volition that you use for operating the normal muscles, the harder you try presumably the better it works, but when you're trying to control the involuntary nervous system the harder you try the worse it works. You have to learn how to talk to the body, tell it what you want it to do, have confidence in it, allow it to do it and detach yourself from the results. If you don't do that it won't work. If you keep worrying about it or thinking about it won't do it. It's like forcing yourself to go to sleep, which doesn't work very well either. And about the time you give up trying to force yourself to go to sleep then you go to sleep.

Through trial and error a subject can learn to control these functions, just as infants learn to control their hands from visual, tactile and kinesthetic feedback, by trial and error. Any variable that can be measured can serve as a basis for such training.

It was once thought that muscles in the gut and arteries are not susceptible to voluntary control. This was because people had not received adequate feedback to know when these "involuntary" muscles were contracting or relaxing. A simple example, which you can test yourself with a little patience, involves the muscle of the iris of the eye. By providing feedback with a mirror, many people can learn to contract or dilate that muscle voluntarily. The average learning time is about an hour. Self-regulation may provide control over tensions in the following areas: voluntary muscles throughout the body (I learned to wiggle my ears with feedback from a mirror); portions of the bowel; blood pressure; heart rate; selective blood vessels (as in your hands to make them warmer or cooler, or in your head to relieve migraines); brain waves; skin resistance, and more.[103]

Mechanisms for self-regulation

Biofeedback is helpful for treating the pain component of many diseases. Pain is usually associated with tension. It may result from the primary disease process, as with inflammation of joints in arthritis, or from inadequate blood supply caused by spasm in the arteries or blockage of blood vessels, as in arteriosclerotic heart disease. Pain can also lead to the vicious circles of anxiety → tension → muscle spasms → pain → more anxiety → etc. For example, with tension one may get headaches caused by spasms of muscles attached to the skull.

Relaxation may also help with breathing problems. Asthmatics may also find themselves in vicious circles: wheezing → anxiety → tension in the body → constriction of airways → more wheezing → more anxiety → etc.

In these situations, a twofold healing process may be activated through relaxation. First, relaxation breaks the vicious circles detailed above. Second, releasing tension in various muscles may interrupt the primary disease processes. When bronchioles relax, we breathe easier, literally and metaphorically. If arteriospasm is reduced by relaxation, more blood will reach the affected tissues, and the pain will ease. Other mechanisms that have not been so well studied may also be involved at the primary level, such as reduced inflammation due to hormonal, immune, or other biochemical alterations that are enhanced through relaxation.

Implications for self-healing
Illnesses may be initiated when people are sensitized in particular organ systems. Some seem to have skin, bowels or other parts that are more sensitive than usual. In such cases, these parts of the body respond first to tension. They may have had spontaneous internal feedback learning (unassisted by external feedback loops) via sensations of bowel tension, skin sweating, rash, or other subtle cues. They may have been sensitized cognitively (by the examples of relatives with organic or psychosomatic illnesses) to pay attention especially to these parts of the body.their use of language may program their unconscious minds to tense up particular parts.

Initially, control is initiated through anxieties and tensions that produce pain or other problems. In therapy, improvement of these same conditions is facilitated under hypnotic or other suggestion - which reverse the direction of previously learned controls, producing relaxation rather than tension.

One psychologist provided an exotic example of this sort of self-control, teaching himself to beat his heart in any desired rhythm (*Brain/ Mind* 1983a). Another unusual example is the practice of *tumo* in Tibet, in which meditators develop the ability to stay warm in sub-zero weather, and can raise the temperature of their extremities at will to above-normal levels (H. Benson 1983a).

Yoga adepts, after years of practice, have been known to demonstrate highly unusual levels of control over many aspects of their bodies. Other people may practice yoga or other forms of meditation for these purposes or may spontaneously develop unusual control over body functions in the course of meditation. These unusual feats are not the ultimate goals, per se, of the meditative practices. They do, however, serve for some people as ways of motivating and demonstrating mental focus, which is a landmark of meditation. They also provide feedback to those meditating, proving that they are advancing in their spiritual practices.

The unconscious mind appears capable of taking control and regulating various body functions, given the proper mind-sets. If self-regulation can be learned with biofeedback, the body can potentially also be induced by suggestion to make the same changes, even without such training. Hypnosis can elicit unusual control over the body, without preliminary practice. We must be cautious, therefore, in assessing any therapy that addresses problems which are subject to self-regulation.

Biofeedback and spiritual healing
There are several ways in which biofeedback may be associated with spiritual healing.

Control over body functions similar to that achieved in biofeedback may be a part of spiritual healing. A variety of illnesses associated with the physiological mechanisms discussed above could be alleviated by patients learning to control their own bodies.

Many people clearly have the potential to learn self-regulation, but we are far from clear on the mechanisms that might activate these self-healing potentials. We must therefore be cautious in crediting spiritual healing with changes that could be the result of self-regulation, activated by suggestion, self-hypnosis, etc. This does not rule out the possibility that spiritual healing directly activates some of the mechanisms that suggestion alone does not. Spiritual healing and suggestion may complement each other, with the two in concert being more effective than either alone.

A special case of biofeedback is that of electroencephalogram (EEG) biofeedback. Numerous studies have confirmed that it is possible to enhance relaxation by increasing the level of alpha brain waves. Deeper relaxation and meditative states may be achieved with increases in the slower delta and theta waves.[104]

The *mind mirror* of C. Maxwell Cade and Geoffrey Blundell is a device that displays on a panel of lights the amount of brain-wave activity at various frequencies as it occurs simultaneously in both brain hemispheres. Cade found that the more effective healers have symmetrical activity in the two brain hemispheres. This provides a potential mode of biofeedback that might help people to develop their healing abilities through a visual display of their EEGs.

Demonstrations of *allobiofeedback* provide scientific proof that one person can remotely influence the body of another. The researchers measured the skin resistance (GSR) of a subject, displaying this on a meter that was placed in front of a healer in a distant room. Using this feedback, the healer was able to alter the subject's GSR through distant healing. This experiment was repeated with different healers and subjects, and produced highly significant results.[105] This mechanism provides another potential model for teaching healing.[106]

It has also been shown that the brain-wave patterns of healer and healee become synchronized during healings. Bruce MacManaway (1983/ 84) observed that this effect is strengthened when several healers work on one subject simultaneously. While this has not been used yet as biofeedback, it appears to suggest another piece of supporting evidence, or possibly another pathway for spiritual healing to occur.

Biofeedback as taught by Elmer and Alyce Green may also lead to marked transformations in consciousness and spirituality (Green/ Green 1984; Green 1986).

My own understanding of this, similar to that of Green and Green, is that a person gains awareness about his inner awareness in the process of biofeedback. Included here is a confidence in the validity of inner awarenesses. Initially, the focus is on physiological reactions to the biofeedback. With time, confidence in awareness of intuitive and spiritual perceptions is also strengthened.

My clearest personal experience of this type of biofeedback has been in using my own muscle testing for kinesiology to get feedback about my intuitive awarenesses. As I practiced this in casual settings as well as in psychotherapy and healing, I have had the further feedback of life experiences to confirm when I was correct in my intuitions. Exercising these inner awarenesses - to predict whether a cantaloupe will taste good, if it is worth stopping for a garage sale, or whether to offer healing and psychological advice - have all been wonderfully instructive. Extending this to higher spiritual awarenesses has then been easier, as in acknowledging spiritual messages in dreams and in everyday life.

UNUSUAL HUMAN ABILITIES

God's miracles belong to those who can concentrate on one thing and limit themselves.

— Baal Shem Tov

There are many well authenticated reports of physical feats that are beyond normal human abilities. These reports demonstrate that the human body may be able to accomplish unaided some of the same effects that are achieved through spiritual healing. They may also shed some light on the processes that are involved in self-healing. Vladimir Kuznetsov proposes the term *anthropomaximology* for the study of unusual physical powers.

An example is Jack Schwarz, who has an unusual degree of control over some of his bodily functions. He was carefully scrutinized in the act of piercing his flesh with large needles (Green 1981). Not only did he report that he felt no pain, but no bleeding was noted upon withdrawal of the needles, the wound closed within minutes, and healing occurred within a day or two without infection or scarring. This control was apparently only possible when he anticipated the injury. He said:

> Now if you would take the needle and you would sneak behind me and put it in my buttocks or anywhere else I would jump up too and scream out, but if you told me you were going to do that, then I already knew that I had to be alert to control it, so no pain would be felt because I was aware that disharmony would take place that the skin would be destroyed and that therefore blood might come forth. Then I have to start to work right away on it. I detach myself from this physical body and from the outside. I get the image that the blood will keep flowing and that in a way you make it flow so fast that it hardly actually can even get out of your vein.

Others have developed such abilities in contexts of religious practices.

The Parmann Project has reported on a group of Sufis in Jordan who pierce their bodies with spikes, swords and knives as an act of religious faith. They report no pain, bleeding, injuries to internal organs or subsequent infections, and claim that healing occurs within minutes. Some may only pierce the flesh of their arm or cheek, while others may pierce their abdomen through and through. They claim that this ability is conferred with 100% success by masters who transfer the self-healing ability through a blessing and a ritual handshake (Al Dargazelli). I have seen photographs and videotapes of these piercings, and I met a western psychologist, Professor Howard Hall of Case Western University, who observed them and videotaped them first hand and confirmed that these are not magicians' stage tricks.

Alfred Stelter mentions two individuals with unusual abilities. The first is Therese ~Neumann, a devout countrywoman who demonstrated *stigmata (wounds on the body that appear spontaneously at places where Christ's body was wounded during crucifixion). Many similar cases have been reported over several centuries. What was unusual in Neumann's case was that she apparently could survive without more than a token intake of food and water over many years.

The second person Stelter describes was a Dutchman, Mirin Dajo, who was able to let people pierce his body completely through with swords without suffering any pain, and with immediate closure of the wound upon withdrawal of the blade. He too was scrutinized by scientists, and even X-rayed. All examinations confirmed that no tricks were involved. A similar adept, Daskalos, is described by Markides (1991).[108]

Rustum Roy describes a type of Qigong practice called *bigu*, with which people are able to live for periods of months and years with an intake of less than 300 calories daily.[109]

Max Freedom Long (1976; 1978) relates how South Sea islanders are able to walk on hot lava without being harmed. He also describes in detail a person who handled fire and very hot objects, but suffered no burns. This man could even touch a red-hot iron poker with his tongue. He claimed that he was able to do this by "becoming one with the fire," and added that he could do it only if knew he had not injured anyone in any way or caused sorrow to anyone.[110]

Firewalking was also a fad in the US during the 1980's. Many thousands of ordinary people (including myself) learned to enter an alternative state of consciousness (ASC) in a brief workshop, and then walked on coals as hot as 800-1,200°F with no pain or damage to our feet. Only a handful of people have ever been burned in the process.[111]

The practice of *trial by fire* is used in some cultures as a form of popular justice. The accused are required to touch a very hot object with some part of their body, to place a hand in boiling water, or some other variant on this theme. The belief is that if they are innocent, they will remain unharmed.

Berthold Schwarz describes a Pentecostal church in the U.S. where members pass burning acetylene torches over their skin (and also handle poisonous snakes and ingest strychnine) with no ill effects. These activities are meant to demonstrate their religious faith. Several of Schwarz's observations may provide clues to the mystery of firewalking. He reports that the hair and clothes of the faithful are not scorched when their limbs or faces are exposed to flames. One member held his hand, dripping with fuel oil, in flames for ten seconds, and the oil did not catch fire – while an iron poker dipped in the same oil caught fire immediately. The faithful reported that concentration and faith are required for them to perform these feats.

Max Freedom Long describes a woman who could walk on sword blades without being cut, and who gave similar explanations for her abilities.

Michael Murphy and Rhea White present a marvelous collection of peak experiences and psi experiences reported by professional and amateur athletes. They describe highly unusual feats of agility, strength and endurance that far transcend ordinary human abilities.

CASE: Patsy Neal, Professor of Physical Education, describes a remarkable experience while competing in the Free-Throw Championship at the National AAU Basketball Tournament during her freshman year at college. She had practiced diligently for this event and came into the tournament confident she could score well. However, she found herself too nervous to score in the early competition rounds. The night prior to the last round she prayed for assistance and did her best to image herself being calm even though she was performing in front of the crowd – but could not dissipate images of failure. Falling asleep, she had a dream:

> I was shooting the free-throws, and each time the ball fell through the goal, the net would change to the image of Christ. It was as though *I* was flowing into the basket instead of the ball. I felt endless, unhampered…and in some way I was connected to the image of Christ that kept flowing from the basket. The sensation was that of transcending *everything*. I was more than I was. I was a particle flowing into *all* of life. It seems almost profane to try to describe the feeling because the words are so very inadequate.

Next day, the feeling persisted after waking. She felt like she was floating through her day rather than just living it. When she shot her free-throws that evening in the finals, she felt she was probably the calmest she had ever been in her life.

> I didn't…see or hear the crowd. It was only me, the ball, and the basket. The number of baskets I made really had no sense of importance to me at the time. The only thing that really mattered was what I *felt*. But even so, I would have found it hard to miss even if I had wanted to.
>   … I know now what people mean when they speak of a "state of grace." I was in a state of grace, and if it were my power to maintain what I was experiencing at that point in time, I would have given up everything in my possession in preference to that sensation. (P. Neal, p. 167)

She scored 48 out of 50 baskets, winning the championship.

  Many other extraordinary atheletic accomplishments are reported by Oriental athletes, who view sports as a meditative practice. Their athletic performances are routinely conducted while they are in alternative states of consciousness, which invite transcendent physical experiences. Until recently Western athletes also reported ASCs (which accompany exceptional physical performances) but only as rare, unsought occurrences. Today, athletes often speak of getting into a *flow* state, where they are exclusively aware of the physical activity in which they are engaged. Tiger Woods' fierce concentration on his golf strokes is a legendary example of this sort of focus. They also commonly speak of peak experiences. These are directly analogous to meditative states.

> *They can because they think they can.*
> – Virgil

How do they do that?

Such extraordinary feats are difficult to comprehend, or sometimes even to believe. Stelter hypothesizes that firewalking may involve the production by the body of a substance that psychically coats the feet to protect them from the hot coals. He takes as his paradigm the materializations of *ectoplasm* by mediums, which have been observed under sufficient scientific scrutiny to leave little doubt, in his opinion, that they are in fact real. [112] However, no direct evidence for such materializations in firewalking has yet been reported.

Others have suggested that a layer of sweat on the foot may protect the skin, much as a drop of water will scoot across a hot griddle when a layer of steam is formed under it. I feel that this explanation is untenable, because most firewalkers have dry skin on their feet, and because in any case, steam scalds the skin, and evaporates quickly at high temperatures. Another hypothesis is that ash forms an insulating layer over the hot coals. This does not appear likely, as coals with ash on them can still burn people, including some of the firewalkers. In the latter instances, several of the burned firewalkers indicate that they were unable to hold the safe, firewalking state of consciousness in their minds while crossing the bed of coals. If they relinquished this special alternative state of consciousness even for a moment, their feet were burned.

Of the thousands of firewalkers in America, only a handful have been burned, according to Larissa Vilenskaya (1986b; 1991), a psi researcher and firewalk instructor. In my own experience, I could not hold my hand closer than six inches from the coal bed without feeling serious pain from the heat. Yet my feet and ankles felt no heat when I walked across the coals. The fact that some have been burned during firewalks appears to confirm that those who *are* successful demonstrate an unusual ability. Schwarz's reports on the clothing and oil that did not ignite while in contact with the bodies of the fire handlers may support Stelter's hypothesis regarding an emanation of ectoplasm that prevents the fire from harming the body. Perhaps a substance or an energy field is produced that protects against heat.

Most of the above reports have several factors in common. The subjects all claim that they engage in mental exercises in order to be able to achieve the physical feats of being uninjured by sharp objects or by hot materials. They visualize themselves as being at one with the heat or blade, tenaciously hold onto a belief that they cannot be harmed, or enter alternative states of consciousness (ASC). In their *conscious* awareness, they hold firmly to their belief that they are capable of these unusual physical feats.

Further evidence for the ability to change one's body through beliefs and visualizations can be found in exceptional athletic accomplishments. Unusual athletic prowess is often associated with an ASC. The ASCs described by Murphy and White appear similar to, if not identical with, the mystical states described by meditators. [113] Common characteristics include a sense of being one with a higher sentience, or knowing in a profound way one's relationship with the world. This all seems to point to the existence of an alternate reality, which may overlap with the trans-dimensional realities that Lawrence LeShan associates with spiritual healing. [114] The ASC seems to enable people to alter their body's capabilities. Strength, speed, coordination, and dexterity all seem to be enhanced. It is not clear whether the ASC is required before the physical feats can be accomplished, or whether it is merely a concomitant to the extraordinary performance. The former seems more likely, judging from the available reports. When we change the ways in which we perceive and relate to the world, we apparently can alter our relationship with the world. This new relationship includes altered functioning of the body in the context of our physical environment (Benor 1985).

Enhancement of the body's physiological mechanisms during ASCs apparently can include improved abilities to recuperate from a variety of bodily dysfunctions, and by implication from various diseases as well (Dossey 1991). The athletics-ASC appears to include an anesthetic component, as it is well known that athletes may not feel pain *until after their performance* if they are injured during sports events. Reports of people who painlessly pierce their flesh with swords and needles indicate that the body can be prevented from responding to injury with pain and from becoming infected, and can mend itself very rapidly and completely. The parallels with spiritual healing are clear – our state of mind can profoundly influence our bodily functions.

I can add to these reports my own experiences in playing racquetball. I decided to apply principles of relaxation whenever I had an injury. Since racquetball is played at high speeds in a closed court, I was often bruised by balls that struck me with considerable force. I decided that the next time a ball hit me, I would immediately pause, breathe deeply and relax. I found that the pain went away almost instantly. There was redness at the place of impact, but there was very little subsequent discoloration, and what there was cleared up in two days – in contrast with the week or more that it had taken previously for such bruises to resolve.

I feel that the greatest part of my success (which was often repeated, with ever-increasing competence) derived from my conscious relaxation at the time of injury. I have asked myself whether perhaps the blows I sustained during this period were less severe than the earlier ones, and in at least one case I can definitely state that this was not so. My partner unexpectedly turned and hit the ball toward the back wall instead of the front, a shot that requires extra force to carry the ball on the rebound to the front wall. The ball struck me a resounding blow on the cheek that stunned me and alarmed my partner. But after applying my (by then well-practiced) routine, I was able to relax and even joke about the unexpectedness of his move. The pain rapidly abated and I experienced no subsequent black-and-blue discoloration whatsoever.

The feats of the Sufis described in the Parmann Project may be an exception to the ASC hypothesis, though this remains to be studied further. It is possible that they represent rapidly induced ASCs, similar to rapidly induced hypnotic inductions. The statement by the South Seas fire-handler that he needed to be sure he was not hurting others before he could "be one with the fire"[115] parallels the observations of Eastern mystics that the state aimed for in meditation is one of detachment from worldly concerns. Seemingly, in order to achieve such exceptional feats, some adepts must be totally absorbed in the task at hand, and unencumbered by even an unconscious hint of the nagging, unfinished business of the everyday, sensory-reality world.

Athletes echo this observation in another context, reporting that during peak athletic experiences they are completely absorbed in their actions. They are not thinking *about* what they are doing. They are *simply doing it*. Similarly, total absorption in a mental focus is probably a major contribution of meditation to the achievement of healing states. This absorption appears to facilitate and enhance the body's functions, be they physical action or self-healing.

A transpersonal component is also reported with peak experiences. There is a feeling of being one with the flow of whatever you are doing; being an integral part of a greater whole; or being aware of the scene as though you are viewing it in its entirety, rather than just from your own personal vantage point. This might be described as a sort of dance, in which the dancers are so much a part of the action that they seem to function as a unified organism.

> *O body swayed to music, O brightening glance,*
> *How can we know the dancer from the dance?*
> — W. B. Yeats

Athletes may even feel that they are somehow united with their sports equipment (such as a bow and arrow), or animal trainers with their horses or show dogs during competitive events, and that these interactions that reach beyond their physical boundaries are somehow an extension of themselves.

Again we see a parallel with qualitative aspects of spiritual healing. One of the ways in which healers describe the healing state of awareness is that they become one with the healee and, at the same time, one with the All (LeShan 1974a)

Many questions remain to be clarified, such as: Are there more specific states of consciousness that are conducive to healing? Does the effectiveness of an ASC relate to the personality type of the individual (e.g. in regard to Jungian polarities and extraversion/ introversion)? Are mental images subject to enhancement through group inputs, as in group meditation or to increases in potency over time through morphogenetic fields (Sheldrake)? Are there self-healing capabilities that can be conferred rapidly by particular adepts without the benefit of ASCs?[116]

These questions invite us to explore further in the realms of self-healing and healer healing.

SPECIAL BRAIN AND BODY FUNCTIONS

> *Human beings, by changing the inner attitudes of their minds, can*
> *change the outer aspects of their lives.*
> — William James

Several special functions of the brain and body are helpful in understanding and in beginning to explain aspects of healing. This section will briefly examine the perception of pain, special functions of the skin, and brain hemispheric functions.

Pain

> *Illness is the doctor to whom we pay most heed;*
> *to kindness, to knowledge we make promises only;*
> *to pain we obey.*
> — Marcel Proust

C. Norman Shealy (1987), reviewing the *Nuprin Pain Report* – a survey of pain in the US in persons aged 18 and older – notes that in the course of a year 73% of the general population had one or more headaches; 56% had backache; 51% had joint   pain; 46% had stomach pain; 40% had menstrual pain; and 27% had dental pain. An estimated four billion workdays were lost annually, for an average of 23 days per person per year.[117]

 Perception of physical pain is not a simple process, since many factors are involved. These fall into three broad categories defined according to the physical origins of the pain the degree of sensitivity to pain and spiritual factors related to pain.

1. Pain perception is initiated by stimulation of nerve endings in the various organs of the body. Sources of stimulation can include:

a) mechanical factors – trauma ranging from chronic external pressure to acute blows or cuts; internal trauma from heavy use of the musculoskeletal system beyond its natural capacities; and swelling or other deformity of organs and tissues from factors such as edema (excessive body fluid), infection, and direct trauma to nerves;

b) chemical or metabolic factors – caustic external substances or toxins that damage tissues or cause muscle spasms; and accumulations of physiological toxins within the body;

c) thermal or electromagnetic stimulation – reactions range from unpleasant sensations, through muscle spasms, to coagulation of tissues;

d) *infections* – direct inflammation of nerves or indirect pain via swelling of tissues and organs;

e) *neoplastic* – tumors with invasions of tissues and nerves, or indirect pain via swelling of, or encroachment upon, tissues and organs, especially nerves and bones;

f) degenerative factors – wearing out of tissues and articulating surfaces, with pain felt as the body "complains" about overuse;

g) immune system responses – swelling or inflammation of tissues because of allergic reactions that produce inflammation (rheumatoid arthritis is included here because it is thought to be caused by the body's allergic reaction to parts of itself, as though they were foreign intruders);

h) neurophysiological factors – malfunctions of the central and peripheral nervous system, leading to tension in muscles, which eventually tire or spasm, producing pain, which in turn creates the vicious circle considered previously; and

i) *psychological factors* – muscle spasms with tension or conditioned responses; metaphors for emotional problems; and *phantom limb* phenomena following amputations. This category is given a finer analysis in the following section.

2. Pain perception is more than a simple chain of cause and effect of physical and psychological relationships. One person may have little reaction to a given painful stimulus, while another may writhe in agony under the (apparently) same stimulus or condition. Psychological factors influencing pain perception may involve:

a) innate differences in pain thresholds – one person may have less sensitivity to certain stimuli than another;

b) general state of the nervous system (whether affected by tiredness, anxiety, or other emotional factors) – this may relate to altered sensitivity thresholds, or to the amount of energy a person has for coping with the added stress of pain;

c) specific psychological factors – for example, people may tolerate post-surgical pain well if they know that the operation has resulted in a cure of their illness, or they may tolerate the same pain poorly if they hear that the surgery brought only a diagnosis of incurable disease;

d) cultural conditionings – which teach a person to be stoic or vociferous in dealing with pain;

e) attention factors – in the height of an emergency or exciting situation (accident, sports event), while engrossed in achieving some immediate objective, a person might not feel pain despite a severe injury. Only later, when attention is focused on the wound, is the pain perceived. People who have a goal to work toward may focus all their attention on this and even deliberately ignore their pain, subsequently finding that they also feel the pain less;

f) mood factors – may influence responsivity to pain (anxiety and depression may increase pain, tranquility and joy decrease it);

g) rewards associated with the expression of pain – may influence the frequency of its occurrence and the severity of its expression.

A person who unconsciously enjoys some benefit (secondary gain) from a pain, such as avoidance of unpleasant tasks or extra attention from family members, is likely to experience more pain. People who anticipate compensation following accidents are likely to relinquish their pains slowly, if at all. [118]

> *I enjoy convalescence. It is the part that makes illness worth while.*
> – George Bernard Shaw (1921)

h. phantom limb phenomena – persistence of perceptions in a part of the body (limb, breast) that has been amputated, often associated with pains that are experienced as though the limb were still present.[119] Paraplegics (paralyzed from the waist down) may have phantom limb pains even when their spinal cords have been completely severed so that no ordinary sensations are felt from beyond the level of the nerves that were cut (Melzack/ Loeser). Similarly, phantom limb sensations are reported in people with congenital absence of limbs (Melzack et al.); and

i. fantasy pains – sensations seemingly created by the mind, where no objective causes can be identified. These are essentially body metaphors for anxieties, emotions, and traumatic experiences.

3. Transpersonal or spiritual awarenesses may contribute to how we experience and comprehend our pains.

a. Pain may be a stimulus for us to pray, or to question why we are suffering, and to ask God for help in understanding and dealing with our injury or illness. At the very least, pain may be the unconscious mind's way of forcing us to take a break from stresses or lifestyles that are in some way harmful.

Many people who have serious health issues come to feel that their illness led them to re-examine their lives, and to make enormously enriching decisions for better relationships and more emotionally satisfying and rewarding careers, not to mention healthier lifestyles. This life-transforming process may come as a response to the physical challenges that force us to face our mortality and ask questions about the meaning of life.

b. We may come to feel a spiritual causality that underlies and guides major life challenges, sensing that we might have been deliberately invited or pushed into such experiences by our higher self, by spirit or angelic guides, or by the Infinite Source – as a way of deepening our spiritual quest in life. Pain may be related to lessons chosen by our higher self or soul for our spiritual growth. When we are free of pain we tend to be complacent, and coast along, enjoying life but not learning very much. When we are in pain we are challenged to find new solutions to our problems, to plumb the depths of our being, and to push beyond the limits of our ordinary capabilities and awarenesses.

> *We are not human beings having a spiritual experience, but spiritual beings having a human experience.*
> – Pierre Teilhard de Chardin

c. Pain may be a residual from a previous incarnation, which invites us to explore this dimension of our existence, and to resolve ancient emotional scars.[120]

Assessments of pain

Clinicians do not agree on methods for the assessment of pain. Pain is a completely subjective experience, and there is no direct, objective way to measure it. Subjective evaluations rely on people's self-assessments, which may be as varied as human experience itself. Stoics and people with apparently high thresholds for experiencing pain may report minimal discomfort from injuries and stresses that others may find very painful, either because they have low pain thresholds, or because of characterological or habitual emotional intensity.

Cultural factors may play a role here. During my medical training I was challenged by the differences in apparent pain tolerance of Caucasian, Black and Hispanic women who were in labor. The Hispanic women would moan and scream with pain much more than the Caucasian or Black women. My initial impulse was to call for more pain medicine. The nurses, who had worked in the delivery room for a good while longer than myself, cautioned me against this. Pain medicine can often be sedating and can prolong labor if given injudiciously. Assessment of pain by anyone other than the people who are themselves experiencing it is therefore fraught with potential inaccuracies due to cross-cultural differences.

Serial assessments of pain with standardized testing instruments, in which people serve as their own controls for several treatment interventions, would appear to offer the best approach for testing treatments for pain. In this way one can have some degree of assurance that a change in the test response represents a real difference in pain levels related to a treatment given, rather than to differences between various people's responses to pain. This assumes, however, that a chronic pain condition will be painful to the same degree at different points in time, and that there will be no carry-over effect from one treatment period to the next. To minimize the latter possibility when self-control studies are used, it is therefore usual to leave a week or two between treatments to decrease any carry-over effects, and to alternate interventions with control periods over several trial epochs.[120]

Two types of pain assessment are in common use. The first relies on self-assessment questionnaires that have been given to many people in order to derive standardized norms for responses. This gives researchers a rough idea of the intensity of pain levels reported by subjects in a given study. This assumes that there are no cultural or other differences between the standardization groups and the experimental study subjects that might make the standardization irrelevant to the study group. Standardized pain questionnaires are available for this purpose, such as the McGill-Melzack Pain Questionnaire (MMPQ - see Melzack 1975).

Another test of this type is the Visual Analogue Scale (VAS). The VAS requires that people put a mark on a line of standard length (commonly 10 cm), where one end of the line represents no pain and the other end "the worst possible pain." It has been shown that this test is generally as reliable as any other pain assessment (Revill; Scott/ Huskinsson). The advantage of the VAS is that is very quickly administered and scored, compared to other types of tests.

The second approach is to measure objective physiological variables that tend to parallel the subjective experience of pain, such as muscle tension and skin resistance. Although these provide objective measurements, they are not all strictly related to pain, and may be influenced by other factors – such as anxiety, muscle strain, tiredness, and the like.

There is thus no measure of physical pain that is both direct, entirely reliable and and free of confounding influences. My personal impression is that the VAS is as good as any of the available methods, and by far the easiest to use.

Even more difficult to assess is emotional pain. A Visual Analogue Scale can readily be used for tracking pain in individuals over a period of time (F. Shapiro), but comparing and contrasting emotional pain between different people is fraught with problems.

> *Why is it that I'm most aware of my body only when it's not working properly?*
>
> – Ashleigh Brilliant (no. 1985)

The conventional medical view is that pain is usually a symptom of physical dysfunction. The physiological cause of the pain must therefore be identified and treated in order to relieve or eliminate the pain. When specific physical causes for the pain cannot be identified, or when the pain does not respond to pain medications, many doctors raise their hands in surrender, and refer the patient to a psychotherapist.

With luck, the patient may find a therapist who knows to ask, "What is your pain saying?" Often the answers lie in emotional conflicts that produce chronic tensions in the body, which end up being expressed as pain. In such situations, the pain is acting as a call from the unconscious mind, to bring attention to those factors that are producing chronic tensions. Often, the mind-body connection for the pain is metaphoric, as described above. Michael Greenwood points out that pain may be a doorway into places where the ego doesn't normally want to go. It can may be a doorway into places where the ego doesn't normally want to go. It can be a way for the unconscious mind to speak to us through our bodies, to insist that we attend to dis-ease in our emotional life before chronic tensions result in dis-ease could gallop out of control in our physical body.

When a wholistic therapist can help us find the inner meanings of our symptoms, we can also find the reins which enable us to regain control and redirect our lives. The responsibility of the therapist is to guide people to identify the causes of their own pains.

> *...Physicians are released from the need to pretend they know what to do, or to diagnose and treat what they cannot entirely understand – and patients can reclaim their own authority and learn to honour their own intuitions and hunches. Both are freed to follow whatever direction seems appropriate to the needs of the moment; and at that point, true healing can begin.*
> – Michael Greenwood 1998 (p. 55)

Pain and CAM therapies

> *Sickness and disease are in weak minds the sources of melancholy; but that which is painful to the body, may be profitable to the soul. Sickness puts us in mind of our mortality, and, while we drive on heedlessly in the full career of worldly pomp and jollity, kindly pulls us by the ear, and brings us to a proper sense of our duty.*
> – Richard E. Burton

Acupuncture is well known and well researched as a treatment for pain relief.[122]

While no research has been published as yet on self-healing for pain through acupressure techniques, there is a wealth of clinical literature supporting this modality.[123] My personal experience in helping people to deal with pain using one of these approaches, WHEE,[124] has convinced me of its effectiveness.

CASE 1: A psychiatric resident came to work one day with that look on her face which said, "No loud noises, please, and no bright lights! I'm having a serious migraine attack." After a weekend in bed, with all of her migraine and pain medications, she estimated the severity of pain was still at a level of "8" out of a possible worst level of pain at "10." Within three minutes of tapping on acupressure points, while reciting a simple affirmation, her pain was down to a much more tolerable "3."

CASE 2: A secretary in the clinic where I worked was hobbling around with pain in both knees due to osteoarthritis. She had suffered these knee pains for 17 years, and when I offered to help her, the pain was at a level of "7." Within 10 minutes of using WHEE, the pain was down to a "2."

Spiritual healing is especially effective in relieving the physical pain that is experienced with acute and chronic conditions.

Controlled studies have shown that spiritual healing is effective for tension headache (Keller Bzdek) and backache (Dressler; Redner et al.). Healing can prolong the time between doses of pain medication required after surgery (Meehan 1990); but it does not seem to be as good as standard pain medications for postoperative pain (Meehan 1985/ 1993). Healers report anecdotally that pains of every sort respond well to healing.

My impression is that the easing of pain by healers is attributable both to spiritual healing and to suggestion, but that healing is actually the more potent factor. Many anecdotal reports are available of patients who respond to spiritual healing after suffering from chronic, severe pains due to objectively verifiable illnesses, when previously they could not obtain relief from numerous chemical, physical and psychotherapeutic treatments over long periods of time. Presumably these patients would have experienced some reductions in pains from the conventional measures if they were amenable to relief of pain via suggestion. However, their subsequent response to a healer could still be due to special rapport, particular expectations, religious beliefs and faith in transcendent powers, or countless other factors of suggestion that might have been present in the spiritual healing situations.

Chronic pain is a problem in and of itself, but it also has numerous secondary effects. It is physically and emotionally draining and often produces depression. When pain is a manifestation of serious illness, such as cancer, it can also raise anxieties and fears about death. Spiritual healing can help with these secondary problems.

> It is not death or pain that is to be feared, but the fear of pain or death.
>
> – Epictectus

Phantom limb pain has also been reported to respond to healing, where no other conventional techniques have helped (Leskowitz 1997).

From the above it is obvious that one cannot easily evaluate healees' responses to healers in terms of what actually happens to their physical pain. Diverse factors may cause either an increase or decrease in pain.[125] Only through studying numerous similar cases of painful conditions treated by healers, including experimental and control groups, can one hope to arrive at some assessment regarding the efficacy of healing in treating pain.[126] For instance, it would be helpful to have a study of hypnosis compared with spiritual healing, for surgical pain.

Anecdotal reports abound on the benefits of spiritual healing in the treatment of emotional pain. However, I know of few formal studies in this area. Melodie Olson and Nancee Sneed report that Therapeutic Touch was helpful in alleviating post-traumatic stress following Hurrican Hugo in the US. Rhona Campbell reports dramatic benefits achieved with SHEN therapy for families of victims of the Dunblane school massacre in Ireland. My personal experience as a psychotherapist and healer is that healing eases emotional pain dramatically.

Perspectives of healers regarding both physical and emotional pain may differ considerably from those of allopathic medical practitioners and conventional psychotherapists. Within the belief system of many healers, pain may be viewed as one of life's most valued lessons.[127]

> *Suffering presents us with a challenge: to find goals and purpose in*
> *our lives that make even the situation worth living through.*
> — Victor Frankl

Pain calls us to examine what is out of harmony and therefore producing tension in our lives. In my practice of psychotherapy combined with spiritual healing, I find that the healing encounter may facilitate identification of sources of distress underlying pain. Psychotherapy then helps to sort out solutions to the emotional conflicts.

Pain (and illness in general) may also cause us to pause and ask what we are doing with our life, or to consider what life is all about. In doing so, we may be able to connect with our personal spiritual awareness. Ram Dass observes that all acts of healing are ultimately our selves healing our higher Self.[128]

Sometimes physical pain may have known causes, but may be unresponsive to physical, psychological, and healing interventions. Certain injuries, as well as neurological, degenerative and cancerous causes for pain, simply have no cure. In these cases, spiritual healing can be an enormous help in palliating and learning to live with the pain.

To some readers, much of the above may seem far-fetched. It may challenge your belief systems to consider that your body may speak to you through pain and other symptoms.

Others may feel blamed if someone asks them what their unconscious mind is saying through their pain (or other symptoms) – interpreting the questions as accusations that they are imagining the pain. Doctors may unwittingly precipitate such feelings when no physical cause can be found for pain, and they therefore suggest psychological counseling.

> *There was a faith healer of Deal,*
> *Who said, "Although pain isn't real,*
> *If I sit on a pin*
> *And it punctures my skin*
> *I dislike what I fancy I feel!"*
> — Anonymous

Pain, whatever the cause, is always real. But even when the primary cause is clearly physical, psychological components may influence the way we respond to it, or contribute to perpetuating or worsening the pain. Counseling can uncover such factors, and can relieve the pain or help us manage it.

In my personal experience and in the lives of many I have met – both as friends and as clients – I have found that pain can deepen our appreciation for life. It certainly heightens our empathy for others who are in pain and distress.

> *Your heart is not living until it has experienced pain...*
> — Hazrat Inayat Khan

Special skin functions

The skin may serve as far more than a mere barrier between people and their environments, or a simple sensory organ. It is also an important interface for communicating with others. Facial expression is probably the most prominent means of expressing our approval or disapproval, likes and dislikes, and the full spectrum of our feelings. Blushing and blanching may also reveal emotions of which we we are unaware.

Touch is an extremely potent mode of communication, though relatively little research has been done in this area. Caressing and soft touch are important to the normal development of infants, although studies on humans have not been conducted to differentiate this single factor from social attention in general. Studies with apes indicate that touch is vital to normal development (Harlow). Apes raised without a soft surface to cuddle up to will become psychologically disturbed.

> *The greatest sense in our body is our touch sense. It is probably the chief sense in the process of sleeping and waking; it gives us our knowledge of depth or thickness and form; we feel, we love and hate, are touchy and are touched, through the touch corpuscles of our skin.*
> – J. Lionel Taylor

Many psychotherapists comment on how good people feel when they are touched. Massage and aromatherapy[129] are among the most popular of complementary therapies. The nonverbal message of interpersonal openness, acceptance, and caring conveyed by touch has a potent effect on clients. Their perception of the therapist is altered from that of a distant, analytical, uninvolved professional to one of a caring, compassionate and accessible person.

This observation has also been successfully applied by salespersons and others for whom making contact is important. It is well known that even a casual contact by touch between a salesperson and customers will significantly increase the number of sales.

It is very sad that the fear of being sued for sexually inappropriate behavior has led legislators in many states to rule that touching must be prohibited in the psychotherapeutic encounter.

Touch, skin sensitivity and spiritual healing

One possible mechanism whereby laying-on of hands healing may be effective is simply through the power of touch, unrelated to spiritual healing. Conversely, part of the potency of touch may reside in spiritual healing effects, which may occur even without the conscious knowledge or intention of the practitioner.[130]

Studying the skin may further our understanding of healing. Sensations experienced by healers and healees during touch and distant healings have not been explained. These include sensations of heat, cold, tingling, "electricity-feeling," vibrations, and others. The skin may actually have special sensory receptors for healing energies. Moreover, the skin could conceivably emit such energies.

Cases of paranormal perception of color via the skin, commonly termed *dermal-vision*, have been reported over the past two decades.[131] Subjects typically describe the color of an object without receiving any visual cues, when the object is either touching or merely close to their skin. With practice they can even identify various sensations that they associate with different colors. Red may be "stickier" than blue, or yellow may be "rougher" than another color. Lab tests of abilities to identify colors by this method have shown significant results. Some people have even achieved sufficient sensitivity to be able to read large letters using their skin as the sole sensor.

Yvonne Duplessis has taken this research a step further (1985). She found that subjects could identify colors from as far as several feet above the colored target. Different colors appeared to radiate to different heights, and the relative heights differed consistently according to whether the testing was done in daylight or artificial light. Even more interesting, *wood and metal sheets interposed above the targets did not block or alter the sensations or the heights at which they could be perceived.*

These dermal perceptions are *synesthesias* or cross-sensory perceptions. The colored light impinging on the skin probably stimulates nerve endings that are normally used for sensing touch. When the light rays are perceived by the skin sensors, they are translated by the brain into perceptions that are familiar from previous sensations under other types of stimuli. Subjects who feel the light on their skin use the "vocabulary" of touch to describe the light, because that is the range of sensations they are used to receiving and interpreting through their skin.

Another explanation for dermal vision is that in the embryo stage of development, the ectoderm (outer cell layer) is the origin for neural and sensory organs as well as for skin. The skin may therefore possess latent sensory abilities usually thought to reside only in the specialized sense organs (e.g. eyes, ears) which originated during their development in the embryonic skin.

This may explain feelings of heat, cold, tingling and "color" reported by healers and healees during healing. The skin may be stimulated by healing energies, but the brain may be interpreting the stimulation in its more familiar vocabulary of touch sensations, as with dermal optics (Benor 1996).

A spiritual dimension to dermal optics was reported by Si-Chen Lee and colleagues in Taiwan. They found that children between 6 and 13 years old can be trained in finger-reading. These children could identify complex Chinese ideograms and reproduce them with great accuracy.

Using sophisticated measuring devices,[132] they found that blood flow to certain parts of the brain, as well as electroencephalogram patterns shifted at the time their best subject reported she was perceiving the images through her fingers.

They were surprised to find that "when certain special words related to religion - such as Buddha, Bodhisattva, or Jesus (in Chinese), 'I am that I am' (in Hebrew, meaning God) - were presented for finger-reading, these youngsters saw extraordinary phenomena, including bright light, a bright and smiling person, a temple, the Christian cross, or heard the sound of laughter. These responses are completely different from responses to other, ordinary, non-religious words." If the spiritual words were in separate pieces (e.g. "Bud" and "dha"), the children read the characters alone and did not identify these as spiritual names.

Viktor Adamenko, a former Russian researcher now living in Greece, goes much further afield in speculating on possible properties of the skin (1972). He suggests that the skin may act as an antenna. This hypothesis might explain the following reports:

1. People have claimed that they heard peculiar sounds or smelled a sulphurous odor prior to the arrival of meteorites.
2. High-frequency transmitters can produce auditory sensations of humming, whistling, or crackling, at frequencies that are clearly outside the range of normal hearing. The frequencies of 425, 1310 and 2982 megacycles seem particularly likely to produce such effects.

Adamenko feels that smell may be dependent on the resonation of molecules. Minute vibratory "sounds" may be what we sense, rather than particular configurations of molecules acting via chemical stimulation of sensory nerve endings in the skin of the nasal mucosa. If one part of the skin is sensitive to such electromagnetic resonation, the rest of the skin may be similarly sensitive.

He further suggests that the perception of sounds associated with meteorites may be due to low-frequency oscillations produced by the meteorites. This hypothesis is supported by the following unusual experiment, reported by Adamenko:

> If two subjects tightly grasp wires connected to a radio receiver which has no loudspeakers, and lean ear to ear, they can hear music and words picked up by the receiver. Each subject's eardrums apparently function as a loudspeaker for the other because of the low-frequency current picked up via the wires. If the two subjects hold hands, the sound disappears. The human body appears to function to some degree as a radio receiver.

Sound and spiritual healing
Certain kinds of sound can produce healing effects. Lu Yan Fang Ph.D., of the National Electro-Acoustics Laboratory in China, recorded infrasonic sound emitted from the hands of qigong masters[133] during external qi healings. She was able to produce healing effects with synthetic infrasonic sound at similar frequencies, and reported benefits for pain, circulatory disturbances and depression. On the basis of these explorations, the infrasonic emitting machine is now being studied in America.

The frequency emitted by this machine is similar to that of alpha brain waves. This suggests that infrasonic sound emitted by the healer may be an active force in bringing about changes in nervous system activity. It would be of great interest to determine how the healer emits the infrasonic sound.

It is still too early to know whether infrasonic sound conveys the full effect of spiritual healing. Anecdotal reports that I have heard indicate that only partial healing can be achieved with devices that produce infrasonic sound. My expectation is that the human instrument is far more subtle and potent than any mechanical substitute.

I would also question whether the infrasonic devices act purely in and of themselves, or whether they might be variations on radionics devices (instruments which project healing without emitting any known form of radiation[134]), and are known to produce effects that are linked to the operators of the devices. That is, the radionics devices seem to amplify the healing powers of the operators, projecting them to any location around the globe. Clearly, infrasonic waves could not project healing effects at a distance of more than a few yards, so they cannot provide the sole vehicle for the entire range of known and scientifically demonstrated healing effects.

Various reports hint that parts of the skin may be involved in complex interactions with sound. An article in the journal *Brain/ Mind* (1983, V.8) discusses a discovery in the field of audio recording called *holophonic sound.* Developed by the Italian scientist H. Zuccarelli, this method includes a reference tone along with the recorded sounds, so that an interference pattern is created in sound waves. This seems to add extra dimensions to recorded sound, making it appear more realistic. Listeners report that they can sense a directionality in such recordings that far exceeds the quality of stereophonic recordings. Subsequent investigations have demonstrated that *the ear emits a tone that seems to function as a reference tone for itself.*

A report by Walter and Mary Jo Uphoff (1980) indicates that during *thoughtography* (the production of pictures on film via psychokinesis),[135] sound waves are sometimes detectable emanating from the head of the subjects. This was a serendipitous observation made by scientists who were investigating a Japanese youth, *Masuaki Kiyota.* The scientists were looking for radioactive emission from his body, to explain his ability to produce pictures on film that was shielded by metal. They did not find any evidence of such radiation, but their microphones picked up an unexplained noise during taping of the experimental sessions. Subsequent investigations showed that the sounds were in the vicinity of 30-34.5 megahertz, that they occurred only during periods when Kiyota was concentrating in order to produce PK phenomena, and that they appeared to originate in the left frontal lobe of his brain.

Theories to account for the production of sounds from ear and brain have not yet been proposed. Nevertheless, the discovery of this phenomenon opens up further possibilities for investigating the means by which a healer may influence a subject, particularly in view of the evidence for energy fields or energy bodies surrounding the physical body. Healers may influence healees' biological energy fields via such emissions. The healees' adjusted energy fields could in turn influence their physical conditions, resulting in healing effects.[136]

BRAIN HEMISPHERIC FUNCTIONS

> *The left cortex, by itself, seems never to be happy until it either knows everything, or is defended against everything it does not know.*
> — Elmer Green (1986)

Widespread investigations are currently being conducted to clarify the distinctly different functions of the right and left hemispheres of the brain.[137] (In this discussion, the subjects studied are assumed to be right-handed. For left-handed people, the brain hemispheres involved in various functions may be reversed to varying degrees.) Experiments have shown that the functions of analytical, logical, intellectual thinking and expression of language are carried out in the brain's left hemisphere. The right hemisphere of the brain performs intuitive, artistic, symbolic and analogical thinking functions. (See Table II-4.)

Every 90-120 minutes the dominant activity in the brain hemispheres alternates from one side to the other. Although Eastern meditation experts have known of these shifts for millennia, Western science has only recently become aware of them. When hemispheric functions are predominating on a particular side, the nasal passage on the opposite side is markedly more open. That is, when your left nostril is open, your right hemisphere is "in gear," and conversely for the opposite nostril and hemisphere. This is called the *ultradian rhythm* of the brain.[138]

Our brains tend to focus primarily on one hemispheric mode or the other when we are engaged in a specific task, and we tend to have characterological preferences for one or the other mode of functioning. We are all familiar with extremes of such types – for instance, the typical left-brain character is unemotional, logical, and always analyzing what is going on. These are people who have difficulty answering when asked what they are feeling about a given situation, and they are commonly accountants or scientists by profession. Their right-brain preference counterparts, the emotional, intuitive, impressionistic folk, are commonly poets or artists who may have problems dealing with facts and figures.[139]

> *Thank God for making reality, and for giving us means of escaping from it.*
> – Ashleigh Brilliant (no. 2132)

Fredric Uphoff, a psychiatrist at Harvard University, has explored simple ways in which to identify for yourself whether you have strongly divided functions between your left and right brain hemispheres. Think about a problem or memory that disturbs you (with feelings of hurt, anger, or remorse, etc.). Now, use your right palm to completely cover your right eye, and your left palm to cover all but a little of the ear-side of your left eye. This will allow a little light in from the left side of your left eye, which will stimulate and activate your right hemisphere. Spend a few moments exploring your feelings regarding the issue you have chosen to focus on. Then reverse the process and cover your left eye entirely, leaving only a little of the ear-side of your right eye uncovered, and spend a few minutes exploring how you feel about the same issue.

About 60 percent of people will notice a distinct difference, sometimes quite a strong one, between the responses of their right and left hemispheres to this type of stimulation while focusing on an emotionally distressing issue. For most, the left, thinking hemisphere is more rational and can sort out how to deal with the issue, while the right brain tends to be emotional, and when it is activated, they may feel quite upset about the issue.[140]

Schiffer finds that some people he sees in psychotherapy have distinct personalities that are evoked when the left and right brain hemispheres are stimulated. In some of his clients there is a very wounded, angry, immature, self-destructive personality that is more often evoked by stimulating the right brain, and a more mature, composed, rational, constructive personality, evoked in the left brain.

Table II-4. Brain Hemispheric Functions	
Left	**Right**
Rational/ Logic/ Cognition	Intuitive/ Emotion/ Feeling
Differential	Existential
Detail-oriented/ absorbed	Gestalt-oriented, bored
Time sense (past, present, future)	Present-oriented
Paced by rules (acts with time awareness)	Impulsive (acts on present awareness)
Directed/ controlled by rules	Spontaneous
Bound	Expansive
Aims/ Goals oriented/ Planned progress	Instant gratification/ Impatient
Cautious/ Inhibited	Over-reacting
Product	Process
Temporal/ Partializing	Spatial/ Wholistic
Sequential aspects of math (e.g. algebra)	Spatial aspects of math (e.g. geometry)
Sequential (slow)	Parallel (fast)
Discrete	Continuous
Successive (either/ or)	Simultaneous (both/ and)
Focal	Diffuse
Explicit	Tacit
Objective	Subjective
Convergent approach	Divergent approach
Conscious	Unconscious
Language comprehension abstract	Language comprehension concrete
Speech content	Voice intonation
Rhythm	Melody, pitch
Linguistic	Pantomime, kinesthetic, musical
Grammatical	Visuo-spatial
Abstract models	Perceptual-synthetic
Synthesis	Creativity
Relatively narrow arousal level range over which hemisphere can function	Relatively wide arousal level range over which hemisphere can function
Evolutionarily newer	Evolutionarily older

Adapted from: Thomas H. Budzynski 1986.

This knowledge can allow the therapist to selectively access the wounded personality and thus facilitate releases of psychological traumas. The constructive personality is encouraged to provide support and control over the life of a person who may otherwise be dominated by the emotions of her wounded side, and may therefore be self-destructive.

CASE: Schiffer gives the example of "Harold," a brilliant newspaper reporter in his fifties, who was extremely ambivalent about his relationship with his girlfriend. Harold's mother had had unrealistic expectations of him in his childhood, and had rejected him when he could not satisfy her need for him to bring her vicarious glory through successes that were beyond his capabilities. In his right brain hemisphere, Harold carried severe hurts from this experience. In therapy he was able to identify what he called his *immature self*, which constantly anticipated rejections such as he had experienced from his mother. These feelings were particularly strong whenever he was close with his girlfriend. Schiffer was able to help Harold strengthen his *mature self* and release the hurts of the *immature self*, so that Harold was no longer living in the past. Harold went on to overcome his doubts and fears that his girlfriend might hurt him in the same way as his mother had.

Schiffer patented special eyeglasses with shaded tinting from right to left, which can stimulate the appropriate brain hemisphere to activate the more constructive personality, and promote its healing contribution to the patient's life. You can make a simpler version of these glasses with two pairs of safety goggles and some duct tape, to explore your own right/ left hemispheric awarenesses.

Daniel Goleman's bestseller, *Emotional Intelligence*, points out how Western society has emphasized left-brain functions to such a degree that right-brain functions are now given far less importance. He argues persuasively that right-brained, intuitive and feeling awarenesses are vital to the development of our self-image, and may often be more accurate in assessing social and relational situations. This book is very highly recommended reading for anyone who is interested in this subject.

Not all researchers agree about the importance of right/ left brain function distinctions. For instance, some point out that while artistic functions are initiated in the right hemisphere, verbal expressions of creativity involve the left hemisphere as well. I believe that these criticisms do not invalidate the observations of discrete right and left brain functions, which are distinguishable but may sometimes act in synchrony or harmony with each other, and at other times may conflict.

> *We should be passionate about our profession, and professional about our passion.*
>
> – M. Leon Seard II

Eye Movement Desensitization and Reprocessing (EMDR) is a new psychotherapeutic approach that appears to be related to the integration of right and left hemispheric activities (F. Shapiro 1995; 1997). EMDR is an extremely potent method for treating stress disorders. In classical EMDR therapy people are instructed to focus upon their negative experiences, negative feelings and self-critical beliefs and disbeliefs about themselves, while moving their eyes rhythmically from left to right and back a number of times. For reasons that have not as yet been explained, the negative feelings attached to the traumatic memories are diminished within minutes. When the negative feelings have been dissipated, positive feelings and affirmations are implanted and enhanced using the same technique.

It is hypothesized that in EMDR, the back and forth eye movements help to integrate the thinking and feeling aspects of our experiences. This may be similar to what happens during dreams when we have rapid eye movements (REM). It has been postulated that REM periods during sleep reflect the integration of recent and long-term memory. Perhaps EMDR will further clarify the function of REM.

People with the most severe emotional post-traumatic stress disorders (PTSD) deriving from horrendous war experiences or rape, as well as people with lesser stress reactions, have been helped by EMDR.

Following the initial development of EMDR, it was found that alternating stimulation of the right and left sides of the body by touch and sound could produce the same effects. A common way to do this is to pat your hands on right and left thigh as you sit in a chair, or to fold your arms and alternate patting each bicep. (The latter has been called the *butterfly hug*.) This is particularly helpful for people who experience nausea, similar to seasickness, from moving their eyes back and forth. It is also helpful in treating children, for whom the touch aspect is self-comforting and a helpful form of self-healing.

You can easily experience for yourself how this process works. (While it is possible to do this on your own with memories of serious emotional trauma, it is essential that you have a counselor or psychotherapist to assist you in sharpening your focus for this work, and in dealing with the memories and feelings that may be released, which sometimes can be intense.)

To provide a safer, less traumatizing method for clients in my practice, I have added an affirmation to EMDR that eliminates the intense releases of emotions (Benor 2001a).

When you feel comfortable and supported in releasing feelings, you can proceed with this exercise.

First focus your awareness on a mildly unpleasant anxiety, such as a fear of heights, spiders or snakes. Ask yourself, "On a scale of 0-10 (with 10 being the worst you could feel, and 0 being not bad at all), how bad do you feel when you recall this memory?" Then fold your arms and alternately pat the biceps under each hand over a period of 1-2 minutes. Now reassess how bad you feel, on the same scale of 0-10. Many people experience a distinct decrease in their negative feelings.

There are further methods for dealing with more serious problems, for which you are strongly advised to obtain professional support.

I have explored this method with my psychotherapy/ healing clients and with my own personal stresses and painful past experiences. The rapidity and thoroughness of the clearing of negativity and acceptance of positivity is astounding. I have helped many clients achieve major transformations in their fears and emotional defenses within minutes.

The curious paradox is that when I accept myself just as I am, then I can change.

— Carl Rogers

Laural Parnell finds that during the course of EMDR treatment clients may have transpersonal and psychic experiences, opening their minds into creativity and deeper awarenesses of love, forgiveness, and enlightenment.

I have also encountered similar transpersonal awakenings in my practice with EMDR, and now with WHEE. I was pleasantly surprised to find that in addition to helping people release chronic anxieties, phobias and poor self images, WHEE produces an incredible feeling of calmness. In some people this is so profound that it is unsettling, as they have not known such peace for a long time. In addition, as people reach a deep state of acceptance of themselves and of others, they may feel a spiritual opening – a profound sense of knowing that they are okay, lovable, free of sin/ guilt, and in touch with the Infinite in a personal way.

Brain and body laterality and spiritual healing

The tendency for one side of the brain, connected with the opposite side of the body, to process and express different sets of functions is referred to as brain and body laterality.There are several different ways in which this may relate to spiritual healing.

For one thing, there appear to be projections of the qualities of brain laterality to the body. Intuitives report that the right side of the body expresses masculine energy, and the left side of the body feminine energy (Schulz). The right side of the body is linked to the left brain, whose functions are specialized in linear thinking. Linear thinking is more characteristic of men than of women. Conversely, intuitive and feeling expressions, more common in women, are functions of the right brain. The right brain links to the left side of the body, hence the association of the left side with feminine characteristics.

Mona Lisa Schulz, a neurologist with very strong intuitive gifts, reviews fascinating research to support such divisions of the two sides of the body into masculine and feminine functions. For instance, in hermaphrodites, (people who have dual sexual characteristics), the male sexual organs are usually on the right, while the female organs are on the left.[141] The right testis generally develops first, whereas it is the left ovary that is the first to develop (Mitwoch). Bowel cancers develop in men more often on the left side and in women more often on the right (Schulz). Pre-menopausal women who are right-handed get breast cancers more often on the left, while postmenopausal women are more prone to cancers on the right. Women who are left-handed have the opposite frequencies (J. Howard et al.; M. Kramer et al.). Schulz notes that pre-menopausal women are more involved with nurturing activities of raising families, and nurturing is more associated with the emotional, right side of the brain

Psi abilities may also be linked with right brain functions, because they are more likely to occur in nonlinear states of consciousness.[142] They are often experienced as intuitive perceptions. Some studies have supported the view that intuitive functions reside in the right hemisphere,[143] while others suggest that psi functions may be associated with either hemisphere, depending on the sensory function(s) associated with them (Maher/ Schmeidler 1977). Researchers are still debating the interpretations of these findings (Broughton 1978; Maher/ Schmeidler 1978).

Western society has overemphasized left brain thinking as the best way to analyze situations and to function in the world, and as the only road to success – particularly through linear achievements on tests and in employment. At the same time we have denigrated intuitive pursuits, relegating them to "less serious" activities such as artistic hobbies. These are seen as "unscientific" or – if highly valued – as un*reason*able. (Even our language biases us to left brain priorities.)[144]

> *We ought to learn to become human beings rather than human doings.*
> – Anonymous

Notwithstanding the historical reasons behind this tradition,[145] the fact remains that most of us who are raised in Western cultures have deeply ingrained habits and prejudices toward left brain functions and against right brain ones. This may help to explain why psi powers seem so alien to us. It may also be why spontaneous expressions of psi abilities are less commonly reported in a Western context than in non-Western cultures. Eastern teachings emphasize intuitive, holistic modes of perceiving the world, and in some cultures this awareness has been carried to the opposite extreme. Meditative contemplation and passive receptivity have been stressed to the neglect of logical, linear thinking and planning.

This Eastern approach has produced a wealth of information about inner states and spiritual development, but it has been at the cultural expense of inertia and apparent ineptness – by Western standards – in dealing with material problems. However, one aspect that is overlooked in these analyses through Western eyes is that many of the non-industrialized, intuitive-sensitive cultures live in harmony with their environments. Though they are subject to the vagaries of weather and availability of food supplies, prior to being "modernized" they do not despoil their worlds through excesses of exploitation and control.

What seems both logically and intuitively reasonable is that human beings should develop a balance between their hemispheric functions, both in terms of their inner world and in terms of their interaction with the environment.

> *In a strange way, analog associations are never wrong: they are just nearer or farther from the central truth, as though accuracy moves in resonant rings of propinquity that can get warped when too far from the center. To notice analogs and heed them accurately, one must true up the inner gyroscope and walk into the echoing halls of intuition toward a central truth along the resonant labyrinth of the right brain hologram. Seeking truth in here is scary for those who shun dreams, neglect their dark side, disown shadow. But the analog domain can become rich and beautiful, a place of inspiration and creation. Its analog richness, however, should always be examined and paralleled against the left brain's logic, to see whether the whole is split and divided against itself... or if its view of reality is congruent and harmonious.*
>
> – Katya Walter (p.174)

Recent research suggests that healing is correlated with an integration of both hemispheric functions. The work of Maxwell Cade and Geoffrey Blundell on the *mind mirror* has demonstrated that effective healers show symmetrical patterns of EEG (brain wave) activity during healings. Some even are able to maintain this balance while engaged in casual conversation and other activities unrelated to healing. This lends support to speculations that brain hemispheric synchronization is relevant to healing ability. It was also found that EEG frequency patterns of the healer and the healee would occasionally synchronize during healings, but it is unclear whether this is related to hemispheric synchronization.[146]

Mind mirror studies of yoga and meditation adepts, along with studies of people who are successful in their chosen careers, also show a balanced hemispheric pattern. Meditation may be one method for bringing the brain hemispheres into synchronous activity. This state may reflect a more comprehensive mode of brain function, and this may explain why people who are able to activate both hemispheres simultaneously are able to do things that others, who are limited to a single primary hemispheric mode, can't do.

Further research is needed to clarify these early observations and speculations.

SELF-HEALING PROGRAMS

> *Every day, in every way, I am getting better and better.*
> – Emile Coué

There is a plethora of self-help approaches available for treating and curing one's own disease and dis-ease. Some of these primarily involve attitudinal changes. If you attend more to positive developments than to negative ones, in your life, or even if you simply make a point of smiling more, you will feel better.

Many books, such as Norman Cousins' *Anatomy of an Illness,* describe active self-help methods. Cousins' method of laughing himself to health is highly original. When diagnosed with scleroderma, a medically incurable illness, he refused to accept his medical death sentence. He watched numerous humorous films starring Laurel and Hardy and other comedians and managed to release whatever negative energies were causing and maintaining his disease – making an otherwise unexplainable recovery.

Self healing is not an uncommon experience. Other approaches have included behavior modification, biofeedback, autosuggestion, visualization and numerous relaxation techniques. Most of the books in this category relate principally to relaxation of emotional and physical tensions.[147]

Meditation can promote relaxation and have other, far-reaching effects. It can often bring about subtle, qualitative alterations leading to the development of more positive attitudes towards oneself and others.[148] These effects are difficult to describe, and even more difficult to quantify and measure.[149]

Self-healing can accelerate recuperation from most illnesses. I will discuss heart disease and cancer as the most challenging of these. (AIDS is similarly problematic, but it has not yet been as well researched.)[150]

Self-healing with cancer

Conventional treatments for cancer include surgery, chemotherapy, and radio-therapy as therapeutic and palliative interventions, with pain killers prescribed to treat the most common and most feared problem. All of these treatments carry severe side effects. Chemotherapy and pain medications in particular may impair quality of life, which is a sad prospect when one's remaining time is limited.

It is astounding to note that many of the chemotherapy agents administered routinely have not been studied in controlled experiments to demonstrate whether they are beneficial in prolonging life. If these agents are shown to *shrink* tumors it is assumed that they are beneficial. In fact it has never been clarified in controlled trials whether people with cancer would survive as long if they did not receive chemotherapy. It is considered unethical to conduct studies in which some people with cancer would not be given what *may be* effective treatments.

Screening for cancer is touted as offering the prospect of early identification of the disease, which can allow for earlier, presumably more effective intervention. However, this is not always the case. For instance, with cancer of the cervix this is only a partial truth. Surgery is frequently recommended for mild to moderate abnormalities on cervical smear tests. It is far from certain that this is necessary, and the surgery carries a small but significant risk of complications.[151]

The costs of cancer screening are considerable. In women under 55, for instance, it has not been shown that regular mammograms increase the success rate of diagnosing cancers.[152] There is also the added factor of the increasing risk of cancers with repeated exposure to x-rays.

Daniel Greenberg summarizes twenty years of experience in the American "War on Cancer," which was declared by President Richard Nixon and Senator Edward Kennedy and affirmed by the National Cancer Act of 1971. The results achieved with about $520 billion of research, mostly on the physical treatment of cancer, are unimpressive. Fears and desperation on the part of people with cancer, rigid approaches on the part of conventional medicine, and profit motives of the drug industry are the active forces in the politics of cancer, just as they were at the start of this "war." Greenberg points out that Congress was inspired and misguided by the success of the American moon-landing in 1969 and sought to conquer cancer as it had conquered the problems of lofting space vehicles into orbit. "…A few sensible voices cautioned that the Manhattan Project and the Apollo program were engineering feats based on existing scientific understanding. Cancer, they pointed out, was not understood…" Though there has been a slight reduction in cancer mortality below age 65, the overall incidence of deaths from cancer in the US has risen from 335,000 in 1971 to 553,000 in 2000. Minority groups were also noted to be suffering greater incidence and mortality rates for cancer. Greenberg points out that Congress has continued to pour funds uncritically into this "war," despite the lack of any evidence that it is being won.

However there is increasing evidence that through self-healing approaches, it is possible to ameliorate symptoms of cancer, reduce the morbidity involved in toxic cancer radiotherapy and chemotherapies, and in some cases, to increase survival time or even effect total remissions of the disease.

Until recently the diagnosis of cancer has held a very negative prognosis. Patients could expect to suffer from the pain associated with the disease, from toxic therapies, and from fear of recurrence or impending death. Self-healing methods offer a variety of approaches to deal with these stresses and fears.

It is generally assumed that cancer is a scourge to be fought in every possible way – to be extirpated, poisoned, irradiated, and eliminated at any cost. However, when people with cancer are invited to discuss their illness they often show another side to this picture.

> *...Most people experiencing cancer or other life-threatening illness will tell you they came alive under the crisis of the diagnosis. Priorities were suddenly revalued. The petty and infantile were discarded for the meaningful and fulfilling. Relationships that had been taken for granted were heightened. Other relationships, long dead, were discarded.*
>
> – W. Brugh Joy (1990, p.149)

Psychological explorations are now uncovering ways in which people allow their illnesses to develop, as well as ways to help people deal with them.

Bernie Siegel, a surgeon in New Haven, Connecticut who treats many people with cancer, is a naturally gifted counselor and a very loving human being. He advocates wholistic approaches to involve cancer patients more fully in their own treatment. He even coined the term *respant* (for *responsible participant*) to replace *patient*. He asks his respants the following questions:

1. Do you want to live to be 100?
2. What has happened to you in your life in the year or two prior to the illness?
3. What does the diagnosis mean to you?
4. Why did you need this illness?

In discussing the answers to these questions with his respants, Siegel helps them to discover why they may have allowed cancer to develop, how they can change their unhealthy attitudes and how they can find new reasons to live. Typically, they found themselves in a job or in a personal relationship that was unbearable, but they couldn't see any acceptable way of leaving. In group therapy they often come to realize that they have allowed the cancer to develop as a socially acceptable form of suicide.

One of Siegel's most potent techniques is to ask respants to draw pictures of themselves, of the cancer, and of their cancer therapies. From the drawings he can assess whether the respant is a good risk for surgery, whether chemotherapy and/or X-ray therapy are likely to be successful, what conflicts might underlie the illness, and what hopes there are for recovery (Siegel 1986). Siegel found that only a few exceptional people will elect to work with his approach to overcome their disease through active efforts on their own part.

Another pioneer in psychological treatments for cancer is Lawrence LeShan,[153] who has been exploring for forty years how intensive psychotherapy can help people suffering from a variety of terminal cancers. LeShan describes life patterns and a personality type that seem particularly susceptible to cancer. Common catalysts for developing illness can include a loss of *raison d'être* (reason for *being*) and an "inability to express anger or resentment... in their own defense." LeShan feels that a sense of joy and purpose in life is essential for improvement.

LeShan reviews cancer mortality rates around the world, finding that many studies support the predictions drawn from his observations. He reports in detail on a number of individuals who experienced a remission of their cancer linked with shifts in their attitudinal patterns during psychotherapy. These clinical observations strongly suggest that people may contribute to the development and/ or remission of their own cancer.

Siegel and LeShan are only two of many explorers in this field of self-healing. Several common denominators in their approaches are emerging. Self-healing therapies require that people regularly practice relaxation, meditation, imagery or other techniques,[154] and that they attend to the basic lifestyle factors of diet,[155] exercise, and avoiding toxins (alcohol, tobacco, recreational drugs and various environmental toxins). Deeper self-healing may be achieved if they can identify and deal with the stresses and conflicts that may have contributed to the development of the cancer.

How can these methods succeed? How is it possible that psychological interventions will halt or reverse the development of cancers of all sorts?

The *surveillance theory* hypothesizes that cancerous cells are constantly appearing in every individual, but that in most people they are quickly destroyed by the body's immune system (Frank 1975). Combinations of physical factors such as radiation exposure, genetics, diet, and contact with carcinogenic substances can predispose certain individuals to develop clinical cancer. O. C. Simonton et al. describe a number of helpful psychotherapeutic techniques including relaxation, focusing on positive mental images and goals, exercising, and working with family support systems. Visualization techniques invite people to develop mental images of their immune system fighting the cancer (e.g. they may see white blood cells as white knights, sharks, or soldiers. attacking the cancer cells and destroying them).

O.C. Simonton et al. (1980) reported from their pioneering explorations:

> In the past four years, we have treated 159 patients with a diagnosis of medically incurable malignancy. Sixty-three of the patients are alive, with an average survival time of 24.4 months since the diagnosis. Life expectancy for this group, based on national norms, is 12 months. A matched control population is being developed and preliminary results indicate survival comparable with national norms and less than half the survival time of our patients. With the patients in our study who have died, their average survival time was 20.3 months. In other words, the patients in our study who are alive have lived, on the average, two times longer than patients who received medical treatment alone. Even those patients in the study who have died still lived one and one-half times longer than the control group.

Three years later, the status of the disease in the patients still living was as shown in Table II-5:

Table II-5. Status of four-year cancer survivors

	No. of patients	% of total
No evidence of disease	14	22.2
Tumor regression	12	19.9
Disease stable	17	27.0
New tumor growth	20	31.7
Totals	63	100.0

All of these patients were at one time considered medically incurable.

Although this research is interesting, the reported data are deficient in several respects. Specific types of cancers are not tabulated; comparison groups are very loosely defined; and patients were self-selected for the study. Mitigating these criticisms are reports of self-controlled cases in which discontinuation of Simonton techniques led to more rapid tumor growth and, conversely, resumption of therapy led to slowed growth and/ or regression of tumors.

Jean Bolen summarizes the results of Simonton's treatment of 152 patients in Table II-6.

Simonton and Matthews-Simonton (1981) replicated the above-mentioned study with patients who had advanced breast, lung, and bowel cancers. They reported that group therapy and counseling increased the mean survival time to twice what is expected for patients with these cancers in the US. However, no statistical analyses supported their findings, and again, selection factors may have biased the results.[156]

Some therapists have found that visualizing aggressive imagery of fighting the disease does not work as well as meditation for harmonizing oneself with both one's inner self and one's environment (S. Levine). There is the story of a Quaker who attended a workshop on developing imagery for fighting cancer. He felt like a failure when he simply could not muster up aggressive imagery of his body *fighting* against the cancer, because this completely contradicted his pacifist principles, and he thought he would have to give up on these methods. But after sleeping on the problem, he was pleased to awaken the next day with the mental imagery of small but strong gnomes who came along and firmly grabbed the cancer cells and carried them to the kidneys for elimination.

Larry Dossey (1992, p. 197) presents similar observations:

> The message being delivered today to many sick persons is... that only if they demonstrate an antagonistic, robust "fighting spirit" will they have a chance to "beat cancer" or recover from heart disease or some other malady. But there are other ways to "fight"... These ways require giving up the hubristic, arrogant, and narcissistic belief that the universe revolves around our own condition and should invariably dance to our tune. They require that we cease dictating our own terms to the universe, that we hush our petulant little "I want it thus," that we stop our incessant efforts to beat the world into line. This cessation can ideally create a vacuum or an emptiness into which healing *can* flow.

Table II-6. Two-year study of patients treated by O. Carl Simonton, MD

	Uncooperative, does not follow instructions	Uncooperative, rarely follows instructions	Usually follows instructions	Follows instructions and shows some initiative	Full cooperation, follows instructions implicitly, is enthusiastic about getting better	Totals
Patient response	- -	-	+ -	+	+ +	
Excellent: Marked relief of symptoms and dramatic improvement of conditions	0	0	0	11	9	20
Good : Relief of symptoms and general condition improved	0	2	34	31	0	67
Fair: Mild relief of symptoms	0	14	29	0	0	43
Poor: No relief of symptoms	2	17	3	0	0	22
Totals	*2*	*33*	*66*	*42*	*9*	*152*

What is advocated in these psychological approaches to treating cancer is an attitude of asking for and expecting help via inner resources of self-healing, and via one's higher self/ cosmic energies/ Divine intervention. This sort of surrender to a higher power is quite the opposite of giving up hope, which is a more common response to a diagnosis of cancer.[156]

Positive imagery works not only with combating the illness but also with managing the toxic side effects of some therapies. Nausea from chemotherapy and radiotherapy may be markedly reduced through imagery which builds expectation that the body is working in concert with these agents to heal the cancer. People who draw pictures of their radiotherapy as magic bullets aimed to strike each cancer cell find that they weather their radiotherapy in better shape than expected.

How can mental exercises change the course of cancers? It is possible that visualizations increase the activity of the body's immune system. Steven Locke and Mady Hornig-Rohan review 1,453 professional articles on this subject in an annotated bibliography, and Jeanne Achterberg (1985) presents a most readable and thorough discussion on the subject. Achterberg finds that this art has been honed to such a degree that the course of illness in people with cancer can now be predicted through analysis of their visual imagery regarding the state of their cancers and the functioning of their immune systems.[158] Sadly, very few cancer therapists have used these tools in research or clinical practice.

Developing on the work of Simonton and colleagues, other researchers have explored the effects of psychosocial factors in influencing cancer and heart disease. Just a few of the many available reports are reviewed here.

Amanda Ramirez et al. have investigated the possibility that stress might worsen the prognosis of women who have had surgery for breast cancer.

Adverse life events and difficulties occurring during the postoperative disease-free interval were recorded in 50 women who had developed their first recurrence of operable breast cancer and during equivalent follow-up times in 50 women with operable breast cancer in remission. The cases and controls were matched for the main physical and pathological factors known to be prognostic in breast cancer and socio-demographic variables that influence the frequency of life events and difficulties. Severely threatening life events and difficulties were significantly associated with the first recurrence of breast cancer.

Highly significant correlations were found between adverse life events and the development of the cancers.[159]

Another fascinating and encouraging report on self-healing for cancer comes from David Spiegel, a psychiatrist at Stanford University. Together with several colleagues he set up a weekly support group for 86 women who had metastatic breast cancer, to provide instruction in self-hypnosis for pain relief. At the end of a year the women who participated in the group intervention were coping better with their pain than 36 women who did not have a similar support group. Much later, the investigators heard reports of people who seemed able to prolong their lives through relaxation and imagery, so ten years after the study they checked up on how these 86 women had fared. They were amazed to find that the entire control group had died within four years, but a third of the treated group were still alive at four years and three had survived ten years.[160] The effects of treatment had become apparent 20 months into the study, which was 8 months after the end of the therapy group.[161]

Fawzy et al. (1993) replicated Spiegel's study, with 35 patients who had malignant melanomas (skin cancers) in early stages of development. There were lower rates of recurrence and death for the treatment group, compared to a randomly chosen group of patients with melanomas who did not receive this treatment.

Both Spiegel's and Fawzy's studies were criticized for including too few patients, for poor randomization procedures, and for using control subjects who exhibited unusual courses of illness. The last is the most telling criticism, because when the treated subjects' survival times are compared with national norms there are no differences, while those in the control groups had shorter survival times than the national norms.

J. L. Richardson et al. found that cancer patients who had been given education and support, designed to enhance medical compliance, survived longer than controls who had not had these interventions. However, the longer survival times were not correlated with the degree of medical treatment compliance. The researchers' impressions were that the critical factors increasing survival were the greater social support and sense of being in control of their situation, along with improved self-care habits.

Linn, et al. studied effects of individual counseling on people with advanced cancers. This randomized study found enhanced *quality* of life, although no significant *prolongation* of life. These researchers concluded that psychosocial interventions late in the course of cancer could not be expected to affect survival time. This study did not include the full range of psychosocial support and education provided in the studies of Spiegel et al. and Fawzy et al.

Dean Shrock et al. studied the effects of a series of six Health Psychology classes on breast cancer and prostate cancer patients. Each class was two hours long, offered repeatedly in its series over the course of a year. Participants could attend as often as they wanted, together with family and others in their support network. From 5 to 50 participants attended any one class. In addition to giving lectures and answering questions, group leaders also encouraged discussion and socialization. A guided imagery audiotape was provided, including exercises in relaxation and imagery to enhance immune functions. Participants were also encouraged to engage in joyful and meaningful activities, and not to be critical of themselves if they failed to adhere to the program schedule or heed the advice provided.

Participants in this study were selected from a larger, more heterogeneous group than in those previously mentioned. The group of experimental subjects was composed of all those who attended at least 5 classes, and it included 21 women with stage I breast cancer (mean age 57 years) and 29 men with stage I prostate cancer (mean age 68). Controls were matched by tumor registrars at the hospitals where the experimental subjects were receiving treatment. The control group included 74 women with breast cancer (mean age 60) and 65 men with prostate cancer (mean age 71), closely matched for age at diagnosis and date of first diagnosis to the experimental subjects.

The death rate at five years was significantly higher in the control group (p < .04). Medical treatments did not account for the differences between groups, and survival time of the controls were comparable to those of national norms.[162]

Schrock and colleagues propose that several mechanisms, which are not mutually exclusive, may explain the positive effects of psychosocial interventions in prolonging survival of people with cancer:

1. People are encouraged to comply with effective conventional medical advice and treatments.

2. Suggestions for improvement may increase self-healing. These interventions may act as potent placebos.

3. Increased social support, with the opportunity to share and vent emotions in a safe setting, can reduce stress while increasing hope and enhancing feelings of being more in control of one's life. All of these factors can enhance immune responses.[163]

4. Strengthening hope can enhance immune functions, possibly through neuorimmune or neurohormonal pathways.[164]

5. The factor most often cited by participants in these cancer psycho-educational programs is that they encounter others – both peers and health caregivers – who listen to them, support them, and care about them (Berland; Schrock).

David Spiegel (2001) summarizes this research, noting that five[165] out of ten of the trials found that various forms of psychotherapy enhance survival of patients with cancer.

Five studies found no increase in survival with various forms of psychotherapy. Goodwin et al. found reduced distress and pain, but no increase in survival with supportive-expressive group psychotherapy for women with metastatic breast cancer. The benefits were greatest among those who showed the most initial anxiety and depression. Linn et al. also showed positive psychological effects, but no somatic ones. Three of these studies reported only transient psychological benefit (Edelman et al.) or none of any kind (Cunningham et al.; Ilnyckyi et al.).

Spiegel notes:

> The difference between the findings of the two studies may be explained by changes in treatment during the past several decades. First, the medical treatment of breast cancer has improved substantially, and the notable reduction in breast-cancer mortality that began in the late 1990s undoubtedly reflects the earlier detection of cancer, the use of selective estrogen-receptor modulators, and the development and use of more effective chemotherapy.
>
> Second, psychosocial support for patients with cancer has also improved substantially. Emotional support for patients with cancer is far more readily available than it was decades ago. Because medical and surgical treatments are better now and emotional support has improved, the effect of formal psychosocial intervention on survival time that was found in earlier studies is difficult to replicate.

Another factor influencing the severity of patients' response to cancer is a history of previous traumatic stress. Lisa Butler and colleagues found that where people had experienced severe stress earlier in life, there was greater likelihood of responding to the cancer with avoidance, and anxieties about the cancer were likely to be more intrusive.

Future research might therefore focus on those people with cancer who are more anxious, and who have previously experienced serious life stresses.

Believe that life is worth living, and your belief will help create the fact.

– William James (1890)

Self-healing for cardiovascular disease

Dean Ornish, an Internist at the University of California, San Francisco, developed a group therapy approach to treat severe heart disease, which even helps to avoid cardiac bypass surgery.[166] Ornish finds that relaxation, meditation, low fat diet, exercise and group therapy not only can arrest the progress of heart disease, but can actually reverse the damage in cardiac arteries.[167] After one year of participation in his group, many people reversed the atherosclerotic arterial hardening that was causing their cardiac symptoms. Previously, it had been considered impossible to see such changes without medication or surgery. Further studies have shown that improvements are progressive if people persist with the self-healing regimen.[168] A measure of the success of this program is that insurance companies are now compensating people who participate in it.

H. J. Eysenck (1992) summarizes a series of studies[169] supporting the following hypotheses:

1. Psychosocial factors (personality, stress) play an important role in the development of cancer and coronary heart disease.

2. These factors are different for cancer and heart disease, and can be measured in healthy people as well, leading to the postulation of personalities that are particularly prone to cancer or coronary heart disease.

3. The cancer-prone personality is characterized by suppression of emotion and inability to cope with interpersonal stress, leading to feelings of hopelessness, helplessness, and eventually depression.

4. The coronary-heart-disease-prone personality is characterized by strong reactions of anger, hostility, and aggression.

5. Appropriate behavior therapy (stress management) can act prophylactically to make people who are prone to cancer or coronary heart disease less likely to develop other diseases.

6. Similar types of treatment can prolong the lives of patients with inoperable cancer.

7. Risk factors (psychosocial, genetic, behavioral etc.) are synergistic, not additional.

8. Cancer and coronary heart disease are each influenced differently by consumption of coffee, cola, and alcohol, in line with theoretical expectation.[170]

Eysenck (1992) argues convincingly against criticisms of these studies by other researchers (Pelosi/ Appleby; Pettingale et al.):

> ...The results of a prospective, multidisciplinary study of women with early breast cancer... indicated that psychological responses to cancer diagnosis, assessed three months postoperatively, were related to outcome five years later (Greer, et al.). Recurrence-free survival was significantly commoner among patients who reacted to cancer by denial or "fighting spirit" than among patients who responded with stoic acceptance or feelings of helplessness or hopelessness. Ten years since our cohort of patients was recruited, we have re-examined the association between psychological response and outcome. Although there was a higher mortality rate in the second than in the first five years, a favorable outcome is still commoner among those whose responses were categorized as fighting spirit and denial (11/ 20, 55%) than among those who showed stoic acceptance or helpless/ hopeless response (8/ 37, ...22%) ... p = 0.024...

Worthy of brief mention here are early reports indicating that imagery, relaxation, and meditation can be effective in treating AIDS as well as cancer (Ironson et al.).

Psychoneuroimmunology (PNI)
A whole new medical specialty, *psychoneuroimmunology (PNI)* is developing around these findings.[170] PNI combines relaxation, meditation and imagery and a support group. PNI confirms the broad extent of the mind's influence over hormones, antibodies, white cells and other factors that are essential to health and to coping with illnesses such as cancer and AIDS (P. Solomon). As explained earlier, white cells contain some of the same neuropeptides present in the nervous system, and we find that the immune system interacts far more intimately with the nervous system than was previously appreciated. Some suggest that the immune system is actually an extension of the nervous system.[171] This might help to explain the body's "memory" for immunizations and infections over many years.[172]

Although much is known about the processes involved in the immune system's protection of our bodies from disease, it is not clear what factors are responsible for regressions of cancers. Possible mechanisms could include:

1. *starvation* of the cancers' blood supply through selective constriction of blood vessels that nourish the tumor;
2. *activation of immune mechanisms,* including antibodies and white blood cells, which can attack the cancer with enhanced vigor;
3. *alteration of hormonal and/ or other physiological conditions conducive to tumor growth* - such factors may also be associated with emotional states of fear, anxiety, depression and despair;
4. *restructuring* of the body via *visualization* of new self images; and
5. other psi *and bioenergy self-healing mechanisms.*

Mechanisms (4) and (5) could support the hypothesis that there is an energy template for the body that can be altered through mental imagery.[173]

The medical community is unfortunately unreceptive, for the most part, to approaches relying on psychological techniques, and which place a substantial responsibility for recovery upon the respant. Doctors are accustomed to prescribing physical and chemical measures for cancer therapy. Psychotherapy and self-help approaches for cancer sound incredible to them, and are thought to be placebos (used here as a distinctly pejorative term to mean a non-effective treatment rather than a self-healing approach) within the conventional allopathic system.

Doctors often fear that their patients will delay conventional therapies past the point at which they could be effective, or reject them entirely, because of their distaste for undergoing mutilating, painful and toxic treatments. Many physicians believe that patients who resort to spiritual healing are grasping at less threatening, but ineffective straws.

Critics of conventional cancer therapies have observed that treatment of cancer has become an industry. Like any established institution, this industry tends to perpetuate itself and to resist approaches that might encroach on its territory.

Another factor plays into this conflict between conventional therapies and self-healing approaches. The fear of death in patients and in medical staff is poorly managed.174 Doctors are trained to diagnose and cure disease, and they often feel that they have failed when they find themselves confronted by a medically incurable illness. They are likely to ignore the obvious, as is pointed out by Bernie

Siegel: "Life is invariably fatal. A doctor ought to be aiming to improve quality of life, not simply to prolong it."

Self-healing CAM therapies face a major challenge in proving their worth through objective research. The selection of patients with cancer who are willing to participate in complementary cancer therapies is problematic. I was surprised to hear that in various studies the percentage of cancer patients willing to try such self-healing therapies ranged from a high of 10-20% to a low of less than 1%. Much of the research to date has therefore been based on a highly self-selected group of patients who agree to apply the new methods. The prognosis for those who consent to participate may already be better than expected, because these patients tend to be *fighters*, have a greater will to live, and perhaps are less depressed. This feeds the doubts of skeptics, who do not want to encourage false hopes in cancer patients who might not be predisposed for success in self-healing.

Sadly, all of these factors have combined to severely limit the availability of PNI for patients with cancer, cardiovascular disease, AIDS and other illnesses.

Much of Western medicine is focused on putting more days into our lives, at any cost. But a major shift toward putting more life into our days can be brought about through better attitudes toward serious and fatal illnesses. Cancer and other life-threatening illnesses can be challenges that lead to positive emotional changes. Hervé Guibert observes that cancer is "An illness in stages, a very long flight of steps that led assuredly to death, but whose every step represented a unique apprenticeship. It was a disease that gave death time to live and its victims time to die, time to discover time, and in the end, to discover life."

People with fatal illnesses may come to a state of mind in which they feel grateful for the positive changes the illness has brought into their lives. I myself found it difficult at first to believe reports of this kind of positive acceptance. It is only in working closely with people who are struggling with cancer and AIDS that I've come to understand this. When we realize that there is very limited time left to live, we are forced to choose carefully how we budget our precious remaining minutes on this earth. Many problems that may have seemed important before, now shrink to insignificance – when we ask ourselves if we truly want to spend our limited remaining time attending to them. Sorting out relationships becomes much more important – with our own past and with significant others in our lives. It becomes easier to let go of old emotional dross and urgent to put our personal relationships into the best possible order. Sorting out unresolved issues and saying goodbyes can be a great blessing to friends and family as well.

When we process all of these issues, our *quality of life* is dramatically improved. We feel much more alive when every minute is being lived to the maximum, when we are no longer wasting time on outdated *shoulds* and *shouldn'ts* – old habits that may have been programmed into our personal life computer many years earlier by our child selves or by parents, teachers, religious institutions and others who couldn't know then where we would be today.

Spiritual questions arise as we ask ourselves what may await us when we close our eyes for the last time and release our final breath. We may find comfort in the religious teachings and practices of our upbringing or of our personal choice. Recent studies suggest that we may be blessed with pre-death visions of spiritual vistas that seem as real – if not more real – than anything we have experienced in the flesh (Morse/ Perry 1994). We may look forward to being welcomed by the spirits of those who have preceded us across that mysterious divide between life in the flesh and pure spirit existence.

> *And almost every one when age,*
> *Disease, or sorrows strike him,*
> *Inclines to think there is a God,*
> *Or something very like Him.*
> — Arthur Hugh Clough

Death is only frightening to those who run away from it. Reports by people who have had near-death experiences, spirit communications, and reincarnation memories uniformly confirm that the transition is painless, and that the spiritual dimensions are far more pleasant than life in the flesh.[175]

Despite all of the above, few of us rush to abandon our physical existence. We hang onto life, because that is what we know. Healing is largely a matter of making the best of the life we have been given.

SPONTANEOUS REMISSIONS OF ILLNESSES

> *Give it a name, any name, and we feel we understand what we're talking about.*
> — Anonymous

Tilden Everson and Warren Cole (1966) reviewed the medical literature on cancer from 1800, and identified 176 cases *of spontaneous remission.* They suggest that modern isolated "cures" of cancer via unorthodox therapeutic measures might actually be spontaneous regressions of cancer. That is, the natural progression of the disease in some instances might include remissions that could be unrelated to therapeutic interventions. They propose that the following factors might contribute to such remissions: endocrine influences; fever and infection; allergic or immune reactions; disruption of the nutrition of the cancer; removal of the carcinogenic agent; unusual sensitivity to therapy that is normally inadequate; complete surgical removal of the cancer (where it had been presumed that the removal was incomplete); and incorrect histologic (microscopic) diagnosis of malignancy.

Although estimates of the frequency of spontaneous regression of serious illnesses are greatly speculative, all sources agree that it is extremely rare, possibly in the range of one case per 80,000 to 100,000.

Everson and Cole had to rely on retrospective reports from a variety of sources, spread over many decades. Duration of the spontaneous remission was of necessity determined by the publication date of the report, except in the cases where death was recorded.

Brendan O'Regan and Caryl Hirshberg (1993), using computer-assisted library searches, undertook the Herculean task of reviewing 3,500 cases of *spontaneous remission,* many from more recent years. About three-quarters of these remissions were from cancers. They point out that spontaneous remissions may occur without allopathic treatment; may be associated with treatments by allopathic or complementary therapies; or may be associated with spiritual cures –sometimes labeled as *miracle cures*. They most often occur gradually, over days or months, but may also occur rapidly, within minutes or hours. An oddity of these reports is the general lack of explorations to identify how these unusual cures occurred.

> *You see things; and you say "Why?" But I dream things that never were; and I say "Why not?"*
>
> – George Bernard Shaw (1921*)*

According to O'Regan and Hirshberg, spontaneous remission has been largely overlooked by medical science for several reasons:

1. remissions are usually identified after the fact, which makes the processes involved in these unusual cures difficult to study;
2. quality of reports varies in so many respects that it is difficult to assess their frequency or accuracy;
3. doctors suspect that there must have been errors in the initial diagnosis;
4. clinicians are reluctant to report such remissions – wary of skepticism, and afraid of being criticized for poor initial diagnosis or other similar errors;
5. clinicians treating physical conditions often omit details of patients' personal histories, and clinicians addressing psychological aspects of illness rarely include documentation about the physical conditions; and
6. skeptics suspect that all such remissions will be temporary.

The survey of O'Regan and Hirshberg is a monumental work. However, it focuses heavily on remissions of physical illness, with minimal consideration given to psychological aspects of remission. The next reference amply redresses this deficit.

Caryl Hirshberg and Marc Ian Barasch reviewed *remarkable recoveries* from a broad spectrum of illnesses. Great attention was given to people's descriptions of their beliefs about illness, how they received their treatments – both conventional and complementary – and how they understood their transformations. I have selected a few examples from among their many helpful observations. The study contains numerous other discussions and fascinating individual accounts of personal health challenges that were met with courage, and were dealt with through a spectrum of wholistic healing approaches.[176]

Hirshberg and Barasch noted that certain characteristics appeared frequently among the large number of people they interviewed:

1. They had a strong sense of their *selfhood*.
2. They demonstrated qualities of *congruence*, being true to their beliefs, ideals, values and life goals in the emotional, cognitive and behavioral aspects of their lives.
3. They did not cluster in particular personality styles. "[I]t may be more a matter of finding an individual 'right path' than having the 'right stuff.'" (p.152)
4. They were *determined to improve*, and *assertive* in exploring therapeutic alternatives and implementing them.

5. They refused to accept dire prognoses from their doctors, sometimes even deciding to fight their illnesses to spite their doctors' predictions. This kind of *constructive denial* might also extend to a refusal to equate a serious diagnosis, such as cancer, with death.
6. They developed reasons to live and to enjoy life.
7. They had spiritual experiences, often associated with profound personality changes, as a result of their illnesses.

In the foreword to this outstanding book, Larry Dossey observes (p.xii):

> Because remarkable recoveries often occur unbidden and out-of-the-blue, they appear to be a blessing, a grace. We do not know the buttons to push to make them happen; we cannot compel them to our bidding. This means we cannot control them. Control has become immensely important to generations of scientifically trained physicians. Could it be that we modern doctors, so desperate to control nature, have shunned these marvelous events because they are so uncontrollable?

This book contains a wealth of information for anyone who is interested in spontaneous remissions and remarkable recoveries from illnesses. It strongly suggests that self-healing is at work when people have unusual recoveries from illness. Clearly, many of the mechanisms in these self-healing experiences do not take place within the conscious awareness of the people experiencing them, nor are they evident to those studying them, and in that sense these remarkable recoveries appear to be "spontaneous." However, in broad terms it can be hypothesized that some of the factors related to the occurrence of such remissions include: changing one's attitudes and beliefs about one's illness; releasing blocked emotions; finding joy, and changing one's relationships, life course and styles of handling emotions – particularly in situations of stress and conflict – in order to facilitate release of tensions, conflicts and resentments. As people come more fully into awarness of the need to relate differently to the world, they may achieve states of acceptance and forgiveness in which tensions and conflicts are not generated.[177]

A final strong recommendation for further reading is the personal account of Marc Barasch (1993) in his search for ways to deal with a thyroid tumor. This is accompanied by brief summaries of the stories of many others who faced the challenges of serious illness and transcended them. This is a masterful presentation, full of helpful information, and a good read besides.

> Almost all the journeyers I interviewed discovered that new life can grow from the same painful roots that may have contributed to their disease. For if some disease springs in part from an early-thwarted need for love and relatedness, a soul-growth denied, then the roots of illness are, paradoxically, the very roots of life.
>
> – Marc Ian Barasch (p. 99)

So-called spontaneous remissions may represent self-healing, perhaps through some of the mechanisms suggested by the above-mentioned authors, or through spiritual healing, which Everson and Cole did not examine and O'Regan and Hirshberg considered only in an extremely limited scope. They made no attempts to investigate psychological correlates of cancer regressions. This would be impossible in any case in such retrospective studies, since psychological (not to mention PNI and psi) factors of disease have not been in the forefront of medical awareness, and thus have been under-reported.

Once we become aware of spontaneous remission, we must ask whether remissions reported by various therapists are anything more than this. The reported rates of improvement with Simonton-type techniques and other PNI approaches appear to exceed the rate for spontaneous remission, but because subjects self-select for these treatments, it is difficult to be certain of this.

Conventional cancer treatments usually include chemotherapy. Modern medicine has readily embraced this mode of treatment despite its terrible morbidity, including nausea, vomiting, diarrhea, hair-loss and more.

It is rather shocking to realize that this drastic method of treatment has been widely used even though controlled studies of chemotherapy have in most cases been methodologically flawed in ways similar to the Simonton studies. Robert Oye and Martin Shapiro found that:

> ...Of 80 studies, 95% reported response to chemotherapy as an end point. Of 38 studies demonstrating 15% or greater objective response, 76% reported significantly greater survival of responders than of non-responders. Of 21 studies containing statements supporting treatment effectiveness, 95% based this claim at least in part on the superior survival of responders compared with nonresponders. Because responders may have lived longer without treatment, such comparisons are not valid and may lead to overly optimistic views of chemotherapy effectiveness.
> ...No study confirmed survival of responders as superior to that of a favorable subset of untreated patients.
> ...None of the studies systematically examined quality of life in the patients treated with chemotherapy.

For all the researchers know, the responders in these studies might have done equally well without the treatment (or perhaps even better!). Non-responders might be selectively poisoned by chemotherapy, and might therefore do worse than responders, rather than vice versa. To prove chemotherapy effective, a group of treated patients with a positive prognosis should be compared with a similar group that is untreated. The medical profession, having assumed a priori that chemotherapy is effective, considers such a study unethical. They are also afraid of being sued by patients who could complain that they were not given the best available treatment.

This is condemning evidence against the common-practice standard of acceptability in Western medicine. It is distressing that cancer patients are being subjected to the torment of treatments that have not been properly demonstrated to be effective.

One may only hope that spiritual healing, clearly a non-invasive, non-toxic therapy, will be increasingly used in the treatment of cancer, along with the currently more accepted modalities. This is not to say that healing must replace chemotherapy and radiotherapy. Healing can be effective in combination with these treatments, certainly in reducing toxic side effects and probably in potentiating the actions of these more accepted treatments – assuming that they are in fact effective themselves.

A FEW WORDS IN SUMMARY ABOUT PSYCHOTHERAPIES

The variations on the themes of psychotherapy are as infinite as the creativity of therapists and the countless manifestations and resolutions of the suffering of mankind. It is impossible to say in all cases which treatment method may be the best for any given problem, because health problems are manifested through the complex interplay of genetic endowments, personalities, relationships and cultural settings within which they occur.[178]

In many ways, the person who is the instrument of the therapy is as important as the methods that she applies. The more work therapists have done on themselves in their own paths through life, the better instruments they will be in helping clients to change. Ram Dass (1996, p.75) observes, "The mistake of therapists is in thinking they do something *to* other people. I don't have that sense of doing anything *to* anyone else. I have a sense that I am an environment, and people do it to themselves."

> *People are healed by different kinds of healers and systems because the real healer is within.*
> – George Goodheart

The indefinable *chemistry* of relationships between therapists and clients also influences the clients' openness to growth and change. In the most profound therapeutic relationships, therapists open their own hearts, and learn and grow as much as their clients do.

These observations apply all the more in spiritual healing, where the subtle energy interactions and spiritual dimensions of the encounter can add to the complexity of the therapeutic relationship. Swami Satchidananda (1996, p.227) advises, "If we don't experience that God in us, we will never see God in anyone else because we have no eye to see." Everyone must work on the shadow aspects in every level of their being, in order to provide as clear a channel as possible for healing.

THE MIND AND THE BRAIN

> *The brain is the organ through which we think that we think.*
> – Ambrose Bierce

Where the mind actually resides is far from obvious. The structure and processes of the brain are by necessity much easier to define. It is clear that if the brain is awry physically, biochemically or electrobiologically, the expression of mind is distorted or impaired. Doctors have discovered much about how the brain functions through examining people whose brains have been injured by trauma, vascular disease, tumors, infections or surgery. The resultant psychological and physical deficits reveal the functions of the damaged or missing portions of the brain. Further information can also be obtained during neurosurgery – which is usually performed under local anesthetics because the brain does not hurt when it is probed. Neurosurgeons can carefully stimulate selected portions of the brain electrically and obtain information about their function by observing patients' responses.

Biochemical studies of the brain have shown that it performs numerous chemical and hormonal processes that are maintained in a delicate, homeostatic balance. Even minor chemical changes can produce serious brain dysfunctions. Medicines and drugs can likewise alter brain functions, for better or worse.

Electroencephalograms and new computerized electromagnetic and radioactive imaging devices[179] allow researchers to study the living brain in incredible detail and with special techniques also to assess changes in its functions during various mental and emotional processes. Studies of humans have been supplemented with numerous experiments on animals, whose brains are sufficiently analogous to human brains to permit deductions and inferences as to how the human brain works.

Using these methods, detailed physical, biochemical and electrical maps have been drawn of how the brain functions during a variety of mental activities and emotional states. These studies could suggest that "mind" is purely a function of the brain (Dennett). They point out that particular reactions are elicited, including motor responses, sensory perceptions and emotional tones, when particular areas of the brain are stimulated electrically,[180] or if particular drugs or hormones are present in the brain (Bergland). They therefore conclude that consciousness is a product of brain bioelectrical activities.

Yet there is also strong evidence suggesting that mind is not necessarily the product of brain. Among the more interesting of these, consider the following:

1. During anesthesia, when people's conscious awareness is asleep, they may still hear and respond to what is taking place in the operating room (Cheek 1962). Cases are reported in which a surgeon made negative comments such as, "Too bad! There's nothing more we can do. The cancer has spread too far," and within moments the patient's heart stopped beating. Conversely, suggestions may be given under anesthesia that patients will have less post-surgical pain and other complications. Sometimes they respond so well to these suggestions that they may be discharged from the hospital earlier than expected (Evans/ Richardson).

2. Cases of out-of-body (OBE) viewing of the operating room during surgery while patients are under anesthesia have been reported (Fenwick; Rogo 1978).[181]
In such OBE experiences, patients feel themselves floating as a point of consciousness or a ghost-like being near the ceiling of the operating room, looking down at their physical body, on which the surgical team is still operating. They will often be able to recall in minute and accurate detail various actions that occurred and words that were said during their operations (sometimes to the embarrassment of their surgeons!).

3. Research on reports of near-death and reincarnation experiences suggest that there is more to the mind than the brain that exists in one's current life can account for.[182] For example, children and adults who live in countries where they have no access to newspapers or media have reported details of previous lives that have been verified – when there was no known way in which they could have obtained the information in question. In occasional instances these reports include the use of languages that the speakers have never learned.

4. There are people who have grown up with unidentified hydrocephalus, which has left them with such large ventricles (fluid filled-spaces within the brain) and such a thinned cerebral cortex that they should be imbeciles (as it is assumed that an intact cerebral cortex is required for thinking), yet they have become successful university students (Lewin).

The alternative view is that the mind exists outside of the brain, or overlaps several dimensions to include the brain, which acts as a transducer for mind across the boundaries between dimensions.

In this view, mind resides on some non-physical plane(s), but expresses itself via transformations of energy or information through the brain. The brain contains an estimated 10 to 14 billion nerve cells, with a constant interplay of electrochemical messages between its countless interconnections. It is possible that the brain may readily be influenced by outside energies that can modulate some of this ongoing intercellular activity. A minimum of energy input might be required to influence any of the multitudes of brain cells that are frequently standing on the threshold of emitting impulses. Thus the brain would act like radio or TV receiver.

All the body is in the mind, but not all the mind is in the body.
– Swami Rama

Philosophical speculations have gone even further. Consider the following quotation from the psychologist Keith Floyd: "Contrary to what everyone knows is so, it may not be the brain that produces consciousness but rather, consciousness that creates the appearance of the brain matter, space, time and everything else we are pleased to interpret as the physical universe."

While such statements based on evidence from neurobiology and psi research might appear speculative, well substantiated research from quantum physics suggests similar conclusions.[183] Quantum physics has shown that the consciousness of the observer determines that which is observed. Consciousness therefore appears to shape matter. While this doesn't prove that the consciousness is primary and brain secondary, it lends support to this possibility.[184]

The physicist does not discover, he creates his universe.
– Henry Margenau

These questions are highly complex. The evidence for theories of mind influencing brain, and possibly even creating reality both internally and externally, deserve far more consideration than is practical in the context of this volume. It may eventually prove impossible to arrive at definitive answers to some of these questions, but in my opinion, the theory of mind being the primary agency is consistent with the greater weight of evidence.[185]

TRANSPERSONAL PSYCHOTHERAPY

Much of what we think is extraordinary in another plane is just the ordinary - not understood or experienced.

— Ted Kaptchuk

Most conventional psychotherapists are trained to help people suffering from distress in their inner psychological worlds. Some therapists extend treatment to involve relationships with other people, as in couples and family therapy. Spiritual awareness is usually relegated to ministrations of the clergy, and is dismissed by many psychotherapists as fantasy, wishful thinking, the beliefs and habits resulting from religious upbringing or a manifestation of the denial of death. The most damning criticism of religion by psychology is that there is no way to prove it is intrinsically valid rather than a mental construct.

We tend to overlook the fact that psychology is based on unprovable basic assumptions, just as religions are.[186] In fact, there are probably more theories in psychology than there are religions. Frances Vaughan (1995) observes, "Psychology, like exoteric religion, is an expedient rather than a final teaching."

Ordinary people (who are not trained in specific academic disciplines that specialize in *parts* of human experience) will usually view spirituality as an important lining to the fabric of their lives, inseparable from their other experiences.

> *...The older I became, the more the intimation grew that the deepest longing in the universe of the unconscious, in fact the greatest of all the urges in the collective unconscious, was the strange, irresistible longing to become more conscious: that and not the unconscious, was the real life-giving mystery...*
>
> – Laurens van der Post (1994, p. 21)

A new, *transpersonal* branch of psychology has emerged that includes meditative techniques, alternative states of consciousness and integration of spiritual, mystical and religious teachings and rituals.[187] These practices heighten awareness of aspects of their beings that traditionally have been relegated to the realm of religion in Western culture. Transpersonal awareness suggests that each of us is a part of a vast whole – an intricate network of which we are usually but dimly aware. If we see our lives in relation to the All just as the life of a cell is in relation to our whole body, then our lives may take on a deeper meaning. Such awarenesses are better experienced than articulated in words. They partake of the essence alluded to by F. David Peat in discussions about the elements of the unconscious, in which he suggests that there is a higher self:

> [T]he archetypes leave their footprints in the mind and project their shadows across thought. While it is not possible to observe the archetypes directly, their movements can be sensed through the numinous images, myths, and happiness that enter consciousness...

At the very least, transpersonal approaches can provide an expanded perspective from which to view our own problems.[188] Anxiety or depression may not appear so onerous when they are placed in these temporal, spiritual or priority frameworks. These dimensions of therapy can also provide discipline, inspiration, courage, hope and community with other people or higher powers.

> Break*down* may be a break*through.*
> – Anonymous

For some, transpersonal approaches can be transformative, especially when we have "hit bottom." We may emerge from "the dark night of the soul" through transpersonal therapy into completely new modes of interacting with the world.

To illustrate how transpersonal awareness can be accessed for healing let us consider a few salient examples of such approaches. The most common of these is meditation.

Meditation leads us inward to Alternative States of Consciousness (ASCs) in which we can find relaxation, peace, release from worldly cares, emotional release of buried hurts, serenity, inspiration and connection with our higher selves and with the Divine. Because these ASCs and inner worlds are beyond the descriptive powers of linear words and concepts, it is difficult to articulate them. Of the many writers on meditation I particularly recommend Daniel Goleman and Ken Wilber.

Daniel Goleman (1977; 1988) follows classical Eastern meditative practices in describing two paths for meditation.

The *path of concentration* involves focusing undivided attention upon an object, either in the world outside or within the mind. With practice, one reaches successively deeper meditative stages *(jhanas)*. The first is a merging with the object. "Rapture at the level of the first *jhana* is likened to the initial pleasure of excitement at getting a long-sought object; bliss is the enjoyment of that object." (1977, p.14). At the second *jhana* the meditator stops focusing on the object and identifies with the rapture, freeing the mind of all concrete thoughts. At the third level the meditator attains equanimity, or an even-mindedness that exists beyond the rapture and produces an encompassing bliss. Going deeper, the fourth *jhana* brings cessation of all thought and sensation, and even of breathing. "The meditator's mind at this extremely subtle level rests with one-pointedness in equanimity." (p.17)

Further stages on the path of concentration are formless. The meditator's concentration is imperturbable and cannot be disturbed. He comes out of the meditative state according to his intention, which he determines prior to entering the meditation. At the fifth *jhana* the meditator becomes aware of the space that the object of focus occupies, with only the dimmest remnant of perception of the object itself remaining at the periphery of his concentration. The sixth *jhana* extends awareness into the infiniteness of space. Then, abandoning the focus on space, the meditator reaches infinite awareness. The seventh *jhana* is the void. The eighth and final stage is awareness of the peacefulness of the void, without even the desire to attain this peacefulness. Only the faintest residual mental processes remain.

On the *path of insight* the meditator focuses awareness on perceptions of body, feelings, mind or mind objects but does not analyze them in any way. Should a thought about a perception occur, then the thought itself becomes the subject of concentration. Without judgment, the meditator releases each perception after contemplating it. A degree of facility in concentration is required for insight practices, so that these will follow naturally upon the practices of the *path of concentration*.

Any of these techniques of *mindfulness* will break through the illusions of continuity and rationality that ordinarily sustain our mental life. In *mindfulness*, the meditator begins to discern the random units of mental perception from which his reality is built. From these observations emerge a series of realizations about the nature of the mind. Through this process, *mindfulness* matures into *insight*. The practice of insight begins at the point where mindfulness continues without interruption or time lag. In *insight meditation* awareness fixes on its object so that the contemplating mind and its object of contemplation arise together in unbroken succession. This point marks the beginning of a chain of insights – mind knowing itself – which ends in the *nirvanic state*.

The first step in mindfulness is to realize that the mind is distinct from the phenomena it contemplates. Next, the meditator notices that she is not willing these processes but that they proceed on their own. She realizes that the "I" does not really exist. Reality shifts with endless perceptions from moment to moment, and she experiences only the state of impermanence. The constantly changing nature of reality leaves nothing to which one needs to remain attached. Eventually a state of detachment is reached in which the mind is perceived as a source of suffering.

> *We are all serving a life-sentence in the dungeon of self.*
> – Cyril Connolly

As the meditator continues through this development of awareness, various visions and rapturous feelings begin to arise. Goleman labels this *pseudonirvana,* because it is really only a stage on a longer path. Though the meditator may be tempted to enjoy these distractions, he must simply focus on his attachment to them, rather than on the feelings themselves.

More difficult stages follow, in which the disappearance of awareness becomes more distinct than one's perceptions of both the object and one's contemplation of it. At this point, all awareness loses its attraction and cessation of mental processes appears to be the most attractive goal. Painful feelings may assail the body and suffering may become intense. As the meditator continues simply to note these feelings, they eventually cease. Contemplation then becomes automatic and the focus clears. Each transient moment is simply noted and released, and no deliberate effort is required to maintain a detached meditative state. Goleman describes what follows:

> [A] consciousness arises that takes as its object the signless, no-occurrence, no-formation: *nirvana*.... Awareness of all physical and mental phenomena ceases entirely.
> [N]irvana is a "supramundane reality," describable only in terms of what it is not. Nirvana has no phenomenology, no experiential characteristics. It is the unconditioned state. (p.31)

With *nirvana* a natural moral purity emerges which eliminates all emotional attachments. *Jhana* suppresses rather than eliminates these factors. "…Entering the nirvanic state is... 'awakening'; …subsequent stages are… 'deliverance'." (p.33) With deliverance, the meditator relinquishes ego attachments to achievements, pleasures, emotions and possessions. Moral misbehavior is no longer within the spectrum of his conduct. Deliverance is experienced in an initial, partial state, and then it becomes permanent. Fully developed, the meditator becomes an *arahant* – an awakened being or saint.

The paths of contemplation and insight may be different for Eastern and Western meditators, and I will discuss this further below.

A second analysis of meditation may help to clarify some of the intricacies of this finest of human endeavors and greatest of human challenges.

> *Who is brave? The person who conquers his own spirit.*
> – Jewish saying

Ken Wilber (1980) is a world expert on meditation. He views consciousness as extending beyond ordinary awareness – largely through the unconscious mind – into transpersonal and cosmic awarenesses.[189] This is in contrast to conventional psychology, which views the unconscious as a storehouse of material that may be perceived consciously or subliminally and is then screened and repressed. The unconscious is considered as the *automatic pilot* for repetitive responses and behaviors – both physiological and psychological. Within this framework, meditation is acknowledged by psychologists as a tool that can be used to penetrate repressions, stop filtering, and de-automate responses. Wilber's approach is much less mechanistic; he emphasizes that meditation is, most importantly, a path towards transcendence.

Wilber details how a child grows through various maturational levels during psychological development. At a given level the child *translates* emotional drives and cognitive needs into various behavioral expressions. At a given level of development, the child is capable of analyzing and understanding inner and outer experiences within the range of their comprehension, at that particular level of development. As the *translations* that characterize a given level of development become outmoded due to conceptual and emotional maturation, the child's consciousness is *transformed* into a higher level of organization and functioning. "There is differentiation, dis-identification [with outmoded coping mechanisms], transcendence and integration" (p.93).

These maturational processes of *translation* and *transformation* are like the risers and steps in a staircase. The periods of translation are plateaus where a person explores and consolidates a given level of awareness. Then comes a rise through transformation to a new level, which is qualitatively different from the previous level. This is followed by successive alternating steps of translation and transformation as a person's awareness matures and deepens. Adults may continue to develop and deepen their awareness, or may stop at a given step.[190]

Throughout the ages, many religious and mystical traditions have invited people to explore varieties of ways to facilitate the transformation process which reaches into higher steps of spiritual awareness.

Meditation is the path to transformation that has been explored in the most systematic way. Meditation can take a person into deeper levels of awareness, through a variety of approaches. Meditation masters can frustrate and block the customary *translations* and undermine emotional resistances, while introducing symbols that embody aspects of the higher levels of consciousness, which are then used as the focus of meditation. Practicing the higher meditative translations helps to induce spiritual transformation. Such translations may include awareness of timelessness, avoidance of attachments, uniting with objects outside oneself, accepting unconditionally everything that enters consciousness, and holding awareness of love in one's consciousness.

Concentrative meditation stops the activity of translation. By concentrating on a particular image, word, chant or other focus, the mind is occupied and stops its wandering. Receptive *observing meditation* defocalizes attention, focusing the mind to observe its own mental processes but not engaging in any of them – simply letting them drift by. Both place meditators at a higher level of awareness than their customary conscious translations, while breaking down the lower order of translations.

Wilber identifies three classes of meditation:

1. Meditation may focus on the body, as in various forms of yoga, with the goal of transmuting body energies into lower subtle regions of awareness.
2. Meditation may focus on higher subtle regions beyond the crown chakra.
3. The meditator may focus on "inquiry into the causal field of consciousness itself, inquiry into the I-ness or the separate-self sense, even in and through the Transcendent Witness of the causal region, until all forms of subject-object dualism are uprooted." (p.96)

Any of these paths can lead to the highest states of meditative consciousness. Ultimately, individual consciousness unites with the cosmic consciousness.

> And so proceeds meditation, which is simply higher development, which is simply higher evolution – a transformation from unity to unity until there is simply Unity, whereupon Brahman, in an unnoticed shock of recognition and final remembrance, grins silently to itself, closes its eyes, breathes deeply, and throws itself outward for the millionth time, losing itself in its manifestations for the sport and play of it all. Evolution then proceeds again, transformation by transformation, remembering more and more, until each and every soul remembers Buddha, as Buddha, in Buddha – whereupon there is then no Buddha, and no soul. And that is the final transformation... (p.99)

Wilber believes that the ultimate healing is Unity with the All, or *Atman* (in Buddhist terminology). He views psychological growth in terms of its progress towards this goal. However, unconscious resistances to meditative progress are many and strong. This makes the practice of meditation a challenge that may require years of practice to master. Most commonly,

> Because man wants real transcendence above all else, but because he cannot or will not accept the necessary death of his separate-self sense, he goes about seeking transcendence in ways, or through structures, that *actually prevent* it and *force symbolic substitutes*. And these substitutes come in all varieties: sex, food, money, fame,

knowledge, power – all are ultimately substitute gratifications, simple
substitutions for true release in Wholeness... (p.102-3)

Wilber is describing *Eros*, the drive to wish, desire, seek, grasp, possess, and so
forth. Eros is dealt with through concentrative and receptive meditations.

A major anxiety encountered during meditation is *Thanatos,* the fear of dying
and thus of losing one's awareness of self. This occurs to some extent with each
advancement and growth from one meditation level to another. It is a natural fear,
quite distinct from psychopathological anxieties and fears. This fear is inherent in
developing a growing sense of being a separate self, and it finds expression at
each level of development according to the translations appropriate at that level.
The challenge is to transcend this fear in order to ultimately relinquish all sense of
self and unite with the All.[191]

> ...Only at the end of psychological growth is there final enlightenment
> and liberation in and as God, but that is the *only* thing that is desired
> from the beginning...
>   The point is that each stage or level of growth seeks absolute Unity,
> but in ways or under constraints that necessarily prevent it and allow
> only compromises: substitute unities and substitute gratifications...
> (p.101)

The climb up the stairway to spiritual awareness can be accompanied by resur-
gences of repressed traumatic memories and resultant emotional releases. Wilber
cites M. Washburn, who suggests that only the receptive type of meditation opens
directly into the unconscious. This absorptive meditation focuses so completely
on the object of concentration that everything else, including unconscious material, remains outside of the meditator's awareness during the meditative practice.
In absorptive meditation, unconscious materials are confronted only after the
meditative object is relinquished or the meditative practices are concluded.
Wilber feels that this advantage of receptive meditation definitely applies in accessing the shadow aspects of the unconscious but not in exploring the emergent,
higher aspects of the unconscious that develop as a result of meditation.

In view of the greater emphasis placed upon "clearing the psychological
shadow" in the West, it would seem to me that this could be an important consideration in choosing a path of meditation – these assertions are verified.

Deeper meditative practices can take us into realms of consciousness that are
hard to define or describe. Eastern meditative masters have been teaching meditation for many hundreds of years, and they find that students of meditation
regularly go through specific phases of awareness as they deepen their meditative
practices. Eastern terms for these stages can be difficult for westerners to understand, as you may have found with Goleman's explanations. Wilber (1980)
proposes a map of this inner territory in terms that represent extensions of the
stages of growth as defined in developmental psychology.

Wilber proposes that human consciousness develops in a stepwise fashion
through what he calls the *outward arc*, and that meditation can extend consciousness into dimensions beyond our ordinary awareness through the *inward arc*. (See
figure II-5, from Wilber 1980, p.5)

Figure II-5. The complete life cycle

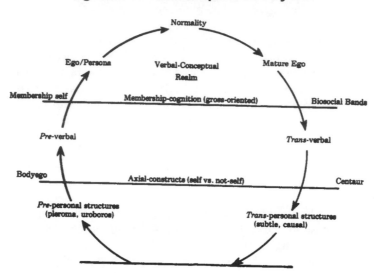

Conventional psychology has identified stages of cognitive development (Piaget); psychosexual development (S. Freud); emotional/ affective development; formation of family relations; moral maturation, and more. Wilber considers all of these to be on the *outward arc* of human consciousness (per his diagram), even though these processes may extend to the end of a person's physical existence.

Wilber has developed his own terminology for the developmental stages that he considers significant.[192] While the terminology refers to Western conceptual frameworks, it may be no less challenging than the Eastern terms it replaces!

He starts with the *Pleromatic Self* of the fetus and newborn infant, who does not differentiate between the self and the material world. Consciousness is autistic, relating to the world without any appreciation of space or time and assuming itself to be the center of the universe.

The first task of the infant is to differentiate between self and others, usually through the relationship with its mother. This leads into the next stage of the *Uroboric Self* (named for the mythic serpent that is pictured eating its own tail). The infant develops a dim and poorly differentiated awareness of self as differentiated from the mother's breast. There is still no sense of time, nor any real appreciation of the nature of others as existing for any reason other than to satisfy the infant's needs.

In the stage of the *Typhonic Self* the infant develops awareness of its *axial,* physical body as separate from its physical environment. In this stage only objects that are present remain within the infant's awareness. Out of sight is truly out of mind. In the early *typhonic* stage the self simply *is* in whatever state it finds itself. Next, the child's awareness of a *Pranic Self* develops through the experience of basic emotions. In the earliest stages there is only a primitive awareness of hunger, tension, anxiety, anger and satiation/ pleasure, while causality is still beyond conceptual awareness.

The infant develops its ability to conceptualize imagery when it is around seven months old, and it begins to separate out objects in its environment, though it still does not connect them causally. They simply are or are not there. Classes of objects may be identified according to individual parts, with only partial understanding of categorization. This is called *prelogical* (Freud), *part-identity* or *parataxic* logic (H. Sullivan). In this *primary process* thinking, self and objects in the outside world may be confused.

The infant then develops an *image-body* awareness. The baby is highly sensitive to the quality of caring received, and is vulnerable to adopting a positive or negative self-concept, depending upon the treatment it receives from its mother. As imagery can be invoked internally, this imagery can also evoke emotions, and imagined anxieties become possible. Wishes and desires may also be fulfilled by imagined pleasures.

As the infant learns to distinguish itself as being separate from objects, the self *transcends* those objects and can then operate upon them through the mental structures that have differentiated at that level of development.

The *Membership Self* evolves as language learning introduces new capabilities, including an expanded appreciation of time, a deeper and more complex emotional life, and basic elements of self-control – all in all, a higher order of self-awareness. The details of development at this level are very much shaped and limited by the participation of the individual in a particular family and culture. This has been identified as *secondary process* (Freud); *syntaxical mode* (H. Sullivan); and *realistic thinking* (Piaget).

This stage takes a relatively long time to develop. In the intermediate period there exists a mixture of logic and magical thinking, termed *precausal* (Piaget); *prelogical* (S. Freud); *paleological* (Arieti); *autistic language* (H. Sullivan); and *"forgotten language of childhood"* (Lacan 1968a; b). Thinking at this level is mostly auditory and verbal.

As logical awareness matures, children achieve a greater degree of consensual reality testing within their culture. While this is clearly advantageous and necessary, each step forward may require considerable readjustments. For instance, an awareness of oneself as being separate from others enables one to engage in more realistic interactions with them, but this individuation may be frightening at first.

The *Mental-Egoic Stages* introduce further elaborations of self-awareness. A thinking-self develops as a self-concept or *ego*. Wilber identifies an *early ego* (age 4-7), *middle ego* (7-12), and *late ego* (from 12 years to the start of the inward arc, if and when the person commences on this path, usually after age 21).

Using the language of Transactional Analysis (I. Stewart/ Joines), Wilber describes how subdivisions of functions evolve within the ego. One of these is an emotional *child* part that is highly interactive with others. This is the aspect of the self that seeks immediate pleasure and avoids pain, that wants to be accepted by parents and parent-figures, and that fights and rebels against authority for its independence while at the same time seeking the security of external limits. An *adult* part assumes the tasks of logical analysis and prioritizing inner and outer needs and wants, relative to costs. A *parent*, or *super-ego* part internalizes attitudes and behaviors that are approved or forbidden by parents and society.

Every individual has to modify his behaviors in response to his environment. Aspects of the self that are uncomfortable to the conscious self may be repressed in unconscious parts of the mind. The repressed parts of the self constitute the *shadow*, and the remaining, "fraudulent" self or "social mask" is termed the *persona* (Jung).

Wilber examines the transitions from one stage of development to another, and finds that the self must dis-identify with its current structure in order to identify with the next higher level.

> [B]ecause the self is differentiated from the lower structure, it *transcends* that structure (without obliterating it in any way), and can thus *operate* on that lower structure using the tools of the newly emergent structure (p.80). [A]t each point in evolution or remembrance, a *mode* of self becomes merely a *component* of a higher-order self (p.81).

Each level has a *deep structure*, which defines the inner nature, functions and limitations of that level, and a *surface structure*, which is the outward expression of the deep structure. Wilber uses the analogy of a building, in which each floor represents the structure of a given level. The rooms, their contents, and the activities that go on within them represent the surface structures of the self. He calls movement within surface structures *translation*, and movement from one deep structure to another *transformation*. Translation involves various expressions within the same level. In lower levels, the oceanic awareness of the *uroboric* self is transformed, as the axial self-image develops into an awareness of bodily pleasure. At a higher level, a little girl may experience anxiety on the level of the *typhonic* self if she receives insufficient attention from her mother. This could be experienced as physical tension, emotional irritability or crying – all of which are translations of the original discomfort. Endless translations occur within the range of capabilities at any given level.

If the stress continues in the little girl's experience, a transformation may be precipitated. A *regressive* transformation would be for the girl to withdraw into herself and stop communicating with the outside world, shutting off her emotions from her own awareness, and seeking satisfaction through doll play and fantasy. A *progressive* transformation could be to develop explanations to rationalize the distress and soften anxieties, tensions and emotional pain. The latter involves transformation into the mental levels. The child could say, "I must be a bad girl if Mommy doesn't want to pay attention to me. I'll have to work very hard to be good and do everything Mommy wants." Or she could displace frustration and anger onto objects in her environment, or engage in a myriad of possible translations within the mental level. All of these would be unconscious processes.

When direct expressions of needs are diverted through defensive translations, developmental progress is distorted and may be arrested. Normally, when feelings arise and seek expression, a *sign* comes into conscious awareness regarding the discomfort at that level, and appropriate action is taken to relieve the discomfort. When a category of need was blocked at a previous level, its expression cannot be sought directly at a later level because it is kept out of conscious awareness. The unconscious continues to work overtime to repress memories of the distressing material and thereby to diminish anxiety and pain. At the same time, the unconscious mind will send *symbols* regarding the buried conflict into awareness, hoping that the conscious mind at its new level of awareness will find more productive ways to sort out the discomfort. These symbols can take the form of irrational thoughts, inappropriate behaviors or physical symptoms. People forget how they translated their original stresses into defensive reaction patterns, and even *that* they did so. Psychotherapy can help people to translate symbols back into their original signs, complete with the feelings that were involved. This then enables a completion of the translational development that was blocked by the inner conflict.

When the body, ego, persona and shadow harmonize into a unified whole, a *Centauric Self* emerges. At this existential level the lower levels are not ignored but are viewed dispassionately as past experiences. The person is no longer distracted, dominated or driven by symbols from lower levels. This is the level of existential psychology in which the whole person is integrated and the total is more than the sum of the parts – having progressed beyond ego and persona levels of development/ awareness. It is here that the *spontaneous will* (Farber) of the whole self originates. Beyond the *membership* level of self, but still linked with body awareness, are the "realms of being that transcend conventional, egoic, institutional, and social forms" (Wilber 1990, p.56). Existing in the *now*, fully aware that all time is *present*, is another characteristic of this level.

> *[T]he nowness of everything is absolutely wondrous.*
> – Dennis Potter (1994)

Transpersonal aspects of the centauric level have parallels with the pre-personal levels of development as defined by Freud, but these two states are clearly distinct. Wilber emphasizes that psychoanalysis has mistakenly presumed that transpersonal awareness represents a regression to infantile, wish-fulfilling fantasies – of an all-knowing, all-caring parental figure that is mistakenly projected as a God-figure. Wilber marshals reasons and evidence to refute this assertion.

Wilber points out that imagery and fantasy provide modes for transition through the existential and into the transpersonal. Lower fantasy is focused on the body-self, while higher, mature fantasy looks toward higher modes of awareness and being, which transcend physical existence. Symbolic imagery is the language used by our brain to translate transpersonal perceptions into awarenesses that we can begin to appreciate, though we may not comprehend them in their entirety.

Coming from a totally different source, in the study of shamanism, Mircea Eliade (1969) comments, "…The symbol reveals certain aspects of reality – the deepest aspects – that defy any other means of knowledge. Images, symbols, and myths are not irresponsible creations of the psyche; they respond to a need and fulfill a function, that of bringing to light the most hidden modalities of being."

Wilber notes that as the individual opens to the centauric levels, intuition and higher energies become more easily available to conscious awareness. Intuition may also exist on lower, psi levels and may extend to the awareness of a Divine presence.

All of the stages described above belong to the *gross realm* of being that Buddhism considers "the realm of ordinary waking consciousness." As we stretch to experience the transcendent from the gross realms, we move into regions that are even more difficult to describe.

Wilber identifies *subtle realms* that are beyond words. The *lower subtle* is associated with the brow chakra, or *third eye*, and connects to psi and astral awareness. The astral realm includes out-of-body experiences and aura perception, which Wilber acknowledges are often considered to be elements of psi awareness.

The *high subtle* realms start at the crown chakra and extend into seven transcendent levels. In the first four we may encounter intuitional inspiration, spirit guides, angels, devas and the like, extending to archetypes of God. Wilber views all of these phenomena as parts of one's own higher self. The highest three realms are entirely beyond the descriptive power of language. In these realms, consciousness differentiates itself completely from the lower mind and self.

> ...[I]t is God as an Archetypal summit of one's own Consciousness... At its peak, the soul becomes one, literally one, with the deity form... with God. One dissolves into Deity, *as* Deity – that Deity which, from the beginning, has been one's own Self or highest Archetype... (p.69)

The *Causal Region* lies beyond the high subtle realm. The *low causal* is "the pinnacle of God-consciousness, the final and highest abode of Ishvara, the Creatrix of all realms." At this level:

> ...[the] deity-Archetype itself condenses and dissolves into final-God, which is here seen as an extraordinarily subtle audible-light... from which the individual... Archetype emerged in the first place. Final-God is simply the ground or essence of all the archetypal and lesser-god manifestations which were evoked – and then identified with – in the subtle realms. In the low-causal, all of these archetypal Forms simply reduce to their Source in final-God, and thus, by the very same token and in the very same step, one's own Self is here shown to *be* that final-God, and consciousness itself thus transforms upwards into a higher-order identity with that Radiance. Such, in brief, is the low-causal, the ultimate revelation of final-God in Perfect Radiance and Release. (Wilber 1990, p.71)

In the *high causal* region:

> ...all manifest forms are so radically transcended that they no longer need even appear or arise in Consciousness. This is total and utter transcendence and release into Formless Consciousness, Boundless Radiance. There is here no self, no God, no final-God, no subjects, and no thingness, apart from or other than Consciousness as such. (p.72)

Beyond this level:

> ...Consciousness totally awakens as its Original Condition and Suchness... which is, at the same time, the condition and suchness of all that is, gross, subtle, or causal. That which witnesses, and that

which is witnessed, are only one and the same. The entire World Process then arises, moment to moment, as one's own Being, outside of which, and prior to which, nothing exists. That Being is totally beyond and prior to anything that arises, and yet no part of that being is other than what arises.

And so: as the center of the self was shown to be Archetype; and as the center of Archetype was shown to be final-God; and as the center of final-God was shown to be Formlessness – so the center of Formlessness is shown to be not other than the entire world of Form. "Form is not other than Void. Void is not other than Form," says the most famous Buddhist Sutra... At that point the extraordinary and the ordinary, the supernatural and mundane, are precisely one and the same...

This is also... the Ultimate Unity, wherein all things and events, while remaining perfectly separate and discrete, are only One. Therefore, this is not itself a state apart from other states; it is not an altered state; it is not a special state – it is rather the suchness of all states, the water that forms itself in each and every wave of experience, as all experience. It cannot be seen, because it is everything which is seen; it cannot be heard, because it is hearing itself; it cannot be remembered because it only *is*. By the same token, this is the radically perfect integration of all prior levels – gross, subtle, and causal, which, now of themselves so, continue to arise moment to moment in an iridescent play of mutual interpenetrating. This is the final differentiation of Consciousness from all forms in Consciousness, whereupon Consciousness as Such is released in Perfect Transcendence, which is not a transcendence from the world but a final transcendence as the world. Consciousness henceforth *operates*, not on the world, but only as the entire World Process, integrating and interpenetrating all levels, realms, and planes, high or low, sacred or profane. (p.73-4)

Wilber's observations point to another important contribution of meditative practice. Transition from one meditative level to another requires a release of previous patterns of belief. This *letting go* of habitual patterns of self-perception and of relating to others is often experienced as a little death. Our little deaths help to prepare us for our physical death.

> *Death is only what shoves life along its way. It is a doorway to something new. Nothing is annihilated or lost or forgotten. All is carried on to the next place and... is shared and remembered. It is a great trick to learn to use this doorway. You must face, confront your death, prepare to die. This changes your place among the webs, gives you courage, shows you how living is a matter of attention.*
> – Kay Cordell Whitaker (p.42)

The observations of Marie-Louise von Franz (1987), a gifted Jungian teacher and writer, parallel those of Wilber:

*All of the symbols which appear in death dreams are images that are
also manifested during the individuation process. (p. xiii)*

Wilber (1980) continues to explain how Buddhist tradition holds that immediately
after the time of physical death each person is opened to ultimate Consciousness.
The average person is not prepared for this level of awareness and holds on to
perceptions of their personality, earthly thoughts, and so on. These draw them
away from the infinite light.

> Contracting in the face of infinity, he turns instead to forms of
> seeking, desire, karma, and grasping, trying to "search out" a state of
> equilibrium... [T]hese karmic propensities couple and conspire to
> drive the soul away from pure consciousness and downwards into
> multiplicity, into less intense and less real states of being (p.164).

A person can step off this wheel of life, death and rebirth through dedicated meditation. The potential is there at every moment, since consciousness is constantly
shifting at every instant from ordinary awareness to infinite awareness. "This
moment-to-moment phenomenon we call 'microgeny' – the micro-genetic involu-
tion of the spectrum of consciousness" (p.175). The greatest challenge to the soul
is to remember – to not get distracted by everyday attractions and challenges in
the physical world, and to hold the awareness of the transcendent worlds.

Sometimes the statements of experienced meditators can bring us to a sense of the
deeper truths that emerge between the lines of words, resonating with deeper truths
in our lives that dwell outside of our ordinary awareness:

> *...This noting of mental states encourages a deeper recognition of what
> is happening while it is happening. It allows us to be more fully alive to
> the present rather than living our life as an afterthought. It enables us
> to watch with mercy, if not humor, the uninvited swirl of "mixed
> emotions" not as something in need of judgment but as a work in
> progress.*
>
> – Stephen Levine 1997 (p.35)

> *...Healing awareness is a noninterfering attention that allows natural
> self-healing responses to take place...*
> *...When consciousness itself becomes the object of attention, the
> necessary conditions for healing may become apparent...*
>
> – Frances Vaughan (1995, p.59)

> *...[E]ach technique needs to be done with balance and heart for the
> practice to take one beyond the method itself. For one not to be only a
> meditator but to become the meditation itself...*
>
> – Stephen Levine (1991, p.14)

...[T]he self as a subject cannot be known without turning itself into an object, thereby separating itself conceptually form the whole, apart from which it does not exist. One may nevertheless persist in treating oneself as if one were a distinct separate entity looking for its true nature. Just as the eye cannot see itself, the Self cannot find itself. As soon as I see myself as an object, I have made myself into an entity which exists only as a concept in my mind. The ego, insofar as it is known or perceived as an object, becomes the object of an unknown and superordinate subject, namely the Self. This self can be experienced, but cannot be known as an object.

            – Frances Vaughan (1995, p. 53)

Those who justify themselves do not convince. To know truth one must get rid of knowledge. Nothing is more powerful and creative than emptiness.

            – Lao Tsu

[M]editation is the practice of the art of dying, of letting go into the vast unknown.

         –   Stephen Levine (1997, p. 62)

The earth is rapidly entering a new field of consciousness that is bringing it back into resonance with primal rhythms of creation. This new consciousness is rooted not in the historical human understanding of God but in an intelligence that resides within the very animating current of the universe. It is rooted in the informational reality of a universal Presence whose awareness and memory is awakening inside human time, awakening and gazing forth from within each vested interest, each player in this planetary field, helping people to understand the greater context in which they move the board, the other players, the rules of the Primate into Universal Species game.

         – Ken Carey (1991, p. 101-102)

Another avenue to transpersonal awareness is through bioenergy therapy. John Pierrakos is in many ways representative of this group of therapists.[193] He discusses here his views of the mind-body connection (1974; 1976):

With Reich, I recognize that the human character has three layers of development: the innermost, where spontaneously decent impulses originate; a middle layer, which Reich identified with the Freudian repressed unconscious, and where negative and destructive impulses germinate; and the outermost layer, the external behaviour that the person interposes between the inner impulses and the outside world. Willfulness appears most strongly in this outer shell, maintaining the facade of manners and mores required by society. But volition penetrates through the interior layers too, because of the person's psychosomatic identity; and as it can work to perpetuate blocks, so can it work to remove them.

Bioenergetic therapy begins with the practitioner exploring the characterological symptoms that are perceptible both on the surface and below it. Vocal tones, body postures and gestures, skin texture and resilience, hair quality, eye luster, and other evidence reveal the location of blocks, their intensity, their interrelationships, something of their etiology, and their overall configuration – the type of character structure.

Pierrakos uses specific physical exercises to deal with specific psychological issues (similar to Reich's and Lowen's) in helping clients to understand their body *armoring* and defensive tensions, to deal with buried emotional traumas and to loosen up so that core energies can be mobilized. He emphasizes the element of willfulness in holding on to illness, when people elect to maintain their symptoms (despite their discomfort) rather than face the core emotions that may lie behind them.

He proceeds with discussion of integration of elements that extend beyond the individual person, into the *trans*personal.

I found that almost all patients increasingly sensed a lack of deep fulfillment as they progressed toward the freeing of their functioning and improved their life situations. They showed this invariably as a yearning for greater unification with external reality.

[T]he human energy system is by nature a creative design of forces working bidirectionally to integrate the self within and fuse the self with the environment.

In other words, our bioenergies coordinate our inner world of the body and mind, while at the same time linking us energetically with the environment.

[T]he mass of the living energy is the quantity of the person, and the consciousness of the living energy is the quality of the person. We do not therefore have a body and a spirit; we have a vital substance that in structure is the body and in function and perception is the spirit. The substance, under its two aspects, composes the core of the human being. The physiological body is energy slowed down into a denser, stable form rather as ice is water solidified. It swims in the energy body and is distinct from it only in degree of energetic vibration, not in substance.

This definition accords with the findings of the physical sciences. We know that man is made of billions of cells that cohere structurally and functionally in an ascending order of complexity, from cells to tissues, from tissues to organs, from organs to systems, from systems to the entity who is the self. Under a microscope with the power to multiply, say, 500,000 times, the body would look rather like a galaxy, the cells spread out with spaces between them but uninterruptedly exchanging energies.

Pierrakos is speaking here of the same hierarchy that Gary Schwartz described earlier in linear terms, functioning as a system that is linked by imagery.

...Every minute cell knows exactly what it is doing – it is aware, and it acts as an individual. The same is true of all the structural components, up to the complex that is considered the seat of feeling, thought, and decision, the brain. But consciousness is not only the operation of faculties of the mind. It is the unified whole of the power of knowing, from the cell's to the mind's and more: it includes the innate movement of the core outward from the self, the movement of the soul.

The core of the person reaches toward infinity...

Pierrakos is not using *energies* as a metaphor to link the elements in the hierarchy. He speaks from personal perceptions of energies. He can see auras, the halos of color, which are the energy fields that surround all objects (especially living ones).[194] He describes several ways in which he correlates auras with his therapy:

> Any significant blocks disturb the entire energy system, not just the regions where they are located. This shows in the centrifugal outflow that makes up the aura.
>
> The organism as a whole, then, exhibits the three-beat pulsatory rhythm, just as does each miniscule cell – the assertive phase that carries energy outward from the body, the receptive phase that pulls energy into the body, and the rest phase that completes the cycle.
>
> The flow rate ranges from a low of about 15 pulsations per minute to 40 and above when the person is highly charged, as in sexual communion.[195]
>
> In an armored person, conversely, the energy flow in both directions is visibly sluggish at the sites of blocks, and the overall rate of pulsation in a neutral state is unnaturally high or low.

The phenomenon of the aura, which is an apparent visual perception of the energy component of matter, confirms the existence of energetic aspects to physical bodies. In Chapter 3 there is a wealth of evidence confirming the presence of such fields, suggesting that they may represent an energetic embodiment of our transpersonal selves. Pierrakos's core therapy integrates many levels of perception and awareness in both the therapist and the healee.

If each of us has a bioenergy self as well as a physical self, this could explain a variety of transpersonal theories and experiences, including the out-of-body experience, survival of a spirit self beyond physical death, ghosts, channeling, and reincarnation. This is reflected in several ways in transpersonal psychology.

Many transpersonal therapists are now addressing clients' awareness of past life experiences in their practice. Though this may seem far-fetched, there is ample evidence to support the therapeutic benefits of such work.[196]

The most remarkable evidence for spiritual residues that reach across linked lifetimes were gathered by Ian Stevenson (1995; 1998), a psychiatrist at the University of Virginia. He found an impressive series of birthmarks that correlate with physical traumas recalled from past lives by the people who bear these marks. For instance, a man had a small birthmark on the right side of his head and a larger one on the left side. This corresponded with his detailed memories of committing suicide by shooting himself in the head. Stevenson verified that a person fitting these past life memories had in fact killed himself in just the manner described.

Within this framework of understanding, problems in our current lives may reflect physical and emotional traumas that have left scars in the surviving consciousness or in the energy body from past lives.[197]

> *Every problem is an assignment from your soul. Therefore, acknowledge that a purpose is being served by your problem, your wound, your illness, your disability, your terminal condition, and try to align with it; that is, seek what it is trying to teach you. Remember that from the soul's perspective, a change in consciousness is of far greater value than a "cure." Therefore, follow King Solomon's wise injunction: "With all your getting, get understanding." Make that understanding the object of your quest and be optimistic that you will be rewarded.*
>
> – Robin Norwood (1994, p.205)

Psi and spiritual healing in psychotherapy

Several pioneering therapists are now incorporating aspects of psi into their work.[198] This is an enlightened step, bridging a gap that heretofore has been filled primarily by many types of psychic *readers* (Benor 1986). Some of these readers do creditable jobs but many seem to offer "shoot-from-the hip" insights without the benefit of psychotherapeutic processing of the materials. This can be unsettling and upsetting to clients who are unprepared for intense emotional releases, and who are left without the benefits of counseling to sort out their emotions.

As a psychiatrist/ healer I am very interested in exploring cross-fertilizations between the practices of psychics and psychotherapists (Benor/ Mohr 1986). Let me share some of my early impressions.

One of the areas where healing can be helpful in psychotherapy is the alleviation of anxiety. This facilitates the process of therapy, making it easier for careseekers to deal with distressing emotional material. One of the nicest aspects of spiritual healing in this regard is that it is not habit-forming and has no dangerous side effects – in contrast with many of the medications that are used to treat anxiety.

There is a secondary level of anxiety that responds particularly well to healing. This type of anxiety may arise *from* people's basic conflicts and concerns. When people become upset or ill they tend to become anxious about being dis-eased. I call this level of worry *meta-anxiety*, because it functions at a level of abstraction that is once removed from the original problem. Meta-anxiety frequently becomes part of a vicious circle of tension → worry about the tension → more tension → more worry → worry about the worry, and so on. At times this cycle can lead to panic. This is the level where one may say, "I can't stand this tension!" or "I'm going crazy!" or even, "If this depression continues, I'm going to kill myself." If therapists are uncomfortable with their clients' emotionality, they may consciously or unconsciously convey their uneasiness to their clients, whose meta-anxiety may then escalate to unmanageable proportions. Conversely, if therapists are not upset by strong emotional releases, they can help their clients endure the anxiety-laden process of facing their fears and emotional hurts, restructuring their unconscious mind's defenses, and getting on with the issues at hand. Their clients will thus be reassured that they need not panic, since they will not be struggling alone.

> *It isn't what happens that bugs you, it's the things that you say in your head about what happens that makes all the machinery get messed up, and leads to varieties of disease.*
>
> – Wallace C. Ellerbroek (1978, p.38)

Suggestion in all its forms can alleviate meta-anxiety, whether it be through a visit to a physician or healer; a diagnosis that transforms one's nameless fears into medically recognized syndromes (even if the obscure medical terminology is incomprehensible!); or simply the belief that the healer is healing us. Healing may thus be effective in part because of its relief of meta-anxiety through suggestion.

My clinical impression from speaking with many other healers, as well as from the experience gained in my own healing practice, is that *healing is specifically effective in relieving meta-anxiety, above and beyond the suggestion component.* I have witnessed powerful emotional releases during healings, especially with *Reiki* and *Mariel* (Lombardi) techniques. When patients experienced these releases during healing, they did not come close to the meta-anxiety levels that I would have anticipated from similar emotional releases in a conventional therapy environment. Even patients who had previously denied having emotional difficulties, and had refused psychotherapy, have been helped though these techniques.

In these cases, the repressed emotions simply well up and pour out during healings. Sometimes they are assimilated without discussion or apparent conscious processing of the traumas. At other times spontaneous insights and understanding develop, on their own or with the aid of counseling from the healers.

I propose that several mechanisms may contribute to these effects. First, healers and healees trust that whatever happens during healing is directed by a higher power, and is therefore sure to be beneficial. Second, healers and healees communicate on very deep levels during healing (probably including telepathy and/ or clairsentience) so the healees do not feel alone with their anxieties, and can draw directly and deeply on the healers' confidence in their ability to deal with these powerful emotions. Third, and most important, the healing process itself appears to help healees deal more effectively with their primary-level emotions, thus eliminating the meta-anxiety and panic.

Many healers report that one of the most noticeable effects of healing is a feeling of relaxation, with deep breathing and a sense of warmth or tingling. Controlled studies of healing for anxiety produced highly significant results,[199] confirming the anecdotal reports. Clearly, this effect can help healees to break vicious circles of anxiety → tension → pain → etc. This seems to be an effect of spiritual healing per se, above and beyond those provided by conventional interventions already mentioned, such as suggestion.

The usual assumption in psychotherapy is that people are cured once the problems that are bothering them are eliminated. But another possibility exists – as this apocryphal story illustrates:

CASE: John met his friend Henry at their ten-year high-school reunion. Discovering that Henry was unmarried, John asked him why. With some embarrassment,

Henry revealed that he avoided serious relationships because he feared the woman would discover that he was a bed-wetter. He felt he could not endure such mortification. John then told Henry about his successful psychoanalysis for much more difficult problems, and recommended several good therapists.

When Henry arrived with his wife at the twentieth high-school reunion, John pulled him aside, saying, "I guess the psychoanalysis got rid of the bed-wetting?" "No," replied Henry. "Now I'm proud of it!"

People completing therapy may simply have learned to accept and live with their difficulties. Healers (who tend to invoke broader cosmologies than most psycho-therapists and conventional doctors) may introduce new perspectives that permit clients to accept rather than fight against their symptoms. Spirituality may teach patience, tolerance, forgiveness, willingness to transcend one's travails and to help others, and more – while encouraging clients to refrain from excessive self-criticism.[200]

A psychological problem can also be transformed into an asset. Psychology refers to this process as sublimation. For example, mentally ill people can transform their fantasies into artistic creativity (technically termed *regression in the service of the ego*), and hyperactive people can channel their energies into productive work. Katya Walter makes a strong case for combining our logical and linear potentials as *analinear* awareness:

> …Logic has often labeled those who gather in the liminal twilight bordering the dark unconscious as deviates on the fringes of society, as romantics and degenerates and witches and spellbinders and dangerous lunatics escaped from the linear highways of traditionally sanctioned thought. Yet these people can enrich us even as they are despised for going beyond the pale and over the linear edge. They stride into the boundless nightways of creation where darkness bestows creative riches and hidden truth.
>
> Seers and artists and shamans could be an integral part of our society. Dark resonance could be acknowledged and discussed and harmonized within the culture, and in oneself. Dreams could be understood and heeded. Drugs could be dropped for the true high of a meaningful life that is not just touched by god, but nestled in god. (p.145)

Healers are good at suggesting ways to sublimate problems, by opening healees to an awareness of the lessons that an illness may bring to the sufferer. They refocus healees' outlook from *fighting* their illness to *listening to what it is saying*. They also may introduce alternative cosmologies such as reincarnation and astrology. These may at least provide people with explanations for their problems, and give them hope that things can change with understanding, patience, altered behavior, and the shifting of planets in the heavenly spheres. On deeper levels, these cosmologies help to remind us of our interrlationship with the All.

Sometimes physical symptoms may not respond to healing because they are rooted in such deep and pervasive disorders of the subject's being that to relinquish them would require intolerable changes in underlying emotional conditions.

This account for some failures of spiritual healing – as healees may simply not be ready to relinquish their symptoms. In such cases healers can at least help people bear their cross of suffering. Some of the more potent healers have effected dramatic changes even in such difficult cases.

On the other hand, many healers I have spoken with shy away from clients who have emotional problems because the healers have little understanding of psychological processes. The more enlightened healers refer these healees to counselors or psychotherapists, while unenlightened healers simply ignore emotional problems. Sadly, many unenlightened doctors and nurses do the same.

Further psychotherapeutic benefits of healing appear to include the more rapid establishment of a deeper rapport between therapist and healee; greater trust in the therapist, which allows for more expedient and deeper exploration of conflicts; enhanced management of stresses through the addition of healing processes to the treatment; accessibility of a collective consciousness or higher self through which to seek solutions to problems; and encouragement of personal growth, which includes a deeper awareness of one's responsibility to mankind and nature as a whole.

The healing of psychological disturbances that are unconnected with physical problems is scantily reported in the anecdotal literature. Bob Hoffman (St. Clair) is an American healer specializing in emotional problems. Alberto Villoldo and Stanley Krippner (1987) describe a Brazilian surgeon who is now a healer working primarily with schizophrenics and epileptics. Kyriakos Markides describes a very remarkable Cypriot healer, the late Daskalos, who addressed emotional problems. I am personally familiar with a growing number of other, less well-known psychotherapists/ healers who are very capable, sometimes actually gifted, in treating emotional problems. Through the addition of healing to the therapy, they seem able to facilitate much more rapid development of insight and emotional change in their clients.[201]

No scientific studies of these types of healing have yet been reported. Therefore we cannot say with certainty whether the application of healing for anything more than reduction anxiety or depression is truly effective, though this seems highly likely.

The combination of healing with psychotherapy raises many controversial issues. Let me share some questions that I am struggling with as I expand my practice of psychotherapy with spiritual healing. I believe people must understand the roots of their problems in order to receive the full lessons of their illness. Yet there are potent healers (such as the late Harry Edwards)[202] who primarily address the physical component of illness, and bring about rapid, dramatic, physical improvements without the benefit of psychological understanding. Some have suggested that insight, along with spiritual growth, will naturally follow of its own accord and in its own time. I feel that this is an important question to study, with far-reaching implications. I also would like to study healers and healees who do and do not address psychological components of illness, to learn whether there are quantitative and/ or qualitative differences in their healings.

Healers also offer dimensions of spiritual healing and counseling for the dying. A good death in itself is seen as the final healing.[203]

All of the factors mentioned above are at play in any therapeutic interaction. Suggestion is one of the most important of these, and one that makes many contributions to healing, so it has been discussed in greater detail. Spiritual healing, likewise, is an inevitable aspect of therapeutic interactions (Benor 1995a).

COLLECTIVE CONSCIOUSNESS AND SPIRITUAL AWARENESS

Diverse evidence suggests that our minds can reach beyond the realm of our own individual consciousness.

Carl Jung described what he called the *collective unconscious*, as it was mirrored in the dreams and mental imagery of his psychoanalytic patients. This awareness was evident in the universal manifestations of *archetypal images* that often were not meaningful to his patients until Jung pointed out their mythical significance, at which point the messages from their unconscious minds were clarified, and their emotional problems were alleviated.

> I vividly recall the case of a professor who had had a sudden vision and thought he was insane. He came to see me in a state of complete panic. I simply took a 400-year-old book from the shelf and showed him an old woodcut depicting his very vision. "There's no reason for you to believe that you're insane," I said to him. "They knew about your vision 400 years ago." Whereupon he sad down entirely deflated, but once more normal.
>
> – Carl Jung (1964)

It appears that mythic, archetypal imagery resides in a collective conscious of mankind, and is available as a vehicle for expressing and processing emotions and conflicts. There may be layers and layers of interconnectedness. Marie Louise von Franz (1980) suggests that there is a core layer of the mind in which universal consciousness resides, a layer in which all of mankind participates, and that extending out from this core are increasingly differentiated and localized layers that are limited in their scope of awareness.

This all sounds very grand, but how can we explain the collective unconscious?

The most basic elements contributing to the collective unconscious are the psi powers of telepathy, clairsentience (perceiving objects in the world without outer sensory access to them), precognition (knowing the future), and retrocognition (knowing the past).[204] If we can communicate with others telepathically, and they with us, then our minds have the potential to link with others in a network that forms a collective consciousness.

Spontaneous psi interactions between people often occur during dreams, and psi perceptions often come to us as metaphoric imagery. The similarity between dream imagery and psi imagery suggests that both may occur in the same parts of the mind, in the deeper layers of our awareness, below conscious perception and cognition. It is likely that our unconscious minds are in more immediate and intimate contact with the world beyond ourselves than our conscious minds are aware of. It also seems probable that our psi awareness is frequently (perhaps even constantly) functioning below our conscious awareness. If this is so, then we are intimately linked to the minds of everyone else in the world, in a vast inter-connected network. Precognition and retrocognition extend our connections of awareness backwards and forwards in time, so our consciousness can connect with anywhere and *anywhen*. In essence, there is a cosmic data bank to which we all have access – though each of us sees only portions of it, and these are gener-ally perceived indistinctly.

You might think that such speculations are far-fetched, but various experiments have confirmed that it is possible to bring these psi perceptions into conscious awareness. For instance, remote viewing studies by Robert Jahn and colleagues at Princeton University School of Engineering have shown that subjects sitting in a laboratory can accurately describe what is transpiring at distant locations, before the verifying observers choose the locations and go there to validate the psi perceptions (Jahn/ Dunne).[205]

Rupert Sheldrake hypothesizes that specific files in the cosmic data bank are reserved for the use of each living species. Individuals within a species contribute information to their species' file, and can also read information that has been ac-cumulated within the file. This would explain such phenomena as the migration of birds, which can fly accurately to their species' nesting grounds without in-structions from others of their species.

Laboratory experiments support Sheldrake's theories. The most striking demon-strated an ability of purebred laboratory mice to learn mazes. In the US, mice from one such strain were taught to run a maze, and successive generations learned this faster than their forbears. This was at first explained away as social learning transmitted from parents to offspring. However, years later, scientists in England tested mice of the same strains who were very distant cousins of the original US mice that had learned the mazes. Though having common ancestors, the English mice were not direct descendants of the US mice. Nevertheless, some of the English mice ran the same mazes correctly on their first trial. Sheldrake's theory of a species-specific intuitive data bank could explain these findings.

Sheldrake also suggests that data on the body shape, size, and functions of each species are stored in some of these files, which he calls *morphogenetic fields*. These could serve as cosmic information centers that track the development of species over time.

Spiritual awareness seems to reside in a similar cosmic library. We can tap into this resource if we first clear our inner computer screen, as in meditation, or if we pray to be linked into the grid. Prayers and rituals that are repeated many times may become morphogenetic paths towards spiritual awareness. This subject is discussed further in Volume III.

PREVIEW OF AN ENERGY HEALING MODEL

Let us briefly review the discussion so far of mind-body links.

Interactions between the mind and the body are pervasive and complex. At the simplest level, we see that emotions are expressed by the body in nonverbal com-munication.[206]

At a more organic level, memories may be stored in association with, if not actually within various tissues and organs of the body – particularly in muscles and tendons, as witnessed in the emotional releases that are common during massage and other *bodymind* therapies.[207] Several psychophysiological mechanisms for this storage are possible. Psychological conditioning can imprint information in the body through nerves, muscles, and hormones. Emotional stress may produce localized or generalized physical tensions, accompanied by pains or other malfunctions in many parts of the body, such as muscle and joint aches, hypertension, asthma or ulcers.

Conversely, problems in the body may also influence our awareness and emotions. Illnesses caused by known physical agents and processes may be accompanied by emotional and physical tensions. If these are chronic, they can produce pains that lead to vicious circles of anxiety → tension → pain → anxiety → etc. Such tensions may present as simple muscle tightness (e.g. headaches, backaches, etc.), or they may exacerbate other illnesses, as in the case of emotional disturbances that worsen existing diabetic metabolic disorders, or set off thyroid dysfunctions.

Many aspects of these discomforts may be relieved through a variety of conventional psychotherapy techniques, including talking psychotherapy, suggestion (generated by oneself or by others), placebos, hypnosis, relaxation techniques, meditation, biofeedback, and medications (e.g. tranquilizers, pain medicines and muscle relaxers).

In addition to the bodymind mechanisms that have been discussed in this chapter, numerous complementary therapies (discussed in Chapter II-2) demonstrate that the mind may influence the body through *subtle energy* aspects of the body. That is, there are subtle biological energy fields around and within the body that may be influenced by the mind, and that may reciprocally influence the mind. These fields appear to control various functions of the physical body.

Many conventional medical practitioners find it difficult to understand subtle energy medicine. This may be in part because people tend to focus on one particular mode of complementary therapies, or even on a partial aspect of a method, and forget that other factors may simultaneously be playing an equally important role. Biological energy interventions have been ignored by conventional medicine, and it has been assumed that spiritual healing is no more than massage, soothing touch, or suggestion. The subtle energy aspect of healing has been largely overlooked.

>*If all you have is a hammer, then everything looks like a nail!*
>   – Abraham Maslow

It may be that aspects of mind function as an energy field, with the brain serving as a transducer for this field. Healers go even further and suggest that the energy field is where a person's *being* resides, and that this is a template for the physical body. Looking at it from the other side, the body can be seen as the expression of a person's spirit. It is like a sort of metaphysical garment that is worn while receiving a lifetime of lessons (which may include illnesses) and then discarded, to be replaced in future lifetimes by other garments that are appropriate to further lessons. These spiritual and philosophical aspects of subtle energies and healing are discussed in Volumes III and IV of *Healing Research.*

Self-healing may be brought about by a change of mind that alters subtle energy fields, which subsequently causes changes in the body.

If we accept that spiritual healing may be projected by healers in the form of energy fields,[208] we can postulate that it might act on the body in further ways. It could release old, maladaptive mental and emotional patterns; permit natural, healthy patterns to reassert themselves; and/ or insert new, healer-inspired, healer-generated or healer-transmitted patterns in the bodymind of the healee.

Moving from purely psychological problems to psychosomatic ones, we find additional levels of complexity. Spiritual healing may be directly effective in alleviating body tensions and releasing memories stored within the body, bypassing the conscious mind.

> *It appears possible that consciousness may extend beyond the brain to include the whole body.*
> – DB

There will be further discussion of biological energy fields in Chapter II-3, following a review of many of the established techniques of wholistic energy medicine in Chapter II-2.

CHAPTER 2

Wholistic Energy Medicine

The part can only be known
when the whole is apparent.
— Ted Kaptchuk (1983, p. 142)

Healing may be defined as the movement toward wholeness – through enhanced and harmonized awareness and function of body, emotions, mind, relationships, and spirit. The ancient Germanic and English roots of the word "healing" derive from *haelen*, meaning "to make whole." To emphasize this point, I use the term *wholistic healing* to indicate a focus on whole-person care.

At its best, wholistic medicine[210] is whole-person healing. This appeals to people who are discouraged by conventional, allopathic medicine's heavy focus on the body – addressing only the *physical* aspects of illness, often to the exclusion of any other level of healing. Ruth Benor, worked with many women who were challenged with breast cancer. Their nearly universal complaint was that their breasts were being well cared for, but the doctors and nurses and x-ray therapists seemed to forget that there was a woman attached to the breasts that they were probing and x-raying and needling and cutting and reconstructing, while prescribing toxic chemicals and radiotherapy to fight the disease that they perceived was attacking the body.

Whole-person care has often been addressed under the popular term *holistic care*. Sadly, this term has degenerated in many therapeutic contexts as welll as in the professional and popular literature. Often it has come to refer only to the use of bits and pieces of a few complementary/ alternative medicine (CAM) therapies (such as a smattering of techniques from acupuncture, meditation, herbalism, massage and others) – which are often offered in abbreviated and diluted versions of the original practices, ignoring their rich roots in diverse ancient and modern treatment philosophies. Too many allopathic therapists go on weekend courses to learn about these modalities, and immediately start applying fragments of the methodologies from these traditions. In effect, the *methodologies* are viewed as the whole therapy. The fuller essences of the therapeutic practices are discarded, and much of their benefits are lost.

We have spent too much time criticizing healers because they are not doctors and not enough time criticizing doctors who are not healers.
— Jesuit Father Louis Beirnaent

Complementary therapies offer extensive systems for conceptualizing *dis-ease* and disease. These systems differ substantially from the traditions of Western, allopathic medicine in their approaches to problems of physical, psychological, and spiritual health and illness.

Rudolph Ballentine (2001) has an excellent discussion on conventional medicine's heavy emphasis on *effects* of underlying problems that manifest as symptoms and illnesses, and *effects* of discrete medical and surgical interventions that are meant to address these surface manifestations of deeper issues. In our focus on the goal of *curing* illness, we too often overlook the healing effects of *caring* that make the journey towards wholeness a healing one.

Conventional Western medicine has concentrated on treatments of the body, viewing psychological issues as peripheral to medical practice. I was distressed in medical school when I attended a well-baby clinic. The pediatrician was an absolute joy to observe. He obviously loved helping the babies and mothers who came to him for guidance, reassurance and clarifications of their maturation and health issues. Equally, the mothers, babies and children loved coming to visit him. This was such a breath of fresh air to me – in the otherwise dehumanizing process of medical education that focused on diagnosing and curing illnesses rather than treating people with dis-ease. My distress was over the attitudes of my fellow-students. They felt it was a waste of time sitting around with babies who were mostly healthy and mothers who were often anxious over problems which were not life-threatening.

Wholistic medicine views people as complex organisms whose minds, emotions, relationships, and spiritual selves are as much a part of whatever they are experiencing as their physical bodies are.

Volume II of *Healing Research* explores how consciousness can influence states of health and illness, acting directly through neurological, hormonal and immune mechanisms as well as through bioenergies. Psychological *dis-ease* manifests as *disease*. Physical problems are often a wake-up call from the unconscious mind, for the conscious mind to become aware of inner disharmonies and conflicts.

It is not surprising that about half the prescriptions written by family practitioners go unfilled or unused. People realize (consciously or unconsciously) that the symptoms the physician is addressing are not the real issue. What they really need is something that the doctor is not providing.

Wholistic healing helps people to become aware of their whole selves – including body, emotions, mind, relationships, and spirit – and then to discover the disharmonies that are manifesting as problems in their lives, so that they can sort out how to address them. In many cases it is not just a matter of treating the symptoms of physical pain, fatigue, or trauma; these symptoms invite us to explore the underlying tensions that have created them, as discussed in Chapter II-1.[211]

Facilitating self-healing and whole-person care is a creative challenge to wholistic health caregivers. They must be educators as well as prescribers and providers of direct interventions. This is in sharp contrast with the physician's traditional roles of *prescribing and administering treatments* within the prevalent model of Western allopathic medicine. These issues will be discussed in greater depth in later sections of this chapter.

Strengths of allopathic medicine

Wholistic health care need not conflict with good allopathic medical care.

The strengths of conventional allopathic practice are in making precise diagnoses and prescribing specific therapies. To arrive at a diagnosis, doctors rely on the history of symptoms, on physical examination, and on the results of laboratory tests that may be quite sophisticated. Preventive interventions have also been a major contribution of modern medicine, particularly in improving hygiene and sanitation.

For many years allopathic medicine rejected complementary therapies because there had been little or no rigorous, Western-style research to validate the efficacy of these approaches. Western doctors (including myself) thought that these were spurious interventions – no better than placebos that could lead to improvement through the potent powers of suggestion.[212]

> *Formerly, when religion was strong and science weak, men mistook magic for medicine; now, when science is strong and religion weak, men mistake medicine for magic.*
> – Thomas Szasz (1973)

Allopathic medicine recommends *evidence-based* practice. Ideally, new therapies should be carefully researched before they are accepted into the medical armamentarium to help fight against disease. Doctors and nurses are cautious against making the *Type I research error* of accepting as valid a therapy that is not truly effective.[213] We know that therapies may be effective simply because patients and doctors *expect they will work*, whether or not they are intrinsically beneficial. This is called the *placebo effect*. Roughly 30% of patients suffering from almost any illness will show some symptomatic improvement with any treatment whatsoever. This appears to be due to the effect of psychological expectations, working in combination with the patients' own self-healing capacities.

Conventional medical practitioners have regarded placebo responses as something of a nuisance, feeling that they interfere with efforts to determine the effects of what Western medicine considers *real* therapeutic interventions, particularly when medications are involved.

Various research strategies have been devised to test the effectiveness of treatments, taking into consideration the placebo response.

Research approaches

Randomized controlled studies: To guard against Type I errors, researchers have devised the *randomized controlled trial* (*RCT*). Before it can be accepted as a legitimate therapy, a treatment modality (medication, surgical procedure, psychotherapeutic method, or complementary therapy) must pass a battery of stringent RCTs. A group composed of patients who have the same diagnosis and severity of illness is randomly divided into sub-groups. One of the subgroups is given the therapy under study, and another group is given a known placebo. A third group may be given a therapy of proven intrinsic value (a medication, massage, etc.). The groups receiving comparison treatments are called *control* groups. Therapists, researchers and subjects in the study are kept *blind* to which of the treatments (experimental therapy, placebo, or intervention of known value) is being given to any one subject. This minimizes the effects of suggestion, which might influence subjects to feel better or worse in response to the expectations of the therapists or researchers, or according to their own expectations of improvement with a given therapy.[214] Assessments of symptomatic change, whether negative or positive, are likewise made by diagnosticians who are blind to the particular therapy being given, for similar reasons. Where therapists and subjects are blind to the treatment given, it is called a *double blind* study.

Therapies are administered within a standard protocol that is determined prior to the start of the study, so subjects within treatment groups will receive similar doses and durations of interventions. This assures that the treatments under study are of known quality and quantity, and it allows other researchers to replicate the experiment under a similar protocol.

Statistical analyses are prepared based on the results of the study. These provide estimates of the possibility that the results of the RCT might have occurred by chance. The most common statistical standard for a treatment to be accepted as a valid finding rather than a chance occurrence is that it must be effective beyond the statistical probability of five times in a hundred. That is, there is less than a chance of 5 times in 100 that the results could have occurred randomly. (This is expressed as *p less than .05*, or $p < .05$). Naturally, if the same results would only occur by pure chance less than one time in a hundred ($p < .01$) or one time in a thousand ($p < .001$), and so on, they are that much more impressive.

> *The aim of science is not to open the door to infinite wisdom,*
> *but to set a limit to infinite error.*
>   – Bertolt Brecht (1939)

At the end of the study, subjects in the various groups are checked to see that there were no significant differences between the groups in respect to any important variables. For instance, there might have been a group in which the subjects had more severe symptoms than in another group, which would have biased the comparison between groups in respons to the different therapies that each received.

The initial randomization of subjects into the various groups is meant to guard against this possibility. Assigning subjects randomly to each group makes it statistically more likely that equal numbers of subjects with any given symptom will be assigned to each group, and therefore that the groups will be closely equivalent at the start of the study.

In some studies the same subjects are consecutively given active treatments and placebos, also under double-blind conditions. Subjects thereby serve as their own control group, thus eliminating the risk of variations in the composition of different groups. The difficulty with this approach is that there may be effects of a treatment that could carry over from one period of intervention to the next, thereby confounding the final results. In addition, subtle factors might bias each treatment period differently. For instance, there could be a change in personnel or other factors that differ for various subjects over a period of time. There might thus be more (or less) sympathetic clinical or research personnel present in either the treatment or control periods, which could bias the results through suggestion effects that would differ in the different treatment and control periods.

Despite the best efforts of scientists to establish a research protocol that will pro-tect against Type I research errors, it is still possible that errors may occur. For example, there could be confounding differences between groups which are not identified, and which bias the responses of some or all of the subjects for better or worse. This could mislead researchers into believing that the therapy caused (or failed to cause) various effects, when in reality the observed effects were due to unequal distribution of symptom severity between groups (or some other biasing influence – perhaps age or sex), which led to the different responses between the groups. If such an error leads to the rejection of a therapy as being ineffective when it *is* actually a potent intervention, it is classed as a *Type II research error*, which is an error of *rejecting as false something that is actually true*.

Notwithstanding its stated good intentions and best efforts, the actual practice of evidence-based medicine remains elusive. Conventional medicine generally over-looks the fact that the majority of accepted medical treatments have not been subjected to this careful scrutiny. Furthermore, medical research is challenged by the enormous complexity of the human organism, which eludes the best efforts of studies that are intended to clarify its nature. It is impossible to account for every relevant variable that might influence a given symptom or illness. Many studies, even when performed to the highest scientific standards, remain open to questions and criticisms regarding confounding variables that might have accounted for or at least influenced the observed results.

There is also a growing trend in America for medical advertising and promo-tional companies to commission medication studies. This introduces serious issues of researcher bias in performing and reporting the research.[215]

Even without all of the above methodological problems, the results of studies are frequently open to more than one interpretation. The practice of medicine there-fore remains as much an art as a science.[216]

The tendency in conventional medicine is to err in the favor of caution, and not to accept new therapies until there is a convincing body of evidence with minimum risk of Type I research errors. Even leaving aside consideration of complementary therapies, many are questioning the validity of relying so heavily and exclusively on controlled studies, pointing out that the focus of RCTs is too narrow.[217]

The U.S. Food and Drug Administration licenses the prescription and sale of new medications and therapies on the basis of such research. The costs of build-ing a body of evidence for FDA approval amount to hundreds of millions of dollars for each treatment. Needless to say, only pharmaceutical companies and other organizations with enormous financial resources can afford such expenses.

It is not suggested that RCTs should be abandoned. There are, however, other research approaches that can round out the picture, particularly with CAM thera-pies.

Observational studies: Anecdotal evidence from reports of individual therapists is also useful in sorting out which therapies are of benefit. From these fertile observations we harvest a rich trove of suggestions to expand our understanding of how treatments work. However, there are countless difficulties in accepting any individual person's positive response to a treatment as evidence for the efficacy of that treatment. Possible confounding variables contributing to an individual's improvement may include: spontaneous waxing and waning of symptoms over the normal course of illness; constitutional or psychological strengths of that particular person which may exceed the average; unknown variables of diet, activity, or other therapeutic interventions; changes in psychological stresses or in social support; and so on.

Anecdotal reports are strengthened when a series of subjects' responses to treatments is presented. If several people had similar results, it is more likely that the observations are valid.

A further caution, however, with anecdotal evidence is that the professional training, views and personal experience s of the reporting observer may bias the report.

Nevertheless, anecdotal evidence provides the necessary initial observations of a new therapy, and if these reports suggest that the therapy may be helpful, they encourage further study.

In addition, anecdotal reports are usually rich in details of a personal nature – details that tend to be lost when the responses of large numbers of people are statistically analyzed. [218]

Qualitative studies: Qualitative studies analyze individual responses to treatments, while still guarding against Type I errors. Small numbers of people with a common problem are given a particular therapy and their reports are analyzed in great individual detail. Analyses of these details provide a basis on which to build theories about *how a therapy may work to make a person better.* [219]

Surveys of patients' satisfaction with treatments: Surveys provide yet another avenue for assessing therapeutic benefits. Doctors tends to consider these research methods of lesser value, due to the biased belief that self-assessments will be riddled with Type I errors. Surveys are frequently dismissed as "purely subjective evidence." Yet it is the consumers of health treatments who are increasingly voting with their feet and dollars for the therapies that they find helpful, and increasing numbers of people are choosing complementary therapies. [220]

Research in wholistic therapies: All of the above-mentioned types of research on spiritual healing are discussed in *Healing Research* Volume I.

In Volume II of *Healing Research,* we focus on research that explores effects of a broad spectrum of additional complementary therapies, with a particular focus on biological energies that may be involved in these therapies. Heavy emphasis will be given to RCTs, to establish as clearly as possible that these modalities produce measurable effects and are not placebos.

Growing numbers of rigorous studies demonstrate that CAM therapies are effective, and it is surprising that many conventional doctors and scientists are as yet little aware of them. Without having investigated the available scientific evidence, many criticize CAM as being unsupported by research, compared to conventional medical treatments. In fact, today the situation is quite the opposite. Rupert Sheldrake systematically reviewed a range of conventional scientific papers, to see how many included blinds or double-blinds that would control for experimenter bias. He found none in the physical sciences, 0.8 percent in the biological sciences, 24 percent in conventional medicine, only 5 percent in psychology and animal behavior studies, and 85 percent in parapsychological studies. No comparison is available for CAM studies in general. For spiritual healing the studies with blinds comprise more than 25 percent.[221]

While the RCT is viewed by many as the golden standard for examining the efficacy of therapies, it has not proven entirely satisfactory for clinical subjects (where statistics may overlook important qualitative aspects of treatment), and the RCT may not be adequate or appropriate for the study of many aspects of complementary therapies. This is because complementary therapies are individualized to the personalities and circumstances of the individual respant (*responsible participant* – Siegel 1990) much more than allopathic therapies are.

In conventional medicine, an atherosclerotic heart is seen as a muscle whose blood supply is compromised by clogged arteries. The primary therapy is focused on cleaning out the arteries, preventing blood clots, or even replacing the heart. Attention may be given to preventive dietary factors such as monitoring cholesterol levels and salt intake, and to lifestyle factors such as smoking and exercise – but the focus remains on the physical aspects of the disease.

In wholistic integrative care, attention may also be given to various vitamins and minerals that may be of help; to the stresses that may be raising blood pressure; to emotional heartaches that may be manifesting in physical heart symptoms; to biological energies related to the heart and to the rest of the body (addressed through spiritual healing, acupuncture, craniosacral therapy, homeopathy, flower essence or other CAM therapies); and to spiritual issues, such as concerns over the possibility that the heart disease may prove fatal.

Randomized controlled studies often do not take these additional factors into consideration. It may in fact be inappropriate to use control groups, because each person is so different from every other person that the treatments indicated in complementary therapies may be completely individualized for every patient, despite the similarity of the medical diagnosis. There will be further discussion of these differences in approaches and of individualized treatments in the final section of this chapter.

Skeptics suggest that complementary therapies have not been explored through controlled studies, and should therefore be approached with the utmost caution – but here they are applying a double standard. The current high standards for research have evolved over recent decades. Many conventional therapies, about 85 percent of those in common use in allopathic medicine, have not passed the rigorous tests that would have been demanded of them had they been discovered today.[222]

Despite all of these cautions and warnings, an impressive and growing body of controlled research on complementary therapies is available, as reviewed in this chapter.

Although much of the evidence available shows that complementary therapies are effective, some health care professionals remain skeptical. This is mostly a problem of adjusting to new concepts and treatments (Dossey 1998b; 1999).

> *New options are always suspected, and usually opposed, without any other reason but because they are not already common.*
> – John Locke (1690)

Qualitative vs. quantitative assessments

> *Not everything that counts can be counted and not everything that can be counted counts.*
> – Albert Einstein

Rigorous research methods have their limitations. While quantitative studies help to analyze *average reactions* to treatments, many important details are missed when we focus on the abstract picture. Double-blind, randomized, controlled studies may provide precise evidence relating to narrow, general questions, but they do not give a complete picture of clinical therapies. The very precision of their focus makes them blind and insensitive to many qualitative aspects of treatment.

> *According to the latest official figures, 47% of all statistics are totally worthless.*
> – Ashleigh Brilliant (no. 875)

As mentioned earlier, observational case reports and qualitative studies provide valuable contributions to our understanding of how various complementary therapies can be of benefit. Though often subject to Type I errors, they flesh out the dry bones of the limited, bare facts that are garnered from controlled studies (Lukoff et al.).

Two quotations highlight these limitations of rigorous research:

> *The scientific picture of the world is inadequate for the simple reason that science deals only with certain aspects of experience in certain contexts. All this is quite clearly understood by the more philosophically-minded men of science. But most others tend to accept the world picture implicit in the theories of science as a complete and exhaustive account of reality.*
> – Aldous Huxley (1946, p.35-36)

> *Science strives to reduce our experience of symbols. Experiences are colorful, multi-faceted, and fuzzy along the edges; symbols are bland, one-dimensional, and precisely-bounded. Real world observations can be bulky and ill-shaped and can have both strong and tenuous ties with a myriad of other real world observations; abstractions are built of simple, smooth-faced elements, uncoupled from other constructs...*

*Scientifically, we give up the shifting and elusive mystery of the world,
but, in exchange, we gain the standardised and reproducible abstrac-
tions from which we can build determinate explanations.*
                                           – Michael Katz (p.85)

Qualitative studies explore the subjective experience of dealing with illness. Single case studies offer in-depth explorations of many dimensions of illness and
treatments that are often overlooked by quantitative studies that focus on externally measurable symptoms. With single subjects, however, it is difficult to know
how much of the result may be attributed to the individual personality of the subject or other factors. When similar responses are found in groups of people with
similar problems, we have greater assurance that we are dealing with subjective
experiences that are common to a given illness or treatment.

There are valid points on both sides of this argument. Conventional medicine
works hard to research and validate its own therapies. Until recently, most of the
complementary therapies did not subject their treatments to such scrutiny, and
there is therefore a modest body of research to validate their efficacy. On the
other side of the argument, complementary therapy practitioners complain that it
is impossible to assess many of their interventions within standard Western research designs. Homeopathic remedies, for instance, are prescribed to each person
on an individualized basis. People suffering from the same illness or syndrome
may express similar symptoms, but their personalities and life experiences will be
different, and therefore the underlying causes of their illnesses may also differ. A
standardized therapy applied to a group of subjects for the purpose of research
would not be a fair test of homeopathy because some people would not receive
the correct remedy for their constitutional makeup, personalities, and life experiences. Despite these challenges, in recent years a substantial body of research on
complementary therapies has been coalescing.[223]

Integrative medicine and whole person care

To analyze holism is unholistic.
The whole is more than the sum of its parts.
                                           – Tony Pinchuck and Richard Clark

Integrative care combines the best of conventional medical approaches and
wholistic energy medicine, to offer the maximal benefits to patients and therapists. When practiced wholistically, this is *whole-person care.*

An atmosphere of competition has developed between various allopathic and
complementary health care practitioners, each claiming that their interventions
are better in particular ways than those of other therapists. In some instances sick
people have been faced with the dilemma of having to choose between conventional and complementary therapies. some allopathic doctors have refused to treat
patients who seek therapies they consider to be of unproven value,, and complementary therapy practitioners may feel that their approaches are incompatible
with allopathic medicine. Many people who find complementary therapies helpful
simply don't tell their doctors that they are receiving these treatments (Adler/

Fosket), and if they do tell them, they may encounter a very mixed reception (M. Richardson et al.).

> *How can I prove I'm not crazy to people who are?*
> – Ashleigh Brilliant (no. 958)

Conventional, allopathic medicine has for many decades established a monopoly over the practice of health care in the West. In the eyes of the public, the presumed superiority of this approach had the appearance of legitimated, established fact. This viewpoint has been supported by legislation that is heavily influenced by medical lobbying (Brody, et al.). But while legislation is necessary to protect the public from unethical practices and practitioners, many feel that such laws also serve to restrict the access of the public to therapies that are outside the scope of mainstream medicine. For example, homeopathy was very widely practiced in the US at the end of the 19th Century, but medical doctors successfully lobbied to enact laws restricting homeopathic practice. Such restrictive lobbying continues today.[224] Medical practitioners who refer patients to CAM practitioners or who practice CAM methods have been censured by some state medical societies for diverging from conventional medical practice. Were such laws to be rigidly enforced for all innovative practices, there could never be any new developments or progress in medical care. The public has responded to these restrictive measures by lobbying for enactment of *access to treatment laws* (M. Cohen).[225]

The main strengths of conventional medicine lie in its rigorous research methodology; its precision in diagnosis; its effective treatment of infections and of other illnesses that respond well to medications, hormones and surgery; and the promise of medically indicated genetic manipulations.

Nevertheless, there remain vast numbers of sick people for whom conventional medicine offers only limited understanding and treatment options. In some cases, as in cancer chemotherapies, the side effects of conventional treatments may diminish the quality of life even more than the illness they are meant to treat.[226] Side effects of tranquilizers, antidepressants, painkillers and sleeping pills, among many other frequently prescribed medications, may also be unpleasant or even dangerous.

A very sobering summary of the dangers of conventional medications is presented by J. Lazarou and colleagues. They reviewed 39 prospective studies from U.S. hospitals between 1966 and 1996, and summarized the incidence of negative drug reactions leading to hospital admissions, or occurring while people were hospitalized – many of which were serious enough to be permanently disabling or fatal. They did not include errors in medication administration, or incidences of overdose, abuse, or allergic reaction.

> *It may seem a strange principle to enunciate as the very first requirement in a Hospital that it should do the sick no harm.*
> – Florence Nightingale (1863)

Lazarou and colleagues found an incidence of 6.7 percent serious adverse reactions, and 0.32 per cent fatal reactions in hospitalized patients. They estimated that in 1994 there were 2,216,000 serious adverse drug reactions in hospitalized patients, with 106,000 deaths. This places adverse drug reactions between the fourth and sixth most common cause of death.[227]

This is not a problem restricted to the US. In New Zealand, a study carried out by Harvard School of Medicine showed that one in four people with serious health problems suffered effects of medical errors. This was particularly likely to occur when several physicians were involved in treating the same person (Stuff.co.nz).

Medical errors may also contribute to negative effects and fatalities, for an estimated 44,000 to 98,000 additional annual casualties due to negligent medical care, as reported by the Institute of Medicine.[228] These numbers exceed the annual fatalities from highway accidents, breast cancer, and AIDS. It is a sobering statistic that we are 9,000 times more likely to die under medical care than from wounds inflicted by firearms (Mercola).[229] Len Horowitz, a biting critic of the dangers of medical treatments, calls this *iatrogenocide*.

In contrast, the anticipated annual death rates from consumption of vitamins, herbal products, homeopathic remedies and flower essences are near zero.

This is not to say we should be complacent and ignore the few serious side effects that have been reported, nor that we shouldn't be on the alert and searching for any further serious side effects of these approaches. For instance, improper use of acupuncture needles, and inappropriate use of force in spinal manipulations can cause injuries. Kava is an herb which has been used successfully for treatment of anxiety. Recently, it has been discovered that Kava can cause liver damage, which is sometimes fatal. We are also just beginning to learn that there are also herb and supplement interactions with conventional medications.[230] Adverse effects, where apparent, are listed under each therapy. Nevertheless, the CAM therapies remain indisputably safer by far than medical treatments.

Confirmation of the fatal dangers involved in medical practice comes from the statistics of mortuaries in Israel during periodic doctors' strikes. There were 15 to 50 percent fewer deaths during these periods (Fonorow).[231]

A further problem associated with allopathic medical practice is the enormous cost of medical treatments, which is of growing national concern in every country in the world.

Likewise of great concern are the costs of days lost from work due to health problems that have not responded to medical care are.

Complementary therapies can help with many of the chronic health problems for which conventional medicine offers limited benefits, such as back pain[232] and other chronic pains; arthritis; neurological disorders (from accidental injury or cerebral palsy,[233] or from diseases such as multiple sclerosis (Gardener), myopathies, etc.); emotional disorders; chronic fatigue syndrome;[234] and many more. These are ailments that cost the health care system enormous sums because they require multiple consultations, expensive diagnostic tests, costly medications and other interventions – and in many cases they are incurable. Health care authorities have responded to the mounting costs with bureaucratic legislation that addresses only the time/ wages and therapy cost factors, leaving both health caregivers and patients dissatisfied. These problems are not new. William Shakespeare quipped: "[You] can get no remedy against this consumption[235] of the purse."

CAM therapists address the whole person rather than just a set of symptoms. This is appreciated by many people who complain that conventional doctors don't take the time to speak with them beyond asking about their immediate complaints. To some extent this is due to the narrow focus of medical practitioners on *physical* aspects of illness. In addition, managed care has steadily lowered the fees of doctors, who have responded by abbreviating the amount of time spent per patient visit, in order to compensate for the drastic reductions in their income.

> *I am not a mechanism, an assembly of various sections.*
> *And it is not because the mechanism is working wrongly that I am ill.*
> *I am ill because of wounds to the soul, to the deep emotional self.*
> *And the wounds to the soul take a long, long time, only time can help*
> *And patience, and a certain difficult repentance.*
> *Long, difficult repentance, realization of life's mistake, and the freeing*
> *of oneself*
> *From the endless repetition of the mistake*
> *Which mankind at large has chosen to sanctify.*
> – D. H. Lawrence

On the other hand, the weaknesses of complementary therapies include a limited appreciation of precision in diagnosis and research; lack of follow-up to determine why some patients treated do not improve; and lower standards of peer supervision and review.

Both allopathic and complementary therapists may have limited appreciation of psychological factors that can contribute to the development of illness, and limited training in dealing with them. Most conventional therapists and many CAM therapists may likewise be lacking in spiritual awareness. But for increasing numbers of complementary therapists, particularly spiritual healers, the spiritual aspects of awareness are the most important in assessing health and illness.[236]

There is also a growing appreciation that CAM can be cost-effective. The fact that complementary therapists charge less than allopathic physicians is only one contributing factor in this regard. Their primary cost-effectiveness derives from successfully treating illnesses and getting people better more quickly.[237]

Despite the difficulties involved, complementary and allopathic therapists are learning to understand each other and to interweave their therapeutic modalities so that people who need help can receive the best combinations of therapies. This is not to deny that there are still significant differences in philosophies and practices between the various approaches. We are learning to cooperate and collaborate across these professional divides, respecting that each approach has its strengths and weaknesses, its successes and failures. Each has a piece of the puzzle to contribute to our comprehension of the human condition. Working together, our understanding will be more complete. It is in this spirit that the discussions of various therapies are presented in this volume of *Healing Research*.

Wholistic care
Wholistic care seeks to bring people to a state of wholeness in body, emotions, mind, relationships and spirit. The main tenets of this approach are as follows:

- It is important to address the people who have the illness rather than merely treating their problems.

- Psychological dis-ease must be addressed as well as disease.

- Caring is at least as important as curing, and often moreso.

- The therapist is as important as the therapeutic modality used in the treatment.

- The recipients of care are full participants in their own care and treatment.

- Spiritual dimensions are important aspects of healthy adjustment in the world.

Wholistic medicine is a growing, humanizing movement in the health field. It emphasizes treatment of that aspect of the whole person rather than addressing just that part of the person which is diseased. This is not an innovation so much as a return to the bedside manner that doctors today have too little time to cultivate – under increasing pressures to provide "efficient" medical care.

 The focus of wholistic medicine on philosophies and theories of practice rather than on methodologies, discussed at the start of this chapter, is clearly relevant here as well.

 Some integrative clinical practices address various aspects of each patient separately, with a physician treating the body, a counselor or psychotherapist addressing psychological issues, a social worker dealing with relational problems, and clergy team member attending to spiritual matters. The advantage of this approach is that each of the therapists gains a more thorough knowledge of the patient according to their area of expertise. The doctors, who are paid very high wages, are encouraged to be as efficient as possible with their diagnoses, prescriptions and therapies, and are often discouraged from participating more actively in wholistic aspects of care. They very often feel that they cannot spend the hour or more per visit that the other practitioners routinely give.

 While this sort of teamwork subdivision of labor within wholistic care can have economic advantages, it may at the same time leave patients feeling that they are still being parceled out in bits, without being fully heard or understood by any one of their therapists. The therapists may also be dissatisfied if there is little time or opportunity to communicate with each other. When the members of the team that is hitched to a patient's wagon all pull in different directions, even if only by a narrow angle of deviation, it does not serve the patient or the team as well as when there is a fully integrated effort.

 Other integrative, wholistic practitioners address illness as an expression of the whole self – the body expressing through symptoms the stress and distress experienced in emotions, thoughts, relationships, and spirit. This is not a new concept in health care – though it may be unfamiliar to many Western practitioners. Brooke Medicine Eagle (1989, p.61) explains:

> ...We now understand our own health as something created through
> the patterns of our lives; and are beginning to understand disease not

as something bad or evil that "comes to get us", but as a symptom of an imbalanced way in which we walk on Mother Earth. With this understanding we can begin the process of healing ourselves through proper nutrition, physical exercise, new beliefs, and a more healthy environment, as well as through the balancing of energies and the right use of medicines that stimulate the body's innate healing capacities.

Personal responsibility and prevention are major aspects of wholistic treatment. The respant is encouraged to participate in the treatment, especially with regular exercise, proper diet, avoidance of substances injurious to health (tobacco, alcohol, commonly allergenic foods that we tend to crave – such as chocolate, etc.), and application of active stress-reduction techniques (meditation, biofeedback, relaxation exercises, etc.). In essence, wholistic medicine advocates self-healing.

Since wholistic medicine views the person as a unity of body, emotions, mind, relationships, and spirit, disease is seen not as something to be fought or extirpated, but as a problem to be understood. Illness is a dis-ease or disharmony of people within themselves, in their relationships with significant others, or in their interaction with their environment. While this is easy to say, it may be difficult to conceptualize – particularly when a patient has complex problems on several or all of these levels. Figures II-6 and II-7 illustrate this kind of complexity.

Richard Moss (1987), a wholistic, spiritual doctor, states:

> ...If we want to understand the disease, we must understand it as part of life itself seeking expression through a system that is unable to contain or conduct that life except in a diseased mode. To try and label the disease as the problem misses this fundamental point.
> [W]hat we call disease cannot be separated from the total consciousness of the individual. The healthy person isn't someone without the disease; the disease is not some abnormal addition to be eliminated. On the contrary, disease is a part of our wholeness. No matter how miserable we appear from a humanistically biased perspective, all individuals are already whole – now and always. Each of us is a complete system and the energies of being take a particular form of expression in each of us in accordance with our own unique dynamics.

Wholistic care for dis-ease people involves exploration of the roots of the disharmonies in their lives. Moss adds, "[F]ar from being some dark and terrible force, diseases such as cancer are the transformational impulses seeking expression in us..."

This approach can require major changes in the general attitudes of health practitioners as well as their clients. In a wholistic practice, people will no longer bring their bodies into the doctor's office for repairs, leaving the responsibility for the cure to the health practitioner and waiting patiently for something to happen through agencies beyond themselves.

The wholistic practitioner becomes a counselor and midwife during the gestation and birthing of healing strategies and in the growth and development of new ways for people to relate to their illnesses. In its truest essence, wholistic medicine is about helping people to be whole and to take responsibility for creating and maintaining their health.[238]

Figure II-6. Four aspects of health[239]

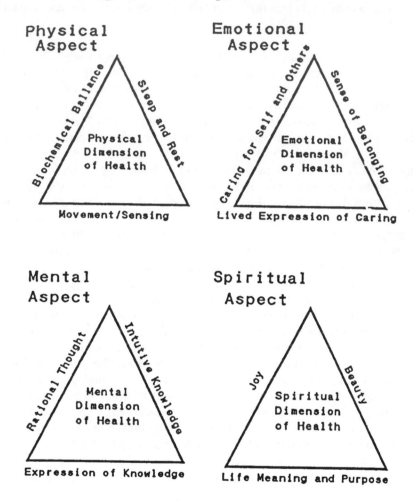

[I]llness and loss of inner strength appear together so frequently one could say that they are really different aspects of the same thing.

Consequently, then, any medicine which does not assist us to recover our inner strength and fails to teach us how to look after ourselves in the end only creates a self-serving dependency – or to be frank, a co-dependency. Though we may seem to get well from such treatment, in fact the root imbalance will remain and we will configure new illnesses, one after another, until either death or true healing occurs. In this way, our present system of medicine actually betrays us while appearing to help.

– Michael Greenwood (1998, p.47)

Wholistic approaches are growing in popularity within an atmosphere of general agreement that health care in the US and in many other countries is in serious – and some would even say in dire – need of reform. Consumers, medical administrators, legislators, and insurance companies are unhappy with the high costs of medical care. Doctors are unhappy with the pressures put upon them to economize, when these pressures are often applied under bureaucratic regulations that are insensitive to the needs of individual patients and practitioners (N. Edwards et al.; A. Murray et al.).

Figure II-7. Interpenetrating process of healing[240]

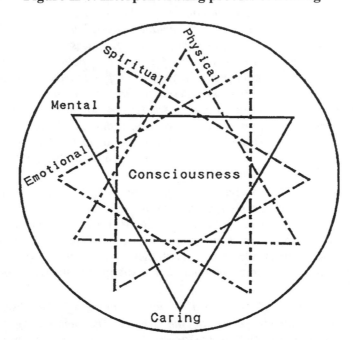

The remedies being applied address economic and administrative issues but tend to overlook many of the relevant human issues. Administrators regulate the types and durations of treatments allowable under insurance programs. Doctors are forced to shorten their interventions to work within these limitations, and at the same time they are faced with inordinate burdens of paperwork, not to mention endless telephone arguments with bureaucratic administrators over regulations, to justify treatments that are essential for the welfare of their patients.

The public is unhappy with medical services that address bits and pieces of their bodies separately but often ignore them as people, and with a medical administration that views their problems as statistics and fails to address them individually.

Growing numbers of doctors and nurses are exploring ways to humanize this system, and many of them have shifted to treating patients within wholistic frameworks. Holistic Medical Associations and Holistic Nursing Associations can be found in the US, Canada and several other countries.[241] Training and certification in Holistic Medicine[242] and Nursing[243] are now available in the US. The public has been seeking help from a wide variety of practitioners outside the conventional medical system, and people are now pressing doctors and insurance companies to include these treatments and attitudes within their medical treatment options. These trends are encouraging, although the overall picture in health care still seems rather bleak – for both practitioners and patients.

> *...The predominant style of medicine too often runs counter to the patient's own healing requirements: They need to develop autonomy, but are instead infantilized, kept in the dark; they need to actively affirm their uniqueness, but are reduced to passive recipients of normative "protocols"; they need time, but are rushed onto a virtual conveyer belt; they need to build up their immune system, but are given therapies that may debilitate it; they may crave life's messy vitality, but are instead sequestered in a sterile ward; they need a helpful vision of the future, and are instead provided with often pessimistic ("realistic") prognoses; they may need to reacquaint themselves with their bodies (particularly the diseased parts, where emotional issues may be "somaticized"), but instead receive drugs that block function and sensation, or surgeries which may remove these parts altogether.*
> – Marc Ian Barasch (p.202)

The *how* of treatments may be as important, or even more important than the *what*. A physician giving conventional treatment can be just as wholistic in his approach as any complementary therapist, if the treatment is given from the heart, with caring and compassion. Conversely, a CAM therapist can be just as unwholistic as the crustiest allopathic practitioner, if the therapist mechanistically treats the presenting symptoms, without paying attention to the whole person.

> *The utterances of the heart – unlike those of the discriminatory intellect – always relate to the whole. The heartstrings sing like an Aeolian harp only to the gentle breath of the premonitory mood, which does not drown the song but listens. What the heart hears are the great things that span our whole lives, the experiences which we do nothing to arrange but which we ourselves suffer.*
> – C.G. Jung (1977)

One of my favorite New Yorker cartoons features a patient at the receptionist's desk, asking: "Does the doctor hug?"

Complementary therapies can be vehicles for wholistic care

Acupuncture, homeopathy, spiritual healing, and other CAM approaches, when practiced in the fullness of their traditions, address the person who has the disease as a unitary, whole organism – not focusing merely on the presenting symptoms. Chinese medicine, Native American medicine, and medical practices in many other cultures go even further, considering individual people as elements of their communities and their environments, and many even view them as parts of the entire cosmos.

In contrast with wholistic practices, conventional medicine is particularly poor at dealing with death and dying. Allopathic medicine is oriented toward fighting disease. I was taught as a medical student that if a person under my care died, I was probably to blame because I hadn't diagnosed her problem correctly or hadn't prescribed the correct treatment. I was not taught to help people deal with impending death. There should be no *blame* imposed on caregivers when people under their care reaches the end of their life, though there is clearly an ethical and moral obligation to ask whether treatments given or not given could have contributed to their demise.

To anyone not aware of the death-avoiding habits of western medicine, the above may be difficult to appreciate. Let me point out how this fear of death impacts the medical care of people who are in the hospital and nearing their time to die. In most of the hospitals where I worked, people who were beyond the benefits of medical interventions were placed in the rooms farthest from the nurses' stations – ostensibly with the intention of sparing them the disturbance of the noise and bustle of the nursing station. However, I believe an even stronger motivation was to spare the nurses and doctors the discomfort of constantly facing what they view as their failure.

Medicolegal issues also contribute to our anxieties and difficulties in dealing with the realities of death. Doctors are afraid of being sued by relatives for not having done absolutely everything possible to preserve and prolong life. Therefore, people who are in the terminal stages of their illnesses may be given cardiac resuscitation and other heroic interventions when they are actually ready (and sometimes even eager – due to the discomforts of their illnesses and of hospital treatments) to make their transition out of their physical bodies.

> *[W]hen should health care end? It is no secret that as much as 30 to 60 percent of our health care dollar is spent in the last few days of a person's life. The dirty little secret is that most of it is spent in irrational procedures that do nothing significant to prolong life. In short, we are doing all we can do, not all that we should do.*
>
> *Listening to death-related visions has the potential to dramatically reduce wasteful medical procedures that are often painful to the patient. These procedures are often used on dying patients without their consent and without any hope of prolonging life. The purpose of much of this last-minute medicine is only to make us doctors feel as though everything possible has been done to prevent death, even when death is imminent. The result, writes Dr. William Knaus, of George Washington University, is "to give treatment of no benefit and tremendous cost, depriving others of treatment while dignity disappears."*
>
> – Melvin Morse (1995, p.136)

Spiritual healing and various other CAM approaches may be of great help to respants and also to caregivers in dealing with death. Within the philosophies that guide these approaches, death is perceived as a natural part of life. Within many of these traditions, death is not the end of one's personal existence. The spirit survives the death of the physical body, continues its path of lessons, and may return to the physical world in another incarnation.[244] Helping a person to die a good death is every bit as much a healing as helping them overcome an illness.

Integrative care brings together conventional and CAM therapies
Some allopathic physicians work together with complementary therapists.[245] In other cases the doctors themselves administer acupuncture, homeopathy, or other complementary therapies. Complementary therapists are critical of some of the doctors who do this, pointing out that it takes 1-2 hours to properly complete an initial acupuncture or homeopathic interview – a time investment few physicians are willing or able to make. CAM practitioners also criticize doctors who claim that they can practice a new therapy after attending only a weekend course – when complementary therapists may study for months and years to learn the basic theories and practices of these approaches. Complementary therapists point out that it is not just methodology that must be mastered (such as where to insert acupuncture needles). Practitioners must also develop an understanding of energetic patterns of illness and vast complexes of interventions (e.g. acupuncture points for different types of pain; herbal and homeopathic remedies; chakra[246] interventions, etc.), as well as an appreciation for the unique individuals who will be treated.

Ideally, the doctor will take a thorough course in the treatment philosophy and method, and will arrange to practice the modality to its fullest potential, allowing adequate session time in which to do so.

It is impossible for any one person to master all of the complementary therapies, but to maximize integrative care it is helpful for doctors to know *about* as many complementary therapies as possible, in order to refer patients to appropriate therapists.

The successful marriage of medical and complementary therapies requires close collaboration between the various practitioners. Like other marriages, these relationships may require a fair amount of effort to make them work well. A number of experiments are being developed to investigate these collaborations.[247]

Complementary/ Alternative Medicine (CAM) Therapies

Conventional medicine is increasingly responsive to public demand for complementary therapies,[248] and centers providing CAM therapies are becoming more widely available. American medical schools are also introducing courses and graduate programs on complementary therapies[249] in the wake of surveys showing that since 1990 almost as many billions of dollars have been paid to complementary therapists as to medical doctors (Eisenberg et al. 1993; 1998). The British Medical Association (1993) has acknowledged that many doctors are including acupuncture, homeopathy, osteopathy, chiropractic and herbalism in their practices, and has recommended that more collaborative research be undertaken.[250] Long-term trends show a growing use of CAM over the last 50 years (Kessler et al). Above all, consumer satisfaction appears to be the most influential factor in the increased CAM use in the West (Eisenberg 1993; 1998).[251]

Figure II-8. Witch Doctor?

By Martin Honeysett (with permission of Century Publishing, London)

There are many instances in which CAM therapies may be sufficient in and of themselves to treat disease states. Some therapists advocate that these methods be employed routinely as *alternatives* to conventional medicine, when conventional doctors are not open to including them in their practices or are actually opposed their utilization. A few CAM therapists feel that *alternative medicine* should in fact be the label for these therapies, because their therapeutic philosophies differ substantially from Western medical views.[252]

Though the term *alternative* might serve to emphasize differences in attitudes and approaches, I feel it reflects an unfortunate polarization that can only be detrimental to respants' care in the long run. There is also the danger that an alternative therapist who is untrained in medical diagnosis could unwittingly cause harm by overlooking problems in interactions between treatments or serious problems for which allopathic medicine might provide relief or even a cure.

The prevalent view in the West has been that conventional, allopathic medicine is the only reliable method of addressing illness.[253] However, this view is changing as professionals and the public learn more about complementary therapies. Many of these therapies, such as acupuncture, Ayurvedic medicine, Native American medicine, and yoga, have been practiced for many hundreds of years in their cultures of origin. These systems of medicinal practice have evolved with worldviews that differ substantially from those of allopathic medicine (Krippner 1999).

The West has much to learn from other cultures and their medical practices. While some of these may appear alien to us, such as using acupuncture needles for pain management, others may appear more sensible and may be transposed more easily into Western medical cosmologies. For example, Ken Bearhawk Cohen describes a Native American tradition concerning the activation of inner healing abilities:

> When personal gifts ('medicine' in Native terminology) are not used, they rot inside, causing sickness. "Healing," says… Seneca elder Twylah… Nitch, "is sometimes not a matter of taking something in – an herb or other medication, but of letting something out, having the confidence to express yourself'." (K. Cohen 1999b, p.237).

Doctors have lobbied state and Federal governments to enact legislation that would limit or outlaw many complementary therapies, but it seems clear that such restrictions would not be in the best interests of the public. This is apparently not a new problem – Benjamin Rush, U.S. Surgeon General and signer of the Declaration of Independence recommended:

> The Constitution of this Republic should make special provision for Medical Freedom as well as Religious Freedom. To restrict the art of healing to one class of men and deny equal privileges to others will constitute the Bastille of medical science. All such laws are un-American and despotic. They are fragments of a monarchy and have no place in a Republic.

The National Health Freedom Coalition is promoting State laws that permit the practice of unlicensed CAM therapies without danger of prosecution for "practicing medicine without a license."[254] Minnesota and California have passed such laws and other states are considering them.

There are many knotty issues involved in health laws.

One obstacle to the acceptance of complementary therapies is related to issues of training and certification of practitioners. For some complementary therapies there are professional boards that set varying levels of standards for training and certification (for example osteopathy, chiropractic, acupuncture, naturopathy, homeopathy, Therapeutic Touch and Healing Touch). For others, there may be a wide variation of training and practice standards. Some states license some but not all practitioners (Chez et al.), and this is a growing trend. Licensure ensures that CAM therapists have studied a certain number of months or years, that they have mastered a certain body of knowledge, and that they uphold certain standards of practice.

In many complementary therapies, however, the *person of the therapist* is a vital aspect of the therapy. This is particularly true of the practices that involve adjustments of biological energies (such as acupuncture, craniosacral therapy, and spiritual healing). While training and certification in these methods can assure the public that practitioners know *about* their modality and its ethical applications, these standards do not guarantee that the therapist is a *good* or a *potent* practitioner. Herein lies a major, serious challenge for those of us who want to protect the public on the one hand, and to assure full availability of integrative care on the other.

Bioenergies and CAM

Subtle biological energies are essential elements of many complementary therapies. They are particularly important in spiritual healing, and also function in the meridians of acupuncture, the subtle manipulations of craniosacral osteopathy, the energy patterning of water in homeopathy, and so on. Spiritual healers rely directly upon energy medicine interventions,   but many Western scientists investigating complementary therapies (other than healing), and indeed many CAM practitioners themselves, de-emphasize the energy aspects of these treatments. It is less challenging to Western worldviews to attribute the efficacy of complementary therapies to mechanical interventions (e.g. insertion of acupuncture needles, or osteopathic manipulations of bones and joints) or chemical agents (e.g. homeopathic preparations) than to invoke explanations involving subtle energies that cannot be measured on conventional instruments.

Spiritual healing is viewed by conventional science as one of the "fringe" modalities of complementary medicine, operating at the extreme limit of credibility, because there isn't even a partial explanation to make spiritual healing comprehensible and acceptable within conventional scientific frameworks. Nevertheless, the numerous studies reviewed in Volume I of *Healing Research* reveal that the opposite is in fact the case. With the exceptions of hypnosis and psychoneuroimmunology, there have been more controlled studies of spiritual healing than of any other complementary therapy.

Spiritual healing is emphasized in this volume for two reasons. First, it appears to be a common denominator in all of the complementary therapies (Benor 1995a). Not only are subtle energies involved in these therapies, but there are also therapeutic factors including subtle energies inherent in the persons who administer them. Many complementary therapists who are particularly sensitive can detect subtle energies with their hands or through mental imagery. They may also be able to administer subtle energies through their hands. I have heard many grateful recipients of massage and reflexology treatments report to me that their therapist had warm, tingly hands. Many such therapists are totally unaware that they are channeling subtle energies during their treatments.

The second reason for focusing on spiritual healing in this volume is to frame it within the context of a multitude of subtle energy therapies. Each therapy contributes another facet of understanding to the mystery of healing, and similarly, spiritual healing helps us to understand aspects of various complementary therapies.[255]

Another criticism of complementary therapies is that their professional standards are not on a par with those of medical practice. Not all of these therapies have profession-wide (rather than school-specific) standards for training and practice, and only a few are licensed by various states.

Spiritual healers in Britain who were registered with the *Confederation of Healing Organisations* worked under a unified Code of Conduct. This Code required healers to recommend that healees see their allopathic doctors prior to having healing.[256]

Healers and other complementary therapists generally are untrained in medical diagnosis and allopathic medicine. Likewise, most medical doctors are unaware of energy medicine. Nevertheless, practitioners of both modalities are gradually learning to work with each other – and the greatest beneficiaries will be the respants in their care.

Each complementary therapy offers treatments that can help with some problems some of the time. While each therapy has its own methodologies and theories of health and illness, there are common denominators across the various approaches that will be discussed at the end of this chapter.

Let us begin with a review of CAM therapies.

I have ordered the therapies alphabetically. A more logical order might have grouped various therapies by their derivations (as with acupuncture, applied kinesiology, reflexology, and shiatsu), or according to similarities in practice (as with homeopathy and flower essences). However, this would make it more difficult for readers to locate discussions of individual therapies. I have indicated the related therapies at the end of each discussion, so that the associations are clear.

Though some of these have not yet been well researched, I prefer to consider a broad spectrum of practices in order to gather as much evidence as possible from the information available at this time – to help us begin to understand these approaches, both individually and collectively. These clinical methodologies and anecdotal reports of efficacy, along with their explanatory theories, may help us understand how self-healing and energy medicine can bring about improvements in health.[257]

A brief discussion of some of the problems that are effectively addressed by CAM therapies follows the descriptions of the various modalities.

ACUPUNCTURE

> Now for some words about the theory of acupuncture. But bear in mind that one must not mistake an explanation for the reality. And this is where we are very often uptight. We want things explained. Then we think we can behave as though that explanation is the reality. The explanation of anything is nothing more than a technique or a system that is used to make it comprehensible within the circumference of our own understanding, and when your understanding grows and is enlarged then we find that there is a need for new explanations. And this is where the American medical man is going to have difficulty, trying to understand how acupuncture works....To understand acupuncture we must empty ourselves of all of our theoretical scientific concepts. The American medical man will say, "This is an unreasonable thing. He must make it understandable to me in my terms." And yet he would think that the Oriental acupuncturist was terribly unreasonable if he asked him to explain Western medicine in terms of five elements, yin and yang and Tao.
>
> [I]f we are going to understand or try to understand something new, we must be able and willing to learn the language in which it is written. I'm talking about the vocabulary, not national language

itself. In the Tao it says, this is the important key: that we must learn to unlearn our learning. And that's the secret to understanding acupuncture.

– Khigh Alx Diegh

Acupuncture is based on ancient Chinese observations of subtle energy lines called *meridians* that run from the head to the fingers and toes. This energy is called *qi* (pronounced *kee* or *chee*, with alternative English spellings: *Ki* or *Chi*). Each meridian is related to one or more of the organ systems, and diseases are caused by excesses or deficits of energy, or blockage of energy flow in the meridians. Points of special sensitivity exist along the entire length of each energy line. Stimulation of these acupuncture points can influence the related organ systems by altering energy flow in the meridians. The therapist can stimulate the acupuncture points in several ways: by inserting needles, applying finger pressure, moxibustion (burning *moxa* herbs) with the stalks held against the acupuncture points, applying mild electrical current, laser rays, or through mental projection of healing to the points.

Some meridians correspond to physical organs (e.g. heart, lungs), while others are correlated with functions for which allopathic medicine has no exact parallels (e.g. the *triple warmer)*. The *triple warmer* is a body system that is named but poorly defined. It is that aspect of the body that controls the water-regulating organs (kidney, stomach, small and large intestine, spleen and bladder). The *upper warmer* governs the head and chest; the *middle warmer* the spleen and stomach; and the *lower warmer* the liver and kidneys.

Even where a physical organ corresponds to a specific line, the meridian reference is to energy functions of the line more than to its body functions (per Western physiology). For instance, a Chinese acupuncturist who speaks of the kidney meridian may be referring to its role in storing life energy (*jing*); its influence on development, maturation, and or reproduction; its effects on marrow, bones and teeth; or its interactions with respiration.[258]

The various meridians have specific times of day when they are more and less active. Treatments may therefore be given for specific problems at particular times, even at unusual hours of the night (W. McGarey; Thie).

For many years, allopathic medicine maintained a very skeptical or even dismissive attitude towards Eastern explanations of acupuncture, because no anatomical structures were known that might support Eastern theories of energy lines traversing the body. The meridians do not correspond in any way to the well-mapped peripheral or autonomic nervous system, and until recently no other communication network in the body had been demonstrated that could support such theories. It seemed patently ridiculous to Westerners that needles inserted at acupuncture points on the foot or arm could influence internal organs at considerable distances from the sites of treatment. It was presumed that acupuncture treatments were effective purely on the basis of placebo responses or other aspects of suggestion. Yet some acupuncturists claim that they can sense acupuncture points with their fingers, and others claim that they can manually detect when the meridians have a proper flow of Qi or are blocked (e.g. Upledger[259]). A few sensitives who see auras also claim that they can see acupuncture meridians and acupuncture points.

In addition to treatment by acupuncture, Chinese medicine also recommends self-healing through various movement and imagery exercises focused on facilitating bioenergy flow (K. Cohen 1997; Jahnke). Roger Jahnke explains that there are three states of Qi: *jing*, related to earth energies; *Qi*, related to life energies; and *shen*, related to spiritual dimensions. People are seen to be an intimate part of the world around them. Energies within the body interact with and resonate with those of the environment and of the worlds of spirit.

Western explorations of acupuncture

Traditional acupuncture identifies the acupuncture points in relation to anatomical maps. A point will be over a bony prominence, or measured in finger-width distances from such anatomical landmarks.

Recently, Western science has found several ways of confirming the validity of acupuncture points and meridians.[260] Numerous studies have shown that acupuncture points have a much lower electrical resistance than surrounding areas of the skin. This difference is on the order of a few thousand ohms compared to millions of ohms. Simple resistance meters are now in common use to confirm the locations of acupuncture points. These measurements are variable within short periods of time, particularly in respect to the width of individual points, but also to some extend in their locations.[261] It seems that this variance reflects shifting organismic energetic states rather than inherent inaccuracies in the measurements.

Clinical studies have demonstrated correlations between predicted changes on various meridians and the activity of the organs traditionally associated with those meridians. For instance, conductance measured nearly 20 times higher at the Liver 8 acupuncture point (located at the knee) in people with demonstrated liver disease (acute hepatitis or cirrhosis), as compared with a control group with no liver disease (Bergsmann & Woolley-Hart 1973). Sullivan et al. found that people with lung disease that had been verified with chest X-rays demonstrated 30% lower electrical conductance at acupuncture lung points (Sullivan et al. 1985).

New scientific methods have also been developed to demonstrate the existence of the meridians. Jean-Claude Darras, a physician and president of the *World Union of Acupuncture*, and P. de Vernejoul, a physician who heads the Department of Biophysics of Neckar Hospital in Paris, injected radioactive chemicals at acupuncture points and followed the course of distribution of these materials with a Geiger counter at the body surface. They demonstrated that connections exist between acupuncture points, along lines identical with the meridians described by acupuncturists. Similar research completed decades earlier had been rejected due to difficulties in verifying the findings.[262]

Kirlian photography, an electrophotographic technique, reveals an enhanced Kirlian aura at acupuncture points (Dumitrescu).[263]

Instruments for clinical use that assess electrical potentials at various acupuncture points, and through which electrical stimulation of acupuncture points may be applied, are growing in popularity.[264] One of these is the Voll instrument, on which a reading of "50" indicates a healthy state, while lower readings point to degenerative diseases, and higher readings are associated with injury or inflammation (Sancier 1993; Voll). William Tiller (1997), Professor Emeritus at Stanford University, suggests that the intuitive perceptions of the instrument operators may be crucial to the success of readings taken with such devices. The amount of pressure exerted by the operator's hand in touching the acupuncture point can influence the reading, so there is room for the operator's intuitive awareness to find subtle expression in the process of taking the measurements. This effect is often completely unconscious on the part of the operator, whose perception is that she is leaving it entirely to the instrument to do the assessments.[265]

Hiroshi Motoyama (1981), a Japanese biologist trained in Buddhist traditions, developed another instrument for quantitative measurements of the electrical currents along acupuncture meridians. He calls this an "apparatus for measuring the function of the meridians and corresponding internal organs," or "AMI" for short. Using the AMI he can diagnose illnesses, sometimes even before the disease is otherwise perceptible. Western scientists are now beginning to confirm Motoyama's findings, using the AMI.

Electroacupuncture assessments are being used to identify remedies for the treatment of physical and psychological problems. Baseline measurements are made of skin resistance at acupuncture points associated with a given problem. The person being tested is then given various remedies or nutrients to hold. It is assumed that the therapeutic substances interact with the bioenergy field. Repeat measurements are made. Healthier readings indicate treatments that are likely to be helpful. The use of these devices has not been adequately researched.

Lively explorations of acupressure techniques are likewise proceeding in the US, especially as self-healing for the treatment of psychological problems.[266] These methods are rapidly and potently effective for the relief of pains, anxiety, emotional traumas and negative self-beliefs. They can also enhance sports performance.

Other energy centers in the body that have been identified by Chinese medicine are called *chakras* (the Sanskrit word for *wheels*).[267] There are many chakras around the body, but the seven major ones that are along the central axis of the body are the most important. They project as vortices of energy to the front and back of the body, as well as upwards and downwards. (See Table II-7.)

The chakras are said to be regions of the body where energies from other dimensions are transformed into forms that are suitable for vitalizing the physical body.[268]

Motoyama also developed an electronic device that verifies the existence of chakras. He associates the seven major chakras with nerve plexuses in the autonomic nervous system. Others associate the major chakras with the hormone-secreting endocrine glands, suggesting that one function of hormones may be to convey information recorded as energy patterns imprinted from sources outside the body to distant parts of the body – in addition to their known biochemical functions.

Elaborate images are used in Eastern teachings to depict the chakras, associated with the various physical body functions and levels of psychospiritual development that are attributed to each chakra. Some are simple petals in floral designs, with increasing numbers of petals from the base to the crown chakra. Others include Sanskrit symbols with animal and human figures from Eastern mythologies and religious cosmologies.

Table II-7. The Chakras

Name	Location of chakra	Level *Endocrine gland* NERVE PLEXUS	Influence on
Crown *Sahasrara*		Apex of skull *Pineal*	Higher brain centers, spiritual connection
Brow/Third Eye *Ajna*		Brow *Pituitary* DEEP BRAIN CENTERS	Deeper brain centers, eyes, ears, nose, nervous system, visualization
Throat *Visuddha*		3rd cervical *Thyroid* PHARYNGEAL	Voice, breathing, digestive tract, expression, clairsentience
Heart *Anahata*		4th thoracic *Thymus* CARDIAC	Heart, blood, autonomic nervous system, circulation, closeness of relationship
Solar Plexus *Manipura*		8th thoracic *Spleen/pancreas* SOLAR PLEXUS	Stomach, liver, gall bladder, awareness of place in cosmos
Sacral *Svadhisthana*		1st lumbar *Gonads* SPLENC	Reproduction, relating on sexual levels
Base/Root *Muladhara*		Base of spine *Adrenals* COCCYGEAL	Spine, kidneys, levels of energy

Frances Vaughan (1995) reports that Carl Jung (1976) found correspondences between the archetypal images that his patients reported as they individuated in psychotherapy, and symbolic images that are found in classical representations of the stages of psychological development associated with the chakras.

Some healers instruct healees in awareness of their chakras as a way of initiating self-healing. I have learned to do this, but I found at first that it was quite difficult to learn to trust my subjective sensations, because there was no direct feedback to confirm that I was on target. Over the years, with various meditative practices and life experiences, I have come to a greater trust in my chakra perceptions.

Acupuncture theories

Acupuncture as practiced in the West is often mechanistic, as. it has been difficult for allopathic medicine to acknowledge that therapeutic concepts outside the realm of Western science might provide a valid method for dealing with disease.

Ted Kaptchuk provides an excellent discussion on aspects of health that allopathic medicine seems helpless to treat, but which respond well to Traditional Chinese Medicine (acupuncture combined with herbal therapies). He also expands on the comments of Khigh Alx Diegh (quoted at the beginning of this section), explaining Chinese views of health and illness.

> For instance, the Chinese do not ask what causes a particular illness. They ask, "Which patterns within the individual and his environment are in harmony and which are in conflict?" Therapy is not aimed at

correcting symptoms so much as at bringing the person to greater harmony with the cosmos.

…The Chinese description of reality does not penetrate to a truth, it can only be a poetic description of a truth that cannot be grasped. The Heart, Lung and Kidneys… are not a physical heart, lung or kidneys; instead they are personae in a descriptive drama of health and illness. For the Chinese, this description of the eternal process of Yin and Yang is the only way to try to explain either the workings of the universe or the workings of the human body. And it is enough, because the process is all there is; no underlying truth is ever within reach. The truth is immanent in everything and is the process itself…

Chinese medicine also views the body holographically, assuming that a part will reflect the whole.[269] Thus the tongue, teeth, upper palate, face, ear, hand, foot, or pulse may be used to diagnose or treat disorders anywhere in the body. For example, a beefy, red tongue may indicate congestion or blockage of energy, and a pale tongue can mean a lack of energy – not necessarily in the vicinity of the tongue but perhaps in other specific parts of the body, or everywhere in the body. Tenderness in points on the foot, hand or ear may likewise indicate disorders in distant body parts or in organs related to these points.

Stimulation of the indicated points may bring symptomatic relief. The stimulation is to release blocks, to enhance energy flows, or to decrease excessive energy activity.

It is not recorded how the meridians and *chakras* were identified in some distant millennium. From reports of sensitives (such as Motoyama and others) who state that they can see auras, and from practitioners who report that they can sense these energy points by touch, one may readily postulate that it must have been an anonymous aura-seeing sensitive who originally mapped out these systems.

My own experience of learning elementary touch healing techniques confirms it is possible to sense gross energy changes in the body with touch. It does not seem to me far-fetched that people with more highly developed sensitivities could have a more refined ability to sense these energies. I can also personally verify that it is possible to influence one's own *chakras* for self-healing. Other healers echo these observations.[270] There are some who claim that in modern times the meridians and acupuncture points that most require attention may differ from those that were codified in past centuries. That is to say, there may have been a collective, evolutionary shift in human acupuncture energies.

Whether the visual chakra phenomena are objectively or consensually verifiable has yet to be determined. A survey of the literature reveals variations in descriptions of the chakras by individual sensitives. Perhaps the variations relate to different physical or energy states in the various people observed, or perhaps the differences are due to individual factors in the observers. Most likely all of the descriptions are affected by the difficulties in translating inner intuitive perceptions of energies and/ or other realities into images and words of our outer-world, sensory reality. Because the chakra and meridian energies that are sensed clairsentiently differ so entirely from anything familiar to Western science, it may be that all the related descriptions are, at best, rough analogies.[271]

Yin and *yang* are polar opposites that must be balanced in order for life to proceed in harmony. The term *yin* denotes the shady side of the slope, and may be associated with qualities of femininity, openness, passivity, receptivity, introversion, diminution, repose, weakness, and coolness.. *Yang* is the sunny side of the slope, and may be associated with the sun, masculinity, strength, brightness, assertiveness, movement, extroversion, growth and excitation.

In the body, the front is yin relative to the back; the upper portions of the body are yang relative to the lower parts; the inner organs are more yin than the outer aspects such as hair and skin. Yang disorders are characterized by fever, hyperactivity, heat and strong movements; yin illnesses include weakness, slowing down, feeling cold and lethargy.

Yin and yang complement each other. If yang is excessive, then yin will be too weak, and conversely.

In Chinese cosmology, causality is unimportant. It is the *pattern* of relationships which defines reality, and all reality is relative to the context which is under consideration.

> The philosopher Zou Yen...describes this idea this way: "Heaven is high, the earth is low, and thus [Heaven and Earth] are fixed. As the high and low are thus made clear, the honorable and humble have their place accordingly. As activity and tranquillity have their constancy, the strong and the weak are thus differentiated... Cold and hot season take their turn... [Heaven] knows the great beginning, and [Earth] acts to bring things to completion... [Heaven] is Yang and [Earth] is Yin."
> Any Yin or Yang aspect can be further divided into Yin and Yang...
> – Kaptchuck (p. 9)

Chinese cosmology also explains health and illness according to the balance of five elements in a person's life, each associated with a set of body organs (C. Moss):

- Fire – heart, small intestine, triple heater, master of heart; blood vessels, tongue, complexion;
- Earth – stomach, spleen, mucous membranes, mouth;
- Metal – lung, colon, skin, nose;
- Water – kidney, bladder; back, bones, ears;
- Wood – liver, gallbladder, muscles, tendons, eyes.

These can be better understood as five processes or phases (Kaptchuk). Each phase controls another and is in turn controlled by yet another. These can be more descriptively characterized, as follows:

- Wood – windy, shouting, anger, sour, goatish;
- Earth – damp, singing, pensiveness, sweet, fragrant;

- Water – cold, groaning, fear, salty, rotten;
- Fire – hot, laughing, joy, bitter;
- Metal – dry, weeping, grief, pungent, rank.

Causality derives from the ways in which each of these five element processes relates to the others, through extremely complex relationships. Opinions vary widely on these interrelationships, and they have not stood up to systematic scrutiny, even within Chinese historical traditions. Nevertheless, they continue to be part of Chinese medical tradition (Kaptchuk).

Environmental influences on health are addressed in the Oriental system of *Feng Shui,* which will be discussed later in the sections on environmental medicine.

Meridians, chakras and spiritual healing

Observations from the tradition and practice of acupuncture may explain various aspects of spiritual healing.

Some healers focus assessments and treatments on specific *chakras* during healings. These reports make sense in the light of Chinese explanations regarding the functions of the chakras in regulating energies in adjacent organs, and not only in the nerves or glands immediately next to each chakra.

Diurnal waxing and waning of activity along particular meridians (Thie) may be correlated with positive and/ or negative responses to spiritual healing and othermedical treatments. It may be that at particular hours of the day, certain organ systems have greater or lesser sensitivity to healing and other therapies.

Yefim Shubentsov, an ex-Soviet healer living in Boston,[272] reports that healers may have more potent abilities at particular hours of the day or night. In reports by Western scientists from several decades ago, it was found that direct current fields on the body surface varied according to time of day, lunar phase and solar flares (Burr; Ravitz). This area of research has not been well explored.

Motoyama's electrophysiological verification of the meridian and chakra systems are relevant to the study and understanding of healing. The energy systems thus elucidated could possibly revolutionize our understanding of the functions of the body. If energy levels and flows within the body can be objectively measured, we can verify whether they are effected via bioenergy inputs associated with healing. This would then give us objective, measurable readouts for the changes brought about by healing, which could in turn provide a biofeedback mechanism whereby healing might be more precisely and effectively taught for the promotion of self-healing and healer-healing. This approach might also facilitate spiritual development through awareness of bioenergetic connections with higher aspects of oneself.

The human body can be conceptualized in ways that differ even more radically from traditional Western cosmologies. For example, the concept of *yin* and *yang,* and the linking of human illness with man's place in the cosmos may prove to be useful approaches for understanding and promoting health care.

The theory of acupuncture assumes the body is a sort of hologram. In a holographic picture, one can cut away any part of the negative, and this section of the negative will still contain the whole picture.[273] Each part of the picture, therefore, contains the whole picture. If the physical and/ or energetic body are holograms, this would help to explain how acupuncture diagnosis can be based on the appearance of the tongue or condition of the teeth, and how treatments may be applied to points on the ear, hand, or foot that correspond to each of the various organs of the body.[274]

Partisans of allopathic medicine believe that this is the best system of treatment. Yet allopathic medicine is helpless when confronted with many illnesses. Sufferers from allergies, arthritis, cancer, multiple sclerosis, strokes, addictions, and other health problems bear ample testimony to this fact. There is much to be gained by exploring the alternatives that acupuncture and Chinese medicine offer. Furthermore, acupuncture has far fewer side effects than many of the treatments used in allopathic medicine.

If allopathic medicine wishes to include the full benefits of a Chinese system of treatment, it must study the related concepts and traditions. It cannot demand that the approaches of acupuncture be made to conform to Western systems.

Research:[275] It was difficult at first to design acupuncture studies that conform to Western research protocols because Eastern methods of diagnosis and treatment differ substantially from those used in the West. Traditional acupuncture individualizes treatments to each person, and therefore does not lend itself to randomized controlled studies that require a standard treatment for each member of a group of subjects with the same diagnosis. Another challenge is in providing a control group. Some studies have accommodated the requirement for applying a standard treatment to subjects who share a Western medical diagnosis, and have used control subjects who receive *sham* acupuncture, with needles inserted at points that are not known to produce beneficial effects.[276]

One of the best known uses of acupuncture is in the treatment of pain. Studies have demonstrated its efficacy as a remedy for the following health problems: tension headaches;[277] migraines (Hesse et al.); facial pain (Hansen/ Hansen; Johansson et al.); dental pain (Ernst/ Pittler; L. Lao et al. 1995); craniomandibular disorders (List/ Helkimo; List et al. 1992); neck pain;[278] back pain;[279] lumbar disk protrusion (Longworth/ McCarthy); tennis elbow (Haker/ Lundeberg; Molsberger/ Hille); osteoarthritis;[280] renal colic (Y. Lee); dysmenorrhea (J. Helms 1987); fibromyalgia (Berman et al. 1999; Deluze et al.); peripheral nerve pain (Kreczi et al.); knee injuries from chronic trauma (L. Wang et al. 1985); and chronic pain (Ezzo et al. 2001).

While individual studies may produce only modest results, a series of studies analyzed as a group provides more substantial proof. One such meta-analysis of acupuncture studies confirms that it is an effective treatment for chronic pain (Ter Riet, et al. 1990a). Another meta-analysis was made of 14 randomized controlled studies of acupuncture for chronic pain (M. Patel et al. 1989). Pooled results according to the location of pains, the type of study, and the type of journal publishing the data showed statistically significant numbers. A more critical meta-analysis of 51 studies of acupuncture for pain (Ter Riet et al. 1990a) produced the impression that the quality of even the better studies was mediocre, and the results appeared contradictory. Reviews of 22 studies of acupuncture for neck and low back pain (Ter Riet et al. 1989a), and of 10 studies for migraine and tension headaches (Ter Riet et al. 1989b) showed that the numbers of subjects studied were too small, and poor methodologies made it impossible to assess the results. D. Bhatt-Sanders reviews eight studies of acupuncture for rheumatoid arthritis, five of which reported significant pain relief. He notes, however, that methodological problems make it difficult to accept these results.

Another well publicized use of acupuncture is for medical and surgical procedures. Studies have shown significant benefits from acupuncture in controlling the pain and discomforts of gastroscopy (Cahn et al.) and colonoscopy (H. Wang et al. 1992), and for postoperative pain following lower abdominal surgery in women (Christensen et al. 1989).

In one study, real and sham acupuncture treatments were given to 26 people with stable angina pectoris (heart pains) that had been unresponsive to medical treatments (Ballegaard et al.). Subjects were randomized and did not know which treatment they were receiving. Assessments were then made of frequency of angina attacks, medication requirements (nitroglycerin), and performance on exercise tests. Cardiac work capacity was also found to be significantly increased by acupuncture treatments ($p < .001$).

The way in which acupuncture produces analgesia has not yet been identified. It is strongly suspected that acupuncture stimulates the production of natural opiates (endorphins) in the body, because the effects of acupuncture analgesia are decreased when a chemical antagonist to opiates (naloxone) is injected prior to acupuncture treatments for pain (Pomeranz/ Stux). Electroacupuncture induced the production of different endorphins, depending on the frequency of the electrical pulse used.

Studies have shown significant relief of nausea and vomiting with acupuncture after surgical anesthesia,[281] chemotherapy (Dundee et al. 1989; J. Shen et al.), morning sickness during pregnancy,[282] and motion sickness (S. Hu et al. 1995).[283]

One extraordinary though little recognized contribution of acupuncture is in the treatment of strokes. Significant effects have been reported in improving muscle strength in leg and arm paralysis (W. Zhang et al. 1987; Naeser, et al.). The latter study clarified that benefits were obtained only when less than half of the motor pathway areas of the brain were damaged. Walking and balancing abilities were improved, activities of daily living (ADL) scores were higher, and days in hospital and nursing homes were halved, with estimated savings of $26,000 per patient (K. Johansson et al. 1993). Significant recovery of muscle functions and ADL scores were noted in another study, but with no decrease in hospital stay (Sallstrom et al.). When treatment was started within 36 hours of the onset of the strokes, those whose condition was poorer at the start of the study showed significant improvements in neurological functions and ADL scores, while those with better initial conditions showed no significant benefits from acupuncture (H. Hu et al. 1993). This would appear to contradict the evidence from the study by Johansson et al., which showed that with more severe strokes there was less improvement. Kjendahl et al. performed a study using 6 weeks of therapy for strokes and a one-year follow-up, which showed clear benefits. Further research is definitely warranted.

Traditional acupuncture has been used widely in the treatment of respiratory diseases. Reviewers are generally positive in their conclusions (Vincent/ Richardson; Virsik et al.), though the more critical reviewers point to mixed findings. J. Kleijnen et al. (1991) reviewed 13 studies on acupuncture for asthma, rating each according to 18 methodological criteria. Positive results on pulmonary function tests, improvement of symptoms, and reduction in the need for medications were reported in the 5 studies that were rated as the weakest from the standpoint of methodology. Of the 8 studies that were considered to have the best research design and reporting, only 3 concluded that acupuncture had beneficial effects. David Aldridge and Patrick Pietroni agreed with this assessment, and criticized the studies for addressing acupuncture as a needling method rather than as a full treatment modality. Many variables may have influenced these clinical results. For instance, duration of needling is probably a factor. One researcher recommends 40 minutes as the optimal time (J. Zang).

The following is a sampling of studies on asthma, showing similarly mixed results. A Chinese study of 192 patients showed marked improvements (J. Zang). A double-blind placebo comparison crossover study of 15 patients with stable illness found no objective or subjective improvements (Tandon et al.). A study of 9 patients found significant reductions in medication use (Sternfield et al.). A study of 12 patients showed that acupuncture could reduce experimentally induced bronchospasm in patients who had bronchial asthma. There were improvements in some pulmonary functions, though a medication spray was more effective (Tashkin et al. 1977). In a study of 19 children, exercise-induced asthma improved with acupuncture (Fung et al. 1986). A Danish report found modest enhancements in air flow rates and reduced medication requirements when patients were treated over a 5 week period (Christensen et al.). A study of 10 patients over 5 weeks showed enhanced pulmonary function and cessation of asthmatic episodes (Berger/ Nolte). A well designed study of 20 patients observed over 4 weeks showed no prolonged effects for chronic asthma (Tashkin et al. 1985). Morton et al. believe that those with allergic or drug-induced asthma may respond better than those with exercise-induced asthma.[284]

Chronic obstructive pulmonary disease (COPD) is a horrible illness in which lung tissues are destroyed by chronic infections, leaving sufferers unable to exert themselves due to oxygen starvation. It has no effective conventional treatment. A study of acupuncture for 26 people with COPD demonstrated improvements in ADL and well-being, with longer walk distances but no objective changes in pulmonary functions (Jobst et al. 1986).

In a critical review of acupuncture as a treatment for pulmonary diseases, Jobst (1995) concluded that it can ameliorate symptoms and potentiate effects of medication so that lower doses can be used, and it is also safe, with no side effects.

A review of German-language acupuncture research identified 14 studies dealing with ear, nose and throat (ENT) problems, of which only 2 were randomized, single-blind studies (Kubiena). Acupuncture was helpful for allergic rhinitis, sinusitis (especially in children), Menière's disease (middle ear problems) in younger people, trigeminal neuralgia, facial paralysis, and susceptibility to recurrent infections. Benefits were noted in reduction of pain, less need for medications, and more rapid recovery.

Of two studies on acupuncture as a treatment for allergic rhinitis, one (with 22 asthmatic subjects) showed that half of those studied were freed of symptoms and another third had moderate symptomatic improvements (Lau et al.). A second study concluded that any improvements were probably due to suggestion (Czubalski et al.).

Other applications of acupuncture showing significant effects include: facilitating labor and delivery (Romer et al.); relief of menopausal symptoms (Wyon et al. 1995); treatment of depression (H. Luo et al. 1985; X. Yang et al. 1994); enhancement of physical performance (Ehrlich/ Haber); treatment of enuresis (Serel et al.), and of frequent, urgent and painful urination (P. Chang 1988; Phillip et al.); treatment of nocturia (Ellis et al. 1990) and tinnitus (Park et al.); weight reduction (Ernst 1997); and chronically dry mouth (Blom et al. 1992).

Acupuncture is also finding a wide range of applications in the treatment of addictions. In severe alcoholics who had not responded to other therapies, treatment was given to 40 patients at acupuncture points that are recommended for treatment of substance abuse, and at "nonspecific" points in a control group of 40 similar patients (Bullock et al. 1989). In the treatment group, 21 subjects completed the program, while in the control group only 1 did. Significant positive effects were still evident in the treated group after 6 months. The control group demonstrated a greater need for alcohol, with twice as many drinking episodes and twice as many admissions to a detoxification center. In another study of 54 long-term (average 20 years) alcoholics, significantly more patients completed the treatment (Bullock et al. 1987). For 32 cocaine addicts (average use 13 years), abstinence in the treated group was significantly greater than in a group treated with amantidine,[285] and marginally better than in patients treated with desipramine[286] (Margolin et al. 1993). In 651 smokers, acupuncture plus group therapy brought about significant reductions in smoking (Clavel et al. 1985). Twice as many smokers were able to quit when acupuncture was added to nicotine replacement therapy (Haxby). White et al. (1999) review acupuncture as a therapy to help people stop smoking. Brewington et al. present a good overall survey of acupuncture for drug detoxification, including anecdotal and research reports (they did not address its long-term efficacy in dealing with addiction). They conclude that there is good evidence for the use of acupuncture in this application.

A meta-analysis (Ter Riet et al. 1990b) of controlled studies of acupuncture for addictions to nicotine (15), heroin (5) and alcohol (2) points out that research designs in most of these studies were deficient. There were far fewer studies with positive rather than negative results for nicotine, and too few good studies with significant results for the other addictions to provide encouragement.

Moxibustion has been found to be effective in correcting breech presentations, where babies have not turned head-down just before birth (Crdini/ Weixin).[287]

Acupuncture is also used in animals. One study has shown it helpful in the treatment of diarrhea of bacterial origin in pigs (Hwang/ Jenkins).

Several studies have shown that acupuncture is cost-effective in the following contexts: in general practice in reducing requirements for laboratory examinations, use of prescription medications, and hospitalizations (Helms 1993); in a managed care setting in reducing clinic visits, physical therapy, phone consultations, and prescription medicines for 6 months following a brief course of treatment (R. Erickson); and in reducing anti-inflammatory medication use and recourse to surgery in prospective patients for elective knee replacement operations (Christensen, et al. 1992).

There are thousands of non-controlled clinical reports on the efficacy of acupuncture for various problems, but these are too numerous to summarize and assess here. [288]

Eastern Cosmologies

Here are a few summarizing observations on a few of the cosmologies that are associated with the Eastern systems of medical belief and practice. The most widely known of these is the concept of *yin* and *yang*, which identifies special relationships between mind and body, between subtle biological energies of the patient and the manipulations of the acupuncturist, and between mankind and the greater universe beyond the individual and collective that is humanity.

1. All objects have a balance of *yin* (receptive, passive, feminine, empty, small, relaxed, mysterious, etc.) and *yang* (forceful, active, masculine, full, large, excited, revealed, etc.) aspects. Health and harmony require a balance of yin and yang, and full awareness of one polarity requires an awareness of its opposite. An object or action may be yin in relation to one thing but yang in relation to another. This Oriental relativity of everything to everything else allows for acceptance and harmonizing of theories and practices as *both-and*, rather than contrasting and rejecting theories and practices – as in the Western *either-or*, dichotomizing approach. [289]

2. The physical body is intimately associated with several non-material bodies. An *etheric double* connects it to the *astral* body. The astral body is concerned with desires and emotions. Motoyama likens this to the Western concept of soul. The Eastern *causal* body is compared to the spirit, which is the non-physical portion of man linking him to God. [290] While many acupuncturists focus primarily on the physical body, much as their Western counterparts do, it is fascinating to find the observations above on Eastern spiritual awareness that closely corresponds to those in the West.

3. The chakras are the points of connection and interaction between the various energy bodies and the physical body.

4. Many clairsentient people report that they see the glowing, wheel-like portions of the aura which correspond precisely to the *chakras* described by the Indians and Chinese (B. Brennan 1988; Kunz 1991). A few of the more gifted clairsentients report that they can see lines corresponding to the meridians, with bright spots at the acupuncture points. Some sensitives report that they see many more meridians and acupuncture points than are described in classical Chinese teachings.

5. A variant of acupressure, *Shen Tao,* attributes its efficacy to visualizations of energy flows from the acupuncturist to the patient when the acupuncture points are touched with the therapist's finger.

6. There is a diurnal waxing and waning of energy movements in each meridian (W. McGarey; Thie) as well as monthly and seasonal ebbs and flows of energies. In line with these diverse fluctuations in environmental and internal energies, there are optimal as well as unfavorable times for treatments of given illnesses. Unless this diurnal variability is taken into account, it may be difficult for Western science to obtain fully consistent measurements of acupuncture energies and valid assessments of the efficacy of acupuncture treatments.

7. The cosmology of acupuncture has a holographic aspect to it, not only within the individual, but also between the individual and the entire cosmos. Each person is a microcosmic parallel to the macrocosm and is in constant resonance with it.[291]

8. There are basic elements that form the building blocks for all matter: wood, fire, earth, metal and water. Each object and living thing is composed of its own unique balance of these elements. The elements are interrelated, and imbalances in one element can produce imbalances in associated elements, causing disease. Treatments are prescribed according to the elements that are diagnosed to be out of balance.

9. Acupuncture can be of help in a wide variety of illnesses. Some of these diseases are familiar to us, including the equivalents of the entire range of Western diagnoses such as cancer (Sun), but others illnesses are alien to Western cosmologies – such as *energy blocks, excess dampness, deficits or excesses of internal heat*, etc. (A. Campbell). Psychological disorders also respond well to acupuncture[292] and acupressure[293] treatments. Animals respond to appropriate acupuncture techniques as well.

10. Herbal remedies are recommended in treatments of illnesses. Allopathic medicine seeks to understand these substances in terms of their chemical ingredients, which may have effects similar to Western medications. There may be additional energy medicine aspects to herbal remedies, similar to those of homeopathy.[294]

11. Prevention of illness is achieved by maintaining balance and harmony within ourselves and with the cosmos.

12. Indirectly related to acupuncture, it is worth noting that Chinese healers use a method of healing called *Qigong* (K. Cohen). Qigong masters instruct healees in self-healing meditations and physical exercises, identified as *internal qigong*. Qigong masters also project healing through elaborate movements of their own bodies and limbs, called *external qigong (waiqi)*.[295]

Qigong healing combined with acupuncture may enhance the effects of the acupuncture (Chou).

In summary, we can say that Chinese medicine has been effective in treating many millions of people over many centuries. It draws its theories and practices from a culture that gives greater weight to patterns and relationships than to linear, causal explanations.

> *Chinese medicine is not less logical than the Western system, just less analytical.*
> – Charles Krebs (p.46)

Training and licensing: Over 50 schools in the US teach acupuncture and Oriental medicine, and there is a National Accreditation Commission for Schools and Colleges of Acupuncture and Oriental Medicine, which accredits 30 of these schools and has a licensing exam which is recognized in most states that license acupuncturists. Included are a master's degree with a three year course of education for acupuncture (1,700 hours), and a four-year course for Oriental Medicine (2,100 hours) including both acupuncture and herbalism (B. Mitchell). There are briefer postgraduate courses (220-400 hours) in medical acupuncture for physicians (Helms; G. Kaplan). The American Academy of Medical Acupuncture, the professional organization for medical and osteopathic doctors who practice acupuncture, developed a proficiency examination and is working towards board certification.[296]

Currently, 36 states and the District of Columbia regulate the practice of nonphysician acupuncturists, with widely varying standards, and legislation is pending in about a dozen more states. Another estimated 7,000 US physicians have trained in acupuncture.

The National Institute of Health (NIH) acknowledged (1997) the potential benefits of acupuncture with the observation: "The data in support of acupuncture are as strong as those for many accepted Western medical therapies. One of the advantages of acupuncture is that the incidence of adverse effects is substantially lower than that of many drugs and other accepted medical procedures used for the same conditions."[297]

Adverse effects: Both mechanical and infectious adverse effects may occur with acupuncture (Ernst 1999b; Yamashita et al.). Most of the serious complications are due to the improper use of needles. Re-use of needles that have not been properly sterilized may introduce bacterial infections, hepatitis B and AIDS. All of these infections are preventable by the use of disposable needles. Puncture of the lung may produce pneumothorax (air in the chest cavity that may severely hinder breathing), and puncture of the heart may produce cardiac tamponade (bleeding into the pericardial sac that prevents the heart from filling with circulating blood) – both of which can be fatal. Spinal cord injuries have also been reported (Yamashita et al.). Minor injuries from broken needles have also occurred. Electroacupuncture carries an additional risk of interference with cardiac pacemakers.

To put this into perspective, there are about 9,000 licensed acupuncturists in the US, performing millions of treatments every year. In a review of the literature over the past 33 years, about 200 adverse effects, including seven deaths, were reported in the English medical literature of 27 countries, according to Lixing Lao, a licensed acupuncturist and Professor of Complementary Medicine at the University of Maryland Medical School. Contrast that with over 100,000 deaths every year in the US alone from side effects of medications that were properly prescribed, and tens of thousands more fatalities from medical errors.

Less serious problems may also result from acupuncture treatments. Drowsiness may be produced when a relaxation response is too strong. Light-headedness, fainting (possibly due to extreme relaxation), nausea, vomiting, and psychological reactions may occur. As with many complementary therapies (notably homeopathy and spiritual healing) there may be exacerbations of some symptoms, such as pain, prior to the lessening of these symptoms. Occasionally convulsions have occurred, and one instance of death due to a severe asthma attack has been reported.

Clinical efficacy: Clinical efficacy appears most likely when the diagnosis in the Traditional Chinese Medicine system of assessment is clear and distinct. Acupuncture is of proven benefit for treatment of pain in primary illness – such as rheumatoid arthritis, migraine and tension headaches – as well as for pain and discomforts from trauma and surgical procedures, and pains that arise from chronic tensions. It can alleviate nausea and vomiting from morning sickness during pregnancy, motion sickness and chemotherapy, and can be useful in treating lung infections, and addictions, and in recuperation from strokes. It may be of help in treating many other problems, for example in slowing muscle wasting due to disuse (as when a person is bed-ridden or in a cast), diminishing post-surgical scarring, and hastening labor and delivery, but these benefits have yet to be substantiated by research.

Acupuncture therapists must administer most treatments, but self-healing with acupressure is commonly used, for example in reducing cravings for cigarettes and other habituating substances, and in the meridian based therapies.

See also derivatives of acupuncture: Applied Kinesiology, Meridian Based Therapies (under massage); Reflexology; Shiatsu.

ALEXANDER TECHNIQUE

Give me a lever and a firm place to stand and I will move the earth.
– Archimedes (287-212 BC)

The Alexander Technique (AT) is a series of exercises that people practice under careful supervision of a teacher to correct injuries as well as damage from habitual misuse and abuse of their musculoskeletal systems. The benefits are derived from learning new ways of using one's muscles and correcting one's posture. Pupils are guided through prescribed movements while standing, seated or lying down. The teacher may apply light pressure to guide the body towards healthier movements, as well as to enhance kinesthetic awareness (awareness of the position and action of muscles and joints).

The Alexander technique has been particularly helpful with neck and back pain of postural or traumatic origins, breathing disorders, arthritis, repetitive strain injury, and a variety of stress related disorders.

Tricia Hemingway, an AT teacher, shared the following:

> Although the impression generally given is that the Alexander technique is primarily mechanistic, the most important aspect of the technique is *direction. Direction* is the intent of the teacher to allow the life force within the teacher to be available to the life force within the student. Direction is best grounded by being still and doing nothing, letting the hands sense what might come through intuitively to the teacher and letting the hands rest lightly on the student's body at whatever locations they are guided to intuitively. Then, only the lightest of touch and the conscious, and of course intuitive guidance, of the teacher can facilitate response and generate change in a student. No physical manipulation is used, simply guided movement.

> During lessons the hands of the teacher may become very hot or vi-
> brate and students often experience releases of emotions during the
> lessons. Students commonly report a sense of well being during and
> after sessions and improvement in whatever dysfunctions brought
> them for Alexander training.

The similarities between Hemingway's approach and spiritual healing are obvious. Not all Alexander teachers use direction, which is taught by only one school
in England.

Alexander teachers who learn the methods of direction are expected to do so by
undergoing the lessons themselves. They take three years learning to release their
own body and emotional blocks before they are ready to sense, handle and guide
the direction as teachers. Not to be forgotten are the mechanical skills more
commonly associated with the Alexander technique, which teachers are required
to polish to a high proficiency as well.

Research: I know of no research that supports the efficacy of this method, though
clinical anecdotes suggest it is very helpful – when students take responsibility
for doing the exercises regularly. This can be challenging, as many people come
for treatments expecting the therapist to "fix" them.[298]

There are no established standards for practice or licensing of AT in the US.

Adverse effects: None known.

Training and licensing: The Alexander Technique is not regulated or licensed.

Clinical applications: The Alexander Technique can help with musculoskeletal
and joint pains; post-injury and post-surgical rehabilitation; enhancing athletic
and artistic performance; asthma; headaches; irritable bowel syndromes; depression; and boosting poor self-esteem and self-confidence.

A teacher is required for assessment and instruction in the various exercises,
which are then practiced as self-healing.

See also: the *Feldenkrais Method* later in this chapter.

ANTHROPOSOPHIC MEDICINE

Healing is not a matter of mechanism but a work of the spirit.
                                    – Rachel Naomi Remen

Rudolf Steiner, an Austrian philosopher and scientist (1861-1925), devised a
spiritually oriented scientific model for psychological development. He applied
scientific principles to spirituality in agriculture (biodynamics), social theories
(threefold social order), education (Steiner Schools) and in the arts. Together with

Ita Wegman, Steiner developed a course for physicians intended to develop and promote healing as an art rather than applying it as a mechanistic technology.

His model, anthroposophic medicine, combines three avenues of therapeutics: naturopathy, homeopathy and conventional medicine (Bott 1984; 1996). Doctors who use these approaches are found particularly in Holland, Germany, Switzerland and Sweden, with a few practicing in other countries as well., They have developed some of their own homeopathic remedies and other wholistic techniques. Spiritual awareness is a major aspect of interventions used in this method.

There is no separate licensing for medical or osteopathic doctors practicing Anthroposophic Medicine.

Research: There are studies supporting some of the claims regarding the efficacy of Anthroposophic medicine (Hildebrandt/ Hensel). This discipline must be assessed according to its individual components.[299]

Training and licensing: A medical license is required prior to specialty training in Anthroposophic medicine. Training is available in medical schools in the US, Germany and Switzerland.

Adverse effects: See individual treatment modalities.

Clinical applications: Anthroposophic medicine is a very broad approach that can be helpful with most health problems.

The doctor makes assessments and may prescribe various medications, as well as self-healing exercises.

See also: Naturopathic Medicine.

APPLIED KINESIOLOGY (AK)

Where is the wisdom we have lost in knowledge
and where is the knowledge we have lost in information
— T.S. Eliot

Applied Kinesiology was developed by George Goodheart, a chiropractor. AK is based on the principle that certain muscles reflect conditions of internal organ systems because they share the same acupuncture meridian lines. If a given muscle system is weak it is because the associated parts of the body need a rebalancing of energy. Thus internal conditions may be assessed through muscle tone and strength, and the balance of strength between particular muscles.[300]

Treatment for disorders identified by AK is applied to acupuncture points and meridians by touch and massage, along with movements of the hands near the body. Chiropractors using AK also recommend spinal manipulations.

Similar techniques may be used to detect conscious and unconscious emotional conflicts. These methods were developed by psychiatrist John Diamond (1996), a psychiatrist, and they are collectively known as *Behavioral Kinesiology*. After establishing the client's "baseline strength" (described below), the examiner will ask a question. If there is anxiety about the question, the client's arm becomes weak. This acts as a sort of bioenergetic meter that provides immediate feedback about physical and psychological states.

You can try this yourself with the help of a friend. Extend your arm out to your side, parallel with the floor. Have your friend test the strength of your arm muscles by pressing down on your wrist (firmly, but not so hard as to "break" your position) to establish your baseline strength to resist his pushig down. Think silently to yourself of a situation that makes you feel sad. (Don't tell your friend what you are doing, so there will be no question that your arm is being pressed down either more or less firmly according to your friend's expectations.) Note whether your muscle strength is different when your friend pushes down a second time, as you are focused on sadness. Then rest your arm a moment, and have your friend press down on your wrist again while you're thinking of something that makes you happy. Note the strength of your arm. See the endnote for the most common responses to this sort of testing.[301]

Muscle testing can also be used to explore emotional conflicts and early psychological experiences, with muscle strength or weakness indicating *yes* and *no* answers to questions posed by the therapist. You can do this yourself without the help of a friend, using smaller muscles. For example, hold the tips of your right thumb and little finger together, forming an "O" or ring. Hook your left thumb through this ring, just where the thumb and finger are touching, and see how firmly you have to pull in order to break the grip of these fingers. Now, ask yourself, "What is my *yes*?" and repeat the process, noting any change in the strength of your grip. Repeat the process, checking the strength of your grip while you are asking yourself, "What is my *no*?" Most people will find there is a distinct difference in the strength of their grip with a *yes* and a *no*.[302] Another experiment is to gently rub your first finger back and forth across the nail of your thumb, while asking "What is my *yes*?" and "What is my *no*?" Note any differences in what you feel with your finger. Extend this to practice with other questions. You might say out loud, "Today is ___ " (stating the correct day), and explore the feeling of your finger running across your thumbnail. Then say, "Today is ___ " (stating the wrong day), and again check your sensation.[303]

Having established your *yes* and *no* responses concerning neutral issues, you can proceed to ask yourself questions about your physical or psychological well-being. Simpler questions might concern whether various foods or medicines are likely to be helpful or harmful. We often find that the foods we particularly crave are the ones that AK will indicate are bad for us. Chocolate, coffee and white sugar are frequent culprits.[304] You may also explore more complicated questions, such as whether to engage in certain experiences or not, or whether psychological factors could be contributing to a stress state or illness. Any question at all can be posed, as long as it is simplified to allow a *yes* or *no* reply or series of replies.

This process of inner exploration is similar to the hypnotic technique of ideomotor responses. Ideomotor responses have been known for at least 100 years. The hypnotist might say, "Your unconscious mind can communicate through gestures. Rest your hands on your knees. Your right index finger will rise if the answer to a question is 'Yes,' and your left index finger will rise if the answer is 'No.' This provides access to the 95 percent of the brain that is outside of conscious awareness and to the vastness of our transpersonal selves. The great advantage of kinesiology is that it does not require hypnotic induction, and can be used by people for their own problems.

One must be cautious in interpreting the results of kinesiology. As with any diagnostic procedure (intuitive or physical), there is always a percentage of false positive and false negative findings. Several ways to reduce the risk of error include:

1. Use common sense and reasoning to analyze information;
2. Examine your introspective, emotional, and intuitive responses to the information provided through kinesiology;
3. Record the precise words used in asking the questions, so they can be re-evaluated in the light of later analysis; and
4. When there are questions about results obtained with AK, use multiple readings and supplement them with readings by others, preferably by clinicians who are experienced and expert in the use of these methods.

The help of a knowledgeable clinician can be invaluable. Clinicians trained in kinesiology know the ways in which innate characteristics and learned patterns of behavior tend to cluster and manifest – both physically and psychologically. They may identify psychological issues that we ourselves are blind to – particularly around traumatic experiences which we have buried in our unconscious mind. They may recognize blocks or overactivities in various meridians that would not be apparent or even suspected by anyone who is unfamiliar with these patterns, and good therapists will know ways to help unravel the complex structures of defenses built up over a lifetime of human interactions.[305]

Addressing meridian problems may shortcut the process of therapy. For instance, overactivity in a meridian produces active responses under certain emotional conditions, and conversely, underactivity in the meridian produces passivity when you are faced with similar emotional problems. If "John" has a problem in his Governing Vessel meridian, it may incline him towards embarrassment. If he has overactivity in the meridian, his behavior will be colored by a sense of superiority, with a tendency to judge others negatively. If his meridian is underactive, he will tend to feel inferior and to withdraw from social interactions (Altaffer).

Kinesiologists report consistency in their own clinical assessments of these meridian activity diagnoses, but the research in this area, reviewed below, shows very mixed results.

Where there is any doubt or question you must proceed with the greatest caution when using these techniques. Your unconscious expectations, hopes, wishes and fears may all influence your self-explorations. The same may apply for therapists, whose own unresolved issues may make them blind to particular problems their clients may have.

Skeptics will question whether AK could represent anything more accurate than guessing or chance, and research is beginning to address this issue. Kenneth Sancier and Effie Chow used sophisticated measuring devices to confirm that AK produces significant changes in muscle strength under stringent testing conditions..

A very cogent discussion by one skeptic, including a review of selected research, suggests that kinesiology is strictly a variation of *ideomotor response*, based on unconscious movements of muscles, guided solely by the unconscious beliefs of the subject (Hyman 1999).

While Hyman presents this as a fatal flaw, I see this as no criticism of the method or reliability of kinesiology, but rather as a bridge of understanding between kinesiology and hypnotherapy – which has used ideomotor responses for many decades to explore unconscious awarenesses. Typically, the hypnotherapist will suggest to the subject as part of the trance induction that the right index finger will rise "spontaneously" to indicate an answer of *yes*, and the left index finger will rise to indicate *no*. The enormous advantage of kinesiology is that most people can learn to use this for themselves, whithout the help of a therapist.

Hayman's cautions regarding the possibilities that wishful thinking, fears or other cognitive processes could intrude and bias the responses are well worth heeding.

AK is proving enormously helpful in diagnosing and treating children and adults with learning, hyperactivity, attention deficit, and traumatic neurological disorders. This is particularly impressive in light of the relatively limited improvements in these disorders achieved through conventional medical and psychotherapeutic approaches.

Charles Krebs is an inspiring example of the benefits of AK. Krebs was an athletic marine biologist who enjoyed deep sea diving. In 1982 he suffered a severe case of *the bends* (cerebrospinal damage from too rapid decompression after a deep-sea dive) and ended up a paraplegic. By dint of enormous willpower and persistence he regained almost full use of his legs, but he still had poor coordination, as well as frequent urinary and bowel incontinence. Residual brain damage also left him unable to cope with the intellectual demands of marine biology. Though he could read and remember facts, he could not organize them into patterns in his mind, so he had to abandon his career. Meditation and emotional releases of rage and frustration helped Krebs to bring back most of his lost functions, but his legs remained poorly coordinated even two years after his accident. A single session of AK produced remarkable improvement in the coordination of his legs, as it helped to identify previously unidentified and unresolved emotions that were influencing his physical condition.

Meanwhile Krebs shifted careers, and began working with students who had learning disabilities. He went on to study AK and to develop techniques for reducing learning disabilities, building on the work of other kinesiologists (Krebs/ Brown).[306] Today there are an impressive variety of AK approaches that can help to overcome learning disabilities.[307] Krebs describes many cases of people who have been helped through these methods.

Krebs theorizes that many learning disabilities derive from poor communication between the right and left brain hemispheres across the *corpus callosum* (nerve pathways connecting the right and left brain hemispheres). The vast majority of these blocks are due to emotional traumas but some may also be due to organic brain problems. AK diagnoses and treatments of learning disabilities are directed toward re-establishing the severed connections across the corpus callosum.

Following are two typical cases in which Krebs found AK helpful in diagnosis and treatment of learning disorders.[308]

Case: Julie, aged 15, "could not abstract arithmetical concepts that a primary school student could manage easily." In tenth grade "she could not add up numbers greater than 10. She did not know how to carry a digit and couldn't add, subtract, or do fractions." She had nevertheless been allowed to advance with her peers through school, mostly because of her charming personality. Krebs was able to help Julie with a total of 10 hours of exercises that connected up her logical thinking functions to the point where she could understand the concept of carrying numbers in doing addition. With a further five weeks of remedial tutoring during her summer holiday, Julie caught up with her class in school, mastering all of her subjects including algebra.

Case 2: Steven was nine when he came to Krebs for help with spelling problems. Krebs noted:

> [T]he alphabet was little more comprehensible than alphabet soup.
>
> I took him through the alphabet to see what letters caused him stress and found the letter K was enormously loaded for him. I did an [AK] emotional stress correction and took him through the age recession procedure to find out why, when he saw the letter K, he would get so stressed. A major emotional stress was revealed at age five. His mother confirmed our findings, saying, "Oh, I remember. When Steven was five, K was the first letter that he learned and he scratched it into the side of his grandmother's cedar wardrobe."
>
> You can bet that grandma didn't congratulate Steven on mastering one letter in the alphabet. She justifiably hit the roof, and the whole emotional context of the event had been locked into that letter for Steven ever since. And since there are Ks in many words and scattered through even elementary reading material, was it any wonder that this boy had been having all sorts of problems with reading and spelling tasks?

Theories: I suspect that some of these phenomena may be caused by suggestion via subtle cues provided by practitioners, and by the beliefs and expectations of the persons tested. Beyond the effects of suggestion, however, there are interactions of the therapist and respant on intuitive and biological energetic levels. Both information and energetic patterns that can facilitate healing may be interchanged during the therapeutic encounter. Kinesiology provides feedback to the respant and therapist via the body movements of the respant, and this makes it possible to explore the causes and potential treatments for problems. These theories would lend themselves readily to further controlled studies.[309]

I believe that Krebs' theory that benefits from AK may derive from enhanced right and left brain communications may have merit. This is more clearly evidenced in other therapies, such as EMDR and WHEE.[310]

AK effects appear to represent another energy medicine phenomenon, relating to interactions of organismic and substance energy fields.[311] There is also some speculation about neurological mechanisms for kinesiology.[312]

Research: G. Leisman and colleagues (1989) demonstrated electroencephalographic (EEG) changes in the brain that correlated with strong and weak kinesiology muscle test responses. Leisman et al. (1995) identified electromyographic differences between muscles when they were testing weak due to internal issues and muscles that were tired from exertion. An unpublished thesis by Susan McCrossin adds experimental support for the hypothesis that kinesiology can alter brain functions. Five learning-disabled adults were studied using a sophisticated electroencephalogram called the Steady-State Visually Evoked Potential (SSVEP), and they were found to have activity primarily in the occipital lobes at the back of the brain. After AK treatments, their brains registered increased activity in the frontal lobes, similar to the brains of normal adults.

Krebs proposes that AK interventions are based on subtle energies. He believes that there are subtle energetic "circuit breakers" that can be switched off due to emotional and physical traumas. AK provides the methods to identify these broken circuits, and to reconnect them.

AK also appears to provide a method for identifying foods and medicinal substances that might be harmful or helpful to an individual person.

CASE: Victor suffers from frequent headaches, abdominal bloating, tiredness and irritability. He has seen his physician, who could not identify any organic problems. He is reluctant to take pain-killers for his headaches, and frustrated that no remedy is available for his other symptoms. The AK examiner first shows Victor a method of muscle testing with one arm. Next, the examiner places in Victor's other hand a series of substances (foods, chemicals, etc.) that may be causing his symptoms through toxicity or allergy, and again tests the muscle strength in his arm with each substance. If Victor's body senses that the substance is toxic or allergenic, there will be an immediate response of weakening in his arm against the pressure of the examiner. Conversely, food and medicinal substances that the body senses are salutary produce a strengthening in his arm. Victor discovered he had a wheat intolerance, and his symptoms cleared when he avoided bread and other wheat foods.

Clinical controlled studies of these methods have produced mixed results. Daniel Monti et al. explored muscle testing with "congruent (true) and incongruent (false) self-referential statements," showing significant correlations with muscle strength. W. H. Schmitt and G. Leisman reported that immune globulins for specific allergens were correlated with muscle testing results for allergies to those substances. K. Peterson reports success in diagnosing phobias. G. Jacobs et al. find that AK can enhance clinical and laboratory assessments for thyroid abnormalities, but they do not recommend AK as a replacement for standard tests. J. Kenney et al. could not validate muscle tests for nutritional deficiencies with lab tests for the same deficiencies.

Test-retest reliability may be a problem with AK, though G. Jacobs et al. report good inter-rater reliability.[313] R. Ludtke and colleagues found there were no correlationd between muscle testing of four Health Kinesiology[314] examiners, using wasp venom and placebos. Others report similar problems with test-retest reliability.[315]

Thus the use of AK has many anecdotal reports in its support, but we must await further controlled studies to rule out alternative explanations such as chance results, suggestion effects[316] and clinical intuition on the part of the practitioner.[317]

AK effects can also extend into the bioenergetic, transpersonal and spiritual realms. Here one may have to take greater leaps of faith, with less solid feedback to verify the answers to questions asked, although formal experimentation is still feasible. For instance, intuitive therapists are increasingly using AK on themselves (not on the client) to aid them in diagnosing problems and suggesting remedies. This approach relies on the therapists intuitive and psychic abilities. A therapist may use AK to check whether a particular psychotherapy intervention is appropriate, by posing questions such as, "Is Tom ready to deal with his addiction to alcohol at this time?" This method will tap the resources of the therapist's training and clinical acumen, and it can bring various intuitive processes into conscious awareness.[318] Intuitive therapists supplement their own AK responses with parallel responses of clients to these clinical explorations. However, even greater caution is warranted here, because it is easy to digress on tangents that are purely the creations of fantasy, or mental projections of the client or therapist, or caused by other psychological defense mechanisms.

One study of AK reports very unimpressive results in this sort of assessing for nutritional status (Kenney, et al.).

I have personally found AK techniques clinically useful in helping clients to explore their unconscious beliefs and conflicts.

Cautions: While AK may help the unconscious mind speak about its problems and conflicts, the messages may not be clear or may be misinterpreted for a number of reasons. Information from the unconscious mind often rises to consciousness through the vehicle of imagery, and it is often less than entirely clear. Even gifted intuitives are not accurate in their analyses all of the time. Furthermore, if the patient has fears, ambivalence, or a habit of avoidance of issues that are related to the focus of the AK work, these may color the responses. In other words, the AK response may come from a place of psychological defense, rather than from a place that is seeking the changes required for healing. The unconscious mind may continue to resist releasing whatever feelings it has buried, to avoid re-experiencing the initial discomforts that led to the defensive habit.

In using AK for transpersonal explorations, one must be even more cautious. Our ordinary consciousness is limited in its ability to communicate with these realms, and there are often distortions in the communications that get through – which adds another potential layer of error to those that may be introduced by the unconscious mind.

Training and licensing: There are no general standards for training and no licensing requirements for Applied Kinesiology.

Clinical applications: Applied Kinesiology is limited in its applications only by the inventiveness of the clinician and the client. It is helpful as a primary approach in exploring contributing factors for physical and psychological problems. It can help to suggest traumatic psychological roots and toxic environmental factors that may be contributing to states of dis-ease and disease. It can suggest whether clients are ready for particular therapeutic approaches and remedies. It can sharpen the focus of affirmations or other therapeutic interventions, with a query such as, Is this the best focus for treatment at this time? Common-sense cautions against false positives and negatives must be applied in intuitive work, as in any diagnostic system.

A therapist is required for assessment and treatment, but individualized self-exploration and self-healing approaches are commonly used.

AROMATHERAPY

> *When the lotus opened,*
> *I didn't notice and went away empty-handed.*
> *Only now and again do I suddenly sit up from my dreams*
> *to smell a strange fragrance.*
> *It comes on the south wind,*
> *a vague hint that makes me ache with longing,*
> *like the eager breath of summer wanting to be completed.*
> *I didn't know what was so near,*
> *or that it was mine.*
> *This perfect sweetness blossoming in the depths of my heart.*
>   – Rabindranath Tagore

Aromatherapists report that the effects of aromatic oils containing any of a wide variety of essences (essential oils) can be quite potent and specifically beneficial for a range of ailments. For instance, lavender is used to soothe and calm; lemongrass and rosemary to uplift and refresh; eucalyptus and tea tree are antiseptic; and orange is soporific. Studies have shown that essential oils are absorbed through inhalation and through the skin. Some therapists also recommend oral use.[318]

Aromatic oils, diluted in water, are heated in decorative, candle-powered burners to evaporate the liquid and spread the therapeutic odors.

Aromatherapy is often combined with massage, in which case the aromatic essences are added to the massage oils.[319]

Some claim that in addition to inducing relaxation, essential oils can also contribute to spiritual awareness (Worwood). The burning of incense and the use of aromatic oils in religious rituals is a common practice in many cultures around the world.[320]

Research: While it is still early days in aromatherapy research, many studies suggest benefits for a variety of problems. Sadly, the quality of these studies varies widely, with many lacking in details of reporting or statistical analyses. The following benefits have been reported:

- *pains* – reducing spinal pains from trauma, enhancing muscle tone and flexibility, and reducing costs of treatment (Weintraub 1992a; b); reducing pain and disability in ulcerative colitis and Crohn's disease (Joachim); controlling pain in children with HIV (Styles); treating pain in a critical care unit (Wolfson/ Hewitt); decreasing painfulness and size of hyperkeratotic plantar lesions (*corns*), (M. Khan et al.); headache pain (Gobel et al.);
- *anxieties and emotional distress* – lowering indicators of anxiety such as increased heart rate, and EMG measures of muscle tension and skin resistance (McKechnie et al.); treating anxiety in palliative care (Wilkinson); relaxing the elderly (Fakouri/ Jones);
- *premature infants* – increasing weight gain, reducing time in hospital, and saving about $,000 in expenses per child (Field et al.); reducing complications in neonates whose mothers used cocaine during pregnancy, increasing weight gain, and enhancing maturation (Field 1993);
- *reducing depression* in children and adolescents with depression and adjustment disorders (Field et al.);
- *reducing depression and enhancing immune cell activity* (Komori et al.);
- *enhancing antimicrobial*[321] *and antifungal activity* (Janssen 1987);
- *sedative effects* with lavender, neroli, rose and sandalwood, and stimulation with various compounds[322] in animals (Buchbauer);
- *alopecia areata* - highly significant effects in treating a patchy baldness that is estimated to afflict about one percent of the population (I. Hay et al.);
- *activating and depressing brainwave activity* (Torri et al.);
- *analgesic effects* in rats with lemongrass had (Lorenzetti et al.);
- *anti-anxiety effects* with oil of neroli citrus in cardiac surgery patients (Stevensen 1994);
- *reducing anxiety in patients attending a palliative care center* aromatherapy with chamomile can (Wilkinson 1995);
- *agitation in senile dementia* may respond to melissa (Ballard et al.);
- *eliminating head lice* with coconut oil, anise oil and ylang ylang oil (Mumcoglu et al)[323]

On the subject of spiritual aromatherapy, which seeks to release deep patterns underlying physical and emotional problems, see Berkowsky.

Theory: Our olfactory sense connects to the deeper, more primitive parts of the brain, associated with the brain's emoti onal centers. By stimulating these portions of the brain it may be possible to alter various mind-body connections, much as psychoneuroimmunology does.[324]

Adverse effects: Several cautions need to be observed in the use of essential oils. Stock solutions are extremely concentrated and only a few drops are used, diluted in many times the quantity of water. The concentrated stock solutions can be caustic to the skin and certainly to the mouth and throat. There have also been toxic, allergic and photosensitive reactions in smelling the oils, and taken internally some can be toxic to the liver. One must also be cautious in purchasing oils, as their manufacture is not standardized or regulated, and various companies may include preservatives or extenders that could produce allergic or other reactions.. There may be also be interactive effects of essential oils with some medications (Wade et al.).

Training and licensing: Training is through workshops. Aromatherapy is not licensed, but as massage it is regulated under laws dealing with massage.

See also: Aromatherapy as massage.

AUTOGENIC TRAINING (AT)

It breathes me.
— Wolfgang Luthe and J. H. Schultz

Wolfgang Luthe and J. H. Schultz developed a profoundly potent method of relaxation in which clients repeat to themselves six key phrases that address various somatic functions. These are: "My hands and arms are heavy," "My hands and arms are warm," "My heartbeat is regular," "It breathes me," "My stomach is warm," and "My forehead is cool." These sentences can be recited a number of times until, for instance, one's hands actually become warm. This is a form of self-healing that involves relaxation and acquiring control over various physiological processes.[326]

Popular especially in Europe, AT has been used for years in treatment of anxiety, hypertension and other stress-related states. Many physical conditions have also responded to this method. Autogenic training shades into transpersonal therapy,[327] in the state of passive observation that is at the core of this approach and in the phrase, "It breathes me," which is recited mentally while breathing.

I am impressed that the combination of meditative concentration with focus on the body is more potent than either method used alone.

There are no established standards for practice or licensing of Autogenic Training in the US.

Theory: It is possible that primarily relaxation and reduction in anxiety states secondarily produce the perceived and/ or actual improvements that are seen with this therapy in physical conditions. AT therapists propose that the general statements are a form of auto-suggestion that may directly influence the body, for example by reducing hypertension or releasing the spasm in peripheral arterioles in cases of Raynaud's disease or migraine.

Research: Extensive early research conducted in Europe (without control groups) suggests significant effects of AT on psychological stress and depression (Luthe/

Schultz 1970a; 1970b). Combined with the cathartic model of Luthe (taught in Europe but not in the US), controlled studies have shown medium effect sizes for physical problems such as angina, asthma, childbirth, headaches (including migraines), hypertension, infertility, recovery from myocardial infarction, and Raynaud's disease, and for psychological problems such as pain, stress/ anxiety, and eczema. Large effect size was shown for insomnia (Linden 1994; Stelter). A review of AT by Kanji and Ernst found it limited for use in anxiety and stress.

Preliminary evidence from Kirlian photography indicates that AT may also affect energy states (V. Hunt; Stelter).[328]

Adverse effects: Emotional releases are possible during AT exercises. These may cause fear or retraumatize if the person is not alerted to anticipate this possibility and does not have therapeutic support to deal with the surfacing materials.

Training and licensing: AT training and practice are not regulated.

Clinical applications: Autogenic Training can be profoundly helpful with stress and stress related illnesses, including (but not restricted to) asthma, irritable bowel syndrome, hypertension, migraines, and muscular pains. When practiced to its full potential, it provides an excellent entry into psychotherapy.

A teacher is required, to instruct in the techniques and to provide guidance and support. Most of the practice is in the form of self-healing, which continues after the basic course of instruction (usually 8 weekly sessions) is completed. This may become a lifelong practice that leads to ever-deepening benefits.

See also: Biofeedback; Meditation; Relaxation; Self-Hypnosis; Yoga.

AYURVEDIC MEDICINE

*Ayus means **life** and veda means **knowledge/ science** in Sanskrit, combining as "**a science of life.**"*

Ayurveda is the natural medicine system of India, which has been practiced for at least five millennia. Ayurveda assumes that health and illness depend upon proper balances in consciousness and lifestyles. Its practices include yoga, specialized diets, and herbal remedies. Several hundred American doctors incorporate Ayurvedic methods in their practices (Workshop on Alternative Medicine).

Theories: Ayurvedic medicine teaches that illness is caused by imbalances in three *doshas* (physiological principles) that govern the body's functions. *Vata*, composed of air and ether elements in air energy, moves one towards change. *Pitta*, or fire energy, gives strength, intelligence and direction. *Kapha*, composed of water and earth elements in water energy, contributes steadiness, calmness and reliability.

Ayurveda identifies three body types, each associated with a dosha, and each associated with particular metabolic and personality characteristics, along with susceptibilities to certain illnesses. The *vata* type is slender of build and change-able in moods and activities, intuitive and creative but not good with practical applications. Vata people tend to have constipation, premenstrual symptoms, and various anxieties. The *pitta* type is of medium build, fair-skinned, steady and regular in routines, and generally predictable. Pitta people are intelligent and quick-witted, but they are perfectionists and can have short tempers. They are susceptible to stomach problems such as ulcers, and may also have hemorrhoids. The *kapha* type is solidly built and strong. Kaphas are laid-back, relaxed, affec-tionate and slow to anger. They are prone to have allergies and tend to be overweight.

Every person has varying ratios of the three *doshas*, each of which is concen-trated in a certain part of the body. *Vata* is energy that enlivens the physical body, facilitating breath and circulation of blood. Vata predominates in the pelvis, par-ticularly in the large intestine, as well as in the bones, thighs, ears, and skin. *Pitta* encourages the metabolism of food, water and air, and energizes the body's en-zymes. Pitta resides in the stomach and small intestine, blood, eyes, and sweat glands. *Kapha* is contained in the structural elements of the body – the bones, muscles, and fat – providing form and protection for the various organs. It is prominent in the chest, lungs, and spinal fluid.

When people of these body types have balanced doshas that are harmonious with their constitutional characters, they are healthy. Illness is the result of imbal-ances in the doshas. Physical and emotional stresses, poor diet, injudicious lifestyles, seasons, and time of day can all influence health.

Classical Ayurvedic diagnosis relies on the doctor's palpation of the radial pulse (in the wrist). Ayurvedic doctors learn to recognize an enormous range of subtle variations in pulses that can reveal the relative strengths and weakness in the doshas, as well as suggesting therapeutic interventions. Additional diagnostic as-sessments are based on the appearance of the tongue, eyes and nails. Treatments can include herbal remedies, lifestyle changes (diet, sleep, exercise programs, and outdoor exposure time under the sun), meditations and mental/ spiritual healing. It is assumed that harmful waste products accumulate in the body and may contribute to ill health. These can be reduced through massage, herbal remedies, heat treat-ments and enhancement of elimination through various forms of internal cleansing.[329]

Research supports the benefits of many of these approaches, particularly medita-tion and yoga[330] exercises. Ayurvedic methods have been effective in promoting healthier blood pressure, cholesterol, and stress reactions, all factors that are predic-tors of cardiac risk (Murphy 1992; C. Schneider et al.). They are also useful in preventing and treating cancers of the breast, lung and colon (H. Sharma et al. 1990); for enhancing mental health (C.N. Alexander et al. 1989b); and for slowing the effects of aging (C.N. Alexander et al. 1989a; Glaser).

Mentalin, an Ayurvedic herebal combination of ginger, bacoba, and gotu kola, has been shown to help in the treatment of Attention Deficit Hyperactivity Disor-der (A. Agrawal, et al.; Kulkarni).

Adverse effects: Side effects of herbs or interactive effects of herbs with conven-tional medications are possible.

Training and licensing: In India there are about 200 schools that teach Ayurvedic medicine. A five-year course leads to a Bachelor of Ayurvedic Medicine and Surgery (BAMS), and a two-year internship is required prior to commencing practice. Graduate studies that include research are rewarded with a Master of Ayurvedic Science (MASc) degree, recently changed to Doctor of Medicine in Ayurveda (MD in Ayurveda).

In the West, there are no established standards for Ayurvedic education or licensing. For the most part, Western Ayurvedic practitioners are health caregivers who have taken courses of various durations and depth (often very brief and superficial).

Clinical applications: Ayurvedic medicine is a complete system of treatment. It can be particularly helpful in treating problems of digestion, allergies, chronic infections (e.g. acne), obesity, hypertension, emotional imbalance, fatigue and addictions.

Integrative use of Ayurvedic medicine can be helpful, particularly with chronic illnesses. It may reduce the need for some medications, and it may also predict that certain medicines are better than others for treating the various characterological types. For instance, a *pitta* type is likely to be extra-sensitive to aspirin, so another treatment for pain management might be advised. There is potential for conflict here with conventional medical practices, so dialogue between practitioners is needed as well as further research. One report indicates that preventive use of Ayurvedic medicine can reduce the costs of conventional medical care (Orme-Johnson/ Herron).[331]

Most Ayurvedic practice is performed under the care of a doctor, though some self-healing exercises may be included.

See also: Naturopathic Medicine.

BARBARA BRENNAN HEALING

Barbara Brennan was an astrophysicist who left her job with NASA in the mid-70s to work on strengthening her clairsentient and healing gifts, which had been present since childhood. She founded a now prestigious school of healing that has been attended by many doctors and other caregivers The Brennan school has a strong emphasis on psychological and energy approaches, including intuitive assessments of energy field abnormalities based upon the theory and practice of bioenergetics. Practitioners must work on their own psychological and physical issues, learning through personal experience as well as in didactic, demonstration and supervisory sessions.[332]

Brennan's books (1987; 1993) are classics in the healing literature, containing excellent illustrations.

Adverse effects: No harmful effects have been reported See discussion of potential general negative effects from rapid improvements under Spiritual Healing.

Training and licensing: The training is modular, over four years, with a major focus on self-healing for the healer. This method is not licensed.

See also: Spiritual Healing, Volume I of *Healing Research*.

BIOFEEDBACK

> *[H]umankind has more talents and more potential for self-regulation than we usually use or take credit for... Mind over body, inside the skin, is a special case of mind over nature.*
> – Elmer Green and Alyce Green (1977, p. 62)

Though biofeedback was discussed as a form of self-healing in Chapter II-1, it deserves separate mention here as one of the important complementary therapies.[333]

Some parts of our bodies have no sensory connections, so we are unaware of their state and therefore cannot control them. However, when we use instruments to tell us what is going on in these parts of our body, we can gain some measure of control over them. For instance, if an instrument attached to electrodes on our skin shows us on a dial, or lets us hear by the pitch or loudness of an auditory tone how tense our muscles are, we can then consciously direct our muscles to relax. If we monitor our skin temperature with an electrode taped to one hand, we can relax and dilate the blood vessels in our skin, thereby warming the hand. Another window for feedback is through the electrical resistance of our skin, which changes with our states of physical and emotional tension. Likewise, if we can monitor our own brainwaves, we can learn to enter a state of deeper relaxation by adopting the mental state that produces alpha or theta brainwaves.

Research has shown biofeedback to be effective in the treatment of hypertension (C. Patel), asthma, migraines, Raynaud's disease (spasms of small arteries in the hands when they get cold), irritable bowel syndrome, urinary and fecal incontinence, epilepsy, chronic pain, anxiety, attention deficit disorder, and more (Workshop on Alternative Medicine). Peavey et al. showed that biofeedback-induced relaxation could influence the phagocytic (germ-destroying) activity of white blood cells.

Carol Schneider reviewed studies demonstrating that biofeedback is cost-effective.

Training and licensing: Many biofeedback practitioners are health caregivers who hold other professional licenses (psychologists, counselors, etc.). The Biofeedback Certification Institute of America (BCIA) requires 200 hours of training at an approved institution[334] for those who have no primary certification, and 30 supervised clinical hours for licensed clinicians. Written and practical exams are required. Most states classify biofeedback as a subcategory of mental health treatment, though it is not separately licensed.

Clinical applications: Biofeedback is of benefit in the treatment of problems for which self-regulation of the body can be achieved, such as disorders of the musculoskeletal, digestive, and nervous systems (especially for pain reduction), and for problems of the cardiovascular system. While its most common uses are for muscle relaxation, hypertension, and migraines, it can also be used for irritable bowel syndromes and ulcers, Raynaud's disease, incontinence, irregular heartbeats, epilepsy, and hyperactivity in children. Brainwave biofeedback has been widely used for deepening meditation.

Biofeedback is a helpful adjunct to conventional medical treatments for the above-mentioned problems. Biofeedback adds an important dimension to conventional treatments, empowering people to feel that they can help themselves – both in curing their illness and in a much broader, general sense of enhanced self-confidence.

Biofeedback is initiated and supervised under the treatment of a therapist, but the practice is performed as self-healing.

BODYMIND THERAPIES

> The most important question to ask in addressing a person's illness is
> "What do you think your body is saying?"
> – D.B.

Many complementary therapies integrate work on the body with work on psychological issues. The body holds on to memories of events and emotions. These may be experienced as muscle tensions, pains, neurohormonal problems, and various diseases. Massage, spinal manipulation, or biological energy interventions can access these memories, often resulting in emotional releases. Let me share several examples from my personal practice of psychotherapy combined with spiritual healing.

Case: I observed "Greta," a middle-aged healee with arthritis receiving spiritual healing at a healing center in England. She had had several treatments over a period of weeks with modest, temporary relief, but the pains in her hands kept returning and were interfering in her salaried work and in her work around home. As she spoke with the healer about her experiences during the previous week, I noticed that her fists were clenched.

I asked Greta, "What do you think your hands might be saying?"

Unclenching her fists and looking at her palms, Greta indicated that she didn't know what I meant. I shrugged and she continued speaking with the healer. In less than a minute her hands were again balled into fists. I repeated my question, getting a similar response.

The third time I asked the question, Greta held up her fists, looked at them, and asked in an angry tone, "Are you trying to say that I'm angry?" The incongruity of her tone was obvious to the three of us and we all laughed.

This incident led Greta to explore some chronic, frustrating situations in her life that she was angry about. The discussion, the emotional release, and the healing combined to relieve her of all symptoms of arthritis within a few weeks.

I used healing with "Jean," a middle-aged woman who came to me with back pains and fatigue that had been bothering her for several years. Within two sessions, as I was giving a laying-on of hands treatment, she spontaneously recalled incidents of sexual abuse in childhood which she had completely forgotten.

The healing, combined with psychotherapy, helped her work through her anger, hurt, and (unjustified) guilt over the sexual abuse. In the course of the treatment, her back ceased to hurt and she gradually regained her energy.

I am impressed that therapies which include touch and manipulation of the body work exceedingly well in combination with psychotherapy. In my experience, the two taken together are more potent than either approach used alone.

Bodymind therapies and psychotherapy

While most reviewers focus on the *body* side of bodymind therapies, several highly effective bodymind approaches that focus on the *mind* are rapidly growing in popularity.

1. *Eye Movement Desensitization and Reprocessing* (EMDR) is an extraordinarily potent method that helps people to deal with discrete, severe emotional distress and with crippling patterns of belief (e.g. "I am unlovable," "I can't handle social situations," etc.). Healees focus upon their problems while moving their eyes repeatedly from right to left and back under the guidance of a therapist. Even severe, debilitating emotional traumas such as post-traumatic stress disorders (PTSDs) from wartime experiences or rape may be released, and the person can be restored to normal psychological functioning with a relatively brief course of treatment (F. Shapiro). People with PTSD who have been crippled with panic attacks and nightmares for decades have been restored to normal functioning using this method (Goldstein/ Fenske).

Although the name of this therapy implies that eye movements are the effective healing process, people may respond equally well to alternating stimulation by sound or tapping on the right and left sides of the body. It is therefore speculated that right-left brain integration may be the underlying process in this therapy.

2. Various acupressure approaches facilitate profound psychological transformations. See under Meridian Based therapies.

3. A spectrum of approaches have been developed for uncovering psychological issues through massage and specific exercises.[335]

Research: An extensive body of research confirms that EMDR is helpful in treating stress, particularly Post-Traumatic Stress Disorder (PTSD).[336]

Adverse effects: Emotional releases are possible during bodymind therapies. These may cause fear or could be retraumatizing if the person is not alerted to anticipate this possibility and has no therapeutic support.

Clinical applications: Bodymind therapies are particularly helpful for treating problems of emotional stress, musculoskeletal disorders, clarifying emotional factors that may underlie or complicate physical problems of all sorts and in enhancing self-confidence.[337]

A therapist is essential for instruction and guidance in bodymind exercises. Some self-healing exercises are usually included.

See also: Alexander Technique; Bioenergetics; EMDR; Feldenkrais Method, Massage; Meridian Based Therapies; Rubenfeld therapy.

BREATHWORK

Make time as the long march of this day unfolds to pause... breathe...
collect and focus yourself...
Wake up from the cultural trance that you have been hypnotized into...
                                        – Michelle Levey and Joel Levey

Ordinary breathing may be shallow and less than fully effective. Yoga and other bodywork therapies often recommend expanding one's breathing capacity to provide better oxygenation of body tissues. Lung volume is increased by exercises for expanding the chest and lowering the diaphragm.

The breath is often used as a focus for meditation, with myriads of variations in techniques.[338] Some therapists recommend chest breathing over diaphragmatic breathing, while others recommend the reverse.

Mental focus upon breathing can form a basis for meditation, as this natural metronome is always available to us and is an excellent focus for concentration.[339]

When we shut down our awareness of our feelings, the body may tense up in various places, particularly in the chest. If we expand the chest and breathe deeply, we open up our awareness of our feelings.

Eastern teachings suggest that we inhale cosmic energies (*prana*) along with the air that enters our lungs. Various techniques and practices encourage and facilitate these energy flows.[340]

Therapeutic breathwork is a separate category of therapy. Rapid breathing may induce alternative states of consciousness, which can be used to facilitate and deepen psychotherapies and bodywork therapies such as *holonomic* therapy (Grof/ Halifax) and *rebirthing* (Orr/ Ray). These techniques help people to retrieve very early memories, often related to traumas suffered around the time of birth and while still in the womb.[341]

It is fascinating that in the framework of breathing therapies it is uncommon to find subjects suffering from hyperventilation symptoms (dizziness, tingling and numbness of hands, abdominal pains and panics).

Adverse effects: Intense feelings that have been long buried and forgotten may surface with breathwork. It is advisable to have an experienced therapist for this form of healing.

Training and licensing: Breathwork is a technique used by various therapists in addition to their other approaches, but some specialize in breathwork alone. There are no standards for practice or certification of breathwork therapies. This is not a licensed modality.

Clinical applications: Therapeutic breathwork provides a potent, rapid opening into deep, early memories of emotional traumas. It can bring about rapid changes in emotional problems.

Breathwork is done under the supervision of a therapist, both for guidance with the technique and for support with emotional releases.

CHELATION THERAPY

See: EDTA Chelation

CHIROPRACTIC AND OSTEOPATHIC MANIPULATIONS

The new emphasis on outcomes research is changing the ground rules. There is less interest in theories. Today the bottom line: Is the treatment effective? Is it reproducible? What is the cost?
                                                            – Mootz, DC

Chiropractic

D. D. Palmer, a "magnetic healer" who practiced at the turn of the century, developed a system of chiropractic therapy based on the thesis that the nervous system controls the body, and therefore that any malfunction must be due to blockage of the nerves involved in that part of the body. Treatments are based on spinal adjustments, with the presumption that misalignments of the vertebral column (subluxations) cause pinching of the nerves and thus block their control of the body. Diagnosis is accomplished with manual palpation of the body and exploration of musculoskeletal movement and with x-rays of the spine. Manipulations are described as *high-velocity, short-amplitude* manual interventions. Chiropractic has split into many and varied schools, some following a *straight* focus upon spinal manipulation and others adopting a *mixed* program that may include kinesiology, nutritional counseling, and other such techniques (Gillet/ Liekens; Schaefer/ Fay).

An estimated 12 million Americans receive spinal manipulative therapy annually.

Theory: Release of the pressure on the nerves pinched in a misaligned spinal cord is presumed to restore normal functioning to the body. The potential applications of chiropractic for the treatment of musculoskeletal disorders are obvious. Conventional medicine treats pinched nerves with surgery. This is different from the subluxations treated by chiropractors, as nerves can also be pinched by "slipped" disks (cartilage that protrudes from between the vertebral joints and impinges on the spinal cord or nerve roots).

Many chiropractors also claim to be able to treat various body organ diseases through spinal manipulations, but few have demonstrated causal connections between their interventions and the claimed results. The new and promising specialty of chiropractic neurology may begin to fill in some of these gaps. There is speculation that chronic irritation of peripheral nerves can produce changes in the biochemistry of the peripheral nerves, the spinal cord, and the brain, which in turn send abnormal messages to the body, thereby causing disease processes.

Bruce Lipton suggests that the true theories of D. D. Palmer were altered in order to conform to prevailing medical and cultural paradigms, and that the original conceptualization of D. D. Palmer was one that focuses on spirit and body consciousness:

> D. D. Palmer was very sensitive to scientists' displeasure concerning concepts related to spirit and vital forces. In formulating the original science of Chiropractic, he coined the terms Universal Intelligence and Innate Intelligence to refer to the inherent organizing intelligence of the Universe and of life...
>
> In the early years of Chiropractic I used the terms Innate (Spirit), Innate Intelligence (Spiritual Intellect), Universal Intelligence (God) because they were comprehensive, and the world was not prepared to receive the latter terms just mentioned in parentheses. It may be even now premature to use them. (Palmer, p. 542).
>
> [T]he basic philosophy of Chiropractic, as defined by D. D. Palmer (before its modification by B. J. Palmer), perceives the flow of information from an externalized source, Universal Intelligence. An eternal "metamerized" portion of that intelligence, referred to as Innate, is needed by each individualized being (pages 494 and 496, The Science, Art and Philosophy of Chiropractic). Although Innate is not localized, its seat of control is the brain. From the brain, Innate's intelligence travels down the spinal cord, and from the spinal cord outward to the periphery, a pathway referred to as Above>Down>Inside>Out (A-D-I-O).
>
> Bruce Lipton (2003)

Research: See under Osteopathy in the next section.

Training and licensing: The Council for Chiropractic Education sets criteria for training. US chiropractic colleges have entry requirements including a minimum of 60 semester or 90 quarter hours towards a BA or BS degree at a recognized accredited institution. The usual five years of chiropractic training include two years of basic sciences (anatomy, biochemistry, physiology, microbiology, etc.); two years of clinical and radiological diagnosis, biomechanics, orthopedics, rehabilitation, neurology, cardiology, nutrition, and chiropractic diagnosis and manipulations; and a year of supervised practice in an internship. Educational standards are set by the Council on Chiropractic Education (CCE),[341] and exams are administered by the National Board of Chiropractic Examiners, with each state setting its own licensing requirements. Postgraduate education is available, with two-year residencies in orthopedics, radiology, neurology, pediatrics, family practice, sports medicine, rehabilitation, meridian/ acupuncture, and research.

Guidelines for practice are currently being clarified by various groups.[342] As of 1993 over 45,000 chiropractors were licensed in the US. Practitioners are trained in 17 chiropractic colleges that produce a total of 2,000 graduates every year. There are also chiropractic colleges in Australia, Canada, England, France and Japan.

It is instructive to consider the efforts of the medical profession in the US to limit the licensing and practice of chiropractic. For many years doctors were warned by their medical societies not to associate with or refer patients to chiropractors. However, a successful lawsuit by chiropractors charging the American Medical Association (AMA) and other medical associations with restraint of trade brought about a dramatic change in 1987 (Wilk et al.). Chiropractors are now working much more closely with doctors.

The benefits of chiropractic (compared to medication and other conventional treatments) for back, neck, and other pains include: avoidance of habituation to drugs, addressing (presumed) causes rather than symptoms, and cost effectiveness.

Osteopathy

Osteopathy was developed by Andrew Taylor Still (1828-1917), an allopathic doctor who served in the American Civil War. Still was motivated by the death of several of his children from spinal meningitis to seek methods that went beyond symptomatic relief, which at the time was all that medical practice could offer. In 1874 he launched the system he had spent many years developing through diligent study of human anatomy and physiology. Though he had intended osteopathy to be an extension of medical practice, it developed over the years into a separate system. This was largely due to the fact that conventional doctors opposed and ridiculed his system, and actually drove him out of his home state of Kansas. He founded the American School of Osteopathy in Kirksville, Missouri in 1892.

Osteopathy involves techniques of spinal assessment and manipulation that address the body as a functioning unity. The focus is on posture, respiration and the status of the skeleton and connective tissues. While the primary tool of osteopathy has been physical manipulation (and this continues to be the case in the UK), in the US osteopathy also incorporates many other approaches, including physical and occupational therapy, orthotic and prosthetic devices, fitness, pharmacology, surgery, biofeedback, psychotherapy, and the whole range of conventional medical treatments. In essence, the practice of most osteopathicphysicians trained today is almost identical with the practice of conventional medical doctors.

The remainder of this discussion will focus on the manipulative aspects of osteopathy and chiropractic. Cranial osteopathy and craniosacral therapy, which represent distinct and largely separate advances over conventional osteopathy, are discussed below.

The goal of osteopathy is to remove pressure on nerves that are presumed to be pinched by spinal deformities, and to release other tensions in the musculoskeletal system and fascia (connective tissues), thus restoring the body to its natural state of healthy functioning. Doctors of Osteopathy (DOs) have treated many health problems through spinal manipulations.

Classical osteopaths use a variety of manual manipulative approaches, individually or in combination with each other or with allopathic medical interventions (Workshop on Alternative Medicine):

1. *Soft tissue massage* – relaxes muscles and enhances circulation of blood and lymph.
2. *Isometric and isotonic methods* – relaxes and restores of normal joint mobility.
3. *Articulatory methods*, or manipulation without impulse improves joint mobility.
4. *High-velocity, low-amplitude methods*, or manipulation with impulse - realigns vertebral joints.
5. *Myofascial release methods* address muscles and fascia through direct and indirect techniques (Barnes 1990).
6. *Functional methods* - address dysfunctions diagnosed by the manual assessments of the practitioner.
7. *Strain and counterstrain methods* – identify sore spots that are related to specific abnormalities in joint mobility or muscle spasm. These *trigger points* are soothed by positioning the body in specific ways for brief periods.
8. *Craniosacral (also called Cranial) methods* - are described later in this chapter.

Research in Chiropractic and Osteopathic Manipulations: Controlled studies confirm that spinal compression does bring about changes in nerves.[343]

Chiropractic studies: The reliability of some types of chiropractic examinations has been confirmed with reproducibility of diagnoses in several other studies.[344]

In controlled studies, chiropractic has been found to be: helpful in treatment of back pain of mechanical origin;[345] and better in these problems than a placebo for pain, though no better than physiotherapy for decreasing disability or duration of disorders (Parker et al); effective in treating headaches (manipulations vs. antidepressants);[346] and of significant value in treating other disorders.[347] Reviews of research series produced mixed impressions. One meta-analysis of 44 studies of chiropractic spinal manipulative therapy (SMT) for back pain showed positive results in 38 of the studies (R. Anderson et al. 1992); however it was difficult to compare one study with another due to omissions of details such as the length of time after treatments when assessments were made, and specific measures used to assess results. A review of 21 randomized studies spanning 20 years (Abenhaim/ Bergeron) showed modest evidence of short-term benefits but no clear long-term benefits. A major problem was the lack of precision in diagnoses, which made it impossible to assess the results. In another review (Assendelft et al. 1993), 4 out of 5 studies reported favorable results, but methodological weaknesses were again cited. A review of chiropractic manipulations for neck pain (Aker et al.) suggests some efficacy. Pain that does not involve neurological impairment appears to be the most responsive (Coulter et al.).

A review spanning 75 years and considering more than 350 reports on spinal manipulations for visceral disorders shows no convincing research evidence for claims of positive results from such interventions.

Case reports show osteopathic manipulations can be effective in treatment of carpal tunnel syndrome.[348] Of historical interest are reports that osteopathic treatments were beneficial during the influenza epidemic of 1918 (Anonymous 1919; R.K. Smith).

Chiropractic has been shown to be cost-effective in one analysis (Manga et al.) but of questionable value in another – where severe deficits in research method-ologies were noted (Assendelft/ Bouter).

Spiritual healing may be a helpful complement to chiropractic and osteopathy, as with other manual therapies. Some chiropractors have included applied kinesiology[349] in their repertoires. This is another biological energy intervention. Edgar Cayce, an extraordinarily gifted clairsentient diagnostician and a prescriber of unusual, but highly effective treatments, included chiropractic among his recommended therapies (Stearn 1967; Sugrue). The late Bruce MacManaway, a gifted natural healer from Scotland, also based much of his healing technique on spinal manipulations.

The limited scope of the existing research is at first glance surprising, in view of the vast popularity of osteopathy and chiropractic over the past century. Because studies of the efficacy of these manipulations have not been published until re-cently, and because until recent years, training in chiropractic in some schools was very brief and insubstantial, conventional medicine has held a generally negative view of this discipline. This has been something of a Catch-22. Because of this skepticism, conventional medicine has not invested in the study of this modality, which medicine then criticizes because it lacks a basis in research.[350]

Osteopathic studies: Studies addressing the mechanisms of action in osteopathy have begun to provide theoretical support for this treatment. Research supports the theory that compression of nerve roots near the spine may cause blockages (Sharpless et al.); that experimentally compressed nerves produce toxic protein substances (Luttges/ Gorswald); that nerve cells near spinal dislocations (*subluxa-tions*) are irritable (*facilitated segments*) and tend to stimulate muscles and viscera excessively;[351] that muscles and joints may reflect the conditions of visceral or-gans (Eble) and therefore can provide a basis for manual diagnosis (Kelso et al.); and that manual manipulations can restore balance in neuromuscular and visceral function (Buerger/ Greenman; Korr 1978).[352]

Only a modest number of rigorous studies show that osteopathic diagnoses are consistent between practitioners[353] and that osteopathy produces beneficial effects beyond those of a placebo.[354] Studies of clinical efficacy are modestly impressive with back pain (Hoehler et al.), carpal tunnel syndrome (Sucher), paresthesias (unusual sensations) due to peripheral nerve dysfunctions (Larson et al.), burning pain in an extremity (D. Levine), postoperative recovery (Jarski et al.), postopera-tive collapsed lungs (Sleszynski/ Kelso), and hypertension (Morgan et al.). One controlled study showed significant relief of back pain with reduced need for pain medicine (G. Andersson et al.), while other studies showed osteopathic manipulations were no better than short-wave diathermy or placebo for relieving back pain.[355] . Assessments of treatment depend upon measurements taken before and after the interventions.[356] Inter-rater reliability requires careful coordination, and it has been demonstrated in several studies.[357]

It is unclear to what extent chiropractic and osteopathic manipulations resemble each other or differ. Many of the studies do not include controls for suggestion and touch, so a considerable measure of suggestion may be involved in the benefits attributed to these treatments. These effects may also be augmented (largely unconsciously) by spiritual healing in the form of laying-on of hands. The study by Dressler of *Light Touch Manipulative Technique* illustrates this point.

Spiritual healing, chiropractic and osteopathy
The reported effects of chiropractic and osteopathic manipulations may also be augmented (without the awareness of the therapists) by spiritual healing in the form of laying-on of hands. Numbers of chiropractors and osteopaths have told me that their hands get warm during manipulations, which is typical of spiritual healing. In fact, some of the reported benefits of manipulations may be due to spiritual healing effects. The study by Dressler of *Light Touch Manipulative Technique,* and the benefits described by Network Spinal Analysis illustrate that this is possible.

Many and varied are the possible combinations of healing and manipulative therapies. Deliberately applied spiritual healing may be a helpful complement to chiropractic and osteopathy, as with other manual therapies. Conversely, chiropractors may develop their own healing gifts, as has Eric Pearl in California. The late Bruce ~MacManaway, a gifted natural healer from Scotland, also based much of his spiritual healing technique on spinal manipulations.

Some chiropractors include applied kinesiology[358] in their repertoires. This is another biological energy intervention.

Chiropractor Donald Epstein developed a technique called *Network Spinal Analysis.* This involves very light touch in its early stages, and it is clearly a form of spiritual healing (D. Epstein 1994). More conventional chiropractic manipulations may be used after the initial course of light touch treatments. A retrospective survey of 2,818 people treated at 156 treatment centers in the US, Canada, Australia and Puerto Rico showed a 67-71% positive response rate. Significant improvements in physical and mental/ emotional states, stress levels, and life enjoyment were reported by the majority of the respondents (Blanks, et al.).[359]

Research*:* No studies have been published on the clinical efficacy network spinal analysis. However, a British study of Light Touch Manipulative Technique, a method that closely resembles Network Spinal Analysis, showed significant effects for back pain (Dressler).

Adverse effects: There are significant risks associated with manipulative therapy (mostly with chiropractic), although the incidence of serious negative effects is low.[360] These have included spinal injuries, with some fatalities[361] and strokes (Klougart et al. 1996; K. Lee et al.). The percentage of negative effects from spinal manipulations is lower than the percentage of side effects from medications used to treat the same problems. Excessive use of x-rays is a potential long-term hazard that has not been adequately evaluated. Contraindications that might predispose patients to injuries include absent odontoid process (the bone that stabilizes the skull on the top of the spine), anticoagulant therapy, spinal disc lesions, cancers, and osteoporosis (Ernst 199a; Grieve). Another potential danger is misdiagnosis, particularly of early neurological diseases.

Training and licensing: Doctors of Osteopathy (DOs) in the US have now joined the mainstream of allopathic medicine, and have incorporated medicine and surgery in their training and practices. In the US they are licensed along with Medical Doctors (MDs) under similar, if not identical medical examinations.

The National Board of Osteopathic Medical Examiners follows the criteria of allopathic medical examinations in the US. There were over 32,000 DOs in the US in 1993, with 16 schools graduating another 1,500 each year. Today there are 19 osteopathic schools in the country, with 129 hospitals accredited by the American Osteopathic Association (AOA). The AOA is also the professional body that represents osteopaths and promotes research. The American Academy of Osteopathy promotes the exploration and teaching of manipulative techniques.

Though for several decades osteopaths in the US tended towards conventional medical practice, in the past few years there has been a revival of interest in osteopathic manipulations amongst students of osteopathy.[363]

In the UK, osteopathic practitioners do not have conventional medical training. UK osteopaths have remained focused on physical manipulation in their therapy, and do not study medicine (Belshaw). Osteopathy has been acknowledged by the British Medical Association as an accepted therapy.[364]

Clinical applications: Chiropractic and osteopathic manipulations can help with many musculoskeletal disorders, sciatica, and other spinal nerve root problems, particularly back and neck aches.

Early evidence that spinal manipulations alleviates back and neck pains suggest that when applied by competent practitioners, these might be the treatments of first choice for these conditions. These treatments could well be combined with the pain management techniques of relaxation, imagery, hypnotherapy and spiritual healing, plus conventional pain medications and muscle relaxants.

See also: Craniosacral Therapy.

COLONIC IRRIGATION

Irrigation of the colon is recommended for detoxification in Eastern medicine, and also by the gifted clairsentient healer Edgar Cayce. (S. Duggan). It is believed that particles of feces that cling to the walls of the colon (large bowel) may putrefy and produce toxins that are then absorbed into the body. Irrigation of the colon with water inserted in the rectum removes these particles.[365] Irrigation may similarly help to reduce overgrowths of yeasts (*Candida*) in the large bowel.

It is widely believed in the CAM community that toxins are released by the body through the gut, kidneys, sweat, breath, and biological energies as a part of various natural healing processes, as well as through holistic therapies such as fasting. Colonic irrigation is believed to facilitate this process by enhancing the cleansing of the body's wastes. It is also believed that colonic irrigation may be of use in treating liver or kidney disease, by relieving the body of toxins that these organs might otherwise have to process.

Adding nutrients to the enema water is believed to help in healing the intestinal wall if it is irritated.

Colonic irrigations are often offered by chiropractors and naturopaths.

I have seen no research to validate this treatment method, and there are no standards for practice or certification for this therapy.

Adverse effects: While this is generally a safe therapy, several deaths have been reported from excessive use of coffee enemas (Eisele/ Resy).

Training and licensing: Colonic irrigation is practiced by various health care practitioners without any licensing requirement.

Clinical applications: Conditions that may benefit from colonic irrigation include intestinal disorders (particularly sluggish bowel function); toxins in the body; infections; illnesses such as arthritis, chronic fatigue syndrome and other ailments with an allergic component; and skin problems.

Colonic irrigation can be given by a therapist, usually using sophisticated modern equipment. Water enemas can be taken without supervision, though introductory instruction and careful technique are important.

CRANIOSACRAL THERAPY/ CRANIAL OSTEOPATHY

> *...I use intrusive techniques only when I know more subtle diagnostic techniques won't be needed later during that session...*
> *...I have admitted to myself that these are intuitive phenomena which I can not explain scientifically. I am not afraid of them and I trust myself, which is probably the most important part of the whole process.*
> – John E. Upledger

> *Work in the cranial field is largely perceptual. The heart of clinical practice is listening. This demands both stillness and humility on the part of the practitioner. In this inquiry all one can do is to enter into a stillness and see what our journey brings.*
> – Franklyn Sills (2001, p. 3)

A variant of osteopathic therapy using craniosacral manipulation was developed by William G. Sutherland in the early 20th century. Though slow to be accepted, this method has recently become more popular. It is based on the observation of a palpable, rhythmic bioenergy pulsation around the head and body, with a normal frequency of 6-12 cycles per minute, which is unrelated to breathing or heart rate. (This is not to be confused with brain waves, some of which pulse at 3-30 cycles per *second.*) The rate of craniosacral pulsation can be slower or faster than normal due to various malfunctions of the body, though it is rarely faster than 60 beats per minute.

Therapists correct abnormalities in this rhythm through light touch applied with their hands on the patients' head and/ or sacrum, *combined with visualizations of the integrity of each bone of the skull and of its proper interdigitation with neighboring cranial bones.* Further visualizations can achieve temporary cessation of craniosacral pulsation through the mental intent of the osteopath (F. Sills 2001).

Craniosacral manipulation is used for common ailments but its special contribution lies in its purported ability to alleviate problems for which conventional medicine may offer limited treatment options. These include pains in the back and neck; fibromyalgia; frozen shoulder and carpal tunnel syndromes; arthritis; scoliosis; chronic ear infections; hormonal abnormalities; migraines; post-injury/ illness symptoms of head injury, meningitis and encephalitis; behavioral, developmental and learning disorders in children (sometimes attributed to cranial birth injury); and sacral injuries. Craniosacral therapy can likewise be helpful in treating chronic neuralgia syndrome; hypertension; temporo-mandibular joint (TMJ) pain; strabismus (crossed eyes); amblyopia (lazy eye); migraine headaches; cluster headaches; trigeminal neuralgia; chronic fatigue syndrome; tinnitis; vertigo; asthma; lymphedema (swelling due to blocked lymph vessels); plantar faciitis (inflammation of the tissues on the bottom of the foot); shin splints; tennis elbow; and golfer's elbow (Digiovanna/ Schiowitz).

Craniosacral therapists rest their hands lightly upon the healee's skull and visualize that the bones of the skull can flex and move with the vis*ualized* movements of their hands, and that the meningeal coverings of the brain stretch out as their (visualized) hands rise many inches in the air away from the head. These interventions, most of which are not actually physical manipulations, produce distinct subjective sensations within the head and spinal cord that are difficult to describe, including heat and tingling. At times the therapist will place a hand on the sacrum to sense the biological energies at the base of the spine and to facilitate the energy flow in the lower part of the body.

I attended a basic course in craniosacral therapy in England, where I learned, both as therapist and healee, to perceive the sensations that these practitioners describe. Many subjective sensations were similar to those I experience when giving and receiving healing, yet some of the sensations were uniquely characteristic of craniosacral manipulations. For example, with manipulations of my cranium involving very light touch or with the therapist's hands near to but not touching my head, I felt sensations that I can only approximate by saying that it was as if something within my head were being stretched.

I have had numerous conversations with craniosacral osteopaths in England, and I am bemused by their firm insistence that they are engaging in a mechanical manipulation rather than an energy field intervention. The prevailing hypotheses among craniosacral therapists suggest that the brain causes fluctuations of pressure in the cerebrospinal fluid, though no mechanism for the production of such fluctuations has been reasonably postulated. It is claimed that the pressure passes through the dura (tissue layer covering the brain) to cause palpable expansions and contractions of the cranial bones across their sutures, and then passes down the spinal canal to the sacrum, influencing the spinal nerves along the way. The fascia (connective tissues between muscles and organs) are proposed as the agent for transmission of these pulsations to the limbs.

Evidence has been found to support only limited aspects of these mechanistic hypotheses, based on measurable motions of cranial bones (Dove).

A growing number of craniosacral therapists are combining manipulations with psychotherapeutic work, as *somatoemotional release*.[366]

Sadly, most of the younger US osteopaths are no longer practicing craniosacral manipulations, having transformed their profession to copy the conventional medical model. Here and there one can find an older osteopath who still uses these helpful manipulations. I find it hopeful that numbers of osteopathic students are again showing interest in this aspect of their studies.

Theories of John E. Upledger

John E. Upledger[367] is a strong proponent of craniosacral therapy,[368] who theorizes that physical and/ or emotional trauma can create an *energy cyst* within the body.[369] He hypothesizes that ordinarily a blow to the body produces heat that is dissipated by the body. (This is similar to the heat produced by a hammer pounding nails.) If the body is unable to dissipate the heat, it may be encapsulated as a localized concentration of energy. This *energy cyst* can obstruct normal body energy flows (of bioelectricity and acupuncture Qi); produce or exacerbate abnormal energy flows; compromise mobility of tissues, especially fascial layers; and produce energy interference waves. Energy cysts can create dysfunction or pain, and drain the body's energy. Upledger can palpate a "fullness" on the "upstream" side of acupuncture meridians where they are blocked by a cyst, and an "emptiness" beyond the block. Working with acupuncturists, he also found that pulse diagnosis abnormalities were restored to normal after treatments that released the cysts.

Infections or gross physiological malfunctions such as heart attacks can also leave energy cysts in the body. Upledger believes that several factors may determine whether or not a cyst is formed in response to a traumatizing energy. The trauma may be of such magnitude as to overwhelm the body's ability to dissipate it; previous trauma may compromise the ability of that part of the body to dissipate it; and intensely negative emotional states may hinder its dissipation.

Upledger believes that local bioenergy regions of the body (as well as energy cysts) may function autonomously, with associated memory, intelligence and emotion.

> *God will forgive you, but your nervous system will not.*
> – Hans Selye

The *facilitated segment* of the spinal cord is another concept from osteopathy, which describes an excessive sensitivity of nerves at particular spinal cord levels.

A spinal cord segment with a low threshold for excitation may act as a *neuronal lens,* concentrating and focusing energy from the whole nervous system into particular areas of the body. This may keep the muscles and organs of that area in an excessively stimulated state. Hyperactive organs then become more susceptible to irritants, and they may malfunction and cause pain, as with ulcers. Such hyperactivity can readily be identified by rubbing the skin of the back along the spine. Facilitated regions will redden more quickly and more intensely than normal ones. This has been termed the *red reflex.*

Upledger describes how to release the tensions in facilitated segments:

> Once you have located a facilitated segment... sit the patient up and examine for tissue change, mobility loss and "red reflex." Place a finger on each side of the spinous process at the affected level. Place the flattened palm and fingers of the other hand lightly over the front of the body at the same level and follow the motion that occurs. The tissues will begin to move back and forth. Gradually you will feel the restricted vertebrae mobilize. It will feel as though you are rolling a barrel hoop around the patient's body. Eventually you will feel a release... At this point, reevaluate for the presence of the facilitated segment; it may be gone. If it is still present, repeat the process... You take away the secondary effects first and then the underlying cause... (Upledger/ Vrederoogd).

Upledger finds that if he positions the body in such a way that the craniosacral rhythm halts abruptly, he can establish the precise position that is most appropriate for the release of an energy cyst. This is done through a process of deduction and intuition. When the rhythm stops, the therapist keeps his hands immobile until it resumes. When the body position is exactly correct for the release of an energy cyst or for somatoemotional release, the craniosacral rhythm suddenly stops. The rhythm also stops abruptly when subjects speak of or think about an issue which is emotionally significant. The pulsations can thus function as "significance detectors," when combined with particular body positions of patients that are associated with their problems. [370]

Sensations of heat accompany the release of a cyst, which Upledger interprets as a dissipation of stored negative energies. Upledger finds that he must hold the limb still until processes such as the release of heat are completed and the craniosacral rhythm resumes its normal rate and amplitude. Occasionally the limb may move ever so slightly after the release, and the craniosacral rhythm ceases again. The process is then repeated. When the treatment is finished, the patient's entire body relaxes and she reports a sense of completion.

Case: A skier who had suffered a shoulder injury five years prior to treatment illustrates Upledger's approach. She suffered from chronic pain and her injury had not responded to numerous conventional medical treatments. Upledger moved her arm till he found a position where the craniosacral rhythm stopped, and then performed the steps described above. She then released anger which she had felt at another skier who had caused her to fall. After the cyst was released she discussed the incident, and her craniosacral rhythm halted till she got in touch with her anger, which had remained undischarged for five years. Once she forgave the other skier, the encysted energy remnants of the accident fully dissipated.

Upledger (1987) proposes that this sort of pathological process in the body can set up interference waves of energy. A therapist who is aware of such processes can palpate the interference waves to localize them, since they emanate as arcs from the focus of disturbance. This holds true for active pathological processes, but not for older ones.

Biological energy processes may evolve in ways that are unique to each organismic system. Upledger (1995a) suggests:

> [W]ithin each of us is the program for a natural process that, once begun, must be completed or it remains incomplete in a sort of frustrated state of suspended animation. This may occur when a fetus does not go through a normal vaginal delivery, such as during a Cesarean section delivery, or in a situation wherein the newborn is not allowed to bond with the mother. It may occur when, although the female has ovulated many times, there are no offspring. Now age 40 is here and the supply of ova is running low, panic for pregnancy ensues. It may occur when an abortion is performed and the pregnancy does not go to completion. (p.159)

Upledger suggests that such frustrated biological processes may cause energetic imbalances that can become symptomatic. One way to clear these is to have the healee use guided imagery to picture the processes continuing to their natural completion, as they would have done if they had not been interrupted.

Of particular relevance to spiritual healing are Upledger's observations that he can intuitively know things about the patient, and can deliberately apply his mind to obtain a diagnosis. He holds specific questions in his mind and the information needed to clarify a diagnosis comes to him.[371]

Upledger finds that a group of therapists can facilitate somatoemotional release, but he recommends that a team leader be designated to direct this process. The emotional release connected with the dissipation of a cyst may occur immediately or over the following hours or days. Upledger advises against interrupting treatment when the rhythm is stopped (which can produce discomfort), and against scheduling sessions more than two weeks apart (which may lead to regression).

Upledger comes close to calling himself a healer, as is evidenced by his statement at the beginning of this section, and by some of his more recent observations as well. Upledger (1995a) reports that experienced craniosacral practitioners can identify obstructions in chakras and acupuncture meridians and can use energy release techniques to correct them. He also notes that people can project negative emotional energies (such as fear, anger, guilt or frustration) into other people. This is of particular concern for both allopathic and complementary therapists of all modalities, and is a caution for therapists to clear themselves on all psychological and energetic levels in order to avoid harming healees unintentionally.

As described by Upledger (1986), there appear to be major overlaps between craniosacral therapy and spiritual healing.

> ...The use of CranioSacral Therapy, at its most advanced levels, requires the suspension of therapist ego and personal judgments. The therapist cannot take sides, he/ she should only observe, blend, connect with inner wisdom, and facilitate and support the therapeutic process as the patient/ client's inner wisdom navigates through the complexities of denials, suppressions, and rationalizations. (p.154)

> ...It would appear, from clinical observations and experiences, that every cell and every tissue in the body has its own consciousness and its own memory. Therefore, a liver or a muscle or a bone or any other tissue or cell can retain the energy of a past experience. This energy can compromise the functional vitality of that tissue or cell, to some degree, and in so doing may create symptoms and/ or disease. The patient's inner wisdom knows of all of these retained tissue memories. It also knows which ones are causing the most difficulty, which ones are requiring the most adaptive energy expenditure and which ones are the most desirable to discharge at any given time. When the therapist blends and connects with the patient/ client's inner wisdom, the inner wisdom first assesses the therapist's skills and particular talents and then presents to the therapist those retained memories that, in the inner wisdom's judgment, this therapist might best be able to work with and clear. It is very frequent that craniosacral therapists feel tested by "inner wisdoms." (p.154)

The healee's inner wisdom can be accessed through the cranial subtle energy rhythm. A suggestion is given to the healee that his cranial rhythm will stop its pulsations as an indication of a "yes" response to a question from the therapist. This allows the therapist to use this response in questioning the healee's unconscious mind, even if the healee is in a coma, is an infant, or for some other reason is unable to respond verbally (Upledger 1995a).[372]

Craniosacral therapy patients may sometimes move spontaneously into unpredictable, unusual body positions. At such times their cranial rhythms cease to pulsate. If their body position is supported and held, they may then experience somatoemotional releases of long-buried and forgotten memories that had been repressed in their unconscious minds.[373]

Lessons from craniosacral therapy

Very few osteopaths go as far as Upledger in acknowledging there is a biological energy component to craniosacral therapy. This method was developed from a tradition of mechanical adjustment of joints and realigning of posture, and this background inculcates a mechanistic mode of thinking in its practitioners. It is no surprise that a theory that was derived from a branch of osteopathy should have a mechanistic basis. The fact that cranial bones do move rhythmically suggests that a mechanical explanation for some of these observed phenomena may one day be confirmed. However, the following points appear problematic:

1. The movements of cranial bones appear to me inadequate to explain the observed clinical phenomena.:

2. It is physically impossible for flexion to occur across the frontal bones in adults, after these bones have fused across the suture that was open in childhood, or in the occipital bone, which never had a suture - yet cranial osteopathy claims that there is flexion across these sutures.

3. Craniosacral rhythms palpated on the limbs seem unlikely to be transmitted physically from the spinal cord, across the body by fascia.

4. The sensations of heat, tingling, etc. experienced by patients during somato-emotional releases are postulated by Upledger to represent the release of bioenergy stored in energy cysts in the healee's body. Healers interpret similar sensations as energies passing from or through the healer to the healee.

5. The therapist mentally influencing craniosacral pulsations in the healee and correcting physical misalignments of bony joints merely by therapists holding their hands lightly on or near the body appear to be yet further spiritual healing intervention.

My personal experience in learning this technique was that the sensations in my hands were very similar to those I experience in healing, though there are distinctions that I would find hard to convey to anyone who hasn't had similar training. I am puzzled that neither I nor other healers sense *pulsations* of biological energies during spiritual healings, while these are regularly reported by craniosacral osteopaths. I, too, felt them when I was studying this method, but not when I have subsequently engaged in spiritual healing.

Upledger's assertions that the heat sensed during his treatments originates in the patient rather than in the therapist deserve further comment. I tend to discount this also on the basis that clients in psychotherapy who release pent-up emotions do not report a focalized sensation of heat at the time of their abreactions. This would bear more careful investigation, however, before one could rule out Upledger's hypothesis with greater certainty. It may be that his observations are valid for emotions linked with physical trauma, or that psychotherapists (including myself) simply have not queried patients about such sensations in the context of psychotherapy.

At present it would seem that the best theory to explain craniosacral therapy involves an energy field within and around the body, which is palpable and which interacts with the minds of the healee and the therapist. In other words, this would seem to be a variant of spiritual healing.

My intuitive impression is that craniosacral therapists' visualizations of manipulations of individual cranial bones facilitates their resonance with the energy field(s) of the healee. This may enable them to resonate with parts and/ or functions of the body in order to diagnose and treat problems through energy interactions. Parallel reports (from Autogenic Training, biofeedback, therapies involving imagery, and yoga) of the efficacy of visualization combined with physical activity suggest that this is likely. Visualization may serve as a meditative focus and/ or as a way for the therapists to manipulate bioenergies.[374]

Research: I have found no published research on the clinical efficacy of cranio-sacral manipulations. David Dressler, a therapist who practices the *Light Touch Manipulative Technique* somewhat similar to osteopathy, showed that this method was an effective treatment for back pain. Dressler also observes that his work might be labeled as healing.[375]

Cranial manipulations and spiritual awareness

The writings of Franklyn Sills (2001) are, in my opinion, among the finest in the literature on spiritual healing. His concise, clear descriptions of what he does and how he does it are an inspiration to practitioners to strive for the highest levels of wholistic healing. Here are a few examples:

> Work in the cranial field is largely perceptual. The heart of clinical practice is listening. This demands both stillness and humility on the part of the practitioner. In this inquiry all one can do is to enter into a stillness and see what our journey brings. The foundation of this endeavor is the experience of our own perceptual and inner process. An appreciation of our inner world is crucial for efficient clinical practice. This awareness of our own interior world is critical in the creation of a safe and efficient healing relationship. In this process, we will come directly into relationship to our own human condition and our own suffering. This is a huge undertaking. It means truly inquiring into who we are. The ground of this exploration is a commitment to learn about ourselves… (p. 3)

Cranial field therapy requires that the therapist focus completely in the present moment. Sills acknowledges the wisdom of The Buddha in reaching towards and into the stillness that facilitates healing.

> He simply and profoundly stated that *there is suffering and it must be understood*. This simple statement is the ground of therapeutic inquiry. (p. 4)

Sills continues with a discussion on dealing with suffering:

> …if we hold onto things, onto fixed positions, onto self-construct, self-view, and past history, there will be suffering… Most of us, most of the time, tend to see the present through the filters of the past. But if we can find a way to truly live in the present, in the present time-ness of things, then there is the possibility of not suffering. There may be pain, but there needn't be suffering. Within the cranial context, it is seen that suffering is relinquished when the system truly aligns with the present time-ness of things. It is an alignment to something else beyond the fear that seems to hold our sense of selfhood together. It is a realignment to a universal, an Intelligence much greater than our human mentality. To something still, yet potently present. This occurs when the oppositional forces of our past experience are reconciled

within us, in states of balance and stillness. Within the Stillness, known only in this present moment, something else can occur beyond the suffering held. It is as simple as that. (p. 8-9)

Adverse effects: None are known.

Training and licensing: There are various schools of craniosacral therapy. Training has not been standardized between them, and this therapy is not licensed.

Clinical applications: While research has yet to confirm many of the claimed benefits of craniosacral therapy, clinical reports indicate that it can be of great help in treating hormonal abnormalities; migraines; post-traumatic symptoms of head injury; meningitis and encephalitis; behavioral, developmental and learning disorders in children (sometimes attributed to cranial birth injury); and sacral injuries.

A therapist trained in craniosacral therapy is essential for this treatment. This appears to be a form of spiritual healing, and the personal qualities of the therapist may be as important as the technique.

CREATIVE ARTS THERAPIES AS HEALING

> *Today, like every other day*
> *We wake up empty and scared.*
> *Don't open the door of your study*
> *And begin reading.*
> *Take down a musical instrument.*
> *Let the beauty we love be what we do.*
> *There are hundreds of ways to kneel*
> *And kiss the earth.*
>
> – Rumi

The creative arts have provided avenues to healing throughout recorded history. Through storytelling, metaphor, poetry, myth, drama, dance, humor and art we can access wellsprings of self-healing energy that lies within all of us.

Music Therapy uses recorded and live instrumental music, singing, toning, chanting and drumming to restore emotional and spiritual balance and to stir healing energies. Music can be soothing or energizing, commonly attributed to the associations and moods that it evokes emotionally. A variety of music that is conducive to relaxation and meditation, as well as to invoke various moods is available at most record shops.

Participating in playing music adds dimensions to its healing potentials. Drumming, chanting and singing can usher us into alternative states of consciousness in which pains may be relieved and healing on very deep levels can occur. Participating in a group that uses any of these musical modalities can enhance their potency. Many traditional cultures make extensive use of music for healing, both individually and collectively. Music Therapy may be used for specific therapeutic purposes.

Alfred Tomatis developed a complex system using sound to treat children who have auditory processing problems, dyslexia, learning disabilities, attention deficit disorders, autism, and difficulties in sensory integration and motor skills. In adults this method has helped in depression, improving communication skills, speeding the learning of foreign languages, and enhancing creativity and job performance. It can also be used in a more general way to improve self-confidence, raise levels of energy and motivation, and produce a sense of well-being.[376]

Figure II-9. Movement and dance are taught in combination with healing by Lilla Bek, a UK healer

Photograph by Tony Sleep

Some healers use vocal tones or particular music in conjunction with their healings. They feel that the tones and/ or rhythms help healees alter their body and/ or energy field vibrations in healthy ways. For instance, it is said that Tibetan music and chants are tuned to particular healing frequencies, perhaps related to the vibrational levels of the chakras.

> [T]he person is instructed to follow the tone of the gong down into the void itself, into the nothingness. When it reaches that void and nothingness from which all things arise – the creative void – they completely let go of whatever they are envisioning. The way we do it, you are lying on your back and you hold your left hand up over your abdomen as long as you can hear the sound. If you can no longer hear the sound, drop it. Say, "I give up." What we have found – and we can't prove this – is that at the moment of surrender, the mental-material interface somehow clicks in. In other words, what was real in the mental realm, to some small extent becomes real in the material

realm. Of all the methods we have tried, focused-surrender has turned out to be our most effective induction.

– George Leonard

While the obvious spiritual aspects of liturgical music are familiar to most of us, a further spiritual use of music has been developed by Therese Schroeder-Sheker (1994; 2001) in the form of *music thanatology*, which is intended to help people make the transition into dying.[377]

Research is beginning to confirm some of the clinical reports in this area. A study by Mark Rider and Jeanne Achterberg showed changes in white cells in response to music. Adarsh Kumar and colleagues showed that melatonin production was increased significantly following music therapy in patients with Alzheimer's disease, with further increases at six weeks. Norepinephrine and epinephrine levels also increased significantly at four weeks but returned to baseline by six weeks.

Recent evidence suggests that drumming can enhance immune system functions (Bittman et al.).

One unusual sound therapy developed by Robert Monroe (Hutchinson 1986) involves presenting binaural beats to the brain. When tones that differ by a given number of beats per second are presented to each ear, auditory beats are produced by the brain itself at a frequency equal to the difference between the presented beats. For example, if a tone of 100 Hz is played in one ear, and a tone of 110 Hz in the other, the brain will produce an auditory beat of 10 Hz. While this is lower than the threshold for perceived sound, it is at the frequency of alpha waves, which are present when the mind is in a relaxed state. Research is beginning to show that binaural beats of this kind can promote relaxation.[378]

Felicitas Goodman (1987; 1990) found that rhythmic sounds helped to create alternative states of consciousness that were particular to specific body postures.

Dorothy Retallach studied the effects of various forms of music upon the growth of plants. She found that plants grew better when exposed to soft music, and grew less with loud, hard-rock music.

It has been found that infrasonic sound emanates from the hands of Qigong healers. Various electronic instruments have been developed that produce infrasonic sound at the same frequencies, and Chinese researchers report that these can also bring about healing for many problems.[379]

Clinical applications: Music has been particularly useful in promoting relaxation. While broad claims have been made by various healers regarding the benefits of tonal vibrations in spiritual healing, most of these have yet to be substantiated.

Obviously no therapist is needed to help us simply enjoy ourselves and relax with music, but trained therapists may be able to markedly deepen the beneficial effects of tones, rhythmic beats and music. They can help by selecting appropriate pieces, toning their voices to utilize their essence as healers, and convening music therapy groups that can enhance vibrational healings.

Ilana Rubenfeld, trained as an orchestra conductor, clarifies the links of music to therapy:

...As the conductor/ bridge, I was making the music happen, but also stepping aside from it, letting it happen on its own, listening to it happen, *hearing* it happen. I became an insignificant part of the music's energy, and also essential to it. I had re-created it, but it had also re-created me.

The same state to ego and egolessness, or insignificance and essence, is true in regard to cosmic energy, of which music is a magnificent expression, for we are all insignificant, essential parts of the cosmic sphere, part of the ascending spiral. And it is true in regard to my therapeutic work with people.

When I'm with clients, I feel that I am in that egoless state. I am still Ilana, yet different: nonjudgmental, totally accepting, loving. I can be both a partner in the therapeutic experience and step aside from it. You sing your own song. I am a vital guide to help you hear and understand it, and to accept your body as your musical score.

The tools I use for my therapeutic work – to let you hear your authentic self – are my brain and my hands... (p.5-6)

Art Therapy invites participants to draw, paint, sculpt, collage, and use other media to express feelings, explore psychological issues, and resolve conflicts. Projecting problems onto artistic media allows people to identify and sort through their issues in new and creative ways.[380]

Dance and Movement Therapy invite the body to participate in rhythmic movements that can be soothing or stimulating, according to our needs and moods.[381]

Storytelling can be healing in several ways. A therapist may use stories to illustrate or suggest ways in which change might occur. People find that telling their life story, and particularly relating the problems that surround (and may have contributed to) their illness, may relieve their symptoms. Stories (either created by the participant or told by others) offer stages upon which to explore conflicts and play out options for their resolution[382] These elements can also be used to clarify therapists' process (counter-transference).[383] Poetry adds a metaphoric dimension to these processes.[384]

John McEnulty provides a lovely example of storytelling as a transformative process:

There is a teaching method developed by the Educational Center in St. Louis. It is called the Maieutic Method after Socrates' belief that all he could do was to help someone birth what was already within them, that he himself had nothing to teach. So the teaching was always about finding what was within.

There are three questions to the method: (1) What is the actual story? (2) Where do you find the story in your life? (3) Where do you find the story in the world?

We hear the story and talk about what actually happened in the story, perhaps information about the story, its background, to ground ourselves in the elements of the story itself.

Then we agree that whatever anyone finds within that they feel is connected to the story is valid. There is no criticism, no right or wrong. How you relate to the story, how you find it in your life is your own precious and unique meaning.

Each person shares how they relate to the story. So the life experiences of each participant deepen and enrich the others who are revealing who they are.

The final sharing is of where we find the story in the world. The same rule applies. Your vision is yours and is precious and valid, not to be contradicted or criticized by anyone else.

The beauty of this method is the love and tolerance that it creates, the safety for each person to express what is within and to grow in understanding through the opportunity to hear other viewpoints and recognize them as valid.

It goes beyond the moral of the story, or the lesson to be learned. It connects directly with the individual and their special way of seeing. It allows each person to reach within and find their own consciousness, process of awareness.

It leads to individual and group awareness of the rich complexity of the human experience.

Where do you see yourself in this story?

Journaling can also be an outlet for feelings and a great aid to sorting out our problems. Writing out one's story and feelings has a cathartic effect, allows a person to consider the problems at a distance, provides perspective as one reviews journaled materials from the past, and much more. Journalin may be helpful even with the most profound of emotional distresses, such as suicidal ideation and bereavement.[385]

All of these modalities may speak to us in ways that transcend language and logic.[386]

Psychodrama, originated by Jacob L. Moreno, invites participants to stage their life situation, relationships and conflicts – inviting them to perceive them in new ways and to explore innovative approaches to sorting them out. Profound transformations are often achieved quite rapidly.[387]

Research: I have not reviewed the research in this area.[388]

Humor can bring healing in difficult situations. Norman Cousins is famous for having cured himself of scleroderma, a serious, progressive illness that has no cure in conventional medicine. The therapy he administered to himself was to watch as many funny movies as he could find. He literally laughed himself back to health.[389]

> *A merry heart does good like a medicine, but a broken spirit dries the bones.*
>
> – Proverbs 17:22

Humor pokes fun at the rules we live by. It makes us laugh when we appreciate incongruities and inconsistencies in our customary ways of doing things. Humor can thus help to point out our frailties and false pretenses, relieving the related feelings of guilt, frustration or anger. Humor allows us to explore new possibilities by breaking the rules and taking us outside of our usual frameworks for perceiving situations.

Research: Early research suggests that humor can produce measurable effects on the cardiovascular, respiratory, and immune systems, [390] in addition to reducing psychological stress reactions.[391]

Poetry speaks to the heart of our human experiences. It can help people to find words for the feelings and conflicts they are struggling with. [392]
  Imagery and metaphors invite us to see new connections between various elements in our lives, and to explore creative ways of reweaving the patterns of our relationships with ourselves, with significant others in our lives, and with the world at large.*[393]*

> *And a man said, Speak to us of Self-Knowledge.*
> *And he answered, saying:*
> *Your hearts know in silence the secrets of the days and the nights.*
> *But your ears thirst for the sound of your heart's knowledge.*
> *You would know in words that which you have always known in thought.*
> *You would touch with your fingers the naked body of your dreams.*
>
> *And it is well you should.*
> *The hidden well-spring of your soul must needs rise and run murmuring to the sea;*
> *And the treasure of your infinite depth would be revealed to your eyes.*
> *But let there be no scales to weigh your unknown treasure;*
> *And seek not the depths of your knowledge with staff or sounding line.*
> *For self is a sea boundless and measureless.*
>
>   – Khalil Gibran

Discussion: Metaphor, storytelling, myth, drama, humor and poetry have resonated through the ages with human joys, hurts, angers, loneliness, elation, bliss, and despair – in short, with all the permutations of the human condition.. While we may have difficulty describing adequately in words our subjective reactions to the creative arts, we can acknowledge their resonations through shared metaphors and myths. Every society has a creation myth among the roots of its belief system. Classical Greek dramas and tragedies still speak potently across several millennia, and national myths guide and inspire us in deeply significant ways. Today the publishing, media, and entertainment industries provide us with enormously varied and often rich expressions of shared understanding through these doorways to our inner being.

These media can be tools and avenues for healing our emotional wounds, both individually and as social collectives. Consider what the TV series *The Holocaust* and the film *Schindler's List* have done to heal some of our residual wounds from the Nazi atrocities, and what *Roots* did to raise awareness about the sufferings of African Americans. Consider the warnings against the dangers of biological engineering that are suggested by *Jurassic Park*, and the encouragement to deal with fears of death that has been offered by stories about surviving spirits through the ages, as well as in modern films like *Ghost* and *Always*, and the many angel TV series.

> When I... discovered that the nightmares and other aspects of my obsessive-compulsive disorder were written of in biblical stories and mythology, I was able to understand and integrate my illness as an experience in soul growth rather than as a meaningless bout with madness. A wound with meaning is much easier to heal than a wound that is meaningless or that, worse, is interpreted as divine punishment of other evidence of personal unworthiness.
> – Joan Borysenko (1993, p.93)

In my psychotherapy practice I often recommend books for inspiration and to let clients know that they are not alone in facing their life's challenges. I may tell stories or jokes to illustrate or counterpoint issues that we are discussing. In consulting with couples or families who are in conflict, particularly when the trouble has gone on for a long, bitter time, here is one of my favorite stories:

> George finds himself at the Pearly Gates, where St. Peter opens his ledger to determine in which direction he must go. St. Peter shakes his head in bewilderment, saying, "I've never seen anyone like this! Your good deeds and your sins are precisely balanced. I cannot see even a hair's difference that would say whether you belong in heaven or in hell. I'm going to have to ask God what to do." Returning shortly, St. Peter tells George that under these unusual circumstances, God has suggested that he should be given his choice of where he would rather be.
>
> George asks to be taken first to see hell. He is surprised to see tables piled high with the most sumptuous foods. The people sitting around the tables have large ladles with very long handles tied to their hands. No matter how hard they stretch and turn and twist, they are unable to reach the bowl of the ladle with their mouths.
>
> "What terrible torture!" says George. "I certainly don't want to stay here. Take me to heaven."
>
> Arriving in heaven, he is even more surprised to see the very same tables piled high with the same sumptuous foods, and the people around the tables holding ladles of the same length... but in heaven they are using them to feed each other.

Joy is a common denominator of the effects that the healing arts can have on our lives. Lawrence LeShan (1989), a psychologist who has worked and written extensively on dealing with cancer, emphasizes that to maximize health and increase chances of survival, people must have joy and passion in their lives. Research is beginning to confirm that joy is a factor in cancer survival. Baseline assessments show that greater joy was a predictor of longer survival in 36 women with breast cancer (S. Levy et al.).

> I slept and dreamt that life was joy.
> I awoke and saw that life was service.
> I acted and behold, service was joy.
> — Rabindranath Tagore (1861-1941)

CRYSTALS

> *Fifty-five crystal spheres geared to God's crankshaft is my idea of a satisfying universe. I can't think of anything more trivial than quarks, quasars, big bangs and black holes.*
> — Tom Stoppard

Some healers feel that crystals augment or focus their healing powers, either by storing healing energies for later use or by concentrating and magnifying them.[394] Others believe that the crystals themselves carry vibrations that are therapeutic, and some claim that electrical currents augment crystal vibrations (Oldfield/ Coghill). While crystals appear to augment spiritual healing effects, it is difficult in many instances to know whether this is due to anything more than suggestion.

Sensitives report that crystals have brighter auras than many other inanimate objects, and that they interact with the energy fields which surround living things

My personal experience is that I can palpate energy fields around some crystals and gemstones with my hands. I must admit that despite my own tactile confirmation of apparent crystal energies, I was skeptical that they had healing effects much beyond those of placebos, until I saw the study by Shealy described below.

Research: C. Norman Shealy, a neurosurgeon who began investigating complementary therapies for use in pain management, demonstrated highly significant effects of crystals on depression.[395]

Adverse effects: Healers report that it is possible to have negative effects from too strong an exposure to crystals, or to other types of misguided uses of crystals.

Theories: A basis for the healing powers of crystals is suggested by their use as signal receivers and current rectifiers in crystal radio sets, quartz watches, and other devices. It may be that they can serve similar focusing functions for the presumed unconventional energies that may be involved in healing.

Training and licensing: There are no formal training programs or licensing for crystal therapy.

Clinical applications: I know of no research to confirm the use of crystals for particular problems other than depression, though they are used by some healers to augment healing for many ailments. Here are a few examples:

- *Amethyst quartz:* Harmonizes relationships
- *Fluorite:* Neutralizes irritating energies
- *Opal (gem quality):* Opens and stimulates chakras to higher functions

Crystals (e.g. clear quartz) may be used for self-healing, but the selection of particular crystals by a healer may be a great help. Crystals may also carry the healing vibrations of self-healing intent, or of a healer who "programs" them.

CURANDERISMO

> *...Even when a curandero uncovers specific causes of illness he is still likely to focus on sin and the will of God as critical factors which have affected the susceptibility of the patient and predisposed him to illness.*
>
> – Ari Kiev (1968 p. 34)

Curanderismo originated in Spain and spread to every Latin American country, where it integrated with local healing and herbal lore and practices. Traditions therefore vary in each country. Its original Catholic spiritual orientation has blended over time with local traditions. Curanderas (women were the original practitioners) and curanderos may invoke the help of God, Christ, saints, indigenous gods and healing powers of nature – particularly of medicinal herbs. Where economic resources are limited, and where there is a distrust of allopathic medicine, curanderismo provides natural healing approaches. This method is also widely practiced in the US, where it is influenced by Mexican traditions. As with clients of other complementary therapy practitioners, people who seek the help of curanderas may hesitate to mention this to their Western physicians, anticipating that these practices will be denigrated or dismissed as folklore placebos.

The are various types of curanderismo practitioners who deal with different aspects of the traditional techniques.

Yerberas prescribe herbal remedies, whose properties are enhanced by the practitioners' knowledge of where and when to gather the plants for maximal potency (M. Moore).

Sobardoras offer massage and laying-on of hands treatments. They treat *empachos* (biological energy blocks) in the body (particularly in the gastrointestinal tract) or in the spirit.

Parteras are midwives who provide pre-natal and post-natal care, and may also baptize babies. Prayer is a vital aspect of their practice, and herbs may also be used.

Consejeras provide counseling that may cover personal, relational, and spiritual issues. The *platica* is a heart-to-heart discussion. The *consejaras* encourage healees to pour out their souls, in a process called *desahogar*, which may go on for many hours, over several days.

Treatment may include *the limpia*, a spiritual cleansing, which is accomplished by sweeping around the body with a bundle of herbs or a feather to remove negative biological energies. An egg may also be rubbed over the body to absorb negative energies.

Various levels of competence and natural calling are acknowledged among curanderas. The highest level practitioners offer all of the above-mentioned services. Any practitioner may use herbs, feathers, crystals, chants, rattles, and drums in their ministrations. All practitioners are encouraged to heal themselves so that their energies can be as pure and strong as possible.

Curanderismo is thoroughly wholistic, addressing issues related to body, emotions, relationships, and soul.

Diagnoses used in this modality may have no precise equivalents in Western terminology or conceptualizations. *Bilis* (rage) becomes a problem when angers are not expressed, and it is caused by over-secretion of bile. *Mal aire* (bad air) causes disease by inhalation of germs. *Mal puesto* (hexing or cursing) can cause severe malaise or even death. *Mal ojo* refers to illness caused by staring.[396] This term is used to describe problems caused by giving excess attention, especially to a child. *Mala suerte* (bad luck) is a destructive force that people bring into their own lives through negative thinking, poor self-esteem and fears. *Susto* (soul loss) occurs with severe emotional traumas, following which people feel that they are not really themselves any more. The process of soul retrieval may restore a person's integrity. *Espanto* is a fright received from seeing a ghost or from being severely jarred emotionally, which causes the soul to flee in fear.[397]

Adverse effects: See potentials for harmful effects under herbalism; spiritual healing.

Training and licensing: Training is traditionally by apprenticeship, with students initiating the process as they sense an inner calling to become a healer, or with experienced curanderos approaching people they feel have a gift that can be developed (K. Whitaker). This is an entirely individual process, and setting of standards would appear inappropriate, as this would destroy the uniqueness of the mentoring/ apprenticeship relationship. For similar reasons, it would be difficult to license such practitioners. There is no official licensing.

Clinical efficacy: While I have not found any controlled studies of curanderismo, anecdotal reports abound about how Latin Americans have responded well to these approaches, which resonate with them because they find them *culturally congruent*.[398]

Curanderismo is but one of many shamanistic practices. Every culture has its folk practitioners, [399] and it is impossible to list them all. It is important, however, for health caregivers to become familiar with local subcultural health practices. As one example, in the Los Angeles area there was a group of Cambodian child immigrants who were found to have bruises on their backs. Physical abuse was suspected and the parents were investigated. However it was found that the bruises resulted from the practice of rubbing the back with a coin to treat viral respiratory illnesses. Both children and parents, however, were traumatized by the child welfare investigations and allegations of possible child abuse.

Curanderismo is given by a healer, but it may include elements of self-healing prescribed by the healer.

See also: Shamanism.

DEAN ORNISH THERAPY FOR HEART PROBLEMS

See: Psychoneurocardiology.

EDTA CHELATION

History records no more gallant struggle that that of humanity against the truth.
> – Ashleigh Brilliant

Chelation therapy (Chele = Greek for claw) relies on molecules that bind positive ions, just as the pincers of a crab might grab a pebble. Chelated molecules found in nature include chlorophyll (binding magnesium) and hemoglobin (binding iron). Chelation treatment with intravenous calcium disodium ethylene diamine tetra-acetic acid (EDTA) can be used to remove toxic chemicals from the body, such as lead. A broader application is to treat atherosclerotic cardiovascular disease. EDTA binds calcium from arteriosclerotic plaques, moving the calcium into the blood stream to be excreted through the kidneys. This therapy has not been accepted by conventional medicine as yet, although it has been approved for treatment of hypercalcemia (excessively high levels of calcium circulating in the blood) and digitalis toxicity. The manufacturer's patent expired in 1969, and the cost of obtaining approval from the U.S. Food and Drug Administration (at a conservative minimum estimate of $250,000 or more) is prohibitive.

Chelation is given as an outpatient procedure by intravenous infusion over a three hour period, once or twice weekly over several months. It has been shown to be safe if administered slowly under medical supervision.

Doctors and grateful patients have reported dramatic benefits from this treatment in clearing arteriosclerotic blockage of arteries in the extremities, common in diabetes; in reducing cholesterol levels; lowering blood pressure; encouraging recovery from strokes; addressing angina and other problems of ischemic heart disease (due to blocked arteries); and preventing cancers. Its most common use today is for treating heart disease, and it is often used in wholistic practice as an alternative to cardiac surgery.

Research: A wealth of anecdotal reports supports the growing popularity of this treatment.[399] Three controlled studies that showed negative results[400] have been severely criticized for their faulty methodology (Chappell et al. 1996). Olszewer et al., studying 10 subjects, found suggestive improvement in exercise capacity with chelation. A fortuitous finding in one 18-year follow-up study was that people who received EDTA chelation had a lower mortality rate from cancers (Blumer/ Cranton).

Adverse effects: In a RCT of 153 subjects, Guldager et al. found no significant adverse effects in the treated subjects vs. the control group.

Training and licensing: While legal action has been initiated in several states to outlaw these uses of EDTA chelation, the courts have for the most part permitted its use, in view of the evidence and testimony of satisfied patients. Treatment must be given under the supervision of a physician.

Clinical applications: Numerous anecdotal reports suggest that EDTA chelation can slow or even reverse arteriosclerotic cardiovascular disease.

ELECTROMAGNETIC (EM) AND MAGNET THERAPIES

> *[O]ne can easily understand that man is... penetrated by the two-fold stream of universal fluid, and that he must have his poles and his surfaces in the same way as do all other substances of nature which are more or less penetrated, according to their own characteristics, by this same universal fluid.*
>
> – Franz Anton Mesmer

Local and general electromagnetic treatments are reported to be effective in resolving a wide range of health problems.

Local applications of simple magnets: Small magnets and weak electromagnetic fields have been reported to relieve musculoskeletal stress responses and soft tissue injuries, chronic pain, arthritis, neurological problems, and infections, and to enhance the mending of bone fractures.[403] The magnets may be applied locally in bands around their wrists, elbows, ankles, or knees, or used generically in the form of magnetic insoles or mattress pads. Paul Rosch, an acknowledged expert on magnet therapy, has been impressed to find that any magnets at all may be helpful, regardless of their strength or degree of sophistication (R. Lawrence et al). James Oschman and Candace Pert (2000) point out that magnetic fields can help with both soft and hard tissue problems simultaneously, though each may require different pulsation frequencies.

The new medical specialty of *bioelectromagnetics* is developing out of intensifying research on the effects of EM fields when they are applied externally to the body. Several categories of EM therapies are evolving, each with different effects and applications.

Thermal effects of EM radiation are used to create heat, which can be beneficial in treating muscles and tissues that have been damaged by trauma and disease. Laser and radio frequency (RF) surgery are also in this category.

Pulsed electromagnetic fields (PEMFs) have been found to promote healing for a variety of problems.[404] PEMFs can enhance Immune system activity, particularly to increase natural killer cells that are effective in responding to viruses and cancers (Cadossi et al. 1988a; b).

Physical healing of fractures that are slow to mend may be facilitated by PEMFs; by alternating current fields; by DC fields and by combinations of these fields. Some therapeutic devices of these types have been approved by the U.S. Food and Drug Administration. Remarkably, failures in bone healing have been corrected using these methods, with full bone mending achieved after periods of as long as forty years with no prior improvement (Bassett 1995). There are also reports that EM fields may aid in soft tissue healing (Sisken/ Walker).

Microwave resonance therapy is in wide use in Russia, where it is reported to be beneficial for arthritis, hypertension, pain, neurological problems and cancer chemotherapy side effects (Devyatkov et al.). The benefits of this therapy are thought to be mediated by changes in cell membranes or in the chemicals that communicate information within the body. It is speculated that EM therapies work through information that promotes healing, and that this information may be transmitted within the total body EM field.

Nerve stimulators are used for:

1. Pain relief and physical therapy, with FDA approval for a variety of transcutaneous electrical nerve stimulation (TENS) devices;
2. Emotional disorders that respond to transcranial electrostimulation (TCES), including depression, insomnia and anxiety;[405]
3. Repair of damaged nerves, particularly in the wrist (Wilson et al.).

A Swedish radiologist named Björn Nordenström reports dramatic cures of tumors treated with application of DC currents to the tumors and the surrounding tissues via electrodes (Nordenström; Taubes). Nordenström hypothesizes that tumors create local electrochemical imbalances within the body that function somewhat like an automobile battery. The tumor creates a positive charge due to accumulation of damaged and dead cells at its center. The center of the tumor then becomes acidic, creating an electrochemical gradient relative to the surrounding tissues. By applying external electrical current of opposite polarity Nordenström reports that he can arrest and reverse the cancerous growth. Becker and Marino also discuss applying electrical currents to limit tumor growth (per Humphrey/ `Seal).

Soft tissue wound healing can be accelerated using this therapy if wounds are slow to heal (Lee et al.; Vodovnik/ Karba), particularly in the case of skin ulcers. Various types of EM stimulation may be used directly, or EM current may be used to drive active metallic ions into tissues. Silver has been particularly effective in promoting healing with minimal scarring.

PEMF instruments that emit 27 MHz have been shown to reduce swelling, accelerate wound healing, stimulate nerve regeneration, and enhance recovery from injuries (Sisken/ Walker 1995). PEMFs also produced significant reductions of pain due to injuries of cartilage, tendons, and bone (Sjaust/ Hurtler) and in osteoarthritis (Trock et al. 1993; 1994). Early evidence suggests that part of the improvement may have been due to regeneration of damaged cartilage under EM stimulation (Aaron/ Plass; Brighton et al.).[406]

Low energy emission therapy (LEET), which is applied through an electrode held in the patient's mouth, produced significant improvements in stress (Higgs et al.) and insomnia (Pasche et al.; Reite et al.).

An unpublished report by Valerie Hunt et al. presents another angle of investigation. EM measurements and parallel analyses by a sensitive who sees auras (Rosalyn Bruyere) were obtained for volunteers who underwent treatment by Rolfing[407] and for matched controls. Rolfing involves deep massage of muscles and joints, during which old memories, feelings and altered states of consciousness may be evoked. EM and acoustic monitoring of chakras and acupuncture meridians correlated significantly with Bruyere's descriptions of aura changes that occurred during and following the structural integration treatments. Recognizable wave forms were consistently observed when Bruyere reported seeing primary and secondary colors. The sequence of wave frequencies recorded over chakras was almost uniformly correlated with the sequence of colors in the spectrum, and with colors traditionally associated with the different chakras. These range from red at the base chakra to violet at the brow.

Hunt also used Kirlian photography to detect significant differences between structural integration subjects and controls, but the meaning of these results is as yet unclear.

Valerie Hunt (1992) also reports on a study of telemetry electromyography. Using surface electrodes she recorded high frequency[408] EM activity under the following circumstances:

> ...during meditation; emotional states; pain; energy fields transactions between people; laying-on-hand healing of post polio, brain disturbances, and tissue regeneration; Mu[409] Room manipulation of electromagnetic atmosphere and during imaging. Data were analyzed by Wave Shape Analysis, Fast Fouriere Transform, Cross Plot Analysis, Chaos Pattern, and color comparison of Wave Shape and Voice Spectrogram Analysis with aura readers' reports.

Hunt finds that the patterns in EMG recordings that had previously been assumed to represent only "noise" between large waves actually carry an enormous amount of information about the subject. From her readings, she claims she can identify subjective states, sometimes including mental imagery of the subject.[410]

Brain stimulators: A number of transcranial magnetic stimulators (TMS)[411] are able to produce relaxation and deep, meditative states (Hutchinson 1986; Klawansky), which have beneficial physical and psychological effects, particularly for depression.[412] Symptoms of Parkinson's disease responded to TMS (Malley/Stone). TMS may enhance healing through relaxation – by releasing tensions, encouraging greater openness to healing, or by initiating other health-promoting mechanisms that are inherent in meditative states. They may also activate neurohumoral mechanisms in the brain.

Minute doses of ionizing radiation may significantly increase survival rates of people with Hodgkin's lymphoma (Sakamoto). Interestingly, when radiation was directed to only half of the body, tumors outside the irradiated region also disappeared. Enhanced immune system activity was also demonstrated.

A number of helpful reviews of bioelectromagnetic therapy have been published.[413]

Theories: Electromagnetic fields exist within each cell, tissue, and organ, and within and around the body as a whole. These are viewed by conventional medicine as the result of electrochemical properties and activities of the cells and tissues. CAM therapists suggest that the bioelectrical fields may have a regulating function upon and within the body.[414] See further discussion on the organizing properties of bioenergetic fields in Chapter II-3.

Oschman and Pert (2000) note that possible pathways for action of EM fields in enhancing soft tissue injury repairs may include: "enhancement of capillary formation, decreased necrosis, reduced swelling, diminished pain, faster functional recovery, reduction in depth, area, and pain in skin wounds, reduced muscle loss after ligament surgery… and increased tensile strength of ligaments, and acceleration of nerve regeneration and function recovery."[415]

Research: Controlled studies are beginning to confirm that static magnets can help various problems, such as post-polio pain (Vallbona et al.),[416] musculoskeletal pains (Hinman et al), and pains of diabetic neuropathy (Weintraub 1999). All of these are usually difficult to treat with conventional pain management approaches.[417]

Static and pulsed magnetic fields can enhance bone healing[418]

Pulsed electromagnetic fields (PEMFs) enhance healing in damaged musculoskeletal tissues, with reduces in inflammation, increases in vascularization, and greater collagen and bone growth through proliferation of osteoblasts, chondroblasts and fibroblasts.[419] This can be helpful in the prevention and treatment of osteoporosis (C. Rubin et al.; Tabrah et al.) and for osteoarthritis (Trock et al. 1993; 1994). PEMFs can also help with symptoms of multiple sclerosis (T. Richards et al.; Sandyk 1992c), Alzheimer's disease (Sandyk 1992a) and Parkinsonism (Sandyk 1992b).

Much broader discussions on electromagnetic effects, both positive and negative, are presented in Chapter II-3, within a general description of the fields and energies that may be present in and around the body.

Adverse effects: I have heard anecdotal reports of negative effects, such as worsening of pains and arthritis with misuse of simple magnets. Though as yet controversial, there is strong suspicion that chronic or excessive exposure to EM radiations can have negative effects. This is discussed in Chapter II-3.

Training and licensing: There is no formal training for electromagnetic or magnet therapies, nor is there any licensing.

Clinical applications: Electromagnetic therapies are particularly helpful in wound healing and relieving chronic pain. Their effectiveness for inducing relaxation and treating stress-related illnesses and depression has yet to be firmly established.

A trained therapist is required for administration and supervision of EM therapies. Simple magnets may be worn over parts of the body in need of healing, but initial guidance of a therapist may also be helpful in applying these as well.

ENVIRONMENTAL MEDICINE (CLINICAL ECOLOGY)

The very same skills of separation, analysis, and control that gave us the power to shape our environment are producing ecological and so-cial crises in our outer world, and psychological and spiritual crises in our inner world. Both these crises grow out of our success in sepa-rating ourselves from the larger fabric of life."
— Fred Kofman and Peter Senge (1993)

In the 1940s Theron Randolph pioneered the identification of food allergens that can cause many symptoms, including fatigue, headaches, muscle weakness and pains, gastrointestinal upset, emotional lability, depression, and irritability. Par-ticular dietary culprits include corn, wheat, milk and eggs. Randolph adopted Herbert Rinkel's elimination diet, which requires that people avoid the suspected allergenic food for 4-10 days and then deliberately ingest it to see whether there is a negative reaction. Illnesses and symptoms for which this approach has been helpful include arthritis, asthma, hay fever, eczema, colitis, migraines, urinary disorders, attention deficit hyperactivity disorder, anxiety, depression, irritability, fatigue, distractibility, memory loss, chronic fatigue syndrome, and enuresis.

Various common chemicals encountered in the environment may also produce debilitating symptoms. The top culprits include industrial solvents, pesticides, formaldehyde, natural gas, car exhaust fumes, cosmetics, laundry soap, and the like. Some people are incredibly sensitive to these substances, and may develop problems at exposure levels that most other people would easily tolerate without symptoms. In the case of severe reactions, people may become *universally aller-gic* to multiple chemicals. These people may even be unable to tolerate being in the same room with anyone using perfume or after-shave lotion, may not be able to travel in certain vehicles because of the exhaust fumes, and may even be sensi-tive to electromagnetic fields. In extreme cases they may have to live in a rural setting without electricity. Testing for such allergies may require environmentally controlled units in which exposure to toxins can be monitored and controlled. It also requires an alert diagnostician to detect the presence of such allergies. It is estimated that only a small percentage of people who suffer from them are ever identified.[420]

Environmental medicine acknowledges that different people may have similar symptoms with widely varying causes, as well as widely differing symptoms from the same cause. Susceptibility varies not only between individuals but also in the same individual over periods of time. One common pattern is an initial *preadapted, nonadapted* or *"O"* (zero) phase, with initial exposure causing a brief bout of symptoms. This may be followed by an *adapted* or *masked* phase in which the body copes with the allergen without expressing symptoms. With con-tinued exposure and other stresses, more severe symptoms may occur in what is called the *exhaustion* phase. Contributing factors may include: genetic predisposi-tion, nutritional factors, and general health problems (particularly relating to the immune system, digestive system, and emotional stress).

Environmental medicine investigations may also reveal more blatant evidence of chemical poisonings. A striking example is that of sudden infant death syndrome

(SIDS), which has been a mystery since 1950. For no apparent reason, babies between one and six months old have been found dead in their cribs, and SIDS is the leading cause of death in this age group. Lendon Smith and Joseph Hattersley present strongly suggestive evidence that SIDS may in fact be caused by poisonous gasses emitted from mattresses when chemicals used as fire retardants and plastic softeners are metabolized by fungi. The fungi grow in the mattresses due to sweating, urination, and the body heat of the infant. A plastic mattress cover that is impermeable to gasses can prevent these crib deaths. Not a single death has occurred in 100,000 babies sleeping on mattresses that are protected in this way. An inexpensive alternative is to raise the head of the bed by two inches, which leads any gasses to gravitate to the bottom of the crib and away through the bars. A rolled towel can prevent the baby from sliding down the slight incline. (This will not work in a bassinet or baby carriage.). Having the baby sleep face-up is a further preventive measure.

We can't yet cure all diseases, but we're already expert at causing many of them.

– Ashleigh Brilliant

Electromagnetic (EM) pollution is one of the more common but less appreciated subjects of environmental medicine research. There is a growing awareness that environmental EM fields may have deleterious effects.[421]

Beyond the negative health effects of electromagnetic pollution, there can be further problems in buildings that have sealed windows and closed ventilation circuits, where toxic chemicals can build up in the air. These can create a *sick building syndrome* in people who work and live in such environments over a period of time. Symptoms can include headaches, allergies, arthritis, anxiety, tensions, and emotional lability.[422]

Subtle energy environmental medicine

Subtle energies are palpably present in *places* as well as in living organisms. Most of us have had the experience of entering a church or going to a place of natural beauty where we sensed a positive atmosphere, or *positive vibrations*. Likewise, most of us may have entered a room or a place in nature where we felt *negative vibrations*. Some of these vibrations may be the energetic residues of positive human interventions, such as prayer, meditation, and joyous experiences, or of anger, grief, and pain that have been suffered in these locations. Other sources of positive and negative vibrations can derive from earth energies. For example, a dowser might identify negative energy lines that run under a particular part of a room. People who spend a lot of time over such a point might suffer impairments of their biological energy fields, predisposing them to various illnesses such as arthritis, cancer, and emotional upsets.[423]

Self-healing can be extremely helpful to people who suffer from environmental allergies. See imagery and bioenergy exercises in Chapter II-5.

Case: A 54 year-old artist came to me for help because he was had so many allergies that his life was severely restricted. He couldn't tolerate stopping in a gas station or being around people with perfume, and couldn't eat many foods, which produced skin rashes and stomach upsets. By using simple visualizations of an energy shield protecting him from the allergens he reduced his sensitivity significantly. Meridian based therapies eliminated further allergies, enabling him to live a much more normal existence.

Feng Shui is a Chinese system for identifying and accommodating subtle environmental energies. It is very close to Chinese Medicine in its principles.[424] Various elements are considered in analyzing the subtle energies of a room or building, such as the position of doorways, windows, and stairs; magnetic compass orientation; color schemes; and the dates of birth of the occupants. Analyses are made based on a system of the *five elements* (fire, earth, metal, water, and wood), and according to a standard map, or *bagua,* that identifies areas within a room that are associated with aspects of the occupants' lives. (See Figure II-10.)

Figure II-10. The Bagua

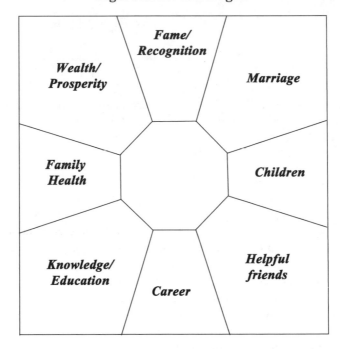

Global ecological healing

Health care workers have mostly focused on treating the *effects* of pollution and environmental toxins, but there is a growing awareness of the need to address these problems on a national and planetary level, both directly and through political reforms. This subject diverges too far from the general focus of this book, so I have recommended some reference works in the endnotes.[425]

Training and licensing: There is no formal training or licensing in environmental medicine.

Clinical applications: Environmental medicine can be enormously helpful in diagnosing and treating aspects of chronic fatigue syndrome and multiple allergy syndromes. In its more subtle aspects, it can enhance the esthetic and energetic ambience of work, home and play environments. Subtle environmental interventions can improve health and are said to bring good luck as well. In the Far East, no builder would begin construction of a house without consulting an expert in subtle environmental energies.

Consultation with a therapist trained in this field can be invaluable in identifying and dealing with environmental irritants. Self-healing is also possible for those who have the mind-set and patience for detective work, and typical methods include carefully watching your diet and exposure to potential allergens.

THE FELDENKRAIS METHOD

Learning must be undertaken and is really profitable when the whole frame is held in a state where smiling can turn into laughter without interference, naturally, spontaneously.
– Moshe Feldenkrais (1985, p. xiii)

Moshe Feldenkrais (1972; Feldenkrais/ Kimmey), an Israeli physicist of Russian origin, developed methods of movement that enhance people's awareness of how they live in their bodies. I was very impressed with how keenly he observed the most minute aspects of posture and movement, and how he could detect the smallest misalignments of posture or the tiniest signs of strained motion in his pupils' bodies. In exercises of *awareness through movement*, Feldenkrais practitioners guide pupils through sequences of simple motions, such as walking or reaching out with their hands, and use these exercises as the basis for teaching body awareness. *Functional integration* adds the light touch of the practitioner to shift pupils' movements towards healthier patterns. Changes in unproductive habits depend upon pupils' altered awareness and actions rather than upon the teachers' manipulations.

Research on the Feldenkrais method has shown improvements in the health of people with chronic rheumatoid arthritis (Narula), and enhanced physical movements in healthy people (Jackson-Wyatt et al.; Greta/ Kegerries). Clinical reports of its efficacy can be found in review articles on pain management and physical therapy.[426]

Adverse effects: No harmful effects have been reported See discussion of potential general negative effects from rapid improvements under Spiritual Healing.

Training and licensing: There are Feldenkrais practitioners in many countries, including about 1,000 in the US and Canada. Training lasts 3-4 years. There are no standards for training or licensing in this method.

Clinical applications: The Feldenkrais method is helpful in sports; the performing arts; physical therapy; musculoskeletal pain management; neurological damage, and the like.

A therapist is essential for instruction and guidance in Feldenkrais exercises. Self-healing exercises are usually taught and included in the therapy.

See also: Alexander Technique; Bodymind Therapies; Rubenfeld therapy.

FITNESS

> *Walking is man's best medicine.*
> – Hippocrates

Physical fitness is one of the best preventive medicines. It is an aspect of health care that each of us can adapt to our own particular inclinations, abilities, needs and circumstances. Exercise keeps the cardiovascular and musculoskeletal systems in good tone, provides a release for physical and psychological tensions, and is an excellent natural antidepressant.

Rhythmic exercises can be a form of meditation, and a regular exercise regimen promotes mental and emotional discipline.

Particular methods of exercise can promote self-healing, such as Yoga, T'ai Chi Ch'uan, and Qigong. Some aspects of these practices appear to incorporate biological energy activations and healing effects that go well beyond the simple exercise of heart and muscles.[427]

Exercise can also provide a doorway into spiritual awareness, via peak experiences (Murphy/ White). People who exercise regularly report that at some point in their physical exertions they may enter a perceptual space where they are exquisitely aware of every cell and muscle in their body, and of their relationship to everything around them. This has been called *experiencing the flow*. Equestrians report that they become one with their mounts. Time seems to slow down in the flow of peak experiences, and you are able to savor every tiny nuance of movement. It is as though you know exactly how everything within and around you works together harmoniously. Having had a peak experience, you may come away knowing that you are an intimate part of something far vaster than your little, physical self.

Research has confirmed that regular exercise is particularly helpful for prevention of cardiovascular problems. Exercise can be a treatment for depression that is equivalent in efficacy to antidepressant medications (Babyak et al.).

Adverse effects: Muscle, tendon and joint pains and injuries are possible with too vigorous exercises. Consultation with a trainer is advised when beginning a course of fitness training or when developing a strenuous exercise program.

Training and licensing: Sports medicine is practiced by physicians. Fitness education and training is not a licensed profession.

Clinical applications: Graded exercises are advised for building muscle strength and cardiac tone.

By definition this is a self-healing method. The guidance of a fitness instructor may be helpful in developing an exercise program.

See also: Qigong; T'ai Chi Ch'uan; Yoga.

> *Spiritual fitness: Exercise daily – walk with the Lord.*
> – Anonymous

FLOWER ESSENCES

> *To see a world in a grain of sand*
> *And a heaven in a wild flower*
> *Hold infinity in the palm of your hand*
> *And eternity in an hour.*
> – William Blake (1803)

Edward Bach,[428] a Harley Street physician, identified flowers whose essences have curative powers. The essences from these flowers are prepared in somewhat similar manner as homeopathic remedies, except that they are not succussed (shaken) and cannot be diluted more than a few times before they lose their potency. As in homeopathy, there are two methods that are used to identify applications for flower essences. The first is through clinical testing on healthy people and on patients with dis-ease/ disease. The second relies on the intuitive perceptions of gifted sensitives who are able to identify medicinal properties of plants clairsentiently (Barnao/ Barnao; B. Lee).

The flower remedies are intended to correct psychological problems as well as disharmonies between the personality and the higher self and soul. This method could be likened to a transpersonal homeopathy. Flower essences are widely used, and while they are available over the counter (Bach; Scheffer), consultation with a flower essence specialist can provide much more sophisticated prescriptions than a layperson is likely to choose. For instance, within the Bach remedies there are five different essences that could be used for treatment of depression, depending on associated feelings such as agitation, withdrawal, anger and other parameters.

Rescue Remedy, a combination of five Bach flower essences, is a popular treatment for stress and trauma, and it is available in drops or as a topical cream. This preparation can be a good personal introduction to the efficacy of flower remedies. Taken orally it calms anxiety and panic, counteracts emotional and physical shock, reduces pain and swelling following injuries, and more. Applied topically it reduces the pain, swelling and blistering of burns and other injuries.

Case: A personal experience with our cat, Cuddles, illustrates the effectiveness of this remedy. One day, a very aggressive stray cat settled into our quiet neighborhood in Devon, on the Southwest coast of England. It bullied Cuddles in our back yard and even came in through the cat-flap at night, got into fights with Cuddles, and had the audacity to spray all over our CD rack! Cuddles was traumatized by the intrusions and aggressive attacks, and became excessively anxious and clinging. For two days she would not separate from us other than to relieve herself in very brief trips outside. She was constantly under foot, tripping us up in the kitchen to the point where she was getting stepped on and we were in danger of falling over her. We decided to give her some Rescue Remedy, and after one dose her behavior changed dramatically. She became calmer, stopped clinging to us, and went outside in a manner more like her usual behavior. She needed several doses daily over a period of several weeks until the situation with the stray was resolved.

In the past few decades, numerous new essences have been developed from plants, gems and minerals on several continents..[429] Plants from places that are unpolluted with pesticides, chemical fertilizers or toxic wastes are more potent.

There are books that detail the indications for many of the flower essences. When the therapist recommends a remedy it is often helpful to have clients read the descriptions of the therapeutic indications and anticipated results, to help develop cognitive insights that can then enhance their responses to the essences.[430]

A recent development is the topical application of flower essences for treatment of various physical and psychological problems.[431] It is hypothesized that the vibrational energies of the flower essences interact with acupuncture points, thereby influencing the body's bioenergies. It may be that the flower energies also interact in a more general way with the bioenergy field, not necessarily through acupressure points. This application opens new ways of studying localized pains and other symptoms. By referring to flower essence topical maps of the body (D. Kramer 1995a; 1995b) it may be possible to identify psychological conflicts that underlie symptoms at a particular body location.

Flower essences may also be prescribed intuitively in cooperation with the client. The therapist will take a history and recommend essences on the basis of their known therapeutic effects, and will also use intuition to select additional essences. In addition, clients may be encouraged to pick essences for which they sense a particular affinity. While this may seem unusual in terms of conventional practice, several factors recommend this approach. First, there are no negative side effects of these essences – they either are beneficial or produce no apparent effects – so there is no risk involved. Second, there may be subtle reasons for taking certain essences that are not apparent to logic or forethought.

Skeptics may criticize such practices, saying that the benefits claimed for this treatment are due to nothing more than suggestion. I believe that suggestion is an excellent adjunct to any therapy, and can enhance people's responses to treatments of all sorts. The fact that suggestion may be present does not rule out the possibility that the flower essences are also effective in and of themselves.

The essences are far more than chemicals that interact with the physical body. In the realms of energy medicine, the flower essences appear to have their effects at the psychological and spiritual ends of the continuum of wholistic interventions.

Steve Johnson, who developed the Alaskan flower essences, observes:

Flower essences catalyze evolution in consciousness. They help us identify emotional and mental qualities within that need to be awakened or strengthened, and stimulate our spiritual growth, which is the ongoing process of grounding our spiritual selves into our physical bodies.

Flower essences are unique in that they are a source of intelligent healing energy that is available to both empower and educate the person taking them. They are empowering because they do not do our healing work for us, but with us – they are powerful catalysts for growth and change but they respect our free will. They are educational because they reveal the causal level of our problems and difficulties. Flower essences illuminate the inner landscape of our psyches and direct our awareness to the conflicting issues and patterns of resistance that are contributing to our dis-ease. They then offer us the precise levels of support we require to resolve our conflicts and release these discordant energies, gently and completely, from our lives. They are like gentle teachers showing us who we really are, and reminding us of our oneness with all life.

The gift of the plant kingdom is spiritual consciousness. Flowers are the most evolved part of this kingdom and carry positive, life-affirming patterns of conscious energy. These patterns originate in the higher dimensions and are expressed into our physical world through the specific form of each plant... (p. 5)

Research: Jeffrey Cram (1999a; b) reports controlled, double-blind studies on various combinations of flower essences that are commonly used for treating stress. These include the Bach five-flower essence[432] and Yarrow formula.[433] Math exercises were the stressors in in one study, and exposure to fluorescent lights in another. Electromyograms, which are used as a measure of stress, showed significant decreases of muscular tension over the mastoid processes and the chest[434] following treatment with the essences, as compared with the placebo.

Adverse effects: Flower essence practitioners claim there are no adverse effects from these remedies, other than disappointment if they are not as effective as one had hoped.

Training and licensing: The various flower essence traditions are taught in workshops that are not standardized. Flower essence therapy is not licensed.

Clinical applications: Flower essences may be of benefit in treating most physical and psychological problems, in a manner and range similar to homeopathy. Flower essences lend themselves particularly to treatment of psychological and spiritual aspects of illness.

Healers can enhance the efficacy of herbal remedies by giving healing to the remedies themselves.

While you may take essences as recommended in books, and while Rescue Remedy is helpful in dealing with physical and emotional stress, the guidance of a flower essence practitioner can markedly enhance and deepen the effects of essences, through knowledgeable selection and combinations of the remedies. There are also many ranges of essences, so a layperson may not be aware of the particular ones that might be most helpful.

See also: Homeopathy.

> *And the day came when the risk to remain tight in a bud was more painful than the risk it took to blossom.*
> – Anais Nin

HAIR ANALYSIS

Mineral analysis of hair samples is believed by some CAM practitioners to provide an index of states of health. Hair analysis has been fairly well accepted for identifying heavy metal toxicity, but in other applications there have been problems in standardization of measurements (Seidel et al.).

Research: I am aware of no research to confirm the validity of hair analysis other than in heavy metal poisonings.

Adverse effects: Relying on an unproven method of analysis in assessing problems and making therapy decisions is dangerous.

HEALING TOUCH (HT)

Healing Touch, developed by Janet Mentgen, was similar in its initial practice to Therapeutic Touch, but HT healers have diverged from TT to include chakra diagnosis and treatment; the use of pendulums to augment intuitive awareness; meditation, other forms of self-healing, spiritual awareness; and a variety of other approaches. Healing energy is perceived as being channeled through the healer from a universal source.

Research: HT is the second most researched healing modality, after Therapeutic Touch. HT has been shown in quantitative and qualitative studies to help in treatment of pain (fibromyalgia, post-surgical, cancer); shorter hospitalization after coronary bypass; chemotherapy (pain, mood, fatigue, BP); anxiety (in PTSD of abused women; nursing students), depression, mobility after knee replacement; improvements in chronic spasticity; enhanced immune function in AIDS; behavioral improvement in Alzheimer's Disease and in dementia; enhanced quality of life, and improved interpersonal wellbeing in hospice.

Adverse effects: No harmful effects have been reported See discussion of potential general negative effects from rapid improvements under Spiritual Healing.

Training and Licensing: Healing Touch International offers training and certification courses.

See also: Spiritual healing; Therapeutic Touch, Volume I of *Healing Research.*

HERBAL REMEDIES

See: Herbal Remedies under Nutrition.

HOMEOPATHY

> *...Hahnemann stumbled upon a phenomenon that is barely beginning to be understood by modern physics, a dynamic that might be likened to spirit, information or meaning in matter...*
> – Edward Whitmont (1993, p. 7)

Samuel Hahnemann (1755-1843), a physician of German origin, developed a system for treatment through a sort of immunization process. He believed that the body could learn to deal with symptoms of an illness if it was given minute quantities of substances that produce similar symptoms in a healthy person.

Hahnemann developed this approach after noticing that when he ingested quinine in order to observe its effects on a healthy person, he developed intermittent bouts of fevers, chills and weakness. These symptoms are very similar to those of malaria, for which quinine is a remedy.

Homeopathic evaluation begins with a detailed listing of symptoms. These are organized into personality types and diagnostic categories that make little sense in terms of conventional medicine. Homeopathic remedies are prescribed for *syndromes* rather than for individual symptoms. These include the presenting illness, personality factors in the patient, past traumas of a physical and/ or emotional nature, relationships with others (particularly parents), likes and dislikes, and much more. The syndromes are then organized into *remedy symptom clusters*.

The patient is not placed in a diagnostic box defined by the patho-physiological or psychological causalities that are presumed to produce the illness according to conventional Western concepts of disease. For instance, symptoms such as inertia or lack of will are viewed in allopathic medicine as defects of character or motivation. In homeopathy, these symptoms are approached as further aspects of disharmony, in addition to other empirically derived symptom clusters for which specific remedies may be effective treatments.

The remedies prescribed are minute doses of substances that would cause similar symptoms to those presented by the patient if these remedies were given to healthy people . Under the stimulus of these substances, the body can learn to handle the symptoms competently instead of being overwhelmed by them as it had been previously. Oddly, this method is successful even when a person is currently suffering from the very same symptoms that are being treated. A clear example is found in the treatment of laboratory rats poisoned with lead. When given homeopathic microdoses of lead, the rats excreted greater amounts of lead in their urine than did untreated rats (Fisher/ Capel). Similarly, homeopathic arsenic provides protection against arsenic poisoning (Mallick et al).

Homeopathic remedies are developed in two ways. In *conventional homeopathy*, agents that might be therapeutic are given to healthy people in order to study their clinical effects (T. Allen). This is termed *proving.* The symptoms produced are then presumed to be treatable in ill people by giving them diluted solutions of these substances. *Intuitive homeopathy* relies on the clairsentient perceptions of highly sensitive individuals who are able to intuitively assess the therapeutic properties of the substances.[435] While clinical effectiveness of intuitive remedies have been reported, research to substantiate their efficacy has so far been limited to a single study, which had negative fidings (R. McCarney, et al.). [436]

Two broad approaches to treatment
Classical homeopathy advocates the prescription of a single remedy, which may be given in one large dose. They choose the remedy very carefully, considering in particular the personality type of the client. This may bring about major changes in symptoms, in underlying illnesses, in psychological awareness, and even in personality, over a period of several months. A repeat dose of the high potency remedy, taken weeks or months later, may be added in some cases. A gentler approach may also be taken within classical homeopathy, prescribing less potent doses of the single remedy, which is then repeated over several weeks or months.

Allopathic-style homeopathy prescribes one or more remedies in repeated doses over periods of days or weeks, with periodic reassessments and adjustments or substitutions of other remedies.

In both approaches, additional remedies are added as the original symptom patterns shift and new patterns arise. The effects of homeopathic remedies can be antidoted (counteracted or stopped) by drinking coffee.

A case example will help to illustrate how homeopathy is prescribed for a specific problem in a particular person.[437]

Case: "Patricia" was an intense, loquacious, passionate person who was very jealous and frequently angry and sarcastic with her lover. She had a history of migraines, pharyngitis, tonsillitis, and colitis. She hated having anything tight around her throat. She frequently woke with a feeling of being suffocated at night, especially when she was falling asleep. She came for help because her PMS symptoms (irritability, jealousy, depression, headache, hot flushes) had become a major problem for her, and they were threatening her relationship. She also mentioned in passing that she always had diarrhea before her menses.

Patricia's homeopath recognized that this pattern of symptoms points to the remedy Lachesis (a snake venom remedy), which has among its profile of indications the following items that appeared to fit Patricia's profile: [438]

Mental – Passionate, intense people; Jealousy; Loquacity,
  Anger Sarcasm.
Head – Migraine headaches.
Throat – Pharyngitis; tonsillitis; Intolerance to tight collars,
  turtlenecks, necklaces.
Gastrointestinal – Colitis; Diarrhea before menses
Urogenital – Premenstrual syndrome, including irritable,
  jealous, depressed, headache, flushes of heat.
Chest – Wakes with suffocating feeling at night, especially on
  falling asleep.

Patricia was given one dose of 200C Lachesis. When she came back for her next appointment in a month, she reported that her PMS symptoms just didn't happen this month, and that oddly she also did not have diarrhea before her menses. Upon inquiry, she also noted that she was waking much less rarely with that old feeling of suffocation, and that she just wasn't feeling as jealous anymore. (Steele)

While such combinations of symptoms as a treatable entity appear strange in conventional medicine, this is no reason to reject homeopathy. It is, rather, a criticism of the narrowness and exclusivity of conventional medical thinking and practice.

  It is of historical interest that the practice of homeopathy originally spread rapidly in Europe, the US, Asia, and South America. It was very popular and widely used in the US at the end of the 19th century. It was credited with more than halving the mortality rate from cholera in London in 1854, and from yellow fever during a US epidemic in 1878. There were 22 homeopathic medical schools and over 100 homeopathic hospitals in the US prior to the publication of the Flexner Report in 1910. This report, which was promoted through lobbying by medical doctors, established guidelines for funding allopathic medical schools and led to a rapid decline in the practice of homeopathy, almost to the point of its disappearance in the US. (Naturopathic medical treatment met the same fate.) In Great Britain, the practice of homeopathy was also much reduced but not eliminated. Several homeopathic hospitals remain, and the Royal Family's support of homeopathy has helped to encourage its use.

  In recent years, clinical research demonstrating the efficacy of homeopathy has helped bring about a resurgence in its popularity in the US, Europe, Asia and Latin America. Several American states have homeopathic licensing boards for physicians.

Homeopathic remedies are usually prepared by dissolving small amounts of a medication, mineral or allergen in a mixture of alcohol (generally 87% ethanol) and water. Water may also be used alone, or it is sometimes mixed with other preservatives (especially for alcohol-intolerant patients). Serial dilutions of 1/ 10 or 1/ 100 and greater are prepared, and then *potentized* by *succussion* (shaking). The solutions are identified by their degree of dilution. For example the designation of 6c (or C6) means that the substance was diluted by 1/ 10 successively 6 times; 30c is diluted 30 times, etc. Dilutions of as little as one original volume per million (1M) are available. *In contrast with conventional medications, the greater the homeopathic dilution, the greater the potency of the preparation.*[439] For modern commercial purposes mechanical vortexing is used rather than hand-held succussion, as in earlier days. While it might appear from a Western scientific standpoint that the process of vortexing can be standardized, there are sensitive homeopaths who feel that the attitudes of company personnel who manage the vortexing may make a difference in the qualities of the remedies.

Clinical studies (W.E. Boyd 1946) and laboratory tests (Davenas et al.; Resch/ Guttman) demonstrated that a succussed remedy was effective, whereas an unsuccussed one was not. Ten seconds of succussing suffices to potentize a solution. Heating potentized solutions to 70-80 degrees Centigrade inactivates them (Davenas et al.). Another unusual observation is that loss of potency in aging solutions can be reversed by repeated succussion (R. Jones/ Jenkins).

Potency can be demonstrated in remedies that are so dilute that they could not contain even a single molecule of the original substance (Davenas et al.; R. Smith/ Boericke 1968). Studies using nuclear magnetic resonance have also shown alterations in homeopathic solutions (T. Young).

Another counter-intuitive observation is that the more dilute the remedy, the more potent are its clinical effects. This is very different from conventional medications, where we are used to seeing greater potency with *less* dilute medications. Jacques Benveniste (2000) and other homeopaths suggest that there is a bioenergetic pattern carried by water which brings about the observed healing effects.

A further strange but repeatedly observed phenomenon is that there the efficacy of homeopathic treatments rises and falls repeatedly as the remedies are progressively diluted. That is to say, an effect observed with initial dilutions disappears when greater dilutions are used, then reappears when even greater dilutions are applied, etc. This waxing and waning of effectiveness continues in a regular pattern with increasing dilutions.[440]

Another class of homeopathic remedies is prepared from materials associated with disease. These include *nosodes* (from infected tissue), *sarcodes* (from noninfected tissue in an organism that has an infection), and *isopathy* (from infectious agents). Homeopathy was widely used to prevent and treat infections prior to the discovery of antibiotics (Shepard), and recent studies confirm that homeopathy can indeed prevent infections.

Many homeopaths feel that immunizations are a common contributor to chronic illness. It is believed that they can contribute to later development of neurological diseases, arthritis, chronic fatigue syndrome, and more. Conventional medicine does not accept this view (Glickman-Simon). A homeopathic approach to preventing latent side effects of immunizations is to prescribe homeopathic preparations of the immunization substances prior to and following conventional immunizations (Pasche 2000).[441]

Let's look at two more case studies that demonstrate homeopathy in practice.

Case No. 1: A nine year old boy was brought to the homeopath by his mother because he was being disruptive in school – humming and singing, getting out of his seat, standing on his chair, not paying attention to his teacher, and staring out the window over extended periods. He lacked motivation, disliked and avoided schoolwork, and refused to do homework. At home he was messy and disorganized, never shared toys with others, and was unfriendly and sometimes aggressive with his peers. His mother reported that if he read a problem from a book he would be unable to do it, but when he heard the problem spoken by someone he could solve it correctly. Surprisingly, he was still getting good grades at school. The presumptive diagnosis was that he had an attention deficit hyperactivity disorder (ADHD).

The boy was never angry, and had no strong cravings (e.g. would eat whatever his mother fixed). His mother felt that he was abnormal because nothing seemed to excite him.

In the homeopathic interview, the child was cooperative and pleasant but seemed only partly present. However, when talking about his best friend, he became quite animated. His mother was astounded by this, saying: "Aside from seeing that boy in church, he has played with him only once in the whole year."

His mother had had no problems with the pregnancy or delivery, but she had smoked marijuana for 11 years and had stopped only when she learned that she was pregnant.

Homeopathic *Cannabis indica* (marijuana) in a single, very potent (1M) dose was prescribed because of the history of cannabis use by the boy's mother in very early pregnancy, combined with his present time-perception distortions and general spaciness. (The basic homeopathic principle holds that the correct homeopathic prescription should be for a substance which produces symptoms similar to those exhibited by the patient.) Within a month the boy's ability to focus improved dramatically; he did homework without reminders, and showed enthusiasm for particular foods.

Over the course of a year his behavior remained improved, but then it began to deteriorate. Once again he was not completing his work, and he seemed less motivated. Another single 1M dose was given, resulting in a renewed remission of his symptoms.[442]

The art of homeopathy is to select out key factors that are amenable to interventions of this sort. Other homeopaths might have prescribed different remedies, addressing different constellations of factors. A good homeopath will have an encyclopedic knowledge of the clusters of effects of various substances, so that the remedies can be matched to the symptom clusters of the patient. Computer programs can be a great help in suggesting remedies, as it is impossible for any one person to know the entire homeopathic pharmacopoeia.

Homeopathy can be a very intricate, wholistic art, as illustrated in the next case, in which the symptom complex addressed by the remedy, Calcium Carbonate, includes physical, psychological, biological energies and metaphorical patterns.

Case No. 2: Edward Whitmont (1993, p., 74) beautifully illustrates the blending of symptom, substance and symbol in the clinical case of a man of about 40, whom I will call "Henry," who suffered from acne.

After taking a detailed history, Whitmont prescribed a single dose of calcium carbonate (extracted from oyster shells) at a dilution of C1,000. This produced temporary spasms of the finger muscles, similar to tetany. This is a typical symptom of parathyroid gland dysfunction, which would produce lower blood calcium levels. The spasms evoked memories from Henry's childhood, when his mother had taped his fingers to his bedside in a position that resembled that of the spasms he experienced from the homeopathic calcium carbonate. His mother had done this to prevent him from masturbating. During the treatment, vivid memories arose in Henry of his anger and shame connected with this experience. As a child he had completely repressed these memories in his unconscious mind. This somehow was translated into his skin condition and a boisterous personality. With the release of these memories, the spasms in his fingers also released, and this healing process furthered his progress in psychotherapy.

> …Shame, anger, finger spasm, parathyroid hormonal activity, calcium metabolism, the dynamic field of the 9oyster (in homeopathic practice the "personality of the *Calc. Carb.* Type can be likened to an oversensitive but heavily defended person, akin to an oyster without or with too thick a shell) and the functioning of the skin all appear here as different transduction codes of one and the same dynamic field process. (Whitmont 1993, p. 74-75)

As Whitmont eloquently points out, it may be impossible to clarify many of the complexities of linked energetic and imagery components that produce these effects. Every remedy has its particular spectrum of effects – its *personality*. When a person has a cluster of symptoms and personality traits that match those of a particular remedy, then that remedy can effect a clearing of those symptoms, and it may also alter the accompanying personality traits. The art and challenge of the practice of homeopathy is to ask the right questions in order to identify the relevant symptom clusters. If the homeopath did not ask the patient about specific related symptoms, many of which might not be at all obvious or likely to be reported spontaneously, the best remedy could easily be missed.

Self-help with homeopathy: Some homeopaths encourage patients to prescribe for themselves, and health food stores carry many common remedies in lower potencies as well as books on homeopathy for the layperson. However, while people may benefit from particular over-the-counter remedies for certain problems, these preparations may easily miss the mark with more serious or pervasive problems, as would a prescription from a therapist who does not have thorough training in homeopathy. Computers may be a great help in identifying symptom clusters and potentially relevant remedies.

Intuitive prescription of homeopathic remedies, in which the therapist allows their unconscious mind and psi powers to scan for relevant details, may offer distinct advantages in selecting the best remedies from amongst the thousands that are available. Similarly, muscle testing and other intuitive approaches may be used for self-help to identify appropriate remedies. Dowsing and radionics, two other systems of intuitive assessment, are sometimes used for the same purposes.[443]

Research: *Clinical research* on homeopathy is complicated by the fact that the remedies are prescribed on an individualized basis for each person. Although two patients may have the same *medical diagnosis*, such as a streptococcal sore throat, each might expect to receive a different homeopathic medication depending upon their symptoms, personalities, and life experiences. In contrast, conventional medicine usually prescribes the same medication for all patients with a given diagnostic problem. Despite these difficulties, some homeopathic research has managed to conform to the requirements of randomized controlled studies.

The majority of comparative reviews of series of controlled trials conclude that significant clinical efficacy for homeopathic remedies has been demonstrated,[444] although three critical reviews conclude that there is only limited evidence for clinical efficacy.[445] The study that is generally acknowledged to be the most carefully designed and executed is that of David Taylor-Reilly et al. (1986), which shows a 50% reduction in the need for antihistamine medication in the treatment of hay fever.[446] Other studies have shown significant effects of homeopathy in treating arthritis (Gibson et al.); asthma (Reilly et al. 1994); Attention Deficit Hyperactivity Disorder (Lamont); fibrositis (Fisher et al. 1989); influenza (Ferley); and childhood diarrhea (G. Jacobs et al. 1994; 2000). Another study of arthritis showed that standardized doses of *Rhus Toxicodendron*, were ineffective for this condition (Shipley et al. 1983). However, the research protocol that prescribes the same dose of homeopathic medication for every patient is contrary to basic homeopathic practice. Other studies confirm that homeopathy can prevent infectious diseases,[447] and a single report shows some efficacy in treatment of attention deficit disorders (Lamont).

Research on treatment using minute doses of homeopathic medications has shown that they do produce observable effects. Within the context of Western scientific practice, it has been hard to accept that serial dilutions of substances can possibly have any medicinal effects, particularly since dilutions beyond C30 cannot contain even a single molecule of the original substance. Skeptics propose that even in double-blind controlled studies there must have been hidden suggestive effects to produce such results. It is therefore reassuring to find studies on cells in laboratory cultures, bacteria, yeasts, plants and animals that also show significant effects.[448]

The principles of homeopathy may also be relevant to other areas of medicine. A rigorous meta-analysis was made of 135 studies on the protection of organisms from poisoning by environmental toxins, using dilutions of C30 or greater (Linde, et al. 1994). This meta-analysis included studies of animals (70%), plants (22%), isolated organs (5%), and cell and embryo cultures (3%). Of the 26 studies that met the reviewers' stringent criteria for design and reporting, 70% showed positive effects.[449]

Even more fascinating and also relevant to the energy medicine thesis of this book, is a study by P. C. Endler of homeopathic dilutions of thyroid hormone that produced significant effects on climbing behavior in frogs. In this study the remedy was entirely encased in a glass tube that was simply held near the frogs. This suggests even more clearly that homeopathy is a subtle energetic intervention.

In the treatment of human health problems, a major consideration in prescribing homeopathic remedies is the personality of the subject. B. Brewitt et al. used the Myers-Briggs Type Indicator (MPTI) to look for personality types that might be more prone to using and benefiting from homeopathy. In their homeopathy user sample of 125 people (29 healthy; 76 HIV+, mostly homosexual) they found significantly higher personality test scores on the intuitive vs. the sensing scales, as compared to general population norms for these tests (p < .001). Similarly, they found higher scores for feeling over thinking (p < .001), despite the predominance of males in their sample. It is unclear to what degree these findings reflect homeopathy preference and to what extent they may reflect attitudes of homosexual men.[450]

Basic research shows that the water in very dilute homeopathic solutions differs significantly from plain water and from water with salts dissolved in it (Benveniste website; Migron).

The above-mentioned research clearly just begins to scratch the surface of the mystery of energy healing that could transform our understanding of the world when we finally solve it.

Theories: Homeopaths assert that the material world, living organisms, and consciousness are all intimately connected. Particular material substances have constellations of characteristics that become evident when they are used to treat people (animals, plants, etc.). When a group of healthy people ingest a homeopathic substance they will experience a range of symptoms, thus *proving* the characteristics of that substance. These symptoms may be either physical or psychological (P. Bailey).

The fact that very high dilutions of homeopathic substances are potent (even when diluted beyond the point where not even a single molecule of the original substance could remain in the solution) has been very challenging to explain – within CAM theoris as well as in conventional scientific explanatory frameworks.

Water may be a much more complex substance than is generally realized, and two Italian physicians have put together an excellent discussion of this subject. The first is Paolo Bellavita, an Associate Professor of General Pathology at Verona University School of Medicine with postgraduate training in biotechnology at the Cranfield Institute of Technology in England, and the second is Andrea Signorini, a medical doctor who also graduated from the Verona Homeopathic School.[451] They propose that the effectiveness of homeopathic remedies may be explained on the basis that water imprinted with energies and/ or information conveys the effects of the remedy, rather than homeopathic remedy effects being due to chemical reactions with the remedy substance. Bellavita and Signorini base their theories on new understanding that is emerging from the study of *complexity theory*. In brief, complexity theory suggests that complex biological systems are more than the sum of their parts. Complex systems, such as those that are modeled on fractal equations, may produce effects that are not predictable on the basis of theories concerning their individual elements. Processes within complex systems may not be reproducible experimentally, as they do not follow linear patterns of interaction. Complex systems may also assume different states, partly depending on the qualities (not just the quantities) of the energies and other components that combine to compose the system.[452]

> *A mind that is stretched by a new idea can never go back to its original dimensions.*
>
> – Oliver Wendell Holmes

David Taylor-Reilly, a physician who completed a Research Fellowship in homeopathy in Glasgow and has personally been a teacher of homeopathy to many physicians in the UK, postulates that homeopathic clinical efficacy may be due to stimulation of the immune system (Taylor-Reilly/ Taylor). To support his hypothesis he cites evidence from experiments with minute doses of various substances that are toxic to the immune system in larger doses, but which produced stimulation of the immune system in microdoses. To explain the efficacy of solutions in which none of the original substance is present, he suggests that information may be stored within the semicrystalline structure of the water that is used as diluent. This last point is echoed by C. Smith.

Others hypothesize that it is not the substance itself that produces the effects (even in initial dilutions that still contain molecules of the substance) but rather a field effect or vibration of that substance (G. Barnard/ Stephenson; Tiller 1983). William Tiller, a Stanford University Professor Emeritus of Material Sciences and Engineering, suggests that this type of vibration acts upon the etheric body.[453] While his writing is difficult to follow for anyone who has not studied quantum physics, it is nevertheless fascinating that quantum physics may be able to explain bioenergy medicine.

> A key postulate is that the condition of health occurs when each type of physical chemical in the *physical* body has a chemical counterpart in the *etheric* body at the appropriate concentration ratio, CE_j/ CP_j, of the j species. Disharmony leading to disease is thought to occur when this ratio is out of balance. Balance may be restored by either increasing or decreasing the j chemical constituent at the physical level; i.e., by manipulating CP_j. Present allopathic medicine utilizes the "increase" mode. The "decrease" mode is not generally possible, although recent studies with blood filtration is a step in the proper direction. Balance may also be restored by increasing or decreasing a chemical constituent at the etheric level; i.e., by manipulating CE_j. Homeopathic remedies deal with the increase mode and no apparent method exists at this level for the decrease mode. A potentized remedy is, in fact, the etheric counterpart of the physical constituent that has reached toxic proportions in the body and has produced the specific symptoms. Thus, by combining both allopathic and homeopathic procedures in the increase mode, all values of the ratio CE_j/ CP_j are possible so that the balanced condition may always be produced.
>
> This can also be looked at from an energy point of view in that each atom is an absorber and radiator of a specific spectrum of energies of the EM or ME variety. Thus, for optimum tuning between the etheric and physical bodies so that energy is most efficiently used, the proper chemical radiators must be available in each body and at a concentration such that the absorption cross-sections for the important specific radiations… are properly impedance matched.

Although many Western scientists find the theories of homeopathy alien to their conventional medical thinking, Daniel Eskinazi (1999) suggests that several aspects of the theories of homeopathy are paralleled by observations that have been made within the context of conventional biomedicine. For instance, several low-dose vs. high-dose responses are well recognized. Very small doses of allergens are used to desensitize people to stronger exposures to the same substances. Therapeutic doses of aspirin lower temperature, while toxic doses can produce hyperthermia, even to a life-threatening degree (L. Goodman/ Gilman). An unusual note from China is that exposure to low levels of radiation offers some protection for animals that are subsequently exposed to higher doses of radiation (Luckey). Another observation is that stimulation of various systems occurs with low doses of some toxic substances, while higher doses of the same substances produce inhibitory effects.[454]

Eskinazi also points out that many of the lower potencies of homeopathic remedies contain active molecules of the medication and have been shown to produce significant clinical effects.

Conversely, in conventional medical research there have been observations of clinical effects with doses so low that no active molecules could have been present. In these studies, serial dilutions of conventional medications are commonly conducted to the endpoint at which no greater effects are noted in the experimental subjects as compared to the controls – in order to establish what is the lowest possible dose that could be used. Researchers assume that studies of even lower concentrations are pointless, and do not explore this possibility. In one study, the lowest concentration[455] of leukotriene (which induces the release of a hormone) produced a stronger effect than a higher dilution. Greater dilutions were then tested and a further peak of activity was identified (Gerozissis et al.). Eskinazi also found other studies in which very low dilutions of conventional preparations were effective. [456]

In the worlds of bioenergetic phenomena, there may be some types of causality that are completely outside the realm of conventional medical concepts. Homeopathy suggests that there can be energetic predispositions to illness that are hereditary, which are known as *miasms*. It is postulated that certain diseases can cause persons who have that disease, *or their descendents*, to develop particular illness patterns or predispositions to illnesses. Examples of diseases that produce miasms include scabies, syphilis, gonorrhea, tuberculosis, cancer, leprosy, rabies, typhoid, ringworm and malaria. Thus, a history of these diseases in patients or their families may be an important element to consider in deciding upon particular homeopathic remedies.

Further metaphysical theories were proposed by the late Edward Whitmont. Whitmont was an amazingly gifted physician, homeopath, and Jungian therapist. The breadth and depth of his understanding of the multi-dimensional aspects of healing is truly awe-inspiring. He added enormously to our appreciation of the mechanisms of action of homeopathic remedies.

Whitmont (1993) proposes that homeopathy is clearly an energy medicine, as evidenced by the following facts:

1. It is effective in potencies that are beyond the thirtieth dilution (the *ultramolecular* range, where not even a single molecule of the original substance remains).

2. Remedies are imperishable. Whitmont had bottles of remedies that were over a hundred years old and were still potent.

3. Any material with which the remedies come in contact becomes a *vehicle* for their medicinal properties.[457] For instance, if a bottle that contained an ul-tramolecular dilution of a remedy is refilled with water, it will transmit the medicinal properties to the fresh water.

4. The effects of remedies radiate to distances of over thirty feet, and can be confirmed through applied kinesiology muscle testing. For instance, if a person has a particular physical dysfunction, their arm muscles will be weak when they are mentally focused on that dysfunction. If a remedy that is helpful in treating that dysfunction is brought near to the person, their muscle strength will be significantly increased.[458]

5. Whitmont points out that correspondences between remedies and dis-ease or disease (in homeopathy and other therapies) may be metaphoric as well as symptomatic.[459] He gives the example of metallic gold. Part of its potency as a remedy may lie in the correspondence of gold with the sun. Intuitively, both gold and the sun are associated with the human heart. Homeopathic gold is indicated as a treatment for excesses in expressions of personality traits, as in an over-scrupulous conscience, a tendency to focus on darker sides of issues and problems, and in vulnerabilities to burnout and tendencies to black depressions. Homeopathic applications of gold include the treatment of disorders of the heart, circulation, bones and joints.

Whitmont also provides excellent discussions on the collective unconscious, pointing out that if we explore the realms of psychotherapy, in dreams and synchronistic occurrences we will find ample evidence that the mind of man has access to all knowledge, through all time. This capacity enables us to diagnose our own illnesses and to identify the root causes of our problems.

Whitmont wisely notes that many physical problems have their origins in emotional traumas. Memories of these traumas are encoded within specific states of consciousness.[460] Therefore accessing and releasing these memories may require alternative states of consciousness, often achieved by invoking emotions that are similar to those that were felt during the original traumas. If the traumas were very severe or occurred during pre-verbal years, and if they have been expressed through the body in physical pathology, homeopathic remedies may be helpful in accessing and releasing them – when they may otherwise be inaccessible.

Whitmont proposes that we can best understand the human condition and homeopathic treatment as manifestations of a holographic universe, in which every living and non-living thing is interconnected with every other thing through subtle and *intricate* dimensions of existence.[461]

Homeopathic remedies, whether based on animate or inanimate matter, restore the innate patterns of people whose physical, psychological or spiritual order has gone awry.

> *...Homeopathy... demonstrates that every possible illness that can affect living organisms has a corollary in some substance that is part of the earth's organism. External substances replicate psychosomatic*

> *patterns and are able to induce pathology when foisted upon the or-*
> *ganism. However, they are also able to cure when applied in the*
> *appropriately diluted or "potentized" form. In a mosaic of unknown*
> *scale, the various states of human consciousness and the ingredients*
> *of the human drama are encoded in various mineral, plant and animal*
> *substances – the unit "particles" of our earth. They slumber in these*
> *materials waiting for their unfolding on the human level.*
>
> – Whitmont 1993 (p.22)

Whitmont points out that within a holographic universe, everything in the cosmos may influence a given organism. Conversely, a given organism is an intimate part of everything in the cosmos. Illness and health are therefore seen from perspectives that differ from those of allopathic medicine and the reductionistic philosophies that underpin it. Holographic understanding so of the universe suggest that in the unfolding of enfolded orders of reality, illness in individuals or groups (such as in epidemics) may serve as challenges that unsettle established orders and make new developments possible. The same may be true of natural disasters.

Whitmont suggests that life is characterized by *entelechy*, which is an Aristotelian term denoting an *inherent goal-directedness*. Though the ultimate goals are often beyond our appreciation, the influence of entelechy is seen in our avid pursuit of excitement and drama and in our vigorous rebellion against boredom. Illnesses are mechanisms for disrupting stultifying patterns. Death – either in miniature (as when we relinquish old patterns of being and behaving) or in major expressions (as when a physical existence on earth comes to an end), is a clearing of the way to invite new patterns and experiences to develop.

This briefest of summaries in no way does justice to the enormous range of wisdom integrated by Whitmont, nor to his style – which is erudite and frequently poetic in its metaphoric richness.

The intuitive and metaphoric applications of homeopathy are being explored by other homeopaths. These are sometimes referred to as the *imponderable* remedies.

Colin Griffiths describes a new intuitive approach that is called *meditative proving*. A group of 13 homeopaths gather for the proving. Only one of them, the *Chair* for that session, knows what the remedy is. All of the participants except for the Chair take the remedy and report their physical, emotional and general states. The Chair then records their observations over a 3-4-hour period of group meditation.

> What became readily apparent was the way a dynamic field seemed to
> be set up in the group as a whole, as though the provers resonated on a
> deeper level, and were able to spontaneously elicit unique insights
> into aspects of the remedy that normally would take years of slow and
> meticulous research. The ensuing empathy created by a group in a
> state of stillness can create a situation of direct cognition bypassing
> our normal rational states of awareness and eliciting a far more direct
> and dynamic identification with the actual object under consideration
> - the remedy in this case.

This proving method is tentative in nature but sufficiently germane to excite new explorations in homeopathy. We would therefore request our fellow homeopaths to invoke freedom from prejudice as their first therapeutic ideal, and put these proving insights to the test of empirical experience.

Griffiths proceeds to discuss the homeopathic remedy that was developed from a piece of concrete taken from the Berlin Wall when it was torn down. The wall was built of concrete, incorporating bricks and other debris that had been gathered after the bombings of World War II. The piece of the wall that was used to develop the remedy was brought to Britain by a German woman who had lived in the UK since childhood. It was given to Griffiths as a curiosity, and it lay in a drawer for about a year till he presented it to a psychic sensitive and homeopath for her intuitive impressions.[462] She instantly felt fear, panic and distress, though she was totally unaware of the source of the little piece of concrete. This encouraged Griffiths to have a homeopathic company prepare a remedy from the stone. When the sensitive was given a dose of a 30c dilution of the Berlin wall preparation she felt that it was so extraordinarily potent that she strongly advised it should be kept separate from other remedies because it might mutate them or antidote them.

The Berlin wall was built in 1961, separating Communist-dominated East Germany from West Berlin, which was a Western enclave buried deep within East Germany. The wall was the product of Communist fears about the infiltration of Western influences, and the source of enormous tensions and conflicts between East and West. Thousands died in attempts to escape to the West, hoping for freedom and reunification with families that had been torn asunder by the war and its aftermath. With the coming of *glasnost* the wall was torn down, releasing large floods of people who had been trapped and powerless to oppose the governing authorities.

Griffiths and other homeopaths have found that the remedy prepared from this highly symbolic material is helpful for treating people who are suffering in various ways from oppression, suppression, depression or repression. An example from Griffith follows.

A 28-year-old woman had been taking homeopathic remedies for several years to treat depression and a number of other complaints. One day she came to the clinic in deep misery, feeling that nothing was right with her, or had ever been right before, or would ever be right thereafter. She felt deprived in her inner life and her relationships, and in particular she felt short-changed by her parents, who had separated when she was a little girl. She complained of always giving and not receiving in return, of being alienated from her loved ones, and of marking time to no purpose. She longed to be protected from the world, feeling that she had never really wished to grow up, and pining for the security of her family and the place of her birth, in Berlin.

The woman was given a single dose of Berlin Wall 30c, and after 3 days she reported that she was quite changed.

> ...She had resolved a number of difficult issues with both her boyfriend and her father and, in the case of the latter, felt that she had

established the first proper communication for years. She had also been offered a decent job, after years of doing indifferent work. She felt as though a wall had been broken through that had stood between herself and the rest of the world. She has not needed to come since.

The obvious alternative explanation of suggestion as the causal agent in this case awaits clarification via controlled studies of such metaphoric remedies.[463]

Debate on homeopathy in the scientific community

In 1984 Jacques Benveniste, a scientist at the Université Paris-Sud (INSERM), submitted a paper to the journal *Nature* describing effects upon white blood cells of antibodies in homeopathic dilution. Because the study was performed to adequate standards of scientific rigor and because it came from a respectable laboratory, it could not be ignored. However, because it contradicted the worldview of John Maddox, the editor of the journal (a journalist with expertise in physics), he demanded that the study be independently replicated before publication. Benveniste complied. After four years he submitted successful replications from laboratories in Canada, Israel, and Italy, and Maddox had no choice but to publish the combined reports (Davenas). However, he appended an "editorial reservation" expressing incredulity regarding these observations, and promised a prompt investigation of the experiments.

> *Scientists, especially when they leave the particular field in which they have specialised, are just as ordinary, pigheaded and unreasonable as anybody else, and their unusually high intelligence only makes their prejudices all the more dangerous...*
> – Hans J. Eysenck (p.108)

Maddox invited Walter Stewart and James Randi (an American stage magician), both confirmed disbelievers and avid debunkers of psi phenomena, to join him in observing replications of Benveniste's work in his Paris laboratory. Three open replications and one with "blinds" were all confirmatory. Three further replications with blinds showed no significant results. Maddox reported that Benveniste had not paid attention to sampling errors, and expressed incredulity that Benveniste had previously rejected some biological samples that did not respond to his system of study, and had found periods of months at a time when the experiments did not work at all. Benveniste complained that Maddox's investigation had been performed by people who were completely unfamiliar with biological research methods. He claimed that they had introduced into the process "a tornado of intense and constant suspicion, fear and psychological and intellectual pressure unfit for scientific work..." Maddox provided no evidence that he had checked with the other laboratories which had replicated the study, nor did he invite the consultation of scientists who were competent in biological research. In July 1988, Maddox rushed to publish his report, which claimed that "'high dilution' experiments (are) a delusion."

The pressure tactics employed by Maddox and his colleagues have been widely decried in the complementary medical literature (e.g. Anthony 1988; MacEoin), where it has been pointed out that biological laboratory studies are subject to variability, and that the *Nature* team was not in any way competent to assess this kind of research.

We would do well to keep in mind the advice of Carl Sagan (1991):

> *It is the responsibility of scientists never to suppress knowledge, no matter how awkward that knowledge is, no matter how much it may bother those in power. We are not smart enough to decide which pieces of knowledge are permissible and which are not.*

Ignoring the hysterical reaction of Maddox, whose "boggle threshold" was obviously exceeded, we can discover in this incident some further hints about aspects of homeopathic effects and energy medicine. Psi phenomena[464] can be inhibited by the presence of negative observers. For instance, fluctuations during laboratory protein flocculation tests (Takata) and industrial experiments on water (Piccardi), were both found to be associated with sunspot activity (Gauquelin 1969).[465] Any of these factors might be influential in homeopathic studies as well.

Initial repetitions of the original study on degranulation of basophils (which influence white cells) produced mixed results (Benveniste 1991), and left many questions unanswered. More recent repetitions by Benveniste and others appear to confirm the original reports.[466]

Lessons from homeopathy
In earlier years the fact that relatively few controlled homeopathic studies had been done led to a suspicion that homeopathy might be riddled with Type I research errors, and could include a significant proportion of experimenter/ placebo effects. Despite masses of clinical reports claiming successes with homeopathic remedies, even in treating chronic conditions that had not responded to wide varieties of other treatments over months and years, skeptics could always question whether the positive results were due to factors other than the remedies. A growing body of controlled trials demonstrating significant effectiveness of homeopathic therapies is gradually remedying this situation. The effects of homeopathic remedies on non-human subjects provide especially strong evidence against the placebo hypothesis.

Various empirical observations on the behavior of homeopathic remedies suggest that we need to keep our minds open to entirely new ways of conceptualizing energy medicine therapies, even if the evidence runs counter to our everyday experience. The potency demonstrated in solutions that cannot contain even a single molecule of the original substance suggests that the potentizing material either *chemically* patterns the solution in which it is prepared, or patterns an *energy template* onto the diluent or onto the diluent's energy field. Three facts suggest that the latter explanation is more likely:

1. potency is observed when none of the potentizing substance is present;
2. stale solutions may be revitalized by succussion; and
3. the potency of remedies waxes and wanes with increasing dilutions.

Evidence from other branches of energy medicine which is detailed in this volume also suggests the influence of energy interactions in the treatment of disease.

To say... that a man is made up of certain chemical elements is a sat-
isfactory description only for those who intend to use him as a
fertilizer.

– H. J. Muller

Spiritual healing and homeopathy

Spiritual healing overlaps with homeopathy in several areas.

Spiritual healing can alter the spectrophotometric properties of water – apparently producing an energy effect upon the water.[467] One must wonder whether
this is comparable to the changes in water that occur with homeopathic remedies.
The similarity would be closer if succussion of remedies was done by hand, but it
is done with automated shaking machines.

Kirlian photographs of water that has been treated by healers, water left in
churches, and water drawn from "healing" springs produce an altered image as
compared to "normal" water (Dean 1987; 1989).[468]

Elsewhere in this chapter I discuss the use of electroacupuncture devices for
intuitive assessments, and in Chapter II-4 I review the use of *radionics* devices
that can project spiritual healing effects. Various dials are set on the machine to
attune it to healing bioenergy frequencies. Similar devices have been developed
for the preparation of homeopathic remedies (M. Rae). Spiritual healing works
through the mental intent of the healer. It is speculated that the operators of the
radionics devices may be using their intuitive gifts unconsciously to tune these
devices and to project healing.

Radionics may have other overlaps with homeopathy. In India, a system of radionic diagnosis with projection of healing via homeopathic remedies has been
practiced for several decades (Rae; Narayani/ Ananda). The operator uses a series
of cards with coded homeopathic patterns to imprint tablets with the homeopathic
remedy vibrations. While this process may stretch the belief systems of Western
science, it is supported by anecdotal reports of excellent responses.[469] Later in
this chapter we will consider the processes of visualization whereby the mind
may influence the body, and in Chapter I-3 we reviewed psychokinesis (mind
influencing matter) research. These may be further mechanisms or contributing
factors in energy-medication phenomena. It may be possible to imprint a remedy
effect on water through imagery or mental intent.

The report of the late Sigrun Seutemann (Stelter) in which she noted changes in
the auras of patients who had been given homeopathic treatments, and similar
reports of other sensitives (including Cayce) regarding the efficacy of homeopathic treatments add further clues that energy phenomena may be involved in
these processes.

We may also find that as we move into treatments involving realities beyond
sensory perception (LeShan 1974a; 1976), evidence from individual case studies
may merit greater credence due to the *nature of knowing* in other realities. Intuitive perceptions provide immediate, direct psychic perceptions of people's
conditions and of changes in their conditions. As we gain further experience from
intuitive explorations of our world, we may come to trust intuitive observations as
valid evidence for healing effects. The case is of course stronger when multiple

observers participate in intuitive observations so that such explorations can be consensually validated.

Electromagnetic and other analogues of homeopathy

Jacques Benveniste now reports that he can record EM analogues of homeopathic and conventional medications that are clinically effective. Samples of the active therapeutic ingredients are placed between two electrodes, one of which emits white noise while the other records the signals that are modulated by the substance. The recorded frequencies remain effective after they are transmitted electronically.

Jean Monro and Ray Choy are British doctors who specialize in allergic disorders (Shallis 1988; C. Smith/ Best). They use allergens serially diluted in homeopathic doses to diagnose and treat people with unusual allergies, for example sensitivity to very large numbers of allergens. They report that if a particular dilution of an allergen produces symptoms when it is placed on the skin, even greater dilutions of the same allergen placed on the skin will cure the same symptoms. Patients keep a vial of the effective therapeutic dilution for use at home, and find equally positive effects when the treatment is applied in their natural environments. They report nearly instantaneous relief of symptoms, suggesting that this may be an energy field effect. Double blind trials are said to have produced the same results, though I have not seen reports from any such experiments.

Some people are so extraordinarily sensitive to allergens that they develop symptoms when a vial of allergenic solution is brought into the room without their knowledge (Shallis 1988). A solid aluminum shield around the vial completely inhibits this reaction, while aluminum mesh with smaller than one-centimeter holes provides partial protection.[470]

Cyril Smith, working with Choy and Monro, reported that a variable electrical oscillator could be tuned to particular frequencies that would produce the same symptoms and to other frequencies that would relieve them. After applying the therapeutic electrical frequency to vials of water, this water could be used therapeutically as well. Its potency was retained for up to six weeks (C. Smith et al.).[471]

Overlaps of various imprints of healing effects in water

These are fascinating reports, but fuller descriptions are needed for assurance that we are not being misled by placebo effects. It is unclear from Shallis's summary whether these types of allergic responses to water that has been imprinted are seen only in unusually sensitive people or also with more common, less severe allergies. If their results were confirmed, these studies could provide important contributions to our appreciation of energy medicine.

Radionics specialists report that they are able to sense *vibrations* that are typical to specific states of health and illness, and that they are able to project corrective vibrations through their radionics devices when illness is found. Radionics treatments appear to function similarly to the electromagnetic imprintings of water. It would be helpful to study whether one could distinguish between mental and electromagnetic imprinting of water by researchers. There are radionics specialists who utilize homeopathic remedies along with radionics treatments, to correct the disharmonies that have been identified.

A healer related to me that she once went on holiday and forgot to take along her homeopathic remedy. She visualized to herself that she was holding the actual remedy (though she was actually holding only a glass of mineral water), and she felt that her "treated" water produced the same effects as the actual remedy. Similarly, a world-renowned homeopath (who asked to remain unnamed) reported that he had once been phoned by a friend and colleague from Africa with an urgent request for a remedy to treat an illness. Unable to provide the remedy expeditiously, the homeopath mentally imaged the remedy and his friend reported a rapid, very positive response.

Whether these reported results are valid or are only placebo effects awaits clarification through further studies.

Adverse effects: Intense emotional releases, accompanied by intense physical reactions may occur with homeopathic remedies, particularly when high doses are given – as in classical homeopathy. Negative effects can be antidoted with coffee.

Training and licensing: There are a variety of homeopathic training programs, and training is not standardized in the US. The National Center for Homeopathy in Alexandria, Virginia is a professional training and support organization. The Council for Homeopathic Certification (CHC) is the sole board certifying competency in homeopathy practice without regard to professional training.

In the US until recently, homeopaths were rare and were viewed with extreme skepticism by the medical community. They are now growing in numbers and acceptance, although many health authorities in the US are reluctant to grant licenses to practice homeopathy except to medical doctors. This is ironic, as MDs who have minimal training in homeopathy may be licensed to practice, while homeopathic doctors with years of training and experience may not.

Homeopaths are currently licensed in only three states.[472] In most other states, the practice of homeopathy is restricted to physicians, although unlicensed lay homeopaths may be found practicing in many states. Minnesota and California include homeopaths in their CAM Freedom of Practice Acts.

In the UK, homeopathic practitioners are accredited by their schools, the most prestigious being the Royal Society of Homeopaths. Many UK doctors have trained in homeopathic medicine after finishing conventional medical school, and there are several homeopathic hospitals around the country. In the UK; homeopathic remedies are covered under the National Health Service; and close to half of all general practitioners (primary care physicians) refer patients to homeopaths.

Homeopathic remedies are available in the US and Britain over the counter in lower potencies. Arnica is very popular, and is useful as first aid in cases of physical and emotional trauma.

Clinical applications: Homeopathy may be beneficial in treating most physical and psychological problems, including many for which conventional medicine has no cures. In the UK, homeopathy is well accepted and there are hospitals there that are devoted primarily to homeopathic treatment.

While there are self-help books for homeopathic remedies, and substances such as arnica are popular and anecdotally effective treatments for stress and other common ailments, a homeopathic therapist can help patients benefit much more extensively and deeply from this treatment.

Many of the patients who respond well to homeopathy are often served poorly by allopathic medicine, which addresses symptoms such as anxiety and depression in a rather heavy-handed way, using tranquilizers and antidepressants to tone down or suppress the symptoms, but not getting to the underlying problems and also producing many unpleasant side effects.

Counseling and psychotherapy can help with these problems, but it may take many months and years to bear fruit. Homeopathy offers profoundly transformative changes, and often with startlingly rapidity, when a remedy is found that resonates with the person's situation. Conversely, the emotional releases that may be brought about by homeopathy can be worked out through psychotherapy, as may various chronic resistances and entrenched patterns of behavior. The best method may be a combination of the two modalities.

I can certainly testify to the potency of this combination in my private practice of psychotherapy. Clients taking homeopathy and flower essences are able to unearth inner conflicts more rapidly; are better able to tolerate the anxieties of emotional releases; achieve more rapid resolution of their mood disorders; are better able to improve their relationships, and more.

See also: Flower Essences.

HYDROTHERAPY

See: Water Therapies.

HYPNOTHERAPY

Your unconscious mind can listen
To me without
Your knowledge
And also deal with something else at the same time
    – Milton Erickson (in Rossi 1976, p.38)

The basics of hypnotherapy are discussed in Chapter II-1, but this modality deserves separate mention here as one of the important complementary therapies.[473]

Hypnotherapy has not gained as wide acceptance as one might expect, considering that it has been used in various forms and applications for 200 years. The greatest obstacle to its use today in allopathic medicine is that not all patients respond to hypnosis. While everyone has some measure of hypnotizability, the levels range from profoundly deep to almost negligible (Bates). For a good hypnotic subject, this treatment offers a spectrum of benefits with virtually no side effects, though it requires an investment of a period of time to learn the induction techniques.

Various clinical tests (most of which are essentially forms of mini-induction of hypnosis) and a questionnaire are helpful in assessing hypnotic potential.[474]

When people are responsive to hypnotic inductions, the benefits of this treatment can be enormous. Hypnotherapy can help in pain management;[475] migraines (Cedercreutz); hypertension (Deabler et al.); irritable bowel syndromes;[476] fibromyalgia (Haanen et al.); accelerating healing of burn wounds (Ewin 1979; Patterson et al.) and bone fractures (Ginandes/ Rosenthal); halting traumatic and surgical bleeding,[477] decreasing bleeding in hemophiliacs,[478] and stabilizing diabetes (McCord 1968b); menstrual problems (Erickson 1977); enhancing breast development (Staib/ Logan; R. Willard); managing children's distress during unpleasant procedures (Wall/ Womack); insomnia (H. Stanton); and reducing the side effects of chemotherapy (L. Walker et al. 1988). It is also useful in treating warts[479] and allergies (Madrid et al.); obesity (Bolocofsky et al.; M. Andersen); asthma,[480] and tobacco addiction (Barabasz). Hypnotherapy greatly facilitates psychotherapy, providing a quick window into repressed memories and feelings, and strengthening willpower to apply oneself to constructive tasks (Wolinski).[481]

Adverse effects: Hypnotherapy must be used with caution. A potential danger is that pain could be reduced, when it might in fact be an urgent warning of body malfunctions. Ignoring the pain could delay seeking medical treatment. If appendix or cancer pains are ignored, for example, the result could be fatal. Another risk is that during hypnotherapy a subject may open up repressed feelings too rapidly and be overwhelmed with feelings that they have worked very hard to keep out of their conscious awareness.

Stage hypnotists lead people to do silly things that may be embarrassing, which can be damaging to a person's self-confidence and self-image.

Considering all of the potential risks, one must be cautious in selecting a hypnotherapist. The public is cautioned to check the training, experience and other qualifications of hypnotherapists prior to seeking treatment.

Training and licensing: There are many and varied courses available in hypnotherapy. Treatment is best provided by therapists who are competent to treat the given problem through other means as well, because responses to hypnotherapy are so variable. Various professional associations provide guidelines for training and practice.[482] Hypnosis is not regulated by law, and people who are unlicensed in any other helping profession may advertise that they practice hypnotherapy. The public is cautioned to check the training, experience, and other qualifications of hypnotherapists prior to seeking treatment.

Hypnotherapy must be used with caution. One possible negative effect is that pain could be reduced, when it might in fact be an urgent warning of bodily malfunctions. Ignoring the pain could lead to dangerous delays in seeking treatment. If appendix or cancer pains are ignored, for example, the result could be fatal. Another risk is that during hypnotherapy a subject may open up repressed feelings too rapidly, and be overwhelmed with feelings that they have worked very hard to keep out of their conscious awareness. Stage hypnotists lead people to do silly things that may be embarrassing, which can be damaging to a person's self-confidence and self-image. Considering all of the potential risks, one must be cautious in selecting a hypnotherapist.

Clinical applications: Hypnotherapy can be of great help in treating pain; many illnesses in which a measure of self-regulation is possible (such as asthma, irritable bowel syndrome, hypertension, and fibromyalgia); hormonal disorders, and more.

A hypnotherapist will help the subject find the best ways to enter hypnotic states, and can be of great assistance in exploring contributions to health and illness from the unconscious mind. Once this method has been mastered, self-hypnosis can be of enormous benefit.

See also: Suggestion, Placebo Effects (self-healing) in Chapter II-1.

IMAGERY

See: Visualization; also Metaphor (under the arts, in Creative Therapies).

LEECHES

Leeches were used for bleeding over several centuries in Europe in the treatment of many ailments, such as heart disease and infections (Dossey 2002a). American leeches were deemed less effective than the European varieties, and this led to a thriving import trade, which at times even depleted European supplies.

Leeches suck blood through wounds that they create by biting, and the blood flow is maintained with anticoagulants the animals secrete.

While bleeding is no longer accepted as a treatment for most of these ailments, a few applications have been found in which leeches are still useful. When fingers or toes are sewn back on after they have been accidentally amputated, residual swelling can cut off the blood supply to the digit. When skin is grafted, when breasts are reconstructed after mastectomies, and when there is severe injury with a black eye, there is often swelling that can impede wound healing. Leeches are used for treatment of pain in many parts of the world. While it was thought that this is a metaphoric treatment of "sucking out the pain," recent research shows leeches can reduce pain of osteoarthritis (Michalsen et al). In these limited applications leeches have been found to be useful adjuncts to conventional care.

Adverse effects: Leeches can invade the body, and historical notes caution against letting them enter the vagina, through which they can invade the uterus, or the throat, where they may cut off the airway. There can be prolonged oozing after the leech is removed, and if the animal is not removed carefully, parts of its mouth may remain behind and cause infections. Anyone with a bleeding tendency is not a candidate for treatment with leeches.

See also: Maggots.

LESHAN HEALING

In Type 1 healing, the healer goes into an altered state of consciousness in which he views himself and the healee as one entity. There is no attempt to "do anything" to the healee… but simply to meet him, to be one with him, to unite with him…

— Lawrence LeShan (1974a, p. 106)

This method was developed in the late 1960s by Lawrence LeShan, a clinical and research psychologist who specializes in psychotherapy for people with cancer. LeShan was initially a skeptic, as noted earlier, and believed that healing was at best some combination of wishful thinking, suggestion and avoidance of facing up to one's problems. He set out to observe some of the more prominent healers in order to expose their charlatanism, but was surprised to find some of them had potent abilities to bring about unusual arrests or remissions in various diseases, occasionally with such rapidity as to be considered instantaneous or "miraculous."

He carefully observed some of the better healers, noting the following common denominators in their practices:

1. They were able to focus or *center* their minds;
2. They found ways to join with the healees in a profound way; and
3. They felt themselves and the healees to be "one with the All."

LeShan practiced meditation in order to center his own mind, and then began offering healing as he had observed it, with very positive results. He subsequently went on to teach others to develop their healing gifts. For over three decades Joyce Goodrich has taught the LeShan method, while LeShan has continued to focus on self-healing through psychotherapy for people with cancer and other serious illnesses.

LeShan healing focuses primarily on distant/ absent/ *Type 1* healing. Healers are taught a range of meditative and imagery approaches to help them center themselves, focusing on the image that they are one with the healee and one with the All. Healers are encouraged to work in pairs.

Goodrich has been working for years to develop collaborative research on LeShan healing, with modest success.

Research: Studies of LeShan healing for depression and anxiety have been with small groups, which did not demonstrate clinical effects.

Adverse effects: No harmful effects have been reported See discussion of potential general negative effects from rapid improvements under Spiritual Healing.

Training and licensing: Basic and advanced training are offered by Joyce Goodrich, PhD. There is no licensing for healing.

See also: *Spiritual Healing* – Volume I of *Healing Research.*

LIGHT AND COLOR THERAPIES

The heavy dark falls back to earth
And the freed air goes wild with light,
The heart fills with fresh, bright breath
And thoughts stir to give birth to colour.
           – John O'Donohue

Full-spectrum light can influence innate cycles of waking and sleeping. These cycles of consciousness are also cycles of tidal hormonal ebbs and flows. Hormones are secreted in greater and lesser amounts, corresponding with our body's needs at different times of day and night. For instance, melatonin is a hormone secreted by the pineal gland in the brain under stimulation of the body by light This is the body's timing messenger, relaying information to all parts of the body about the circadian (daily) cycle. In response to this message, levels of other hormones such as adrenal steroids are raised and lowered – to help us deal appropriately internally with the external energies that shift as day alternates with night.

Each species has a circadian rhythm that is close to 24 hours long. These rhythms continue even in total darkness. In the natural cycle, which alternates the light of day and the darkness of night, these rhythms are entrained and conform to the 24-hour solar day.

Light is helpful in healing. Full spectrum light is effective in treating *seasonal affective disorder* (*SAD*), a depression experienced by some people during the short days of winter. Exposures to full spectrum light of 40-60 minutes just after sunrise or before sunset, which in effect extends a person's experience of daylight, can prevent or reverse SAD depression.

Colored light is said to convey healing vibrations, and particular colors are used to treat particular problems.[483] Many of these colors correlate with the basic colors associated with the chakras.[484] As you will recall from our previous discussion, there are seven major chakras along the midline of the body. The root chakra, at the base of the spine, is classically identified with red; the sacral chakra, below the navel, with orange; the solar plexus chakra with yellow; the heart chakra with green; the throat chakra with blue; the "third-eye" chakra, on the forehead above the nose, with violet; and the crown chakra, at the top of the head, with indigo or white. Various healers have advocated different systems of color treatments. For example, healees might be exposed to light of the color associated with the chakra that is in the region of the body that needs healing.

These recommendations are often based on the color perceptions of healers who see the biological energy field and the chakras as colors.[485] The different colors indicate a healthy, stressed, or diseased state.[486]

Other systems of color diagnosis (Birren; Luscher) and color/ light therapy have been developed through empirical observations of the health benefits of shining particular colors upon specific parts of the body (Ghadiali; Dinshah), and of shining light into the eyes (Spitler).

One area of light therapy has a well established physiological mechanism. Blue light has been found to cure neonatal jaundice by facilitating the metabolism of excess bilirubin, and this method is widely used in hospitals around the world (Lucey).

It is also known that ultraviolet light kills bacteria. Niels Finsen was awarded a Nobel Prize in 1903 for treating tuberculosis of the skin with ultraviolet light.

Jacob Liberman (1991; 1995) extends light, color and vision therapy to effect profound healings on physical, emotional, mental, and spiritual levels. Particularly impressive are his summaries of his findings that constricted visual fields in children with learning disabilities are correctable with colored light therapy (R. Kaplan; Liberman 1986).[487]

Research: Research has confirmed that full spectrum light is an effective treatment for seasonal affective disorder.[488]

Liberman reviews evidence from controlled studies showing that blue light may help in treating arthritis (S. McDonald), and full spectrum light combined with particular colors on the walls may enhance learning and improve behavior of children in schools.[489] An unexpected finding was that children in these circumstances also had fewer dental caries (Ott 1985), a result supported by a study of full spectrum light in hamsters (Sharon et al.). Liberman adds his clinical observations that red light may relieve migraines.

While these uses of color have no known causal relationship to disease processes, they are reported empirically to have helped many patients. Scientists in Russia (Krakov) and America (Gerard) have found that red stimulates the sympathetic nervous system, while blue stimulates the parasympathetic system. Harry Wohlfarth showed that maximal increases in blood pressure, pulse and respiration could be obtained with yellow light; modest increases with orange; and minimal increases with red. Maximal decreases in these measurements could be obtained with black; modest decreases with blue; and minimal decreases with green.

The color of bubble-gum pink has been found to have a calming effect on violent behavior. While the mechanisms for this effect are unknown, criminals and juvenile delinquents placed in rooms painted pink demonstrate far less aggression and violence.[490]

Healers may recommend that clothing of particular colors be worn to help alleviate speific problems. Colors may also be used in visualizations of subtle energy projection. For instance, in Therapeutic Touch healers will visualize green or yellow light to energize the healee, and blue to calm and soothe (Krieger 1979; 1993).

Krieger (1973) suggests a simple experiment you can try for yourself. Picture in your imagination that you are in a church on a sunny day. Sense that your face is bathed in the light coming through a stained-glass window. Sense the feeling of each color in turn as you move from one spot to another. Check with other people what their experiences are with this imagery.

Color therapy appears to be a fertile ground for future research.

Adverse effects: Excessive use of full spectrum lighting can make people uncomfortable, and anecdotal reports indicate it may precipitate manic reactions in people with bipolar disorders.

Training and licensing: There is no formal training or licensing for light and color therapy.

Clinical applications: Light therapy is of proven value in seasonal affective disorder and in neonatal jaundice. Light and color treatments appear to have much broader ranges of applications, but these remain to be substantiated with research.

Light and color therapies require the guidance of a therapist. Self-healing through the proper use of appropriate lights and colors can then be implemented.

LOVE

> *Love and intimacy are the root of what makes us sick and what makes us well. I am not aware of any other factor in medicine – not diet, not smoking, not exercise... not drugs, not surgery – that has a greater impact on our quality of life, incidence of illness and premature death.*
> – Dean Ornish (1998)

Though discussing love as a therapeutic technique might seem to trivialize this profound and complex emotion, it must be acknowledged that love is one of the most powerful forces for healing.

Most importantly, healers feel that respants must love themselves in order to be healed (Siegel 1986). Much of our dis-ease and disease derives from self-doubt, self-criticism, and self-hate. These attitudes and emotions can block the flows of our bioenergies. They create disconnections from nurturing environmental energies, and stagnations within the body that can either allow or cause illness to manifest. From this perspective, illness is like an alarm set off by the bodymind to alert us that our energies are not flowing properly. Often this is a direct result of feeling unloved.

Love as a factor in therapy was never even mentioned in my medical school training. In contrast, it is a word that is heard quite often in discussions at the American Holistic Medical Association, where I once heard Leo Buscaglia speak. Famous for his teachings and books about love, he told of how he had once been invited to speak at a hospital. When he submitted the title of his lecture, "Love," he was contacted by the hospital and was told politely that this probably would not be acceptable as a topic in a medical setting. When he changed the title to "Unconditional Positive Regard," they had no trouble approving it.

Caregivers are better at promoting healing when they have a loving attitude. My first supervisor in psychiatric residency training, Joe Golden, advised me, "If you cannot find something in your patient that you love, you should not be treating that person." I didn't realize at the time what a profound piece of advice that was. After thirty years of psychotherapy and healing practice, I am now more sure than ever that this is true.

Spiritual dimensions of love can be powerful adjuncts for healing. People who have near-death experiences often report that they were transformed by being in the presence of a "Being of Light" that was unconditionally accepting (i.e. totally loving). They felt that they were then able to forgive and accept themselves and others, when they had never before been able to do so.

Research: Although research on human love is fraught with difficulties, the effects of love have been studied in laboratory animals (Nerem et al.). In one experiment, rabbits were fed cholesterol supplements for a number of weeks. One group was also given love (handled, stroked, talked to, played with) and another group was merely given the minimal physical care that is usual for laboratory animals. When the arteries of both groups were examined at the end of the trial period, the rabbits that had received loving attention showed 60% lower levels of arteriosclerotic changes.

Love has traditionally been associated with feelings in the heart. It is fascinating to find that research is confirming effects of feelings of love upon the heart muscle. Studies by Glen Rein and Rollin McCraty[490] show that when people learn to meditate on love their electrocardiograms (EKGs) show a significantly increased coherence in their heartbeats. When they enter this meditative state, they are also able to alter the winding of DNA. As a demonstration of an intentional effect upon living matter, this is by definition a form of healing.

If two people sit opposite each other a few feet apart while they are both in this state of cardiac coherence, and the first projects loving thoughts and feelings toward the other, the electroencephalogram (EEG) recorded in the frontal lobes of the second person will reflect the heartbeat rhythm of the first person. However, some people's EEGs do not become entrained in this way. A further reflection on the power of love is that those who *do* respond in this situation report that their parents showed a caring attitude toward them in their childhood, while those who *do not* respond report that their parents did not demonstrate a caring attitude.[491]

Adverse effects: The English language is lacking in words to distinguish "unconditional positive regard" love from sexual love. This is where love, as in sexual activity between therapists and clients, has given love a bad press. Laws in many states now prohibit psychotherapists and psychiatrists from touching their patients, as a precaution against slipping from one expression of love into another. This is a serious impediment in the conduct of psychotherapy, as touch can be a potent healing intervention.[492]

People who have not known unconditional acceptance as children may have difficulty when they encounter a loving person, be it a therapist, a family member, or a friend. Their automatic pilot may have been programmed in childhood to distrust others, in anticipation that they will be rejected or hurt. It may take counseling or psychotherapy to change and overcome such defensive programming.

Training: While it may seem unusual to suggest that love should require or even be subject to training, I believe this should be a part of therapist's training.

Caregiving that is offered through the heart has a completely different feel, effect and potency from healing offered through the head. It is possible to learn to open one's heart through unconditional acceptance, empathy and respect, as well as to connect with one's heart center energetically and to link through spiritual healing with others.

Clinical applications: Love is an essential element in care-giving and healing.

See also: Massage, Touch.

MAGGOTS

There are in fact two things, science and opinion; the former begets knowledge, the latter ignorance.

– Hippocrates (*Law, Book I*)

Maggots are fly larvae that eat decaying flesh. They refuse to eat live flesh, and have therefore been helpful in treating infections through many centuries. They will quickly clear out pustular wounds, leaving clean tissues that heal rapidly.[493] Prior to the development of antibiotics, maggots were used as the primary treatment for pustular wounds (Dossey 2002).

Ronald Sherman, MD, a professor of surgery at the University of California, has brought back this ancient method, which has proven invaluable for the treatment of chronic infections that are not responsive to antibiotics. This can happen when the infections are due to antibiotic-resistant bacteria or when the blood supply to the tissues is compromised (e.g. in diabetes and atherosclerotic disease) and the body is unable to bring an adequate dose of antibiotics to the wound, even though the bacteria are sensitive to them.

Of the many species of flies, the greenbottle blowfly, *Lucilia sericata,* is the most effective. The flies are raised in labs where their eggs are sterilized so that they will not add new infectious organisms to wounds. The eggs are packed into the wounds, leaving an open airway so the hatched maggots can breathe. Maximal benefits are found in one to three days after the maggots hatch. Rarely is it necessary to repeat the treatment more than once to achieve full debridement (clearing away of dead flesh) in even the most difficult wounds. The maggots also secrete ammonia, which slows the growth of bacteria. It is believed that they also secrete substances that enhance wound healing, because the results achieved with maggots are often realized faster than would be anticipated with antibiotics (Sherman 1998; Sherman et al.).

Doctors have been amazed, and patients have been delighted with the results. During treatment there is a rapid decrease in pain and foul odors. Patients who were candidates for amputations of their limbs due to chronic skin ulcers (common in diabetes), and bone infections (osteomyelitis) have been spared the surgery, and their legs and arms have been saved. Other applications have included treatment of bedsores, venous ulcers due to varicose veins, burns, wounds from surgery or trauma, and wounds with bacterial infections that are resistant to antibiotics.

This is one of the many lessons we can garner from traditional medical approaches. It is a safe and non-toxic therapy. This is particularly relevant in today's concern over the hundreds of thousands of deaths that are caused annually by the side effects from medications, including antibiotics.

Adverse effects: Patients and medical personnel often have to overcome a revulsion at the sight, or even at the thought of using maggots in this way. While it was initially feared that there might even be psychological trauma from using maggots, patients have almost uniformly been very favorable in their response to the treatment – especially when they observe the rapid, positive results.

See also: Leeches.

MASSAGE AND MANUAL THERAPIES

The hands of those I meet are dumbly eloquent to me. There are those whose hands have sunbeams in them so that their grasp warms my heart.

– Helen Keller

Touch is one of the most potent means of communicating care (Montagu 1971). It relaxes muscles and releases the tensions that form part of the familiar vicious circle of tension → spasm → pain → anxiety → tension, etc. Massage is one of the oldest of all known therapies, with records acknowledging its benefits found in China dating to 4,000 years ago, and others written by Hippocrates in the 4th century BC. Two brothers named George and Charles Taylor, both New York physicians who studied in Sweden, introduced massage as a therapy in modern America in the 1850s. Because of the time constraints of medical practice, massage was initially delegated to physical therapists and nurses. These, in turn, have likewise succumbed to the pressures of time, relinquishing massage to the hands of massage therapists. A move back toward integrating massage with psychotherapy is growing amongst psychotherapists, who are finding that touch markedly enhances therapeutic rapport, relaxation, exploration of bodymind memories, and more.[494]

Western massage approaches emphasize mechanical interventions, including gliding strokes (*effleurage*), kneading (*pétrissage*), rubbing/ friction and percussion (*tapotement*), vibration, compression, and range of motion. A variety of other therapeutic approaches may also be combined with massage. It is estimated that more than 80 different types of massage are practiced, many of them adapted from other cultures. The following list describes a few of these, ranging from methods that primarily address the body, to those that focus upon subtle energies, and others that include psychological components (*bodymind* therapies).

1. *Swedish massage*, the most common variety, directs long, gliding strokes and kneading to superficial layers of the muscles, usually from the periphery towards the heart. It induces relaxation, relief of muscle tensions/ spasms, improved circulation and enhanced range of motion.

2. *Deep-tissue massage* directs pressure across the grain of the muscles with slow strokes and greater pressure than (1), for the same effects and purposes.

3. *Sports massage* combines (1) and (2) to treat athletic strains and injuries.

4 *Manual lymph drainage* uses light strokes to enhance lymph flow when there is edema, inflammation or circulatory problems due to nerve damage. Research has shown that lymphedema massage is superior to mechanical methods in reducing swelling after radical mastectomy, and also lowers treatment costs.[495]

5. *Neuromuscular massage, myotherapy* (Witt 1984), and *trigger point massage*[496] address specific muscles that may be in spasm due to emotional or physical stress, or may have *trigger points* that initiate pain. Sometimes pressures on nerves from various tissues can also be relieved.

Figure II-11. Healing and other complementary therapies, such as massage and aromatherapy, work well together.

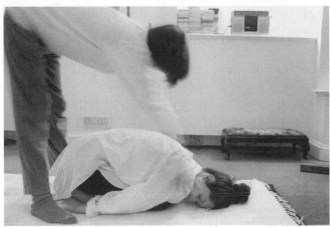

Photograph by Tony Sleep

6. *Traditional Chinese massage* has been practiced for about 2,000 years. It may include rubbing and tapping with the palms and finger tips, pinching, lifting and/ or twisting pinched flesh, and other techniques. In addition to treating musculoskeletal problems, this massage may be given for headaches, stomach aches, dysmenorrhea, upper respiratory infections, asthma, enuresis, and more.[497]

The next therapies in the list involve very light pressure or massage at discrete points on the body, rather than deep tissue massage.

7. *Aromatherapy* is named after the aromatic oils that are used to lubricate the skin during the massage, which is usually similar in method to (1).
Aromatherapists report that the effects of these oils can be quite potent and specifically beneficial for a variety of ailments, in and of themselves.[498]
   The American Massage Therapy Association (AMTA) has an online massage database where further information can be found.[499]

8. *Structural Integration* (*Rolfing*) is deep massage directed to fascia (connective tissues) rather than to muscles. Rolfing is based on the theory that fascia hold and maintain tensions of misalignments in the body that are adopted unconsciously in response to emotional stresses and defenses (Rolf; Schultz/ Feitis). This theory is drawn from the architectural model of Buckminster Fuller's *tensegrity mast*, in which wires under tension hold solid elements together. In the human body, the fascia parallel the wires and the bones resemble Fuller's solid elements (Robie).
   Research has shown rolfing to be helpful in treating cerebral palsy (J. Perry et al.), stress and other symptoms from whiplash and low back pain (Rolf 1977), and anxiety (Weinberg/ Hunt), and in influencing various other physiological and psychological variables (Silverman et al.).
   Hellerwork (Heller/ Henkin) and *Aston Patterning* are both offshoots of rolfing that are somewhat less forceful in their physical manipulations of body tissues.

9. *Pressure point therapies/ Meridian-based therapies* act through particularly sensitive pressure points on the body, using the pressure of the practitioner's fingers. The pressure points often correspond to the meridian and acupuncture point systems.[500] These therapies, with the exception of (b) below, often rely on touch rather than massage, although pressure or tapping at the acupressure point may be used. The touch may be quite light or very firm, depending upon the therapy. These therapies rely on subtle energy medicine interventions rather than on massage of muscles, tendons and fascia for their effects.[501]

a. *Acupressure* may be used instead of acupuncture needles anywhere on the body. Several variations are practiced. *Shiatsu* (Japanese) and *tsubo* use sequences of pressure from one end of every meridian to the other.[502] This is similar to healing, in that therapists project Qi energy through their fingers as they apply pressure. *Jin shin jyutsu* and *jin shin do* (both Japanese) apply pressure along selected meridians according to the problems being treated.[503]

Several variants of acupressure facilitate profound psychological transformations through treatment applied to specific points on the head, chest and hand, combined with affirmations that focus the mind on issues a person would like to address.[504]

> There's an ancient Chinese medical text that names three levels of healing[:] ...Address a person's complaints to diminish her pain, ...understand someone's nature, [and] assist a person in fulfilling his or her destiny.
> – Harriet Beinfield and Efrem Korngold

While these approaches are highly innovative in terms of allopathic medicine, they are simply rediscoveries of long-forgotten, traditional healing lore.

b. *Reflexology* (*zone therapy*) addresses points on the feet that correlate with the rest of the body, including internal organs. This is a form of massage, as firm pressure is used. The pressure stimulates healing through meridian energy lines rather than relaxing the specific muscles and tissues that are being touched.

Reflexology can help in treating a broad variety of health problems (Botting) in a manner similar to that of acupuncture, from which it is derived.

Some reflexologists claim they are able to diagnose problems by assessing tender zones in the feet that correspond to the parts of the body that are diseased.

Recently, awareness has been growing that reflexology can be a potent intervention for emotional problems as well (Trousdall), sometimes inducing emotional releases during treatments (Mackereth).[505]

Research: A randomized controlled study shows reflexology is effective in treatment of premenstrual syndrome (Oleson/ Flocco).[506] A study of diagnosis by reflexology demonstrated no success (A. R. White et al.).

c. *Polarity Therapy* was developed by Randolph Stone, a chiropractor, osteopath and naturopath, in the early 19th century. He studied healing methods in China and India, and settled in India, where he developed this method. It is based on energy interventions in the patterns of chakras and in the specific directions of flows of energy in and around the body. In this method, particular points on the body are pressed with the fingers. Exercise, diet and psychological states are also addressed, the latter through *positive thinking*.[507]

d. *SHEN Therapy* was developed by Richard Pavek, an American scientist. This method addresses emotional tensions that manifest in physical symptoms, using light touch at particular points on the body. It has been helpful in treating anorexia, bulimia, migraine, pains of all sorts, panic attacks, post-traumatic stress disorder, pre-menstrual symptoms, irritable bowel syndrome, and more. This is one of the few bodywork therapies that has developed research methods to demonstrate and clarify its possible mechanisms of action. Pavek (1984-5) showed that decreases in white cell count during the course of chemotherapy of four patients could be reversed significantly with *SHEN* treatments to the thymus gland. Pavek (1986) also reported that *SHEN* therapy provided long-term relief of premenstrual symptoms in 11 out of 13 women. Although *SHEN* therapy did not significantly shorten the hospitalization time of 6 people with major depression (compared to 6 randomized controls), Pavek found significant changes in emotional expressiveness, dreams, and interpersonal relations of the subjects receiving *SHEN* therapy (M. Beal/ Pavek).

e. *The Bowen Technique* is another form of gentle massage with healing. Sharing from my brief introductory course in this method, let me take a moment to flesh out the description of this interesting type of hands-on therapy. The Bowen Technique was developed in the 1950's by Tom Bowen, a gifted Australian intuitive. The methods he developed are claimed to be effective 85-90% of the time with 1-3 treatments. Bowen was able to treat serious problems very rapidly, seeing up to 13,000 people in a year. The Bowen method is available in Australia, England and the US.

This method involves a very gentle rolling of particular muscles under the hands of the therapist. A standard set of manipulations is used to treat most problems. Particularly responsive are musculoskeletal problems, even when they have been present for many years and are unresponsive to conventional medical treatments and other complementary therapies. For example, frozen shoulders respond so well that when Bowen therapists are demonstrating the method at public meetings they routinely invite people with this problem to receive treatments. Many are permanently cleared of all pain and limitation of motion within minutes. Others may take a few days to demonstrate changes, and one or two more treatments often bring further improvements. Numerous other conditions have responded dramatically, including anxiety, pains of all sorts, asthma, emphysema, irritable bowel syndrome, hiatus hernia, skin conditions, hyperactivity, depression, and more. This method helps the patient on organic, emotional and psychological levels simultaneously.

Diagnosis is unnecessary with the Bowen method because the body is allowed to readjust itself and return to health rather than being pushed to change in particular ways. Conditions other than the presenting problem (which often are not even mentioned to the therapist by the client) may improve as well. Here is an example from the experience of my course instructor.

> I treated "David," an elderly man who came in bent over and moaning, obviously suffering with serious back pain. In a thick Yiddish accent he explained that he had been to numbers of other therapists over many months without benefit. I gave him a standard treatment and he went out hobbling just about as much as when he entered, as do many clients of Bowen therapists.
>
> The Bowen method is so simple and quick that it isn't uncommon to have clients feel they have been duped when they are asked to pay for what seems to be of no immediate benefit, involving so light a touch for so brief a period, often not particularly directed to the site of discomfort. We always book two appointments a week apart, knowing that a second treatment at that interval is often necessary. I reminded him of his second appointment and knew from the look on his face as he departed that he was thinking, "I'm not *that* foolish that I'm going to return and pay you good money again for nothing."
>
> The next week he returned at the scheduled time, walking normally and beaming. He came in and said, "I'm all better. I have to show you." Whereupon he turned his back, dropped his trousers and underpants and bent over. I could understand his bending over to show me his back was better, but not the rest of his show. He gleefully announced, "My hemorrhoids!" Still bewildered, I told him I didn't see any hemorrhoids. "Of course!" he said. "They're gone! I suffered with them for years. And I didn't even tell you about them! If I was Christian, I'd think you were Jesus returned to help the sick."
>
> – Julian Baker

Unlike other forms of healing, which may be complementary to a wide variety of therapies, the Bowen method is recommended as a complement only with homeopathy, Bach flower remedies and counseling/ psychotherapy.

Lest you think that this is purely a mechanical therapy, the Bowen method has been reported effective with the use of a proxy patient[508] in cases where the person with the illness cannot be treated directly.

Research: A pilot study suggests that the Bowen technique can be helpful in the treatment of frozen shoulders (B. Carter).

I will mention three other therapeutic methods to round out the above list of therapies. These are subtle energy interventions rather than forms of massage, but they may involve light touch and are therefore often listed in conjunction with massage. Treatments may also be given without touch.

f. *Therapeutic Touch* (*TT*), Healing Touch (HT) and *Reiki* are sometimes categorized as massage techniques, though they do not involve physical manipulation of the body. These and other spiritual healing approaches are combined with massage by some practitioners.

See also: Reiki; Therapeutic Touch; Spiritual Healing.[509]

10. *Trager psychophysical integration* involves gentle, rhythmic rocking, bouncing, and shaking movements, to free up chronic tensions in muscles and joints. It was developed by a Hawaiian physician named Milton Trager (Trager; Trager/ Guadagno-Hammond), out of his experience as a trainer for boxers. Trager treatments address emotional patterns that have lodged in body tensions. The principles of *hookup* (a meditative state) and, *mentastics* (physical movements) are also taught to increase enjoyment in movement. Clinical successes have been reported in treating cerebral palsy (P. Witt/ Parr) and many other conditions, including chronic musculoskeletal pains, headaches, temporomandibular joint (TMJ) pain, spinal cord injuries, and neurological impairments from spinal cord injuries, polio and strokes.

11. *Bioenergetics*, a method originating from the work of Wilhelm Reich, uses focused manual pressure by the therapist, various positionings of the body, focused breathing, and other physical exercises. All of these are designed to release emotional tensions and *armoring* (physical stiffening) of the body that result from emotional traumas and stresses. Emotional releases may be intense, with accompanying emergence of memories of old traumas that were long buried, and insights about how the unconscious mind kept these from conscious awareness through body armoring. Variations on bioenergetics have been developed under the names of *neo-Reichian therapy, Lowenwork* (Lowen), *core energetics* (Pierrakos), and *radix*.[510]

12. There are other variations on the theme of massage that are less well known and less commonly available in many parts of the world.[511]

Research lags well behind the enormous popular acceptance of these bodymind therapies.

A general observation must be made regarding frequent critical observations by reviewers of controlled studies on these manipulative techniques. Conventional medicine has accepted that physiotherapy is effective for musculoskeletal disorders, but there is little scientific data to support this general agreement in the profession. Beckerman et al. reviewed 180 randomized studies on the efficacy of physiotherapy for a wide range of problems in the back, neck, shoulders, and knees. Approaches covered included spinal manipulation, exercises, traction, ultrasound, and laser therapy. Here, too, there was severe criticism of the low quality of the studies, which made it impossible to assess their overall benefits.

I will add a few personal observations. In the stress management workshops I lead for doctors, nurses and others, massage is one of the most appreciated modalities. I also had a course of treatment with Lowen-type bioenergetics that I found most helpful in getting past my intellectual defenses and releasing long-buried feelings.

Components of massage
Several distinct components contribute to the efficacy of massage.

In relaxing a patient physically and psychologically, the three modalities of touch, massage, and (in aromatherapy) aromatic oils all address the tensions that contribute to the familiar vicious circle of tension → spasm → pain → anxiety → tension, etc.[512] In addition, some aromatherapists claim that the oils they use can also interact with subjects' biological energy fields. In any case, the biological energies of the person giving the massage may convey spiritual healing effects.

Touch is one of the most potent means of intervening to offer healing. Because this method of communication is non-verbal it reaches deep into people's awareness at levels that resonate with nurturing that they may have experienced early in their lives. Touch conveys caring, facilitates rapport, and builds trust – all of which help people to relax under the hands of their massage therapist and to open to receiving healing.[513]

Massage[514] relaxes muscles. When muscles and joints are painful due to tiredness, physical strain, or injuries, massage acts directly upon the problem areas. Sometimes massage can relieve *trigger points* of sensitivity in muscles and tissues that appear to set off more generalized muscle tensions and spasms (Weintraub 1992b). There may be emotional traumas that are associated with painful muscles and joints, as the physical body participates in storing emotional memories. When there is a general level of physical tension due to emotional stress, massage can relax the overall tension of muscles in the body. Systems of deep massage have been developed to facilitate emotional releases along with releases of physical pains (J. Perry et al.; Rolf).

Aromatic oils are used in aromatherapy to smooth the contact between the therapists' hands and the clients' skin. They also have medicinal benefits based on the qualities of the substances used in preparing the oils (see discussion above on aromatherapy.)

Spiritual healing may be an aspect of any complementary therapy, particularly those that include touch.

Research: While abundant testimonials suggest a very high success rate (85-90%) for the various bodywork therapies, with complete resolution of phobias and other problems, little research is available on these modalities and I have found no controlled studies.

Adverse effects: While I have not seen reports of harm from massage or bodymind therapies, common sense cautions apply to using massage or other physical manipulations too vigorously, with a potential for physical harm from the manipulations. Other potential negative effects may arise from rapid releases of emotional traumas that have been locked into the body.

Training and licensing: In the US, training in massage varies enormously from one school to another, as do licensing standards in various states. A National Certification Exam has been established under the Psychological Corporation.[515] A Commission on Massage Training Accreditation and Approval recognizes more than 60 training programs, with curricula of 500 hours or more covering anatomy, physiology, and the theory, practice and ethics of massage. The US Massage Therapy Association, the most established of the professional massage associations, has over 20,000 members. It publishes the *Massage Therapy Journal*. The

Federation of Therapeutic Massage and Bodywork Organizations is an umbrella group including the AMTA, the American Oriental Bodywork Therapy Association, the American Polarity Therapy Association, the Rolf and the Trager Institutes.[516]

National organizations have been unable to agree on standards for training and licensing. Massage therapists are licensed in about half of the states.

Massage therapists are lobbying for the licensing of massage in a growing number of states in the US. Healers have objected to this in some cases because the laying-on of hands is considered to be a sub-category of massage, and would therefore require licensing under this rubric. This would require of healers that they study manipulative massage for licensing, even though this is outside of their practices of spiritual healing – which in most healing practices involves only light touch and no manipulation.

Some US states prohibit psychotherapists from touching clients, unfortunately limiting the combined use of these approaches. (These laws are intended diminish sexual temptations in the therapeutic encounter.) This is a very unfortunate loss to careseekers, who could benefit enormously from massage used together with psychotherapy. A few psychotherapists are now acquiring training in hands-on therapies so that they will have a license to touch their clients.

Clinical applications: Massage in its many variants can be enormously helpful in addressing musculoskeletal problems. It is also useful as a relaxation method in treating almost any condition. For instance, it can be enormously beneficial for women during labor, and for neonates, particularly in premature births.. In its bodymind applications, it can facilitate emotional releases and restructuring of the mind as well as the body, thus easing the progress from dis-eased and diseased states towards health. Anxiety, phobias, panic attacks, depression, sensory deprivation with prolonged illness or hospitalization, and lack of self-confidence can all respond well to these methods. Massage is also lovely for inducing relaxation, not only as a treatment but also as a preventive to stressed states, and just for the pleasure of physical stimulation.

A therapist is essential for a full massage, though it is possible to massage a limited number of one's own muscles. Once you are familiar with some of the simpler methods of massage, you may share and exchange this pleasurable healing technique with others. Many of the meridian-based therapies, and some of the bioenergy healing approaches can be practiced as self-healing.

See also: Bodymind Therapies.

MEDICAL INTUITION (Intuitive Assessments)

The intuitive mind is a sacred gift and the rational mind is a faithful servant. We have created a society that honors the servant and has forgotten the gift.

— Albert Einstein

Intuition is an inner knowing that alerts and informs us about things we would not otherwise know through ordinary sensory perception, memory, or reasoning.

Many health caregivers report that they occasionally intuitively know various bits of information about people who come to them for help. Some who are more sensitive may intuit what a diagnosis is (before completing the examination and laboratory tests), or even identify the underlying physical and psychological causes in the distant past for patients' current physical or emotional problems.[517]

In almost every group of doctors and nurses I have spoken with, many report that they have had inexplicable hunches about patients who needed urgent attention – at times when there were no sensory indications that this might be the case. They report that attending to their intuitive hunches, they have sought out these patients and found that indeed they were in serious and urgent need of help. Such incidents are rare occurrences, but so distinctly odd and impressive that they are clearly recalled. Most health caregivers who have had such experiences are unwilling to discuss them because they anticipate that their colleagues will not believe them – especially if they aren't sure themselves whether this was a real hunch or just an odd coincidence.

A few have more highly developed intuitive abilities, and find that such experiences are common, though not regular. They simply know that the patient before them has heart disease, kidney disease, or whatever – even before she opens her mouth to state her problems. They may also intuit specific medications that could be of help, such as the correct antibiotic for a given infection – prior to receiving the laboratory report on bacterial culture sensitivity to antibiotics.

With very highly developed intuition, it is possible to intuit what is wrong and what will be helpful for almost every patient. Several fascinating books have been published by medical intuitives, some of whom are doctors.[518]

For some, the intuitive knowing comes as an inner feeling, like an itch that urges them to "scratch their minds" to discover what is tickling their awareness. For others, it comes in the form of words or mental images. Another avenue for intuitive knowledge is through the senses, most commonly by perceiving an aura of color around the patient that reveals the state of their body, emotions, mind, relationships, and spirit. Some intuitives report smells or tastes that appear when patients have particular physical conditions or emotional problems, and yet others mirror in their own bodies the sensations that are troubling their patients.

Some intuitives can see into the past to identify the causes for present problems. They may also see into the future, to discover the outcome of treatments.

The more highly gifted intuitives work with only the name of the subject they are diagnosing, sometimes using additional information such as their birth date and city of residence. They can diagnose the condition of anyone in the world, from any distance. A far more common ability is intuitive diagnosis through sensations in the hands of the healer as they are moved around the body of the subject. Sensations in the hands of intuitives, which are apparently caused by interactions with the biological energy fields of the subjects, can provide information relating to states of health, psychological dis-ease, and illness, which the intuitives then interpret.

Medical intuitive abilities are no different from the sensitivities of psychics, which have been thoroughly studied by parapsychologists. Extensive studies, including meta-analyses, all showing statistically significant results, confirm that telepathy, clairsentience, psychokinesis (PK), precognition, and retrocognition can all be demonstrated. Everyone has a measure of these abilities, as has been shown in extensive studies of ordinary people. However, in most people these abilities are weak and produce effects that can be identified only through statistical studies of the intuitive abilities of large groups. Interestingly, the results obtained in trials of non-believers are frequently significantly *lower* than chance, suggesting that the subjects' unconscious minds process the psi awarenesses and produce results that are consistent with their beliefs.[519]

Theories: Several varieties of intuition are apparent (Benor 2002d).
Automatic responses from previous experiences and memory

> *In seeking knowledge, the first step is silence, the second listening, the third remembering, the forth practicing, and the fifth is teaching others.*
> – Ibn Gabirol

When we learn a skill such as driving a car, we initially have to practice each component of turning on the engine, releasing the parking brake, putting the car in gear, steering as we step on the gas pedal, scanning for road clearance and hazards, braking, and so on. As we become proficient in all of these maneuvers, they become habitual and we can do them with little thought. Our automatic responses may be so good that we could be lost in thoughts and suddenly realize that we have driven some distance and cannot recall any conscious adjusting of the steering, braking, or other controls of the car.

The same processes of automating responses occur as we learn other skills, such as clinical medical and nursing interventions. Going through a medical history and examination is initially a complex process, involving myriads of details of information and procedures. The more experienced we are with these, the more they become automatic.

Clinicians are able to draw from their mental databases of knowledge in order to respond to situations rapidly and efficiently, often with little thought. Surgical bleeding occurs, and the surgeon instantly reaches for a clamp and stops it. The patient gags or retches, and the nurses' hand is immediately reaching for the nearest handy towel or basin.

This is a basic level of intuition, in the sense of recognizing a problem and knowing what to do without having to consciously analyze the details and respond through conscious, logical deductions in order to respond to a situation.

Cognitive pattern recognition

> *Let us train our minds to desire what the situation demands.*
> – Seneca

A patient presents with depression, gravelly voice, and thick hair and the doctor, who hasn't seen a case of hypothyroidism this severe since reading his medical school textbooks many years earlier, instantly recognizes that this is a case of hypothyroidism.

A surgeon asked me to see a 23 year-old patient after his appendectomy because he was depressed. His parents reported he had always been something of a loner. As I spoke with him, I felt uncomfortable because his eyes would not meet mine. The diagnosis of Asperger's syndrome came to mind, from having seen children 5 to 10 years old with such presentations - particularly the avoidance of gaze. Further questioning confirmed this to be a very likely diagnosis. I hesitated before sharing this impression, because it suggests an incurable problem, with the patient likely to remain autistic and distant from everyone. The parents, however, were extremely grateful because at last they understood their son's problems and could plan how to deal with them.

Clinical pattern recognition may be more subtle. Clinical sensitivity often leads doctors, nurses and other caregivers to recognize when something is going wrong or going well. Postoperative nurses will often report a sense of a patient "not being right," although objective signs and symptoms are within normal limits. Often, these sorts of intuitive awarenesses prove correct, and an internal bleed or other problem develops soon after the nurse's intuitive "alarm bells" start to ring. At other times, the nurse will sense that all is well, and the patient will have an uneventful postoperative course (King and Clark 2002).

Studies that consider the use of intuition in nurses with varying levels of experience confirm this is a valid modality for decision making. There is a progressive development of trust in intuition - according to levels of experience, from nurses who are beginners, through those who are competent, proficient, and expert [520].

Pattern recognition appears to be (at least in part) an extension of learned knowledge, honed to a fine, automated tool. As clinicians learn more and become more experienced, they can perceive increasingly subtle patterns of appearance, behaviors, monitored body data (from sophisticated instruments), and laboratory studies which alert them to unusual changes and dangers in their patients .

This is the art and science of medical and psychiatric practice. It is medical detective work, the gathering of evidence and seeking the underlying pattern that explains the underlying dynamics (physical, psychological, spiritual) that solve the riddle of what caused the problems. Dreyfus and Dreyfus (1986) discuss pattern recognition as a factor in intuitive awareness.

This level of intuition, pattern recognition, is congruent with the prevalent materialist paradigms that guide and inform conventional medical and nursing practice. Intuition, however, can reach far beyond this level.

Inspiration and creativity

> *When you are inspired by some great purpose, some extraordinary project, all your thoughts break their bonds;y our mind transcends limitations, your consciousness expands in every direction, and you find yourself in a new, great and wonderful world. Ðrmant forces, faculties and talents become alive, and you discover yourself to be a greater person by far than you ever dreamed yourself to be.*
>
> – Patanjali (c. 1st to 3rd century BC)

Poets, writers, actors, painters, sculptors and others in the arts speak of inspiration that sparks their creativity. Inspiration may come as an idea in words - as though a voice speaks to them from another dimension, planting a new idea or a new way of perceiving or explaining something they are working on. Many speak of a *muse* that feels like a wise entity with a distinct personality, visiting from some other dimension when they are quiet and receptive to its whisper. The muse may show them directly what is helpful or may speak through imagery - sometimes in dreams. Among those acknowledging such inspiration are the scientists André Ampère, Karl Gauss, Henri Poincaré, Michael Faraday, Lord Kelvin, Albert Einstein, Nikola Tesla and Thomas Edison, and many poets, authors, actors, musicians and artists.[521]

Where does the muse reside? Various explanations have included psychic abilities,[522] a collective consciousness,[523] spirit guides and Divine inspiration.[524]

How we listen to the muse is also important. It makes a big difference if we listen only through our head/ left brain/ linear awareness, through our heart/ right brain/ gestaltic awareness, or whether we listen with both.

Research: Very few controlled studies have been published on intuitive diagnosis, but numerous workshops and courses in psychic development are advertised for the public. The following studies examined whether one such course, *The Silva Mind Control,* produced any positive results. Robert Brier and colleagues tested several graduates of this course, finding non-significant results overall. However, several children were included among their subjects, and when the individual adult subjects were studied separately, it was found that some achieved modestly significant results ($p < .05$). Alan Vaughan, studying a single subject, found no significant results for her intuitive diagnoses.

There areeveral tabulations of distant intuitive impressions (without control groups or statistical analyses). C. Norman Shealy, a neurosurgeon who has been a pioneer in the study of medical intuition and a past president of the American Holistic Medical Association, published several series of studies on medical intuitives, including the very gifted Carolyn Myss. In one series (Shealy 1975; 1988) which required identification of the site of pain on the body, two of the intuitives studied achieved 75 percent accuracy and another reached 70 percent.

Nils Jacobson and Nils Wiklund studied a single subject after a similar course called Swedish Mind Dynamics, with no significant results in 10 diagnoses.

A series of 2,005 paired diagnoses by naturally gifted intuitives and doctors was briefly summarized by Karel Mison of Prague, in the Czech Republic. While the overall diagnostic agreement was 29 percent, one subject achieved 85 percent.

There are several controlled studies of energy field diagnosis. Susan Marie Wright's doctoral dissertation (1988) studied two healers' energy field diagnoses of the location of pain in the body of 54 subjects, with highly significant results ($p < .0008$ and better). Gary Schwartz et al (1995) studied the abilities of 20 ordinary people to identify when the experimenter's hand was held above their own hand, with modestly significant success ($p < .02$). In a second study of 41 subjects (Schwartz et al. 1996), where most of the subjects were familiar with their experimenter., highly significant results were obtained ($p < .00005$).

A caution in research on medical intuition is highlighted by two pilot studies I did with healers who see auras (Benor 1992). The healers simultaneousl observed the same people with known medical diagnoses. Their observations differed substantially from each other. It appeared that each healer was looking at the subjects through a different window of perception.[525]

Figure II-12. Intuition

In contrast with the studies mentioned above, research by Linda Rosa et al, published in the prestigious *Journal of the American Medical Association* showed negative results for energy field diagnosis. This is an extraordinary study in several respects. First, it was a science fair project of a 10-year-old girl. Second, the negative findings of this study were interpreted by the journal editor, George D. Lundlberg, as proof that Therapeutic Touch healing is a worthless method of treatment. These findings and the editor's conclusion were widely publicized in the popular media, and widely criticized in the alternative medicine media. I do not see much point in belaboring this study, which is critically reviewed in Chapter I-4.

Adverse effects: No harmful effects have been reported See discussion of potential general negative effects from rapid release of buried emotional hurts and rapid improvements under Spiritual Healing.

Training and Certification: C. Norman Shealy MD and Carolyn Myss are now setting up the American Board of Scientific Medical Intuition to certify medical intuitives. See also after Medical Dowsing.

MEDICAL DOWSING

...Little appeared to be known of basic and primary causes, and it seemed impossible to diagnose departures from the normal in the very earlies stages. The average doctor was mainly engaged in baling out leaking boats.

– Aubrey Westlake (p. 3)

Dowsers have long been known for using intuition to locate water and other materials underground, and some dowsers develop medical intuitive diagnostic and healing gifts as well.

Dowsers use rods and pendulums to allow their unconscious minds to speak through unconscious movements of their hands and arms. This is similar to the ideomotor movements of hypnosis and applied kinesiology.[526] A dowser will hold a question in his mind and allow the instrument to answer it with movements that indicate a "yes" or a "no." Dowsers will walk across a field, focusing on the question, "Where is there water?" The dowsing rod will move in a distinct way to indicate when they pass over underground water. Dowsers can also get intuitive information from a distance, using a map to locate water or other substances.[527]

I am impressed that the feedback derived from field and map dowsing provides an excellent way for many people to develop their intuitive gifts.

Many healers in other traditions, such as Healing Touch, use pendulums to get in touch with intuitive knowledge for diagnosis and healing.

In Britain there are also practitioners of *radiesthesia* and *radionics* who are essentially dowsers who use instruments with dials, affectionately called *black boxes*, for dowsing and distant healing. These practices have been outlawed in America by the Food and Drug Administration, which has been very vigilant and at times merciless in prosecuting people who promote the use of these instruments.[528]

Research: While no controlled studies on medical dowsing have been published, there is a promising body of research on field and map dowsing, reviewed in Chapter II-4.

Discussion: While genuine intuitive abilities can be of great help to therapists and people seeking diagnosis and treatment, one must be cautious in interpreting intuitive impressions. There is a distinct margin of error in this practice, as with all physical, psychological, and laboratory-based examinations. Also, intuitive impressions bear a strong imprint of the intuitive diagnostician. That is, different medical intuitives will perceive different impressions, even when examining the same subject at the same time (Benor 1992). While skeptics would view this as proof that medical intuition is faulty, I believe the truth is that it is simply more individualized – both to the particular medical intuitive and to the subject. Each intuitive appears to look into the being of the subject through a different window, providing a unique perspective on their condition.

Medical intuition is a vital element in numerous complementary therapies, often moreso for experienced therapists than for beginners. For instance, acupuncturists may learn to identify where acupuncture points are through their fingertips. Craniosacral therapists sense the rhythms of craniosacral biological energies, and may diagnose specific problems anywhere in the body through this process. Homeopathic and Flower essence practitioners and herbalists may intuitively identify which remedies are needed, and very advanced practitioners may intuit the specific problems that a new plant or other element can treat. Any therapist may intuitively think to ask a particular question or suggest a particular avenue for understanding or dealing with a problem that may be unusual, but which nevertheless precisely hits the mark and brings about new awareness of or changes in physical or psychological conditions (Benor 2001a).

Various approaches for self-assessment of health problems are growing in popularity. These include a spectrum of muscle-testing methods[529] and imagery techniques. In the late 18th Century, hypnotherapists were able to induce profound trances which they called *somnambulism, or plenary hypnosis*, an altered state of consciousness in which people were able to diagnose their own physical and spiritual problems (Ellenberger). I believe that medical dowsing is a sub-category of medical intuition. While these approaches may provide useful information, we must be cautious in interpreting and relying on these materials, as they can be distorted by our wishes, fears, beliefs or particular life experiences (Hayman). In addition, each intuive may perceive different aspects of a person's problems (Benor 1992).

Theories to explain intuitive awareness of problems that exist outside oneself include collective consciousness,[530] psychic perceptions,[531] energetic resonations, a holographic universe, and spiritual awareness.[532] These overlap broadly with various theories that seek to explain aspects of healing.[533] Intuitive self-awareness is is well described in the literature on hypnosis (D. Cheek 1994).

Training, certification and licensing: It is possible to develop and enhance medical intuitive abilities. The therapist's ability grows naturally through the practice of laying-on of hands healing. Meditation and imagery exercises can enhance it as well, and these approaches can also improve distant diagnostic abilities.
 There is no general standardization of training or practice for medical intuition or dowsing, although several methods of healing, such as Therapeutic Touch, Healing Touch, and Barbara Brennan School of Healing, teach specific techniques. C. Norman Shealy, MD is working towards developing methods and standards for certification.

Clinical efficacy: Medical intuition can be an enormously helpful supplement to integrative care, both in identifying problems, and in selecting and guiding treatments.
  While conventional wisdom recommends consulting a highly gifted intuitive to help in identifying causes of mysterious medical symptoms, developing our own intuitive capacities to identify the roots of our problems is also enormously helpful. In fact, this is one of the most effective of the self-healing approaches. It helps us connect with deep sources of inner wisdom – not just in our unconscious mind, but also through a deeper, spiritual awareness of the world beyond. **See also:** Applied Kinesiology; Medical dowsing; Radionics and Radiesthesia; Remote viewing[534]

MEDITATION

> *...Question put to a Zen monk, while walking down a busy street. I was amazed by the way he took up the shock and the repercussions of the traffic and of the shoving crowds. After a while I said to him, "How do you get this way – self-controlled, orderly, integrated?" Because in those days I was searching for these qualities within myself.*

He said, "Well, if I'm different from anyone else, I must lay credit to one thing."
"What is that?" I asked.
He replied, "I never leave my place of meditation."
                                                        – Marcus Bach

Meditation appears to be a gateway to *alternative states of consciousness (ASCs)* in which self-healing and spiritual healing may occur.

How to meditate, and the experience of meditation
Meditation is not a way of mentally focusing upon a task as in ordinary states of consciousness, where the will is engaged in order to achieve a particular end. It is an opening up to allow a process to happen. The process is simply given a space or channel through which to occur. There is an intentionality associated with meditation for healing, but it is passive rather than active. As one would not push a river to flow, so the healer does not *push* the energy to flow for the healing, nor does he push healees to improve faster than they are ready to be healed. It is as though a stream of energy is invited to flow through the meditator, and meditation clears away obstructions to this flow.

The effect of meditation has been likened to looking at the stars at night and at noon. During the daylight hours the competing stimuli of the sun's rays block the weaker light of the stars, making them invisible. At night, as in the meditative state, the process of turning off the overwhelming stimuli occurs and the stars are clearly visible.
                                                        – Marianne Borelli

For many of us, Meditation is hard work, because we do not know how to let go of our thinking in order to experience *being*. There are many different ways to mediate, and I will discuss just a few of the better known approaches here.

  Lawrence LeShan (1974b) presents an excellent discussion of practical aspects of meditation that are relevant to healing, ranging from the why and how of this practice to the social significance of its use. He identifies several paths and varieties of meditation:

1. *Intellect:* meditation "uses the intellect to go beyond the intellect, the will and directed thought processes to transcend themselves." (p.33)
2. *Emotions:* there are "meditations that loosen the feelings and expand the ability to relate to others, to care and to love... some meditational schools concentrate on learning to love the self, some on learning to love others, some... to love God. Ultimately all arrive at the same place, loving all three." (p.35)
3. *Body:* "...one learns to be aware of one's body and bodily movements and to heighten this awareness through practice, until, during... meditation, this awareness completely fills the field of consciousness to the exclusion of anything else." (p.36)
4. *Action:* meditation "consists of learning how to 'be' and to perceive and relate to the world during the performance of a particular skill... Various skills have been used: archery, flower arrangement, Aikido and karate (two methods of unarmed combat) in the Zen tradition and rug weaving in the Sufi tradition. Singing and prayer have been used in the Christian tradition." (p.37)
5. *Structured:* meditation "carefully and precisely defines what the inner activity is

that you are working toward… Any straying… is corrected as soon as you become aware of your wandering." (p.41)

6. *Unstructured.* "…you think about a subject and simply stay with the subject and your own feelings about it." (p.42)

LeShan suggests specific meditations for each of the above-mentioned categories, recommending graded series and ways of varying meditations to suit individual needs. It is possible to do much of this on a self-taught basis, though the guidance of an expert may be desired with some types or in some stages of meditation. LeShan also details several distinct states of inner consciousness.[535]

Patricia Carrington reviews studies of meditation and related states. She has many practical suggestions on how to meditate, emphasizing the use of *mantras* (words repeated mentally). She discusses many functions and benefits of meditation, focusing most heavily on aspects of personal growth and psychotherapy. She summarizes her views:

> Meditation… is a time when the organism shifts gears from the active to the receptive mode; from a state of ego dominance to a state where the ego is subordinate and can be partially dispensed with; from a state of automatization to one of deautomatization. It may also be a time when the organism experiences a shift from the dominance of one cerebral hemisphere to a state of concordance or harmony between both hemispheres of the brain; and perhaps a time when it experiences a shift from limited contact with some as yet unidentified energy source toward a more deep fundamental contact, or 'flowing with,' that source. (p.315)

Figure II-13. Stephen spends his morning on a snowy mountain peak in silent meditative communion with the rising sun

Cartoon by Joe Sumrall, from *Lighten Up*

Arthur Dykeman presents a lovely experiment that demonstrates how simple it is to enter another reality through meditation. He had college students simply stare for a while at a blue vase to get a sense of "being one with the vase." A number of subjects reported marked experiences of altered states of consciousness within a short while.

Research: Physical benefits of meditation include reductions in pain (Kabat-Zinn et al. 1986); improvements in stress responses (Glueck/ Stroebel; Goleman/ Schwartz), diminished levels of substance abuse (Sharma et al. 1971), and other behavioral parameters;[536] reduced pulse and blood pressure;[537] changes in respiration rate, oxygen consumption and carbon dioxide elimination; reduced muscle tension and blood lactate levels (associated with anxiety and hypertension); higher skin resistance (indicating relaxation); subjective experiences of "feeling better" in various ways;[538] lower cholesterol (M. Cooper/ Aygen); reduced blood cortisol levels, when these are elevated due to stress (MacLean, et al.); and reduced prostate specific antigen with prostatic cancers (Saxe et al.). Meditation has been demonstrated to be a cost-effective treatment for chronic pain (Caudill et al.). An extensive overview of meditation research has been compiled by the Maharishi International University, covering over 500 studies and including a meta-analysis (Orme-Johnson/ Farrow),[539] and three other reviews: two by Michael Murphy and Steven Donovan covers over 600 studies, and a briefer, annotated bibliography by Bogart (1991).[540]

Because meditation influences mental activities, its effects upon brainwaves have been studied extensively using electroencephalograms (EEGs).[541] Alpha waves (9 to 13 cycles per second) and theta waves (5 to 8 cycles per second) are frequently found during meditation. Much has been made of alpha and theta brainwave biofeedback as a method of learning to enter alternative states of consciousness, and benefits similar to those of meditative states are therefore anticipated when people train themselves to produce these brainwave frequencies. However, the results are far from conclusive.[542] Maxwell Cade and Geoffrey Blundell developed an EEG machine that displays the amount of brainwave activity from 0.5 to 32 cycles per second in each of the cerebral hemispheres, using a panel of LED lights. They are impressed that the most effective meditative and healing state is one in which the *activity in the right and left hemispheres is balanced.*

Early research with brain imaging devices confirms that there are measurable changes in brain activity with meditation (Newburg et al.). [543]

Meditation is a clearing of all extraneous preoccupations from the mind, and as such it can be of great benefit to healees because it allows them to focus exclusively upon the task of self-healing. It also facilitates release of worries, anxieties and fears related to serious illness. Meditation in and of itself also appears to convey benefits on physical, mental, emotional and spiritual levels.

For healers, meditation appears to provide a gateway to states of being in which spiritual healing can be facilitated. Some also feel that quiet meditation by the healee facilitates distant healing, especially when it coincides with the sending of healing.

The practice of meditation has been found to be cost effective, in that those who meditate regularly have significantly reduced health care use (McSherry; Orme-Johnson 1987).

I have mentioned only a few of numerous teachers who discuss meditation and its benefits.[544] A fuller knowledge of this important branch of human exploration can be of benefit not only in developing greater self-knowledge and awareness but also in learning to heal ourselves and others of the ills that can mark or accompany our progress along the paths of our existence.

Lessons from meditation
The improvements in physical conditions that result from meditation may be explained as relaxation effects that reduce physical and emotional tensions. These changes then bring about neurophysiological and neurohormonal changes that improve physical problems.

If we allow that biological energies may be shaped by consciousness, then we can see how these can provide another pathway for relaxation to influence the body. Meditation can alter our energy fields, which in turn can improve body functions. Furthermore, in helping us to connect with our higher selves, meditation may strengthen our access to energetic aspects of ourselves which can facilitate healing.

The subjective experiences of meditation have far-reaching effects and implications. Meditation can open the mind into awarenesses that transcend the individual self. Our ordinary states of consciousness rely on our outer senses and thought processes, which are grounded in the experiences of physical existence. Inner experiences of emotions are tied to our physical being and our relationships with others in our physical environment.

In meditative states we can become aware of transpersonal realms that extend beyond the individual self. These may be explained as:

1. Fantasies, wishful thinking, denial of death, or other projections of the physical-based mind;
2. Awarenesses of realms of experience that legitimately extend beyond our perceptions of the ordinary, physical and psychological world (These are extensively discussed in Chapter II-1 and Volume III); or
3. The result of activity within particular parts of the brain, which create the subjective experience of unusual experiences.

The first hypothesis is difficult to support, in view of the similar reports of transpersonal experiences from cultures all around the world.

A logical argument can be made for the third hypothesis. The similarities of meditative experiences and other altered states of consciousness in cultures around the world could be an indication that these are simply products of the biochemical and bioelectrical processes of the brain.

However, an argument can equally well be made for the second point of view. The similarities of meditative experiences and other altered states of consciousness in cultures around the world could be an indication that these are consensual perceptions of realities in other dimensions.

It is my personal impression and belief that there are other dimensions of reality that we can reach through spontaneous psi experiences[545] and altered states of consciousness, such as those achieved through meditation. My subjective experiences, particularly in spiritual healing interactions, is that these intuitively perceived realities feel more valid and real on deeper levels than the outer realities. I will discuss these issues in much greater depth in Volume III.

Meditation offers profound healings in and of itself, and can enhance and deepen the effects of spiritual healing.

Effects of meditation on healers and healees
In *healees:*

1. Meditation may act directly to normalize respiration, blood pressure and other neurohormonal concomitants of anxiety. These effects alone may be beneficial, regardless of which disease processes may be present. Reduced anxiety and relaxation may also lead to subjective relief from pain.

2. Meditation may powerfully sharpen the focus of inner energies – as a single-minded projection of self-healing – to deal with whatever disease processes are present or to correct hormonal and/ or energy imbalances or disharmonies. In ordinary consciousness the mind may be distracted and mental energies may be scattered and therefore less than optimally focused on healing. With meditation, all of the healee's mental energies can be directed towards healing, thereby achieving more potent effects. This may be analogous to karate, where physical energies are narrowly focused on a target along with mental intent, which maximizes the effect of the applied energies. The mental intent is vital to the success of the karate. Meditation may be a mental karate, enhancing internal applications of healing energies.

As self-healoing, his enhanced focus may be similar to the enhancement of control over body processes achieved under hypnosis.

There are many points of similarity between meditation and hypnosis, such as concentrating on one subject to the exclusion of all others; focusing on rhythmic, repetitive stimuli; and relinquishing investment in outwardly-directed conscious thought. In the context of spiritual healing there is the further similarity of placing one's self in the hands of a skilled therapist.)

3. Meditation may teach healees to focus mentally and to visualize themselves free of disease, in the process of self-healing. This could be a form of positive thinking, de-emphasizing the illeness aspects and enhancing the awareness of the healthy aspects of one's life.

4. Meditation may enable healees to tap healing resources from other levels of reality. Healees may achieve this on their own, or may be aided in linking through meditation with a healer who can facilitate connections with other dimensions.

In *healers:*

For many healers, the meditative state facilitates healing, and may even be a prerequisite for activation of healing. Important components of this state include:

1. Reduction or elimination of sensory and mental distractions may permit a more efficient, forceful utilization of healing powers or energies. This could permit activation of portions of the healer's mind that are ordinarily unused, by shutting off the constant noise of observing, thinking and emotional activities. Perhaps this involves shifts from left-brain to right-brain functions, or a more balanced

coordination of the right and left brain hemispheres.[546] It may also involve the activation of deeper, less conscious portions of the mind.

2. Mental concentration may facilitate a greater ability to focus the transfer of energies from within the healers or through them to the healees. The analogy to karate is again applicable.

3. (1) may lead healers into a mode of *being* rather than *doing,* in which they can set aside preconceptions, associations and thoughts, and just commune with their healees. It may facilitate an unconditional acceptance of the healees, which is the sine qua non of psychotherapy..

4. (1) may enable healers to be more in contact with and to deliberately utilize forces and energies in the realms of realities that are otherwise not available to them. Healers may then channel these cosmic forces of nature through themselves to the healees (LeShan 1974a; 1976).

5. (1) and (3) may facilitate the release of perceptions of a disease-reality and may permit the establishment of a health-reality via (2-4). This process, which may include visualization, may lead to a restructuring of healees' bodies so that they can relinquish disease processes and begin to be healed, or, in special cases, be instantaneously transformed to a state of health.

> *When the mind is still, tranquil, not seeking any answer or solution even, neither resisting nor avoiding, it is only then that there can be a regeneration, because then the mind is capable of perceiving what its true and it is the truth that liberates, not our effort to be free.*
> – Krishnamurti

It is fascinating to me that some healers do not seem to require a state of meditation for successful healings to occur. They seem able to invoke a healing state automatically. Some of these healers easily enter an altered state of consciousness in which they can converse freely without disturbing the healing process. Perhaps these healers are open to healing awareness most of the time, so that they don't have to shift out of ordinary awareness to enter a healing state.

Many healers report that the frequent releases of conscious focus that they practice during healing also carries over into everyday life. It is particularly common for healers to be easily distractible and to have memory problems.

One strong healer that I know personally finds that her long-term memory does not record much of the data processed in conversations that take place during healings, although she is able to discuss any topic intelligently and coherently while she is healing.

Subjective and psychotherapeutic benefits of meditation

The self-healing aspect of meditation requires a great deal of further research. It is clear however that meditation can be used in very practical ways to address focal problems. For instance, if you are stuck with an issue that you can't resolve, using a creative imagery meditation can open up possibilities that you have overlooked.[547]

It is common to practice meditation while focusing upon an external object, such as a lit candle, a plant, or some other aspect of nature. With even a modest meditation period of 30-60 minutes you may find yourself so strongly identifying with the object that you feel you *are* the object, and can sense many aspects of its essence. You can equally well focus on some inner part of yourself, such as an ache or pain, an illness, or a psychological conflict. With the support and guidance of a therapist (you are strongly advised not to do this on your own), you may immerse yourself totally in a symptom or issue. By totally connecting with a problem, rather than avoiding its unpleasantness, you may find that its negativity is rapidly and markedly diminished. A variety of meditations can be helpful in this way.[548]

Going deeper, you can invite your pain, illness, or other problem to speak to you, and to tell you what it wants to say in words – rather than just in symptoms. Symptoms may often be messengers from your unconscious mind, inviting you to explore or release old issues.[549]

> It is only with the heart that one can see rightly; what is essential is invisible to the eye.
>
> – Antoine de Saint-Exupéry

These are very different sorts of meditations than those associated with more prolonged traditional meditative practice. These are deliberate forms of therapy, intended to help particular problems.

Deep therapeutic changes are also often reported with regular meditation that is practiced for spiritual development. Meditators frequently claim that with prolonged practice they find that very profound positive changes occur in their personalities, their outlooks on life, their interpersonal relationships, their physical health and so forth.

> He who looks outwardly, dreams. But he who looks within, awakes.
>
> – C.G. Jung

These changes often resemble the results achieved through successful transpersonal psychotherapy. Recent research supports these claims (Wilber/ Engler/ Brown).

For many years I was puzzled by this spontaneous resolution of problems during meditation that did not deliberately focus on the problems – but in fact seemed designed to focus the mind *away* from these, along with the avoidance of all other intrusions on the meditative focus.

In psychotherapy the goal is usually to uncover conflicts and emotions that have been buried in the unconscious mind. The repressed problems reveal themselves though troublesome reactions and behaviors that are disproportionate to the stresses in one's present life. The work of psychotherapy is often long and arduous, requiring meticulous conscious analysis of associations from conflictual material and projections of feelings upon others, tracing back to the roots of these problems in the depths of well defended repressions. Alternatively, behavioral approaches seek to restructure cognitive responses and reactions to inner and outer stimuli that are troublesome.

Newer techniques permit the rapid release of symptoms and hurts – even when we have carried them with us for years. As mentioned above, you may immerse yourself totally in a symptom or issue (with the support of a therapist) and surprisingly, this often leads to release of suffering – rather than to greater suffering (that logic suggests might result from focusing on the problems).[550]

In meditation one does not follow associations, or look for repressed material, or push to release emotions that have not been expressed in times past. In fact, it would seem that meditation seeks to teach the exact antithesis of such endeavors – which is to set aside all associations and feelings and not to invest them with attention or importance. This appears at first glance to be similar to, if not identical with pathological processes such as denial and repression that produce so many of the psychological problems that I work very hard to get clients (and myself) to overcome.

I finally realized that this puzzle is only an apparent paradox, and is related to the questions that are asked about meditative practices and processes. It appears problematic only as long as one focuses on what occurs in *psychopathology*. If we ask instead what is occuring in psychotherapy and meditation that is *positive*, the similarities begin to emerge and the apparent contradictions disappear. Both meditation and psychotherapy teach people to let go of their attachments to prior belief systems and unhealthy habits of self-criticism and doubt. Psychopathology can be seen as a dis-ease engendered by a disparity between an individual's present situation and the way she believes her situation to be (based on experiences from the past), or the way she wishes it to be (based on hopes, aspirations, anxieties or fears regarding the future). In this context, the task of psychotherapy is either to help her identify and release her rigidly maintained guidelines from the past or relinquish her unrequited wishes or worries about the future. Similarly, meditation helps people to let go of all of their conflicts that do not exist in the immediate here and now.

Newer psychotherapy techniques also permit the rapid release of symptoms and hurts – even when we have carried them with us for years. You may immerse yourself totally in a symptom or issue, and surprisingly, this often leads to release of suffering – rather than to greater suffering.

Meditation may take one even deeper, opening into transcendent awareness in which everything is in the eternal *Now* and physical existence is but a moment in a vaster awareness.

> *Now is the only time over which we have dominion.*
> – Tolstoy

Some holistic therapists believe that meditation alone is sufficient as a way of dealing with stresses and emotional problems. While this may be true in many cases, psychotherapy may be necessary in other instances, particularly when there are strong emotional releases during meditation. Jack Kornfield (1993, p. 249) observes, "Just as deep meditation requires a skilled teacher, at times our spiritual path also requires a skilled therapist. Only a deep attention to the whole of our life can bring us to the capacity to love well and to live freely."

While meditation may be practiced purely for its spiritual benefits, Kornfield suggests other benefits:

> The purpose of spiritual life is not to create some special state of mind.
> A state of mind is always temporary. The purpose is to work directly
> with the most primary elements of our body and our mind, to see the

ways we get trapped by our fears, desires, and anger, and to learn directly our capacity for freedom. As we work with them, the demons will enrich our lives. They have been called "manure for enlightenment" or "mind weeds," which we pull up or bury near the plant to give it nourishment.

To practice [meditation] is to use all that arises within us for the growth of understanding, compassion, and freedom. Thomas Merton wrote, "True love and prayer are learned in the hour when love becomes impossible and the heart has turned to stone." When we remember this, the difficulties we encounter in practice can become part of the fullness of meditation, a place to learn and to open our heart. (p. 99-100)

Meditation may have different effects upon people raised in Eastern and Western cultural traditions, and it may involve different practices and processes as well. In Western culture we emphasize individuation, while in the East people are primarily expected to function as a part of their social group. As Joseph Campbell (1972) points out:

The word 'I'... suggests to the Oriental philosopher only wishing, wanting, desiring, fearing, and possessing, i.e., the impulses of what Freud has termed the id operating under pressure of the pleasure principle...

The virtue of the Oriental is comparable, then, to that of the good soldier, obedient to orders, personally responsible not for his acts but only for their execution. And since all the laws to which he is adhering will have been handed down from an infinite past, there will be no one anywhere personally responsible for the things that he is doing...

In a related observation, Jack Kornfield (1993) reports:

...When I worked in Asian monasteries there was very little attention to what might be called personal, or psychological problems. In fact, upon returning from America, one of the great masters commented that he had seen a kind of suffering over here that he wasn't so familiar with – "they call it psychological suffering, whatever that is."

It would be fascinating if sensitives who perceive mental and emotional layers of the aura would observe meditators from the East and the West, and report on any differences they note in the energy fields of meditators – over the immediate and the long term practice of meditation.

Some may use meditation as a means of avoidance or escape, rather than as a form of cleansing, which is sometimes termed a *meditational bypass.*. Jack Kornfield calls these meditators *skippers*. I know many who have reached very refined levels of development on spiritual dimensions, but who have neglected to work through or release much of the dross in their physical/ psychological/ emotional levels.

Meditation offers further psychotherapeutic elements. These include encouraging an appreciation of one's place in the cosmos; placing psychological conflicts in new and more healthy perspectives; and introducing an inner peace that derives from the deeply satisfying, spiritual, noetic experience of being one with the All.[551]

It is conceivable that practicing meditation from childhood, or in other ways learning the art of being in the present (Tart 1986b; Wilber 1981), may help one avoid unnecessary conflicts caused by self-imposed, unsatisfying comparisons between conditions in time-present and other temporal contexts, wishes or fears. It is unclear to me whether the ideal of total self-differentiation without conflicts is attainable. Satprem (1981) leads us to believe that this is possible in gifted individuals, and Kornfield and Irina Tweedie provide excellent descriptions of the processes and challenges encountered on such paths.

The subject of potential negative reactions to meditation deserves further study. It is my impression that people who are emotionally unstable, or whose personal boundaries between themselves and the rest of the world are not very firm, may find the experience of meditation frightening. The impairments in psychological boundaries in their ordinary states of consciousness, due to their emotional instability, is often troubling to them and to others around them. The loss of conscious awareness during meditation may arouse further anxieties.

This sort of anxiety may lead a person to become anxious about being anxious, which I term *meta-anxiety*.[552] If unchecked, it can escalate to panic proportions. It is quite possible that some of the negative reactions to meditation are due to meta-anxiety around fears of losing control rather than to effects of the meditation in and of itself.

For all of the discussion *about* meditation, it is impossible to appreciate its nature and benefits without trying it for yourself. I highly recommend this practice to anyone interested in self-healing and spiritual development.

Adverse effects: Though it is a rare occurrence, there have been occasional reports of serious negative experiences with meditation. People who are prone to emotional instability are advised to use meditation only under professional supervision. Meditation may intensify obsessiveness (A. Ellis 1984); produce insomnia and depression (Lazarus); elicit psychosomatic symptoms (Otis); precipitate psychotic decompensation;[553] and bring about withdrawal from engagement with normal life activities and relationships (Maupin).

Short of such severe effects, which are not very common, mild negative experiences are not uncommon (Braith et al.; D. Shapiro) and simple *emotional releases* are common during meditation. It appears that as a person relaxes, their psychological defenses also relax. Emotional hurts that were long buried may then surface to consciousness, with an accompanying release of the buried feelings. At times this brings full recognition of the earlier precipitating traumas, but it may also occur as a release of feelings without attached memories.

These potential problems are best dealt with by experienced meditation teachers (Kornfield 1993).

It is worth mentioning that teachers are human and are still learning the challenging lessons of life. None is perfect. In fact, some are so far from perfection that one may wonder how they presume to teach others. One should not to assume that everyone who claims to be a meditation teacher is competent to do so with people who may have serious life issues to deal with. Meditation instructors, as with any therapist, should be screened by prospective students – as suggested at the end of this chapter. This is not to say that due to their imperfections we cannot learn from flawed teachers. Brugh Joy (1990, p.102) reminds us, "You are not there to verify facts about the teacher. You are there to experience some aspect of your Self."

There is no general credentialing and no standard training in the teaching of meditation. Eastern religions and Transcendental Meditation specify clear requirements for instructors. Several stress management programs at universities have developed courses for the therapeutic use of meditation.[554]

Clinical applications: Meditation is an excellent avenue to relaxation, and it can contribute to prevention and treatment of most stress-related illnesses. It is excellent for development of spiritual awareness.

See also: Chapter II-1 on self-healing and on meditation as a transpersonal therapy; Chapter I-1 on healer and healee reports of subjective experiences of healing; Volume III of *Healing Research* on research in spiritual dimensions; Chapters IV-2 and IV-3 on dissections of the spiritual healing experience.

MERIDIAN BASED THERAPIES (MERIDIAN PSYCHOTHERAPY)

*There is only one corner of the universe you can be certain of improving...
and that's your own self."*

– Aldous Huxley (1944)

Included among these approaches are *Thought Field Therapy* (*TFT*),[555] *Emotional Freedom Technique* (*EFT* – G. Craig), *the Wholistic Hybrid of EMDR and EFT (WHEE-* Benor 2001a), *Touch and Breathing* (*TAB* – Diepold), Be Set Free Fast (*BSFF* – Nims), *Tapas Acupressure Technique* (*TAT* – Fleming) and numbers of other variations on this theme. Healees focus on their psychological problems while using their fingers to apply pressure to acupuncture points on their head, chest, and/ or hand. Within minutes they usually find that their irrational fear or the hurt of old emotional traumas is released, and long-held disbeliefs and negative beliefs are transformed. These approaches can markedly alleviate and sometimes even cure chronic pains and allergies.[556] Positive beliefs can then be instilled through the same techniques, to replace whatever negativity has been released.

Muscle testing of applied kinesiology[557] can be used to guide clients to the roots of their problems, and to set up the mental focus for pressure point treatment.[558]

Often, mental processing of the roots of their problems is not necessary, although in many cases people do spontaneously come to understand how their problems developed and how they were maintained by choice or through psychological and relational reinforcements. This contradicts the teachings of many varieties of mainstream psychotherapy, which insist that without cognitive awareness and understanding of the roots of our problems we cannot achieve true healing.

CASE: Joe was afraid of heights, which interfered with his life in a variety of ways. If an elevator was not working, he could not climb the stairs if there was an open stairwell where he could see the stairs below him, and he couldn't go down a flight of stairs without suffering a panic attack. He had to take tranquilizers to travel by plane, and this made him groggy when he landed, necessitating extra days' stay during business trips to clear his mind. Repairing anything in his home that required standing on a chair or ladder was something he avoided at all costs.

At a stress reduction workshop, I introduced WHEE, which is rapidly and potently effective in dealing with stresses of all sorts. WHEE differs from other meridian based therapies because it includes major components of EMDR.[559] Joe skeptically participated, not really expecting to have any response. He alternated tapping on his right and left eyebrows, after repeating an affirmation, "Even though I'm afraid of heights, I love and accept myself wholly and completely, and God loves and accepts me wholly, completely and unconditionally."

Before starting to tap, Joe estimated his initial level of anxiety when thinking about heights was 15 on a scale of zero to ten. Within 5 minutes, after four rounds of tapping, he was down to zero – much to his amazement.

Next, using the same technique, he installed a positive affirmation: "I can look down from a height and feel comfortable." After several rounds of tapping he brought this from a zero to a level eight. He just couldn't believe this would really work, so we had him go out and climb the stairs. He reported back in amazement that he felt only mild anxiety going down the stairs, and none going up – even though it was an open stairwell. With repeated tapping, he strengthened the positive affirmation to a level ten.

He subsequently used this technique himself to overcome his fear of flying as well. Needless to say, WHEE transformed his life in many ways.

One of the greatest benefits of these approaches is that they can be practiced by the client for self-healing. Once people know the methods, they can proceed, if they wish, to do a systematic house-cleaning of old emotional and habitual debris that they may have carried around for years.

> *'Tis not enough to help the feeble up,*
> *But to support them after.*
> – William Shakespeare *(Timon of Athens)*

My personal experiences with these therapeutic modalities is that they are profoundly effective in releasing old hurts and the accompanying chronic physical problems, and in installing positive beliefs. EMDR may also spontaneously bring people into a deep state of spiritual awareness. I was at first skeptical that these results could be more than superficial or temporary improvements because I had been biased by my conventional psychotherapy training to believe that psychological insight and conscious understanding of problems are necessary for healing to take place. The astounding results achieved with these therapies testifies that one can release old hurts and move on to healthier psychological functioning without conscious understanding of the roots or developmental processes of the problems.

Research: While there is a solid database of research for EMDR,[560] there are only anecdotal reports of successes with the meridian based therapies.[561]

Clinical applications: I am personally impressed that the meridian based therapies are among the best and most potent of self-haling interventions. They are helpful with emotional stress and distress, limiting beliefs, self-defeating attitudes, addictions (food, smoking, drugs), acute and chronic physical pains and allergies.

See also: EMDR, Applied Kinesiology.

NATIVE AMERICAN MEDICINE

> *...When we come into the Earthwalk, we come in with truth encoded in us. But we can lose sight of that. The only ones who do not know who they are are the two-leggeds. So sometimes we have to open up and receive messages from the Spirit to remember...*
> – Grandmother Twylah Nitch

It is difficult to speak of Native American medicine generically when there are about 500 distinct Nations or tribes, each with its own traditions and practices that date back over an estimated 12,000 to 40,000 years. There is also the universal Native American tradition of honoring individual innovations, which are derived in varied clinical situations according to the intuition of each individual healer.

Common denominators in Native American medicine include a belief in a *life force* (called *ni* in Lakota) or *divine breath,* and a concept of disease seen "in terms of morality, balance, and the action of spiritual power rather than specific, measurable causes" (K. Cohen 1999b). Illnesses are felt to occur when individuals are not in harmony with themselves, their relationships with other people, and the natural world. Diagnosis may be derived by speaking with the person and their family and community, or through divination, prayer, and consultation with nature guides and spirit guides. Treatments may include counseling to identify internal problems (such as negative thinking); dream interpretation; herbal medicines; chanting or other rituals (drumming, dances, fasts, sweat lodge ceremonies, laying-on of hands); and asking the help of spirits of the natural world, or of the Great Spirit. Diagnosis and treatment is a highly individualized art, so it is impossible for outsiders simply to copy rituals and expect that they will work for anyone but the original practitioner.[562]

Native American medicine is not exclusive of other practices, and can be used in harmony with Western treatments.

Adverse effects: No harmful effects have been reported See discussion of potential general negative effects from rapid improvements under Spiritual Healing and other considerations under Shamanism.

Training and certification: There are no standards for practice or certification. Training is by calling and apprenticeship and highly individualized to the gifts of the individual medicine man or woman.

Clinical applications: Native American medicine is a complete system of therapy. While it is particularly helpful for Native Americans, it has also been shown to be effective in treatment of many disorders in people who are not of this tradition (e.g. Boyd).

A medicine man will guide and lead the healee through appropriate ceremonies, and can recommend various practices and herbs for healing. Self-healing exercises and practices may be prescribed.

See also: Shamanism.

NATUROPATHIC MEDICINE

Naturopathy helps a person to establish a positive state of health.
— D.B.

Naturopathic medicine has been practiced in the US since the early 1900s. At the height of its popularity, there were over 20 naturopathic medical schools. In 1910, the Flexner Report established guidelines for funding medical schools. This was a political coup for allopathic doctors, as the Flexner recommendations gave preference to schools approved by the American Medical Association. This led to a rapid decline in the practice of naturopathy, almost to the point of its disappearance in the US.[563] In the past 20 years naturopathy has seen a marked revival. There are 3 naturopathic medicine schools and about 1,000 naturopathic doctors (NDs) practicing in the US today.

Naturopathic approaches include nutrition and life-style counseling, herbal remedies, homeopathy, flower remedies, acupuncture, traditional Chinese medicine, hydropathy, and various manipulative therapies. The major focus is on supporting, stimulating and strengthening the self-healing potentials within the body. Treatments are directed at causes rather than at symptoms. The doctor is seen as a teacher who aims to promote and maintain optimal health in the whole person.[564]

Research: Rigorous research in naturopathic treatments is in its infancy. For instance, a study of naturopathy for treatment of abnormal cells in the cervix[565] showed a return to normalcy in 38 out of 43 women with abnormal Pap smears (Hudson 1993).

Training and licensing: Naturopathic training in the US involves a four-year, 4,100-hour course at a recognized school. Subjects covered include basic biological sciences, diagnosis, pathology, microbiology, pharmacology, nutrition, public health and clinical practice. Naturopathic physicians (ND or NMD) are licensed after passing a nationally standardized formal examination[566] for provision of primary health care, in a dozen states, [567] and in most of the Canadian provinces. In other states anyone may claim to be a naturopathic practitioner, even with minimal training. There are also Naturopathic doctorate programs.[568]

The Council on Naturopathic Medical Education (CNME) accredits schools and training programs and is recognized by the US Department of Education. The American Association of Naturopathic Physicians (AANP) is the US professional association.

In the UK, the General Council and Register of Naturopaths (GCRN) is the professional organization for Naturopaths, who are not covered by statutory regulation. Training also varies, with some Naturopaths graduating from 4-year courses and others with far less training.

Growing numbers of medical and osteopathic physicians and many nurses in the US and UK are incorporating many of the same approaches in their practices. The American Holistic Medical Association (AHMA) promotes these practices and the American Board of Holistic Medicine (ABHM) offers Board examinations in Holisitc Medicine. The American Holistic Nurses Association (AHNA) similarly promotes naturopathic practices integrated with conventional nursing.

Clinical applications: Naturopathy encourages a healthy lifestyle and is certainly helpful in promoting and maintaining health and preventing disease. As naturopathy may include a very broad range of treatments, one must assess its efficacy according the successes of the individual treatments applied.

A naturopathic doctor can be enormously helpful in prescribing and recommending therapies for most illnesses. Self-healing practices may also be recommended.

Integrative care is developing gradually, with naturopathy complementing conventional medicine particularly in herbal and nutritional interventions[569] ,as well as in other CAM approaches.

See also: Anthroposophic Medicine, Ayurvedic Medicine, individual CAM therapies.

NUTRITIONAL AND HERBAL THERAPIES

> *2000 BC: Here, eat this root.*
> *1000 AD: That root is heathen. Here, say this prayer.*
> *1850 AD: That prayer is superstition. Here, drink this potion.*
> *1940 AD: That potion is snake oil. Here, swallow this pill.*
> *1985 AD: That pill is ineffective. Here, take this antibiotic.*
> *2000 AD: That antibiotic is no longer effective. Here, eat this root.*
> – Anonymous

Diets

Numerous specialized diets have been recommended by various types of practitioners for health maintenance and for treatment of illnesses. While some are simply fads, others have been supported by research demonstrating their efficacy.

One obvious recommendation is to eat organically grown fruits and vegetables that do not contain pesticides or preservatives, and meat from animals that have not been given growth hormones, antibiotics or other chemicals. Such chemicals could be toxic – if not immediately, then on a cumulative basis.

Other cautions include avoiding irradiated[570] and genetically modified foods,[571] foods cooked in Teflon (over 600 degrees)[572] and foods stored in plastics.[573] Water from municipal supplies is often recycled without clearing out the metabolized products of the myriads of drugs taken by people who excrete these into the sewage system – providing those who drink this water with a cocktail of unknown chemicals (Batmanghelidj). Bottled water alone may be unhealthy over the long run (C. Day). Another suggestion is to avoid foods that have been cooked in Teflon (at over 600 degrees) or aluminum cookware, as these may be unhealthy.

The general field of nutrition is too vast to summarize adequately here. I can only discuss a few salient problems and studies. [574]

Elimination diets can help to identify food allergies. An initial restriction of intake to non-allergenic foods such as rice for a week may allow the body to clear itself of allergens and of the various related symptoms. Specific allergies can then be identified through serial additions of single food items, spaced over several days. Avoidance of the offending foods, and implementation of various desensitization procedures can then be instituted. Desensitization may include meridian-based therapies, which involve a self-healing acupressure technique.[575]

We commonly think of allergic reactions as direct responses of our digestive systems to something we eat or drink. Sometimes other organs may also respond with allergic reactions, such as our skin (with hives and other rashes)' airways and lungs (wheezing, asthma, or even complete shutting off of our breath from sever swelling of the airways); eyes (with itching, redness); muscles (weakness, fatigue, fibromyalgia); and mind (confusion, memory problems, tiredness, attention and hyperactivity disorders).

Elimination of allergens and/ or toxins may help in treating many of these problems (Colborn et al.). For instance, there are numerous anecdotal reports that mercury in dental amalgam may produce signs of toxicity, which can be relieved by removal of the offending fillings (Huggins; Kidd). In Attention Deficit Hyperactivity Disorder, elimination of allergenic foods may reduce symptomatology (Egger, J. et al.; Shannon 2000; 2001).

Fasting is helpful in several ways. It can clear toxins, as in the initial phase of an elimination diet. Fasting is in itself a discipline, and it can produce alternative states of consciousness that are conducive to meditative and spiritual experiences.

Vegetarian diets can promote better health in several ways. Especially today, when pesticides and other chemical pollutants are accumulating in our environment, this may be very wise advice. Many of the synthetic chemical pollutants are not metabolized by plants or excreted by animals. Animals who eat chemically polluted vegetation accumulate these substances in their bodies, and the levels in their flesh may be much more concentrated than those found in the environment. When we eat the flesh of these animals, the toxins accumulate in our bodies as well.

Vegetarian diets can reduce our fat and cholesterol intake, which is helpful in treating cardiovascular disease.

Organically grown vegetable, poultry, fish and meat products are a precaution against ingesting pollutants and toxic chemicals. Healers sensitive to bioenergetic vibrations report that organic foods have far greater vitality than those grown with chemical fertilizers, pesticides and hormones.

Specific benefits of vegetarian diets have been observed. They can reduce our fat and cholesterol intake, which is helpful in treating cardiovascular disease. They are widely recommended in wholistic approaches to cancer therapy.

Significant improvements in rheumatoid arthritis were demonstrated with four months on a vegetarian diet, followed by gradual reintroduction of non-vegetable foods, with careful observation to see whether they caused any reactions over the course of a year (Kjeldsen-Kragh et al.). In the field of cancer there are promising studies suggesting the efficacy of some diets. The most common recommendation is to avoid red meat.

Vitamins: *Ordinary (rational) doses of vitamins* prevent vitamin deficiency diseases. They may also helpful in treating certain conditions, such as learning disabilities in children (Carlton et al.).

Recommended dietary allowances (RDAs) for vitamins were established in 1943 by the US National Research Council. These standards represent the minimal doses required to prevent vitamin deficiency syndromes such as scurvy and rickets. Since 1945, food manufacturers have been required by 22 states to enrich certain foods with vitamins.

In recent decades there has been a growing awareness that various supplements can alleviate and prevent many more diseases than was previously appreciated. Now, various governmental agencies[576] are in the process of updating and replacing RDAs with Dietary Reference Intakes (DRIs). These will include Estimated Average Requirements (EARs) and Tolerable Upper Intake Levels (ULs). Where recommended doses have not been established, Adequate Intake levels (AIs) are provided, based on the best available estimates.[577]

Megavitamin therapy has been recommended for a variety of problems. It is speculated that some people are less efficient at absorbing some vitamins, so they may require larger doses to achieve normal metabolic function. Megavitamin doses may also be recommended for specific problems. For instance, doses of 4-6,000 units of vitamin C are anecdotally reported to prevent and to hasten recovery from viral upper respiratory infections.

Other supplements: *Coenzyme Q_{10} (CoQ$_{10}$)* may prevent and help treat cardiac problems because it facilitates metabolism, particularly in heart muscle. In cardiac disease, heart muscle is often deficient in this enzyme. Significant improvement in cardiac function and survival time were achieved when 100 mg/day of CoQ$_{10}$ was given (Langsjoen et al.). In another study, there was less fluid accumulation in the lungs and fewer hospitalizations were required for people with congestive heart failure when CoQ$_{10}$ was given (Baggio et al.).

Galantamine, derived from the snowdrop *(Galanthus nivalis)* and related species appears to enhance intelligent, purposive consciousness, and it is being explored as a treatment in early Alzheimer's.[578]

Orthomolecular medicine is a growing specialty in the use of megavitamin and mineral supplement therapies (Gaby 1999).

A sample of problems treated with vitamins, minerals and enzymes

Osteoarthritis, which most of us suffer as our bones and joints degenerate with age and wear, has been shown to respond to treatment with several natural substances. In clinical studies, 900-4,000 mg. of niacinamide taken daily increased the range of motion in joints and decreased pain and stiffness within four weeks of starting treatment, with further improvements as the therapy was continued (Kaufman 1949; 1955). A double-blind study of general symptoms and mobility in arthritis confirmed significant improvements with niacinamide (Jonas et al. 1996). Another double-blind study compared niacinamide (in the dose specified above) with ibuprofen, an anti-inflammatory agent (1.2 gm. daily). After eight weeks the effects of glucosamine were significantly more pronounced than those of ibuprofen (Vaz). It appears that glucosamine not only reverses symptoms but also stimulates repair of arthritic joints. Glucosamine sulfate at doses of 500 mg. three times a day produced significant relief of pain, swelling, and joint tenderness in a double-blind, controlled study (Pujalte et al.).

Allergies: Research on various nutritional and herbal therapies has shown promise in treating allergies (Sheehan/ Atherton; Sheehan et al.); reducing incidence of kidney stones (G. Johansson et al.; Prien/ Gershoff); treating digestive disorders (Bensoussan et al.; Workshop on Alternative Medicine); addressing women's endocrine problems (Workshop on Alternative Medicine), diabetes (Vuksan et al.), cancer (E. Hoffman; Saxe et al.), gingivitis (R. Vogel et al. 1976; 1978), anxiety,[579] depression,[580] and schizophrenia.[581] This area of research is blossoming rapidly, and only a few examples of further potential uses are given here.[582]

Fatigue is a classical symptom suggesting a need for supplementary vitamins. A double-blind study confirmed that taking vitamin B_{12} (5 mg. twice a week) significantly enhanced overall well-being and happiness, and suggestive results were found for fatigue and appetite loss (Ellis/ Nasser). Potassium magnesium aspartate (1 gm. twice a day) also produced significant relief of fatigue.[583]

Theories: One of the theories behind some of the megavitamin therapies is that oxidants in the body may predispose certain people to cancers. Some vitamins and minerals are anti-oxidants. While anti-oxidants may help prevent cancers, there has also been speculation that they might interfere with chemotherapy or radiotherapy. A review of research on this subject has not confirmed these fears (Lamson/ Brignall).

Conventional medicine has been skeptical about nutritional approaches, and most medical schools provide little or no education in nutrition and nutritional therapies. Hospital diets are notoriously unhealthy, in some cases not even providing the minimum daily requirements of nutrients and vitamins to sustain health, much less to assist in recuperation from illness and surgery (Fulder 1994).[584]

This is too vast a subject to even touch upon adequately in this book, and further reading is highly recommended.

Herbal remedies

In Europe herbal medicine, called *phytotherapy* has been extensively researched over the past decade. For instance, milk thistle (*Siloybum marianum*) is known to help in treating alcoholic cirrhosis of the liver (Feher; Ferenci et al.). Bilberry extract (*Vaccinium myrtillus*) alleviates veinous insufficiency in the legs (Corsi 1987; Guerrini 1987); relieves cramps and other symptoms of varicose veins (Gatta 1982); and reduces symptoms such as pain and itching of hemorrhoids due to venous insufficiency after pregnancy (Baisi 1987; Teglio et al. 1987). Valerian (*Valeriana officinalis*) helps people to fall asleep and also deepens sleep.[585]

St. John's Wort (*hypericum perforatum*) is the most widely used antidepressant in several countries in Europe because it is both potent and relatively free of side effects (Hornig). A meta-analysis of 23 studies of this herb as a treatment for mild to moderate depression showed that 61 percent of users improved on a low dose of *hypericum*, while 75 percent improved with a higher dose (Linde et al. 1996). Another meta-analysis, with more rigorous criteria for inclusion of the 9 studies reviewed, also concluded that St. John's Wort was superior to a placebo (Ernst 1995). People with somatic symptoms such as decreased activity, fatigue, and sleep disorders, as well as people with seasonal affective disorder, were particularly likely to benefit. An extract of St. John's Wort containing the effective ingredient hyperforin[586] proved as effective as amitriptyline[587] in mild to moderate depression and had fewer side effects (Wheatley). Compared to imipramine[588] (Vorbach et al.) and fluoxetine[589] (Schrader) this same extract had equal efficacy and fewer side effects in treating mild to moderate depression. These studies focused on short-term effects, as have most of the studies of conventional antidepressants. Further work remains to be done in order to establish the efficacy of *hypericum* in long-term treatment of depression.[590] St. John's Wort combined with valerian produced better effects than diazepam[591] in treatment of anxiety.

Ginkgo biloba has been shown to slow the progress of dementia in Alzheimer's disease. Ginkgo is an ornamental as well as a medicinal tree, which was domesticated in China thousands of years ago and now grows only under cultivation. A meta-analysis of 40 studies of *ginkgo biloba* found 8 that conformed to high standards (Kleijnen/ Knipschild), and confirmed that mild to moderate memory impairment was improved. P.L. Le Bars et al. found that Egb 761, an extract of *Ginkgo biloba*, stabilized and improved the cognitive and social functions of demented patients over 6-12 months. In a placebo-controlled, double-blind, randomized study, the treatment group scored significantly higher on the cognitive subscale of the Alzheimer's Disease Assessment Scale ($p < .005$), and on the Geriatric Evaluation by Relative's Rating Instrument ($p < .003$). Though modest, these changes represent a significant contribution to the wellbeing of people with Alzheimer's Disease.[592] Paul Solomon et al. (2002) found that there were no significant effects of ginkgo in treating senile dementia, with adequate doses in a controlled study. This study was limited to only 6 weeks, and the review of the literature does not include the above references.[593]

Green tea is widely touted as a tonic and remedy in the East. Reviews of research (Mckenna et al.; T. Wolfe) suggest that it may be associated with lower serum cholesterol and triglycerides (Imai/ Nakachi); lower rates of strokes and cerebral hemorrhage (Sato et al.); and lower rates of recurrence of stage 1 and stage 2 breast cancer (Nakachi et al.). Meta-analyses of series of cancer studies were less conclusive (Bushman; Kuroda/ Hara).

Boxwood (*Buxus sempervirens*) extract, in doses of 990 mg daily, slowed the progression of HIV+ disease in a double-blind controlled study that was terminated before its 18-month planned duration because the researchers considered it unethical to deny the control group benefits of the active treatment (Durant et al.).

Ginger (*Zingiber officinale*) is used as a medicine as well as a spice. It has been shown to have antiemetic properties in motion sickness (Mowrey/ Clayson), seasickness (Grontved et al.), postoperative vomiting (Bone et al.), and vomiting in pregnancy (Fischer-Rasmussen et al.). Several other studies failed to confirm the efficacy of ginger for nausea.[594]

Echinacea (*E. angustifolia, E. pallida, E. purpurea*), or the purple coneflower, was introduced by Native Americans to the European settlers as a tonic for many ills. A meta-analysis of 26 clinical studies showed that for 22 out of 34 measured factors echinacea proved better than a placebo in enhancing immune functions (Melchart et al. 1995), and other studies confirm its efficacy in the treatment of upper respiratory infections.[595] Animal and laboratory studies confirm that it can enhance immune system activity.[596]

Garlic (*Allium sativum*) has been used for several millennia in Mediterranean countries and China as a seasoning and a medicine, and it has many popular medicinal uses today.[597] Over a thousand studies have explored its efficacy in treating various ailments (H. Koch/ Lawson). In Europe it has been approved as a preventive treatment for atherosclerosis and for elevated serum lipids. Meta-analyses confirm its efficacy for hyperlipidemia (Silagy/ Neil 1994a; Warshafsky et al.), and for hypertension (Silagy/ Neil 1994b). Several other studies have failed to confirm its efficacy.[598]

PC-SPES a combination of eight Chinese herbs (PC indicating prostate cancer; *spes* = Latin, *hope*) has been helpful in treating prostate cancer in men who had undergone no hormone treatment or were resistant to hormone treatment.[599] The blood level of PSA (prostate-specific antigen), which is used as a measure of the development of prostatic cancer, decreased by over 50 percent in 9 out of 12 subjects of both types studied. Estrogenic side effects included gynecomastia (breast enlargement), loss of libido, and nausea. These appear to be less serious than the side effects of androgen therapy (one of the standard conventional medical treatments), which also produces decreased bone density, muscle degeneration, and depression.

Mentalin, an Ayurvedic combination of ginger, bacoba, and gotu kola, has been shown to help in treating Attention Deficit Hyperactivity Disorder.

Extensive studies have been made of the use of herbal remedies in China, Japan, and Korea (the more rigorous ones using animal subjects), and ##of Ayurvedic herbal remedies in India, and a few studies have been done on North American Indian herbal remedies. Searches for the active pharmaceutical ingredients in herbal remedies have been initiated,[600] and integration of herbal remedies with conventional medical practice is well on its way.[601]

This is an area of growing interest in wholistic medicine. There have been many other studies of herbal remedies, but reviewing them all is beyond the scope of this book.[602]

Regulation of herbal remedies
Until recently, US laws discriminated against herbal remedies by requiring applications of such complexity, with so much supporting research and clinical data, that costs for approval of a new remedy could run between $140-500 million. Botanicals are not patentable, and therefore no manufacturer can afford this sort of outlay. Research on medications in the US is primarily funded by pharmaceutical companies, so there are very few labs where scientists investigate herbal remedies. To remedy this problem, the Food and Drug Administration reclassified herbal remedies as food supplements. The Dietary Supplement and Health Education Act of 1994 permits claims regarding compound structure and function, but outlaws claims regarding diagnostic and therapeutic specificity. While this facilitates access to herbal remedies, the lack of standards and regulation has spawned a bewildering number of varieties of commercial products. The prohibition against stating a therapeutic indication creates an awkward situation wherein people buy products that are not labeled for their target symptoms and illnesses. Quality control is also often lacking in production.[603] Many producers do not standardize the potencies or the remedies, and some do not standardize doses of their products. Many suggest that their products are of benefit for physical and psychological problems, but provide no research to substantiate their claims.

The European community is also developing regulations for herbal products.

Education and Training: There are no standards as yet for herbal education or licensing in the US. Training courses may last from one weekend to 400 hours.

Most conventional physicians are inadequately trained in nutritional medicine,[604] but naturopathic doctors and some medical physicians specialize in this area. The field of nutritional medicine is so vast and complex that there is little agreement within conventional or CAM groups as to what might constitute adequate standards of training and clinical competency. The American Herbalists Guild is the leading professional organization (Tierra 1992). There are standards for Registered Dieticians and Licensed Dieticians (under the Commission on Dietetic Registration of the American Dietetic Association). RD and LD practitioners will advise about specialized diets, for instance for patients with hypertension or diabetes, but they will not diagnose illnesses.

Theories: Traditional healers relate to herbal remedies in a wholistic fashion. They do not consider that they are simply giving a chemical. The remedy is part of a ceremonial and ritual healing process that addresses body, heart, community, harmonization with nature, and spirit. A traditional herbalist once suggested, "It's not just the herb that helps, it's what you tell the herb to do!"

> *The Rebbe used to say that it is not the medicine that heals but faith in God's loving-kindness.*
> – Rabbi Kolonymus Kalman Shapira (p.xv)

Conventional medicine and pharmaceutical companies seek to extract active ingredients from herbal remedies for patenting. While this may develop new pharmaceuticals, and may standardize doses of remedies, it can also miss the unique combinations of ingredients in herbal remedies that make them effective.

In my personal and clinical experience, adding healing and prayer to medications of any sort, herbal or allopathic, enhances their efficacy and diminishes side effects. While many would see this simply as evidence of the power of suggestion, I believe that healing actually adds to the potency of the medication.

Adverse effects: While generally much safer than conventional medications, side effects may also be caused by nutritional supplements, megavitamin therapy, and herbal remedies.[605] Some of these are dose related. For instance, very high doses of vitamin E can greatly increase the body's requirements for vitamin K. If sufficient vitamin K is not available, clotting disorders may result. Patients may also have allergic reactions to any substance, even if it is a natural product.

Adverse effects may occur with natural remedies combined with conventional medications. There can be interactions and incompatibilities such as additive biochemical effects may become toxic; interferences of one remedy in the effects of the other; and interferences in absorption or elimination of one by the other.[606]

Having pointed out all of the above, the evidence is overwhelmingly clear that herbal remedies have fewer side effects and produce far fewer fatalities than conventional medicines.[607] Spiritual healing can lessen side effects of conventional medication. For example, a nurse working in a hospital cancer unit where she didn't feel safe revealing her spiritual healing interventions gave healing to the IV bottles that carry the chemotherapy. Her patients had noticeably fewer side effects such as headaches, nausea, and vomiting. I would anticipate that spiritual healing could potentiate the effects of herbal remedies and also reduce their side effects.

Clinical applications: Nutritional and herbal therapies can be of enormous benefit for health promotion and weight adjustments, and an adjunct to treatment of most illnesses. They can help people build resistance to illness, provide building blocks for repair and recuperation, and enhance general wellbeing. Specific vitamins, minerals and other food elements can be curative for particular illnesses. We are only beginning to appreciate the enormous benefits of these remedies. The interested reader is highly encouraged to pursue further readings in this area.

While many people recommend diets that have helped them and others they know about, a nutritional or herbal consultant can suggest special diets, vitamins, minerals, and herbal remedies that may be unfamiliar to the non-specialist.

The last word on our understanding of nutrition

Here's the final word on nutrition and health. It's a relief to know the truth after all the many conflicting medical studies.

1. The Japanese eat very little fat and suffer fewer heart attacks than the British or the Americans.

2. The French eat a lot of fat and also suffer fewer heart attacks than the British the Americans.

3. The Japanese drink very little red wine and suffer fewer heart attacks than the British or Americans.

4. The Italians drink excessive amounts of red wine and also suffer fewer heart attacks than the British or Americans.

5. The Germans drink a lot of beer and eat lots of sausages and fats and suffer fewer heart attacks than the British or Americans.

CONCLUSION: Eat and drink what you like – speaking English is apparently what kills you.

- Anonymous

See also: Naturopathic Medicine, Ayurvedic Medicine.

PET THERAPY AND ANIMAL HEALINGS

> *Pets heal as well as heel.*
> – Anonymous

Anecdotes and case studies abound on the benefits of having pets.[608] In the UK, pets are allowed in many hospice wards, and in the US pets who are trained for therapy interventions are allowed in hospitals.[609]

Case: Kay Sassi, who suffered severe depression had shock therapy and medications for two years after a suicide attempt. She left her home only to see her therapist.

> …Sunshine… a small white poodle with wild, untrimmed hair and an incredibly loving spirit… was my only companion during those years, and the only living being that could connect with me.
>   She'd sit on my lap, quiet, as I rocked her for hours in my room. I held her, hugged her, hummed, and whispered to her, and cried into her fur. At night, when it seemed the whole world slept on without me, I'd bring her into my room and she'd keep watch with me against whatever I imagined was out there. She was the only truly safe being in my world.

> I'm in my forties now. Years of good health and deep faith have given me
> what I couldn't imagine at twenty. Sunshine left us a long time ago. Maybe
> she didn't "heal" me but she saved me so that with time and strength, I
> could heal myself. (McElroy 1996, p. 78)

Anecdotal reports indicate that dogs, cats, horses, dolphins and other animals may
be able to participate as very gifted and potent healers.[610] Psychological and
physical problems have been reported to improve with their help. People who
swim with dolphins have also reported that they feel a deep joy and spiritual up-
lifting (Sandoz).

Pets can help indirectly with healing. Their intimate relationships with their
owners may lead them to develop problems when their owners are stressed. They
can thus alert a wholistic healer to issues that could be addressed in their owners.

Of note are books and therapists who can help with bereavement over the loss of
a pet – an often neglected aspect of counseling (McElroy; Traisman).

Research: I know of no controlled pet therapy studies. Anecdotal reports are beginning to confirm that there are distinct psychological and physical benefits to
pet ownership. One longitudinal anecdotal study showed that dogs and cats enhanced wellbeing indices on assessments of the activities of daily living (Raina et
al.). However, the mere presence of a pet is not a guarantee of enhanced health.
The level of bonding with the owner appears to be the crucial factor. Benefits
include decreased anxiety and loneliness, lowered blood pressure, increased survival following heart attacks, and more. Most people find a pet that is intuitively
compatible with their needs.

Pet therapy is a an intervention that is growing in popularity. Animals, particularly dogs, may be certified as therapy animals and accompany their owners on
visits in hospitals and hospices, as well as serving as co-therapists in clinics.

Equestrian therapy has a long history on several continents with a strong reputation for enhancing self-image and self-confidence, particularly for physically and
psychologically handicapped children.[611]

Adverse effects: No harmful effects have been reported, though common sense
precautions are in order. While many people welcome pets immediately, some
have pet phobias and must be approached in a healing manner.

Training and licensing: Proper training and certification for the animal owner is
as important as for the animal.

OSTEOPATHY

See: **Chiropractic and Osteopathic Manipulation; Craniosacral Manipulation.**

POLARITY THERAPY

Polarity Therapy was developed by Randolph Stone (1986; 1999), an osteopath, naturopath and chiropractor. This form of healing balances energies between various points on the body. It addresses positive (top/ head, right) and negative (bottom/ feet, left) polarities of energies in the body. Massage, light touch, and near-the body healing are also used.

Research: I have found no research on polarity therapy.

Clinical applications: See Spiritual Healing.

Adverse effects: No harmful effects have been reported See discussion of potential general negative effects from rapid improvements under Spiritual Healing.

Training and licensing: The American Polarity Therapy Association certifies Associate therapists who have completed 155 hours of training and Registered therapists who have completed 675 hours. This method is not licensed.

See also: Chapter I-1

PROBIOTICS

Probiotics is the use of bacteria to achieve positive effects in the body.

Countless bacteria and yeasts live harmlessly in our gut, as well as on our skin and mucous membranes. Some of these are very helpful, repaying us, so to speak, for being their hosts.[612] The intestinal tract contains bacteria and yeasts that participate in digesting food, produce vitamins B3 and B6 (Alm et al.); produce lactase to digest milk (Alm et al); and recycle estrogen (Speck). In breast milk, microbes contribute to food absorption and immunity in babies (Rasic). Our normal microbial population produces antibacterial chemicals that can deactivate or kill pathogenic bacteria by altering local acidity levels, by producing substances that are antibacterials for the invading organisms, or by metabolizing nutrients that would otherwise be available to pathogenic bacteria (Friend/ Shahani).

We are usually unaware of these harmless symbiotes until something happens to upset our relationship with them. The most frequent cause of problems is a course of antibiotics, which kills off many of these harmless and helpful organisms along with the pathogens that are causing disease. The void left by the absence of the ordinary inhabitants of the gut or vagina leaves a fertile ground for overgrowth of survivors or of new invaders. A common problem following treatment with antibiotics is *candidiasis*, an overgrowth of *candida* yeast in the gut and vagina.

Research in probiotics is still in its infancy. Early research shows promise in the treatment of antibiotic-induced diarrhea (D'Souza) and diarrhea in children (Rosenfeldt et al.).[613]

Clinical applications: Probiotics, or replacement of friendly bacteria that have been killed off with antibiotics, has been shown to be helpful in treating colitis, irritable bowel syndrome, allergies, migraine, rheumatic and arthritic problems, candidiasis, cystitis, acne, eczema and psoriasis. Probiotics may prevent diarrhea in children following courses of antibiotics (Elmer). There is even a suggestion that certain cancers may respond to probiotic treatment (Reddy), and that the side effects of radiation therapy may be alleviated or prevented (Simon).

See also: Nutritional and herbal remedies.

PSYCHONEUROCADIOLOGY
(THE DEAN ORNISH PROGRAM)

> *The best doctors in the world are Doctor Diet, Doctor Quiet, and Doctor Merryman.*
> – Jonathan Swift (1738)

The practice of psychoneurocardiology involves relaxation, meditation, imagery, group support/ therapy, dietary, and exercise programs. Developed by Dean Or-nish, this method has been shown to enhance cardiovascular functions and to provide an effective treatment for some cardiovascular conditions – even when they are severe.

A measure of the success of this therapy is that insurance companies provide coverage for it.

See: Discussion of psychoneurocardiology in Chapter II-1.

PSYCHONEUROIMMUNOLOGY (PNI)

> *[L]ist the five major stresses that were going on in your life in the six months preceding the onset of the disease[E]xamine how you partici-pated in that stress, either by creating the stressful situation or by the manner in which you responded to it...*
> – O. Carl Simonton, Stephanie Matthews-Simonton,
> and James Creighton (1978, p. 112-113)

The practice of PNI includes relaxation, meditation, imagery, and group support/ therapy. First and foremost, PNI empowers respants to feel they can participate in treating their own illness. This is an enormous contribution to healing because people with cancer and other immune problems often feel utterly helpless and frustrated with having to rely on others to treat them.

PNI has been reported to slow and sometimes even to reverse and halt the growth of cancers.

PNI can also help to address pain and side effects of chemotherapy and radiotherapy.

Research: An enormous body of research confirms that the mind can influence the immune system.[614] Some even speculate that the immune system is a part of the mind. This hypothesis is consistent with the fact that many neurochemicals found in the nerve cells of the brain, serving as chemical messengers between nerve cells, are also found in immune cells. This suggests that these chemical messengers serve as well to communicate between the nervous system and the immune system. This may also explain the memory inherent in the success of immunizations.

Clinical applications: PNI appears to prolong life and sometimes to lead to remissions of cancers. It may also be helpful in treating various allergy problems, such as multiple allergy syndromes.

Training and licensing: There is no certification or licensing for this therapy, which may be practiced by many types of caregivers.

See also: Detailed discussion of PNI in Chapter II-1, Relaxation, Meditation, Visualization, Psychoneurocardiology.

PSYCHOTHERAPY

> *The Unconscious is not unconscious, only the Conscious is unconscious of what the Unconscious is conscious of.*
> – Francis Jeffrey

Psychotherapy is an essential aspect of every wholistic therapy; it is the part of each treatment modality that addresses the person who has the illness. Sadly, many medical schools do not prepare doctors to deal with this aspect of treatment, and even psychiatrists today may have no training in psychotherapy.

Psychotherapy is a deeper form of counseling, which relies not only on cognitive counseling but also makes extensive use of the relationship between the therapist and the client as an instrument for healing. *Transference*, the projection of anticipated responses by the client onto the therapist, and *counter-transference*, the emotional responses of the therapist towards the client are also a major focus in psychotherapy.

Research: Enormous bodies of research confirm the benefits of a broad spectrum of psychotherapies – from behavioral, throiugh rational emotive, psychosomatic, and into psychodynamic variations on this theme. Quantitative and qualitative studies have shown significant benefits of various forms of psychotherapy in treatment of anxiety, panic, obsessive compulstive disorders, depression, marital and family issues, schizophrenia and more..[615] I am not aware of studies of efficacy of transpersonal psychotherapy.

Clinical applications: While many of us grow and mature with age and experience, psychotherapy can add many dimensions to our personal growth. Psychotherapy provides support, insight regarding intrapsychic (within the careseeker) and interpersonal issues, education for new ways to understand issues, and opportunities for restructuring and repatterning one's ways of perceiving and relating to the worlds within and without. It is particularly helpful in identifying and dealng with blind spots and shadow issues – areas in our lives that we tend to avoid noticing and would often rather ignore.

Psychotherapy can help with problems in areas such as emotions, relationships (with spouses/ partners, parenting) and psychosomatic disorders. Transpersonal psychotherapy helps with spiritual issues.

Psychotherapy is second only to healing in its dependence on the person who is the caregiver as much as it relies on whatever methodologies and approaches used in the therapy.[616]

If we accept that the body is intimately related to the emotions, mind, relationships and spirit, then it is clear that psychotherapy can help people to deal with any physical problem. Among its benefits are enhanced abilities in the following crucial areas of the proactive management of disease:

- accepting the illness;
- adapting to living with the illness;
- dealing with the illness, through
- relaxation techniques
- meditation
- imagery
- psychoneuroimmunology
- exploring and dealing with psychological contributors to the illness;
- exploring and dealing with relational aspects of the illness;
- dealing with secondary gains;
- exploring transpersonal and spiritual issues.

Training and licensing: Psychotherapy may be done by social workers, psychologists, nurses, physicians and other caregivers. Psychotherapy is usually defined as involving more training and promoting therapy in greater depth than *counseling*. Some use these terms interchangeably. The person who is the therapist is often more important than the label or the training.

Psychotherapy and counseling are defined and licensed differently in different states. In addition to a professional degree or certificate, hundreds of hours of supervised therapy with careseekers are usually required for licensing. In some branches of psychotherapy the therapists are also required to undergo their own therapy – to clear themselves as much as possible of blind spots and shadow issues that could intrude in their ministrations to clients.[617] While ongoing supervision is not required, many find this also helpful in their continued personal and professional growth and in continuing to guard against transference errors.

See also: Psychotherapy in greater detail in Chapter II-1; brief summaries of varieties of psychotherapy in Appendix A; self-healing exercises in Chapter II-5 of the popular edition of this book.

QIGONG

> *Qigong is a wholistic system of self-healing exercise and meditation, an ancient, evolving practice that includes healing posture, movement, self-massage, breathing techniques, and meditation.*
> – Ken Cohen (2000, p.4)

The *Qigong* (pronounced *chee-gong*) system of physical exercises was developed in China some time prior to the 6th Century BC, to address the flows of bioenergy in the body and to exert a calming effect on the mind through meditative focus. *Qi* means "life energy" and *gong* means "work" and "the benefits acquired through perseverance and practice" (K. Cohen 2000, p.3). Qigong self-healing is excellent for treating many physical problems, and anecdotal reports claim dramatic improvements in chronic diseases, including cancer. Roger Jahnke has a lovely and thorough discussion of various forms of qi, with advice on how to enhance their flow and potency, and a spectrum of exercises for self-healing. Qigong exercises are used frequently as a complement to the qigong healings (*waiqi, external qigong*) that are given by trained masters.[618] External qigong healing is similar to the many forms of spiritual healing detailed in *Healing Research*, Volume I.

There are thousands of different styles of qigong. A few rough categories can be delineated (K. Cohen 2000):

By form:	*Jing gong* – Tranquil qigong, without movement
	Dong gong – Active qigong, with movement
	Ruan gong – Soft qigong
	Ying gong – Hard qigong

By application:	*Yi gong* – Medical or healing qigong
	Wu gong – Martial or sports qigong
	Fo gong – Buddhist qigong
	Dao gong – Daoist qigong

Research: A wealth of research, almost entirely from China, is summarized by Kenneth Sancier, in his monumental *Qigong Database*.[619] Unfortunately, the quality of this research is questionable.

Training and licensing: There are no standards for training or licensing in qigong. Qigong is a healing art, rather than a system of treatment. Because there are so many styles of qigong, it is difficult to see how standards could be established.[620]

Clinical applications: Qigong practices can improve relaxation, muscle tone and breathing. It can contribute to improvements in stress-related illnesses such as musculoskeletal pains, hypertension, asthma and cancer. By enhancing biological energy flows it can strengthen the body's abilities to deal with many other illnesses – in ways that cannot be explained within Western medical theories. It can also facilitate the development of spiritual discipline and improved sense awareness.

Qigong can be integrated with conventional care in many applications. External qi, when used for healing, can complement any therapy. T'ai Chi Ch'uan and Qigong exercises are excellent as preventive medicine and for maintaining muscle tone and normal flows of biological energies. They may also be helpful in rehabilitation following injuries or illnesses.

While initial instruction is usually necessary in these techniques, their practice is self-healing.[621]

See also: T'ai Chi Ch'uan; Yoga.; research on infrasonic sound emitted by qigong masters (Chapter II-3).

RFLEXOLOGY

See: Massage.

REIKI

The process of attunement or initiation is what sets Reiki apart from every other form of laying on of hands or touch healing. The attunement is not a healing session, it creates the healer...
                                                    – Diane Stein (p. 17)

Developed in Japan by Dr. Mikao Usui in the mid-nineteenth century, this system is one of the most popular and widely used healing methods in the Western world.

Usui trained twenty-two Reiki masters. It appears that each of these masters was empowered with individualized gifts and healing symbols, which could differ from those of the other masters in subtle or substantial ways.

Reiki is growing in popularity, with many thousands of healers now practicing around the world. Graduated levels of instruction are offered. Reiki-I teaches beginners a pattern of hand positions on the head and torso. Reiki healers initially adhere to this pattern, to assure that they will not overlook aspects of healee's problems, or introduce energy imbalances by addressing only the symptomatic sites on the body of the healee. A pain in the head, for example, might be due to local muscle spasms from fatigue, but it might also be due to poor posture, emotional imbalances such as anger or depression, systemic dysfunctions such as hypertension, hormonal shifts such as in premenstrual tension and more. An essential part of level one teaching involves an *induction, attunement/ empowering* of healing abilities in the student by the master.

Reiki II teaches distant healing, and Reiki-III is an induction to Master level. Japanese ideograms are used as power symbols that embody and transmit healing, and various Reiki traditions use different symbols (Stein).

Research: Very limited research has been done on Reiki, with only a few of these studies suggesting healing benefits.[622]

Training and licensing: Training is by weekend workshops. There are numerous different schools, each with its own variations of practices. Originally, masters were carefully selected by teachers but in recent years a person can attend three weekend workshops and become a master. In some cases masters have very limited innate healing ability, training, and experience.

Modest fees are charged for Reiki I and II courses, and fees of several hundred to several thousand dollars may be charged for Reiki III training.

Reiki is not a licensed therapy.

Adverse effects: No harmful effects have been reported See discussion of potential general negative effects from rapid improvements under Spiritual Healing. Because there is very brief training for Reiki healers, one is cautioned to seek references if healing is needed for serious problems.

Clinical applications: See spiritual healing.

See also: Spiritual Healing, Volume I of *Healing Research.*

RITUALS

> *Rituals are formalized patterns which, like classical dance steps, require particular behaviors but may also allow for individual interpretations and variations of the practitioners.*
>
> – D.B.

Rituals create windows of drama through which we can draw support, enact our conflicts, explore intuitive and creative solutions to challenges, seek inner inspiration and guidance from our higher selves (from collective consciousness and spirit), celebrate our progress, and offer our thanks. Community involvement, prayers and religious elements may be included in healing rituals, as they all lend power to the healing experience. Modern society has distanced itself from much of the healing available in rituals, as we have distanced ourselves from religious practices and from the wise habit of living in proximity to several generations of family. We tend to limit this healing modality to the doctor's white coat and stethoscope hanging out of her pocket or around her neck.[623]

These creative approaches may facilitate healing, in and of themselves or as aspects of other therapies. They may seem to share more with the artist's palette and the tones of the lute than they do with the needles of the acupuncturist or the remedies of the herbalist, but their healing power has been recognized and respected since earliest times.

In traditional societies, shamans make extensive use of healing rituals. These may include prayers, chanting, drumming, dancing, feasts, ingestion of ritual drugs, smoking, libations, fasting, sacred art, sweat lodges, pilgrimages to traditional sacred sites, vision quests, and invitations to spirits and the Divine to participate. While many Western caregivers view these as magical beliefs that are more in the realm of wishful thinking than anything resembling an effective treatment, there are many reports of successful, even dramatic healings, through these rituals.[624]

See also: Creative art therapies as healing; Shamanism.

SHAMANISM

> *[S]hamans were the world's first physicians, first diagnosticians, first psychotherapists, first religious functionaries, first magicians, first performing artists, and first story-tellers…*
> – Stanley Krippner and Patrick Welch (1992, p. 27)

Shamanism is practiced in every known culture. The shaman acts as a counselor, physician, spiritual healer, community authority and priest. Shamans call upon psi powers for diagnosing and treating illness, counseling, predicting the future, and guiding their society in spiritual matters. Technically speaking, shamans are more diverse in their skills, training, and interventions than *medicine men*, who are specialists in diagnosing and treating illness.

A rich literature is available on healing in indigenous, non-industrial cultures, which is usually practiced under the hands of shamans.[625] The most comprehensive discussion on shamanism and healing is by Krippner and Welch. They point out that although Western scientists have been eager to borrow herbal knowledge from shamans, they have ignored teachings in diagnosis and treatment for physical and psychological problems. The presentation by Krippner and Welch is enormously helpful in increasing our appreciation of the spectrum of healing practices and beliefs around the world.

Shamans may use herbs, rituals (such as dancing, chanting, sand painting), divination, spiritual healing, and prayer. They often invite the participation of the entire family of the person who is sick, and may even involve a broader segment of their community in the healing ceremony. Their healing ceremonies may last for many hours or even for several days.

Traditional shamanic education consists of three parts: expansion of one's ability to see beyond the ordinary five senses; destabilization of the body's habit of being bound to one plane of being; and encouragement of the ability to voyage into "otherworldly" dimensions and return with spirit guidance for individual and community healings, advice on dealing with serious challenges and predictions about the future..

Case: JoEllen Koerner, PhD, RN, FAAN is a nursing executive of international repute. Major problems in birthing over five generations in her family culminated in her daughter, Kristi, coming close to death with kidney stones following the birth of her second child. Kristi's pain was so excruciating and debilitating that she had given up the will to live. Conventional medicine was unable to help.

> During my thirty-five-year nursing career, I have been present to many people in their suffering. I had witnessed Kristi experience childbirth and C-sections, but I had never witnessed anything quite so difficult. Her body trembled with the pain. Her breath was short and gasping rather than deep and rhythmic. Her hands clutched the sheets, and her ashen face was drenched with perspiration. It was more than I could bear to witness – and there was absolutely nothing I could do for her. (Koerner, p. 98)

Koerner turned to a Lakota medicine man, Wanigi Waci, who intuited that Native American healing could help Kristi. He arranged for a series of healing ceremonies. Koerner was an active participatnt in these rituals, which drew on the spiritual strength of the Lakota tribe as well as on her own. These shamanic healings brought about dramatic improvements in Kristi, both physically and emotionally.

The rituals and prayers for shamanic healing often are focused on the individual as part of the community. The prayers bring healing to the community as much as to the person who is ill.

It is refreshing today to see Western scientists seeking the wisdom of so-called "primitives." These ancient cultures may be less advanced than ours in technology, but they are far more advanced in application of psi skills, especially intuitive awareness and healing. They are attuned to spiritual dimensions of awareness, which include the participation of all living things in the ecobiological system of our planet (commonly termed *Gaia*), and in the cosmos beyond. We may learn new ways of healing from them that complement our modern medical methods. The shamans, in turn, may learn from us to distinguish between the essential elements of their teachings and superstitious beliefs that may have little therapeutic benefit. Thus we may all gain insight into how healing works.

Much of the literature on shamanism (e.g. Harner) and eastern medicine (e.g. Kaptchuk) elaborates worldviews in which human beings constitute a small part of the cosmos, linked with nature via a vast web of psi and spiritual interactions. Descriptions of these interconnections vary widely, and to Western eyes they may seem so alien as to constitute mere superstitious beliefs. Nevertheless, people living in each culture believe wholeheartedly in their cosmologies and respond to elements within them.[626] A shaman draws upon imagery and beliefs from her or his culture in order to facilitate spiritual healings. In fact, it may be impossible for a healer from one culture to heal some patients from another, because of their dissimilar frames of reference.[627] The converse is likewise true. Healers from a different culture from those of the healee may bring about dramatic healings, partly because of the charisma that is attributed to healers from distant places.[628]

> *Jesus said, "No prophet is accepted in his own village; no physician heals those who know him."*
> – Gospel of Thomas (31)

We may take profound lessons from cross-cultural studies that are relevant to our own systems of medical care.

> There are shamanic healing methods that closely parallel contemporary behavior therapy, chemotherapy, dream interpretation, family therapy, hypnotherapy, milieu therapy, and psychodrama. It is clear that shamans, psychotherapists, and physicians have more in common than is generally suspected…
> – Stanley Krippner and Patrick Welch (p. 37)

If we allow that healing in various cultures may appear entirely different from healing in modern Western society, we may then be in a better position to re-examine the attitudes of patients toward their healings in our own culture. Western investigators tend to discount patients' beliefs as unimportant or inessential to the actual processes of healing. If we can agree that alternative views may apply to healing in other cultures, should we not consider the possibility that the perspectives of medical patients in our own culture are relevant to their success in healing, even if this view differs from that of our scientist subculture?[629]

Research: I have found no controlled studies on shamanic healings. Therre are rich descriptive studies of shamanism in the anthropological and sociological literature.

Training and licensing: Training is by apprenticeship. Shamans may identify children or adults with potentials for developing shamanic gifts, or people may feel a calling to learn to be shamans. Aprenticeships develop the unique spectrum of abilities of the individual apprentice over periods of many years.

Westerners have come to shamans to learn their methods of healing. They are usually told that it is not about learning methods but about developing their own gifts.

Michael Harner has developed a school for shamanic healing, translating shamanism into Western culture. Growing numbers of healthcare professionals are participating in these courses and integrating shamanic practices in their work.[630]

There is no licensing specifically for shamans as such, but they are generally regarded as religious leaders and accorded the same authority and protection under the law as other religious priests and ministers.

Clinical applications: Shamanism can address all psychological and physical problems. Many shamans recognize that allopathic medicine has much to offer, particularly in the treatment of infectious diseases and trauma. Shamanic treatments can be complementary to conventional medical care.

Adverse effects: No harmful effects have been reported Where herbs are used, see cautions under herbal and nutritional remedies. See also discussion of potential general negative effects from rapid improvements under Spiritual Healing.

See also: Spiritual Healing; Rituals.

SHEN HEALING

SHEN therapy was developed by Richard Pavek, an American scientist. This approach addresses emotional tensions which manifest in physical symptoms, using light touch at particular points on the body.

Training and licensing: I am impressed with the integrity of the training, which requires therapists to undergo their own therapy to "clear the channels" so that they can be as effective as possible in their own practice.

Clinical applications: SHEN healing has been specifically helpful in treating a number of conditions, including anorexia, bulimia, migraine, pains of all sorts, panic attacks, post-traumatic stress disorder, pre-menstrual symptoms and irritable bowel syndrome.

Adverse effects: No harmful effects have been reported for SHEN healing See also potential general negative effects from rapid improvements under Spiritual Healing.

See also: Spiritual Healing, Volume I of *Healing Research*.

SPIRITUAL HEALING

> *Healing is not a matter of mechanism but a work of the spirit.*
> – Rachel Naomi Remen

Spiritual healing (which is often called simply *healing*) is any sort of purposeful intervention by one or more persons wishing to help another living thing to change via the sole processes of focused intention or the laying-on of hands. Healers may invoke outside agents such as God, Christ, other "higher powers," spirits, universal or Cosmic forces or energies; special healing energies or forces emanating from themselves; psychokinesis (mind over matter); and self-healing powers or energies latently present in the healees.

The laying-on of hands may involve light touch or holding the hands near to but not touching the body. It may also be given through a wish, simple intent, meditation, or prayer for the healing of the subjects. Healing may be sent from any distance, with no direct contact between healer and healee.[631]

Spiritual healing is a natural gift, much like playing the piano. Everyone has some ability, but only a few are truly gifted. A mother kissing away a child's hurt may be giving healing along with her physical and emotional comforting. Most of us can learn to improve our healing gifts with practice. Some are better off (or their potential healees are better off) if they don't engage in healing, because they lack the sensitivity, emotional balance or the required discerning judgment to engage in what can be an unsettling experience of transformation.

While healing may be given specifically as spiritual healing, it is also a component of most other therapies – though it may be an unmentioned or even unconscious part of the therapeutic interaction.

Historically, shamans and medicine men have practiced healing in every known culture throughout the ages. Shamans are not only healers. In their wider social and spiritual role, they mediate between the natural world and the worlds of spirits.[632]

A variety of popular forms of healing are practiced today.

Research: This is one of the most thoroughly researched forms of CAM, with numerous studies (including several hundred doctoral dissertations) showing effects on hemoglobin, skin wounds, hypertension, immune system function, pain, and anxiety.[633]

In Britain, the organiz ation of healers into self-regulating and certifying bodies was a major contribution to the acceptance of healing. [634]

Clinical applications: Spiritual healing can be used alone or as a complement to all other therapies. It may, in fact, be a component of many other therapies – even without the conscious awareness of therapists or their clients. It is usually given by a healer, though self-healing is also possible.

Adverse effects: No harmful effects have been reported from spiritual healing. There may be emotional releases during treatments, as with many of the other CAM therapies. These are often experienced as less traumatic with healing treatments, since spiritual healing is also excellent for treatment of physical and emotional stress and pain and helps to deal with the stress of emotional releases.

Physical pain may increase briefly following the initial healing treatments, but this is generally viewed by healers as a positive response, a sign that there is a shift in the bioenergetic pattern of the pain. With further healing treatments the pain then reduces below the initial levels of intensity.

Relief of pain and other symptoms may sometimes be rapid and experienced by the healee as a dramatic shift. While to many this is pure relief, to others it may be a challenge, as they have to adjust their lives to being without their symptoms.

Healers who are not sensitive to psychological issues may not know how to counsel careseekers who are too rapidly relieved of their symptoms.[635]

Training and Licensing: There are no generally accepted standards for training or licensing in spiritual healing. This may be a gift from birth or developed at any time later in life, and can be enhanced through training. There are widely varying courses in the several types of healing reviewed in this book, with Reiki offering weekend courses; Barbara Brennan School of Healing requiring four years of training; and other modalities ranging in between.

In Britain, the organization of healers into self-regulating and certifying bodies was a major contribution to the acceptance of healing. [636]

See also: Barbara Brennan Healing, Healing Touch, LeShan Healing, Native American Healing, Network Spinal Analysis, Polarity Therapy, Qigong, Reiki, Shamanism, SHEN Healing, Therapeutic Touch, Volume I of *Healing Research.*

T'AI CHI CH'UAN

T'ai Chi Ch'uan is a highly ritualized series of movements that was developed from martial arts practices in China. Unlike the combative martial arts, this method is more like a very slow dance. It is excellent for developing and maintaining muscle tone. In addition, it enhances the flow of biological energies.[637]

Research: While no controlled studies are available, various anecdotal reports, case studies, and clinical observations indicate that T'ai Chi can help in treating problems of balance, cardiovascular system, immune system, mood, relaxation, respiration, stress hormones, and weight bearing ability (Krapu).

Adverse effects: None known.

Training and Licensing: There are no Western standards for training or licensing in T'ai Chi Ch'uan. It is essentially a healing art. In China there are established standards for training and practice.

Clinical applications: T'ai Chi practices can improve relaxation, muscle toning and breathing. They can contribute to improvements in stress-related illnesses such as hypertension and musculoskeletal pains. By enhancing biological energy flows, they can strengthen the body's abilities to deal with many other illnesses – in ways that cannot be explained within the context of Western medical theories. T'ai Chi can also facilitate spiritual discipline and higher sense awareness.

T'ai Chi Ch'uan exercises are excellent as preventive medicine, because they maintain muscle tone and normal flows of biological energies. They may also be helpful in rehabilitation following injuries or illnesses.

While initial instruction in these techniques is usually necessary, their practice is effective as self-healing.

See also: Qigong; Rituals; Yoga.

THERAPEUTIC TOUCH (TT)

> *[I]n the final analysis, it is the healee (client) who heals her- or himself. The healer or therapist…acts as a human energy support system until the healee's own… system is robust enough to take over.*
>
> – Dolores Krieger (1993, p. 7)

TT was developed by Dolores Krieger, PhD, RN, a professor of nursing at New York University, and Dora van Gelder Kunz, a gifted clairsentient and healer. It has been taught to a conservatively estimated 80,000 nurses and other health practitioners in America and around the world, and it is now taught in more than 90 nursing schools in America.

TT teaches people to *center* themselves and to develop their awareness of biological energy fields around the body. Students learn to scan the body, passing their hands a few inches away from the body from head to toe, and front to back. They note any asymmetries or abnormal energy sensations and address these energetically, by holding their hands above these body parts. They may image that they are conveying energy to the healee if energy depletions are noted, or that they drawing energy from the healee if excesses of energy are found. Healers may project images of particular colors to correct or counteract energy imbalances. The aura may be *combed* or *smoothed* if negative energies are to be removed.

Kunz warned that only the most advanced healers should give treatments to the head, as they may inadvertently cause sever energy imbalances. The source for the healing energy may be imaged as coming from the healer or from a universal source of energy.

In some of her more recent writings, Krieger is suggesting that TT can open healers and healees into greater transpersonal awareness (Krieger 2002).

Research: TT is the most thoroughly researched of the spiritual healing methods. TT has been shown in controlled studies to help in treatment of pain, anxiety, depression, enhanced arthritis, immune function, hypertension, wellbeing in palliative care, and disruptive behavior in Alzheimer's Disease.

Many qualitative studies have also been published on TT.[638]

Adverse effects: No harmful effects have been reported See discussion of potential general negative effects from rapid improvements under Spiritual Healing.

Training and licensing: Training and certification is available through the Nurse Healers Professional Associates, Inc. Weekend introductions to TT are also offered, and relatives of ailing people may be taught to offer TT. As with other forms of spiritual healing, there is no licensing.

Clinical applications: See under Spiritual Healing.

See also: Spiritual Healing, Volume I of *Healing Research.*

TIBETAN MEDICINE

The tradition of Tibetan medicine dates back fifteen hundred years. It was influenced by Chinese and Indian traditions but it has a distinct character of its own. It was also practiced extensively in Mongolia and parts of Russia. There are many variations within the Tibetan tradition, which are passed down through the lineages of the ancient practitioners.

Tibetan medicine is based on a cosmology of *Chi* (space, air),[639] *Schara* (subtle energy, bile), and *Badahan* (the material world, phlegm). Ten essential elements influence all of existence: awareness, willpower, compassion, structure/ temperature, gas/ liquid/ solid, plants, gender, animals, man, and mind. The basic triad and the ten elements combine in various proportions to determine the nature of everything in the world.[640]

Every individual is responsible for maintaining his or her own health and preventing illness. Each person must achieve this through an understanding of their relationships within their family, community, society and the cosmos, and through proper nutrition, lifestyles, adaptation to seasonal changes, and awareness of their characterological predispositions. For example, different foods and food combinations are recommended for each season. Emotional and mental "digestion" are also stressed, and spiritual awareness is considered of great importance.

Diagnosis is made according to the triadic types. *Chi* people are tall and lean, with dry skin and thin hair. They tend to be intelligent but not practical, anxious and changeable, and they may lack perseverance. They are not comfortable in parenting roles. They prefer sweet, light, hot foods. They are susceptible to illnesses but tolerate and adapt well to being ill. They tend to have psychological and neurological disorders, as well as arthritis. They have strong desires but low energy. Illness occurs more in fall and winter, and later in life.

Schara people are of medium build and strong, with a pink complexion but tend to have freckles, moles and acne. Hair grays and thins early. They tend to be intelligent and critical thinkers, strong-willed, and gravitating toward leadership positions, where they may focus more on programs than on the people they are meant to serve. In family life they are passionate, demanding, authoritative, and dominating. They prefer sweet and bitter foods. They are prone to infections, ulcers, liver and pancreatic diseases, skin allergies, rashes and infections, and cancers. Illnesses tend to occur in late spring or summer, more often during early and middle adulthood.

Badahan people are heavy-set and tend toward obesity, with pale moist skin and thick hair. They are stable, loving, and compassionate but tend not to assume leadership positions. They are pleasant, good listeners, slow to react, and unimaginative. They are devoted to their partners and families and like to have a comfortable marital nest. They favor sour, strong tastes. Their resistance to illness is high, but when sick they have low endurance. They are particularly sensitive to emotional stresses from deprivations, metabolic disorders, asthma, cardiovascular problems, diabetes, pulmonary disorders, and tumors. Their susceptibility to illness is higher in late winter or early spring, and they tend to suffer illnesses early in life.

Mixtures of these three types are more common than pure types. In addition to reading the physical types, practitioners place great emphasis on reading the pulses at the wrists. Various pulses reveal the entire state of health and illness of the person (not only their cardiovascular condition). Three fingers are used to sense the pulses, each finger applied with a different pressure. I have heard reports of amazing diagnostic assessments with this method, relating to physical and psychological problems.

In addition to recommending nutritional and lifestyle changes, herbal remedies, and massage, the physician must approach healees with compassion. Mental focus and concentration are essential to proper practice. The goal is to awaken the healee's self-healing abilities, which are further enhanced with breathing exercises that facilitate the flows of biological energies through the body. Spiritual teachings may be included in the treatment when the physician is also a lama or priest, but only after physical and emotional problems have been addressed.

Adverse effects: No harmful effects have been reported Where herbs are used, see cautions under herbal and nutritional remedies. See also discussion of potential general negative effects from rapid improvements under Spiritual Healing.

Training and Licensing: There are no professional organizations or certifications for Tibetan Medicine practitioners. There is no licensing for Tibetan Medicine.

Research: A few studies suggest that a standardized combination of 25 herbal and mineral ingredients may be helpful in treating peripheral vascular diseases (Drabaek et al.; Smulski/ Wojcicki)[641] as well as in arresting the progress of dementia (Panjwani et al.).

Clinical applications: Tibetan medicine is a complete system of treatment that is applicable to most illnesses. It has been used as integrative care in parts of the West since the 1930s (Badmaev).[642]

A therapist is required for the practice of Tibetan medicine.

VISUALIZATION/ IMAGERY

> *Mind no longer appears as an accidental intruder into the realm of matter; we are beginning to suspect that we ought rather to hail it as the creator and governor of the realm of matter.*
>
> – Sir James Jeans

Visualization is the deliberate holding of images in the mind's eye with the intent of imprinting these images upon one's own mental and physical states or upon those of others. Visualization is an important element in self-healing. Many healers also emphasize this method as a part of centering and treatment in spiritual healing.

Advanced practitioners of meditation tell us that all of what we experience in life is brought into being through our expectations, wishes and needs.

> *But to the eye of the man of imagination Nature is imagination itself. AS A MAN IS, SO HE SEES.*
>
> – William Blake

William Blake and other visionaries have been called *mystics*. They say that if we release our everyday expectations and wishes we may experience the world very differently.[643] The word *mystic* derives from the same root as *mystery*, harking back to the Greek mystery cults in which esoteric knowledge was kept as a secret of the priesthood.

Visualization is a component of so many healing approaches that it deserves special consideration and emphasis here.

Westerners would like to define visualization and related healing processes in a scientific manner. Robert Jahn and Brenda Dunne (1987) observe:

> [W]e find ourselves fishing in a metaphysical sea with a scientific net far better matched to other purposes. Inevitably, much of the anomalous information we seek will slip through this net, leaving us only skeletal evidence to retrieve, but it is on that alone that we can base systematic analysis and scientific claim.

It is in this spirit that we approach these areas of healing, such as visualization, that are more difficult to define. We must continue personal and clinical explorations of these elements that could slip through our more rigorously constructed net of scientific study and elude our observation, while striving to develop new nets that may retain them for closer scrutiny.

Numerous self-healing books present a variety of applications for visualization. They all point out that visualizing yourself in a new state of being or in a new activity, and mentally practicing the experience of being in that state can vastly enhance your actual ability to achieve these altered physical states. Visualizing yourself practicing a sport can produce marked gains in skills and ability in that sport (Mahoney/ Avener; Murphy/ White). Visualizing one's body improving from illness to health seems to be in another realm because it involves physiological and structural changes rather than alterations of behavioral patterns and athletic achievements. Research is beginning to confirm that imaging physical changes can actually alter many conditions in our bodies.

The simplest use of imagery is for reducing tensions. You may find it relaxing to picture yourself on a holiday, enjoying fresh surroundings and pleasurable activities. You might image yourself on a beach or by a pool, savoring a cool drink after a refreshing swim. You'll find that your body will relax as you relax psychologically.

More complex imagery approaches might involve problem-solving exercises focused on issues that are causing you tension. You could allow yourself to imagine as many ways as possible of dealing with someone whom you find oppressive or abusive. Your visualizations could take the form of vengeful interactions, or – more constructively – of successful confrontations and problem resolution. You might bring up memories of pleasant and satisfying experiences with that person, to remind you during times of stress and distress that good things are still possible. Such visualizations may introduce hope in situations where you feel despair, provide immediate emotional satisfaction, and suggest creative solutions that you might not have considered previously.

Figure II-14. Visioning happiness

© ASHLEIGH
BRILLIANT 1991

POT-SHOTS NO. 5551.

THE
MEMORY
OF A
HAPPINESS

CAN LAST
MUCH
LONGER
THAN
THE
HAPPINESS
ITSELF.

Imagery can provide healing for various physical problems. Pain responds particularly well to this method. If you have a headache or other pain and you image that a compress of exactly the right temperature is being gently applied to the painful spot, the pain may diminish. Picturing the pain as a color (often an angry red or a dark black), you might think of lighter colors and find that the pain lightens along with the shifting mental picture.

Multiple mechanisms may contribute to pain reduction through visualizations. The psychological effects of suggestion may reduce pain perception or emotional responses to pain. Muscle spasms may be reduced through muscle relaxation. Further effects may be possible through shifts in physiological conditions that are facilitated by the imagery – for example through neurohormonal mechanisms or possibly through alterations in biological energy fields that influence physical conditions or pain perception.

Visualizations can also be effective in treating severe illnesses, as has been shown in recent experiments. For example, visualization is used in self-healing for cancer (Achterberg; Simonton et al.). Healees picture their bodies fighting off their disease in every way possible. Classical examples include: seeing their white cells as white knights attacking cancer cells, imaging the blood vessels that feed the cancer as pipes with spigots that the healee shuts off; and so on. Conversely, respants can picture themselves as being healthy (in particular organs and in general) and doing things they like (such as sports; visiting with family and friends; working). Each respant must find the specific images that work for her. Intensive practice has often produced improvement in quality of life and occasionally has brought about arrests or even complete remissions of cancer.

Jean Bolen's summary of Simonton's results shows that when patients applied themselves diligently to the visualization exercises their improvement was more marked. Similar methods have been helpful in improving quality of life and length of survival with AIDS (Solomon) and with heart disease.[644]

Critics have pointed out that this research may represent a circular system, in that patients with a better prognosis may tend to volunteer for these new therapies. They may have more energy, better spirits, more will power or other factors that permit them to apply themselves more vigorously or successfully to these methods.

While it was initially proposed that visualization could be effective in slowing the development of cancer by influencing the immune system, this was only a conjecture. Rider et al. showed that visualizations could alter immune globulin A (IgA) in saliva, which was a step in confirming this hypothesis. Other studies of self-healing have confirmed changes in this and other immune markers as a result of imagery exercises (Fawzy et al 1990; O'Leary).

Many find that self-generated imagery is the most potent, as it holds the structure and associations that are most suitable for the individual person's specific needs. Others find that imagery suggested by a therapist may be more helpful to them, as it can introduce new elements that they may not have considered themselves. Even better, a therapist may suggest new approaches that people can then individualize to meet their own needs.

One measure of the validity of a method is its predictive value. Therapists working with imagery report it is possible to determine the status of people's illnesses from their visualizations, and even to predict the course of the illness, especially with cancer.[645] The unconscious mind reveals a person's physical condition via the imagery in their fantasy visualizations and drawings. Jean Achterberg (1985, p. 188) presents scales for scoring these visualizations. Fourteen critical dimensions include: ...vividness, activity and strength of the cancer cell; vividness and activity of the white blood cells; relative comparison of size and number of cancer and white blood cells; strength of the white blood cells; vividness and effectiveness of medical treatment; choice of symbolism; the integration of the whole imagery process; the regularity with which they imaged a positive outcome; and a ventured clinical opinion on the prognosis, given the previously listed thirteen factors.

These factors were derived from a study of about 200 cancer patients. They "...were found to predict with 100% certainty which patients would have died or shown evidence of significant deterioration during the two-month period, and to predict with 93% certainty which patients would be in remission." (Achterberg, 1985, p. 189)

Gerald Epstein (1981; 1989), a psychiatrist in private practice, helps people to self-heal a wide range of illnesses with imagery exercises. His approaches are very direct and mechanistic. For instance, a patient may have an enlarged prostate, which is the gland between the bladder and the penis that produces seminal fluid. This can constrict the urethra, making it difficult to start and stop urinating, causing dribbling, etc. Epstein might prescribe the practice of mental imagery, such as picturing the prostate encased in a net that the patient draws tight, constricting the swollen gland to encourage it to shrink. At the same time, the patient could visualize that he is massaging his prostate, encouraging the flow of urine and semen through the urethra. Though there is no known spontaneous mechanism whereby an enlarged prostate will shrink, Epstein's patients have had success with such exercises.

In another example, a pregnant woman whose baby is lying with its feet towards the cervix in the last month of pregnancy is in danger of delivering the baby feet-first. This can be dangerous because the umbilical cord is at risk of being constricted by the head as it descends through the birth canal. Because of this danger, caesarian delivery is often recommended. Epstein might suggest to the woman that she image herself entering her own body, going to the baby through the cervix, and helping it to turn to the more common and safer head-down position.

Epstein does not emphasize exploration for psychological causes underlying physical conditions, although he does accept that emotional and social factors may become apparent in the course of treatment. He feels that if illness is present it should be addressed directly, and the rest will follow as required by the individual.

My own preference tends strongly toward exploring underlying psychological causes behind physical problems. Before assuming that a symptom, however troublesome, should be encouraged to diminish or disappear, I recommend to my respants that they ask their symptoms what lessons they might be offering. A neck pain may be a metaphor for someone in your life who is "a pain in the neck." A cough, stomach ache or indigestion may be the unconscious mind's way of bringing to your attention that you are having to "swallow down" feelings that you are uncomfortable with or fearful of expressing.[646] I believe that if underlying causes are not addressed then there is an increased likelihood that the same problem will return, or that other symptoms will develop in its place.

However, not everyone is open to such psychological explorations. For some it may be enough to be relieved of their symptoms and illnesses. It is always possible that a symptom may have outlived its psychological utility and may be hanging on as an old habit. It is also possible that respants' unconscious mind may be inviting them to engage in the process of mastering their physical problems as a pathway to greater personal or spiritual awareness.

These beliefs are not supported as yet by research. I would be delighted to see studies on whether the treatment of symptoms brings about as much long-lasting relief as the search for underlying causes in combination with symptomatic treatments.

How do they do that?
It has been known for decades that the mind may influence the body through the nervous system and the endocrine system, and in the past decade it has been found that the mind may also influence the immune system. Visualizations have been shown to enhance the functioning of neurohormonal, antibody, white cell and other body defense mechanisms. Dozens of proteins called neuropeptides are found in the brain. These are presumed to serve as chemical messengers between brain cells. Interestingly enough, all of these very same neuropeptides are also found in the immune system. The immune system therefore appears to be far more closely integrated with the mind than we had formerly realized, and they may even function as a unit. We are thus beginning to find more links that will help us understand the interactions of mind and body, as well as pathways by which the mind can influence the body through visualizations.[647]

Clinical applications: Visualization can help with pains, allergies, and musculoskeletal and gastrointestinal disorders. Sports performance can be enhanced.

Visualizations in spiritual healing
Visualization by the healee is reported by many healers to be an essential element for spiritual healing. Helpful imagery may include inhaling healing energies along with the air that fills the lungs; picturing a colored light connecting one's own heart with the healer's heart; imaging healing energies surrounding the whole body and focusing on the parts that are in need of healing, and so on.

Healers may visualize healees as whole and well in order to bring them to that state. A number of gifted natural healers suggest that this is truly a mind-over-matter effect in which the picture of wellness in the healer's mind imposes itself on the energy field and/ or on the body of the healee, restructuring the aspects of the healee's being that need healing.

While conventional medicine views the physical body as a structure that can only change with physical interventions, CAM practitioners believe the body can respond to psychological and bioenergy inputs. Many CAM therapies assume that there is a bioenergetic "template" or guiding plan that organizes and maintains body form and functions. By changing the bioenergy structure of the template, it is possible to remove disease patterns and insert healthy ones.

Oszkar Estebany reported that he visualized himself giving laying-on-of-hands treatment to healees during distant healing. He did not project images or "push" the healees to change.

During distant healings, Vladimir Safonov visualizes the healee sitting in a chair in his presence. He passes his hands around the imagined body of the healee, obtaining the same sensations in his hands as though the healee were present.

Suzanne Padfield visualizes the healee in perfect health (Herbert 1975). She images herself beside the healee's bed, telling the healee that he is getting well. She projects this image and this thought into the healee's mind. When she receives an image of cloudiness, she projects an image of clearness to counteract it. Padfield warns that it is important for healers to let go of the picture of illness that they observe diagnostically, so that they will not experience similar symptoms.[648]

Dean Kraft says that he likes to understand the physiological mechanisms of disease processes in order to bring about healing more effectively.[649] For instance, he visualizes increased blood flow to the affected skin in cases of shingles; cellular disintegration of tumors; and so forth.

Philippine psychic surgeon Tony Agpaoa frequently saw a murkiness within the healee at the place where he was ill (Stelter). He would then visualize this murkiness moving out of the body via one of the orifices. If the murkiness did not come out he would perform psychic surgery to heal the sick parts.[650]

Many healers report spontaneous visual perceptions of white or colored light surrounding the healee during a successful touch or distant healing. This has led to the common healing practice of deliberately visualizing light around the healee. Some healers visualize particular colors for particular effects (e.g. Krieger 1979;1993).

Lawrence LeShan (1974a) made a careful study of common denominators amongst gifted healers. He found that they tend to visualize that they are united in some way with the healee, and that both healer and healee are united with the "All." By using these visualizations LeShan learned to be a healer himself, and he has been able to teach others to develop their healing gifts in a similar way. An alternative state of consciousness is the third common denominator. This comes without effort to most gifted, natural healers, and is attained through mental concentration by healers who study in order to develop their gifts.

Healers may also visualize themselves sending or channeling energy to the healee, trusting that the healee will utilize the energy as needed for healing.

Vladimir Safonov (1981) suggests that people may achieve rejuvenation by visualizing themselves in scenes from their earlier years. [651]

The use of words, and particularly metaphors, in healing is well known from studies of suggestion and hypnosis. Words can create images and expectations that become templates for change.[652]

V. P. Zlokazov et al. hypothesize that psychokinesis (PK) may be more prevalent in people with a "high level of generated images" (proficiency in visualization).

Visualization by the healee is also reported by many healers to be an essential element for spiritual healing. Helpful imagery may include inviting white light to enter one's body, particularly bathing those parts in need of healing; inhaling healing along with the air that fills the lungs; picturing a colored light connecting one's own heart with the healer's heart; and so on.

Tony Agpaoa (Stelter) and F. W. Knowles (1954; 1956) reported that a positive attitude is required for the healee to maintain the gains achieved with the help of the healer. Conversely, if a healee sees himself in a negative light, this may impede healing.

Osteopath John Upledger and biofeedback specialist Elmer Green have shown that traumatic physical and emotional experiences may leave their imprints in the body, in the form of energy cysts that can cause a host of chronic symptoms (Upledger 1987).[653] Upledger reports that he can visualize these cysts within the body during craniosacral therapy, and can bring about cures through their release.

Craniosacral therapy employs visualizations of the therapist manipulating the bones of the skull and the meninges lining the skull and spinal cord to clear away scars and facilitate the flow of cerebrospinal fluid. Physical manipulations are not used. The osteopath's hands are held lightly on the patient's body while they visualize the desired motions of the bones and tissues. Visualizations are also used to alter the subtle energy pulsation of the craniosacral rhythms.

Visualizations are also sometimes helpful in working with plants. Luther Burbank was reportedly able to get a cactus to grow without spines by using various processes including visualization (Tompkins/ Bird 1973). [654]

Machaele Small Wright (1997) suggests that we can visualize ourselves as garden projects, inviting nature spirits to help us grow spiritually.

An imagery exercise

All of the words in the world will not convey the power of visualization, just as it is impossible to know the taste of cactus fruit from words that describe this uniquely delicious morsel. Only by actually tasting that fruit can we truly know the essence of its taste. So let me suggest an experiential exercise that you can do to sense how potent visualization can be.

Pick a time to do this when you feel confident that you are in a good psychological space. It should also be a time when you will not be interrupted for at least an hour or more. Find a comfortable chair that will support your back firmly, and settle yourself into the chair with your feet firmly planted on the floor. You might want to read the following instructions onto an audio tape so that you can have their guidance as you move through the exercise, without having to interrupt yourself to find the steps of instruction on these pages.

Picture to yourself that you are on a holiday, with no obligations or cares. You start out from your country inn, taking a pleasant walk through a beautiful countryside on a clearly marked, winding path. See the bushes and flowers and trees along the path. Feel the crunch of the earth under your feet; the warm sun and pleasant breeze on your skin. Smell the smells of the earth and the fragrance of lush vegetation. Hear the rustle of the breeze through the leaves of the trees, and the twitter of birds.

As you round a turn in the path, you come upon a cottage, where a wise being dwells. He is sitting by his doorway, and welcomes you warmly. He invites you to sit down and enjoy a fresh drink, and offers to answer any questions you may have.

You ask him questions that you've pondered about your life and your relationship. You take as long as you need to pose all your unsolved problems, listening carefully to his answers.

Take some time to reflect on his observations, clarifying with this wise being any issues that remain unclear.

Feeling sated with his wise replies, you thank him, take your leave, and start back along the path.

You are surprised at how differently you feel on the path back, and how quickly you reach the inn.

Consider the answers you received to your questions. Were they helpful? Where did they come from?

Many people find such exercises incredibly enriching, stimulating inner resources which they never knew they had within them.[655]

Research on visualization with spiritual healing is scanty. Matthew Manning, a famous British healer, was challenged in a laboratory experiment to protect red blood cells from the harmful influence of a dilute saline solution, which ordinarily causes them to burst (Braud et al. 1979). He visualized a white light surrounding the cells, and thus helped them to survive significantly better than cells that did not receive his treatment.

S. Wilson/ Barber describe a "fantasy-prone personality," which includes proficiency in visualization and is highly correlated with psi abilities.[656]

Discussion: Visualization appears to be a powerful method for self-healing and spiritual healing. Visualizations are important aspects of several of the spiritual healing modalities. I am impressed that those modalities which include visualizations may offer certain advantages to the healing process.

Craniosacral therapy is a very effective introduction for therapists to energy medicine practices. The therapist visualizes the bones of the skull flexing and moving at their sutures, and projects the bioenergy image of halting the craniosacral rhythm pulsations for a brief period and then allowing them to restart.

In Therapeutic Touch, healers may visualize various colors being projected to the healee, in accordance with their perceptions of the healee's needs for enhancing, reducing or unblocking bioenergy flows.

Visualization may also help healers focus on or resonate with healees.

Self-healing techniques may utilize ritualized movements combined with self-healing thoughts or meditations. In *Qigong, T'ai Chi* and *Yoga* there is a focus on very specific, ritualized movements of the body. These represent another form of connection with the body that can help to bring about healing. In *Autogenic Training,* general phrases are recited that focus attention on the body, as in "My right hand is warm." In psychoneuroimmunology and psychoneurocardiology, there is a meditative focus on images of aspects of the body – such as white cells or antibodies – while holding an intent for a change in the body. I believe that the potency of these treatments derives in some measure from their focus on visualizing the body while being in a meditative state.

It appears that consciousness can focus and direct the therapists' healing through intent, as supported by the many studies of spritual healing, and as reported anecdotally by many CAM bioenergy therapists. It seems reasonable to speculate that intent can shape the actions of bioenergies – both in the process of a healer manipulating these energies and .in their effects as templates for physiological processes in healees.

Perhaps it is not visualization alone that is effective in self-healing, and it may be that any meditative and sensory connection with the body will have the same self-healing effect. We have much to clarify yet in this fascinating modality.

Studies of group visualizations

How we see the world is to some extent shaped and even determined by what our family and culture tell us to perceive. Consensual validation serves to maintain beliefs about reality. There are strong processes of indoctrination within each culture that imprint upon children the prevalent beliefs about the world, so they will *see things in ways that are congruent with their society.* In Western culture the prevalent beliefs are materialistic. They condition us to believe that the body is independent of the influence of the mind, and that it is primarily through physical and biochemical treatments that a person may be healed.[657] These beliefs may actually create the reality that they propound. [658]

Consensual validation may also be used to alter our everyday reality. Charles Tart (1969) describes experiments involving mutual hypnosis between two subjects. That is to say, one person hypnotized another and then instructed that person to hypnotize him. Under these conditions both parties were able to share identical visualizations that appeared real to them. In one instance a third person entered the room and was also able to participate in the consensually visualized experiences. This supports the view that it is possible to create a separate reality via visualization.

An unusual series of consensual imaging is explored in *Conjuring up Philip* (Owen/ Sparrow). In this experiment, a group of people explored whether they could produce psychokinetic (PK) effects if they pretended to communicate with an imaginary personality in a seance. They made up details describing a fictitious person named "Philip." They then held regular seances over a period of many months in which they explored communications with this patently imaginary spirit. To their surprise, they began to get mediumistic information in the form of table-rapping which purported to be from that entity.[659] The information obtained was entirely consistent with the fantasy story they had created.

The visualization of Philip took on a very real quality for the participants. It worked best when they were relaxed and when conversation with Philip revolved around topics and questions that were comfortable and familiar to the group. If topics were raised that made members uncomfortable (such as Philip's sex life) then Philip might answer evasively, or not answer at all, or answer with scraping sounds or vibrations in the table instead of distinct raps. All of these responses were consistent with their previous experiences of conversation with an independent, discarnate entity.

Careful scrutiny of recorded sessions revealed that the personality of Philip varied according to the presence and/ or absence of particular members of the group at the seance. The information he conveyed was limited to the knowledge that was available to those present at any given time.

Communication effects would occur *when the above conditions were met and when a jovial spontaneous, unfocused atmosphere prevailed.* If deliberate, conscious efforts were made to produce Philip communications, they did not occur.

Communication with Philip proceeded as described *so long as all of those who were present believed in Philip's existence.* If his existence was called into question by a visiting skeptic or if his communication became the focus of conscious awareness and analysis by the participants, *few or no communications would occur.*

Discussion: It seems that three elements in the group members were essential to the production of *Philip effects:* first, an unfocused, relaxed intentionality; second, the visualization or conceptualization of a discarnate entity named Philip; and third, a total belief in the existence of "Philip."[660]

Others have obtained communications in this fashion from allegedly real spirits (Batcheldor). In the light of the Philip experiments it is unclear whether these other studies represent channeling of discarnate spirits or creations of the fantasies of the experimenters.[661]

Such experimentation may contribute a great deal to our understanding of healing. Observations of this kind may help us understand how the healer may create and consolidate a new vision of a healthier reality with the healee. This may help to explain why it is often more effective to consult a healer than to practice self-healing. People may need an authority figure who gives them permission to relinquish their habitual consensual reality of being ill, and who can help them build a new reality. I will discuss this further below.

I know of no replications of Tart's mutual hypnosis work.

Meditative visualization practices
Eastern meditative practices help to develop independence from everyday, linear, sensory reality.

Alan K. Tillotson studied *Ayurvedic medicine* in Nepal. He reports the following sequence for training of spiritual healers in Nepal, according to the *Chanda Maharosina Tantra,* an ancient book on healing. The initiate, after suitable preparation in *vajrayan* Buddhist meditation and six years training in standard

Ayurvedic medicine, embarks on another six-year course of intensive studies. His first year is spent in isolation in a monastery cell. He comes out once daily to bathe and eat and to obtain instruction and guidance, but otherwise remains totally alone.

He sits for long hours before figures of a many-limbed god called Chanda Maharosina – the god of dread and anger – until the student can clearly visualize every part of the god with his eyes closed. Next, he practices visualizing the same figure with his eyes open, to the point where he can actually see this figure in three-dimensional form in front of him. He then merges the figure's energy field with his own and becomes Chanda Maharosina himself. This figure becomes the symbol for a destroyer of everyday perceptions and realities, and it is capable of channeling *prana* (bioenergy) to the meditative disciple who worships him. This process may take a year to learn, but many are unable to achieve proficiency in this training.

Chanting aimed at stimulating the chakra system is practiced simultaneously with the visualization of the god. A rosary is held in the right hand while the mantras are chanted for hours. The rosary is usually made of human skull bones. All these techniques are used to gain control of prana.

Vajrayana Buddhists do not believe in the reality of the iconographic figure – they see the universe as a mental construct only. They seek to master the power of mind through meditation and visualization, and those who succeed are given further training. This consists of daily meditation and exercises in mobilizing prana for use in healing. With proficiency in these techniques, the initiate can alter the realities of another person's state of health, especially nerve disorders such as paralysis.[662]

These reports suggest that visualization may be a template for ordering and altering physical reality. It would be helpful to have careful observations, and better yet, formal studies of the practitioners of these theories and methods.

Another report is from Alexandra David-Neel, who studied Eastern philosophies at the Sorbonne and spent 14 years in Tibet, where she became a lama. Her attention was drawn to visualizations when she met an apparition of her Master while she was far away from him. Later, on meeting him in person, he explained that he had deliberately projected himself to where she was to see how she was doing.

In response to her query, her Master said she could learn to do this, and he instructed her in the prescribed practices. She reports a number of curious visualizations and/ or materializations that she learned. For example, she visualized a short, fat monk repeatedly for a few months. Gradually his form came to appear real, as though he were a guest living in her home. When she went on a trip, he accompanied her. He gradually began to perform actions that she had not commanded, but which were appropriate to the situation he was in. Though the illusion was mostly visual, she sometimes felt he rubbed against her or touched her. Gradually his appearance changed – he looked leaner, and then also began to appear sly and malignant. These were changes that were beyond David-Neel's control. She also reports that another person was able to see the monk and actually mistook him for a live person. She finally decided that she wanted to be rid of this apparition of her creation. It took her six months to dissolve the phantom.

David-Neel reports:

> ...Tibetans disagree in their explanations of such phenomena: some think a material form is really brought into being; others consider the apparition as a mere case of suggestion, the creator's thought impressing others and causing them to see what he himself sees.

However, Tibetans report that such materializations may have physical solidity and may interact in a physical way with physical beings and objects in the world. David-Neel also reports that she was told the following by another adept:

> [B]y means of certain kinds of concentration of mind, a phenomenon may be prepared in connection with a particular event which is to take place in the future. Once success is obtained with the concentration, the process goes on mechanically, without further cooperation of the man who has projected the energy required to bring about the phenomenon.

She was also told that in some cases, once such a plan had been put into effect, it might be impossible for the originator of the plan to change it.

Discussion: The limits of visualization and materialization are unclear. David-Neel's reports add to the indications that far more may be possible than Western worldviews generally acknowledge. Relevant to healing, her evidence suggests that it may be possible to create new realities – perhaps even materializations of items such as tissues required for healing a wound, or other restructuring of the body. Her last observation on the impossibility of altering certain visualizations may indicate some sort of natural law of imaging realities into existence that could explain why particular disease realities cannot be helped through healing.

Visualizations of being in other realities
It is certain that visualizations can help us to alter our psychological reality. We often assume that our past casts its shadow on our present lives, influencing our behaviors through the habits we developed in response to our early experiences. Many also assume that their past experiences are etched in stone, and though they might wear a little smoother with time or might be ignored, they cannot be changed in any substantial manner. Within this belief system, we are burdened with our past errors of commission or omission and can only ask for forgiveness or absolution but cannot change them.

Recent studies show that visualizations can be used to change our relationships with our past experiences. For instance, if an unhappy childhood has left you feeling unloved and unlovable, you might find it hard to believe that anyone in your current life could love you. This is a common problem that keeps people from developing satisfying, close and intimate relationships. One way to heal such crippling childhood scars is to visualize that you are nurturing and loving your *inner child* – that part of each of us which continues to crave cuddling and loving and reassurance – teaching that all is safe and all will be well. By engaging in such imagery practices you can alter the feeling-experiences of your inner child so that this part of yourself is more trusting and more open to receiving love in your current life (C. Black).

Visualizations may also influence our awareness in transpersonal dimensions that extend outside our bodies. D. Scott Rogo (1978) suggested that the form people assume during *out-of-body experiences* (OBEs) may be determined by their state of mind. People having OBEs may perceive themselves as ghost-like figures with human forms; as balls of light; or as points of consciousness located in physical space.[663]

The Tibetan Book of the Dead, an ancient Eastern religious text, emphasizes that the last thoughts in your mind before death influence your fate when you leave your body (Rinpoche). Elaborate visualization exercises and prayers for the dying and for their relatives are prescribed to help project the souls of the dying into the higher and purer dimensions.

There appears to be a suggestion here that our state of mind at the time of death can project us into the sort of spiritual reality that corresponds to that state of mind. This might lend a transpersonal reality to the words of John Milton (1667):

> *The mind is its own place, and in itself*
> *Can make a heaven of hell, a hell of heaven.*

People who have had *near-death experiences* (NDEs) report that they encounter a Being of Light who is all-knowing, unconditionally accepting and loving.

In NDEs (Moody; Ring) and in pre-death visions (Osis/ Haraldsson; Morse 1994) people report seeing the spirits of relatives coming to welcome them. In deathbed visions people also report that they see Christ, God, or a being of light.

Western sensitives who counsel the dying will often suggest that they should look towards the light as they are breathing their last breaths, so that they may find their way more easily across the barriers between realities and into the next dimension.

Some healers report they are aided by spirits during healing (e.g. H. Edwards; Turner 1970). Paul Beard (1966; 1980) carried this several steps further, throgh investigations of channeled reports which indicated that spirits in the afterlife may create whole environments for themselves through their beliefs, expectations and visualizations. A person who disbelieves in life after death may, upon entering the world of spirits, congregate with others of similar beliefs. Together they may visualize into existence whole earth-like suburban communities. Such a person may go on for a long time mowing his astral turf before he reaches enlighten-ment.[664]

Discussion: The consistent reports of healers, mediums and people close to death suggest that either there is a widespread human need to project imagery of an af-terlife, or that spirit levels of existence are real and perceivable through intuitive senses. I believe that the latter is true because of the consistent, coherent reports of an afterlife from very diverse sources in many cultures around the world.

Visualizations as "thought forms"
In other dimensions of existence visualizations reportedly shape and mold the substance of those realms.

Annie Besant, the second president of the Theosophical Society,[665] and C. W. Leadbeater were gifted clairvoyants who explored intuitive awareness early in the 20th Century. They described *thought forms* that appear in an individual's aura in association with what that person is thinking. Besant and Leadbeater depict a variety of examples of these forms, along with their interpretations of them, though they say it is impossible to render the thought forms from clairvoyant vision accurately in drawings.   Here are some of their explanations:

What is called the aura of man is the outer part of the cloud-like substance of his higher bodies, interpenetrating each other, and extending beyond the confines of his physical body, the smallest of all. Two of these bodies, the mental and desire bodies, are those chiefly concerned with the appearance of what are called thought forms. Every thought gives rise to a set of correlated vibrations in the matter of this body, accompanied with a marvelous play of color, like that in the spray of a waterfall as the sunlight strikes it, raised to the n-th degree of color and vivid delicacy. The body under this impulse throws off a vibrating portion of itself, shaped by the nature of the vibrations – as figures are made by sand on a disc vibrating to a musical note – and this gathers from the surrounding atmosphere matter like itself in fineness from the elemental essence of the mental world. We have then a thought-form pure and simple, and it is a living entity of intense activity animated by the one idea that generated it. If made of the finer kinds of matter, it will be of great power and energy, and may be used as a most potent agent when directed by a strong and steady will.

Each definite thought produces a double effect – a radiating vibration and a floating form. The thought itself appears first to clairvoyant sight as a vibration in the mental body... The mental body is composed of matter of several degrees of density...

There are... many varieties of this mental matter, and it is found that each one of these has its own especial and appropriate rate of vibration, to which it seems most accustomed, so that it very readily responds to it, and tends to return to it as soon as possible when it has been forced away from it by some strong rush of thought or feeling. When a sudden wave of some emotion sweeps over a man, for example, his astral body is thrown into violent agitation, and its original colors are for the time almost obscured by the flush of carmine, of blue, or of scarlet which corresponds with the rate of vibration of that particular emotion. This change is only temporary; it passes off in a few seconds, and the astral body rapidly resumes its usual condition. Yet every such rush of feeling produces a permanent effect: it always adds a little of its hue to the normal coloring of the astral body, so that every time that the man yields himself to a certain emotion it becomes easier for him to yield himself to it again, because his astral body is getting into the habit of vibrating at that especial rate.

[L]ike all other vibrations, these tend to reproduce themselves whenever opportunity is offered them; and so whenever they strike upon another mental body they tend to provoke in it their own rate of motion. That is – from the point of view of the man whose mental body is touched by these waves – they tend to produce in his mind thoughts of the same type as that which had previously arisen in the mind of the thinker who sent forth the waves. The distance to which such thought-waves penetrate, and the force and persistency with which they impinge upon the mental bodies of others, depend upon the strength and clearness of the original thought. In this way the thinker is in the same position as the speaker.

[T]his radiating vibration conveys the character of the thought, but not its subject.

[E]lemental essence, that strange half intelligent life which surrounds us in all directions, vivifying the matter of the mental and astral planes... thus animated responds very readily to the influence of human thought, and every impulse sent out, either from the mental body or from the astral body of man, immediately clothes itself in a temporary vehicle of this vitalized matter. Such a thought or impulse becomes for the time a kind of living creature, the thought-force being the soul and the vivified matter the body. Instead of using the somewhat clumsy paraphrase, "astral or mental matter ensouled by the monadic essence at the stage of one of the elemental kingdoms," theosophical writers often, for brevity's sake, call this quickened matter simply elemental essence; and sometimes they speak of the thought-form as an "elemental." There may be infinite variety in the color and shape of such elementals or thoughtforms, for each thought draws round it the matter which is appropriate for its expression, and sets that matter into vibration in harmony with its own; so that the character of the thought decides its color, and the study of the variations and combinations is an exceedingly interesting one.

If the man's thought or feeling is directly connected with someone else, the resultant thought-form moves towards that person and discharges itself upon his astral and mental bodies. If the man's thought is about himself, or is based upon a personal feeling, as the vast majority of thoughts are, it hovers round its creator and is always ready to react upon him whenever he is for a moment in a passive condition...

If the thought-form be neither definitely personal nor specially aimed at someone else, it simply floats detached in the atmosphere, all the time radiating vibrations similar to those originally sent forth by its creator. If it does not come into contact with any other mental body, this radiation gradually exhausts its store of energy, and in that case the form falls to pieces; but if it succeeds in awakening sympathetic vibration in any mental body near at hand, an attraction is set up, and the thoughtform is usually absorbed by that mental body.

Franklin Loehr, who studied healing effects on plants, summarizes succinctly what has been repeated by others: "A thought is a thing." By this he meant that thoughts produce effects in the physical world.[666]

Robert Leichtman (1984), a clairsentient physician in Baltimore, writes about the emotions in parallel with Besant and Leadbeater:

> Emotions are a type of subtle, invisible energy, much like electricity or light, although different in quality. The easiest way to visualize them… is as streams of living energy that circulate throughout the planet. This emotional energy is alive, active, and has specific characteristics of shape, size, and color. As a living force, it exists independently of human beings, but of course we are influenced by it, conscious of it, and able to use it.
>
> Together, these living streams of emotional energy form a vast "sea" of emotions that permeates the entire planet… Literally, this sea of emotions is the collective emotional consciousness of all life forms on the planet. Within this sea, there are many grades and types of emotions, all of which can be contacted by human beings for better or for worse.

Leichtman finds that there are positive and negative emotions of many sorts which appear to be polar opposites of each other. They all have varying elements of intensity, form, magnetism, plasticity and motion. He believes that emotions should be used for *touching* others, i.e. "…to heal conflict and negativity…" Incorrectly used, he believes, emotions are superficially experienced as *feeling:*

> [W]e are seeking only the *appearance* of wealth, comfort, and status, not the *qualities* of compassion, peace, and wisdom. Because we are only interested in feeling the surface of life, our life ends up empty.
>
> The "feeling" approach to emotions also commonly leads to the perpetual quest for some kind of ultimate sensation – which of course does not exist.

These observations by Leichtman suggest that one may be able to draw upon or in other ways interact with the energies or aggregates of thought/ feeling forms that either exist naturally in our environment or are collected over periods of time from human (and other?) sources, or both. He seems to corroborate Besant and Leadbeater's observations on thought forms.

Last, I will mention that there are a number of reports of sensitives who say that they perceive in another dimension some sort of "ring of information" or "*Akashic records*" that contain all knowledge.[667] This might represent a subtle energy repository for thought forms that exists in the aura of the earth, or perhaps may be a linear description for "super-psi," through which all knowledge is available. In other words, if we all possess psychic abilities – which can reach anywhere and anywhen – there may be a realm we can visit psychically, in which all knowledge resides.

Observations on visualization in self-healing and spiritual healing
The evidence regarding visualizations is intrinsically subjective. This area has not yet been sufficiently researched for us to describe with any confidence what

might be the intermediary processes between mental/ emotional projections of visualizations and any potentially more objective source for these perceptions.

The most methodical applications of visualization are in self-healing for serious illnesses and in craniosacral therapy. These applications have the convincing weight of numerous reports supporting them, many of them gathered by people familiar with research techniques. The observations of gifted or practiced sensitives, though lacking consensual validation in the individual reports, appear to have sufficiently consistent common denominators to merit modest credence as well.

Let us first analyze visualization from the vantage of the healee. Common experience and the explorations of psychotherapy reveal that habits are hard to change. People tend to see themselves in certain ways, and they act in accordance with these perceptions – which are comfortable to them because of their familiarity. Relatives and friends come to have certain anticipations regarding their behavior, based on previous interactions with them. If they start to change, their own habits of perception and behavior, along with the expectations of others, will often get in their way. It is usually much easier to stick with the familiar and known. Even when change may be for the better, people tend to resist it both in themselves and in others. For instance, a man who has been obese and is dieting may be teased by the rest of his family about his efforts to lose weight. A wife who tends to be habitually late in getting ready to go places with her husband may be on time for once. Instead of complimenting her, he may say, "Well! What on earth happened to you today?"

These are only persistent habits of *behaving* – so how much more difficult must it be to change habits of *being*. This requires alteration of self-perceptions that have become so automatic that they are second nature. A perfect example is when a chronic pain is eliminated and the relieved sufferer feels odd, as if something has been removed from her life, rather than restored to it. After healing relieved her pain, one healee said, "I feel as though I'm walking around without my shoes or skirt." Following successful healings, people have actually managed to retrieve their lost pains by tensing their bodies where they used to hurt, because it is so unfamiliar to have body free of pain.

There are many ways that visualizations can help to shift our self-awareness.

Self-healing visualizations involve *mental* practice of patterns of behaving that anticipate subsequent *physical* changes. Through these auto-suggestions healees may be opened to new elements of behavior that are partial steps in the desired direction of the healing they seek. For example, people suffering from cancer might well feel depressed. Because of debility from the disease itself, combined with the weakening side-effects of chemo- and X-ray therapy, they may become even more depressed. Depression has its own vicious circle of: lack of energy → hopelessness → reduced socializing and weakened attention to daily living routines → fewer satisfactions in social and other aspects of life, weakened PNI and other systems → worsening depression, etc. By visualizing themselves engaging in desired positive activities, they can prepare themselves to work their way out of such vicious circles. In mechanistic terms, we may see this as "starting to put your mind in gear," or "partializing" the problem into manageable steps. They may then more readily engage in social or intrapsychic actions that produce positive changes in their lives, creating a *sweetening spiral* – which is the opposite of a vicious circle.[668] Both their inner and outer lives may be transformed. Feeling better, they will then have more energy to do more ☐ to feel still better.

We can postulate that healees may use visualizations to open themselves to changes of a more radical nature, which are brought about by healing energies. Visualizations may serve as templates for them to literally restructure themselves by reshaping their bioenergy fields. This postulate is consonant with the visualization practices described above. It is also supported by theories and research on *Life-fields* (Burr) and/ or *Thought-fields* (E. Russell 1971;1973), which suggest that the mind may influence the body through biological energy fields that are present in all living things.[669]

Healers appear to be able to help healees to let go of old images or visions of themselves and to insert and adjust to new ones. A number of factors are probably at play, either individually or more likely in concert.

The first of these is the power of suggestion. Healees usually come with the expectation that the healer is going to help them change. Thus, both through the self-selection of those who are looking for and/ or willing to accept changes, and through the build-up of hope with a visit to the healer, the stage is set for real change to occur. Sitting in a waiting room or in a crowded revival meeting tent may likewise enhance healees' readiness to relinquish outdated self-images.[670]

Healers may pray, move their hands around healees' bodies, and touch them, or they may engage in more dramatic rituals (especially in revival meetings and shamanistic healings). All of these procedures will enhance the healees' anticipation of and readiness for a lasting change, which they will accomplish in part by letting go of their old visualizations of themselves.[671]

The second important factor in healing is the belief that another person can bring about the desired changes. "Placing themselves in a healer's hands" may permit healees to relinquish their mental grip on their sick self-images, allowing new, healthy, restructuring images to take hold.

It requires a major act of faith to dare to hope for success through such techniques. Even though this is difficult, our mind is capable of such shifts, as was waggishly pointed out by Franklin Loehr:

> One day I sat upon a chair.
> Of course the bottom wasn't there.
> Nor legs, nor back. But I just sat,
> Ignoring little things like that.

The healer may hold the image of a new state of being for the healee in her mind's eye, as with Loehr's chair, until the healee is ready and able to hold it himself. Visualization may be one of the key factors in bringing about healing. It may be that the visualization is transmitted by the healer to the healee telepathically as a *template* for change. It may be easier for the healee to accept a new template transmitted by a healer than to build one from scratch.

Healers often attribute their healing gift to agencies beyond themselves. These may include God, Christ, angels, spirits, the "higher self" of the healer or healee, or cosmic forces and energies. Many healers engage in healing rituals. These may aid the healer to let go of the image of the sick patient sitting before him, and to visualize an image of the healee in a healed state. This is obviously a parallel to the healee's reliance on the healer or on the healer's external aids as agents of change. Without such adjuncts, both the healer and healee may be too bound to the self-perpetuating "reality" of their senses and memories of past experiences.

The introduction of higher powers into the process of healing may also encourage healees to relinquish their sick *templates*, by invoking an authority higher than the societal teachers who created their disbeliefs in their own ability to change themselves.

With the support of these external aids, healers and healees may be able to put their minds, their beings and their healing energies to work through mechanisms that function in other dimensions but which influence our everyday reality. Rituals and beliefs may be mental "keys" or release mechanisms on the doors that lead to such alternative realities.

The degree of success in visualization achieved by the healer and healee may be one factor that accounts for part of the spectrum of success and failure observed in healings, which can range from mild, partial and slow changes to radical, total and sometimes near-instantaneous transformations. This theory predicts that a class of potent healers may be identified whose greatest strength lies in their powers of visualization. With healees, either an ability to visualize or a pronounced suggestibility would be complementary characteristics.[672]

The whole-and-well visualization might also act as an effective mechanism for releasing images of sickness that retard self-healing.

Although many healers visualize their healees as whole and well, they often do not do this as a focused, volitional act. It is more commonly a "wishing the healee well" and "leaving her in the hands of a higher power." Healers report that they can achieve surprisingly potent healing through visualizations of sending energy in a general way like this, without mentally specifying its intended action – saying in effect, "Thy will be done." Quite often the specific condition that brought the healee for a treatment is not affected. Yet other conditions, which were sometimes not even mentioned to the healer or not even in the conscious awareness of the healee at the time of the healing, may be the very ones that will respond to the treatment. It is not uncommon to hear a healee say something like, "Though I came to have healing for my heart condition, it was the patch of psoriasis on my elbow that cleared up." This seems at face value to contradict my thesis that visualization is an effective part of healing. However, it may be that visualizing the healee as whole and well allows the healing energies to act where they are most needed, much as an antibiotic injected into the body would. It would be of great interest to study whether such scattered healing responses occur more frequently with healers who use a general rather than a focused approach to healing. It may also be that extraneous factors such as time of day, geomagnetic activity, or other variables interact with healing to influence which ailment responds to the treatment. [673]

Leaving the healing process "in the hands of God" may activate collective unconscious images of the healer's society. Rupert Sheldrake suggests that such images may accrue power with repeated applications, thus building up what he calls *morphogenetic fields*.[674] The collective unconscious of mankind may store the visualized healing images of God from individual healings performed throughout time. This stored imagery may somehow provide access for individual healers to tap into a shared healing force or a healing awareness. Thus, while God could be an external source, the effects attributed to God could be drawn from the collective sum of healing by all healers through all time.

The healers' beliefs in what they do are often sincere and confident – with an inner certainty that transcends linear logic. Trusting in outside agents may strengthen their belief that healing will work, which may in turn enhance the potency of their visualizations.

If mind can influence matter, and if the mind of one person can affect the mind and body of another, by what process(es) does this occur? Besant and Leadbeater describe clairsentient perceptions of what appear to be parts of an etheric energy process. One must ask whether their observations represent objective, physical world" phenomena. Alternatively, they could be mental images constructed in the minds of the perceivers to give "substance" of a more familiar sort to clairsentient perceptions deriving from unfamiliar processes that in other dimensions.

At this stage of our knowledge we can only speculate that thoughts and feelings may shape aspects of dimensions of which we are only dimly aware in our conscious minds, and which we must therefore distort when we try to use linear language and concepts to describe them.

Whether there is objective validity to spiritual healers' claims and descriptions of higher sentient beings such as spirit guides and angels is another question that we cannot presume to answer with any certainty at this stage. It is widely felt that there are entities and/ or sentiences on other planes of existence who can help us. It could be postulated that these are simply cosmic energies that can be tapped into, which healers and mystics have anthropomorphically transformed into caring entities. In either case, processes of visualization may facilitate the healers' mediation between their healees and the Infinite Source.

I would also reiterate an intuitive observation that visualization combined with some sort of physical intervention is more potent than visualization alone. We see hints of this in *hatha* (exercise) *yoga* and *pranayama* (breath) *yoga;* Chinese *Qigong* healing; craniosacral therapy; biofeedback; autogenic training; homeopathy; and the "passes" of touch healing.

Though much of this discussion has focused on spiritual healers, I believe that similar visualizations are utilized by many other complementary and conventional therapists, often without their conscious awareness.

Negative contributions of visualization in healing

Visualizations may also hinder healing. If people cannot or will not relinquish their self-images of being sick, it may be difficult for them to be healed. If they do not believe that they can recover, they may simply remain ill. Doctors and healers can influence these tendencies for better or worse. W. C. Ellerbroek, working with people who had venereal herpes (which has been notoriously resistant to medical treatment) reports: "I refrained from telling patients they were intractable, and they all got well…"

In a broader context, visualizations of a consensual reality may build, maintain, and perpetuate that shared reality. Social evolution may thus depend upon the creation of inspiring images that encourage, create, energize and shape changes into being new realities.

> *"Human nature" is self-validating. Whatever answer we live with will come to approximate the truth.*
>
> – Gregory Bateson

Many healers feel that healees possess within themselves a healthy template, or a part of themselves that remembers what wellness is. Others go further, saying that our *conscious* mind is only aware of a small portion of the many realities in which we live, and that much of the time we are actually participating in other dimensions of our existence, in a vaster reality. Brugh Joy (1988), the American physician-turned-healer, shared the following:

> My experience with this miracle called being is that there is an orchestration to it beyond our wildest imaginations, and that you and I are actually beings much different than we think we are. And... when you begin to trust that there is a richer, vaster resource that orchestrates the process of manifest reality you would never think of directing it through the little ego awareness, the one that thinks it understands what's going on. For that would be like the subatomic particle in the molecule in the cell of the hair on the dog wagging the dog. That's what the outer mind is. We are 99.9999% comatose.

If visualization can shape or even create reality, then group consensus must maintain it. Through self-validating spirals we tend to hold on to our "truths" and to defend them against outside influences that may alter or negate them. Yet with time there is a gradual drift in consensual beliefs. This may mean that prevalent beliefs shape the possibility that a particular treatment is effective, and that over time the efficacy of this treatment may grow with the strength of collective belief in its potency. Likewise where there are negative beliefs about healing, the efficacy of the very same treatment may fade and it may not work as well, if it works at all.

  Modern science is reluctant to relinquish its view of the world, and this is one reason why spiritual healing has not enjoyed wider acceptance in the West. Spiritual healing suggests that the material world is not as solid or stable as we told by scientists. It feels threatening to us to be challenged to alter our view of reality. Many would prefer to deny the challenging evidence that is rapidly accruing for the potency of healing than to re-examine their cherished beliefs about physical matter, the body and bioenergy.[675]

  Group visualizations may create *local, temporary* consensus realities. These can make it difficult to conduct repeatable studies of bioenergy medicine. Heraclitus observed, "We cannot step into the same river twice," and this may be a more basic truth than we ever realized. Differing consensus realities shared among different groups of people may explain part of the difficulty in replicating psi and healing effects. It may be impossible to reproduce a given reality when it is shaped by multitudes of factors in the diverse participants in the creation of local consensus realities – many of them outside of our conscious awareness. A replication of an experiment, even when procedural protocols are identical, can never be completely identical to the original as far as subtle biological energies are concerned. There will be differences in the energies of the experimenters and subjects as well as in the laboratories; in geomagnetic and sunspot activity; in the times of day at which interventions are instituted; in the extensions of all of these factors into geobiological interactions; and probably in hundreds of other variables that are impossible to control.

> You are led
> through your lifetime
> by the inner learning creature,
> the playful spiritual being
> that is your real self.
> Don't turn away
> from possible futures
> before you're certain you don't have
> anything to learn from them.
> You're always free
> to change your mind
> and choose a different future,
> or a different
> past.
>   *– Richard Bach*

Adverse effects: No harmful effects have been reported. However, a logical caution would appear to be that engagement in negative imagery should be avoided, as when one is angry at someone. There is the possibility of producing negative bioenergy effects.

Training and certification: Imagery work is taught in workshops and has no certification or licensing.

Clinical applications: The best research on visualization has focused on its uses for self-healing for cancer and atherosclerotic cardiovascular disease.[676] Less rigorous studies suggest that it can improve quality of life when people are seriously ill, enhance sports performance, and facilitate the processes of psychotherapy. Its applications seem limited only by the clinical vision of therapists and respants. There seem to be no physical or psychological problems that cannot be aided to some extent through imagery work. In my own clinical work I have been able to help clients with anxieties and fears, old emotional traumas and severe allergies to make significant changes in their lives by using imagery.

Imagery techniques are readily learned and used as self-healing. A skilled, experienced therapist can markedly broaden the range and scope of possible techniques and applications of visualization for respants to consider.

It appears likely that bioenergy therapists may significantly enhance the effects of their treatments through the use of visualizations. Additional benefits are predictable if both caregivers and careseekers practice visualization techniques.

See also: Discussions in Chapter 1.

VITAMINS

See: Vitamins, under Nutrition.

WATER THERAPIES (HYDROTHERAPY)

Water at research establishments concerned with probing its characteristics should never be so intensively analysed and measured. The "water corpse" brought in for investigation can in no circumstances reveal the natural laws of water. It is only with natural free-flowing water that conclusions can be drawn and ideas formulated. The more profound laws are, however, hidden within the organism of earth.

– Viktor Schauberg (in Alexandersson, p. 52)

Water has been used throughout recorded time in a variety of ways to treat an enormous range of problems (Buchman; Thrash/ Thrash).

Drinking water in large quantities is advocated as an element of some therapies to detoxify the body by flushing out wastes. It is assumed that many therapeutic procedures – particularly those involving major shifts in bioenergies – release toxins that are bound up in the body, and that washing them out with quantities of water facilitates healing.

Hot baths, showers and saunas may be used to detoxify the body through sweating, in a similar fashion. A prominent example of this is found in the Native American *sweat lodge ceremony*.

Colonic irrigation with water (Donovan) is widely practiced to clear the colon of wastes that may accumulate due to sluggish bowel function, build-up of toxins in the body, infections, and illnesses.[677]

Ice is used to reduce swelling after injuries, and baths may relax tired and strained muscles.

Swimming supports the body's weight and can therefore provide a gentle way to exercise, particularly for people who are recuperating from injuries and debilitating illnesses.

Flotation tanks contain water with inert salts that buoy the body up, creating a feeling of weightlessness. Combined with the sensory deprivation of a quiet, dark, enclosed tank, this therapy provides an atmosphere in which meditative states are markedly enhanced (Hutchinson 1984), sometimes resulting in *peak experiences* (Lilly).

Steam in shamanic ceremonial sweat lodges may contribute to altered states of consciousness that promote spiritual awareness.[678]

Research: No controlled studies support the above-mentioned uses of water in and of itself as a therapy.

The body is composed of 65 percent water. There is evidence from homeopathy and flower essences[679] that healing vibrations can be imprinted in water. There is speculation that the water in our bodies may transmit the healing vibrations of various therapies to whatever parts of the body are in need of treatment.

Research has shown that spiritual healing can alter the UV and IR spectrum of water, and that healing intent and psychological states of people who hold water .can alter its effects on the growth of plants.[680] This lends further support to the hypothesis that water may become a vehicle for healing.

Negative effects of water

Common sense must apply in drinking water. It is possible to drink so much that necessary body chemicals are washed out of the system, creating dangerous imbalances in the body.

Drinking water may carry infections and toxins. One of modern medicine's greatest contributions to health care has been in the development of water supplies that are safe to drink.

Sadly, most water supplies today are potentially dangerous to our health. They may contain pesticides, fertilizers and countless drugs that are flushed down the toilet. Recycled water is purified of common chemicals such as chlorine and some fertilizers. The cocktail of medicinal drugs and pesticides that find their ways into the water system escapes purification because these are complex and diverse chemicals which would be enormously expensive to detect, much less to eliminate from the water supply.

Clinical applications: Water therapies have been used for relaxation and as adjuncts in treatment of musculoskeletal and psychological problems.

Most water therapies are self-healing in nature.

YOGA

> *The old Yoga teaching was… non-authoritarian[A] person has only to learn to listen within – to become aware of, and finally at-one with, his own "God" – in order to find all the direction he needs for his life on earth[I]n the course of time… every man would recognize some form of its truth as applicable to himself and would begin the journey to his own atonement with God.*
>
> – Joan Cooper (1979, p. 42)

One of the oldest forms of self-healing is yoga, a series of disciplines built up through many centuries of Hindu practices.[681] *Yoga* comes from the same root as *yoke*, applicable here in both its senses: to link together and to "place under discipline or training" (H. Smith, p. 31). Yoga practices unite one's spirit with God.

Huston Smith presents a clear and concise description of these approaches, which are more varied than is generally appreciated in the West. He begins with

Hinduism, which recognizes there are four main paths that a person may choose for spiritual development, depending on his personality and preferences:

1. *Jnana yoga* is the path of knowledge, which is the most direct but also the most difficult. On this path students first study the texts of past masters. Second, they observe themselves to learn the distinction between the masks of personality they have developed and their deeper Self, which is eternal. Finally, they shift their identification to that deeper, eternal part of their being.

2. *Bhakti yoga* aims "to direct toward God the geyser of love that lies at the base of every heart." This is the most popular variant of yoga in India. First, a student clarifies that the God he loves is not himself.

> [H]is aim will not be to perceive his identity with God but to adore him with every element of his being...
> All we have to do in this *yoga* is to love God dearly – not just say we love him but love him in fact; love him only (loving other things because of him), and love him for no ulterior reason (not even from the desire for liberation) but for love's sake alone... (p. 37)

The practice of Bhakti yoga includes constant repetition of God's names; the exploration of the manifold nuances of students' love for God; and the steadfast worship of God in an idealized image of each student's choice – from among a myriad that were created and worshipped through the ages. As man is familiar with love towards man, the personification of God in a concrete image is viewed as a helpful intermediary step in developing love and devotion to God the infinite.

3. *Karma yoga* is the path towards God through work, which may be practiced philosophically or through love.

> ...the point of life is to transcend the smallness of the finite self. This can be done either by shifting the center of interest and affection to a personal God experienced as distinct from oneself or by identifying oneself with the impersonal Absolute that resides at the core of one's being. (p. 41)

In *karma yoga,* students must work without any thought of self, in order to move closer to God.

> ...Every act of his diurnal routine is performed without concern for its effect upon himself. Not only is it performed as a service to God; it is regarded as prompted by God's will, executed for God's sake, and transacted by God's own energy which is being channeled through the devotee. "Thou art the doer, I the instrument." (p. 42)

4. *Raja yoga* brings students closer to God through scientific experiment. They practice mental and physical exercises with the aim of moving toward awareness of the infinite Being that underlies their body, their conscious, and their uncon-

scious. Eight steps are recommended to reduce distractions in daily activities, in the body, in breathing, in the senses and in thinking. Breathing exercises help to channel *prana* (cosmic energy); *hatha yoga* (physical exercises) disciplines the body; and meditation disciplines the mind.

In the West, *hatha yoga* exercises have been popular for the benefits they provide to physical health, such as maintaining fitness, reducing hypertension, improving diabetic control, and the like.[682] Breathing exercises *(pranayama)* have helped in treating asthma and other pulmonary conditions.

The energy aspect of these practices has been largely ignored in modern Western applications, but this was not so in the original Hindu teachings. Breathing exercises are said to increase flows of healing energies into and throughout the body. Hatha yoga exercises and meditations open channels within the body to energy flows that purify the body and spirit, bringing practitioners to states of *samadhi* (enlightenment; union with God).[683]

Eastern traditions point out that particular physical exercises and *kriyas* (postures) are conducive to developing and experiencing specific states of consciousness (Khalsa/ Khalsa).

A store of energy *(kundalini)* is said to reside near the base of the spine, coiled like a snake, available but dormant in most people (Greenwell; J. White 1979). When the suitable levels of meditation and spiritual development are reached, this energy rises through the spine to the head, bringing with it enlightenment. If the yoga practitioner is not properly prepared, however, this transformation may bring with it a host of physical and emotional disorders (Greenwell; Sannella).[684]

The experience of *kundalini* is so powerful that it dramatically and profoundly transforms those who experience it. Christopher Hill observes: "[B]elief in... *kundalini*, whatever it is, must be based on direct experience and not on some teacher's parroting of cultural brainwash."

The *chakras,* or energy centers in the body, were described in Sanskrit writings on yoga. The bioenergies may be channeled by the yoga adept to heal others (Motoyama 1981; Perrin). It seems likely that these are the same energies that are focused in the Chinese self-healing and healer-healing practices of *Qigong*, which are used to treat numerous illnesses.[685]

Spiritual aspects of health form an integral part of yoga and other Eastern healing systems. For instance, reincarnation is an accepted belief in Hindu religion. This belief provides a framework within which people can cope with some of their difficulties in life and with their fears of death.[686]

Integrative care and Eastern approaches

Medical practice in the West has focused on manipulations of the material world and consequently on the *physical* aspects of disease.

In contrast, the healing arts in the East have focused on *energy medicine* and on harmonizing all aspects of life. One does not negate the other, and both can help to heal.

In *hatha yoga* and *pranayama* we again find a combination of meditative and physical exercises. This combination appears especially effective for self-healing.

Some Christians have hesitated to be involved in yoga because it has religious overtones that are not accepted in their church. Christina Jackson has developed yoga exercises that are harmonized with Christian prayers.

There are also numerous Western methods of exercise for self-help and for developing awareness that involve harmonizing of body, emotions, mind, and spirit. Many of these have considerable overlaps with yoga.

Rebirthing (Orr/ Ray), *Holotroopic Breathwork* (Grof/ Halifax), and other breathing methods have been developed to help people release old memories that are buried in the unconscious mind, and sometimes locked into physical pathology. These methods may also bring out memories of past life traumas.

Bodywork psychotherapy uses physical exercises to promote physical health and facilitate emotional release.[687]

Meditation is widely recommended in the West for health enhancement and spiritual development. Many meditations use the biological metronome of breathing as a focus for concentrating the mind. Variations on the theme of pranayama suggest that meditators visualize healing energies entering their body along with their breath, and then picture the release of tensions and other expressions that they are ready to let go of.[688]

Adverse effects: While generally a gentle and safe practice, there have been injuries reported with exercises that are too vigorous or advanced. The supervision of a trained yoga teacher is advised in developing a program of yoga practice.

Training and certification: There are no Western standards for training, certification or licensing in these practices.

Clinical applications: Yoga practices can improve relaxation, muscle toning and breathing. Hatha yoga exercises are excellent as preventive medicine, and helpful in maintaining muscle tone and normal flows of biological energies. They may also be helpful in rehabilitation following injuries or illnesses. Yoga can contribute to improvements in stress-related illnesses such as hypertension and musculoskeletal pains. By enhancing biological energy flows it can strengthen the body's abilities to deal with many other illnesses, in ways that cannot be explained within Western medical theories. It can also facilitate spiritual discipline and higher sense awareness.

While initial instruction in these techniques is usually necessary, their practice is self-healing.

See also: Qigong; T'ai Chi Ch'uan.

Problems Addressed Effectively by CAM Modalities

ALLERGIES

CAM therapists may identify allergies as causal agents in chronic illnesses where conventional medicine would not consider this a possibility. These may include health problems such as anxiety and panic attacks, depression, headaches, attention deficit hyperactivity disorder (ADHD), learning disorders, arthritis, asthma and other respiratory problems, sinusitis, menstrual problems, digestive disorders, and chronic fatigue syndrome. Symptoms that may suggest allergies include rashes, abdominal pains, nausea, vomiting, diarrhea, headaches, irritability, chronic fatigue and even epileptic fits.

Multiple allergy syndrome may occur alone or in combination with chronic fatigue syndrome and candidiasis. For no apparent reason, people may develop hypersensitivity to numerous chemicals and foods. It seems as though their immune systems are working overtime in response to many chemicals which they had previously handled without difficulties.

Treatment begins with identification of allergens and avoidance of these substances for a period of time so that the immune system can recover its normal functions. CAM modalities that may be helpful in identifying allergies include applied kinesiology; medical dowsing and electroacupuncture according to Voll (Sancier 1993); and in treating allergies meridian based therapies,[689] homeopathy, nutritional counseling, Anthroposophic medicine, and Ayurveda.###

CANDIDA YEAST INFECTIONS

Candidiasis often develops after a course of antibiotics that kill the normal bacteria in the gut and allow yeasts to grow there instead, or with steroids that weaken the immune system. Candidiasis may present with any of the following symptoms:

- "feeling lousy" without reason, being irritable or easily angered;
- craving yeasty foods (bread, alcohol, fermented cheeses) and sweets;
- eating these foods may provide temporary relief, but this may be followed by a worsening of symptoms,
- abdominal pains;
- premenstrual syndrome, menstrual irregularities, and pain;

- symptoms resembling hypoglycemia (fatigue, sharp hunger spells, weakness, trembling, drowsiness, cold sweats, dizziness, headaches, blurred vision, palpitations, rapid pulse, and irritability);
- vaginal infections and local discomfort during intercourse;
- prostatitis or impotence;
- loss of libido;
- persistent fungus infections of the feet, crotch, toenails, or skin;
- fatigue that is worsened when exposed to molds (basements, gardening); and
- heightened sensitivity to tobacco smoke, perfumes, and other chemicals.

Treatment may involve avoidance of foods that promote yeast growth – which are often the very foods that are craved; avoidance (to a reasonable extent) of antibiotics; taking the anti-yeast (prescription) drug nystatin; eating yogurt; taking capsules of lactobacilli to replace the normal flora that are killed off by antibiotics; drinking special herbal teas (taheebo, la pacho, pau d'arco); and having cleansing enemas (Trowbridge/ Walker).

CHRONIC FATIGUE SYNDROME (CFS)

CFS and fibromyalgia often begin with a viral illness such as a severe flu. Symptoms persist for weeks and even months, and may include severe weakness, insomnia, headaches, muscle aches, and depression. When muscle aches predominate, the usual diagnosis is fibromyalgia, but the dynamics and treatments are similar in either case. Sufferers are doubly and triply afflicted because nothing in conventional treatment tends to help, and malingering is often suspected (Klimas; Stoff/ Pellegrino). The resulting weakness may be so severe that sufferers cannot even get out of bed. Symptoms typically persist for months and years.[690] Candidiasis, fibromyalgia and multiple allergies may be present concurrently.

 Helpful treatments include spiritual healing, acupuncture, homeopathy, massage, whole-food and allergy diets, identifying allergens and psychotherapy.[691]

 Conventional medicine has been slow to acknowledge CFS because no clear cause has been identified, nor is there any definitive diagnostic test for it.

> …Presently, modern medicine does not proceed on clinical observation and experience alone but relies almost exclusively on objective laboratory data. Where CFS is concerned, it's hard to see the beast. Given the limitations of our present medical technology, we can only follow its footprints.
>
> – Jesse Stoff and Charles Pellegrino (p.60)

Multiple allergy syndrome may occur on its own or in combination with chronic fatigue, fibromyalgia and candidiasis. In these conditions, reason people develop hypersensitivity to numerous chemicals and foods for no apparent reason. It seems as though their immune systems are overwhelmed and unable to deal with chemical stresses which they had previously handled without any difficulties. (See discussion of allergies, above).

While some wholistic medical doctors are familiar with these syndromes, many who are afflicted with these problems are disappointed to receive little or no help from their family physicians, and find relief only from CAM therapists. CAM therapies that may be helpful include addressing allergies (as suggested above), adding vitamin and herbal remedies; acupuncture; meridian based therapies, relaxation, imagery techniques, and spiritual healing to deal with the allergies as well as the stress and depression that accompany CFS.

FIBROMYALGIA (FM)

Fibromyalgia often presents with many of the same symptoms as chronic fatigue syndrome and multiple allergy syndrome. It involves chronic pains in muscles all over the body, with weakness and tiredness on exertion. People with FM may be unable to manage more than a bare minimum of self-care without utter exhaustion.

Treatments are similar to those of CFS and multiple allergy syndrome. Careful pacing of exertion, with budgeting of energies allotted to tasks is essential.

CANCER

We treat dogs and cats better than we treat people with terminal illness in our society. When our pets areafflicted with major debilitating and painful terminal illnesses we put an end to their suffering with a merciful sleep into death.

Western medicine has difficulty accepting its limitations to cure human disease. The possibility that cancer will prove fatal leads conventional medicine to treat cancer aggressively – fighting it and waging war against it, cutting it out wherever possible, poisoning it with toxic chemicals and bombarding it with x-rays.[692]

The prolongation of life at all costs becomes the goal of treatment, often carried to extremes, well past the point that the person with cancer might wish. Quality of life is not given as high a priority as fighting off what is viewed as the grim reaper. While some chemotherapy and radiotherapy can be extremely helpful in slowing or reversing the growth of cancers, there are many times that highly unpleasant side effects are produced – seriously diminishing the quality of life (Gralla).

People with cancer are often frightened and bullied into accepting treatments that produce major side effects which seriously diminish the quality of their remaining months and days on earth. When they elect to refuse these treatments, some doctors may take extreme measures. In some places, if a child has a terminal illness and the parents refuse to accept a doctor's recommendation for toxic therapies, the child may even be removed from the parents' care by the child welfare department at the doctors' insistence and forced to undergo the treatment (Hillary).

CAM therapies for cancer more often focus on the whole person rather than just on the disease (S. Downer; M. Leerner 1994), as with CAM therapies for other illnesses. There are no studies to show which therapy is best. Here is a modest list of CAM therapies commonly used in treatment of cancer: Nutrition (E. Hoffman; M. Jacobs); herbs (R. Moss); macrobiotic diet (Sattilaro); self-healing for cancer;[693] living and dealing with cancer;[694] exceptional cancer patients;[695] hypnosis (Newton); psychoneuroimmunology (PNI);[696] spiritual healing;[697] family involvement in cancer therapy (S. Matthews-Simonton)

NEUROLOGICAL PROBLEMS

Strokes leave people with perceptual, cognitive and motor deficits. Acupuncture can markedly enhance recuperation from strokes.[698]

Phantom limb pain is pain that is perceived to come from a limb or other body part that has been amputated. This is particularly responsive to spiritual healing.[699]

Multiple sclerosis is a condition in which plaques of white matter proliferate in the nervous system, extending from the myelin sheaths of the nerves, and disrupting nervous system function. The course of the illness is highly variable and unpredictable, with periods of worsening symptoms alternating with periods of quiescence of the disease. Rates of progression are also quite variable.

Conventional Western medicine is limited in the treatments that it has to offer.

CAM therapies have not been well documented in their applications for the treatment of MS. Nevertheless, I have heard several reports of marked improvement, even in severely advanced cases, which have responded well to a combination of spiritual healing (Gardener) and intensive psychotherapy. The new meridian-based therapies appear particularly promising in facilitating the use of psychotherapy in these cases. I am impressed that some of the reports appear to indicate improvements that go well beyond those that occur with the periodic waxing and waning of symptoms typical of MS.

Coma following head trauma and various infections is reported anecdotally to respond well to craniosacral therapy and spiritual healing in some cases.

Complementary/ Alternative Medicine (CAM) Issues

ETHICAL ISSUES IN CAM

Ethical issues may be more complex for CAM practitioners, as compared with conventional medical practitioners. The following are some of the key issues that apply to most therapists.[700]

Competence – Some CAM therapies, such as massage, acupuncture, chiropractic, and homeopathy, involve knowledge-based and specific intervention-based treatments. In these cases, objective criteria for competence can be established. In other CAM therapies, such as healing and craniosacral therapy, competence is more difficult to establish because the energetic interventions are subtle and impossible to measure, and procedures may vary enormously between one practitioner and another.

In all of these interventions, the person of the therapist is to a lesser or greater extent a variable in the intervention.[701] For instance, in acupuncture, it is not just the insertion of needles that brings about changes, but also *how* the needles are inserted. Herbalists in traditional cultures suggest that it is not just the plant essence that heals, but *what you tell the plant to do*. Intuitive assessments by sensitive therapists and practitioners can lead to much deeper and more effective interventions in all CAM therapies.

To standardize the subtler dimensions of these treatments it may be necessary to establish that competence in CAM therapies must include an apprenticeship with certified teachers, along with a thorough, formal demonstration of knowledge and technical skills.

Negotiating therapy contracts with clients – In CAM therapies it is important that informed consent be established before any procedures begin. With healing and other CAM approaches there is often an expectation that rapid, even miraculous cures can be achieved in a single treatment. Few people coming for their initial assessments know much about these approaches, so appropriate time should be invested to explain how they work and what results to expect from the therapist and the interventions. Expectations of client responsibilities in using these therapies should also be spelled out.

Respect for autonomy and consent – Compared with conventional medicine, CAM clients are often given more autonomy in choosing therapeutic modalities, as well as greater responsibility for their own treatment. CAM therapies may be therapist-generated, as in acupuncture and homeopathy, but they may also rely heavily on client participation, as in nutrition, fitness, Qigong, meditation, relaxation, meridian based therapies, and imagery approaches. Self-assessment and self-healing are essential aspects of many interventions.

Records of treatment – Proper record keeping is essential for continuity of care, as well as for legal purposes. This can also provide databases for evaluation and research.

Research – Responsible use of CAM approaches requires that therapists assess the efficacy of their interventions, both to know that what they are doing is effective and to monitor any side effects or adverse effects that may occur. This research need not be complicated. Much can be learned from systematic review of records of treatment, case presentations, and qualitative studies.

Continuous professional development – There are frequent advances that enhance treatment potentials in most therapies. Therapists should stay current with developments in their own areas of specialization, and to the extent that is possible, in other CAM methodologies as well. In addition to cognitive updates, personal development is particularly important wherever the therapist is an essential component in the treatment. Clearing emotional dross, clarifying blind spots that result from prior emotional traumas, and staying alert to issues of transference and counter-transference will markedly enhance the therapy. This process requires personal psychotherapy and/ or other CAM therapy interventions for the therapist. This is one of the most important aspects of ethical practice.

Collaborations and referrals to other health caregivers – No single therapy is appropriate for every person or every problem. It is important to know the limits of any CAM approach and when to refer to other therapists for treatment of aspects of problems that are beyond one's own competence or the limits of one's therapeutic modality. Making appropriate referrals is an art that requires at least a basic knowledge of other therapies, and of the competencies and personalities of specific therapists. Collaborating with other therapists is an even greater challenge. We don't know very much about the range of efficacy of individual CAM therapies, much less about combinations of these modalities. For many problems, such as arthritis, backaches, chronic fatigue syndrome, fibromyalgia, and cancer, multimodal approaches seem to be more effective than single therapies. It takes both self-confidence and humility to be able to admit one's own limitations and to work productively with other therapists in helping people faced with complex problems.

Special duties towards children – Children may not be able to articulate or explain their problems, and their judgment usually is not sufficiently mature to allow them full responsibility for making healthcare decisions. However, their cooperation is often vital to the success of treatment. Therapists have to rely to a great extent on parental impressions about their children's problems, and parents will also carry out or supervise treatments at home. Therapists must also remain alert to the possibilities of children's problems being caused – directly or indirectly – by their parents. On the mild end of the spectrum, tensions in the home may contribute to children's tensions, which may cause or worsen their illnesses. On the severe end of this spectrum, parents may be directly harming their children through emotional, physical, or sexual abuse. CAM therapists should take responsibility for reporting suspected abuse to the appropriate authorities, just as conventional therapists do.

Respecting confidentiality – Clients expect that therapists will maintain confidentiality regarding their problems and treatment records. Written permission should be obtained before releasing information or records to anyone.

Maintaining professional boundaries – Clients are needy and vulnerable when they come for help. Therapists must not take advantage of clients to satisfy their own ego, emotional or sexual needs (Jehu).

Professional etiquette, respect for colleagues – People who come for CAM therapies often have chronic problems and may have seen a series of conventional and CAM therapists already. While clients may have justifiable complaints, their stories often represent just one side of a situation and may be distorted by misperceptions, faulty or selective memory, or psychopathology. While therapists should not totally discount or discredit clients' stories, judgment should be withheld until the other side can be heard.

Availability of effective complaint mechanisms – Responsible professional associations must establish procedures for clients to file complaints, and for review and discipline of therapists' conduct.

The practices of conventional medicine, nursing, psychology, and social work all have established ethical standards. Physicians take the Hippocratic oath, and the principle of "first do no harm" is repeatedly emphasized in their training. CAM therapies would do well to develop similar codes of ethics.[702]

CERTIFICATION AND REGULATION OF CAM PRACTITIONERS

Regulation of complementary therapy practitioners is a complex issue. Some modalities such as acupuncture, chiropractic, and homeopathy have professional organizations that set standards for the education and practice of their members. Many other therapies are represented by no professional organization, and have no generally accepted standards for education or practice.

There are three broad forms of regulation for healthcare practitioners:

1. *Licensing* – requiring that practitioners meet standards imposed by the state;
2. *Certification* – protecting the title of people who meet specified standards, but not restricting others from practicing without using the title; and
3. *Registration* – requiring only that practitioners file their names, qualifications, and addresses.

While it is desirable to protect the public from incompetent, unethical, and/ or fraudulent health care practitioners, many state laws have been written in language that favors allopathic medicine, stating that no one may practice as a health care professional outside of the norms of local medical practitioners.[703]

State laws governing medical practice have been enacted in consultation with medical doctors over the past 100 years. Medical doctors have actively used these laws to promote the exclusive legal legitimation of allopathic medicine, and have sought to deny practitioners of other therapies the right to practice. In the early 1900s, medical doctors were successful in eliminating competition from homeopathic and naturopathic physicians through such legislation. Since then they have endeavored to limit the practices of other complementary therapists as well. In addition, some local medical societies strongly discourage their member physicians from introducing CAM in their practices, by applying restrictive recommendations based on legal definitions of proper practice. These legal limits state that doctors are judged to be practicing properly or improperly according to the "standard medical practices of their local colleagues or of the school in which they were trained." While this provides the courts with some standard for judging whether a doctor was liable in a malpractice suit, it is not a suitable basis for restricting the use of other methods. Were such standards rigidly applied, there would be very little progress in medical treatment, and what therre was would be very slow.

> *When everyone is wrong, everyone is right.*
> – Nivelle de la Chaussée (1747)

These restrictive laws were successfully challenged by chiropractors in 1985. Other complementary therapies have been accepted by several states – often as the result of constitutional challenges of existing laws by practitioners and the public. A restrictive attitude is still prevalent in the majority of states, though this is steadily improving.

It is difficult to find the best balance between protecting the public from harm on the one hand, and excessively restricting complementary therapy practices on the other. Therefore complementary therapists are challenged to improve their own internal professional regulation and to support their claims of efficacy for their modalities with research evidence. Where they have done so, they have often achieved better recognition and acceptance within the existing laws.[704]

Spiritual healing is not yet among the modalities that have professional licensing boards in America. In fact, there is even dissention and schism between healers trained and practicing in different traditions, such as Therapeutic Touch and Healing Touch, and the various Reiki lineages and schools.

Complementary therapists complain that physicians can take weekend courses in CAM methodologies (e.g. acupuncture for pain control) and then be allowed by law to practice these modalities, while CAM practitioners who have years of training and experience are denied this right because they don't have a medical degree. Ironically, in some states restrictions are applied just as vigorously against pioneering physicians who engage in the practice of complementary therapies. Doctors have been hounded by members of their own medical societies on the grounds that they are practicing therapies that are not accepted by their peers – often with no consideration of the evidence for the efficacy and relative safety of these therapies.

> *If a little knowledge is dangerous, where is the man who has so much as to be out of danger?*
> – T. H. Huxley (1877)

INSURANCE AND LEGAL ISSUES

Insurance coverage for CAM treatments and malpractice coverage for practitioners

With increasing awareness that the public is paying billions of dollars annually out of pocket for CAM therapies (Eisenberg et al. 1993; 1998), a growing number of insurers now include payment for some CAM services in their policies. Several states now have laws requiring health insurers to include CAM benefits (Firsbein). Acupuncture, chiropractic, and massage are the most commonly covered modalities. This is a reflection of the general rate of usage of these modalities, as well as an acknowledgment of the professional membership organizations that their practitioners have formed.

Growing numbers of states mandate insurance coverage for licensed CAM therapies such as chiropractic and massage.

The numbers of insurance claims against CAM practitioners is much lower than the number of claims against medical practitioners (Studdert/ Eisenberg et al.). This is probably due to the facts that CAM therapies have much lower rates of serious complications and that closer, more personal and trusting relationships often develop between CAM practitioners and their clients. It may also be that awareness regarding the possibility of litigation has yet to grow in this area to the extent that it has in conventional medical practice.

Malpractice insurance is now available for many CAM practitioners. Again, there are more insurers offering coverage for the more commonly used and accepted modalities, such as acupuncture and chiropractic.[705]

Legal status of CAM therapies

CAM practitioners and the public may have difficulty understanding why the medical profession has been slow to develop programs of integrative care, when so many practitioners and recipients of CAM therapies report that they are beneficial. Several issues are at play here.

Private medicine in the US has viewed CAM therapies as competition for the healthcare dollar. The AMA has lobbied against the acceptance and legal recognition of CAM practitioners, starting with homeopathy and naturopathy in the early 1900s. These discriminatory practices continue today. For instance, the AMA has discouraged hospitals and medical schools form providing Continuing Medical Education credits for conferences on CAM.[706]

> *Our ideas are only intellectual instruments that we use to break into phenomena; we must change them when they have served their purpose, as we change a blunt lancet that we have used long enough.*
> – Claude Bernard (1865)

Three primary objections to physicians' involvement with CAM have been proposed:

1. *There is no good evidence for the efficacy of CAM therapies.* This is patently ridiculous, considering the wealth of evidence summarized in this book.

Critics suggest that CAM research is not up to the level of conventional medical research. This is likewise untrue. This claim is largely a product of ignorance caused by the limited access conventional doctors have had to this body of research.

There is a major problem with publication bias against CAM in the conventional medical literature. This has limited the dissemination of information in the medical community, thus perpetuating the division between CAM and allopathic approaches and impeding the development of integrative care. [707]

2. *Use of CAM therapies may delay the application of more effective therapies beyond the point where these are able to help.* This might be true if people with medically treatable illnesses used CAM therapies exclusively in place of conventional therapies.

This is a spurious argument in cases where CAM is used within a program of integrative care. It is also far from clear that all conventional therapies are of proven efficacy. Furthermore, the side effects of many conventional therapies (particularly with cancer, pain and depression) may diminish quality of life to such an extent, while offering minimal hope of palliation or cure, that respants may seek out CAM therapies that can enhance quality of life.

3. A doctor who refers a patient to a CAM practitioner may be liable for malpractice claims if the patient suffers harm at the hands of the CAM practitioner. This is a very complex legal issue (Studdert/ Eisenberg et al.).

A doctor could be liable if his referral of a patient to a CAM practitioner is negligent. For instance, if the doctor knows that an acupuncturist does not sterilize needles after use or does not use disposable needles, the doctor could be held liable if the referred patient gets hepatitis B or AIDS as a result of treatment by that acupuncturist. If the doctor maintains a supervisory relationship with the CAM practitioner there would be a clear liability, and the same might apply if the doctor and the CAM practitioner work within the same institution or under the same health management plan.

A doctor might conceivably be held liable for referring a patient to a particular type of CAM practitioner when another type of CAM therapy is significantly more appropriate.

In all of these cases, the injured party would have to demonstrate a causal relationship between the alleged substandard referral and the injury.

On the whole, the liability rate for physicians referring patients to CAM therapists is likely to be low, considering the low rate of malpractice claims against CAM practitioners.

4. The AMA has often objected to physicians' use of CAM on the basis that these therapies are not standard local practices. Because the AMA has successfully lobbied to have many state legal codes reflect this standard for deciding upon the suitability of care, this complaint often carries the force of law. The illogic of the complaint is again patently obvious. If it were rigidly applied, there would be very little progress in the practice of medicine. Few new treatments would ever be discovered or developed.

The AMA has promoted legislation to outlaw the practice of medicine without a license. All states license chiropractors, and growing numbers license acupuncturists, massage therapists, naturopaths, and homeopaths. Most do not license other CAM practitioners. A therapist who offers to diagnose or treat a disease without a license can be subject to prosecution. The law does not consider it an adequate defense if patients testify to the efficacy and benefits of the therapy, or claim that no harm has come from the therapy. Even research evidence supporting the efficacy of the therapy often may not be accepted as a legal defense against claims of practicing medicine without a license.

Here is an example of this policy in practice.

> This is the true story of a man who cured himself of a near-fatal cancer after conventional medicine had mutilated and then abandoned him. He spent the next thirty years helping others with the disease. In the struggle to keep his clinic open, he faced raids and robberies, a near-fatal beating, a kidnapping, and a prison sentence many called justice gone wrong. He is in jail for a second time as this book goes to press in 1998, for the offense of treating cancer patients. The therapies that made up his treatment protocol were an eclectic assortment that covered the gamut and drew from the best of thte available natural cancer remedies. The details of this therapies, and the history and vicissitudes of the non-traditional health care movement that his life personifies, are woven through his story.
>
> Is effective non-toxic cancer treatment being suppressed? Hundreds of people who wrote to the court in Jimmy Keller's defense in 1991 thought so. Many wrote that he had kept their cancers in remission when nothing else would... (E. Brown, book jacket)

True, the therapies used by Keller were not researched, but there was no evidence he was causing direct harm, and many reported that he had been helpful to them.

> *The legal criminality of the social system and its institutions, of government, and of individuals at the interpersonal level is tacit violence.*
> – Johan Galtung

Several CAM therapy groups, aided by grateful recipients of their treatments, are lobbying state governments for changes in such restrictive laws. Minnesota has passed the most progressive legislation, allowing great freedom for CAM practitioners,[708] Followed by California, and other states are considering similar legislation. This seems a far better approach than was used in the case of chiropractors, who had to sue the AMA for restraint of competitive trade in order to obtain governmental approval for their right to practice.

Some laws, however, state that referrals to CAM therapists can be made only after the failure of all reasonable conventional medical treatments. This places people with cancer at risk for delaying treatments of their choice past the point where they may be effective.

Licensed CAM practitioners are tried by the courts according to the standards of their CAM schools of practice, just as physicians are tried according to the standards of their individual medical schools.

CAM practitioners whose methods of treatment are not licensed are tried according to standards of conventional medical care or lay healthcare standards.

Considering that the public pays more visits to CAM practitioners than to conventional medical doctors, there are bound to be shifts in the degree of collaboration and in legal status of CAM practices. Currently, patients visiting CAM practitioners often may not tell their physicians about their medically unaccepted treatments – which could lead to harmful interactive effects of therapies.

David Studdert, David Eisenberg and colleagues (1998) suggest:

> Physicians who currently refer patients to practitioners of alternative medicine or who are contemplating doing so should not be overly concerned about the malpractice liability implications of their conduct[I]t may be useful to ask the following questions. First, is there evidence from the medical literature to suggest that the therapies a patient will receive as a result of the referral will offer no benefit or will subject the patient to unreasonable risks? Second, is the practitioner licensed in my state? (Some added comfort can be derived from knowing that the practitioner carries malpractice insurance.) Third, do I have any special knowledge or experience to make me think that this particular practitioner is incompetent? And fourth, will this be the usual kind of referral (i.e. basically at arm's length, without ongoing and intrusive supervision of the patient's management)?
>
> If the answers to the first and third of these questions are no and the answers to the second and fourth questions are yes, then this should remove many of the concerns a physician has that the referral decision itself will be construed as negligent. This conclusion holds even if the patient suffers an injury caused by the alternative medicine practitioner's negligence. That practitioner should be held accountable for his or her autonomous actions and should be judged according to standards set by fellow practitioners.

The legal status of spiritual healing differs in several respects from that of CAM therapies in which herbs or other substances are prescribed or which use physical interventions such as massage or physical manipulation. When healing is given without touch, either with the healer's hands held near to but not touching the body, or through distant healing, it is unlikely that any causal connection could be established between a claimed negative effect and the healing treatment. Even where light touch is used in spiritual healing, the same constraint would apply.

However, this would not provide a defense against charges of delaying treatment that might have been of greater benefit, of sexual misconduct, or of other commonsense damages.

Some spiritual healers protect themselves legally by being ordained as religious ministers, which allows them to practice healing without fear of legal restraints. Others may be covered by their professional practitioner licenses, such as nursing, medicine, psychology, social work or the like. The danger here is that some professional organizations may object to spiritual healing or other CAM modalities that are outside the normal range of practices for their members. In some states, practitioners have been called before their professional boards and some have even lost their licenses for practicing CAM therapies.

INTEGRATIVE CARE:
WHICH THERAPY FOR WHICH PROBLEM?

Holistic Medicine – New map, old territory.
                                                    – Patrick Pietroni

It is a challenge both to practitioners and to people seeking help to decide which therapy is most appropriate for which health problem. We are barely beginning to understand the spectrum of efficacy of individual therapies, let alone being able to make informed choices between them. The case is a little clearer for the question of allopathic medicine vs. CAM therapies, though the research base is no stronger.

Conventional treatments

Allopathic medicine has a major contribution to make with treatments for certain problems. However, many conventional medical treatments have distinct disadvantages:

1. *Infections* caused by bacteria (e.g. bacterial pneumonia and meningitis), by spirochetes (e.g. syphilis), by rickettsia (e.g. Rocky Mountain spotted fever), and by some other organisms often respond well to treatment with antibiotics. Specific antibiotics must be given in recommended doses for specific periods of time if they are to be effective.

However, if they are taken for too brief a period or in doses that are too low, antibiotics may worsen the problem by selectively killing the weaker infectious organisms, leaving the patient with a *super-infection* of antibiotic-resistant organisms.

Bacteria can develop resistance to antibiotics. Viral illnesses do not respond to antibiotics, yet many people ask their doctors for antibiotics when they have the flu or other viral infections, and many doctors find it easier to give an antibiotic than to argue against these requests. This leads to a very serious public health problem. It is becoming increasingly difficult to deal with infections caused by drug-resistant strains of bacteria. This has become a serious concern with tuberculosis and venereal diseases in particular.

Allergic reactions may limit the use of antibiotics in certain individuals, and can present a danger to health and even to life when the reactions are severe. Severe allergic reactions constitute a significant portion of the many deaths in the US annually caused by medications (which were properly prescribed).

Antibiotics given for an infection in one part of the body may eliminate other useful or apparently harmless bacteria in another part of the body. Gastrointestinal and mucous membrane infections with yeasts and other organisms may result from administration of antibiotics that eliminate the benign organisms that normally dwell on these tissues.

Homeopathic medicine offers an alternative to antibiotic use that has not yet been adequately explored or researched.

2. *Medications* may help in treating many problems such as pain, cardiovascular disease, epilepsy, arthritis, anxiety, depression, schizophrenia, and more. New

medications are constantly being developed. In some cases medications can cure problems completely, as in single episodes of depression that are relieved by antidepressants and do not recur. In other instances, symptomatic relief is possible. For instance, physical symptoms of viral illnesses can be alleviated – even though the infections are not eliminated. Though herpes and AIDS are not cured by taking medication, quality of life can be substantially improved and life may be prolonged.

The downside of medications is that every drug may produce side effects in some people some of the time. When these effects are mild, the benefits of medicinal therapy may outweigh the costs. However when side effects are severe, quality of life may be compromised to the point that the medications cause as much distress as the illnesses for which they are prescribed – or more. This is particularly true of *cancer chemotherapy* (and *radiotherapy*). While these treatments may prolong life, their negative effects must be weighed carefully against their benefits. With some cancers the prolongation of life can be considerable. With others the efficacy of these treatments may be minimal, and the impairment to quality of life is sufficient to raise serious questions as to whether the treatments are of real benefit to the patient. Their use actually could be a symptom of the patient's and the doctor's denial of the fatal nature of the illness (R Moss 1995).

The annual rate of deaths from serious negative reactions to medications is about 100,000, as was mentioned at the beginning of this chapter (Lazarou et al.).

I remain hopeful that some day CAM therapies such as spiritual healing, relaxation, and imagery will be used to help reduce the side effects of medications (as in chemotherapy, or with drugs used to treat pain, depression, and anxiety). This would be far preferable to the current practice of prescribing further medications to control the side effects of the primary treatment.

3. *Surgically correctable problems* can be addressed by conventional medicine with excellent results, as in: treatment of injuries resulting from physical trauma; draining or excision of localized infections (e.g. lancing boils, appendectomy, gall bladder surgery); removal of localized growths (e.g. cysts, benign and cancerous tumors); orthopedic corrections; corneal replacements; insertion of cardiac pacemakers and bypass surgery; skin grafts and other cosmetic surgery; caesarian sections; joint prostheses; organ transplants; and more.

In some cases, however, there is serious doubt as to whether surgery is even necessary, as in hysterectomies for heavy bleeding or mildly abnormal Pap smears, or with caesarian sections for brief episodes of fetal distress.

Any kind of surgery can be dangerous to one's health. It is estimated that up to 20 percent of people who are hospitalized develop secondary problems during their hospitalization, such as infections, poor results from anesthesia or surgery, allergic reactions to medications, problems due to medical errors, and the like. Because medicine is an art as well as a science, there will always be some errors in diagnosis and treatment, and some of these may prove fatal.

Surprisingly, even serious surgical interventions may become faddish. Numbers of procedures have been developed and used to treat thousands of people, only to be proven over time to be ineffective. Examples include internal mammary ligation for angina (Cobb et al.); radical mastectomy for breast cancer (Nuland); extracranial-intracranial artery bypass surgery (EC/ IC Bypass Study Group); splenectomy for all ruptured spleens (Nuland); prostatectomy for all prostate cancers (Nuland); and recently, arthroscopic knee surgery (Moseley et al.). Thousands of people have been treated with unnecessary and sometimes ineffective surgery.

The questionable advisability of surgical interventions is particularly relevant where CAM therapies may be helpful, especially considering the low incidence of side effects with these therapies. For example, CAM treatments (such as the Ornish approach) can eliminate the need for cardiac bypass surgery for atherosclerotic cardiovascular disease - (which is well supported by research), and EDTA chelation (which is still considered controversial, but nevertheless carries negligible risks).

4. *Hormone replacement* can be life-enhancing (as in menopause) or life-saving (as in diabetes, hypothyroidism' Addison's disease, and more). Treating hormonal hyperfunctions can also be life-saving (as in hyperthyroidism, Cushing's disease, and others).

Hormone treatments also have side effects, and sometimes they are quite serious. For many years women were encouraged to use hormone replacement therapy during menopause, with the promise that this would slow the processes of aging and reduce the risks of heart attacks and arteriosclerosis. Recently however, it has been shown that hormone replacement therapy does not reduce the risk of heart attacks and that it can increase the incidence of thrombosis of the leg veins (with the risk of pulmonary embolism due to clots from the legs being carried to the lungs). It may also increase the need for biliary surgery.[709]

5. *Genetic manipulations* promise to help with many health problems, as in the tailoring of new antibiotics and other drugs, the correction of inborn errors of metabolism, and more.

However, the potential for negative or even disastrous effects, especially in long-range terms, poses a serious concern. Nature has selected the current pool of genes through many years of trial and error, with the errors weeding themselves out. If we introduce new genetic changes, the complexity of biological systems will in many cases exceed our limited abilities to foresee the consequences of our tampering – with the distinct possibility that unforeseen harmful effects will occur.

6. *Diets* can be helpful in treating various problems, but very few doctors are trained in nutrition. Here too, there have been examples of serious medical errors. For many years, doctors strongly recommended low-fat diets to reduce the risk of cardiovascular disease, but this now proves to have been poor advice (Taubes 2002). Similarly, low fiber diets for chronic diverticulitis have proved to be ineffectual (Nuland).

7. *Prevention of illness* is another major contribution of allopathic medicine.

Improved sanitation to prevent the spread of infectious diseases has probably saved more lives around the world than any other medical intervention.

Immunizations have lowered the incidence of numerous serious illnesses, and in the case of smallpox, have actually eliminated the illness globally.

On the negative side, some people have severe (and occasionally even fatal) immune reactions to immunizations. There is an increasing suspicion voiced by many CAM practitioners that immunizations may have long-term negative effects on the immune system. This has yet to be confirmed by rigorous research, although several surveys are supportive.[710] Perhaps the new generation of cell-free immunizations, which eliminate a major source of allergic reactions, will be better in this regard.

Identification and elimination of insect vectors and animal hosts for illnesses have provided further avenues for prevention.

Another disadvantage of preventive allopathic interventions is that the pesticides used to limit carriers of diseases may produce serious toxic effects and side effects in people and in the environment. Pollution of the planet with pesticides is a particularly serious problem. For example, increasingly toxic levels of DDT are killing enormous numbers of birds and fish, and are working their way up the food chain to human consumption.

8. *A specific diagnosis* is required before treatment can be prescribed. This is a mainstay of what is considered good and ethical medical care. This principle is based on a linear, cause-and-effect analysis of physiology and of disease processes. It is assumed that a person is endowed at conception with specific genetic programs. These are then influenced by nutrition, physical and emotional environments, traumas, infections, toxins, allergies, neoplastic and degenerative processes. The belief and hope of allopathic medicine is that eventually every health problem will be understood in terms of physical and biochemical processes, and that once this has been achieved, then mechanical, biochemical, or genetic interventions will be devised to prevent and/ or treat all problems.

Knowing what your own problem is – giving it a name and a focus for addressing it – may provide healing in and of itself. Without a diagnosis, you may worry that anything is possible. Even when you receive a diagnosis of severe illness, there is still the relief of being able to begin to do something about the problem.

> *We are half dead before we understand our disorder, and half cured when we do.*
>
> – Charles Caleb Colton

In allopathic medicine, diagnosis focuses upon symptoms and diseases, with therapies prescribed accordingly. Conventional medicine prides itself on its thoroughness in this regard. Specialists are available to address various elements of the body, diverse disease processes, and an enormous spectrum of treatment interventions. Research is emphasized as a basis for establishing diagnoses and for identifying effective interventions.

While these practices and standards have advanced and refined medical knowledge, they have posed some difficulties in clinical applications. One of the most frequent complaints about medical doctors is that they take little time to listen to people's problems. They focus on the disease the person has, rather than on the person who has the disease.[711] Bearing witness to this dissatisfaction is the high percentage of prescriptions that go unfilled (estimated to be as high as 50 percent), and the enormous number of people who are now utilizing complementary therapies – and are willing to pay billions of dollars annually out of pocket for these treatments. In many cases, conventional medicine is simply missing the target with its mechanistic diagnoses and interventions.

9. Doctors are clothed in a mantle of enormous respect, which has been earned by the profession as a whole through dedicated care provided over many decades.

Doctors take upon themselves a heavy burden of responsibility when they care for patients. Their diagnoses and treatments must be accurate – within the limitations of human ability. They provide care around the clock, every day and night of every year. No other profession regularly requires and provides 24-hour coverage. Moral and ethical standards have been established, and they have been generally maintained at a high level.

The process of professional peer review has been highly developed, with hospital and medical licensing boards having the power to censure doctors or even to recommend the removal of their license to practice, in cases of negligence and misconduct.

Doctors usually have high standards of confidentiality and professional conduct. It is expected that intimate disclosures will be protected.

The key role of doctors as guardians of healthcare standards has been enacted into law in every state.

The downside to conventional medical care is that errors are inevitable in any human activity, and when medical errors or misconduct lead to injuries and suffering, doctors are liable to be sued. The high rates of malpractice litigation in the US have produced an atmosphere of defensive medicine. In many situations doctors may be inclined to act with caution or even fear – lest they be sued for acts of commission or omission. Defensive medicine leads to over-use diagnostic procedures (some of which carry serious risks), and to a tendency to intervene with invasive procedures lest the lack of intervention eventually provide grounds for a lawsuit claiming medical negligence. Some specialists have been sued so frequently, often for unavoidable problems such as childbirth injuries, that their insurance premiums have skyrocketed. Many obstetricians and gynecologists have chosen to leave their practices rather than have to pay hundreds of thousands of dollars annually for insurance premiums.

Sadly, the danger of malpractice litigation has grown to the point that many doctors practice in an atmosphere of distrust and fear. This has eroded the healing nature of the doctor-patient relationship.

Direct disadvantages of conventional medicine
There are two very practical matters and two philosophical issues that are highly problematic in medical care.

1. *Costs* of medical care in the US are excessive by the standards of every other developed nation in the world. Medications comprise one of the most expensive items.

These costs are becoming bones of contention between employers whose profit margins are squeezed by the costs of employee health programs and employees who are now being expected to pay increasing proportions of their own healthcare costs. Ironically, the higher costs are not purchasing better care. By all international assessments, the US ranks relatively low on the list of health ratings.

2. *Deaths caused by conventional medical care*, due to medical errors and side effects of medications properly prescribed, place medical care between the first and fourth leading cause of death in the US – depending on the source of the estimates.[712]

3. *Death* is seen by many conventional medical practitioners as the end of existence, an evil to be fought at all costs.

While prolonging life is one of the primary goals of modern medicine, there comes a time in every life when this struggle is no longer appropriate.

Doctors are often trained (as I was) to believe that if a person under their care dies it may be the doctors' fault – because they either failed to make the correct diagnosis, did not prescribe the correct treatment, or prescribed a treatment that had disasterous effects. While this may be true in some instances, doctors have to consider this possibility in every instance, because in many cases they cannot know what the cause of death was, even after an autopsy.

Many doctors have not been taught how to deal with death. Because of their discomfort and feelings of failure when the death of a patient looms or has occurred, they may often avoid dealing with this issue altogether.[713]

3. *Life after death* is considered no more than wishful thinking and any discussion of this subject is often dismissed or relegated to the clergy.

While the average medical practitioner may not be familiar with these aspects of human experience, wholistic practitioners frequently address such spiritual matters, and some are specifically trained to do so.[714]

> *Man's extremity is God's opportunity.*
> *– William Blake*

CAM treatments

Complementary therapists often approach healthcare in ways that differ substantially from the views and methods of allopathic medicine.

1. *CAM theoretical constructs are more wholistic.* Most complementary therapies address the person who has the illness rather than the illness the person has. These approaches are based on the belief that a person functions as a unitary organism and cannot be understood from the examination of its individual parts. In fact, many of the CAM therapies include people's relationships with other people and with their environment as essential elements in the course of their assessments and treatments.

2. *Biological energies* are assumed to play an essential role in normal physiology and in pathological processes. Interventions may be made through acupuncture points and meridians, chakras, energy medicines, and biological energy interactions with the therapist. Mental imagery can influence the body's energy patterns, as well as its neurohormonal and neuroimmunological systems.

3. *Diagnosis may relate to symptoms* but they are usually considered in the context of the entire person, and assessment may include analysis of the clients' relationships and environment. Treatments may be given to the whole person rather than focused on individual symptoms or on any one part of the body.

One of the most serious risks in complementary therapies perceived by Western medicine is that a medical problem that is potentially treatable through another modality – such as allopathic medicine – might be missed, and delay of conventional medical treatment could allow the illness to worsen.

The converse is also true, but almost totally ignored by Western medicine. For instance, acupuncture can halve the time for recovery after a stroke. Were the same standards of negligence to apply for failure to prescribe an effective CAM therapy, more people would enjoy the benefits of a variety of wholistic modalities.

4. *Diagnoses and treatments may vary between practitioners*. Just as each respant is unique, so is each therapist. The *person* of the practitioner may be as important as her *practices*. It is generally held that different approaches may be equally effective within systems of wholistic care, but this has yet to be substantiated in research. The question will probably always remain as to whether there aren't better treatments available than the one(s) prescribed.

5. *Treatments may produce side effects briefly*, as in emotional releases with deep massage, or symptoms that appear when a homeopathic remedy is started. These are usually transient and are viewed as *releases* of old, maladaptive patterns. People usually tolerate these responses much better than side effects of allopathic medications because practitioners let them know that they will be transient; that they are meaningful; that they are not harmful; and that they indicate progress.

6. *Psychological aspects of illness* are considered integral to many of the complementary approaches. Many people understand that their thoughts, memories, and emotions play important roles in the development of their health problems, and in the degree to which they are able to tolerate and deal with them. Similarly, many respants are able to accept that shifts in their attitudes, psychological conflicts, and relationships can bring about improvements in their condition.

7. *Exercise, nutrition and other aspects of lifestyle* are addressed by complementary therapists. This makes good sense and feels good to people who appreciate that they can contribute to the maintenance of their own health. People feel empowered when they can participate in their own treatments, and cures.

One danger, however, is that some people may begin to hope and believe that they can treat themselves without the help of conventional healthcare professionals. This is particularly true in the age of the Internet, since surfers can locate information on any conditions and multitudes of treatments for them. Here, a little knowledge may truly be a dangerous thing. I have seen many people misdiagnose themselves and their family members and apply inappropriate remedies through limited knowledge. Consumer Reports confirmed this problem in a survey of 46,000 subscribers (May, 2000) which found a higher rate of success when treatments were supervised by therapists than when they were self-prescribed.

8. *Respants are encouraged and empowered to explore and use self-healing approaches*. Many people are pleased to help themselves and not to be completely dependent upon a therapist. Others seek the expertise of a knowledgeable practitioner to advise them on approaches to self-care.

9. *Spiritual belief and practices* are important aspects of some of the complementary therapies.

> *All illness is curable, but not all patients.*
> – Keith Mason

One of the most common points of satisfaction is the fact that CAM therapists take more time to listen and to talk with clients. Respants also appreciate being addressed as people rather than as agglomerations of symptoms or walking containers of biochemicals. They feel that the psychological and spiritual aspects of their health problems are important, and they feel better understood when these are considered as integral aspects of their overall health.

10. *Chronic illnesses and conditions* such as backaches, arthritis, multiple sclerosis, and the like respond well to complementary therapies such as spiritual healing, homeopathy, and osteopathy. Sadly, because of our society's history of reliance on allopathic medicine, many people turn to CAM therapies late in the course of their illnesses, when it is actually less likely that they will have a strong effect. When CAM treatments are given early on in the course of illness, most therapists feel that they have a better chance of helping.

11. *Particular illnesses may be more effectively and/ or more safely treated by complementary therapies.* For instance, the newer anti-inflammatory and pain medications called NSAIDS, which are used in the treatment of osteoarthritis, may produce tens of thousands of cases of severe side effects annually – such as renal failure and gastrointestinal bleeding. On the other hand, glucosamine supplements have no serious side effects and they have comparable salutary effects to NSAIDS (Lopes). Chronic ear infections in children are often treated with antibiotics, with all of the potential risks mentioned above. Surgery for implantation of ear-tubes carries further risks. In comparison, significant numbers of cases of ear infection in children improve without treatment and with greater subsequent immunity to reinfection (van Buchen et al);[715] and with elimination of allergens from their diet (Dees/ Lefkowitz), with no serious risks involved.

For further discussion of problems where CAM may be of great benefit, see the section on particular problems that respond well to CAM modalities.

See Table II-8, *Complementary Therapies compared to Conventional Medicine*, for a summary of the differences between complementary therapies and allopathic medicine.

Two separate issues are relevant to any discussion of the benefits of complementary therapies.

Complementary therapies can be cost-effective. Most CAM therapies contribute substantially to health promotion and disease prevention at various work sites.[716] A study at a general practitioner's office in England showed that spiritual healing reduced expenses for 25 patients with chronic illnesses by $1,600 for the group over a period of six months (Dixon 1993). Disputing the cost-effectiveness of CAM therapies, A. White and E. Ernst noted a dearth of rigorous studies to support such claims.

Complementary therapies promote hope and positive attitudes toward illness and health management. Many of the CAM therapies include self-healing components. These empower respants with the feeling that they can contribute to their own healing.

CAM therapists stress caring rather than curing. This attitude focuses on the present, exploring all possible ways for enhancing quality of life *now*. Allopathic medicine, which focuses heavily on fighting disease, looks toward the future – to avoid death at all costs, even if this means seriously diminishing quality of life in the present.

CAM therapists offer hope by encouraging explorations of the spiritual dimensions of awareness. From this perspective, death can be seen as a transition to an afterlife rather than as the end of all existence.

Conventional practitioners caution against introducing false hopes of cure that can lead to severe disappointment, disillusionment, and despair. In ethical CAM practice, as in ethical allopathic practice, treatments are offered with the suggestion that they may help – not with promises of cures.

Table II-8. CAM Therapies compared to Conventional Medicine	
Diagnosis	
Diagnosis may be unnecessary	Diagnosis required
Diagnosis by intuitive perceptions that supplement history and observations	Diagnosis by history, physical examination, and laboratory examinations
Syndromes – patterns of symptoms that involve body, emotions, mind, spirit	Symptoms – primarily physical; emotions, mind, spirit are considered secondary
Diagnoses may vary between diagnosticians	Diagnoses should be consistent between diagnosticians
Treatments	
Wholistic approach includes body, emotions, mind, relationships and spirit.	Discrete elements of therapies are introduced, focus is mostly on the body.
Treatments may be specific or non-specific, may involve bioenergies, and may be focused by actions or by the mind of the therapist.	Treatments are discrete and specific within physical parameters. They are considered "objective," i.e. independent of the person giving them.
Interventions to uncover underlying causes of problems, restore harmony	Treatments to repair malfunctioning or damaged organism
Respant (responsible participant) takes active role in self-healing as possible	Therapist diagnoses, prescribes and/ or administers treatments
Theory	
Symptoms and diseases are indications of disharmonies in body, emotions, mind, relationships and spirit.	Symptoms and diseases are evidence of malfunctions of the physical body.
Spiritual aspects may be viewed as the most important elements of health.	Physical aspects are the most important; spiritual issues are relegated to clergy.
Mind and body are unitary parts of one entity and constantly interact directly with one another.	Mind and body are separate; only words, symbols, and sensory exchanges are vehicles for their interactions.
Healing action effective from any distance	Action is local, distance diminishes force
All of time is present in the now, and treatment may be directed to "anywhen."	Time is linear, with past, present, and future; treatments are given in the present.
Physical death is a transition to spiritual dimensions.	Physical death terminates existence.
Death is a natural part of existence, and healing into death is a good healing.	Death is to be avoided and fought against at all costs.
Explanations are "both/ and"	Explanations are in either/ or"
Research	
Individual case reports and qualitative studies preferred, RCTs (with compromises in usual CAM practices)	RCTs are the gold standard; qualitative studies and observation based on individual cases are inferior.

Another criticism of CAM interventions is that respants may feel guilty if they do everything prescribed but their disease continues to deteriorate. They may also come to feel they are somehow to blame for creating or maintaining their illness. This is sometimes a problem with CAM bodymind fundamentalists, who insist that our mind-set or attitudes entirely determine what happens to us. I believe this approach is unrealistic, in view of the multiple factors that combine to determine one's state of health, including genetic endowment, exposure to infectious organisms, allergens, environmental toxins, and normal degenerative processes in the body. Many of these factors are clearly beyond any individual's control.

The opposite danger is of introducing *negative suggestions* with nocebo responses that discourage hope, and this is far more common in allopathic medicine. Most doctors present statistics in a negative way, such as, "In a cancer of your type the life expectancy is about three years." This sets up the expectation that the patient won't survive beyond three years, which is similar to the casting of a hex. Some patients may take these suggestions on board and expect to die after a certain length of time and therefore program themselves to do so.[717]

Statistics are just averages of data from many individual cases. The CAM practitioner or the more wholistically oriented doctor might say, "While this is a serious illness, a certain number of people who have it live longer than others. No one but God knows how long any of us will live. I might get hit by a bus and you might live much longer than me even though you have this serious illness. Let's see how we can help you be one of those people who lives longer."

Research: There has been little research to clarify which CAM approach is best for which problem.

In one survey (A. Long et al), single-modality providers were queried about the target problems that respond to their treatments. Modalities with 2 or more responses included: aromatherapy, Bach flowers, Bowen technique, chiropractic, homeopathy, hypnotherapy, magnet therapy, massage, nutrition, reflexology, Reiki and yoga. The most common conditions responding to particular therapies were the following (parentheses indicate lack of research support for claims):

Stress/ Anxiety – aromatherapy, Bach flowers, hypnotherapy, magnet therapy, massage, nutrition, reflexology, (Reiki), and yoga

Headache/ Migraine – aromatherapy, (Bowen technique), chiropractic, hypnotherapy, massage, nutrition, reflexology, (Reiki), and yoga

Back pain – (Bowen technique), chiropractic, magnet therapy, massage, reflexology, and yoga.

Contraindications were therapy-specific, as in avoiding massage in cases of skin disease.[718]

While evidence comparing CAM and conventional therapy is limited, what is evident is that the safety of CAM approaches is on the whole is far greater than the safety of conventional treatments.

While much remains to be clarified on this subject, there are often clear advantages to the uses of CAM therapies (T. Chappell).

The best of both worlds can be found in *integrative care*, where conventional and complementary therapists work together or where conventional therapists learn to use CAM therapies. Attesting to the growth of this approach is the fact that about half of the medical schools in the US now offer courses in complementary therapies (Wetzel et al.; Pelletier 2000). There is now an American Board of Holistic

Medicine, which was initiated by the American Holistic Medical Association, and an American Holistic Nurses' Association.[719].

People are spending more and more of their healthcare dollars on CAM therapies. Out of 831 adults who used both CAM and conventional medical care in 1997, 79% believed that the two approaches combined were better than either one alone (Eisenberg, et al. 2001). Many cancer patients undergoing conventional treatments in the UK also seek CAM therapies (Downer et al.). They choose healing, relaxation, visualization, diet, homeopathy, vitamins, herbalism and other therapies.

How does one decide which therapy to use for which problem?
When there are obvious indications that a particular problem can be competently handled by allopathic medicine, such as a bacterial infection or a fracture, the initial choice is easier. However, there is no reason why treatments that help to deal with shock and pain, such as rescue remedy (a Bach flower remedy), arnica (homeopathic), or spiritual healing, should not be used at the same time. Similarly, my personal experience is that the pain of bruises, cuts, fractures and burns can be markedly lessened by applying these treatments, and that physical healing is more rapid – with no conflict in adding the healing to conventional treatments.

Complementary therapies may be helpful additions to allopathic treatments for almost any health problem. In some cases, however, there may be diverse or even conflicting recommendations from practitioners of these two approaches – and from different complementary therapists as well.

If your problems are more complex, particularly in the case of serious and chronic illnesses, complementary therapies may be the treatments of choice. One of the most thoughtful resources in exploring these clinical questions is the summary of the (London) Marylebone Health Centre's experience in exploring integrative care (Pietroni/ Pietroni). The physicians at this center explored how they could integrate conventional medical care with Chinese medicine, massage, counseling, relaxation, imagery, and spiritual awareness (in a clinic housed within a church). The summary of their work is broad, deep and very well presented.

Other excellent resources include the following:
Alternative Medicine (Burton Goldberg Group) gives succinct summaries of complementary therapies as modalities and also discusses various illnesses and therapies that may be helpful; and
Alternative Medicine: Expanding Medical Horizons (NIH – Workshop on Alternative Medicine) provides discussions of complementary therapies and extensive research references.[720]

A spectrum of CAM therapies can be helpful in the treatment of psychological problems (Bassman). Ruth Benor Sewell makes more specific recommendations for CAM therapies that may be most appropriate for people with different strengths in their characterological preferences, according to the Jungian polarities.[721] She suggests that there may be similar characterological preferences for complementary therapies in treating various problems. For instance, people with strong intuition (and weak outer sense attachments) may prefer imagery, music and story telling to deal with pain, while people who have opposite preferences may benefit more from yoga, massage and Autogenic Training.[722] (See Figure II-15.)   While these suggestions are as yet unsupported by research, they would be easy to explore.

In the more limited area of using CAM in surgery, a variety of approaches were found to be helpful for related psychological and physical problems (Norred).

We still have so much to learn about integrative care. The challenges are great, but the benefits that are already apparent clearly indicate that the efforts will be worthwhile.

Figure II-15. Stress management approaches

For all
Devotional time
Prayer
Chanting
Sacred ceremony
Rituals

Journal writing
Guided imagery
Reflexology
Self-hypnosis
Autogenic Training
Alexander technique
Breathing exercises
Counseling
Time Management
Biofeedback
Thought-stopping techniques
Raising humor

Thinking

Intuition
(Inner senses)

Sensation
(Outer senses)

Drawing
Yoga
Massage
Autogenic training
Progressive muscular relaxation
Handicrafts
T'ai chi
Counseling
Biofeedback
Humor
Time management skills
Alexander Technique
Movement, Dance
Meridian-Based Therapies

Feeling

Counseling
Massage
Aromatherapy
Meditation
Journal writing/poetry
Visualization
Art therapy
Music
Movement, dance, song
Meridian-Based Therapies

Visualization
Meditation
Guided imagery
Self hypnosis
Music
Story telling
Art therapy
Counseling
Raising humor
Song
Dance

* Adapted for each primary functions, from Sharp 1987.

NATURAL HEALING ABILITIES AND NORMAL RHYTHMS OF THE BODY

The art of medicine consists of amusing the patient
while nature cures the disease.

– Voltaire

Having discussed an enormous spectrum of psychological approaches and CAM modalities for healing, it is worth emphasizing again the vast natural healing abilities that we all possess. It is unclear where the body's memory of normalcy resides,[723] but it is certain that within each one of us there are vast capacities for self-healing, when we honor and encourage our self-regulating mechanisms to resume their normal functions.

To do nothing is sometimes a good remedy.
— Hippocrates

Spiritual healers suggest that the biological energy body contains the templates for all of the body's functions. This could explain how organs and tissues know to grow to a certain size and shape but no farther; how cuts, bruises and burns are repaired by the body; and how fingertips can regenerate after they are amputated (even including the same fingerprint).

> *Our body is a machine for living. It is organized for that. It is its nature. Let life go on in it unhindered and let it defend itself, it will do more than if you paralyze it by encumbering it with remedies.*
> — Leo Tolstoy

If the energy body is the template for the physical body, this could also help to explain how psychological factors and emotional traumas might alter the biological energy field, thus producing secondary subjective discomforts and even changes in the physical body (as in anger that seems to produce arthritis).[724]
Taking this several steps further, spiritual awareness and spiritual healing suggest that each of us is an expression of spiritual templates that manifest through the energy body, and are in turn expressed through the mental, emotional, and physical bodies.[725]

> A person is neither a thing nor a process, but an opening or clearing through which the Absolute can manifest.
> — Martin Heidegger

As a part of this discussion, we should also consider the factor of *time*.
First of all, it is important to take time to contemplate what is actually going on when disharmonies develop in body, emotions, mind, relationships, and spirit, rather than rushing in and trying to fix things according to the swift logic of clinical diagnosis. When we provide a healing atmosphere within which to heal, time can allow self-healing to occur.
Second, there are biological rhythms of several varieties that may facilitate or impede healing (Touitou/ Haus). The study of shifts in body rhythms over time has been termed *chronobiology*.
In women, the menstrual cycle may determine certain periods of sensitivity, receptivity, or resistance to therapeutic interventions.
Some believe that there are regular biorhythms – cycles of biological activity that correlate with a person's date of birth, as cycles with a fixed series of numbers of days in the life of the person (Thommen). I have found no research evidence to support the influence of such regular biorhythms on health.
Astrological factors may also be relevant to medical problems and treatments within the discussion of time as an influence on healing.[726]
Circadian rhythms are physiological shifts that occur, like the tides, within the 24-hour diurnal cycle. Production of hormones such as adrenal steroids and melatonin may rise and fall in regular patterns over the course of a day. Acupuncture (and its

derivatives) is said to be more effective for treating certain problems at particular times of the day or night, related to the greater activity at those times of the meridians associated with the affected body areas.

Ultradian rhythms are shifts in brain hemisphere dominance that occur in cycles of 90 to 120 minutes. These have not been studied in relationship to physical healing, but they could influence a person's receptivity or resistance to suggestion and other healing interventions.[727]

Considering all of these factors, it is easy to conceive that each individual may have times of greater and lesser receptivity to healings of every sort. Repeated visits to complementary therapists, which are commonly spaced at weekly intervals, may provide more windows in time for greater therapeutic efficacy.[728]

THE PERSONHOOD OF THE THERAPIST

The doctor's arrival is the first part of the cure.
– Anonymous

I have been examining the questions raised in *Healing Research* since I began my 13 years of adult education and throughout my entire professional career – which has spanned over 35 years. I am impressed that the person of the therapist is one of the most important ingredients in the level of satisfaction that people derive from their treatments, second only to the *chemistry* between therapist and client.

Qualities in the therapist that are important for good healing to occur include openness, caring, compassion, ability to empathize, unconditional acceptance, integrity, and rich life experiences.

When therapists have undergone treatments for their own problems, they are better able to appreciate the processes of healing in their respants and to empathize with them.

Even more important in bioenergy medicine is the clearing of psychological dross such as old emotional traumas, anxieties, fears, prejudices, ego involvement and other shadow issues. These have the potential to impede and impair the administration of healing energies.

No man's knowledge here can go beyond his experience.
– John Locke (1690)

Another book, or at least an editorial, feels like it is percolating around this subject, so I will say no more here beyond emphasizing that therapy does not occur only in a therapist's office. All of life is a process of healing and every single thought and action has the potential to contribute to this healing journey.

The creative spirit creates with whatever materials are present. With food, with children, with building blocks, with speech, with thoughts, with pigment, with an umbrella, a wineglass or a torch. We are not craftsmen only during studio hours. Any more than man is wise only in his library. Or de-

vout only in church. The material is not the sign of the creative feeling for life: of the warmth and sympathy and reverence which foster being; techniques are not the sign. The sign is the light that dwells within the act, whatever its nature or medium.

— M. C. Richards

CHOOSING YOUR DOCTOR AND OTHER THERAPISTS

It's not enough for your doctor to stop playing God. You've got to get up off your knees.

— Marvin Belsky

Choosing a generalist or specialist and developing a treatment team to deal with chronic or difficult problems can be a challenge. Here are some factors that you may wish to consider:

- Establish a relationship with a primary care physician who gets to know you and who you know over a period of time, to develop mutual understanding and trust.
- Clarify your problems and learn as much as possible about them. If you are dissatisfied with the information or treatment you receive, the Internet offers a very broad range of sites with information about most problems.[729]
- Prioritize your needs and wishes for the people who will treat you.
- Seek clarity of diagnosis for your problems, in words you understand. Don't hesitate to ask clarifying questions, and insist on clear, and comprehensible answers.
- If you want your caregivers to take charge of your problems and prescribe treatments without providing explanations, tell them so.
- If you want your caregivers to be your advisors, making decisions for treatment in consultation with you, be clear with them about this.
- Caregivers should:
    - Care for you as a person, and not only focus on treating your symptoms and illnesses
    - Be open to your questions
    - Understand the contributions to your problems made by stress, and by psychological and relational issues
    - Have a spectrum of other caregivers available to refer you to for specialized interventions
    - Be open to your seeking second opinions
    - Be open to your exploring a variety of approaches for dealing with your problems
    - Be open to consulting with other therapists

- Convenience of location
- Availability for urgent consultations
- Costs

Getting personal recommendations from satisfied respants is probably your best way of making an initial choice of caregiver. A wise and trusted caregiver can then be a resource for further consultations and interventions, as well as further referrals to other therapists who can provide further modalities.

   If you develop uncomfortable feelings about your therapist, seek a second opinion. Trust your intuition if the advice you are getting or the manner in which you are being treated feels wrong to you. Should you have more serious questions about the behavior or ethics of your caregiver, consult their professional associations regarding standards for practice in general, or to ask for information on the specific person you are concerned about.[730]

THE TRANSPERSONAL IN WHOLISTIC MEDICINE

> *No one can touch the full potential for healing by believing that one treatment is good for the body but in conflict with the soul, or vice versa... The fullest potential exists when the inner conse-cration and the outer action unify.*
>
> – Richard Moss

Transpersonal perspectives[731] can re-frame challenges within their worldviews, helping you to deal with them in more creative and satisfying ways. For instance, many transpersonal therapists are now including work on awareness of birth,[732] pre-birth,[733] and past life[734] experiences in their treatments. Though this may seem far-fetched, there is ample evidence to support the belief systems surround-ing such work.

> *[W]e not only choose our responses, but perhaps more importantly, we choose the labels we give them. A rose by any other name is not a rose.*
>   *The moment you step outside of your problem to observe it, you create a larger context for it. Observing or witnessing this becomes a key activity in therapy...*
>
> – Steven Wolinsky (p. 101)

The old/ new methods of meditation are finding applications in modern psychotherapy, as the practice of wholistic medicine shades into and blends with transpersonal psychology.

   In the past century there has been an increasing opening in Western society to awareness of an interdependence and interconnectedness between individuals as well as between humankind and all of creation. This awareness exists on many levels of consciousness, from linear deductions about limitations on natural resources and the consequent need for their better allocation and distribution, to the need to manage environmental pollution, to a growing sense of the need for global community, to awareness of interpersonal connections on other levels of reality (including karmic), to a more experiential appreciation of interconnections with the All.

The transpersonal includes insights from intuitions, meditation, altered states of consciousness, spirit guidance, and the like, which can point to a holographic organization of the cosmos.[735] "As above, so below," is a succinct statement of the concept that every single thing you do, think, feel, and *are* is an important part of the All. By clearing your inner self you enhance the state of the All, since you are part of it.

In terns of linear logic this appears at first to be superstitious nonsense. However, quantum physics[736] teaches that the observer and the observed are inseparable. Each of us is far more integrally connected with the universe than we generally believe in our materialistic Western culture.

> *Clinical science has always viewed the state of a system as a whole as merely the result of interaction of its parts. However, the quantum potential stood this view on its ear and indicated that the behavior of parts is actually organized by the whole.*
>
> – Michael Talbot (p.41)

Along with transpersonal awareness of oneness with the All comes a reverence for nature, concern for our fellow man, and awareness about the excesses of modern materialism, which places a higher premium on personal gains and emphasizes regional economic, political and sectarian interests and exploitation of natural resources over global concerns for all life.

Chief Seattle observed in 1854:

> *The shining water that moves in the streams and rivers is not just water but the blood of our ancestors. If we sell you land, you must remember that it is sacred, and you must teach your children that it is sacred and that each ghostly reflection in the clear water of the lakes tells of events and memories in the life of my people. The water's murmur is the voice of my father's father.*
>
> *The rivers are our brothers, they quench our thirst. The rivers carry our canoes, and feed our children. If we sell you our land, you must remember, and teach your children, that the rivers are our brothers, and hours, and you must henceforth give the rivers the kindness you would give any brother.*

When making important decisions, Native American elders would always consider the consequences their actions would have upon the seventh generation following their own. Contrast this with Western time frames for governmental concern in decision making!

The awareness of our oneness with nature has not escaped the observation of Western naturalists, poets, artists and mystics. Sadly, our society is allowing them ever fewer resources to further their explorations of how we can live in harmony with our environment, and how we can teach our children these vitally important lessons. Instead, an ever greater emphasis is placed on promoting the global consumer society. Schools are increasingly cutting or even eliminating their budgets for teaching the arts and humanities, from elementary school through university.

> *In any weather, at any hour of the day or night, I have been anxious to improve the nick of time, and notch it on my stick too; to stand on the meeting of two eternities, the past and the future, that is precisely the present moment, to toe that line.*
>
> – Henry David Thoreau (1854)

I recall a time not many years ago when I viewed discussions of spiritual awareness as "preachy" and found myself put off by what seemed more like evangelical scientisms than scientific observations. I have no intention to preach here – only to share what I and others have observed by letting our intuitive awareness complement our sensory awareness. If evidence from further studies suggests that some of these observations are inaccurate, I am open and eager to explore further alternatives. The personal experience, however, of opening to greater awareness in transpersonal realms carries a feeling of inherent truth to it. This can only be appreciated through experiencing it.

There has recently been a tide of millennial predictions that we may be coming to the end of an age of materialism, and should be soon moving onward and upward into more spiritual ways of organizing our affairs. Whether these awarenesses and predictions are merely wishful thinking or contain elements of precognitive perceptions remains to be seen. But perhaps such a dream can be actualized if enough people lend themselves to the cause (Benor 1985).

I will discuss the subject of spirituality in much greater detail in Volume III. In the present volume we will continue with our explorations of energy medicine.

INTEGRATIVE CARE: HARMONIZING CAM AND ALLOPATHIC THERAPIES

> *The problem is not that there are problems.*
> *The problem is expecting otherwise*
> *and thinking that having problems is a problem.*
>
> – Theodore Rubin

We have reviewed many ways in which biological energies can manifest in illness, and have discussed how they can be used through various CAM approaches to promote healing. Our understanding of these vastly expands our appreciation of energy medicine as a part of wholistic healing.

Blending allopathic and CAM approaches can be a challenge (Faass). For a summary of the theoretical and practical differences between these approaches, see earlier Table II-8.

One of the most important differences in these two approaches concerns the process of determining what is wrong with a person in the first place. Allopathic medicine emphasizes precision in diagnosis, and this approach has facilitated enormous advances in medical research and treatment. With clear and precise diagnoses it is possible to identify specific physical and psychological malfunctions, and to clarify what causes them and how to treat them. Students of medicine, nursing and the counseling arts are trained to identify various symptom clusters that manifest within particular processes of dysfunction and disease. They rely on patients' historical reports, focused questioning by the examiner, physical examination and laboratory studies. Objective criteria are emphasized, and multiple examiners are expected to arrive at similar if not identical diagnoses after considering given sets of data.

CAM therapies are much broader in the range of data collected for patient assessments. Symptom clusters that are meaningful in CAM diagnosis may have no relevance to conventional medical practitioners. The color of a person's tongue, a tooth that is in need of dental care, and sensitivity to hot and cold may be relevant to acupuncture diagnosis for seemingly unrelated conditions. Similarly, discomfort with tight collars and lack of motivation to engage in activities may be highly relevant to the choice of a homeopathic remedy. CAM practitioners often focus on people's subjective experiences of their illnesses; their relationships with family, friends, colleagues, home and work environments, and society as a whole; their spiritual life, and other factors that may influence bioenergies.

Diagnoses may vary much more widely between individual CAM practitioners than between allopathic physicians. This is particularly true if therapists are working within different modalities, but diagnoses may also vary between practitioners of the same modality. It is as yet unclear to what extent this is or is not correlated with efficacy of treatment. The explanation commonly accepted by CAM therapists is that there are many roads to health and all of them can be effective in releasing patterns of illness and promoting patterns of health. The therapist is also a part of the treatment, which introduces another source of variability in treatment effects and outcomes.

Many conventional medical practitioners have minimal training in dealing with non-physical issues that affect health and illness. I was shocked to find that many medical schools do not include training in bedside manner and public relations. It is apparently assumed that basic common sense will always prevail, and that doctors and nurses must possess these skills innately. Not only is this far from the truth, but the experience of going through medical or nursing school can discourage and even deaden the inborn interpersonal sensitivities which caregivers-in-training bring in with them. In conventional medical training the emphasis is placed very heavily on physical diagnosis and interventions. Patients' eagerness to discuss the psychological and social aspects of their problems is often viewed as a hindrance in the caregivers' attempts to obtain a complete and accurate medical history, focused on physical issues. Doctors and nurses tend to cut short such discussions, which in any case may take more time than they feel they can devote to a given patient under the pressures of their job parameters.

Conventional caregivers, who focus on the physical causes of problems, naturally prescribe physical interventions. Medicines and surgical procedures are the primary tools they are trained to use. Patients are presumed to be ignorant of the true causes of their problems, and it is seen as the caregivers' job to cure them.

CAM practitioners usually spend much more time exploring the complex issues surrounding the problems that cause patients to seek their help. They tend to label the people they treat as *clients* rather than *patients*. CAM therapists see their roles as teachers who can help people to develop better lifestyle appreciation and habits. They seek non-physical roots of problems, and develop self-healing strategies and practices with which clients can address their own health issues.[737]

It is not surprising that in the US, more visits are paid annually to CAM practitioners than to physicians. Many find that simply telling their story to a respectful and caring listener is a healing interaction. Spiritual healers and other CAM therapists are often good listeners, and many will deliberately promote self-healing practices. Qigong, meridian based therapies, and psychoneuroimmunology are particularly helpful in this regard.

Another contrast in the focus of CAM and allopathic approaches is in *caring* vs. *curing*. In conventional medicine, practitioners are taught and encouraged to strive toward a cure as the ideal goal. Death thus becomes an enemy to be fought, as it represents ultimate, irretrievable failure. By comparison, for many CAM therapists, particularly spiritual healers, a good death is considered a good healing.

Compounding their other difficulties, doctors and nurses often work under unhealthy, dehumanizing conditions. They function under the combined pressures of long work hours; night call, night duty, and rotating shifts; very brief time allotments for each patient; economic and administrative requirements to see increasing numbers of patients; a besieged mentality generated by the ever-present danger of malpractice litigation; lack of peer support; and no training or experience in stress management techniques for their own needs. In fact, medical personnel are encouraged to ignore their feelings or to swallow them down. Throughout the challenging years of their training and practice, these stresses accumulate and take multiple tolls. Family life is stressed by job pressures, so there may be less than optimal support or nurturance at home. In the competitive atmosphere of modern professional training, asking for help is felt to be a weakness. It is no surprise that doctors have a very high rate of alcohol and drug abuse and even of suicide.

One of the major benefits offered by CAM therapies is stress management and healing techniques for the practitioner. I know many health caregivers who were first introduced to CAM methods through their own personal need for help. Some of the clearest introductions I've had to CAM therapies have been through enjoying their benefits for my own stresses and stress-related pains and other symptoms. I've been especially pleased with the results of spiritual healing and meridian and chakra based therapies.

There has been interest in working together on both sides of the divide. CAM therapists have offered to help doctors with patients who have difficult problems, and doctors have invited CAM therapists to work in their clinics and private offices. The results of such collaborations have been mixed. They seem to work best when they evolve gradually, from shared experiences of helping patients together. In that way, each side gets to understand how the other side works, and therefore has more realistic expectations when closer working relationships are forged. The richness of these therapeutic interactions is often highly stimulating and deeply satisfying to all participants. While a number of large clinics for integrative care have been started, some of these have not lasted for long. The greatest obstacle to success seems to be financial in nature. The high overhead expenses of maintaining large conventional medical facilities require that more patients be seen than most CAM therapists can comfortably manage without limiting their interventions to the point that their added benefit would be lost. More frequently successful are the working relationships in which doctors refer to CAM therapists in their own offices. However, the element that is often missing in these referral relationships is the close collaboration and mutual learning that occur when therapists with varied expertise and approaches work in closer collaborations organization.

When the CAM-allopathic marriage does work, both sides usually benefit and all involved learn a great deal from each other. As in any working relationship, the personalities and good will of the participants are major determinants in the success of the partnership. This marriage, like any other, needs the nurturing of time budgeted for discussions and clarifications of the working relationships. The people who benefit the most from integrative care are the respants, who enjoy the best of both CAM and allopathic therapies.

Acknowledging the engagement, if not yet the marriage of CAM with conventional medical care, The Federation of State Medical Boards (Euless, Texas) introduced "Model Guidelines for the Use of Complementary and Alternative Therapies in Medical Practice" in April 2002. They recommend that state medical boards should be given the options of adopting, modifying, or ignoring these guidelines:

> 1. The guidelines are grounded in an evidence-based approach. Conventional and alternative medicine are placed on an equal ground, and the limitations of both approaches are acknowledged.
> 2. Conventional and alternative therapies are addressed accurately and with parity. Patients can choose the therapies they want and physicians will not be disciplined based solely on their use or recommendation of CAM.
> 3. The guidelines are the vocabulary and evidence-based approach of the National Center for Complementary and Alternative Medicine (NCCAM). By adopting the definition of CAM used by NCCAM, the Federation established a link to the major NIH center responsible for evaluating alternative medicine in the United States. (Horrigan/ Block)

This mixed marriage will require exhaustive pre- and post-nuptial contracts in order to make it a success. To help smooth the problems of diagnostic differences between the two systems, Alternative Link (http:/ / www.alternativelink.com) devised over 4,000 codes covering a wide range of CAM procedures and supplies, which are categorized as Alternative Billing Concept (ABC) codes. These codes have been given a trial run at a several medical centers with integrative programs. Their adoption on a nationwide scale will significantly advance the development of integrative care (Dumoff).

CHAPTER 3

The Human Energy Field

> *Big fields have little fields*
> *Upon their backs to fight 'em;*
> *And little fields have lesser fields*
> *And so ad infinitum.*
> — *Edward W. Russell*

Heat and other measurable energies emanate from the human body. These may be what healers sense when they pass their hands around the body to assess its condition. It may also be that laying-on of hands healing works through these known, conventional energies.

Many people can sense these bioenergy fields. You might just take a moment to explore this yourself. Hold your hands opposite each other, separated by about an inch. Slowly move them to about 18 inches apart, then back to their starting position. Repeat this about ten times. Pay attention to any sensations in your palms and fingers. (The endnote at the bottom of this paragraph describes what many people experience.) Now, rapidly make fists with your hands and then open them, about 20 times. Repeat your initial explorations. If you can find several people who are willing to explore this with you, repeat this process with each of them in turn, with one of your hands near one of theirs. Then reverse hands through all the possibilities of right opposite right, right opposite left, and left opposite left.[738]

Gifted, sensitive people may develop a detailed tactile vocabulary and learn to interpret these sensations as indications of specific energy blocks, illnesses, and psychological states.

Some of the fields that healers sense appear to involve energies that conventional science has difficulty in assessing. For instance, there are gifted sensitives who report that they can see an aura, or halo of color, around the body. A few very gifted sensitives can perceive the physical body itself as a complex energy field. In effect, they seem to have "X-ray eyes" with which they can observe the bioenergetic aspects of organs and biological processes as they occur in the living body. Some of these healers report that they can see the standard acupuncture meridians as well as many other meridians that are not mentioned in conventional acupuncture texts.

Healers can diagnose people's physical, mental, emotional, and spiritual conditions by examining their auras. Healers may perform various manipulations on the auric fields that "cleanse," "unblock," and/ or heal these abnormalities in the aura, thus producing secondary healings in the physical body, the mind, the emotions and the spirit.

Some healers claim that it is in these fields and in a *higher self* that the true essence of our being resides. Many healers believe that the fields are shaped by the non-material spirit and soul, and the physical body is shaped by a *higher self*, which is an energetic aspect of the person, in and through these fields.[739]

Let us start our discussion of the human energy fields with a review of reports on the auras that are sensed by healers. We will then consider studies exploring energies that may account for many aspects of auras.

AURAS

The real voyage of discovery consists not in seeing new landscapes, but having new eyes.

– Marcel Proust

Gifted clairvoyants[740] have reported that they see colored auras or halos around all objects – both living and "inanimate."[741] (Gifted intuitives report that all matter, even rocks, are sentient.) They tell us that the auras of living things change according to their physical, mental, emotional and spiritual states, as well as in response to interactions with their surroundings. Various healers have reported differing observations of auras.[742]

The late Dora Kunz, a gifted clairvoyant and healer, learned to make medical diagnoses by sitting with a physician named Shafika Karagulla and describing the auras she saw when Karagulla described her patients' medical conditions (Karagulla/ Kunz 1991). Kunz (1981) explained: "That's how I learned, for instance, that little red bricks in the aura mean that the person is on insulin."[743] After learning to identify the meaning of her aura perceptions, Kunz could then diagnose people's illnesses from their auras. She identifies three concentric layers of the aura: the *vital* (*etheric* – relating to the physical body); the *astral* (emotional); and the *mental*.[744]

Kunz, like other clairvoyant healers, also identifies health problems by observing the appearance of the *chakras* (Karagulla/ Kunz 1991). The chakras are focal energy concentrations within the energy field. Seven major centers along the midline of the body appear as cones of swirling energy that interpenetrate the auras through all their layers. (See Table II-7.) Distortions in chakra color and form correlate with illness in that region of the body.[745] It is interesting that Kunz locates the second (splenic) chakra well to the left of the midline of the body, and the fourth (heart) chakra slightly to the left. Most other clairvoyants report that these chakras lie along the midline of the body.

Sensitives like Kunz have learned to systematically correlate these fields with specific conditions of the organism. They can diagnose states of health in any living organism at a glance.

Dolores Krieger (1979), Professor of Nursing at New York University, developed the Therapeutic Touch (TT) method of healing in collaboration with Dora Kunz. TT healers pass their hands around the body of healees, holding them several inches away from the skin, to obtain intuitive impressions about states of health and illness from tactile sensations of the aura. Areas in which there are physical problems may feel warmer, cooler, tingly, or different in some other distinctive way from normal areas of the body.[746]

I can personally attest to the efficacy of this method for locating problem areas, though I am not sufficiently gifted or practiced in this method to be able to identify much more than the general location of a physical problem with my hands, and even this only works for me some of the time. I find it easiest to identify asymmetries in the right and left sides of the body that can provide clues as to the areas where problems reside. Chronic problems often produce a diminished intensity of sensations, while acute problems may feel hot, tingly or prickly. I am far more sensitive to picking up emotional components of dis-ease than physical ones, which is consonant with my specialization in psychiatry.

Barbara Brennan, an astrophysicist who now teaches aura reading and healing, observes at least seven concentric levels to the aura. Each is related to a distinct aspect of a person's being:

1. *etheric* – physical body;
2. *emotional* – emotions;
3. *mental* – thinking;
4. *astral* – I-thou emotions and desires;
5. *etheric template* – higher will;
6. *celestial* – higher feelings;
7. *ketheric* – higher concepts.

Each level envelops all of those below it. [747]

Brennan (1993) discusses additional energy levels within the aura. She calls these the *hara,* which relates to intentions; and the *core star,* which represents the divinity within us.

Brennan (1987; 1993) reports that the auras of people who are physically close to each other interact, which indicates bioenergetic exchanges between people.

Gordon Turner (1970), a British healer, was gifted with the natural ability to see auras (and spirits). He described clear changes in the auras of healees during healings:

> [T]he process of spiritual healing can be traced through the auric field and, although there are variations in pattern according to the nature of the disorder and the personality of the person concerned, there does appear to be some similarity in the phenomena observed in all cases. When a healer places his hands upon a patient there is an immediate blending together of their auras. Within a few minutes all other col-

ours that were previously observable become subordinated by a prevailing blue, which extends greatly beyond normal and seems to fill the room in which treatment is being carried out. Physical vision is not impaired by this and it is still possible to see furniture in the room or the patient's features; but more than a moment's concentration on them causes the auric colour to become fainter and frequently to vanish altogether. It is still possible to see the colours that had denoted symptoms, but these float away from the body of the patient and become surrounded by a yellow coloured light which seems to be spinning. What follows is for all the world like the action of a "spiritual penicillin." The yellow light gradually overcomes the duller colour of the disease and it becomes flattened out and much less intense. Only about five minutes is required after the healing for the aura to return to normal and, if the cure has not been instantaneous, the disease colours return in lessened intensity according to the degree of benefit evoked by the healing, but still surrounded by the yellow light seen during the healing. When the healing is complete, the colours that signified the original disorder become flattened and very small, like minute scars. These may remain in the auric field for a varying length of time, from weeks to years, according to the gravity of the disorder.

Turner's description is consistent with the reports of Philippine healers who claim that they can tell by looking at the auras of prospective healees whether they have been treated previously by other healers.[748] In some instances they even claim to be able to identify *which* healer did the healing. They do not report which parts of the aura are used in this process. [749]

  Healers frequently direct their attention to the chakras, in addition to the parts of the body that are symptomatic. The chakras provide information about the condition of the body area adjacent to each chakra, and also give healing access to these local tissues and organs. These observations are in complete agreement with the Chinese descriptions of *chakras.*[750]

Research:[751] Susan Marie Wright developed an energy field assessment (EFA) questionnaire, to identify particular qualities observed during assessments of the biofield. Her study was set up to develop the validity and reliability of the EFA in assessing the location and intensity of pains, as well as in identifying generalized fatigue and depression.

  The 52 people studied (34 women, 18 men) suffered from chronic lower back or cervical pain, fibrositis/ fibromyalgia, osteoarthritis, and other musculoskeletal pains, excluding cancer and rheumatoid arthritis. They included 37 subjects from a chiropractic office and 15 from a rheumatology practice. The duration of pain symptoms ranged from 2 to 480 months (mean 83.4 months).

  The following results were reported:

  Significant correlations were found between the sensed field abnormalities and subjects' reports of pains in the neck, upper back, and lower back ($p < .0008$ to $p < .0001$).

There were not enough subjects with pains at other locations for the study to achieve the experimental criterion of a p < .01 level of significance with the statistical analysis used.

My own rough scan of the matchings and mismatchings of the experimenter assessments with subjects' reports of pain locations shows a fairly close correlation. (See Table II-9) "The investigator was more likely to miss energy field disturbance in the presence of pain than to attribute energy field disturbance to an area where there wasn't pain..." (p. 84).

Table II-9. Subjects' and Experimenters' reported locations of pain		
Site	Subjects	Experimenters
Head	4	4
Right shoulder	10	8
Left shoulder	7	7
Chest	4	2
Right elbow	1	0
Left elbow	2	1
Abdomen	1	2
Right hand	2	3
Left hand	3	5
Pelvis	2	0
Neck	25	28
Upper back	21	34
Right arm	3	4
Left arm	2	2
Low back	36	43
Right leg	9	5
Left leg	9	10
Right knee	6	7
Left knee	4	9
Right ankle	4	0
Left ankle	2	0

Wright allows that the healers' awareness of the fact that subjects were being examined in a chiropractor's office would suggest that they were feeling pain in the spine. She balances this with the observation that identification of specific location of pain along the spine was statistically successful.

Wright notes that subjective experiences of pain vary widely between people, despite the presence of apparently similar objective pathology. She suggests that in future studies it might be helpful to include assessments of *organic pathology*, as this might correlate more highly with energy field disturbances than do subjective experiences of pain. Further suggestions include replications with larger samples and inclusion of a control group of subjects who are pain-free.

While this study is strongly supportive of healers' claims of being able to sense the biofield, there were several weaknesses in the methodology. [752]

Two experiments (Schwartz et al 1995) were performed to establish whether ordinary people who were blindfolded could detect the hand of an experimenter that was held several inches above one of their hands. (Subjects had made no claims of healing abilities.)

The first of these experiments included 20 subjects, the majority of whom were not previously familiar with the experimenter.

In each trial, the blindfolded subjects used either their left or right hand to sense the presence of the experimenter's hand, and the experimenter used either his left or right hand to test the subjects' abilities. Experimenters sat opposite the subjects, holding their palms together with their hands placed in their lap. This was intended to maintain an equal temperature in both of their hands. During the trial, experimenters held their left or right hand palm down, 3 - 4 inches above the subject's right or left hand. When an experimenter had her or his hand in place, they would say "ready." Subjects then reported which of their hands they felt was covered by the experimenter's hand. Experimenters withdrew their hand after the subject's choice was stated. Subjects then rated their confidence in their guess on a scale of 0 to 10. Experimenters recorded the guesses and confidence estimates and returned their hands to their laps. Intervals between trials were about 30 seconds.

At the end of the series of 24 trials, subjects completed a questionnaire about the sensations they believed were associated with correct guesses, and they made an estimate of their total percentage of correct guesses.

Results: Mean correct guesses by subjects were above chance (58.5 per cent, p < .02), while estimates of performance were 12 percent lower (not significant). Subjects' mean confidence ratings were higher for correct guesses than for incorrect ones (p < .004). This suggests that they were partially aware of whether their guesses were correct.

The second experiment included 41 subjects, most of whom were familiar with the experimenter who tested them. The same procedures were followed as in Experiment 1.

Results: Subjects' guesses were 69.8 percent correct, which is significantly above chance (p < .00001). Again, estimated performance was 12 percent lower than actual performance.

Combined results from both experiments: Results were highly significant (p < .00005). Both groups also had higher confidence ratings regarding correct guesses compared to incorrect ones (p < .007). Subjective sensations that were reported when subjects felt more confident of their guesses included temperature (usually warmth), tingling, and pressure.

Out of the 61 subjects, 47 were able to identify the correct side (left or right) at better than chance levels, with an overall correct rate of 66 percent (p < .00001).

Authors' discussion: The authors point out that precautions were not taken to block auditory cues (such as using headphones with white noise), so it is possible that very subtle auditory cues might have influenced the results. Likewise, micro-breezes could have influenced the subjects' perceptions. The authors suggest that the subjects' hands might be covered with glass to prevent this in future studies. Similarly, grounded wire mesh screens could be used to determine whether electrostatic or electromagnetic effects contribute to subjects' perceptions. Other variables that should be examined include the distance and rate of movement of the experimenter's hand (which could produce electrostatic effects); the intention of the experimenter; and the caringness of the relationship between experimenter and subject.

This study clearly demonstrates that ordinary people can sense when another person's hand is near their own. This supports claims by healers that they are able to sense an energy field around the body.

This study does not prove that biological energies exist outside of the known and currently accepted electromagnetic spectrum. As noted by the authors, effects of heat, electrostatic energy, or electromagnetic resistance could have produced the results in this study. No conclusions can be drawn relevant to healing, other than that healers might experience sensations in their hands and healees might experience sensations in their bodies due to effects of known physical energies.

> *As a hands-on therapist, what you touch is not merely the skin – you contact a continuous interconnected webwork that extends throughout the body.*
>
> – James Oschman, 2000 (p. 47)

In contrast with the last two studies, the next one is of interest primarily due to its publication in a prestigious American medical journal, and its demonstration of the readiness of conventional medical journals to present what they perceive to be negative results of healing studies.[753]

In 1966 Linda Rosa's nine-year-old daughter Emily studied TT healers' abilities to sense biological energy fields, for a fourth grade science fair project. Fifteen TT healers were tested over several months at their offices or homes (Rosa et al 1998).

In the experiment, healers were asked to lay their hands on a table, palms up and 25-30 cm. apart. The experimenter sat opposite the subjects, screened from sight by a tall barrier. The healers inserted their arms through holes at its base, and as a further precaution a towel was placed over their arms so that they could not see the experimenter through the armholes. Each healer was tested 10 times, and was allowed to prepare mentally for as long as they wanted before each set of trials. The experimenter positioned her right hand 8-10 cm. above one of the healer's hands (chosen by coin toss) and then alerted the healer, who identify which of the healer's hand the experimenter was covering.

To reach a significance level of $p < .04$, healers had to identify the targeted hand correctly 8 out of 10 times. In the first series only one healer scored 8, but on a retest the same healer scored only 6.

Healers' explanations for their failures included the following:

1. A tactile "afterimage" made it difficult for healers to distinguish the actual hand from the "memory" perception. However, the initial trials in each series did not produce scores greater than chance either.

2. Healers' left hands are usually more sensitive receivers of biological energies than their right hands, which are usually more potent projectors of such energies. Out of 72 trials with healers' right hands, 45 (62 percent) demonstrated incorrect responses. Out of 80 incorrect responses, 35 (44 percent) were with the left hand. These differences are not statistically significant.

3. In a practice trial prior to the experimental test series, healers performed better if they were given feedback as to which hand was being tested. Rosa et al. feel that feedback should not be necessary, but concede that allowing it would eliminate this objection.

4. The healers felt that the experimenter should be more active, by intentionally projecting her energy field. Rosa et al. feel that this should not be necessary, as no such demand is placed upon patients whose energy fields are being sensed by TT healers.

5. Some healers reported that their hands felt so hot after several trials that they either had difficulty or were unable to sense the experimenter's field. Rosa ct al. observe that this contradicts statements by TT healers who claim that they can deliberately manipulate patients' energy fields during the course of a typical 20-30-minute TT session. This objection is also contradicted by the fact that only 7 out of 15 first trials produced correct responses.

In 1997 a second series was completed in a single day and recorded on videotape by a TV broadcasting crew. In this experiment healers were permitted to sense the experimenter's field, and each selected which hand the experimenter would use for the test. Healers correctly identified which of their hands was being tested in 53 out of 131 trials (41 percent). The range of correct responses was 1-7.

Healers made the following objections at the end of the study:

1. One healer said the towel over his hands was distracting.
2. One healer said her hands were too dry.
3. "Several" healers complained that the televising of the proceedings interfered with their concentration and increased stresses.[754] Rosa et al. believe that the presence of a TV crew should not distract or stress healers more than the usual hospital settings in which many TT healers practice.

The result of 123 correct responses out of 280 trials (44 percent) in the two series obviously does not support claims by healers that they are able to sense energy fields. No significant correlation was found in this study between healers' performance and their levels of experience.

Rosa et al. conclude that TT healers have no ability to sense the biological energy field because the 21 TT healers studied did not succeed in identifying which of their hands was being tested. "To our knowledge, no other objective, quantitative study involving more than a few TT practitioners has been published, and no well-designed study demonstrates any health benefit from TT."

They also point out that "In 1966 the James Randi Educational Foundation offered $742,000 to anyone who could demonstrate an ability to detect an HEF[755] under conditions similar to those of our study. Although more than 40,000 American practitioners claim to have such an ability, only 1 person attempted the demonstration. She failed, and the offer, now more than $1.1 million, has had no further volunteers despite extensive recruiting efforts."

George D. Lundlberg, M.D., editor of the *Journal of the American Medical Association,* adds the following comment on this study in the issue in which it appears:

> The American public is fascinated by alternative (complementary, unconventional, integrative, traditional, Eastern) medicine. Some of these practices have a valid scientific basis; some of them are proven hogwash; many of them have never been adequately tested scientifically. "Therapeutic Touch" falls into the latter classification, but nonetheless is the basis for a booming international business as treatment for many medical conditions. This simple, statistically valid study tests the theoretical basis for "Therapeutic Touch": the "human energy field." This study found that such a field does not exist. I believe that practitioners should disclose these results to patients, third-party payers should question whether they should pay for this procedure, and patients should save their money and refuse to pay for this procedure until or unless additional honest experimentation demonstrates an actual effect.

I wrote to Lundberg, informing him that a doctoral dissertation examining the sensing of auras by healers had showed positive effects. Phil Fontanarosa, MD, senior editor of *JAMA* replied that my letter "did not receive a high enough priority rating for publication in *JAMA*" and indicated no interest in this dissertation.

It is surprising that a study done by a 9-10 year old girl could be published in a prestigious medical journal. Editorial standards of such publications usually require that all research be performed by a medical practitioner or qualified scientist.

Three of the co-authors of this article are self-identified skeptics and the last two are members of an organization called Committee for the Study of the Paranormal. This organization is known to be dedicated to discounting all evidence for parapsychological phenomena. The methods it uses do not always meet the highest scientific standards, and many observers find them to be deliberately misleading. Several examples of such methods are also evident in the study by Rosa et al.

An example of misdirection in this study can be found in the statements by Rosa et al. that "Of the 74 quantitative studies, 23 were clearly unsupportive."[756] The authors make no mention of the remaining 51 studies, which one would guess from their analysis must be supportive. I know of several such studies, and Rosa et al. cite some of these in footnotes nos. 76-86 of their article, inclusive. *No discussion of the positive findings is presented, and I find no reference in the text to footnotes 76-86.*[757] The authors' statement, "To our knowledge, no other objective, quantitative study *involving more than a few TT practitioners* [my italics] has been published☐" is again misleading. Most studies of healing involve only one or a few healers. This is cannot be taken as a valid as criticism of the general research methods in this field, which have in fact produced significant results in many cases. The conclusion of the sentence, "☐and no well-designed study demonstrates any health benefit from TT" is clearly untrue.

Due to these omissions and falsehoods, at first reading the article looks quite convincing in its damnation of published TT research. It would appear that these omissions function to support the authors' and editor's skepticism, and one must wonder whether they were deliberate.

Rosa et al. and the JAMA editor assume that there is no validity to healers' claims that they are able to sense energy fields or to influence them. They therefore dismiss any complaints by healers regarding factors in the test situation which might influence their ability to sense such a field.

Healers' objections that the stress of performing in front of TV cameras could have a negative influence appear to me a valid criticism of the second part of this study. While the ambiance of a hospital ward might seem stressful (particularly to outsiders), it is composed of elements that are familiar to nurses and are therefore not as distracting as the unfamiliar presence of a TV crew.

There is evidence that one can influence one's own energy field and the process of healing by controlling one's mental state and intent. In one study, several nurses were able to produce significant results with TT when it was given with the intent to heal, as opposed to simply going through the motions of the therapy while doing arithmetic in their heads (Keller 1983; Quinn 1989). It has also been observed that skin resistance in the hands can be altered by changes in mental state.[758] This would produce a concomitant change in the electromagnetic field around the hand. Kirlian photography has demonstrated that when people have positive feelings for each other their energy fields merge, and conversely, when they feel negatively towards each other their energy fields retract.[759] I can add anecdotal evidence from workshops that I give on developing one's healing gifts. One person can project energy from a hand or foot and another person can identify when the first one discontinues this projection of energy. I personally support healers' suggestions that it is possible for experimenters to withdraw or to not project their energy fields, thus making it difficult for a healer to identify the energy field.

A further objection that can be raised in connection with this study is that part of the experience of sensing energy fields is dynamic. When I sense someone's field I move my hand towards and away from their body, as well as across their body. This provides far stronger sensory perceptions than simply holding my hand still near the body.

I would also suggest that the presence of a skeptic during a study of parapsychological phenomena or healing practices could dampen or inhibit the effects under study. While this must appear to skeptics as an unfair proposal, this is in fact the nature of parapsychological effects. They are very much influenced by the mental states of participants and observers. Skeptics are likely to obtain negative effects, believers positive ones. This has been amply supported by studies of *sheep* (believers) and *goats* (disbelievers) in psi research.[760] In the testing of energy fields, two studies of sensitives' abilities to see auras produced negative results (Ellison; Gissurarson/ Gissurarson).

The sweeping dismissal of TT as a valid therapeutic method by the authors of the Rosa et al. article and by the editor of the journal, based upon the evidence of limited research carried out by a 9-10 year old girl, is patently ridiculous. This study simply explored the ability of healers to sense the energy field of one experimenter under specific test conditions. In no way did it test healing abilities.[761]

Discussion of energy field sensing

Various energies that are well recognized in conventional science could account for some of the observed bioenergy phenomena. Schwartz et al. (1995) note that direct current (DC) skin electrical potentials can normally be measured on the hands. It's possible that the amount of sweat on the skin could modulate these DC potentials, and this could also alter the amount and quality of the heat radiated from the skin. Blood flow in the skin and muscles of the hands conduct cardiac electrical and sound patterns as well as generating heat, which is radiated as infrared pulses. The muscles in the limbs produce electromyographic (EMG) pulses. Movements of the limbs generate electrostatic fields. All of these energies combine to form a complex, dynamic energy pattern around the hands and other parts of the body.

Chien et al. (1991) also identified emanations of heat energy, which they measured as infrared signals in therapeutic touch healings.

Conversely, the hands contain nerve endings which can detect pressure, temperature, and the stretch of tendons and ligaments. These receptors could, theoretically, also respond to other energies. Electrostatic fields might produce subtle stretches or pressures which these receptors might be able to register. Minute breezes could also be detected through temperature, pressure, and/ or stretch receptors. Perceptions of electrical or magnetic signals have not been empirically established as yet.[762]

Other energy field interactions

Gary E. Schwartz and colleagues (Russek/ Schwartz) note that the various measurable energies of two people may interact when they are physically close together. For instance, electrical cardiac energy interactions measured by an electrocardiogram (ECG) occur and they may vary with the degree of openness that the participants feel toward interpersonal communication. This team also found that the ECG patterns of two people sitting near each other are reflected in each other's electroencephalogram (EEG) patterns.

Valerie Hunt (1977) reported on aura changes during rolfing. Rolfing is a form of vigorous, deep massage that is used to loosen up tense areas of muscles, tendons and joints. Rolfing produces intense releases of emotions that are often associated with physical tensions. It is theorized that emotions are stored in the body either through conditioning or via an actual imprinting of memories in the body per se.[763] In Hunt's study, electronic readings of changes in muscle tension were recorded during Rolfing treatments. Rosalind Bruyere, a gifted clairvoyant, simultaneously described the auric changes she observed in therapists and patients. Clear correlations emerged between the changes noted by Bruyere and those measured by bio-electronic sensors. Bruyere found particular visible changes in chakras that developed progressively through the series of rolfing sessions.[764]

Other scientists question the validity of visual aura perceptions.

Arthur Ellison was a Professor of Electrical and Electronic Engineering at London City University and a parapsychologist. He performed an experiment in which a sensitive who claimed to be able to observe auras reported the colors of the aura that he saw between the fingers of Ellison's hands, which were held close to but not touching each other. Next, he placed a cardboard box with a small window in it as a screen between himself and the sensitive. Only the space between his hands was visible to the sensitive, and his hands were screened. When he told the sensitive that his hands were next to the window, the sensitive confirmed that he could see the aura. When he told the sensitive that he had removed his hands, the sensitive reported that he saw no aura. Ellison then had the sensitive continue to report when he saw the aura and when he did not, and meanwhile Ellison led him to believe that at certain times he was holding his hands up and at other times not. In fact, he held his hands flat on the box below the window for the whole period of the experiment, or even removed them and placed them in his lap. The sensitive nevertheless continued to report that he saw an aura at the window at times when Ellison *indicated* that his hands were there. Ellison concludes that the aura "…was produced by what is sometimes called 'unconscious dramatization' and bore no relationship to 'reality' by way of the position of the fingers." He speculates that auric matter reportedly seen by sensitives may be a reflection of visual fatigue, after-images, and/ or projections from the mind of the perceiver. Generalizing from this single case study, he suggests that such projections may be the mind's way of transforming unconsciously imaged material into the conscious mind (A. Ellison 1962). His conclusion is that the aura is a projection of the imagination of the alleged sensitive.

In a similar study, Loftur Gissurarson and Asgeir Gunnarsson challenged several people who reported that they could see auras to identify which one of four barriers a man was standing behind. They presumed that the auras would project beyond the edges of the barriers. Only chance scores were achieved.

I was surprised to find that no one had studied whether several sensitives would perceived the same colors in the aura if they all observed a patient at the same time. I set up a pilot experiment on making assessments based on auras with the help of Dr. Jean Galbraith,[765] an English general practitioner. Eight sensitives simultaneously observed a series of people with known diagnoses. The sensitives drew and interpreted their perceptions of the subjects' auras. The overlaps between the drawings and interpretations of the sensitives were small compared to the differences between them. Yet when the patients who had been observed heard the diverse interpretations they resonated with seven out of the eight.

In a second pilot project with four healers who are more gifted and more experienced, we again found diverse observations of the auras and broadly differing interpretations of what they perceived. In addition, we found concurrences among the healers in observations regarding energy field abnormalities that bore no relationship to clinical diagnoses. The *interpretations* of the latter field abnormalities differed from one healer to another (Benor 1992).

How can we understand the varying reports about auras?
My conclusion is that aura readings, as with other psi perceptions, are filtered through the unconscious mind and the perceptual apparatus of the sensitive. Psychic perceptions arrive in the deeper awareness of the mind, and only partially filter into conscious awareness. The data are thus colored by the individual during the processes of perception, translation into visual imagery, and cognitive/ verbal interpretation.

Barbara Brennan[766] suggests that the difference between reports may relate to healers' resonation with different layers of the aura. The innermost aura layer, which relates to the physical body, will appear different from the next aura layer, which relates to the emotional body; and similarly for the mental and spiritual layers. Many healers may not be aware that they are perceiving a particular sub-section of the aura. I believe that Brennan's assessment is probably correct for some instances of such discrepancies.

However, some sensitives intuitively or clairsentiently perceive the condition of a person's health without seeing their aura. The information may come to them as audible words, smells, tastes, bodily sensations, or direct, intuitive *knowing*.[767] This suggests to me that my original interpretation of the data may be more valid. It may also be that each of these explanations is partially valid.

Evidence from other areas of study may shed some light on the phenomenon of aura perceptions.

There are reports that a sense organ (eye, ear, etc.) can sometimes convey in-formation obtained by unusual stimulation, of a kind that is not ordinarily perceived by that particular sense (Romains). This is technically termed *synesthe-sia*. An example of this fascinati8ng capability is that many people (about one woman in twenty, and fewer men) can *hear* color.[768] That is to say, various sounds produce mental sensations of color.

Research on dermal optics, or the sensing of color through the skin, may provide further information about aura vision (Duplessis 1975; 1985). It may be that auras are manifestations of such synesthesias, with dermal or clairsentient perceptions that are translated by the brain into visual imagery. Several clairsentients have told me that they perceive auras even with remote viewing or when looking at photographs and videotapes of subjects. One sensitive reported that when she looked at a picture of a woman who was drinking water from a Japanese temple, she saw a white light around the water, indicating that it had healing properties.

Yvonne Duplessis (1985) found that the skill of perceiving the color of pieces of paper through sensations in the hands could be learned. The distance of the hand above the paper beyond which a color could not be perceived varied consistently in each subject for each color. The height threshold for the same color also varied, consistent with the illumination of the target colors by natural or artificial light-ing. This research appears to parallel in a general way the studies of body aura perception with the hands. It may also provide a caution to investigators to note whether studies are done in natural or artificial light.[769]

Carlos Alvarado and Nancy Zingrone explored the visual imagery styles of peo-ple who experience synesthesias (crossed-sensory perceptions, such as perceiving certain sounds in response to seeing certain colors).[770] Those who perceive sy-nesthesias have very vivid visualization abilities. While this enables them to produce internal imagery that appears very real to thcm, investigators may still find it difficult to clarify and assess what actually occurs in the process of synes-thesias.

I tested a musician who reported that he "heard" colors, by playing various tones on a tape recorder and having him select paint color chips that approximated the colors he perceived. He found the task exhausting, and required many repetitions of the tone and careful sorting of the paint colors. He often ended up dissatisfied that he could not find precisely the right match. He believed that he was absolutely consistent in his perceptions, so I re-tested him two months later. His color selections were 90 percent consistent, but several tones produced distinctly different colors the second time. He was very surprised at this finding, as he had not been aware of shifts in his color hearing.

Tactile perception of the energy field is much more commonly experienced and reported by healers and ordinary people than are synesthesias.

Synesthesias demonstrate that the mind may interpret sensory inputs from one sensory modality as subjective perceptions that are experienced in another modality. This supports the speculation that bioenergy aura perceptions could be translated into various sensory perceptions.

Overall, clairsentience appears to me the more likely explanation for auras.

The process of diagnosis within the frameworks of other complementary therapies may overlap with the clairsentient perceptions reported by healers. Robert Duggan, a gifted acupuncture practitioner, reports:

> When I first learned to read the pulse as used in relation to the practice of acupuncture, I thought I was observing what occurred on the wrist of the other person. Later, I realized that what I observed was what occurred in my fingertips as I experienced my fingertips in the presence of the other. Another practitioner placing finger on wrist would experience a very different phenomenon.

Other experienced acupuncturists report that they can sense and reliably identify the locations of acupuncture points with their fingers and can tell when the meridians have a proper flow of Qi or are blocked (e.g. Upledger). This tactile sensitivity supports the claims of healers that it is possible to sense the human energy field through one's hands.

Further support for the existence of energy fields comes from of *phantom limb* sensations following amputation.[771] People often report that they continue to experience pain and other sensations where an amputated limb used to be, even though it no longer exists physically. It can be most distressing to feel a physical itch they cannot scratch! Conventional medicine interprets this as persistent brain or mental habits/ images that produce fantasy sensations of the limb. It is further speculated that the nerve ends from the amputated limb may still send messages to the brain, which interprets these as though they were coming from the now non-existent limb. Healers suggest that phantom limb perceptions may be energy field phenomena. Healers may be able to sense the presence of an energy limb after the physical limb has been removed. Spiritual healing given to the energy limb may reduce or eliminate the phantom limb sensations (Leskowitz 1997).

Phantom limb phenomena parallel the phantom leaf effects of Kirlian photography.[772]

How can we explain the intensity of skeptics' criticisms of healing (and other psi phenomena)?

The willingness of a major medical journal to publish a study done by a 10-year-old girl; the exaggerated criticism of spiritual healing levied by the editor of that journal; and the degree of publicity surrounding this study are remarkable. all These (and similar critical reactions to reports of healings and healing research suggest that there is considerable resistance to accepting evidence supporting the validity of intuitive assessments and spiritual healing, and a great readiness to accept evidence, however flimsy, that suggests these are not valid phenomena. It is apparent that intuitive awareness and spiritual healing push the boundaries of Western scientific paradigms, and it is a natural reaction to resist change.[773]

Discussion of aura phenomena

We still have much to clarify about the perception of auras. The visible aura described by sensitives does not appear to be a wholly consistently or objectively observable phenomenon – both within and between individual aura perceivers. Gifted sensitives report they see the aura all of the time, but many others see the aura only some of the time. The differences in aura perceptions between sensitives is striking.

There are some who propose that the visible aura is nothing more than a visual after-image (Fraser-Harris). They note that it is normal to see colors if you close your eyes after staring at an object. The colors perceived in this case will be primary complements to the real-world colors that they reflect. You may test this yourself by staring at something with a single strong color, in bright light, for about a minute. Then close your eyes. Your brain will now perceive the after-image of the object in its complementary color (e.g. if the object is red, you will see green with your eyes closed).[774] Given the fact that the eyes flit around constantly as we gaze at objects, Fraser-Harris hypothesizes that some alleged aura phenomena are blurred after-images from the edges of the objects being gazed at.

This theory might account for a small portion of reported aura phenomena, specifically those connected with the aura that is seen immediately adjacent to the body. However it cannot account for the portions of the aura described as the chakras, or the portions extending many inches and even several feet away from the body, nor for interactions of auras when people are physically close to each other. It also cannot account for sensitives' correlations of the aura with physical, mental and emotional processes, which they perceive in colors that not only differ from the primary color complements of the object observed, but change constantly as well.

Some have suggested that auras might be instances of bioluminescence, or the emission of visible light from living organisms (like the lights of fireflies). Carlos Alvarado surveyed reports of such luminous phenomena around the body and found that they are qualitatively distinctly different from the auras described by sensitives.

Western science relies more on electronic sensors denigrates human sensors as being too full of "noise" to provide reliable readings. In my opinion, the human biocomputer is the most sensitive of all sensors. Symptomatic exploration with aura readers may offer us the most valuable information available, with the caveat that we must be cautious in accepting any single human "reading."

This last caution would apply equally to Ellison's study of a single subject's report of aura perception, from which he deduces that auras as described by healers do not exist

Charles Tart (1972b) and others suggest there may be psychological constructs of psi perceptions or of projected mental imagery, thoughts or feelings that manifest in the conscious mind as auras. I have found support for this view in reports of a number of healers who perceive auras. For instance, the late Olga Worrall (1982) was one of the better-studied healers in America, and she claimed that she could perceive auras with her eyes closed. She speculated that the visual information was detected by her *third eye*, a spot between the eyebrows alleged by many mystics to be the sense organ for clairvoyance. Other healers have told me that they perceive auras with their *third eye* or some other "inner perception."

Harry Oldfield (Oldfield/ Coghill), an English healer, and Valerie Hunt, an American scientist, have developed methods of videotaping the aura. Sensitives who have seen these videotapes report that they closely resemble the auras they perceive visually. Hunt's methods involve processing the tape after the recordings are made. Oldfield and Hunt have not revealed their methods as of the date of this publication, and this unfortunately leaves their work open to question.[775]

Why some people perceive auras and others do not is unclear. One hint comes from the work of James Peterson, who studied descriptions by children of "the colors they saw around things." He found that many children had such perceptions, although they might differ in range and quality from one child to another. He adds (1975):

> In my experience, clairvoyant children have been very reluctant to talk about their unusual vision, usually because their reports have been rebuffed, condemned or ridiculed. Even a kind parent is likely to say the experiences aren't "real." And a concerned and sensitive teacher might well call the perceptions "imaginary." More stern adults may scold the clairvoyant child for lying. The sum of it all is apt to be confusion, self-doubt, even self hate. (One seven-year-old, Stacy, told me she hated herself because her visions distracted and disturbed her so much.) And it's not only adults who can disturb the clairvoyant child. Peers are quite likely to make fun of the one who "sees things," often less gently than adults.

Imagine the strain on a child who is scolded by her parents, disciplined by a teacher, and ridiculed by friends – all because she sees things they don't. To cope with the stress, the child may work at convincing herself that what she sees isn't really there at all. Or she may simply learn to keep quiet about what she sees.

Peterson reports that children were often very relieved that they could discuss their perceptions with him. An adult who Peterson interviewed also confirmed that she would have been much happier if, as a child, she been able to find someone who understood her clairvoyant perceptions. Peterson speculates that children may actually lose these psi abilities, partly through their attempts to conform to expected social norms, and partly due to physiological maturation. He concludes with a plea for sensitivity to the needs of such children, who require and deserve understanding on the part of the adults in their lives.

A decrease in aura sensing ability with maturation may be similar to observations of a peak age for photographic memory in children. This peak occurs around age ten, with gradual waning of memory abilities thereafter (Feldman). Further studies should clarify whether social rather than developmental factors contribute to or cause these changes.

> *When I was the age of these children I could draw like Raphael; it took me many years to learn how to draw like these children.*
> – Pablo Picasso

While we don't yet have research to demonstrate the functions of the aura, Barbara Brennan (1987) and other healer report that the innermost layer of the visible aura is a template and matrix for the anchoring of body matter. Changes in the aura that indicate disease processes may become apparent as unusual aura colors several months prior to the appearance of the physical problems. Brennan and John Pierrakos "…observed that an energy field matrix in the shape of a leaf is projected by the plant prior to the growth of a leaf and then the leaf grows into that already existing form" (Brennan 1987).

John Pierrakos (1971; 1987) is a New York doctor who sees auras and specializes in bioenergetics. He claims that the aura represents *both* a life-field that is a sort of template for the physical body, and also a product of life processes within the body – indicating a dual nature for the aura. This explanation seems the most convincing to me.

In effect, the aura may be a part of the energy aspect of physical, material life processes. This would correlate with Albert Einstein's theory of relativity. Quantum physics has amply confirmed that matter and energy are interconvertible. Newtonian medicine has been slow to accept that the human body can be addressed as a form of biological energy.

> *What is Matter? Never mind.*
> *What is Mind? No matter.*
> *– Punch* (1855)

On the basis of conventional science, it would be hard to differentiate between healers' claims that they can influence the *etheric body* which in turn influences the physical body, and the alternative explanation that healers influence the physical body *directly* and the etheric body reflects these changes. Clairsentients, however, are unanimous in their observations that it is the etheric body that changes first, preceding the resulting physical changes in some cases by many weeks or months. Changes indicating illness that are observed in the aura do not have to manifest in the physical body. They can be altered and cleared by self-healing and healer-healing.

Several sensitives have reported that they can predict the impending death of a person by the presence of a black aura or by the total absence of an aura. Such observations have been made not only in assessing patients who are ill, but also when a sensitive has noticed such auras around a group of people boarding a plane that subsequently crashed. This raises many fascinating questions regarding the phenomenon of death, precognition, and predestination of events (all of which lies beyond the scope of our present discussion). It supports the hypothesis of the aura as a construct of the mind that brings psi perceptions into conscious awareness.

Some sensitives suggest that relationships exist between various portion(s) of the aura and the astral body of the *out-of-body experience* (OBE),[776] and also with "higher" or non-physical aspects of man's being. These suggestions should not be beyond the reach of investigation, though at present they remain speculative. One could, for instance, explore further how different sensitives agree and disagree in their readings of *spiritual* aspects of the aura; what different sensitives perceive when a person is dying and their spirit separates from the body; whether such observations correlate with other assessments of spirituality, meditative practices, and more.

What seems clear is that a biological energy field exists around the body that is visible to some people, probably more though clairsentient perception than through visual perception. Others can sense such fields with their hands.[777] This ability is much more common than the ability to perceive auras visually.

Let us now turn to a discussion of the energy fields on and around the body that are measurable with various instruments and technical devices.

KIRLIAN PHOTOGRAPHY

> *If you conduct a study and the data doesn't agree with your theory,*
> *the scientist throws away the theory.*
> *The quack, on the other hand, throws away the data.*
> — David Bresler

The late Russian scientist Semyon Davidovich Kirlian and his wife Valentina developed an electrophotographic technique in the 1940s for recording auras around animals, plants, and inanimate objects. No light or lenses are used in this process. Objects photographed are placed directly against the film in a darkroom and a pulsed electric current of high voltage and low amperage is passed through both the object and the film.[778]

For diagnostic purposes, Kirlian photographs are usually made of the palm, fingertips, foot or toes. The shape, density and color of the Kirlian aura have been found to correlate with states of health and disease in plants, animals and humans. This is a new field for research that may help us greatly to understand the energy nature of life. In Eastern Europe numerous practitioners utilize this diagnostic technique (which they have termed *bioelectrography*). Sadly, Western medical science has not invested in this promising mode of diagnosis, and most Western researchers have had to finance their work out of pocket.

Relevance of Kirlian photography to healing
1. Various states of physical and emotional health and disease in plants, animals and humans can be identified using this method.[779] Kirlian photographs in color add dimensions to the readings, but they also add to the variability of the process

and considerably increase costs. Generally speaking, illness, tiredness, or physical and emotional imbalances may be reflected in a narrow, thin, broken and irregular aura. The field is broken into *streamers*[780] (See Figure II-16, below.) A healthy state usually correlates with a broad, robust, dense and unbroken aura (See Figure II-17, on the next page.)

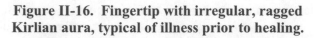

Figure II-16. Fingertip with irregular, ragged Kirlian aura, typical of illness prior to healing.

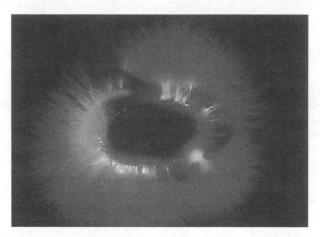

These criteria are applicable for many conditions, but with cancer the corona may be dense and unvarying, in contrast to normal auras, which show cyclical variations with time (Mallikarjun).

A careful study correlating Kirlian auras with illness was performed by Dr. Ramesh Singh Chouhan and P. Rajaram, Professor of Obstetrics and Gynecology, in Pondicherry, India. Using black and white Kirlian fingertip images, they studied fifty normal peri- and post-menopausal women to obtain a normative baseline for such images in this population. They then studied the Kirlian photographs of 100 women aged 45 - 60 years whose only illness was cancer of the cervix. In all cases biopsies and/ or vaginal cytology were also examined. No anti-cancer therapies had been started prior to the initial Kirlian photography. The study focused on "increase in intensity and character of the emission pattern" that correlated with the stages of the cancer.

The film was processed on an automatic processor and the electrogram was then analysed densitometrically for the intensity of the emission... Palmar sweating/ hyperhidrosis was seen only in 6% of the subjects. 60% showed dryness of the skin to touch. Analysis of electrograms revealed that there is a definite increase in the intensity of emission in cancerous and precancerous stage as against normal. The coronal midzone increase is linear to the advancement of disease. The streamer density was plotted on a graph after densitometric measurement. Though slight fluctuation was seen in the intensity of individual images they all fit into a pattern which could be distinct to each stage of the disease… Correlation with histopathologic and clinical staging was 100%…

In cases where follow-up evaluations were made, staging of disease progress by Kirlian photography correlated closely with clinical and laboratory results for staging of the disease. An unpublished extension of this series to include 1,000 cases confirmed the results (Chouhan).

Figure II-17. Fingertip with regular, robust Kirlian aura, typically seen in healthy people and following healing.

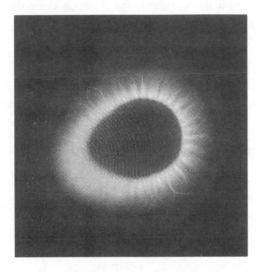

2. Valerie Hunt et al. found correlations of Kirlian photography with results of structural integration treatments (rolfing, or deep body massage). Those treated showed a significant finding: greater numbers of white bubbles in their Kirlian auras after rolfing (p < .02).[781]

3. Healers' and healees' Kirlian auras may change reciprocally from before to after a healing treatment.[782] Typically, healers' auras are robust prior to healing and less so afterwards; and conversely for healees' auras. If a healee's aura is ragged prior to healing, it may be more full after the treatment is received. Autogenic training, a system of self-healing, is also said to alter Kirlian images (Roman/ Inyushin; Steel).

  Hans G. Engel is a Los Angeles physician who is also a healer. With the collaboration of Thelma Moss at the University of California, Los Angeles, he obtained Kirlian photographs for each person he healed, and for himself, prior to and following each treatment session over an 18-month period (Engel/ Cole). An assistant selected a representative 120 paired samples from thousands of pictures taken before and after every phase of treatment, representing every type of response to giving and receiving healing. The pairs of *befores* and *afters* were randomly arranged on pages of an album.

After these 120 pairs were mounted, each pair to a page, the set was given to three judges in turn. These three were individuals working in the laboratory but not involved in the energy healing experiment. They were asked to evaluate the corona discharge on the pictures according to three standards: darkness (i.e., intensity), length of emanations, and gaps in the pattern, to a total of 360 evaluations.

There was a strong tendency of all judges to score the therapist's corona discharge as more intense before than after treatment; however, they did not find that patients showed a significant increase in the corona discharge after therapy… neither of these results was found to be statistically significant. Concordance between the judges' evaluation was subjected to blind, independent rating; statistics reveal significant correlation (p = 0.01) in their collective interpretations.

4. Kirlian and others claim that they can identify illness in plants or animals through their Kirlian images even prior to the appearances of outward signs of disease that are visible or detectable by other measurements. Rosemary Steel studied the clinical correlations of Kirlian hand images, finding links with specific physical and emotional problems. This suggests that there may be a holographic representation of the whole person in the hands.[783]

5. A correlation is reported between some aspects of Kirlian photography, and acupuncture points and acupuncture treatments.[784] Particularly bright flares appear at acupuncture points and their intensities are altered with acupuncture treatments. Steel finds that her interpretations of Kirlian hand images correlate well with hand maps of acupuncture and kinesiology.

6. Dumitrescu has an electrophotographic technique that he calls *Electronography*. He has demonstrated flares emanating from parts of the body that correspond with acupuncture points.

7. Plants and food products that have been grown organically (without pesticides) and are fresh typically demonstrate much brighter and broader Kirlian auras than those grown with chemical fertilizers and pesticides. Food products treated with preservatives and especially those that are irradiated show particularly dull and narrow auras (Oldfield/ Coghill).

8. Water that is given healing and water from holy springs demonstrates a very bright Kirlian aura (Dean 1987; Steel).

9. In rare Kirlian photographs of leaves that have had portions cut away, the Kirlian aura of the missing segment may still appear. This has been labeled *the phantom leaf effect*.[785] This effect has been difficult to replicate but it has been reported in a sufficient number of laboratories to confirm its existence. The parallels between phantom leaf Kirlian photographs and phantom limb effects[786] are consistent with a theory of energy fields that exist within and around living organisms.

10. Interactional effects have been found in Kirlian auras of pairs of people who are photographed simultaneously on the same film. In exposures of their fingertips (held adjacent but not touching) their Kirlian auras will coalesce if they have positive feelings for each other. Conversely, if they have negative feelings for each other the auras withdraw from each other.[787]

Problems with replication of research results

The interpretation of these Kirlian photographic halos is still a controversial subject.

As with many other aspects of energy medicine, Kirlian phenomena have not been consistently replicable by all investigators, or under all circumstances by the same investigators. This has unfortunately contributed to the rejection of a potentially useful tool for medical diagnosis.

Numerous technical factors may influence the appearance of the Kirlian images. These include voltage; electrical pulse width and rate; frequency of signal pulse; moisture (e.g. sweat) and dirt on objects photographed; atmospheric gases; pressure of object on film; exposure time; film type; flatness of film; angle of objects relative to the film; barometric pressure; atmospheric temperature (Poock); grounding of subjects – which may be influenced by leather vs. rubber-soled shoes or the type of chair the subject sits in (Steel) – as well as parameters of film development such as the specific chemicals used, their concentration, temperature, and the freshness and agitation of processing solutions. Because these parameters have not been standardized or consistent among investigators, it has been difficult to obtain consistent results in different laboratories.

In addition, psychological/ emotional factors in the subject and in the other persons present in the laboratory may influence the photographs (K. Johnson 1974; Steel). It appears possible that the operator of the equipment or other observers may influence the Kirlian photographs, and believers may obtain positive results while disbelievers do not.

Yvonne Duplessis (1985) found that in color sensitivity tests of dermal optics, perceptions shifted according to whether the subject was tested in daylight or under artificial light. Sensitives have told me that the size and nature of the room in which Kirlian photographs are made and in which other energy medicine phenomena are observed may influence the results. Jacob Liberman makes a strong case for deleterious bioenergetic effects of ordinary fluorescent light bulbs, which is the most common type of lighting in scientific laboratories. We must take such cautions seriously when investigating phenomena that differ substantially from conventional subjects of study in Western science. These factors may contribute to some of the variability that is repeatedly found in replications of subtle energy studies.

Some researchers believe that the operator of the Kirlian equipment may contribute an energetic component to the Kirlian photographs, thus adding yet another confounding factor to the list of variables that can influence these pictures.

Other researchers contest the validity of all of the above-mentioned positive findings, citing conflicting theories and confusion in experimental parameters (Canavor/ Wiesenfeld).

Implications of Kirlian photography

It is unclear as yet what Kirlian pictures actually represent. The majority of scientists studying Kirlian photography believe that the image reflects the biological energy state of the subject. If wse assume this to be a valid theory, then interactional effects between Kirlian auras of several persons suggest that there are field interactions among living things when they are in close proximity with each other. This suggests a possible basis for how spiritual healing may work. Sadly, other than the limited experiments cited above, no controlled studies have been published to support this view.

Some skeptics think that Kirlian images represent only the photographic effects of electric currents or magnetic fields that flow through and/ or around the object being photographed. They do not believe the pictures correlate with any unconventional fields or emanations from the subjects, or that they reflect their internal states. They suggest that variations in photographs of the same subject *simply reflect technical variabilities* in the system. Fluctuations in skin moisture has been particularly implicated as a variable that could produce these effects.[788]

Others (e.g. Konikiewicz) see skin moisture as an intermediary condition influenced by neurohormonal states (as when one "gets into a sweat" with anxiety or other emotions), which could provide a recognized indicator for limited internal mind-body conditions.

Where spiritual healers' Kirlian auras are less robust after giving treatment, and healees' auras are more robust after receiving healing, it is suggested by Kirlian researchers that an energy transfer may have occurred from healers to healees. One avenue for studying the bioenergy transfer hypothesis suggests itself for investigation. One would expect to see more robust Kirlian auras after healings in those healers who claim to channel external energies (particularly those who report they feel energized by the process) than in those healers who report they are projecting their own bioenergies. It would also be of interest to see simultaneous Kirlian photographs on the same plates or motion pictures of healer-healee Kirlian images to detect any direct interactions that might confirm energy transfers between healers and healees. The difficulty is that this procedure would be likely to interfere with the healing treatment.

> *A scientist wished to study the neglected natural phenomenon of the cat's purr. He implanted electrodes in the cat's brain and throat and connected them to sophisticated electronic devices. His efforts were in vain. The cat refused to purr.*
>
> – Anonymous

It is imperative that investigators fully describe parameters such as instruments, photographic film, developing techniques and other relevant factors if the confusion reigning in this area at present is to be sorted out. In addition to the known factors mentioned above, I would suggest paying attention to the many factors that could potentially influence healing research (listed in Chapter IV-3), and especially to geomagnetic activity, time of day, and lunar phases (per Chapter II-4).

Although it is clear that extraneous factors do alter Kirlian photographs, there appears to be much more to Kirlian effects than mere artifact. There is a growing body of anecdotal literature evidencing relationships between Kirlian images and states of health and disease in animals and plants.

The Kirlians, Oldfield/ Coghill and Hunt developed instruments for direct, live aura observations. These should be able provide even more detailed data. Russians investigators report that in Kirlian aura motion pictures there are discharges, flares, and other pulsatory, dynamic phenomena (Ostrander/ Schroeder).

There are also similarities between Kirlian photography and aura perceptions in the ability to identify acupuncture points.

The phantom leaf effects seem to support contentions by sensitives that an energy body surrounds the physical body of all living things. The interactions between Kirlian auras of people who are photographed simultaneously also support this claim. These observations imply that the Kirlian image represents an interaction of electric current with leaves and the people and their biological fields.

The reports of sensitives and Kirlian photographers are similar in *predicting* the development of physical illness, according to changes observed in the auras. This suggests that: **1.** the Kirlian aura and the aura perceived by healers may be similar or identical in origins; and **2.** the aura may be an organizing energy field, so that a disharmony in the field is secondarily reflected in the physical body.[789]

Interactional effects between Kirlian auras of several persons also suggest that there may be energy field interactions amongst living things that are in proximity with each other. The same is true for interactional effects between the operator of the Kirlian instrument and the subjects being photographed. The energy field interaction hypothesis of how spiritual healing works may find support here.

Sensitives suggest that the energies concentrated at acupuncture points are exchanged between the body and the energy fields around it, as well as with energies flowing within the body. The reports of more intense Kirlian aura activity at acupuncture points supports these claims.

Though the validity of all the observations on Kirlian photography is still moot, they are consistent with observations from other energy medicine areas reviewed in this book. The presence of an energy field surrounding living things has been reported repeatedly by sensitives who see auras, and by healers who feel them.[790]

No studies have been reported to verify that the Kirlian aura is similar to or identical with aspects of the aura that sensitives perceive. An observation of Jack Schwarz (who sees auras) that only a small portion of one of the aura bodies that lies close to the physical body is represented in Kirlian photography is the only relevant comment I have seen.

Other diagnostic methods have been developed using photography. For instance, Alain Masson has developed a "biotonic instrument" that produces aura photographs using an electric generator and chemicals (phyllosilicates) present in beeswax. The results are dependent on the operator of the instrument.

Konstantin Korotkov has developed a computerized display of colors around people, based on EM readings at various acupuncture points. This display is often confused with Kirlian photography. The Korotkov instrument colors are *arbitrarily assigned* by the inventor as a visual display correlated with electroacupuncture readings – in contrast with the natural occurrence of the aura in Kirlian photography.

Possible applications for Kirlian photography

Kirlian photography appears to hold the promise of providing a system for screening and diagnosing energy states of health and disease.

Much as the *A.M.I. instrument* of Hiroshi Motoyama assists in evaluating activity in acupuncture meridians, and the *Mind Mirror* of Maxwell Cade helps to clarify mental states via electroencephalograms, *Kirlian devices* could provide a method for assessing the effects of healing. It could also provide a feedback device for students who are learning to heal.

Now that we have surveyed a range of evidence for a biological field that can be perceived by sensitives and healers, and fields in Kirlian photography that appear to overlap with these, let us examine reports from other studies of biological energies.

LABORATORY MEASUREMENTS OF BIOLOGICAL ENERGY FIELDS

> *The universe in which we find ourselves and from which we can not be separated is a place of Law and Order. It is not an accident, nor chaos. It is organized and maintained by an Electro-Dynamic Field capable of determining the position and movement of all charged particles.*
>
> *For nearly half a century the logical consequences of this theory have been subjected to rigorously controlled experimental conditions and met with no contradictions.*
>
> – Harold Saxton Burr (1972)

Recognized energies

Conventional science recognizes four energies or forces:

1. *The strong nuclear force* binds neutrons and protons in the atomic nucleus. It is relatively strong but acts only over short distances.

2. *The weak nuclear force* also contributes to nuclear structure and to radioactive decay. Both (1) and (2) have little effect outside the nucleus.

3. *The electromagnetic (EM) force* pervades all of our cosmos, from atomic structures, to chemical molecular interactions and electrical power. It is also active in stars, including our own sun.

4. *Gravity* is weaker than the others over short distances and is active in proportion to the mass of an object. On the planetary, solar, and cosmic scales it is the dominant force. Although its effects are measurable, its nature is least understood amongst the four forces. We can measure its effects with great precision, but as yet we have no clear theories to explain *how* it works.

In our everyday world it is the electromagnetic (EM) force that we have harnessed to fill our energy needs, and with which we are most familiar.

Studies of healers and psychics are inconclusive, reporting correlations of healing effects with EM fields in some cases[791] but not in others (Balanovski/ Taylor; Taylor/ Balanovski). Theoretically, the fields might explain some aspects of local psi effects, but they cannot explain psi effects that do not appear to diminish over enormous distances, and that transcend time. We will consider these studies in detail below.

It may be that some form(s) of energy exist that we have not yet identified, and which may have EM components or aspects (Rein 1992). Albert Einstein speculated:

> It is possible that there exist human emanations which are still unknown to us. Do you remember how electrical currents and "unseen waves" were laughed at? The knowledge about man is still in its infancy.

Mind may interact with energy and matter in ways we have yet to understand. The following sections explore such possibilities.

Electromagnetic fields and the body

Let us start by reviewing research on the energies that are recognized by conventional science, looking first at studies of EM fields that are present in and around the body.

Electrochemical reactions in nerve cells create electrical impulses that are used for communication amongst nerve cells, and between nerve cells and the various organs and tissues of the body. The electroencephalogram (EEG) is used to identify the summed fluctuations in EM activities of countless brain cells. EEG brainwaves are recorded with electrodes placed on the scalp.

When muscles contract they create EM impulses that can be measured on the surface of the body by an electromyogram (EMG).

The electrocardiogram (ECG or EKG) is used to record the contractions of the heart muscle, which produces the most powerful EM activity found in the body.

These EM activities have been thoroughly studied over the course of many decades. There are other EM fields within and around the body whose presence and functions have not been studied as thoroughly and are therefore not as well understood. They have also been ignored by mainstream science for reasons that are not entirely clear or obvious.

Findings with much broader implications have resulted from careful measurements of biological EM fields. Harold Saxton Burr (1944; 1972) taught at the Yale University Department of Medicine for over four decades. He developed reliable methods for measuring differences in electrical potentials between points on the bodies of animals and plants. Using this method he established that every living system has a complex direct current (DC) EM field that can be measured with electrodes on its surface. Organisms studied included slime molds, plant seeds, trees, amphibian eggs, amphibians, rodents, humans, and many other organisms. These EM fields vary over time, and are highly correlated in regular patterns with growth, development, physiological processes (e.g. ovulation), disease (e.g. malignancies), wound healing and emotional conditions. Patterns of variation were noted with external factors, such as correlations with atmospheric and earth potentials as well as with lunar cycles and sunspots.

Labeling this phenomenon the "L-field" (*Life-field*), Burr speculated that it provides a template for the maintenance of relative structural and biochemical constancy. Molecules and cells are replaced through the normal turnover of chemical materials throughout the life of the organism. It appears that the organism requires a mechanism to assure that appropriate replacements will be made in an orderly fashion, to provide for continuity of physical integrity and to maintain the health of the organism. Burr's L-fields may provide the necessary templates for this process. Similarly, he speculated that the L-fields may also function as organizers for growth and development of the organism. For instance, Burr found that frog eggs demonstrate an electrical polarity that predicts which side of the egg will develop into a head and which will become a tail.

Leonard Ravitz, an American physician, took Burr's research a step further. He reviewed numerous measurements of electrodynamic states in humans in a wide variety of conditions,[792] and found that field perturbations accompanied many physical symptoms. They also correlated with schizophrenia and depression.

He confirmed that periodic field shifts correlated with lunar and solar flare cycles, and extended the connection several steps further. He noted periodic shifts in human potentials and those of plants and other animals which all occurred in the same time intervals. Furthermore, behavioral and physiological changes in people over time could be predicted on the basis of anticipated periodicities in environmental field shifts. Human behavior correlated most closely with quantitative shifts in field intensity, while somatic changes correlated more with polarity vector readings.

> *I sing the body electric.*
> – Walt Whitman (1855)

Ravitz argues that the polarities measured relate to global organismic fields of living organisms, and are not directly dependent on nerve transmissions or other somatic elements such as ionic shifts in the body as a whole. [793]

In other studies, Robert Becker and Andrew A. Marino extensively investigated the effects of EM fields on the mammalian body. They believe that the fields observed by Burr and his followers cannot be adequately explained as the products of underlying physiological mechanisms such as cellular metabolism (Becker/ Marino; Becker/ Selden). Becker and Marino see no adequate explanation that would account for how metabolic activity could be converted into the observed electrical potentials.

Becker and colleagues review a large number of experiments (some their own and some by others), and build a convincing argument for their hypothesis of an organizing function for DC fields within the body. In one experiment, they built a model of a salamander, including a wire analog of the salamander's central nervous system. They then measured a similar electrical pattern in the model as was found in a live salamander. This and other evidence suggested that the DC fields (which are probably associated with the nervous system rather than the body in general) are products of general physiological processes in the nervous system, particularly in *glial* (supportive) cells. Prior to this, no clear functions had been attributed to glial cells.

Becker and colleagues postulate several functions that may be served by the DC current system in the body. First, they think that it may help to integrate the entire activity of the brain, whose functions are too complex, in their opinions, to be accounted for by the digital neuronal model alone.

Second, the DC fields may integrate processes of organ growth. This hypothesis is supported by research on the *planarian* flatworm, a rather winsome creature measuring less than a centimeter in length, with large spots on its head resembling eyes. (When viewed under the microscope, the planarian appears to be looking back at the person viewing it.) When cut transversely into pieces it regenerates an entire worm from any piece, preserving the same electrical polarity of head and tail in the regenerated worms as was present in the original (Marsh/ Beams).

The electrical orientation of the worm is also maintained by the pieces. That is to say, the head of the worm is positively charged and so are the ends of the pieces that were oriented towards the original head. But if an externally generated current is applied to the pieces in reverse to the original polarity, a tail will usually develop where the head should be and vice versa. This is the clearest demonstration I have seen of an organizing property for DC fields.

Becker and Marino found further evidence for the organizing properties of DC currents that are applied from outside the body. In their own experiments, small DC currents markedly enhanced healing of human fractures that had previously refused to knit (as sometimes occurs for unknown reasons). With externally applied fields they also produced complete regeneration of limbs of frogs (including the joints) and partial regeneration of limbs of rats. This had been considered impossible prior to their work

An empirical observation reinforces the evidence presented above. If the fingertip is sheared off in an accident at a point distal to the first joint, and the end of the finger is left unsutured to heal on its own, often an entire fingertip will regenerate, complete with a fingernail and a fingerprint identical with the original. This occurs more often in children under the age of ten. It is hypothesized by Becker that an organizing field must exist to account for this.

A completely different line of research is suggested by the observation that biophotons are emitted by living organisms. These minute quanta of energy may be triggers for some aspects of bioregulation.[794] (See further discussion on light emitted from the body below.)

With the helpful clinical EM treatments that are now being developed, further studies are proceeding on biological EM fields within and around the body. These are discussed in chapter II-2. To recapitulate briefly, pulsed EM fields (PEMFs) can help with healing in cases of chronic failure of mending in fractures, in osteoarthritis, pain, depression, and many other syndromes.

The precise mechanisms by which EM fields influence living organisms has yet to be established, and several hypotheses are being pursued.[795] A likely point of manifestation for EM effects is the cell membrane. Minute EM forces might alter the transporting mechanisms that shuttle material across these membranes by modifying chemical receptors (Adey 1992; Tenforde/ Kaune).

Naturally occurring EM fields, such as those in nerve cells, might also be modulated by external EM fields. It is postulated that specific EM frequencies may trigger particular cellular biological processes that facilitate physical healing (Sisken/ Walder). Alternatively, EM fields may facilitate bioenergy flows and healing (Oschman 1993).

Energy fields near the body

The late Canon Andrew Glazewski, a British theologian, scientist and healer, proposed a theory based on more than forty years of investigations in healing. He observed that each person emits a unique pattern of infrared (IR) radiation, due to wave interferences that are peculiar to the individual. He also noted that EM and sound patterns must surround the body, as they are products of physiological functions. Such radiations, he postulated, must carry information relating to the body of origin, and they may thus form a basis for a spiritual healer to analyze and diagnose. The crests and waves of the interference patterns could account for the various sensations (such as heat, tingling and vibrations) described by healers when they are giving touch and near-the-body healing. He theorized that some day it may be possible to analyze this biofield with suitable instrumentation, but that scientific equipment of this kind will never surpass the human hand in sensitivity or the mind in its ability to interpret such sensation.[796] He also makes an unsupported observation that the field around the body rotates once in twenty-four hours.[797]

J. Bigu points out that a very complex set of known energies and fields may emanate from the body to produce the visual aura which has been reported by sensitives.[798] These energies may include: electrical, magnetic, radio frequency and microwave, infra-red, ultra-violet, X-ray, gamma ray, beta ray, neutrino, chemical, mechano-acoustical scattering, diffraction and refraction auras. The perceived aura may represent a sensory or psi perception of these fields individually or in combination(s), perhaps in the form of interference patterns.

The same is obviously true for the bioenergy fields perceived as tactile sensations.

Jan Szymanski (1986), of Warsaw, Poland identified a stationary electromagnetic field (EF) as well as a quasi-stationary or slow-changing field around the body. This can be detected from a distance of several centimeters from the body and it appears to correlate with aspects of normal and pathologic physiology. His instrument is a "high sensitivity static-electricity meter" with a probe that is held five centimeters above the surface of the skin. Measurements "at 40 skin measuring points" were performed on 9 *bioenergotherapists* (Eastern European term for healers) and 20 "common persons" inside a Faraday cage, which excludes extraneous EF. Szymanski found that:

> 1. [P]ersons with various ailments show relatively high potential difference, from -3V to +3V at various points of their body but positive potentials generally prevail;
> 2. Healthy persons with a good general feeling show more often negative potentials and there are not high potential differences between various points of their bodies (-1V to +1V only)...

3. All the bioenergotherapists, 7 men and 2 women, showed with almost no exception negative potentials only (-1.1 V to -0.2V); the only positive potentials, if any, could be observed exclusively around their heads and were very low (less than +O.5V)...; and

4. [A]ttention has been given to the quasistationery EF of the therapists' hands. It was found that only negative potential could be detected... mean value -0.5V to -0.6V[C]ommon persons have shown... the mean value... 0.0V to -0.1V.

Szymanski found that EF potentials of the hands may change slowly or rapidly. In common people 10% fluctuations may be noted over a period of two hours. In two bioenergotherapists, after performing single brief treatments of patients, EF potentials of their palms dropped 200 - 300%, to about -1.5V. During treatments, the bioenergotherapists' hands produced EFs measuring "to some scores of Hz, the EF intensity at a distance of about 3 cm being 0.1 to 3V/ m."

He speculates that healers may be able to diagnose problems by detecting alterations in the fields around patients' bodies, and to treat them by influencing the patients' EFs with their own.

John Zimmerman, at the University of Colorado School of Medicine, reports that he can identify a magnetic field around the entire body by using a modified EEG (Brain/ Mind 1985). Zimmerman (1990) documented that EM pulsations emanate from TT healers' hands at frequencies shifting from 0.3 to 30 Hz. The most common frequency is in the range of 7 to 8 cycles per second, which is also one of the more common brain rhythm frequencies.

These findings were confirmed in Japan through studies of various healers and martial arts experts. Seto et al. (1992) found that extremely strong biomagnetic fields could be measured near the hands of experts in a wide range of healing and martial arts, such as meditation, Qigong and yoga. Fields measured up to 0.0010 gauss, or approximately 1,000 times more intense than the cardiac field, which is the strongest field in the body, and 1,000,000 times stronger than the brain's electromagnetic fields.

Chinese researchers report that infrasound (sound waves below audible levels) is regularly emitted from the hands of qigong healers. Mechanical emitters of infrasonic sound can reproduce many of the beneficial effects of qigong healing.[799]

Significant decreases in gamma radiation counts have been measured around the bodies of people receiving Polarity Therapy (Benford et al.).

SQUID (superconducting quantum interference device) technology can detect EM fields around the body (Zimmerman 1990; Zimmerman et al.). The SQUID is particularly sensitive to the EM currents that are created by ions in the blood as they stream through blood vessels. Alterations in these currents can be mapped in the blood flow through the brain during particular mental activities. This process has led to entirely new ways of studying activity in the brain. Newer technology will make it possible to identify whether certain parts of the brain are activated during healing. J. Zimmerman (1990) reported that biomagnetic pulses from the hands of a Therapeutic Touch healer could be measured with a SQUID magnetometer. Pulses between 0.3Hz and 30 Hz were found, with the greatest activity between 7 - 8 Hz. Non-healers were found to produce no such pulses.

A. Seto et al. confirm that the hands of qigong healers (as well as those of people who practice yoga, meditation, and martial arts) emanate EM pulsations between 8 - 10 Hz, with an intensity about 1,000 times greater than that of ordinary human biofields. This is within the range of alpha brainwaves, and within the frequency that is found to be most beneficial in enhancing physical healing of wounds: 2 - 50 Hz.(Sisken/ Walker).

While there is as yet no study demonstrating direct effects of EM pulsations from healers' hands upon healees' EM pulsations, J. Oschman (1997) suggests that the entrainment of bioelectrical EM pulsations is theoretically quite feasible. Physicists have noted that EM pulsations of similar frequencies in different EM devices have a tendency to become coupled to each other. This could occur in living organisms as well. Early research with EEGs (summarized below) appears to confirm this speculation.

There are some interesting investigations of EM effects on living systems that are currently underway. It is speculated that biological systems may be exquisitely sensitive to EM fields, and that they may be able to distinguish meaningful signals from the cacophony of EM "noise" that is constantly present in the environment (Adey/ Bawin). There is further speculation that arrays of cells, or even arrays of molecules which are polarized within cells, could act as EM sensors for detecting meaningful signals. These would be similar to the arrays of antennas that are used in radio telescopes to detect faint signals from heavenly bodies that may be billions of light years away.[800]

> Bodywork and other repetitive practices such as yoga, Qigong, tai chi, meditation, therapeutic touch, etc. may gradually lead to more structural coherence (crystallinity) in the tissues, facilitating both the detection and radiation of energy fields (Oschman & Oschman 1997). Arrays of water molecules associated with the macromolecules are probably involved as well.
>
> The process has been described as the formation of "coherence domains" in liquid crystal arrays (Sermonti 1995). The mechanism involves that stabilization of the positional and orientational order of millions of rod-shaped molecules, as in cell membranes, connective tissues, DNA, muscle, the cytoskeleton, the myelin sheath of nerves, and sensory cells (Oschman 1997). Stabilization spreads from molecule to molecule, throughout the system. Del Guidice (1993) describes the process as one in which individual molecules "lose their individual identity, cannot be separated, move together as if performing a choral ballet, and are kept in phase by an electromagnetic field which arises from the same ballet."
>   – James Oschman 2000 (p. 221-222)

Elmer Green and colleagues (1991) at the Meninger Institute followed up on an unusual observation from the meditation literature, which was recorded in 1882 (Barker). It was recommended that Tibetan student monks sit on a marble bench that is isolated from the ground by glass, and stare at their image mirrored in a copper wall with the north pole of a bar magnet suspended from a string over their heads. Green et al. constructed a room with copper walls and replicated this arrangement, attaching sensitive instruments to the walls to measure any EM effecs.

Studying ten meditators in 45-minute sessions they found no body-potential surges reaching as high as 4 volts. In contrast, healers who meditated in the copper-walled room produced surges of 4 to 221V (median 8.3V) lasting 0.5 to 12.5 seconds (median 3.6 sec.).

During non-contact healing sessions the same healers demonstrated body-potential surges between 4 and 190V. Most of the surges had a negative polarity.

These surge values are 1,000 times greater than EM changes observed with emotional responses, 100,000 times greater than EKG voltages, and 1,000,000 times greater than EEG voltages.

Others are also studying EM biofields.

The Institute of Heartmath in California has developed a meditation and bio-feedback system for teaching people to develop coherent EM patterns of heartbeats. People who learn to develop heartwave coherence often find that they also develop healing abilities. Conversely, some healers have been found to have this pattern without having had the training. During healings, healers' and healees' heart rhythms become entrained (Childre; McCraty et al.).

Linda Russek and Gary Schwartz found that the EEG in the anterior region of subjects' brains would become entrained to the ECG rhythm of the experimenter. Experimenter and subject sat facing each other, with their eyes closed, without touching. The effect was more pronounced in those subjects who felt that they had been raised by loving parents than in subjects who felt that their parents had not been loving.

In these studies we see early evidence of EM interactive effects between healers and healees. These suggest that there may be an EM aspect in bioenergy fields and that the fields of healers and healees may interact during healing. It is unclear whether there is a single EM healing energy being measured along segments of its full spectrum, or whether there are several different healing energy fields.

A last item in this category is reported by William Tiller, Professor Emeritus in Physics at Standford University. Tiller[801] has developed an Intentionally Imprinted Electrical Device (IIED). The IIED can be imprinted with the intention to alter the acidity (pH) of water. With a blinded protocol, he has sent imprinted devices to distant laboratories, where they either increased or decreased the acidity of water according to their programming. This is a clear demonstration of intentional effects on an EM device. Confounding these reports, however, is the fact that the same effects were obtained in a laboratory in England *prior to the arrival of the devices in the mail*[802] – suggesting that intentionality alone may be able to produce these effects.

Discussion

It is definitely too early to say with any clarity or certainty what fields are sensed or activated by healers.

> *Whoever undertakes to set himself up as judge in the field of truth and knowledge is shipwrecked by the laughter of the gods.*

> – Albert Einstein

EFFECTS OF ENVIRONMENTAL EM FIELDS

Geomagnetic effects on biological systems are well recognized but as yet they are little understood. The molten core of the earth contains a high percentage of iron. This produces EM fields around the earth, including the magnetic polarity that is reflected in compass needles. The sun also radiates EM fields that fluctuate with solar activity. When solar flares erupt, these fields can be so strong that radio and TV communications are disrupted.

Living organisms are influenced by EM fields in ways that have yet to be clarified and explained. For instance, there are certain naturally occurring EM frequencies around the earth, and it is speculated that they are relevant to biological systems. One is the Schumann resonant frequency of 7-8 cycles per second, a regular EM pulsation produced by standing waves that bounce back and forth between the surface of the earth and the ionosphere.[803] Biological systems on earth appear to have adapted to these constant EM pulsations. In one study, when people were shielded from environmental EM radiations, their biological rhythms of sleeping and waking and the regular fluctuations of various hormone levels were disrupted (Wever 1968; 1974).

Gross magnetic fields and chronic environmental EM pollution may have negative effects on health.

M. F. Barnothy reviews the literature on the effects of magnetic fields on living things to 1964, and Vinokurava reviews related Russian research. In the laboratory, gross magnetic fields produce headaches, fatigue and other symptoms of malaise. These were disturbances of sufficient severity to warrant concern and recommendations for removal of the subjects from exposure to such fields. Vinokurava also reviews research on naturally occurring fields, such as that of the sun. Specific brain centers (hypothalamus) and types of brain cells (glia) were noted to respond to magnetic influence.

Deliberate exposure to EM fields at the frequency of EEG theta waves altered short-term memory (Michaud/ Persinger)

Robert Becker and colleagues (Becker/ Marino; Becker/ Selden) review a variety of evidence strongly suggesting there are serious health risks associated with environmental EM pollution from power lines, transformers and other such equipment. Environmental medicine has also clarified that combinations of EM fields from household appoliances and electrical wiring in the walls can be irritating or harmful. These may include phones (especially cell phones used without earphones), electric blankets, and various computer and entertainment equipment. It is a wonder that the public is not more aware of and concerned about these issues. Personnel exposed to the enormously powerful magnetic fields surrounding scanners for imaging the inside of the body also would appear to be candidates for related health problems, although early research does not support this.

Reichmanis et al. and B. Wilson found a relationship between depression and overhead power lines.

Svetlana Vinokurava (1971) also reports on the effects of magnetic fields on living things. She found that strong fields produced negative symptoms, including headaches, fatigue, loss of appetite and insomnia. Physical changes included edema, decreased pain sensitivity, heart pains and itching. Other studies showed that magnetic fields increased the phagocytic capacity (ability to eliminate foreign bodies) of white blood cells; decreased non-specific immunity to bacteria and viruses and increased cell mutations.

Anecdotal reports suggest that in its simplest expression, EM radiation from fluorescent lights may cause fatigue and headaches. People with multiple allergy syndromes often complain that they do not tolerate fluorescent lighting. In more complex exposures, EM radiation appears to contribute to more serious symptoms, including arthritis, allergies, and susceptibility to infections.

Evidence is now emerging in Western countries indicating that long-term EM pollution may contribute to a variety of illnesses, such as heart disease and depression (Perry/ Pearl); various allergies, including to EM radiations themselves Shallis 1988; Smith/ Best); chronic fatigue syndrome; psychological effects, and more.[804] Much of this evidence is as yet partial and in need of further confirmation, as some studies have shown no negative effects.[805]

Of particular concern is evidence that children[806] and adults (H. Brown/ Chattopadhyay; Speers) who are exposed to environmental EM fields may be prone to developing cancer. This is further supported by laboratory studies showing that cancer cell growth in vitro is enhanced with exposure to EM fields.[807]

Cyril Smith, a Senior Lecturer in the Department of Electronic and Electrical Engineering at Salford University in England, in collaboration with Ray Choy and Jean Monro, two doctors specializing in allergic disorders, explored the reactions of people who are hypersensitive to EM radiation (C. Smith et al.; Shallis 1988). One person was so sensitive that she would convulse whenever she was within 200 meters of overhead power lines.

This team reports that a simple laboratory oscillator can bring out the allergic symptoms, and that other frequencies could neutralize them. They found that frequency was far more of a factor than signal strength. Patients identified frequencies that produced symptoms identical to those that they developed with exposure to specific chemical allergens, such as food, gasoline fumes and perfume. Although blinds are mentioned, they are not described – which leaves these reports open to questions about experimenter effects. I have not seen the originals of these reports to know about specific freauencies for specific problems.

While a great deal of skepticism has been expressed about the dangers of environmental EM radiation, simple tests of EM influence on non-human subjects have also produced negative effects. These have demonstrated significant detrimental effects on purified water (Dibble/ Tiller), alkaline phosphatase (a liver enzyme; Kohane/ Tiller 1997), and fruit fly larvae (Kohane/ Tiller 2000). Samples protected by a Faraday cage and placed inside an incubator were successfully shielded from measurable EM effects, as compared to samples placed on a shelf adjacent to the incubator (all $p < .001$).

Various devices have been developed that allegedly can protect a person from negative environmental EM effects. Shealy et al. (1998) demonstrated in a controlled study that the Clarus Qlink could indeed offer significant protection against environmental EM disturbance of the EEG.

Replications and extension of studies on EM effects appear to be urgently needed. Without these there is the clear possibility that some results may represent placebo effects.[808]

SPIRITUAL HEALING AND ELECTROMAGNETISM

> *... He [C. G. Jung] would sit on the stone day after day wondering whether*
> *he was the one sitting on the stone; or was he the stone that felt it was be-*
> *ing sat upon? This problem raised by the speculation was never solved.*
> *But he had no doubt that he was in some secret relationship with the stone.*
> *Also that the dialogue thus begun was in terms of a greater, more perma-*
> *nent and irreducible reality as represented by the stone...*
>   – Laurens van der Post 1974

Spiritual healing appears to have some similarities or actual points of overlap
with EM effects.

Studies by Robert Miller showed that both healers and strong magnets could
alter water in such a way that its surface tension was decreased, and this water
enhanced plant growth. In separate studies, Justa Smith and Hoyt Edge demonstrated that both a healer and an extremely strong magnetic field could enhance
the activity of the enzyme trypsin.[809] Much further work remains to be done in
order to clarify the relationship between electromagnetism and healing.[810]

John Zimmerman studied the magnetic fields around the bodies of healees. Regardless of where on the healee's body Therapeutic Touch healing was being
applied, he observed alterations in the entire body field. Some of these signals
appeared to parallel brain wave frequencies. This seems similar to the work of
Motoyama on acupuncture meridians and chakras.[811]

Benford et al. found that Polarity Therapy decreased the amount of gamma radiation emitted by healees' bodies.

Unusual EM phenomena have been noted around people who have psi experiences. Boguslaw Lipinski studied the teenage children who reported that they saw
the Virgin Mary appear frequently in a church in Medjugorje, in the former
Yugoslavia. Healings are also said to have occurred when people prayed there
before and after these apparitions (O'Regan). Lipinski was following up on reports by Professor Henri Joyeaux, of the Cancer Institute at the University of
Montpellier in France, which claimed that the alpha waves in the EEGs of these
children increased in amplitude at the beginning of an apparition. Lipinski hypothesized that an increase in concentration of ambient ions (electrically charged
air molecules) might be responsible for the altered EEG patterns. Using a portable
electroscope (ion detector) he did in fact record exceedingly high readings of up
to 100,000 ions per cubic centimeter.

When Lipinski shielded the instrument with a metal sleeve to prevent registration of ions from the air, high readings continued. Ordinarily this could only be
caused by such a high radioactivity that physical damage and fatalities would be
expected. He hypothesizes an unknown type of energy causing these effects. The
highest reading was *before* the visionaries arrived, and Lipinski later recorded an
unexplained high reading at his home. He cannot explain why others obtained
only brief positive electrostatic recordings at the site or none at all. He postulates
that he may have contributed to the effect as the operator of the instrument.

Lipinski also discovered an unusual effect on a tape that was used to record a
conversation at the home of the children. Upon replaying the tape after returning

home, he noted a low frequency sound (15 - 20 cps) that had not been noticed at the time of recording. He presumes that it was caused by a magnetic pulsating field of unknown source.

Others have used Geiger counters to record reduced background readings during healing sessions (Benford; R. Taylor 2000).

Lu Yan Fang, Ph.D., of the National Electro Acoustics Laboratory in China, recorded infrasonic sound emitted from the hands of qigong masters during external qi healings. She was able to produce healing effects with synthetic infrasonic sound at similar frequencies, and reported benefits for pain, circulatory disturbances and depression. On the basis of these explorations, the infrasonic QGM is now being studied in America.

Fritz Grunewald, a German engineer, studied a medium named Johannsen around 1920 (Stelter). He reported the following:

> ...Johannsen could do simple feats of psychokinesis such as depressing one side of an evenly balanced scale. Grunewald found that each time, just before the scale descended, the magnetic field strength in the medium's hands – which he held out toward the object to be moved – grew markedly weaker, only to increase after the psychokinetic act. It looked as if something which had produced the strong magnetism in Johannsen's body – perhaps the turbulent cold plasma postulated by Sergeyev – displaced itself outward and released psychokinetic effects.

> A few times Grunewald, by means of iron filings strewn on glass plates, was able to obtain pictures of the magnetic field within Johannsen's hands. In this way, he found several magnetic centers in the hand's magnetic field which Grunewald believed were evoked by electrical eddies in the medium's hands – another startling similarity to Sergeyev's theories of turbulent cold plasma. But strangely, the magnetic centers seemed at times to lie outside the medium's hand. We must recall the hypothesis that the biofield can move outside the body.

Photons and ultrasound may be produced in dividing cells, perhaps during shifts between liquid and crystal states of the involved molecules. Such mechanisms may underlie mitogenetic radiation Gurwitch, below.

I have heard anecdotal reports of other researchers working along similar lines, but I have not seen publications of their results.

Discussion
The above observations are highly speculative.

> *Where is the life we've lost in living?*
> *Where is the wisdom we've lost in knowledge?*
> *Where is the knowledge we've lost in information?*
> — T. S. Eliot, The Rock

UNCONVENTIONAL FIELDS AND RADIATIONS

Scientists have identified a variety of unusual fields and radiations that can be found on and around humans and other living things. While the existence of these fields has not been accepted by conventional science, the evidence suggests that there may be fertile ground for further study in these reports.

Measurements of conventional EM fields around the body in relation to their effects on healing have not produced consistent results. Glen Rein suggests that self-healing and healer-healing may be mediated by unconventional EM fields, postulated to exist when two opposing EM fields neutralize each other's conventionally measured EM effects. Drawing on writings of David Bohm (1980; Bohm/ Peat), he suggests that such fields may act through higher dimensional energies, or that they may be described as repositories of information rather than as fields.

The existence of such energies has been investigated by a number of scientists, in addition to Rein: "They have been called non-Hertzian energy... scalar energy, longitudinal waves, motional fields, time-reversed waves, radiant energy, gravitational waves... free energy and cosmic energy to name a few. It is presently unknown whether these energies are identical or distinct from non-Hertzian energy..." (Rein 1992). These energies cannot be measured using conventional EM devices.

The body may respond to the influences of such fields through its positive and negative ions; through the liquid crystals in cell membranes, bones and other tissues; through bioenergetic patternings in body fluids; and/ or through subatomic biopotentials in the atomic nuclei.

One device that is theorized to produce non-Hertzian fields is a specially designed Möbius strip that traps EM fields. Such Möbius strip devices are commercially available in certain wristwatches, and they are alleged to generate non-Hertzian fields as well as EM fields between 7 to 8 Hz. Rein showed that this kind of device could influence the growth rates of nerve cells (1988) and immune cells (1989) in tissue culture.

Because there is as yet no instrument for measuring non-Hertzian fields, it has been impossible to test directly Rein's hypothesis that these may be the mediators for the effects of healing. Rein took a step towards clarifying this issue himself when he introduced a device that was alleged to produce non-Hertzian fields. He used this device to study the hands of a healer who was producing measurable conventional magnetic field patterns:

> ...prior to addition of the device, the magnetic pattern was repetitive containing numerous sharp, small positive peaks. Upon addition of the device, the magnetic field pattern was substantially altered. The new pattern was qualitatively similar in shape but gradually increased in overall magnitude. These results suggest that non-Hertzian quantum fields enhanced the magnetic field emitted from Laskow's hand during holoenergetic healing.

These observations echo reports by healers who say that healing involves interactions between energy fields that surround the bodies of both healers and healees.

Dubrov (reviewed in Krippner 1980) speculates that all living things may emit gravitational waves, which could possibly be produced by the rhythmic movements of cellular molecules. Of related interest are speculations on the relationship between psi and gravity (Gallimore; Herbert 1979b).

Various unusual energies are said to be produced by a range of unorthodox electronic gadgets, some of which are based on the inventions of Nikola Tesla and Antoine Priore (Bearden 1980; Laurie). These instruments supposedly produce combinations of EM and gravitational waves which are said to travel faster than the speed of light, cause levitation of objects, and produce rapid cures of illnesses. If verified, these reports may explain some or all of the effects of healing. The role of the observer is said to be a crucial aspect of these phenomena, and therefore healing may reciprocally help to explain some of their unusual aspects.

In Eastern Europe and America there are Psychotronic Associations that study these devices. The USPA publishes a journal of their reports.

Physicists are now postulating (M. King) that enormous energy resources are available from empty space, which in turn would indicate a source for healing energy. Edward Russell (1971) hypothesizes that the thoughts (*T-fields*) of one person can telepathically affect the biofields (*L-fields*)[812] of another person, and that this may explain a host of psi and healing phenomena.

Burr further speculates that *L-fields* act as guiding principles in the evolution of living things, or bridges between the spiritual and the material worlds. There may be overlaps in this regard with Sheldrake's theory of *morphogenetic fields*.

Otto Rahn reviews numerous experiments on what he has labeled *mitogenetic radiation*. This effect was first discovered by A. G. Gurwitsch[813] of the USSR in 1923. Its name originates from the biological system in which it was noted – the growing tip of an onion root. When one onion root was pointed toward the tip of another (See Figure II-18), the second root demonstrated increased cell division (mitoses) in the segment towards which the first root was pointed.

Figure II-18. Onion roots used to test mitogenetic radiation

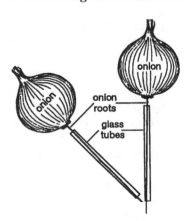

Gurwitsch and associates found numerous organisms and tissues that emitted this kind of radiation, including bacteria; yeast; eggs of annelid worms; chickens (during the first two days of incubation); blood; intact contracting muscle; neoplasms; and more. Non-radiating organisms and tissues included adult animal tissues (except brain); blood, muscle; blood of cancer patients and of starving rats, and more. The common denominators for active emitters seem to be that they are either undergoing glycolysis (sugar metabolism) or proteolytic processes (breaking down of proteins).

Intermittent, pulsed mitogenetic radiation was found to be more powerful than steady radiation. The effects of mitogenetic radiation are generally positive and growth –enhancing, especially in bacteria and yeasts, and cultures of these organisms eventually came to be used as indicators instead of onion roots. Gurwitsch also cites a study in which wounds in tadpoles healed more rapidly when this form of radiation was applied (Irichimowitsch/ Liosner/ Woronzewa). From these and other experiments he concluded that the mitogenetic rays are actually UV light, in the range of 1800 to 2600 ängströms.

Rahn also observed evidence for radiations that had negative effects. For instance, he found that radiations from menstrual blood could alter the cell forms of microorganisms in the laboratory or even kill them. This effect was stronger in summer than in winter. He also reviews several reports about particular women whose presence affected bacterial cultures negatively during their menses. He noted that in other instances laboratory workers of both sexes had negative effects on a particular strain of yeast. Rahn determined that this effect was related to emanations from their fingers, which could kill a particular yeast strain at a distance of a few millimeters within a period of five minutes. With other yeasts the effect was less severe.

A variety of researchers have reported similar positive results with mitogenetic radiation, but several attempts at replications were negative. These studies therefore were abandoned. It is not clear whether the entire series took into account all of the factors mentioned by Gurwitsch and others.[814] For instance, it may be that certain experimenters are able to obtain positive results while others are not, as in the *sheep/ goat* effect[815] and some aspects of radionics (Day/ de la Warr). It may also be that seasonal effects and geobiological[816] or other influences contribute to these variations.

With the observation in mind that pulsed UV light may transmit bioenergetic information, it is fascinating to survey other pilot studies that consider similar phenomena.

In Eastern European countries there has been a strong interest in the fields surrounding the body. V. M. Inyushin is a respected Russian scientist who researched biological fields that he and others believe consist of "bioplasm." He quotes Victor Adamenko (1972) in explanation of this theory:

> ...until recent times, three states of matter were known, solid, liquid, and gaseous, differing principally in the degree of packing of the molecules. Then the "fourth state of matter" was discovered, called plasma, in which the particles are ionised and charged, with free electrons mixed with them; we may have hot plasma such as occurs in stars, and cold plasma, which according to the doctrines of bioplasm, can be found in living organisms. Because the particles are charged,

they can affect the electrical fields used in Kirlian photography, and so become visible on the photographic film.[817]

Inyushin reports that bioplasma emits ultraviolet (UV) light, which he has been able to detect using photo-cells, and to record on special photographic film using cryogenic (ultra-cold) techniques to eliminate hot objects as extraneous sources of UV light.

He also found that sensitive photomultipliers were able to pick up UV emanations near the eyes of animals and humans. Variations were noted in the intensity of these emanations, related to emotions and diurnal cycles. Yet these radiations seem to consist of more than just UV light. Inyushin reports that he was able to obtain exposures on "special emulsions particularly sensitive to 'hard' components of radiation" even when metallic screens were interposed between the emulsions and the subjects' eyes so that no UV radiation could reach the film. This was successful even with exposures as brief as one-thousandth of a second.

Inyushin also reports on experiments in which healthy chicken tissues were placed in two containers next to each other, with quartz windows in the adjacent faces of the containers (Krippner 1975). When tissues in one of the containers were infected with a toxic virus, with every precaution taken not to contaminate the second one, the tissues in the second container nevertheless demonstrated identical changes, and died just as those in the first container did. Regular glass blocked this effect. This suggests that UV light may be involved in "transmitting" disease, because UV light penetrates quartz but not regular glass.

This type of experiment has been repeated a number of times using frog hearts separated by quartz glass, with similar transmission of the effects when one of the hearts was physically damaged. The second heart developed identical damage, even though it was protected from physical damage.[818] Of tangential interest is the fact that this experiment worked with spring and summer frogs but not with winter frogs.[819] At times pulsations of UV light were observed coming from the infected or poisoned heart tissues, suggesting an association of these emanations with certain stages of biological processes, infection or toxicity.

Larissa Vilenskaya (1982) refers to further observations by Inyushin. He found that two onion roots will produce a UV interference pattern when pointed in the same direction. Such observations led him to experiment with weak, pulsed laser light. He found that this could stimulate seeds to germinate faster.

Viktor Adamenko (1982) confirms yet another aspect of the pulsed emissions of UV light in mitogenetic radiation (Rahn). He reviews evidence that pulsating light appears to have salutary effects in arthritis and asthma; that pulsed stimulation of acupuncture points is more effective than steady stimulation; and that pulsed illumination of plant seeds enhances the growth of plants grown from these seeds.

Chinese researchers also report that brief pulses of light were found to emanate from a psi subject during clairvoyant perception experiments (Yongje et al.).

Russian researchers report on UV emanations from healers' bodies, especially their hands and eyes.[820] This suggests that UV light might be the source of healing energy that we are seeking. However, *UV light does not penetrate beyond the most superficial layers of the body's surface.* A. P. Dubrov (1982) hypothesizes that UV light may cause alterations in biological systems via interactions with the biological field of the organism.

Inyushin postulates that there are emissions from the tissues that act as carriers of information, possibly analogous to telepathy at a molecular level (Krippner 1975):

> A structure in the bioplasmic field is produced which acquires temporary stability, conveying mitogenic information from the living organism. This structure endures for up to five minutes, long enough to make an impression on the film emulsion. Telepathy, or biological communication, can be looked upon as a product of resonances in the bioplasmic bodies of two organisms.

He further states (Inyushin 1972):

> We envisage microbioplasmons or excitons carrying a 3-D hologram, conveying with it information relevant to the bioplasmic field of the entire organism.

The Russians have emphasized the information-carrying properties of these apparent energies. Kaznacheyev (1982) details studies of luminescence of blood with a photomultiplier. He postulates that "...blood in the human organism might be not only a carrier of nutrient substances, but also a carrier of information that might be 'written' on it in the form of a hologram that is given to tissues and organs through ultra-weak radiation in the ultraviolet or/ and other ranges of the electromagnetic spectrum" (Vilenskaya 1983). UV radiation could imprint patterns in blood elements at the surface of the skin, and this would explain how UV light emanating from a healer could be a vehicle for healing in humans. It would be difficult to see how this could apply to animals, however, as their fur would block UV patterning of blood in skin capillaries.[821]

Gennady Sergeyev (1981) reports on measurements of biological radiations in a healee prior to, during, and following a healing given by Nina Kulagina. He noted changes in the frequency of emissions from the healee.[822]

The Russian researchers do not propose how the UV emanations might originate, although they seem to imply that they are the result of ordinary metabolic processes.

Yvonne Duplessis (1985) studied the phenomenon of dermal optics, which is another aspect of information sensing. She found that people could learn to identify colors through sensations that they experienced when holding their hands on or even several inches above colored papers. Most remarkable of all, she found that *they could still do this when the colored papers were covered with metal plates.* Various colors were regularly detected at different heights above the papers, even with the metal plates intervening. The height at which individual colors were perceived differed systematically according to whether daylight or artificial light illuminated the laboratory. Duplessis' work suggests that there are energies involved in color perception that we cannot as yet identify, and that the skin may pick up information from the environment in ways that we do not understand.

Dietrich Luedtke mentions that laser light can pick up and transmit information from a liquid through which it passes. The informational component of the laser beam is not blocked by solid substances, even though the light component is blocked.

In the mid-nineteenth century, German industrialist Karl Von Reichenbach investigated energies associated with magnets (W. Mann 1973; 1983). He found that sensitive people could feel sensations of cold or "pulling" when a magnet was passed near their body. Some also saw luminous emanations in the dark from the poles of strong magnets and from crystals. (Some healers today report similar perceptions with magnets.) Reichenbach called this magnetic force *od* or *odyle*. Searching for other sources of odic energy, he found that much of the material world could, under suitable circumstances, produce it.

W. Edward Mann (1973; 1983) summarizes Reichenbach's findings on the properties and potentials of *odyle*:

1. Odyle is a universal property of all matter in variable and unequal distribution in space and time.

2. It interpenetrates and fills the structure of the universe. It cannot be eliminated or isolated from anything in nature.

3. It quickly penetrates and courses through everything.

4. It flows in concentrated form with heat, friction, sound, electricity, light, the moon, solar and stellar rays, chemical action, and organic vital activity of plants and animals, especially man.

5. It possesses polarity. There is both negative odyle, which gives a sensation of coolness and is pleasant; and positive odyle, which gives a sensation of warmth and discomfort.

6. It can be conducted, with metals, glass, resin, silk and water being perfect conductors.

7. It is radiated to a distance and these rays penetrate through clothes, bed-clothes, boards and walls.

8. Substances can be charged with odyle, or odyle may be transferred from one body to another. This is affected by contact and requires a certain amount of time.

9. It is luminous, either as a luminous glow or as a flame, showing blue at the negative and yellow-red at the positive[and] can be made to flow in any direction.

10. The aura around the body is produced by odyle, because living things contain odyle which produces a luminosity. Over 24 hours there is a periodic increase and decrease of odylic power in living things.

These observations were confirmed and extended by other researchers. The most famous of these was Wilhelm Reich, a physician and psychoanalyst who trained with Sigmund Freud. Reich (1986) was impressed that in sex as in many other functions of living organisms there is a basic, four-beat rhythm consisting of mechanical tension; bioelectric charge; bioelectric discharge; and relaxation. This is most dramatically seen in orgasm but it is also evident in rhythmic pulsations of the heart, lungs, intestines, and other body systems. Reich (1960) postulated that there is a basic energy that he called *orgone* behind this pulsation.

Reich reported finding *bions* (basic units of orgone) in many different preparations. Bions were microscopic vesicles that appeared to be organized at times into cells like protozoa, yet were distinctly different in their behaviors and properties. Reich found that cancer cells were immobilized when placed near bions. Investigators reported that their eyes were irritated with prolonged observation of bions, which suggested that bions radiated an irritant energy which Reich labeled *orgone radiation*. Certain bions could also produce discoloration, pain and inflammation of the skin when held on a glass slide in a person's palm. They also fogged photographic film. They induced the ability to see auras in people who previously had not possessed this ability. Organic insulating substances such as paper, cotton and cellulose absorbed orgone energy and could then discharge an electroscope. Such experiments led Reich to believe that the electroscope measures orgone and that static electricity is not electricity at all, but orgone.

Reich constructed a box with metal walls on the inside and organic material (such as wood) on the outside. He anticipated that orgone radiating from bion cultures would be kept within the box by the metal inner layer, while the outer layer would prevent external orgone radiation from entering. When bion cultures were placed in the box, bluish moving vapors and yellow points and lines were produced (Gallert). These visual phenomena persisted in the box even after it was ventilated, dismantled and thoroughly washed. This led to the use of such boxes as orgone accumulators. Alternate layering of metal and organic materials in the walls of the boxes increased their effectiveness as accumulators of orgone energy.

Further experimentation with orgone boxes showed that a thermometer placed above an accumulator would register 0.2 to 1.8 degrees Centigrade higher than room temperature, which suggested that orgone might be a physical energy.

Orgone also was found to have biological effects. Protozoa grew more slowly inside an accumulator, but faster when placed above one. Mice with malignant tumors who spent half an hour daily in an accumulator survived markedly longer than untreated mice. Reich also used various orgone-storing and transmitting devices to treat a variety of human illnesses.

Reich believed that orgone energy flows relatively slowly through the body, and that in some people there are blocks to the flow due to chronic tensions. When unacceptable emotion is elicited by life's circumstances, the neurotic person will unconsciously block the full, conscious, unpleasantness of the feeling, diverting it into tensions in particular parts of the body. These are comparable to body armoring, designed by the unconscious to protect the conscious mind (the *ego*) from external and internal dangers.[823]

Reich's ultimate goal was to help patients achieve an unblocked flow of energy from head to pelvis. Followers of Reich continue to focus on relaxing the physical armoring at particularly tense points. They find that this can change the patient's emotional defensive patterns.[824] One study supports this theory. A sensitive who sees auras observed patients treated by rolfing, which is a variant of Reich's methods (Hunt 1977; 1995). She reported clear changes in the patients, closely correlated with changes noted simultaneously in EM monitoring devices.

Reich's experiments with apparatus that seems to demonstrate a biological energy have been repeated by other experimenters (Gallert;: Mann). Others independently reported similar findings of apparent energies that can be blocked in the body, radiated by living organisms and transmitted by wood and silk.[825]

Two controlled studies on orgone treatments were published in German. Clinical controlled studies have yet to be published in the US due to the harassment of the FDA, so at present experimenter effects cannot be ruled out in most of the available research.[826] Nevertheless, anecdotal reports continue to suggest that there may be considerable value in orgone therapy. For instance, Myron Brenner (1991), a psychiatrist in Baltimore, reports that orgone treatments were helpful in treating chronic infections that had not responded to conventional treatments. Other therapists continue to use and study the approaches of Reich (DeMeo).

Mann briefly reviews the sad and unfortunate response of the American medicolegal establishment to Reich's work. He was hounded to jail in the early 1950's for espousing views and recommending treatments that ran counter to accepted beliefs and practices, and his books were publicly burned. He died after two years in jail. The existence of this sort of threat partially explains why these and other such unconventional energy-related phenomena have not been better studied.[827]

Further types of energies, which have been observed using unconventional methods, are suggested by other experiments.

In England, L. E. Eeman explored bioenergy transmissions within single individuals and between various people, using copper wires as conductors. With single individuals, copper gauze mats were placed under a subject's head and buttocks (at the base of the spine). A wire from each mat was held in either of the subject's hands. With the head (H) mat wire held in the left hand (L) and the spine mat wire (S) in the right hand (R) subjects reported feeling relaxed within a few minutes. Eeman called this configuration a relaxation circuit. (See Figure II-19.) If the wires were held in the opposite hands (H-R and S-L) the person soon felt tense, restless and uncomfortable. Eeman called this a tension circuit.

**Figure II-19. One subject in a relaxation circuit,
showing copper gauze mats and wire connections.**

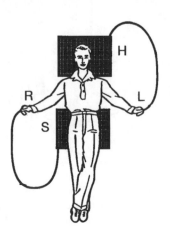

Eeman assumed that these effects are due to polarities of unknown energies in the respective parts of the body. He arbitrarily designated them as positive and negative, presuming that opposite *charges* attract and like charges repel. (See Figure II-20) He later discovered that left-handed subjects have a reversed polarity relative to right-handed people.

In another experiment, Eeman connected several subjects in one circuit. He found that if positives were connected to negatives, an even more marked sense of relaxation was produced, and conversely for the like-charged connections. Subjects regularly fell asleep for a few minutes in relaxation circuits, awaking invigorated,

Figure II-20. Classical diagram of human polarities

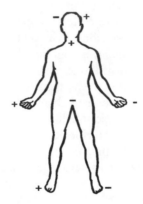

with a feeling of having rested well. Numerous subjects can be connected in series using similar mats and wires. (Fig. II-21.)

Figure II-21. Two subjects in series

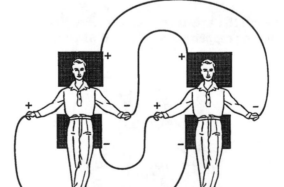

Eeman identified several different types of individual according to their characteristic functions as "valves" in his energy circuits: emitters, conductors, resisters and relayers. Further, he found that many illnesses were relieved by

and relayers. Further, he found that many illnesses were relieved by spending some time in a relaxation circuit. Conversely, normal subjects could sense the symptoms of ill people within the same circuit. A drunk in the circuit produced a mild sense of intoxication in sober participants. Only a few attempts at controls for suggestion were reported in Eeman's experiments, and the controls did not diminish the reported effects.

Eeman also discovered that if he placed a medicine such as aspirin in a liquid solution and connected it into the relaxation circuit, subjects responded as though they had taken the medicines. For instance, fevers could be lowered this way using aspirin.[828]

Eeman hypothesizes that people radiate a carrier wave that transmits information from one person to another. Conversely, the bodies of others can resonate with the originator of a state or sensation.

Aubrey Westlake (1973) suggested that the energies Eeman was investigating might be transmitted by materials other than copper wires. Eeman checked this hypothesis and found that silk was also effective as a conductor.

Leslie Patten and Terry Patten (1989) review many further experiments performed by Eeman and others. In one of these, an acute illness appeared to be ameliorated through the influence of another person in a circuit who had recuperated from that illness. This suggests that antibodies may have an energy field component. Placing left-handed people in circuits with right-handed people introduced tension, which was dissipated if lefties' heads and feet were placed next to the feet and heads, respectively, of the righties' heads and feet. The Pattens' review contains many other interesting observations on these apparent energetic phenomena.

Julian Isaacs and Terry Patten report on a double-blind controlled study of biocircuits' effects on EEGs, EMGs and GSRs. The EEGs and EMGs demonstrated significant relaxation responses. Subjective reports differentiated between real and placebo circuit effects on relaxation and other sensations.

Some of Eeman's approaches and findings appear to be echoed in the healing methods of *Polarity Therapy*, where healers intuitively sense body polarities and rebalance those that are disharmonious (R. Gordon; F. Sills 1989).

Recent research by William Tiller (2003a; b), Professor Emeritus of Physics at Stanford University shows that an intentionally imprinted electrical device (IIED) can be used to alter the acidity of water. The devices were imprinted in one laboratory, then mailed to another laboratory hundreds of miles away, with identical control devices. Each was marked with a code so that the second laboratory researchers were blind to which was the imprinted device. Intents imprinted in these devices to either increase or decrease the acidity of water were able to significantly alter the water acidity in the predicted directions. This suggests that intent may include a force or energy that can influence matter. As Tiller notes, this is very similar in action to a healing intent that brings about physical changes in biological systems. Even more fascinating is the imprinting of intent to alter water in a laboratory in England - prior to the arrival of the IIED in the mail (Tiller 2003c).

LESSONS FROM BIOLOGICAL ENERGY FIELD STUDIES

There is convincing evidence from the numerous research and anecdotal reports reviewed in this volume and in Volume I of *Healing Research* that biological energy fields are found around all living things.[829] There would appear to be many levels of fields, including those that are found in cells, organs, and the entire living organism.

The reports reviewed suggest that these fields interact with environmental energies and with inputs from several types of more local external fields, which I will describe briefly here.

Electromagnetic fields: Minute inputs of external EM energy facilitate physical self-healing of some physical disorders, such as fractures. Chronic exposures to mild fields and shorter exposures to stronger fields appear to be deleterious.[830]

The work of Burr, Ravitz and others correlating L-fields with physiological and geobiological processes suggests that all living things resonate with each other and with geological and cosmic fields. Their hypotheses on the *organizing* nature of DC fields, though logical, are still speculative. These fields may be produced as a result of biological processes involved in metabolic and/ or neuronal activity, as postulated by Glazewski.

The studies cited by Burr in which predictions are made of behavioral and physiological changes in living organisms, which can be anticipated through periodicities in external field shifts, lend more support to the hypothesis that external fields may influence biological systems. This is especially true where such periodicities are noted across numerous species. However, alternative hypotheses are also possible. Seasonal changes in the length of day, atmospheric ionic concentrations, or other, unknown factors may account for some of these cross-species periodicities. That is, factors such as changes in the length of the day may trigger physiological adjustments that secondarily influence the fields produced by the organism.

The evidence from experiments with flatworms seems to prove conclusively that fields can organize body processes. Becker's work with salamander limb regeneration adds weight to these arguments, as does the example of the perfect regeneration of severed fingertips.

An alternative explanation for the fingertip regeneration, however, is that there are organizing fields generated from within the body that maintain its integrity. These may be summations of minute atomic and/ or molecular fields from protein molecules or from clusters of individual cells, which may be expressed via processes that are just starting to be clarified under *chaos (complexity) theory* (Gleick).[831] Organizing fields could also be generated by the glial cells which surround nerves, as suggested by Becker and his co-authors. Chaos theory explains how simple, repetitive summations of mathematical equations can produce regular patterns that are commonly found in nature, for example in the shapes of plants. It is possible that similar summations of biological EM fields might organize various aspects of body structure and functions.

That external fields may reorganize body processes is demonstrated by the healing of fractures (Becker) and by the successful treatment of cancer with DC currents (Nordenström). This, in turn, suggests a possibility that EM healing effects may operate through body/ organ energy fields. Some self-healing and spiritual healing effects might also be mediated by EM effects within the body, perhaps initiated by neurohormonal mechanisms triggered by suggestion or by spiritual healing.

Becker's work with mechanical models suggests that the nervous system is a source of DC fields. It may also be that the nervous system acts as an antenna or channel for external fields. Gary Schwartz and colleagues confirmed that the human body can act "as a strong antenna and/ or receiver for electrostatic body-motion" at a distance of 5 to 25 cm. from an electronic sensor. Schwartz and colleagues also note that with hypnoanalgesia, a suggestion can be given that a person's tactile perception will be anesthetized as though a glove were covering one hand. Not only does the suggestion reduce pain perception, but it also reduces electromagnetic field gradients over the entire hand. This is particularly interesting, because the analgesia does not follow the patterns of the nerves in the hand. That is, several nerves running to the hand begin producing a weaker EM field, starting at the wrist. This shows that the mind can influence EM aspects of bio-energy.

Some people appear hyper-allergic to EM fields, become severely symptomatic when exposed to certain EM frequencies. Conversely, alleviation of allergic reactions have been reported through exposure to particular EM frequencies (C. Smith et al 1985)

The enhancement of bone knitting and chronic wound healing with DC inputs is marvelous in and of itself. This phenomenon makes it clear that there are latent regenerative potentials in the body. Sadly, this discovery has also illustrated the initial reluctance of the medical establishment to explore unconventional findings.

In summary, at this stage of our study of bioelectromagnetics, we can say that there appears to be an organizational level within the body at which EM fields can at least transmit information about body growth and physical healing. The EM fields may act as templates for growth and physiological functions. It is conceivable that this EM level could act as an antenna or resonating field for healing that is directed from outside the organism. It may also mediate mind/ body or spiritual self-healing.

Spiritual Healing and EM effects: If the fields around living things have organizing properties, then healing may act via these fields. In touch healing or near-the-body healing, the agent or channel of healing may be EM, UV, infrasound or other emanations from healers' bodies. Alternatively, healing could function via resonations, transdimensional coupling or other sorts of interactions between the fields of the healers and those of the healees. Such field interactions might explain the sensations that are experienced by healers and healees (warmth, tingling, etc.) during healings.

EM effects might also be produced indirectly via telepathic influence on the healees, who then activate their own self-healing powers through their bodies' EM fields.

Eeman's observations of polarities in the body overlap with the work of Burr, Ravitz and Becker. Eeman's experiments with interconnections of polar points on the body using various wires or silk as conductors appear well worth further

study. The existence of a type of energy other than the EM spectrum is suggested
– particularly if effects of medications and resonations with the illness of someone in the biocircuits can be sensed by others linked in the biocircuits.

Reich's orgone energy may be similar to Eeman's energies, in that it can be
transmitted via wires. Reich's observations on the induction or enhancement of
aura perception via exposure to orgone radiations are most interesting. Perhaps
exposure to such energy sensitizes one to experiencing its effects.

Ultraviolet light and biophotons: The report by Rahn demonstrating that mitogenetic radiations enhanced wound healing in a salamander appears at first glance
to point to UV light as a likely agent for healing effects. Kaznacheyev proposes
that blood may transmit information to tissues and organs via the UV light that it
emits. This provides yet another alternative means (in addition to interactions
with organizing fields) through which UV light from external sources might affect internal organs, despite the fact that the original light cannot penetrate deeper
than the skin. In addition, UV light may act upon total-body fields, which then
influence physical processes. The observation that water may demonstrate
changes in its UV range after healing treatments supports this possibility (Dean
1983; Schwartz et al.). It may be that water in the blood or body tissues is patterned by UV light or by subtle energies.

The reports by Rahn and Adamenko (1982) regarding the efficacy of pulsed
light may indicate another fertile area for exploration in the relationship between
field effects and healing. Perhaps more successful healers have oscillations in
their fields that enhance their effectiveness. The vibrations of healers' hands and
the sensations of vibration and tingling that are experienced during healing by
healers and healees alike may be related to such field oscillations.

Eeman's observations on the transmission of the effects of medicines and immunity via wires connecting people in his healing circuits seem revolutionary.
They may point to an efficacy of medications that does not function via chemical
effects but rather through field or healing energy interactions with the fields and
energies of the body. This is supported by Smith and Best's reports on electromagnetic patterning of allergies, and by subtle energy observations from the
modalities of homeopathy, other complementary therapies, radionics, Kirlian photography and recent research with crystals and lasers.

Distant healings: We cannot explain distant healings as the result of EM effects
because the strength of EM fields decreases with distance from their source.
Therefore the strength of EM signals could not be sufficient to influence healees
across many miles, though healing effects have been confirmed at such distances
in randomized controlled trials.[832]

One might hypothesize that healers influence healees' EM fields directly via PK.
This possibility is supported by studies demonstrating significant psi effects registered on EM equipment, such as random number generators, showing psi effects
over great distances. This is not meant to explain distant healing per se, since psi
effects over great distances have yet to be explained too. It does suggest, however, a possible way in which EM fields may be involved in distant healings.
Intentionality would appear to be the causal agent in this case.

Distant healing effects may be explained eventually as *tunneling* through other dimensions, or through as yet unidentified processes.[833]

The sensations felt by healees during distant healings are hard to explain on the basis of field interactions.[834] It is possible that these sensations are independent of healer-healee field interactions, and the field hypothesis still holds. One would have to postulate an unknown energy source in this case, because healing seems to work regardless of distance. Alternatively, the sensations may be produced by processes that are triggered by self-healing within the healees' bodies, regardless of whether it is initiated through touch or distant healing.

In summary: A substantial body of evidence suggests the existence of bioenergies that are not recognized within conventional science. Western science assumes that there are no energies beyond the basic four discussed earlier. However, in quantum physics there is a growing acknowledgement of the role of consciousness in selecting processes that determine which of several quantum pathways are followed. The precise mechanisms by which consciousness could interact with matter and energy have not yet been clarified.

The East Europeans' theories on bioplasma and UV rays seem at variance with Western scientific thinking. For many years they have been more open than the West to studying healing phenomena and to utilizing healers in clinical settings. In part this is due to the economic straits in the East that make healing and other CAM therapies attractive (Grigoriantz).

My own best guess is that there are biological energies that are as yet unidentified by conventional science. These energies may overlap in some respects with EM energy. Alternatively, they may produce EM energy secondarily during phase shifts of whatever brings about healing, possibly through various dimensions of reality beyond our familiar three dimension – much as heat may be produced when liquids change to solids, or as a byproduct of electrical transformers.

It seems certain that healing energy interacts with the mind and emotions of all participants in experiments on healing effects. These bioenergies may link with the mind or be an aspect of mind. The general acknowledgement of such a mind/energy or mind-energy link could conceivably advance the search for a unified field theory in quantum physics.[835] Consciousness may eventually become a variable in the equations of a future elaboration of quantum physics.

Living organisms are probably the most sensitive sensors for these energies, though people may require practice to perceive them consciously and to identify them reliably. Our extreme sensitivity leaves us open to distractions and distortions from extraneous "noise," such as geomagnetic forces.[836] Rather than rejecting biological sensors on this basis, I see room to refine their focus and their ability to screen helpful signals. For instance, we might schedule our measurements to take into account geomagnetic fields, sunspots and other influences that alter biological systems, so that we can increase the reliability of human sensors. Multiple sensors can be used to seek common denominators of perceptions, which would likewise help to sift out some of the "noise."

The above-mentioned reports and speculations on fields and energies are only a meager beginning in our attempt to explain the mechanisms of self-healing and spiritual healing. Clairsentients and mystics have been talking about visible and palpable *energy bodies* around the physical body for several millennia. Our western materialistic conditioning makes it hard for us to accept such reports from a gifted few, when the rest of us "normal" folk cannot validate them for ourselves. How much moreso with observations of mystics about astral bodies and other levels of existence. Readings on instruments that indicate various quantifiable physical forces and energies seem much more believable. However, even with so-called objective measurements we have not arrived at definitions and explanations of our world that are beyond question. We often forget that we must add our own interpretations to these instrument readings in order for them to have any meaning. Furthermore, mechanistic science starts with axioms of belief just as energy medicine does. Both provide models that are useful, each in their own domains, but they all will inevitably be altered with further study.

See Table II-10 for a comparison of the world of quantum physics and the world of Newtonian physics, and Table II-8 for a comparison of CAM therapies with conventional medicine, or – in the light of our discussion in this chapter, we might say this is a comparison of energy medicine with Newtonian medicine.

Table II-10. Various ways to define the world	
Quantum physics $\qquad$ $E = mc^2$ $\qquad$ **Newtonian physics**	
Particles and energies are interconvertible.	Matter and energies (mechanical, electromagnetic, gravity) are distinct.
Action can occur from any distance.	Action is local, and effects diminish with distance.
Holographic world	Linear/ spatial world
Observer may determine reality.	Mind is separate from the physical world, a product of the brain.
Time is reversible.	Time is a linear stream.

Hopefully, researchers will confirm and extend these pioneering works that have enhanced our comprehension of mankind's energetic relationship with the universe. We may then see the development of instruments that measure biological fields reliably, or we may learn to refine the human biological instrument itself. Then we can develop frameworks that more satisfactorily explain spiritual healing.

Western scientific paradigms will have to change to accommodate these findings, and quantum physics appears to be moving already in this direction. Particularly in its observational theories we find hints that mind may interact with matter, and thus we may find within quantum theory a reciprocal basis for understanding healing.[837]

We should not delay the use of *biological energy medicine* or *vibrational medicine* techniques (Gerber) till definitive theories are developed and validated. There is already sufficient empirical evidence that these techniques are effective.

> *Our life is frittered away by detail... Simplify, simplify.*
> $\qquad$ – Henry David Thoreau (1854)

CHAPTER 4

Geobiological Effects

> *Men often stumble over the truth*
> *but most of them pick themselves up*
> *and hurry off as if nothing had happened.*
> *– Winston Churchill*

In the preceding chapter we examined a variety of fields and forces that exist in and around the body. Some are within the electromagnetic (EM) spectrum that is recognized by conventional science. Other energy phenomena seem to contradict the basic laws of conventional science, and provide strong hints that the accepted energy spectrum must be expanded to include several new types of fields and energies.

In this chapter we shall examine fields in the natural environment that may interact with biological energy fields. Some of these can be measured by electromagnetic devices, while others are only perceptible to particularly sensitive people.

We shall start with various geobiological[838] effects that have been observed by dowsers and supported by scientific research. Then we shall consider evidence for astrological influences that may interact with biological systems.

RADIESTHESIA (DOWSING) AND RADIONICS

> *At one of his trials, Jurion was testifying about patients he had cured by dows-*
> *ing remedies when, suddenly and savagely, the judge turned on him to shout*
> *sarcastically: "This tribunal is not objecting to your curing people but to your*
> *treating them."*
> *– Christopher Bird*

The Chinese have studied the effects of *feng shui* from at least the ninth century AD. Experts in this field can sense earth energies and advise people about the selection of sites for houses and graves, or about positive and negative vibrations at a certain location that may bring good or bad luck.[839] According to this system, certain architectural structures and configurations within a home are health-promoting and others may have deleterious effects on inhabitants' health. Strategically placing mirrors, plants, and other objects can correct bad energy configurations. Various parts of a home and areas within each room relate to different aspects of one's life. (See figure II-9, The Bagua, in Chapter II-2.)

Sacred geometry is the study of how aesthetically and spiritually pleasing shapes of rooms and buildings can influence the way we feel within those spaces. Thomas Moore terms this *"Genius loci,* the spirit of a place." It has been recognized for ages that certain proportions of length, width and height are inherently aesthetically pleasing. Mystical properties have been attributed to particular measurements, some of which appear repeatedly in nature, as in the chambers of a snail shell and the structure of plant leaves (Lawlor).

I have not made a study of sacred geometry, as I have not found research to validate the reported effects on health. Sacred geometry was also applied by ancient cultures to the study of the planet Earth (W. Becker/ Hagens).[840]

Beyond aesthetics of ambience, there are intuitive perceptions of positive and negative subtle energies that are inherent in any location. You have probably experienced a sense of positive energies when visiting particular places in nature, or perhaps some houses of worship. Conversely you may have sensed negative energies in other places in nature or in particular buildings that appear to induce a sense of gloom, tension or foreboding. People who are sensitive to subtle energies have many explanations for these perceptions. The simplest is that the presence or lack of healing energies can produce such sensations. These energies may occur naturally in particular locations or they may be the result of prayers or healing activities that are conducted there. Electromagnetic and chemical pollution may produce negative feelings in a given place.[841] In addition, our intuitive and bio-energy awarenesses can connect with the vibrations of a place, giving us an inner knowing of its positive or negative nature.

One way of detecting earth energies is through dowsing. *Dowsing,* or *geomancy,* has been used in Western culture for centuries. The earliest published report, *De re Metallica* by Georgius Agricola, dates from 1556.

Dowsers are gifted people who are able to locate water, oil and other minerals in the earth with the aid of various simple instruments. While dowsing may appear odd to many readers of this book, dowsers' abilities have been used to great advantage in numbers of situations. Dowsers have helped in the U S Army Corps of Engineers and the military to clear minefields and to locate enemy installations underground (H. Baldwin), and by various civilian utility companies to locate buried pipes and power lines.

Various devices are used by dowsers. Some use forked sticks or Y-shaped, flexible plastic rods, which they hold, flexed in front of them in a state of tension, while walking back and forth over the land they are exploring. The dowser holds the image of the desired material in his mind, and when he passes over it, the forked branch will bend sharply downward. Others use L-shaped wires held parallel in each hand, encased in a loose metal or plastic sleeve so that they are free to swivel. When passing over the sought material the wires will diverge or converge from their initial parallel positions. Some dowsers use a pendulum, which they typically hold over the ground or over a map of the territory while the dowser is thinking about a specific question relating to the material in the ground.

Dowsers may use their intuitive powers to answer any yes/ no questions, including those relating to health and illness. Various types of pendulum motion give the dowser answers. For instance, a swing away from the body and back may indicate a "yes" and a swing parallel to the body a "no," or a clockwise turn may indicate "yes" and counterclockwise, "no." The pendulum may also be swung above a radial chart to indicate the degree to which a factor is present, such as the rate of flow of an underground stream, the severity of an illness, or the required strength of a medication. Dowsers report that they themselves are not consciously manipulating the devices, although many acknowledge that their unconscious minds are probably providing the impetus through their muscles. The more sensitive dowsers rely on sensations such as heat in their hands, pains in various parts of their bodies, smells, etc. as indicators, and do not use any mechanical device.

Map dowsing
Many dowsers claim that they can dowse for items within a territory by using a map. The map seems to function as a *witness,* which in dowsers' terminology is an object that connects the dowser psychically with whatever she wants to focus upon. In some instances dowsers claim greater accuracy when they are facing in a particular compass direction – either for map or field dowsing.

Others may use *radionics* devices (sometimes affectionately called *black boxes*) for diagnosis and treatment. These have a range of dials and compartments for specimens from the patient. In an earlier model of the box, a rubber diaphragm was rubbed with a finger until a particular sensation was felt, which indicated that the device was tuned to the vibration of the item that was being sought mentally by the dowser. More modern devices have electrical dials for assessing health problems of patients, described below.

The distance of dowsers from the object of their dowsing is no obstacle to success in locating it or in projecting healing. Many dowsers find they are equally effective in dowsing a map of the territory as they are in the field, and this is equally true with radionics devices, which may be located many miles from the target person.

Dowsing for diagnosis and treatment
Dowsers may ask their pendulum or other device to identify illnesses in people, animals and plants. They arrive at the answers through a series of Yes/ No queries or through swinging the pendulum over radially distributed lists of problems, percentages of deficits, doses of medication and the like. When the patient is not present, dousers usually prefer to use a *witness,* which can be any object closely associated with the healee, in order to link with her. The witness may, for example, be a lock of hair, a drop of spittle, urine or blood on a piece of blotting paper, a photograph, or an object belonging to the healee. Lacking these, the healee's name written on a piece of paper may suffice.

Devices with electronic dials plus visual and/ or tonal outputs have accompanied dowsing into the modern age. The devices may utilize sealed vials of toxic and medicinal materials in place of the dowser's mental image as a focus for tuning. A person with chronic tiredness, for example, will be told to hold an electrode attached to such a dowsing device. As the dowser puts each of a series of vials of toxins in the diagnostic chamber, he places an electronic probe on an acupuncture point. The dial will give a reading indicating whether the healee's body contains the given chemical at deficient, normal or toxic levels. Similarly, tests can be made for allergens or vitamin deficiencies, and for predicting the efficacy of therapeutic agents.

With all of these devices, the operator appears to be an essential link with the instrument, though many dowsers who use them tend to project the responsibility for the results entirely onto the devices. This is patently impossible with the rubber diaphragm radionics device, as the boxes have no intrinsic circuitry that can do more than provide mental focus and/ or feedback to the operator. Some radionics practitioners propose that these devices, in and of themselves, hold and/ or project healing energies (of an as yet undetermined nature), once they are tuned by the practitioner.

One unique contribution of dowsing to the field of energy medicine is the ability to identify illnesses that are caused by underground streams or other sources of negative earth energies, called *geopathic zones*. These are said to stress people who spend time over them, for example when sleeping or working regularly above a geopathic zone. Moving one's bed or workstation away from these zones has been reported to cure a variety of problems, such as insomnia, arthritis, chronic fatigue syndrome and more. Alternatively, spikes or pipes can be driven into the ground at particular points along the negative energy line to neutralize its effects, or to transform its emanations to positive energy.

Radionics practitioners claim that they can tune their devices to send healing vibrations to correct a wide variety of problems that are causing illness or harm to plants, animals and humans. Radionics treatments consist of tuning the dials on the device to vibrational frequencies that are corrective for chemical deficiencies, allergies, infections and toxicities. Radionics specialists have also reported successes in treating infections, possession by errant or malevolent spirits,[842] and infestations of insect pests in crops. The recipient of radionics treatments is a passive subject to the ministrations of the radionics operator.

Radionics devices have also been developed to produce homeopathic remedies. They utilize vibrational patterns printed on cards to transfer therapeutic vibrations to the carrier solution or to the sugar pills that are used for homeopathic treatments (M. Rae).

Sensitive medical dowsers may gradually develop conscious powers of clairsentience so that eventually they rely on their instruments less or not at all. Then they can simply ask their questions mentally, and the answers come to them intuitively. Some also develop healing abilities that operate independently of their devices.

Some skeptics have suggested that dowsers may simply be well-versed in geology and/ or keen observers of various cues that they can translate into intuitive impressions (as in pattern recognition based on accumulated unconscious knowledge), which are projected onto their devices. Others have hypothesized that dowsers may be extra-sensitive to various EM or other known radiations.

Your reasoning is excellent - it's only your basic assumptions that are wrong.

– Ashleigh Brilliant (no. 601)

Let us examine the research evidence, starting with field dowsing and extending into medical dowsing.

Research

Field dowsing is the term commonly applied to the locating of materials and objects in the greater world using intuitive means.

The classical use of dowsing is to locate underground streams for wells. Under sponsorship of the German government, physicist Hans-Dieter Betz studied dowsers in Sri Lanka over a 10-year period. In 691 drillings they achieved a success rate of 96 percent, compared to the 30-50 percent success rates anticipated when drillings in this area are based on geological recommendations. Even more impressive was the fact that the dowsers predicted the depth at which water would be found and the amounts of flow, within a 20-30 percent margin of error, *prior to drilling.*

A. M. Comunetti (1978) discovered that Hoffman-La Roche, a major drug company in Basle, relied on two sensitive employees to dowse for underground sources of water for their chemical plants around the world. Comunetti tested these dowsers in the corridors of the multi-story Basle factory for their abilities to identify a source of water that was several floors below. Even with blindfolds or blinkers (which prevented them from seeing the walls or the floor of the corridors) they were reliably able to identify the location of the source of water. As Comunetti had each of the dowsers approach the area of the water source from both directions, it became apparent that one dowser was sensitive to the borders of the water zone, and the other to the body of the zone.

Continuing his investigations, Comunetti (1979) set up a series of parallel pipes along the floor of a warehouse. The pipes were clustered together so that a stream of water could be directed through each of them individually, in parallel. The pipes were made of glass, 5 cm in diameter and 2 meters long. One was clear and the others were filled with sand. This enabled the experimenter to vary the amount of flow systematically, up to 10 liters/ minute. The dowsers walked along a platform that was 8.8 meters long, and raised 2.1 meters above the water source. One dowser could identify when water was flowing in the sandy pipes but not in the clear one. The other could not sense a flow of water, even when he knew the water was turned on. When a layer of sand 10 - 15 cm thick was placed on top of the pipes, both dowsers felt the flows much more clearly.[843] Comunetti tested the dowsers with blindfolds (gas masks with blackened glasses), both walking and riding on a cable-trolley that was remote-controlled. The dowsers knew the location of the pipes but not when the water was turned on and off – that was determined by the toss of a coin for each trial. Intervals between trials were 2 to 4 minutes. The dowsers were successful in 4 out of 8 series of between 10 and 11 trials each (p < .011 - 006).

Comunetti initially intended to vary the position of the water pipes. In exploratory trials he found that there was a linger effect at the initial location that lasted for 5 - 15 minutes. That is to say, the dowsers would identify the previous location of the water pipes during the first 5 to 15 minutes after the pipes had been moved.[844] J. B. Rhine, a methodical parapsychology investigator, challenged two dowsers to identify whether water was flowing in two hidden underground pipes over which they walked carrying dowsing rods. The dowsers scored significantly lower than chance in one series of trials and somewhat above chance in another series. There was a decline in success rate as the experiment progressed.

Remi Cadoret asked dowsers to locate a penny that was hidden under one of 25 tiles. The dowsers produced results that were statistically marginally significant in a series of trials. In another experiment dowsers used a map corresponding to a grid in Cadoret's back yard to locate a buried penny. Again, marginally significant results were obtained.

Karlis Osis, at the Parapsychology Laboratory of Duke University, tested a dowser who worked for a gas company. Osis placed 18-inch long segments of pipes randomly in ten trenches he had dug in the ground, and covered them with boards. In tests where Osis was blind to the location of the pipes, the results were marginally significant; for the entire series, the results were highly significant. Osis also tested the dowser for the ability to locate money hidden under one of 25 tiles. Results were marginally significant.

D. H. Pope reported on results of experiments by a lecturer in biology at Harrogate Training College in England. A dowser was challenged to locate a coin under pieces of cardboard. Despite the fact that only 63 trials were run, the results were highly significant. Unfortunately, sensory cues were not entirely ruled out. Stage magicians have demonstrated that such cues can very often reveal hidden objects to a person who is seeking them. When people know the location of a hidden object, they very often provide non-verbal indications, such as glancing at the location or tensing up as the magician moves closer to it.

L. A. Dale et al. found only random results in a study of 27 dowsers who tried to locate natural sources of water and to estimate depth and rate of flow.

Benson Herbert[845] (1979a), an English parapsychologist, pointed out that the pendulum used by dowsers does not move of its own accord but rather due to minute motions of the dowsers' hands or via their breath. Herbert clearly demonstrated this by holding the string of the dowsers' pendulums in a fixed clamp and/or under a glass bell. In such cases the dowsers were unable to make the pendulum sway. Benson tested a dowser by asking him to identify under which of two paper wrappings a coin and a rock were placed. Only random results were produced. Herbert was doubtful that any psi effects are involved in dowsing.

N. B. Eastwood found that if dowsers' hands and forearms were covered with aluminum foil their ability to dowse with forked twigs was blocked, but their dowsing ability with pendulums and rods was unchanged. Foil over the chin and jaw blocked only the pendulum, and foil over the upper face and upper abdomen blocked only the rods.

Dowsing of EM fields has been studied to explore whether dowsers might obtain information on EM wavelengths.

Zaboj V. Harvalik (1973a; b) was a professor of physics retired from the University of Arkansas and a former adviser to American Army Advanced Concepts

Materials Agency. He describes a series of tests with a German master dowser, Wilhelm de Boer. The dowser walked perpendicularly to the current flow of 5 milli-amperes, which was gradually reduced in successive tests to 2.5 micro-amperes, and de Boer was still able to identify the signal by dowsing for it. Rest periods of 5 to 10 minutes were needed between every 10 to 12 runs. He was successful 100% of the time when his left side faced the negative electrode, and unsuccessful 100% of the time when his left side faced the positive electrode.

In another experiment, Harvalik blindfolded de Boer and had him walk in circles past one of two generators (operating in the 7-m and 5-cm bands, on 1.0 watt and 0.2 watts, respectively). The generators were switched on and off at random. Forty runs were made with the generators on. The position of the generator coils was varied so that as the dowser passed the generators, he sometimes crossed the magnetic vectors and sometimes did not. The dowser was able to reliably identify when he crossed the radiation beam. A copper mesh screen interrupting the beam prevented him from receiving a signal. If the copper screen was used as a mirror to deflect the beam into his path, the dowser did note a signal.

No blinds are described by Harvalik, nor are the numbers of trials or successes given. It is implied that the dowser was entirely accurate. The only discrepancy noted was on an indoor trial where the beam was pointed vertically towards the ceiling and the dowser reported a weak signal. This was explained as a possible detection of reflected signals.

Harvalik then proceeded to test de Boer with partial screening of the dowser's body by copper wire mesh. The screening totally interrupted the dowser's ability to identify the signal when it was placed before his solar plexus, and partially obstructed his ability when his head was shielded. Harvalik postulates that the presence of two parts of the body where dowsing sensors are apparently located may enable dowsers to discriminate gradients of magnetic fields. The sensing of EM fields from two points on the body might provide indications of the materials and objects for which they are dowsing, as the EM fields (or other bioenergy vibrations) of objects in the environment may have different "tonal qualities" when perceived through the two separate sensors. With auditory perceptions, it is possible to set up an interference pattern within the brain by inputting different sound frequencies into each ear. Having two sensors for dowsed vibrations may set up interference patterns that provide identifying clues to the dowser as to the nature of the items that are being perceived.

Having two sensors could also provide perceptions that are similar to the depth perception that is possible when two eyes view an object from different angles. This may explain their reputed abilities to identify the depth at which minerals are located, just as stereoscopic vision enables depth perception.

Harvalik (1978) repeated the blocking experiments with fourteen dowsers, using a low-power, high-frequency EM field and pieces of aluminum sheet placed over the kidneys and brain. In 694 trials they were able to guess correctly whether the field was on or off 661 times. This is one of the most convincing studies, as it was conducted with a double-blind design and the field was switched on and off on a random schedule. It is unclear, however, whether the dowsers were aware of the experimental hypotheses about the locations of sensitive body zones, so one still has to view with caution the blocking aspect of this study.

Harvalik concludes from a long series of studies that sensitive dowsers can respond to changes in magnetic fields of .000001 gauss per second, and exceptional dowsers can detect changes 100 times weaker (G. Hansen).[846]

Sol Tromp (1949), a Dutch geology professor and director of the Bioclimatological Centre of Leiden, also tested dowsers' sensitivity to EM fields with a tangent galvanometer and a coil of wire. Elaborate precautions were taken to limit extraneous cues. These included using noiseless switches on the electrical equipment, blindfolds, and cotton earplugs, as well as keeping the experimenter who was recording responses blind to whether the current was on or off. Using U-shaped rods, dowsers were able to detect alterations in the strength of the EM field at gradients under 0.1 gauss per meter. They could identify shifts and changes in the field, but not field strength per se. In the first 20 trials sensitive dowsers had an 80% rate of accuracy, but after this they complained of fatigue and their success rate subsequently declined.

Tromp noted that some dowsers were able to detect EM fields with the aid of pendulums when they had failed with the U-shaped rods. Pendulum dowsers were also able to identify differences in field strength.

Yves Rocard,[847] a physics professor at the École Normale in Paris, also confirmed that dowsers could identify alterations in a DC EM field using rods (of a different configuration from those used by Tromp). He found that at the level of the chest their sensitivity was in the range of 0.3 - 0.5 milli-ohms/ meter (approximately 0.0003 - 0.0005 gauss/ m) when the dowsers were walking at normal speed (1 - 2 meters/ second). Gradients above a certain level (not specified in the article) were not detected and were presumed to produce *saturation* of the dowsers. Magnets attached to the forearms of the dowsers also blocked their perceptions of fields. Responses were poorer with the use of pendulums. Hansen (1982), my source for the review of this French study, makes no mention of blinds.

R. A. Foulkes, testing only one dowser, failed to replicate Rocard's work.

P. Kiszkowski and H. Szydlowski found that it was impossible to reproduce Rocard's results when they replicated his experiments. They then explored dowsers' sensitivity to AC EM fields at voltages of 15 or 150 Hz using aluminum electrodes 10 cm in diameter. They found that different dowsers were able to detect EM fields over different parts of their bodies. The dowsers did not know when the current was switched on. When electrodes 12 cm in diameter were held near the hand of a dowser, the pendulum often swung in a particular direction which was often parallel to the direction of the electric fields. Positive results were noted in the range of 0.1 to 10,000 Hz with a field strength of 1 V/ m. Factors that were found to influence the results included the duration of the sessions and the time of day. After two hours of experimentation they could not obtain reproducible results.

König et al. also explored dowsers' responses to EM fields. The dowsers were required to identify one of the following:

1. Where an EM field was located within a given area;
2. When a field from a known source was switched on or off; or
3. Which of several EM devices was switched on.

The last two produced clearer results, as only yes/ no responses were required. Following the format used by Fadini,[848] spools of half a meter in diameter with 24 windings of wire were mounted on wooden supports about 1.5 meters high. No shielding was used over the leads, so stray currents of about 10^{-6} Volts/ m were detectable at distances of 0.5 to 1 m around the coils. Subjects who felt that they could tell the difference between on and off conditions were challenged to identify which one of a row of 8 coils was switched on. In the initial trials the subjects were blind to which coil was on but the experimenter was not. The dowsing rods moved for most subjects when they were still 1 - 2 meters or more away from the coils.[849] The series of 8 coils is preferable because the repetitive testing procedure with only one coil is fatiguing to the dowsers. In this series situation a frequency of 30 Hz was used, and the current (which determined intensity) was varied. Under single-blind conditions the correct coil was identified in 23 out of 46 trials (p < .0001).

People who trained to develop their sensitivity to EM fields spontaneously developed an ability to dowse for water. However, the experimenters could not identify EM fields around the water sources identified by dowsers.

Duane Chadwick and Larry Jensen, two electrical engineers at Utah State University, asked ungifted subjects to mark places along a prescribed path where their dowsing rods indicated a reaction. Chadwick and Jensen then measured EM variations along the path. Various dowsers' marks clustered significantly around particular locations and these were more likely to be areas with a gradient of 0.5 gamma per foot (0.000016 gauss/ m). Statistics for correlation between clustered and other measured locations are not presented in their report.

W. H. Jack, an instructor in parapsychology at Franklin Pierce College in New Hampshire, asked twelve ungifted subjects to use dowsing rods to detect whether a current of 0.1 amp was or was not flowing through an electrical wire. His subjects achieved significant results, but proper blinds were not included in the study.

Colin Godman and Lindsay St. Claire report on attempts to demonstrate the effectiveness of dowsing by using it to map underground caves and locating men who were hidden in them. Results were partially successful but no quantification of the data was built into the study design.

J. L. Whitton and S. A. Cook tested 27 people, two of whom claimed dowsing abilities, using weak EM fields produced by alternating current. They tested another 11 people (none of whom claimed dowsing ability) using a direct current coil. Using L-rods, only chance results were obtained.

E. Balanovski and J. G. Taylor (1978) found dowsers insensitive to magnetic fields of 100 gauss, and to high-frequency, low-power electromagnetic fields.[850]

Electrodermal responses during dowsing

Dowsers often complain of severe physiological reactions, such as dizziness, nausea, and pains, when they are exposed to negative earth energies. Changes in the voltage gradient of a person's skin reflect stress (which provides the physiological basis for lie detector tests). Recordings of *electrodermal activity* (EDA) during dowsing have thus provided measures of dowsing-related stress responses.

Tromp connected the wrists of dowsers to an Eindhoven string galvanometer to record skin potential. Insulated grips were provided for the loop-shaped rods. Alterations in EDA were noted immediately after a magnetic field was turned on. Similar readings were obtained with dowsers walking through "dowsing zones." Tromp presents evidence to counter the possibility that the altered galvanometer measurements were due to emotional reactions or induction potentials. For example, similar measurements were recorded with dowsers walking through "dowsing zones" without rods. Less sensitive people demonstrated similar, though slower and less marked EDA when walking through such zones. Tromp found that sensitive dowsers had a baseline skin resistance that was much lower than that of other people. Sketchy mention is also made of EDA that was recorded when dowsers moved rods over the heads and feet of subjects.

Kenneth Roberts, a historical novelist, reports a study by American electrical engineers of the EDA of Henry Gross, a famous dowser. They noted changes in his EDA during several trials at map dowsing, and a 100-millivolt change when he walked over underground water. A subsequent series of map dowsing trials did not produce significant results. In another series of tests, skin potential changes of 100 to 200 millivolts were noted in a Canadian dowser, Desrosiers, when he walked over a known water vein. Desrosiers worked without instruments, dowsing through sensations of pain in the soles of his feet and in the small of his back. Non-dowsers showed only 10 - 30 millivolt changes when walking over the same territory.

Berthold E. Schwarz (1962; 1963) noted some inconclusive changes in the EEG of Henry Gross during dowsing performed in the laboratory, as well as irregular respiration, decreased skin resistance, increased pulse rate and blood pressure.

Underground dowsable energy lines (*ley lines*) and geopathic stress

Dowsers can detect lines of energy within the earth that are unrelated to EM energies and undetectable except through the person of the dowser (Devereaux/ Forrest). Many call these *ley lines,* though some prefer the term *dowsable earth lines.* The Chinese refer to these as *dragon paths* or *dragon currents.* Mapping ley lines is a hobby for some, has produced fascinating historical information. Many ancient roads and modern tracks of wild animals follow ley lines. Ancient holy places were often built at points of confluence of several ley lines. In Germany and Austria a regular grid of energy lines running 3 to 4 meters apart has been identified. This is called the *Curry net.*[851]

There may be harmful earth radiations above ley or *Curry lines* that are alleged to contribute to or even cause disease. The danger points, called *geopathic zones,* are above intersections of two or more lines or of ley lines with underground water streams.

Ilse Pope discusses geopathic stress in German and Austrian patients with various disorders:

> In 1929 a German scientist named Freiherr von Pohl was curious about anecdotal reports connecting ley lines with illness. He convinced Dr. Blumenthal of the Berlin Centre for Cancer Research to review the 54 cancer deaths in Vilsbiburg, a village in Southern Germany with a population of 3,300. This is an unusually high number over the brief period when records were kept of cancer deaths. Frei-

herr von Pohl drew onto the map of Vilsbiburg all the subterranean water veins which had a strength of above 9 on the Pohl Scale... This scale, which went up to 16, Freiherr von Pohl had worked out over his many years of research into the phenomenon of earth radiation. After three days his plan was compared to the records of the district hospital and it was found... that every single cancer death had occurred exactly above the lines which Freiherr von Pohl had drawn as being above the strength of 9 and therefore cancer producing... When Freiherr von Pohl was called back to Vilsbiburg 18 months later because another ten people had died of cancer, the beds of these ten people again were exactly on the lines he had drawn on the map.

These results were so impressive that they were published in the *Journal of the Centre for Cancer Research*. While no blinds are mentioned, the last 10 cases occurred in predicted zones.

Dr. Rambeau, the President of the Chamber of Medicine in Marburg, heard of Freiherr von Pohl's work. Using a geoscope, "an instrument used by the Geological Institute to locate geological fault lines," he mapped the geological fault lines in the villages around Marburg. He found that "the beds of all his severely ill patients were above these geological fault lines." He could not locate a house that was not over a geopathic zone in which a person had lived for a long time just prior to the development of cancer, and felt that cases of cancer did not occur on neutral ground. No controls or blinds are mentioned.

In Stettin, Dr. Hager studied the 5,348 cancer deaths that occurred between 1910 and 1931. All were associated with dowsed subterranean water lines. *Only 1,575 premises were associated with one cancer death each. All the rest involved multiple deaths.* All premises with more than 5 cancer deaths (199 people in 28 houses) were located on crossings of water veins. Five premises were associated with more than 10 cancer deaths each (Pope; von Pohl).[852]

Kaethe Bachler, an Austrian teacher, compiled an excellent review of dowsing. She studied the influence of geopathic lines on children with learning disabilities. She reports that moving the beds or school desks of such children (when these were located over water or *Curry crossings)* often resulted in improved school performance. She also found correlations between cancer and such geopathic zones. No controls or blinds are mentioned.

O. Bergsmann, a Viennese consultant in medicine, explored the effects of geopathic stress on 24 laboratory parameters. These included electrodermal response; heart rate; systolic blood pressure; orthostatic changes in blood pressure (changes when people rise from recumbent positions); time required to warm fingertips that were cooled in a standard manner; tendon reflex time; muscle electrical potentials; blood sedimentation rate; circulating immunoglobulins; and levels of calcium, potassium, zinc, serotonin, tyrosine, and tryptophan in the blood. Three dowsers identified areas of geopathic stress and neutral areas in eight hospital rooms around Austria. The stress areas involved crossings of water lines or crossings of water and earth energy lines. Bergmann studied the 24 parameters in 985 people. Each subject was given the battery of tests three times: after sitting for 15 minutes in a neutral area, after 15 minutes in a stress area, and after another 15 minutes in a neutral area. Subjects did not know which were the stress areas.

Results showed significant changes in 12 parameters. The serotonin level is the only test identified specifically by the reviewer of this German report (G. Schneck). Serotonin levels change with mood and sleep, and changes in this variable may be related to sleep disturbances and depressions reported by people suffering from geopathic stress.

Herbert Douglas (1974) investigated 34 cases of arthritis. he dowsed underground veins of water that crossed precisely under the affected part of each arthritic's body. In 18 out of the 34 cases he was able to convince the patients to move their beds. In each case there was partial or complete improvement within one day to three months following the relocation. No controls or blinds were instituted in this study, so effects of suggestion cannot be ruled out.

Vlastimil Zert of Czechoslovakia reports that tree tumors are also found more frequently over geopathic zones, and other studies have shown various further anomalies occurring over geopathic zones.

In one very interesting summary of dowsing research, Herbert L. König et al. mention that infrared radiation from human bodies is altered when they stand above geopathic zones.[853]

Petschke (1953a; b) performed extensive experiments on laboratory blood test results in relation to geopathic zones. In 62 series he observed differences in results when tests were run over a neutral zone, in a dowsing zone, and at a crossing of dowsing zones – all carried out in the same area, only a few meters apart. He found that the blood sedimentation rates[854] were either accelerated or retarded over dowsing zones and over crossings, relative to the rates over neutral zones.

E. Hartmann (1967; 1976) repeated these tests in the homes of people who had died of cancer. He had several sedimentation tubes that were placed 6 cm apart in a rack, with some of the tubes over the point in the bed where the cancerous organ would have been positioned and others outside of this zone. The sedimentation rates in the tubes over the geopathic zones deviated markedly from those that were not over these zones. Germination of seeds of vegetable such as cucumbers and corn was suppressed over these zones. No blinds or controls are mentioned.

Changes in the weather were also noted to alter the sedimentation rates in the above-mentioned studies.[855]

E. F. Scheller studied ionizing radiation anomalies that he found at particular locations which he felt were injurious to health. Wherever there was an elevated level of radiation he found that blood samples developed fibers, granules, globules, and vesicles. The *Scheller test* for darkfield microscopic examination of red blood cells was developed in the belief that this could identify people at risk for the development of cancer because of geopathic stress.

Hartmann (1972a) found that "reaction times" (unspecified) were 1 to 10 percent slower over geopathic zones. Hartmann (1970) observed 3 groups of 4 mice (3 female, 1 male). The first cage was kept over a geopathic zone, the second over a neutral zone half a meter away, and the third in a Faraday cage (which blocks EM radiation) 2 meters away. Over a 6-month period there were 124 mice born in the neutral zone, 118 in the Faraday cage and 56 in the geopathic zone. No blinds are mentioned.

Hartmann (1972b) injected rats subcutaneously with Yoshida tumors. He studied 12 series involving 3 rats in each of 3 cages, following each series over a period of 3 to 4 weeks. In the initial 4 series one cage was placed over a geopathic zone, one over a neutral zone and the last in a Faraday cage. The cages were 1 to 1.3 meters apart. Just after their inoculation the rats in the Faraday cage were given two exposures of 15 minutes each to high-frequency radiation.[856]

In the last 8 series a fourth cage with 3 mice was placed in a second neutral zone about 30 cm from one of the control cages, as a check on whether small distances unrelated to geopathic zones could produce observable differences in tumor growth. In the last 8 series the rats in the Faraday cage received no EM exposure after their inoculation.

Tumor growth was estimated by palpation followed by molding in plastiline and weighing. In the first series the rats over the geopathic zone had the most rapid growth of cancer, those over the neutral zone had slower growth, and those in the Faraday cage the slowest growth. In the second series the rats in the Faraday cage had the fastest growth, followed by those over the geopathic zone, and those over the neutral zones had the slowest growth.

Magnetic field intensity was measured over the various points. A probe that was passed over the geopathic zone in one direction registered a decrease in magnetic field intensity of about 80 percent compared to other places in the room. No blinds are mentioned in this study.

Hartmann (1967; 1976) found magnetic anomalies over a geopathic zone, using a dual compass. J. Wüst measured magnetic anomalies over such points with a local variometer and a field balance, and Wüst and Petschke report that the EM resistance in the ground was substantially increased at such points. S. W. Tromp (1954) found that ground conductivity over geopathic zones was increased but also noted resistance peaks in some of these areas. G. Lehman (1960) found significantly lower gradients in electrostatic fields over geopathic zones. Lehman also noted increased conductivity in the air over dowsed water veins. F. Bürklin found that lightning strikes were more frequent at low-voltage power transmission poles that were located at geopathic zones. A grounding wire provided protection for these poles.

Brüche (1954) found that radioactivity over water veins could be elevated or decreased, and that this seemed related to weather conditions. Endrös identified infrared and microwave emissions over underground water veins. Stängle developed a scintillation counter using sodium iodide, which he mounted on wheels and used for measurements of radioactivity over geopathic zones. He studied the sites identified by von Pohl (where people living over geopathic zones had died of cancer) and found radiation intensities close to twice as high as over adjacent areas. The scintillation curves in these areas were similar to curves obtained over underground water veins. Hartmann (1970; 1976) found that gamma radiation varied at heights of 12 to 25 cm over geopathic zones (usually producing 10 to 30 percent higher radiation counts). He noted periodic rises and falls at intervals of 15 minutes and 3 hours. Again there were variations correlated with the weather. Lead shielding of the instrument probe decreased the counts over geopathic zones, but not to the same degree as it did over normal areas. Shielding with paraffin-graphite blocks of about 10-cm thickness increased the counts.

J. Wüst (1959) showed that VHF radio transmitters performed differently over geopathic zones. Hartmann (1967; 1976) found VHF anomalies around sick beds, unrelated to geopathic zones. Physician D. Aschoff (1967; 1976) studied VHF field intensities in the rooms of 125 people with chronic health problems that had been unresponsive to conventional treatments. Of 85 who moved from areas of high VHF intensity to areas of low intensity, 28 reported immediate improvements.

Hartmann (1967; 1976) developed a VHF transmitter and receiver with which he measured the DC resistance between the hands of subjects. He found that the time course of body resistance varies when subjects are over geopathic points, as compared to when they are over neutral points. These findings are also related to weather conditions.

Various devices have been developed for neutralizing negative earth energies. Hartmann (1967; 1976) claimed excellent results with *bioresonators* that he developed for this purpose. H. L. König (1968a) studied the elastic, double brass coil that is at the core of this instrument. He found that its natural mechanical resonance is around 10 Hz, which means that is biologically active. Therefore it could easily be activated by vibrations in the floor. However, König is skeptical that this could neutralize other EM fields and thus eliminate geopathic stress.

Discussion

Dowsers have had difficulty convincing scientists that their perceptions are anything more than lucky guesses. As with other forms of psi and intuitive perception, they are irregular in their successes.

The research in dowsing is not well publicized and most scientists are unaware that any has been done at all. The studies summarized here strongly suggest that dowsing produces significant results, although suggestion cannot be ruled out in many of the studies, due to lack of controls and blinds.

Why dowsers scored significantly lower than chance in the series by Rhine is unclear. Perhaps this poor result was related to the attitudes and interactions of the dowsers and experimenters. Declines in success are typical of many psychological and psi experiments. They may be related to factors of fatigue and boredom with experimental tasks, as well as with the dowsers' perception of a lack of true need for the application of their psi abilities in many laboratory conditions.

It is unfortunate that Pohl's and König's reports on medical dowsing do not review the German literature critically, and that Bachler shows little appreciation for scientific methods in her reports. Dr. Blumenthal's investigations appear to be the most rigorous, especially his last ten cases, in which locations where cancers developed were predicted ahead of time.. The opposite seems the case with the work of Rambeau, Hager, Bachler, Douglas and Zert. These investigators presumably knew that a cancer death had occurred or that a learning-disabled child lived in a particular house, and dowsed there for that reason. When dowsers are seeking correlations with dowsed phenomena and they know the expected outcome, their unconscious minds might bias the results in the direction they anticipate. A more scientific procedure would be to give a dowser a randomized list of addresses to dowse, including equal numbers of houses where residents have health problems and others which are problem free. However, even in this case experimental results may reflect only the clairsentience of the dowser. That is to say, the dowser might psychically (and unconsciously) detect the fact that a person with cancer had been in particular rooms, and the dowsing results could then be influenced by this awareness. Further evaluations, as in the last ten cases of Dr. Blumenthal, would be even more convincing. With this model, however, precognition on the part of the dowsers could still influence the results.

The fact that *multiple* cancer deaths occurred in particular homes is strongly suggestive of a geopathic effect. Other factors, such as EM radiation or other known environmental stressors, would still have to be ruled out in these cases.

The studies of electrodermal responses of dowsers help to confirm their subjective claims and add support to the theory that they may be responding to unconventional energies.

Surprisingly enough, these are the only scientific studies of dowsing that I could locate. It seems incredible to me that so few serious investigations have been made of a potentially valuable method of searching out natural resources, identifying harmful influences on physical health and mental conditions, and providing healing therapy.

More on medical dowsing
Medical radiesthesia is an area that has been even more meagerly explored than field dowsing. Here again, a plethora of anecdotal evidence is available, attesting to dowsers' successes in:

1. Identifying areas of geopathic stress where underground energies appear to emanate a negative influence;
2. Locating and diagnosing plant, animal and human diseases;
3. Selecting medications and determining dosages that are appropriate for treating the diagnosed problems;
4. Suggesting innumerable biological and horticultural applications, the range of which is limited only by the dowsers' innovativeness in asking "either/ or" or "yes/ no" questions. For instance, a common use of dowsing in agriculture is to match soil components with seed, and to recommend appropriate mineral and fertilizer additives.

The first of these applications was discussed above. The other three differ little from other sorts of clairsentience, and seem to represent the dowsers' use of the pendulum or wand to make their psi impressions consciously perceptible. I know of no formal research to clarify whether dowsing has any intrinsic advantage over clairsentience without dowsing devices, but a wealth of anecdotal reports on the efficacy of dowsing and radionics suggest this is a fertile area for further study.

The Chinese have a rich tradition of folklore that describes states of health and disease, harmony and disharmony, as related to *dragon lines* and other earth forces (S. Skinner).

Christopher Bird, who had a wide-ranging interest in parapsychology, prepared a very attractive, well-illustrated book on dowsing. He mentions a number of items that are relevant to spiritual healing (unfortunately these are not reviewed with scientific rigor, but they are nevertheless interesting and suggest rich possibilities for further research):

1. Abbe Alexis Bouly was a well-known dowser in France. He was able to identify specific types of bacteria in a laboratory using a pendulum. As with dousing results achieved using a radio receiver, orientation of the dowser to different compass points could influence the readings.
2. Father Jean Jurion, inspired by Bouly, successfully extended the investigation of dowsing to the diagnosis of medical problems that were puzzling to doctors.[857]

Aubrey Westlake, a British physician, investigated dowsing and radionics over the course of many years. He postulates several levels of sensitivity at which a dowser may function:

1. The physical level, at which the operator appears to function like a radio receiver tuned to presumed vibrations of various substances.
2. The level of divination, in which the dowser utilizes sensory and psi faculties. Here the dowser appears to have a wider range of perception, and is not restricted to utilizing sensory and psi faculties. At this level, dowsers are not restricted by their orientation within the earth's magnetic field or other such factors. (Westlake considers this to be another physical level of dowsing.)
3. The level of consciousness, where the sensitive "…appeared to be on a mental level of full consciousness and became independent of the limitations of both time and space, in the sense that it was possible to recover the past, and neither witnesses[858] nor actual remedies were required and orientation was unnecessary."
4. Westlake also identifies "…still higher levels, of clairvoyance and clairaudience, but not in the ordinary psychic sense, as the vision and the speech were inward and not outward. It is the inner vision and the still, small voice that is apprehended in full consciousness and not the apparition or the trumpet of the seance room under trance conditions."

Westlake notes that in (2) and (3) a technique of question and answer is often very helpful. Yes/ no dichotomies are put to the pendulum, which provides answers. This can be an extremely helpful aid in clarifying medical diagnosis and treatment, yet Westlake feels that this should not be used as a *mechanical* approach to treatment. In his practice he does not focus on diagnosis, except in very broad terms:

> One deals with a sick person, a person who is out of balance, out of harmony physically, mentally, emotionally, spiritually - the object of therapy is to restore that person to a harmonious functioning as a whole.

Westlake notes that the *witness*

> …is subjected to forces tending to restore the patient's health pattern by the removal of blockages, restoration of flows and a rise of con-

sciousness. This is mystery enough, but the main mystery is the nature of the relationship of the blood spot to the patient, as for all practical purposes the blood spot and the actual patient can be regarded as identical.

This is consistent with LeShan's theories on the mythic level of reality (1974a; 1976), in which a part of an object and the entire object may be identical in some essential, functional way.[859]

There are anecdotal reports of broad disparities in results when several dowsers simultaneously or serially gave readings on the same subjects (for both diagnosis and treatment). Dowsers explain these objections away by claiming that each individual dowser picks up on different aspects of the subject's problems, filtering them through the various aspects of their various devices and prescribing accordingly. They assert that there are many ways to shift an organism from disharmony towards greater wholeness.

Westlake found that radiesthetic readings often indicated an improved condition when the patient was close to death or even dead already. He believes this indicates that the radiesthetic readings relate to the condition of the *auric* body rather than the *physical* body. Under normal conditions the physical and etheric bodies coincide closely enough that a reading on one reflects the condition of the other. At the time of death, when the energy body is separating from the physical body, the reading reflects the condition of the auric rather than the physical.[860] Death may be a release from suffering for many people, in which case the etheric, spirit part of the person that the dowser is reading might register as being improved.

In a similar manner radionics treatments may affect the auric body rather than the physical, and the auric body could then secondarily influence the physical. Dowsing for the condition of the aura could provide a warning of illness prior to its appearance in the physical body. Radionic treatments may also facilitate separation of the auric from the physical when death is near, thus theoretically hastening death. This can be seen as a form of healing, especially when the healee is suffering, weary and ready to die.

RADIONICS

Treating healees at a distance using a radionics device is a clear example of absent healing. Radionics practitioners claim a greater precision than healers, who do not project vibrations specific to the identified problems. They also claim that their devices may be effective in storing and projecting healing energies, and that they can tune a device and leave it to project specific healing vibrations as long as necessary. All of these claims require further investigation and substantiation.

Langston Day and George de la Warr report their extensive observations on the users of radionics devices that were developed in England a few decades ago. In connecting with a healee, Day and de la Warr wrote, "For at least one second he [*the operator*] must hold in his mind a single thought – as a result of which his solar plexus emits a wave-form which resonates with the blood specimen."

Relevant to healing, Day and de la Warr observe the following:

1. There appears to be a resonation between an object and any part of the object, including a picture of it. This enables the operators to make contact with patients via specimens of blood, urine, etc. that they place in the radionics device.

2. If a subject is rapidly rotating during the operation of the device this blurs the results. Linear directional motion of the subject did not seem to have adverse effects.

3. A magnet placed near the specimen, and rotated to a specific orientation relative to the specimen and to the earth's magnetic field, would markedly enhance the sensitivity of the device.

4. De la Warr developed a photographic diagnostic device based on these principles. It could produce pictures of the target object using a *witness*. In addition, with proper setting of the dials, it could produce photographs of the future potential or the past of that object. For instance, from a seed the device could produce a picture of the flower of that species. From a blood specimen of a pregnant woman he obtained pictures of the fetus in stages of development that were both earlier and later than its age at the time of the picture. The more displaced the images were in time, however, the hazier they appeared. The specific person who inserted the film in the camera was as critical to the success of its operation as was the operator of the dials.[861] Only a few operators were able to obtain photographs of this sort.

5. Plants removed from their original place of germination grew best if their original orientation to Earth's magnetic field were maintained at their new location.

6. De la Warr's instruments, when suitably tuned, produced distant healings of a gradual (not instantaneous) nature.

7. Though these devices seemed effective in curing bacterial infections, they failed to kill bacteria in laboratory cultures. De la Warr attributed this to a selective intelligence inherent in the cosmic forces that are involved in these processes, which would work for the greatest good.

8. These devices could be used to clear plants of insect pests. If an aerial photograph of a field were used as a *witness*, with a section of the field marked off with a pen and the operator's intention focused upon it, the insect pests from the area indicated in the photograph could be eliminated. Many experiments were done that verified this use of radionics (E. W. Russell).

9. Spring water and water consecrated by a cleric produced markedly different registrations on these devices than did untreated tap water.

Day and de la Warr speculate on the mechanisms involved in these processes. They feel that there is a resonance between the parts and the whole of an organism, and also between the whole of an organism and other members of its species. The influences of magnetic fields seem to be involved, but there may be other "fundamental rays" involved that have yet to be identified. Day and de la Warr also comment on emanations that seemed to originate in the operator's solar plexus. This was deduced from the fact that a sheet of perspex (heatproof glass) placed in front of the solar plexus partially cut off the emanations. (How this was calibrated is not indicated.)

Much of their book is devoted to stories of the difficult times that Day and de la Warr had in trying to get the scientific community to pay attention to their experiments. The general skepticism has even led to outright refusal to consider their experiments as anything more than trickery. This resulted in part from the fact that proper controls were not instituted in the experiments.

Despite these problems, Day and de la Warr's observations seem to warrant further investigation. For instance, Cleve Backster reports results that are similar (L. Watson 1975). Backster placed wires from a polygraph into a human semen sample. The donor, who was sitting about forty feet away, was then asked to sniff amyl nitrite, which is very noxious. Two seconds later his sperm showed a response. Control specimens from other donors did not respond.[862]

Lyall Watson (1975) similarly reports that when one sample of tissues from a donor is damaged with concentrated nitric acid, a second sample at a distant location often can be shown to react as well, using electronic monitoring. Watson speculates that this is a cellular response, which originally evolved as a species-specific means of communication, possibly for defensive purposes. In single-cell organisms it would be the primary means of inter-individual communication. In plants and animals it is overshadowed by other inter-organism mechanisms, but is still present as a residual ability.[863]

Edward Russell (1973) presents an excellent review of radiesthesia and radionics. The following are some items of note:

1. Experiments demonstrated that a screen of cardboard covered with tin foil is impervious to human energy fields. (No mention is made of blinds or other controls for suggestion.)
2. Ruth Beymer Drown was able to produce photographs of the internal organs of patients using radionics devices. An anesthetized patient could not be successfully photographed in this way.
3. T. Galen Hieronymous obtained a patent in America for a device with which he could grow healthy green plants in the dark (as compared to control specimens, which were pale and seemed to lack chlorophyll). Energy was conducted to the plants via wires.

Anthony Scofield (1988-89) is a lecturer in animal physiology at the University of London. He has investigated the influence of geopathic lines both in his own dowsing and in the practice of a wide range of other dowsers. He feels that the so-called geopathic zones may in many cases be created either by the ill person or by the dowser who is seeking them. Ley lines are presumed to be vertical "walls" of energy that stand above geopathic zones, yet when Scofield examined rooms in a building that were below rooms in which geopathic lines had been dowsed, he was not able to identify similar lines that theoretically should have been present beneath those rooms where such lines were dowsed. He notes further that he has found some lines (called "black lines") that make him feel ill when he dowses them.

Scofield has also created energy lines by visualizing them, and other dowsers have subsequently been able to identify them by dowsing. Scofield's observations are anecdotal and suggest a variety of experiments that would be easy to perform.

Scofield notes that *Curry lines* have been identified in Germany and Austria by dowsers in those countries, but not in Britain by British dowsers. When a German dowser visited England she was able to demonstrate Curry lines and local dowsers could identify them as well. However, after she left the local dowsers could no longer identify them.

Sig Lonegren, another dowser, also observes that the results of dowsing depend on the question that the dowser holds in his mind during the procedure. He points out that historically, *ley lines* correspond with the energy lines that have been identified between ancient sacred sites, and that these may be qualitatively different from other energy lines.

The Chinese identified *dragon lines* that seem similar, if not identical, to ley lines in their effects on health and illness. The Chinese have extensive systems, called *feng shui,* for concentrating or accumulating positive earth energies as well as for neutralizing negative ones.[864]

THEORIES OF RADIESTHESIA AND RADIONICS

If we assume that dowsing is essentially successful clairsentience, this raises some interesting points.

Numerous attempts have been made to increase subjects' abilities to demonstrate psi powers reliably. Feedback has been highly successful in bringing many psychophysiological mechanisms under the control of the conscious mind.[865] Using this method, practitioners have been able to alter their heart rate, blood pressure, skin temperature and more. All of these physiological processes were previously thought to be controlled exclusively by the autonomic (unconsciously regulated) nervous system. Extending the experience of biofeedback into research in extra-sensory perception, it was hoped that if feedback were given for successful psi perceptions, then subjects would be able to learn to perform better with their psi abilities.[866] Neither receptive nor expressive aspects of psi have responded more than minimally to feedback in average people. If we assume dowsing is a clairsentient skill, it would appear that this is the psi area in which feedback has come the closest to being successful for large numbers of people.

There seems to be a contradiction here between laboratory evidence of biofeedback as a method to enhance psi effects and the feedback observed with dowsers' devices in their practices. Why the former should be unsuccessful while the latter appears highly functional is as yet unclear. This may support the hypothesis of the importance of *need* as a vital factor in the expression of psi and healing.In other words, people may be more successful in producing psi and healing effects when they feel there is a true need for the use of their abilities – rather than demonstrating them to meet the needs of a laboratory researcher. Another possibility is that people who self-select to become dowsers are highly intuitive.

The same seems to apply in spiritual healing. People have been highly successful in learning to develop their healing gifts, in a wide range of courses that teach how to heal.

Dowsers' subjectively report that they tune in to vibrations of the thing that they are seeking. When it comes to treating disease by radionics, which is in fact a mode of healing, dowsers claim that they can return to normal the vibrations that have gotten "out of tune"; reimpose a healthy vibration; or identify missing elements that are needed to reharmonize total body vibrations. It seems reasonable to propose that radiesthetic devices are aids to clairsentience and that radionics is actually a form of spiritual healing, which the practitioners of radionics attribute to the devices they use. The reports on dowsing add to evidence from other research covered in this book, supporting the growing awareness of bioenergy forms of medicine.

The evidence from published reports of dowsing strongly suggest that this topic seriously warrants further study. Such study must take into account the intrinsic differences between dowsing and conventional science. For instance, we ought to give careful consideration to dowsers' explanations and theories of dowsing. For instance, it seems to be a general property of psi that it is expressed more readily in response to true, serious needs, rather than according to the demands of laboratory situations. The need factor may explain why there is a higher percentage of significant results in studies of spiritual healing than in studies of other psi effects.

There are also numerous reports from psychics and healers that skepticism and negativity in observers can inhibit the expression of their psi gifts. Non-believers will of course see this as an excuse for the inability to produce psi under scrutiny, and will interpret this as proof that psi consists of nothing more than wishful thinking, selective reports of random successful guesses, self-delusion motivated by ego or desire for fame and fortune, or deliberate fraud.

While I don't agree with the skeptics' interpretations of the evidence or of dowsers' motivations, I do agree that there is reason to ask for more research. Until more and better controlled studies are run, dowsers have only a limited scientific basis on which to lay their claims. More work is needed of the caliber of Harvalik's, Hager's, Von Pohl's and Tromp's explorations.

Research of medical dowsing would be very easy to set up with rigorous controls. This task awaits only the people to do it.

William Tiller (1971) is a professor in the Department of Materials Science and Engineering at Stanford University. He studied at Oxford University on a Guggenheim Fellowship, during the course of which he extensively investigated radiesthesia and radionics. He defines radiesthesia as

> ...sensitivity to radiations covering the whole field of radiations from any source, either living or inert. As such, this would appear to include clairsentience and telepathy. Radionics is the use of instruments to augment the sensitivity to radiations.

Tiller observes that pendulums, dowsing rods and radionics devices all serve to reduce the signal/ noise ratio. They help the average individual who is not blessed with the gifts of concentration that are apparently inherent in gifted healers, who can enter meditational states very rapidly and easily. He feels that psi abilities are not required for dowsing so much as a well-disciplined mind and sensitive emotional structure, although psi abilities may develop with prolonged practice of dowsing, to the point where the devices are no longer required. Tiller proposes:

> ...A basic idea in radionics is that each individual organism or material radiates and absorbs energy via a unique wave field which exhibits certain geometrical, frequency and radiation-type characteristics. This is an extended force field that exists around all forms of matter whether animate or inanimate... The fundamental carrier wave is thought to be polarized with a rotating polarization vector.
> ...The information concerning the glands, body systems, etc., ripples the carrier wave and seems to be associated with a specific phase modulation of the polarization vector of the wave and also with frequency modulation of the wave for a specific gland. Regions of space associated with a given phase angle of the wave constitute a three dimensional network of points extending throughout all space. To be in resonance with any one of these points is to be in resonance with the particular gland of the entity. The capability of scanning the wave-form of the gland exists for the detection of any abnormalities.

Tiller then explains spiritual healing as follows:

> Likewise, if energy having the normal or healthy waveform of the gland is pumped into any one of these specific network points, the gland will be driven in the normal or healthy mode. This produces a tendency for its structure to reorganize itself in closer alignment with the normal structure; i.e., healing of the gland occurs. Cells born in the presence of this polarizing field tend to grow in a healthier configuration, which weakens the original field of the abnormal or diseased structure and strengthens the field of normal or healthy structures. Continued treatment eventually molds the healthy organ structure and the condition is healed.

Tiller integrates Eastern cosmologies into his explanations of how dowsing works.[867] His recent work, exploring how intention can be imprinted on electronic devices, also supports the reports of Scofield regarding imprinting of ley lines through mental focus (Tiller 2003a; b).

Larry Dossey (1989) suggests that our everyday expectations may mislead us to believe that some kind of energy must intervene in order for perceptions or physical changes in the world to occur. Nevertheless, awareness and action at a distance may occur without energetic exchanges, according to the theories of modern physics, psi research and reports of mystics through the ages.

Discussion

Field dowsing appears to have a basis in an energy form that can be blocked by various types of metal shields, and possibly by other materials as well, just as EM energies can be blocked. It may be that the human body is far more sensitive to EM radiation than has previously been appreciated by conventional science, as evidenced by Harvalik's and Tromp's experiments. The parapsychological studies of remote psi perception[868] suggest a close parallel with dowsing, which would seem to be a kind of instrument-assisted clairsentience.

Critics have objected that movements of the various mechanical devices that are used in dowsing (pendulums and rods) are not automatic but rather controlled by the dowsers themselves. Critics imply that the dowsers are deluding themselves and/ or others, or even defrauding others, in representing these devices as instruments that are effective in and of themselves. There is validity to these criticisms insofar as the instruments are concerned, but this mechanistic Occam's razor cuts at a point too close to the device. Since clairsentience may manifest itself via unconscious processes within the dowsers' minds, a different hypothesis may therefore be proposed. If the dowsers themselves are the instruments that identify whatever they are seeking, their devices can be seen as feedback devices that identify what their unconscious minds are perceiving, rather than the devices themselves locating things directly in the outside world through inherent properties of the devices. In other words, the dowsers are the receivers for the information, and the instruments are like dials that provide readings from the dowsers' unconscious.

Other factors may help to explain why various devices work well for dowsers in facilitating their psychic impressions.

Numerous healers report that it is more comfortable to work in a group, or to "turn the healing over to a higher power" rather than to focus on doing the healing themselves. By taking less responsibility for making the healing happen, they become less ego-involved in offering healing. This allows them to be more totally immersed in the healing state, not worrying about how they are doing with the healing – which would become a distraction from being fully engaged in the healing process.

Similarly, in meditation practices it is a common joke that when you are thinking about how well you are meditating you have lost your focus on the meditation itself.

Applied Kinesiology[869] is very similar to dowsing. It relies on changes in muscle strength to access unconscious, intuitive, and psychic impressions.

It would thus appear that dowsing is well within the spectrum of approaches that help people to access their intuitive and psychic awarenesses.

There is so far only limited and not very convincing evidence that map dowsing of distant locations is effective. If solid evidence is produced for map dowsing, this would suggest that a type of energy other than EM may be involved in field dowsing because of the diminution of strength of EM signals with distance. It would also indicate that clairsentience rather than sensitivity to energies emanating from dowsed items is the mechanism for dowsing.

The significant studies of Harvalik, Hager, Osis Von Pohl, and Tromp provide strong evidence for dowsing abilities. However, it is unfortunate that relatively little rigorous research has been done to establish the validity of dowsing and to explore the range of its efficacy. Numerous anecdotes attest that dowsers have successfully located natural water sources, forgotten water mains, buried electrical lines or gas pipes, oil and other minerals, missing people, archaeological remains, and land mines, and have determined the missing minerals in poor soil conditions. Dowsers have also identified the quantities of underground resources that will be found, such as the rates of flow of well and spring waters. The evidence for radionics effects is much weaker.

Research questions
Why are there differences between varying perceptions when several dowsers explore the same geographical or medical territory? How can we explain the disparate findings of British and German dowsers regarding Curry lines? The skeptic will say that it is the different projections of the imaginations of the dowsers that produce these discrepancies. In fact, there is probably a component of this sort in most dowsing, but I suspect that there are two further explanations. First, clairsentient perceptions are often colored by the perceiver, as are all data that filter through to consciousness from the unconscious mind.[870] Second, some of the geopathic zones and medical diagnoses may be projections of the minds of the dowsers, as when Scofield seemed able to visualize a dowsable line into existence, which other dowsers could then identify. Much research will be needed to clarify which hypothesis is more relevant, and to what degree.

Dowsing as a wholistic therapy
If we accept that wholistic healing is the harmonizing of energies within healees, then this should also be the goal of radionics treatments. Within this framework of healing we may more easily accept that there is indeed a range of prescriptions that might each achieve positive therapeutic ends, although the results might differ. This is similar to the variations seen with many of the CAM modalities, where assessments and responses to treatments by different caregivers applying the same modality may differ.

Although these explanations are consistent with energy medicine theories, they leave me most uneasy. The chances seem quite high that we may fall prey to Type I research errors, and allow ourselves to be convinced of "facts" that are in fact not true.

In considering the specificity of radionics from within its own conceptual framework, I have a further uneasiness. The very specificity of the modality, which is alleged to be beneficial, may also be a dangerous pitfall. If the dowsers ask the wrong questions or fail to ask the right questions, they may obtain limited or erroneous information and may therefore make poor or misleading recommendations or interventions. My pilot studies of aura perceptions, in which several sensitives observed the same patients with known medical diagnoses,[871] seem to indicate that intuitive diagnosticians may perceive only *part* of the picture. It remains to be clarified whether dowsers and radionics practitioners can guard against this danger by asking the question, "Is there anything more I should ask or know?"

Healers who direct their unconscious minds or higher selves to identify health problems and to prescribe and/ or administer the necessary vibratory treatments may be less prone to such errors. These healers' energies may also be directed toward a wider spectrum of problems. On the other hand, it may be that the broader spectrum approach is not as potent for some or all specific problems. It may also be that different energy medicine practitioners convey different forms or qualities of subtle energy intervention, and that each tunes in to the particular aspects of their healees' problems with which they resonate and/ or that they are best suited to address, and provide the interventions that their healees are most ready to receive from them.[872]

The current state of radionics and dowsing practices leaves so many questions unanswered that they seem to be more an art than a science. In seeking medical advice from dowsers on serious problems, I suggest: 1. Select a dowser with a good track record, preferably based on trustworthy personal recommendations from satisfied healees. This is the usual way of selecting a healer. 2. In any case, you should not rely only on your intuition to determine whether the intuitives and healers you consult seem to match your expectations and needs. You must also use common sense to assess whether they present themselves professionally, ethically, and sensibly. When in doubt, as with medical consultations, a second opinion may provide a measure of protection against misreadings due to idiosyncrasies of individual dowsers. However, although it might seem logical and prudent to consult a number of experienced dowsers separately and to follow the consensus of opinions, this can sometimes be confusing because different intuitives may perceive different parts of the problem.

Conversely, if we are too cautious, we may lose the benefits of intuitive diagnoses and treatments that are particular to specific dowsers.

In the end, we have to make our own decisions (using logic along with intuition) as to what will cure our ills – whether we consult conventional or CAM practitioners. We might learn from dowsers to increase our own intuitive skills, perhaps with the aid of their devices. At times I have personally found a pendulum or bent wire rod helpful in letting my unconscious express an opinion. Learning to communicate with my unconscious has been, in and of itself, a form of healing.

Dowsers have not been able to demonstrate their abilities consistently in the laboratory. Skeptics suggest that reports of successful dowsing are old wives' tales, with occasional lucky "hits" or selective reporting of chance accurate predictions, while inaccurate ones are ignored. Dowsers I have spoken with say that the powers of their trade are not to be used frivolously and that their work is accurate when used for legitimate, real-life needs. It is less successful when used in parlor games or laboratories.

Dowsable energy lines in Gaia, our planet

It has been suggested that ley lines on the earth are analogous to acupuncture meridians on the body (S. Skinner). Further observations suggest that our planet may be a huge, living organism in its own right. Fascinating observations have been gathered to support this view.

James Lovelock (1979; 1988) pointed out homeostatic interactions between life on earth and its geological evolution. Over many eons, algae, bacteria and plants have altered the balance of gasses in the atmosphere and have stabilized the planetary temperature. Lovelock proposes that the earth's flora and fauna have transformed the planet into an extension of life at an interactional level. He named this ecosystem Gaia, after the Greek earth goddess.

> You... interact individually in a spiritual manner through a sense of wonder about the natural world and from feeling a part of it. In some

ways this interaction is not unlike the tight coupling between the state of mind and the body...

>
> – Lovelock (1988, p. 211)

Every living creature has homeostatic mechanisms that maintain its internal environment within required ranges of temperature, hydration, nutrition, etc. required for life. If temperatures rise, the organism sweats, breathes faster or pants. Lovelock proposes that aspects of the planet earth suggest that it too has homeostatic mechanisms that maintain various conditions within particular ranges. For example, oxygen and nitrogen contents in the air remain at fixed values despite man's gross alterations of the environment – in decimating or eliminating large numbers of life forms and in polluting on a massive scale. Temperatures also remain within particular limits over many centuries.[873]

John Barrow and Frank Tipler have gone so far as to hypothesize that this ecological stability implies an inherent guiding cosmic intelligence. They speculate that this transcends mankind's influence by so great a factor that it overshadows all of human endeavor, making us no more than a tiny speck in the vastness of the universe. More modest views hold that man is analogous to an organ of the planet, acting much as nerve and brain cells. Others view man as a cancer, growing unchecked, fouling and destroying the earth-body that nurtures mankind.

> By avarice and selfishness, and a groveling habit, from which none of us is free, of regarding the soil as property... the landscape is deformed.
> – Henry David Thoreau

Those who live close to nature and are intuitive describe an awareness of sentience in trees, water, wind and earth. They believe it is a logical extension to suggest that healing may be effective at planetary levels, either through species-specific, collective fields, through the ecosystem as a unit, or piecemeal through successive transformation of small units at a time.

Though our focus has been on the scientific aspects of radiesthesia and radionics, these practices touch upon the spiritual as well.[874] I will close with the observations of Rev. J. C. C. Murray:

> [R]adiesthesia reveals most clearly the fact that there is no hard and fast frontier between matter and spirit. The artificial divisions created by centuries of materialism taken as a matter of course until very recently, have been abolished. In their place, we begin dimly to see a continuum of vibration, of radiation, extending unbroken from the heart of so-called "dead" matter, right up through the octaves of the rays of flesh and blood and the etheric processes of the mind, to a region beyond the human spectrum in which powers from another dimension begin to be apparent. It is therefore more than possible that just here the long battles between science and religion will find their truce at last and that the radiations found and plotted out by man's intellect will coalesce with and intermingle with those discerned by the

spirit. We shall discover something of the unity of creation, a unity which must be reflected in His works. We seem to be presented once again with that strange pattern of the ascending spiral which leads without a break from the heart of the stone to the heart of immortality.

COSMOBIOLOGY AND ASTROLOGY[875]

At present we can only suspect a general relationship of some kind between the whole of the human species and the whole of the electromagnetic phenomenon that includes the sun, other stars and the galaxies.

– Robert Becker (Attributed)

Astrology interested us, for it tied men to the system. Instead of an isolated beggar, the farthest star felt him and he felt the star. However rash and however falsified by pretenders and traders in it, the hint was true and divine, the soul's avowal of its large relations and that climate, century, remote natures as well as near, are part of its biography...

– Ralph Waldo Emerson

Claims have been made over thousands of years that the sun, moon and planets influence our lives. Western science has considered all this to be mere superstition, but in the last few decades research has confirmed that the positions of the moon and the planets, as well as solar flare activity, are correlated with biological fields and with the behaviors of plants, animals and man.

After H. J. Eysenck and D. K. B. Nias, I distinguish here between the following disciplines:

1. Cosmobiology – seeking correlations between the positions of heavenly bodies as related to limited, discretely observable phenomena such birth, surgical bleeding, personality characteristics, and death by murder or suicide; and
2. Astrology – seeking correlations between the positions of heavenly bodies, astrological signs, and aspects of people's lives such as compatibilities in their relationships with others, propitious and unpropitious days for various activities, and predictions of the future.

The research evidence supporting most of the claims regarding astrology as a science is not substantial, although there are some overlaps with cosmobiology.

The evidence for cosmobiological influences on living systems is impressive. This research was very carefully reviewed and confirmed by H. J. Eysenck, Professor of Psychiatry at the London University Institute of Psychiatry, in collaboration with his colleague at the same institute, D.K.B. Nias.

An excellent place to begin our scientific review of astrology is the work of Michel Gauquelin (1969). With the help of his wife Françoise, Gauquelin has done more than any other person to establish the validity of particular correlations between planetary positions at time of birth and people's success in their professions.

His first study examined 576 members in the French Academy of Medicine. These were men who had achieved outstanding success in medical research. Gauquelin found that their birth times correlated beyond chance with the rising of Mars and Saturn, or with the passing of these planets through the mid-heaven. As a control group he checked the same correlations for people whose names were randomly chosen from the electoral register, who had been born during the same time period as the doctors. The astrological correlations for the control group were only at chance values.

Gauquelin repeated the study with a second group of 508 French doctors who were involved in significant research, and found similarly significant correlations.

To rule out the possibility of an anomaly peculiar to his initial test populations, Gauquelin (1969) charted the positions of the sun, moon and planets at the time of birth for 25,000 prominent people in five European countries. He found that success in one's chosen career was significantly correlated with positions of the moon and of several planets at the time of birth.

Separating out 3,647 successful people involved in the sciences and 5,100 in the arts, Gauquelin found that Saturn was ascendant significantly more frequently than chance at the time of birth of the scientists, or had just passed the mid-heaven. The artists were significantly less likely to have been born with these correlations. Mars and Jupiter were correlated significantly more frequently with the births of military leaders.

Such correlations were found only for the births of people who had distinguished themselves in their careers, and not for ordinary people. Clarifying this point further, Gauquelin checked the birth dates of soldiers whose careers had been truncated by crippling injuries or death, but who had received military decorations for bravery. These soldiers also showed significant correlations between their birth times and the positions of Mars and Jupiter. This suggested that the crucial factor in determining success or failure was not a matter of destiny but rather of the innate characteristics of the individual.

Gauquelin also tested this theory with successful figures in sports. Those who had a firm determination to succeed showed similar significant correlations, whereas those who lacked ambition and vigor showed no such correlations.

This was a turning point in his conceptualizations about the relationships between heavenly bodies and human experience. It became clear that *it was not the choice of career that was related to time of birth, but the personal characteristics correlated with certain times of birth that made for success in particular careers.*

Gauquelin et al. (1979) then classified famous people according to personality characteristics evident in their biographies, including 1,409 actors, 2,089 sportsmen, and 3,647 scientists in his subject group. Distinguishing factors included introversion and extroversion, tough-mindedness, and emotional instability. Sybil Eysenck rated each of the subjects according to these personality criteria, while remaining blind to their birth times. Irrespective of profession, the personality variables correlated significantly with the relevant planets' presence in the critical zones in the sky at the time of birth. The traits that correlated with particular planets included the following (Eysenck/ Nias):[876]

Mars – active, aggressive, quarrelsome, dynamic, fearless, daring, willful;
Jupiter – ambitious, authoritarian, assertive, debonair, independent, bantering, vain;
Saturn – formal, reserved, conscientious, cold, precise, melancholy, timid, industrious; and
Moon – amiable, sociable, good-hearted, generous, imaginative, easily influenced, poetic, tolerant.

Once it was established that there were indeed relationships between time of birth and personality, the obvious question presented itself: How could the planets and the moon influence personality?

To begin teasing out answers to this question, Gauquelin studied the relationships between the times of birth of successful people and of their parents. He found highly significant correlations between planetary and lunar positions at the time of birth of children and those of both of their parents. The correlations are twice as strong for each parent with their child when both parents have birth times under similar heavenly bodies as their child. The correlations apply for Mars, Venus, Jupiter, Saturn and the moon. No relationships were found with the sun or other planets. *These correlations hold for natural births but not for births induced by chemicals or by or caesarian section, nor for births assisted with forceps.*[877] Rather than concluding that the heavenly bodies influence a person's career, Gauquelin suggests an alternative hypothesis: People are born at the time which is appropriate for their dispositions.

What sort of signals could pass between people and planets? Gravity is a force that knows no limits, while electromagnetic forces diminish rapidly with distance. Gauquelin checked the correlations of births on days when planetary geomagnetic fields were disturbed. Such disturbances may occur in relation to sunspots or without known cause. He found that children were more likely to have planetary correlations with birth times corresponding to their parents' correlations with planetary birth times on days when earth's magnetic fields were disturbed. There is no hypothesis as yet to explain this association.

Being the meticulous scientist that he is, Gauquelin replicated the study on children and parents twice, examining groups of more than 15,000 couples with their children. All of the previous findings were confirmed.

Gauquelin (1980) did not find correlations between births under heavenly bodies and mental illness.

It would thus appear that either cosmic influences may result in a particular time of birth for each individual, or that births are initiated to coincide with propitious conjunctions of heavenly bodies. Eysenck and Nias suggest that it is the baby who chooses the time to initiate the birth process. They note, however, that this is a very complicated proposition because labor commences 5-15 hours prior to birth. Labor averages 9 hours in first births and 5 hours in subsequent births, and is 25% shorter when it occurs at night rather than during the day. Eysenck and

Nias do not even consider the multitudes of factors influencing conception, which add further complexity to their hypothesis.

Gauquelin's studies do not question or refute the claims of astrologers that heavenly bodies continue to influence people's destinies. However, there is no research evidence as yet to support these claims.

Eysenck and Nias carefully consider the responses of skeptics to Gauquelin's research. They find that criticisms by such groups as the Belgian Committee for the Scientific Investigation of Alleged Paranormal Phenomena (Committee Para) and the American Committee for the Scientific Investigation of Claims of the Paranormal (CSICOP) have serious biases, of the kind that is not consistent with forthright scientific inquiry. They have claimed that it is impossible to assess time of birth with sufficient accuracy to permit this sort of analysis. What they consistently ignore is the fact that the control groups do not show these effects, while groups of people whose births conform to the stated criteria repeatedly demonstrate the effects to a significant degree. The Gauquelins emphasized this point again and again, using samples from several countries, and repeatedly demonstrate that people who excel in their professions show these effects while other people do not.[878]

Eysenck and Nias go so far as to state:

> We have looked carefully at the arguments concerning statistical evaluation and experimental design, and we have inspected with great interest the debates between the Gauquelins and their critics on various points. We have come to the definite conclusion that the critics have often behaved in an irrational and scientifically unusual manner, violating principles they themselves have laid down, failing to adhere to their own rules, failing to consult the Gauquelins on details of tests to be carried out, or failing to inform them on vital points of the results. We have not found any similar misdemeanor on the part of the Gauquelins, who seem to have behaved throughout in a calm, rational and scientifically acceptable manner, meeting criticism by appropriate re-analysis of the data, by the collection of new data, however laborious the process might have been, and by rational argument. We do not feel that the "scientific" community emerges with any great credit from these encounters. (p.202)

Solar effects

Relationships between heavenly bodies and other biological systems have also been observed (Gauquelin 1970). Gauquelin found negative health effects associated with solar flare activity, including heart attacks, deaths from tuberculosis, eclampsia (hypertension in pregnancy) and epidemics.

He reviews research of other scientists demonstrating the following findings:

1. An inorganic chemical reaction may be influenced by sunspot activity. Giorgio Piccardi, Director of the Institute of Inorganic Chemistry at the University of Florence, is credited with clarifying the mysterious variability in a process for removing *scale,* a calcareous deposit, from industrial boilers.

...Household saucepans are an example of this... and, in industry, boilers follow the same rule. These calcareous deposits would impair their function if a procedure had not long existed for descaling them. The procedure is simple: at regular intervals *physically treated* water is put into the boiler. This special water, called "activated water," removes the carbonate of limestone when it is heated; instead of forming a hard and thick crust, like ordinary water, it removes the crusts already formed in a kind of scum. The procedure is very simple, but at the present time the way it works is completely incomprehensible to scientists...

...a glass phial containing a drop of mercury and low-pressure neon, is gently moved about in the water. As the buoy is moved, the mercury slides on the glass; the double layer of electricity between the mercury and the glass splits and produces a reddish glow through the neon. The water which comes in contact with the buoy thereby becomes "activated"...

Many scientists were skeptical that the process described above could affect the water, especially as there were no observable chemical changes detectable in the activated water. Furthermore, activated water was not reliably effective, and results might vary with the time of day, or the date. When Piccardi found that the variability in the effectiveness of the activated water was reduced by placing a metal screen over his laboratory test tubes, he was encouraged to seek an outside influence for this phenomenon. In a decade of exploration he gathered convincing evidence that this variability correlated with minor sunspot activity, which caused short-term changes; major sunspot activity, which caused eleven-year cycles of changes; and months in the year (March and September) when the earth's course through space intersects galactic lines of EM force at a particular angle, which caused lesser changes.

2. Human serum albumin changes its chemical properties in correlation with a number of solar factors. Maki Takata (1938), a Japanese doctor, developed a test in which serum albumin flocculates (clumps) when a particular chemical reagent is added to it. The degree of flocculation correlates with women's ovarian hormonal cycles, and this test was therefore useful in gynecological evaluations. In men the degree of flocculation remains constant. In 1938, after many had been successfully using the flocculation test for several years, doctors began to report extreme, unpredictable and unexplained variability in their results with this test. Takata confirmed that this was true even in testing men.

Takata methodically examined the new responses of serum albumin in his test, discovering that identical, simultaneous rises and falls in reactivity were noted in serum from patients in distant parts of Japan and in several other countries as well. In 1951, after thirteen years' work, he found conclusive proof that the variations were related to the sun. Flocculation indices rose markedly just prior to sunrise, and when the test was performed in a high-flying airplane. They fell during a solar eclipse or when the test was performed in a deep mine shaft. It was also discovered that the sudden variability in 1938 correlated with a periodic increase in solar flare activity. The particular aspect of solar radiations responsible for these changes is not known. Laboratory exposure of people to X-rays, gamma rays or neutrons produced effects that were similar to but not as marked as those of the sun.

3. German scientists G. Caroli and J. Pichotka demonstrated that both inorganic (*Piccardi type*) and organic variabilities (such as the Takata test) occurred during the same time periods.

4. Russian scientist N. Schulze found that sunspot activity correlates with reductions in numbers of white blood cells in healthy people.

Gauquelin's observations on correlations of inorganic and organic reactions with sunspot activity present a mystery as well as a caution. Students of subtle energies may themselves be subject to variability related to sunspots. This may help to explain why healing works on some occasions and not on others.

A variety of subtle energy observations appear similar to those reviewed by Gauquelin.

Burr and Ravitz report extensive correlations between geophysical conditions and changes in the biological fields of plants and animals.[879] A. J. Becker (1990) found that sunspot activity correlated modestly with aggravated assaults and with cases of murder and non-negligent manslaughter. Victor Yagodinsky reports solar and magnetic effects on virus and bacteria.

The underlying mechanisms linking these reactions with the sun have yet to be elucidated. Viktor Adamenko (1972a) reports on a study by Velkover demonstrating that certain characteristics of bacteria could reliably be used to predict solar flares one week before they occur. Adamenko proposes several possibilities to explain this effect:

1. The bacteria may respond directly to solar EM or corpuscular emanations;
2. They may respond to changes in the earth's magnetic field; or
3. They may react to some unknown emanation that has specific biological effects.[880]

From the accumulated evidence, it is evident that solar influences upon biological systems exist. These are subtle but distinct and measurable. Further work is clearly warranted to clarify the extent and nature of these effects, which may well be relevant to bioenergy therapies.

Lunar influences

Lunar influences on various aspects of life are legendary, though many consider such reports to be no more than myth and fable. Yet various studies suggest that there may well be correlations between phases of the moon and earthly events.

In the most thorough analysis of these possible effects, Dean Radin and Jannine Rebman review reports on lunar correlates with human behaviors. These include *anecdotal reports* of: problems at or near the full moon, including increased postoperative bleeding (Guiley); psychiatric disturbances (Daquin, in Oliven; Guiley), and alcoholism (Oliven). Research shows significant correlations with homicides (Geller/ Shannon), psychiatric hospital admissions (H. Friedman et al.; Weiskott/ Tipton), and various other crises (Snoyman/ Holdstock). Other studies show *inconsistent correlations* with madness (J. B. Chapman), homicides (Pokorn/

Jackimczyk), and other findings that could be simply coincidental, as in calls to fire and police stations (Frey et al). A meta-analysis in 1985 concluded there was insufficient evidence to support correlations of lunar phase with lunacy (Rotton/ Kelly), but a later reconsidered opinion suggested that an effect was present but was very small, on the order of 25.7% vs. the 25% expected by chance. A review of 20 studies on lunar phases and suicide was also unconvincing (S. Martin et al).

Radin and Rebman then summarize their study in Clark County, Nevada on the correlations of lunar phase with 37 variables, including weather (sunlight, maximum, minimum and range of daily temperatures, precipitation, wind speed, humidity, and barometric pressure); geophysics (daily planetary geomagnetic indices, sunspot number, and radio flux); abnormal behavior (911 telephone emergency service crisis calls, suicides, admission to a county mental health department for observation and for treatment); crime (homicides); death rates (total, motor vehicle, and other accidents); financial behavior (average of residuals of 250 de-trended mutual funds); and "Pick 3" state lottery payouts (6 individual states and their average).

They point out that there are actually five ways to measure lunar cycles,[881] which may account for some of the variability and conflict in research reports.

Radin and Rebman present a series of analyses of data collected throughout the entire year of 1993.

1. Linear correlations were calculated for the moon phase with each variable. Then averages were calculated for periods of 1-15 days before and after the full moon, and a correlation was calculated on a 29-step sine curve of the lunar phase vs. the 29-element average variable array.
2. Correlations of maximum and minimum values with the time of the full moon were calculated, with particular focus on maximum deviations found relative to the full moon.
3. The mean values of data were calculated for each item 14 days prior to the full moon and compared to the means for 14 days following the full moon.[882]

Positive correlations were noted between lunar phases and psychotic behaviors ($p < .04$); total deaths ($p < .0276$); death rate for motor vehicle accidents for men ($p < .0016$); and stock prices ($p < .0117$).[883] Correlations were also found with the geophysical variables of daily planetary magnetic indices ($p < .0180$); sunspot numbers as reported by NOAA ($p < .0000$); and 10.7-cm solar radio flux ($p < .0000$). The average of 6 states' lottery payout percentages showed a significant negative correlation ($p < .0076$).

Of particular interest are findings that result when correlations with maximum and minimum values are calculated. The minimum of sunlight occurred on the day of the full moon ($p = NS$), and correlations were noted with the full moon for minimum temperature ($p < 10^{-9}$); maximum temperature ($p < 10^{-9}$); precipitation ($p < .009$); barometric pressure ($p < .003$); crisis calls ($p < 10^{-9}$); strange behaviors ($p < .029$); homicide overall ($p < .004$; male homicide *increases* $p < .0000$; female *decreases* $< .012$); male deaths ($p < .007$); female deaths ($p < .046$); and female motor vehicle accidents ($p < 10^{-5}$).[884]

Abrupt changes were also found in the rates of suicides (rising with the waxing moon, dropping sharply at the full moon); total deaths (dropping 7-9 days before and 2-6 days after the full moon); and crisis calls (rising sharply on the day of the full moon).

Complex spectral analyses of the data confirmed that the results are unlikely to represent chance anomalous findings.

Discussing the results, Radin and Rebman note that two types of theories explaining lunar effects include the variable of tidal effects influencing biological systems and lunar/ weather interactions[885] (Geller/ Shannon; Lieber/ Sherin). Critics suggest that the tidal fluctuations involve such small gravitational changes that effects on humans are unlikely (I. Kelly et al), although effects on fish and on small mammals have been demonstrated (Lieber). Other critics observe that there are correlations between lunar phase and behavior does not necessarily mean that these are related in a causal manner (Rotton/ Kelly). A simpler correlation might be with stormy weather, which is related to moon phase (Guiley), and can have a negative influence on mood (Persinger/ Levesque).

It is also apparent that the magnitude of these changes is small in terms of numbers and percentages, despite their statistical significance. Thus the increase in psychiatric admissions from one day prior to the full moon to one day afterward was only a tenth of a person, and the increase in deaths from one week prior to the day of the full moon was only one person. Crisis calls increased by only 1.5%.

There are many other reports of phenomena on Earth which correlate with positions of heavenly bodies.[886] Here are a few of these:[887]

1. At or near the time of the full moon there are more homicides (Lieber/ Sherin; Lieber 1978); aggravated assaults, as well as a wide variety of other crimes (Tasso/ Miller); psychiatric admissions (Weiskott/ Tipton) and emergency room admissions. A slight but not significant increase in suicides was noted at the time of the full moon (Garth/ Lester) and the new moon (P. Jones/ Jones).

One difficulty in these studies is to determine at which point a meaningful causal relationship might have existed between moods, mental states, behaviors, and consequences of these behaviors. For example, a crime or emotional breakdown might have occurred hours after a particular conjunction of heavenly bodies.

2. Lunar influence seems to be demonstrated in a classical study on oysters. When Frank Brown (1954; 1959) transported a dozen oysters from the seashore in Connecticut a thousand miles away from their native ocean beds and placed them in a laboratory in Illinois that was shielded from outside light, the oysters had some unknown means of identifying when the local tides would be high. After an adjustment period of about 10 days they opened their shells during these hours, even though no clues from outside light or ocean water could reach them.

3. Brown found that a rat which remained in a cage under unchanging light and temperature was half as active when the moon was above the horizon as it was when the moon was below the horizon (Brown/ Terracini).

4. Brown measured the activity of four hamsters for two years, recording their use of an activity wheel. Lights were turned on and off at regular intervals. The hamsters learned to anticipate the timing of the changes in lighting, decreasing their activity just prior to the lights coming on, and increasing it just before they went

off. They also demonstrated significantly greater activity for four days following the full moon and for several days following the new moon (Brown/ Park).

M Klinowska studied a male hamster for a year and could not demonstrate correlations of activity with lunar phases. The difficulty with these studies is that they included small numbers of animals.

Arnold Lieber proposes that biological effects of lunar influences may be due to altered permeability of cell membranes and blood vessels. He does not present adequate evidence to support his hypothesis.

Variations in plant growth in several studies also have suggested lunar effects.

N. Kollerstrom found that potatoes grew 25 percent better if planted when the moon was in earth signs of the zodiac than when it was in water signs.

F. Brown and Chow found that the amount of water absorbed by bean seeds (controlled for temperature) was greater during the full moon. Jan Joy Panser, a biologist, found that water intake and germination of seeds correlated with moon phases (Spiritual Frontiers).

Harold S. Burr (1944; 1972), Professor Emeritus of Anatomy at Yale, and Leonard Ravitz (1962; 1970), a Neurologist at Duke University, measured direct current EM fields on a wide variety of animals and plants. They found that there were periodic variations in these measurements that were consistent across the entire range of measured species, and that correlated with atmospheric and geomagnetic potentials, lunar cycles, and sunspots. These scientists were able to reproduce their findings many times, but their experiments still await replication by others.[888]

Vlail Kaznacheyev (1982a) noted that frog hearts studied in the laboratory responded differently in different seasons to various experimental procedures.

Geomagnetic energies appear to be possible sources for many of these observed effects. For instance, the research on biological resonations with the Schumann standing waves was mentioned in Chapter II-3.[889]

All of these plant and animal studies await replication before any firm conclusions can be drawn. However, they appear to suggest that biological systems – including human beings – are sensitive to and influenced by geomagnetic and other geobiological energies.

Psi and geobiological effects
George B. Schaut and Michael Persinger, at Laurentian University in Canada, found that telepathic transmissions were more likely to succeed on days when there was low Earth geomagnetic activity, relative to attempted transmissions on preceding or following days. This effect was not observed with precognitive reports. Several confirmations of these observations were published.[890] They suggest that extremely low frequency (ELF) bands may be carriers for telepathy.

Sanley Krippner (1975) retrospectively reviewed results of his dream telepathy experiments. He found statistically significant differences in successful telepathic transmissions, correlated with phases of the moon. The second quarter, around the time of the full moon, was the most favorable.

A Russian psychiatrist, Dr. Soomere, reported findings exactly opposite to those of Krippner (from Krippner 1975). There were significantly fewer cases of spontaneous telepathy in his series during the full moon.

In another experiment, Krippner (1975) found results similar to Soomere's, thus contradicting his own initial findings. There were fewer successes with a test of clairvoyance during the full moon.

An unidentified editor of the journal *Spiritual Frontiers* reports on a number of healing studies related to geobiological effects:

1. Dr. Setzer performed a double-blind study on the effects of water left in church sanctuaries on the growth of radish plants, compared to the growth of radishes given tap water. Those that got the church water grew more, overall, but at an erratic rate that was related to moon phases. A high degree of correlation was noted but no numbers or statistics are presented. Water "taken from church close to the second and fourth lunar quarters (when the gravitational pull of the moon is increasing) always produced spectacular plant growth[W]ater… close to the first and third quarters produced growth less than or no better than the [control] plants…"

2. Edward Brame, an industrial scientist, found that water kept in churches during services showed an alteration in its infrared spectrophotometric pattern on Sundays near the full and new moon, and no effect at the half moon.

Discussion

Evidence is accumulating that the positions of heavenly bodies may be correlated with physiological processes of living organisms, as well as with various biochemical and industrial processes. The nature and import of these correlations are still a matter for conjecture. In some instances we may hypothesize causality (e.g. ionic radiation from solar flares, or tidal gravitational effects of the moon), though in others (e.g. positions of planets) the concatenation of heavenly and earthly events may be tied to different levels of causalities.[891]

Influences of the moon and of solar flares on health appear to be negative. This may have to do with gravitational effects, especially in the case of the moon. *How* these forces influence living organisms is as yet entirely unknown. The sun may emanate a field and/ or rays that affect biological systems either directly or secondarily, after interacting with the Earth's atmosphere or fields (perhaps by shifting atmospheric ionic balances). Gravity, EM fields, cosmic rays, or other unidentified rays or fields may be involved.

Although we view lunar effects as being caused by the moon, we must recall that they are usually maximal when the moon and sun are aligned in gravitational opposition. A solar contribution may therefore be relevant to lunar geobiological effects.

It is worth noting that "activated" water, which cannot be distinguished chemically from normal water, has a different interaction with calcareous deposits compared to the effects of normal water. This suggests that the effective alteration in activated water may be the result of an energy field alteration. Spectrophotometric analysis of activated water might reveal changes similar to healer-treated water.[892]

The manifestation of bacterial sensitivity to sunspot activity a week prior to the appearance of the sunspots suggests that there may be various forms of energy emitted by the sun that are detectable by living organisms but as yet unidentified by modern science. Interference in psi perceptions by geomagnetic activity like-wise suggests that there may be an unidentified energy that is common to both, or that telepathy is somehow related to electromagnetism (despite the fact that it does not diminish with distance between participants). Alternatively, the effects upon psi may be secondary to effects upon the brains or other physical features of the participants.

Kaznacheyev's observations on seasonal variability in frogs' hearts may relate to geobiological influences, or to hormonal differences due to seasonal variations in frogs. These might be related to temperature or life cycle fluctuations and unre-lated to direct influences of heavenly bodies.

Of relevance to spiritual healing research is the caveat that healing responses may fluctuate with geobiological conditions. This would mandate that appropriate controls be instituted in all experiments. The simplest method would be to pair experimental and control trials as closely as possible in time. At the least, such influences should be retrospectively sought and factored out of the data. This may potentially be another factor that could explain some of the seemingly irregular expressions of healing and psi effects.

Ecopsychology

In a more immediate sense, we are closely related to the planet Earth. Theodore Roszak coined the term *ecopsychology* to indicate this relationship. He focuses on our innate need to commune with nature both physically and psychologically.

This review of bioenergies suggests that our relationships to Gaia are even more intimate than we may have supposed, due to our energetic relationships with the cosmos. We are an integral energetic part of the ecobioenergetic system of our planet.[893] I discuss this subject further, as well as our spiritual relationship with Gaia, in the next two volumes of *Healing Research*.

Conclusion

If a man will begin with certainties, he shall end in doubts; but if he will be content to begin with doubts, he shall en d in certainties.
– Francis Bacon (1605)

Volume I of *Healing Research* presents rich anecdotal evidence that spiritual healing can accelerate recuperation from a variety of illnesses, and research evidence confirming many significant effects of healing on humans, animals, plants, bacteria, yeasts, cells in laboratory culture, enzymes, DNA and more.

It is therefore evident that through touch and mental intent we can influence the physical and psychological state of other people and of non-human organisms.

Volume II of *Healing Research* has explored a broader spectrum of healing phenomena. Here we have seen that there are a variety of ways in which we can both cause and heal ourselves of psychological and physical problems. Western medicine has assumed that such self-healings are brought about by the mind influencing the body – primarily through relaxation, with the concomitant harmonizing of functions of the nervous system and hormones. Recent research is beginning to add an appreciation of how the mind can also influence immune functions.

Complementary therapies are now being studied systematically, under rigorous research conditions. We are finding that many of the claims made over decades and centuries can be confirmed scientifically. Gradually, these therapies are being integrated into Western medical practice.

Studies of complementary therapies add to our understanding of how biological energy medicine works. The simplest explanation I have found is Einstein's Theory of Relativity, expressed in the equation $E = mc^2$. *Quantum physics* has confirmed that matter is interconvertible with energy. A living organism may be viewed as a physical object or as an energetic being. *Newtonian medicine* has barely begun to absorb the imports of this insight, while bioenergy practitioners have been saying for several millennia that the body can be understood and treated as energy.

The discipline of *biological energy medicine* is growing out of this understanding, shaped by health care practitioners with various beliefs and practices relating to bioenergies. We are just in the earliest stages of exploring how these biological energies function. Various complementary therapies suggest that there are biological energy lines, energy centers, and energy fields that interact with the body, emotions, mind, relationships and spirit. There are many ways in which we can actively interact with these bioenergy systems in the interest of health management.

Excess flows or blocks to flows of energies in the meridians are identified by acupuncture and its derivatives (acupressure, applied kinesiology, reaflexology, shiatsu), Therapeutic Touch, and other healing methods . Craniosacral therapists find bioenergy pulsations – especially around the head and spinal cord, but also around the rest of the body – which inform them about the state of the healee and the progress of the healing. Homeopathy and flower essences are given with the explanation that they convey a patterned biological essence in the water or in other vehicles that are used to administer these remedies. Spiritual healers report that they can sense (mostly through touch or visual perceptions) a bioenergy field around the body. Many people who are not healers can also sense these fields.[894]

Many bioenergy therapists believe that the biofield acts as a template for the physical body, and is also a reflection of the current condition of the body. Two lines of evidence support this assertion. First, the various treatments that influence the energy body can bring about changes in physical and psychological conditions. Second, some spiritual healers report that they can see abnormalities in the bioenergy field prior to the development of physical illness, often preceding the manifestation of physical evidence of disease by several weeks and months. The function of the biofield as a template also could explain how the physical body maintains its integrity during growth and during repairs following injuries.

Bioenergy therapists also suggest that the biofield is influenced by a person's emotions, mind, relationships (with others and with the environment), and spirit.

At this stage in our explorations of bioenergy medicine, it is still difficult to be clear or certain regarding the patterns we are beginning to explore.

> *We are like flies crawling across the ceiling of the Sistine Chapel. We cannot see what angels lie underneath the threshold of our perceptions. We... live in our paradigms, our habituated perceptions... the illusions we share through culture we call reality, but the true... reality of our condition is invisible to us.*
>
> – William Irwin Thompson (p.81)

Elements of spiritual healing appear to be common denominators in all of these complementary therapy frameworks (Benor 1995a).

Spiritual healing is practiced through an apparent exchange of bioenergies between healer and healee. These exchanges may promote healing by: 1. adding energies to a healee's depleted bioenergy system; 2. removing excesses of energies; 3. removing blocks to energy flows within the healee's bioenergy system; 4. converting bioenergy patterns of illness into patterns of health; 5. influencing the body directly, through interactions with the nervous, hormonal, and/ or immune systems; or 6. through combinations of the above.

Some or all of the above mechanisms may include exchanges of information that accompany exchanges of bioenergies. In fact, we may come to understand bioenergies as combinations of information with energy.

Once we conceive of ourselves as energy organisms, we become more aware of vast, known and potential interactions with our environment. While our conventional instruments tell us that an electromagnetic field cannot have *material* influence beyond a measurable distance, the laws of physics tell us that EM fields extend to infinity. We may be influenced by vibrations of sound, of light, and of the entire electromagnetic spectrum that exists outside of our usual sensory awareness. As energy denizens of the cosmos, we are in constant energetic communication and interaction with all that is.

Homeopathy suggests even more profound resonations with our environment. Energetic patterns of various mineral and plant substances interact with the bioenergy patterns of humans and animals in ways that can harmonize physical and psychological functions and promote healing. The world – including plants, animals, minerals and universe around us are not just composed of non-human, inanimate or "dead" matter. Each and every element in the universe, including thoughts, words and metaphors, can have an influence on us – and we on them.

In summary, we see that there appear to be diverse biofields that can be accessed and manipulated through the practices of the various energy medicine specialties. The minds of healee and healer appear to be active elements in these bioenergy interactions with the body. Our beliefs and disbeliefs may influence our states of health and illness. Healing energy fields may enter into the processes of spiritual healing and self-healing through visualizations and through therapeutic ministrations of health professionals, even without the knowledge of the participants. Intentions of healers and healees may reshape disease processes through bioenergies and intentions.

We are just in the earliest stages of sorting out how biological energy approaches can be integrated with conventional medical care. The enormous complexities of both systems make this a monumental task.

Considering the sensitivity of bioenergy and consciousness interactions, the *how* of integrative medicine may be even more important than the *what*.

> *[B]ecause the whole is so much greater than the sum of the parts –*
> *the relationship between the parts becomes the biggest part of all.*
> – Stephen Covey (in DiCarlo p.220)

Our bioenergetic connections and interactions with our environment make us much more intimately a part of our environment than Western culture generally accepts. The evidence presented in Volumes I supports the evidence reveiewed in this volume, which suggests that all life on this planet is a part of the ecobiological entity called *Gaia* and of the wider universe beyond.

Volume III extends the review of research in the fields of bioenergies and consciousness into the spiritual dimensions. It examines scientific evidence supporting reports from healers, mystics, and healees regarding the spirit and spiritual awareness. These are aspects of healing that are not yet included in much of mainstream energy medicine, but which are often reported as essential in spiritual healing.

Volume IV explores theories that may explain some elements of energy medicine and of healing processes, along with a detailed synthesis of our present-day understanding of healing. Some people object to the suggestion that there are biological energies that provide the substratum for spiritual healing and other complementary therapies. These skeptics demand that proof of such energies must be registered on some instrument in order to verify their existence. The best instrument for this purpose appears to be the human organism, which is an exquisitely delicate sensor and instrument for interventions with subtle energies. Volume IV reviews this and other theories that attempt to explain healing. Various reasons why healing has not been accepted by conventional, Newtonian, medicine are also discussed in detail. Volume IV also includes my personal experiences in learning to open myself to the infinite possibilities of spiritual awareness and healing.

> *...It is we who, with our minds, determine the final shape of reality. Which is not to say that the world is "all in the mind." It would be more accurate to suggest that the mind is all in the world. That it is part of the world, in fact, because we are intimately involved.*
> – Lyall Watson (1989, p. 40)

Appendix A

VARIATIONS ON THE THEME OF PSYCHOTHERAPY

There are enormous variations in psychotherapy approaches from one school of practice to another. Here are just a few examples.

Bioenergy therapy Therapies that address the person as energy that interacts with the physical body, where the energies provide information about the body and offer avenues of access to shift the body towards greater harmony and health.[896]

Bodymind therapy Psychotherapy that invites awareness of what the body is saying about our past and present relationships with ourselves and each other.[897]

Cognitive therapy relies on clients' thinking functions to identify misperceptions and self-destructive behavior patterns. The therapist introduces new perspectives, and encourages clients to practice applying these in every day life.[898]

Cognitive behavior therapy (A. ~Ellis 1962; Ellis/ Grieger) combines elements of both the cognitive and behavioral approaches, which are symptom and goal oriented.

Creative arts therapies Music, art, movement, dance, metaphor, poetry, journaling, psychodrama invite explorations that stage our issues and conflict in new and innovative ways, inviting us to explore and re-evaluate our relationships to ourselves, to others and to the cosmos.

Dream analysis Invites explorations of dramatic hints about our inner selves that are thrown up on the screen of our consciousness, inviting us to explore issues our unconscious minds consider important to our lives.[899]

Energy Psychology (See Meridian Based Therapies).

Eye Movement Desensitization and Reprocessing (*EMDR*) teaches clients to move their eyes back and forth laterally, or to alternate stimulating the right and left sides of their body as they focus on a problem.[900]

Gestalt Therapy (Perls) invites clients to put words to aspects of their behaviors, the images in their dreams, their sub-personalities, and their anticipated reactions of others. Clients can then dialogue back and forth with their inner self to discover the sources of their discomforts.

Hypnotherapy uses potent suggestions to explore the depths of clients' consciousness, and to introduce and strengthen new beliefs and behavior patterns.[901]

Imagery/ Visualization/ Metaphor Imaginary stages upon which we can explore old and new ways to deal with our lives creatively.[902]

Jungian analysis (Jung) focuses mostly on dreams and archetypal imagery to sort out clients' belief systems. *Jungian analysis* can also extend into transpersonal realms, if the analyst is open to this. In my experience, psychoanalysis can help with existential issues, and is particularly useful for psychotherapists who wish to understand the workings of their own minds in order to be more helpful to their clients.[903]

Meditation Practice of mental discipline that allows one to not focus on stressful issues, promotes physical, psychogical and spiritual health in many ways.[904]

Meridian Based Therapies (also called *Energy Psychology*) invite clients to tap on acupressure points while mentally focused on a problem. Some of these therapies also have clients simultaneously recite an affirmation while tapping on these points.[905]

Metaphor See Imagery.

Mind-Body Therapy Therapy that addresses body issues through conscious and unconscious interventions. (See also Bodymind Therapy)

Neurolinguistic Programming or NLP (Bandler/ Grinder) introduces elements of hypnotic suggestion and conditioning to bring about focused, rapid changes in clients' beliefs, emotional responses, and behaviors.[906]

Primal Scream Therapy (Janov) encourages intense releases of emotions so clients will stop holding in negative feelings that could inhibit or even cripple them in their relationships.

Psychoanalysis is offered in several variations, all focused on uncovering inner psychological processes, and requiring sessions once (or preferably several times) weekly for many years. Deepening insight, rather than achieving behavioral change, is the goal of psychoanalysis. **Freudian analysis* (A. Freud; ~S. Freud) focuses on early childhood traumas, and uses the client's associations and dreams to guide therapists as they help clients to recognize the conflicts in their unconscious mind. The process of transference, or projection of beliefs and expectations onto the therapist, also reveals the inner workings of the clients's mind.[907]

Psychodrama invites clients to act out their conflicts with others who may have similar problems, but who may respond differently in the same situation. This allows clients to release buried feelings, acquire new insights about their responses to various situations, and explore new options for response.[908]

Psychoneuroimmunology Combination of relaxation, meditation, imagery and group support that enhances immune functions.

Psychosynthesis (Assagioli) invites clients to find spiritual inspiration to help them deal with their problems. It combines a broad spectrum of techniques, including creative arts, gestalt therapy, and others.

Relaxation Relaxing the body and mind individually and collectively promotes health.[909]

Rogerian therapy (~Rogers) assumes that clients have all the tools they need to sort out their own problems, and requires only the listening ear and empathy of the therapist to bring these out. The principal agent for change is the therapist's unconditional acceptance.

Transactional Analysis (~Stewart/ Joines) translates psychoanalytic terminology into everyday language that can alert clients to aspects of themselves and others that may be in conflict. For instance: your inner *parent* may plague you with injunctions about what you should and shouldn't be doing; your inner *child* may rebel against these injunctions; and your *adult* self may have a difficult time deciding how to resolve this inner conflict, and how to behave in this situation. TA combines insight, emotional clarity, and behavioral changes to help clients recognize and deal with their own self-defeating habits.

Transpersonal psychotherapy introduces a variety of spiritual elements into psychotherapy, such as meditation, prayer, and discussions of spiritual issues.[910]

Visualization See imagery.

The *Wholistic Hybrid of EMDR and EFT (WHEE)* combines the Eye Movement Desensitization and Emotional Freedom Techniques, utilizing the alternating stimulation of both sides of the body while reciting an affirmation.

Stress levels associated with problems the clients focus on rapidly diminish with all of these approaches. Clients can then install positive affirmations to replace the negative feelings and beliefs they have relinquished (Benor 2001a).

Notes

Foreword

[1] C. Norman Shealy, MD, PhD is a neurosurgeon specializing in holistic therapies for pain and other problems. Dr. Shealy's research on healing for depression and clairvoyant diagnosis is reviewed in Chapters 4 and 5 of *Healing Research, Volume I – Spiritual Healing: Scientific Validation of a Healing Revolution i*

Introduction

[2]. The term *healee* is used to designate a recipient of healing.

[3] Many quotes counterpoint the text and invite readers to consider intuitive ways of understanding and appreciating the linear discussions. I have collected these over many years from a wide variety of sources. Wherever possible, I have included the original source. Often, suchquotes are cited without reference, so I am unable to point the reader to the original source.

e more commonly used *alternative,* which tends to be polarizing.

[4] **Spiritual healing** is used here as a generic term for treatments using the laying-on of hands, intent, and/ or prayer – such as Therapeutic Touch, Healing Touch, Reiki, external Qigong, and many others. These are extensively discussed, and 191 controlled studies of healing are reviewed in *Healing Research, Volume I.*

[5] More on **physicists and mystics** in Chapters III-10; IV-2, IV-3; Capra; Dossey 1982; 1993; Jahn/ Dunne 1987.

[6] This is a composite clinical picture from several people who struggled with these problems.

[7] Parapsychology as related to healing is discussed in Chapter I-3.

[8] **Psi phenomena** are discussed in detail in Chapter I-3. See the **glossary** for explanations of terms.

[9] Healing has also been called *psi* healing, *faith* healing, *mental* healing, *paranormal* healing, etc. More on the many names for healing in I-Introduction.

Chapter 1

[10] See extensive discussion of biological energies in the following chapters of this volume.

[11] Though subsequent studies failed to replicate these results, the research methods used in the later experiments apparently did not follow the same careful assessment procedures for identifying Type A subjects (Dienstfrey; Sys et al.).

[12] Many clinicians have lost interest in the Type A personality, feeling that the research literature is not clear-cut in supporting this typology. I believe this is a mistake

[13] I have found this much-cited notion of addressing the person who has the disease attributed to Sir William Osler and to Hippocrates (references lost).

[14] Dossey 1998a; Hirshberg/ Barasch; O'Regan/ Hirshberg; Roud

[15] See discussion on personality development – as a basis for understanding meditation – later in this chapter.

[16] The Jungian functions have been translated into the Myers-Briggs psychological test, and are quite useful in psychotherapy (Jung 1967; Sharp).

[17] J. Goldberg; Johnson.

[18] See more on **Jungian polarities** and **shadow** under *reasons healing has not been accepted*, in Chapter IV-3. More on treatment of shadow in Bly 1988; Goldberg 1993; Johnston.

[19] Healing is specifically helpful for chronic state anxiety. See **studies of healing for anxiety** by C. Ferguson; Fedoruk; Gulak; Heidt; Quinn, summarized in Chapter I-4. See discussion of **healing for meta-anxiety** in Chapter IV-3[20] I highly recommend Dethlefsen; Dahlke; Harrison; Hay; Rossi 1986a; and Steadman for discussions on **how emotional conflicts and tensions lead to illness and how awareness and abreaction can be curative.** See also Knaster.

[21] Ader; Ader/ Cohen; *Advances;* G. Baker; R. Booth; Chopra; Dienstfrey (of particular interest, detailing aspects of mind within the body); Pert 1986; Pert/ Dienstfrey; Pert, et al.; Solomon 1993 (102 postulates).

[22] On **psychosomatic medicine**: Sadock/ Kaplan; Knaster; Ornstein; Sobel. On precise descriptions of psychosomatic diagnoses: American Psychiatric Association, Diagnostic and Statistical Manual.

[23] There are varying views on differences and similarities between psychotherapy and counseling. I see psychotherapy as being treatment that brings people to a greater depth of awareness and more profound changes in their understanding, behaviors and relationships than counseling does. However, in psychotherapy (second only to spiritual healing), the person who is the therapist is as important (often even more important) than the methodologies used in the therapy. There is therefore an enormous overlap between the two approaches.

[24] **Body memories** are discussed later in this chapter.

[25] Eeman termed the presentation of physical symptoms that are based on emotional traumatic memories *myognosis.*

[26] Hypnosis is discussed later in this chapter.

[27] Janov is a little hard to take when he touts his method as the only one that is worthwhile. His arrogant manner and readiness to make brash, poorly supported claims have left the vast majority of professionals resistant to what I see as quite penetrating observations regarding the process of intensive psychotherapy.

[28] Benson 1972; 1975; 1996.

[29] Lowen 1958; 1975; 1980.

[30] Pierrakos 1974; 1975; 1986.

[31] See discussion of **massage** in Chapter II-2.

[32] A variety of **orgone energy devices** were invented by Reich and are still in use by his followers, as will be discussed in Chapter II-3.

[33] See discussion of massage techniques in Chapter II-2.

[34] See discussion of Network Spinal Analysis and the Bowen technique in Chapter II-2.

[35] Many people will notice that the feelings connected with the negative memory are markedly less intense.

[36] On **Research in psychotherapy** see references in Chapter 2.

[37] More on PNI, including a review of research, later in this chapter.

[38] *(Advances* 1993, 9 [3])

[39] More on the work of Ornish below.

[40] See section on suggestion later in this chapter.

[41] Eisenbud 1970; Mintz/ Schmeidler; Ullman 1953; 1959; 1974; 1977.

[42] See discussion of psi research in Chapter I-3.

[43] Internal feedback loops are discussed under *Self-healing* and *Biofeedback*, later in this chapter.

[44] For more on **feedback loops** of interdependent, complementary needs and behaviors **surrounding illness**, as well as systems theory analyses of these problems, I highly recommend Bateson 1972; von Bertalanffy 1966; B. Brown 1985; Haley 1976; G.E. Schwartz 1984; Taub-Bynum; Watzlawick/ Weakland 1974.

[45] Dossey; Sherrill/ Larson; an entire issue of the *Journal of the American Medical Association (JAMA)* was devoted to problems of publication bias (March 9, 1990).

[46] Kaja Finkler (1985) provides an excellent example of such social factors and belief systems in operation among Mexican spiritualist healers and their adherents.

[47] **Visualization** is discussed in Chapter II-2.

[48] See Volume III of *Healing Research* for research and discussions of spiritual dimensions.

[49] Other references on **changing persistent patterns of perceiving and behaving**: Greenwood/ Nunn; Laing 1970; D. Quinn; Watzlawick/ Weakland/ Fisch. Other references on **systems theory**: Abu-Mustafa; Flood; Kauffman; J. G. Miller; Mithaug; Russek/ Schwartz; G. Schwartz 1982; 1984b; 1987; 1989; 1994; 1996; G. Schwartz/ Russek 1996a; b; von Bertalanffy; Yates. See further discussions on **systems theory**, on **information as an explanation for healing** and on **chaos** in Chapter IV-2.

[50] John Pierrakos, below, discusses the unity of this apparent hierarchy, when conceived and perceived through the bioenergies that interlink all of these levels.

[51] A recent addition to the list is to cover the skin with duct tape for several days, finding that the warts come off when the tape is removed.

[52] A **placebo** is an inert substance or other treatment which, in and of itself, does not have any therapeutic effect through chemical or other action. Its efficacy lies in the suggestion tendered by the therapist or perceived by the healee in association with the treatment. The belief of the healee that she/ he is receiving a potent treatment activates self-healing mechanisms. About a third of all people will respond to nearly any treatment whatsoever. Classically, sugar pills were used to study these effects. More on placebo responses later in this chapter.

[53] More on placebos below.

[54] See St. Clair, Chapter III-5 on **spirit guides.**

[55] See Spraggett, Chapter III-11 on **spiritual healing by Katherine Kuhlman**.

[56] In his article he discusses suggestion and placebo effects, Lourdes and holy water, Christian Science, psychic surgeons, and more.

[57] James Randi and William Nolen are dismissive in this way about healing; Paris Flammonde does the same with radionics (discussed in Chapter 4).

[58] Though Frank's emphasis is on religious conversion, the same **factors of suggestion engendered by the social setting** almost certainly apply to the physical healings observed in revival meeting settings. See also Calestro for a discussion of these issues, emphasizing suggestion; Inglis 1981 for contagious hysterical symptoms (many of which sound like cases of hyperventilation). For discussions of **self-healing by auto-suggestion:** Lambillion; J. Schwarz 1972. Other references on self-healing: Borysenko; Borysenko/ Borysenko; E. Brown; L. Gilmore; Goleman/ Gurin; Harrison; Hay; Knaster; Pelletier; Steadman. See also Beck; Peper on healer and healee beliefs in Therapeutic Touch. (More on this subject at the end of this chapter.)

[59] See Rosenthal/ Rubin for a review of 345 studies on the **experimenter effect.** Solfvin 1982, reviewed in Chapter 1-4, and Spindrift, reviewed in Chapter 1-5, have gone much further in their research on experimenter effects in psi and healing, suggesting that experimenters may influence their studies through psi. If these studies can be replicated, they could throw into question the validity of the methods used in randomized controlled trials. That is, they would imply that experimenters could influence the results of controlled studies via psi, despite all implementation of blinds and controls. Wiseman/ Schlitz performed a classical study of psi experimenter effects, showing that the experimenter's beliefs and disbeliefs could shape the results of studies conducted with otherwise identical protocols. Sheldrake (1999) suggests that experimenter effects should be considered in all scientific research, as they may bias findings even with non-human subjects.

[60] Appelbaum; Kiev (1964, 1968); Moerman; Finkler 1985.

[61] For further **discussions on varieties of healings in other cultures**, see also R. Beck 1967; Boshier; Boyd; Calderon; Ding-ming (Chinese); Dirksen; Dobkin de Rios 1984a; b; Eliade; Finkler 1980; 1981; Freidson; Garrison; Geisler 1984; 1985a; 1985b; Golomb; Gonzalez; Grossinger; Halifax; Heinze 1984; 1985; Kapur; Katz; Kerewsky-Halpern; Kleinman 1973; 1980; Koss; Krippner 1980; E. Crippner/ Welch (outstanding discussion on shamanic healings); Landy; Levi-Strauss; Moerman; Morley/ Wallis; Mullin; Murphet 1972; 1978; J. Neal; Oubre; Peters; Peters/ Price-Williams; *Phoenix,* Romanucci-Ross et al.; Sandner; Sandweiss; Singer;

Slomoff; Webster; Winkelman; A. Young. For a description of Hawaiian Huna healings, which involve a heavy dose of suggestion administered with psi skills, see M. Long (Chapter 1); S. King 1983. For blends of Eastern and Western psychotherapeutic approaches see Ajaya; Kakar; Elbert; Russell; Sheikh/ Sheikh; and for a Western blend see Shealy/ Myss 1988.

On **healing within religious contexts:** Ikin; MacNutt.

Prince discusses **differences between psychoanalysis and faith healing.**

For reviews of studies on religion and health: Levin 1988; 1993a; 1994 (extensive refs); Levin/ Schiller; Levin/ Vanderpool 1987 (extensive refs); 1989; 1992. Also Jarvis/ Northcutt; Schiller/ Levin; Witter et al.

For a discussion of **conscious and unconscious fears of healing** see Chapter IV-3, "Reasons Healing Has Not Been Accepted" (Benor 1990).

For **color effects on health and human behavior** see Plack; Schick. **Light and health** is discussed by Lieberman; Ott.

[62] **Placebo responses** are reviewed by H. Beecher 1955; 1959: 1961; Harrington; Honigfeld; Moerman 2002; A. Shapiro 1960a; 1960b; 1971; White, Tursky/ Schwartz. Cobb et al. review surgical procedure as placebo. S. Wolf looks at the pharmacology of placebos. See also Uhlenhuth; Uhlenhuth et al. **Health improvements in people on waiting lists:** Bergin 1971; Bergin/ Lambert; Lambert.

[63] See more on metaphors in psychotherapy below, under *hypnosis.* J. Harrison; Hay.

[64] See more on nocebo effects under **the will to live,** below.

[65] **Many further factors that can influence healing** are discussed in Chapter IV-3.

[66] Healing effects on water are reviewed in Chapter I-2.

[67] It is paradoxical and distressing to find studies on *hope* which entail the killing of animals. See also Dossey 1991 on *hope* in medical practice.

[68] For more on **hex and voodoo** see Dossey 1991; Chapter IV-3. For **giving up on life** see Seligman; for **the will to live** see Hutschnecker. For the evil eye as a possible hypnotic phenomenon see Machovec. For nocebo effects, see Lown.

[69] A wide range of **hypnotic phenomena and effects** are described by: Ahser; Barber 1969; 1984; Bellis; Black, et al.; Bowers; de Saussure; Cheek 1994; Dingwall; Eurley; Frankel; Gilian; Hilgard; Honiotest; Lynn/ Rhue; C. Patel 1993; Playfair 1975a; 1985b; Sinclair-Geiben/ Chalrners; H. Spiegel/ Spiegel; Staib/ Logan (breast growth); Surman, et al.; Tinterow; Ullman/ Dudek; Wickramasesekera; Willard (breast growth); Williams (breast growth). Excellent professional discussions on **hypnotherapy** are presented by Rhue, et al.; Rossi; Rossi/ Cheek; Spiegel/ H. Spiegel; and for the layperson, see Caprio/ Berger; Kendall/ Hunt. **Research** presented in Fromm/ Nash. Bandler/ Grinder present **Neurolinguistic Programming,** a variant of hypnosis. Haley 1973 discusses the hypnotic suggestions of Milton Erickson, including very rapid indications of trance, and suggestions without apparent trance. Wallas introduces **hypnotic suggestions** through stories. Aronson discusses hypnotic alterations of space and time perception. Hypnotic alterations of immune responses are described by Black et al.; G. Smith McDaniel. Hypnosis for hemophilia is described by Fredericke; LaBaw. Newton uses hypnosis in the treatment of cancer; Garcia describes negative suggestion causing dermatitis; Gitlin induced abilities to hear weak electrical fields; Inglis 1981 mentions a case of execution by hypnosis. For suggestion under anesthesia see Evans/ Richardson; Pearson. See also Chapter III-3 on reincarnation memories under hypnosis. Eisenbud 1983 discusses fears of hypnosis and psi, which may have led to discontinuation of hypnotically induced psi in the late 19th century.

[70] Dreaper; Sinclair-Gieben/ Chalmers, Ullman 1959.

[71] Aronoff et al.; British Tuberculosis Association; Collison.

[72] Bensen; Clawson/ Swade; McCord 1968a.

[73] This is discussed in detail in Chapter III-3. For past life hypnotic regressions see Weiss 1994; 1995; 1996. See Netherton for accessing past life memories without hypnosis during counseling; Kelsey/ Grant for accessing past life memories through a psychic/ intuitive consultation; Gershom 1992; 1996 for troublesome past life memories that spontaneously intrude in current lives.

[74] For reviews of **ESP with hypnosis,** see Edmunds; Honorton/ Krippner 1969; van de Castle 1969. For original French literature on telepathic hypnotic induction, see Janet 1886; Richet 1886.

[75] Skin vision has also been called *dermal optics.*

[76] Shaposhnikov does not describe his selection procedures for subjects sufficiently to clarify whether his report is in contradiction of Wilson/ Barber's. Shaposhnikov may have selected subjects similar to those of Wilson/ Barber.

[77] Rush criticizes Vasiliev's criteria for deciding whether the subject was asleep due to tele-pathic hypnotic induction, or due to naturally occurring sleep. The coincidence of the timing between induction and occurrence of sleep is convincing in my opinion, but to put Rush's criti-cism to rest would require further studies. Eisenbud 1983 reviews some of this work, pointing out how the fear of psi may have interfered with proper explorations in these areas.

[78] Not to be confused with the American, Herbern Benson

[79] See Chapter III-7 on **psychic surgery**.

[80] **Hawaiian kahuna healings** described by M. Long in Chapter I-1 are also similar in many respects to hypnotherapy.

[81] For discussions on the range of **splits observed with multiple personality,** see Allison; Braun; Coons; Crabtree; Putnam.

[82] Eye Movement Desensitization and Reprocessing (EMDR), discussed briefly later in this chapter and Chapter II-2, is also very helpful in treating multiple personality disorders. See Schreiber; Thigpen/ Cleckley for fascinating novelized stories of people who had therapy for MPD.

[83] Gretchen Sliker has done a magnificent job of delineating these sorts of personality splits in "normal" people.

[84] See also the discussion on multiple personality disorder below.

[85] Glioma

[86] Braun 1983a; b; S. Miller 1989; Putnam 1986; 1996; Putnam et al.

[87] Alvarado 1989; Braun 1983a; Coons; Lamore et al.; Loewensten/ Putnam.

[88] See Fitzherbert for a discussion of **hypnosis, healing and spirituality.**

[89] NLP, reviewed earlier in this chapter.

[90] Becker/ Selden report that DC fields around a subject's hand are altered during hypnosis. I have not seen this confirmed by others.

[91] F. Alexander; J. Goldberg 1991; Hay; Harrison; Hodgkinson; Justice; Knaster; Lankton/ Lankton; K. Mason; Steadman.

[92] F. Alexander 1950; Goleman/ Gurin; Seguin; Wittkower/ Warner

[93] For **the mind and immune system** see more under **psychoneuroimmunology (PNI)**, dis-cussed later in this chapter.

[94] The body as energy is discussed in detail in Chapter II-3.

[95] For imagery in psychotherapy see Achterberg; Haley; Lankton/ Lankton; Rossi.

[96] See discussion on super ESP in Chapter 1-3.

[97] See Newberg et al on brain imaging that shows particular areas of the brain that are active in meditative and spiritual experiences.

[98] Cuddon; Knowles 1954; 1956.

[99] E.g. Leshan 1974a; b; Motoyama 1978a.

[100] More on **channeling** in Chapter III-5.

[101] For **possession as a part of the spectrum in multiple personality disorder** see Allison; Crabtree; Kenny and discussion in Chapter III-6..

[102] More on **biofeedback** in B. Brown; Kiefer; A. Wise.

[103] Basmajian; Birk; B. Brown 1979; Green/ Green 1977; G. Jonas; N. Miller.

[104] Cade/ Coxhead; Green/ Green; Wise

[105] See the review of **allobiofeedback** in Chapter I-4.

[106] Braud; Braud/ Schlitz; Braud et al.; Radin et al.; Schlitz/ Braud, reviewed in Chapter 1-4.

[107] See discussion of kinesiology in Chapter II-2.

[108] See Thurston 1952 for a thorough **review of stigmata, levitation,** heat tolerance, biolumi-nescence, absence of cadaveric deterioration **and more**, drawn from reports of religious mystics and their associates over the centuries. Gitlin also covers some of these topics, but cites no specific references. Briefer descriptions can be found in Dietz; Jovanovic; Larly/ Lifschutz; Lifschutz; McCaffery; Rickard 1981(a-c); Sieveking 1982. Starr reports a highly unusual case of a stigmatist whose young child also developed stigmata. Holmes also briefly reviews some "flesh piercers" and stigmatists. See Al-Dargazelli for details of Jordanian dervishes who pierce their bodies without pain, bleeding, infection or other damage.

[109] Survival without eating for a number of days is also reported by Choedrak.

[110] Being free of guilt over harming anyone as a requisite for unusual abilities is echoed by Pierce 2002.

[111] For other accounts of **firewalking and fire handling** phenomena see: McClenon; Nae-geli-Osjord 1970; Nordland; *Psi Research 1983,* V 2(4); 1985, V 4(2); Ianuzzo, for a review and discussion of 33 such reports; Mezentscv; B. Schwarz 1970; Stillings 1985; Vilenskaya 1983c for a report on Tolly Burkan, an American who teaches firewalking in a four-hour group session; 1991 for a superior review and discussion with voluminous references. Barnuow men-tions heat insensitivity in children raised in the wild by wolves. For a skeptic's discussion see Leikind; McCarthy, who describes non-parapsychological theories to explain firewalking.

[112] More on **ectoplasm** under mediumistic experiences in Chapter III-5.

[113] See Chapter II-2 for more on meditation; III-9 for more on mystical states.

[114] See Chapter IV-2 for more on LeShan's realities.

[115] Echoed by Pearce, 2002 in other unusual physical performances

[116] There is much more on **theories explaining healing** in Chapter IV-2.

[117] This average is obviously high, reflecting the enormous number of days lost by people with chronic pain problems – who are averaged in with ordinary people who have no major pain problems.

[118] See discussions of secondary gain, above.

[119] **Phantom limb pain** has been reported after surgical removal of breasts, tongue, eyes, and penis. See Biley; Kao et al.; Kroner et al. For treatment with spiritual healing see Leskowitz 1997; Melzack, R.; Melzack/ Loeser; Melzack et al.; Philcox et al; R. Sherman.

[120] More on **reincarnation** in Chapter III-3.

[121] The pattern is alternated in some variations of Treatment/ Placebo/ Treatment/ Placebo; or Treatment/ Placebo/ Placebo/ Treatment. This also helps to tighten the blinds on the clinicians who are assessing the outcomes, as it makes it more difficult to guess whether subjects are receiving active or comparison treatment at any given time.

[122] See reviews of research on acupuncture for pain relief in Chapter II-2.

[123] See Meridian Based Therapies (MBTs), Chapter II-2.

[124] WHEE is the Wholistic Hybrid of EMDR and EFT, Benor 2001. More on this below, in the section on EMDR.

[125] For pain management see Ajrawat; Bowman; Brena/ Chapman; Bresler/ Trubo; Doran New-ell; Farrel/ Twomey; Geiser et al.; Glover et al.; Inglis 1978: Jamison et al.; Kori et al.; S. Levine; Madison/ Wilkie; McCaffery; Meares; Miller 1990; Pomeranz/ Chiu; Shattock; Shealy: J. Witt; Wolfe/ Millet.

[126] Studies on healing for pain include: headaches – Keller/ Bzdek; back pain – Castronova/ Oleson; Dressler; post-surgical pain – Meehan 1985; 1990; dental surgery – Wirth et al. 1993b; chronic, idiopathic – Sundblom et al., all reviewed in Chapter I-4.

[127] Discussed earlier in this chapter under **transpersonal psychotherapy**; also in Chapter III-8, III-12; IV-3.

[128] "Self" (spelled with capital "S" – The part of our self that is aware of a transpersonal, spiri-tual dimension, of which we are an integral part.

[129] More on **aromatherapy and massage** in Chapter II-2.

[130] References on **touch:** Alagna et al.; Barnett 1972; Bean; Burnside; C. Carpenter; Clay; L.K. Frank; Harlow; Kerewsky-Halpern; Krieger; Montagu 1953; 1971; Oldor 1982; 1984; T. Pre-

ston; Waddeil; Weininger 1953; 1954: S.J. Weiss 1978: 1979; Wyschgrod. For **massage** see M. Beck; Chaitow; Field 1997; Hollis; Tisserand; for **aromatherapy/ massage** see Vickers.

[131] Duplessis 1975; Romains; Ostrander/ Schroeder 1976; Sacks; Sako/ Homma; Sako/ Ono.

[132] Trans-cranial Doppler measurements of the mean cerebral blood flow velocity (cBFV) bilaterally in the middle cerebral arteries. They also identified specific electroencephalographic (EEG) brain wave patterns during her dermal optic reading experiments.

[133] Qigong is a Chinese form of healing, discussed in Chapter II-2. See research on infrasonic healing devices in Chapter I-4.

[134] See Chapter II-4 for more on radionics devices.

[135] See discussion on **thoughtography** in Chapter IV-3.

[136] See discussions on **biological energy fields** in Chapter II-2; II-3; IV-2, 1V-3.

[137] Naranjo/ Ornstein; Ornstein/ Thompson; Schiffer; Springer/ Deutsch (16pp. refs).

[138] **Ultradian rhythms** – Osowiec 1992; 1993; 2000; Rossi 1986b; Wernitz; Wernitz et al. 1983; Wernitz et al. 1987 (selective hemispheric activation through nostril breathing). **Chronobiology (overall study of biorhythms)** - Halberg; Kleitman (rest/ activity); Luce; Naitch.

[139] See further discussions on **brain and mind structures and functions** in Bergland; Bolles; Budzynski (comprehensive table of' cerebral hemispheric functions); Corliss; Damasio; Diagram Group; Dossey 1989 (excellent discussion on non-local mind); Gazzaniga; Ornstein; Penfield; Penfield/ Roberts; Ripinski-Naxon; Rossi; Sperry; U.S. News Books; Vitale; J.R. Wilson 1981. Liddon discusses the dual brain and religion. An **unusual brain function,** recently discovered, is navigation ability, partially mediated apparently by a magnetic sense – described by R. Baker. See also Jaynes for fascinating speculations on right and left brain functions in historical context. On **brain and mind – united or separate** – see Springer/ Deutsch for a broad discussion; Eccles/ Robinson; Popper/ Eccles for the views of a prominent neurophysiologist and philosopher. Hampden-Turner has one of the best surveys on "Maps of the Mind." Lewin reviews cases of
hydrocephalus where very little cerebral cortex remained, but mental function was at college levels. For the **body as part of mind – and person** – see Dethlefsen/ Dahlke; Dienstfrey; Dychtwald; Leshan/ Margenau (psychologist/ healer and physicist); Pierrakos 1974; 1975; 1976; 1987; Polhemus.

[140] About 30 percent of people note a strong difference with one eye or the other partly open; 30 percent note a mild difference; 40 percent note no difference. When the left outer quadrant of the left eye is stimulated by light, the right cerebral hemisphere is activated. This may shade the experience with emotional tones. When the right outer quadrant of the right eye is stimulated, the left hemisphere is activated. Your perception of the experience may be more analytical and less emotional from this perspective.

[141] Mittwoch; Overzier 1963; 1967.

[142] As in dreams, or in the laboratory-induced ganzfeld state (discussed in Chapter I-3).

[143] Andrew 1975; Braud 1975; Broughton 1976; Ehrenwald 1976b; Kreitler/ Kreitler 1973; Rao 1977.

[144] Some might see in this a sinister (pun intended) plot for masculine domination in the world – the word, *sinister*, deriving from the Latin for "left."

[145] See I-introduction; III-12; IV-3.

[146] Charman; Dilbeck et al; Duane/ Behrendt; Gringerg-Zylberbaum et al; Orme-Johnson et al; Seto et al; Sugano et al; Zimmerman

[147] See section on biofeedback earlier in this chapter.

[148] See more on **meditation** in Chapter II-2.

[149] See many more avenues to self-healing in the popular edition, Chapter II-5.

[150] Additional references on **self-healing:** Benson 1979; Bristol; E. Brown; Burkan/ Keyes; Challoner 1972; Cousins 1976; de Langre; de la Pena; Edlin; Fischer-Williams et al.; Fontes; Fosshage/ Olsen; J. Frank 1975; Libet/ Gerard; Goddard; Houston; Hulke; Inglis 1965; 1978; Jafolla; B. Joy 1979; Keyes/ Burkan; Kinnear; Lambillion; R.A. Moody 1978; Ornish; Otto/ Knight; Oyle; Ponder; Reilly/ Brod; J. Rogers; Rossi; Roud (spectrum); Sattilaro (macrobiotic diet for cancer); Schneider (blindness); Shattock 1979, 1982; Stanway; Stapleton; Wade. On

self-healing for AIDS: Badgley; Bamforth. Edlin/ Golanty 1982 present a pleasant, easy-reading volume on health and normal physiology. On **autogenic training** see also Luthe 1963; 1971; 1977; Luthe/ Schultz; Schultz/ Luthe. On **biofeedback** see Basmajian. Cost-effectiveness of biofeedback is detailed by Schneider. **"Spontaneous remissions"** are discussed by Everson/ Cole; O'Regan/ Hirshfield – and reviewed later in this chapter.

Caring for the ill at home, a self-care and potentially self-healing situation, is considered by L. B. Murphy.

[151] One out of every six people who are hospitalized is likely to acquire an infection in the hospital. Between 40,000 and 100,000 people die in US hospitals annually due to medical errors. More on this in Chapter II-2.

[152] Problems with routine electronic monitoring of babies when their mothers are in labor is another instance where intervention may be harmful. Medical staff tend to over-react at any signs of fetal abnormality, increasing the frequency of caesarian surgeries way beyond reason. The risks to children and their mothers and the costs are clearly higher than the benefits of the monitoring.

[153] LeShan 1977; 1989; 1996. On **finding joy** in life see also Dalai Lama.

[154] See section on visualization in Chapter II-2.

[155] Dietary approaches to self-healing are briefly discussed in Chapter II-2.

[156] See detailed discussions of PNI in S. Simonton 1994; S. Simonton/ Sherman.

[157] More on surrender in Eysenck, discussed below; earlier in this chapter under *acceptance*; Chapters III-8; IV-3.

[158] For more on **psychological correlates, predictors and treatments of cancer** see Booth 1973; National Cancer Institute (NCI) 1978; Achterberg/ Lawlis 1978; 1989; Achterberg et al.; Cunningham; Funch/ Marshall; Goldberg; S. Harrison 1987; Holden 1978; Lawlis 1994; LeShan 1989; MatthewsSimonton; Moyers; Quander-Blaznik; Roggenbuck; Shealy/ Myss; Shmale/ Iker; Siegel 1986; 1990; Surawicz et al.; Thomas/ Greenstreet.

For discussions of **exceptional cancer patients** see Gawler; Roud; Sattilaro. See S. Matthews-Simonton for **family involvement in cancer therapy.** Riley presents a classical study on correlations of stress in mice with development of cancer; Cassileth et al. 1984; Lerner 1985 reviews complementary cancer therapies from a skeptic's viewpoint. Serious questions regarding conventional cancer therapies are raised by Bailar; Cairns; G.L. Engel.

On **living and dealing with cancer** see J. Canfield, et al.; Conway; A. Frank; Halvorson-Boyd/ Hunter; Holland/ Rowland; Korda; M. Lerner 1994; Leviton; N. Levy; Rando; Remoff; Schlessel-Harpham; Shinoda-Bolen 1996.

For more on **stress/ life event inventories related to illness** see Avison/ Turner; Brown/ Harris; Craig/ Brown; Dohrenwend/ Dohrenwend; C.G. Ellison; Kaplan et al.; Landerman et al.; Lin/ Ensel; Mirowsky/ Ross; Morris/ Blake/ Buckley; Pearlin; Ramirez 1988; Selye; Tausig; Wetherington/ Kessler.

For related **stress management methods for cardiovascular problems** see Ornish.

See also the discussion of mechanisms for PNI earlier in this chapter under "Conditioning/ Reinforcement"; Footnote xxII2-11.

Personal stories of dealing with cancer: Barasch; Hirshberg/ Barasch; Lawlis 1994; Moyers; Roud; Sattilaro; D. Watson.

Complementary therapies for cancer: Chapter II-2.

[159] Comparing "pairs of women who had at least one adverse stressor during the disease free interval or the equivalent follow-up time… a significant relative risk was associated with the experience of a severe life event (p < 0.004)."

(P < .004 is a shorthand way of saying that the probability that these results could have occurred by chance is less than four times in 1,000.)

"…There were nine times as many pairs in which only the women who had a relapse had experienced a severe stressor… as there were pairs in which only the control had (p < 0.001).

[160] "…At 10 year follow-up, only three of the patients were alive, and death records were obtained for the other 83. Survival from time of randomization and onset of intervention was a

mean 36.6 months in the intervention group compared with 18.9 months in the control group, a significant [p<0.0001] difference."
[161] Kogon et al. reviewed Spiegel's work and suggest that factors other than the treatments employed may have produced the observed results.
[162] See also the critical review and discussion of Fawzy et al. 1995 on psychosocial interventions in cancer treatment; discussion of Reele on quality of life effects.
[163] Andersen et al.; Block; B. H. Fox; Futterman et al.; Gross; S. Kennedy et al.; Temoshok 1985; 1987.
[164] Pert et al. 1985; C. Wood; Levy et al. 1987; 1990.
[165] Fawzy et al. 1993; Kogon et al.; Kuchler et al. 1999; Ratcliffe et al.; M. Richardson et al.; Spiegel et al. 1989.
[166] Cardiac bypass surgery has been developed for people whose hearts are being starved of oxygen by hardened, narrowed arteries which are blocked by arteriosclerosis. Bypass surgery is a complicated procedure that carries considerable risk and discomfort to patients. Veins from the leg are transplanted to the heart to carry blood around the blocked portions of the diseased cardiac arteries. A significant percentage of patients develop further blocks following the surgery, and repeat operations may be necessary.
[167] Ornish 1990, 1992, 1998; Ornish et al. 1983; Ornish et al. 1998.
[168] Jiang et al.; Linden et al.; Markovitz; Siegman/ Denbroski. See also Denoliet; Gould et al.
[169] Eysenck 1991a; b; 1992b; Eysenck/ Grossarth-Matticek; Grossarth-Matticek/ Eysenck 1990; 1991a; b; Grossarth-Matticek/ Vetter.
[170] For more on psychological factors and cancer see: Chen et al.; Sklar/ Arlsman; for cardio-vascular disease see Denoliet et al.; Friedman/ Rosenman 1959; 1991; Jiang et al.
[171] Some are designating the cardiac programs as *psychoneurocardiology*.
[172] Achterberg; Booth; Booth/ Ashbridge; Pert; Solomon.
[173] See the extensive annotated bibliography of 1,300 related reports on **psychoneuroimmunology** (PNI) in Locke/ Hornig-Rohan; good reviews on PNI in Achterberg/ Lawlis 1980; 1984; G.H.B. Baker; Coates; Cohen et al. 1994; Cooper; Dreher; Fawzi; Guillemin; Hermanson; Ironson et al.; C. Lewis et al.; Locke et al.; Pert; S. Phillips; Rabin; Simonton 1998; Simonton/ Sherman. Interesting articles: Olness et al.; Rider/ Achterberg; Rider et al.; Schleifer et al.; S. Simonton 1998; Simonton/ Sherman; Solomon. Popular discussions of this subject are presented by Dienstfrey; P. Pearsall; Wingerson. Two journals regularly feature articles on PNI: *Advances: The Journal of Mind-Body Health* and
Psycho-Oncology Journal of Psychological, Social and Behavioral Dimensions of Cancer; Chichester; Wiley. More on this form of self-healing under **visualization**, Chapter II-2. See also hypnotic effects on the immune system, as in Black et al.; Goldberg; Ikemi; Mason/ Black; C. Smith et al. 1985. For **cardioimmunology** see Ornish 1990; Ornish et al. See L. Stevens on **imagery for diabetes**. See Chapter III-12 for correlations of religious affiliation/ practice and faith with health.
[174] See Chapter II-2 on auras; Chapter II-3 on **biological energy templates for the body**.
[175] See discussion of **fear of death** in Chapters III-2, 8, 11; **fears of healing** in Chapters IV-3; on **denial of death among nurses see** Hocking.
[176] Fascinating research is available on all of these pre-death and post-death experiences, reviewed and discussed in detail in Volume III of *Healing Research*.
[177] Bedford; Roud; Sattilaro; Wilbur 1993.
[178] For **remarkable recoveries** see also Dossey 1998a; Levoy; Roud.
[179] I have sometimes wondered whether a psychologically-minded mathematician might develop equations for the various infinities of human experiences.
[180] CAT, PET and MRI scans
[181] Churchland; Gazzaniga; Oakley.
[182] In out-of-body (OBE) experiences, people perceive themselves to be located outside of their physical body. This may occur during sleep, surgery or life-threatening accidents. Some people can do this deliberately, in which case it is often called *remote viewing*. See Chapter III-1 **on**

out-of-body experiences, and Chapter III-2 on similar reports during **near-death experiences,** and Chapters I-3 and IV-3 on **remote viewing**.

[183] Netherton; Stevenson; Wambach, reviewed in Chapter 1II-3.

[184] See discussions of **modern physics in Chapters** III-10; IV-2.

[185] While it is too complex to expand upon here, see discussions in chapters III-10; IV-2; Capra; Jahn/ Dunne 1987; F. Wolf; Zukav 1979.

[186] For discussions on **mind and brain** see above.

[187] All of science is built on basic assumptions that are ultimately unprovable. Some branches of science, however, are better supported than others by consistent bodies of observations and research. See Ferrer for an outstanding discussion of the limitations of transpersonal psychology in these regards.

[188] For **transpersonal therapy and philosophy** see Allison; Arasteh; Assagioli; Bear Hawk; Satprem 1968; Beasley; Berman; Bolen 1979; Dass/ Gorman; Dethlefsen; Dahlke; Donahoe; Ferguson; Ferrer; Foundation for Inner Peace; Goleman et al.; Green 1986; Green 1984; 1986; Grof/ Halifax; Harner; Hillman; Jung 1967a; b; Khan; Krystal; S. Levine 1984; 1986; Lukoff; Maslow; Matthiessen; R.T. Moss 1981; 1986; 1987; Needleman; Neher; Pearce; Elbert Russell; Tart 1975b; Taub-Bynum; Underhill; F Vaughan; von Franz 1980; 1987; Walsh; Walsh/ Vaughan; Watts; Weber; Wilber 1979; Wilber et al. 1986; Wolman/ Ullman.

On **death and dying:** Gersie 1991; Kubler-Ross 1969; 1975; 1982; 1983; Mullin. See also Chapter II-2, *The Transpersonal in Holistic Medicine.*

[189] More on **transpersonal awareness** in Boorstein 1996; 1997; Cortright; Firman/ Gila; Grof/ Grof; R. Mann; J. Nelson; J. Perry; Steere; Wullimier; and in detailed discussions in Volume III.

[190] See **Wilber's cosmologies** in Chapter IV-2; personal experiences in meditation in Wilber 1999.

[191] **Stages of development of faith** are discussed in Chapter III-11 and in Benor 2003.

[192] An important theoretical side note: Freud, Rank, and others have postulated that the fear of death leads people to kill, or sacrifice, others. Symbolically, through the death of others, these killers attempt to put off their own death.

[193] Wilber develops his own levels and does not adhere strictly to the levels described in the various conventional developmental theories.

[194] Pierrakos has an even broader perspective, and his methods are closer to healing per se than many others in this category.

[195] See discussion on **auras** in Chapter II-3. Many psi sensitives can see these.

[196] These rates of pulsation are similar to craniosacral rhythms, discussed in Chapter II-2. Perhaps they relate to the same biological energy field phenomena.

[197] See extensive research evidence for survival of the spirit and for reincarnation in Volume III of *Healing Research.*

[198] On clinical applications and research in meditation see Chapter II-2.

[199] Beasley; Benor 1996; Benor in Chapter I-1; Benor/ Mohr; Berman; Eisenbud 1946; 1970; Krystal; Taub/ Bynum.

[200] Gagne/ Toye; M.Green; Heidt 1979/ 1981; O'Laoire; Quinn 1982; 1984; Simington/ Laing.

[201] **Many facets of healing** are discussed in greater detail in Chapter IV-3.

[202] We have formed an International Association for Healing and Psychotherapy in England for mutual support and personal learning/ growth, and are working on a similar organization in America. See also the International Association for Spiritual Psychiatry, Jean-Marc Mantel, M.D., P.O. Box 288, Haifa 34980, Israel; tel. 972-4-8262843; fax 972-4-8251395; e-mail spiram@netvision.net.il; web site http:/ / rdz.stjohns.edu/ iasp

[203] See description of Edwards in Chapter I-1.

[204] See Ruth Benor, Chapter I-1 on healing unto death; also Chapter III-8 on spirituality and death.

[205] **Psi powers** are discussed in chapter I-3. More on the collective unconscious in Chapters IV-2 and IV-3.

[206] More on remote viewing in Chapter I-3.

[207] Non-verbal communication can be as simple as gestures punctuating conversation (Weitz), or may include unconscious psychological communications (Fast). If chronic, it may lead to physical changes in body morphology (Lowen 1958; 1975).

[208] Bodymind therapies are discussed in Chapter II-2.

[209] For **biological fields** see Chapters II-3; IV-3; Benor 1984; Brennan 1987; 1993; Gerber.

Chapter 2 – Wholistic Energy Medicine

[210] I use the term *wholistic medicine* to include nursing as an integral part of medical practice. Nurses have, in fact, made as many advances into wholistic care as doctors have, if not more.

[211] I pondered hard and long on whether to keep Chapters 1 and 2 as a single chapter – to emphasize the wholeness of self-healings and caregiver-assisted healings. The separation of these approaches in clinical practice is unfortunate. For ease of accessing discussions and references I have conceded to popular views and reluctantly separated these chapters.

[212] On the **history of medicine:** H. L. Coulter; Illich (patients' disempowerment); Inlander et al. (descriptive); Starr (medicine and power); Lappé (antibiotics).

[213] The code of conduct of the American Medical Association declares that it is unethical for medical doctors to use or abet in the use of a treatment that has no scientific basis, promotes false hope, or delays "proper" care.

[214] **Placebo effects** and **suggestion** are discussed in greater detail in Chapter II-1.

[215] On **market influences on the practice of medicine** see Angell; Kassirer; Ludmerer; Rothman; Sullivan; Wolfe; Wynia

[216] On **problems and limitations of evidence-based medicine** see Feinstein/ Horwitz; Grimes; McTaggart.

[217] Eddy; Feinstein/ Horwitz; Jadad/ Renne; Kiene 1996a; b; Levin et al. 1997; Lukoff 1998.

[218] N. Black discusses the role of observational studies in health care; White/ Ernst 2001 presents the case for non-controlled studies. See also: Greenhalgh; Greenhalgh/ Taylor; Walach 1998.

[219] On **qualitative studies** see: Bowling; Braud/ Anderson; Britten; Fitzpatrick/ Boulton; Greenbalgh/ Taylor; R. Jones; McDowell/ Newell; Mercer, G. et al.; M. Patel 1987a; b; Pope/ Mays; J. Richardson.

[220] An excellent instrument for patient self-assessment of outcomes is the SF-36, per Farr et al.; Ware, et al.; Medical Outcomes Trust.

[221] This figure is taken from the summary of research presented in Chapter I-4. I have not noted the studies that included blinds in such a way that they could easily be counted. The figure of 25 percent represents only those studies that were rigorously designed. This is an underrepresentation of the percent of blinded studies, as many of the studies reviewed were given lower rankings due to faults other than lack of blinding.

[222] Grimes; Nuland; R Smith.

[223] On issues surrounding **CAM research** see: Bloom; D. Callahan; Eddy; Feinstein; Fitter/ Thomas; Gifford; Hart 2001; Jonas/ Levin; Long et al. 2000; Peacock; Ribeaux/ Spence; J. Richardson; Schneider/ Jonas; Thomas/ Fitter; Vickers 1999; Vickers et al.; White/ Ernst 2001; Workshop on Alternative Medicine. On **CAM legal issues** see P White. On **grounded theory/ qualitative research** see Glaser/ Strauss; J. Levin 1997 (for CAM); Reinharz; Strauss/ Corbin.

[224] See further discussion of medical restrictions below, under Homeopathy.

[225] The **National Health Freedom Coalition** has been a pioneer in promoting legislation that is permissive to the practice of CAM, with major successes in Minnesota and California www.nationalhealthfreedom.org/

[226] Moss 1995 questions whether chemotherapy is of proven value.

[227] The ranking of causes of death varies with several forms of gathering statistics for each cause. On **adverse drug reactions** see: Bates; Lazarou et al.; Pittet/ Wenzel; G. Roach. For more on the **limits and problems of conventional medicine** see Angell/ Kassirer; Dossey

1998c; Forster et al; Grimes; Illich; Inlander; Laurence/ Weinhouse; McTaggart; R. Smith 1991.

[228] This is not a new finding. In 1964, the Yale New Haven Medical Center reported in the Annals of Internal Medicine that deleterious effects of negligent medical care occurred in 20 percent of admissions, with major negative effects in 4.7 percent (Pear). An assessment by the The Nutrition Institute of America estimates that medical errors are the leading cause of death in the US
http:// curezone.com/ forums/ m.asp?f=237&i=338 **

[229] On **medical errors** see also Bates, et al.; Brennan 2000, Brennan T.A., et al.; Corrigan; J. Eisenberg; Kohn L.T., et al.; Leape; Milamed/ Hedley-Whyte; Momas E.J., et al.; T. Moore; Peterson/ Brennan; Weiler, et al.; and the Internet citation of J. M. Eisenberg. The estimate of medical deaths vs. firearm deaths was calculated by Joseph Mercola 2000. See also: www.mercola.com/ 2000/ jul/ 30/ doctors_death.htm
On avoiding harmful effects of medication see Wolf et al.

[230] See discussion of adverse effects under Acupuncture; Kava and herb-medication interactions under nutritional and herbal therapies, below.

[231] Even more sobering are the ethical issues surrounding big business and government-led efforts to cover up such problems (V. Coleman 1996).

[232] On treatments for back pain see chiropractic, osteopathy, massage.

[233] On treatment for cerebral palsy see craniosacral therapy, later in this chapter.

[234] See discussion of chronic fatigue syndrome at the end of this chapter.

[235] There is a pun here, as *consumption* was also used as a term for tuberculosis in Shakespeare's time.

[236] **Spiritual aspects of health and illness** are considered in great detail in Volume III.

[237] Spiritual healing – Dixon; acupuncture – Christensen, et al. 1992; R. Erickson; Helms 1993; K. Johansson et al. 1993; spectrum of CAM therapies – Pelletier 1991; 1993.

[238] Further readings in **holistic medicine:** Albright/ Albright; Allison (introductory, broad); R. Anderson 2001a; b; Bakken; Balch/ Balch; Bassman (CAM for psychological problems); Benson 1975; Berman; Borysenko; Beckner et al.; Brenner 1978; 1981; Brewin/ Garrow; Brutsche (asthma); Carlson; Carper; Castelman; M. Cohen (legal issues); Chopra; Chordas/ Gross; Church/ Sher; C. C. Clark; Deliman/ Smolowe; B. Dossey, et al.. 1992; L. Dossey 1982; 1984; 1991 (excellent, detailed general discussions); S. Downer (CAM use in cancer); Ebell/ Beck (fibromyalgia); D. Eisenberg et al 2001 (survey of public views of CAM vs conventional medicine); Ernst 1998; 2002; Ernst et al.1995; 2001; Fabrega; Fadiman et al.; Favazza; Featherstone/ Forsythe; Freeman/ Lawlis; Fritts; Fugh-Berman (good pro/ con discussion of CAM); Fulford; Geis 1980; Gevitz; Golan; B. Goldberg (outstanding, well-organized summaries of CAM); Goleman/ Gurin; J Gordon 1996; Gottlieb; Graham; Grossinger; Jaffe/ Bressler; Grossman; Hastings et al.; Hess; Hilfiker; A. Hill; Inglis/ West; Ivker/ Anderson/ Trivieri; Jamal; Jonas 1999; Jonas/ Levin; Katzman (weight loss); Kenyon; Krieger 1981; Kessler, R et al (trends in CAM use); Kohatsu (treatment modalities and target symptoms); Krivorotov 1981; Kronenberg F/ Fugh-Berman (CAM for menopausal symptoms); Kunz 1985; Lappé (antibiotics); Lewith et al. 1996; Lewith/ Jonas/ Walach; Macintyre (ME/ CFS); G. McGarey (self-healing); Liverani et al.; A. Margolin (RCT issues); Mason, et al.; Melchart et al 2000; Micozzi 1996; 1999; Moher; Monte/ Editors of EastWest Natural Health; Murray/ Pizzorno (dietary/ minerals/ herbs); Novey (excellent, detailed general overview); Null 1998; K. Olsen (ignore cautions against use of TT in treating cancer); Pagano (psoriasis); Pearce; Pelletier 1979; Pelletier/ Astin (reimbursement for CAM care); Pietroni; Pietroni/ Pietroni; Pizzorno/ Murray; Pizzorno/ Murray/ Joiner-Bey (pocket summary); Poulton; Rakel; J. Richardson; D. Riley/ Berman; Robb; U. Roberts; Rush 1981; Salmon; J. Sanford 1977; Shealy/ Freese; Shealy/ Myss; Siegel 1990; Siegel/ Siegel; Sierpina; Smolowe/ Deliman; Sobel; D. Spencer/ Jacobs; Spiegel; J. Spiegel/ Machotka; Thompson; van der Lugt/ Firth; Verhoef; Vuckovic; Weil 1995; Woodham/ Peters (comprehensive, nicely illustrated, popular explanations). Nerem et al. consider social factors in atherosclerosis.

On **holistic nursing** see B. Dossey et al.; Guzzetta; Keegan; McMahon/ Pearson; J. Watson; Wren/ Norred. See Benor (in Salmon); Benor2000a for a discussion on the place of healing within wholistic medicine. On self-healing see: Bair; Belli/ Coulehan; Benor 2000b; Borysenko; Dowsrick; Ornish; Siegel; Tipping. On **self-healing for cancer** see: Dowrick; Jampolsky; Kubler-Ross; Metzner; B. Siegel; Wilber (1998).

On **self-healing for cancer** see: Dowrick; Jampolsky; Kubler-Ross; Metzner; B. Siegel; Wilber (1998).Breakey has a *Guide* to *Health-Oriented Periodicals*; Allais et al. – databases in holistic medicine.

For a thorough discussion on the **cosmology of wholistic approaches,** Bennan is indispensable.

Holistic methods of research see A. Hart; A. Long et al.; Reason; Ribeaux/ Spence; Tunnell; Vithoulkas.

On healing and other psi phenomena see Etzel, et al.; discussion in Chapter I-3. See Gerber for a well illustrated review of **vibrational medicine,** not specifically focused on spiritual healing and with less rigorous scrutiny of research. Evidence for spiritual healing from anecdotal reports and research is reviewed in Chapters 1-1; 1-4; 1-5.c.

Dissatisfaction with conventional medicine: Graedon/ Graedon; John Henry (side effects, negative interactions of medications); Laurence/ Weinhouse; McTaggart; M. Walker.

Dangers of synthetic hormones in our food: Cadbury.

Women's issues in CAM: Hudson 1993; 1999; Laurence/ Weinhouse; Northrup 1998.

Dangers of not taking responsibility for your health: Cancilla.

[239] Figure from Swift, Gayle, A contextual model for holistic nursing practice, *Journal of Holistic Nursing* 1994 12 (3), 265-281, Copyright © 1994 by Gayle Swift, reprinted by permission of Sage Publications, Inc.

[240] Figure from Swift, Gayle, A contextual model for holistic nursing practice, *Journal of Holistic Nursing* 1994 12 (3), 265-281, Copyright © 1994 by Gayle Swift, reprinted by permission of Sage Publications, Inc.

[241] Several of these are listed in Appendix B.

[242] The American Board of Holistic Medicine has examinations in holistic medicine.

[243] The AHNA Holistic Nurse Certification Program (with examination) is described in B. Dossey 1997. The 4-part program covers holistic caring/ healing nursing modalities over 18-24 months. Certification may be by examination without formal training.

[244] Much more on dying and death in *Healing Research Vol. III.*

[245] **Integrative care by caregivers:** Astin et al. 1998; Botting/ Cook; Elder et al.; LaValley/ Verheof; Pelletier et al. 1997 (managed care, insurance providers, hospitals); **by careseekers:** Aldridge 1989; Astin 1998; Cassileth, B. et al.; Downer et al.; Fulder/ Monro; Thomas, K.J. et al.; Younus/ Collins.

[246] **Chakras** are discussed under acupuncture, later in this chapter.

[247] See particularly Pietroni/ Pietroni, and the following journals: *Alternative Therapies, Journal of Alternative and Complementary Medicine, Journal of Complementary and Alternative Medicine, Journal of Holistic Nursing.*

[248] Angus Reid; Eisenberg et al. 1993; 1998; Gevitz; Landmark Report.

[249] The American Medical Student Association (AMSA) has put together a comprehensive listing of medical school courses, electives, and interest groups relating to complementary, alternative, and/ or integrative medicine http:/ / www.amsa.org/ humed/ CAM/ umbrella_search.cfm

[250] The numbers of people using CAM therapies is truly impressive. For instance, a review of cancer therapy patient surveys showed a rate of use ranging from 7% to 64% (mean 31%) worldwide (Ernst/ Cassileth). See also Goldbeck-Wood, et al.; Harris/ Rees; Landmark.

[251] See Chapter I-5 for a brief discussion on **surveys of healee assessments of their treatments** in several countries. These show a very high rate of consumer satisfaction with healing.

[252] Acupuncture, homeopathy, Ayurveda, naturopathy and Native American healing are good examples of treatment systems with well developed philosophies.

[253] There are extremists who even assert that there is no evidence for any benefits from CAM or wholistic approaches. See Dossey 1998b for a discussion of some of these.

[254] http://www.nationalhealthfreedom.org/index.htm

[255] Because of these overlaps in effects of the various therapies, there are also overlaps in the discussions about them.

[256] See Appendix B for **British healing organizations.** The CHO is undergoing a major reorganization at the time of writing of this book.

[257] Other good **surveys of complementary therapies** are presented by Freeman/ Lawlis; B. Goldberg Group; Hastings et al.; Fadiman; L. Freeman; Gordon; Inglis/ West 1983; Jonas/ Levin; Micozzi; Mills/ Bone, Novey; Spencer. On CAM for surgical patients see Norred. On CAM use in conventional medical practice see Kaptchuk/ Eisenberg.

[258] General references on clinical acupuncture: Chang; Connelly; Helms; Kaptchuk; Maciocia 1989; Maciocia; Manaka/ Urquhart; Mole; Porkert; Serizawa; Stux/ Pomeranz. On qi: Jahnke. For more on research in acupuncture see: American Foundation of Medical Acupuncture. On **electrical correlates of acupuncture points** see Helms 1995. On differences between acupuncture diagnoses by various examiners see Hogeboom. Reichmanis et al. *Brain/ Mind Bulletin* 1982, 7(14), 2, describes the use of **acupuncture as a preventive measure** in maintaining health. For recommendations of Qigong as a health promoter see: *China Sports Magazine;* K. Cohen (outstanding ref); Connor; Dong 1984; 19X5; Kuang et al.; Lee (breath); Shen; Takahashi/ Brown; Vilenskaya 1985a; b. On acupressure see: Anhui Medical School Hospital; Bauer; Gach 1981; 1990; Namikoshi; St. John 1982; Serizawa; Teeguarden; Irwin/ Wagenvoord 1976; Thie. On foot and hand **reflexology** see Byers; Carter; Carter/ Weber; Dougans; Gillanders; Kaye/ Matson; Kunz/ Kunz; Liang; L. Norman; Segal; Wills. On **ear acupressure** see Chan; on tongue diagnosis see Lu; Maciocia 1987; on face reading see Mar. On **massage and Qi** see Feldman/ Yamamoto. On metamorphic technique see Namikoshi. Eisenberg mentions that Qigong healing directed to acupuncture points provides apparent potentiation of both slowing and unblocking effects. Acupuncture for pain relief that correlated with endogenous brain opiates is described by Christensen/ Noreng; Sjolund Eriksson; Pomeranz Chia. Courtenay mentions emotional abreactions with acupuncture and curtailment of addictions. K. Cohen; Hammer discuss **acupuncture treatment for emotional problems.** Goss describes manipulation of acupuncture points in order to disrupt body functions, and even to kill, as a martial arts technique. See also **Chinese qigong healing** research in Chapter I-4. **Unusual feats with Qigong** are described by Yan; Zeng. On chakras see below. On **Traditional Chinese Medicine** see Beinfield/ Korngold; Chi; Fratkin; Gascoigne; Hadady; Hammer; Hicks; Kaptchuk; Y. Liu; Omura; Pitchford (diet); J. Ross; Tang (research). On **Chinese herbal and nutritional medicine** see Maciocia; Maoshing/ McNease; Naeser.

[259] Upledger's work is described below under *Craniosacral Therapy.*

[260] On **physical characteristic of acupuncture points** see R. Becker 1976; Helms 1995; Hyvarien/ Karlson; Roppel/ Mitchell.

[261] The work of Burr (1972); Ravitz (1962; 1970) and others on **DC fields in the body** may also be related. Becker (1982; Becker/ Selden) has also postulated bioelectrical mechanisms by which related energy fields could be understood in Western terms. See Chapter II-3.

[262] De Vernejoul et al.; Kim Bong Han; Requena; Rose -Neil.

[263] More on **Kirlian photography** in Chapter II-3.

[264] Konstantin Korotkov is promoting a device that is programmed to produce images of color around the body, correlating with acupoint electroassessments (Gurvits et al). Other popular devices include the MORA (Morel) and Voll (Voll) instruments.

[265] More on electrodermal testing in Ali (allergy); Krop, et al. 1985; 1997 (allergies); S. Sullivan (cancer); and more below on intuitive perceptions unassisted by external devices.

[266] More on these acupressure techniques under **bodymind therapies**, below.

[267] Sanskrit dates back 3,000 years in India, which shows that acupuncturists have been aware of these energy centers for a very long time.

[268] On **therapy focused on chakras** see Anodea; B. Brennan; Clinton (discussed below under Meridian Based Therapies); Krieger 1993; Myss 1996; Page; Sherwood 1988; F. Vaughan; J.

White, 1990 (review of a spectrum of views); Wilber. **Imagery activation of chakras** – Gallegos 1983; 1990; 2000. My own clinical impression is that the chakras are very real gateways to energy dynamics in the body.

[269] More on **holographic theory** in Chapter IV-2.

[270] See **Healers' views and descriptions** of their work in Chapter 1-1.

[271] On **chakras** see: Bruyere; Karagulla/ Kunz; Kunz 1991; Judith; Leadbeater; Motoyama 1978a; Page 1992; Vollmar. An example of variations between descriptions of chakras is provided by Leadbeater (echoed by Kunz), who describes the third chakra as being shifted to the left of midline and associated with the spleen rather than over the solar plexus.

[272] See description of Shubentsov in Chapter I-1.

[273] More on holograms and holographic organization of the body in Chapter IV-2.

[274] Iridology, a system of diagnosis of body conditions through examination of the iris of the eye, represents another body hologram. On **iridology** see: Colton; V. Davidson; E. Hall; B. Jensen; Kriege; D. Johnson 1984; H. Wolf.

[275] The greatest part of this review is taken from the annotated bibliography of Birch/ Hammerschlag, in which studies are reported to have shown "significant" effects, with no statement about the criteria used in designating them as "significant." For updates on acupuncture research see http:/ / www.nlm.nih.gov/ pubs/ cbm/ acupuncture.html

[276] For discussions of acupuncture research methodology see Lewith/ Machin; Resch/ Ernst; White et al. 2001.

[277] Ahonen et al.; Carlsson et al. 1990; Melchart et al. 2001; Vincent 1990.

[278] Coan et al.; Petrie/ Langley; Smith et al. 2000; White/ Ernst 1999

[279] Ernst/ White 1998; Gunn/ Milbrandt; MacDonald et al.; Smith et al. 2000; Thomas/ Lundeberg; Tulder et al.).

[280] Christensen et al.; Dickens/ Lewith; Ezzo et al. 2001; Thomas et al.

[281] Barsoum et al.; Fan et al.; Ghaly et al.; R. T. Ho et al. (1990); with acupressure, see Fan et al.

[282] Carlsson et al.; Dundee et al. 1988; Hyde 1989.

[283] See A. Vickers 1996b for a review of acupuncture as treatment for nausea and vomiting; Lee/ Done for a meta-analysis of non-pharmacologic treatments for nausea and vomiting. .

[284] On acupuncture for asthma see also Linde et al. 2000.

[285] Amantadine is a medicatin used to treat addictions.

[286] Generic name for Tofranil, an antidepressant.

[287] Many treatments, including spiritual healing and hypnotherapy, are suggested for inducing babies to turn in utero just prior to birth.

[288] An outstanding summary of articles on acupuncture is at http:/ / www.nlm.nih.gov/ pubs/ cbm/ acupuncture.html

[289] Jahnke; Kaptchuk; K. Walter.

[290] Moyama 1978; 1992; B. Brennan 1987.

[291] More on **holographic reality** and **cosmic awareness/ unity** in Volume III and Chapter IV-2 and IV-3.

[292] C. Cohen; Hammer; Page; Seem/ Kaplan.

[293] Callahan; Craig; Diepold; Durlacher; Fleming.

[294] More on **homeopathy** later in this chapter.

[295] For details of **Chinese cosmologies and acupuncture** practices see Beinfield/ Korngold; (Chinese); Donden; Hammer (psychology); J. Helms (for physicians); Kaptehuk; Mann 1972; O'Connor/ Bensky 1981; Palos 1972; Plummer; Unschuld. **Controlled trials of acupuncture** are contradictory to Chinese cosmology but have been completed for limited aspects of acupuncture treatment. See for example Bullock. For **macrocosm/ microcosm discussions** see Bohm 1957; 1980, and Weber 1978 on Bohm; Motoyama 1978; Tiller 1974; Weber 1979 excerpted in Chapter IV-2.

On **kundalini** phenomena see Chinmoy; Galbraith 1998; 1999; 2000; Hill 1990; Khalsa; Lockley; Muktananda; K. Thomas; J. White 1990; discussions in Chapters III-9; IV-3.

Gopi Krishna focuses primarily on the nervous system as the source of kundalini experiences. He suggests that many of the related physical sensations could be explained by stimulation of nerve plexes corresponding to the chakras, and that visions could be explained by stimulation of the optic centers in the brain: "...The Indian sage Sri Aurobindo maintains that the chakras are primarily psychic energy points in the middle of the etheric body. The scholar Joseph Campbell said in a 1975 *Psychology Today* article... that the chakras are psychological teaching devices without any physical reality merely metaphors. Yogi Bhajan maintains that they have multilevel reality as etheric energy transducers that interact with physical electromagnetic energy fields... Christopher Hills... says[kundalini] is consciousness. The energetic effects experienced in the chakras and their associated psychologies arc secondary byproducts, not kundalini itself."

Ken Wilber (1990) discusses the chakras from the vantagepoint of cosmic awareness in Eastern traditions and suggests that "...the chakras do *appear* real to the separate self who constructs these knots in his flight both from death and from a prior unity with all manifestation. The flight from death generates time, while the flight from unity generates space. Now, the self created world of time and space is, by all accounts, the world of samsara, the rope of our own bondage and suffering, and the chakras are but the knots in these binding ropes of misery."

Christopher Hill points out: "Belief in such power or for that matter kundalini, whatever it is, must be based on direct experience and not on some teacher's parroting of cultural brainwash."

[296] The AAMA follows the guidelines for physician training that were established by the World Federation of Acupuncture-Moxibustion Societies, under the guidance of the World Health Organization.

[297] It is a sociological curiosity that in its early introductions into the West, acupuncture found a more ready acceptance in the US and healing was more readily accepted in Britain. This illustrates the processes of dissemination of information related to aspects of energy medicine. These treatments may be more or less available to individuals due to preferential allocations of research resources and input of prominent personalities in the sciences, government and media (through advertisement, politics and faddism), irrespective of the inherent benefits of the therapeutic modalities themselves.

[298] More on the **Alexander Technique** in Alexander; Austin/ Ausubel; Barker; Barlow; Dennis; Gelb; Gray; F.P. Jones; Maisel; C. Stevens (overview); Westfeldt; www.alexandertechnique.com/ teacher.htm

[299] See under naturopathy; homeopathy.

[300] Altaffer; Craig; Callahan; Diamond 1978; 1985; 1996; Durlacher, Gallo; Whisenant.

[301] Sadness usually produces weakness, happiness strengthens the muscles. Occasionally an individual will have the reverse response. A woman I worked with once shared her experience: "I grew up in a tough neighborhood. I taught myself to be tough if I was sad and never to cry, because if I cried they made fun of me." Her arm was much stronger when she was sad.

[302] The *yes* is usually stronger. This is sometimes called the *bidigital O-ring test*, or *BDORT*.

[303] The *yes* usually feels smoother.

[304] See Goldstein 1976; C. Holden 1974 for similar views. I conducted a pilot study with the help of Sushma Sharma, a physiotherapist/ acupuncturist in London. We found apparent differences between responses of people who are more sensitive to subtle energies and people who are less sensitive. The less sensitive people had less strong responses. I am impressed that qualitative reports on subjects and procedures must be included with quantitative assessments of energy medicine therapies. See Monti et al. for a study of AK for congruence of muscle strength with beliefs.

[305] Altaffer; Craig; Callahan; Diamond 1978; 1985; 1996; Durlacher; Gallo; Whisenant.

[306] Beardall; J. Bennett; Kendall/ Kendall; Roppel/ Mitchell.

[307] Dennison/ Dennison; Parker/ Cutler-Stuart; Stokes/ Whiteside; Utt 1991a.

[308] Cases taken from Krebs, p.256-258.

[309] For more on **applied kinesiology** see Barton Beardall 1980a; 1981; 1982; 1983; 1985; Dennison/ Dennison 1987; 1989; Dewe/ Dewe; Diamond 1979; 1980; Gallo; Kendall; LaTourelle/ Courtenay; Shepard; Thie; Walther 1981; 1988.

[310] Eye Movement Desensitization and Reprocessings (EMDR) and the Wholistic Hybrid of EMDR and EFT (WHEE) – the latter being one of the Meridian Based Therapies (MBTs) - are discussed below.

[311] For more on **kinesiology** see Walther.

[312] Motyka/ Yanuck; Schmitt/ Yanuck.

[313] Jacobs' statistical methods are questioned by Ludtke et al.

[314] Health Kinesiology is a variation on Applied Kinesiology.

[315] Problems with kinesiology testing: Garrow (milk allergy); Hass et al. (normal persons); Hsieh/ Phillips (dynamometer – criticized by Ludke et al.); J. Kenney et al. (nutritional deficiencies); Lawson/ Calderon; Motyka/ Yanuck; Motyka et al.; K. Peterson (phobias). See also McCarney, et al. on pendulum dowsing for homeopathic remedies.

[316] On **suggestion** see Chapter II-1.

[317] On **intuitive assessment** see Chapter I-4; Benor 1992; 2001b.

[318] See Chapter I-3 on **parapsychological studies** and Chapters I-4 and IV-3 on **intuitive diagnosis**.

[319] Dermal absorption of aromatic oils – Bronough; Collins et al.; Hotchkiss; Jäger et al.; inhalation – Buchbauer; Falk; Kovar et al.

[320] Massage is discussed below.

[321] For the spiritual uses of aromatherapy see Worwood.

[322] Baylier; Janssen; Moleyar/ Narasimham; Panizzi et al.

[323] Including alpha-pinene, geraniol, isoborneol, isoeugenol, methylsalicylate, nerol and thymol.

[324] On **aromatherapy** see: Buckle (review); Damian/ Damian; d'Angelo; P. Davis (target problems, profiles of oils, methods, safety factors and sources); Firsher-Rizzi; Lavabre; Lawless; Micozzi; L. Miller/ Miller (for advanced practitioners: healing Ayurvedically with aromatherapy – diets, body types, chemistry, application and blending); PDR (Young Living Oils – topical and oral use, history, science, profiles of oils, target disease processes – physical, emotional and spiritual); S. Price/ L. Price; Remedy Guides; J. Rose; Schnaubolt; Stevensen, C.; Stevenson; M. Tisserand; R. Tisserand (plant medicines for prevention, treatment, strengthening immune system; topical and oral, research, case histories, and profiles of oils); Tisserand/ Balacs (history, research, chemistry, and profiles of oils); Torri et al.; Valnet; Vickers 1996; and see *International Journal of Aromatherapy, Appendix* A; Wilkinson; Worwood (personality, mind, mood and emotion). An excellent website with descriptions of oils and a symptoms guide is http:/ / www.fragrant.demon.co.uk/ .

[325] See discussions of PNI later in this chapter, also in Chapter II-1.

[326] Luthe; Schultz/ Luthe.

[327] **Transpersonal psychotherapy** is described in Chapter II-1.

[328] See further discussions on mind-body controls and on self-healing later in this chapter, especially under Yoga, Osteopathy, Meditation, and Visualization. See Chapter II-3 for more on Kirlian photography.

[329] More on **Ayurveda** in Ballentine 1999; Chopra 1990; V. B. Dash 1991; 1993; Dash/ Junius; Frawley; Frawley/ Lad; Karambelkar (also Athraveda); Rama 1979; 1980; Sharma/ Dash; Svoboda; Thakkur. On **subtle energies and Ayurveda** see Collinge 1998.

[330] More on **meditation** in Chapter II-1, and on **yoga** later in this chapter.

[331] See also Tibetan Medicine, later in this chapter.

[332] Brennan 1987; 1993; Lowen; Pierrakos. **Bioenergetics** is discussed under massage.

[333] On **biofeedback** see Amar/ Schneider; Basmajian; Brown; Byers; Cade/ Coxhead; Danskin/ Crow; Evans/ Arbanel; Fischer-Williams; Green/ Green; Karlins/ Andrews; Lubar/ Lubar; Schwartz et al. On cost effectiveness and 3rd party reimbursement see Shellenberger/ Amar; Shellenberger et al.

[334] Such as the Association for Applied Psychophysiology and Biofeedback (AAPB).

[335] See Alexander technique; Bioenergetics; Bowen therapy; Feldenkrais method; Rubenfeld technique; and many variations on the theme of massage.

[336] Research on EMDR is summarized at http:// www.emdr.org/

[337] On a spectrum of **bodymind therapies** see Achterberg; Achterberg/ Lawlis 1980; 1984; F. Alexander; Ballantine/ Ajaya; Benson 1975; Boadella; Borysenko; Braddock; Malcolm Brown; Caldwell 1996a; b; Chopra 1989; Christiansen; Cousins 1991; Dethlefsen/ Dahlke; Ford; Goldberg 1991; Goleman/ Gurin; Hanna 1987; 1988; Harrison; Hay; Heckler; Hendricks/ Hendricks 1991; 1993; D. Hodgkinson; D. H. Johnson (bodywork, breathwork); Justice (well referenced); Kabat-Zinn 1990; Keleman; Kurtz; Kurtz/ Prestera; P. Levine; Locke/ Colligan; Lowen 1970; Masters/ Houston; Masunaga (meridian-activating exercises); Menkin; Mindell; Moyers; North; Oschman/ Oschman 1997; 1998; Peper/ Holt; Pesso; Pierrakos; W. Reich 1986; Rosen/ Brenner; Rosenberg et al.; Rossi; Rossman; Saraswati (breath); Siegel; E. Smith; Steadman.

[338] See a spectrum of breathing meditations in Chapter II-5.

[339] More on **meditation** in Chapter II-1.

[340] Ballantine; D. H. Johnson (breathwork, bodywork); Prasad (breath, energies); Rama/ Ballantine (breath energies); Sky.

[341] On birth memories with breathwork see K. Taylor; and on hypnotic pre-birth and birth memories see Cheek 1974; 1975; 1986; 1992.

[342] There are accrediting bodies in other countries as well: e.g. the Council on Chiropractic Education (Canada), European Council on Chiropractic Education, and Australasian Council on Chiropractic Education. Many other countries have chiropractic licensing boards.

[343] Bigos et al.; Haldeman et al.; Hansen.

[344] Lutges et al.; MacGregor/ Oliver; MacGregor et al. 1975.

[345] Boline et al.; Gonella et al.; Haas et al.; Love/ Brodeur; Mior et al.; Mootz et al.; Nansel et al.; Wiles; leg length, critique of tests – Lawrence; radiographic interpretation – Frymoyer et al.

[346] Studies of chiropractic for back pain: Bergquist-Ullman; Cherkin; Di Fabio; Godfrey; Hadler et al.; Kirkaldy et al.; Koes; Koes et al.; J. Matthews et al.; Meade et al.; Ottenbacher/ Difabio; Shekelle et al. 1991; 1992; Waagen et al. Patient satisfaction – Cherkin/ MacCornack.

[347] Positive findings – Boline et al.; Nilsson et al.; negative findings – Bove/ Nilsson.

[348] On **chiropractic practices** see Redwood; Network Chiropractic – D. Epstein. On **chiropractic research** showing benefits see: Thoracic pain syndromes – Barker; headaches – Boline; Vernon; migraines – Parker et al.; muscle soreness following exercise – Molea et al.; paraspinal cutaneous pain tolerance – Terrett/ Vernon. For infant colic – Klougart et al. 1989; dysmenorrhea – Thomason et al.; Kokjohn et al.; hypertension – Yates et al. See Brunarski for a review of 50 studies. On lack of efficacy in allergic diseases see the review by Renaud/ Pichette. Other studies of spinal manipulation: Hochler et al.

[349] Sucher 1993a; 1993b; 1994; Sucher/ Hinrichs.

[350] Applied Kinesiology was discussed above.

[351] In part this is a vicious circle. Because chiropractic and other complementary therapies have been excluded from mainstream medicine, they do not conform to the same standards as conventional medicine. Until recently, chiropractic and other complementary therapies likewise had not taken the initiative or assumed the responsibility for regulating their practices to high professional standards.

[352] Denslow et al.; Korr 1955; 1978

[353] Thermographic studies with peripheral nerve problems – Kappler/ Kelso; Larson; correlating manual diagnosis in cadavers with autopsy data – Reynolds et al.; Ward; cerebral evoked potentials from paraspinal muscles with unilateral back pain – Zhu et al.

[354] W.L. Johnson; W.L. Johnson et al. 1982(a); (b); 1983.

[355] This has placed DOs at a disadvantage with insurance companies, many of which refuse to compensate for manipulative interventions by DOs. Funding for most osteopathic research has had to come from the private sector.

[356] Coxhead et al.; Doran/ Newell; Farrell/ Twomey; T Gibson et al.; Glover et al.; Hochler et al.; Sims-Williams et al.

[357] Cyriax 1980; 1982; Mennell; Stark.

[358] Beal et al. 1980; 1982; Johnston 1982; Johnston et al. 1982a; b; 1983; Kelso, et al.; McConnell (low agreement).

[359] Applied Kinesiology is discussed above.

[360] For more on chiropractic: Agency for Health Care Policy and Research; www.chiro.org; *Journal of Manipulative and Physiological Therapeutics; Journal of the Neuromusculoskeletal System;* Lederman; Redwood.

[361] Ernst 1999a; F. C. Powell et al.; Stevinson et al.

[362] Assendelft et al. 1996; Coulter et al.; Dabbs/ Lauretti.

[363] The ICD-9 lists codes for various osteopathic manipulations performed by licensed doctors.

[364] On osteopathy see DiGiovanna/ Schiowitz; Kuchera/ Kuchera; Magoun; Still; R. Ward. More on **craniosacral therapy and cranial osteopathy** later in this chapter.

[365] Ballantine 1999; Donovan; R. Gray (with herbs); Maury (France – homeopathic detox); Samiti (yoga); N. Walker.

[366] Manheim et al.; Upledger 1992; 1995a; 1995b.

[367] Upledger/ Vrederoogd; Upledger 1986

[368] The Upledger Institute identifies its work as CranioSacral Therapy™.

[369] *Energy cyst* is a term originated by Elmer Green (Upledger/ Vredevoogd). This theory was presaged many centuries ago in the yoga sutras of' Patanjali, in the concept of *samskaras* or scars in the energy body that may impede proper body energy flows and physiological functions. On other origins of craniosacral therapy see Dove.

[370] These techniques have overlaps with Applied Kinesiology.

[371] This appears to be an example of psychic/ intuitive assessment. More on psychic abilities in Chapter I-3.

[372] There is a clear similarity here to the methods of **Applied Kinesiology**, also discussed in this chapter.

[373] This is a further overlap of craniosacral therapy with spiritual healing. Very similar descriptions of spontaneous physical movements during spiritual healing are described in Chapter I-1.

[374] More on visualization later in this chapter.

[375] A controlled study of "I.ight Touch Manipulative Technique" by Dressler, is reviewed in Chapter I-4. See also controlled trial of cervical spine manipulation for migraine by Parker et al.

[376] Madaule; Tomatis 1992; 1997. Several pilot studies are reviewed at www.tomatis.com.

[377] Detailed discussions of the **therapeutic effects of music** are presented by K. Aldridge; Amatas; T. Andrews; Berendt; D. Campbell 1991; 1992; 1997; Droh; Eagle 1976; 1978; 1984; Ensminger; Gardner-Gordon; Gaynor; Gilmore et al.; J. Goldman (spiritual development); Kerkvliet; Lingerman; McClellan; Merritt; Munro/ Mount; Mullooly, et al.; Purdy (blues); Randall; Redmond; Schullian/ Schoen; Sprintge; Tomatis; Watson/ Drury; Zimmerman, et al.

[378] D. Foster; Lane et al.; Le Scournec et al.; Oster; and many more references at http:/ / www.monroe-inst.com/ research.

[379] See Chapter I-4 for clinical studies of some of the infrasonic sound devices.

[380] The American Art Therapy Association site has many resources www.arttherapy.org

[381] The American Dance Therapy Association is an excellent resource for training, information, research, with many regional offices http:/ / www.adta.org.

[382] On **storytelling** and **writing**: Adkins (spoken autobiography); Bapko/ Krestan (women); Bly/ Woodman (fairytales); Brand; Brun et al.; M. Burns (incest); C. Coates; Coles; Combs/ Freedman; Cushman; Dion (chronic illness); A. Ellis 1965; E. Estes (abandoned child); Farley/ Farley (gifted children); Feinstein/ Krippner; R. Gardner (children); Haddock; Keen/ Valley-Fox; N. King; J. Kremer; L'Abate; Laing 1976; Lankton/ Lankton (imbedded trance inductions); S. Larsen; Lerner/ Mahlendorf; Mairs (bridging inner/ outer worlds); McKinney; R. Mills/ Crowley (child); O'Hanlon; C. Pearson; Peay; Riordan; R. Rubin; Sheikh 1986; Sheikh/ Sheikh (journaling, imagery); Shrodes; J. Smyth et al.; Spear et al. (job loss); Stemberg (women); Stone/ Winkelman; Wallas 1981; 1988; Wenz/ McWhirter; .L. Whitaker 1992 (mother-daughter). **Spiritual explorations:** Caprio; Caprio/ Hedberg; Fling; J. Houston 1987; Noonan; Reuther (women); Savary/ Berne (dreams); Smith/ Counsel. **Techniques:** Capac-

chione; K. Chase; Cohen et al.; N. Goldberg 1986; 1990; Klauser; Muhl (automatic writing); Rico; Ross (writer's blocks); Ueland; White/ Epston.

[383] On **the therapist's process:** M. Bean; Lett; Wadeson.

[384] On **poetry:** Alexander (adolescents, depression); Bachelard; Belli/ Coulehan; Berger/ Giovan (forensic); R. Bowman (PTSD); Bowman/ Halfacre (sexual abuse of adolescents); Bowman et al. (shattered dreams); R. Brown et al.; Demaria (group, abuse); Dyer (children of alcoholics); J. Fox 1985; 1992; Gendler (bibliotherapy); Gorelick 1989a; b (schizophrenia); Harrower; Heller; D. Hodges 1993 (hospice); Houlding/ Holland (psychiatric); Howe; Hynes/ Hynes-Berry (classic work, includes bibliotherapy); Jung; 1972 [?]; Kir-Simon; Klein (AIDS); A. Kramer (group process); Lantz/ Harper (Logotherapy); Leedy; A. Lerner (1981; 1982 – group); Lester/ Terry; Lifshin (mother-daughter); Mazza (adolescents); Meiffren (adolescents); J. Montefiore (feminist); Morrice; M. Morrison; Ostriker (women); Pietropinto (group); Rolfs/ Super; Rothenberg (1990); Sass (schizophrenia); Siegelman (metaphor); Silver (case-schizophrenia); *Voices of the Living* (Journal – AIDS); M. Williams (sexual abuse); Wisechild (incest); *Writing for Our Lives* (journal on women's healing poetry). **Spiritual:** Estes 1992; J. Houston 1987; Hynes; Ritblatt/ Ter Louw. **Techniques:** Bchn; Kennedy/ Kennedy; Kock (child); D. Metzger; Yochim; **Research:** Pannebaker.

[385] Most of the following references are taken from the outstanding annotated bibliography on poetry and bibliotherapy by Paula Platt.

On **journaling:** Adams 1990; 1993 (general); 1994 (men); C. Baldwin 1990; 1991; Bass/ Davis (sexual abuse); Biffle 1989; 1990 (workbook); Brady (child sex abuse); Capacchione 1979; 1982 (children); J. Chapman; Hagan 1990; 1991; Hannah (Jungian, active imagination); Kast (joy); P. Lucas (bereavement); Maldee (guided autobiography); Pleasse (parenting/ addiction); Progroff; T. Rainer; Solly/ Lloyd. **Spiritual:** M. Kelsey; Solly/ Lloyd (12-step); D. Wakefield.

[386] On **creative arts therapies in general:** D. Aldridge (AIDS); *Creative Life Lines for Survivors* (Journal); Dickerman (tarot); Goldstein-Roca/ Crisafulli; Gorelick; D. Grayson (AIDS); D. Johnson; Jung 1933; Knill (theories); R. Landy; N. Rogers; Rossiter; Sass (schizophrenia). **Spiritual:** Cady et al. (women).

[387] American Society of Group Psychotherapy & Psychodrama http://www.asgpp.org/; Psychodrama worldwide community http://psychodrama.org/; Psychodrama bibliography http://www.asgpp.org/02ref/index.htm

[388] Junge/ Linesch.

[389] On **humor** see Bellart; Berger; Berk/ Tan; Bosker; Buxman; Carlyon/ Carlyon; N. Cousins 1981; 1989; Ditlow; Dossey 1996; J. Dunn; Erdman; Flipse; L. Green; Holden 1994; A. Hunt; A. Klein; Kuhn; M. Kushner; Lefcourt et al.; Loomans/ Kolberg; R. Martin; A. Matthews; McGee-Cooper; McGhee 1994; 1999; Nahemow; Paulson; Robinson; N. Schmitt; Seaward; J. Simon 1988a; b; Strickland; C. White/ Howse; P. Wooten.

[390] L. Berk 1989; L. Berk/ Tan; L. Berk et al. 2001; N. Cousins; Dillon; Fry 1971; 1977; 1979; Lefcourt 1986; 1990; R. Martin; McGhee.

[391] **Professional literature on humor:** W. Kelly; A. Klein; McDougall; R. Moody; Parfitt; Parkins; V. Robinson; Shem.

Patients' literature on humor: L. Grizzard; J. Henry; T. Jackson; Nehmer; D. Stewart.

[392] Coulehan; J. Fox; National Association for Poetry Therapy; Osna-Heller; Weissman.

[393] More on **mythic levels of awareness** in Chapter IV-2. See also imagery in visualization, later in this chapter and in Chapter II-1.

[394] Hodges; Lombardi; Lorusso/ Glick; Mella; R.S. Miller; Oldfield/ Coghill; Vogel.

[395] Shealy is reviewed in Chapter I-4.

[396] *Mal ojo,* caused by staring, is often confused in common usage, as well as in translation, with *mal puesto,* as "the evil eye, which is the casting of a hex or curse."

[397] Much of this summary was taken from Harding. See also Avila/ Parker; Kiev; M. Moore; Perrone et al.; K. Whitaker. Castaneda has described the experiences of an apprentice curandero in his popular stories of the legendary *Don Juan.*

[398] See Servadio for a discussion of the cultural congruence of a healer in the Italian countryside.

[399] See discussion of **shamanism** in Chapter I-5.

[400] Michael Schachter provides an excellent overview of the method and its historical background, and a discussion of criticisms of chelation therapy. M. See also Ali et al. (105 refs); M. Walker.

[401] M. Ali et al. (105 refs); Chappell/ Stahl; Chappell et al. 1994; Clarke et al.; Cranton; Hancke/ Flytlie; Schachter.

[402] Guldager et al.; Olszewer et al.; Van Rij et al. See also Chappell 1994; 1996; Kitchell et al.; Sloth-Nielson et al.; and the systematic review of Ernst 1997.

[403] On **biomagnetic therapies** see Andra/ Nowak; Becker 1990; Bersani; Bilotta (osteoporosis); Cadossi (chronic venous ulcers); Coghill 2000(b); Conca (drug withdrawal, depression); Davis/ Rawls; Dovganiuk (chronic venous insufficiency); Erman (anxiety, insomnia); Hahnemann; Jorgensen et al. (pelvic pain); Kircaldie (drug withdrawal, depression); Lawrence et al.; Lee et al. 1993 (soft tissue repair); Lubennikov (enhancing immune functions and post-op recovery in cancer); Null 1998; Oschman 2000 (excellent general discussion); Pascual-Leone et al. (addictions, drug resistant depression); Phila/ Kloth (sports injuries); Philpott/ Taplin; Sandyk (Alzheimer's disease; chronic pain; epilepsy); Sandyk 1995 (MS); Sandyk 1995 (Parkinsonism); Salzberg (surgical wounds, decubitus skin ulcers); Sisken/ Walker (soft tissue injuries); Stiller et al. (chronic venous ulcers); Trock (osteoarthritis); Vallbona (post-polio pain); Wahlstrom (fresh bone fractures); Whitaker/ Adderly; and *BEMI Currents - Journal of the Bio-Electro-Magnetic Institute*. See discussion on **negative effects of EM fields** in Chapter II-3.

[404] Blank 1993; 1998; Brighton/ Pollack; Levin; Ramel/ Norden; Workshop on Alternative Medicine.

[405] Klawansky; Nias; Shealy et al. 1992.

[406] For more references on PEMF therapies contact Richard Markoll, Bio-Magnetic Therapy Systems, 1200 Clint Moore Road, Boca Raton, FL 33487.

[407] See Rolfing under Massage.

[408] 350Hz to 20 KHz.

[409] Mu metal is impervious to EM fields.

[410] Further applications of electrotherapeutic devices are briefly reviewed in Chapter II-2.

[411] These have been called *transcranial magnetic stimulators (TMS)*.

[412] George et al.; Klein et al.; Pascual-Leone et al.

[413] Adey 1992; Adey/ Lawrence; Blank; Blank/ Findl; Brighton/ Pollack; Brighton et al.; Liboff/ Rimaldi; Marino; O'Connor/ Lovely; Oschman 2000; Popp et al.; Ramel/ .Nordenstrom; Workshop on Alternative Medicine.

[414] See much more on bioenergy fields and the body in Chapter II-3.

[415] Quoted items have been extracted from a bulleted list in Oschman/ Pert. No references for these theories are cited in this fascinating book.

[416] Magnets were 300-500 Gauss.

[417] Website with over 300 references to magnet and EMF therapies: http:/ / www.5pillars.com/ content/ MagneticResearch/ magneticresearch.cfm

[418] Barker et al.; Bassett et al.; Brighton et al. 1981; Darandeliler et al.; Sharrard; Weinberger et al.; Yan et al.

[419] These are various cells that maintain and repair bones, cartilage and connective tissues. See: Aaron; Bassett; Darendeliler/ Darendeliler; Foley-Nolan et al.; C. Rubin et al.; Tabrah et al.; Trock et al. 1993; 1994.

[420] On **environmental medicine see** Crook 1988; 1991; Dadd 1984; 1986; L. Grant; Kidd (toxins); Milburn/ Oelbermann; Randolph/ Moss; Rapp; Rea.

[421] See discussion on **negative effects of EM fields** in Chapter II-3.

[422] On **sick building syndrome** see Bower; Busch; Dodd; Girdlestone; Lotz; Rousseau et al.; Steiner.

[423] More on **negative and positive earth energies** and on **dowsing**in Chapter II-3 and II-4.

[424] More on **Chinese Medicine** under acupuncture. On Feng Shui see: K. Cohen 1998; Feuchtwang; Lip; Rossbach 1983; 1987; Rossbach/ Lin Yun; Wydra.

[425] On planetary ecological healing see: L. Brown et al.; N. Moss; Schauberger; Starke; Waste-busters; outstanding website: www.worldwatch.com; social change at www.newciv.org.

[426] DeRosa/ Porterfield; Jackson 1991; Lake; Shenkman/ Butler.

[427] More on Yoga, T'ai Chi Ch'uan and Qigong later in this chapter. See E. Chang for the exercise manual of the Republic of China.

[428] In inner circles pronounced as in *batch*; elsewhere pronounced as for the composers of that name.

[429] See Appendix II-B, posted at www.WholisticHealingResearch.com for a list of many of these brands of flower essences.

[430] On flower essences see: Barnard; Barnard/ Barnard; Chancellor (England); Cole (essences supporting each chakra); Flower Essence Pharmacy (outstanding ref, out of print); Harvey/ Cochrane (brief, world-wide, includes spiritual sources); D. Cunningham; Gottlieb; Gurudas; Howard; S. Johnson; Kaminski/ Katz (repertory & materia medica); D. Kramer 1995; 1996; J. B. Lee; Mansfield 1995; Marciniak (unity of Creation); G. Mason; Mason/ McIntyre (plants also as herbs, homeopathy, aromatherapy); Meyer/ Shor; Pettit; Remedy Guides; Scherer; Sheehan; Tressider (Bach, psychological); I. White; M. Wood, M. S. Wright (listening to nature).

[431] D. Kramer 1995a; 1995b; email@livingessences.com.au

[432] Bach remedy trade named *Rescue Remedy*, containing Rock Rose (to "bring about stabilization and calmness"), Clematis (to "draw one back into present time"), Clematis (to "balance and soothe away impulsiveness and irritability"), Cherry Plum (to "bring about inner peace and stillness which allows us to ease the contraction felt in the body"), and Star of Bethlehem (to "help us regain our composure" and "for learning and mastery of our lives").

[433] Yarrow Special Formula includes Yarrow, Arnica, and Echinacea.

[434] At the level of the heart, C6

[435] See chapter I-3 on clairsentience, or intuitive perception of the world that does not rely on our five outer senses.

[436] See chapter I-3 on clairsentience, or intuitive perception of the world that does not rely on our five outer senses.

[437] Case description courtesy of J. Steele.

[438] Description of remedy spectrum of efficacy taken from R. Morrison

[439] Anonymous joke: "Did you hear about the homeopath who forgot to take his medicine? He died of an overdose."

[440] Scofield reviews numerous studies demonstrating this sinusoidal periodicity (meaning periodic that increases and decreases) with increasing homeopathic dilutions. See also Davenas et al.

[441] More on the controversy over negative effects of immunizations at the end of this chapter.

[442] Case related to me by a UK homeopath.

[443] Dowsing and radionics are discussed in Chapter II-4. See Boyd 1923; 1925; *British Homeopathic Journal* 1923, 1925, 1928, 1933.

[444] See **research on homeopathy** in: Bellavite/ Signorini; V. Brown/ Ennis; Callinan; M. Castro; Fisher/ Capel; R.G. Gibson et al.; Hahnemann; Jonas/ Jacobs; Kayne; Lewith et al. 2001; Linde et al. 1999; O'Neill; Riley, et al. 2001; Scofield; Singh/ Gupta; C. Smith 1988; Smith/ Boericke 1966; 1968; M. Taylor/ Reilly 2000;Taylor-Reilly et al. (1986); Taylor-Reilly/ Taylor; Vithoulkas; A.D. Watkins. **Controlled studies** are reviewed in Boissel; Feder et al. 2002; Jonas/ Jacobs; Kleijnen et al.; Kollerstrom; Scofield; Taylor-Reilly. Suggested references on the **practice of homeopathy:** Anderson et al. 1978; Anschutz (tissue salts); Boericke/ Dewey (tissue salts); Buegel; *British Homeopathy Journal;* Chapman (tissue salts); Choudhury; C. Coulter 1981; Hahnemann; Herscu (children); Jonas/ Jacobs; *Journal of the American Institute of Homeopathy;*Manning/ Vanrenen; Maury (France-first detox); H. Roberts (intro text); Sacks; Scheussler 1987 (tissue salts); D. Shepherd (intro); Stephenson; Vithoulkas 1979 (intro); Vithoulkas 1980 (major work); Whitmont 1980. Hastings et al. has additional recommendations. **Self-help with homeopathy:** Cummings/ Cullman; Dale Lessell (travelling companion); Lockie; Lockie/ Geddes (women); Remedy Guides; D. Ullman 1988 (children)

[445] Linde et al. 1994 review 89 out of 119 studies that contained adequate information for their meta-analysis, applying the most stringent criteria of any survey. They graded 26 of these as good studies. They conclude that homeopathy cannot be considered a placebo, but they could not find sufficient evidence that it is beneficial for any specific clinical condition. See also earlier reviews by Hill/ Doyon; Kleijnen, et al. 1991 and "state of the art/ science summary in Consensus Statement from Commonweal Conference, and later reviews of Linde and colleagues.

[446] See also Taylor, M.A. et al. 2000 for overview of four trials of homeopathy in allergic rhinitis.

[447] Castro/ Nogueira; J. English; A. Fox; Gibson; Jonas; Krishnamurti; Rastogi/ Sharma; Taylor-Smith.

[448] Review of 25 studies – Stephenson 1955; reviews of 100 studies – Belon; Bastide; effects on white blood cells of mice – Davenas 1987; release of arsenic in rats – Cazin; on white blood cells in humans – Fisher 1987.

[449] See also Linde et al. 1997.

[450] See also discussion by R. Benor on **personality types and CAM modalities** at the end of this chapter.

[451] Bellavita/ Signorini is highly recommended for its thorough review of homeopathic research, in addition to the theories presented.

[452] More on **complexity theory, information as healing,** and **chaos theory** in Chapter IV-3.

[453] See more about **Tiller and his theories** in Chapter II-4 under *radionics*; about healing in Chapter IV-2; and about the etheric body in Chapter II-3 under *auras*. Tiller (2003a; b) also discusses how quantum physics can explain spiritual healing

[454] Calabrese/ Baldwin; Pollycove; van Wijk et al.

[455] 10^{-10} mol/ L

[456] Adams et al.; Brenneman/ Gozes; Junier et al.; Watson/ Hessinger; Williamson et al.

[457] See more on **water as a vehicle for healing** in Chapters I-2 and I-4; **a summary of vehicles for healing energies** in Chapter IV-3.

[458] See Applied Kinesiology earlier in this chapter.

[459] See more on **metaphor and imagery in healing** in Chapter II-1; II-2; IV-3; and on **mythic dimensions of healing** in Chapters III-8; IV-2.

[460] On **state-specific consciousness** see Tart, reviewed in Chapter IV-2.

[461] For more on **holographic realities** see Chapter IV-2.

[462] This sort of intuitive reading of an inanimate object is called **psychometry**, a form of extrasensory perception discussed in Chapter I-3.

[463] Other intuitives have developed such remedies, in the context of homeopathic and flower essence therapies. Madeline Evans has an excellent book on homeopathy, including essential, esoteric and chakra relevance.

[464] See **psi phenomena** in Chapter I-3.

[465] More on solar influences on biological systems in Chapter II-4.

[466] See the latest on Benvenisti's work at www.digibio.com/ cgi-bin/ node.pl?nd=n0

[467] See Chapter I-2 on **IR and UV measurements of healing changes in water.** Dean; Dean/ Brame; S. Schwartz et al.

[468] **Kirlian photography** is discussed later in this chapter.

[469] Overlaps with sacred geometry (Chapter II-4), vehicles for healing (IV-3), and healing rituals (IV-3) are suggested here as well. More on **healing through metaphor and imagery** in IV-2.

[470] It is of note that the people described by Shallis who suffered from extreme allergies sometimes were also able to produce electrical effects, such as electric shocks given to other people and damage to electrical appliances. Many also have a variety of psi abilities.

[471] More on **allergies** in the discussion of **environmental medicine**, later in this chapter.

[472] Governing bodies are: Arizona Board of Homeopathic Medical Examiners; Connecticut Dept. of Health Homeopathic Licensure; Nevada State Board of Homeopathic Medical Examiners.

[473] Ajaya 1976; Ballantine 1986.

[474] **Clinical hypnotic susceptibility tests:**

Harvard Group Scale of Hynotic Susceptibility – J. Green et al.; Kirsch; Kirsch et al.; Kurtz/ Strube; Shor/ Orne.

Stanford Hypnotic Susceptibility Scale (considered the standard for such testing) – C. Perry et al.; Kurtz/ Strube. On difficulties with this test, including negative responses to the testing – Crawford et al.; E. Hilgard 1974.

Hypnotic Induction Profile – Frischolz et al.; Perry et al.; Spiegel/ Spiegel.

Paper/ pencil test:

Absorption test – Roche/ McConkey; Woody et al.

[475] Hilgard/ Hilgard; Wadden/ Anderton.

[476] Harvey et al.; Whorwell; Whorwell et al. 1984; 1987

[477] Bensen; Clawson/ Swade; McCord 1968a.

[478] Dubin/ Shapiro; Fredericks; LaBaw.

[479] Dreaper; Sinclair-Gieben/ Chalmers; Surman et al.; M. Ullman; M. Ullman/ Dudek.

[480] Aronoff et al.; British Tuberculosis Association; Collison; Ewer/ Stewart; Murphy, et al.; Wadden/ Anderton.

[481] For further reading on hypnotherapy see Cheek 1994; Frankel; Gilian; Rossi 1976; 1986a; H. Spiegel/ Spiegel.

[482] American Society for Clinical Hypnosis; Society for Clinical and Experimental Hypnosis; International Society for Hypnosis; American Boards of (Psychological, Medical, Dental) Hypnosis.

[483] Breiling; Light Years Ahead Productions; Vasquez (psychotherapy).

[484] See more on chakras in the section on acupuncture, later in this chapter.

[485] On **color therapy** see: Amber; Beasley; Brennan 1987; 1993; L. Clark; Dinshaw; R. Heline; Hunt 1940/ 1971; 1965; Kunz; Luscher; C. Page; Wilson/ Bek.

[486] See Benor 1992 on aura diagnosis, discussed in Chapter II-3.

[487] More on **light therapy** in Babbitt; Breiling; Coghill 2000(a); Dinshah (on Ghadiali's work); Ghadiali; Kime; Spitler.

[488] On **full spectrum light therapy** see: Boulos et al.; Campbell et al. 1995a; b; c; 1997; Dijk et al.; Eastman et al.; Moore-Ede; W. Schwartz; Terman et al. 1989; 1991; 1995. For more on seasonal affective disorder see:

http:/ / www.aafp.org/ afp/ 980315ap/ saeed.html http:/ / www.aafp.org/ patientinfo/ sad.html

Archives of General Psychiatry 1998;

http:/ / www.websciences.org/ sltbr/ jama.htm http:/ / www.depression.com/ types/ types_07_seasonal.htm

For SAD in children see:

http:/ / www.aacap.org/ commun/ pressrel/ sad.htm http:/ / www.aacap.org/ journal/ june/ 816.htm

[489] Ott 1985; Wohlfarth 1984a; b; 1985; Wohlfarth/ Wohlfarth 1982.

[490] Pellegrini et al.; Schauss 1979; 1985.

[491] 1993a; 1993b; 1994.

[492] More on EEG resonations between healers and healees in Cade/ Coxhead ; Charman ; Dilbeck et al; Duane/ Behrendt; Fahrion, et al; Grinberg-Zylberbaum et al; Orme-Johnson, D et al; Seto, A et al; Sugano, H et al; Zimmerman.

[493] See discussion of touch below, under Massage.

[494] Dossey 2002; Root-Berenstein/ Root-Berenstein; Sherman; Sherman et al.; Zimmer

[495] See references on bodymind therapies, above. Note also the impediment to including touch and massage in psychotherapy imposed by laws that are meant to prevent sexual malpractice within the therapeutic relationship.

[496] C. S. West; Wittlinger/ Wittlinger; Zanolla et al.

[497] Prudden 1977; 1984; 1987.

[498] Many more variations on the theme of massage are described in Dunn/ Williams; Knaster; Koch 2001a; b; c. See D. Nelson on wholistic, spiritual touch.

[499] See Aromatherapy, earlier in this chapter.

[500] www.amtamassage.org/

[501] Acupuncture is described later in this chapter. The meridian-based therapies (MBTs) include Thought Field Therapy (Callahan 1985; 1991; 1996; Callahan/ Callahan 2000; Durlacher; Gallo), Emotional Freedom Therapy (Craig); and Touch and Breathe (Diepold). More on MBTs in Fling 1999; Gallo 1999; 2000; Gallo/ Furman; Gallo/ Vincenzi; M. Gordon 1998; 1999; Hartman-Kent; Lake/ Wells; Mountrose/ Mountrose; Pratt/ Lambrou; K. Zimmerman.

[502] I feel it is important to include these subtle energy interventions here, within the massage overview, despite the obvious redundancy. This is not only for the sake of thoroughness in discussing manual therapies. It is also to emphasize that many of the manual therapies may include elements of subtle energy healing – even without the awareness of the practitioners.

[503] On **Shiatsu** see Cowmeadow; Ridolfe; Ridolfe/ Franzen.

[504] For a discussion of **acupressure** see under acupuncture.

[505] These Meridian Based Therapies (MBTs) were discussed earlier, under acupressure.

[506] On emotional and physical releases during reflexology see also P. Griffiths; Sahai.

[507] For further discussion of **reflexology** see under acupuncture.

[508] For more on **Polarity Therapy** see R. Gordon; Seidman; Siegal; R. Stone 1986; 1999.

[509] A **proxy** is a person who receives the energy medicine intervention in place of the person for whom the treatment is intended. The proxy serves as an antenna or a form of living clairsentient *witness*, enabling the bioenergy therapist to connect with the person in need. More on the use of a witness under *Radionics* in chapter II-4.

[510] See extensive review of spiritual healing in Volume I.

[511] Radix therapy was developed by Charles Kelley and is described at http:/ / www.radix.org.

[512] Eutony (Gerda Alexander); Hakomi (Ron Kurtz); Hawaiian massage (Kahuna); Metamorphic Technique (Robert St. John; Gaston St. Pierre); Thai massage; Zero balancing (Fritz Smith).

[513] This tension cycle is discussed in Chapter II-1

[514] On **touch** see Montagu 1953; 1971; D. Nelson.

[515] Massage is often termed *manipulation*, which is confusing because there are separate therapies that combine spinal manipulation with massage.

[516] The Psychological Corporation is an company that develops assessment tools.

[517] On **massage** see: M. Beck; Bentley (head); Cassar; Chaitlow; Chia; Downing; Hollis; Inkeles; Knaster; Lidell; Maanum/ Montgomery; Sohn/ Finando; Vickers.

[518] Benor 1992 (reviewed in Chapter I-4); Orloff; Shealy 1975; 1988; 1995; M. Schultz. See also brief mention of intuitive assessments using devices that read electromagnetic potentials at acupressure points, under Acupuncture (earlier in the chapter).

[519] Karagulla; Karagulla/ Kunz; Myss; Shealy; Orloff; M. Schulz.

[520] **Psi abilities** are reviewed in Chapter I-3.

[521] King and Clark 2002; Offredy 1998; Polge 1995.

[522] For instance, poets A. E. Houseman, Longfellow, and John Masefield; authors Kipling, George Eliot, Oscar Wild; actor Sir Alec Guiness; musicians Stravinsky, Mozart, and Tchaikovsky; artists William Blake, Picasso, and Klee – all mentioned in Inglis/ West 1986.

[523] **Psi abilities**, including telepathy, clairsentience, pre- and retro-cognition, and psychokinesis (PK) are discussed in Chapter I-3.

[524] See discussion on **collective consciousness** in Chapter II-1.

[525] Spirit guides and **spiritual awareness** are extensively considered in Volume III.

[526] More on aura perceptions and assessments in Chapter II-3.

[527] AK and hypnotic ideomotor movements were discussed earlier in this chapter.

[528] Much more on dowsing in Chapter II-4.

[529] More on **dowsing and radionics** in Chapter II-3.

[530] See Applied Kinesiology, earlier in this chapter.

[531] **Transpersonal psychology** is discussed later in this chapter and in Chapter II-1.

[532] Psi perceptions are discussed in Chapter I-3. See especially **remote viewing** in Graff; McMoneagle 1993; 2000; Morehouse; Schnabel; Targ/ Harrary; Targ/ Katra; Targ/ Puthoff.

[533] Volume III reviews research in spiritual dimensions of healing. Of particular interest for intuitive assessments are the channeled perceptions that may provide suggestions to help identify the causes of illness and various cures that can help. In the basic sciences, Besant/ Leadbeater 1908 is particularly interesting – includes clairsentient perceptions of the elements in the periodic table before they were identified by conventional science.

[534] **Theories to explain healing** are discussed in Chapter IV-2.

[535] Remote viewing is discussed in Chapter I-3.

[536] See review of **LeShan's realities** in Chapter IV-2; also Table IV-2. LeShan (1974a) and Joyce Goodrich (1978) teach a method of spiritual healing that is based on achieving a focused, meditative state, described briefly earlier in this chapter.

[537] Murphy 1992b lists studies on visual sensitivity, auditory acuity, other aspects of perception, reaction time and other motor skills, concentration, empathy, creativity, and more.

[538] Bensen 1975; Cooper/ Aygen; Schneider, et al.; and Murphy 1992b.

[539] See numerous references for behavioral effects, pain relief, skin resistance changes, and subjective improvements in Murphy 1992b.

[540] See briefer, annotated bibliography at http:/ / www.WholisticHealingResearch.com/ References/ Meditation.htm

[541] Murphy 1992a; 1992b; Murphy/ Donovan. See also meditation in schizophrenia (Lukoff et al. 1986).

[542] See also **biofeedback** in this chapter for further studies with EEGs.

[543] See lists of EEG studies in Murphy 1992b.

[544] See Horgan for discussion of brain imaging and mystical states of consciousness.

[545] More on **meditation** in *Advances* (journal); Ajaya 1976; M. Ali 1990 (stress management); Austin; Ballantine 1986; Banquet; Coxhead; Crookall (breathing); Dass; Goleman 1977; Gunaratana; E. Harrison; Heron; Hopkins; Kabat-Zinn; Kabat-Zinn, et al. 1985; 1986; Kuvalayananda; Lazar et al. (brain mapping); Leichtman/ Japiske; S. Levine (beautiful descriptions of healing through meditations); Lingerman; Macbeth; Magaray; Mahesh; K. McDonald; McLaird; Moin; Pennington; Rama/ Hymes (breath); Ramacharaka 1904 (breath); Rinbochay et al.; Roth; Sarayadrian; Schwarz 1977; Shapiro/ Walsh; R. Singh; B. Smith 1963; Strand; Tart 1986b; Trungpa; Wallace (TM); Wangchen; Washburn; Wilber; Engler/ Brown; Wolinski (overlaps with hypnotherapy, psychotherapy). Several articles discuss meditation and ESP: Honorton; Osis/ Bokert 1971; Rao/ Puri 1977. Naranjo/ Ornstein produced a lovely book on **meditation.** Naranjo discusses mystical views of meditation. This presentation helps readers to grasp the spirit of meditation, some of its uses within the contexts in which it was developed, and relevant applications today. Ornstein discusses points of **comparison and integration of meditation with modern psychologies**, but Kornfield, LeShan, or Carrington are even better in this regard. D. Rozman recommends an integration of meditation with exercises in sharing and problem-solving in a family format, and suggests ways to introduce, encourage and develop meditational practices in children of all ages. On **research in meditation** see C. Alexander, et al.; Benson 1972; Glaser, et al.; R. Monroe, et al.; M. Murphy; Murphy/ Donovan; Orme-Johnson/ Farrow 1976; 1977. For discussions on **psychotherapy and meditation** see Claxon; Engler; Goleman; Kornfield (outstanding); Smith/ Dass; Wilber, Engler/ Brown (similarities); E.W Russell (differences). On personal experiences of meditation: Perrin; Satprem 1981; Tweedie. On EEG and meditation: Blundell; Peper/ Ancoli.

Searchable database of meditation research:

http:/ / www.noetic.org/ ions/ medbiblio/ biblio.htm

[546] See discussion of psi awarenesses in Chapter I-3.

[547] See Chapter II-1 on right and left brain functions, especially Naranjo/ Ornstein; Budzynski.

[548] Here is a sample meditation for seeking creative solutions to problems: Picture to yourself that you are in the center of an enormous flower with many petals, such as a lotus or dahlia. Ask yourself, "What can I do about this problem?" Take any answer which pops into your mind and place it on a petal near you, without analyzing or criticizing it. Answers may be mundane, silly, foolish, or brilliant inspirations. Don't give in to temptations to abandon any one of them or to analyze them. Return and ask yourself the same question again and again, placing each answer on its own petal. When you feel this process of inner exploration has run its course, stop asking your question. Sit back and examine each item on its own petal. I have often found this to be an extremely productive meditation.

[549] See EmotionalBody Process in Benor et al 2001; 2002; S. Levine (1986); The Sedona method at http://www.sedona.com .

[550] See EmotionalBody Process in Benor et al 2001; 2002

I have seen very penetrating insights arise from such meditations, in myself and in clients I have worked with.

[551] See the Meridian Based Therapies; EMDR; and the Sedona Method (http://www.sedona.com) as examples of techniques for rapid release of problems.

[552] See LeShan 1974a, reviewed in Chapter IV-2, on **alternative realities**; discussion on **mystical experiences** in Chapter III-8.

[553] More on **meta-anxiety** in Chapter II-1.

[554] Carrington 1977; Gersten; Lazarus; Walsh/ Rauche.

[555] U. of Pennsylvania; U. of Massachusetts.

[556] R. Callahan; Hooke; Leonoff.

[557] In addition, with the Tapas Acupressure Technique, roots of psychological problems in past lives may be discovered and released. Much more on past lives and past life therapy in Volume III.

[558] Applied kinesiology was discussed earlier in this chapter.

[559] See discussion on applied kinesiology, below. No literature is available as yet on TAT. See Appendix B for information on courses.

[560] EMDR, Eye Movement Desensitization and Reprocessing, is described under Bodymind therapies

[561] For research on EMDR see http://www.emdr.org/

[562] For a wealth of clinical observations on Emotional Freedom Technique see http://www.emofree.com

[563] On **Native American Medicine** see Beck/ Walters; K. Cohen 1999a; b; Lyon; V. Vogel; Yellowtail/ Fitzgerald.

[564] A similar fate befell the Homeopathic schools and practitioners as a result of the Flexner Report.

[565] On **naturopathic medicine** see Airola; Boyle; Coulter 1973; Kirchfield/ Boyle; Lininger et al.; Marz; R. Moss; Murray/ Pizzorno 1989; 1991; Pizzorno/ Murray; Sullivan. See **research on herbal medicine** in the section on nutrition, later in this chapter.

[566] Uterine cervical dysplasia.

[567] Naturopathic Physicians Licensing Examination (NPLEx).

[568] Alaska, Arizona, Connecticut, Hawaii, Maine, Montana, New Hampshire, Oregon, Puerto Rico, Utah, Vermont, Washington. Florida also has some naturopaths practicing under a sunsetted licensure law.

[569] Two years of basic medical sciences: anatomy, physiology, biochemistry, pharmacology, pathology, and microbiology/ immunology (total of 1025 hours) are blended with 2 years of naturopathic philosophy and therapeutics, plus 869 hours of clinical education and 1,500 hours of clinical training.

[570] I have always been amazed that medical schools offer next to no training in nutritional therapies.

[571] Meeker-Lowery/ Ferrara; Mercola 2001.

[572] Mercola June 2, 2001

[573] See study of birds killed by exposure to heated Teflon at http:// www.ewg.org/ reports/ toxicteflon

[574] Mercola April 16, 2003.

[575] On **nutrition and herbal medicine** for starters I recommend Airola; American Academy of Family Practitioners; Artschwager (herbal); Balch/ Balch; Baldwin; Ballentine 1978; 1987; 1999; Bendich/ Deckelbaum (preventive nutrition); Bennett (diets for specific conditions); Bland; Block (concise, w/ 280 refs); Blumenthal et al. (herbals); Bratsman/ Kroll (herbal); Braverman 1987; 1993 (amino acids); Braverman et al.; Cass; Cass/ McNally; Colbin (macrobiotic); Cousens (spiritual development); Ensminger et al.; Fredericks; Goldberg; Hastings et al.; E. Hoffman (cancer); IBIS (herbs, nutrition); M. Jacobs (cancer); T. Johnson (database of ethnobotany); Klos; Kushi (Macrobiotics); Lu (Chinese); McGuffin et al. (herbal); Mills/ Bone (researched herbal remedies); Moerman (Native American); R. Moss (herbs for cancer); Murray/ Pizzorno (dietary/ minerals/ herbs); National Research Council; Null 1997; PDR (herbal); Peirce/ Gans (herbs); Philpott/ Kalita (allergies); Pitchford (Chinese Medicine); Preconception Care; Prevention Magazine (vitamins); Rampton/ Stauber (food industry problems); Randolph/ Moss (allergies); Regelson/ Colman (aging); J. Robbins; Saifer/ Zellerbach (detoxification); Sattilaro (personal experience with macrobiotic diet for prostatic cancer); Schauss et al. (children); Schultex (ethnobotany); Schulz et al. (herbal); Werbach; J. Wright 1984 (therapy cases); Zand (children herbal). On **orthomolecular medicine** see Gaby/ Wright; Hoffer/ Walker; M. Murray; Werbach. For herbal medicine see below. Subscription information service **website**: Intramedicine. **Marijuana**: B. Zimmerman/ Bayer.

[576] Meridian based therapies are discussed under acupuncture and massage.

[577] The Food and Nutrition Board of the Institute of Medicine in the National Academy of Sciences, together with the national health service in Canada.

[578] See also *Schüssler salts,* also known as *Biochemic Tissue Salts,* re minerals that may be helpful in the prevention and treatment of illness.

[579] Getsios et al.; Raskind et al.; Wilcock et al.

[580] **Ginseng** – Bhattacharya/ Mitra; Vuksan et al.; **kava (*DANGEROUS!!* – see caution below)** – Kinzler et al.; E. Lehman; R. Reichert; Warnecke; Woelk et al. (vs. benzodiazepines). **Caution:** recent research suggests that Kava may cause liver damage, with 4 fatalities reported. Its use has been banned in Germany and the UK.

[581] **Adenosylmethionine** – K. Bell et al.; Criconia et al.; DeVanna/ Rigamonti. **Ginko biloba** – D. Brown 1994a. **Omega-3 fatty acids** – A. Stoll; **St. John's Wort** – see below. **Valerian** – D. Brown 1994b.

[582] **Glycerine** – Leiderman et al.; Kanofsky et al; Osmond/ Hoffer; J. Wright.

[583] For an excellent brief overview of benefits and risks of herbal medicine see B. Barrett et al.

[584] Formica; J. Hicks; Shaw et al.

[585] Fulder has recommendations for nutritional items that a person may take as preventives when they have to spend more than a brief period in a hospital.

[586] Leathwood et al.; Leathwood/ Chauffard; Lindahl/ Lindwall.

[587] LI 160/ **hyperforin extract of St. John's Wort** – Delle et al.; Laakmann et al.; W. Muller et al.

[588] An antidepressant, brand name Elavil.

[589] An antidepressant, brand name Tofranil.

[590] An antidepressant, brand name Prozac.

[591] More on St. John's Wort in Buist; Cass; Clouinard et al.; Gelenberg et al.; Nangia et al.; Vorbach et al. (vs. imipramine); Wheatley (vs. amitriptyline).

[592] A tranquilizer, brand name Valium.

[593] Later studies continue to confirm the efficacy of *ginkgo* for dementia: Hofferberth; Kanowski et al.; Le Bars et al.; Maurer et al.; Rai et al.

[594] For a review of laboratory and clinical studies on ginkgo leaf see DeFeudis 1991; 1998.

[595] Failures of ginger for treating nausea are reported in motion sickness (J. Stewart et al.; Stott et al.; C. Wood et al.); and postoperative nausea/ vomiting (Arfeen et al.).

[596] Hoheisel et al., and also see German studies referenced in Barrett et al.

[597] Elsasser-Beile et al.; Luetig et al.; Melchart et al. 1995; 1998; See et al.

[598] Fulder; Heinerman; Koch/ Lawson (excellent book). Garlic for cancer: Hoffman

[599] Berthold et al.; Isaacson et al.; Neil et al. 1996; Simons et al.; and a meta-analysis of garlic for hypercholesterolemia by Stevinson et al.

[600] Darzynkiewkz et al.; De La Taille et al.; Kameda et al.; E. Small et al.; Zunin.

[601] Bensky/ Gamble 1986; Hsu et al. 1982; 1985.

[602] Sun 1988; Unschuld 1992; Wong et al. 1991.

[603] On **herbal remedies** see *American Botanical Council (324 herbs – clinical and research data),* American Botanical Council (CD ROM); *American Herbal Association Quarterly Newsletter;* Barrett et al. (excellent, concise summary); Bisset/ Wichtl; Blumenthal (German Commission); Bratsman/ Kroll; Brinker (contraindications, drug interactions); Bruneton; Buhner 1996 (Native American); Buhner 2000 (herbal antibiotics); N. Coon; Culpepper; deSmet et al. 1997; 1999 (adverse effects); Dincin; Eskinazi 1998; Frawley/ Lad (Ayurvedic); Grieve (British); Hadady (Asian); D. Hall (plant personalities); *Herbal Society of America*; D. Hoffmann (European/ American); J Lake (psychological problems);.Leung/ Foster; McGuffin (safety); Messegue (French); National Institutes of Health; Newall et al.; Physicians' Desk Reference (PDR) for Herbal Medicines; Rector-Page (self-healing per symptoms); Remedy Guides; Rose 1976; A. Rosenberg; Santillo; V. Schulz et al.; Tierra 1983; 1992; V. Vogel (Native American); R. Weiss; Werbach/ Murray (concise); Wichtl; M. Wood 1986; 1997 (Chinese, homeopathic, Native American).

Vogel (Native American); R. Weiss (trans. from German); Werbach/ Murray (concise); Wood (Chinese, homeopathic, Native American).

[604] Reference chromatograms are available for most of the commonly used herbs. See O'Mathúna on problems with unregulated production.

[605] More than half of physicians surveyed by the Association of American Medical Colleges complained that their education in nutrition and nutritional therapy was inadequate. Less than a third of medical schools have courses in nutrition, and there is rarely any extension of the course in clinical education. The Physicians' Committee for Responsible Medicine has designed a resource for medical students to fill this gap.

[606] De Smet 1997; 1999a; b.

[607] (Brinker; Chan/ Cheung; Complete Geerman Commission E Monographs; Ernst 2002; Fulder (regrettably, Fulder does not reference his notes on this aspect – or others – of CAM therapies); *HealthNotes Clinical Essentials*; Meletis/ Jacobs.

[608] **Adverse herbal effects**: Bone; D'Epiro; Ernst 1998; Farnsworth; Tyler.

While these are clearly of concern, they do not begin to approach the numbers or severity of adverse medicinal effects, which include 100,000 deaths annually from properly prescribed medications in the USA alone: Bates et al.; T. Brennan et al.; Classen et al.; Lazarou et al.; Litovitz/ Manoguerra; D. Phillips et al.

[609] S. Barker; Beck/ Meyers; California Veterinary Medical Association; Cusack; Huebscher; Ory/ Goldberg; Owen; Pastronek/ Glickman; Vormbrock/ Grossberg.

[610] On pets as therapists see Delta Society; McElroy.

[611] On **Pet Therapy** see Cusack; Ory/ Goldberg; Patronek/ Glickman. McElroy 1996; 1998 (spiritual dimensions of pets); W. Thomas (nursing home). On dolphin healing see Dobbs; Sandoz; Upledger 1995b.

[612] See The International Alliance for Animal Therapy and Healing (IAATH) at http:// www.iaath.com/ pg/ about/ contact.htm

[613] Much of this discussion comes from Burton Goldberg Group 1997.

[614] Further studies are cited in the articles mentioned above.

[615] See PNI research in Chapter II-1.

[616] **Research in psychotherapy:** Anderson/ Lambert (efficiency over time); Lambert et al (survey); Bergin/ Garfield (outstanding overview); Elkin (with medications); Froyd et al (outcomes); Howard et al (cost effective); Hubble et al (overview); Lambert et al (efficiency over time); Thase (with medications); Wampold (overview).

Meta-analyses: Andrews/ Harvey; Landman/ Dawes; Nicholson/ Berman; Shapiro/ Shapiro; Smith et al. 1980.
Online resources for psychotherapy research: APA Online (Efficacy) http:/ / www.apa.org/ practice/ peff.html; Evidence-Based Mental Health Collections http:/ / ebmh.bmjjournals.com/ collections/ ; Lambert (review of reviews) http:/ / www.cwru.edu/ affil/ div29/ lambert.htm; Lambert/ Okiishi (outcomes) http:/ / www.clipsy.oupjournals.org/ cgi/ content/ abstract/ 4/ 1/ 66; Network for Research on Experiential Psychotherapies http:/ / experiential-researchers.org/ ; Counseling and Psychotherapy Research http:/ / www.cpct.co.uk/ cpct/ ; Narrative Psychology Resource Guide http:/ / maple.lemoyne.edu/ ~hevern/ narpsych.html; Qualitative Research Resources on the Internet http:/ / www.nova.edu/ ssss/ QR/ qualres.html. This field is so vast as to defy reasonable summary here.**

[617] More on the personhood of the therapist near the end of this chapter; with extensive discussion of psychotherapy in Chapter II-1; a brief summary of types of psychotherapy in Appendix A.

[618] The projection of therapist problems upon clients is called *transference.*

[619] Chai; Frantzis; *China Qigong;* Sui; M. Walker.

[620] Some of these studies are reviewed in Chapter I-4. See also Kuang (hypertension).

[621] A 2-year training program is offered at Zou Du University in the Hai Ding District of Beijing, and four quarterly classes are offered annually at Tianjin University in Heibei province. Briefer courses are offered elsewhere in China. China has certified qigong practitioners since 1989, requiring confirmation of effective treatment of 30 people with similar illnesses, with longitudinal observation to assure that the therapeutic effects are lasting. Candidates are encouraged to build up their cases in an internship at a qigong hospital.

The primary professional association is the China Research Society of Qigong Science in China.

[622] More on qigong in K. Cohen (1997); Connor; Jahnke; A. Lu (1997);

[623] Dressen/ Singg; Schlitz/ Braud 1986; Wetzel.

[624] Carl Hammerschlag and Howard Silverman suggest a lovely variety of rituals that can be helpful in a wide range of situations.

[625] See outstanding examples of healings through rituals in Body; Koerner.

[626] Technically, a medicine man is defined as a native healer. **Shamans** are **medicine men,** but not all medicine men are shamans. Shamans serve in many other capacities within their culture, in addition to performing their duties as healers They may mediate disputes, officiate at religious holidays and rites of passage, etc.
References in related disciplines which deal with **shamanic healing,** and with **healing in the context of Western sub-cultures and other cultures**: Achterberg 1985; Arvigo; Atkinson; Ayishi; R. J. Beck; Bhandari, et al.; F. Bloomfield; Boshier; Boyd; Calderon; S. Campbell; Constantinides; Dieckhofer; Dirksen; Dobkin de Rios 1972; 1984a; b; Eliade (a classic); Fabrega; Raquel Garcia; Raymond Garcia; Garrison; Geisler 1984; 1985; Glick; Golomb; Halifax; Hammerschlag; Harner (a classic); Heinze 1984; 1985 (excellent surveys); Helman; Hiatt; Hill; Hood; Hultkrantz; Humphrey; Joralemon; Kakar; Kaptchuk/ Croucher; Kapur; Katz; Kerewsky-Halpern; S. King; Kleinman (essential to a cross-cultural understanding of diagnosis and treatment); Kleinman/ Sung; Koss; Krippner 1980b; Krippner/ Villoldo; Kuang, et al.; Landy; J. Long; M. Long 1976; 1978; Machover; McClain; McClenon; McGaa; McGuire; C. Miller; Morley/ Wallis; Myerhoff; J. Nash; Orsi; Osumi/ Ritchie; Oubre; Packer; Peters/ Price-Williams; R. Prince 1972; Rauscher 1985; St. Clair 1970; 1974; Sandner; Scharfetter; P. Singer; Singer, et al.; Sneck; Sobel; Swan 1986; Takaguchi; Torrey; Peters; Ullrich; Villoldo/ Krippner; Webster; Winkelman; M. Young 1976; Zimmels.

Mexican: M. E. Brown; Rubel; Rubel et al.; J. C. Young.

Native American: Boyd; Farrer; Hand; Koerner; McGaa; W. Morgan; Morse et al.; Naranjo/ Swentzell; Powers; Reichard 1939; 1950; Topper; Yellowtail; M. Young.

Psi healing: Achterberg and Heinze. For excellent discussions on factors in the healers' cultures which help to explain their effectiveness see: Gevitz; Harwood; Hufford; Kakar;

Kleinman; Lanty; Romanucci-Ross, et al.; R. H. Schneider; Servadio (reviewed in Chapter 4); Terrell; Trotter; Unschuld.

[627] E.g. Chesi 1980; 1981; Finkler 1985.

[628] Berman; Finkler 1985; Kiev 1964; 1968; Kleinman 1980; Phoenix; Servadio.

[629] For examples of cross-cultural healings see Boyd; M. Long.

[630] Berman is especially cogent in arguing these points. In sociology and anthropology, these polarities of attitudes towards other cultures are termed:

Emic - Explanation that acknowledges that peoples from cultures other than our own, behaving in manners that are different from ours, usually have their own legitimate cultural explanations for their beliefs and behaviors. (Contrasted with *etic*)

Etic - Explanations based on Western convictions that modern science can provide "objective" explanations for every phenomenon - within the frameworks of Western scientific paradigms. (Contrasted with *emic*)

[631] See Harner training at http://www.shamanism.org/

[632] Research confirms that absent healing can influence people, animals, plants, bacteria, and yeasts – as reviewed in detail in Chapters I-4; I-5; and briefly in IV-3.

[633] More on **shamanism** in earlier in this chapter and in Chapter I-5.

[634] See annotated healing research bibliography in *Healing Research*, Volume I.

[635] The Confederation of Healing Organisations in Britain includes 16 healer groups with around 6,000 members. Their Code of Conduct prescribes that they will not diagnose, and will suggest that healees see a doctor first for their problems. These have been strong labor unions, and effective in lobbying the government to accept healing. See Appendix B for names of healing organizations.

[636] See discussions of **secondary gain** in Chapter II-1 under *self-healing* and *suggestion.*.

[637] The Confederation of Healing Organisations in Britain includes 16 healer groups with around 6,000 members. Their Code of Conduct prescribes that they will not diagnose, and will suggest that healees see a doctor first for their problems. These have been strong labor unions, and effective in lobbying the government to accept healing. See Volume I, Appendix B for names of healing organizations.

[638] Cheng; Jou; W. Berk.

[639] See partial list of qualitative studies of TT (and other healing modalities) at http://www.WholisticHealingResearch.com/Research/Studies.htm#qsh

[640] The Tibetan definition of chi differs from the Qi (same pronunciation) of Chinese medicine.

[641] Summary taken primarily from Badmaev.

[642] Several other German studies are cited in Badmaev.

[643] On **Tibetan Medicine** see Badmaev; B. Clark; Kunzang/ Rechung Rinpoche; Wangyal; Donden. On psychological aspects see T. Clifford. See also **Ayurvedic Medicine** earlier in this chapter.

[644] I see **mystic** as a Western term that expresses our unfamiliarity and discomfort with the realms that these explorers of internal worlds are describing – immersed as we are in the materialistic, Cartesian dualism that separates mind from matter. The research and theories reviewed in this book put mysticism in a different light, and make such reports of inner realms more easily comprehensible and acceptable. See more on **mystical experience** in Chapter III-8.

[645] Ornish; Denoliet; Gould; Jiang, et al.; Linden, et al.; Markovitz; Siegman/ Denbroski. See further discussions of healing for cancer through PNI in Chapter II-1.

[646] Achterberg 1985; Kübler-Ross 1981; Siegel 1986.

[647] Benor 2002b; Dethlefsen/ Dahlke; Hay; Harrison; Steadman.

[648] On **visualization techniques in psychotherapy and self-healing** see Achterberg 1985; Assagioli; Bek/ Pullar; Bresler/ Trubo; Brigham; Caudell; J. Day (children); Epstein 1981; 1989; 1994; Gawain; Glouberman; Goleman; Gurin; Hillman; King 1981; Hillman 1975; Jaffe; Lusebrink; McLaird 1982; Mehl; Morrison; Moyers; J. Schwarz 1978; Samuels/ Samuels; Sheikh 1983; 1984; 1986; Sheikh/ Shafler; Sheikh/ Sheikh; Sheikh Solmnon; Sontag 1979 (TB, cancer); 1983 (AIDS); S. Taylor; Vernon; L. Walker et al.; Zahourek. Desoille on the "Directed

Daydream" technique is similar (M. Watkins). On physiological determinants of visual images see Hedges. On visualizations in ESP see Stanford 1969. On vivid visualuations that may be confusing see Schatzman; Wilson/ Barber. On Simonton's work see Chapter II-1, section on self-healing; Simonton/ Simonton 1981; Simonton et al. 1980; Spiegel et al. 1989. On the mind and the immune system see Chapter II-1, under *Psychoneuroimmunology.*

[649] See **telesomatic reactions** in Chapter IV-3.

[650] See description of Kraft's healing work in Chapter I-1.

[651] More on **psychic surgery in** Chapter III-7.

[652] The healing work and views of Edwards; Estebany; Ivanova in Mir/ Vilenskaya; Knowles 1954; 1956; Lombardi; and Safonov are described in Chapter I-1.

[653] See **suggestion and hypnosis** in Chapter II-1; **metaphor in healing** under creative arts in this chapter; Chapter IV-2.

[654] Reviewed above under Osteopathy.

[655] For further observations on **visualization in healing** see Achterberg 1985; Benor 1985; Sheikh; also Bibb/ Wood; F King 1982; Krystal; Plume (in St. Clair 1979); Sanford; Schultze/ Luthe; Shubentsov; Turner 1974. On visualization and psi, see George/ Krippner.

[656] Another such exercise is described in Benor et al 2001.

[657] More on the fantasy-prone personality in Chapter I-3.

[658] See discussion on the history of spiritual healing and paradigm shifts, in I-introduction.

[659] A clear example of this imprinting is seen in the 20 percent of children who see auras – till they enter school, at which point the percent drops to close to zero (Peterson 1975; 1987).

[660] In table rapping, those sitting around the table hold a yes/ no question in their minds, with the anticipation that it will be answered by a spirit through paranormal raps that are heard from the table. Typically, one rap signals YES, and 2 raps mean NO. While skeptics suggest these raps are most likely produced by the participants in some covert physical manner, research suggests otherwise. The oscilloscope recordings show that the raps have a crescendo profile, which is physically impossible. In contrast with this, ordinary raps start with a jar to the table and then have a decrescendo profile – as the vibrations from the initial physical tap on the table dissipate. More on this in Chapter III-5.

[661] In similar ways, sightings of various **apparitions and nature devas** (van Gelder) or interactions with apparent **discarnate influences** (Eaton) may be projections of the perceivers, sometimes called "Thought forms." More on this in Chapter III-4, under Apparitions. Some sightings of UFOs and of the Loch Ness monster may also be thought forms of this sort.

[662] More on **mediumistic channeling and spirits** in Chapters III-4; III-5; and III-6.

[663] See C. George for a detailed report on these ancient writings.

[664] More on OBEs in Chapter III-1.

[665] More on these spirit and spiritual aspects of healing in Volume III. Edwards is described in Chapter I-1; Turner in I-1 and III-5. See Besant/ Leadbeater; A. Hicks; Leadbeater.

[666] The Theosophical Society was formed by H.P. Blavatsky in India in 1871, "through which the West and the world in general would be instructed in 'true Spirituality.'" http:/ / ts-adyar.org/ history.html

[667] See also discussion of effects of intentionality imprinted on electrical devices in Tiller 2003a; b.

[668] On the **ring of knowledge phenomenon** see: Agpaoa (in Stelter); Brennan 1993; Brown/ Plume (in St. Clair 1979); Cain (in Sykes; Wooding): Cayce (in Stearn; Sugrue); Rev Brown, Rev Plume (in St. Clair 1979); Mr Gray (in Montgomery 1973); Jung; Teilhard de Chardin's description of a world-field of thoughts and conceptions of all living things, which he termed the "noosphere."

[669] The very lack of a common term for the opposite of a "vicious circle" is an example of social resistance to altering reality. See more on self-perpetuating circles and spirals in Chapter II-1 under systems theory.

[670] More on these fields in Chapter I-3.

[671] For good discussions of such **powers of suggestion** see Bishop; Playfair 1987. See discussion in Chapter II-1.

[672] See discussion on **rituals** above and in Chapter IV-3.

[673] I would expect other clusters of healers and healees to be found with strengths in different areas as well, which would similarly be reflected in the processes and/ or results of their healings. Cooperstein has made a start at clarifying these points, as reviewed in Chapter I-5.

[674] **Numerous factors that may influence healing** are considered in Chapter IV-3.

[675] See Chapter IV-2 for a discussion of **morphogenetic fields.**

[676] See a more extensive discussion on **reasons that healing and psi have not been accepted** in Chapter IV-3; Benor 1990).

[677] in combination with relaxation, meditation, dietary and lifestyle changes, and group therapy

[678] See colonic irrigation, earlier in this chapter.

[679] On **water therapies** see: Ballantine/ Batmanghelidj; Batmanghelidj; Boyle; Flanagan/ Flanagan; Kloss; Thrash/ Thrash.

[680] See homeopathy and flower essences, above.

[681] Healing effects on water are reviewed in Chapter I-4.

[682] On **yogic practices** see: Aurobindo; Ballantine/ Ajaya; Brena; J. Cooper; Funderburk; Hewitt; Iyengar; P.Y. Johnson; C. Kent; M. Lee (Hatha yoga therapy); Masunaga (meridian-activating exercises); Patel; Phelan: Rama 1980; Ramacharaka 1904; 1930; 1934; Samskrti/ Veda; Vishnudevananda; Schatz; Shearer; Taimni; Vivikananda; E. Wood; and *Yoga Journal.* On **yoga research** see Udupa; Udupa et al.; R. Monro et al. (extensive bibliography). Goodman 1986; 1990 explored subjective experiences with particular postures, relevant to *kriyas.* On **movement therapy** see Fisher/ Stark.

[683] Arthritis – Schatz; asthma – Nagendra/ Nagarthna; chronic pulmonary obstruction – Tandon; hypertension – Frumkin et al.; C. Patel 1973; vision – Hider;

[684] A few advanced practitioners of yoga have cooperated with Western scientists, allowing measurements of their bodily functions while they enter unusual meditative states and/ or simply demonstrate control over their bodies. Some have exercised their egos along with their bodies, employing their unusual control over body functions to entertain or astound audiences.

[685] Masons speak of the energy, or Spirit, that rises through the spinal column. The Hopi Indians of North America have always known about kundalini (Kripinanda pp.1-3).

[686] See discussion of Qigong under Acupuncture, earlier in this chapter.

[687] See Chapter III-3 on **reincarnation research** and **past life therapy.**

[688] Feldenkrais; Lowen 1971; 1975; 1978; Pierrakos.

[689] More on **meditation** earlier in this chapter.

[690] All the Meridian Based Therapies can be used to treat allergies. See especially NAET; List of MBTs at:

http:/ / www.wholistichealingresearch.com/ References/ MBTs.htm

[691] It is estimated that close to 4 billion pounds are lost annually in the UK due to CFS (http:/ / news.bbc.co.uk/ 2/ hi/ health/ 3014341.stm).

[692] See also Merchant et al. re chlorella for firbomyalgia.

[693] Bailar; Cairns; G.L. Engel.

[694] Dowrick; Jampolsky; Kubler-Ross; Metzner; B. Siegel; Wilber (1998).

[695] Barasch; J. Canfield, et al.; Conway; A. Frank; Halvorson-Boyd/ Hunter; Hirshberg/ Barasch; . Holland/ Rowland; Lerner 1994; Leviton; N. Levy; Lawlis 1994; Moyers; Rando; Remoff; Roud; Sattilaro; Schlessel-Harpham; Shinoda-Bolen 1996, D. Watson..

[696] Gawler; Hirshberg/ Barasch; Roud; Sattilaro

[697] See PNI in Chapters II-1; II-2.

[698] See Chapters I-1; I-4; I-5.

[699] H. Hu et al. 1993; K. Johansson et al. 1993; Kjendahl et al; Naeser, et al; Sallstrom et al; W. Zhang et al. 1987.

[700] Leskowitz 1997; Melzack, R.; Melzack/ Loeser; Melzack et al.; Philcox et al; R. Sherman

[701] Many of the captions in this section were suggested by J. Stone.

[702] See more on the **personhood of the therapist** below.

[703] On professional ethics see Brody et al.; M Cohen; Ernst 1996; Gillon; Pope/ Vasquez (psychotherapy); Stone/ Matthews.

[704] Blevins (outstanding succinct summary, 138 refs); Brinegar/ Schmitt; Carroll/ Gaston; Capan et al.; Cato Institute; Clouser/ Hufford; Coulter; Cox/ Foster; Dorn/ Manne; Feldstein 1977; 1988; Follard et al.; Friedman/ Friedman; Fulder/ Munro; Gaumer; Gilliam; Hamowy; Havighurst; Kessel; L. King; Kochman; Korte; Kovner; Lenard et al.; Lowell; Nichols; Paul; Pearson; Pruitt; Safriet 1992; 1994; Shepard; Starr; Wasley; L. Wilson; S. D. Young.

[705] A sad example of persecution of CAM therapies is presented in E. Brown.

[706] See www.WholisticHealingResearch.com for a few companies that offer insurance coverage for CAM modalities and malpractice insurance for CAM practitioners. The numbers of such insurers is growing rapidly. See also discussion of Pelletier/ Astin.

[707] CME credits are required for the annual renewal of physicians' medical licenses. By discouraging the granting of credits for CAM courses, the AMA blocks doctors from learning about - and then recommending or using these therapies

[708] See Ernst 2000 for a study of journal reviewer bias against CAM; D. Haley for a more general discussion of medical biases; and Mahoney 2001 on medicine as a business rather than a helping profession.

[709] See National Health Freedom Action www.nationalhealthfreedom.org

[710] Grady et al.; Hulley et al.; Petitti.

[711] See Stratton et al. for a survey; www.mercola.com has a variety of discussions on suspected negative effects of immunizations. On legal rights to refuse immunizations see Mercola: http:/ / www.mercola.com/ article/ vaccines/ legally_avoid_shots.htm

[712] This phrasing attributed to Sir William Osler.

[713] References earlier in this chapter.

[714] Dealing with death is discussed by Jackson, M.; Lee, J.; Foos-Graber, A.; James, J. W. and Cherry, F.; Rinpoche, Sogyal Rondo, T. A.; Rose, Z.; St. Aubyn, L.; Sarnoff; Schiff, H.; Seibert, Dinah, et al.; Shem; Staudacher, C. See also Moyers, B./ Moyers, J. for PBS documentary on end-of-life issues.

[715] Dealing with death wholistically is discussed in depth in *Healing Reserch,* Volume 3.

[716] Amazingly, this has been known for about 30 years and is very well accepted in Europe, but US physicians continue to prescribe antibiotics for children's ear infections.

[717] Pelletier 1991; 1993; 2000; Pelletier et al. 1997.

[718] Dying through negative suggestion is discussed in Chapters II-1; III-8; IV-3.

[719] Eight tables detail many further findings, with 58 references including relevant RCTs and modality reviews.

[720] Canada, England, and Australia also have holistic conventional caregiver associations.

[721] Other useful CAM references: Horrigan; M. Lerner.

[722] See discussion on **Jungian polarities** in Chapter II-1.

[723] Other helpful resources on choosing complementary therapies: Brewitt; Eisenberg 1997; R. Moss 1996; Sinclair; Woodham/ Peters.

[724] Conventional medicine assumes these templates reside somewhere in the genes, but no evidence has been found as yet to confirm this hypothesis.

[725] More on the **biological energy body** in Chapters II-3, II-4, Volumes III and IV.

[726] More on spiritual templates in Chapters III-8, 9, 10, 11; IV-2, 3 and on bioenergetic templates in II-3, 4.

[727] See Chapter II-4 for research in **astrological factors** that may influence healing.

[728] See discussion of right and left hemispheric functions in Chapter II-1; M. Erickson's use of hypnotic suggestions during the window of increased suggestibility between right and left hemispheric dominance (Rossi 1982; 1986a, b).

[729] On **Chronobiology** see: Halberg; Kleitman (rest/ activity); Naitch. **Ultradian rhythms** – Osowiec 1992; 1993; 2000; Rossi 1982; 1986a, b; Wernitz; Wernitz et al. 1983; Wernitz et al. 1987 (selective hemispheric activation through nostril breathing).

[730] See Resource Guide at WholisticHealingResearch.com for many organizations and therapeutic modalities that may be of help to you.

[731] Some of the CAM modalities have professional associations, a number of which are listed in the Resource Guide. To verify board certification of a physician, call the American Board of

Medical Specialties at (800) 776-2378; for a surgeon or anesthesiologist call either the American Board of Surgery at (215) 568-4000 or the American Board of Anesthesiology at (919) 881-2570. Other resources: the Board Certification Directory, The American Medical Directory, and The Directory of Medical Specialists. For information on physicians who have a history of documented incompetence check the Questionable Doctors Directory, published by the Public Citizen's Health Research Group, Washington, D.C.

[732] See discussion of Transpersonal psychology in Chapters II-1; Mystical experience in III-9.

[733] Chamberlain 1998; 2000; Cheek 1974; 1975; 1986; 1992; Grof; Gabriel; Klaus/ Klaus; Maurer; Nilsson.

[734] Lipson; Nathaniels; Piontelli; Verny.

[735] See extensive research evidence for survival of the spirit and for reincarnation in Volume III of *Healing Research*.

[736] See discussion on **holography** in Chapter IV-2; also Bohm 1957;1980; Weber.

[737] See discussions on the observer as part of the observed in Chapters III-9; IV-2; also Bohm 1957; 1980; Capra; Jahn Danne; LeShan 1974a; Zukav.

[738] In effect, they are teaching their clients to be "respants" (Siegel 1986).

Chapter 3 – The Human Energy Field

[739] People experience a variety of sensations in doing these explorations, ranging from feeling nothing to sensing a very light pressure (like a very soft bubble or like two magnets opposing each other), as well as heat, tingling, vibrations, prickliness, cold, and other sensations. Most people who report these perceptions find that they are distinctly different with different people and that they vary over time.

Rapidly opening and closing your hands may make them respond more strongly and sensitively.

You can explore further, by putting your hands over a broken green twig to get a sense of the sensations of injury, or over part of a person's body that has pain in order to sense what the bioenergy of pain feels like to you. Different people may report totally different sensations when they pass their hands over the same pain spot.

Going further yet, you may have someone mentally image that they are projecting energy through their hand as you hold your hand opposite theirs. Tell them to cease the projection at some point without letting you know when they do this. See if you can identify when they stop projecting.

These are some ways in which you can begin to develop your personal awareness and sensitivity to bioenergy and to healing.

Healers may have a natural gift that makes them more sensitive to these perceptions, or they may work diligently to develop them. Many healers find that one hand is more facile at sensing different energies and the other more open to projecting or channeling energies for healing.

[740] More on **research on spiritual dimensions** in Volume III.

[741] Clairvoyants perceive psychic information as visual imagery.

[742] So-called inanimate objects also have auras. Sensitives report they also are sentient, with rocks being some of the wisest – as they connect through their collective conscious with elements that have been in existence for many eons.

[743] For discussions of **auras** see Besant/ Leadbeater; Bek/ Pullar; Bhatacharyya; Brennan 1987; 1993; Leadbeater; Kilner; Karagulla/ Kunz; Kunz; Ostrom; Ouseley; Rampa; Regush; Regush/ Merta; J. Schwarz 1980; Scott; Tart 1972; Weed; Wilson/ Bek. For skeptic's views see Fraser-Harris. Aspects of the aura are also discussed under Visualization in Chapter II-2. On effects of **color** on human behavior see Plack/ Schick.

[744] This does not mean that all clairvoyants see red bricks in the aura when a person is on insulin. That was Kunz's own personal visual code.

[745] Kunz 1981; 1991; Karagulla 1967; Karagulla Kunz.

[746] More on chakras in Chapter II-2 under Acupuncture; Brennan; Bruyere; Lansdowne; Motoyama 1981; Page.

[747] Others report similar **palpable aura** observations: Brennan 1987; 1993; Safonov 1981; Seu-temann (in Meek 1977); Shubentsov; Vilenskaya 1976. See Chapter I-1. Healing Touch, a derivative of TT, also includes sensing of the aura with the hands.

[748] The differences in perceptions between gifted aura seers are difficult to understand. It would be helpful to have Kunz and Brennan observe the same people simultaneously and compare what they see. See Benor 1992, reviewed later in this chapter, on explorations of multiple aura sensors viewing the same subjects at the same time.

[749] See descriptions of **Philippine healers** in Chapter III-7.

[750] On other **intuitive aura readers** see Cayce 1945; Merta; Pierrakos 1971; 1987; Turner 1970. J. Schwarz 1980 and Brennan provide the clearest written description of the many and varied layers of the aura. Polarity therapy differs substantially from the above in descriptions of the energy fields, per F. Sills.

[751] See brief discussion of chakras in Chapter II-2 under Acupuncture.

[752] The following three summaries are taken from Chapter I-4.

[753] See full details of this study in Chapter I-4.

[754] See a detailed discussion of **reasons why healing and psi have not been accepted** in Chapter IV-3; earlier versions in Benor 1990; Dossey 1993.

[755] It is odd that the authors do not mention the actual number of subjects who made this complaint.

[756] HEF = human energy field

[757] p. 1007, column 1, para 3.

[758] I must say that I am grateful to Rosa et al. for identifying a host of TT dissertations which I had not been aware of. Even with these references in hand, I was only been able to locate 3 of them in the hard copy of *Dissertation Abstracts International*. It was only on CD ROM disk that I was able to locate most of them.

[759] See discussion of **electrodermal responses** in Chapter II-1; studies of healing effects on electrodermal responses earlier in this chapter; Bagchi/ Wenger.

[760] See discussion of **Kirlian photography** in Chapter II-3.

[761] See discussion on **sheep and goat effects** in Chapter I-3.

[762] This is a rather lengthy response to a very limited study. I feel it is warranted in view of the serious weight given to this study by the editor of the prestigious journal in which it appeared.

[763] *Dowsers (people who can identify water and other materials and information with the use of various devices) have been shown to respond to electromagnetic energy, as discussed in Chapter II-4.*

[764] *Brain/ Mind* 317178; Brennan 1987; 1993; V Hunt. See Rolfing in Chapter II-2 under Bodymind Therapies. See also discussions under Kirlian photography and also under energy fields, later this chapter. Changes in the Kirlian auras have also been correlated in some studies with various physical changes in the subjects. Bio-energy theories are discussed in Chapter IV-2; discussions of energies and fields in IV-3.

[765] The evidence of **body storage of memories** from practitioners of Rolfing is similar to Upledger's results with craniosacral osteopathy (discussed in Chapter II-2); of Lowen and of Pierrakos with bioenergetics therapy; and of Bandler/ Grinder with Neurolinguistic Programming, regarding storage in the body of tensions generated by emotional traumas (discussed in Chapter II-1).

[766] Formerly Jean Roberton.

[767] Personal communication 1990.

[768] My personal experience of intuitive perceptions is that it may take a while to learn to become more consciously aware of them, and even longer to learn to differentiate true perceptions from one's own imagined or projected images. See a brief description of a healee's varied sensory perceptions in Freed 1991.

[769] On **synesthesias** see Baron-Cohen, et al.; Cytowic; Hodson; Jersild; Lemley; McKeller; A. Richardson; Rizzo.

[770] For a remarkable bibliography of synesthesia in art and science s see Van Crampen et al.

[771] More on synesthesias below.

[772] See more on **phantom limbs** in Chapter II-1; Kao et al.; Leskowitz 1997; R. Melzack; Melzack/ Loeser; Melzack et al.; R. Sherman.

[773] See Kirlian photography later in this chapter.

[774] See Benor 1990, and further expansions in Chapter IV-3 for detailed discussions on **reasons why people reject psi and spiritual healing**.

[775] Complementary primary colors are red-green; orange-blue; and yellow-violet.

[776] Some even suggest that their tapes may be faked, but I have spoken personally with both of them and I would doubt that this is the case. In a demonstration of Oldfield's video camera (not performed by Oldfield himself) I was suspicious that the energies being picked up were either reflected light or heat, as the images appeared to vary with the angle of my body in front of the camera.

[777] See more on **OBEs** in Chapter III-1.

[778] See further discussions of **scientific analysis of the aura** in Bagnall; Caymaz; Tart 1972.

[779] **Similar electrophotographic techniques were** developed by others as early as 1896 (mentioned in Clausure; Dakin; Johnson 1975; Krippner 1980; Tiller 1974), but these were not developed into a system of diagnosis as was the work of Kirlian.

[780] Adamenko 1970; Anonymous 1973; Chouhan; Davis/ Lane; Dumitrescu; Emboden; Krippner 1980; Krippner/ Rubin; D. Mayer; Oldfield/ Coghill; Omura; Ostrander/ Schroeder 1970; Pehek et al.; Steel 1988; Stillings 1983; Tiller 1976.

[781] Dumitrescu 1978; 1983; T. Moss 1972, 1974; 1979; Oldfield/ Coghill; Ostrander/ Schroeder 1978.

[782] The specific significance of the bubbles is not apparent.

[783] Davis/ Lane; Johnson 1975; Konikiewics; T. Moss 1972, 1974; 1979; Ostrander/ Schroeder 1974; Pietrzycka-Wilczewska Wilczewski; Steiner.

[784] See Chapter II-2 on Chinese maps of the body represented in the hand and other body parts; Chapter IV-2 on **holographic aspects** of the body; and Monte on Chinese and other Eastern cosmologies which view the body as an integrated energy system.

[785] Dumitrescu 1978; 1983; Mayer; Omura.

[786] Dumitrescu 1978; 1983; C. Hills; Krippner 1979; T. Moss 1979; Oldfield/ Coghill; Stillings; Tiller 1974. This may provide support for theories of organizing fields (per Burr; Ravitz; Sheldrake).

[787] See **phantom limb** effects earlier in this chapter and in Chapter II-1.

[788] Further references on **Kirlian photography** include: *Experiments and theories* – Boxler/ Paulson; Boyers/ Tiller; L. Burton; Burton et al.; Canavor/ Wiesenfeld; Choudhury et al.; Chudacek/ Matousek; Emboden et al.; Engel/ Cole; Gennaro et al.; Koot; P. Mandel; Marinho; T. Moss 1972; Mucha; Murstein/ Hadjolian; Omura; Pehek; Pushkin/ Adamenko; Snellgrove; Stevens et al.; Tiller 1976; van Hasselt et al. *Techniques and applications* – Gris/ Dick; Kirlian/ Kirlian 1961; Konikiewicz; Krippner 1980; Leach; Medical World News 1973; Omura. Oldfield/ Coghill describe equipment which can produce dynamic Kirlian photos. R. White 1988 has an extensive bibliography. Websites: http://www.intraforum.com/kirlian/ http://www.psy.aau.dk/bioelec/ www.kolumbus.fi/pekka.kaariainen/gdv/gdv1.htm

[789] Canavor/ Wiesenfeld; Leavitt; Montandon.

[790] See more on **organizing fields** later in this chapter.

[791] See discussion of auras, preceding.

[792] Guseo; Schwartz et al. 1995; 1996; C. Smith et al.; Shallis 1988. See brief review under Homeopathy in Chapter II-2.

[793] Ravitz 1951; 1962; 1970.

[794] Rupert Sheldrake (1981) makes a further observation that seems to support the hypothesis proposed by Burr and Ravitz that the L-Field has an organizing property: "...the spherical egg cells of the alga *Fucus* have no inherent electrical polarity and their development can begin only after they have been polarized by any one of a variety of directional stimuli including light, chemical gradients and electrical currents: in the absence of any such stimuli, a polarity is taken up at random, presumably owing to chance fluctuations."

This phenomenon may be due to polarization of an energy field, especially if it can be brought about by light.

An alternative explanation I see is that the findings with eggs and *Fucus* cells might involve chemical changes in these organisms that only secondarily are manifested as an electrical polarity.

[795] Chwirot et al.; Mathew/ Rumar; Popp et al. 1984; 1988; 1992.

[796] These are taken from Workshop on Alternative Medicine, which also mentions the following resources: Blank; Brighton et al. 1979; 1991; Liboff/ Rinaldi; Marino 1988; O'Connor et al. 1990; O'Connor/ Lovely; Popp et al. 1992; Ramel/ Norden.

[797] A variety of body emanations which may be sensed as an aura or field around the body are discussed by Bigu, cited earlier in this chapter.

[798] This might be related to the observation from acupuncture that the various meridians are active at different times of the day.

[799] See details below under fields; laboratory measurements of biological energies.

[800] X. Peng/ G. Liu 1991; X. Niu et al.; Z. Yuan. See reviews of these studies in Chapter I-5.

[801] Oschman 2000 summarizes these studies nicely. For original literature see Bassett; Frohlich 1968a; b; 1970; 1974; 1988.

[802] 2003a; b; 2004.

[803] Tiller 2003c.

[804] Schumann predicted and then identified these standing waves. See Schumann/ Konig; Sentman 1995.

[805] See Barnothy; Becker (1990); Ghandi for reviews of **biological effects of magnetic fields**; Beck 1986 on **mood effects of ELF fields**; Beck/ Byrd for a bibliography on **psychological effects of electromagnetic fields**; discussions in Chapter IV-3. Discussions of negative effects of EM fields in R. Becker 1990; Brodeur; Smith/ Best.

[806] EM fields and childhood cancers – N. Day et al. 1999.

[807] R. Becker 1990; Becker/ Marino; Liboff; Maxey (review); Savitz; Wertheimer/ Leeper 1979; 1982.

[808] Phillips; Phillips et al.

[809] Further reviews of **EM effects on living organisms** can be found in Beal 2000; Blank; Gerber; Presman; Laub; Smith/ Best; Whitton; Wiseman. Davis et al. present an annotated bibliography on biological effects of magnetic fields. Guseo reports benefits of pulsing EM fields for multiple sclerosis. Taubes reviews the work and theories of Nordenstrom on weak electrical fields in diagnosing and healing various illnesses, including cancer. He mentions a self-published book by Nordenstrom describing his work. Lipinski reports on high concentrations of positive and negative ions during prayers at a shrine. Beck 1984 briefly reviews a variety of geomagnetic and EM effects on living things.

[810] See studies by Smith; Edge; reviewed with **controlled studies of healing** in Chapter I-4.

[811] EM and other **effects of healers on the physical world** are reviewed in Chapter I-2.

[812] See the work of Motoyama in Chapter II-2.

[813] Burr 1974; Ravitz 1962; 1970.

[814] Also spelled Gurvitch.

[815] See **factors which may influence psi healing** in Chapter IV-3.

[816] The *sheep/ goat* effect, in which believers in psi (sheep) demonstrate psi effects at rates higher than chance, and disbelievers (goats) at rates poorer than chance, is discussed in Chapter I-3.

[817] See the following chapter on geobiological effects.

[818] For more on **bioplasma** and the biofield see also Adamenko 1971; Cassirer 1973; Sergeyev/ Kulagin; Zhvirblis.

[819] Kaznacheyev 1976; 1982a; b.

[820] These experiments are reviewed also in Krippner 1980; T. Moss 1974; Ostrander/ Schroeder 1974.

[821] On **ultraviolet emanations from healers** see Vilenskaya 1981, re Krivorotov; Vilenskaya (in Uphoff/ Uphoff 1980, re Kulagina). On failure to find photon emissions other than those caused by heat see Kenyon.

[822] This parallels a similar hypothesis that homeopathic medicines may be effective due to particular energy patterning in the remedy solutions rather than due to chemical substances in these remedies. Should such research be validated, this might open up a whole new theoretical approach to the investigation of effects of medications via their vibrational interactions with the physical and energy bodies. See Chapter II-2.

[823] Sergeyev et al. 1972 describe some of the characteristics of one of their measuring instruments. Sergeyev/ Kulagin report on measurements taken with their equipment of normal people and of PK adepts. These reports seem to me too sketchy to evaluate properly, though I am not an expert in the electronics or mathematics involved.

[824] This parallels the *energy cyst* discussed by Upledger in Chapter II-2.

[825] Brennan 1993; Lowen; Pierrakos; Rolf.

[826] Of interest on **body energies** are Boirac; Eeman; Laub; Whyte. On difficulties in correlating these with psi phenomena see Kenyon.

[827] Two controlled studies of orgone healing: Hebenstreit; Müschenich/ Gebauer. For a bibliography of orgone research see http:/ / www.orgonelab.org/ bibliography.htm

For an academic dissertation bibliography, mostly from US universities, see http:/ / www.orgonelab.org/ bibliog.htm – and on-line articles are linked to http:/ / www.orgonelab.org/ Pulse5.htm. Mann mentions several references that appear relevant and interesting: Gallert; Brunler; Whyte. See Chapter I-2 for mention of further studies relating to energies possibly involved in healing, as manifested in healers' effects on water and crystals, and Chapter IV-3 for effects on photographic film. See also M. Brenner.

[828] The US Food and Drug Administration continues to hound practitioners of radionics. Radionics is reviewed in Chapter II-4.

[829] For other reports on **vibrational aspects of medications** see Choy; Monro; Shallis; C. Smith, reviewed earlier this chapter, and **homeopathy** in Chapter II-2.

[830] Unlike electrons and electromagnetic fields, biofields can be explored directly by most people, as described earlier in this chapter.

[831] See effects of electromagnetic fields in Chapter II-2.

[832] Also called *complexity theory*.

[833] See reviews and analyses of these studies in Chapter I-4.

[834] See discussions of other **theories to explain healing** in Chapters IV-2; IV-3.

[835] See for example the review of Goodrich in Chapter I-4; Turner in 1-5 regarding sensations perceived during distant healing.

[836] See discussion on **quantum physics** in Chapter IV-2.

[837] Geobiological effects are discussed in Chapter II-4.

[838] More on quantum physics and spiritual healing in Chapters III-10; IV-2; IV-3. I am particularly impressed with the explorations of healing by William Tiller (2003a; 2003b), a physicist who is researching the imprinting of intent on electronic devices that are able to alter the acidity of water.

Chapter 4 – Geobiological Effects

[839] A few words about my choice of the term, **geobiological:** I've seen a variety of reports of apparent human interactions with forces attributed to Earth and other heavenly bodies. The term *geobiological* is intended to be as neutral as possible in designating these interactions, leaving us free to speculate on their nature. (I started out with *geomagnetic* but this implied that magnetic fields were the source of these effects, which is clearly a premature presumption.) *Dowsing* is included in this section rather than with fields and forces in the preceding chapter, because it may be more than or different from a mere sensitivity to fields, and perhaps even a special case of clairsentience (if this is not a field phenomenon too).

[840] *Feng-shui* means *wind and water*, referring to heaven and earth. See H. Lin; Rossbach; S. Skinner.

[841] On **architecture, sacred space, and healing**: C. Alexander 1979a; 1979b; Dubrov 1978; Grabow/ Christopher; Riggs; Schimmelschmidt; Wright/ Sayre-Adams.

[842] Busch; Dodd; Girdlestone; Lotz; D. Pearson; Rousseau et al.; Steiner. See more on electromagnetic pollution of buildings in Chapter II-2 under Environmental Medicine.

[843] More on negative spirit influences in Chapter III-6.

[844] This is consistent with Mermet's observation that identification of water appeared to be more distinct the deeper the stream lay in the earth.

[845] Linger effects with spiritual healing have been reported in controlled studies of mice, reviewed in Chapter I-4.

[846] Not to be confused with Harvard's Herbert Benson.

[847] Krippner 1980 reviews findings similar to Harvalik's.

[848] Rocard 1964 (French); Rocard (in Barnothy); reviewed in D.J. Montgomery.

[849] 1971a; b; 1972.

[850] With a 70 mA (rectangular) current at 6 Hz, producing a magnetic field of 4×10^{-6}T (.04 G) at the center of the coil, 6 out of 30 trials had positive results. With a frequency of 200 Hz, 6 out of 15 trials were positive. In one double-blind test a subject was able to identify the field at 59 Hz with a 30 mA current (1.7×10^{-6}T, = .017 G). The intensities given were measured at the center of the coils, and decrease rapidly with distance. Dowsers walked past the coils at a distance of 0.5 - 0.75 meter, at which distance no more than 90 percent of the intensity is measurable.

[851] The best review of **dowsing research** is in G. Hansen 1982 (many of the cited references are from Hansen); the best overall survey is in Bird. Other helpful references: Barrett 1897-98; 1910; 1913; Bergmann (German); Comunetti 1978; 1979; Eastwood; Enright; G. Graves; Lethbridge; Lonegren; Ross/ Wright; P. Underwood; von Pohl.

[852] Named after Dr. Manfred Curry, who studied these lines.

[853] See further studies below on the geopathic sites identified by von Pohl.

[854] König et al. are the source for the next series of reports that I review, which extends to the end of this section.

[855] Sedimentation rate - blood test indicating a disturbance in health, often due to infection or an immune system problem.

[856] See Schinle et al. for human behavioral responses to changes in the weather.

[857] 21 cm. high-frequency radiation with 1.75 Hz modulation, with a power density of 1 mW/cm^2

[858] Note the quote at the opening of this chapter.

[859] Physical objects belonging to the person who is being analyzed from a distance by a dowser.

[860] See discussion on **LeShan's views** in Chapter IV-2.

[861] See research on spiritual dimensions in Volume III.

[862] This suggests that **thoughtography** (producing pictures on film using PK) may have been the method of production for the pictures taken with the de la Warr camera. See further discussion on thoughtography in Chapter IV-3.

[863] More on **Backster's plant communication experiments** in Chapter I-4, the section on plant research.

[864] Similar mechanisms may unite colonial insects such as bees, ants, and termites (Marais; L. Thomas).

[865] Other references of interest on general investigations of **dowsing and radiesthesia** include: Bachler; Garret/ Besterman; Hansen; Krippner 1980. Melville describes crystal gazing. S.A. Schwartz describes psi-assisted archaeology. On medical radiesthesia: Baerlein/ Dower; Beasley (especially interesting for applications of dowsing with energy bodies, homeopathy, etc.); de France; Lethbridge; Locker; Mermet; Reyner et al.; Russell 1973; Tansley et al.; Trinder; Wethered; White/ Krippner; Williamson. Tromp has an extensive bibliography. On geomancy (*feng shui*): S. Skinner.

[866] Biofeedback is discussed in chapters II-1 and II-2.

[867] More on psi abilities in Chapter I-3.

[868] More on Tiller's theories in Chapter IV-2; Tiller 2003a; b.

[869] **Remote viewing** is reviewed in Chapter I-3. See Jahn/ Dunne; Puthoff/ Targ; Utts.

[870] See applied kinesiology in Chapter II-2.

[871] See discussions on parapsychology in Chapter I-3; L. Rhine 1961; 1967. See also Chapter II-2 for a discussion on the differences between several aura perceivers who viewed the same subjects (Benor 1993).

[872] See under **auras**, earlier in this chapter.

[873] These and many other questions are considered in greater detail in Chapter IV-3.

[874] Lovelock is distinctly opposed to a hypothesis of guiding intelligence in the universe. Others have taken his theory further, considering that there may be a conscious, creative and guiding intelligence that has produced the universe.

[875] See Volume III for research on **spiritual dimensions of healing.**

[876] I have included astrology under geobiological effects because it appears to represent an influence of cosmic nature upon the organism; or, conversely, the interaction between the individual and the cosmos. The contiguity of astrology with dowsing may appear unusual, but it seems to me that both involve the elements of individual sensitivities to and interactions with the environment.

[877] See Eysenck/ Nias p. 189 for a more comprehensive list.

[878] See Gauquelin 1973 for similar descriptions. See also Innes 1981; West/ Toonder for reviews of evidence for **astrology relevant to healing;** Bogart (psychotherapy, spiritual); Forrest; Greene/ Sasportas (psychological). On **geomagnetic influences on psi phenomena** see: Adams 1985; 1986; Andrews/ Arango/ Persinger; Braud/ Dennis; Currier Downer; Dubrov 1978; Friedman/ Becker/ Bachman; Gearhart/ Persinger; Hubbard/ May; Klinowska; N. Kollerstrom; Makarec/ Persinger; Neison/ Dunne; Persinger/ Krippner; Presman 1970; Rounds; Sweeney; Tart 1988; Wiseman 1987. See also Footnote 20. On **lunar effects** see: E.A. Andrews; Gunning; Currie; Downer; Klinowska; N. Kollerstrom; Lieber; Rounds.

[879] There is great difficulty involved in conducting this sort of research in America because the 1974 Privacy Act prohibits the release of data from private records. The American CSICOP study which sought to replicate the Gauquelin findings could not obtain sufficient data on outstanding sports figures, and it included numerous athletes who were not of international class in the sample pool. For more criticisms of the CSICOP investigations see Rawlins 1981; Curry 1982.

[880] See review of Burr; Ravitz in Chapter II-3.

[881] Other references on similar geophysical effects include: Blackman Catalina; Friedman, Becker/ Bachman; Osborn; Ossenkopp/ Ossenkopp; Tasso/ Miller; Weiskott/ Tipton.

[882] The *synodic* cycle is the most familiar, measuring 29.53 days from one full moon to the next. The *anomalistic* cycle is 27.55 days, from apogee (greatest orbital distance from the Earth) to apogee; the *sidereal* cycle is 27.32 days (the period of a lunar orbit relative to a fixed-star background from a point on Earth); the *tropical* cycle is also 27.32 days (period of a lunar cycle relative to a given celestial longitude); and the *draconic* cycle of 27.21 days (period of a lunar cycle crossing the plane of the Earth/ sun orbit).

[883] Paired *t*-test, r = 0, two-tailed. "...*t*-scores and probabilities...[are] 'adjusted'. The adjustment is necessary because the data used in these correlations are smoothed twice; once due to the moving average transformation applied to the raw daily data, and then again when averaged by the day of the lunar cycle. This double-smoothing decreases the variation of the individual datapoints, and thereby decreases the standard deviation of each data series assumed by correlation. This, in turn, inflates the *t* score, and the probabilities. Through Monte-Carlo simulations, we determined that to provide a more accurate estimate of the probability of the correlation given the smoothing transforms, the adjusted standard deviation should be approximately doubled. Thus, the *t* scores and probabilities reflect this adjustment of the standard deviation."

[884] One-tailed.

[885] Two-tailed.

[886] Including changes in positive and negative ions in the air.

[887] Lieber does not cite references. Eysenck and Nias review many of the same findings more briefly, and cite references.

[888] Taken from the reviews of Lieber; Eysenck/ Nias.

[889] Geomagnetic fields (per se) have been studied in great detail, as summarized by Chapman/ Bartels; Jacobs 1987; Matsushita/ Campbell. See also the bimonthly journal *Geomagnetism and Aeronomy*, which is focused on research of geomagnetism, the ionosphere and atmospheric radio noise

[890] Schumann/ Konig; Sentman 1995; Wever 1968a; b.

[891] Lewicki/ Schaut/ Persinger; Persinger 1985; Persinger/ Schaut; Spottiswoode; Wilkinson/ Gauld.

[892] For brevity's sake and for easier reading I discuss these phenomena as though an influence of heavenly bodies upon earthly events is actually demonstrated, though I feel that in most cases this is far from solidly established.

Notes - Appendix A

[893] See Chapter I-2 for more on healing effects in water.

[894] On *Gaia* see Ausubel; Christie/ Warburton; Glenn/ Gordon; S. Singh;

[895] See discussions of many different energy medicine approaches in Chapter 2.

[896] More on bioenergy therapy in Chapters II-1, II-2.

[897] More on bodmind therapy in Chapters II-1, II-2.

[898] More on behavior therapy in Chapter II-1.

[899] More on dream analysis in Chapter II-1.

[900] More on EMDR in Chapter II-2.

[901] More on hypnotherapy, below and in Chapters II-1; II-2.

[902] More on imagery/ visualization in Chapters II-1, II-2.

[903] More on Jungian explanatory systems in Chapter II-1.

[904] More on meditation in Chapters II-1, II-2.

[905] See discussion of meridian based therapies in Chapter II-2..

[906] More on NLP in Chapter II-1 and II-2.

[907] More on psychoanalysis in Chapter II-1.

[908] More on psychodrama in Chapter II-2.

[909] More on relaxationin Chapters II-1.

[910] More on transpersonal therapy in Chapters II-1; II-2; Volume III.

References

A

Aaron RK/ Plass AHK. Stimulation of proteoglycane synthesis in articular chondrocyte cultures by a pulsed electromagnetic field, *Trans. Ortop. Res. Soc.* 1987,12, 273

Aaronson, BS. Color perception and affect, *American J Clinical Hypnosis* 1971, 14, 38-42.

Abell, George O. The mars effect, *Psychology Today* 1982 (July), 8-13.

Abenhaim, L/ Bergeron, AM. Twenty years of randomized clinical trials of manipulative therapy for back pain: a review, *Clinical and Investigative Medicine - Medicine Clinique et Experimentale* 1992 15(6), 527-535.

Achterberg, Jeanne. *Imagery in Healing: Shamanism and Modem Medicine*, Boston/ London: New Science Library/ Shambala 1985.

Achterberg, J/ Lawlis, GF. *Imagery of Cancer,* Champaign, IL: Institute for Personality and Ability Testing 1978. (Lit. rev.)

Achterberg, J/ Lawlis, GF. *Bridges of the Bodymind: Behavioral Approaches to Health Care*, Champaign, IL: Institute for Personality and Ability Testing 1980.

Achterberg, J/ Lawlis, GF. *Imagery and Disease: Diagnostic Tools?* Champaign, IL: Institute for Personality and Ability Testing 1984

Achterberg, J/ Rider, MS. The effect of music-mediated imagery on neutrophils and lymphocytes, *Biofeedback & Self Regula-tion* 1989, 14, 247-257.

Achterberg, J/ Simonton, OC/ Matthews-Simonton, S. (eds), *Stress, Psychological Factors and Cancer,* Ft. Worth, TX: New Medicine Press 1976.

Achterberg, J et al. Psychological factors and blood chemistries as disease outcome predictors for cancer patients, *Multivariate Experimental Clinical Research* 1977, 3(3), 107-122.

Adamenko, Viktor. Electrodynamics of living systems, *J Paraphysics* 1970, 4(4), 113-121. (Reprinted with permission of the Editor, Paraphysical Laboratory; (Downton, Wilts. UK)

Adamenko, Viktor. Seminar on the problems of biological plasma, *J Paraphysics* 1971, 5(4), 105-110. (Technical)

Adamenko, Viktor. Living detectors, *J Paraphysics* 1972a, 6(1), 5-8.

Adamenko, Viktor. The phenomenon of skin electricity, *J Paraphysics* 1972b, 6(1), 9-12. (Reprinted with permission of the Editor, Paraphysical Laboratory, Downton, Wiltshire, England)

Adamenko, Viktor G. Attempted human control of a bioelectric field, *Psychoenergetic Systems,* London: Gordon & Breach 1974, l(l),35-36.

Adamenko, Viktor. Give the 'green light' to red light!, Translator Larissa Vilenskaya) *Psi Research* 1982, 1(1), 97-106. (Orig. Russian, *Tekhnika molodezhi* 1981, No.6.)

Adams, DH et al. Transforming growth factor-β induces human t lymphocyte migration in vitro, *J Immunology* 1991, 147, 609-612.

Adams, K. *Journey to the Self: 22 Paths to Personal Growth*, New York: Warner 1990.

Adams, K. *The way of the J: A J Therapy Workbook for Healing*, Lutherville, MD, 1993.

Adams, K. *Mightier Than the Sword*, New York: Warner 1994.

Adams, M. Variability in remote viewing performances: Possible relationships to the geomagnetic field, *Proceedings of Presented Papers, 28th Annual Convention of Paraps-ychology Association* 1985, 1, 451-462.

Adams, M. Persistent temporal relationship of ganzfeld results to geomagnetic activity, appropriateness of using standard geo-magnetic indices, *Proceedings of Presented Papers 29th Annual Convention Para-psychology Association* 1986, 471-485.

Ader, Robert (ed). *Psychoneuroimmunology*, New York: Academic 1981.

Ader, Robert/ Cohen, Nicholas, Behaviorally conditioned immunosup-pression and murine systemic lupus erythematosus, *Science* 1982, 215, 1 534-l536.

Ader, R/ Felten, DL/ Cohen, N. *Psychoneuroimmunology*, 2nd Edition, New York: Academic 1991.

Adey, W R. Collective properties of cell membranes, in Norden, B/ Ramel, C. (eds) *Interaction Mechanisms of Low-level Electromagnetic Fields in Living Systems, Symposium, Royal Swedish Academy of Sciences, Stockholm*, New York: Oxford University 1992, 47-77.

Adey W R/ Bawin SM. 1977 Brain interactions with weak electric and magnetic fields, *Neurosciences Research Program Bulletin* 15(1):1-29

Adkins, BJ et al. The spoken autobiography: A powerful tool in group psychotherapy, *Social work* 1985, 30, 435-439.

Adler, SR/ Fosket, J. Disclosing complementary and alternative medicine use in the medical encounter: a qualitative study in women with breast cancer, *J Family Practice* 1999, 18(6), 453-458.

Advances - Journal featuring psychoneuroimmunology, meditation, spiritual awareness, for health care policy and research report on chiropractic practice and research, www.chiroweb.com/archives

Agrawal, A et al. Effects of "Mentat" on memory span, attention, galvanic skin resistance (GSR) and muscle action potential (EMG) among normal adults, *Pharmacopsychoecologia* 1990, 3, 39-42.

Ahonen E et al. Acupuncture and physiotherapy in the treatment of myogenic headache patients: Pain relief and EMG activity, *Advances in Pain Research Therapy* 1983, 5, 571-576.

Ahser, R. Respectable hypnosis, *British Medical J* 1956 1, 309-313.

Airola, Paaro. *Are You Confused? De-Confusion Book on Nutrition and Health*. Phoenix, AZ: Health Plus 1971.

Airola, Paaro. *Everywoman's Book,* Phoenix, AZ: Health Plus 1979.

Ajaya, Swami. *Yoga Psychology*, Honesdale, PA: Himalayan 1976.

Ajaya, Swami. *Psychotherapy East and West: A Unifying Paradigm,* Honesdale, PA: Himalayan Institute 1984.

Ajrawat, P S. *Pain*, 1997. www.painspecialist.com.80/pain.htm

Akerele, O. *The WHO Traditional Medicine Programme: Policy and Implementation: International Traditional Health Newsletter*, Geneva, Switzerland: World Health Organization 1985, 1, 1.

Alagna, FJ et al. Evaluative reaction to interpersonal touch in a counseling interview, *J Counseling Psychology* 1979, 26, 465-472.

Albright, P/ Albright, B Parker (eds). *Mind, Body and Spirit,* Findhorn: Thule 1981.

Al-Dargazeli, Shetha. New findings in healing research, *Doctor-Healers Network Newsletter* Winter 1993-94.

Aldridge, D. Europe looks at complementary therapy, *British Medical J* 1989, 299, 1211-2.

Aldridge, D Hope. Meaning and the creative arts therapies in the treatment of AIDS, *The Arts in Psychotherapy* 1993, 20, 285-297.

Aldridge, David, *Spirituality, Healing and Medicine, Return to the Silence,* London/ Philadelphia: Jessica Kingsley, 2000.

Aldridge, David/ Pietroni, Patrick C. Clinical assessment of acupuncture in asthma therapy: discussion paper, *J the Royal Society of Medicine* 1987, 80(4), 222-224.

Aldridge, K. The use of music to relieve pre-operational anxiety in children attending day surgery, *Australian J Music Therapy* 1993, 4 19-35.

Alexander, Christopher. *The Timeless Way of Building*, New York: Oxford University 1979a.

Alexander, Christopher. *A Pattern Language*, New York: Oxford University 1979b.

Alexander, CN et al. Transcendental meditation, mindfulness and longevity: an experimental study with the elderly, *J Personality and Social Psychology* 1989a, 57, 950-964.

Alexander, CN et al. Transcendental meditation, self-actualization, and psychological health: a conceptual overview and statistical meta-analysis, *Soc. Behav. Pers.* 1989b, 6(5) 189-247.

Alexander, F Matthias. *The Resurrection of the Body,* New York: Delta 1969.

Alexander, F M. *The Use of the Self,* New York: Dutton 1932/ Centerline 1984.

Alexander, F Matthias. *The Universal Constant in Living,* New York: E.P. Dutton 1941; Centerline 1986.

Alexander, Franz. *Psychosomatic Medicine,* New York: WW Norton 1950.

Alexander, K. Communicating with potential adolescent suicides through poetry, *The Arts in Psychotherapy* 1990, 17, 123-130.

Alexandersson, Olof, *Living Water: Viktor Schauberger and the Secrets of Natural Energy,* Bath, England: Gateway 1990.

Ali, M. Correlation of IgE antibodies with specificity for pollen and mold allergy which changes in electrodermal skin responses following exposure to allergens (Abstract), *American J Clinical Pathology* 1989, 91(3), 357.

Ali, Majid. *The Cortical Monkey and Healing,* Bloomfield, NJ: Institute of Preventive Medicine 1990.

Ali, Majid et al. Improved myocardial perfusion in patients with advanced ischemic heart disease with an integrative management program including EDTA chelation therapy, *Townsend Letter* 1999, Jan, 92-102. (105 refs)

Allais G, Voghera D, De Lorenzo C, Mana O, Benedetto C. Access to databases in complementary medicine, *J Alternative Complement Med* 2000 Jun; 6(3): 265-74.

Allen, TF. *The Encyclopedia of Pure Materia Medica: A Record of the Positive Effects of Drugs upon Healthy Human Organisms,* New Delhi: B. Jain 1982.

Allison, Nancy (ed). *The Illustrated Encyclopedia of Body-Mind Disciplines,* New York: Rosen 1999.

Allison, Ralph/ Schwarz, Ted. *Minds in Many Pieces,* New York: Rawson Wade 1980.

Alm, L. et al. Effect of fermentation on B vitamin content of milk in Sweden, *J Dairy Sciences* 65, 353-359.

Altaffer, Thomas. *Energetic Homeostasis,* http://home.att.net/~tom.altaffer/index.htm.

Alvarado, Carlos S. Observations of luminous phenomena around the human body: A review, *J the Society for Psychical Research* 1987, 54, 38-60.

Alvarado, Carlos S/ Zingrone, Nancy L. Individual differences in aura vision: relationships to visual imagery and imaginative-fantasy experiences, *European J Parapsychology* 1994, 10, 1-30.

Amar, PB/ Shneider, C. (eds) *Clinical applications of biofeedback and applied psychophysiology* Wheat Ridge, CO: Association for Applied Psychophysiology and Biofeedback 1995.

Amatas, CA.*Study of the effect of music on postoperative patients in the recovery room,* Unpublished master's thesis, University of Kansas 1964.

Amber, Reuben B. *Color Therapy,* Santa Fe, NM: Aurora 1983.

American Academy of Family Practitioners for Physicians, *Curriculum in Clinical Nutrition,* Kansas City, MO: AACP.

American Botanical Council. HERBCLIP (CD-ROM), Austin, TX: Herb Research Foundation 1998.

American Botanical Council. *The German Commission E Monographs,* PO Box 21660, Austin, TX 78720 (800) 373-7105 1999.

American Foundation of Medical Acupuncture. Clinical research in medical acupuncture: a literature review, *Biomedical Research on Acupuncture: An Agenda for the 1990s, Conference Summary,* Los Angeles, CA: 1993

American Psychiatric Association, *Diagnostic and Statistical Manual of Mental Disorders: Third Edition (DSM-IV),* Washington, DC: American Psychiatric Association 1980.

Andersen, BL et al. A biobehavioral model of cancer stress and disease course, *American Psychyologist* 1994, 49, 389-404.

Andersen, MS. Hypnotizability as a factor in the hypnotic treatment of obesity, *Interna-tional J Clinical and Experimental Hypnosis* 1985, 33, 150-159.

Anderson, David, et al. *Homeopathic Remedies for Physicians, Laymen, and Therapists*, Honesdale, PA: Himalayan International Institute 1978.

Anderson, E.M., & Lambert, M.J. (). A survival analysis of clinically significant change in outpatient psycho-therapy. *Journal of Clinical Psycho-logy* 2001.

Anderson, R et al. A meta-analysis of clinical trials of spinal manipulation, *J Manipulative and Physiological Therapeutics* 1992, 15(3) 181-194.

Anderson, Robert A. *Clinician's Guide to Holistic Medicine*, USA: McGraw Hill, 2001a.

Anderson, Robert A. The Scientific Basis for Holistic Medicine: Annotated Ab-stracts, 2001 Edition, American Health Press, 2001b.

Anderson, Sherwood. Attributed.

Andra, Wilfried/ Nowak, Hannes. *Magnetism in Medicine: A Handbook*, New York: Wiley-VCH 1998.

Andrew; IC. Psychokinetic influences on an electromechanical random nwnber generator during evocation of 'left-hemispheric' vs. 'right-hemispheric' functioning, In: Morris, R0 et al (eds): *Research in Parapsychology 1974*, Metuchen, NJ: Scarecrow 1975, 58-61.

Andrew, K. Psychokinetic influences on an electromechanical random number generator during evocation of 'left-hemispheric' vs. 'right-hemispheric' functioning, In: Morris, JD (ed). *Research in Parapsychology*, Metuchen, NJ,1974.

Andrews, ES. Moon talk: The cyclic pe-riodicity of postoperative hemorrhage, *J the Florida Medical Association* 1961, 46, 362-266.

Andrews, G/ Harvey, R. Does psycho-therapy benefit neurotic patients? A re-analysis of the Smith, Glass, & Miller data, *Archives of General Psychiatry* 1981, 38, 1203-1508.

Andrews, Ted. *Sacred Sounds: Trans-forma-tion through Music and Word*, St. Paul, MN: Llewellyn 1992.

Angell, M/ Kassirer, JP. Alternative medi-cine: the risks of untested and unregulated remedies (editorial), *New England J Medicine* 1998, 339(12), 839-841

Angus Reid Group Poll, Canada www.Angusreid.com/ (612) 904-6970

Anhui Medical School Hospital, *Chinese Massage Therapy: A Handbook of Thera-peutic Massage*, Boulder, CO: Shambala 1983/ Tokyo: Japan Publications 1981.

Anodea, Judith. *Wheels of Life*, St. Paul, MN: Llewellyn 1990.

Anonymous, Osteopathy's epidemic re-cord, *Osteopathic Physician* 1919, 36, 1.

Anonymous, Finger-tip halos of Kirlian photography: another failure to replicate, *J Psychology* 1979, 103 159-162.

Anschutz, EP. *Guide to the Twelve Tissue Remedies of Biochemistry*, Philadelphia, PA:

Anthony, H M. Some methodological prob-lems in the assessment of comple-mentary therapy, *Stat. Med.* 1987, 6, 761-771.

Anthony, Honor M. Homeopathy: The controversy in "Nature," *Complementary Medical Research* 1988, 3(1), 79-87.

Antman, EM et al. A comparison of re-sults of meta-analyses of randomized control trials and recommendations of clinical experts: treatments for myocardial infarction, *J the American Medical Asso-ciation* 1992, 268(2), 240-248.

Antoni, MH et al. Cognitive-behavioral stress management intervention buffers distress responses and immunologic changes following notification of HIV-1 seropositivity, *J Consulting and Clinical Psychology* 1991, 59(6) 906-915.

APA Online. The Efficacy of Psychother-apy 1994 http://www.apa.org/practice/peff.html

Apostol, Andrei. Dowsing in geology: An experience from Romania, *Psi Research* 1985a, 4(3/ 4) 199-211.

Apostol, Andrei. Dowsing and earthquake prediction, *Psi Research* 1985b, 4(3/ 4), 212-218.

Appelbaum, Stephen A. The laying on of health: personality patterns of psychic healers, *Bulletin of the Menninger Clinic* 1993, 57(1), 33-40.

Arasteh, A Reza. *Growth to Selfhood: The Sufi Contribution,* Boston/ London: Routledge and Kegan Paul 1980.

Arietti, S. *The Intra-psychic Self,* New York: Basic 1967.

Aronoff, Gerald M et al. Hypnotherapy in the treatment of bronchial asthma, *Annals of Allergy* 34, 356-362.

Aronson, B. Hypnotic alternatives of space and time, *International J Parapsychology* 1968, 10, 5-36.

Arpita, Physiological and psychological effects of Hatha Yoga: a review of the literature, *J the International Association of Yoga Therapists* 1990, 1(I/ II), 1-28.

Artschwager, Kay Margarita. *Healing with Plants in the American and Mexican West,* Tucson: University of AZ 1996.

Aschoff, D. Cited in Hartmann 1967; 1976.

Assagioli, Roberto. *Psychosynthesis,* London: Turnstone 1965.

Assendelft, W/ Bouter, LM. Does the goose really lay golden eggs? a methodological review of workmen's compensation studies, *J Manipulative and Physiological Therapeutics* 1993, 16(4) 161-168.

Assendelft, WJ et al. The efficacy of chiropractic manipulation for back pain: blinded review of relevant randomized clinical trials, *J Manipulative and Physiological Therapeutics* 1992, 15(8) 487-494.

Assendelft, WJ et al. Complications of spinal manipulation: a comprehensive review of the literature, *J Family Practice* 1996, 42, 475-480.

Astin, JA. Why patients use alternative medicine: results of a national study, *J the American Medical Associationi* 1998, 279, 1548-1553.

Astin, JA/ Marie, A/ Pelletier, KR/ Hansen, E/ Kaskell, WL. A review of the incorpor-ation of complementary and alternative medicine by mainstream physicians, *Archives of Internal Medicine* 1998, 158(21), 2303-2310.

Astin, JA et al. A review of the incorporation of complementary and alternative medicine by mainstream physicians, *Archives of Internal Medicine* 1998, 158, 2303-2310.

Atkinson, JM. Shamanisms today, *Annual Review of Anthropology* 1992, 21, 307-330.

Aurobindo, Sri. *The Mind of Light,* New York: Dutton 1953.

Aurobindo, Sri. *The Synthesis of Yoga,* Pondicherry, India: Aurobindo Ashram 1957.

Austin, James H. *Zen and the Brain: Towards an Understanding of Meditation and Consciousness,* Cambridge, MA: MIT 1998.

Austin, JH/ Ausubel, P. Enhanced respiratory muscular function in normal adults after lessons in proprioceptive musculoskeletal education without exer-cises, *Chest* 1992, 102(2),486-90.

Avila, E/ Parker, J. *Woman Who Glows in the Dark,* New York: Tarcher/ Putnam 1999.

Avison, WR/ Turner, RJ. Stressful life events and depressive symptoms: Disaggre-gating the effects of acute stressors arid chronic strains, *J Health and Social Behavior* 1988, 29,253-264.

Axline, Virginia. *Dibs in Search of Self,* New York: Ballantine 1976.

Ayisi, Christian Harry. African cosmology and the paranormal, *Proceedings of the 4th International Conference on Psychotronic Research 1979,* 289-299.

B

Babbitt, E D. *The Principles of Light and Color* East Orange, NJ: Self-published 1896.

Babyak M/ Blumenthal JA/ Herman S et al. Exercise treatment for major depression: maintenance of therapeutic benefit at 10 months, *Psychosomatic Medicine* 2000, 62, 633-638.

Bach, Edward. *Heal Thyself: An Explanation of the Real Cause and Cure of Disease,* Essex, England: CW Daniel 1988. (Orig. 1931)

Bach, Marcus. The religious experience in the healing process, *J Holistic Health* 1977,

Bach, Richard. *Illusions: The Adventures of a Reluctant Messiah* Delacorte Press/ Eoleanor Friede 1977.

Bachelard, G. *The Poetics of Space,* Boston: Beacon 1958.

Bachler, Kathe. *Earth Radiation,* Manchester, England: Wordmasters 1989.

Bacon, Francis. *The Advancement of Learning* 1605.

Badgley, Laurence. *Healing AIDS Naturally,* San Bruno, CA: Human Energy 1987.

Badmaev, Vladimir. Tibetan medicine, In: Jonas/ Levin p. 252-274.

Baer, R/ Bustillo M. Susto and mal de ojo among Florida farmworkers: emic and etic per-spectives, *Medical Anthropology Quarterly* 1993, 7, 90-100.

Baerlein, E/ Dower, ALG. *Healing with Radionics: The Science of Healing Energy,* Wellingborough, England: Thorsons 1980.

Baggio, E et al. Italian multicenter study on the safety and efficacy of coenzyme Q_{10} as adjunctive therapy in heart failure (interim analysis), *Clinical Investigation* 1993, 71, S145-149.

Baginski, B. *Reiki: Universal Life Energy,* CA: Life Rhythms 1988.

Bagnall, O. *The Origin and Properties of the Human Aura,* New Hyde Park, NY: University 1970. (Orig. 1937)

Bahn, R (ed). *The Practice of Poetry: Writing Exercises for Poets Who Teach,* New York: HarperCollins 1992.

Bailar, John C/ Smith, Elaine M. Progress against cancer? *New England Medical J* 1998 (8 May), 1226-1232.

Bailey, Philip M. *Homeopathic Psychology: Personality Profiles of the Major Constitutional Remedies,* Berkeley, CA: N. Atlantic Books/ Homeopathic Education Services 1995.

Baime, Michael J. Meditation and mindfulness, in Jonas/ Levin 1993, 522-536 (93 refs).

Bair, Puran. *Living from the Heart: Heart Rhythm Meditation for Energy, Clarity, Peace, Joy and Inner Power,* New York: Three Rivers 1998.

Baisi, F. Report on clinical trial of bilberry anthocyanocides in the treatment of venous insufficiency in pregnancy and of post-partum hemorrhoids, *Presidio Ospedaliero di Livorno,* Italy 1987.

Baker, GHB. Psychological factors and immunity, *J Psychosomatic Research* 1987, 31(l), 1-10.

Baker, Julian. Personal communication 1996.

Baker, Robin R. *Human Navigation and the Sixth Sense,* New York: Simon & Schuster 1981.

Bakken, Kenneth L. *The Call to Wholeness: Health as a Spiritual Journey,* New York: Crossroad 1985.

Balanovski, E/ Taylor, JG. Can electromagnetism account for extra-sensory perception? *Nature* 1978, 276, 64-67.

Balch, James F/ Balch, Phyllis A. *Prescription for Nutrirional Healing: A Practical A-Z Reference to Drug-Free Remedies Using Vitamins, Minerals, Herbs, and Food Supplements,* Garden City Park, NY: Avery 1997. (many refs)

Baldwin, C. *Life's Companion: J Writing as a Spiritual Quest,* New York: Evans 1990.

Baldwin, C. *One to One: Self-Understanding Through J Writing,* New York: Evans 1991.

Baldwin, HSM. Dowsers detect enemy's tunnels, *The New York Times* 1967 (13 October), p 17.

Ballard, Clive G et al. Aromatherapy as a safe and effective treatment for the management of agitation in severe dementia: the results of a double-blind, placebo-controlled trial with Melissa, *J Clinical Psychiatry* 2002, 63, 553-558

Ballegaard, S et al. Acupuncture in severe, stable angina pectoris: a randomized trial, *Acta Medica Scandinavia* 1986, 220(4), 307-13.

Ballentine, Rudolph. *Diet and Nutrition: A Holistic Approach*, Honesdale, PA: Himalayan 1978.

Ballentine, Rudolph, *Theory and Practice of Meditation,* Honesdale, PA: Himalayan 1986.

Ballentine, Rudolph, *Transition to Vegetar-ianism, an Evolutionary Step,* Honesdale, PA: Himalayan 1987.

Ballentine, Rudolph, *Radical Healing: Integrating the World's Great Therapeutic Traditions to Create a New Transformative Medicine*, New York: Three Rivers 1999.

Ballentine, Rudolph, Radical healing and the rebirth of science, *Townsend Letter for Doctors & Patients* 2001, 28-36.

Ballentine, Rudolph/ Ajaya, Swami, *Yoga and Psychotherapy: The Evolution of Consciousness*, Honesdale, PA: Himalayan 1976.

Bamforth, Nick. *AIDS and the Healer Within,* New York/ London: Amethyst 1987.

Bandler, Richard/ Grinder, John. *Frogs into Princes: Neurolinguistic Programming,* Moab, Utah: Real People 1979.

Banquet, JP. EEG and meditation, *J the American Medical Association* 1972, 224, 791-799.

Bapko, C/ Krestan, J. *Singing at the Top of Our Lungs: Women, Love, and Creativity*, New York: HarperCollins 1993.

Barabasz, AF et al. A three year clinical follow-up of hypnosis and restricted environmental stimulation therapy for smoking, *International J Clinical and Experimental Hypnosis,*

Barasch, Marc Ian, *The Healing Path: A Soul Approach to Illness*, New York/ London: Arkana/ Penguin 1993.

Barber, Theodore X. Physiological effects of 'hypnosis', *Psychological Bulletin* 1961, 58, 390-41.

Barber, Theodore X. *Hypnosis: A Scientific approach*, New York: Van Nostrand 1969.

Barber, Theodore X. Changing unchangeable bodily processes by (hypnotic) suggestions: New look at hypnosis, cogni-tions, imagining, and the mind-body problem; Also in: Sheikh, Anees A. *Imagination and Healing,* Farmingdale, NY: Baywood 1984.

Barber, Theodore X/ Wilson, Sheryl C. Hypnosis, suggestion and altered states of consciousness: experimental evaluation of the new cognition-behavioral theory and the traditional trance-state theory of 'hypnosis', In: Stoyva, Johann et al (eds), *Biofeedback and Self Control* 1977/ 1978, Chicago: Aldine 1978.

Barker, AT. (ed), *The Mahatma Letters to AP Sinnett, 2nd Ed.* (p. 455, Letter no. CXXVII, 13 August 1882), London: Rider 1948 (1st Ed. 1923).

Barker, AT et al. Pulsed magnetic field therapy for tibial non-union: interim results of a double-blind trial, *Lancet* 1984, 1(8384), 994-996.

Barker, ME. Manipulation in general medical practice for thoracic pain syndromes, *British Osteopathic J* 1983, 15, 9

Barker, Sandra B (1999). Therapeutic Aspects of the Human-Companion Animal Interaction, *Psychiatric Times*, Vol. XVI, Issue 2, February.

Barlow, Wilfred. *The Alexander Principle*, London: Arrow 1975.

Barnard, GP/ Stephenson, JH. Microdose paradox: New biophysical concept, *J the American Institute of Homeopathy* 1967,60, 277-286.

Barnard, Julian (ed), *Collected Writings of Edward Bach*, Hereford, England: Bach Educational Programme 1987.

Barnard, Julian/ Barnard, Martine, *The Healing Herbs of Edward Bach: An Illustrated Guide to the Flower Remedies*, Hereford, England: Bach Educational Programme 1988.

Barnes, John F. *Myofascial Release*, Paoli, PA: MFR Seminars 1990.

Barnett, Kathryn. A theoretical construct of the concepts of touch as they relate to nursing, *Nursing Research* 1972, 21(2) 102-110.

Barnothy, Madeline F (ed). Biological *Effects of Magnetic Fields,* New York: Plenum Press 1964.

Barnuow, V. Paranormal phenomena and culture, *J the American Society for Psychical Research* 1945,40, 2-21.

Barrett, Bruce, et al. Assessing the risks and benefits of herbal medicine: an overview of scientific evidence, *Alternative Therapies* 1999, 5(4), 40-49.

Barrett, WF. On the detection of hidden objects by dowsers, *J the Society for Psychical Research* 1910, 14, 183-193.

Barrett, WF. The psychical versus the physical theory of dowsing, *J the Society for Psychical Research* 1913, 16, 43-48.

Barrett, WF/ Besterman, T. *The Divining Rod*, New Hyde Park, NY: University Books 1968.

Barrow, John D/ Tipler, Frank S. *The Anthropic Cosmological Principle*, New York: Oxford University 1986.

Barrows, CM. Suggestion without hypnotism, *Proceedings of the Society for Psychical Research* 1896, 12, 21-44.

Barton, J. *Encyclopedia of Mind and Body, Volumes I, II, III, IV, V, VI, VII*, Shade Cove, OR: Biokinesiology Institute 1981.

Bartrop, R et al. Depressed lymphocyte function after bereavement, *Lancet* 1977, 1, 834-836.

Basmajian, JV ed. *Biofeedback: Principles and Practice for Clinicians*, 3rd Ed, Baltimore: Williams and Wilkins 1989.

Bass, E/ Davis, L. *The Courage to Heal: A Guide for Women Survivors of Child Sexual Abuse*, New York: Harper & Rowe 1988.

Bassett, C. 1995 Bioelectromagnetics in the service of medicine, In: Blank M (ed) *Electromagnetic Fields: Biological Interactions and Mechanisms, Advances in Chemistry Series 250*, Washington DC: American Chemical Society, 1995, 261-275

Bassett, C et al. PEMF treatment of ununited fractures and failed arthrodeses, *J American Medical Association* 1982, 247, 623-628.

Bassman, Lynette. *Complementary treatments for mind, mood, & emotion*, Novato, CA: New World 1998.

Bastide, M. Immunological exsamples of UHD research, In: Endler, PC (ed), *Ultra High Dilution: Physiology and Physics*, Dordrecht, Germany: Klewer Academic Publishers 1994.

Bates, BL. Individual differences in response to hypnosis, In: Rhue, JW et al (eds), *Handbook of Clinical Hypnosis*, Washington, DC: American Psychological Association 1993, 23-54.

Bates DW et al. Incidence of adverse drug events and potential adverse drug events: implications for prevention, *J the American Medical* 1995, 274,29-34.

Bateson, Gregory. *Steps to an Ecology of Mind*, New York: Ballantine Books 1972.

Batmanghelidj, Fereydoon. *Your Body's Many Cries for Water: You Are Not Sick, You Are Thirsty!*, Falls Church, VA: Global Health Solutions 1995.

Bauer, C. *Acupressure for Everybody*, New York: Henry Holt 1991.

Baylier, MF. Bacteriostatic activity of some Australian essential oils, *Perfumer and Flavourist* 1979, 4(23), 23-25.

Beal, James. *Presentation at ISSSEEM Annual Meeting*, Boulder, CO 1992.

Beal, James, *BioElectromagnetics-2000 Health Effects Update*, EMF Interface consulting, www.emfinterface.com 2000.

Beal, MC et al. Interexaminer agreement on long-term patient improvement: an exercise in research design, *J the American Osteopathic Association* 1980, 79, 432-440.

Beal, MC et al. Interexaminer agreement on patient improvement after negotiated selection of tests, *J the American Osteopathic Association* 1982, 81, 322-328.

Beal, M/ Pavek, R. *An uncompleted controlled study of SHEN and major depression*, Milwaukee County Mental Health Centre 1985.

Bean, M. The importance of touch in patient care, *Imprint* 1980, *27(5)*, 46-71

Bean, M. The poetry of countertransference, *The Arts in Psychotherapy* 1992, 19, 347-358.

Bear Hawk, Ken (alt. for Cohen, Ken). *The Four Winds: Native American Teachings,* PO Box 234, Nederland, CO 80446, USA.

Beard, Paul. *Survival of Death: For and Against,* London: Hodder & Stoughton 1966.

Beard, Paul. *Living on,* London: Allen & Unwin 1980.

Beardall, AG. *Clinical Kinesiology, Volumes I, II, III, IV, V,* Lake Oswego, OR: Beardall, DC 1985.

Bearden, Thomas E. *The Excalibur Briefing,* San Francisco: Strawberry Hill 1980.

Beasley, Victor, *Subtle-Body Healing,* Boulder Creek, CA: University of the Trees 1979.

Beck, AM/ Meyers, NM. Health enhancement and companion animal ownership, *Annual Review of Public Health* 1996, 17, 247-257.

Beck, PV/ Walters, AL. *The Sacred: Ways of Knowledge, Sources of Live,* Tsaile (Navajo Nation), AZ: Navajo Community College 1977.

Beck, Robert C. Occult influences in health and disease, *Archaeus* 1984, 2(1), l-7.

Beck, Robert C. Mood modification with ELF magnetic fields: Preliminary investiga-tion, *Archaeus* 1986, 4, 47-53.

Beck, Robert C/ Byrd, Eldon A. Bibliography on the psychoactivity of electromagnetic fields, *Archaeus* 1986, 4, 54-77.

Becker, A J. Geomagnetic activity and violent crime, *Subtle Energies* 1990 1(2), 65-79.

Becker, M. *A Theory and Practice of Therapeutic Massage,* New York: Milady 1988.

Becker, Robert O. Search for evidence of axial current flow in peripheral nerves of the salamander, *Science* 1961, 134, 101.

Becker, Robert, Acupuncture points show increased DC electrical conductivity, *American J Chinese Medicine* 1976, 4, 69.

Becker, Robert O. An application of direct current neural systems to psychic phenomena, *Psychoenergetic Systems* 1977, 2, 189-196.

Becker, Robert O. *Cross Currents: The Perils of Electropollution, The Promise of Electromedicine,* Los Angeles: Tarcher 1990.

Becker, Robert O/ Marino, Andrew A. *Electromagnetism and Life,* Albany: State University of New York 1982. On line at http://www.ortho.lsumc.edu/Faculty/Marino/EL/ELTOC.html

Becker, Robert O / Selden, Gary. *The Body Electric: Electromagnetism and the Foundation of Life,* New York: William Morrow 1985.

Becker, WS/ Hagens, B. The rings of Gaia, in Swan, JA (ed), *The Power of Placei,* Wheaton, IL: Quest 1991, 257-79

Beckerman, H et al. The efficacy of physiotherapy for musculoskeletal disorders: overview of the current state of knowledge, *European J Physical Medicine and Rehabilitation* 1993, 3(6), 236-241.

Beckner, Mac/ Berman, Brian/ Kiley, Robert. *Complementary Therapies on the Internet,* London: Churchill Livingstone 2002

Bedard, Jim, *Lotus in the Fire: The healing Power of Zen,* Boston: Shambhala 1999.

Beecher, Henry K. The powerful placebo, *J the American Medical Association* 1955, 159, 1602-1606.

Beecher, HK. Experimentation in man, *J the American Medical Association* 1959, 169,461-478.

Beecher, HK. Surgery as placebo, *J the American Medical Association* 1961, 176, 1102-1 107.

Beinfield, Harriet/ Korngold, Efrem, *Between Heaven and Earth: A Guide to Chinese Medicine,* New York: Ballantine 1991.

Beinfield, Harriet/ Korngold, Efrem. Eastern medicine for western people, *Alternative Therapies* 1997, (4)3, 80-88; 119.

Beirnaent, Louis (Jesuit Father). Quoted from meeting of the International Congress of Parapsychology, St. Paul, France, May 1945.

Bek, Lilla/ Pullar, Philippa. *The Seven Levels of Healing,* London: Century 1986.

Bell, KM et al. S-adenosylmethionine blood levels in major depression: changes with drug treatment, *Acta Neurologica Scandinavia* 1994 (Supp), 154, 15-18.

Bellavite, Paolo/ Signorini, Andrea. *Homeo-pathy: A Frontier in Medical Science,* Berkeley, CA: North Atlantic 1995.

Belli, A & Coulehan, J eds. Blood and Bones: Poems by Physicians, Iowa City: University of Iowa 1998.

Bellis, JM. Hypnotic pseudo-sunburn, *American J Clinical Hypnosis* 1966, 8, 310-312.

Belon, P. Homeopathy and immunology, *Proceedings of the 42nd Congress of the LMHI, Arlington, VA 1987,* 265-270.

Belshaw, Chris. *Osteopathy: Is it for You?* Longmead, England: Element 1993.

Belsky, Marvin and Gross, Leonard, *How to Choose and Use Your Doctor,* Harper-Collins 1979

BEMI Currents - J the Bio-Electro-Magnetic Institute, 2490 W. Moana Lane, Reno, NV 89509-3936, Tel. (702) 827-9099.

Benford, M Sue, "Spin Doctors": A New Paradigm Theorizing the Mechanism of Bioenergy Healing, *J Theoretics* 1999, 1(2), www.Joftheoretics.com .

Benford, M Sue, et al. Gamma radiation fluctuations during alternative healing therapy, *Alternative Therapy* 1999, 5(4), 51-56.

Bennett, George, *Handbook of Clinical Dietetics,* Rev. 2nd Ed. Belfast: Navan 1995

Bennett, Henry L. The mind during surgery: The uncertain effects of surgery. *Advances* 1993, 9(1), 5-16. (30 refs)

Bennett, HZ. *Write from the Heart,* Nataraj Publications 1995.

Bennett, J. Dynamics of correction of abnormal function, From *Terrence Bennet Lectures,* RJ Martin (ed), Sienna Madre, CA: privately published by RJ Martin, DC 1977.

Benor, Daniel J. Fields and energies related to healing: Review of Soviet and Western studies, *Psi Research* 1984, 3(1), 8-15.

Benor, Daniel J. Believe it and you'll be it: Visualization in psychic healing. *Psi Research* 1985, 4(1), 21-56.

Benor, Daniel J. A psychiatrist examines fears of healing, *J the Society for Psychical Research* 1990, 56, 287-299; excerpted in Dossey 1993.

Benor, Daniel J. Intuitive diagnosis, *Subtle Energies* 1992, 3(2), 37-59. http://wholistichealingresearchcom.readyhosting.com/Articles/IntuitDx.htm

Benor, Daniel J. Spiritual healing: a unifying influence in complementary therapies, *Complementary Therapies in Medicine* 1995a, 3(4), 234-238. http://www.WholisticHealingResearch.com/Articles/Unifying.htm

Benor, Daniel J. Medical student health awareness, *Complementary Therapies in Medicine* 1995b, 3(2), 93-99.

Benor, Daniel J. Further comments on 'loading' and 'telesomatic reactions', *Advances* 1996a, 12(2), 71-75.

Benor, Daniel J. Psychotherapy & spiritual healing, *Human Potential* 1996b (summer) 13-16. http://www.WholisticHealingResearch.com/Articles/PsychotherSH.htm

Benor, Daniel J. Wholistic integrative care, 2000a, Wholistic healing http://www.WholisticHealingResearch.com/Articles/WholisIC.htm

Benor, Daniel J. Self-Healing: Brief psycho-therapy with WHEE (Wholistic Hybrid of EMDR & EFT), and other approaches 2001a. http://www.wholistichealingresearch.com/Articles/Selfheal.htm

Benor, Daniel J. Intuitive Assessments: an overview 2001b Benor, Benor, Daniel J. *Healing Research: Volume I, Spiritual Healing: Scientific Validation of a Healing Revolution,* Southfield, MI: Vision Publications2001c. http://wholistichealingresearchcom.readyhost-ing.com/Articles/IntuitAssessOverv.htm

Benor, Daniel J. Intuition (Editorial), *International J Healing and Caring – On line* 2002a, 2(2), 1-17.

In a word (Editorial), *International J Healing and Caring – On line* 2002b, 2(1)1, 1-15.

Benor, Daniel J. The body (Editorial), *International J Healing and Caring – On line* 2002c, 2(3), 1-17.

Benor, Daniel J. Intuition (Editorial), *International J Healing and Caring – On line* 2002d, 2(2), 1-11.

Benor, Daniel J. Developing faith in the transcendent: Approaches and stages of development (Editorial), *International J Healing and Caring – On line* 2003, 3(2), 1-27.

Benor, Daniel, von Stumpfeldt, Dorothea, and Benor, Ruth, EmotionalBodyProcess, Part I. Healing through Love, *International Journal of Heahng and Caring – On Line* www.ijhc.org 2001, 1(1). http://www.ijhc.org/Journal/0601articles/love-I-1.html

Benor, Daniel, von Stumpfeldt, Dorothea, and Benor, Ruth, EmotionalBodyProcess, Part II: *International Journal of Heahng and Caring – On Line* www.ijhc.org 2002 2(1), January,.

Benor, Daniel/Mohr, Margaret, The overlap of psychic 'readings' with psychotherapy, *Psi Research* 1986, 5(1,2), 56-78

Benor, Ruth, A holistic view to managing stress, In: Fisher RA/ McDaid, P (eds), *Palliative Day Care,* London: Arnold 1996, 126-138,

Bensen, Vladimir B. One hundred cases of post-anesthetic suggestion in the recovery room, *American J Clinical Hypnosis* 1971, 14,9-15.

Bensky, D/ Gamble, A. *Chinese Herbal Medicine: Materia Medica,* Seattle, WA: Eastland 1986.

Benson, Herbert, The physiology of meditation, *Scientific American* 1972, 226, 84-90.

Benson, Herbert. *The Relaxation Response,* New York: Morrow 1975.

Benson, Herbert, et al. Body temperature changes during the practice of Tummo (heat) yoga, *Nature* 1982, 295.

Benson, Herbert, *Timeless Healing: The Power and Biology of Belief,* New York: Scribner 1996.

Bensoussan, A et al. Treatment of irritable bowel syndrome with Chinese herbal medicine: a randomized controlled trial, *J the American Medical Association* 1998, 280, 1585-1589.

Bentley, Eilean, *Step-by-Step Head Massage,* London: Gaia 2000.

Benveniste, Jacques et al. L'agitation de solutions hautement diluees n'induit pas d'activite specifique, *Comptes Rendus Academie Science Paris* 1991, 312(II), 461-466.

Benveniste, Jacques. Understanding digital biology http://www.digibio.com/cgi-bin/node.pl?nd=n3 1998. (accessed 5/3/03)

Benveniste, Jacques. Website with many references on research from Benveniste's lab http://www.digibio.com/cgi-bin/node.pl?nd=n4

Berendt, Joachim-Ernst. *Nada Brahma: The World is Sound - Music and the Landscape of Consciousness,* New York: East-West 1987.

Berger, Arthur Asa, *The Art of Comedy Writing,* New Brunswich, NJ: Jason Aronson 1997.

Berger, A/ Giovan, M. Poetic intervention with forensic patients, *J Poetry Therapy* 1990, 4, 83-92.

Berger, D/ Nolte, D. Acupuncture in bronchial asthma: body plethysmographic measurements of acute bronchospasmolytic effects, *Complementary Medicine, East and West* 1977, 5, 265-269.

Berger, RE/ Persinger, MA. Geophysical variables and behavior LXVII: Quieter annual geomagnetic activity and larger effect size for experimental psi (ESP) studies over 6 decades, *Perceptual and Motor Skills* 1990, 73 1219-1223

Bergin, A E. The evaluation of therapeutic outcomes, In AE Bergin/ SL Garfield (eds). *Handbook of psychotherapy and behavior change,* New York: Wiley 1971, 217-270.

Bergin, A E/ Lambert, M J. The evaluation of therapeutic outcomes, In AE Bergin/ SL Garfield (eds). *Handbook of psychotherapy and behavior change: An empirical analysis,* New York: Wiley 1978.

Bergin, Allen E/ Garfield, Sol L (eds). *Handbook of Psychotherapy and Behavioral Change,* 4th ed. John Wiley & Sons 1993.

Bergland, Richard. *The Fabric of Mind,* Middlesex, England: Viking/ Penguin 1985.

Bergquist-Ullman, M/ Larsson, U. Acute low back pain in industry, *Acta Orthopaedica Scandinavica* 1977 170 (Suppl) 1-117

Bergsmann, O. *Risk Factor Place, Dowsing Zone and Man: Scientific Study Investigating Place-Related Influences in Man,* Vienna 1990 (German - book review by Schneck).

Bergsmann, O/ Woolley-Hart, A. Differences in electrical skin conductivity between acupuncture points and adjacent skin areas. American J Acupuncture 1973, 1:27-32

Berk, L. Eustress of mirthful laughter modifies natural killer cell activity, *Clinical Research* 1989, 37, ll5.

Berk, L/ Tan, S. Neuroendocrine influences of mirthful laughter, *American J Medical Sciences* 1989, 298, 390-396.

Berk, Lee S et al. Modulation of neuroimmune parameters during the eustress of humor-associated mjirthful laughter, *Alter-native Therapies* 2001, 7(2), 62-76 (93 refs).

Berk, William R. (ed), *Chinese Healing Arts: Internal Kung Fu,* Burbank, CA: Unique 1986.

Berkowsky, Bruce, wwwl.samarabotane.com/Dr_BruceBerkowsky/index.htm.

Berland, W. Unexpected cancer recovery: why patients believe they survive, *Advances* 1995, 4, 5-19.

Berman BM et al. Is acupuncture effective in the treatment of fibromyalgia? J Fam Pract 1999, 48, 213- 218.

Berman, Morris. *The Reenchantment of the World,* New York: Bantam 1984.

Bernard, Claude. *An Introduction to the Study of Experimental Medicine* 1865.

Bersani, Ferdinando (ed), *Electricity and Magnetism in Biology and Medicine,* New York: Plenum 1999.

Bertalanffy, Ludwig von. General systems theory and psychiatry, In: Arieti, Sylvano (ed): *American Handbook of Psychiatry Vol. I, Chapter 51* New York: Basic Books 1974, 1095-1117.

Besant, Annie/ Leadbeater, CW. *Thought-Forms,* Wheaton, IL: Theosophical/ Quest 1971. (Orig. 1925, reprinted with permission of The Theosophical Publishing House, Adyar, Madras 600 020, India)

Best, S. Lunar Influence in plant growth: a review of the evidence, *Phenomena,* May 1978.

Betz, Hans-Dieter. Unconventional water detection: field test of the dowsing technique in dry zones, part 1, *J Scientific Exploration* 1995, 9(1), 1-43. (Also as: 2nd ed. GTZ Deutsche Gesellschaft fur Technische Zusammenarbeit 1993)

Bhattacharya, SK/ Mitra, SK. Anxiolytic activity of Panax ginseng roots: an experimental study, *J Ethnopharmac-ology* 1991, 34, 87-92.

Bhattacharyya, H. *VIBGYOR: The Science of Cosmic Ray Therapy,* Baroda, India: Good Companions 1957.

Bhatt-Sanders, D. Acupuncture for rheumatoid arthritis: an analysis of the literature, *Seminars in Arthritis and Reheumatism* 1985 14(4), 225-231.

Bibb, Benjamin O/ Weed, Joseph J. *Amazing Secrets of Psychic Healing,* West Nyack, New York: Parker 1976.

Bierce, Ambrose. Attributed.

Biffle, C. *A Journey Through Your Childhood: A Write-in Guide for reliving Your Past, Clarifying Your Present, and Charting Your Future,* Los angeles: Tarcher 1989.

Biffle, C. *The Castle of the Pearl* (rev ed), New York: Harper 1990.

Bigos, S et al. Acute lower back problems in adults, Clinical Practice Guideline,

Quick Reference Guide No. 14, Rockville, MD: US Dept. of Health and Human Services, Public Health Service, Agnecy for Health Care Policy and Research AHCPR Pub. No. 95-0643 1994.

Bigu, J. On the biophysical basis of the human 'aura,' *J Research in Psi Phenomena* 1976, 1(2), 8-43.

Birch, S. Some thoughts on the nature and timing of currently proposed changes in the acupuncture field, Unpublished paper (cited in Workshop on Alternative Medicine).

Birch, Stephen/ Hammerschlag, Richard, *Acupuncture Efficacy: A Compendium of Controlled Clinical Studies*, Tarrytown, NY: National Academy of Acupuncture and Oriental Medicine, Inc. 1996. (Excellent summary, though unclear regarding criteria for statistical significance of studies included in this work)

Bird, Christopher. *The Divining Hand: The Five Hundred Year Old Mystery of Dowsing*, New York: EP Dutton 1979.

Birk, Lee (ed), *Biofeedback, Behavior Medicine*, New York: Grune & Stratton 1973.

Bishop, G. *Faith Healing: God or Fraud?* Los Angeles: Sherbourne 1967.

Bisset, NG/ Wichtl, M. (eds), *Herbal drugs and phytopharmaceuticals: A handbook for practice on a scientific basis*, Stuttgart, Germany: Medpharm Scientific 1994.

Bittman, Barry B et al. Composite effects of group drumming music therapy on modulation of neuroendocrine-immune parameters in normal subjects, *Alternative Therapies* 2001, 7(1), 38-47 (52 refs).

Black, Claudia. *It's Never Too Late to Have a Happy Childhood: Inspirations for Adult Children*, New York: Ballantine 1989.

Black, N. Why we need observational studies to evaluate the effectiveness of health care, *British Medical J* 1996, 312, 1215-1218.

Black, S/ Humphrey, JH/ Niven, JSF. Inhibitions of mantoux reaction by direct suggestion under hypnosis, *British Medical J* 1963, 1, 1649-1652.

Blackburn, IM/ Moore, RG. Controlled acute and folow-up trial of cognitive therapy and pharmacotherapy in out-patients with recurrent depression, *British J Psychiatry* 1997, 171, 328-334.

Blackman, Sheldon/ Catalina, Don. The moon and the emergency room. *Perceptual and Motor Skills* 1973, 37, 624-626.

Blake, Julianne. Attribution of power and the transformation of fear: Empirical study of firewalking, *Psi Research* 1985, 4(2), 62-88.

Blake, William. *Auguries of Innocence* 1803.

Blalock, E. The immune system as a sensory organ, *J Immunology* 1984 132 1067-1069.

Blank, M. (ed), *Electricity and Magnetism in Biology and Medicine: Proceedings of the 1st World Congress for Electricity and Magnetism in Biology and Medicine, Orlando, FL, June 14-19 1992*, San Francisco: San Francisco Press 1993.

Blank, M. Electromagnetic fields: biological interactions and mechanisms, Advances in Chemistry Series 250, Washington, DC: American Chemical Society 1995.

Blanks, Robert HI et al. A retrospective assessment of Network Care using a survey of self-rated health, wellness and quality of life, *J Vertebral Subluxation Research* 1997, 1(4), 15-30 (52 refs).

Blevins, Sue A. The medical monopoly: Protecting consumers or limiting competition? Cato Institute, 1000 Massachusetts Ave. NW Washington, DC 20001 Tel. 202/ 842-0200, Fax 842-3490.

Block, Keith I. Nutritional biotherapy, in Jonas/ Levin 1999, 490-521.

Block, KL. The role of the self in healthy cancer survivorship: a view from the front lines of treating cancer, *Advances* 1997, 13, 6-26.

Blom M/ Dawidson I/ Angmar-Mansson, B. The effect of acupuncture on salivary flow rates in patients with xerostomia, *Oral Surgery, Oral Medicine, Oral Pathology* 1992, 73:293-298.

Bloom, Bernard S et al. Evaluation of randomized controlled trials on complementary and alternative medicine," *International J Technology Assessment in Health Care* 2000, 16(1), 13-21.

Blumenthal, M et al (eds), *The Complete German Commission E Monographs: The Therapeutic Guide to Herbal Medicines*, American Botanical Council 1998.

Blumenthal, M et al. *Herbal Medicine: Expanded Commission E Monographs*, Newton, MA: Integ. Med. Com. 2000.

Blumer, Walter/ Cranton, Elmer M. Ninety percent reduction in cancer mortality after chelation therapy with EDTA, *J Advancement in Medicine* 1989, 2(1/ 2), 183-188.

Blundell, Geoffrey. Personal communication 1989.

Blundell, Geoffrey. The wonderful brain, *Caduceus* (Summer) 1990, 17-21.

Bly, Robert, *A Little Book on the Human Shadow*, San Francisco, Harper & Row 1988.

Bly, Robert/ Woodman, Marian, *The Divine Child*, Belleville, Ont. Canada: Applewood Centre 1991.

Boadella, David. *Lifestreams: An Introduction to Biosynthesis*, London: Routledge and Kegan Paul 1987.

Boericke, W/ Dewey, WA. *the Twelve tissue Remedies of Schuessler*, New York: Aperture 1911.

Boerstler, Richard W. Letting Go: *A Holistic and Meditative Approach to Living and Dying*, Watertown, MA: Associates in Thanatology 1982.

Bogart, Greg. Meditation and psychotherapy a review of the literature, *American Journal of Psychotherapy* 1991 (100 annotated refs) http://jps.net/gbogart/med_article.html

Bogart, Greg, *Therapeutic Astrology: Using the Birth Chart in Psychotherapy and spiritual Counseling*, Berkeley, CA: Dawn Mountain 1996.

Boguslawski, Marie, Therapeutic Touch: a facilitator of pain relief, Borysenko, J. Healing motives: an interview with David C McClelland, *Advances* 1985, 2(2), 29-41.

Bohm, David. *Causality and Chance in Modern Physics*, London: Routledge and Kegan Paul 1957.

Bohm, David. *Wholeness and the Implicate Order* London: Routledge and Kegan Paul 1980.

Bohm, David/ Peat, F David, *Science, Order and Creativity*, New York: Bantam 1987.

Boirac, Emile. *Our Hidden Forces*, New York: Stokes 1917.

Boissel, JP et al. *Critical literature review on the effectiveness of homeopathy: overview of data from homeopathic medicine trials*, Brussels: Homeopathic Medicine Research Group, Report to the European Commission 1996, 195-210.

Bolander, Donald O et al. *Instant Quotation Dictionary*, Mundelein, IL: Career 1990.

Bolen, Jean S. Meditation and psychotherapy in the treatment of cancer, *Psychic* 1973 (July-August), 19-22.

Bolen, Jean Shidona. *The Tau of Psychology: Synchronicity and the Self,* New York: Harper & Row 1979.

Bolen, Jean Shinoda. *Close to the Bone: Life Threatening Illness and the Search for Meaning*, New York: Touchstone/ Simon & Schuster 1998.

Bolles, Edmund Blair. *Remembering and Forgetting,* New York: Walker 1987.

Bolocofsky, DN et al. Effectiveness of hypnosis as an adjunct to behavioral weight management, *J Clinical Psychology* 1985, 41, 35-41.

Bone, ME et al. Ginger root – a new antiemetic: The effect of ginger root on postoperative nausea and vomiting after mayor gynaecological surgery, *Anaesthesia* 1990, 45(8), 669-671.

Bonny, Helen L/ Savary, Louis M. *Music and Your Mind: Listening with a New Consciousness*, Port Townsend, WA: ICM 1983.

Boorstein, Seymor, *Transpersonal Psycho-therapy*, State University of New York Press 1996.

Boorstein, Seymor, *Clinical Studies in Transpersonal Psychotherapy*, State University of New York Press 1997.

546 References

Booth, Gotthard. Psychobiological aspects of 'spontaneous' regressions of cancer, *J the American Academy of Psychoanalysis* 1973, 1, 303-317.

Booth, Roger J/ Ashbridge, Kevin R. A fresh look at the relationship between the psyche and immune system: teleological coherence and harmony of purpose, *Advances* 1993, 9(2), 4-23; Comments on this article pp24-65. (3pp refs)

Borelli, Mariane D/ Heidt, Patricia (eds). *Therapeutic Touch: A Book of Readings,* New York: Springer 1981.

Borysenko, Joan, *Minding the Body, Mending the Mind,* New York: Bantam 1987.

Borysenko, Joan, *Fire in the Soul: A New Psychology of Spiritual Optimism,* New York: Warner 1993.

Borysenko, Joan/ Borysenko, Miroslav, *The Power of the Mind to Heal: Renewing Body, Mind and Spirit,* Carson, CA: Hay House/ Enfield, England: Eden Grove 1994.

Boshier, A. African apprenticeship, In: Angoff, A/ Barth, D (eds). *Parapsychology and Anthropology,* New York: Parapsychology Foundation 1974.

Bosker, Gideon (ed), *Medicine is the Best Laughter,* St. Louis, MO: Mosby 1995.

Bosveld, J. *Topics for Getting in Touch* Johnston, OH: Puddinghouse 1982.

Bott, Victor. *Anthroposophical Medicine,* Rochester, NY: Healing Arts 1984.

Bott, Victor. *Spiritual Scinece and the Art of Healing: Rudolf Steiner's Anthroposophical Medicine,* New York: Inner Traditions 1996.

Botting, D. Review of the literature on the effectiveness of reflexology, *Complementary Therapies in Nursing and Midwifery* 1997, 3 (5), 123-130.

Botting D/ Cook R. Complementary medicine: knowledge, use and attitudes of doctors, *Complementary Therapies in Nursing and Midwifery*2000, 6, 41 – 47.

Bouchardon, Patrice. *The Healing Energies of Trees,* London: Gaia 1998.

Boulos, Z et al. Light treatment for sleep disorders: consensus report VII. Jet lag, *J Biological Rhythms* 1995 10 167.

Bower, John. *The Healthy House: How to Buy One; How to cure a "Sick" One; How to Build One,* Secaucus, NJ: Lyle Stuart/ Carol 1992.

Bowers, KS. *Hypnosis for the Seriously Curious,* Monterey, CA: Brooks/ Cole 1976.

Bowman, D. A veteran's recoverey and the use of poetry therapy, *J Poetry Therapy* 1991, 5, 19-21.

Bowman, DD/ Halfacre, D. Poetry therapy with the sexually abused adolescent: a case study, *The Arts in Psychotherapy* 1994, 21, 11-16.

Bowman, DD et al. Using poetry, fiction, and essays to help people face shattered dreams, *J Poetry Therapy* 1994, 8, 81-90.

Bowman, JM. Experiencing the chronic pain phenomenon: A study, *Rehabilitation Nursing* 1994 19(2), 91-95.

Boxler, C/ Paulson, M. Kirlian photography: a new tool in biological research? *J the Biological Photography Association* 1977, 45(2), 51-60.

Boyd, Doug. *Rolling Thunder,* New York: Delta/ Dell 1974.

Boyd, WE. An investigation regarding the action on diastase of microdoses of mercuric chloride when prepared with and without mechanical shock, *British Homeopathic J* 1946, 36, 214-223.

Boyers, DG/ Tiller, WA. Corona discharge photography, *J applied Physics* 1973, 44, 3102-3112.

Boyle, Wade/ Saine, Andre, *Lectures in Naturopathic Hydrotherapy,* East Palestine, OH: Buckeye Naturopathic 1988.

Braddock, Carolyn J. *Body Voices: Using the Power of Breath, Sound and Movement to Heal and Create New Boundaries,* PageMill 1995.

Brady, M. *Beyond survival: A Writing J for Healing childhood Sexual Abuse,* New York: Ballentine/ Hazelden 1990.

Brain/ Mind Bulletin. Electronic evidence of auras, chakras in UCLA study, 1978 (9 March), 77-78.

Brain/ Mind Bulletin. Life energy patterns visible via new technique, 1982, 7(14), 1.

Brain/ Mind Bulletin. Psychologist makes medical history -beats heart to any rhythm on demand, 1983a, 8(14).

Brain/ Mind Bulletin. Test supports Sheldrake theory, 1983b, 8(15), 1.

Brain/ Mind Bulletin. Morse code experiment supports M-field theory 1985, 10(12), 1.

Brain/ Mind Bulletin. New technologies detect effects of healing hands, 1986a, 10(16), 3.

Brain/ Mind Bulletin. Remission project gathers data on 2,000 unexplained recoveries, 1986b, 11(7), 1; 3.

Braith JA et al. Relaxation-induced anxiety in a subclinical sample of chronically anxious subjects, *J Behavior Therapy and Experimental Psychiatry* 1988, 19(3), 193-8.

Brand, AC. Writing as counseling, *Elementary School guidance and Counseling* 1987, 21, 266-275.

Brand, Paul with Yancey, Philip. *The Gift Nobody Wants,* New York: HarperPerennial 1993.

Brandjes, Sophia. *You Gain Living Skills (Yoga and Living Skills),* Hornsby, NSW, Australia: Gerald Brandjes 1987. (Cartoons reproduced with kind permission of the author and publisher.)

Brandon, David, *Zen in the Art of Helping,* London: Routledge & Kegan Paul 1976.

Branthwaite A/ Cooper, P. Analgesic effects of branding in treatment of headaches, *British Medical J* 1981, 282, 1576-78.

Bratsman, S./ Kroll, D. *Natural Health Bible,* Rockland, CA: Prima 1999.

Braud, William G. The psi conducive syndrome: free response CIESP performance following evocation of 'left-hemispheric' vs. 'right-hemispheric' functioning, *Research in Parapsychology 1974,* Metuchen, NJ: Scarecrow Press 1975, 17-20.

Braud, William G. Allobiofeedback: Immediate feedback for a psychokinetic influence upon another person's physiology *Presented at* PA Convention, Washington DC (August) 1977, In: Roll, WA) (ed). *Research in Parapsychology* 1977, NJ Scarecrow Press 1978, 123-134.

Braud, William G. Conformance behavior involving living systems, In: Roll, WG et al (eds). *Research In Parapsychology 1978,* Metuchen, NJ: Scarecrow Press 1979, 111-115.

Braud, William G. Distant mental influence of rate of hemolysis of human red blood cells. *J the American Society for Psychical Research* 1990a, 84(1).

Braud, William. On the use of living target systems in distant mental influence research, In: Shapin, Betty/ Coly, Lisette (eds). *Psi Research Methodology: A Reexamination,* New York: Parapsychology Foundation 1990b.

Braud, William. On the use of living target systems in distant mental influence research, In: Shapin, Betty/ Coly, Lisette (eds), *Psi Research Methodology: A Reexamination,* New York: Parapsychology Foundation 1990.

Braud, William G/ Dennis, Stephen P. Geophysical variables and behavior LVII: Autonomic activity, hemolysis, and biological psychokinesis: Possible relationships with geomagnetic field activity, *Perceptual and Motor Skills* 1989, 68, 1243-1254.

Braud, William/ Schlitz, Marilyn. A Methodology for the Objective Study of Transpersonal Imagery, *Journal of Scientific Exploration* 1989, 3(1), 43-63.

Braud, William, et al. Experiments with Matthew Manning, *J the Society for Psychical Research* 1979, 50 199-223.

Braud, William, et al. Further studies of the Bio-PK effect: feedback, blocking, specificity/ generality *Presentation at* Parapsychological Meeting 1984.

Braud, William/ Anderson, Rosemarie, *Transpersonal Research Methods for the Social Sciences: Honoring Human Experience,* Thousand Oaks, CA: Sage 1998.

Braud, William/ Schlitz, Marilyn. Psychokinetic influence on electrodermal activity *J Parapsychology* 1983, 47(2), 95-119.

Braun, Bennett G. Neurophysiologic changes in multiple personality due to integration: A preliminary report, *American J Clinical Hypnosis* 1983a, 26 (2), 84-92.

Braun, Bennett G. Psychophysiologic

phenomena in multiple personality and hypnosis, *American J Clinical Hypnosis* 1983b, 26(2), 124-137.

Braverman, Eric. *The Healing Nutrients Within: How to use amino acids to achieve optimum health and fight cancer, Alzheimer's disease, depression, heart disease, and more*, North Bergen, NJ: Basic Health 2003

Braverman, Eric R et al. *The Healing Nutrients Within: Facts, Findings, and New Research on Amino Acids*, New Canaan, CT: Keats 1987.

Breakey, Jeff. *Guide to Health-Oriented Periodicals*, Ashland, OR: Sprouting Publications 1983.

Brecht, Bertholt. *Life of Gallileo* 1939.

Brehin, J. Post-decision changes in the desirability of alternatives, *J Abnormal and Social Psychology* 1956, 52, 378-384.

Breiling, Brian, et al (eds), *Light Yers Ahead: The Illustrated Guide to Full Spect-rum and Colored Light in Mindbody Heal-ing*, Tiburon, CA: Light Years Ahead 1996.

Brena, Steven F. *Yoga and Medicine,* New York: Penguin 1972.

Brena, S & Chapman, S (eds). *Management of patients with chronic pain*, New York: SP Medical and Scientific 1985.

Brennan, Barbara A. *Hands of Light: A Guide to Healing Through the Human Energy Field*, New York: Bantam 1988.

Brennan, Barbara. Personal communication 1989, 1990.

Brennan, Barbara. *Light Emerging*, New York: Bantam 1993a.

Brennan, Barbara. *Healing through the human energy field*, *Caduceus* 1993b, no.21, 16-49;

Brennan, TA et al. Incidence of adverse events and negligence in hospitalized patients: results of the Harvard Medical Practice Study I, *New England J Medicine* 1991, 324, 370-376.

Brennan, Troyen A. The institute of medicine report on medical errors – could it do harm?

Brenneman, DE/ Gozes, I. A femtomolar-acting neuroprotective peptide, *J Clinical*

Brenner, Myron D. Orgonotic devices in the treatment of infectious conditions, *Pulse of the Planet* 1991, 3, 49-53.

Brenner, Paul. *Health is a Question of Balance,* Marina del Rey, CA: DeVorss 1978.

Brenner, Paul. *Life is a Shared Creation,* Marina del Rey, CA: DeVorss 1981.

Bresler, David E/ Trubo, Richard. *Free Yourself front Pain,* New York: Simon & Schuster 1979.

Brevoort, P. The booming US botanical market: a new overview, *HerbalGram* 1998, 44, 33-46.

Brewin, T/ Garrow, J. Commissioning complementary medicine. Evaluations of efficacy of treatments should be consistent, *BMJ* 1995, 311(7008),809.

Brewington, V et al. Acupuncture as a detoxification treatment: an analysis of controlled research, *J Substance Abuse Treatment* 1994 11(4) 289-307.

Brewitt, B et al. Personality preferences of healthy and HIV+ people attracted to homeopathy, *Alternative Therapies* 1998, 4(2), 99; 102.

Brier R.; Savits, B/ Schmeidler, G. Tests of Silva mind control graduates, In: Roll, W.G.; Morris, R.L/ Morris, J.D. (eds), *Research in Parapsychology 1973*, 1974, 13-15.

Briggs, John P/ Peat, F David. *Looking Glass Universe: The Emerging Science of Wholeness,* New York: Simon & Schuster 1984.

Brigham, Deirdre Davis, *Imagery for Getting Well: Clinical Applications of Behavioral Medicine*, New York: Norton 1994.

Brighton, CT/ Pollack, SR (eds). Electromagnetics *in Medicine and Biology,* San Francisco: San Francisco Press 1991.

Brighton, CT et al *Electrical properties of bone and cartilage: experimental effects and clinical applications*, New York: Grune and Stratton 1979.

Brighton, CT et al. A multicenter study of the treatment of nonunion with constant direct current, *J Bone and Joint Surgery* 1981, 63A, 2-12.

Brighton CT, et al. In vitro growth of bovine articular chondrocytes in various capacitively coupled electrical fields, *J Orthopedic Research* 1984, 2, 15.

Brigo, B/ Serpelloni, G. Homoeopathic treatment of migraine: a randomized double-blind controlled study of sixty cases, *Berlin J on Research in Homoeopathy* 1991 1, 98-106.

Brilliant, Ashleigh, *All I Want Is a Warm Bed and a Kind Word and Unlimited Power*, Woodbridge 1985

Brinker, F. *Herb contraindiations and drug interactions*, Sandy, OR: Eclectic Medical 1997.

Brinker, Francis J. *Herb Contraindications and Drug Interactions: with Appendices Addressing Specific Conditions and Med-icines, 3rd ed,* Sandy, OR: Eclectic Medical Publications, 2001.

Bristol, Claude M. *The Magic of Believing,* New York: Kangaroo/ Pocket 1977. (Orig. 1948)

British Medical Association. *Complementary Medicine: New Approaches to Good Practice*, Oxford: Oxford University Press 1993.

British Tuberculosis Association. Hypnosis for asthma -a controlled trial, *British Medical J* 1968, 4, 71-76.

Britten, N. Qualitative interviews in medical research, *British Medical J* 1995, 311, 251-253.

Brodeur, Paul, *Currents of Death The Attempt to Cover Up the Threat to Your Health*, New York: Simon and Schuster 1989

Brody, Howard et al. Ethics at the interface of conventional and complementary medicine, in Jonas/ Levin p. 46-56.

Bronough, RL. In vivo percutaneous absorption of fragrance ingredients in rhesus monkeys and humans, *Food and Chemical Toxicology* 1990, 28(5), 369-374.

Brostoff, J/ Gamlin, L. *Complete Guide to Food Allergy and Intolerance*, New York: Crown 1992.

Broughton, RS. Possible brain hemisphere laterality effects on ESP performance, *J. Society for Psychical Research* 1976, 48, 384-399.

Broughton, Richard S. Comments on 'Cerebral lateralization effects in ESP processing,' *J the Society for Psychical Research* 1978, 72, 384-389.

Brown, Barbara B. *New Mind, New Body,* New York: Bantam 1979.

Brown, Barbara. *Infinite Well-Being,* New York: Irvington/ New Jersey: New Horizon 1985.

Brown, D. *Ginko biloba* extract for resistant depression, *Quarterly Review of Natural Medicine* 1994a (Fall), 211-212.

Brown, D. Valerian root: non-addictive alternative for insomnia and anxiety, *Quarterly Review of Natural Medicine* 1994b (Fall), 221-224.

Brown, Ellen, *Forbidden Medicine*, Murrieta, CA: Third Millenium 1998.

Brown, Frank A. Persistent activity rhythms in the oyster, *American J Physiology* 1954 178, 510-514.

Brown, Frank A. Living clocks, *Science* 1959 130 1534-1544.

Brown, FA/ Chow, CS. Lunar-correlated variations in water uptake by bean seeds, *Biological Bulletin* 1973 145, 265-278.

Brown, FA/ Park, YH. Synodic monthly modulation of the diurnal rhythm of hamsters, *Proceedings of the Society for Experimental Biology and Medicine* 1959 101, 457-460.

Brown, FA/ Terracini, EE. Exogenous timing of rat spontaneous activity patterns, *Proceedings of the Society for Experimental Biology and Medicine* 1959 101, 457-460.

Brown, GW/ Harris, T. *social origins of depression,* Cambridge UK Cambridge University 1978.

Brown, HD/ Chattopadhyay, SK. *Cancer Biochemistry and Biophysics* 1988, 9, 295.

Brown, Lester R et al (eds), *State of the World 2000*, Washington, DC: Earthscan 2000.

Brown, MF. Shamanism and its discontents, *Medical Anthropology Quarterly* 1988, 2 102-120.

Brown, Malcolm. *The Healing Touch: An Introduction to Organismic Psychotherapy*, Mendocino, CA: Life Rhythms 1990.

Brown, R et al. A new criterion for selecting poems for use in poetry therapy, *J Poetry Therapy* 1990, 4, 5-11.

Brown, Vivienne (Sarida). Personal communication 1988, 1989.

Brown V, Ennis M. Flow-cytometric analysis of basophil activation: inhibition by histamine at conventional and homoeopathic concentrations, *Inflamm Res* 2001; 50 (suppl 2), S47-S48.

Brüche, E. Bericht über Wünschelrute geopathische Reize und Entstörungsgeräte, *Naturwiss Rundsch* 1954, 9, 367-377.

Brüche, E. *Problematik der Wünschelrute*, Basel: JR Geigy 1960.

Brun, B et al. *Symbols of the Soul: Therapy and Guidance Through Fairy Tales*, Avon, UK: Bookcraft 1993.

Brunarski, DJ. Clinical trials of spinal rnanipulation: a critical appraisal and review of the literature, *J Manipulative and Physical Therapy* 1985. 7, 243.

Bruneton, J. *Pharmacognosy, Phytochemistry, Medicinal Plants*, Paris: Lavoisier 1995.

Brunler, Oscar. *Rays and Radiation Phenomena*, Los Angeles: DeVorss 1950.

Brutsche, MH. Complementary and alternative medicine in asthma--safety, effectiveness and costs, *Swiss Med Wkly* 2002, 132(25-26)., 329-31. (Review)

Bruyere, Rosalyn L/ Farrens, Jeanne. *Wheels of Light: A Study of the Chakras*, Sierra Madre, CA: Don 1989.

Buchbauer, G. Aromatherapy: Evidence fot he sedative effects of the essential oil of lavender after inhalation, *Zeitschrift fur Naturforschung* 1991, 46 C 1067-1072.

Buchman, Dian Dincin, *The Complete Book of Water Therapy*, New Canaan, CT: Keats 1994.

Buckle, Jane, Use of aromatherapy as a complementary treatment for chronic pain, *Alternative Therapies* 1999, 5(5), 42-51.

Budzynski, Thomas H. clinical applications of non-drug-induced states, In: Wolman/ Ullmann 1986, 428-460. (Table 'Cerebral lateralization' p 435)

Buegel, Dale et al. *Homeopathic Remedies for Health Professionals and Laypeople*, Honesdale, PA: Himalayan 1991.

Buerger, AA/ Greenman, PE. *Empirical Approaches to the Validation of Spinal Manipulation*, Springfield, IL: CC Thomas 1985.

Buhner, Stephen Harrod, *Sacred Plants Medicine*, Boulder, CO: Roberts Rinehart 1996.

Buhner, Stephen Harrod, *Herbal Antibiotics: Natural Alternatives for Treating Drug-Resistant Bacteria*, Newleaf 2000.

Buist, RA. The therapeutic predictability of tryptophan and tyrosine in the treatment of depression, *International Clinical Nutrition Review* 1983, 3(2), 1-3.

Bullock ML et al. Acupuncture treatment of alcoholic recidivism: a pilot study, *Alcoholism: Clinical and Experimental Research* 1987, 11, 292-295.

Bullock, M et al. Controlled trial of acupuncture for severe recidivist alcoholism, *Lancet* 1989, 2989, 1435-1438.

Bunning, E. *The Physiological Clock*, Berlin: Springer 1964.

Bunt, Leslie, *Music Therapy*, New York/ London: Routledge 1994.

Burbank, Luther. Quote from Tompkins, Peter/ Bird, Christopher: *The Secret Life of Plants*, New York: Harper & Row 1972, 134.

Burk, Larry, Psychic/ intuitive diagnosis: two case reports and commentary, *J Alternative and Complementary Medicine* (UK) 1997, 3(3), 209-212 (letter).

Burka, Christa Faye. *Clearing Crystal Consciousness*, Albuquerque, NM: Brotherhood of Life 1988.

Burkan, Tolly/ Keyes, Ken. *How to Make Your Life Work or Why Aren't You Happy?* Twain Harte, CA: Reunion 1983.

Bürklin, F. *Vortrag auf der Jahrestagung des Forschungskreises für Geobiologie*, Neckar: Eberbach 1965.

Burns, M. Writing to heal: therapeutic uses of creative writing by adult survivors of incest, *J Poetry Therapy* 1991, 5, 135-142.

Burnside, JM. Touching is talking, *American J Nursing* 1973, 73, 2060-2063.

Burr, Harold S. The meaning of bioelectric potentials, *Yale J Biological Medicine* 1944, 16, 353.

Burr, Harold. *Blueprint for immortality,* London: Neville Spearman 1972.

Burton, Larry/Joines, William. Some aspects *of* Kirlian photography, In: Roll, WG/Morris, RL/Morris, LD (eds). *Research in Parapsychology 1973.* Metuchen, NJ: Scarecrow 1974, 15-16.

Burton, L et al. Kirlian photography and its relevance to parapsychological research (Summary), In JD Morris, et al (eds). *Research in Parapsychology 1974,* Metuchen, NJ: Scarecrow Press 1975, 107-112.

Burton, Richard E. Attributed.

Buscaglia, Leo, Love, New York: Fawcett Crest/Ballantine 1972.

Busch, Hartwin. How buildings affect living beings, *Caduceus* 1989, No. 7, 15-21.

Bushman, JL. Green tea and cancer in humans: a review of the literature, *Nutrition and Cancer* 1998, 3(3), 151-159.

Butler, Lisa D et al. Traumatic stress, life events, and emotional support in women with metastatic breast cancer: cancer-related traumatic stress symptoms associated with past and current stressors, *Health Psychology* 1999, 18(6), 555-560.

Buttram HE. The National Vaccine Childhood Injury Act - a Critique, Townsend Letter for Doctors & Patients, October, 1998:66-68.

Byers, AP. *The Byers neurotherapy reference library, (2nd ed),* Wheat Ridge, CO: Association for Applied Psychophysiology and Biofeedback1998

Byers, Dwight, *Better Health with Foot Reflexology*, St. Petersburg, FL: Ingham 1987.

C

(Chinese): *A Barefoot Doctor's Manual,* Translation of Ch'ih Chiao: Sheng Shou Ts'e, Philadelphia, PA: Running Press 1977.

Cadbury, Deborah, *The Feminization of Nature: Our Future at Risk*, London: Penguin 1998.

Cade, M/ Coxhead, N. *The Awakened Mind: Biofeedback and the Development of Higher States of Awareness,* New York: Delacorte Press/ Eleanor Friede 1978.

Cade, Maxwell/ Cashford, J. Biometric research into the brain rhythms of healers and the healing process, *Light* 1980 (Spring), 3-15.

Cade, Maxwell/ Coxhead, N. *The Awakened Mind, 2nd ed.* Shaftesbury, UK: Element 1986.

Cadoret, Remi J. The reliable application of ESP, *J Parapsychology* 1955, 19, 203-227.

Cadossi, RG et al. Lymphocytes and pulsing magnetic fields, in Marino, AA 1988a.

Cadossi, RG et al. Effect of low-frequency low-energy pulsing electromagnetic fields on mice undergoing bone marrow transplantation, *International J Immunopathology and Pharmacology* 1988b, 1, 57-62.

Cady, S et al. *Wisdom's Feast: Sophia in Study and Celebration*, San Francisco: harper & Row 1989.

Cahn, AM et al. Acupuncture in gastroscopy, *Lanceti* 1978, i, 182-183.

Cairns, J. The treatment of diseases and the war against cancer, *Scientific American* 1985, 253(5), 51-59.

Calabrese, EJ/ Baldwin, LA. Hormesis as a biological hypothesis, *Environmental Health Perspectives* 1998, 106 (suppl), 357-362.

Calderon, Eduardo. *Eduardo El Curandero: The Words of a Peruvian Healer,* Richmond, CA: North Atlantic 1982.

Caldwell, Christine. The somatic umbrella, *Bridges: ISSSEEM Magazine* 1996a, 7(1), 1, 4-7.

Caldwell, Christine, *Getting Our Bodies Back: Recovery, Healing and Transformation in Body-Centered Psychotherapy*, Boston, MA: Shambhala 1996b.

Calestro, Kenneth. Psychotherapy, faith healing and suggestion, *International J Psychiatry* 1972, 10(1), 83-113.

California Veterinary Medical Association, *Guidelines: Animals in Nursing Homes*, Morage, CA: California Veterinary Medical Association, 1024 Coventry Club Drive, Moraga, CA

Callahan, Daniel, *The Role of Complemen-*

tary and Alternative Medicine: Accommodating Pluralism (Hastings Center Studies in Ethics), Washington, DC: Georgetown Univ. Press 2002

Callahan, Roger J. *Five Minute Phobia Cure*, Wilmington, DE: Enterprise Publishing 1985.

Callahan, Roger. Successful psychotherapy by telephone and radio, *Proceedings of the International college of Applied Kinesiology* 1987.

Callahan, Roger J. *Why Do I Eat When I'm Not Hungry?* New York: Doubleday 1991.

Callahan, Roger J/ Callahan, Joanne, Stop the Nightmares of Trauma:Thought Field Therapy, The Power Therapy for the 21st Century 2000 (order through www.selfhelpuniv.com or (800) 359-CURE)

Callahan, Roger/ Callahan, Joanne, *Thought Field Therapy (TFT) and Trauma: Treatment and Theory,* Thought Field Therapy Training Center, 45350 Vista Santa Rosa, Indian Wells, CA 92210 (no date).

Callahan, Roger J/ Trubo, Richard, *Tapping the Healer Within Using Thought Field Therapy to Instantly Conquer Your Fears*, Anxieties, and Emotional Distress, New York: Contemporary 2001

Callinan, Paul. The mechanism of action of homeopathic remedies: Toward a definitive model, *J Complementary Medicine* 1985, 1(I), 35-36.

Campbell, Anthony. *Acupuncutre, the Modern Scientific Approach,* London: Faber 1986.

Campbell, Don, *Music Physician for Times to Come*, Wheaton, IL: Quest/ Theosophical 1991.

Campbell, Don (Compiler): *Music and Miracles,* Wheaton, 1L: Quest/ Theosophical 1992.

Campbell, Don. *The Mozart Effect: Tapping the Power of Music to Heal the Body, Strengthen the Mind, and Unlock the Creative Spirit,* Avon 1997.

Campbell, Joseph. *Myths to Live By,* New York: Bantam/ Viking Penguin 1972.

Campbell, Rhona. Presentation at SHEN Therapy conference, Galway, Ireland (Dunblane SHEN Centre 12 Dalmorglen Park, Stirling, UK FK7 9JL).

Campbell, Susan Schuster, *Called to Heal: African Shamanic Healers*, Twin Lakes, WI: Lotus 2000.

Campbell, SS et al. Light treatment for sleep disorders: consensus report V. Age-related disturbances, *J Biological Rhythms* 1995a 10 151.

Campbell, SS et al. Light treatment for sleep disorders: consensus report I. Chronology of seminal studies in humans, *J Biological Rhythms* 1995b 10 105.

Campbell, SS et al. Light treatment for sleep disorders, Consensus report III: Alerting and activating effects, *J Biological Rhythms* 1995c 10 129.

Cancilla, Dorothy, *Death by HMO: The Jennifer Gigliello Story*, Dedicated Press, Box 1638, Pacifica, CA 94044 4bobreed@msn.com

Canfield, Jack, et al. *Chicken Soup for the Surviving Soul: 101 Stories of Courage and Inspiration from Those Who Have Survived Cancer,* Florida: Health Communications 1996.

Canter, C/ Nanke, L. Emerging priorities in complementary medical research, in: Lewith, GT/ Aldridge.

Capacchione, L. *The Creative J: The Art of finding Yourself,* OH: Swallow 1979.

Capacchione, L. *The Creative J for Children: A Guide for Parents, Teachers, and Counselors*, Boston: Shambhala 1982.

Capacchione, L. *The Power of Your Other Hand: A course in Channeling the Inner wisdom of the Right Brain*, North Hollywood: Newcastle 1988.

Capra, Fritjof. *The Tao of Physics,* Boulder, CO: Shambala 1975.

Caprio, B. *The Woman Sealed in the Tower*, Mahwah, NJ: Paulist 1982.

Caprio, B/ Hedberg, T. *Coming Home: A Handbook for Exploring the Sanctuary Within*, Mahwah, NJ: Paulist 1986b (separate workbook).

Caprio, F/ Berger, J. *Helping Yourself with Self-Hypnosis*, New York: Prentice-Hall 1986a.

Carbonell, Joyce L. An experimental study of TFT and acrophobia. http://tftrx.com/expstudy.htm .

Cardini, F/ Weixin H. Moxibustion for correction of breech presentation: a randomized controlled trial, *J the American Medical Association* 1998, 280, 1590-1584.

Carey, Ken. *Starseed, the Third Millenium: Living in the Posthistoric World*, HarperSanFrancisco 1991.

Carlson, KJ et al. *Harvard Guide to Women's Health*, Cambridge, MA: Harvard University 1996.

Carlson, Richard/ Shield, Benjamin. *Healers on Healing*, London: Rider 1988.

Carlson, Rick J. (ed). *The Frontiers of Science and Medicine*, Chicago, IL: Henry Regnery 1975.

Carlsson CPO et al. Manual acupuncture reduces hyperemesis gravidarum: a placebo-controlled, randomized, single-blind, crossover study, *J Pain Symptom Management* 2000;20:273-279.

Carlton, Richard M. Rational dosages of nutrients have a prolonged effect on learning disabilities, *Alternative Therapies* 2000, 6(3), 85-91.

Caroli, G/ Pichotka, J. Weitere Untersuchungen zur Beziebung zwischen Blutgerinnung und Wetter, AMGB Series B, 1954.

Carpenter, C. The importance of touch inpatient care, *Imprint* 1981, 28(1), 42, 65-66.

Carper, Jean, *Miracle Cures*, New York: HarperCollins 1997 (herbs, vitamins, other natural remedies).

Carrington, Patricia: *Freedom in Meditation*, Garden City, NY: Anchor/ Doubleday 1978.

Carter, B. A pilot study to evaluate the effectiveness of Bowen Technique in the management of clients with frozen shoulder, *Complementary Therapies in Medicine* 2001, 9, 208-215

Carter, Mildred. *Hand Reflexology*, West Nyack, NY: Parker 1975.

Carter, Mildred/ Weber, Tammy. *Body Reflexology*, West Nyack, NY: Parker 1986.

Casdorph, H Richard. *The Miracles*, Plainfield, NJ: Logos International 1976.

Caspers, H. The cortical DC potential and its relationship with the EEG, *Clinical Neurophysiology* 1961, 13, 651.

Cass, Hyla. St. John's Wort - Nature's Blues Buster: A common sense guide to understanding and using St. John's Wort, New York: Avery 1998.

Cass, Hyla / McNally, Terrence. *Kava - Naure's Answer to Stress, Anxiety and Insomnia: Discover Nature's Ancient Remedy for Modern-Day Stress*, Prima Health 1998.

Cassar, Mario-Paul. *Massage Made Easy*, Toronto: Elan 1994.

Cassileth, Barrie R et al. Contemporary unorthodox treatments in cancer medicine: A study of patients, treatments, and practitioners, *Annals of Internal Medicine* 1984, 101, 105-112.

Cassirer, M. Bioplasmic energy: New science of the Future? *J Paraphysics* 1973, 7(1), 4-7.

Castelman, Michael. *Nature's Cures*, Emmaus, PA: Rodale 1996.

Castro, D/ Nogueira, G. Use of the nosode meningococcinum as a preventive against meningitis, *J the American Institute of Homeopathy* 1975, 68, 211-219.

Castro, M. *The Complete Book of Homeopathy*, London: St. Martins 1990.

Castronova, Jerri/ Oleson, Terri, A comparison of supportive psychotherapy and laying-on-of-hands healing for chronic back pain patients, *Alternative Medicine* 1991, 3(4), 217-226.

Caudell, Kathryn Ann, Psychoneuroimmunology and innovative behavioral intervnetions in patients with leukemia, *Oncology Nursing Forum* 1996, 23(3), 493-501.

Caudill, M et al. Decreased clinic use by chronic pain patients: response to behavioral medicine intervention, *J Chronic Pain* 1991, 7, 305-310.

Canavor, Natalie/ Wiesenfeld, Cheryl: Kirlian imagery: Photographing the glow of life, *Popular Photography* 1973 (Feb.), p 88.

554 References

Cayce, Edgar. *Auras,* Virginia Beach, VA: A.R.E. Press 1973. (Orig. 1945)

Caymaz, Gultekin, Aura visible on X-ray films and color photography, *Proceedings of Fourth International Conference on Psychotronic Research*, Sao Paolo 1979, 17-20.

Cazin, J et al. A study of the effect of decimal and centesimal dilutions of arsenic on the retention and mobilization of arsenic in the rat, *Human Toxicology* 1987, 6, 315-320.

Cedercreutz, C. Hypnotic treatment of 100 cases of migraines, In: Frankel, FH/ Zamansky, HS (eds). *Hypnosis at Its Bicentennial*, New York: Plenum 1978.

Chadwick, D/Gijensen, L. *The Detection ofMagneaic Fields Caused by Groundwater and Me Correlation of Such Fields with Water Doiesing,* Logan, Utah: Utah Water , Research Laboratory, College of Engineering, Utah State University 1982.

Chaitow, LJ. *Soft Tissue Manipulation,* Wellingborough, England: Thorsons 1988.

Chaitow, L/ Trenev, N. *Probiotics*, New York: Harper Collins 1990

Challoner, HK. *The Path of Healing,* Wheaton, IL: Quest/ Theosophical 1972.

Chamberlain, David, *The Mind of Your Newborn Baby,* Berkeley, CA: North Atlantic 1998.

Chan, Kelvin, Cheung, Lily. *Interactions Between Chinese Herbal Medicinal Products and Orthodox Drugs*, Amsterdam: Harwood Academic Publishers, 2000.

Chan, Pedro, E*ar Acupressure,* Wellingborough, England: Thorsons 1981.

Chancellor, Philip, *Handbook of the Bach Flower Remedies*, London: CW Daniel 1971.

Chang PL. Urodynamic studies in acupuncture for women with frequency, urgency and dysuria, *J Urology* 1988 140:563-566.

Chang, Edward C. *Knocking on the Gate of Life*, New York: Gill & Macmillan 2000.

Chang, Stephan Thomas. *The Complete Book of Acupuncture*, Millbrae, CA: Celestial Arts 1976.

Chapman, JB. *Dr. Scheussler's Biochemistry: A Natural Method of Healing*, Rochester, VT: Thorsons 1973.

Chapman, J. *Jing for Joy*, Newcastle 1985.

Chapman, LJ. A search for lunacy, *J Nervous and Mental Disease* 1961 132 171-174.

Chappell, Terry. A white paper on safety and choice in medicine, *Townsend Letter* 2000 (Nov), 92-97.

Chappell, LT et al. EDTA chelation treatment for vascular disease: a meta-analysis using unpublished data, *J Advancement in Medicine* 1994, 7, 131-142.

Chappell, LT et al. EDTAchelation therapy in the treatment of vascular disease, a review, *J Cardiovascular Nursing* 1996, 10(3), 78-86.

Charman, Robert A. Placing healers, healees, and healing into a wider research context, *Journal of Alternative and Complementary Medicine* 2000, 6(2), 177-180.

Chase, IK. About collaborative writing, *J Poetry Therapy* 1989, 3, 97-105.

Chasin, Esther G. *Mitzvot as Spiritual Practices: A Jewish Guidebook for the Soul*, Northvale, NJ: Jason Aronson 1997.

Cheek, DB. The ancsthetized patient can hear and can remember, *American J Proctology* 1962, 13, 287.

Cheek, David B. Sequential head and shoulder movements appearing with age regression in hypnosis to birth, *American J Clinical Hypnosis* 1974, 16(4), 262-266.

Cheek, David B. Maladjustment patterns apparently related to imprinting at birth, *American J Clinical Hypnosis* 1975, 18(2), 75-82.

Cheek, David B. Prenatal and perinatal imprints: apparent prenatal consciousness as revealed by hypnosis, *Pre- and Perinatal Psychology J* 1986, 1(2), 97-110.

Cheek, David B. Are telepathy, clairvoyance and "hearing" possible in utero? Suggestive evidence as revealed during hypnotic age-regression studies of prenatal memory, *Pre- and Perinatal Psychology J* 1992, 7(2), 125-137.

Cheek, DB. *Hypnosis: The Application of Ideomotor Techniques*, New York: Allyn & Bacon 1994.

Cheng, Man-chi'ing. *Cheng Tzu's Thirteen Treatises on T''ai Chi Ch'uan*, Berkeley: North Atlantic 1985.

Cherkin, DC/ MacCornack, FA. Patient evaluations of low back pain care from family physicians and chiropractors, *Western J Medicine* 1989 150, 351-355

Chesi, Gert. *Voodoo: Africa's Secret Power, Trans*lated from German by Ernst Klambauer) Austria: Perlinger 1980.

Chess, Stella/ Thomas, Alexander. *Temperament in Clinical Practice*, Guilford Press.

Chez, Ronald A et al. The physician and complementary and alternative medicine 1999 (in Jonas/ Levin, 31-45)

Chi, Liu Yan. *The Essential Book of Chinese Traditional Medicine, Vols. 1-2*, New York: Columbia University 1988.

Chia, Mantak. *Chi Self-Massage: The Taoist Way of Rejuvenation*, Huntington, NY: Healing Tao 1986a.

Chia, Mantak. *Iron Shirt Chi Kung*, Huntington, NY: Healing Tao 1986b.

Chien CH et al. Effect of emitted bioenergy on biochemical functions of cells, *American J Chinese Medicine* 1991, 19, 285-292

Childre, Doc/ Bruce Cryer (ed). *Freeze-Frame: Fast Action Stress Relief: A Scientifically Proven Technique,* Planetary Publications 1998.

China Qigong. Bei Dai He Qigong Hospital, China (in Chinese).

China Sports Magazine: The Wonders of Qigong: A Chinese Exercise for Fitness, Health and Longevity, Los Angeles: Wayfarer 1985.

Chinese Academy of Sciences: Exceptional human body radiation, Translated from Chinese by JF Paasche, *Psi Research* 1982, 1(2), 16-21.

Chinmoy, Sri. *Kundalini: The Mother-Power* Jamaica, NY: Agni 1974.

Chocron, Daya Sarai. *Healing with Crystals and Gemstones,* York Beach, ME: Weiser 1983.

Choedrak, Tenzin. *The Rainbow Palace*, New York: Bantam 1999.

Chopping, Keith, With kind permission for use of logo, London 1992.

Chopra, Deepak, *Quantum Healing: Exploring the Frontiers of Mind/ Body Medicine*, New York/ London: Bantam 1989.

Chopra, Deepak. *Perfect Health: The Complete Mind/ Body Guide*, New York: Harmony 1990.

Chopra, Deepak. *Perfect Health*, New York: Harmony 1991.

Chopra, Deepak, *Ageless Body, Timeless Mind*, New York: Harmony 1993.

Chordas, TJ/ Gross, SJ. Healing of memories: Psychotherapeutic ritual among Catholic Pentecostals, *J Pastoral Care* 1976, 30, 245-257.

Chou, Chu, Rehabilitation Hospital, Canada - Moniliasis treated by emitted qi and acupuncture therapy (*2nd World Conference for Academic Exchange of Medical Qigong, Beijing 1993* - from Qigong Database of Sancier).

Choudhury, Harimohon. *Indication of Miasm*, New Delhi: Jain 1988.

Choudhury, J K et al. Some novel aspects of phantom leaf effect in Kirlian photography, *J the Institution of Engineers* 1979, 60, 67-73.

Chouhan, Ramesh Singh: *Presentation at Annual Conference of the Scientific and Medical Network, Dartington 1989.*

Chouhan, RS/ Rajaram P. Electrographic images in cervical cancers, Proceedings of the 6th International Congress on Psychotronic Research, Zagreb 1986, 177-181.

Chouhan, RS/ Rajaram, P. Bioelectrography - a non invasive technique for screening and monitoring cancers: A study on carcinoma cervix, *Proceedings of the International Urogynaecological Assoication, Annuan Meeting, Ljubljana 1987.*

Chouinard, G et al. Tryptophan-nicotanimide, imipramine and their combination in depression, *Acta Psychiatrica Scandinavica* 1979, 59, 395-414.

Christensen BV et al. Acupuncture treatment of severe knee osteoarthrosis: A long-term study, *Acta Anaestbesiol Scandinavia* 1992, 36: 519-525.

Christensen, PA et al. Acupuncture and bronchial asthma, *Allergy* 1984, 39, 379-385.

Christensen PA et al. Electroacupuncture and postoperative pain, *British J Anaesthesia* 1989, 62:258-262.

Christiansen, B. *Thus Speaks the Body*, New York: Arno 1972.

Chudacek, I/ Matousek, L. Kirlian photography as a type of plasma photography, *J Photographic Science* 1987, 35, 2~25.

Church, Dawson/ Sherr, Alan: *The Heart of the Healer,* New York: Aslan 1987.

Churchill, Winston. Attributed.

Churchland, Patricia: *Neurophilosophy,* Cambridge, MA MIT 1986.

Chwirot, WB. Ultraweak photon emission and anther meiotic cycle in Larix europaea (experimental investigation of Nagl and Popp's electromagnetic model of differentiaion), *Experientia* 1988, 44, 594-599.

Clark, B. *The Quintessence Tantras of Tibetan Medicine*, Ithaca, NY: Snow Lion 1995.

Clark, Carolyn Chambers et al (eds). *Encyclopedia of Complementary Health Practice,* New York: Springer 1999.

Clark, HM/ Kaufman, ME. Effective management of people with chronic pain, *J Rehabilitation* 1987, 53(4), 51-54.

Clark, Linda. *The Ancient Art of Color Therapy*, New York: Pocket 1975.

Clarke, NE et al. The 'in vivo' dissociation of metastatic calcium: and approach to atherosclerosis, *American J Medical Science* 1955, 229, 142-149.

Classen JB/ Classen DC. Association between type I diabetes and Hib vaccine, causal relation likely, British Med J, 1999; 319:1133.

Clausure, G. De l'effet Bouvier a l'effet Kirlian, *First International Conference on Psychotronics* 1973, 2, 64-66.

Clavel, F. Helping people to stop smoking: randomised comparison of groups being treated with acupuncture and nicotine gum with control group, *British Medical J* 1985, 291:1538-1539.

Clawson, Thomas A/ Swade, Richard H. The hypnotic control of blood flaw and pain: The cure of warts and the potential for the use of hypnosis in the treatment of cancer, *American J Clinical Hypnosis* 1975, 13(3), 160-169.

Claxon, Guy (ed). Beyond Therapy: The Impact of Eastern Religions on Psychological Theory and Practice, London: Wisdom 1986.

Clay, VS. Effect of culture on mother-child tactile communication, *Family Coordinator* 1958, 37,204-210.

Clayton, PJ. The sequelae and nonsequelae of conjugal bereavement, *American J Psychiatry* 1979 1979 136 1530-1534.

Clifford, T. *Tibetan Buddhist Medicine and Psychiatry: The Diamond Healing*, York Beach: ME: Samuel Weiser 1984

Clinton, Asha Nahoma. *Martix Therapy Manual, Level I,* 215 Snowden Lane, Princeton, NJ 08540, AshaC@aol.com

Clive G Ballard, et al. Aromatherapy as a Safe and Effective Treatment for the Management of Agitation in Severe Dementia: The results of a Double-Blind, Placebo-Controlled Trial With *Melissa, J Clinical Psychiatry* 2002, 63, 553-558

Clough, Arthur Hugh. *Dipsychus* 1865.

Coakley, DV/ McKenna, GW. Safety of faith healing, *Lancet* 1986 (February 22), 1(8478), 444.

Coan, R/ Wong G/ Coan PL. The acupuncture treatment of neck pain: a randomized controlled study, *American J Clinical Medicine* 1982, 9:326-332.

Coan RM et al. The acupuncture treatment of low back pain: a randomized controlled treatment, *American J Chinese Medicine* 1980, 8:181-189.

Coates, A et al. Prognostic value of quality-of-life scores during chemotherapy for advanced breast cancer, *J Clinical Oncology* 1992, 10(12), 1833-1838.

Coates, C. Once upon a session: healing stories and the reenchantment of psychotherapy, *Common Boundary* 1990, 8, 12-16.

Cobb, LA et al. An evaluation of internal-mammary artery ligation by a double-blind technic, *New England J Medicine* 1959, 260, 1115-1118.

Cody CL et al. Nature and rates of adverse reactions associated with DTP and DT immunization in infants and children, Pediatrics, 1981; 68(5):650-660.

Coghill, Roger, Protecting ourselves from electric field insult, *Caduceus* 1989 (Summer), 22-23.

Coghill, Roger. *The Healing Energies of Light*, London: Gaia 2000a.

Coghill, Roger. *The Book of Magnet Healing*, London: Gaia 2000b.

Cogprints. http://cogprints.soton.ac.uk/documents/disk0/00/00/20/46/cog00002046-00/CompanionPlacebo.htm

Cohen, B et al. *Managing Traumatic Stress through Art: Drawing from the Center*, Lutherville, MD: Sidran 1995.

Cohen DC / Shoenfeld Y. Vaccine-induced autoimmunity, J Autoimmunity, 1996; 9:699-703.

Cohen, Kenneth S. *The Way of Qigong: The Art and Science of Chinese Energy Healing*, New York: Ballantine 1997.

Cohen, Kenneth. *Taoism: Essential Teachings of the Way and Its Power,* Boulder, CO: Sounds True 1998 (3-casette tape series including a tape on *feng shui*).

Cohen, Ken "Bear Hawk." Native American medicine, in: Jonas/ Levin 1999, p. 233-251.

Cohen, Kenneth S. *Qigong as complementary and alternative medicine*, Instruction manual, Workshop, Boulder, CO, May 2000.

Cohen, Kenneth S. *Honoring the Medicine: Native American Healing*, New York: Ballantine 2003.

Cohen, Michael. *Complementary and Alternative Medicine: Legal Boundaries and Regulatory Perspectives*, Baltimore, MD: Johns Hopkins University 1998.

Cohen, N et al. Pavlovian conditioning of the immune system, *International Archives of Allergy & Immunology* 1994, 105, 101-106.

Colbin, Annemarie, *Food and Healing,* New York: Ballantine/ Random House 1987.

Colborn, Theo et al. *Our Stolen Future: Are we Threatening Our fertility, Intelligence, and Survival? – A Scientific Detective Story*, New York: Penguin 1997.

Cole, Karlie. Where have all the flowers gone? http://www.floweressencemagazine.com/may03/peaceflower.html

Coleman, Vernon, *Betrayal of Trust*, Barnstaple, UK: European Medical J 1996.

Coles, R. *The Call of Stories*, Boston: Houghton Mifflin 1989.

Collinge, William. *The American Holistic Health Association Complete Guide to Alternative Medicine*, New York: Warner 1996.

Collinge, William. *Subtle Energy: Awakening to the Unseen Forces in Our Lives*, New York: Warner 1998.

Collings, J. *Beat Heart Disease without Surgery*, HarperSanFrancisco 1995.

Collins, AJ et al. Some observations on the pharmacology of 'deep-heat', a topical rubefacient, *Annals of Rheumatic Disease* 1984, 43(3), 411-415.

Collison, D. Hypnotherapy in the management of asthma, *American J Clinical Hypnosis* 1968, 11(1), 6-11.

Collison, DR. Hypnotherapy in the management of asthma, *American J Clinical Hypnosis* 1968, 11(1), 6-11.

Collison, D. Which asthmatic patients should be treated by hypnotherapy, *Medical J Australia* 1975, 1, 776-781.

Colton, James/ Colton, Sheelagh. *Iridology: A Patient's Guide*, Wellingborough, England: Thorsons 1988.

Combs, G/ Freedman, J. *Symbol, Story, and Ceremony: Using Metaphor in Individual and Family Therapy*, New York: WW Norton 1990.

Complete German Commission E Monographs: Therapeutic Guide to Herbal Medicines, Austin, TX: American Botani-cal Council, 1998

Comunetti, AM. Systematic experiments to establish the spatial distribution of physiologically effective stimuli of unidentified nature, *Experientia* 1978, 34, 889-893.

Comunetti, AM. Experimental investigation of the perceptibility of the artificial source for the dowsing agent, Progress report, *Experientia* 1979, 35, 420-423.

Connolly, Cyril. *The Unquiet Grave*, New York: Harper Collins 1944.

Connor, Danny. *Qigong: Chinese Movement & Meditation for Health,* London: Stanley Paul 1992.

Consumer Reports, May 2000 46,000 subscribers surveyed re CAM use. More success was noted when treatments were used under therapist supervision than when self- prescribed. continued in no. 22, 11-13.

Conway, Kathlyn. *Ordinary Life: A Memoir of Illness,* New York: WH Freeman 1997.

Cooke, DJ/ Coles, EM. The concept of lunacy: a review, *Psychological Reports* 1978, 42, 891-897.

Coon, Nelson. *Using Plants for Healing,* Emmaus, PA: Rodale 1963; 1979.

Coons, PM. Multiple personality: Diagnostic considerations, *J Clinical Psychiatry* 1980, 41(10), 330-336.

Cooper, Joan, *The Ancient Teaching of Yoga and the Spiritual Evolution of Man,* London: Research 1979.

Cooper, M/ Aygen, M. Effect of meditation on blood cholesterol and blood pressure, *J the Israel Medical Association* 1978, 95 1-2.

Cooperstein, Allan, *The Myths of Healing: A Desciptive Analysis of Transpersonal Healing,* Doctoral dissertation, Saybrook Institute, California 1990.

Corliss, William R. *The Unfathomed Mind: A Handbook of Unusual Mental Phenomena,* Glen Arm, MD: The Sourcebook Project 1982.

Corrigan, Janet, et al (eds). *To Err is Human: Building a Safer Health System,* Washington, DC: National Academy Press 2000.

Corsi, S. Report on a trial of bilberry anthocyanosides (Tegens-inverni della beffa) in the medical treatment of venous insufficiency of the lower limbs, Casa di Cura S. Chiara, Florence, Italy 1987.

Cortright, Brant, Psychotherapy and Spirit; Theory and Practice in *Transpersonal Psychotherapy*, State University of New York Press 1997.

Coué, Emile. *Self Mastery Through Conscious Autosuggestion,* London: Allen & Unwin 1922. ('Every day in every way I am getting better and better.')

Coulter, Catherine R. *Portraits of Homeopathic Medicines: Psychophysical Analyses of Selected Constitutional Types,* Berkeley, CA: North Atlantic 1998.

Coulter, Harris L: *Homeopathic Medicine,* St. Louis, MO: Forman 1972.

Coulter, Harris L. *Divided Legacy: A History of the Schism in Medical Thought,* Vols. 1-4. Washington, DC Wehawken 1973.

Coulter, Harris L. *Homeopathic Science and Modern Medicine,* Richmond, CA: North Atlantic 1981.

Coulter, Harris L/ Fisher, Barbara Loe. A Shot in the Dark, Garden City Park, New York: Avery 1991, 47.

Courtenay, Anthea, Healing and the Whole Man, *The Unexplained* 1980, 1(11), 206-209.

Cousens, Gabriel, *Spiritual Nutrition and the Rainbow Diet,* Boulder, CO: Cassandra 1986.

Cousins, Norman. *Anatomy of an Illness,* New York: Bantam 1981, (Also in: *New England J Medicine* 1976, 295, 1457-1462).

Cousins, Norman. *Head First: The Biology of Hope,* New York: Thorndike 1991.

Covalcski, J/ Goch, L. Malpractice insureres target alternatives, *Best's Review, P/C* (Apr) 1997, 61-63.

Cowan, David/ Guirdlestone, Rodney. *Safe as Houses,* Bath: Gateway 1996.

Cowan, David/ Silk, Anne. *Ancient Energies of the Earth,* London: Thorsons 1999.

Cowmeadow, O. *The Art of Shiatsu,* Shaftesbury, England: Element 1993.

Coxhead, CE et al. Multicentre trial of physiotherapists in the management of sciatic symptoms, *Lancet* 1981, i, 1065-1068.

Coxhead, Nona: *The Relevance of Bliss,* New York: St. Martin's 1986.

Crabtree, Adam. *Multiple Man: Exploration in Possession and Multiple Personality,* New York/ London: Holt, Rinehart & Winston 1985,

Crabtree, Adam. *Animal Magnetism, Early Hypnotism and Psychical Research 1766-1925,* Kraus 1988 (exceptional annotated bibliography).

Craig, Gary/ Fowlie, Adrienne, *Emotional Freedom Techniques: The Manual* (2nd ed), Gary H Craig, PO Box 398, The Sea Ranch, CA 95497, (707) 785-2848 Web site: http:/ / www.emofree.com 1997.

Craig, TKJ/ Brown, GW. Life events: Meaning and physical illness, In: Steptoe, A/ Mathews, A (eds), *Health Care and Human Behaviour* New York: Academic 1984, 7-3 9. (From Ramirez et al)

Cramer, Marc, The rise and fall of the rope trick, *The Unexplained* 1981, 5(56), 1101-1105.

Cranton, Elmer M. A textbook on EDTA Chelation Therapy, *J for Advancement in Medicine* 1989, 2(1/ 2).

Crawford, HJ et al. Transient experiences following hypnotic testing and special termination procedures, *International J Clinical and Experimental Hypnosis* 1982, 30, 117-126.

Criconia, L et al. Results of treatment with S-adenosyl-L-methionine in patients with major depression and internal illnesses, *Current Therapeutic Research* 1994, 55, 666-674.

Crook, William G. *Detecting Your Hidden Allergies*, Jackson, TN: Professional Books/ Future Healt 1988.

Crook, William G. *Help for the Hyperactive Child*, Jackson, TN: Professional 1991.

Crookall, Robert. *Psychic Breathing: Cosmic Vitality from the Air* Wellingborough, England: Aquarian 1979.

Cuddon, Eric. *Paper presented to* British Society of Dowsers, 1963 (28 March).

Cuddon, Eric. The relief of pain by laying-on-of-hands *International J Parapsychology* 1968, 10(1), 85-92. (Also in: Angoff, A (ed): *The Psychic Force,* New York: Putnam's 1970)

Culpepper, Nicholas. *Culpepper's Herbal Remedies*, North Hollywood, CA: Wilshire 1997).

Cummings, NA/ Bragman, JJ. Triaging the 'somatizer' out of the medical system into the psychological system, in Stern, EM/ Stern, VF (eds). *Psychotherapy and the Somatizing Patient*, New York: Hayward 1988 109-112.

Cummings, Stephen/ Ullman, Dana. *Everybody's Guide to Homeopathic Medicines*, Los Angeles, CA: Tarcher 1984.

Cunningham, AJ. The influence of mind on cancer, *Canadian Psychology* 1985, 26, 13-29.

Cunningham, AJ. Information and health in the many levels of man: toward a more comprehensive theory of health and disease, *Advances* 1986, 3(1), 32-45.

Cunningham, AJ. Bringing the mind into medicine, *Today's Life Science* 1991 (Nov), 8-13.

Cunningham, AJ et al. A randomized controlled trial of the effects of group psychological therapy on survival in women with metastatic breast cancer, *Psycho-oncology* 1998, 7, 508-517.

Cunningham, Donna. *Flower Remedies Handbook: Emotional Healing & Growth with Bach & Other Flower Essences*, New York: Sterling 1991.

Currie, R. Lunar tides and the wealth of nations, *New Scientist* 1988 (5 November), 52-55. (From Smith/ Best)

Curry, P. Research on the Mars effect, *Zetetic Scholar* 1982, Spring.

Cusack, Odean. *Pets and Mental Health*, New York/ London: Haworth 1988.

Cushman, A. Once upon a time. . . *Yoga J* 1993, 53-59; 100-101.

Cuzick JR, Holland V, Barth R et al. 1998 Electropotential measurements as a new diagnostic modality for breast cancer, *Lancet* 352:359-363.

Cyriax, J. *Textbook of Orthopaedic Medicine: Volume I. Diagnosis of Soft Tissue Lesions,* 8th ed, London: Balliere Tindall 1982a.

Cyriax, J. *Textbook of Orthopaedic Medicine: Volume II. Treatment by Manipulation, Massage and Injection* 10th ed, London: Bailliere Tindall 1982b.

Cytowic, RE. *Synesthesia: A Union of the Senses,* New York: Springer- Verlag 1989.

Czubalski, K et al. Acupuncture and phonostimulation in poillenosis and vasomotor rhinitis in the light of psychosomatic investigations, *Acta Otolaryngology (Stockholm)* 1977, 84, 446-449.

D

Dacher, Elliott S. *PNI: The New Mind/ Body Healing Program*, New York: Paragon House 1993.

Dadd, Debra Lynn. *The Nontoxic Home: Protecting Yourself and Your Family from Everyday Toxics and Health Hazards*, Los Angeles: Tarcher 1986.

Dakin, HS. *High Voltage Photography,* San Francisco: HS Dakin 1974.

Dale, LA et al. Dowsing: a field experiment in water divining, *J the American Society for Psychical Research* 1951,45, 3-16. (From Hansen)

Daneel, ML. *Zionism and Faith Healing in Rhodesia,* Translated from Dutch by AV February, The Hague, Netherlands: Mouton 1970.

Danskin, David G/ Crow, Mark. *Biofeedback; An Introduction and Guide*, Palo ,Alto, CA: Mayfield 1981.

Darendeliler MA et al. Effects of static magnetic and pulsed electromagnetic fields on bone healing, *Int J Adult Orthodon Orthogn Surg.* 1997, 12(1), 43-53

Darras, Jean-Claude/ de Vernejoul, P. Summary from World Research Foundation: Los Angeles, undated. (Very brief)

Darzynkiewkz, A et al. Chinese herbal mixture PC SPES in treatment of prostate cancer (Review) *International J Oncology* 2000, 17, 729-736.

Dash, Vaidya Bhagavan. *Fundamentals of Ayurvedic Medicine*, New Delhi: Bansal 1982.

Dash, Vaidya Bhagavan/ Junius, Acarya M. *A Handbook of Ayurveda*, New Delhi: Concept 1983.

Dass, Ram. *Journey of Awakening: A Mediator's Guidebook*, New York: Bantam 1978.

Dass, Ram. in Elliott 1996, 61-75.

Dass, Ram/ Bush, Mirabai. *Compassion in Action*, London: Rider/ Random House 1992, p106

Dass, Ram/ Gorman, Paul: *How Can I Help? Stories and Reflections on Service,* New York: Knopf/ London: Rider 1985.

Daut, RL et al, Development of the Wisconsin Brief Pain Questionnaire to assess pain in cancer and other diseases, *Pain* 1983, 17, 197-210.

Davenas, E et al. Effect on mouse peritoneal macrophages of orally administered very high dilutions of silica, *European J Pharmacology* 1987 135, 313-319.

Davenas, E et al. Human basophil degranulation triggered by very dilute antiserum against IgE, *Nature* 1988,333, 816-818.

David-Neel, Alexandra. *Magic and Mystery in Tibet,* New York: Viking/ Penguin 1956.

Davidson, John, *The Web of Life: The Energetic Constitution of Man and the Neum-Endocrine Connection*, Safron Walden, England: CW Daniel 1988.

Davidson, Victor S. *Irisdiagnosis: Diagnosis from the Eyes*, Wellingborough, England: Thorsons 1979.

Davis, Albert/ Rawls, Walter, *Magnetism and Its Effects on Living Systems*, Kansas City, MO: Acres USA 1993.

Davis, GC. Measurement of the chronic pain experience: Development of an instrument, *Research in Nursing & Health* 1989 12, 221-227.

Davis, Leroy D et al. Bibliography of the biological effects of magnetic fields, *Federated Proceedings* 1962 (September-October), Suppl. 12. (393 entries, categorized)

Davis, Mikol/ Lane, Earle, *Rainbows of Life: The Promise of Kirlian Photography,* New York: Harper Colophon/ Harper & Row 1978.

Davis, Patricia. *An A-Z of Aromatherapy,* Safron Walden, England: CW Daniel 1999.

Day, Chet. Why I Now Say No to Distilled Water Only, http://www.mercola.com/article/Diet/water/distilled_water_2.htm

Day, Jennifer. *Creative Visualization with Children*, Shaftesbury, England: Element 1994.

Day, Langston/ de la Warr, George. *New Worlds Beyond the Atom,* London: Vincent Stuart 1958.

Day, N et al. Exposure to power frequency

magnetic fields and the risk of childhood cancer, *Lancet* 1999, 354, 1925-1931.

Dees, SC/ Lefkowitz, D, III. Secretory otitis media in allergic children, *American J Diseases of Children* 1972, 124(3), 364-368.

de France, Le Vicomte Henry. Translated by Bell, AH, *The Elements of Dowsing,* London: G. Bell 1948.

de la Pena, August: *The Psychobiology of Cancer,* New York: Praeger 1983.

De La Taille, A et al. Herbal therapy PC-SPES: in vitro effects and evaluation of its efficacy in 69 patients with prostate cancer, *J Urology* 2000, 164, 1229-1234.

de Langre, Jacques. *Do-In 2: The Ancient Art of Rejuvenation Through Self-Massage,* Magalia, CA: Happiness Press 1981.

de Saussure, Raymond. The magnetic cure, *British J Medical Psychology 1969, 42(2),* 141-163.

de Vernejoul, P et al. Approche isotopique de la visualisation des méridiens d'acupuncture, *Agressologie* 1984,25(10), 1107-1111.

de Vernejoul, Pierre, et al. Étude des méridiens d'acupuncture par les traceurs radioactifs, *Bull. Acad. Natle. Med.* 1985, 169, 1071-1075. (From Gerber)

Deabler, Herdis L et al. The use of relaxation and hypnosis in lowering high blood pressure, *American J Clinical Hypnosis* 1973, 16(2), 75-83.

Dean, Douglas. High voltage photography applied to psychic healing, *Dimensions of Healing, Symposium of The Academy of Parapsychology and Medicine at Los Altos, CA 1972,* 102-109.

Dean, Douglas. An examination of infrared and ultra-violet techniques for changes in water following the laying-on of hands, *(dissertation), Saybrook Institute, CA* 1983.

Dean, Douglas. Personal communication 1987.

Dean, Douglas. *Presentation at Scientific and Medical Network Annual Meeting,* Dartington 1989 (July).

Dean, Douglas/ Brame, E, Physical Changes in Water by Laying-on-of-Hands,

Proceed-ings of the Second International Conference on Psychotronic Research, Monaco 1975, 200-201.

DeFeudis, FV. *Ginkgo Biloba Extract (Egb761): Pharmacological Activities and Clincal Aplications,* New York: Elsevier 1991.

DeFeudis, FV. *Ginkgo Biloba Extract (Egb761): From Chemistry to the Clinic,* Wiesbaden: Ullstein Medical 1998.

Del Guidice, E. Coherence in condensed and living matter, *Frontier Perspectives* 1993, 3, 16-20.

Deliman, Tracy/ Smolowe, John: *Health: Holistic Medicine, Harmony of Body, Mind, Spirit,* Reston, VA: Reston 1982.

Delle, et al. Presentation at 6th World Congress of Biological Psychiatry, Nice, France, June 1997, Abstract 90-56.

Delta Society, *Interactions,*

www.deltasociety.org

Deluze C et al. Electroacupuncture in fibromyalgia: results of a controlled trial, *British Medical J* 1992, 305:1249-1252.

DeMaria, M. Poetry and the abused child: the forest and the tinted plexiglass, *J Poetry Therapy* 1991, 5, 79-93.

DeMeo, James. *Orgone Accumulator Hand-book,* Ashland, OR: Natural Energy Works 1989. DeMeo, James.

Dennett, Daniel. *Consciousness Explained,* (Boston: Little Brown & Co. 1991.

Dennis, Ronald J. Functional Reach Improvement in Normal Older Women After Alexander Technique Instruction, *Journal of Gerontology:Medical Sciences* 1999, 54A(1).

Dennison, P/ Dennison, G. *Edu-K for Kids,* Glendale, CA: Edu-Kinesthetics 1987.

Dennison, PE/ Dennison, G. *Brain Gym Handbook,* Ventura, CA: Educational Kinesiology Foundation 1989.

Dennison, P/ Dennison, GE. *Brain Gym: Teachers Edition, Revised,* Ventura, CA: Edu-Kinesthetics 1994.

Denoliet, J et al. Personality as independent predictor of long-term mortality in patients with coronary heart disease, *Lancet* 1996, Feb 17, 347.

Denslow, JS et al. Quantitative studies of chronic facilitation in human motoneuron pools, *American J Physiology* 1947 150, 229-238.

DeRosa, C/ Porterfield, J. A physical therapy model for the treatment of low back pain, *Physical Therapy* 1992, 72, 261-272.

DeSmet Peter, AGM. *The Safety of Herbal Products* 1999a (from Jonas/ Levin p.108-147).

DeSmet Peter, AGM et al. *Adverse Effects of Herbal Drugs*, Berlin: Springer-Verlag 1997.

DeSmet Peter, AGM et al. *The Safety of Nonherbal Complementary Products*, 1999b (from Jonas/ Levin p.148-166).

Desoille, Robert. *The Directed Daydream,* New York: Psychosynthesis Research Foundation 1966., Translated from French original *Réveil Dirigé)*

Dethlefsen, Thorwald/ Dahlke, Rudiger: *The Healing Power of Illness: The Meaning of Symptoms and How to Interpret Them,* Longmead, UK: Element 1990. (Orig. German 1983, translation Peter Lerresurier)

DeVanna, M/ Rigamonti, R. Oral S-adenosyl methionine in depression, *Current Therapeutic Research* 1992, 52, 478-485.

Devereaux, P/ Forrest, R. Straight lines on an ancient landscape, *New Scientist* 1982 (23 December).

Devyatkov, ND et al. Digest of papers, *International Symposium on Millimeter Waves of Non-Thermal Intensity in Medicine*, Cosponsored by Research and Development Association 'ISTOK' and Research Institute of USSR Ministry of Electronic Industry ('ORION'), Moscow, October 3-6 (Russian; from Workshop on Alternative Medicine).

Dewe, BAJ/ Dewe, JR. *Professional Kinesiology Practice, Volumes I, II, II, IV,* Auckland, NZ: Professional Health Publications International 1990, 1990, 1991, 1992.

Dewhurst-Maddock, Olivea, *The Book of Sound Therapy: Heal Yourself with Music and Voice*, London: Gaia 1993.

Dicarlo, Russell E. *Towards a New World View: Conversations at the Leading Edge,* Erie, PA: Epic 1996.

Di Fabio, RP. Efficacy of manual therapy, *Physical Therapy* 1992, 72(12), 853-864.

Diagram Group (The). *The Brain: A User's Manual,* New York: Perigee/ Putnam 1981.

Diamond, GA/ Denton, TA. Alternative perspectives on the biased foundations of medical technology assessment, *Annals of Internal Medicine.*

Diamond, John. *Behavioral Kinesiology and the Automatic Nervous System*, Valley Cottage: Archaeus 1978.

Diamond, John. BK, Behavioral Kinesiology: How to Activate Your Thymus and Increase Your Life Energy: New York: Harper & Row 1979.

Diamond, John. *Life Energy Using the Meridians to Unlock the Hidden Power of Your Emotions,* New York: Paragon House 1985.

Diamond, John. *Your Body Doesn't Lie,* New York: Warner 1996.

Dibble, WE Jr/ Tiller, WA. Electronic device-mediated pH changes in water, *J Scientific Explorations* 1999, 13, 155.

Dickeman, A. *Following Your Path: Using Myths, Symbols, and Images to Explore Your Inner Life*, new York: Tarcher/ Putnam 1992.

Dickens W/ Lewith GT. (1989) A single-blind, controlled and randomised clinical trial to evaluate the effect of acupuncture in the treatment of trapezio-metacarpal osteo-arthritis, *Compl Med Re,@* 3: 5-8.

Diegh, Khigh Alex. Acupuncture: Origins, theory, history and evolution in practice, Quote from *Conference on Psychic- and Self-Healing (sponsored by the Association for Humanistic Psychology), San Francisco, 1972* (May).

Dienstfrey, Harris. *Where the Mind Meets the Body*, New York: HarperPerennial 1991.

Diepold, John H Jr. Touch and Breathe (TAB): an alternative treatment approach with meridian based psychotherapies, *Paper presented at Innovative and Integrative Approaches to Psychotherapy Conference, Edison, NJ, November 1998.*

Dietz, PA. (Stigmatization produced by Paul Diebel,) *Tidschrift voor Parapsychologie.* 1930/ 31, 3, 145-155 (Dutch). (Abstract in *Parapsychology Abstracts International* 1985, 3(2), No. 01378)

DiGiovanna, E/ Schiowitz, S. *An Osteopathic Approach to Diagnosis and Treatment,* Philadelphia, PA: JB Lippincott 1991.

Dijk, DJ et al. Light treatment for sleep disorders: consensus report II. Basic properties of circadian physiology and sleep regulation, *J Biological Rhythms* 1995 10 113.

Dilbeck, MC/ Banus, CB/ Polanzi, C/ Landrith, GS. Test of a field model of consciousness and social change: the Transcendental Meditation and TM-Sidhi program and decreased urban crime, *Journal of Mind Behaviour* 1988, 9(4), 457-486.

Dillon, K. Positive emotional states and enhancement of the immune system, *International J Psychiatry in Medicine* 1985, 15, 1.

Dincin, Dian, *Herbal Medicine: The Natural Way to Get Well and Stay Well,* New York: Gramercy 1979.

Dingwall, Eric J. The end of a legend: A note on the magical flight, *Parapsychology Review* 1974, *5(2),* 1-3.

Dinshah, D. L*et There Be Light,* Malaga, NJ: Dinshah Health Society 1985.

Dion, S. *Write Now: Maintaining a Creative Spirit While Homeboudn and Ill,* Troy, ME: Nightshade 1993.

Dirksen, Murl Owen. Pentecostal Healing: A Facet of the Personalistic Health System in Pakal-Na, a Village in Southern Mexico, *Unpublished doctoral dissertation,* University of TN 1984.

Ditlow, Florence. Humor as a form of creativity, *J Holistic Nursing* 1993, 11(1), 66-79.

Dixon, Michael, Does "healing" benefit patients with chronic symptoms? A quasi-randomized trial in general practice, J. *of the Royal Society of Medicine* 1998, 91, 183-188.

Dobbs, Horace. *Dolphin Healing,* London: Piatkus 2000.

Dobkin de Rios, Marlene: *Hallucinogens: Cross-Cultural Perspectives,* Albuquerque, NM: University of New Mexico 1984a.

Dobkin de Rios, M. The vidente phenomenon in Third World traditional healing: An Amazonian example, *Medical Anthropology* (Winter) 1984b, 60-70.

Dodd, Debra Lynn. *The Nontoxic Home: Protecting Yourself and Your Family from Everyday Toxics and Health Hazards,* Los Angeles, Tarcher 1986.

Dohrenwend, BS/ Dohrenwend, BP. Life stress and illness, In: Dohrenwend/ Dohrenwend (eds): *Stressful Life Events and Their Contexts,* New York: Prodist 1981, 1-27. (Prom CG Ellison 1994)

Don, Norman S/ Moura, Gilda. Trance surgery in Brazil, *Alternative Therapies* 2000, 6(4), 39-48.

Donahoe, James J. *Enigma: Psychology, the Paranormal and Self- Transformation,* Oakland, CA: Bench Press 1979.

Donden, Yeshe. *Health Through Balance: Introduction to Tibetan Medicine,* (J Hopkins, Translator/ Eli) London: Wisdom 1986.

Dong, Paul. *The Four Major Mysteries of Mainland China,* Englewood Cliffs, NJ: Prentice Hall 1984.

Dong, Paul. Summary Report on Qigong Investigation in Mainland China, *Psi Research* 1985, 4(3/ 4), 133-134.

Donovan, P. Bowel toxemia, permeability and disease: New information in support of an old concept, in : Pizzorno, E/ Murray, MT. 1989.

Doran, DM/ Newell, DJ. Manipulation in treatment of low back pain: A multicentre study, *British Medical J* 1975, ii, 161-164.

Dossey, Barbara (ed). *The American Holistic Nurses Association core curriculum for holistic nursing,* Gaithersburn, MD: Aspen 1997.

Dossey, Barbara et al. *Holistic Nursing: A Handbook for Practice,* Gaithersburg, MD: Aspen 1995.

Dossey, Larry. *Space, Time and Medicine,* Boulder, CO: Shambala 1982.

Dossey, Larry. *Beyond Illness: Discovering the Experience of Health,* Boulder/ London: Shambala 1984.

Dossey, Larry. Deliberately caused bodily damage, *Alternative Therapies* 1988, (5), 11-16; 103-111.

Dossey, Larry. *Recovering the Soul: A Scientific and Spiritual Search*, New York/ London: Bantam 1989.

Dossey, Larry. *Meaning and Medicine: Lessons from a Doctor's Tales of Breakthrough and Healing,* New York/ London: Bantam 1991.

Dossey, Larry. *Healing Words: The Power of Prayer and the Practice of Medicine*, New York: HarperSanFrancisco 1993.

Dossey, Larry. Cancelled funerals: a look at miracle cures, *Alternative Therapies* 1998a, 4(2), 10-18; 116-120 (34 refs).

Dossey, Larry. The right man syndrome: skepticism and alternative medicine, *Alternative Therapies* 1998b, 4(3), 12-19; 108-114 (91 refs).

Dossey, Larry. "You people": intolerance and alternative medicine, *Alternative Therapies* 1999, 5(2), 12-17; 109-112.

Dossey, Larry. Hypnosis: a window into the soul of healing, *Alternative Therapies* 2000, 6(2), 12-17; 102-111.

Dossey, Larry, Maggots and leeches: when science and aesthetics collide, *Alternative Therapies* 2002a, 8(4), 12-16; 106-107

Dossey, Larry. The uncertainties of medicine: a cause for celebration, *Alternative Therapies,* Oct 2002b, 8(5), 32-34

Dougans, I. *Reflexology: Foot Massage for Total Health*, Shaftesbury, England: Element 1997.

Douglas, Herbert. A further look at dowsing and arthritis, *American Dowser* 1974 (February), 14(1), 37-40 (continued in: *American Dowser* 1974, 14(2)).

Dove, Cohn I. The origin and development of cranio-sacral osteopathy, *Holistic Medicine* 1988, 3, 35-45.

Dowling, St. John. Lourdes cures and their medical assessment, *J the Royal Society of Medicine* 1984, 77, 634-638.

Downer, J. *Supersense,* London: BBC Pubs 1988.

Downer, SM et al. Pursuit and practice of complementary therapies by cancer pa-tients receiving conventional treatments, *British Medical J* 1994, 309, 86-89

Downing, George. *The Massage Book*, New York: Random House 1972; 1988.

Dowrick, Stephanie. *Forgiveness & Other Acts of Love*, New York: Viking 1997.

Drabaek, H et al. A botanical compound, Padma 28, increases walking distance in stable intermittent claudication, *Angiology* 1993, 44, 863-867.

Dreaper, it. Recalcitrant warts of the hand cured by hypnosis, *Practitioner* 1978, 220(1316), 305-310.

Dreher, Henry. *The Immune Power Personality: 7 Traits You Can Develop to Stay Healthy*, New York: Plume/ Penguin 1995.

Dreisch, H. *Science and Philosophy of Organisms*, London: Black 1908.

Dressler, David. Light-touch manipulative technique, *J Alternative and Complementary Medicine* 1990 (April), 19-20.

D'Souza, AL et al. Probiotics in prevention of antibiotic associated diarrhoea: meta-analysis, *British Medical J.* 2002; 324 (7350), 1361-1364.

Duane, TD/ Behrendt, T. Extrasensory electroencephalographic induction between identical twins, *Science* 1965, 150-367.

Dubin, Louis L/ Shapiro, Sandor S. Use of hypnosis to facilitate dental extraction and homeostasis in a classic hemophiliac with a high antibody titer to Factor VIII, *American J Clinical Hypnosis* 1974, 17(2), 79-43.

Dubrov, AP. Biogravitation and psychotronics, *Impact of Science on Society* 1974, 24, 311-319.

Dubrov, Aleksander P. T*he Geomagnetic Field and Life: Geomagnetobiology*, New York: Plenum 1978.

Dubrov, AP. A new resonance-field interaction in biology, Translated by Vilenskaya, Larissa. *Psi Research* 1982, 1(2), 32-45.

Duff, Kat. *The Alchemy of Illness,* New York: Pantheon 1993.

Duggan, Robert. Does Russek and Schwartz's language serve future generations? (Response to article by Russek/

Schwartz 1996), *Advances* 1996 12(4), 28-31.

Duggan, Sandra. *Edgar Cayce's Guide to Colon Care*, Virginia Beach, VA: Inner Vision 1995.

Duke, JA. Promising phytomedicinals, *J Naturopathic Medicine* 1991, 2, 58-52.

Dumitrescu, Ion Florin. An electronographic study of psychic states obtained by yoga, *J Holistic Health* 1978, 3, 57-59.

Dumitrescu, Ion/ Kenyon, Julian N (ed). *Electronographic Imaging in Medicine and Biology,* Translated by C.A. Galia from Romanian, London: Neville Spearman 1983.

Dumoff, Alan. New codes for CAM: HHS review could make them a reality, *Alternative Therapies* 2002, 8(4), 32-36.

Dundee, JW. Effect of stimulation of the P6 antiemetic point on postoperative nausea and vomiting, *British J Anaesthiology* 1989, 63:612-618.

Dunn, C et al. Sensing an improvement: an experimental study to evaluate the use of aromatherapy, massage and periods of rest in an intensive care unit, *J Advanced Nursing* 1995, 21, 34-40.

Dunn, Joseph (ed). *Humor and Health Letter,* PO Box 16814, Jackson, MS 39236.

Dunn, Tedi/ Williams, Marian. *Massage Therapy Guidelines for Hospital & Home Care: A Resource for Bodyworkers, Healthcare Administrators and Massage Educators*, Information for People, Inc, PO Box 1876, Olympia, WA 98507-1876 (800) 754-9790 www.info4people.com info@info4people.com 5 p. Refs *Excellent resource*

Duplessis, Yvonne. *The Paranormal Perception of Colon, Trans*lated from French by Paul von Toal) New York: Parapsychology Foundation 1975.

Duplessis, Yvonne. Dermo-optical sensitivity and perception: its influence on human behavior, *International J Biosocial Research* 1985, 7(2), 76-93.

Durant, J et al. Efficacy and Safety of Buxus Sempervirens L. Preparations (SPV-30) in HIV-infected Asymptomatic Patients: A Multicenter, Randomized, Double-Blind, Placebo-Controlled Trial, *Phytomedicine; International Journal of Phytotherapy and Phytopharmacology* 1998, 5(1), 1-10.

Durlacher, James V. *Freedom From Fear Forever,* Arizona: Vaness 1995.

Dychtwald, Ken. *Bodymind,* New York: Pantheon Books 1977.

Dyer, M. Poetry and children of alcoholics: Breaking the silence, *J Poetry and Bibliotherapy* 5, 143-151.

Dykeman, Arthur J. Experimental meditation, in: Tart, Charles T (ed). *Altered Stares of Consciousness,* New York: Wiley 1969.

E

Eagle, CT Jr. Music Therapy Index, Vol. 1. Lawrence, KS: National Association for Music Therapy 1976

Eagle, CT Jr. *Music Psychology Index*, Vol. 2. Denton, TX: Institute for Therapeutics Research 1978.

Eagle, CT Jr/ JJ Minter. *Music Psychology Index*, Vol. 3, Phoenix, AZ: Orynx Press 1984.

Eames, TH. Restrictions of the visual field as handicaps to learning, *J Educational Research* 1936, 19, 460-463.

Eames, TH. The relationship of the central visual field to the speed of visual perception, *American J Ophthalmology* 1957, 43, 279-280.

Early, Loretta F/ Lifschutz, Joseph E. A case of stigmata, *Archives of General Psychiatry* 1974, 30, 197-202.

Eastman, CI et al. Light treatment for sleep disorders: consensus report VI. Shift work, *J Biological Rhythms* 1995 10 157.

Eastwood, NB. Some observations on dowsing and the human magnetic sense, *Lancet* 1987 (Sep 19), 676-677.

Eaton, Evelyn, *I Send a Voice*, London and Wheaton, IL:Quest/Theosophical 1978.

Ebell, MH/ Beck, E. How effective are complementary/alternative medicine (CAM) therapies for fibromyalgia? *J Fam Pract.* 2001, 50(5),400-1.

Eble, JN. Patterns of response of musculature to visceral stimuli, *American J Physiology* 1960 198, 429-433.

Eccles, Sir John/ Robinson, Daniel N. *The Wonder of Being Human: Our Brain and Our Mind,* Boston/ London: New Science Library/ Shambala 1985.

Eddy, DM. should we change the rules for evaluating medical technologies? In: Gelijns, Anette C (ed), *Modern Methods of Clinical Investigation*, National Academy of Science Press 1990.

EC/IC Bypass Study Group. Failure of extracranial-intracranial arterial bypass to reduce the risk of ischemic stroke: Results of an international randomized trial, *New England J Medicinei* 1985, 313(19), 1191-1200.

Edelman, S et al. Effects of group CBT on the survival time of patients with metastatic breast cancer, *Psychooncology* 1999, 8, 474-481.

Edge, Hoyt, The Effect of Laying on of Hands on an Enzyme: An Attempted Replication, In:, *Research in Para-psychology 1979*, Metuchen, NJ: Scarecrow 1980, 137-139.

Edlin, Gordon/ Golanty, Eric. *Health and Wellness,* Boston: Science Books International 982.

Edmunds, Simeon. *Hypnotism and Psychic Phenomena,* North Hollywood, CA: Hal Leighton 1961.

Edwards, Harry, *Thirty Years a Spiritual Healer,* London: Herbert Jenkins 1968.

Edwards, Nigel et al. Unhappy doctors: what are the causes and what can be done? *British Medical J* 2002, 324, 835-838

Edwards, WG. The neutralization of earth rays, *J the British Society of Dowsers* 1964, 28 200-204.

Edwin, DM. Hypnosis in burn therapy, In: Burrows, DR at al. *Hypnosis* 1979, Amsterdam: Elsevier/ North Holland Biomedical 1979.

Eeman, LE. *Co-Operative Healing: The Curative Properties of Human Radiations,* London: Frederick Muller 1947.

Egger, J et al. Controlled trial of hyposensitization in children with food-induced hyperkinetic syndrome, *Lancet* 1992, 339(8802), 1150-1153.

Ehrenwald, Jan. Psi phenomena in search of a neural foothold, *American Society for Psychical Research, Newsletter* 1976, 2, 13-14.

Ehrlich, D/ Haber, P. Influence of acupuncture on physical performance capacity and haemodynamic parameters, *International J Sports Medicine* 1992 13:486-49 1.

Einstein, Albert. Attributed.

Einstein, Albert. *Out of My Later Years,* Rev, reprint ed, Secaucus, NJ: Citadel 1956.

Eisele, JW/ Resy, DT. Deaths related to coffee enemas, *J American Medical Association* 1980, 244, 1608-1609.

Eisenberg, David. *Encounters with Qi: Exploring Chinese Medicine,* London/ New York: WW Norton 1985.

Eisenberg, David M. Advising patients who seek alternative medical therapies, *Annals of Internal Medicine* 1997, 127(1), 61-19.

Eisenberg, David et al. Unconventional medicine in the United States: Prevalence, costs and patterns of use, *New England J Medicine* 1993, 328, 246-252.

Eisenberg, David et al. Trends in alternative medicine use in the United States 1990-1997: results of a follow-up national survey, *J the American Medical Association* 1998, 280(18), 1569-1575.

Eisenberg, David et al. Perceptions about complementary therapies relative to conventional therapies among adults who use both: results from a national survey, *Annals of Internal Medicine* 2001, 135(5), 344-351.

Eisenberg, H. *Inner Spaces: Parapsychological Explorations of the Mind,* Toronto: Musson Book Co. 1977.

Eisenberg, John M. (Director, Agency for Healthcare Research and Quality), *Statement on Medical Errors, before the Senate Appropriations Subcommittee on Labor, Health and Human Services, and Education, December 13 1999, Washington DC. Agency for Healthcare Research and Quality,* Rockville, MD http://www.ahrq.gov/news/stat1213.htm

Eisenbud, Jule. Telepathy and problems of

psychoanalysis, *Psychoanalytic Quarterly* 1946, 15, 32-87.

Eisenbud, Jule. *Psi and Psychoanalysis,* New York: Grune & Stratton 1970.

Eisenbud, Jule. *Parapsychology and the Unconscious,* North Atlantic Books 1983.

Elasser-Beille, U et al. Cytokine production in leukocyte cultures during therapy with echinacea extract, *J Clinical Laboratory Analysis* 1996, 10, 441-445.

Elder, N et al. Use of alternative health care by family practice patients, *Archives of Family Medicine* 1997, 6, 2, 181-184.

Eliade, Mircea. *Images and Symbols,* New York: Sheed and Ward 1969.

Eliade, Mircea. *Shamanism: Archaic Tech-niques of Ecstasy,* Translated by W. Trask, London: Routledge and Kegan Paul 1970.

Elkin, I. The NIMH Treatment of Depression Collaborative Research Program: Where we begun and where we are. In A.E. Bergin/ Garfield

Ellenberger, Henri. *The Discovery of the Unconscious,* New York: Basic 1970.

Ellerbrook, Wallace C. Language, thought and disease, *Co-Evolution Quarterly* 1978, No.l, 17, 38.

Ellerbrook, WC. Quote from *J Energy Medicine* 1980, 1, 64.

Elliott, William. *Tying Rocks to Clouds,* New York: Image/ Doubleday 1996, 61-75.

Ellis, Albert. *Reason and Emotion in Psychotherapy,* New York: lyle-Stuart 1962.

Ellis, A. Some uses of printed, written, and recorded words in psychotherapy, In: Pearson, L (ed). *The Use of Written Communication in Psychotherapy* Springfield, IL: Thomas 1965.

Ellis, Albert. The place of meditation in cognitive behavior therapy and rational emotive therapy, in: Shapiro, D/ Walsh, R (eds), *Meditation: Contemporary and Classical Perspectives*, New York: Aldine 1984.

Ellis, A/ Grieger, R. *Handbook of Rational-Emotive Therapy,* new York: Springer 1977.

Ellis, FR/ Nasser, S. A pilot study of vita-min B_{12} in the treatment of tiredness, *British J Nutrition* 1973, 30, 277-283.

Ellis, N et al. The effect of acupuncture on nocturnal urinary frequency and incontinence in the elderly, *Complementary Medicine Research* 1990, 4:16-17.

Ellison, Arthur J. Some recent experiments in psychic perceptivity, *J the Society for Psychical Research* 1962, 41, 355-365.

Ellison, CG. Religion, the life stress paradigm and the study of depression, In: Levin 1994, 78-121.

Elmer, GW. Probiotics: 'living drugs,' *American J Health System Pharmacists* 2001, 58(12), 1101-1109.

Emboden, William/ Moss, Thelma/ Johnson, Kendall/ Gannon, Joseph. Health and disease in plants as seen through Kirlian photography, *Psycho energetic Systems* 1979, 3, 33-45.

Endler, PC (ed), *Ultra High Dilution: Physi-ology and Physics*, Dordrecht, Germany: Klewer Academic Publishers 1994.

Endros, Robert/ Lotz, Karl-Ernst. Unexplained serious car accidents involving head-on collisions and their explanation by geophysical and biophysical disturbances, *American Dowser* 1986, 26(2), 14-19.

Engel, G. A life setting conducive to illness: The giving up - given up complex, *Bulletin of the Menninger Clinic* 1968, 32, 355-365.

Engel, GL. The need for a new medical model: A challenge for biomedicine, *Science* 1977, I 96~ 129.

Engel, Hans G. Energy Healing, *Research Report* Los Angeles, CA: Ernest Holmes Research Foundation 1978, 1-15.

Engel, HG/ Cole, JP. Documenting the psychic, *Osteopathic Physician* 1976, 2, 66-72.

Engler, Jack. Therapeutic aims in psychotherapy and meditation: Develop-mental stages in the representation of self, *J Transpersonal Psychology* 1984, 16(1), 25-62.

English, JM. Pertussin 30-preventive for whooping cough?, *British Homeopathy J* 1987, 76, 61-65.

Enright, JT. (1995) Water dowsing: the Scheuen experiments, *Naturwissenschaten* 82: 360-369.

Ensminger, Audrey H et al. *Food for Health,* Clovis, CA: Pegus 1986.

Epictectus. *Discourses* A.D. 55-135.

Epstein, Donald M. *The 12 Stages of Healing: A Network Approach to Wholeness,* San Rafael, CA: Amber-Allen/ New World 1994.

Epstein, Gerald. *Waking Dream Therapy: Dream Process as Imatgination,* New York: Human Sciences 1981.

Epstein, Gerald. *Healing Visualizations: Creating Health Through Imagery,* New York/ London: Bantam 1989.

Epstein, Gerald. *Healing into Immortality: A New Spiritual Medicine of Healing Stories and Imagery,* New York/ London: Bantam 1994.

Erickson, Milton H. Control of physiological functions by hypnosis, *American J Clinical Hypnosis* 1977, 20(l), 8-19.

Erickson, RJ. Acupuncture for chronic pain treatment: its effects on office visits and the use of analgesics in a pre-paid health plan - a feasibility study, *American Academy of Medical Acupuncture Review* 1992, 4(2), 2-6.

Ernst, Edzard. St. John's Wort: An antidepressant? A systematic, criteria-based review, *Phytomedicine* 1995, 2(1), 67-71.

Ernst, Edzard. The ethics of complementary medicine, *J Medical Ethics* 1996, 22, 197-198.

Ernst, Edzard. Chelation therapy for periph-eral arterial occlusive disease, *Circulation* 1997a, 96, 1031-1033.

Ernst, Edzard. Acupuncture/ acupressure for weight reduction? A systematic review, *Wien Klin Wochenscr* 1997b; 109: 60-62.

Ernst, Edzard. Rational complementary medicine, *Z Rheumatol* 1998, 57(3),166-7.

Ernst, Edzard. Adverse effects of spinal manipulation 1999a, in Jonas/ Levin p.176-179.

Ernst, Edzard. Adverse effects of acupunct-ure, 1999b, in Jonas/ Levin p.172-175.

Ernst, Edzard. Are reviewers biased against unconventional therapies: a commentary, *The Scientist* 2000, 14(2), 6.

Ernst, Edzard. Iridology: not useful and potentially harmful, *Archives of Ophthalmology* 2000, 118, 120-121.

Ernst, Edzard. The risk-benefit profile of commonly used herbal therapies: Ginkgo, St. John's Wort, Ginseng, Echinacea, Saw Palmetto, and Kava, *Ann Intern Med.* 2002; 136:42-53.

Ernst, E. Intangible principles of good research in complementary and alternative medicine, *Altern Ther Health Med.* 2002, 8(3),22.

Ernst, Edzard/ Cassileth, Barrie R. The prevalence of complementary/ alternative medicine in cancer: a systematic review, *Cancer* 1998, 83(4), 777-82.

Ernst E, Pittler MH. The effectiveness of acupuncture in treating acute dental pain: a systematic review, *British Dental J* 1998; 443-447.

Ernst, E/ Resch, KL/ White, AR. Complementary medicine. What physicians think of it: a meta-analysis, *Arch Intern Med.* 1995, 155(22), 2405-8.

Ernst, E/ White, AR. Acupuncture for back pain: a meta- analysis of randomized controlled trials, *Archives of Internal Medicine* 1998; 158: 2235-2241.

Ernst, E et al. *The Desktop Guide to Complementary and Alternative Medicine,* Edinburgh: Mosby 2001.

Eskinazi, Daniel (ed). *Botanical Medicine: Efficacy, Quality Assurance, and Regulation,* NY: Mary Ann Liebert 1998.

Eskinazi, Daniel. Homeopathy re-revisited: Is homeopathy compatible with biomedical observation?, 1999, 159(17)

Esposito, V et al. Applied Kinesiology Manual Therapeutic Effects on Disc Herniation with Real Time Magnetic Resonance Imaging, *The J Manual and Manipulative Therapy* 1998.

Estebany, Oszkar Personal communication 1982, in Benor 2001c.

Estes, EP. *The Gift of Story: A Wise Tale About What is Enough,* Jugian Storyteller Audio Series, Boulder, CO: Sounds True.

Estes, EP. *Women Who Run with the*

Wolves: Myths and Stories of the Wild Women Archetype, New York: Ballantine 1992.

Etzel, C et al (eds). *Varieties of Anomalous Experience; Examining The Scientific Evidence*, Washington,DC American Psychological Association 2000.

Evans, Carlton/ Richardson, PH. Improved recovery and reduced postoperative stay alter therapeutic suggestions during general anesthesia, *Lancet* 1988, ii, 491-493.

Evans, John. *Mind, Body and Electromagnetism,* Shaftesbury, England: Element 1986.

Evans, Madeline. *Meditative Provings*, Holgate, UK: Rose Press 2000.

Evans-Wentz, WY (ed). *The Tibetan Book of time Dead, or the After-Death Experiences on the 'Bardo' Plane,* New York: Oxford University 1960.

Everson, Tilden C/ Cole, Warren H. *Spontaneous Regression of Cancer,* New York: Saunders 1966.

Ewer, TC/ Stewart, DE. Improvement in bronchial hyperresponsiveness in patients with moderate asthma after treatment with a hypnotic technique, *British Medical J* 1986, 1, 1129-1132.

Ewin, Dabney M. The effect of hypnosis and mental set on major surgery and burns, *Psychiatric Annals* 16(2), 115-118.

Eysenck, Hans J. *Sense and Nonsense in Psychology*, New York: Penguin 1957, 108.

Eysenck, HJ. The prediction of death from cancer by means of personality/ stress questionnaire: Too good to be true?, *Perpetual Motor Skills* 1990,71,216

Eysenck, HJ. Smoking, personality and stress: Psycho-social factors in the prevention of cancer and coronary heart disease, New York 1991a.

Eysenck, HJ. Analysis of mortality data in the 1972 prospective Heidelberg study by Grosssarth-Maticek, covering the period 1982-1986, *Psychological Inquiry* 1991b, 2, 320-321.

Eysenck, HJ. Psychosocial factors, cancer, and ischaemic hearth disease, *British Medical J* 1992, 305,457-459.

Eysenck, HJ/ Grossarth-Maticek, R. Creative novation behaviour therapy as a prophylactic treatment for cancer and coronary heart disease, Part II - Effects of treatment, *Behavioural Research and Therapy* 1991b, 29, 17-31. (From Eysenck 1992)

Eysenck, HJ/ Grossarth-Maticek, R/ Everitt, B. Personality, stress, smoking and genetic predisposition as synergetic risk factors for cancer and coronary heart disease, *Integrative Physiological and Behavioural Science* 1991, 26, 309-322. (From Eysenck 1992)

Eysenck, HJ/ Nias, David. *Astrology: Science or Superstition?,* New York: Penguin/ London: Maurice Temple Smith 1982.

Ezzo, J/ Berman, B/ Hadhazy, V/ Jadad, AR/ Lao, L/ Singh, BB. Is acupuncture effective for the treatment of chronic pain? A systematic review, *Pain* 2000; 86: 217-225.

Ezzo , J et al. Acupuncture for osteoarthritis of the knee: a systematic review, *Arthritis Rheum* 2001, 44, 819-825.

F

Faass, Nancy. *Integrating Complementary Medicine into Health Systems,* Gaithersburg, MD: Aspen 2001

Fabrega, Horacio Jr. *Disease and Social Behavior,* Cambridge, MA: MIT 1974.

Fahrion, Steven L. et. al. EEG amplitude, brain mapping, & synchrony in & between a bioenergy practitioner & client during healing. *Subtle Energies* 1992, 3(1), 19-52

Falk, A. Uptake, distributionn and elimination of alpha-pinene in man after exposure by inhalation, *Scandinavian J Work Environment Health* 1990 16, 372-378.

Fan, CF et al. Acupressure treatment for prevention of postoperative nausea and vomiting, *Anesthesia & Analagesia* 1997, 84(4), 821-825.

Farber, Leslie. *The Ways of the Will*, New York: Basic 1966.

Farell, JP/ Twomey, LT. Acute low back pain: Comparison of two conservative treatment approaches, *Medical J Australia* 1982, 1, 160-164.

Farley, JW/ Farley, SL. Interactive writing and gifted children: communication through literacy, *J for the Education of Gifted Children* 1987, 10, 99-106.

Farr, Charles H et al. Patient outcomes to alternative medicine therapies as measured by the SF-36 - Preliminary report, *Townsend Letter* 1999, 186, 24-25.

Farrer, CR. *Living Life's Circle: Mescalero Apache Cosmovision*, Albuquerque, NM: University of New Mexico 1991.

Fast, Julius. *Body Language,* New York: Pocket Books 1972,

Favazza, Armando It: Modern Christian healing of mental illness. *American J Psychiatry* 1982, 139(6), 728-735.

Fawzy, FI et al. A structured psychiatric intervention for cancer patients. II. Changes over time in immunological measures, *Archives of General Psychiatry* 1990, 47, 729-735.

Fawzy, FI et al. Effects of an early structured psychiatric intervention, coping and affective state on recurrence and survival 6 years later, *Archives of General Psychiatry* 1993, 50, 681-689.

Fawzy, FI et al. Critical review of psychosocial interventions in cancer care, *Archives of General Psychiatry* 1995, Feb, 52.

Featherstone, Cornelia/ Forsythe, Lori. Medical Marriage: The New Partnership Between Orthodox and Complementary Medicine, Forres, Scotland: Findhorn 1997.

Feder, Gene et al. Randomised controlled trials for homoeopathy, *Who wants to know the results? British Medical J* 2002, 324, 498-499 *www.bmj.com/ cgi/ content/ full/ 324/ 7336/ 498*

Fedoruk, Rosalie Berner. Transfer of the Relaxation Response: Therapeutic Touch as a Method for the Reduction of Stress in Premature Neonates (Doctoral dissertation), University of Maryland 1984.

Feher, H et al. Hepatoprotective activity of silymarin therapy in patients with chronic alcoholic liver disease, *Orv. Hetil.* 1990 130 151.

Feinstein, Alvin R. Problems of randomized trials, in Abel U/ Koch, A (ed), *Nonrandomized Comparative Clinical Studies,* Dusseldorf: Symposion Publishing 1998, 3-13

Feinstein, AR/ Horwitz, RI. Problems in the 'evidence' of 'evidence-based medicine,' *American J Medicine* 1997, 103, 529-535.

Feinstein, D/ Krippner, S. *Personal Mythology: The Psychology of Your Evolving Self*, Los angeles: Tarcher 1988.

Feldenkrais, Moshe. *Awareness through Movement*, New York: Harper & Row 1972.

Feldenkrais, Moshe/ Kimmey, M. *The Potent Self: A Guide to Spontaneity*, San Francisco: Harper & Row 1985.

Feldman, David Henry/ Goldsmith, Lynn. *Child Prodigies and the Development of Human Potential,* New York Basic Books 1986.

Fenwick P. Near death experiences in cardiac arrest: visions of a dying brain or visions of a new science of consciousness. *Resuscitation* 2002, 52, 5-11.

Ferenci, P et al. Randomized controlled trial of silymarin treatment in patients with cirrhosis of the liver, *J Hepatol* 1989, 9(1) 105-113.

Ferguson, Cecilia Kinsel. *Subjective Experience of Therapeutic Touch (SETTS): Psychometric Examination of an Instrument*, (Doctoral dissertation) Austin: University of Texas 1986.

Ferguson, Marilyn. The Aquarian Conspir-acy: Personal and Social Transformation in the 1980's, Los Angeles, CA: JP Tarcher/ Houghton Mifflin 1976.

Ferley, JP et al. A controlled evaluation of a homeopathic preparation in the treatment of influenza-like syndromes, *British J Clinical Pharmacology* 1989, 27, 329-335.

Ferrer, Jorge N., *Revisioning Transpersonal Theory: A Participatory Vision of Human Spirituality*, Albany, New York: State University of New York Press, 2002

Feuchtwang, Stephan. *An Anthropological Analysis of Chinese Geomancy,* Vientiane, Laos: Vithagna Press 1974. (highly recommended but out of print)

Field, Tiffany. *Infancy,* Cambridge, MA: Harvard University 1990.

Field, T. *Touch*, Boston: Harvard University 1997.

Field, T et al. Tactile/ kinesthetic stimulation effects on preterm neonates, *Pediatrics* 1986, 77, 654-658.

Field, T et al. Massage reduces anxiety in child and adolescent psychiatric patients, *J the AMerican Academy of Child and Adolescent Psychiatry* 1992, 31 125-131.

Finkler, Kaja. Non-medical treatments and their outcomes, *Culture, Medicine and Psychiatry* 1980, 4, 271-310.

Finkler, Kaja. Non-medical treatments and their outcomes, Part Two: Focus on adherents of spiritualism, *Culture, Medicine and Psychiatry* 1981, 5, 65-103.

Finkler, Kaja. *Spiritualist Healers in Mexico,* South Hadley, MA: Bezgin & Garvey 1985.

Firman, John/ Gila, Ann. *The Primal Wound; A Transpersonal View of Trauma, Addiction and Growth*, State University of new York Press 1997.

Firsbein, J. Picture alternative medicine in the mainstream, *Business & Health* 1995, 13(4), 28-31.

Fischer, K/ Grosshans, S. Trans AR Meuss, Psychology and biography of patients with ulcerative colitis and Crohn's disease: a study (parts 1 and 2*), J Anthroposophical Medicine* 1992, 9, autumn and winter.

Fischer-Rasmussen, W et al. Ginger treatment of hyperemesis gravidarum, *European J Obstetrics & Gynaecology & reproductive Biology* 1991, 38(1), 19-24.

Fischer-Williams, et al. *A Textbook of Biological Feedback,* New York: Human Sciences Press 1981.

Fisher, AC/ A, Stark. *Dance/ Movement Therapy Abstracts: Doctoral Dissertations, Masters' Theses, and Special Projects Through,* Columbia, MD: Marian Chace Memorial Fund of the American Dance Therapy Association 1992.

Fisher, Peter. The influence of the homeopathic remedy *Plumbum Metallicum* on the excretion kinetics of lead in rats, *Human Toxicology* 1987, 6, 321-324.

Fisher, Peter/ Capel, Ifor. The treatment of experimental lead intoxication in rats by penicillamine and plumbum met, *J Ultramolecular Medicine* 1982, 1(1), 30-31.

Fisher, P et al. Effect of homeopathic treatment on fibrositis (primary fibromyalgia), *British Medical J* 1989, 299, 365-366.

Fisher-Rizzi, Suzanne. *Complete Aromatherapy Handebook: Essential Oils for Radiant Health*, New York: Sterling 1991.

Fitter MJ/ Thomas KJ. Evaluating complementary therapies for use in the National Health Service: ' Horses for courses', Part I: the design challenge, *Complementary Therapies in Medicine* 1997, 5, 90-93.

Fitzherbert, Joan. The nature of hypnosis and paranormal healing, *J the Society for Psychical Research* 1971,46,1-14.

Fitzpatrick, R/ Boulton, M. Qualitative methods for assessing health care, *Quality in Health Care* 1994, 3, 107-113.

Flanagan, Patrick/ Flanagan, Gael Crystal. *Elixir of the Ageless: you Are What You Drink*, San Francisco, CA: Vortex 1986.

Fleming, Tapas. *You Can Heal Now: The Tapas Acupressure Technique (TAT), 2nd Ed*, Redondo Beach, CA: TAT International 1999.

Flexner, S. Postvaccinal encephalitis and allied conditions, JAMA, 1930; 94(5):305-311.

Fling, S. The use of psalms in psychotherapy, In: Morrison, M (ed), *Poetry as Therapy*, New York: Human Services 1987.

Flint, Garry A. *Emotional Freedom: Techniques for Dealing with sychological, Emotional and Physical Distress,* 1999.

Flood, RL. *Dealing with Complexity: An Introduction to the Theory and Application of Systems Science*, New York: Plenum 1988.

Flower Essence Pharmacy, *The Flower Essence Pharmacy Catalog* (2 vol.). Little River, CA: The Flower Essence Pharmacy 1997.

Floyd, Keith. *ReVision* 1978, 3/4, 12.

Fonorow, Owen R. Doctors' strike in Israel good for health, *Townsend Letter* 2000 (Aug/ Sep), 93-94 (letter).

Fontana, David. *The Meditator's Handbook*, Shaftesbury, England/ Rockport, MA: Element 1992.

Fontes, Honore. Self-healing: Getting in touch with self to promote healing, In: Borelli/ Heidt *Therapeutic Touch,* New York: Springer 1981, 129-137.

Foos-Graber, A. *Deathing: An Intelligent Alternative for the Final Moments of Life,* York Beach, ME: Nicholas Hays 1989

Ford, Clyde. *Where Healing Waters Meet: Touching Mind and Emotion through the Body*, Barrytown, NY: Station Hill 1989.

Formica, PE. The housewife syndrome: treatment with the potassium and magnesium salts of aspartic acid, *Current Therapeutic Research* 1962, 4, 98-106.

Forrest, Steven. *The Inner Sky: The Dynamic New Astrology for Everyone*, San Diego, DA: ACS Publishers 1988.

Foss, Laurence/ Rothenberg, Kenneth. *The Second Medical Revolution: From Biomedicine to Infomedicine*, Boston: New Science Library/ Shambhala 1987.

Fosshage, James L/ Olsen, Paul. *Healing: Implications for Psychotherapy,* New York Human Sciences 1978.

Forster, AJ et al. The incidence and severity of adverse events affecting patients after discharge from the hospital, *Ann Intern Med.* 2003, 138(3), 1-16.

Foster, DS. EEG and subjective correlates of alpha-frequency binaural-beat stimulation combined with alpha biofeedback, www.Monroeinstitute.org/ research/ alpha-binaural-beat.html.

Foulkes, RA. Dowsing experiments, *Nature* 1971, 229, 163-168. (From Hansen)

Foundation for Inner Peace. *A Course in Miracles,* London/ New York Arkana 1985.

Fox, AD. Whooping cough prophylaxis with pertussin 30, *British Homoeopathy J* 1987, 76, 69-70.

Fox, J. *Finding What You Didn't Lose: Expressing Your Truth and Creativity Through Poem-Making*, New York: Tarcher/ Putnam 1985.

Fox, J. The healing pulse of poetry: the life giving power of your own words, *The Quest* 1992, 65-70.

Fox, John. *Poetic Medicine: The Healing Art of Poem-Making,* New York: Tarcher/ Penguin/ Putnam 1997.

Fox, RH. The role of psychological factors in cancer incidence and prognosis, *Oncology* 1995, 9, 245-255

Frank, Arthur. *At the Will of the Body: Reflections on Illness,* Boston: Houghton Mifflin 1991.

Frank, Jerome. *Persuasion and Healing,* New York: Schocken 1961.

Frank, LK. Tectile communication, *Genetic Psychology Monographs* 1957,56, 211-251.

Frankel, F. Significant developments in medical hypnosis during the past 25 years, *International J Clinical & Experimental Hypnosis* 1987, 35, 231-247.

Frankl, Victor. *Man's Search for Meaning*, London: Hodder Stoughton 1964.

Frantzis, BK. *Opening the Energy Gates of Your Body*, Berkeley, CA: North Atlantic 1993.

Fraser-Harris, DF. A psycho-physiological explanation of the so-called human aura, *British J Medical Psychology* 1932, 12, 174-184.

Fratkin, Jake. *Chinese Herbal Patent Formulas*, Portland, OR: Institue of Traditional Medicine 1986.

Frawley, David. *Ayurvedic Healing*, Salt Lake City: Morson 1990.

Frawley, David/ Lad, Vasant. *The Yoga of Herbs*, Santa Fe, NM: Lotus 1986.

Fredericks, Canton. *Nutrition Guide for the Prevention and Cure of Common Ailments*, New York Simon & Schuster 1982.

Fredericks, Lillian E. The use of hypnosis in hemophilia, *American J Clinical Hypnosis* 1967, 10(1), 52-55.

Freed, Geoffrey. *The Doctor-Healer Network Newsletter* 1991, No. 1, 17.

Freedman, Alfred M/ Kaplan, Harold I/ Sadock Benjamin J. Psychophysiologic medicine, In: *Modern Synopsis of Comprehensive Textbook of Psychiatry IL Second Ed,* Chapter 25, Baltimore, MD: Williams & Wilkins 1976.

Freeman, L. *Best Practices in Complementary and Alternative Medicine: an*

Evidence Based Approach, Gaithersburg, MD: Aspen 2000.

Freeman, LW/ Lawlis, GF. *Mosby's Complementary and Alternative Medicine: A Research-Based Approach,* Chapter 1, p.2-33; Chapter 4, p.45-131, St. Louis: Mosby, 2001.

Freeman, Lynn W/ Lawlis, Frank G. *Mosby's Complementary & Alternative Medicine: A Research-based Approach,* St. Louis, MO: Mosby 2001.

Freidson, Eliot. The social construction of illness, chapter III, In: *Profession of Medicine: A Study of the Sociology of Applied Knowledge,* New York: Dodd, Mead 1970.

Freud, Anna. The ego and mechanisms of defense, In: *Writings of Anna Freud, Vol.2,* New York: International Universities Press 1967. (Orig. 1953)

Freud, Sigmund. The Interpretation of Dreams, in *The Standard Edition of the Complete Psychological Works of Sigmund Freud,* 24 vols, Trans. Strachey, J, London: Hogarth/ Institute of Psychoanalysis 1953-1964.

Freud, Sigmund. *Psychopathology of Every-day Life,* New York: Norton 1971.

Frey, J/ Rotton, J/ Barry, T. The effects of the full moon on human behavior: yet another failure to replicate, *J Psychology* 1979, 103, 159-162.

Friedenberg, R et al. *Detector device and process for degtecting ovulation,* United States Patent 3, 924, 609, December 9, 1975.

Friedman, H/ Becker, RO/ Bachman, C. Psychiatric ward behavior and geophysical parameters, *Nature* 1965, 205: 1050-1052

Friedman, Meyer/ Rosenman, Ray H. *Type A Behavior and Your Heart,* New York: Knopf 1974.

Friedman, Meyer/ Ulmer, Diana. *Treating Type A and Your Heart,* New York: Knopf 1984.

Friedman, Meyer\ et al. Alteration of Type A behavior and its effects on cardiac recurrence in post myocardial infarction patients: summary results of the recurrent coronary prevention project, *American Heart J,* October 1986 112(4).

Friend, B/ Shahani, K. Nutritional and theraputic aspects of lactobacilli, *J of Applied Nutrition,* 36, 125-153.

Frischolz, EJ et al. The relationship between the Hypnotic Induction Profile and the Stanford Hypnotic Susceptibility Scale, Form C: a replication, *American J Clinical Hypnosis* 1980, 22, 185-196.

Frist, Bill. Deciding who is protected against smallpox, http://www.nytimes.com August 9, 2002.

Fritts, M. White House commission examines research on complementary cancer therapies, *J Natl Cancer Inst.* 2000, 92(24),1975-6.

Frohlich H. 1968a Bose condensation of strongly excited longitudinal electric modes, *Physicals Letters* 26A:402-403

Frohlich, H. 1968b Long-range coherence and energy storage in biological systems, *International J Quantum Chemistry* 2:641-649

Frohlich, H. 1970 Long-range coherence and the action of enzymes, *Nature* 228:1093

Frohlich, H. 1974 Possibilities of long- and short-range electric interactions of biological systems, In: Adey W R, Bawin SM 1977 Brain interactions with weak electric and magnetic fields, Neurosciences Research Program Bulletin 15:1-129

Frohlich, H. 1975 Evidence for bose condensation-like excitation of coherent modes in biological systems, *Physics Letters* 51A:21-22

Frohlich, H (ed). 1988 Biological coherence and response to external stimuli, Berlin: Springer-Verlag

Fromm, E/ Nash, MR (eds). *Contemporary Hypnosis Research,* New York: Guilford 1992.

Fromn-Reichmann, Frieda. *Principles of Intensive Psychotherapy,* Chicago: Univ. of Chicago 1950.

Frost, Gavin/ Frost, Yvonne. *Astral Travel,* York Beach, ME: Samuel Weiser 1982.

Froyd, J.E. A review of practices of psychotherapy outcome measurement, *Journal of Mental Health* 1996, 5, 11-15.

Frumkin, K et al. Nonpharmacologic control of essential hypertension in man: a critical reviews of the experiemental literature, *Psychosomatic Medicine* 1978, 40, 294-320.

Fry, W. Mirth and oxygen saturation of peripheral blood, *Psychotherapy and Psychosomatics* 1971, l9, 76-84.

Fry, W. The respiratory components of mirthful laughter, *J Biological Psychology* 1977 l9(2), 39-50.

Fry, W. Mirth and the human cardiovascular system, In Mindess/ Turek (eds) *The Study of Humor*, Antioch University 1979.

Frydrychowski, AF/ Przjemska, B/ Grabiec, S. Light extinction changes in organismic fluids exposed to biofields, *Psychoironika* 1985, 78-80. (Abstract, translated from Polish by Alexander Imich, in: *Parapsychology Abstracts International* 1987, 5(2), No. 2488)

Frydrychowski, Andrzej F/ Przyjemska, Bozens/ Orlowski, Tadeusz. An attempt to apply photon emission measurement in the selection of the most effective healer, *Psychotronika* 1985, 82-83. (Abstract, translated from Polish by Alexander Imich, in *Parapsychology Abstracts International* 1987, 5(2), No. 2489.)

Frymoyer, JWRB Phillips/ Newberg, AH et al. A comparative analysis of the interpretations of lumbar spinal radiographs by chiropractors and medical doctors, *Spine* 1986, 11, 1020-1023.

Fugh-Berman, Adrian. *Alternative Medicine: What Works*, Williams-Wilkins, 1997.

Fulder, Stephen. *How to Survive Medical Treatment: An Holistic Guide to Avoiding the risks and Side-effects of Conventional Medicine*, Saffron Walden, UK: CW Daniels 1994.

Fulder, Stephen. *The Garlic Book: Nature's Powerful Healer*, Garden City Park, NY: Avery 1997.

Fulder, SJ/ Monro, RE. *The Status of Complementary Medicine in the UK*, London: Threshold Foundation 1982.

Fulford, Robert C. *Dr. Fulford's Touch of Life: The Healing Power of the Natural Life Force*, New York/ London: Pocket 1996.

Funch, DP/ Marshall, J. The role of stress, social support and age and survival from breast cancer, *J Psychosomatical Research* 1983, 27, 77-83. (From Ramirez et al.)

Funderburk, James. *Science Studies Yoga: A Review of Physiological Data*, Honesdale, PA: Himalayan International Institute 1977.

Fung, KP/ Chow, OKW/ So, SY Attenuation of exercise-induced asthma by acupuncture, *Lancet* 1986, 2:1419-1422.

Futterman, AD et al. Immunological and physiological changes associated with induced positive and negative mood, *Psychosomatic Medicine* 1994, 56, 499-511.

G

Gabbard, Glen O. Wi*th the Eyes of the Mind,* New York: Praeger 1984.

Gabriel, Michael. *Remembering Your Life Before Birth,* Lower Lake, CA: Aslin 1995.

Gaby, Alan R. Orthomolecular medicine and megavitamin therapy, in Jonas/ Levin 1999, p. 459-471.

Gaby, Allan/ Wright, Jonathan. *Nurtitional Therapy in Medical Practice*, (includes reference manual and audiotapes) gaby@halcyon.com.

Gach, Michael R. *Acu-Yoga: The Acupressure Stress Management Book*, New York/ Tokyo: Japan 1981.

Gach, Michael R. *Acupressure's Potent Points*, New York: Bantam 1990.

Gadsby, JG. Kirlian photography diagnosis: A recent study, *Complementary Therapies in the Medicate* 1993, 1, 179-184.

Gagne, Deborah/ Toye Richard C. The effects of Therapeutic Touch and relaxation therapy in reducing anxiety, *Archives of Psychiatric Nursing* 1994, 8(3) 184-189.

Galbraith, Jean. Spontaneous rising of kundalini energy: pesudo-schizophrenia or spiritual disease? *Network: The Scientific and Medical Network Review* (UK) 1998, 67, 29.

Galbraith, Jean. Is Spiritual experience up spine always a benign process? Can it teach us anything new about spiritual pathways? *Network: The Scientific and Medical Network Review* (UK) December 1999, 71.

Galbraith, Jean. *Erratum,* for Gabraith 1999, *Network: The Scientific and Medical Network Review* (UK) 2000, 72, 29 (corrections in table showing results of survey).

Galde, Phyllis. *Crystal Healing,* St. Paul, MN: Llewellyn 1988.

Gallagher, SM et al. Six-month depression relapse rates among women treated with acupuncture, *Complementary Therapies in Medicine* 2000, 9, 216-218.

Gallegos, Eligio Stephen. Animal imagery, the chakra system, and psychotherapy, *J Transpersonal Psychology* 1983, 15(2), 125-136.

Gallegos, Eligio Stephen. *The Personal Totem Pole: Animal Imagery, the Chakras, and Psychotherapy*, 2nd Ed, Velarde, NM: Moon Bear 1990.

Gallegos, Eligio Stephen. Animal imagery and the personal totem pole process, in: Leskowitz 2000, p.85-94.

Gallert, Mark. *New Light on Therapeutic Energies,* London: James Clarke 1966.

Gallimore, JG. Relationship Between Parapsychology and Gravity, V.3 of Handbook of Unusual Energies, Mokelumne Hill, CA: Health Research 1971.

Gallo, Fred. *Energy Psychology: Explorations at the Interface of Energy, Cognition*, Behavior and Health, CRC Press 1999

Gallo, Fred P. *Energy Diagnostic and Treat-ment Methods*, New York: Norton 2000.

Gallo, Fred/ Furman, Mark Evan. *The Neurophysics of Human Behavior: Explorations at the Interface of Brain, Mind, Behavior and Information*, CRC Press 2000.

Gallo, Fred/ Vincenzi. *Energy Tapping: How to Rapidly EliminateAnxiety, Depression, Cravings, and More Using Energy Psychology*, NewHarbinger 2000.

Garattini, S/ Bertele, V. Efficacy, safety, and cost of new anticancer drugs, *British Medical J* 2002, 325, 269-271.

Garcia, Raymond L. 'Witch doctor?' A hexing case of dermatitis, *Cutis* 1977, 19(1), 103-105.

Gardner, R. *Storytelling in Psychotherapy for Children*, New York: Aronson 1990.

Gardner-Gordon, Joy. *The Healing Voice*, Freedom, CA: Crossing 1993.

Gardener, Jaentra Green. The wave brings us happiness, International J Healing and Caring – On line 2003, 3(2).

Garfield, Leah Maggie. *Sound Medicine: Healing with Music, Voice and Song*, Berkeley, CA: Celestial Arts 1987.

Garrison, Vivian. Doctor, espiritista or psychiatrist? Health-seeking behavior in a Puerto Rican neighborhood of New York City, *Medical Anthropology* 1977, 1, 65-4 80.

Garrow, JS. Kinesiologyu and food allergy, *British Medical J*, 1988, 296, 1573-1574.

Garth, JM/ Lester, D. The moon and suicide, *Psychological Reports* 1978, 43, 678.

Gascoigne, S. *The Chinese Way to Health: A Self-Help Guide to Traditional Chinese Medicine*, Rutland, VT: Charles E Tuttle 1997.

Gaskin, Ina Mae. *Spiritual Midwifery* (book, video), Summertown, TN: Total Video Publications 1998.

Gatta, L. Controlled clinical trial among patients designed to assess the therapeutic efficacy and safety of tegens 160, *Ospedale Filippo del Ponte*, Varese, Italy 1982.

Gauquelin, Michel. *The Scientific Basis of Astrology: Myth or Reality*, New York: Stein and Day 1969.

Gauquelin, Michel. *Astrology and Science*, London: Peter Davies 1970 (Orig. French 1966 - from Eysenck/ Nias).

Gauquelin, Michel. *How Atmospheric Conditions Affect Your Health*, New York: Stein & Day 1971.

Gauquelin, Michel. *The Cosmic Clocks*, New York Granada 1973.

Gauquelin, Michel. *Cosmic Influences on Human Behavior*, New York: ASI 1978.

Gauquelin, Michel. *Dreams and Illusions of Astrology*, Buffalo: Prometheus 1979.

Gauquelin, Michel. *The Spheres of Destiny*, London: Dent 1980.

Gauquelin, Michel/ Gauquelin, Francoise. Star US sportsmen display the Mars effects, *Skeptical Inquirer* 1979.

Gauquelin, Michel/ Gauquelin, Francoise/ Eysenck, SBG. Personality and position of the planets at birth: an empirical study, *British J Social and Clinical Psychology* 1979 18, 71-75.

Gawler, Ian. *You Can Conquer Cancer,* Wellingborough, England: Thorson 1986.

Gaynor, Mitchell. *Sounds of Healing: A Physician Reveals the Therapeutic Power of Sound, voice, and Music,* New York: Random House 1999.

Gazzaniga, Michael S. The split brain in man, *Scientific American* 1967 (August).

Gazzaniga, Michael. *The Social Brain: Discovering the Networks of the Mind,* New York Basic 1985.

Gearhart, L/ Persinger, MA. Geophysical variables and behavior XXXIII, Onsets of historical and contemporary poltergeist episodes which occurred with sudden increases in geomagnetic activity, *Perceptual and Motor Skills* 1986, 62,463-466.

Gebauer, Ranier/ Müschenich, Stefan. Psycho-Physiological Effects of the Reich Orgone Accumulator, *Pulse of the Planet* 1989, 2, 22-24.

Geis, Larry/ Picchi Kelly, Alta/ Kelly, Aidan. *The New Healers: Healing the Whole Person,* Berkeley, CA: And/ Or Press 1980.

Geisler, Patrick V. Batcheldorian psychodynamics in the Umbanda ritual trance consultation, Part I, *Parapsychology Review* 1984, 15(6), 5-9.

Geisler, Patrick V. Batcheldorian psychodynamics in the Umbanda ritual trance consultation, Part H, *Parapsychology Rev.* 1985a, 16(1), 11-14.

Geisler, Patrick V. Parapsychological anthropology II: A multi-method study of psi and psi-related processes in the Umbanda ritual trance consultation, *J the American Society for Psychical Research* 1985b, 79(2), 113-466.

Geisser, ME et al. The coping strategies questionnaire and chronic pain adjustment: A conceptual and empirical reanalysis, *Clinical J Pain* 1994 10(2), 98-106.

Gelb, Michael. *Body Learning: an Introduction to the Alexander Technique,* Delilah 1981.

Gelenberg, AJ et al. Tyrosine treatment of depression, *American J Psychiatry* 1980, 137, 622-623.

Geller, SH/ Shannon, HW. The moon, weather, and mental hospital contacts: confirmation and explanation of the transylvanian effect, *J Psychiatric Nursing and Mental Health Services* 1976 14 13-17.

Gendler, RJ. *The Book of Qualities,* Berkeley, CA: Turquoise Mountain 1984.

Gennaro, Luigi/ Guzzon, Fulvio/ Marsigli, Pierluigi. Translated from Italian by Ornirod, JAJ): *Kirlian Photography: Research and Prospects,* London: East West 1980. (Orig. Rome: *Edizioni Mediterranee* 1977)

George, Christopher S. *The Chamdumahamsana Tantra,* New Haven, CT: American Oriental Society 1974. (Also: PhD thesis, University of Pennsylvania 1971)

George, Leonard/ Krippner, Stanley. Mental imagery and psi phenomena: A review, In: Krippner, Stanley (ed): *Advances in Parapsychological Research 4,* Jefferson, NC/London: McFarland 1984.

George, MS et al. Daily repetitive transcran-ial electrical stimulation (rTMS) improves mood in depression, *Neuroreport* 1995, 6(14), 1853-1856.

Georgopolus, AP et al. Neuronal population coding of movement direction, *Science* 1986, 243 1416-1419.

Gerard, RM. *Differential Effects of Colored Lights on Psychophysiological Functions,* PhD dissertation, University of California at Los Angeles 1958. (Summarized briefly in: Hastings, AC et al.)

Gerber, Richard. *Vibrational Medicine: New Choices for Healing Ourselves,* Santa Fe, NM: Bear & Co. 1988.

Gerozissis, K et al. Leukotrienes C_4 and D_4 stimulate the release of luteinizing hormone-releasing hormone from rat median eminence in vitro, *Brain Research* 1987, 416, 54-58 (cited in Eskinazi 1999).

Gershom, Yonassan. *Beyond the Ashes,* Virginia Beach, VA: 1992.

Gershom, Yonassan. *From Ashes to Healing*, Virginia Beach, VA: 1996.

Gersie, Alida. *Earthtales: Storytelling in Times of Change*, London: Green Print/ Merlin 1988.

Gersie, Alida. *Storymaking in Bereavement*, London: Jessica Kingsley 1991.

Gersie, Alida. *Storymaking in Education and Therapy*, London: Jessica Kingsley 1992.

Gersten Dennis. *Are You Getting Enlighten-ed or Losing Your Mind?: A Spiritual Program for Mental Fitness*, New York: Random House 1997.

Getsios, D/ Caro, JJ/ Caro, G/ Ishak, K. Assessment of health economics in Alzheimer's disease (AHEAD): galantamine treatment in Canada, *Neurology* 2001, 57, 972-8.

Gevitz, N. *The DOs: A social history of osteopathic medicine*, Unpublished PhD dissertation, University of Chicago 1980.

Gevitz, Norman (ed). *Other Healer: Unorthodox Medicine in America,* Baltimore: Johns Hopkins University 1988.

Ghadiali, GE. *Spectro Chrome Metry Encyclopedia,* Malaga, NJ: Spectro-Chrome Inst. 1933.

Ghaly RG et al. Antiemetic studies with traditional Chinese acupuncture: a compar-ison of manual needling with electrical stimulation and commonly used antiemetics, *Aiiaesthesia* 1987, 42, 1108-1110.

Gandhi OP. *Biological Effects and Medical Applications of Electromagnetic Fields*. Englewood Cliffs, NJ: Prentice Hall, 1990.

Gibbs, Scott. Sullivan-Fowler, Micaela, & Rowe, N. *Mosby's Medical Surfari: A Guide to Exploring the Internet and Discovering the Top Health Care Resources*, New York: Mosby 1999.

Gibran, Khalil. *The Prophet*, Alfred A. Knopf 1995.

Gibson, DM. Nosodes and prophylaxis, *Homeopathy* 1958, 8, 111-124.

Gibson, RG et al. Homoeopathic therapy in rheumatoid arthritis: evaluation by dou-ble-blind clinical therapeutic trial, *British J Clinical Pharmacology* 1980, 9, 453-459.

Gibson, T et al. Controlled comparison of short-wave diathermy treatment with osteopathic treatment in nonspecific low back pain, *Lancet* 1985 (1 June), 1258-1261.

Gifford, Fred. "Community-equipoise and the ethics of randomized clinical trials," *Bioethics* 1995, 9(2), 127-48

Gift, A. Visual analogue scales: measurement of subjective phenomena, *Nursing Research* 1989, 38(5), 286-288.

Gilian, S. *Therapeutic Trances: The Cooperation Principle in Ericksonian Hypnotherapy*, New York: Brunner/ Mazel 1987.

Gillet, H/ Liekens, M. *Belgian chiropractic research notes*, Huntington Beach, CA: Motion Palpation Institute 1984

Gillon, R. Medical ethics: four principls plus attention to scope, *British Medical J* 1994, 309, 184-188.

Gilmore, Louise Neild. *The Carer's Handbook: How to Be a Successful Carer and Look After Yourself Too*, St. Leonards, NSW, Australia: Allen & Unwin 1995.

Gilmore, T et al. *About the Tomatis Method*, Toronto: Listening Center 1989.

Ginandes, Carol S/ Rosenthal, Daniel I. Using hypnosis to accelerate the healing of bone fractures: a randomized controlled pilot study, *Alternative Therapies* 1999, 5(2), 67-75.

Ginsberg, C. The Shake-a-leg body awareness training program: dealing with spinal injury and recovery in a new setting, *Somatics* 1986, Spring/ Summer 31-42.

Girdlestone, Rodney. Are you building in a safe place?, *Caduceus* 1989, 7 12-14.

Gissurarson, LR. Studies of methods of enhancing and potentially-training psychokinesis: A review, *J the American Society Research* 1992, 86, 303-346.

Gissurarson, Loftur R/ Gunnarsson, Asgeir. An experiment with the alleged human aura, *J the American Society for Psychical Research* 1997, 91, 33-49.

Gitlin, Murray. *Body and Mind and Their Possibilities: Especially in Occult Experiences,* Philadelphia, PA: Dorrance 1974.

Glaser, JL et al. Elevated serum DHEAS levels in practitioners of the transcendental meditation (TM) and TM-Sidhi programs, *J Behavioral Medicine* 1992 15(4), 327-341

Glazewski, CA. The Human Field in Medical Problems, *Human Dimensions* 1973,5, 14-I5.

Gleick, James. *Chaos: Making a New Science,* New York: Viking/ Penguin 1987.

Glickman-Simon, Richard. The debate over universal immunizations, *integrative Medicine Consult* 2000, 2(12), 136-139.

Glouberman, Dina. *Life Choices and Life Changes Through Imagework: The Art of Developing Personal Vision,* London: Mandala/ Unwin 1989.

Glover, JR et al. Back pain: A randomized clinical trial of rotational manipulation of the trunk, *British J Industrial Medicine* 1974, 31, 59-64.

Glueck, R/ Stroebel, C. Biofeedback as meditation in the treatment of psychiatric illnesses, *Comprehensive Psychiatry* 1975 16, 303-321.

Gobel, H et al. Effects of peppermint and eucalyptus oil preparations on neuro-physiological and experimental algesimet-ric headache parameters, *Cephalalgia* 1994, 4(3), 228-234.

Goddard Henry H. The effects of mind on body as evidenced by faith cures, *American J Psychology* 1899, 10, 431-502.

Godfrey, CM PP Morgan/ J. Schatzker. A randomized trial of manipulation for low-back pain in a medical setting, *Spine* 1984, 9, 301-304.

Godman, Colin/ St Claire, Lindsay. An underground movement, *The Unexplained* 1983, 11 (122), 2421-2425. (From Hansen)

Golan, Ralph T. *Your Health is in Your Hands: A Guidebook for Self-Health Care,* Seattle, WA: GOEK/ Golan 1985.

Goldbeck-Wood, et al. Complementary medicine is booming worldwide, *British Medical J* 1996, 313, 131-133.

Goldberg, B. Hypnosis and the immune response, *International J Psychosomatics* 1985, 32(3), 34-36.

Goldberg, Burton Group, *Alternative Medicine: The definitive guide,* Fife, WA: Future Medicine Publishing 1995 (28 pp refs Outstanding reference book!)

Goldberg, Jane (ed). *Psychotherapeutic Treatment of Cancer Patients,* New York: Free Press/ Macmillan 1981.

Goldberg, Jane G. *Deceits of the Mind and Their Effects on the Body,* New Brunswick, NJ: Transaction 1991.

Goldberg, Jane G. T*he Dark Side of Love: The Positive role of Our Negative Feelings-Anger, Jealousy, and Hate,* New York: Putnam 1993.

Goldberg, N. *Writing the Natural Way: Feeling the Writer Within,* Boston: Shambhala 1986.

Goldman, Jonathan. *Healing Sounds: The Power of Harmonics,* Rev. Ed. Shaftesbury, England: Element 1996.

Goldstein, A/ Feske, U (1994). Eye movement desensitization and reprocessing for panic disorder: A case series, *J Anxiety Disorders, 8,* 351-362.

Goldstein, Murray. National Institute of Neurological and Communicative Disorders and Stroke, *International Review* of *Chiropractic 1976* (September).

Goldstein-Roca, S/ Crisafuli, T. Integrative creative arts therapy: a brief treatment model, *The Arts in Psychotherapy* 1994, 21, 219-222.

Goleman, Dan. *The Varieties of Meditative Experience,* New York: Dutton 1977.

Goleman, Daniel. *The Meditative Mind,* Tarcher 1988.

Goleman, Daniel. *Emotional Intelligence,* New York: Bantam 1995 (28pp notes/ refs.).

Goleman, Daniel/ Gurin, Joel. *Mind/ Body Medicine: How to Use Your Mind for Better Health,* Fairfield, OH: Consumer Reports 1993.

Goleman, D/ Schwartz, G. Meditation as an intervention in stress reactivity, *J Consulting & Clinical Psychology* 1976, 44, 456-466.

Goleman, Daniel/ Smith, Huston/ Dass, Ram. Truth and transformation in psychological and spiritual paths, *J*

Transpersonal Psychology 1985, 17(2), 183-214.

Golomb, L. Curing and sociocultural separation in South Thailand, *Social Science Medicine* 1985,21(4), 463-468.

Gonnella, C. et al. Reliability in evaluating passive intervertebral motion, *Physical Therapy* 1982, 62, 436-444

Gonzalez, Nancy Solien. Health behavior in cross-cultural perspective: A Guatemalan example. *Human Organization* 1966, *25(2)*, 122-125.

Gonzalez, Sara C. A fMRI Study of placebo-induced effects of nicotine in the human brain http://academic.uofs.edu/student/Gonzalez s2/poster.html

Goodman, Felicitas. Body posture and the religious altered state of consciousness: An experimental investigation, *J Humanistic Psychology* 1986,26(3), 81-118.

Goodman, Felicitas D. *Where the Spirits Ride the Wind: Trance Journeys and Other Ecstatic Experiences*, Bloomington & Indianapolis: Indiana University 1990.

Goodman, LS/ Gilman, A. *The Pharmacol-ogical Basis of Therapeutics, 9th Ed*, New York: McGraw-Hill 1996, 764; 819 (cited in Eskinazi 1999).

Goodman, Sandra. *Nutrition and Cancer*, London: Green Library 1995.

Goodrich, Joyce. The psychic healing training and research project, In: Fosshage, James L/ Olsen, Paul. *Healing: Implications for Psychotherapy,* New York: Human Sciences Press 1978, 84-110.

Goodrich, Joyce. Personal communications 1982-1985.

Goodwin, M et al. The effect of group psychosocial support on survival in metastatic breast cancer, *New England J Medicine* 2001, 345, 1719-1726.

Gordon, James. *Manifesto for a New Medi-cine: Your Guide to Healing Partnerships and the Wise Use of Alternative Therapies*, Reading, MA: Addison Wesley 1996.

Gordon, James S/ Jaffe, Dennis/ Bresler, David. *Mind, Body and Health: Toward an Integral Medicine,* New York: Human

Science 1984.

Gordon, Marilyn. *Energy Therapy: Tapping The Next Dimension in Healing*,WiseWord Publishing 1998.

Gordon, Marilyn. *The New Manual for Transformational Healing with ypnotherapy and Energy Therapy*, WiseWord Publishing 1999.

Gordon, Richard. *Your Healing Hands: The Polarity Experience,* Santa Cruz: Unity 1978.

Gorelick, K. Poetry on the final common pathway of the psychotherapies: Private self, self-in-the-world, *J Poetry Therapy* 1989a, 3, 5-17.

Gorelick, K. Rapprochement between the arts and psychotherapies: metaphor the mediator, *The Arts in Psychotherapy* 1989b, 16, 149-155.

Gorter, E. Postvaccinal encephalitis, *JAMA*, 1933; 101(24):1871-1874.

Goss, Michael. The gentle art of murder, *The Unexplained* 1983, ll(121),24l0-2413.

Gottlieb, Bill (ed). Flower remedy/ essence therapy, in *New Choices in Natural Healing*, Emmaus, PA: Rodale 1995a, 37-41.

Gottlieb, Bill (ed). *New Choices in Natural Healing: Over 1,800 of the Best Self Help Remedies from the World of Alternative Medicine*, New York: Bantam 1995b.

Gould, LK et al. Changes in myocardial perfusion abnormalities by positron emission tomography after long-term, intense risk factor modification, *J the American Medical Association* (Sep 20) 1995, 274(11), 894-901.

Grabow, Stephen/ Alexander, Christopher. *The Search for a New Paradigm in Architecture*, Oriel 1983.

Grabowska, MJ. The effect of hypnosis and hypnotic suggestion on the blood flow in the extremities, *Polish Medical J* 1971, 10, 1044-1051.

Grad, Bernard R. Some biological effects of laying-on of hands: a review of experiments with animals and plants, *J. of the American Society for Psychical Research* 1965a, 59, 95-127 (Also reproduced In: Schmeidler, Gertrude (ed) *Parapsychology: Its Relation to Physics, Biology,*

Psychology and Psychiatry, Metuchen, NJ: Scarecrow 1976).

Grad, B et al. The Influence of an Unorthodox, Method of Treatment on Wound Healing in Mice, *International J Parapsyhology* 1961, 3, 5-24.

Grady, D et al. Cardiovascular disease outcomes during 6.8 years of hormone therapy, Heart and Estrogen/progestin Replacement Study followup (HERS II), *JAMA*, 2002, 288(1), 49-57.

Graedon, Joe/ Graedon, Teresa. *The People's Guide to Deadly Drug Interations: How to Protect Yourself from Life-Threatening Drug/ Drug, Drug/ Food, Drug/ Vitamin Combinations*, NY: St Martin's 1995.

Graff, Dale. *Tracks in the Psychic Wilderness; An Exploration of ESP, Remote Viewing, Precognitive Dreaming*, Shaftesbury, England: Element 2000.

Graham, Helen. *Complementary Therapies in Context: The Psychology of Healing*, London: Jesica Kingsley 1999.

Graham, Martha. *Blood Memory* Buschekbooks 2000.

Gralla RJ. Adverse effects of treatment. In: DeVita VT et al eds. *Cancer: Principles & Practice of Oncology.* 4th ed. Philadelphia: Lippincott-Raven 1994, 2338-2347.

Grant, L. *The Electrical Sensitivity Handbook: How EMF's Are Making People Sick*, Prescott, AZ: Weldon 1995.

Graves, Tom. *The Dowser's Workbook*, Wellingborough, England: Aquarian 1989.

Gray, John. *The Alexander Technoique*, New York: St. Martin's 1991.

Gray, Robert. *The Colon Health Handbook*, Reno, NV: Emerald 1981.

Grayson, D. The bridge of hope: the use of creative arts therapies in group treatment for people with AIDS and HIV infection, *J Poetry Therapy* 1995, 8, 123-133.

Green, Elmer. Biofeedback training and yoga: Imagery and healing, *Presentation at Conference on Psychic Healing and Self Healing Sponsored by the Association for Humanistic Psychology*, 1972 (May).

Green, Elmer. *Presentation at Healing in Our Time Conference*, Washington, DC: 1981 (November).

Green, Elmer/ Green, Alyce. *Beyond Biofeedback,* New York: Delta/ Dell 1977.

Green, Elmer/ Green, Alyce. Biofeedback and transformation, *American Theosophist* 1984, 72, 142-152.

Green, Elmer/ Green, Alyce. Biofeedback and states of consciousness, In: Wolman, Benjamin B/ Ullman, Montague (eds). *Handbook of States of consciousness,* New York: Van Nostrand Reinhold 1986.

Green, Elmer E et al. Anomalous electrostatic phenomena in exceptional subjects, *Subtle Energies* 1991, 2(3), 69-94

Green, Hannah. *I Never Promised You a Rose Garden,* New York: Holt-Rinehart & Winston 1964.

Green, J et al. Finding the hypnotic virtuoso-another look, *International J Clinical and Experimental Hypnosis* 1992, 50, 68-73.

Greenberg, Daniel S. A sober anniversary of the 'War on Cancer', *Lancet* 1991, 338, (582-1583.

Greene, Liz/ Sasportas, Howard. *The Development of the Personality: Seminars in Psychological Astrology, Vol. I*, York Beach, ME: Samuel Weiser 1987.

Greenhalgh, Trisha. Narrative-based medicine in an evidence-based world," *British Medical J* 1999, 318, 325-5

Greenhalgh, T/ Taylor, R. Papers that go beyond numbers (qualitative research), *British Medical J* 1997, 315, 740-743.

Greenson, Ralph R. *The Technique and Practice of Psychoanalysis,* New York International University Press 1967.

Greenwell, Bonnie. *Energies of Transform-ation: A Guide to the Kundalini Process,* Cupertino CA: Shakti River/ Transpersonal Learning Services 1990.

Greenwood, Michael. *Braving the Void: Journeys into Healing*, Victoria, BC Canada: Paradox 1998.

Greenwood, Michael/ Nunn, Peter. *Paradox & Healing: Medicine, Mythology & Trans-formation*, Victoria, BC Canada: Paradox 1994.

Greer HS/ Morris, T/ Pettingale, KW.

Psychological response to breast cancer: Effect on outcome, *Lancet* 1979, ii, 785-787. (From Pettingale et al)

Grieve, GP. Incidents and accidents of manipulation and allied techyniques, in: *Grieve's Modern Manual Therapy*, Edinburgh, UK: Churchill Livingstone 1984, p.679.

Grieve, Mrs. *A Modern Herbal*, New York: Dover 1971.

Griffiths, Colin. The Berlin Wall, a remedy proved by group meditation, *Promethius Unbound* 1995, Spring, 25-30.

Griffiths, P. Refloxology, In: Rankin-Box, Denise (ed), *The Nurse's Handbook of Complementary Therapies*, London: Churchill Livingstone 1995.

Grigoriantz, Alexandre. News from Russia, *Doctor-Healer Network Newsletter* Autumn 1993.

Grimes, DA. Technology follies: the uncritical acceptance of medical innovations, *J the American Medical Association* 1993;269:3030-3033.

Grinberg-Zylberbaum, J/ Delafior, M/ Sanchez Arellano, ME/ Guevara, MA/ Perez, M. Human communication and the electrical activity of the brain, *Subtle Energies* 1992, 3(3), 25-41.

Gris, Henry/ Dick, William. *The New Soviet Psychic Discoveries,* New York: Warner 1978.

Griscom, Chris. *Healing of Emotion: Awakening the Fearless Self,* New York: Simon & Schuster 1988.

Grizzard, L. *They Tore Out My Heart and Stomped that Sucker Flat*, New York: Warner 1982.

Grof, Stanislav. *Beyond the Brain: Birth, Death, and Trenscendence in Psychotherapy*, Albany, NY: State University of NY 1985.

Grof, Stanislav. *Books of the Dead: Manuals for Living and Dying*, New York: Thames & Hudson 1994.

Grof, Stanislav/ Grof, Christina. *Spiritual Emergency: When Personal Transformation Becomes a Crisis*, New York: Putnam 1993.

Grof, Stanislav & Grof, Christina . *The Stormy Search for the Self: Understanding and Living with Spiritual Emergency*, Thorsons 1995.

Grof, Stanislav/ Halifax, Joan. *The Human Encounter with Death*, New York: Dutton 1977.

Grof, Stanislav/ Halifax, Joan. *Beyond the Brain: Birth, Death and Transcendence in Psychotherapy*, New York: State University of New York 1985.

Grontved, A, et al. Ginger root against seasickness: A controlled trial on the open sea, *Acta Oto-Laryngologica* 1988, 105(1-2), 45-49.

Gross, J. Emotional expression in cancer onset and progression, *Social Science and Medicine* 1989, 12, 1239-1248.

Grossarth-Maticek, R/ Eysenck, HJ. Coffee-drinking and personality factors in the genesis of cancer and coronary heart disease, *Neuropsycholobiology* 1990, 23, 153-159.

Grossarth-Maticek, R/ Eysenck, HJ. Personality, stress and motivational factors in drinking as determinants of risk for cancer and coronary heart disease, *Psychological Reports* 1991a, 68, 1027-1043.

Grossarth-Maticek, R/ Eysenck, HJ. Cocacola, cancer and coronaries; personality and stress as mediating factors, *Psychological Reports* 1991b, 68, 1083-1087.

Grossarth-Maticek, R/ Eysenck, HJ/ Vetter, H. Personality type, smoking habits and their interaction as predictors of cancer and coronary heart disease, *Personality and Individual Differences* 1988, 9, 479-495.

Grossinger, Richard. *Planet Medicine: From Stone Age Shamanism to Post-Industrial Healing, Vol. I: Origins; Vol. II: Modalities*, Berkeley, CA: North American 1995 (extensively referenced).

Grossman, Richard. *The Other Medicines: An Invitation to Understanding and Using them for Health and Healing*, Garden City, NY: Doubleday 1985.

Grove, DJ/ Panzer, BI. *Resolving Traumatic Memories: Metaphor and symbol in Psychotherapy*, New York: Lexington 1989.

Guerrini, M. Report on clinical trial of

bilberry anthocyanosides in the threatment of venous insufficiency of the lower limbs, *Istituto di Patologia Speciale Medica e Metodologia Clinica*, Universit de Siena, Italy 1987.

Guibert, Herve. Attributed.

Guiley, RE. *Moonscapes: A Celebration of Lunar Astronomy, Magic, Legend and Lore*, New York: Prentice Hall 1991.

Guillemin, Roger (ed). *Neural Modulation of Immunity*, New York: Raven 1984.

Gulak, Jan. Lowering the anxiety levels in persons undergoing bioenergy therapy, Translator Irnich, A. *Psychotronika* 1985, 6-9.

Guldager, B et al. EDTA treatment of intermittent claudication-a double-blind, placebo controlled study, *J International Medical Research* 1992, 231, 261-267.

Gunaratana, The Venerable H. *Mindfulnes in Plain English*, Somerville, MA: Wisdom 1993.

Gunn, CC et al. Dry needling of muscle motor points for chronic low-back pain, *Spine* 1980, 5:279-29 1.

Gurudas, *Gem Elixirs and Vibrational Healing, Vols. I, II*, Channelled by Kevin Ryerson, Boulder, CO: Cassandra 1986.

Gurudas, *Flower Essences and Vibrational Healing*, San Rafael, CA: Cassandra 1989.

Gurvits, BY/ Krylov, BA/ Korotkov, KG. A new concept in the early diagnosis of cancer http://www.kirlian.org/kirlian/korotov/korotkov.htm

Guseo, A. Pulsing electromagnetic field therapy of multiple sclerosis by the Gyuling-Bordacs device: Double blind, crossover and open studies, *J Bioelectricity* 1987, 6(1), 23-35.

Gutman, G et al. Feldenkrais vs. conventional exercise for the elderly, *J Gerontology* 1977, 32, 562-572.

Guzzetta, C. *Essential Readings in Holistic Nursing*, Gaithersburg, MD: Aspen 1998.

H

Haanen, HCM et al. Controlled trial of hypnotherapy in the treatment of refractory fibromyalgia, *J Rheumatology* 1981, 18(1), 72-75.

Haas, MDH et al. Reactivity of leg alignment to articular pressure testing: evaluation of a diagnostic test using a randomized crossover clinical trial approach, *J Manipulative Physiology and Therapy* 1993 16:220-227.

Hadady, Letha. *Asian Health Secrets: The Complete Guide to Asian Herbal Medicine*, New York: Crown 1996.

Haddock, B. Scenario writing: a therapeutic application, *J Mental health Counseling* 1989, 11, 234-243.

Hadler, NMP et al. A benefit of spinal manipulation as adjunctive therapy for acute low-back pain: a stratified controlled trial, *Spine* 1987 12:702-706.

Hagan, KL. *Prayers to the Moon: Exercises in Self-Reflection*, San Francisco: Harper 1991.

Hahnemann, Samuel. *Organor of Medicine, Trans*lated by William Boericke) New Delhi: Hayeet 1974.

Hahnemann, S. *Organon of the Medical Art*, O'Reilly, WB (ed), Redmond, WA: Birdcage 1996.

Haker E and Lundeberg T (1990). Acupuncture treatment in epicondylalgia: A comparative study of two acupuncture techniques, *ClinjPain* 6:221-226.

Halberg, F. Chronobiology, *Annual Review of Physiology* 1969, 31, 675-725.

Haldeman, SD et al. *Guidelines for chiropractic quality assurance and practice parameters*, Aspen Publishers, Gaithersburg, MD 1992.

Haley, Daniel. *Politics in Healing: The Suppression and Manipulation of American Medicine* , Washington DC: Potomac Valley 2001

Haley, Jay. *Uncommon Therapy: The Psychiatric Techniques of Milton H Erickson, MD* New York: Ballantine 1973. (Reprinted by permission of WW Norton & Company, Inc. Copyright 1973 Jay Haley.)

Haley, Jay. *Problem-Solving Therapy*, San Francisco: Jossey-Bass 1976.

Halifax, Joan. *Shaman: The Wounded Healer* New York: Crossroads 1981.

Halifax, J. *Shamanic Voices: A Survey of Visionary Narratives*, New York: Dutton 1994.

Hall, Dorothy. *Iridology: How the Eyes Reveal Your Health and Personality*, New Canaan, CT: Keats 1980.

Hall, Dorothy. *Creating Your Herbal Profile*, New Canaan, CT: Keats 1988.

Hall, EG. Strategies for using Journal writing in counseling gifted students, *Gifted child Today* 1990, 13(4), 2-6.

Halpern, Steven. *Sound Health*, New York: Harper & Row 1985.

Halvorson-Boyd, Glenna/ Hunter, Lisa K. *Dancing In Limbo: Making Sense of Life After Cancer*, San Francisco: Jossey-Bass Publishers 1995.

Hamdan, I. Acidolin and antibiotic produced by acidophilus, *J Antibiotics* 8, 631-636.

Hammer, Leon. *Dragon Rises Red Bird Flies: Psychology and Chinese Medicine*, Barrytown, New York: Station Hill 1990.

Hammerschlag, Carl A/ Silverman, Howard D. *Healing Ceremonies: Creating Personal Rituals for Spiritual, Emotional, Physical, and Mental Health*, New York: Perigee/ Berkeley 1997.

Hampden-Turner, Charles. *Maps of the Mind*, New York: Collier/ Macmillan 1982.

Hancke, C/ Flytlie, K. Benefits of EDTA chelation therapy in arteriosclerosis: a retrospective study of 470 patients, *J Advancement in Medicine* 1993, 6(3), 161-171.

Hand, W (ed). *American Folk Medicine: A Symposium*, Berkeley: University of California 1976.

Hanna, Thomas. *Somatics: Reawakening the Mind's Control of Movement, Flexibility, and Health*, New York: Addison-Wesley 1988.

Hannah, B. *Encounters with the Soul: Active Imagination as Developed by CG Jung*, Boston: Shambhala 1981.

Hannemann, Holger. *Magnet Therapy: Balancing Your Body's Energy Flow for Self-Healing*, Sterling 1990

Hansen PE and Hansen JH. Acupuncture treatment of chronic facial pain - a controlled cross-over trial, *Headache*1983, 23, 66-69.

Hansen, DT et al. Proposal for establishing structure and process in the development of implicit chiropractic standards of care and practice guidelinesI, *J Manipulative Physiology and Therapeutics* 1992 15, 430-438.

Hansen, GP. Dowsing: A review of experimental research, *J the Society for Psychical Research* 1982, 51, 343-367.

Harding, Suzanne. Curanderas in the Americas, *Alternative & Complementary Therapies* (Oct) 1999, 5(5), 309-317.

Harlow, HF. Development of affectional patterns in infant monkeys, In: Foss, BM (ed). *Determinants of Infant Behavior* New York: John Wiley & Sons 1961, 75-88.

Harner, G et al. Comparison of equivalence between the St. John's wort extract LoHyp-57 and fluoxetine, *Arzneim-Forsch/ Drug Research*

Harner, Michael. The *Way of the Shaman*, New York: Bantam/ Harper& Row 1980.

Harrington, A (ed). *The Placebo Effect: An Interdisciplinary Exploration*, Cambridge, Mass: Harvard University Press 1998.

Harris, Philip/ Rees, R. The prevalence of complementary and alternative medicine use among the general population; a systematic review of the literature, *Complementary Therapies in Medicine* (UK) 2000, 8, 88-96.

Harrison, Eric. *How Meditation Heals*, London: Piatkus 2000.

Harrison, John. *Love Your Disease - It's Keeping You Healthy*, London: Angus & Robertson 1984.

Harrison, Shirley. *New Approaches to Cancer*, London: Century 1987.

Harrower, M. *The Therapy of Poetry*, Springfield, IL: Thomas 1972.

Hart, A. Randomized controlled trials: the

584 References

control group dilemma revisited, *Complementary Therapies in Medicine* 2001, 9, 40-44.

Hartmann, E. *Krankheit als Standortproblem*, Heidelberg: Haug Verlag 1967.

Hartmann, E. 20 Jahre private Krebsforschung, *Wetter Boden Mensch* 1970, 10, 517-552.

Hartmann, E. 20 Reaktionszeitmessungen über geopathogenen Zone, *Wetter Boden Mensch* 1972a, 15, 961-963.

Hartmann, E. Tumorwachstum bei Ratten in Abhängigkeit von Standort und Milieu, *Wetter Boden Mensch* 1972b, 16, 988-996.

Hartmann, E. *Krankheit als Standortproblem*, 3rd ed, Heidelberg: Haug Verlag 1976.

Hartmann-Kent, Silvia. *Adventures in EFT*, DH Publications 1999.

Harvalik, ZV. Sensitivity tests on a dowser exposed to artificial DC magnetic fields, *American Dowser* 1973a, 13(3), 85-96.

Harvalik, ZV. Dowsing reactions to polarized electromagnetic radiations, *American Dowser* 1973b, 13(3), 92-95.

Harvalik, ZV. High frequency beams aid in locating the dowsing sensors, *American Dowser* 1973c, 13(3), 95-96.

Harvalik, ZV. Anatomical localization of human detection of weak electromagnetic radiation experiments with dowsers, *Physiological Chemistry and Physics* 1978, 10, 525-5 34.

Harvalik, ZV. A biophysical magnetometer-gradiometer, *Virginia J Science* 1970, 21: 59-60Heron, John, *Confessions of a Janus Brain*, London: Endymion 1987.

Harvey, Clare/ Cochrane, Amanda. *Encyclopaedia of Flower Remedies*, London: Thorsens 1995.

Harvey, RF et al. Individual and group hypnotherapy in treatment of refractory irritable bowel syndrome, *Lancet* 1989, 1, 424-425.

Harwood, A (ed). *Ethnicity and Medical Care*, Cambridge, MA: Harvard University 1981.

Hass, M et al. The reliability of muscle testing response to a provocative 1 chal-

lenge, *Chiropractic Technique* 1993, 5, 95-,100

Hastings, Arthur C/ Fadiman, James/ Gordon, James X. *Health for the Whole Person: The Complete Guide to Holistic Medicine*, Boulder, CO: Westview Press 1981.

Haxby, DG. reaqtment of nicotine dependence, *American J Health Systems Pharmaceuticals* 1995, 52(3), 265-281.

Hay, IC et al. Randomized trial of aromatherapy-successful treatment for alopecia areata, *Archives of Dermatology* 1998, 134, 1349-1352.

Hay, Louise L. *You Can Heal Your Life,* Santa Monica, CA: Hay House 1984.

HealthNotes Clinical Essentials, Vol. I: Drug-Herb-Supplement Depletions/ Interactions, Portland, OR: HealthNotes, 2000.

Hebenstreit, Gunther 1995: "Der Orgonakkumulator Nach Wilhelm Reich. Eine Experimentelle Untersuchung zur Spannungs-Ladungs-Formel", Diplomarbeit zur Erlangung des Magistergrades der Philosophie an der Grung- und Integrativwissenschaftlichen Fakultat der Universitat Wien.

Heckler, Richard. *The Anatomyh of Change: East/ West Approaches to Body/ Mind Therapy*, Boston, MA: Shambhala 1984.

Hedges, Ken. Phosphenes in the context of Native American art, *American Rock Art* 1982, 7-8, 1-10.

Heidegger, Martin. Attributed.

Heidt, Patricia. *An Investigation of the Effect of Therapeutic Touch on the Anxiety of Hospitalized Patients* (Dissertation), New York University 1979.

Heidt, Patricia. Effect of Therapeutic Touch on anxiety level of hospitalized patients, *Nursing Research* 1981, 30(1), 32-37.

Heinerman, John. *The Benefits of Garlic: From Pharoahs to Pharmacists*, New Canaan, CT: Keats 1994.

Heinze, Ruth Inge. *Trance and Healing in Southeast Asia Today: Twenty-One Case Studies*, Berkeley: University of California 1984a.

Heinze, Ruth Inge (ed). *Proceedings of the*

International Conference on Shamanism, St. Sabina Center San Rafael, *CA 1984 (11-13 May)*, Berkeley, CA: Center far South and Southeast Asia Studies, University of California 1984b.

Heinze, Ruth I. *Proceedings of the International Conference on the Study of Shamanism, San Rafael CA 1985*, Berkeley, CA: Center for South and Southeast Asia Studies.

Heline, Corinne. *Healing and Regeneration through Color, Music*, Marina del Rey, CA: DeVorss 1983.

Heller, Joseph/ Henkin, William. *Bodywise*, Bodywise, Berkeley, CA: Wingbow 1991.

Heller, P. The three pillars of poetry therapy, *The Arts in Psychotherapy* 1987, 11, 341-344.

Heller, P. Biblio/ Poetry therapy in the treatment of multiple personality disorder, *Treating Abuse Today* 1993, 3, 10-14.

Helms, JM. Acupuncture for the management of primary dysmenorrhea, *Obstetrics and Gynecology* 1987, 69:51-56.

Helms, J. Physicians and Acupuncture in the 1990s, Report for the Subcommittee on Labor, Health and Human Services, and Education of the Apopropriations Committee, US Senate, 24 June 1993, *American Academy of Medical Acupuncture Review* 1993, 5 1-6.

Helms, Joseph M. *Acupuncture Energetics: A Clinical Approach for Physicians*, Berkeley, CA: Medical Acupuncture 1995.

Helms, Joseph M. An overview of medical acupuncture, *Alternative Therapies* 1998, 4(3), 35-45.

Hemingway, Tricia, Personal communication 1995.

Hendricks, Gay/ Hendricks, Kathlyn. *Radiance: Breathwork, Movement, and Body-Centered Psychotherapy*, Berkeley, CA: Wingbow 1991.

Hendricks, Gay/ Hendricks, Kathlyn. *At the Speed of Life: A New Approach to Personal Change Through Body-Centered Therapy*, New York: Bantam 1993.

Henry, J. *Surviving the Cure*, Cope Inc. Cleveland, (216) 663-0855 1984.

Henry, John. *BMA New Guide to Medicines and Drugs*, New York/ London: Dorling Kindersley 1988.

Herbal Medicine: Expanded Commission E Monographs, Newton, MA: Integrative Medicine Communications, 2000.

Herbert, Benson. Near and distant healing, *J Paraphysics* 1973, *7(5)*, 213-218.

Herbert, Benson. Theory and practice of psychic healing, *Parapsychology Review* 1975, 6(6), 22-23 (excerpted in Benor 2001c).

Herbert, Benson. Systemic hypertension and the relaxation response, *New England J Medicine* 1977, 296(20), 1152-1156,

Herbert, Benson. Automatisms: Signals from the unconscious, Part one: The pendulum and the biophysical effect (BPS), *International J Paraphysics* 1979a, 13(5;6), ll6-121.

Herbert, Benson. Biogravitation: experimental evidence, *Proceedings of the 4th International Conference on Psychotronic Research*, Sao Paulo, Brazil 1979b, 149-152.

Herbert, Benson. The Mind/ Body Effect: How Behavioral Medicine Can Show You the Way to Better Health, New York: Simon & Schuster 1979c.

Hermanson, GH. *An investigation of relationships among imagery of feeling states, imagery of neurtophils/ IgA and immune responsibility as measured by blood neutrophil function and secretory IgA levels*, Unpublished doctoral dissertation, Michigan State University 1983.

Heron, John. *Confessions of a Janus-Brain: A Personal Account of Living in Two Worlds*, London: Endymion 1987.

Herscu, Paul. *The Homeopathic Treatment of Children: Pediatric Constitutional Types*, Berkeley, CA: north Atlantic 1991.

Hesse, J et al. Acupuncture versus metoprolol in migraine prophylaxis: a randomized trial of trigger point inactivation, *J Internal Medicine* 1994, 235: 451-456.

Hewitt, James. *Teach Yourself Yoga*, Sevenoaks, Kent, England 1979.

Hicks, A. *Principles of Chinese Medicine*, HarperSanFrancisco 1996.

Hicks, JT. Treatment of fatigue in general

practice: a double-blind study, *Clinical Medicine* 1964 (Jan), 85-90.

Hider, J. Yoga for the visually handicapped: a kind of tranquility, *Nursing Mirror* 1983, 156, 18-21.

Hildebrandt, G/ Hensel, H (eds). *Biological Adaptation*, Stuttgart, Germany: Thieme 1982.

Hilfiker, David. *Healing the Wounds: A Physician Looks at his Work,* New York: Pantheon 1985.

Hilgard, ER. *Hypnotic Susceptibility*, New York: Harcourt-Brace, World 1965.

Hilgard, ER. Sequelae to hypnosis, *International J Clinical and Experimental Hypnosis* 1974, 22, 281-298.

Hilgard, ER/ Hilgard, JR. *Hypnosis in the Relief of Pain*, Los Altos, CA: William Kaufmann 1975.

Hill, Ann (ed). *A Visual Encyclopedia of Unconventional Medicine,* New York: Crown 1979.

Hill, Christopher. Is kundalini real? In: White, John. *Kundalini: Evolution and Enlightenment,* 1990, 106-119.

Hill, C/ Doyon, F. Review of randomised trials in homeopathy, *Review Epidemiol. Sante. Publ.* 1990, 38 138-147.

Hillary, Eve. *Children of a Toxic Harvest: An Environmental Autobiography,* Australia: Lothian Pub Co 1997)

Hillary, Eve. *Health Betrayal; Staying away from the sickness industry,* Australia: Lothian Pub Co 1997)

Hillman, J. *Re-Visioning Psychology*, New York: Harper & Row 1977, p. 74.

Hills, Christopher. *Nuclear Evolution: Discovery of the Rainbow Body,* Boulder Creek, CA: University of the Trees 1977.

Hinman, Martha R et al. Effects of static magnets on chronic knee pain and physical function: a double-blind study, *Alternative Therapies* 2002, 8(4), 50-55

Hippocrates, *Law, Book I* .

Hirshberg, Caryl/ Barasch, Marc Ian. *Remarkable Recovery: What Extraordinary Healings Tell Us About Getting Well and Staying Well*, New York: Riverhead 1995.

Hixon, Lex. *The Heart of the Korani,* Wheaton, IL: Theosophical 1988.

Ho, RT et al. Electro-acupuncture and postoperative emesis, *Anaesthesia* 1990, 45:327-329.

Hochler, FK/ Tobis, JS/ Buerger, AA. Spinal manipulation for low back pain, *J the American Medical Association* 1981, 245, 1835-1838.

Hocking, Doreen. Denial in terminal care, *Doctor-Healer Network Newsletter,* Winter 1992-93, 15- 18.

Hodges, Doris M. *Healing Stones,* Hiawatha IA: Pyramid 1961.

Hodges, D. For every season: Art and poetry therapy with terminally ill patients, *J Poetry Therapy* 1993, 7, 21-43.

Hodgkinson, Neville. *Will to Be Well: The Real Alternative Medicine*, York Beach, ME: Samuel Weiser 1986.

Hodson, Geoffrey. *Kingdom of the Gods,* Adyar, Madras, India: Theosophical 1970. (From Peterson 1987)

Hoehler, FK et al. Spinal manipulation for low back pain, *J the American Medical Association* 1981, 245, 1835-1839.

Hoffer, Abrham/ Walker, Morton. *Orthomolecular Nurtition*, New Canaan, CT: Keats 1978.

Hoffman, D. *The New Holistic Herbal*, Rockport, MA: Element 1992.

Hoffman, EJ. Enzyme inhibitors for cancer cell metabolism, *Townsend Letter for Doctors and Patients,* May 1997.

Hoffman, EJ. Garlic and allicin and other sulfur-containing compounds as anticancer agents, *Townsend Letter* 1999, Jan, 54-59.

Hoffmann, David. *The Holistic Herbal,* London: Element 1988.

Hoffmann, David. *The New Holistic Herbal*, Rockport, MA: Element 1992.

Hogeboom, CJ et al. Variation in diagnosis and treatment of chronic low back pain by traditional Chinese medicine acupuncturist, *Complementary Therapies in Medicine* 2001,9, 154-166.

Holbeche, Soozi. *The Power of Gems and Crystals,* London: Piatkus 1989.

Holden, Constance. Chiropractic: Healing or hokum? HEW is looking for answers, *Science* 1974, 185, 922-925.

Holden, C. Cancer and the mind: How are

they connected?, *Science* 1978,200, 1363-1369.

Holden, Robert. *Living Wonderfully: A Joyful Guide to Conscious Creative Living - for Today*, London: Thorsons/ Harper-Collins 1994.

Holland, Jimmie C/ Rowland, Julia H (eds). *Handbook of Psychooncology: Psycholo-gical Care of the Patient with Cancer*, New York/ Oxford: Oxford University Press 1990.

Hollenweger, WJ. *The Pentecostals,* Minneapolis, MN: Augsburg 1972.

Hollis, N. *Massage for Therapists*, Oxford: Blackswell 1987.

Holmes, Ernest. *The Science of Mind,* New York: Dodd, Mend 1938.

Holmes, Oliver Wendell. Attributed.

Holmes, Peter. *Jade Remedies: A Chinese Herbal Reference for the West*, Volume 1 & 2, Boulder, CO: Snow Lotus Press 1997.

Holmes, TH/ Rahe, RH. The social readjustment rating scale, *J Psychosomatic Research* 1967, 11,213.

Honigfeld, Gilbert. Non-specific factors in treatment: I. Review of placebo reactions and placebo reactors, *Diseases of the Nervous System* 1964, *25, 145-156.*

Honiotest, GJ. Hypnosis and breast enlargement-a pilot study, *J International Society for Professional Hypnosis* 1977, 6, 8-12.

Honorton, C/ Ferrari, DC. Future telling: a meta-analysis of forced-choice precognition experiments 1935-1987, *J Parapsychology* 1989, 53, 281-308.

Honorton, Charles/ Krippner, Stanley. Hypnosis and ESP: A review of the experimental literature, *J the American Society of Psychical Research* 1969, 63, 214-252.

Honorton, C/ Tierney, L/ Torres, D. The role of mental imagery in psi-mediation, *J the American Society for Psychical Research* 1974, 68, 385-394.

Hooke, Wayne. A review of Thought Field Therapy, *The International Electronic J in the Study of the Traumatization Process and Methods for Reducing or Eliminating Related Human Suffering* 1998, 3(2), article 2, www.fsu.edu/-trauma/v3i2art3.html

Hopkins, Jeffrey. *Meditation on Emptiness,* London: Wisdom 1983.

Hopkins, Jim. Health care tops taxes as small business cost drain, *USA Today* http://www.usatoday.com/news/health/200 3- 04-20-small-business-costs_x.htm

Horgan, John., *Rational Mysticism*, New York, New York: Houghton Mifflin Company 2003, p. 167.

Horiuchi, S et al. Two different histamine-sensitizing activities of pertussis vaccine observed in mice on the 4th and 12th days of sensitization, Japan J Med Sci Biol, 1993; 46:17-27.

Hornig, Mady. Hypericum (St. John's Wort) for treatment of depression, *Alternative Medicine Alert* 1998, 1,1, 4-9.

Horowitz, Len. Mass Murder in Medicine: "Iatrogenocide" http://www.tetrahedron.org/Mass_Murder _in_Medicine.html

Horrigan, Bonnie. Interview of Harriet Beinfield and Efrem Korngold: Eastern Medicine for Western people, Alternative Medicine 1998, 4(3), 80-87.

Horrigan, Bonnie/ Block, Bryna. News briefs, *Alternative Therapies 2002*, 8(4), p. 31

Hotchkiss, S. How thin is your skin? *New Scientist* 1994 141 (1910), 24-27.

Houldin, AD et al. Psychoneuroimmunology: a review of literature, *Holistic Nursing Practice* 1991, 5 10-21.

Houlding, S/ Holland, P. Contributions of poetry writing group to the treatment of severely disturbed psychiatric inpatients, *Clinical Social Work J* 1988, 16, 194-201.

Houston, Jean. *Life Force: The Psycho-Historical Recovery of the Self,* New York: Delta/ Dell 1980.

Houston, Jean. *The Search for the Beloved: Journeys in Mythology and Sacred Psychology*, Los Angeles: Tarcher 1987.

Howard, Judy. *Growing Up with Bach Flower Remedies: A guide to the use of the remedies during childhood and adolescence,* Saffron Walden, UK: CW Daniel 1994.

Howard, J et al. Handedness and breast cancer laterality: testing a hypothesis, *Human Biology* 1982, 54, 365-371.

Howe, F (ed). *No More Masks: an Anthology of Twentieth-Century American Women Poets*, New York: HarperCollins 1993.

Hsieh, CY/ Phillips, RB. Reliability of manual muscle testing with a computerized dynamometer, *J Manipulative Physiological Therapy* 1990, 13,72-82.

Hsu, Ding-ming. *The Chinese Psychic Healing,* Taipei: Parapsychological Assoc. 1984, 6.

Hu, S. P6 acupressure reduces symptoms of vection-induced motion sickness, *Aviation and Space Environmental Medicine* 1995, 66:631-634.

Hubbard, GS/ May, EC. Aspects of measurement and applications of geomagnetic indices and extremely low frequency radiation for use in parapsychology, *Proceedings of Presented Papers, 29th Annual Convention of the Parapsychological Association 1986*, p. 5l9-535.

Hubble, Mark A et al (eds). *The Heart & Soul of Change: What Works in Therapy,* American Psychological Association 1999.

Huebscher, Roxana. Pets and Animal-Assisted Therapy, *Nurse Practitioner Forum,* 2000, 11(1).

Hudson, T. Gynecology and Naturopathic Medicine: A Treatment Manual (2nd ed), Olympia, WA: C.K.E. Publications 1993.

Hudson, Tori. *Women's Encyclopedia of Natural Medicine*, Lincolnwood, IL: NTC/ Contemporary 1999.

Hufford, DJ. Folk medicine in contemporary America, In Kirkland, J et al (ed), *Herbal and Magical Medicine, Traditional Healing Today*, Durham, NC: Duke University 1992.

Huggins, Hal A. *It's All in Your Head: The Link Between Mercury Amalgams and Illness*, Garden City Park, NK: Avery 1993.

Hughes-Calero, H. *Writing as a Tool for Self-Discovery*, Coastline 1995.

Hulke, Malcolm (ed). *The Encyclopedia of Alternative Medicine and Self-Help,* New York: Schocken 1979.

Hulley, S et al. Noncardiovascular disease outcomes during 6.9 years of hormone therapy. Heart and Estrogen/progestin Replacement Study followup (HERS II). *JAMA* 2002;288(1):49-57

Hultkrantz, A. The shaman and the medicine man, *Social Science and Medicine* 1985, 20, 511-515.

Humphrey, CE/ Seal, EH. Biophysical approach toward tumor regression in mice, *Science* 1959, 130, 388.

Hunt, Roland. *The Eighty Key to Colour,* Essex, England: LN Fowler 1965.

Hunt, Valerie. *A Study of Structural integration from Neuromuscular Energy Field, and Emotional Approaches*, Unpublished project report 1977.

Hunt, Valerie. Electromyographic high frequency recording of human informational fields, In: *Energy Fields in Medicine: A Study of device Technology Based on Acupuncture Meridians and Chi Energy,* Kalamazoo, MI: Fetzer Foundation 1989,400-427.

Hunt, Valerie. *Lectures at* Healing Energy Medicine Conference, London 1992. (Taped, from Doctor-Healer Network)

Hunt, Valerie. *Infinite Mind: The Scinece of Human Vibrations*, Malibu, CA: Malibu 1995.

Hurley, J Finley. *Sorcery,* Boston/ London: Routledge and Kegan Paul 1985.

Hutchinson, Michael. *The Book of Floating*, New York: William Morrow 1984 (270 refs).

Hutchinson, Michael. Megabrain: New Tools and Techniques for Brain Growth and Mind Expansion, New York: Morrow 1986.

Hutsehnecker, AA. *The Will to Live,* New York: Prentice Hall 1951.

Huxley, Aldous. *The Perennial Philosophy,* New York: Harper& Row 1944.

Huxley, Aldous. *Science, Liberty and Peace,* New York: Harper & Brothers 1946.

Huxley, Francis. Unusual methods of healing, *J the British Society of Flowers* 1964, l8(l23),4-6.

Hwang, YC/ Jenkins, EM. Effect of acupuncture on young pigs with induced enteropathogenic *Escherichia coli* diarrhea, *American J Veterinary Research* 1988, 49 1641-1643.

Hyde, E. Acupressure therapy for morning sickness: A controlled clinical trial, *J Nurse-Midwifery* 1989, 34:171-178.

Hyman, Ray. The mischief making of ideomotor action, *Scientific Review of Alternative Medicine* 1999, 3(2):34-43. (Psi skeptics' journal) http://www.hcrc.org/contrib/hyman/ideom otor.html

Hyman, Ray. The mischief-making of ideomotor action,

Hynes, AM. Poetry: an avenue into spirit, *J Poetry Therapy* 1990, 4, 71-82.

Hynes, AM/ Hynes-Berry, M. *Biblio/ Poetry Therapy-The Interactive process: A Handbook*, Boulder, CO: Westview 1986.

Hyvarien, J/ Karlson, M. Low resistance skin points that may coincide with acupuncture locations, *Medical Biology* 1977, 55, 88-94.

I

Iannuzzo, Giovanni. 'Fire-immunity': Psi ability or psychophysiological phenomenon? *Psi Research* 1983, 2(4), 68-74.

IBIS Guide to Drug-Herb and Drug-Nutrient Interactions, www.IBISmedical.com/Interactions.html

Ikemi, Y. Psychological desensitization in allergic disorders, In Lassner, J, ed. *Hypnosis and Psychosomatic Medicine* New York: Springer-Verlag 1967 160-165.

Ikerni, Yunjo et al. Psychosomatic consideration on cancer patients who have made a narrow escape from death, *Dynamische Paychiatrie* 1975, 8, 77-92.

Ikin, A Graham. New Concepts of Healing: Medical, Psychological and Religious, New York: Association Press 1956.

Illich, Ivan. *Medical Nemesis: The Expropriation of Health*, New York: Pantheon/ Random House 1976.

Ilnycki, A et al, A randomized controlled trial of psychotherapeutic intervention in cancer patients, *Annals of the Royal College of Physicians and Surgeons of Canada* 1994, 27, 93-96.

Imai, K / Nakachi, K. Cross sectional study of effects of drinking green tea on cardiovascular and liver diseases, *British Medical J* 1995, 310, 122-125.

Inayat, Khan. *The Bowl of Sold: Thoughts for Daily Contemplation* (no date)

Inglis, Brian. *The Case for Unorthodox Medicine,* New York: GE Putnam's Sons 1965.

Inglis, Brian. *The Book of the Back: Where to Seek Help for Your Aches and Pains: All the Treatments from Acupuncture to Yoga,* London: Ebury 1978.

Inglis, Brian. All in the mind?, *The Unexplained* 1981a, 3(34), 670-673.

Inglis, Brian. A shameful affliction, *The Unexplained* 1981b, 3(36), 714-717.

Inglis, Brian. The healing trance, *The Unexplained* 1981c, 4(4), 934-937.

Inglis, Brian. A psychic contagion, *The Unexplained* 1981d, 4(37), 726-729.

Inglis, Brian. Retrocognitive dissonance, *Theta* 1986, 13/ 14(1), 4-9.

Inglis Brian. Mesmerism, in: *Natural and Supernatural: A History of the Paranormal*, Bridport, dorset, UK: Prism 1992, 135-198.

Inglis, Brian/ West, Ruth. *The Unknown Guest: The Mystery of Intuition,* London: Coronet/ Hodder & Stoughton 1987.

Inkeles, Gordon. *Unwinding: Super Massage for Stress Control*, New York: Weidenfeld and Nicolson 1988.

Inlander, Charles B. *150 Ways to be a Savvy Medical Consumer*, Allentown, PA: People's Medical Society 1992.

Inlander, Charles B et al. *Medicine on Trial: The Appalling Story of Medical Ineptitude and the Arrogance that Overlooks It*, New York: Pantheon/ Random House 1998.

Innes, Brian. The signs of success, *The Unexplained* 1981, 3(32), 634-637.

Institute of Noetic Sciences/ Poole, William. *The Heart of Healing*, Atlanta: Turner 1993.

Intramedicine, Inc. subscription website for herbal and supplement information www.intramedicine.com/ default.asp

Inyushin, VM. Report No.5, Translated by

Cassirer & Herbert, *J Paraphysics* 1972, 6(5), 208-212.

Ironson, G et al. Can psychological inter-ven-tions affect immunity and survival? Present findings and suggested targets with a focus on cancer and human immu-nodeficiency virus, *Mind/ Body Medicine* 1995, 5, 85-110.

Irwin, Y/ Wagenvoord, J. *Shiatzu,* Phila-delphia, PA: JB Lippincott 1976.

Isaacs, Julian/ Patten, Terry. A double blind study of the 'biocircuit', a putative subtle-energy based relaxation device, *Subtle Energies* 1991, 2(2), 1-28.

Ivanova, Barbara. Relation of Paraphe-nom-ena to Physical Fields, *International J Paraphysics* 1980, 14 (5&6), 110-112.

Ivanova, Barbara. *The Golden Chalice,* (Mir, Maria and Vilenskaya, Larissa. Eds) San Francisco, CA: HS Dakin 1986.

Ivker, R/ Anderson, R/ Trivieri, L. *The Self-Care Guide to Holistic Medicine: Creating Optimal Health,* New York: Archer/Putnam, 2000.

Iyengar, B. *Light on Yoga*, New York: Schocken 1987.

Iyengar, B. *Light on Pranayama*, New York: Crossroad 1992.

J

Jack, WH. Dowsing for the presence or absence of an electromagnetic field, *New England J Parapsychology* 1978, 1(2), 16-22. (From Hansen)

Jackson, Christina. Movement, breathing and christian meditation: catalysts for spiritual growth, *International J Healing and Caring – On line* 2003, 3(2).

Jackson, ME. The use of Therapeutic Touch in the nursing care of the terminally ill person, Chapter 7, in: Borelli, MD. and Heidt, P (eds). *Therapeutic Touch: A Book of Readings*, New York: Springer 1981, 72-79.

Jackson, O. The Feldenkrais Method: a personalized learning model, in: Lister, M (ed). *Contemporary Mangement of Motor Control Problems: Proceedings of the II-Step Conference*, Foundation for Physical Therapy 1991 131-135.

Jackson, T. *Patient's at Large,* Jackson's Corner, PO Box 504, Pacifica, CA 94044 1984.

Jackson-Wyatt, O et al. Effects of Fel-denkrais practitioner training program on motor ability: a videoanalysis, *Physical Therapy* 1992, 72 (suppl), S86.

Jacobs, GE et al. Diagnosis of thyroid dysfunction: Applied Kinesiology com-pared to clinical observations and laboratory tests, *J Manipulative Physio-logical Therapy* 1984, 7, 99-104.

Jacobs, J et al. Treatment of acute child-hood diarrhea with homeopathic medicine: a randomized clinical trial in Nicaragua, *Pediatrics* 1994, 93(5), 719-725.

Jacobs, J et al. Homeopathic treatment of acute childhood diarrhea: results from a clinical trial in Nepal, *J Alternative and Complementary Medicine* 2000, 6(2), 131-139.

Jacobs, Maryce M (ed). *Vitamins and Minerals in the Prevention and Treatment of Cancer*, Boca Raton, FL: CRC 1991.

Jacobson, NS/ Traux, P. Clinical signifi-cance: A statistical approach to defining meaningful change in psychotherapy re-search, *J Consulting and Clinical Psychology* 1991, 59(1), 12-19.

Jacobson, Nils/ Wiklund, Nils, Investiga-tion of Claims of Diagnosing by means of ESP, In: *Research in Parapsychology 1975*, Metuchen, NJ: Scarecrow 1976, 74-76.

Jadad, AR/ Rennie, D. The randomized controlled trial gets a middle-age checkup, *J the American Medical Association* 1998, 279(4), 319-320.

Jaeger, R (ed). *Complementary Methods for Research in Education*, Washington, DC American Educational Research As-sociation 1988.

Jaffe, Dennis T. *Healing from Within,* New York: Knopf 1980.

Jafolla, Richard. *Soul Surgery,* Marina del Rey, CA: De Vorss 1982.

Jäger, W et al. Percutaneous absorption of lavender oil from a massage oil, *J the Society for Cosmetic Chemistry* 1992, 43, 49-54.

Jahn, Robert G/ Dunne, Brenda J. *The Margins of Reality,* San Diego, CA/ London: Harcourt, Brace Jovanovich 1987.

Jahnke, Roger. *The Healing Promise of Qi: Creating Extraordinary Wellness Through Qigong and Tai Chi,* New York: Contemporary/McGraw-Hill 2002.

JAMA (editorial). Postinfectious encephal-itis, a problem of increasing importance, May, 1929; 92(18):1523-1524.

Jamal, Tranvir. *Complementary Medicine: A Practial Guide,* England: Butterworth Heinemann 1997.

James, JW/ Cherry, F. *The Grief Recovery Handbook: A Step by Step Program for Moving Beyond Loss,* New York: Perennial/ Harper and Row 1988.

James, William. *The Varieties of Religious Experience,* New York/ London: Collier/ Macmillan 1961.

Jamison, RN et al. Cognitive-behavioral classifications of chronic pain: Replication and extension of empirically derived patient profiles, *Pain* 1994, 57(3), 277-292.

Janet, P. Deuxieme note sous le somneil provoqué a distance et la suggestion mentale pendant l'etat somnambulique, *Revue Philosophique de la France et de l'Etranger* 1886, 212-224.

Janov, Arthur. *The Primal Scream,* New York: Dell 1970.

Janssen, AM et al. Antimocrobial activity of essential oils: 1976-1986 literature review, *Planta Medica* 1987, 53(5), 395-398.

Jaynes, Julian. The Origin of Consciousness in the Breakdown of the Bicameral Mind, Boston, MA: Houghton Muffin 1976.

Jeans, James. *The Mysterious Universe,* New York: Macmillan; Cambridge: University Press 1948.

Jeffrey, Francis. Working in isolation: States that alter consciousness, In: Wolman, Benjamin/ Ullman, Montague: *Handbook of States of Consciousness,* New York: Van Nostrand Reinhold 1986, 249-285.

Jehu, D. *Patients as victims: sexual abuse in psychotherapy and counseling,* San Francisco: Wiley 1994.

Jensen, Bernard. *The Science and Practice of Iridology,* Provo, UT: BiWorld 1952.

Jersild, Arthur J. *Child Psychology,* Englewood Cliffs, NJ: Prentice-Hall 1968. (From Peterson 1987)

Jiang, W et al. Mental stress-induced myocardial ischemia and cardiac events, *J the American Medical Association* 1996, Jun 5, 275(21).

Jirout, J. Comments regarding the diagnosis and treatment of dysfunctions in the C2-C3 segment, *Manual Medicine* 1985, 2, 62.

Joachim, G. The effects of two stress management techniques on feelings of well-being in patients with inflammatory bowel disease, *Nursing Papers* 1983 15, 5-18.

Jobst, KA. A critical analysis of acupuncture in pulmonary disease: efficcacy and safety of the acupuncture needle, *J Alternative and Complementary Medicine* 1995 1(1), 57-85.

Jobst, K et al. Controlled trial of acupuncture for disabling breathlessness, *Lancet* 1986, 2:1416-1419.

Johansson, A et al. Acupuncture in treatment of facial Muscular pain, *Acta Odontol Scand* 1991, 49, 153-158.

Johansson, K et al. Can sensory stimulation improve the functional outcome in stroke patients?, *Neurology* 1993, 43:2189-2192.

Johansson, G et al. Effects of magnesium hydroxide in renal stone disease, *J the American College of Nutrition* 1982, 1, 179-185.

Johnson, D. *Body*, Boston, MA: Beacon 1983.

Johnson, Denny. *What the Eye Reveals: An Introduction to the Rayid Method of Iris Interpretation*, Goleta, CA: Rayid 1984.

Johnson, Don Hanlon (ed). *Bone, Breath and Gesture*, Berkeley, CA: North Atlantic 1995.

Johnson, DR. Perspective: shame dynamics among creative arts therapists, *The Arts in Psychotherapy* 1994, 21, 173-178.

Johnson, Kendall. Personal communication 1974.

Johnson, Kendall. The Living Aura: Radiation Field Photography and the Kirlian Effect, New York: Hawthorn 1975.

Johnson, P Youlden. Healing Fingers: The Power of Yoga Pranic Healing, New York: Rider 1950.

Johnson, Steve. The Essence of Healing: A Guide to the Alaskan Flower, Gem, and Environmental Essences, Homer, AK: Alaskan Flower Essence Project 1996.

Johnson, Tim. The Herbage Ethnobotany Database CD-Rom, Second Edition, 2003 http://holisticopia.com/herbage

Johnston, B. One-third of a nation's adults use herbal remedies: market estimated at $3.24 billion, HerbalGram 1997; 40, 52.

Johnston, WL. Interexaminer reliability studies: spanning a gap in medical research. Louisa Burns Memorial Lecture, J the American Osteopathic Association 1982, 81, 819-829.

Johnston, WL et al. Passive gross motion testing, Part III. Esaminer agreement on selected subjects, J the American Osteopathic Association 1982a, 81, 309-313.

Johnston, WL et al. Passive gross motion testing, Part II. A study of interexaminer agreement, J the American Osteopathic Association 1982b, 81, 304-308.

Johnston, WL et al. Interexaminer study of palpation in detecting location of spinal segmental dysfunction, J the American Osteopathic Association 1983, 82, 839-845.

Jonas, Gerald. Visceral Learning, New York: Viking 1973.

Jonas, Wayne B. Do homeopathic nosodes protect against infection? An experimental test, Alternative Therapies 1999, 5(5), 36-40.

Jonas, WB. Magic and methodology: when paradigms clash, J Altern Complement Med. 1999, 5(4),319-21.

Jonas, Wayne/ Jacobs, Jennifer. Healing with Homeopathy: The Complete Guide, New York: Warner 1996 (outstanding table on medical problems and the researched CAM modalities which may be helpful for that problem).

Jonas, W/ Levin, J (eds). Essentials of Complementary and Alternative, Philadelphia: Lippincott Williams & Wilkins, 1999.

Jonas, Wayne et al. The effect of niacinamide on osteoarthritis: a pilot study, Inflammation Reserch 1996, 45, 330-334.

Jones, FP. Body Awareness in Action, New York: Schocken 1976.

Jones, PK/ Jones, SL. Lunar association with suicide, Suicide and Life-Threatening Behavior 1977, 7, 31-39.

Jones, R. Why do qualitative research? (editorial), British Medical J 1995, 311, 2.

Jones, RL/ Jenkins, MD. Plant responses to homeopathic remedies, British Homeopathic J 1981, 70, 120-128.

Jorgensen, WA/ Frome, BM/ Wallach, C. Electrochemical therapy of pelvic pain: effects of pulsed EMFs (PEMF) on tissue trauma, Eur J Surg Suppl 1994; 574: 83-86.

Joshi, YM. Acupuncture in bronchial asthma, J the Association of Physicians, India 1992, 40, 327-331.

Jou, Tsung Hwa. The Tao of Tai Chi Chuan, Rutland, VT: Charles E Tuttle 1980.

Joy, W Brugh. Joy's Way: An Introduction to the Potentials for Healing with Body Energies, Los Angeles: JP Tarcher 1979.

Joy, W Brugh. Presentation at Wrekin Trust/ Confederation of Healing Organizations Conference, London 1988.

Joy, W Brugh. Avalanche, New York: Ballantine 1990.

Judith, Anodea. Wheels of Life: A User's Guide to the Chakra System, St. Paul, MN: Llewellyn 1987.

Juhan, Deane. Job's Body: A Hndbook for Bodywork, Barrytown, NY: Station Hill 1987.

Jung, CG. Psychological commentary on kundalini yoga, Lectures 1, 2, Autumn 1932, Zurich: Switzerland: Spring Publications 1976, 2-33; ibid. Lectures 3, 4, Autumn 1932 1-31.

Jung, CG. Psychology and literature, in: Modern Man in Search of a Soul, New York: Harcourt, Brace, Jovanovich 1933.

Jung, CG, Man and His Symbols, Garden City, NY: Windfall/ Doubleday 1964.

Jung, CG. Psychology and alchemy, In: *Collected Works; Vol. 13.* Translated by RFC Hull, NJ: Princeton University 1967a.

Jung, Carl G. The archetypes and the collective unconscious, In: *Collected Works; Vol. 13.* Translated by RFC Hull, NJ: Princeton University 1967b.

Jung, CG. On the relation of analytical psychology to poetry, in Campbell, J (ed), Hull, R.F., Trans, *The Portable Jung,* New York: Viking 1972 (orig. 1922).

Jung, CG. *The Symbolic Life,* Taylor & Francis (1977)

Jung, CG. *The Collected Works of CG Jung,* 20 vols. Bollingen Series XX, translated by RFC Hull, edited by H Read et al, Princeton, NJ: Princeton University 1953-1979 (Quote from vol. 1, *Nietzsche's Zarathustra,* p.441, from Sharp 1991, p.129).

Junge, MB/ Linesch, D. Our own voices: new paradigms for art therapy research, *The Arts in Psychotherapy* 1993, 20, 61-67.

Junier, MP et al. Inhibitory effect of platelet-activating factor (PAF) on luteinizing hormone-releasing hormone and somatostatin release from rat median eminence in vitro correlated with the characterization of specific PAF receptor sites in rat hypothalamus, *Endicronology* 1988, 123, 72-80 (medline citation from Eskinazi 1999).

Jupp, JJ et al. Estimates of hypnotizability: standard group scale versus subjective impressions in clinical populations, *International J Clinical and Experimental Hypnosis* 1985, 33(2) 140-149.

Justice, Blair. *Who Gets Sick? Thinking and Health,* Houston, TX Peak 1987.

K

Kabat-Zinn, John. *Full Catastrophe Living: Using the Wisdom of Your Body and Mind to Face Stress, Pain, and Illness,* New York: Delta 1990.

Kabat-Zinn, JL. Lipworth/ R. Burney. The clinical use of mindfulness meditation for the self-regulation of chronic pain, *J Behavioral Medicine* 1985, 8, 163-190.

Kabat-Zinn, JL. Lipworth, et al. Four-year followup of a meditation-based program for the self-regulation of chronic pain, *Clinical J Pain* 1986, 2 15-173.

Kakar, Sudhir. *Shamans, Mystics and Doctors: A Psychological Inquiry into India and its Healing Traditions,* Boston: Beacon 1982.

Kameda, et al. PC-SPES for prostate cancer, Presentation at annual meeting of the American Society of Clinical Oncology, May 1999, summarized in *Integrative Medicine Consult* 1999 (Aug), 108.

Kaminski, Patricia/ Katz, Richard. *Flower Essence Repertory: A Comprehensive Guide to North American and English Flower Essences for Emotional and Spiritual Well-Being,* Nevada City, CA: Earth-Spirit 1994.

Kanji, N/ Ernst, E. Autogenic training for stress and anxiety: a systematic review, *Complementary Therapies in Medicine* (UK) 2000, (8), 106-110.

Kanofsky, JD et al. Ascorbate: an adjunctive treatment for schizophrenia, *J the American College of Nutrition* 1989, 8, 425.

Kanziacheyev, Vial. Bioenergetics and biological spectrophotometry, Translated from Russian by Vilenskaya, Larissa) *Psi Research* 1982, 1(2), 26-29.

Kao, J et al. Phantom pain: current insights into it neuropathophysiology and therapy, *Pain Digest* 1997, 7, 333-345.

Kaplan, BH et al. Religion, health and forgiveness: Traditions and challenges, In: Levin 1994, 52-77.

Kaplan, G. The status of acupuncture legislation in the United States: a comprehensive review, *AAMA Review* 1991, 3(1), 7-14.

Kaplan, R. Changes in form visual fields in reading disabled children produced by syntonic stimulation, *International J Biosocial Research* 1983, 5(1), 20-33.

Kappler, RE/ Kelso, AF. Thermographic studies of skin temperature in patients receiving osteopathic manipulative treatment for peripheral nerve problems, *J the American Osteopathic Association* 1984, 83 126.

Kaptchuk, Ted J. *The Web That Has No Weaver,* New York: Congdon and Weed 1984.

Kaptchuk, Ted J / Eisenberg, David M. Vareities of healing, 1: Medical Pluralism in the United States, *Annals of Internal Medicine* 2001, 135(3), 189-195.

Kapur, RL. The role of traditional healers in mental health care in rural India, *Social Science and Medicine* 1979 (January), 138(1), 27-31.

Karagulla, Shafica. Breakthrough to Creativity: Your Higher Sense Perception, Santa Monica, CA: De Vorss 1967.

Karagulla, Shafika/ Kunz, Dora van Glelder. *The Chakras and the Human Energy Fields,* Wheaton, IL: Quest/ Theosophical 1989.

Karambelkar, VW. *Atharveda and Ayurveda,* Nagpur, India: Usha Karambelkar 1961.

Karlins, Marvin/ Andrews, Lewis M. *Biofeedback: Turning on the Power of Your Mind,* New York: Warner 1973.

Karlsson, L/ Scheibner, V. Association between non-specific stress syndrome, DPT injections and cot death, paper presented to the 2nd immunization conference, Canberra, May 27-29, 1991.

Kast, V. *Joy, Inspiration, and Hope,* Austin: Texas University 1991.

Kasl, SV et al. Psychosocial risk factors in the development of infectious mononucleosis, *Psychosomatic Medicine* 1979, 41(6).

Katz, Michael J. *Templates and the Explanation of Complex Patterns,* Cambridge, England: Cambridge University 1986.

Katz, Richard. *Boiling Energy: Community Healing Among the Kalahari Kung,* Cambridge, MA: Harvard University 1981.

Katzman, Shoshanna et al. *Feeling Light: The Holistic Solution to Permanent Weight Loss and Wellness,* New York: Avon 1997.

Kauffman, SA. *The Origins of Order: Self-Organization and the Selection of Evolution,* New York: Oxford University 1993.

Kaufman, W. *The common form of joint dysfunction: its incidence and treatment,* Brattleboro, VT: E. L. Hildreth 1949.

Kaufman, W. The use of vitamin therapy to reverse certain concomitants of aging, *J the American Geriatric Society* 1955, 11, 927-936.

Kaye, Anna/ Matchan, Don. *Reflexology for Good Health: Mirror for the Body,* Hollywood, CA: Wilshire 1980.

Kayne, SB. *Homeopathic Pharmacy: An Introduction and Handbook,* Edinburgh: Churchill Livingstone 1997.

Kaznacheyev, Vlail. Electromagnetic bioinformation in intercellular interactions, *Psi Research* 1982, 1(1), *41-76.*

Kaznacheyev, VP/ Shurin, SP/ Mikhailova, LP/ Ignatovish, NV. Distant intercellular interactions in a system of two tissue cultures, *Psychoenergetic Systems* 1976, 1, 141-142.

Keen, S/ Valley-Fox, A. *Your Mythic Journey: Finding Meaning in Your Life Through Writing and Storytelling,* Los angeles: Tarcher 1973.

Keleman, S. *Emotional Anatomy: The Structure of Experience,* Berkeley, CA: Center 1985.

Keleman, S. *Your Body Speaks its Mind,* New York: Simon & Schuster 1975.

Keller, Elizabeth/ Bzdek, Virginia M. Effects of Therapeutic Touch on tension headache pain, *Nursing Research* 1986, 101-104 (Unpublished M.A. Thesis, University of Missouri 1983).

Keller, Helen. Attributed.

Kellogg, Rhoda/ Knoll, M/ Kugler, J. Form-similarity between phosphenes for adults and pm-school children's scribblings, *Nature* 1965, 208, 1129-1130.

Kelly, IW/ Rotton, J/ Culver, R. The moon was full and nothing happened: a review of studies on the moon and human behavior and lunar beliefs, *The Skeptical Inquirer* 1985-86 10,. 129-143.

Kelly, PT/ Luttges, MW. Electrophoretic separation of nervous system proteins on exponential gradient polyacrylamide gels, *J Neurochemistry* 1975, 24 1077-1079.

Kelly, Peter J. Psychotronics: *A Primer on*

Instruments Using Variable Capacitor Tuning, Lakemont, GA: Interdimensional Sciences 1986.

Kelly, W. Laughter and Learning: Humor in the Classroom, Portland, ME: J.Weston Walsh 1988.

Kelsey, Denys. Many Lifetimes, Garden City, NY: Doubleday 1967.

Kelsey, M. Adventure Inward, Minneapolis: Augsburg 1980.

Kelso, AF et al. A clinical investigation of the osteopathic structural examination, J the American Osteopathic Association 1980, 79, 460-467.

Kendall, Henry. Muscles: Testing and Function, Baltimore: Williams & Wilkins, 2nd ed. 1971.

Kendall, HO/ Kendall, FP. Muscle Testing and Function, Baltimore, MD: Williams & Williams 1949.

Kennedy, S. et al. Immunological consequences of acute and chronic stressors: medicating role of interpersonal relationships, British J Medical Psychology 1988, 61, 77-85.

Kennedy, XJ/ Kennedy, DM. Knock at a Star: A Child's Introduction to Poetry, Boston: Little Brown 1982.

Kenneth, JJ. A psycho-physiological interpretation of the 'aura,' British J Medical Psychology 1933, 12, 343-345.

Kenney, J et al. Applied kinesiology unreliable for assessing nutrient status, J the American Dietetic Association 1988, 88, 698-704.

Kenny, MG. Multiple personality and spirit possession, Psychiatry 1981, 44, 337-352.

Kent, Howard. Yoga Made Easy, Allentown, PA: People's Medical Society 1994. Brandon zen

Kenyon, Julian. 21st Century Medicine: A Layman's Guide to the Medicine of the Future, Wellingborough, England: Thorsons 1986.

Kenyon, Julian. The Dove Project, Holistic Medicine 1989, 4, 81-94.

Kerewsky-Halpern, B. Trust, talk and touch in Balkan folk healing, Social Science Medicine 1985, 21(3), 319-325.

Kerkvliet, G. Music therapy may help control pain, J the National Cancer Institute 1990, 82, 350-352.

Kervran, C Louis. Biological Transmutations, Translated from French) England: Crosby Lockwood 1971.

Kessler, RC et al Long-term trends in the use of complementary and alternative medical therapies in the United States, Archives of Internal Medicine 2001, 135(4), 262-268.

Keyes, Ken Jr/ Burkan, Bruce (Tolly). How to Make Your Life Work, or Why Aren't You Happy?, St. Mary, KY: Living Love 1974.

Khalsa, MSS et al. Kundalini energy, In: White, John: Kundalini: Evolution and Enlightenment, 1990, 254-290. (50 refs)

Khan, Hazrat Inayat. quoted in Welwood, John. Journey of the Heart: Intimate Relationship and the Path of Love, London: Mandala/ HarperCollins 1990.

Khan, M et al. Podiatric treatment of hyperkeratotic plantar lesions with marigold Tagetes erecta, Phytotherapy Research 1996, 10, 211-214.

Khan, Pir Vilayat Inayat. Introducing Spirituality into Counseling and Therapy, Lebanon Springs, NY: Omega 1988.

Khohane, MJ/ Tiller, WA. Biological processes, quantum mechanics and electromagnetic fields: the quandry of human intention, Submitted to Medical Hypotheses 2000.

Khohane, MJ/ Tiller, WA. Energy, fitness and information augmented electromagnetic fields in Drosophila melanogaster, J Scientific Exploration 2000.

Kidd, Robert F. Results of dental amalgam removal and mercury detoxification using DMPS and neural therapy, Althernative Therapies 2000, 6(4), 49-55.

Kiefer, Durand. Meditation and biofeedback, in: White, John. 1972, 322-330.

Kiene, H. A critique of the double-blind clinical trial: part 1, Alternative Therapies 1996, 2(1), 74-80; part 2, Alternative Therapies 1996, 2(6), 39-54.

Kiev, Ari (ed). Magic, Faith and Healing: Studies in Primitive Psychiatry Today, New York: Free Press/ Macmillan 1964.

596 References

Kiev, Ari. *Curanderismo: Mexican-American Folk Psychiatry*, New York: Free Press 1968.

Kilner, Walter J. *The Human Aura*, New Hyde Park, NY: University Books 1965. (Orig. 1920)

Kim Bong Han: Cited in Knippner/ Rubin.

Kime, Z. *Sunlight,* Penryn, CA: World Health Publications 1980.

King, Frances. The word made flesh, *The Unexplained* 1982, 8(85), 1690-1693.

King, Lindy/ Clark, Jill Macleod. Intuition and the development of expertise in surgical ward and intensive care nurses, *Journal of Advanced Nursingi* 2002, 37(4), 322-329.

Moray B. *Tapping the Zero-Point Energy,* Provo, UT: Paraclete 1989.

King, N. Myth, metaphor, memory: archaeology of the self, *J Humanistic Psychology* 1990, 30(2), 55-72.

King, Serge. Imagineering for Health: Self Healing Through the Use oft/ re Mind. Wheaton, IL: Quest/ Theosophical 1981.

King, Serge. Kahuna Healing: Holistic Health and Healing Practices of Polynesia, Wheaton, IL: Quest/ Theosophical 1983.

Kinnear, Willis H (ed). *The Creative Power of Mind,* Englewood Cliffs, NJ: Prentice-Hall 1957.

Kinzler, E et al. Effect of a special Kava extract in patients with anxiety, tension, and excitation states of non-psychotic genesis: double-blind study with placebos over 4 weeks (German), *Arzneimittelforschung 1991,* 41, 584-588.

Kirchfeld, F/ Boyle, W. *Nature Doctors,* E. Palestine, OH: Buckeye Naturopathic 1994.

Kirkaldy-Willis, W/ Cassidy, J. Spinal manipulation in the treatment of low back pain, *Canadian Family Physician* 1975, 31, 535-540.

Kirlian, SD/ Kirlian, VK. Photography and visual observations by means of high frequency currents, *J Scientific and Applied Photography* 1961, 6,33.

Kirsch, I. Hypnotic enhancement of cognitive-behavioral weight loss treatments-another meta-reanalysis, *J Consulting and Clinical Psychology* 1996, 64(3), 517-519.

Kirsch, I et al. Subjective scoring for the Harvard Group Scale of Hypnotic Suggestibility, Form A, *International J Clinical and Experiemntal Hypnosis* 1990, 38, 112-124.

Kir-Simon, W. The poem as therapy: catalyst for the epiphanies of creative growth, *J Poetry Therapy* 1990, 3, 155-166.

Kiszkowski, P/ Szydlowski, H. The low frequency electromagnetic field as a signal carrier in dowsing, *Psychoenergetic Systems* 1981, 4 189-197.

Kitchell, JR et al. The treatment of coronary artery disease with disodium EDTA, *American J Cardiology* 1963, 11, 501-506.

Kjeldsen-Kragh, J et al. Controlled trial of fasxting and one-year vegetarian diet in rheumatoid arthritis, *Lancet* 1991, 338(8772), 899-902.

Kjendahl, A et al. A one year follow-up study on the effects of acupuncture in the treatment of stroke patients int he subacute stage: a randomized, controlled study, *Clinical Rehabilitation* 1997, 11, 192-200.

Klaus, Marshal/ Klaus, Phyllis. *Your Amazing Newborn,* Reading, MA: Addison-Wesley 1985.

Klauser, H. *Writing on Both Sides of the Brain: Breakthrough Techniques for People Who Write*, New York: Harper & Row 1987.

Klawansky, S et al. Meta-analysis of randomized control trials of the efficacy of cranial electrostimulation in treating psychological and physiological conditions, Harvard University School of Public Health: *Report of the Technology Assessment Group, Department of Health Policy and Management* 1992. August 28.

Kleijnen, J/ Knipschild, P. Ginkgo biloba for cerebral insufficiency, *British J Clinical Pharmacology* 1992, 34, 352-358.

Kleijnen, J et al. Acupuncture and asthma: a review of controlled trials, *Thorax* 1991a, 46(11), 799-802.

Kleijnen, J et al. Clinical trials of homeopathy, *British Medical J* 1991b, 302, 316-322.

Klein, Allen. *The Healing Power o9f Hu-*

mor, New York: Tarcher/ Putnam 1989.

Klein, E. et al. Therapeutic efficacy of right prefrontal slow repetitive transcranial magnetic stimulation in major depression, *Archives of General Psychiatry* 1999, 56, 315-320.

Klein, M (ed). *Poets for Life: 76 Poets Respond to AIDS*, New York: Crown 1992.

Kleinman, Arthur M. Some issues for a comparative study of medical healing, *International J Social Psychiatry* 1973, 19(3/ 4), 160.

Kleinman, Arthur. Patients and Healers in the Context of Culture: An Exploration of the Borderland Between Anthropology, Medicine, and Psychiatry, Berkeley/ Los Angeles: University of California 1980.

Kleitman, N. Basic rest-activity cycle in relationship to sleep and wakefulness, in Kales, A. (ed), *Sleep: Physiology and Pathology*, Philadelphia, PA: Lippincott 1969, 33-38.

Klimas, Nancy G. *Disability and Chronic Fatigue Syndrome: Clinical, Legal & Patient Perspectives*, Binghamton, NY: Haworth Medical 1997.

Klinowska, M. A comparison of the lunar and solar activity rhythms of the golden hamster, *J interdisciplinary Cycle Research* 1972, 3, 145-150.

Klos, Jethro. *Back to Eden*, Santa Barbara, CA: Woodbridge 1981.

Kloss, Jethro. *Back to Eden: A Herbal Guide*, Loma Linda, CA: Gordon 1991.

Klougart, N et al. Infantile colic treated by chiropractors: a prospective study of 316 cases, *J Manipulative Physiology and Therapy* 1989 12, 281-288.

Klougart, N et al. Safety in chiropractic practice, part II: treatment to the upper neck and the rate of cerebrovascular incidents, *J Manipulative Physiology and Therapy* 1996, 19(9), 563-569.

Knaster, Mirka. *Discovering the Body's Wisdom*, New York: Bantam 1996 (15pp fine print refs).

Knill, P. Multiplicity as a tradition: theories for interdisciplinary arts therapies-an overview, *The Arts in Psychotherapy* 1994, 21, 319-328.

Knowles, FW. Some investigations into psychic healing, *J the American Society for Psychical Research* 1954, 48(1), 21-26.

Knowles, FW. Psychic healing in organic disease, *J the American Society for Psychical Research* 1956, 50(3), 110-117.

Koch, Heinrich P/ Lawson, Larry D (eds). *Garlic: The Science and Therapeutic Applications of Allium Sativum L. and Related Species, 2nd ed.,* Baltimore, MD: Williams & Wilkins 1996.

Koch, Laura (ed). *Exploring Hospital-Based Massage: Selected Articles from the Hospital-Based Massage Network Quarterly 1995-2000*, Hospital-Based Massage Network (HBMN), 612 College Avenue, Suite 1, Ft. Collins, CO 80524, 2001a 335pp, 8 1/2 x 11 in. (Distributed by Information for People, PO Box 1876, Olympia, WA 98057-1876) - *Discussions on protocols, standards, safety, setting up programs, confidentiality, charting, procedures, insurance reimbursement, self-care for the therapist, applications for categories of problems, and much more.*

Koch, Laura. *Hospital-Based Massage Programs in Review: Data on Over 90 Programs to Network with Colleagues and Support Your Case with Hospital Administrators*, Hospital-Based Massage Network (HBMN), 612 College Avenue, Suite 1, Ft. Collins, CO 80524, 2001b, 8 1/2 x 11 in. (Distributed by Information for People, PO Box 1876, Olympia, WA 98057-1876) - *Briefly describes programs, administrative and financing details, provides names and contact details for administrators*

Koch, Laura (ed). *1001 Sources to Build Your Hospital Massage Program: Extensive Lists of Research, Books and Articles, Networking Contacts and Useful Resources*, Hospital-Based Massage Network (HBMN) 2001c (612 College Ave, Suite 1, Ft. Collins, CO 80524 (970) 407-9232 Distributed by Information for People, PO Box 1876, Olympia, WA 98057-1876) http://www.info4people.com

Kock, K. *Wishes, Lies, and Dreams: Teaching Children to Write Poetry*, New York: Harper & Row 1970.

Koerner, Joellen. *Mother, Heal My Self,* California: Crestport Press, 2003.

598 References

Koes, BW et al. Spinal manipulation and mobilisation for back and neck pain: a blinded review, *British Medical J* 1991, 303 1298-1303.

Koes, LM et al. Randomized clinical trial of manipulative therapy and physiotherapy for persistent back and neck complaints: results of one-year follow-up, *British Medical J* 1992, 304, 601-605.

Kofman, Fred/ Senge, Peter. Communities of commitment: the heart of learning organizations, *Organizational Dynamics*, Autumn 1993

Kogon, MM et al. Effects of medical and psychotherapeutic treatment on the survival of women with metastatic breast carcinoma, *Cancer* 1997, 80, 225-230

Kohane, MJ/ Tiller, WA. On intention-induced increase of in vitro enzyme thermodynamic acitivity, *Subtle Energies* 1997, 8(3), 175.

Kohane, MJ/ Tiller, WA. Energy, fitness and electromagnetic fields in *Drosophila Melanogaster, J Scientific Exploration* 2000, 14(2), 217.

Kohatsu, Wendy (ed). *Complementary and Alternative Medicine Secrets*, Philadelphia: Hanley & Belfus, 2002.

Kohn, LT et al (eds). *To err is human: building a safer health system*, Washington, DC National Academy Press 2000.

Kokjohn, K et al. The effect of spinal manipjulation on pain and prostaglandin levels in women with primary dysmenorrhea, *J Manipulative Physiology and Therapy* 1992 15, 279-285.

Kolata, G. Putting mammograms to the test. Available at http://nytimes.com.

Kollerstrom, Jean. Basic scientific research into the 'low-dose' effect, *British Homeo-pathic J* 1982, 71(2), 41-47.

Kollerstrom, N. Plant response to the lunar synodic cycle, *Cycles* 1980, 3 1(3), 61-63.

Komori, T et al. Effects of citrus fragrance on immune function and depressive states, *Neuroimmunomodulation* 1995, 2, 174-180.

König, Herbert L. Der BIO-Resonator als Höchstfrequenzresonanzpule, *Wetter Boden Mensch* 1968 1981

König, HL et al.The divining rod phenomenon, Chapter 10 in *Biological Effects of Electromagnetism*, New York: Springer 1981 194-217.

Konikiewicz, LW. Kirlian photography in theory and clinical practice, *J the Biological Photographic Association* 1977, 45, 115-134.

Koot, DJ/ Herbert, B. Kirlian photographs, *J Paraphysics* 1971, 5(4), 117 (very brief).

Korda, Michael. *Man to Man: Surviving Prostate Cancer*, New York: Vintage 1997.

Kori, S et al. Kinisophobia: A new view of chronic pain behavior, *Pain Management* 1990, 3(1), 35-43.

Kornfield, Jack. On meditation and the western mind, *Noetic Sciences Review* 1990/ 1991, No. 17, 11-17.

Kornfield, Jack. *A Path with Heart: A Guide Through the Perils and Promises of Spiritual Life,* New York/ London: Bantam 1993.

Korotkov, Konstantin/ Tunik, Leonid (ed). *Light After Life: A Scientific Journey into the Spiritual World* Backbone 1998

Korr, IM. Symposium of the functional implications of segmental facilitation, *J the American Osteopathic Association* 1955a, 54(1).

Korr, IM. The concept of facilitation and its origins, *J the American Osteopathic Assoiction* 1955b, 54(5), 265-268.

Korr, IM. The Andrew Taylor Still memorial lecture, *J the American Osteopathic Association* 1974 (Jan.)

Korr, IM. The Neurologic Mechanisms in Manipulative Therapy, New York: Plenum 1978.

Koss, JD. Expectations and outcomes for patients given mental health care or spiritist healing in Puerto Rico, *American J Psychiatry* 1987, 144(1), 56-61.

Kovar, KA et al. Blood levels of 1,8-cineole and locomotor activity of mice after inhalation and oral administration of resemary oil, *Planta Medica* 1987, 53(4), 315-318.

Kraft, Dean. *Portrait of a Psychic Healer,* New York: G.P. Putnam's Sons 1981.

Krakov, SV. Color vision and autonomic

nervous system, *J the Optical Society of America,* June, 1942.

Kramer, A. Poetry and group process: restoring heart and mind, *J Apoetry Therapy* 1990, 3, 221-227.

Kramer, Dietmar. *The New Bach Flower Body Maps: Healing the Emotional and Spiritual Causes of Illness*, Rochester, VT: Inner Traditions Ltd 1995.

Kramer, Dietmar. *The New Bach Flower Body Maps*, Inner Traditions Ltd, Inner Traditions Ltd 1995a (body maps, companion to 1995b).

Kramer, Dietmar. *New Bach Flower Therapies; Healing the Emotional and Spiritual Causes of Illness*, Inner Traditions Ltd 1995b (discussion of body maps, companion to 1995a).

Kramer, Dietmar/ Wild, Helmut. *New Bach Flower Therapies: Treatment by Topical Application, with a comprehensive atlas of body maps indicating treatment zones*, Rochester, VT: Healing Arts 1996.

Kramer, MA et al. Handedness and the laterality of breast cancer in women, *Nursing Research* 1985, 34(6), 333-337.

Kramer, Nancy Ann. Comparison of Therapeutic Touch and casual touch in stress reduction of hospitalized children, *Pediatric Nursing* 1990 16(5), 483-485.

Krapu, Thomas. www.krapu4.com/taichi/research

Krebs, Charles/ Brown, Jenny. *A Revolutionary Way of Thinking: From a Near-Fatal Accident to a New Science of Healing*, Melbourne, Australia: Hill of Content 1998.

Kreitler, Hans/ Kreitler, Shulamith. Subliminal perception and extrasensory perception, *J Parapsychology* 1973, 37, 163-188.

Kremer, J. shamanic tales as ways of personal empowerment, in Doore, G. (ed). *Shaman's Path: Healing, Personal Growth and Empowerment*, Boston: Shambhala 1988.

Kriege, Theodor. *Fundamental Basis of Irisdiagnosis*, Romford, Essex: L.N. Fowler 1969.

Krieger, Dolores. Therapeutic Touch: the imprimatur of nursing, *American J Nursing* 1975, 7, 784-787; and in The relationship of touch, with intent to help or to heal, to subjects' in-vivo hemoglobin values, In: *American Nurses' Association 9th Nursing Research Conference, San Antonio, TX 1973* Kansas City, MO: American Nurses' Association 1974, 39-58.

Krieger, Dolores. Healing by the 'laying-on' of hands as a facilitator of bioenergetic change: the response of in-vivo human hemoglobin, *Psychoenergetic Systems* 1976, 1, 121-129.

Krieger, Dolores. *The Therapeutic Touch: How to Use Your Hands to Help or Heal*, Englewood Cliffs, NJ: Prentice Hall 1979.

Krieger, Dolores. *Foundations for Holistic Health Nursing Practices: The Renaissance Nurse*, Philadelphia: PA Lippincott 1981.

Krieger, Dolores. *Accepting Your Power to Heal: The Personal Practice of Therapeutic Touch*, Santa Fe, NM: Bear& Co.1993.

Krieger Dolores. *Therapeutic Touch as Transpersonal Healing*, New York: Lantern/Booklight 2002

Krigge, Theodore. *Fundamental Basis of Irisdiagnosis,* Translated from German by Priest, A.W) Essex, England: L.N. Fowlen 1969.

Krippner, Stanley. *Song of the Siren: A Parapsychological Odyssey,* New York: Harper & Row 1975.

Krippner, Stanley. Biological applications of Kirlian photography, *J the American Society for Psychosomatic Dentistry and Medicine* 1979,26, 122-128.

Krippner, Stanley. *Human Possibilities: Mind Exploration in the USSR and Eastern Europe*, Garden City, NY: Anchor/ Doubleday 1980.

Krippner, Stanley/ Rubin, D. *The Kirlian Aura.* Garden City, NY: Anchor 1974.

Krippner, Stanley/ Welch, Patrick. *Spiritual Dimensions of Healing: from Native Shamanism to Contemporary Health Care*, New York: Irvington 1992 (22 pp refs).

Krippner, Stanley. Common aspects of traditional healing systems across cultures, in Jonas/ Levin p.181-199.

Krishnamurti, PS. Report on the use of

influenzinum during the outbreak of epidemic in India in 1968, *Hahnemanian Gleanings* 1970, 37, 225-226.

Krivorotov, Victor. Some issues of bioenergetic therapy, In: Vilenskaya, Larissa. Translator and Editor) *Parapsychology in the USSR, Part HI,* San Francisco: Washington Research Center 1981, 30-41.

Krmessky, Julius. Radiation from organisms, Translated by Irena Vaskova) *J Paraphysics* 1969, 3(4), 102-110.

Kronenberg F; Fugh-Berman A. Complementary and alternative medicine for menopausal symptoms: a review of random-ized, controlled trials, *Annals of Internal Medicine* 2002, 137(10), 805-13.

Kroner, K et al. Immediate and long-term phantom breast syndrome after mastectomy, *Pain* 1989, 36, 327-334.

Kropp, J et al. A comparison of ecological testing with Vega test method in identifying sensitivities to chemicals, foods, and inhalants, *American J Acupuncture* 1985, 13(3), 253-259.

Kropp, J et al. A double blind, randomized, controlled investigation of electrodermal testing in the diagnosis of allergies, *J Alternative and Complementary Therapies* 1997, 3(3), 241-248.

Krystal, Phyllis. *Cutting the lies that Bind,* London: Sawbridge 1986.

Kuang, An-kun et al. Long-term observation on Qigong in prevention of stroke-follow-up of 244 hypertensive patients for 18-22 years, J *Traditional Chinese Medicine* 1986, 6(4), 235-238. (Also in: Kuang A.K. et al. Comparative study of clinical effects and prognosis of 204 hypertensive patients treated with Qigong in 20 years of follow-up and its mechanisms, *Chinese Integration of Traditional and Western Medicine* 1986, 1, 9.) (Chinese with brief English summary)

Kubiena, G. Sinn und Unsinn der Akupunktur in der HNO, *DZA: Deutsche Zeitschrift fur Akupunktur* 1992, 35(1) 16-19.

Kübler-Ross, Elizabeth. *Death: The Final Stage of Growth,* Englewood Cliffs, NJ: Prentice-Hall 1975.

Kübler-Ross, Elizabeth. *Living with Death and Dying,* New York: Macmillan 1981; London: Souvenir 1982.

Kubler-Ross, Elisabeth. *On Children and Death,* New York: Macmillan 1983.

Kubler-Ross, Elisabeth. *The Tunnel and the Light: Essential Insights on Living and Dying With a Letter to a Child With Cancer,* New York: Marlowe & Co. 1999.

Kuchera, W/ Kuchera, M. *Osteopathic Principles in Practice,* 2nd rev. ed, Columbus, OH: Greyden 1994.

Kuchler, T et al.Impact of psychotherapeutic support on gastrointestinal cancer patients undergoing surgery: survival results of a trial, *Hepatogastroenterology* 1999, 46, 322-335.

Kuhn, Clifford C. Healthy humor is good medicine, *Bidges* (ISSSEEM Magazine) 1995, 6(3), 1; 9-10.

Kuhne, Louis. *The Science of Facial Expression,* Mokelume Hill, CA: Health Research 1970.

Kulkarni, SK. Mentat-multicomponent herbal psychotropic formulation, *Drugs of the Future* 1996, 21(6), 585 (see at www.thehimalaysdrugcolcom/ men-0013.htm July 31 2000.

Kumar, Adarsh M et al. Music therapy increases serum melatonin levels in patients with alzheimer's disease, *Alternative Therapies* 1999, 5(6) 49-57 (86 refs).

Kumar, VK et al. Behavioral and subjective scoring of the Harvard group scale of hypnotic susceptibility: further data and an extension, *American J Clinical Hypnosis* 1996, 38(3), 191-199.

Kunz, Dora. Personal communication 1981.

Kunz, Dora (ed). *Spiritual Aspects of the Healing Arts,* Wheaton, IL: Theosophical 1985.

Kunz, Dora van Gelder. *The Personal Aura,* Wheaton, IL: Quest/ Theosophical 1991.

Kunz, Kevin/ Kunz, Barbara. *Hand and Foot Reflexology: A Self-Help Guide,* Wellingborough, Northants, UK Thorsons 1984/New York: Simon & Schuster 1987.

Kunzang, J/ Rechung, Rinpoche. *Tibetan Medicine,* Berkeley/ Los Angeles: University of California 1973.

Kuroda, Y/ Hara, Y. Antimutagenic and anticarcinogenic activity and tea poly-phen-ols, *Mutation Research* 1999, 436, 69-97.

Kurtz, Ron. *Body-Centered Psychotherapy: The Hakomi Method - The Integrated Use of Mindfulness, Nonviolence and the Body*, Mendocino, CA: LifeRhythm 1990.

Kurtz, Ron/ Prestera, H. *The Body Reveals: An Illustrated Guide to the Psychyology of the Body*, New York: Harper & Row 1976.

Kurtz, RM/ Strube, MJ. Multiple suscepti-bility testing: is it helpful? *American J Clinical Hypnosis* 1996, 38(3), 172-184.

Kushi, Michio. *Natural Healing Through Macrobiotics*, Tokyo: Japan Publications 1979.

Kushi, Michio. *How to See Your Health: Book of Oriental Diagnosis*, Tokyo: Japan Publications 1980.

Kuvalayananda, Swami. *Pranayama*, Philadelphia, PA: Sky Foundation 1978.

Kuznetsov, Vladimir. Sport: The main factor in scientific study of hidden human reserves, (Translated from Russian by Kucharev, Anya/ Vilenskaya, Larissa) *Psi Research* 1982, 1(2), 77.

L

L'Abate, L. *programmed Writing: A Paratherapeutic Approach for Intervention with individuals, Couples, and Families*, Pacific Grove, CA: Brooks/ Cole 1992.

La Tourelle, Maggie with Courtenay, Anthea. *Thorsons Introductory Guide to Kinesiology*, London: Thorsons/ Harper Collins 1992.

Laakmann, G et al. St. John's Wort in mild to moderate depression: the relevance of hyperforin for clinical efficacy, *Pharmaco-psychiatry* 1998, 31(supp 1), 54-59.

LaBaw, WL. Regular use of suggestibility by pediatric bleeders, *Haematologia* 1970,4,419-425.

LaBaw, WL. Auto-hypnosis in haemo-philia, *Haematologia* 1975, 9(1-2), 103.-110.

Lacan, J. *Language of the Self*, Baltimore: John Hopkins 1968a.

Lacan, J. The function of speech and lan-guage in psychoanalysis, In: Wilden, A. (ed): *The Language of the Self.* New York: Delta 1968b.

Lacan, J. *The Four Fundamental Concepts of -Psychoanalysis*, London: Hogarth 1977.

Lad, Vasant. *Ayurveda: The Science of Self-Healing*, Wilmot, CA: Lotus Light 1984.

Laing, Ronald D. *The Divided Self*, London: Tavistock 1960.

Laing, Ronald D. *Knots*, New York: Pan-theon/ Random House 1970.

Laing, Ronald D. *The Facts of Life*, New York: Random House 1976.

Lake, B. Acute back pain: treatment by the application of Feldenkrais principles, *Australian Family Physician* 1985. 14(11),1175-1178.

Lake, David/ Wells, Steve. *New Energy Therapies: Rapid Change Techniques for Emotional Healing*, 1999. Available through wells@iinet.net.au

Lake, James. Psychotropic medications from natural products: a review of promis-ing research and recommendations, *Alternative Therapies* 2000, 6(3), 36-60 (112 refs).

Lambert, MJ. Spontaneous remission in adult nerurotic disordes: A revision and summary, *Psycholgical Bulletin*, 1976, 83, 107-119.

Lambert, Michael J et al. The effective-ness of psychotherapy, In Sol L. Garfield &Allen E. Bergin (eds). *Handbook of Psychotherapy and Behavior Change*, New York: John Wiley & Sons 1986, 157-211).

Lambert, M.J et al. The effects of provid-ing therapists with feedback on patient progress during psychotherapy: Are out-comes enhanced? *Psychotherapy Research* 2001, 11, 49-68.

Lambillion, Paul. Being Loving is Being Healthy: Self Healing through the Power of Love, Romford, England: L.N. Fowler 1987.

Lamont, J. Homeopathic treatment of attention deficit hyperactivity disorder: a controlled study, *British Homeopathic J* 1997, 86, 196-200.

Lamont, J. Homeopathic treatment of attention deficit hyperactivity disorder: a controlled study, *Biomedical Therapies* 1998, 16(3), 219-22.

Lamson, DW/ Brignall, M. Antioxidants in cancer therapy: Their actions and interactions with oncologic therapies, *Alternative Medicine Review* 1999, 4(5), 304-329.

Landerman, R et al. Alternative models of the stress buffering hypothesis, *American J Community Psychology* 1990, 17, 625-642. (From CG Ellison)

Landman, JT/ Dawes, RM. Psychotherapy outcome: Smith and Glass conclusions stand up under scrutiny, *American psychologist* 1982, 37,504-516.

Landmark Healthcare, *Landmark Report on Public Perceptions of Alternative Care Sacramento*, CA: Landmark Healthcare 1988.

Landmark Report, (800) 638-4557 www.landmarkhealthcare.com

Landy, David. *Culture, Disease and Healing: Studies in Medical Anthropology*, New York: Macmillan 1977.

Landy, RJ. The child, the dreamer, the artist and the fool: in search of understanding the meaning of expressive therapy, *The Arts in Psychotherapy* 1993, 20, 359-370.

Lane, JD et al. Binaural auditory beats affect vigilance performance and mood, *Physiological Behavior* 1998, 63, 249-252.

Langsjoen, PH et al. Long-term efficacy and safety of coenzyme Q_{10} therapy for idiopathic dilated cardiomyopathy, *American J Cardiology* 1990, 65, 521-523.

Lankton, Carol H/ Lankton, Stephen R. *Tales of Enchantment: Goal-Oriented Metaphors for Adults and Children in Therapy*, New York: Brunner-Mazel 1989.

Lansdowne, Zachary F. *The Chakras and Esoteric Healing,* York Beach, ME: Samuel Weiser 1986.

Lanty, D (ed). *Culture, Disease, and Healing: Studies in Medical Anthropology*, New York: Macmillan 1931/ 1977.

Lantz, J/ Harper, K. Using poetry in logotherapy, *The Arts in Psychotherapy* 1991, 18, 341-346.

Lao, L et al. Efficacy of Chinese acupuncture on postoperative oral surgery pain, *Oral Surgery Oral Medicine Oral Pathology Oral Radiology and Endodontics* 1995, 9, 423-428.

Laotsu, *The Wisdom of Laotsu*, New York: Modern Library 1948.

Lappé, Marc. *When Antibiotics Fail: Restoring the Ecology of the Body*, Berkeley, CA: North Atlantic 1986.

Larsen, S. *The Mythic Imagination: Your Quest for Meaning Through Personal Mythology*, New York: Bantam 1990.

Larson, NJ et al. Functional vasomotor hemiparesthesia syndrome, *Academy of Applied Osteopathy Year Book of Selected Osteopathic Papers* 1984, 70, 39-44.

Lattanzi-Licht, Marcia et al. *The Hospice Choice: In Pursuit of a Peaceful Death, The National Hospice Organization Guide to Hospice Care*, New York: Fireside/ Simon/ Schuster 1998.

Lau, BH. Effect of acupuncture on allergic rhinitis: clinical and laboratory evaluation, *American J Clinical Medicine* 1975, 3, 263-270.

Laub, E. Man as a magnet, *J the British Society of Dowsers* 1958 (March), (cited in Mann, 1973, p 162).

Laurence, Leslie/ Weinhouse, Beth. *Outrageous Practices: The Alarming Truth about How Medicine Mistreats Women*, New York: Fawcett Columbine 1994.

Laurie, Duncan. Virtual state art? The world of psychotronics, *J the US Psychotronics Association* 1988 (November), 1(1), 3 1-39.

Lavabre, Marcel. *Aromatherapy Workbook*, Rochester, VT: Healing Arts 1990.

LaValle, James B et al. *Natural Therapeutics Pocket Guide* 2000-2001, Hudson, Ohio: Lexi-Comp 2000.

LaValley W/ Verheof M. Integrating complementary medicine and health care services into practice, *Canadian Medical Association J* 1995, 153, 1, 45-49.

Lawless, Julia. *Encyclopaedia of Essential Oils*, Shaftesbury, UK/ Boston, MA: Element 1992.

Lawlis, Frank G. *The Cure: The Hero's*

Journey with Cancer, San Jose, CA: Resource 1994.

Lawlor, Robert. *Sacred Geometry: Philoso-phy and Practice*, New York/ London: Thames & Hudson 1982.

Lawlor, Robert. *Voices of the First Day: Awakening in the Aboriginal Dreamtime*, Rochester, VT: Inner Traditions 1991.

Lawrence, D. H. Attributed.

Lawrence, Jerome/ Lee, Robert E. *Inherit the Wind*, English Theatre Guild 1961.

Lawrence, Ron/ Rosch, Paul/ Judith Plowden. *Magnet Therapy: The Pain Cure Alternative*, New York: Prima Health 1998.

Lawson A, Calderon L. Interexaminer agreement for applied Kinesiology manual muscle testing, *Perceptual Motor Skills* 1997, 84,539-546.

Lazar, SW et al. Functional brain mapping of the relaxation response and meditation, *Neuroreport* 2000, 11(7), 1581-1585.

Lazarou, J/ Pomeranz, BH/ Corey, PN. Incidence of adverse drug reactions in hospitalized patients: a meta-analysis of prospective studies, *J the American Medical Association* 1998, 279, 1200-1205.

Lazarus, A. Psychiatric problems precipitated by Transcendental Meditation, *Psychological Reports* 1976, 39, 601-602.

Le Bars, PL et al. A placebo-controlled, double-blind randomized trial of an extract of ginkgo bilboa for dementia, *J the American Medical Association* 1997, 278, 1327-1332.

Le Scouarnec, René-Pierre et al. Use of binaural beat tapes for treatment of anxiety: a pilot study of tape preference and outcomes, *Alterenative Therapies* 2000, 7(1), 58-63.

Leach, AB. Kirlian photography, *British J Photography* 1981, 128, 394-395, 398.

Leadbeater, CW. *Man Visible and Invisible*, Wheaton, IL: Quest 1969. (Orig. 1902)

Leadbeater, CW. *The Chakras*, Wheaton, IL: Quest 1977 (Orig. 1927)

Leadbeater, CW/ Besant, Annie. *Occult Chemistry*, Madras, India: Thosophical 1908; London 1919; Madras 1951.

Leape, LL. Error in medicine, *J the American Medical Association* 1994; 272, 1851-7.

Leavitt, Donald. The photochronology of the Kirlian process, *Popular Photography* 1973 (February), 120-123.

LeCron, Leslie. Hypnosis and ESP, *Psychic* 1970 (August).

Lee, A/ Done, ML. The use of nonpharmacologic techniques to prevent postoperative nausea and vomiting: a meta-analysis, Aneth Analg 1999; 88: 1362-1369.

Lee, Bonita. Vibrational essences - liquid consciousness? *Caduceus* 1996-7, winter, 41-47.

Lee, C. Qigong (breath exercise) and its major models, *Chinese Culture* 1983, 24(3), 71-79.

Lee, J. *At My Father's Wedding: Reclaiming Our True Masculinity*, London: Piagkus 1992

Lee, KH et al. Neurologic complications following chiropractic manipulation, *Neurology* 1995, 45, 1213-1215.

Lee, Michael. *Phoenix Rising Yoga Therapy: A Bridge from Body to Soul*, Deerfield Beach, FL: Health Communications 1997.

Lee, RC et al. A review of the biophysical basis for the clinical application of electric fields in soft tissue repair, *J Burn Care Rehabilitation* 1993, 14, 319-355.

Lee, Si-Chen et al. Finger-reading: Exploring the Information Field, *International J Healing and Caring – On line* 2002, 1, 1-14. http://ijhc.org/members/Journal/2-2articles/SCLee-2-2.asp

Lee, YH et al. Acupuncture in the treatment of renal colic, *J Urology* 1992, 147:16-18.

Leedy, JJ (ed). *Poetry as Healer: Mending the Troubled Mind*, New York: Vanguard 1985.

Lefcourt, Herbert. *Humor and Life Stress*, New York: Springer-Verlag 1986.

Lefcourt, Herbert et al. Humor and immune system functioning, *International J Humor Research* 1990, 3(3), 305-321.

604 References

Leftwich, Robert. Hydrology - some impressions, *J the British Society of Dowsers* 1964, 28(126), 205.

Lehman, E. Efficacy of a special Kava extract (Piper methysticum) in patients with states of anxiety, tension and excitedness of non-mental origin: a double-blind placebo controlled study of four weeks treatment, *Phytomedicine* 1996, 3(2), 113-119.

Leichtman, Robert/ Japiske, Carl. *Active Meditation,* Columbus, OH: Ariel 1982.

Leichtman, Robert R/ Japiske, Carl. The nature and purpose of the emotions, *J Holistic Medicine* 1984, 6(2), 148-160.

Leiderman, E et al. Preliminary investigation of high-dose oral glycerine on srum levels and negative symptoms in schizophrenia: an open-labeled trial, *Biological Psychiatry* 1996, 39, 213-215.

Leikind, Bernard A/ McCarthy, William J. An investigation of firewalking, *Skeptical Inquirer* 1985, 10, 23-34.

Leisman, G et al. A. somatosensory evoked potential changes during muscle testing, *International J Neuroscience* 1989; 45, 143-151.

Leisman, G et al. Electromyographic Effects of Fatigue and Task Repetition on the Validity of Estimates of Strong and Weak Muscles in Applied Kinesiology Muscle Testing Procedures, *Perceptual and Motor Skills.* 1995; 80:963-977.

Leonoff, G. The successful treatment of phobias and anxiety by telephone and radio: a replication of Callahan's 1987 study, TFT Newsletter 1995, 1(2).

Lerner, A. Poetry Therapy, in Corsini, R.J. (ed), *Handbook of Innovative Psychotherap-ies*, New York: Wiley 1981, 640-649.

Lerner, A. Poetry therapy in the group experience, in: Abt, L.E/ Stuart, I.R. (eds), *the Newer Therapies: A Source Book,* New York: Van Nostrand Reinhold 1982, 228-247.

Lerner, A (ed). *Poetry in the Therapeutic Experience*, St. Louis: MMB Music 1993.

Lerner, A/ Mahlendorf, UR (eds). *Life guidance through Literature*, Chicago: American Library Association 1991.

Lerner, Michael. A report on complementary cancer therapies, *Advances* 1985, 2(1), 30-43.

Lerner, Michael.*Choices in Healing: Integrating The Best of Conventional and Complementary Approaches to Cancer,* Cambridge, MA: MIT 1994.

LeShan, Lawrence. *The Medium, The Mystic and The Physicist: Toward a General Theory of the Paranormal.* New York Ballantine 1974a; (UK edition: *Clairvoyant Reality*).

LeShan, Lawrence. *How to Meditate: A Guide to Self-discovery,* New York: Bantam/ Little-Brown 1974b.

LeShan, Lawrence. *Alternate Realities,* New York: Ballantine 1976.

LeShan, Lawrence. *You Can Fight For Your Life: Emotional Factors in the Treatment of Cancer,* New York: M. Evans 1977.

LeShan, Lawrence. *Cancer as a Turning Point: A Handbook for People with Cancer; Their Families, and Health Professionals,* Bath: Gateway 1989.

LeShan, Lawrence/ Margenau, Henry. *Einstein's Space and van Gogh's Sky,* New York: Macmillan 1982.

Leskowitz, Eric D. Phantom limb pain: subtle energy perspectives, *Subtle Energies* 1997, 8(2), 125-154

Leskowitz, Eric D (ed). *Transpersonal Hypnosis: Gateway to Body, Mind, and Spirit*, New York: CRC 2000.

Lessell, Colin B. *The World Travellers' Manual of Homeopathy*, Saffron Walden, UK: CW Daniel 1993.

Lester, D/ Terry, R. The use of poetry therapy: lessons from the life of Anne Saxton, *The Arts in Psychotherapy* 1992, 19, 47-52.

Leuchter AF et al. Changes in brain function of depressed subjects during treatment with placebo, *American J Psychiatry,* 2002, 159(1), 122-129 http://www.placebo.ucla.edu/publications/

Lethbridge, TC. *ESP Beyond Time and Distance*, London: Routledge & Kegan Paul 1965.

Lethbridge, TC. *A Step in the Dark,* London: Routledge and Kegan Paul 1967.

Lett, WR. Therapist creativity: the arts of supervision, *The Arts in Psychotherapy* 1993, 20, 371-386.

Leung, AY/ Foster, S. *Encyclopedia of common natural ingredients used in food, drugs, and cosmetics, 2ⁿᵈ ed.* New York: Johyn Wiley & Sons 1996.

Levenson, E. Psychoanalysis - cure or persuasion? In: Witenberg, E (ed). *Interpersonal Psychoanalysis,* New York: Gardner 1978.

Levenson, F. A holographic model of psychoanalytical change, *Contemporary Psychoanalysis* 1976, 12, 1-20.

Levey, Joel/ Levey, Michelle. *Thought for the Day,* levey@wisdomatwork.com

Levin, Jeffrey S. Age differences in mystical experience, *Gerontologist* 1993, 33 (4), *507-5* 13.

Levin, Jeffrey S. *Religion in Aging and Health: Theoretical Foundations and Methological Froniers*, London/ Thousand Oaks, Ca: Sage 1994.

Levin, Jeffrey S/ Schiller, Preston L. Is there a religious factor in health? *J Religion and Health* 1987, 26 (i), 9~35. (215 refs)

Levin, Jeffrey S/ Vanderpool, Harold Y. Is frequent religious attendance really conducive to better health?: Toward an epidemiology of religion, *Social Science and Medicine* 1987, 24(7), 589-600. (85 refs)

Levin, Jeffrey S/ Vanderpool, Harold Y. Is religion therapeutically significant for hypertension? *Social Science and Medicine* 1989, 29, 69-78. (65 refs)

Levin, Jeffrey S/ Vanderpool, Harold Y. Religious factors in physical health and the prevention of illness, In: Parament, Kenneth I/ Maton, Kenneth I/ Hess, Robert E. (eds). *Religion and Prevention in Mental Health: Research, Vision, and Action,* London/ New York: Haworth 1992.

Levin, JS et al. Quantitative methods in research on complementary and alternative medicine: a methodological manifesto, *Medical Care* 1997, 35(11), 1079-1094.

Levin, Michael. Current and potential applications of bioelectromagnetics in medicine, *Subtle Energies* 1993, 4(1), 77-85 (97 refs).

Levine, Barbara Hoberman. *Your Body Believes Every Word You Say*, Lower Lake, CA: Aslan 1991.

Levine, DZ. Burning pain in an extremity, *Post-graduate Medicine* 1991, 90 175-185.

Levine, P. *Accumulated Stress, Reserve Capacity, and Disease*, Boulder, CO: Rolf 1976.

Levine, Stephen. *Meetings at the Edge: Dialogues with the Grieving and the Dying the Healing and the Healed*, London/ New York: Anchor/ Doubleday 1984.

Levine, Stephen. Who Dies? An Investigation of Conscious Living and Conscious Dying, Bath, England: Gateway 1986.

Levine, Stephen. *Healing into Life and Death,* Garden City, NY: Anchor/ Doubleday 1987.

Levine, Stephen. *Guided Meditations, Explorations and Healings,* London/ New York Anchor/ Doubleday 1991.

Levine, Stephen. *A Year to Live: How to Live This Year As If It Were Your Last*, New York: Bell Tower/ Harmony/ Crown 1997.

Levi-Strauss, Claude. *Structural Anthropol-ogy,* New York: Basic 1963.

Leviton, Patti. *The Miracle of Words: The Power of Words to Heal Body, Mind and Spirit,* Fountain Valley, CA: Synergy Seminars 1998

Levitt, EE. Hypnosis in the treatment of obesity, In: Rhue, JW et al (eds). *Handbook of Clinjical Hypnosis*, Washington, DC: American Psychological Association 1993, 511-532.

Levoy, G. Inexplicable recoveries from incurable diseases, Longevity October 1989, :37-42.

Levy, Naomi. *To Begin Again: The Journey Toward Comfort, Strength, and Faith In Difficult Times,* New York: Alfred A. Knopf 1998.

Levy, SM et al. Prognostic risk assessment in primary breast cancer by behavioral and immunological parameters, *Health Psychology* 1985, 4, 90-113.

Levy, SM et al. Correlations of stress factors with sustained depression of natural killer cell activity and predicted prognosis in patients with breast cancer, *J Clinical Oncology* 1987, 5, 348-353.

Levy, SM et al. Survival hazards analysis in first recurrent breast cancer patients: seven-year follow-up, *Psychosomatic Medicine* 1988, 50(5), 520-528.

Levy, SM et al. Perceived social support and tumor estrogen/ progesterone status as predictors of natural killer cell activity in breast cancer patients, *Psychosomatic Medicine* 1990, 52, 73-85.

Lewicki, DR/ Schaut, GH/ Persinger, MA. Geophysical variables and behavior: xliv days of subjective precognitive experiences and the days before the actual events display correlated geomagnetic activity, *Perceptual & Motor Skills* 1987, 65(1) 173-174.

Lewin, Roger. Is your brain really necessary? *Science 1980*, 210, 1232-1234.

Lewis, CE et al. *The Psychoneuroimmunology of Cancer: Mind and Body in the Fight for Survival*, New York: Oxford University 1994.

Lewith, George/ Aldridge, David (eds). *Clinical Research Methodology for Comple-mentary Therapies*, London: Hodder & Stoughton 1993.

Lewith, G/ Jonas, WB/ Walach, H (eds). *Clinical Research in Complementary Therapies: Principles, Problems and Solutions*, Edinburgh: Churchill Livingstone, 2002.

Lewith, GT/ Machin, D. On the evaluation of the clinical effects of acupuncture, *Pain* 1983 16(2) 111-127.

Lewith, George et al. *Complementary Medicine: An Integrated Approach*, Oxford, England: Oxford Medical 1996.

Lewith, GT et al. Use of ultramolecular potencies of allergan to treat asthmatic people allergic to house dust mite: double blind randomised controlled clinical trial, *British Medical J* 2002; 324: 520-523

Liang, W. An exploration of the clinical indications of foot reflexology: a retro-spective of the clinical application to 8,096 cases, *Reflections* 1997, 18(1), 3-6, taken from 1996 *China Reflexology Symposium Report*.

Liberman, J. The effect of syntonic colored light stimulation on certain visual and cognitive functions, *J Optometric Vision Development* 1986, 17.

Liberman, Jacob. *Ligtht: Medicine of the Future*, Santa Fe, NM: Bear & Co. 1991.

Liberman, Jacob. *Take Off Your Glasses and See*, New York: Crown 1995.

Libet, B/ Gerard, RW. Steady potential fields and neuron activity, *J Neurophysiology* 1941, 4,438.

Libet, B/ Gerard, RW. An analysis of some correlates of steady potentials in mammalian cortex, *Electroencephalography and Clinical Neurophysiology* 1962, 14, 445.

Liboff, AR. Power-line magnetic fields are likely related to leukemia in children (despite the opinion of the American Physical Society), *Alternative Therapies in Health and Medicine* 1996, 2(2), 46-51. (See Park for counterpoint view)

Liboff, AR/ Rinaldi, RA (eds). Electrically mediated growth mchanisms in lving systems, *Annals of the New York Academy of Science* 1974, 238 (Oct. 11).

Liddon, Sim C. *The Dual Brain, Religion, and the Unconscious*, Buffalo, NY: Promethius 1989 (10 p. Refs).

Lidell, Lucinda. *The Book of Massage: The Complete Step-by-Step Guide to Eastern and Western Techniques*, New York: Simon & Schuster 1984.

Lieber, Arnold L/ Agel, Jerome. *The Lunar Effect,* Garden City, NY: Anchor/ Doubleday 1978.

Lieber, AL/ Sherin, CR. Homicides and the lunar cycle, *American J Psychiatry* 1972 129, 69-74.

Lieberman, Jacob. *Light, Medicine of the Future,* Santa Fe: Bear & Co. 1991.

Lifschutz, Joseph E. Hysterical stigmatization, *American J Psychiatry* 1957, 114, 527-531.

Lifshin, L (ed).T*angled Vines: A Collection of Mother-Daughter Poems*, Boston: Beacon 1992.

Light Years Ahead Productions, *Light Years Ahead: The Illustrated Guide to Full Spectrum and Colored Light in Mindbody Healing*, Berkeley, CA: Celestial Arts 1996.

Lilly, John C. *The Center of the Cyclone*, New York: Julian 1972.

Lin, Henry B. *The Art and Science of Feng Shui*, St. Paul, MN: Llewellyn Worldwide 2000.

Lin, Kuo. *A New Methodology of Qigong Applied in Cancer Treatment*, Shanghai: The Scientific Press 1981, p 1.

Lin, N/ Ensel, WM. Life stress and health: Stressors and resources, *American Sociological Review* 1989, 54, 382-399, (From CG Ellison)

Linde, K/ Melchart, D. Randomized controlled trials of individualized homoeopathy: a state-of-the-art review, *J Altern Complement Med* 1998; 4: 371-388 www.ncbi.nlm.nih.gov/entrez/query.fcgi?cmd=retrieve&db=pubmed&list_uids=9884175&dopt=Abstract

Linde, K et al. Critical review and meta-analysis of serial agitated dilutions in experimental toxicology, *Human Experimental Toxicology* 1994, 13, 481-492.

Linde, K et al. St John's wort for depression - an overview and meta-analysis of randomised clinical trials, *British Medical J* 1996, 313, 253-258.

Linde, K et al. Are the clinical effects of homoeopathy placebo effects? A meta-analysis of placebo-controlled trials, *Lancet* 1997; 350: 834-84 www.ncbi.nlm.nih.gov:80/ entrez/ query.fcgi?cmd=Retrieve&db=PubMed&list_uids=9310601&dopt=Abstract

Linde, K et al. Impact of study quality on outcome in placebo-controlled trials of homoeopathy, *J Clinical Epidemiology* 1999; 52: 631-636 www.ncbi.nlm.nih.gov/entrez/ query.fcgi?cmd=retrieve&db=pubmed&list_uids=10391656&dopt=Abstract

Linde, K et al. Acupuncture for chronic asthma (Cochrane Review), The Cochrane Library, Issue 1, 2000. Oxford; Update Software, 2000.

Linden, W. *Autogenic Training*, New York/ London: Guildford 1990.

Linden, W. Autogenic Training: a narrative and quantitive review of clinical outcome, *Biofeedback and Self Regulation* 1994, 19(3).

Linden, W et al. Psychosocial interventions for patients with coronary artery disease: a meta-analysis, *Archives of Internal Medicine* 1996 (Apr 8) 156.

Lindner, Robert. *The Fifty Minute How*, New York: Bantam 1976.

Lingerman, Hal Al. *The Healing Energies of Music*, Wheaton, IL: Quest 1983.

Lingerman, Hal A. *Life Streams: Journeys into Meditation and Music*, London: Quest/ Theosophical 1988.

Lininger, S et al. *The Natural Pharmacy*, Rocklin, CA: Prima 1998.

Linn, MW et al, Effects of counseling for late stage cancer patients, *Cancer* 1982, 49, 1048-1055.

Lionberger, H. *Dissertation Abstracts International*, 1985, 46, 2624B, University Microfilms No. 85-24-008.

Lip, Evelyn. (1987) Feng-Shui: A Layman's Guide to Chinese Geomancy, Union City, CA: Heian International.

Lipinski, Boguslaw. Report on the unknown type of energy recorded in Medjugorje during prayers in March 1985, *Psi Research* 1986, 5(1,2), 239-240.

Lipsey, MW/ Wilson, DB. The efficacy of psychological, educational, and behavioral treatment: Confirmation from meta-analysis, *American Psychologist* 1993, 48 1181-1209.

Lipson, Tony. *From Conception to Birth: Our Most Important Journey*, Newtown NSW, Australia: Millennium 1994.

Lipton, Bruce. The Evolving Science of Chiropractic Philosophy, Part I, *Today's Chiropractic* 1998 (Sept-Oct), 16-19. http://spiritcrossing.com/lipton/chiro1.shtm

List, T/ Helkimo, M. Acupuncture and occlusal splint therapy in the treatmentof craniomandibular disorders, Part II. A one year follow-up study, *Acta Odontologica Scandinavia* 1992, 50: 375-385.

List, T/ Helkimo, M/ Andersson, S and Carlsson, GE. (1992) Acupuncture and occlusal splint therapy in the treatment of craniomandibular disorders, Part 1. A comparative study, *SwedDentj* 16:125-141.

608 References

Liu, Guolong. Department of Physiology, Beijing College of Traditional Chinese Medicine, Beijing - Effect of qigong state and emitted qi on the human nervous system, *1st International Congress of Qigong, UC Berkeley, Calif 1990* (from Qigong database of Sancier)

Liu, Anxi/ Zhao, Jing/ Wang, Xishang/ Zhang, Jun – Dept Biology, Nankai University, China – Effect of waiqi (emitted qi) on singe sodium channel of cultured rate neurons, *3rd National Academic Conference on Qigong Science, Guangzhou, China. 1990* – from Qigong Database of Sancier.

Liu, Guolong. A study by EEG and evoked potential on humans and animals of the effects of emitted Qi, Qigong meditation, and infrasound from a Qigong simulator, (Beijing College of Traditional Chinese Medicine, China - from Sancier 1991)

Liu, Y. *The Essential Book of Traditional Chinese Medicine*, Vols. 1, 2, New York: Columbia University.

Liverani, A/ Minelli, E/ Ricciuti, A. Subjective scales for the evaluation of therapeutic effects and their use in complementary medicine, *J Alternative Complement Med.* 2000, (3), 257-64.

Locke, John. *An Essay Concerning Human Understanding* 1690.

Locke, Steven/ Colligan, Douglas. *The Healer Within*, New York: Mentor 1986.

Locke, Steven E/ Hornig-Rohan, Mady. *Mind and Immunology: Behavioral Immunology 1976-1982*, New York: Institute for the Advancement of Health 1983 (superb annotated bibliography).

Locke, Steven. et al. (eds): *Foundations of Psychoneuroimmunology*, Hawthorne, NY: Walter de Gruyter 1985.

Locker, Leonard. *Healing All and Everything*, Shaftesbury, England: Element 1985.

Lockie, A. *The Family Guide to Homeopathy*, New York: Simon & Schuster 1993.

Lockie, A/ Geddes, N. *The Women's Guide to Homeopathy*, New York: St. Martin's 1994.

Loehr, Franklin. *The Power of Prayer on Plants*, New York: Signet 1969.

Lombardi, Ethel. Personal communication 1981 1984.

Lonegren, Sig. *Spiritual Dowsing*, London: Gothic Image 1986.

Lonegren, Sig. Dowsing the earth energies elephant, *The Fountain* 1988, No. 21, 24-28.

Long, AF et al. Developing a tool to measure holistic practice: a missing dimension in outcomes measurement within complementary therapies, *Complementary Therapies in Medicine* 2000, 8 , 26-31

Long, Max Freedom. *The Secret Science Behind Miracles*, Marina Del Rey, CA: De Vorss 1976. (Orig. 1948)

Long, Max Freedom. *Recovering the Ancient Magic*, Cape Girardeau, MO: Huna 1978. (Orig. 1936)

Longworth, W/ McCarthy, PW. A review of research on acupuncture for the treatment of lumbar disk protrusions and asociated neurological symptomatology, *J Alternative and Complementary Medicine* 1997, 3(1), 55-76.

Lopes, Vas A. Double-blind clinical evaluation of the relative effectiveness of ibuprofen and glucosamine sulfate in the management of osteoarthritis of the knee in outpatients, *Current Medical Research Opinion 1982*, 8, 145-149.

Lorenzetti, BB et al. Myrcene mimics the peripheral analgesic activity of lemongrass tea, *J Ethnopharmacology* 1991, 34(1), 43-48

Lorr, M./ McNair, D. M. *Profile of Mood States (Bi-Polar Form)*, San Diego, CA: Educational and Industrial Testing Service 1988.

Lorusso, Julia/ Glick, Joel. *Healing Stones: The Therapeutic Use of Gems and Minerals*, Albuquerque, NM: Brotherhood of Life 1982.

Lotz, KE. *Do You Want to Live Healthily?* Remscheid: Paffrath-Druck 1982.

Louis, DS et al. Open treatment of digital tip injuries, *J the American Medical Association* 1980, 244, 697-698.

Love, RM/ Brodeur, BR. Inter- and intraexaminer reliability for motion palpation of the thoracic spine, *J Manipulative Physiology and Therapeutics* 1987 10 1-4.

Lovelock, James. *Gaia: A New Look at Life on Earth*, New York: Oxford University 1979.

Lovelock, James. *The Ages of Gaia: A Biography of Our Living Earth*, New York: Oxford University 1988.

Lowen, Alexander. *Pleasure: A Creative Approach to Life*, New York: Penguin 1970.

Lowen, Alexander. *The Language of the Body*, New York: Collier 1971. (Orig. 1958)

Lowen, Alexander. *Bioenergetics,* New York: Penguin 1975.

Lowen, Alexander. *Fear of Life,* New York Collier/ Macmillan 1980.

Lown, Bernard. *The Lost Art of Healing*, New York: Houghton-Mifflin 1996.

Lu, Henry C. *Chinese Classics of Tongue Diagnosis in Color.* Canada: Academy of Oriental Heritage 1980.

Lu, Henry C. *Chinese System of Food Cures: Prevention and Remedies*, New York: Sterling 1986.

Lu, Z. *Scientific Qigong Exploration: The Wonders and Mysteries of Qui.* Malvern, PA: Amber Leaf Press 1997.

Lubar, JF & Lubar JO. Neurofeedback Assessment and Treatment for Attention deficit/Hyperactivity Disorders (ADD/HD), In: J.R. Evans & A. Abarbanel (eds), *Introduction to Quantitative EEG and Neurotherapy (p. 103-143),* New York: Academic Press 1999.

Lucas, P. *the land of Tears is a Secret Place*, Denver: Agape 1992.

Gay Gaer Luce, *Biological Rhythms in Human & Animal Physiology*, New York: Dover 1971.

Lucey, JR. Neonatal jaundice and phototherapy, *Pediatric Clinics of North America* 1972, 19(4),.1-7.

Luckey, TD. Radiation hormesis in cancer mortality, *Chinese Medical J* 1994, 107, 627-630 (medline citation in Eskinazi 1999).

Ludtke, R et al. Test-retest-reliability and validity of the kinesiology muscle test,

Complementary Therapies in Medicine 2001, 9, 141-145.

Luettig, B et al. Macrophage activation by the polysaccharide arabinogalactan isolated from plant cell cultures of Echinacea purpurea, *J the National Cancer Institute* 1989, 81, 669-675.

Lukoff, David/ Turner, Robert/ Lu, Francis. Transpersonal psychology research review: Psychoreligious dimensions of healing, *J Transpersonal Psychology* 1992, 24(1), 41-60 (51 refs).

Lukoff, David et al. A holistic program for chronic schizophrenic patients, *Schizophrenia Bulletin* 1986; 12(2), 274-82.

Lukoff, David et al. The case study as a scientific method for researching alternative therapies, *Alternative Therapies* 1998, 4(2), 44-52 (45 refs).

Lund, EJ. *Bioelectrical Fields and Growth,* Austin: University of Texas 1947.

Luo, H/ Jia, Y/ Zhan, L. Electroacupuncture vs. amitriptyline in the treatment of depressive states, *J Traditional Chinese Medicine* 1985, 5:3-8.

Luscher, M. *The Luscher Color Test,* New York: Washington Squar 1969.

Lusebrink, Vija Bergs. *Imagery and Visual Expression in Therapy,* New York/ London: Plenum 1990.

Luthe, Wolfgang. Autogenic training, *American J Psychotherapy* 1963, 17, 174-195.

Luthe, Wolfgang. Autogenic training, in: Kamiya, J. et al. (eds): *Biofeedback and Self Control,* Chicago/ New York: Aldine-Atherton 1971.

Luthe, Wolfgang. *A Training Workshop for Professionals: Introduction to the Methods of Autogenic Therapy*, Denver, CO: Biofeedback Society of America 1977.

Luthe, Wolfgang/ Schultz, JH. *Autogenic Therapy, Vols. 1-6,* New York: Grune & Stratton 1969.

Luttges, Marvin/ Groswald, Douglas. Peripheral nerve injury, *Presentation at* the 8th Annual Biomechanics Conference on the Spine, University of Colorado, Boulder, CO, December 1977.

Lyerly, SB et al. 'Drugs and Placebos: The

Effects of Instruction upon Performance and Mood Under Amphetamine Sulphate and Chloral Hydrate,' *J Abnormal and Social Psychology* 1964, 68, 321-27.

Lynn, SJ/ JW, Rhue 1987. Hypnosis, imagination, and fantasy, *J Mental Imagery* 11 101-113.

Lyon, WS. *Encyclopedia of Native American Healing*, New York: WW Norton 1996.

M

Maanum, Armand/ Montgomery, Herb. *The Complete Book of Swedish Massage*, New York: Harper & Row 1985.

Macbeth, Jessica. *Moon Over Water: Meditation Made Clear with Techniques for Beginners and Initiates*, Bath: Gateway 1990.

MacDonald AJR et al. Superficial acupunct-ure in the relief of chronic low back pain, *Annals of the Royal College of Surgury* 1983, 65:44-46.

MacEoin, Denis. The Benveniste affair and the denaturing of science, *J Alternative and Complementary Medicine* 1988, 6(9), 16-18 ff.

MacGregor, RJ/ Oliver, RM. A general-purpose electronic model for arbitrary configurations of neurons, *J Theoretical Biology* 1973, 38, 527-538.

MacGregor, RJ et al. A pressure vessel model for nerve compression, *J Neurological Science* 1975, 24, 299-304.

Machovec, FJ. The evil eye: Superstition or hypnotic phenomenon? *American J Clinical Hypnosis* 1976, 19(2), 74-79.

Macintyre, Anne. *M.E.* London: Harper Collins 1988.

Maciocia, G. *Tongue Diagnosis in Chinese Medicine,* Seattle, WA: Eastland 1987.

Maciocia, G. *The Foundations of Chinese Medicine: A Comprehensive Text for Acupuncturists and Herbalists*, New York: Churchill Livingstone 1989.

Mackereth, Peter A. An introduction to catharsis and the healing crisis in reflexology, *Complementary Therapies in Nursing and Midwifery* 1999, 5, 67-74.

MacManaway, Bruce/ Turcan, Johanna. *Healing: The Energy That Can Restore Health,* Wellingborough, England: Thorsons 1983.

MacManaway, Once. Personal communica-tions 1984-85.

MacRae, Janet. Therapeutic Touch in practice, *American J Nursing* 1979 (April), 664-665.

Madaule, Paul. *When Listening Comes Alive,* Moulin 1994.

Maddox, John/ Randi, James/ Stewart, Walter W. 'High-dilution' experiments a delusion, *Nature* 1988, 334 (28 July), 287-290. (Response of J. Benveniste p291).

Madison, JL/ Wilkie, DJ. Family members' perceptions of cancer pain, *Nursing Clinics of North America* 1990, 30(4), 625-645.

Madrid, A et al. Subjective assessment of allergy relief following group hypnosis and self-hypnosis: a preliminary study, *American J Clinical Hypnosis* 1995, 38(2), 80-86.

Magaray, Christopher. Healing and meditation in medical practice, *Medical J Australia* 1981, 1, 338-341.

Magoun, H (ed). *Osteopathy in the Cranial Field*, Kirksville, MO: J Printing 1951.

Maher, Michaeleen/ Schmeidler, Gertrude. Cerebral lateralization effects in ESP processing, *J the Society for Psychical Research* 1977, 71, 261-271.

Maher, Michaeleen/ Schmeidler, Gertrude. The authors' reply to Mr. Broughton, *J the Society for Psychical Research* 1978, 72, 389-392.

Mahesh, Yogi, M. *Transcendental Meditation*, New York: New American Library 1963.

Mahoney, MJ/ Avener, M. Psychology of the elite athlete: An exploratory study, *Cognitive Therapy & Research* 1977, 1, 135-141.

Mahony, Margaret A. *Business Masquerading as a Medical Care: Saving the Soul of Medicine*, San Francisco: Robert D. Reed Publishers 2000

Mainey, Vincent. Confession of a swinging G.P., *J British Society of Dowser's* 1988, 32, 328-338.

Mairs, N. *Voice Lessons*, Boston: Beacon 1994.

Maisel E. *The Alexander Technique: The Essential Writings of F. Matthias Alexander, Selected and Introduced by E. Maisel*, New York: New York University 1989.

Makarec, K/ Persinger, MA. Geophysical variables and behavior XLIII, Negative correlation between accuracy of card-guessing and geomagnetic activity: A case study, *Perceptual and Motor Skills* 1987, *65, 105-106.*

Malacz, WP. Deliberately caused bodily damage (DCBD) phenomena: a different perspective, *J the Society for Psychical Research* 1998, 62, 434-444.

Malde, S. Guided autobiography: a counseling tool for older adults, *J Counseling and Development* 1988, 66, 290-293.

Malley, J/ Stone, T. Therapeutic and "dose-dependent" effect of repetitive microelectro-shock induced by transcranial magnetic stimulations in parkinson's disease, *J Neuroscience Research* 1999, 57, 935-940.

Mallick, Palash et al. Ameliorating effect of microdoses of a potentized homeopathic drug, arsenicum album, on arsenic-induced toxicity in mice, *BMC Complementary and Alternative Medicine* 2003, 3, 7 http://biomedcentral.com/1472-6882/3/7

Mallikarjun, S. Kirlian photography in cancer diagnosis, *Osteopathic Physician* 1978 (May), 24-27.

Malloy, Gail B. Therapeutic touch and type I healing: A continuum, *Consciousness Research and Training Newsletter* 1983, 7(1), 8-11.

Manaka, Yoshio/ Urquhart, IA. *A Layman's Guide to Acupuncture*, New York: John Weatherhill 1972/ 1980.

Mandel, Peter. *Energy Emission Analysis: New Applications of Kirlian Photography for Holistic Health. Bruchsal*, Germany: Institut fur wissenschaftliche Fotografie und Diagnostik, Essen, GermanySynthesis.

Mandell, Marshall. *Dr. Mandell's Lifetime Arthritis Relief System*, New York: Putnam/ Berkeley Group 1985.

Manga, P et al. A study to examine the effectiveness and cost-effectiveness of chiropractic management of low-back pain, Ministry of Health, Government of Ontario 1993.

Mango, MA/ Persinger, MA. Geophysical variables and behavior: LII. Decreased geomagnetic activity and spontaneous telepathic experiences from the Sidgwick collection, *Perceptual and Motor Skills* 1988, 67, 907-910.

Manheim, Carol J et al. *Craniosacral Therapy and SomatoEmotional Releas: The Self-Healing Body,* Thorofare, NJ: SLACK 1989.

Mann, Felix. *Acupuncture: The Ancient Chinese Art of Healing,* New York: Vintage/ Random House 1972.

Mann, Ronald L. *Sacred Healing; Integrating Spirituality with Psychotherapy*, Blue Dolphin Publishing 1998.

Mann, W Edward. *Orgone, Reich and Eros: Wilhelm Reich's Theory of Life Energy*, New York: Touchstone/ Simon and Schuster 1973. (7pp refs)

Mann, W Edward. New evidence for Reich's 'life energy', In: *Fate Magazine. Exploring the Healing Miracle,* Highland Park, IL: Clark 1983.

Manning, AD. The neutralization of harmful rays, *J British Society of Dowsers* 1964, 28(126), 196-200.

Mansfield, Peter. *Flower Remedies*, Boston: Charles E. Tuttle 1995.

Mansfield, Victor. *Synchronicity, Science, and Soul-Making*, Chicago/ La Salle, IL: Open Court1995.

Maoshing, DOM/ McNease, Cathy. *Tao of Nutrition,* Santa Monica, CA: Seven Star Communications 1993.

Mar, Timothy. *Face Reading,* New York Signeo 1974.

Marais, Eugene. *The Soul of the White Ant,* West Drayton, Middlesex, England: Penguin 1973. (Orig. 1937)

Marcus, DM/ Suarez-Almazor, ME. Is there a role for ginger in the treatment of osteoarthritis? *Arthritis Rheum.* 2001, 44(11),2461-2.

Margenau, Henry. Attributed.

Margolin, A. Liabilities involved in conducting randomized clinical trials of CAM therapies in the absence of preliminary, foundational studies: a case in point, *J Altern Complement Med.* 1999, 5(1),103-4.

Margolin, A et al. Acupuncture for the treatment of cocaine dependence in methadone-maintained patients, *American J Addictions* 1993, 2:194-201.

Marinho, Jarbas George. Kirlian photography and evidence of energy transmission from one person to another. (Abstract, translated from Spanish), *Psi Comunicacion* 1976, 2(3/ 4), 65-69.

Marino, AA (ed). *Modern Bioelectricity,* New York: Marcel Decker 1988.

Markides, Kyriakos. The Magus of Strovolos: The Extraordinary World of a Spiritual Healer London and Boston: Arkana 1985.

Markides, Kyriacos C. *Fire in the Heart: Healers, Sages and Mystics,* London: Arkana/ Penguin 1991.

Markova, Dawna. *The Art of the Possible: A Coimpassionate Approach to Understanding the Way People Think, Learn & Communicate,* Conari 1991.

Markovitz, JH. Psychological predictors of hypretension in the Framingham study, *J the American Medical Association* 1993, Nov 24, 270(4).

Marrs, Jim. *The Enigma Files: The True Story of America's Psychic Warfare Program,* New York: Harmony 1999

Marsh, G/ Beams, HW. Electrical control of morphogenesis in regenerating Dugesia tigrinum, *J Cell and Comparative Physiology* 1952, 39, 191.

Martin, Rod. Sense of humor, hassles, & immunoglobulin A: Evidence for stress-moderating effect of humor, *International J Psychiatry in Medicine* 1988, 18, 93.

Martin, SJ/ Kelly, IW/ Saklofske, DH. Suicide and lunar cycles: a critical review over 28 years, *Psychological Reports* 1992, 71, 787-795.

Marz, R. *Textbook in Clinical Nutrition,* Portland, OR: Omni 1997.

Maslow, Abraham. *Religions, Values and Peak-Experiences,* Columbus, OH: Ohio State University 1964.

Mason, AA/ S, Black. Allergic skin responses abolished under treatment of asthma and hay fever by hypnosis, *Lancet* 1958. 1, 877-880.

Mason, Gary. The Flower Essence J. Periodical available from Flower Essence Pharmacy, 6600 N. Hwy 1, Little River, CA 95456. 800-343-8693, fax 707-937-0441.

Mason, Gary. *The Flower Essence Pharmacy Catalog,* Vols. I & II. Little River, CA: Flower Essence Pharmacy 1997.

Mason, Keith. *Thoughts that Harm, Thaughts that Heal,* London: Piatkus 2000

Mason, RC/ Clark, G/ Reeves, RB/ Wagner, B. Acceptance and healing, *J Religion and Health* 1969,8,123-142.

Mason, Su/ Tovey, Philip/ Long, Andrew F. Evaluating complementary medicine: methodological challenges of randomised controlled trials, *British Medical J* 2002,325., 832-834.

Masserman, Jules, H (ed). *Handbook of Psychiatric Therapies,* New York: Grune & Stratton 1966.

Masters, R/ Houston, J. *Listening to the Body,* New York: Delta 1978.

Masunaga, Shizuto. *Meridian Exercises,* Tokyo/ New York: Japan Publications 1987.

Mathews, JA et al. Back pain and sciatica: controlled trials of manipulation, traction, sclerosant, and epidural injections, *British J Rheumatology* 1987, 26, 416-423.

Matthew, R/ Rumar, S. The non-exponential decay pattern of the weak luminescence from seedlings in Cicer arietinum L. stimulated by pulsing electric fields, *Experientia,* in press.

Matthews-Simonton, Stephanie. *The Healing Family: The Simonton Approach for Families Facing Illness,* New York: Bantam 1984.

Matthiessen, Peter. *The Snow Leopard: The Astonishing Spiritual Odyssey of a Man in Search of Himself,* New York: Bantam/ Viking Penguin 1978.

Maupin, EW. On meditation, in: Tart 1969.

Maurer, Daphne/ Maurer, Charles. *The World of the Newborn,* New York: Basic 1988.

Maury, EA. *Drainage in Homeopathy*, Rustington, UK: Health Science Press 1965.

Maxey, ES. Perspective: a lethal subtle energy, *Subtle Energies* 1991, 2(2), 55-72.

May, Brad. *Muscle Testing Miracles*, San Diego, CA: Serenity Systems 1988.

Mayer, Daniel Thomas. Kirlian Photography: History and Philosophical Implications and its Practical Application through Energetic Diagnosis, *Unpublished doctoral dissertation*, SAMRA University, Los Angeles 1984.

Mazarelli, J (ed). *Chiropractic: Interprofessional Research*, Torino, Italy: Edizioni Minerva Medica 1982.

Mazza, N. The use of poetry in treating the troubled adolescent, *Psychotherapy: Theory, Research and Practice* 1981, 8, 195-198.

Mazza, N. Poetry therapy: towards a research agenda for the 1990's, *The Arts in Psychotherapy* 1993, 20, 61-68.

McCaffery, John. *Tales of Padre Pio, The Friar of San Giovanni,* Garden City, New York: Image/ Doubleday 1981 (orig. *The Friar of San Giovanni,* UK Darton, Longman & Todd 1978).

McCaffery, M/ Beebe, A. *Pain - Clinical Manual for Nursing Practice*, St. Louis: C. V. Mosby 1989.

McCarney, R et al. *Can homeopaths detect homeopathic medicines by dowsing?* A randomized, double-blind, placebo-controlled trial, *J Royal Society of Medicine* 2002, 95, 189-191.

McCarthy, Donald/ Keane, Patrice/ Tremmel, Lawrence. Psi phenomena in low complexity systems: Conformance behav-iour using seeds, In: Roll, W.G. *Research in Parapsychology* 1978. Metuchen, New Jersey: Scarecrow Press 1979, 82-84.

McClellan, Randall. *The Healing forces of Music: History, Theory and Practice*, Rockport, MA:/ Shaftesbury, England: Element 1991.

McClenon, James. Fire walking on Mount Takao, *Archaeus* 1983, 1(1),25-28.

McClenon, James. The experiential foundations of shamanic healing, *J Medical Philosophy* 1993 18 107-128.

McClure, Kevin. Fire within and without, *The Unexplained* 1981,4(38), 750-753.

McConnell, et al. Low agreement of findings in neuromusculoskeletal examinations by a group of osteopathic physicians using their own procedures, *Jounrnal of the American Osteopathic Association* 1980, 79, 441-450 .

McCord, Hallack. Hypnotic control of nosebleed, *American J Clinical Hypnosis* 1968a, 10(3), 219.

McCord, Hallack. Hypnotherapy in diabetes - a brief note, *American J Clinical Hypnosis* 1968b, 10(4), 309-310.

McCraty, Roland et al. New electrophysiological correlates associated with intentional heart focus, *Subtle Energies*1993, 4(3), 251-268.

McCrossin, S. Changes in SSVEP topography, digit span performance and reading comprehension in response to acupressure treatment, Unpublished research thesis, Swinburne University, Melbourne, Australia, Oct 1995.

McDonald, Kathleen (Courtin, Robina, Ed). *How To Meditate: A Practical Guide,* London: Wisdom 1984.

McDonald, SF. Effect of visible light waves on arthritis pain: a controlled study, *International J Biosocial Research* 1982, 3(2), 49-54.

McDougall, W. A new theory of laughter, *Psyche*, 1922, 2, 298-300.

McElroy, Susan Chernak. *Animals as Teachers and Healers: True Stories & Reflections*, Troutdale, OR: NewSage 1996.

McElroy, Susan Chernak. *Animals as Guides for the Soul*, New York: Ballantine/ Wellspring 1998.

McEnulty, John, Eman8tions, St. Louis, MO 6/3/2003

McFadden, Steven. *Profiles in Wisdom: Native Elders Speak About the Earth*, Santa Fe, NM: Bear & Co. 1991.

McGaa, Ed/ Man, Eagle. *Mother Earth Spirituality: Native American Paths to Healing Ourselves and Our World,* San Francisco: HarperCollins 1990.

McGarey, Gladys Taylor. *The Physician*

Within You: Medicine for the Millenium, Deerfield Beach, FL: Health Communications 1997.

McGarey, William A. *The Edgar Cayce Remedies*, New York: Bantam 1983.

McGhee, Paul. *How to Develop Your Sense of Humor*, Dubuque, IA:Kendall-Hunt 1994. (Available from publisher: 800-228-0810).

McGhee, Paul. *Health, Healing and the Amuse System: Humor as Survival Training*, 1999. Available from publisher: 800-228-0810.

McGhee, Paul. Humor website http://laughterremedy.com.

McGlashan, Thomas H/ Evans, Frederick J/ Orne, Martin T. The nature of hypnotic analgesia and placebo response to experimental pain, *Psychosomatic Medicine* 1969, 31(3), 227-245.

McGuffin, M et al. *Botanical Safety Handbook*, Boca Raton, FL: CRC 1997.

McGuire, Meredith B. *Pentecostal Catholics*, Philadelphia Temple University 1982.

McIntyre, Anne. *The Complete Floral Healer*, London: Gaia 1993.

McIntyre, Anne. *Flower Power: Flower Remedies for Healing Body and Soul Through Herbalism, Homeopathy, Aromatherapy, and Flower Essences*, New York: Henry Holt 1996.

McKechnie, AF et al. Anxiety states: a preliminary report on the value of connective tissue massage, *J Psychosomatic Research* 1983, 27(2) 125-129 (*Pilot study* - from Workshop on Alternative Medicine).

McKeller, P. Imagery from the standpoint of introspection, In: P. W. Sheehan (ed). *The Function and Nature of Imagery*, London: Academic Press 1972, 36-58.

McKenna, Dennis J. Green tea monograph, *Alternative Therapies* 2000, 6(3), 61-84 (2p. refs).

McKinney, F. Free writing as therapy, *British J Medical Psychology* 1983, 56, 367-370.

McLaird, George. *Meditation/ Visualization: Transformation is an Inside Job*, Marina del Rey, CA: De Vorss 1982.

McMahon, R/ Pearson, A. (eds). *Nursing as Therapy. 2nd ed*, Cheltenham, UK: Stanley Thornes, Ltd. 1998.

McMoneagle, Joe. *Mind Trek; Exploring Consciousness, Time, and Space Through Remote Viewing*, Hampton Roads Publishing 1993

McMoneagle, Joe. *Remote Viewing Secrets*, Charlottesville, NC: Hampton Roads 2000.

McNair, D. M., et al, *EdiTS Manual for the Profile of Mood States*, San Diego, CA: EdiTS 1992.

McNiff, Shaun. *Art as Medicine: Creating a Therapy of the Imagination*, London: Piatkus; Boulder, CO: Shambala 1992.

McSherry, E. Medical economics, In: D. Wedding, ed. *Medicine and Behavior*, St. Louis: Mosby 1990, 463-484.

McTaggart, Lynne. *What Doctors Don't Tell You*, London: Thorsons 1996.

McTaggart, Lynne. *The Field: The Quest for the Secret Force of the Universei*, New York: HarperCollins 2000.

Meade, TW et al. Low back pain of mechanical origin: randomized comparison of chiropractic and hospital outpatient treatment, *British Medical J* 1990, 300 1431-1437.

Meares, Ainslie. *Relief Without Drugs: How to Conquer Tension. Pain and Anxiety*, London: Fontana/ Collins 1967.

Medical Outcomes Trust, 20 Park Plaza, suite 1014, Boston, MA 02116-4313, measuring tools that include patients and health caregivers.

Medical World News, Finger-tip halos of Kirlian photography: Pseudoscience or promising diagnostic tool? *Medical World News* 1973 (25 October), 43-48.

Medical World News, 1973 (26 October), 14(39), 43-48.

Medicine Eagle, Brooke. The circle of healing, in: Carlson/ Shield 1989, 58-62.

Meehan, TC. An Abstract of the Effect of Therapeutic Touch on the Experience of Acute Pain in Post-operative Patient, *Unpublished doctoral dissertation*, New York University 1985.

Meehan, Thérèse Connell. Therapeutic Touch and postoperative pain: a Rogerian research study, *Nursing Science Quarterly* 1993, 6(2), 69-78.

Meehan, TC et al. The effect of Therapeutic Touch on postoperative pain, *Pain* 1990, Supplement p..149.

Meek, GW. *Healers and the Healing Process,* Wheaton, IL: Theosophical 1977. (Quotes reprinted by permission of publisher, copyright George W. Meek, 1977.)

Meeker-Lowery, Susan/ Ferrara, Jennifer. Nuclear Lunch: The Dangers and Unknowns of Food Irradiation http://www.sustainable-city.org/articles/irradiat.htm

Mehl, Lewis E. *Mind and Matter: Foundations for Holistic Health,* Berkeley, CA: Mindbody 1986.

Mehl-Madrona, Lewis. *Coyote Medicine,* New York: Scribner 1997.

Meiffren, M. The use of poetry and ritual with troubled adolescents, *J Humanistic Psychology* 1993, 33, 24-44.

Melchart, D/ Weidenhammer, W/ Thormahlen, J/ Gehring, T/ Saller, R. Quality management and research. A pragmatic concept for evaluation and optimization of complementary medicine within the framework of hospital and practitioner relations, *Z Arztl Forthild Qualitatssich* 2000, 94(9), 751-7.

Melchart, D. et al. Results of five randomized studies on the immunomod-ulatory activity of preparations of echinacea, *J Alternative and Complementary Medicine* 1995, 1, 145-160.

Melchart, D. et al. Echinacea root extracts for the prevention of upper respiratory tract infections, *Archives of Family Medicine* 1998.

Melchart, D et al. Acupuncture for idiopath-ic headache (Cochrane Review). Cochrane Database Syst Rev 2001; 1: CD001218.

Meletis, Chris D/ Jacobs, Thad. *Interactions Between Drugs & Natural Medicines – What the Physician and Pharmacist Must Know About Vitamins, Minerals, Foods, and Herbs,* Sandy, OR: Eclectic Medical 1999.

Mella, Dorothee L. *Stone Power II: The Legendary and Practical Use of Gems and Stones,* Albuquerque, NM: Brotherhood of Life 1986.

Melville, John. *Crystal-Gazing,* London: Nichols, 1903.

Melzack, The McGill Pain Questionnaire: major properties and scoring methods, *Pain* 1975 1, 277-299.

Melzack, R. Phantom limbs, *Scientific American* 1992, 120-126.

Melzack, R/ Loeser, JD. Phantom body pain in paraplegics: evidence for a central pattern generating mechanism" for pain, *Pain* 1978, 4, 195-210.

Melzack, R. et al. Phantom limbs in people with congenital limb deficiency or amputation in early childhood, *Brain* 1997, 120(pt. 9), 1603-1620.

Menkes, JH. Neurologic complications of pertussis vaccination, And Neurology, 1990; 28:428.

Menkes, JH. & Kinsbourne, M. Workshop on neurologic complications of pertussis and pertussis vaccination, Neuropediatrics, 1990; 21:171-176.

Menkin, Dan. *Transformation through Bodywork: Using Touch Therapies for Inner Peace,* Santa Fe, NM: Bear & Co. 1996.

Mennell, J.M. *The Musculoskeletal System: Differentiatial Diagnosis from Symptoms and Physical Signs,* Gaithersburg, MD: Aspen 1992.

Mentgen, J/ Bulbrook, MT. *Healing Touch: Level 1,* Carrboro, NC: North Carolina Center for Healing Touch 1994.

Mercer, G. et al. Researching and Evaluating complementary Therapies: The State of the Debate, Leeds: collaborating Centre for Health Service Research, Nuffield Institute for Health 1995.

Merchant, RE et al. A couble-blind, placebo-controlled (DBPC) crossover study of dietary suplementation with *Chlorella pyrenoidosa* for fibromyalgia syndrome, FASB J 2000, (Mar 13), A728.

Mercola, John. Current health news you can use, *Townsend Letter* 2000 (Aug/ Sep), 40.

Mercola, John. http://www.mercola.com/2000/may/14/doctoraccidents.htm

Meercola, John. The Problems with Irradiated Food: What the Research Says, http://www.mercola.com/article/Diet/irradiated/irradiated_research.htm April 11, 2001 (accessed 7/9/03).

Mercola, John. GMO Crops Are An Accident Waiting to Happen, http://www.mercola.com/2001/jun/2/gmo_crops.htm June 2, 2001 (accessed 7/9/03).

Mercola, John. Store Your Food in Glass Not Plastic, http://www.mercola.com/2003/apr/16/food_storage.htm April 16, 2003 (accessed 7/9/03).

Merker, Mordecai M. Telepathy: A lawyer's analysis of the Indian rope trick, *Parapsychological Review* 1971, 2(6), 20-22.

Mermet, Abbé. *Principles and Practice of Radiesthesia; 2nd ed,* Translated from French by Clement, Mark) London: Stuart & Watkins 1967. (Orig. 1935)

Merritt, Stephanie. *Mind, Music, and Imagery,* New York: Plume 1990.

Mesmer, Franz Anton. *Mesmerism: A Translation of the Original Medical and Scientific Writings of F.A. Mesmer, MD.,* Translated by Bloch, George J.) Los Altos, CA: William Kaufmann 1980.

Messegue, Maurice. Of Man and Plants, New York: Macmillan 1973.

Metzger, D. *Writing for Your Life: A Guide and Companion to the Inner Worlds,* San Francisco: Harper 1992.

Meyer, Patricia/ Shor, Andrea. Helping children with Attention Deficit Disorder through flower essence therapy, *Flower Essence Society Newsletter,* Summer 1995, 5(1&2), 1-6.

Mezentsev, (no f.n.). Firewalkers, Trans, from Russian), *Psi Research* 1982, 1(2), 75-76.

Michalsen, Andreas et al. Effectiveness of Leech Therapy in Osteoarthritis of the Knee: A Randomized, Controlled Trial *Annals of Internal Medicine* 2003, 139(9), 724-730

Michaud, L/ Persinger, M. Geophysical variables and behavior: XXV, alterations in memory for a narrative following applications of theta freuency electromagnetic fields, *Perception & Motor Skills* 1983, 60, 416-418.

Micozzi, Marc (ed). *Fundamentals of Complementary and Alternative Medicine,* New York: Churchill Livingstone, 1996.

Micozzi, Marc S. *Fundamentals of Complementary and Alternative Medicine,* New York/ London: Churchill Livningstone 1996.

Micozzi, Marc (ed). *Current Review of Complementary Medicine,* Current Medicine 1999.

Miettinen, MA. Religious healing from a medical and psychological view, Dissertation, Tampere, Finland: Kirkon Tutimeskeskus, Series A, No. 51 1990.

Migron, Lionel. Icy claim that water has memory, *New Scientist,* 11 June, 2003 http://www.newscientist.com/news/news.jsp?id=ns99993817

Milamed, DR/ Hedley-Whyte, J. Contributions of the surgical sciences to a reduction of the mortality rate in the United States for the period 1968 to 1988, *Annals of Surgery* 1994, 219, :94-102.

Milburn, M/ Oelbermann, M. *Electromagnetic Fields & Your Health,* Vancouver, BC New Star 1988.

Miller, Diane. http://www.nationalhealthfreedom.org/

Miller, J.G. *Living Systems,* New York: McGraw-Hill 1978.

Miller, Light/ Miller, Bryan. *Ayurveda and Aromatherapy The Earth Essential Guide to Ancient Wisdom and Modern Healing,* Motilal Banarasidass 1998

Miller, M/ Rahe, Richard H. Life changes scaling for the 1990s, *J Psychosomatic Research* 1997, 43, 279-292.

Miller, Neal E. Biofeedback and visceral learning, *Annual Review of Psychology* 1978, 29.

Miller, Robert N. Paraelectricity, a primary energy, *Human Dimensions* (undated) 5(1 & 2), 22-26 (Also reported in: Miller 1977).

Miller, Robert. Methods of detecting and measuring healing energies, In: White,

John/ Krippner, Stanley. *Future Science,* Garden City, NY: Anchor/ Doubleday 1977.

Miller, Ronald S. The healing magic of crystals: An interview with Marcel Vogel, *Science of Mind* 1985 (August), 8-13 ff.

Miller, TW. *Chronic Pain (Vol. 1 & 2),* Madison, CT: International University 1990 .

Mills, J.C/ Crowley, R.J. *Therapeutic Metaphors for Children and the child within,* New York: Brunner-Mazel 1986.

Mills, Simon. *The Essential Book of Herbal Medicine,* New York: Viking Penguin 1994.

Mills, Simon/ Bone, Kerry. *Principles and Practice of Phytotherapy,* New York: Churchill Livingstone 1999.

Mills, Simon/ Finando, Steven J. *Alternatives in Healing,* New York: New American Library 1989.

Milton, John. 1637 Source lost.

Milton, John. *Paradise Lost* 1667.

Mindell, Arnold. *Dreambody: The Body's Role in Revealing the Self,* London: Routledge and Kegan Paul 1983.

Mintz, Elizabeth E/ Schmeidler, Gertrude R. *The Psychic Thread,* New York: Human Sciences 1983.

Mior, S. A. et al. Intra- and interexaminer reliability of motion palpation in the cervical spine, *J Canadian Chiropractic Assoc.* 1985, 29 195-198.

Mircea. *Yoga: Immortality and Freedom,* New York: Princeton University 1958

Mirowsky J/ Ross, CE. Social patterns of distress, *Annual Review of Sociology* 1986, 12, *23-45.*

Mison, Karel, Statistical processing of diagnostics done by subject and by physician, *Proceedings of the 6th International Conference on Psychotronic Research* 1986, 137-138.

Mitchell, BB. Legislative Handbook for the Practice of Acupuncture and Oriental Medicine, Washington, DC: National Acupuncture Foundation 1955.

Mithaug, DE. *Self-Regulation Theory: How Optimal Adjustment Maximizes Gain,* Westport, CT: Praeger 1993.

Mittwoch, U. Lateral asymmetry and gonadal function, *Lancet* 1975, 1, 401-402.

Moerman, Daniel E. Anthropology of symbolic healing, *Current Anthropology* 1979, 20(1), 59-80 (3pp refs).

Moerman, Daniel E. Physiology and symbols: The anthropological implications oldie placebo effect, In: Romanucci-Ross, L. (ed): *The Anthropology of Medicine. From Culture to Method* New York: Praeger 1982.

Moerman, Daniel E. *Native American Ethnobotany,* Portland, OR: Timber 1998.

Moerman, D. *The Meaning Response: Rethinking the Placebo Effect,* Cambridge Univ Pr 2002.

Moher, David. MSc The CONSORT Guide-lines: improving the quality of research. Consolidated Standards of Reporting Trials. Interview by Bonnie Horrigan, *Altern Ther Health Med.* 2002, 8(3),103-8.

Moin, Larry. *Meditations for Healing,* Naples, FL: United States Publishing 1994.

Mole, Peter. *Acupuncture: Energy Balancing for Body, Mind, and Spirit,* Rockport, MA/ Shaftesbury, England: Element 1992.

Molea, DB. et al. Evaluation of two manip-ulative techniques in the treatment of postexercise muscle soreness, *J the American Osteopathic Association* 1987, 87, 477-483.

Moleyar V/ Narasimham, P. Antibacterial activity of essential oil components, *International J Food Microbiology* 1992 16(4), 337-342

Molsberger A and Hille E (1994) The analgesic effect of acupuncture in chronic tennis elbow pain, *BritjRbeumatol* 33:1162-1165.

Momas, EJ. et al. Incidence and types of adverse events and negligent care in Utah and Colorado, *Medical Care* 2000; 38:261-71.

Monro, Robin/ Ghoch, A.K/ Kalich, Daniel. *Yoga Research: A Bibliography of Scientific Studies on Yoga,* Cambridge, England: Yoga Biomedical Trust 1987.

Monroe, RAK/ Kalish, D. Yoga Research Bibliography, Scientific Studies on Yoga and Meditation, Cambridge, England: Yoga Biomedical Trust,. 1989.

Montagu, AM. Sensory influences on the skin, *Texas Report of Biological Medicine* 1953, 2, 291-301.

Montagu, Ashley. *Touching: The Human Significance of the Skin*, New York: Perennial/ Harper & Row 1971.

Montandon, HE. Psychophysiological aspects of the Kirlian phenomenon: A confirmatory study, *J the American Society for Psychical Research* 1977, 71, 45-50.

Monte, Tom. Editors of EastWest Natural Health, *World Medicine:A Comperhensive View of Six Traditional Medical Systems* (Chinese, Ayur-Veda, Western Conventional Medicine, Homeopathy, Naturopathy, Greek), New York: Tarcher/ Putnam 1993.

Montefiore, J. *Feminism and Poetry: Language, Experience, and Identity in Women's Writing*, New York: Harper Collins/ Pandora 1987.

Montgomery, DJ. Review of *Le signal du sourcier* by Y. Rocard, In: Physics Today 1964, 17(7), *54-57*. (Cited by G.P Hansen)

Montgomery, Ruth. *Born to Heat,* New York: Popular Library 1973.

Monti, Daniel A. et al. Muscle test comparisons of congruent and incongruent self-referential statements, *Perceptual Motor Skills* 1999, 88, 1019-1028.

Monty, Tom. *World Medicine: The East-West Guide to Healing Your Body*, New York: Tarcher/ Perigee/ Putnam 1993.

Moody, Raymond A. *Life After Life,* New York: Bantam 1975.

Moody, RA. *Laugh After Laugh: The Healing Power of Humor*, Jacksonville, FL: Headwaters 1978.

Mookerjee, Ajit. *Tantra Art: Its Philosophy and Physics*, Basel, Paris, New Delhi: Ravi Kumar 1983.

Moore, Ede et al. *The Clocks that Time Us: Physiology of the Circadian Timing System*, Cambridge, MA: Harvard University 1982.

Moore, M. *Los Remedios: Traditional Herbal Remedies of the Southwest*, Santa Fe, NM: Red Crane 1990.

Moore, NG. Self-regulation in Children,

Alternative Therapies 1996, 6(2).

Moore, S. *Chiropractic,* Rutland, VT: Charles E. Tuttle 1993.

Moore, TJ. *Deadly Medicine*, New York: Simon & Schuster 1995.

Moore, Thomas. *The Re-Enchantment of Everyday Life*. New York: HarperPerennial 1996, pg. 145

Mootz, RD et al. Intra- and interobserver reliability of passive motion palpation of the lumbar spine, *J Manipulative Physiology and Therapeutics* 1989 12, 440-445.

Morehouse, David. *Psychic Warrior; Inside the CIA's Stargate Program: The True Story of a Soldier's Espionage and Awakening*, New York: St. Martin's 1996

Morell, Franz. *The MORA Concept*, Heidelberg, Germany: Karl F. Haug 1990.

Morgan, JP et al. A controlled trial of spinal manipulation in the management of hypertension, *J the American Osteopathic Association* 1985, 85, 308-313.

Morgan, W. Navaho treatment of sickness: diagnosticians, In: Lanty

Morley, Peter/ Wallis, Roy (eds). *Culture and Curing,* Pittsburgh, PA: University of Pittsburgh 1978.

Morrice, JKW. poetry as therapy, *British J Medical Psychology* 1983, 56, 367-370.

Morrison, JH. *The Book of Ayurveda*, New York: Simon & Schuster 1995.

Morrison, James K. The use of imagery techniques in family therapy, *American J Family Therapy* 1981 9(2), *52-56.*

Morrison, M. *Poetry as Therapy,* New York: Human Services 1987.

Morrison, Roger. *Desktop Guide to Keynotes and Confirmatory Symptoms,* Albany, CA: Hahnemann Clinic Publishing 1993.

Morse, J/ Young, D/ Swartz. L. Cree Indian healing practices and Western health care: a comparative analysis, *Social Science and Medicine* 1991, 32 1361-1366.

Morse, Melvin with Perry, Paul. *Parting Visions: An Exploration of Pre-Death Psychic and Spiritual Experiences*, New York: Villard/ Random House 1995.

Morton, AR et al. Efficacy of laser-acupuncture in the prevention of exercise induced asthma, *Annals of Allergy* 1993, 70(4), 295-298.

Moseley, JB et al. A controlled trial of arthroscopic surgery for osteoarthritis of the knee, *New England J Medicine* 2002, 347, 81-88.

Moss, Charles. A. Five element acupuncture: treating body, mind, and spirit, *Alternative Therapies* 1999, 5(5), 52-61.

Moss, Norman. *Managing the Planet: The Politics of the New Millennium*, Washington, DC: Earthscan 2000.

Moss, Richard. *How Shall I Live*, Berkeley, CA: Celestial Arts 1985.

Moss, Richard. *The Black Butterfly: An Invitation to Radical Aliveness*, Berkeley, CA: Celestial Arts 1986.

Moss, Richard. Individual and collective transformations, In: *Church and Sherr* 1987, 165-175.

Moss, Ralph W. *Cancer Therapy: The Independent Consumer's Guide to Non-Toxic Treatment and Prevention*, New York: Equinox 1992.

Moss, Ralph W. *Questioning Chemotherapy*, Brooklyn, NY: Equinox 1995.

Moss, Ralph. *Alternative Medicine Online: A Guide to Natural Remedies on the Internet*, Brooklyn NY: Equinox 1997.

Moss, Ralph W. *Herbs Against Cancer*, Brooklyn, NY: Equinox 1998.

Moss, Thelma S. Photographic evidence of healing energy on plants and people, *Dimensions of Healing. Symposium of the Academy of Parapsychology and Medicine at Los Altos, CA 1972*, pp 121-131.

Moss, Thelma. *The Probability of the Impossible,* Bergenfield, NJ: New American Library 1974.

Moss, Thelma. *The Body Electric,* New York: St. Martin's 1979.

Moss, Vere. Non-physical factors in medical divination and treatment, *J the British Society of Dowsers* 1968, 20, 288-292.

Motoyama, Hiroshi. Tony Agpaoa's psychic surgery and its mechanisms, *Religion and Parapsychology,* Encinitas, CA: Interna-tional Association for Religion and Parapsychology 1978.

Motoyama, Hiroshi. *Theories of the Chakras: Bridge to Higher Consciousness,* Wheaton, IL: Theosophical 1981.

Motoyama, H/ Brown, Rande. *Science and the Evolution of Consciousness, Ki and Psi,* Brookline, MA: Autumn 1978.

Motoyama, H/ Brown, Rande. *Karma and Reincarnation: The Key to Spiritual Evolution and Enlightenment,* Translated from Japanese by Brown Ouichi Rande.) London: Piatkus 1992.

Mott, G. "Lowering of Serum Cholesterol by Intestinal Bacteria Lipids," 1973, 4282-4431.

Motyka, T. Yanuck, S. Expanding the neurological examination using functional neurologic assessment part i: methodological considerations, *Internat. J Neuroscience* 1998.

Motyka, T et al. Expanding the neurological examination using functional neurologic assessment part ii: neurologic basis of applied kinesiology, *International J Neuroscience* 1999.

Mountrose/ Mountrose, Jane. *Getting Through to Your Emotions with EFT,* Holistic Communications 2000.

Moyers, Bill/ Moyers, Judith. *On Our Own Terms,* PBS documentary, www.pbs.org/onourownterms

Mucha, A. V. The aura, *International J Psychosomatics* 1985, 32, 22-24.

Muflln, Glenn H. *Death and Dying: The Tibetan Tradition*, Boston, MA: Arkana 1986.

Muhl, A. *Automatic writing: An Approach to the Unconscious*, 2nd ed, New York: Helix 1962.

Muktananda, Swami. *Siddha Meditation: Commentaries on the Shiva Sutras and Other Sacred TExts*, Oakland, CA: S.Y.D.A. Foundation 1975.

Muktananda, Swami. Sensual excitement, In: White, John: *Kundalini: Evolution and Enlightenment,* New York 1990, 167-168.

Muller, H. J. *Science and Criticism,* New Haven: Yale University Press 1943.

Muller, W. et al. Effects of hypericum extract (LI-160) in biochemical models of antidepressant activity, *Pharmacopsychiatry* 1997, 30 (Supp 2), 102-107.

Mullooly, VR. Levin/ H. Feldman. *Music*

for posoperative pain and anxiety. J the New York State Nurses Assoc, 1988 19, 4-7.

Mumcuoglu KY et al. Essential oils for head lice: The in vivo pediculicidal efficacy of a natural remedy. *Israel Medical Association J* 2002, 4(10), 790-3.

Munro, S/ B, Mount. Music therapy in palliative care, *Canadian Medical Association J* 1978 119 1029-1034.

Murphet, H. *Sai Baba, Man of Miracles,* India: Macmillan 1972.

Murphet, H. *Sai Baba, Avatar,* India: Macmillan 1978.

Murphy, AI et al. Hypnotic susceptibility and its relationship to outcome in the behavioral treatment of asthma: some preliminary data, *Psychological Reports* 1989, 65(2), 691-698.

Murphy, Lois Barclay. *The Home Hospital: How a Family Can Cope with Catastrophic Illness,* New York: Basic 1982.

Murphy, Michael. Scientific studies of contemplative experience, In: *The Future of the Body*, Los Angeles: Tarcher 1992a, 527-529.

Murphy, Michael. Appendix C, Scientific meditation studies, In: *The Future of the Body*, Los Angeles: Tarcher 1992b, 603 611.

Murphy, Michael. Mesmerism and Hypnosis, In: *The Future of the Body*, Los Angeles: Tarcher 1992c, 291-349.

Murphy, Michael / Donovan, Steven. *Physical and Psychological Effects of Meditation*, New York: Tarcher/ Putnam 1995.

Murphy, Michael/ Donovan, Steven. *The Physical and Psychological Effects of Meditation: A Review of Contemporary Meditation Research With a Comprehensive Bibliography,* 1931-1996. San Rafael.CA: Esalen Institute of Exceptional Functioning 1997.

Murphy, Michael/ White, Rhea A. *The Psychic Side of Sports,* Reading, MA: Addison-Wesley 1978.

Murray, Alison et al. Doctor discontent, *J General Internal Medicine* 2001, 16, 452-459

Murray, JCC. Source of quote lost.

Murray, Michael. *Encyclopedia of Nutrition-al Supplements*, Rocklin, CA: Prima 1996.

Murray, Michael/ Pizzorno, Joseph. *Textbook of Natural Medicine, Vols. 1-2*, Seattle: John Bastyr College 1989.

Murray, Michael/ Pizzorno, Joseph. *Encyclopedia of Natural Medicine*, Rocklin, CA: Prima 1991.

Murstein, BI/ Hadjolian, SF. Fingertip aura and interpersonal attraction, *J Personality Assessment* 1977, 41, 255-265.

Müschenich, S/ Gebauer, R.: "Die (Psycho-) Physiologischen Wirkungen des Reich'schen Orgonakkumulators auf den Menschlichen Organismus [The (Psycho) Physiological Effects of the Reich Orgone Accumulator]", University of Marburg (W. Germany), Department of Psychology, Dissertation 1986.

(Short English abstracts in DeMeo 1989; Gebauer/ Müschenich)

Myerhoff, B. Shamanic equilibrium: balance and mediation in known and unknown worlds, In: W. Hand.

Myss, Caroline. *Anatomy of the Spirit: The Seven Stages of Power and Healing*, New York: Harmony 1996.

N

Naegeli-Osjord, Hans. Firedancing and firewalking, *J Paraphysics* 1970, 4(l), 7-12.

Naeser, M. *Outline Guide to Chinese Herbal Medicines in Pill Form*, Boston Chinese Medical 1990.

Naeser MA. et al. Real versus sham acupuncture in the treatment of paralysis in acute stroke patients: a CT scan lesion site study, *J Neurological Rehabilitation* 1992, 6:163-173.

Nagendra, HR/ Nagarthna, R. Yoga for bronchial asthma: a controlled study, *British Medical J* 1985, 291, 1077-1079.

Naitob, P. Chronobiologica approach for optimizing human performance, in: Brown, FM/ Graeber, RC (eds). Hillsdale, NJ: Lawrence Erlbaum Associates 1982, 41-103.

Nakachi, K. et al. Influence of drinking green tea on breast cancer malignancy among Japanese patients, *Japan J Cancer Research* 1998, 89, 254-261.

Namikoshi, Toru. *The Complete Book of Shiatsu Therapy*, New York/ Tokyo: Japan 1981.

Nangia M, Syed, W. Doraiswamy PM. Efficacy and safety of St. John's wort for the treatment of major depression, *Public Health Nutr.* 2001; 3(4A), 487-494.

Nansel, DD. Interexaminer concordance in detecting joint-play assymmetries in the cervical spine of otherwise asymptomatic patients, *J Manipulative Physiology and Therapeutics* 1989 12, 248-233.

Nansel, D/ Slazak, M. Somatic dysfunction and the phenomenpon of visceral disease simulation: a probable explanation for the apparent effectiveness of somatic therapy in patients presumed to be suffering from true visceral disease, *J Manipulative and Physiological Therapeutics* 1995 18(6), 379-397.

Nantikoshi, Toru. *The Complete Book of Shiatsu Therapy,* Tokyo: Japan Publications 1981.

Naranjo, Claudio/ Ornstein, Robert E. *On the Psychology of Meditation,* New York: Penguin 1977.

Naranjo, T/ Swentzell, R. Healing spaces in the Tewa Pueblo world, *American Indian Culture and Research J* 1989 13, 257-265.

Narayani, Mataji/ Ananda, Swami. *The Complete Book of Vibrionic Preparations*, Gujarat, India: Soham Publications 1987 (2 Shriniketan Society, Jetalpur Road, Vadodara 390 005)

Narula, M. Effect of the six-week awareness through movement lessons, *The Feldenkrais Method on selected functional movement parameters in individuals with rheumatoid arthritis,Unpublished Master's thesis,* Rochester, MI: Oakland University 1993.

Nash, June. The logic of behavior Curing in a Mayan Indian town, *Human Organization* 1967, 26(3), 132-140.

Nash, Wanda. *People Need Stillness*, London: Darton, Londman & Todd 1992.

Nathaniels, Peter. *Life Before Birth & A Time To Be Born,* Ithaca, New York: Promethean 1992.

National Cancer Institute (NCI): Oncology Overview. *Selected Abstracts on the Role of Psychological Factors in the Etiology of Cancer,* Bethesda, MD: US Department of Commerce, National Technical Information Service (NTISUB/ D/ 229-004) 1978 (September).

National Institutes of Health Consensus Panel. *Acupuncture,* Bethesda, MD: National Institutes of Health 1997.

National Institutes of Health. international bibliographic information on dietary supplements, including herbal products, www.nal.usda.gov/ fnic/ IBIDS

Neal, James H. *Jungle Magic: My Life Among the Witch Doctors of West Africa,* New York: Paperback 1969.

Neal, Patsy, *Sport and Identity,* Philadelphia, PA: Dorrance 1972.

Nehmer, W. *Have a Heart,* Cudahy, WI: Reminder Enterprise Printing (Author at 5362 Cedardale Dr. West Bend, WI 53095) 1988.

Nelson, Dawn. *From the Heart to Through the Hands: The Power of touch in Caregiving*, Forres, Scotland: Findhorn 2001.

Nelson, J. *Healing the Split: Integrating Spirit into Our Understanding of the Mentally Ill*, Albany, NY: SUNY 1992 (rev. ed).

Nelson, John E. *Healing the Split; Integrating Spirit Into Our Understanding of the Mentally Ill*, State University of New York Press 1994.

Nelson, Roger D/ Dunne, Brenda J. Attempted correlation of engineering anomalies with global geomagnetic activity, *Proceedings of Presented Papers. 29th Annual convention of the Parapsychological Association 1986, 507-518.* (From Brand/ Dennis)

Nerem, Robert M./ Levesque, Murina J./ Cornhill, J. Fredrick: Social environment as a factor in diet-induced atherosclerosis, *Science* 1980, 208, 1475-1476.

Nether, Andrew. *The Psychology of Transcendence,* Englewood Cliffs, NJ:

622 References

Spectrum/ Prentice-Hall 1980.

Netherton, M. and Shiffrin, N. *Past Lives Therapy*, New York: Ace 1978.

New England J Medicine 2000, 342(15).

Newall, CA et al. *Herbal Medicines: A Guide for Health-Care Professionals*, London: The Pharmaceutical Press 1996.

Newburg, Andrew/ D'Aquili, Eugene/ Rause, Vince. *Why God Won't Go Away: Brain Science and the Biology of Belief*, new York: Ballantine/ Random House 2001.

Newberg, Andrew et al. *Why God Won't go Away: Brain Science and the biology of Belief*, New York: Ballantine/Random House 2001

Newhan, Gayle. Therapeutic Touch for symptom control in people with AIDS, *Holistic Nursing Practice* 1989 (Aug), 45-51.

Newman, M. *Health as Expanding Consciousness*, St. Louis: C. V. Mosby 1994.

Newton, Bernauer W. The use of hypnosis in the treatment of cancer patients, *American J Clinical Hypnosis* 1982, 25(2-3), 104-113.

Nias, David KB. Therapeutic effects of low-level direct electric currents, *Psychological Bulletin* 1976, *83(5),* 766-773.

Nicholson, RA/ Berman, JS. Is follow-up necessary in evaluating psychotherapy? *Psychological Bulletin* 1983, 93, 26-278.

Nightingale, Florence. *Notes on Hospitals* 1863.

Nilsson, Lennart. *A Child is Born,* New York: Delacorte Press. 1990.

Nims, Larry Phillip. Be Set Free Fast: Behavioral and Emotional Symptom Elimin-ation Training For Resolving Excess Emotion--Fear, Anger, Sadness & Trauma, (Self-published) 1431 E. Chapman Avenue, Orange, CA 92866,: http:/ / members.aol.com/ eliums/ bsff.html 1999.

Nine Gates Mystery School

Niu, Xin/ Liu, Guolong/ Yu, Zhiming. Beijing College of Traditional Chinese Medicine. Measurement and analysis of the infrasonic waves from emitted qi (*1st World Conference for Academic Exchange of Medical Qigong, Beijing 1988,* from Qigong Database of Sancier).

Noonan, W. healing tales, *Creative Spirituality* 1992, 8, 28-30.

NorAm, Robert M et al. Social environment as a factor in diet-induced arteriosclerosis, *Science* 1980, 208, 1475-1476.

Nordenström, Björn. *Biologically Closed Electric Circuits: Clinical, Experimental, and Theoretical Evidence for an Additional Circulatory System*, self published. Nordic Medical Publications, Grev. Turegatan 2, S-11435 Stockholm, Sweden (Reviewed in Taubes).

Nordenström, Bjorn. Biologically Closed Electric Circuits: Clinical, Experimental, and Theoretical Evidence for an Additional Circulatory System, self published. (Rev. in Taubes.)

Nordlandf Rod. The firewalkers of Fiji: Faith and a nip of 'kava', *Philadelphia Inquirer* ,16 April 1982, p2.

Norman, Laura/ Cosan, T. *Feet First: A Guide to Reflexology*, New York: Fireside/ Simon & Schuster 1988

Norred, Carol. Complementary and Alternative medicine use by surgical patients, *AORN J* 2002, 76(6), 1013-1021.

North, M. *Personality Assessment Through Movement,* Boston, MA: Plays 1972.

Northrup, Christine. *Women's Bodies, Women's Wisdom: Creating Physical and Emotional Health and Healing*, New York: Bantam 1998.

Norwood, Robin. *Why Me? Why This? Why Now?,* London: Century 1994.

Novey, Donald W. *Clinician's Complete Reference to Complementary and Alternative Medicine*, St Louis: Mosby, 2000.

Nuland, SB. Medical fads: bran, midwives and leeches, *New York Times.* June 25, 1995, 15 (reviewing *Assessing the Efficacy and Safety of Medical Technologies*, Washington, DC: Office of Technology Assessment, Congress of the United States; 1978:7. Publication NTIS/ PB-286929).

Nuland SB. Whoops!, *The New York Review of Books*. July 18, 2002, 10-13

Null, Gary. *The Clinicians Handbook of Natural Healing: The First Comprehensive Guide to Scientific Peer Review Studies of Natural Supplements and Their Proven Treatment Values, New York: Kensington 1997.

Null, Gary. The Complete Encyclopedia of Natural Healing: A Comprehensive A-Z Listing of Common and Chronic Illnesses and Their Proven Natural Treatments, New York: Kensington 1998a.

Null, Gary. Healing With Magnets, New York: Carroll & Graf 1998b.

O

Oakley, David (ed). Brain and Mind, New York: Methuen 1985.

O'Connor, John/ Bensky, Dan. Acupuncture, Chicago Eastland 1981.

O'Connor, ME/ Lovely, RH (eds). Electromagnetic Fields and Neuro-behavioral Function, New York: Allan R. Liss 1988.

O'Donohue, John. Anam Cara: A Book of Celtic Wisdom, New York: Cliff Street/ HarperCollins 1998.

Offredy, M. The application of decision-making concepts by nurse practitioners in general practice. Journal of Advanced Nursing 1998, 28, 988-1000

Ogden, Pat. Hakomi integrative somatics: hands-on psychotherapy, in: Caldwell, Christine (ed). Getting in Touch: The Guide to New Body-Centered Therapies, Wheaton, IL: Quest, 153-178.

O'Hanlon, B. The third wave, Family Therapy networker 1994, 18, 19-29.

O'Leary, A. Stress, emotion, and human immune function, Psychological Bulletin 1990, 108, 363-382.

Older, Jules. Touching is Healing, New York: Stein and Day 1982.

Older, Jules. Teaching touch at medical school, J the American Medical Association 1984, 252, 931-933.

Oldfield, Harry/ Coghill, Roger. The Dark Side of the Brain: Major Discoveries in the Use of Kirlian Photography and Electrocrystal Therapy, Longmead, England: Element 1988.

Oleson, T. Flocco, W. Randomized controlled study of premenstrual symptoms treated with ear, hand, and foot reflexol-ogy, Obstetrics and Gynecology 1993, 82(6), 906-911.

Oliven, JF. Moonlight and nervous disorders: a historical study, American J Psychiatry 1943, 99, 579-584.

Olness, K. et al. Self-regulation of salivary imrnunoglobulin A by children, Pediatrics 1989, 83, 66-71.

Olsen, Kristin Gottschalk. The Encyclopedia of Alternative Health Care, New York: Pocket/ Simon & Schuster 1989 (Excellent in the range it covers, esp. with succinct modality summaries and resources. Ignore the cautions suggested against the use of TT in cancer.).

Olson, Melodie/ Sneed, Nancee et al. Therapeutic Touch and post-Hurricane Hugo stress, J Holistic Nursing 1992 10(2) 120-136.

Olszewer, E et al. A pilot double-blind study of sodium-magnesium EDTA in peripheral vascular disease, J Natural Medicine Association 1989, 82(3), 173-177.

O'Mathúna, Dónal. Where to with herbals?, Alternative Therapies 2000, 6(3), 34-35.

Omura, Yoshiaki. International Standards for Kirlian photography research, IKRA Newsletter 1976, 4.

Omura, Yoshiaki. Kirlian photography (high voltage electro-photography) and acupunct-ure: Their application (including single cell micro-electro-photography) to basic and clinical research and diagnosis, Acupuncture and Electro-Therapeutic Research, International J 1978, 3, 273-282.

Omura, Y. Acupuncture Medicine: its Hist-orical and Clincal Background, Tokyo: Japan 1982.

O'Neill, Veronica A. Challenger or charlatan? An overview of homoeopathy, Complementary Medical Research 1988, 3(1), 55-77.

O'Regan, Brendan. Healing, remission and miracle cures, Institute of Noetic Sciences Report 1987b (May), Reprint in: Noetic Sciences Collection 1980-1990: Ten Years of Consciousness Research, Sausalito, CA: Institute of Noetic Sciences 1991.

O'Regan, Brendan/ Hirshberg, Caryl. *Spontaneous Remission: An Annotated Bibliography*, Sausalito, CA: Institute of Noetic Sciences 1993.

Orloff, Judith. *Second Sight: The Personal Story of a Psychiatrist Clairvoyant*, New York: Warner 1996.

Orme-Johnson, DW. Medical care utilization and the transcendental meditation program, *Psychosomatic Medicine* 1987, 49:493-507.

Orme-Johnson, T/ Farrow, J (eds). *Scientific Research in Transcendental Meditation Programme*, Geneva, Switzerland: Maha-rishi European Research University Press 1976. See annotated bibliography also at http://www.WholisticHealingResearch.com/References/Meditation.htm

Orme-Johnson, D/ Dillbeck, MC/ Wallace, RK/ Landrith, GS. Intersubject EEG coherence: Is consciousness a field? *International Journal of Neuroscience* 1982, 16, 203-209.

Orme-Johnson, DW/ Herron, RE. An innovative approache to reducing medical care utilization and expenditures, *American J Managed Care* 1997, 3(1), 135-144.

Ornish, Dean. *Reversing Heart Disease,* New York: Ballantine 1990a.

Ornish, Dean. Can lifestyle changes reverse coronary artery disease?, *Lancet* 1990b, 336, 129.

Ornish, D. *Dr. Dean Ornish's Program for Reversing Heart Disease*, New York: Ivy/Ballantine 1996.

Ornish, Dean. *Love and Survival: The Scientific Basis for the Healing Power of Intimacy*, New York: HarperCollins 1998.

Ornish, D/ Scherwitz, LW/ Billings, JH et al. Intensive lifestyle changes for reversal of coronary heart disease, *J the American Medical Association* 1998, 280 2001-2007.

Ornish, D/ Scherwitz, LW/ Doody, RD et al. Effects of stress management training and dietary changes in treating ischemic heart disease, *J the American Medical Association* 1983, 249, 54-59.

Ornstein, Robert E. *The Psychology of Consciousness,* San Francisco: W.H. Freeman 1975.

Ornstein, Robert/ Sobel, David. *The Healing Brain*, New York/ London: Touchstone/ Simon & Schuster 1987.

Ornstein, Robert/ Thompson, Richard E. *The Amazing Brain*, Boston: Houghton Mifflin 1984.

Orr, Leonard/ Ray, Sondra. *Rebirthing in the New Age*, Millbrae, CA: Celestial Arts 1977.

Ory, MG/ Goldberg, EL. Pet possession and life satisfaction in elderly women, in: Katcher, AH/ Beck, AM (eds). *New Perspectives on Our Lives with Companion Animals*, Philadelphia, PA: University of Pennsylvania 1983, 303-317.

Osbom, RD. The moon and the menial hospital, *J Psychiatric Mining* 1968, 6, 88-93.

Oschman, JL. A biophysical basis for acupuncture, *Proceedings of the First Symposium of the Society for Acupuncture Research, Bockville, MD*, January 1993.

Oschman, J. Energy review, Part 3A, *J Bodywork and Movement Therapy* 1997, 1(3).

Oschman, James L. *Energy Medicine the Scientific Basis,* Harcourt Publishers Limited 2000.

Oschman, James L/ Oschman, Nora H. *Readings on the Scientific Basis of Bodywork, Energetic, and Movement Therapies*, Dover, NH: N.O.R.A. 1997 (PO Box 5101, Dover, NH 03821).

Oschman, James L/ Oschman, Nora H. Researching mechanisms of energetic therapies, *Healing Touch Newsletter* 1998, 8(3), 14.

Oschman, James L/ Pert, Candace. *Energy Medicine: The Scientific Basis*, London: Churchill Livingstone 2000

Osis, Karlis. Some explorations with dowsing techniques, *J the American Society for Psychical Research.* 1960, 54, 141-1 52.

Osis, Karlis/ Bokert, Edwin. ESP and changed states of consciousness induced by meditation, *J the American Society for Psychical Research* 1971, 65, 17-65.

Osis, Karlis/ Haraldsson, Erlendur. *At the Hour of Death,* New York: Discus/ Avon 1977.

Osmond, H/ Hoffer, A. assive niacin treatment in schizophrenia: review of a nine-year study, *Lancet* 1962, 1, 316-320.

Osna Heller, Peggy. 29-page *Annotated Bibliography For Poetry Therapy Students and Practitioners,* 7715 White Rim Terrace, Potomac, MD 20854, (301) 983-3392.

Osowiec, Darlene A. Ultradian rhythms in self-actualization, anxiety, and stress-related somatic symptoms, *Dissertation Abstracts International* 1992, 53, 04B, University Microfilms 92-24529.

Osowiec, Darlene A. Yogic breathwork and ultradian hypnosis, in: Leskowitz 2000, 71-83.

Ossenkopp, Klaus-Peter/ Ossenkopp, Margitta. Self-inflicted injuries and the lunar cycle: A preliminary report, *J Interdisciplinary Cycle Research* 1973, 4, 337-348.

Oster, Gerald. Phosphenes, *Scientific American* 1962, 222, 82-87.

Oster, G. Auditory beats in the brain, *Scientific American* 1973, 229(4), 94-102.

Ostrander, Sheila/ Schroeder, Lynn. *Psychic Discoveries Behind the Iron curtain,* New York: Bantam 1970.

Ostrander, Sheila/ Schroeder, Lynn. *Handbook of Psychic Discoveries,* New York: Berkeley Publishing Corporation 1974.

Ostriker, A. *Stealing the Language: The Emergence of women's Poetry in America,* boston: Beacon 1986.

Ostrom, J. *You and Your Aura,* Wellingborougb, England: Aquarian 1987.

Osumi, Ikuko/ Ritchie, Malcolm. *The Shamanic Healer The Healing World of Ikuko Osumi and the Traditional Art of Seiki-Jutsu,* London: Century 1987.

Otis, LS, Adverse effects of transcendental meditation, in: Shapiro, D/ Walsh, R (eds), *Meditation: Contemporary and Classical Perspectives,* New York: Aldine 1984.

Ott, JN. *Health and Light,* New York: Pocket 1976.

Ott, JN. Color and light: their effects on plants, animals, and people, *J Biosocial Research* 1985, 7, part 1.

Ottenbacher, K/ Difabio, RP. Eficacy of spinal manipulation-mobilization therapy: a meta-analysis, *Spine* 1985 10(4), 833-837.

Otto, Herbert/ Knight, James W. *Dimensions of Holistic Healing,* Chicago, IL: Nelson-Hall 1979.

Oubre, Alondra. Shamanic trance and the placebo effect: The case for a study in psychobiological anthropology, *Psi Research* 1985, 5(1,2), 116-144.

Ourseley, SCJ. *The Science of the Aura* (7th ed.), London: L. N. Fowler 1968.

Overzier, C (ed). *Intersexuality,* London 1963, p.182.

Overzier, C. The classification of intersexuality, *Triangle* 1967, 8(2), 32-41.

Owen, Iris M/ Sparrow, Margaret. *Conjuring up Philip: An Adventure in Psychokinesis,* New York: Harper & Row 1976.

Owen, Olwen Glynn. (2001) Pet Therapy: Paws for Thought, *Nursing Times.* Vol. 97, No. 9, March.

Oye, Robert K/ Shapiro, Martin E. Reporting results from chemotherapy trials, *J the American Medical Association* 1984. 252, 2722-2725.

Oyle, I. *The Healing Mind: You Can Cure Yourself Without Drugs,* Milibrae, CA: Celestial Arts 1975.

P

Pagano, John OA. *Healing Psyoriasis: The Natural Alternative,* Englewood Cliffs, NJ: Pagano Organization 1991.

Page, Christine. *Frontiers of Health,* Saffron Walden, UK: CW Daniels 1992.

Page, Christine. *Mind Body Spirit Workbook: A Handbook of Health,* London: CW Daniels 1999.

Palmer, DD. *The Science, Art, and Philosophy of Chiropractic,* Portland, OR: Portland Printing House 1910. (From Hastings et al; Lipton)

Palmer, Magda. *The Healing Power of Crystals: Precious Stones and their Planetary Interactions,* London: Arrow 1988.

Palos, Steplian. *The Chinese Art of Healing,* New York: Bantam 1972.

Pancoast, S. *Blue and Red Lights*, Philadelphia: J.M. Stoddart and Co. 1877.

Panizzi, L. et al. Composition and antimicrobial properties of essential oils of four Mediterranean Lamiaceae, *J Ethnopharmacology* 1993, 39(3) 167-170.

Panjwani, HK et al. Clinical evaluation of Padma 28 in treatment of senility and other geriatric circulatory disorders: a pilot study, *Alternative Medicine* 1987, 2(1), 11-17.

Parfitt, JM. Humorous preoperative teaching: Effect on recall of postoperative exercise routines, *AORN J* 1990, 52(1).

Park, J et al. Efficacy of acupuncture as a treatment for tinnitus: a systematic review, Arch Otolaryngol Head Neck Surg 2000; 126: 489-492.

Park, Robert L. The great power line scare, *Alternative Therapies in Health and Medicine* 1996, 2(2), 46-51. (See Lieboff for counterpoint view)

Parker, A/ Cutler-Stuart, J. *Switch on your Brain*, Petersham, NSW, Asutralia: Hale & Ironmonger 1986.

Parker, GB et al. A controlled trial of cervical manipulation for migraine, *Australia and New Zealand J Medicine* 1978, 8, 589-593.

Parkins, C. Humor, health, and higher education: laughing matters, *J Nursing Education* 1989, 28, 229-230.

Parnell, Laurel. *Transforming Truama*, New York: Norton 1997.

Parsons, Denys. The black boxes of Mr. George de la Warr, *J the Society far Psychical Research* 1961, 41(707), t2-31.

Pascual-Leone, A. Rubio, B. Pallardo, Catalá D. Rapid-rate transcranial magnetic stimulation of the left dorsolateral prefrontal cortex in drug-resistant depression, *Lancet* 1996; 348: 233-237.

Pascual-Leone, A. et al. Rapid-rate transcranial magnetic stimulation of left dorsolateral prefrontal cortex in drug-resistant depression, *Lancet* 1996, 347, 233-237.

Patel, CH. Yoga and biofeedback in the management of hypertension, *Lancet* 1973, 2(837), 105~1055

Patel, C. Yoga-based therapy, in: Lehrer, P/ Woolfolk, R. (eds). *Principles and Practice of Stress Management, 2nd ed,* New York: Guilford 1993, 89-113.

Patel, MS. Evaluation of holistic medicine, *Social Science and Medicine* 1987a, 24(2) 169-175.

Patel, MS. Problems in the evaluation of alternative medicine, *Social Science and Medicine* 1987b, 25(6), 669-678.

Patel, M. et al. A meta-analysis of acupuncture for chronic pain, *International J Epidemiology* 1989 18(4), 900-906.

Patrizi, A et al. Sensitization to thimerosal in atopic children, Contact Dermatitis, Feb., 1999; 40(2):94-97.

Patronek, GJ/ Glickman, LT. Pet ownership protects against the risks and consequences of coronary heart disease, *Medical Hypotheses* 1993, 40, 245-249.

Patten, Leslie/ Patten, Terry. Biocircuits: *Amazing New Tools for Energy Health,* Tiburon, CA: H.J. Kramer 1988.

Patterson, DR et al. Hypnosis in the treatment of patients with severe burns, *American J Clinical Hypnosis* 1996, 38(3) 200-212.

Pavek, RR. *Handbook of SHEN,* Sausalito, CA: SHEN Therapy Institute 1987,

Pavek, RR. Effects of SHEN Qigong on Psychosornatic and Other Physio-Emotional Disorders, *Proceedings of the First World Conference for Academic Exchange of Medical Qigong, Beijing 1988.*

Pavek, RR/ T, Daily. SHEN physio-emotional release therapy: disruption of the autocontractile, pain response, *Occupational Therapy Practice* 1990 1(3),53-61.

Pavlov, Ivan. *Conditioned Reflexes and Psychiatry,* New York: International Publishers 1941.

PDR for Herbal Medicines, Montvale, NJ: Medical Economics Company 1999.

PDR-People's Desk Reference for Essential Oils, Orem, UT: Essential Science Publishing.

Pearce, Joseph Chilton. *Magical Child: Rediscovering Natures Plan for Our Children*, New York: Bantam 1980.

Pearce, Joseph Chilton. *The Bond of Power: Meditation and Wholeness,* London: Routledge & Kegan Paul 1982.

Pearce, Joseph Chilton. *The Magical Child Matures,* New York: Dutton 1985.

Pearce, Joseph Chilton. *The Biology of Trancendence,* Rochester Vermont: Park Street Press 2002.

Pearlin, LI. The sociological study of stress, *J Health and Social Behavior* 1989, 12, 23-45.

Pearsall, Paul. *Super Immunity: Master Your Emotions and Improve Your Health,* London: Ebury 1987.

Pearsall, Paul. *The Heart's Code: Tapping the Wisdom and Power of Our Heart Energy: The New Findings About Cellular Memories and Their Role in the Mind/ Body/ Spirit,* Connection, New York: Broadway 1999.

Pearson, C. *Awakening the Heroes Within: Twelve Archetypes to Help Us Find Ourselves and Transform Our World,* San Francisco: Harper 1991.

Pearson, D. *The Gaia Natural House Book,* London: Gaia 1989.

Pearson, RE. Response to suggestions given under general anesthesia, *American J Clinical Hypnosis* 1961, 4, 106-114.

Peat, F. *David: Synchronicity: The Bridge Between Matter and Mind,* New York/ London: Bantam 1987.

Peavey, B/ Lawlis, GF/ Goven, P. Biofeedback assisted relaxation: effects on phagocytic capacity, *Biofeedback and Self Regulation* 1985. 10, 33 47.

Peay, P. The singing sword: images guide adolescents' journeys, *Common Boundary* 1990, 8, 7-9.

Pecock, Stuart J. *Clinical Trials. A Practical Approach,* Chichester: Josh Wiley & Sons 1983.

Pehek, John O et al. Image modulation in corona discharge photography, *Science* 1976, 194(4262), 263-270.

Peirce, Andrea/ Gans, John A. *American Phamaceutical Association Practical Guide to Natural Medicines,* New York: William Morrow 1998.

Pellegrini, RJ et al. Leg strength as a func-tion of exposure to visual stimuli of different hues, *Bulletin of The Psychonomic Society* 1980, 16(2),.111-112.

Pelletier, Kenneth R. *Mind as Healer Mind as Slayer,* New York: Delta/ Dell 1977.

Pelletier, Kenneth R. *Holistic Medicine: From Stress to Optimum Health*, New York: Delacorte 1979.

Pelletier, Kenneth. A review and analysis of the health and cost-effective outcome studies of comprehensive health promotion and disease prevention programs, *American J Health Promotion* 1991, 5(4), 311-315.

Pelletier, Kenneth. A review and analysis of the health and cost-effective outcome studies of comprehensive health promotion and disease prevention programs at the worksite: 1991-1993 update, *American J Health Promotion* 1993, 8(1), 50-62.

Pelletier, Kenneth R. *The Best Alternative Medicine*, New York: Simon & Schuster 2000.

Pelletier, Kenneth R/ Astin, John A. Integration and reimbursement of complementary and alternative medicine by managed care and insurance providers: 2000 update and cohort analysis, *Alternative Therapies* 2002, 8(1), 38-48.

Pelletier, Kenneth R et al. Current trends in the integration and reimbursement of complementary and alternative medicine by managed care, insurance carriers, and hospital providers, *American J Health Promotion* 1999, 14(2), 125-133.

Pelosi, AJ/ Appleby, L. Psychological influences on cancer and ischaemic disease, *British Medical J* 1992, 303, 1295-1298.

Peltham, Elizabeth. Therapeutic Touch and massage, *Nursing Standard* 1991, 5(45), 26-28.

Penfield, Wilder. The Mystery of the Mind: A Critical Study of Consciousness and the Human Brain, Princeton, NJ: Princeton University 1975.

Penfield, W/ Roberts, L. *Speech and Brain Mechanisms,* NJ: Princeton University 1959.

Peng, Xueyan/ Liu, Guolong. Beijing

College of Traditional Chinese Medicine, Beijing, China. Effect of emitted qi and infrasonic sound on somatosensory evoked potential (SEP) and slow vertex response (SVR), *1st World Conference for Academic Exchange of Medical Qigong. Beijing 1988* (from Qigong Database of Sancier)

Pennebaker, JW. Confession, inhibition, and disease, *Advances in Experimental Social Psychology* 1989, 22, 211-244.

Pennington, George. *Little Manual for Players of the Glass Bead Game: The Way of Visual Contemplation*, Tisbury, Wiltshire, England: Element 1983.

Peper, E/ Ancoli, S. Two endpoints of an EEC continuum of meditation – alpha/theta and fast beta, In: Krieger 1979. (From Quinn summary of Randolph dissertation)

Peper, Eric/ Holt, Catherine. *Creating Wholeness: A Self-Healing Workbook Using Dynamic Relaxation, Images and Thoughts*, New YHork: Plenum 1993.

Perls, Frederick S. *Gestalt Therapy Verbatin,* New York: Bantam 1969.

Perot, C. Meldener, R. Gouble, F. Objective measurement of proprioceptive technique consequences on muscular maximal voluntary contraction during manual muscle testing, *Agressologie* 1991; 32,10:471-474.

Perrin, Swan. *Leah, A Story of Meditation and Healing,* London & Boston: Wisdom 1988.

Perrone, B et al. *Medicine Women, Curanderas, and Women Doctors*, Norman, OK: University of Oklahoma 1989.

Perry, C et al. The measurement of hypnotic ability, In: Fromm, E/ Nash, M.R. (eds). contemporary Hypnosis Research, New York: Guilford 1992, 459-490.

Perry, John Weir. *Trials of the Visionary Mind; Spiritual Emergency and the Renewal Process*, State University of New York Press 1999.

Perry, J et al. Functional evaluation of Rolfing in cerebral palsy, *Developmental Medical Child Neurology* 1981, 23, 717-729.

Perry, Stephen/ Pearl, Laurence. Power frequency magnetic fields and illness in multi-storey blocks, *Public Health* 1988 102 11-18.

Persinger, Michael A. Geophysical variables and behavior: xxx, intense paranormal experiences occur during days of quiet, global, geomagnetic activity, *Perceptrual & Motor Skills* 1985a, 61, 320-322.

Persinger, Michael A. Subjective telepathic experiences: Geomagnetic activity, and the ELF hypothesis. Part II. Stimulus features and neural detection, *Psi Research* 1985b, 4(2), 4-23.

Persinger, Michael A. Spontaneous telepathic experiences from phantasms of the living and low global geomagnetic activity, *J the American Society for Psychical Research* 1987,81(1), 23-36.

Persinger, MA/ Levesque, BF. Geophysical variables and behavior: XII. the weather matrix accommodates large portions of variance of measured daily mood, *Perceptual & Motor Skills* 1983, 57, 868-870.

Persinger, Michael A/ Krippner, Stanley. Experimental dream telepathy - clairvoyance and geomagnetic activity, *Proceedings of Presented Papers. 29th Annual Convention of the Parapsychological Association 1986, 459-468.*

Persinger, MA/ Schaut, GB. Geomagnetic factors in subjective telepathic, precognitive and postmortem experiences, *J the American Society for Psychical Research* 1988, 82, 217-235.

Pert, Candace. The wisdom of the receptors:Neuropeptides, the emotions and the bodymind, *Advances* 1986, 3(3), 8-16, edited version in: *Noetic Sciences Review*, Spring 1987.

Pert, Candace. *Molecules of Emotions*, New York: Scribner 1997.

Pert, Candace/ Dienstfrey, Harris. The neuropeptide network, *Annals of New York Academy of Science* 1988, 521.

Pert, Candace/ Dreher, Henry E/ Ruff, Michael R. The psychosomatic network: foundations of mind-body medicine, *Alternative Therapies* 1998, 4(4), 30-41 (88 refs).

Pert, Candace et al. Neuropeptides and

their receptors: a psychosomatic network, *J Immunology* 1985 135(suppl. 2).

Pesso, A. *Experience in Action: A Psychomotor Psychology,* New York: SUNY 1973.

Peters, Larry. *Ecstasy and Healing in Nepal,* Malibu, CA: Undena 1981.

Peters, L/ Price-Williams. Towards an experiential analysis of shamanism, *American Ethnologist* 1980, 7(3), 379-413.

Peterson, James. Extrasensory abilities of children: An ignored reality?, *Learning* 1975 (Dec.), 10-14.

Peterson, James W. *The Secret Life of Kids,* Wheaton, IL: Quest/ Theosophical 1987.

Peterson LM/ Brennan, TA. Medical ethics and medical injuries: taking our duties seriously, *J Clin Ethics* 1990, 1, 207-11.

Petrie, JP/ Langley, GB. Acupuncture in the treatment of chronic cervical pain:a pilot study, *Clinical and Experimental Rheumatology* 1983 1: 333-336.

Pettinggale, KW et al. Mental attitudes to cancer, An additional prognostic factor, *Lancet* 1985, 750.

Pettit, Sabina. *Energy Medicine: Pacific Flower and Sea Essences,* Victoria, BC Canada: Pacific Essences 1996 (Box 8317, V8W 3R9).

Petitti, DB. Hormone replacement therapy for prevention: more evidence, more pessimism, *JAMA.* 2002; 288(1): 99-101.

Phelan, Nancy. *A Guide to Yoga,* London: Sphere 1973.

Philipp, M et al. Hypericum extract versus imipramine or placebo in patients with moderate depression: randomized multicentre study of treatment for eight weeks, *British Medical J* 1999, 319, 1534-1539.

Phillip, T et al. Acupuncture in the treatment of bladder instability, *British J Urology* 1988, 61, 490-493.

Phillips, DP et al. Psychology and survival, *Lancet* 1993, Nov 6, 342.

Phillips, J. *Immunology Letters,* 1986, 13, 295.

Phillips, J et al. *International J Radiation Biology,* 1986, 49, 463.

Philpot, William/ Kalita, Dwight K. *Brain*

Allergies: The Psychonurtirent Connection, New Canaan, CT: Keats 1980.

Philpot, William/ Taplin, Sharon. *Biomagnetic Handbook,* Choctaw, OK: EnviroTech Products 1990.

Phoenix: New Directions in the Study of Man. J the *Association for Transpersonal Anthropology* (No date)

Physicians' Committee for Responsible Medicine. *Key Nutrition Issues for Medical Students,* Washington, DC: PCOM (202) 686-2210.

Physiological, physical (postural) and psychological, *American J Chinese Medicine* 1981, 9, 1-14.

Piaget, J. *The Essential Piaget,* Gruber, H/ Voneche, J (eds). New York: Basic 1977.

Picasso, Pablo. Attributed.

Piccardi, G. Phénomènes astrophysiques et évenements terrestres, *Presented at Conference at the Palais de la Découverte,* January 24, 1959,

Pierrakos, John C. *The Energy Field in Man and Nature,* New York: Institute for the New Age of Man 1971.

Pierrakos, John C. *The Core of Man,* New York; Institute for the New Age of Man 1974.

Pierrakos, John C. *The Core-Energetic Process in Group Therapy,* New York: Institute for the New Age of Man 1975.

Pierrakos, John C. *Human Energy Systems Theory: History and New Growth Perspectives,* New York: Institute for the New Age of Man 1976.

Pierrakos, John C. *Core Energetics: Developing the Capacity to Love and Heal,* Mendocino, CA: Life Rhythm 1987.

Pietroni, Patrick. *Holistic Living: A Guide to Self-Care,* London: J.M. Dent & Sons 1986.

Pietroni, Patrick/ Pietroni, Christopher. *Innovation in Community Care and Primary Health: The Marylebone Experiment,* London: Churchill Livingstone1996.

Pietropinto, A. Poetry therapy in groups, in: Masserman, J. (ed), *Current Psychiatric Therapies* New York: Grune & Stratton 1975, 15, 221-232.

Piontelli, Alessandra. *From Fetus to Child: An Observation and Psychoanalytic Study,* London: Routledge 1992.

Pinchuck, Tony/ Clark, Richard. Attributed.

Pirsig, Robert M. *Zen and the Art of Motorcycle Maintenance,* New York/ London: Bantam 1975.

Pitchford, Paul. *Healing with Whole Foods: Oriental Traditions and Modern Nutrition,* Berkeley, CA: North Atlantic 1993.

Pizzorno, JE. *Total Wellness,* Rocklin, CA: Prima 1996.

Pizzorno, JE/ Murray, MT. *Textbook of Natural Medicine,* New York: Churchill Livingstone 1998.

Pizzorno, JE/ Murray, MT (eds*). Textbook of Natural Medicine, 2nd ed.,* Edinburgh: Churchill Livingstone, 1999.

Pizzorno, J/ Murray, M/ Joiner-Bey, H (eds). *The Clinician's Handbook of Natural Medicine.* Churchill Livingstone, 2002.

Plack, JJ/ Schick, L. The effects of color on human behavior, *J the Association for Study of Perception* 1974,9~4-16.

Playfair, GL. *The Unknown Power,* New York: Pocket 1975.

Playfair, Guy Lyon. *If This Be Magic,* London: Jonathan Cape 1985.

Playfair, Guy Lyon. Medicine, Mind and Magic: The Power of the Mind-Body Connection in Hypnotism and Healing, Wellingborough, Nonhasa England: Aquarian/ Thorsons 1987.

Playfair, Guy Lyon. Austria's medical shocker, Fate 1988 (September), 41(9), 42-48.

Pleasse, B. Poetry therapy in a parenting group for recovering addicts, *J Poetry Therapy* 1995, 8, 135-148.

Pokorn, AD/ Jackimczyk, J. The questionable relationship between homicides and the lunar cycle, *American Jof Psychiatry* 1974 131, 827-829.

Polhemus, Ted (ed). *The Body Reader: Social Aspects of the Human Body,* New York: Pantheon 1978.

Polge, J. Critical thinking: the use of intuition in making clinical nursing judgements. *Journal of the New York State Nurses Association* 1995, 26, 4-9

Polyakov, Vadim. Personal communication Russia 1992.

Polycove, M. Nonlinearity of radiation health effects, *Environmental Health Perspectives* 1998, 106 (suppl), 363-368 (cited in Eskinazi 1999).

Pomeranz, Bruce/ Chiu, Daryl. Naloxone blockage of acupuncture analgesia: Endorphin implicated, *Life Sciences* 1976, 19, 1757-1762.

Pomeranz, B/ Stux, G. *Scientific bases of acupuncture,* Berlin: Springer 1991.

Ponder, Catherine. *The Dynamic Laws of Healing,* Marina Del Rey, CA; De Vorss 1966.

Ponson, J. Complementary therapies: making a difference in palliative care, *Complementary Therapies in Nursing and Midwifery* 1998, 4(3), 77-81.

Poock, Gary K. Kirilian photography, an engineer's view, *Techniun. Engjneering Review* (Spring) 1975,28-32 ff.

Pope, C/ Mays, N. Reaching the parts other methodologies cannot reach: an introduction to qaualitative methods in health and health services research, *British Medical J* 1995, 311, 42-45.

Pope, DH. Two reports on experiments with dowsing, *Parapsychology Bulletin* 1950,20, 1-3.

Pope, Ilse. A view of earth energies from Continental Europe, *J the British Society of Dowsers* 1987,32, 130-139.

Pope, KS/ Velasquez, M. *Ethics in Psychotherapy and Counseling: A Practical Guide,* 2nd ed. San Francisco: Jossey-Bass 1998.

Popp, FA et al. Biophoton emission: new evidence for coherence and DNA as source, *Cell Biophys.* 1984, 6, 33-52.

Popp, FA et al. Biophoton emission (multiauthor reveiw), *Experientia* 1988, 44, 543-600.

Popp, FA et al (eds). *Recent Advances in Biophoton Research and Its Applications,* Singapore/ New York: World Scientific Publishing 1992.

Popper, Karl R/ Eccles, John C. *The Self and its Brain,* New York, London: Springer 1977.

Porkert, Manfred/ Ullman, Christian. *Chinese Medicine: Its History, Philosophy and Practice,* New York: William Morris 1982.

Post, Laurens van der. *The Voice of the Thunder,* New York/ London: Penguin 1994.

Potter, Dennis. Television interview with Melvyn Bragg, March 1994.

Poulton, Kay. *Harvest of Light A Pilgrimage of Healing,* London: Regency 1968.

Pourcyrous, M et al. Interleukin-6, C-reactive protein, and abnormal cardiorespiratory responses to immunization in premature infants, Pediatrics, March, 1998; 101(3):461.

Powell, FC et al. A risk/ benefit analysis of spinal manipulation therapy for relief of lumbar or cervical pain, *Neurosurgery* 1993, 33(1), 73-78; discussion 78-79.

Powers, W. *Yuwipi: Vision and Experience in Oglala Ritual,* Lincoln: University of Nebraska 1982.

Prasad, Rama. *Nature's Finer Forces: The Science of Breath and the Philosophy of the Tattvas,* Mokelumne Hill, CA: Health Research 1969 (Orig. London: Theosophical 1889).

Pratt, George J/ Lambrou, Peter T. *Instant Emotional Healing: Acupressure for the Emotions,* New York: Broadway 2000

Preconception Care, *For Tomorrow's Children: A Manual for Future Parents,* Blooming Glen, PA: Preconception Care 1990.

Presman, AS. *Electromagnetic Fields and Life,* New York: Plenum 1970.

Preston, Thomas A. Marketing an operation: Coronary bypass surgery, *J Holistic Medicine* 1985, 7(1), 8-15.

Prevention Magazine Editors. *The Complete Book of Vitamins,* Emmaus, PA: Rodale 1984.

Price, Shirley. *Aromatherapy for Common Ailments,* New York: Simon & Schuster 1991.

Prien, EL/ Gershoff, SN. Magnesium ox-ide-pyridoxine therapy for recurrent calcium oxalate calculi, *J Urology* 1974, 112, 509-512.

Prince, Raymond. Fundamental differences of psychoanalysis and faith healing, *International J Psychiatry* 1972, 10(1), 125-128.

Progroff, I. *At a J Workshop: The Basic Text and guide for Using the Intensive J,* New York: Dialogue House 1975.

Proust, Marcel. Attributed.

Prudden, Bonnie. *Pain Erasure the Bonnie Prudden Way,* New York: M. Evans 1977.

Prudden, Bonnie. *Myotherapy: Bonnie Prudden's Complete Guide to Pain-Free Living,* New York: Ballantine 1984.

Psi Research Eds. More on 'eyeless sight' in: China, *Psi Research* 1983, 2(1), *55-56.* (Original in: *The American Dowser* November 1982)

Psycho-Oncology, J Psychological, Social and Behavioural Dimensions of Cancer, Chichester, England: Wiley 1992.

Psychotronika 1985, 82-83. (Abstract, translated from Polish by Alexander Imich, in: *Parapsychology Abstracts International* 1987, 5(2), No. 2489)

Pujalte, JM et al. Double-blind clinical evaluation of oral glucosamine sulphate in the basic treatment of osteoarthritis, *Current Medical Research Opinion* 1980, 7, 110-114.

Purdy, WR. Code blue: the blues in medicine, *J Poetry Therapy* 1994, 7, 179-187.

Pushkin, VN/ Adamenko, VG. Informational bioelectronics, *J Paraphysics* 1973, 7(1), 4.

Puthoff, H. E./ Targ, R. A, A perceptual channel for information transfer over kilometer distances: Historical perspective and recent research, *Proceedings of the IEEE* 1976, 64, 329-354

Putnam, Frank W. The scientific investigation of multiple personality disorder, In: Quen, JM (ed). *Split Minds, Spilt Brains: Historical and Current Perspectives,* New York: New York University 1986.

Q

Quander-Blaznik, J. Personality as a predictor of lung cancer: A replication, *Personality and Individual Differences* 1991, 12, 125-430.

Quiding, H et al. The visual analog scale in multiple dose evaluation of analgesics, *J Clinical Pharmacology* 1981, 21, 424-429.

Quinn, Daniel. *Ishmael: An Adventure of the Mind and Spirit*, New York/ London: Bantam/ Turner1992.

Quinn, Janet F. *An Investigation of the Effect of Therapeutic Touch Without Physical Contact on State Anxiety of Hospitalized Cardiovascular Patients,* (Doctoral dissertation) New York University 1982; also in: *Advances in Nursing Science* 1984, 6, 42-49.

Quinn, Janet F. Therapeutic Touch as energy exchange: replication and extension, *Nursing Science Quarterly* 1989, 2(2), 79-87.

Quinn, Janet F/ Strelkauskas, Anthony J. Psychoimmunologic effects of Therapeutic Touch on practitioners and recently bereaved recipients: A pilot study, *Advances in Nursing Science,* (June) 1993, 15, 13-26.

R

Droh/ Spintge ed. Angst, Schmerz, Musik in der Anasthesie (p. 16~166). Editiones Roche, Basel, Switzerland 1982.

Rabin, Bruce S. *Stress, Immune Function, and Health: The Connection*, Wiley-Liss 1999.

Radin, Dean I. Beyond belief: exploring interactions among mind, body and environment, *Subtle Energies* 1991, 2(3) 1-41.

Radin, Dean I/ Rebman, Janine, Lunar correlates of normal, abnormal and anomalous human behavior, *Subtle Energies* 1994, 5(3), 209-238.

Radin, Dean et al, Remote mental influence of human electrodermal activity, *European J. Parapsychology* 1995, 11, 19-34.

Radwanowski, Lech J. Geomagnetohydrodynamics, *Proceedings of 4th International Conference on Psychotronic Research.* 1978. 439-452.

Rae, M. Potency simulation by magnetically energised patterns (an alternate method of preparing homeopathic remedies), *British Radionic Quarterly* 1973, March.

Rafael, CA 1985, Berkeley; CA: Center for South and Southeast Asia Studies 1986.

Raffensperger, Carolyn. The precautionary principle: bearing witness to and alleviating suffering, Alternative Therapies 2002, 8(5), 111-115.

Raffensperger, Carolyn et al. Protecting Public Health and the Environment: Implementing the Precautionary Principle, Washington, DC: Island Press 1999.

Ragland, David R/ Brand, Richard J. Type A behavior and mortality from coronary heart disease, *New England J Medicine* 1988, 318(2) .

Rahn, Otto. *Invisible Radiations of Organisms,* Berlin: Verlag Gebruder Borntraeger 1936.

Rai et al. A double-blind, placebo-controlled study of Ginkgo biloba extract in elderly outpatients with mild to moderate memory impairment, *Current Medical Research Opinion* 1991, 12(6), 350-355.

Raikov, Vladimir L. Artificial reincarnation through hypnosis, *Psychic* 1971 (June), (Also described in Ostrander/ Schroeder 1970)

Raina, P et al. Influence of companion animals on the physical and psychological health of older people: an analysis of a one-year longitudinal study, *J the American Geriatric Society* 1999, 47, 323-329.

Rainer, T. *The New Diary: How to Use a J for Self-Guidance and Expanded Creativity*, Los Angeles: Tarcher 1978.

Rakel, David (ed). *Integrative Medicine.* Philadelphia: Saunders, 2002.

Rama, Swami. *Lectures on Yoga*, HOnesdale, PA: Himalayan International Institute 1979b.

Rama, Swami. *A Practical Guide to Holistic Health*, Honesdale, PA: Himalayan 1980a.

Rama, Swami. *Freedom from the Bondage of Karma*, Honesdale, PA: Himalayan 1980b.

Rama, S. *Path of Fire and Light: Advanced Practices of Yoga, Vols. 1 & 2*, Honesdale, PA: Himalayan International Institute 1986 1988.

Ramacharaka, Yogi. *Science of Breath,* Chicago, IL: Yogi 1904

Ramacharaka, Yogi. *Hatha Yoga, or the Yogi Philosophy of Physical Well-Being,* Chicago, IL; Yogi 1930.

Ramacharaka, Yogi. *The Science of Psychic Healing,* Chicago, IL: Yogi 1934.

Ramel, C/ Norden, B (eds). *Interaction Mechanisms of Low-Level Electromagnetic Fields With Living Systems*, London: Oxford University Press 1991.

Ramirez, AJ. Life events and cancer: Conceptual and methodological issues, In: Watson, M/ Greer S/ Thomas C (eds). Psychosocial oncology, Oxford: Pergamon 1988, 51-60.

Ramirez, Amanda J et al. Stress and relapse of breast cancer, *British Medical J* 1989, 298, 291-293.

Rampa, TL. *You-Forever,* Great Britain: Corgi 1965.

Rampton, Sheldon/ Stauber, John. *Mad Cow USA: Could the Nightmare Happen Here?* Monroe, ME: Common Courage 1997.

Rando, Therese A. *How To Go On Living When Someone You Love Dies,* New York: Bantam 1991.

Randolph, Theron. *Human Ecology and Susceptibility to the Chemical Environment*, Springfield, IL: C. C. Thomas 1962.

Randolph, T/ Moss, RW. *An alternative Approach to Allergies*, New York: Lippincott/ Crowell 1980.

Rao, Kanthamani/ Puri, I. Subsensory perception (SSP), extrasensory perception (ESP) and meditation, In: *Research in Parapsychology 1916*, Metuchen, NJ: Scarecrow 1977, 77-79,

Rapbaell, Katrina. *Crystal Healing,* New York: Aurora 1987.

Rapp, Doris. *Is this Your Child?: Discovering and Treating Unrecognized Allergies*, New York: William Morrow 1991.

Rasic, J. *Bifidobacteria and Their Role,* Boston: Birkhauser Verlag, 1983.

Raskind, MA/ Peskind, ER/ Wessel, T/ Yuan, W/ and the Galantamine USA-1 Study Group, Galantamine in Alzheimer's disease. a 6-month, randomized, placebo-controlled trial with a 6-month extension, *Neurology* 2000;54:2261-8. (Abstract at: http://www.galantamine.cc/research/galant amine-research-7.htm)

Rastogi, D/ Sharma, V. Study of homeopathic drugs in encephalitis epidemic (1991) in Uttar Pradesh (India), *Council for Research on Homeopathy Bulletin* 1992, 14, 1-11.

Raswmsley, Marilyn M. Health: A Rogerian perspective, *J Holistic Nursing* 1985, 2, 25-29.

Ratcliffe, MA et al. Eysenck Personality Inventory L-scores in patients with Hodgkin's disease and non-Hodgkins's lymphoma, *Psychooncology* 1995, 4, 39-45.

Ravitz, Leonard J. History, measurement and applicability of periodic changes in the electromagnetic field in health and disease, *Annual of the New York Academy of Science,* 1962-98, 1144-1201.

Ravitz, Leonard J. Electromagnetic field monitoring of changing state functions, *J the American Society for Psychosomatic Dentistry and Medicine 1970,* 17(4), 119-129.

Rawliuns, D Starbaby. *Fate,* 1981, October.

Rea, WJ. *Chemical Sensitivity*, Boca Raton, FL: Lewis 1991.

Reason, Peter. *Human Inquiry in Action,* London: Sage 1988.

Rector-Page, Linda. *How to Be Your Own Herbal Pharmacist*, Sonora, CA: Crystal Star Herbs 1997.

Reddy, G. Antitumour activity of yogurt components, *J Food Protection* 1983, 46, 8-11.

Redmond, Layne. *When the Drummers Were Women*, New York: Three Rivers 1997.

Redner, Robin et al. Effects of a bioenergy

healing technique on chronic pain, *Subtle Energies* 1991, 2(3), 43-68.

Redwood, Daniel. *A Time to Heal*, Virginia Beach: ARE 1993.

Redwood, Daniel. Methodological changes in the evaluation of complementary and alternative medicine: issues raised by Sherman et al. and Hawk et al, *J Altern Complement Med.* 2002, (1), 5-6.

Redwood, Daniel (ed). *Contemporary Chiropractic*, New York: Churchill Livingstone 1997.

Reele, BL. Effect of counseling on quality of life for individuals with cancer and their families, *Cancer Nursing* 1994, 17, 101-112.

Regelson, William/ Colman, Carol. *The Superhormone Promise: Nature's Antidote to Aging*, New York: Simon & Schuster 1996.

Regush, Nicholas. *The Human Aura,* New York: Berkeley Publishing 1974.

Regush, Nicholas M/ Merta, Jan. *Exploring the Human Aura: A New Way of Viewing- and Investigating-Psychic Phenomena*, Englewood Cliffs, NJ: Prentice-Hall 1975.

Reich, Wilhelm. *Selected Writings,* New York: Farrar, Straus and Cudahy 1960.

Reich, W. *The Function of the Orgasm*, New York: Farrar, Straus, Giroux 1986.

Reichard, GA. *Navaho Medicine Man,* New York: J.J. Augustine 1939.

Reichard, GA. *Navaho Religion: A Study of Symbolism,* Princeton, NJ: Princeton University 1950.

Reichert, R. Treatment of anxiety with Kava-kava, *Quarterly Review of Natural Medicine* 1996 (winter), 249-250.

Reichmanis, Maria/ Marino, Andrew A/ Becker, Robert O. Electrical correlates of acupuncture points, *IEEE Transactions Biomedical Engineering* 1975, 22, 533-535.

Reichmanis, M et al. Relationship between suicide and electromagnetic field of overhead power lines, *Physiology, Chemistry and Physics* 1979, 11, 395-403.

Reid, Daniel P. *Chinese Herbal Medicine*, Boston, MA: Shambhala 1987.

Reid, Gary W. *The Complete Book of Rolfing,* New York: Drake 1978.

Reilly, DT et al. Is homeopathy a placebo response? Controlled trial of homoeopathic potency, with pollen in hayfever as model, *Lancet* 1986, 2, 881-886.

Reilly D et al. Is evidence for homoeopathy reproducible? *Lancet* 1994; 344: 1601-1606 http:/ / bmj.com/ cgi/ content/ abstract/ 324/ 7336/ 520Reilly, Harold J/ Brod, Ruth Hagy. *The Edgar Cayce Handbook for Health Through Drugless Therapy,* New York: Jove 1979.

Rein, Glen. *Quantum Biology: Healing with Subtle Energy*, Quantum Biology Research Labs, PO Box 60653, Palo Alto, CA 94306 1992

Remedy Guides. *Interactive Materia Medica*, CD ROM summaries of aromatherapy, Bach flowers, homeopathy, herbal remedies, 2345 W. 103 St. Ste. J, Chicago, IL 60643 www.remedyguides.com

Remen, Rachel Naomi. *Kitchen Table Wisdom: Stories that Heal*, New York: Riverhead 1997.

Remoff, Heather Trexler. *February Light: A Love Letter to the Seasons During A Year of Cancer and Recovery,*New York: St. Martin's 1997.

Renaud, CI/ Pichette, D. Chiropractice management of bronchial asthma: a literature review*, American Chiropractic Association J* 1990, 27, 25-26.

Requena, Yves. *Terrains and Pathology in Acupuncture,* Brookline, MA: Redwing 1986a.

Requena, Yves. Acupuncture's challenge to western medicine, *Advances* 1986b, 3(2), *46-55.*

Resch, G/ Gutmann, V. *Scientific Foundations of Homeopathy,* Berlin: Barthel & Barthel 1987.

Retallack, Dorothy. *The Sound of Music and Plants,* Santa Monica, CA: de Vorss 1973.

Revill, SI et al. The reliability of a linear analogue scale for evaluating pain, *Anaesthesia* 1976, 31 1191-1198.

Reyner, JH/ Laurence, George/ Upton, Carl. *Psionic Medicine: The Study and Treatment of the Causative Factors in Illness,* London: Routledge and Kegan Paul 1974.

Reynolds, HM et al. Quantifying passive resistance to motion in the straight leg raising test of asymptomatic subjects, *J the American Osteopathic Association* 1993, 93, 913-920.

Rhine, Joseph B. Some exploratory tests in dowsing, *J Parapsychology* 1950, 14, 278-286.

Rhine, Louisa E. *Hidden Channels of the Mind,* New York: William Morrow 1961.

Rhine, Louisa E. *ESP in Life and Lab: Tracing Hidden Channels,* New York Macmillan 1967.

Rhue, JW et al (eds). *Handbook of Clinical Hypnosis,* Washington, DC: American Psychological 1993.

Ribeaux, P/ Spence, M. CAM evaluation: what are the research questions? *Complementary Therapies in Medicine* 2001, 9, 188-193.

Richards TL et al. Double-blind study of pulsing magnetic field effects on multiple sclerosis, *J Alternative Complementary Medicine* 1997, 3(1), 21-29

Richards, MC. *Centering,* Middletown, CT: Wesleyan University Press 1989.

Richardson, A. Imagery: Definition and types, In: AA. Sheikh (ed), *Imagery: Current Theory, Research, and Application,* New York: Wiley 1983, 3-42.

Richardson, Janet. The use of randomized control trials in complementary therapies: exploring the issues, *J Advanced Nursing* 2000, 32(2), 398-406.

Richardson, JL et al. The effect of compliance with treatment on survival among patients with hematologic malignancies, *J Clinical Oncology* 1990, 8, 356-364

Richardson, MA/ Nanney, K/ Masse, L et al. Discrepant views of oncologists and cancer patients on complementary alternative medicine, *National Center for Complement-ary and Alternative Medicine, National Institute of health, 6707 Democracy Blvd. #106, Bethesda, MD 20892-5475* (from summary in *Alternative Therapies* 2001, 7(3), 109.

Richet, C. Somnambulisme a distance, *Revue Philosophique de la Pays* et *de l'Etranger,* 1886,21 199-200.

Rickard, Bob.The holy incorruptibles, *The Unexplained* 1981a, 4(39), *774-771.*

Rickard, Bob. A bizarre preservation, *The Unexplained* 1981b, 4(41) 817-820.

Rickard, Bob. Blood and tears, *The Unexplained* 1981c, 4(42), 821-425,

Rico, G. *Writing the Natural Way:Using Right-Brain Techniques to Release Your Expressive Powers,* Los Angeles: Tarcher 1983.

Rico, G. *Pain and Possibility: Writing Your Way Through Personal Crisis,* Los Angeles: Tarcher 1991.

Rider, Mark S/ Achterberg, Jeanne. Effect of music-associated imagery on neutrophils and lymphocytes, *Biofeedback and Self Regulation* 1989 14(3), 247-257.

Rider, MS et al.Effect of immune system imagery on secretory IgA, *Biofeedback and Self Regulation* 1990.

Ridolfe, R. *Shiatsu,* Rutland, VT: Charles E. Tuttle 1993.

Ridolfe, R/ Franzen, S. *Shiatsu for Women,* HarperSanFrancisco 1996.

Riggs, Alf.he effects of earth radiation on the body: Where you work and sleep is crucial to your health, *Caduceus* 1995, 29, 29-31.

Riley, D/ Berman, B. Complementary and alternative medicine in outcomes research, *Altern Ther* 2002, 8(3)., 36-7.

Riley, D/Fischer, M/ Singh,B/ Aidvogl,M/ Heger,M. Homeopathy and conventional medicine: an outcomes study comparing effectiveness in a primary care setting, *J Altern Complement Med* 2001; 7: 149-159 www.ncbi.nlm.nih.gov/entrez/query.fcgi?c md=retrieve&db=pubmed&list_uids=1132 7521&dopt=Abstract

Riley, V. Mouse mammary tumors: Alteration of incidence as apparent function of stress, *Science* 1975, 189, 465-467.

Rinbochay, Lati et al. *Meditative States in Tibetan Buddhism: The Concentration and Formless Absorptions,* London/ Boston: Wisdom 1983.

Rinpoche, Sogyal.*The Tibetan Book of*

Living and Dying, New York: HarperSan-Francisco 1992

Rindge, Jeane Pontius (ed).Quote from *Human Dimensions,* 1977, 5(1,2), 4.

Ring,Kenneth. *Heading Toward Omega,* New York: William Morrow1984.

Riordan, RJ. Scriptherapy: therapeutic writing as a counseling adjunct, *J Counseling and Development* 1996, 74, 263-269.

Ripinsky-Naxon, Michael. The *Neurophysics of Human Behavior: Explorations at the Interface of the Brain, Mind, Behavior, and Information,* Albany: State University of New York 1993.

Ritblatt, S/ Ter Louw, JH. The Bible as biblio-source for poetry therapy, *J Poetry Therapy* 1991, 5, 95-104.

Robb, Sir Douglas. Healing, *New Zealand Medical J* 1971 (August), 74(471), 101-102.

Robbins, John. *Diet for a New America,* Walpote, NH: Stillpoint 1989.

Roberton, Jean. Spiritual healing in general practice, *J Alternative and Complimentary Medicine* 1991 (April), 9(4), 11-13; *9(5),* 2 1-23.

Roberts, Herbert. *The Principles and Art of Cure in Homeopathy: A Modern Textbook,* Rustington, UK: Health Science 1942.

Roberts, K. *The Seventh Sense,* Garden City, NY: Doubleday 1953. (From Hansen)

Roberts, Ursula. *Health, Healing and You,* London: Max Parrish 1964.

Robie, DL. Tensional forces in the human body, *Orthopedics Review* 1977, 6(11), 45-48.

Robinson, V. *Humor and the Health Professions,* Thorofare, NJ: C.B. Slack 1990.

Rocard, Yves. *Le Signal du Sourcien* Paris: Dunod 1964. (French, cited in Hansen 1982)

Roche, SM/ McConkey, M. Absorption: nature, assessment, and correlates, *J Personality and Social Psychology* 1990, 59(1), 99-101.

Rochon, Paula A et al. Are Randomized Controlled Trial Outcomes Influenced by the Inclusion of a Placebo Group? A Systematic review of Nonsteroidal Anti-inflammatory Drug trials for Arthritis Treatment, *J Clinical Epidemiology* 1999, 52, 113-22.

Roesch, KL/ Ernst, E. (Proving the efficacy of complementary therapy: analysis of the literature as represented by acupuncture - review - German), *Fortschritte der Medizin* 1995 113(5), 49-53.

Roger, N. *The Creative Connection: Expressive Arts as Healing,* Palo Alto, CA: Science and Behavior 1993.

Rogers, Carl R. The necessary and sufficient conditions of therapeutic personality change, *J Consulting Psychology* 1957, 21, 95-103.

Rogers, J. *Dying to Live,* Minerva 2000.

Rogers, Martha E. Nursing: A science of unitary man, In: Riehl, J.P/ Roy, C. (eds). *Conceptual Models for Nursing Practice, 2nd Ed.* New York: Appleton-Century-Crofts 1984, 329-337.

Roggenbuck, PE. The good news about cancer, *New Age* 1978, 3, 32-35.

Rogo, D Scott (ed). *Mind Beyond the Body: The Mystery of ESP Projection,* New York: Penguin 1978.

Rolf, Ida. *Rolfing: The Integration of Human Structures,* Santa Monica, CA: Dennis-Landman 1977.

Rolfs, A/ Super, S. Guiding the unconscious: the process of poem selection for poetry therapy groups, *The Arts in Psychotherapy* 1988, 15, 119-126.

Romains, Jules. *Eyeless Sight,* Secaucus, NJ: Citadel 1978.

Roman, AS/ Inyushin, VM. The influence of auto-suggestion, *J Paraphysics* 1972, 6(1), 19-25.

Romanuci-Ross, L/ Moerman, DE/ Taneredi, LR (eds). *The Anthropology of Medicine: From Culture to Method,* South Hadley, MA: Bergin & Garvey 1983.

Romer, A/ Weigel, M/ Zeiger, W/ Melchert, F. Prenatal cupuncture: Effects on cervical maturation and duration of labor, *Geburtshilfe Und Frauenheilkunde* 2000, 60(10), 513-518.

Rondo, TA. *Grieving: How to Go on Living when Someone You Love Dies,* New

York: Lexington/ Macmillan 1988 324 pp

Root-Berenstein, R. Root-Berenstein, M. *Honey, Mud, Maggots, and Other Medical Marvels,* New York, NY: Houghton Mifflin; 1997.

Roppel, RM/ Mitchell, F Jr. Skin points of anomalously low electric resistance: current voltage characteristics and relationships to peripheral stimulation therapies, *J American Osteopathic Association* 1975, 746, 877-878.

Rosa, Linda et al. A close look at Therapeutic Touch (*J the American Medical Association* 1998)

Rose, Jeanne. *Jeanne Rose's Herbal Body Book*, New York: Perigee 1976.

Rose, Jeanne. *The Aromatherapy Book: Applications and Inhalations,* Berkeley, CA: North Atlantic 1992.

Rose, Louis. Someaspects of paranormal healing, *J the Society for Psychical Research* 1955, 38(685) 105-121.

Rose, Louis MD. *Faith Healing,* London: Penguin 1971.

Rose, Xenia.*Widow's Journey A Return to Living*, Human Horizons Series. ISBN 0-285-65098-X

Rosen, Marion/ Brenner, Sue. *The Rosen Method of Movement*, Berkeley, CA: North Atlantic Books 1991.

Rosenberg, Andrew. *Remedy Guides* 2345 W. 103 St. Ste. J. Chicago, IL 60643 (Computer disks for Aromatherapy, Bach Flower, Homeopathy, Herbal Remedies).

Rosenberg, Jack Lee et al. *Body, Self and Soul: Sustaining Integration*, Atlanta, GA: Humanics Ltd. 1985.

Rosenfeldt, V et al. Effect of probiotic Lactobacillus strains in young children hospitalized with acute diarrhea, *Pediatric Infectious Diseases J.* 2002, 2(5), 411-417.

Rose-Neil, Sydney. The work of professor Kim Bong Han, *The Acupuncturist* 1967, 1, 15. (From Gerber)

Rosenman, Richard/ Brand, J et al. Coronary heart disease in the Western Collaborative Group Study, *J the American Medical Association* 1964 189(1), .

Rosenman, Richard/ Friedman, Meyer et al. A predictive study of coronary heart disease, *J the American Medical Association* 1964 189(1).

Rosenthal, Robert. Interpersonal expectations: Effects of the experimental hypothesis, In: Rosenthal, R/ Rosnow, RL. *Artifact in Behavioral Research,* New York: Academic 1969, 181-277.

Rosenthal, R. *On the Social Psychology of the Self-Fulfilling Prophecy: Further Evid-ence for Pygmalion Effects and Their Mediating Mechanisms,* Module 53, pp 1-28. New York: MSS Modular Publications 1974.

Rosenthal, Robert. Replicability and experimenter influence: Experimenter effects in behavioral research, *Parapsychology Review* 1980, 11(3), 5-11.

Rosenthal, Robert/ Fode, Kermit L. The effect of experimenter bias on the performance of the albino rat, *Behavioral Science* 1963 (July), 8(3).

Rosenthal, R/ Rubin, DR. Interpersonal expectancy effects: The first *345* studies, *The Behavioral and Brain Sciences* 1978, 3, 377-415.

Ross, E. *How to Write while You Sleep*, Berkeley, CA: Celestial Arts 1995.

Ross, Jeremy. *Zang Fu: The Organ System of Traditional Chinese Medicine*, Edinburgh, Scotland: Churchill Livingstone Longman 1985.

Ross, T. Edward/ Wright, RD. *The Divining Mind*, Destiny 1990.

Rossbach, Sarah. *Feng Shui: The Chinese Art of Placement,* NY: E. P. Dutton 1983.

Rossbach, Sarah/ Lin Yun. *Living Color: Master Lin Yun's Guide to Feng Shui and the Art of Color,* NY: Kodansha International 1994.

Rossbach, Sarah/Lin Yun. *Interior Design with Feng Shui*, NY: E. P. Dutton 2000.

Rossi, Ernest. *Hypnotic Realities: The Induction of Clinical Hypnosis and Forms of Indirect Suggestion*, New York: Irvington/Halsted/Wiley 1976.

Rossi, Ernest L. Hypnosis and ultradian cycles: a new state(s) theory of hypnosis? *American J Clinical Hypnosis* 1982, 25(1), 21-32.

Rossi, Ernest. *The Psychobiology of Mind-Body Healing,* New York: WW Norton 1986a.

Rossi, Ernest Lawrence. Altered states of consciousness in everyday life: The ultra-dian rhythms, In: Wolman, Benjamin, B/ Ullman, Montague. *Handbook of States of Consciousness,* New York: Van Nostrand Reinhold 1986b, 97-132.

Rossi, Ernest L/ Cheek, David B. *Mind-Body Therapy: Methods of Ideodynamic Healing in Hypnosis,* New York and London: WW Norton 1988.

Rossiter, C. commonalities among the creative arts therapies as a basis for research collaboration, *J Poetry Therapy* 1992, 5, 227-239.

Rossman, Martin L. *Healing Yourself: A Step-by-Step Program for Better Health through Imagery*, New York: Pocket 1989.

Roszak, Theodore. *Ecopsychology: Restor-ing the Earth, Healing the Mind*, San Francisco: Sierra Club 1995.

Roth, Robert. *Transcendental Meditation*, New York: Donald I. Fine, Inc. 1988.

Rothenberg, A. *The Creative Process of Psychotherapy*, New York: WW Norton 1988.

Rotton, J/ Kelly, IW. Much ado about the full moon: a meta-analysis of lunarlunacy research, *Psychological Bulletin* 1985, 97, 286-306.

Roud, Paul C. *Making Miracles: An Exploration into the Dynamics of Self-Healing,* Wellingborough, England Thorsons 1990.

Rounds, HD. A lunar rhythm in the occurrence of blood-borne factors in cockroaches, mice and man, *Comparative Biochemistry and Physiology* 1975, SOC. (sic) 193-197.

Rousseau, David et al. *Your Home, Health and Well-being*, Vancouver, BC: Hartley & Marks 1988.

Roy, Rustum. Qigong effects on health, biological and physical systems, *Eleventh International Congress on Stress,* Kohala Coast, HI December 2000.

Rozman, Deborah. *Meditation for Children,* San Francisco: Celestial Arts 1976.

Rubel, A. Concepts of disease in Mexican-American culture, *American Anthropologist* 1960, 62, 795 814.

Rubel, A/ O'Neill, CW/ Ardon, RC. *Susto: a folk illness*, Berkeley, CA: University of California 1984

Rubenfeld, Ilana. *The Listening Hand: Self-Healing Through the Rubenfeld Synergy Method of Talk and Touch*, New York: Banam 2000.

Rubin, R (ed). *Bibliotherapy Source Book*, New York: Oryx 1978.

Rubin, Theodore. Attributed.

Ruether, R. *Womanguides*, Boston: Beacon 1985.

Rumi, Jelaluddin. Attributed.

Rush, .JH. Review of experiments in mental suggestion by L.L. Vasiliev, *J the American Society for Psychical Research* 1964, 58, 216-221.

Rush, James F. *Toward a General Theory of Healing,* Washington, DC: University Press of America 1981.

Russek, Linda J/ Schwartz, Gary E. Energy cardiology: a dynamical energy systems approach for integrating conventional and alternative medicine, *Advances* 1996 12(4), 4-25 (Comments by others 25-35; Response 36-45).

Russell, Edward W. *Design for Destiny,* London: Neville Speannan 1971.

Russell, Edward W. *Report on Radionics: Science of the Future,* London: Neville Spearman 1973.

Russell, Elbert. Consciousness and the unconscious: Eastern meditative and western psychotherapeutic approaches, *J Transpersonal Psychology* 1986, 18(1), 51-72.

Russell, Peter. *The Global Brain: Speculations on the Evolutionary Leap to Planetary Consciousness*, Los Angeles: Tarcher 1983.

Ruth, S/ Kegerries, S. Facilitating cervical flexion using a Feldenkrais method: awareness through movement, *J Sports and Physical Therapy* 1992 16, 25-29.

S

Sacks, Adam D. Nuclear magnetic resonance spectroscopy of homeopathic remedies, *J Holistic Medicine* 1983, 5(2), 172-177.

Sadock, Harold I/ Kaplan, Benjamin J. *Synopsis of Psychiatry*, New York: Williams & Wilkins 1998.

Safonov, Vladimir. Personal experience in psychic diagnostics and healing, In: Vilenskaya, Larissa. *Parapsychology in the USSR, Part III,* San Francisco: Washington Research Center 1981,42-45.

Sagan, Carl. UCLA Commencement Speech 1991, (quoted in *Network* 1997 (Dec) 65, 33.

Sahai, I. Reflexology -- its place in modern health care, *Professional Nurse* 1993, 18, 722-725.

Saifer, Phyllis/ Zellerbach, Merla. *Detox,* Los Angeles: Tarcher 1984.

Saint-Exupéry, Antoine de. *The Little Prince*, New York: Harcourt 2000.

Sakamoto, K. Fundamental and clinical studies on cancer control with total or upper half body irradiation, *Japanese J Cancer Chemotherapy* 1997, 9, 161-175.

Sallstrom, S et al. Acupuncture in the treatment of stroke patients in the subacute stage: a randomized, controlled study, *Complementary Therapies in Medicine* 1996, 4:193-197.

Salmon, J Warren (ed). *Alternative Medicines: Popular and Policy Perspectives*, London/ New York/ Tavistock: Methuen 1984.

Salzberg, CA/ Cooper-Vastola, SA/ Perez, F/ Viehveck, MG/ Byrne, DW. The effects of non-thermal pulsed electromagnetic energy on wound healing of pressure ulcers in spinal cord-injured patients: a randomized double-blind study, *Ostomy Wound Manage* 1995; 41(3): 42.

Samiti, SMYM. *Hathapradipika of Svatmarama*, Lonavla, Inda: Kaivalyadhama 1970.

Samuels, Mike/ Samuels, Nancy. *Seeing with the Mind's Eye,* New York/ Berkeley, CA: Random House/ Bookworks 1975.

Sancier, Kenneth M. The effect of Qigong on therapeutic balancing measured by Electroacupuncture According to Voll (EAV), *Proceedings of the Second World Conference for Academic Exchange of Medical Qigong, Beijing 1993,* 90-91.

Sandyk R. *Electromagnetic fields improve visuospatial performance and reverse agraphia in a Parkinsonian patient.* Int J Neurosci *1995; 87(3-4): 199.*

Sandyk, R. Resolution of sleep paralysis by weak electromagnetic fields in a patient with MS, *Int J Neurosci* 1997; 90(3-4): 145.

Sandner, Donald. Navaho symbolic healing, *Shaman's Dram* 1985, 1, 25-30.

Sandoz, Bobbie. *Listening to Wild Dolphins: Learning Their Secrets for Living with Joy*, Hillsboro, OR: Beyond Words 1999.

Sandweiss, Samuel H. *Spirit and the Mind,* San Diego, CA: Birth Day 1985.

Sandyk, R. Successful treatment of multiple sclerosis with magnetic fields, *Int J Neurosci.* 1992c, 66(3-4), 237-250

Sanford, John A. *Healing and Wholeness,* New York: Paulist 1977 (not psychic healing).

Sannella, Lee. *Kundalini - Psychosis or Transcendence?* San Francisco: HS Dakin 1976.

Santillo, Humbert. *Natural Healing with Herbs*, Prescott Valley, AZ: Holm 1984.

Saraswati, Swami Dharmananda. *Breath of Life: Breathing for Health, Vitality and Meditation*, Motilal 1996.

Sarayadrian, H. *The Science of Meditation,* Agoura, CA: Aquarian Educational Group 1971.

Sargant, William. *The Mind Possessed,* New York: Penguin 1974.

Sarnoff Schiff, H. *The Bereaved Parent*, Condor/ Souvenir ISBN 0-285-64891-8 146pp

Sass, L. *Madness and Modernism: Insanity in the Light of Modern Art, Literature, and Thought*, Cambridge, MA: Harvard University 1992.

Satchidananda, Swami. In: Elliott, William. *Tying Rocks to Clouds*, New York: Image/ Doubleday 1996, 223-235.

Satir, Virginia. *Peoplemaking,* Palo Alto: Science and Behavior Books 1972.

Sato, Y et al. Possible contributions of green tea drinking habits to the prevention of stroke, *Tohoku J Experimental Medicine* 1989, 157, 337-343.

Satprem. *Sri Aurobindo, or the Adventure of Consciousness,* New York: Harper & Row 1968.

Satprem. *The Mind of the Cells, or Willed Mutation of Our Species,* Translated from French by Francine Mahak/ Luc Venet) NY: Institute for Evolutionary Research 1981.

Sattilaro, Anthony J/ Monte, Tom. *Recalled by Life,* New York: Houghton Mifflin 1984.

Savary, L/ Beme, P. *Dreams and Spiritual Growth: Judeo-Christian Way of Dream Work,* Mahwah, NJ: Paulist 1984.

Savitz, David. 3 milligauss power-frequency magnetic fields are correlated with 20 % of childhood cancers, cited without reference in: R. Becker 1990, p.204-205.

Saxe, GA et al. Can diet, in conjunction with mindfulness-based stress reduction affect the rate of increase in prostate-specific antigen after biochemical recurrence of prostate cancer? *Alternative Therapies* 2001, 7(3), 109-110.

Saywood, Peter. Personal communications 1990.

Schachter, MB. Overview, historical background and current status of EDTA chelation therapy for atherosclerosis, *J Advancement in Medicine* 1996, 9(3), 159-177 (163 refs).

Schaefer, RC/ Fay, LJ. *Motion Palpation and Chiropractic Technic,* Huntington Beach, CA: Motion Palpation Institute 1989.

Schatz, Mary P. *Back Care Basics: A Doctor's Gentle Yoga Program for Back and Neck Pain Relief,* Berkeloey, CA: Rodmell 1992.

Schatzman, Morton. *The Story of Ruth,* New York: Putnam's 1980.

Schauberger, Viktor (ed by Coats, Callum). *The Fertile Earth,* Bath, UK: Gateway 2000.

Schauss, AG. Tranquilizing effect of color reduces aggressive behavior and potential violence, *J Orthomolecular Psychiatry* 1979, 8(4), 218-221.

Schauss, AG. The physiological effect of color on the suppression of human aggression: research on Baker-Miller pink, *International J Biosocial Research* 1985, 72, 55-64.

Schauss, Alexander et al. *Eating for A's,* New York: Pocket 1991.

Schaut, George B/ Persinger, Michael A. Subjective telepathic experiences, geomagnetic activity and the ELF hypothesis. Part I: Data analysis, *Psi Research* 1985,4(l),

Scheffer, Mechthild. *Bach Flower Therapy: Theory and Practice,* Rochester, VT: Thorsons 1987.

Scheibner, Viera. *Vaccination: 100 Years of Orthodox Research Shows that Vaccines Represent a Medical Assault on the Immune System,* Maryborough, Victoria, Australia. Australian Print Group 1993, 230-235.

Scherer, Cynthia Athina Kemp. *The Alchemy of the Desert : A Comprehensive Guide Desert Flower Essences for Professional & Self-Help Use,* Tucson, AZ: Desert Alchemy 1997.

Scherer, Cynthia Athina Kemp, *The Art & Technique of Using Flower Essences,* Tucson, AZ: Desert Alchemy 2002.

Schiff, Jacqui/ Day, Beth. *All My Children,* New York: Pyramid 1972.

Schiffer, Fredric. *Of Two Minds: The Revolutionary Science of Dual-Brain Psychology,* New York: Free Press 1998 www.schiffermd.com.

Schimmelschmidt, Michael. The heart of the house, *Caduceus* 1989, 7, 4-6.

Schleifer, SJ et al. Suppression of lymphocyte stimulation following bereavement, *J the American Medical Association* 1983, 250(3), 374-377.

Schlessel-Harpham, Wendy.*After Cancer: A Guide to Your New Life,* New York: Harper Perennial 1994.

Schlitz, Marilyn J/ Braud, William G. Reiki plus natural healing: An ethnographic/ experimental study, *Psi Research* 1985, 4(3/ 4), 100-123.

Schmale, AH/ Iker, H. Hopelessness as a predictor on cervical cancer, *Social Science and Medicine* 1971, 5, 95-100.

Schmid, Ronald F. *Traditional Foods are Your Best Medicine*, Stratford, CT: Ocean View 1987.

Schnabel, Jim. *Remote Viewers; The Secret History of America's Psychic Spies*, New York: Dell 1997

Schneck, G. book review of Bergsmann, O. *Risk Factor Place, Dowsing Zone and |Man: Scientific Study Investigating Place-Related Influences on Man*, University Publishing House Facultas 1990, reviewed in: *J the British Society of Dowsers* 1993, 239, 236-238.

Schneider, Carol J. Cost-effectiveness of biofeedback and behavioral medicine treatments: A review of the literature, *Biofeedback and Self-Regulation* 1987, 12, 71-92.

Schneider, Carol/ Jonas, Wayne. Are alternative treatments effective? Issues and methods involved in measuring effectiveness of alternative treatments, *Subtle Energies* 1994, 5(1), 69-92.

Schneider, Meir. *Self Healing: My Life and Vision*, New York: Routledge & kegan Paul 1987.

Schneider, RH et al. Health promotion with a traditional system of natural health care: Maharishi Ayur-Veda, *J Social Behavior and Personality* 1990, 5(3),1-27.

Schrader, E. Equivalence of St. John's wort extract (Ze 117) and fluoxetine: a randomized controlled study in mild-moderate depression, *International Clinical Psychopharmacology* 2000, 15, 61-68.

Schreiber, Flora Rheta. *Sybil*, New York: Warner 1995.

Schrock, Dean et al. Effects of a psychosocial intervention on survival among patients with stage I breast and prostate cancer: a matched case-control study, *Alternative Therapies* 1999, 5(3), 49-55.

Schroeder-Sheker, Therese. Music for the dying, *Caduceus* 1994, No. 23, 24-26.

Schroeder-Sheker, Therese. Music thanatology and spiritual care for the dying, *Alternative Therapies* 2001, 7(1), 69-77.

Schullian, D/ Schoen, M (eds). *Music as Medicine*, Henry Schuman, New York 1948.

Schultex, Richard Evans Von Reis. *Ethnobotany*, Portland, OR: Discarides 1995.

Schultz, JH/ Luthe, W. *Autogenic Training: A Psychophysiologic Approach in Psychotherapy*, New York: Grune & Stratton 1959.

Schultz, Louis/ Feitis, Rosemary. *The Endless Web*, Berkeley, CA: North Atlantic 1996.

Schulz, Mona Lisa. *Awakening Intuition: Using Your Mind-Body Network for Insight and Healing*, New York: Harmony 1998.

Schulz, V et al. *Rational Phytotherapy: A Physicians Guide to Herbal Medicine*, Berlin: Springer-Verlag 1997.

Schulze, N. Los globules blancs des sujets bien portants et les taches solaires, Report in: *Toulouse Medical* 1960, 10, 741-57, of work done in Sotchi (R.R.S.S.) and published in *Laboratornoie Delo* 1960 and in *Rapport au Conseil interministériel de l'Académie de Sciences d'UR.S.S.* 1960.

Schumann, WO/ Konig, H. Uber die Beobactung von Atmospheics bei geringstein Frequenzen, *Naturwissenschaf-ten* 1954, 41, 183

Schwartz, Gary E. Psychophysiology of imagery and healing: A systems perspective, In: Sheikh, Anees A,: *Imagination and Healing,* Farmingdale, NY: Baywood 1984.

Schwartz, GE. Personality and the unification of psychology and modern physics: a systems approach, In: Aronoff, J. et al. *The Emergence of Personality*, New York: Springer 1987.

Schwartz, GE. Disregulation theory and psychosomatic disease: a systems approach, In: Cheren, S (ed). *Psychosomatic Medicine: Theory, Research and Practice,* New York: International University 1989.

Schwartz, GE. Soul is to spirit as information is to energy: a theoretical note and poem, *Bridges* 1994, 5, 7.

Schwartz, GE. Levels of awareness and 'awareness without awareness': data and theory, In: Hameroff, SR et al (eds). *Toward a Science of Consciousness: The*

First Tucson Discussion and Debates, Cambridge, MA: MIT 1996.

Schwartz, GE/ Russek, LG. Do all dynamic systems have memory? Implications of the systemic memory hypothesis for science and society, In: Pribram, K.H/ King, JS(eds). *Brain and Values: Behavioral Neurody-namics V,* Hillsdale, NM: Erlbaum 1996.

Schwartz, Gary E/ Russek, Linda GS. *Living Energy Universe,* Charlottesville, NC: Hampton Roads 1999

Schwartz, Gary E et al. Interpersonal hand-energy registration: evidence for implicit performance and perception, *Subtle Energies* 1995, 6(3), 183-200.

Schwartz, Gary E et al. Electrostatic body-motion registration and the human antenna-receiver effect: a new method for investigating interpersonal dynamical energy system interactions, *Subtle Energy* 1996, 7(2), 149-184.

Schwartz, Jack. *Human Energy Systems,* New York: Dutton 1980.

Schwartz, Mark S et al. *Biofeedback,* 2nd ed. New York/ London: Guildford 1995.

Schwartz, Stephan A. *The Alexandria Project,* New York: Delta/ Eleanor Fried/ Dell 1983.

Schwartz, S et al. Infrared spectra alteration in water proximate to the palms of thera-peutic practitioners, In: *Subtle Energies,* 1990, 1, 43-72; (Orig. Los Angeles, CA: Mobius Society 1986).

Schwartz, WJ. A clinician's primer on the circadian clock: its localization, function, and resetting, *Advances in Internal Medicine* 1993, 38, 81.

Schwarz, Berthold E. Physiological aspects of Henry Gross's dowsing, *Parapsychology: The Indian J Parapsychological Research* 1962-3, 4, 71-86.

Schwarz, Berthold E. Ordeal by serpents, fire and strychnine, *Psychiatric Quarterly* 1970, 34, 405-429.

Schwarz, Jack. The Integral Way of Self-Healing and Prevention, *Presentation at Conference on Psychic Healing and Self Healing, Association for Humanistic Psychology,* San Francisco 6 May, 1972.

Schwarz, Jack. *The Path of Action,* New York: Dutton 1977.

Schwarz, Jack. *Voluntary Controls: Exercises for Creative Meditation and for Activating the Potential of the Chakras,* New York: Dutton 1978.

Schwarz, Jack. *Human Energy Systems,* New York: Dutton 1980.

Schwenk, Theodor/ Schwenk, Wolfram. *Water: The Element of Life,* Hudson, NY: Anthroposophic 1989.

Scofield, AM. Experimental research in homeopathy: A critical review, *British Homeopathic J* Part I – 1984a,73(3), 160-180; Part II – 1984b, 73(4), 211-226.

Scofield, AM. Homeopathy and its potential role in agriculture - a critical review, *Proceedings of Agriculture and Horticulture* 1984c, 2, 1-50.

Scofield, Anthony M. Personal communication 1988-9.

Scott, C. *The Initiate in the Dark Cycle,* London: George Routledge & Sons 1938.

Scott, J/ Huskisson, EC. Graphic representa-tion of pain, *Pain* 1976, 2 175-184.

Scully, Dana (Gillian Anderson). *The X-files* 1995.

Seard, M. Leon II. Attributed.

Seattle, Chief, Speech of 1854 http://www.nara.gov/publications/prologue/clark.html

Seaward, Brian Luke. Good vibrations: the healing power of humor, *Bridges* (ISSSEEM Magazine) 1995, 6(3), 5-7.

See, DM et al. In vitro effects of echinacea and ginseng on natural killer and antibody-dependent cell cytotoxicity in healthy subjects and chronic fatigue syndrome or AIDS patients, *Immunopharmacology* 1997, 35, 229-235.

Seem, Mark/ Kaplan, Joan. *Bodymind Energetics: Toward a Dynamic Model of Health,* Wellingborough, England: Thorsons 1987.

Segal, Maybelle. *Reflexology,* North Hollywood, CA: Wilshire 1976.

Seibert, Dinah et al. *Are You Sad too? Helping Children Deal with Loss and Death,* Santa Cruz, CA: ETR Associates 1993.

Seidel, S et al. Assessment of commercial laboratiories performing hair mineral analysis, *J The American Medical Association* 2001, 285, 67-72.

Seidman, Maruti. *A Guide to Polarity Therapy*, Boulder, CA: Elan 1991.

Seligman, M. Submissive death: Giving up on Life, *Psychology Today* 1974, 7, 80-85.

Selye, H. *The Stress of Life,* New York: McGraw-Hill 1956. (From CG Ellison 1994)

Sentman, DD. Schumann resonances, In: Volland H (ed). *Handbook of Atmospheric Electrodynamics,* vol 1,. Boca Raton: CRC Press, 1995, 267-295

Serel, TA/ Perk, H/ Koyuncuoglu, HR et al. Acupuncture therapy in the management of persistent primary nocturnal enuresis, *Scandinavian J Urology and Nephrology.* 2001, 35, 40-43.

Sergeyev, GA. Entropy and health, In: Vilenskaya, Larissa, Translator and Ed): *Parapsychology in the USSR. Part III,* San Francisco: Washington Research Center 1981, 65-66.

Sergeyev, Gennady. Biorrhythms and the biosphere,, Translated from Russian by Larissa Vilenskaya) *Psi Research* 1982, 1(2), 29-31.

Sergeyev, GA/ Kulagin, VV. Psychokinetic effects of bioplasmic energy, *J Paraphysics* 1972, 6(1), 18-19.

Serizawa, Katsusuke. *Clinical Acupuncture: A Practical Japanese Approach*, Tokyo: Japan Publications 1988.

Serizawa, Toru. *Tsubo: Vital Points for Oriental Therapy*, New York/ Tokyo: Japan 1992.

Sermonti, G. The inadequacy of the molecular approach in biology, *Frontier Perspectives* 1995, 4, 31-34.

Servadio, E. Unconscious and paranormal factors in healing and recovery, In: *15th Frederic W.H. Myers Memorial Lecture,* London: Society for Psychical Research 1963.

Seto, A/ Kusaka, C/ Nakazato, S et al. 1992 Detection of extraordinary large biomagnetic fields strength from human hand, Acupuncture and Electro-Therapeutics Research International J 17:75-94

Seto, A/ Kusaka, C/ Nakazato, S et al. Detection of extraordinary large biomagnetic field strength from the human hand during external qi emission, *Acupuncture and Electrotherapeutics Research International* 1992, 17, 75-94.

Shallis, Michael. *The Electric Shock Book,* London: Souvenir 1988.

Shannon, Scott. attention Deficit/ Hyperactivity Disorder, *Integrative Medi-cine Consult* 2000, 2(9), 103-105.

Shannon, Scott (ed), *Handbook of Complementary and Alternative therapies in Mental Health*, San Diego, CA: Academic/ Harcourt 2001

Shapira, Rabbi Kolonymus Kalman.*To Heal the Soul: The Spiritual Journal of a Chasidic Rebbe* (Trans. Starrett, Yehoshua), Northvale, NJ: Jason Aronson 1995.

Shapiro, Arthur K. Attitudes toward the use of placebos in treatment, *J Nervous and Mental Diseases* 1960a, 130 200-211, (86 refs).

Shapiro, Arthur K. A contribution to a history of the placebo effect, *Behavioral Science* 1960b, 5(2), 109-135.

Shapiro, Arthur K. Placebo effects in medicine, psychotherapy and psychoanalysis, In: Bergin, Allen E/ Garfield, Sol L. (eds). *Handbook of Psychotherapy and Behavior Change,* New York; Wiley 1971. 439-473. (9 pp refs.)

Shapiro, DA/ Shapiro, D. Meta-analysis of comparative therapy outcome studies: A replication and refinement, *Psychological Bulletin* 1982, 92, 581-604.

Shapiro, DH. Jr. Adverse effects of meditation: a preliminary investigation of long-term meditation, *International J Psychosomatics* 1992, 39, 62-67.

Shapiro, Deanne H Jr/ Walsh, Roger N (eds). *Meditation. Classic and Contemporary Perspectives,* New York: Aldine 1984.

Shapiro, Francine. *Eye Movement Desensitization and Reprocessing*, New York: Guildford 1995.

Shaposhnikov, A. Some paranormal proper-ties of the human mind, Translated from Russian by Larissa Vilenskaya/ Anya Kncharev) *Psi Research* 1982, 1(2), 93-101.

644 References

Sharma, HM et al. Antineoplastic properties of Maharishi 4, against DMBA-induced mammary tumors in rats, *J Pharmacology, Biochemistry and Behavior* 1990, 35, 767-773

Sharma, HM et al. Maharishi Ayur-Veda: modern insights into ancient medicine, *J the American Medical Association* 1991, 265, 2633-2634

Sharma, Ram K/ Dash, Vaidya, B (eds). *Sharaka Samhita, Vol. 1-3*, India: Jamnagar 1949.

Sharon, IM et al. The effects of lights of different spectra on caries incidence in the golden hamster, *Archives of Oral Biology* 1971, 16(12), 1427-1431.

Sharp, Daryl. *Personality Types: Jung's Model of Typology*, Toronto: Inner City 1987.

Sharp, Daryl. *A Primer of Terms & Concepts*, Toronto: Inner City 1991.

Sharpless, SK/ MacGraegor, RJ/ Luttges, MVA. Pressure vessel model for nerve compression, *J Neurological Science* 1975, 24, 299-304.

Sharrard, WJW. A double-blind trial of pulse electromagnetic fields for delayed union of tibial fractures, *J Bone and Joint Surgery* 1990, 72B, 347-355.

Shattock, EH. *Mind Your Body: A Practical Method of Self-Healing,* Wellingborough, England: Turnstone 1979.

Shaw, DL Jr Et al. Management of fatigue: a physiologic approach, *American J Medical Science* 1962, 243, 758-769.

Shaw, George Bernard. *Back to Methuselah* 1921.

Shealy, Norman, The role of psychics in medical diagnosis, In: Carlson, Rick (ed), *Frontiers of Science and Medicine*, Chicago, IL: Contemporary 1975.

Shealy, C. Norman. The Nuprin pain report, *Holos' Practice Report* 1987, 3(3), 1.

Shealy, Norman, Clairvoyant diagnosis, In: Srinivasan, T. M, *Energy Medicine Around the World*, Phoenix, AZ: Gabriel 1988, 291-303.

Shealy, C Norman. *Miracles Do Happen: A Physician's Experience with Alternative Medicine*, Rockport, MA/ Shaftesbury, England 1995.

Shealy, C. Norman/ Freese, Arthur S. *Occult Medicine Can Save Your Life,* New York: Bantam 1977.

Shealy, Norman/ Myss, Caroline. *AIDS: Passageway to Transformation,* Walpole, NH: Stillpoint 1987.

Shealy, C. Norman/ Myss, Caroline M. *The Creation of Health: The Emotional, Psychological and Spiritual Responses that Promote Health and Healihng,* Walpole, NJ: Stillpoint 1988.

Shealy, C Norman et al. Neuro-chemistry of depression, *American J Pain Management* 1992, 2, 31-36.

Shealy, C Norman et al. Non-pharmaceutical treatment of depression using a multimodal approach, *Subtle Energies* 1993, 4(2) 125-134.

Shealy, C Norman et al. A double-blind EEG-response test for a supposed electromagnetic field-neutralizing device, Part I: Via the clinican experties procedure, *Subtle Energies* 1998, 9(3), 231-245.

Shearer, A. *Effortless Being*, London: Mandala/ Unwin Paperbacks 1989.

Sheehan, Molly. *A Guide to Green Hope Farm Flower Essences*, Meriden, NH: Green Hope Farm 1997.

Sheehan, MP/ Atherton, DJ. A controlled trial of traditonal Chinese medicinal plants in widespread non-exudative atopic eczema, *British J Dermatology* 1992 126 179-184.

Sheehan, MP et al. Efficacy of traditional Chinese herbal therapy in adult atopic dermatitis, *Lancet* 1992, 340 13-17.

Shehani, K. "Role of dietary lactobacilli in gastrointestinal microecology.", *America J Clinical Nutrition* 1980, 2248- 2257.

Sheikh, Anees A (ed). *Imagery; Current Theory. Research and Applications*, New York: Wiley 1983.

Sheikh, Anees. *Imagination and Healing,* Farrningdale, NY: Baywood 1984.

Sheikh, Anees A. (ed). *Anthology of Imagery Techniques,* Milwaukee: American Imagery Institute 1986.

Sheikh, Anees A/ Shaffer, JT(eds). *The*

Potential of Fantasy and Imagination, New York: Brandon House 1979.

Sheikh, Anees A/ Sheikh, Katherina S (eds). *Death Imagery,* Milwaukee: American Imagery Institute 1986.

Sheikh, Anees A/ Sheikh, Katherina S. *Eastern and Western Approaches to Healing: Ancient Wisdom and Modern Knowledge,* New York/ Chichestet John Wiley & Sons 1989.

Sheikh, Anees A/ Solomon, Paul. The triune concept, In: Albright/ Albtight: *Mind, Body and Spirit,* 1981.

Sheinman, Nimrod. Presentation at Mind, Immunity & Health Conference, Sponsored by the Gawler Foundation, Lorne, Victoria, Australia 1998.

Shekelle, PG et al. Spinal manipulation for low-back pain, *Annals of Internal Medicine* 1992 117(7), 590-598.

Shekelle, PG et al. The appropriateness of spinal manipulation of low-back pain: project over-view and literature review, (R-4025/ 1-CCR/ FCER) Santa Monica, RAND.

Sheldrake, Rupcrt. *A New Science of Life: The Hypothesis of Formative Causation,* Los Angeles: Tarcher 1981; rev. ed. 1987.

Sheldrake, Rupert. How widely is blind assessment used in scientific research? *Alternative Therapies* 1999, 5(3), 88-91.

Shellenberger, R/ Amar, P. *Clinical efficacy and cost effectiveness of biofeedback therapy. Guidelines for third party reimbursement,* (2nd edition). Wheat Ridge, CO. Association for Applied Psychophysiology and Biofeedback 1989.

Shellenberger, R et al. *Clinical efficacy and cost effectiveness of biofeedback therapy. Guidelines for third party reimbursement,* Wheat Ridge, CO: Association for Applied Psychology and Biofeedback 1994.

Shem, Samuel. *The House of God,* New York, NY: Dell 1978.

Shen, George J. Study of mind-body effects and Qigong in China, *Advances* 1986, 3(4), 134-142.

Shen, J et al. Electroacupuncture for control of myeloablative chemotherapy-induced emesis: a randomized controlled trial, *J the American Medical Association* 2000, 284(21), 2755-2761.

Shenkman, M/ Butler, R. A model for multisystem evaluation, interpretation, and treatment of individuals with neurologica dysfunction, *Physical Therapy* 1989, 69, 538-547.

Shepard, Stephen Paul. *Healing Energies,* Provo, UT: Hawthorne 1981.

Sherman, RA. Stump and phantom limb pain, *Neurological Clinics* 1989, 7, 249-264.

Sherman, Ronald A. Maggot therapy in modern medicine. *Infectious Medicine* 1998; 15:651-656.

Sherman, RA/ Hall, MJ/ Thomas, S. Medicinal maggots: an ancient remedy for some contemporary afflictions, *Annual Review Entomology* 2000;25:55-81.

Sherrill, Kimberly A/ Larson, David B. The anti-tenure factor in religious research in clinical epidemiology and aging, in: Levin, Jeffrey S. 1994 149-177 (3 1/ 2 pp refs).

Sherwood, Keith. *Chakra Therapy for Personal Growth and Healing,* St. Paul, MN: Llewellyn 1988.

Shinoda-Bolen, Jean. *Close to the Bone: Life-Threatening Illness and the Search for Meaning,* New York: Scribner 1996

Shipley, M et al. Controlled trial of homeopathic treatment of osteoarthritis, *Lancet* 1983.

Shoenfeld Y/ Aron-Maor, A. Vaccination and autoimmunity-'vaccinosis:' a dangerous laison?, *J Autoimmunity,* Feb., 2000; 14(1):1-10.

Shor, RE/ Orne, EC. *Harvard Group Scale of Hypnotic Susceptibility, Form A,* Palo Alto, CA: Consulting Psychologists 1962.

Shrock, Dean et al. Effects of a psychosocial intervention on survival among patients with stage I breast and prostate cancer: a matched case-control study, *Alternative Therapies* 1999, 5(3), 49-55

Shrodes, C. Implications for psychotherapy, in: Rubin, R.

Shubentsov, Yefim. Healing Seminar, Philadelphia 1982 (July).

Siegal, Alan. *Polarity Therapy,* San Leandro, CA: Prism 1987.

Siegel, Bernie S. *Love, Medicine & Mira-*

cles: Lessons Learned About Self-Healing from a Surgeon's Experience with Exceptional Patients, New York: Harper & Row 1986.

Siegel, Bernard. Peace, Love and Healing, London: Ryder 1990

Siegel, Bernard S/ Siegel, Barbara H. Holistic medicine, Connecticut Medicine 1981,45(7), 441-442.

Siegelman, E. Myths and Meaning in Psychotherapy, New York: Guildford 1990.

Siegman, AW/ Dembroski, DW (eds). In Search of Coronary-Prone Behaviour, Hillsdale, NJ: Lawrence Erlbaum 1988.

Sierpina, Victor S. Integrative Health Care: Complementary and Alternative Therapies for the Whole Person, Philadelphia: FA Davis Co., 2001.

Sieveking, Paul. The human glow worms, The Unexplained 1982, 9(105), 2090-2093.

Silbey, Uma. The Complete Crystal Guidebook: A Practical Path to Self Development. Empowerment and Healing, San Francisco, CA: U-Read 1986.

Sills, Franklyn. The Polarity Process: Energy as a Healing Art, Shaftesbury, England: Element 1989.

Sills, Franklyn. Craniosacral Biodynamics, Volume I: The Breath of Life, Biodynamics, and Fundamental Skills, Berkeley, CA: North Atlantic/ Palm Beach Gardens, FL: UI Enterprises 2001.

Silver, C. Jack the giant tamer: poetry writing in the treatment of paranoid schizophrenia, J Poetry Therapy 1993, 7, 91-95.

Simon, G. " Intestinal flora in health and disease.", In: Physiology of the Intestinal Tract, ed. L. Johnson. New York: Raven Press, 1981 1361-1380.

Simonides. In Plutarch, Moralia.

Simonton, O. Carl/ Matthews-Simonton. Cancer and stress: counseling and the cancer patient, Medical J Australia 1981, 1, 679-683.

Simonton, O. Carl/ Matthews-Simonton, Stephanie/ Creighton, IL. Getting Well Again, New York: Bantam 1980a.

Simonton, O. Carl/ Matthews-Simonton, Stephanie/ Sparks, TF. Psychological

intervention in the treatment of cancer, Peychosomatics 19809b), 21(3), 226-233.

Simonton, Stephanie Matthews. see Matthews-Simonton, Stephanie (p. 244)

Simonton, Stephanie. The influence of psychological therapy on the immune system in patients with advanced cancer, Dissertation Abstracts International 1994, 55-05-B:1-86.

Simonton, Stephanie S/ Sherman, Allen C. Psychological aspects of mind-body medicine: promises and pitfalls from research with cancer patients, Alternative Therapies 1998, 4(4), 50-67 (252 refs).

Sims-Williams, H et al. Controlled trial of mobilization and manipulation for patients with low back pain in general practice, British Medical J 1978, ii, 1338-1340.

Sinclair, Brett Jason. Alternative Health Care Resources: A Directory and Guide, W. Nyack, NY: Parker 1992.

Sinclair-Gieben, AHC/ Chalmers, P. Evaluation of treatment of warts by hypnosis, Lancet 1959 (2), 480-482.

Singer, Philip (ed). Traditional Healing: New Science or New Colonialism? Buffalo, NY: Conch Magazine 1977.

Singh, LM/ Gupta, G. Antiviral efficacy of homeopathic drugs against animal viruses, British Homeopathic J 1985, 74(3), 168-174.

Singh, Rajinder. Empowering Your Soul Through Meditation, Shaftesbury, England: Element 1999.

Singh, Sampooran et al. Global Values Education; A Scientific Appraisal, Faith 2001.

Sisken, BF/ Walker, J. Therapeutic aspects of electromagnetic fields for soft-tissue healing, In: Blank, M (ed). Electromagnetic Fields: Biological Interactions and Mechanisms, Advances in Chemistry Series 250, Washington DC: American Chemical Society, 1995, 277-285

Sjaust, Ana/ Hurtler, Cecil. Pulsed signal therapy: Treatment of chronic pain due to traumatic soft tissue injury, Unpublished study, Markoll, Richard, Bio-Magnetic Therapy Stytems, 1200 Cliunt Moore Road, Boca Raton, FL 33487.

Sjolund, Bengt/ Eriksson, Margareta.

Electra-acupuncture and endogenous morphines, *Lancet* 1976 (13 Nov.), 1085.

Skinner, BF. Superstition in the pigeon, *J Experimental Psychology* 1948,38, 168.

Skinner, BF. *Science and Human Behavior,* New York: Macmillan 1953.

Skinner, Stephen. *The Living Earth Manual of Feng Shui: Chinese Geomancy,* London/ Boston: Routledge and Kegan Paul 1982.

Sky, Michael. *Breathing: Expanding Your Power and Energy,* Santa Fe, NM: Bear & Co. 1990.

Sleszynski, SL/ Kelso, AF. Comparison of thoracic manipulation with incentive spirometry in preventing postoperative atelectasis, *J the American Osteopathic Association* 1993, 93, 834-845 .

Sliker, Gretchen. *Multiple Mind: Healing the Split in Psyche and World,* Boston/ London: Shambhala 1992.

Slomoff, Daniel A. Traditional African medicine: Voodoo healings, In: Heinze, Ruth-Inge: *Proceedings of 2ⁿᵈ International Conference on the Study of Shamanism, San Rafael, CA 1985,* Berkeley; CA: Center for South and Southeast Asia Studies 1986.

Sloth-Nielson, J et al. Arteriographic findings in EDTA chelation therapy on peripheral arteriosclerosis, *American J Surgery* 1991, 162, 122-125.

Small, EJ et al. A prospective trial of the herbal supplement PC-SPES in patients with progressive prostate cancer, Presented in part at 1999 American Society for Clinical Oncology Anhnual Meeting, Atlanta, GA.

Smith, LA et al. Teasing apart quality and validity in systematic reviews: an example from acupuncture trials in chronic neck and back pain, Pain 2000; 86: 119-132.

Smith, Bradford. *Meditation,* New York: Lippincott 1963.

Smith, Cyril. Homeopathy - the final solution? *J Alternative and Complement-ary Medicine* 1988, 6(8), 15-16, 20.

Smith, Cyril/ Best, Simon. Electromagnetic Man: Health and Hazard in the Electrical Environment, London: J.M. Dent & Sons 1989.

Smith, Cyril W/ Choy, Roy/ Monro, Jean. Environmental, allergic and therapeutic effects of electromagnetic fields, *Paper at 3rd Annual International Symposium on Man and His Environment in Health and Disease,* Dallas, TX 1985.

Smith, Edward. *The Body in Psychotherapy,* Jefferson, NC: McFarland 1985.

Smith, G. Richard/ McDaniel, SM. Psychologically mediated effect on the delayed hypersensitivity reaction to tubercu-lin in humans, *Psychosomatic Medicine* 1983,46, 65-70. (From Dossey 1989)

Smith, Huston. *The Religions of Man,* New York: Harper/ Colophon 1965.

Smith, Justa. Paranormal effects on enzyme activity, *Human Dimensions* 1972, 1, 15-19.

Smith, Lendon H/ Hattersley, Joseph G. SIDS: Sudden Infant Death "Syndrome," *Townsend Letter* 2000 (Aug/ Sep) 50-54; 126-131 (203 refs).

Smith, ML. et al. *The benefits of psychotherapy,* Baltimore: John Hopkins University 1980.

Smith, RK. Influenza mortality, one hundred thousand cases: with death rate of one-fortieth of that officially reported under conventional medical treatment, *J the American Osteopathic Association* 1920, 19, 172-175.

Smith, Richard. "Where is the Wisdom. . .!" (editorial), *British Medical J* 1991, 303, 798-799

Smith, Rudolph B/ Boericke, Garth W. Modem instrumentation for the evaluation of homeopathic drug structure, *J the American Institute of Homeopathy* 1966, 59, 263-280.

Smith, Rudolph/ Boericke, Garth W. Changes caused by succession on NMR patterns and bioassay of bradykinin triacetate (BKTA) succussions and dilutions, *J the American Institute of Homeopathy* 1968, 61, 197-2 12.

Smith, T/ Counsall, S. Scripture as narrative and therapy, *J Poetry Therapy* 1991, 4, 149-163.

Smolowe, John S/ Deliman, Tracy (eds). *Holistic Medicine: Harmony of Body,*

648 References

Mind, Spirit. Reston VA: Reston 1982.

Smulski, HS/ Wojcicki, J. Placebo-controlled, double-blind trial to determine the efficacy of the Tibetan plant preparation Padma 28 for intermittent claudication, *Alternative Therapies* 1995, 1(3), 44-49.

Smyth, JM/ Stone, AA/ Hurewitz, A/ Kaell, A. Effects of writing about stressful experiences on symptom reduction in patients with asthma or rheumatoid arthritis: a randomized trial, *JAMA.* 1999;281:1304-1309.

Snel, FWJJ/ van der Sijde, PC. The effect of retro-active distance healing on babesia rodhani (rodent malaria) in rats, *European J Parapsychology* 1990-1991, 8 123-130.

Snellgrove, Brian. *The Unseen Self: Kirlian Photography Explained*, Saffron Walden, UK: CW Daniel 1996.

Snoyman, P/ Holdstock, TL. The influence of the sun, moon, climate and economic conditions on crisis incidence, *J Clinical Psychology* 1980, 36, 884-893.

Sobel, David S (ed). *Holistic Approaches to Ancient Ways of Health and Contemporary Medicine*, New York: Harcourt Brace Jovanovich 1979.

Sohn, Tina/ Finando, Donna. *Amma: The Ancient Art of Oriental Healing*, Rochester, VT: Healing Arts 1988.

Solfvin, Gerald F. Psi expectancy effects in psychic healing studies with malarial mice, *European J Parapsychology* 1982b, 4(2), 160-197.

Solly, R/ Lloyd, R. *Journey Notes: Writing for Recovery and Spiritual Growth*,

Solomon, George Freeman. An important and theoretical advance, *Advances* 1993, 9(2), 31-39.

Solomon, Paul. The triune concept, In: Albright/ Albright: *Mind, Body and Spirit*, 1981.

Solomon, Paul R et al. Ginkgo for Memory Enhancement: A Randomized Controlled Trial, *J the American Medical Association.* 2002, 288, 835-840.

Somé, Malidoma Patrice. *Of Water and the Spirit: ritual, Magic, and Initiation in the Life of an African Shaman*, New York: Putnam 1994.

Sontag, Susan. *Illness as a Metaphor: AIDS and its Metaphors*, NY/ London: Penguin 1983 (orig. 1978)

Spear, SP et al. Expressive writing and coping with job loss, *Academy of Management J* 1994, 37(3), 722-733.

Speck, M. "Interactions among lactobacilli and man," *J Dairy Sciences* 59, 338-343.

Speers, M. *American J Industrial Medicine* 1988, 13, 629.

Spencer, JW/ Jacobs, JJ (eds). *Complementary/Alternative Medicine: An Evidence-Based Approach*, St.Louis: Mosby, 1999.

Sperry, RW. The great cerebral commissure, *Scientific American* 1964 (January).

Spiegel, David. A psychosocial intervention and survival time of patients with metastatic breast cancer, *Advances* 1991, 7(3), 10-19.

Spiegel, David. *Living Beyond Limits*, New York: Fawcett Columbine 1993.

Spiegel, David. Mind Matters: Group Therapy and Survival in Breast Cancer, *New England J Medicine,* Volume 2001, 345, 1767-1768.

Spiegel, David et al. Effect of psychosocial treatment on survival of patients with metastatic breast cancer, *Lancet* 1989, 2, 888-891.

Spiegel, Herbert/ Spiegel, David. *Trance and Treatment: Clinical Uses of Hypnosis*, Wahsington, DC: American Psychiatric 1987.

Spiegel, John P/ Machotka, P. *Messages of the Body*, New York: Free Press/ London: Collier/ Macmillan 1974.

Spiritual Frontiers Editor, Research report: Setzer's sanctuary effect, *Spiritual Frontiers* 1980, 12(1), 20-23.

Spitler, HR. *The Syntonic Principle,* College of Syntonic Optometry 1941.

Spottiswoode, SJP. Geomagnetic activity and anomalous cognition: a preliminary report of new evidence, *Subtle Energies* 1990 1(1), 65-77.

Spraggett, Allen. *Kathryn Kuhlman: The Woman who Believes in Miracles,* New York: World Publishing Company 1970.

Springer, Sally P/ Deutsch, George. *Left*

Brain Right Brain, San Francisco: W.H. Freeman 1981 (16pp refs).

Sprintge, Ralph. *MusicMedicine*, St. Louis: MMB Music 1992.

St. Aubyn, L. *Today is a Good Day to Die*, Bath, UK: Gateway 1991 ISBN 0-946551-68-5

St. Clair, David. Spiritism in Brazil, *Psychic* 1970 (December), 2(3), 8-14.

St. Clair, David. *Psychic Healers*, New York: Bantam/ Doubleday 1979.

St. John, Robert. *The Metamorphic Technique: Principles and Practice*, Tisbury, Wilts, England: Element 1982.

Stack, Robin. *Creative Life Lines for Survivors*, PO Box 423, Canter City, MN 55012.

Staib, Allan R/ Logan, DR. Hypnotic stimulation of breast growth, *American J Clinical Hypnosis* 1977, 19(4), 201-207.

Stanford, Rex G. 'Associative activation of the unconscious' and 'visualization' as methods for influencing the PK target, *J the American Society for Psychical Research* 1969, 63, 338-351.

Stängle , Jacob. Strahlungsmessungen uber unterirdischen Quellfuhrungen [Radiation measurements over underground aquifers], *Bohrtechnik-Brunnenbau-Rohrleitungsbau*, 1960, No. 11.

Stängle , Jacob. Sind unterirdische Quellfuhrungen physikalische messbar? [Are underground water courses physically measurable?] *Zeitschrift fur Radiesthesie* 1965, Vol. 1.

Stanton, HE. Hypnotic relaxation and the reduction of sleep onset insomnia, *International J Psychosomatics 1989*, 35(1-4), 64-68.

Stanway, Andrew. *Alternative Medicine: A Guide to Natural Therapies*, New York: Penguin 1980.

Stanwick, M. Aura photography: mundane physics or diagnostic tool? *Nursing Times* 1996, 92(24), 39-41.

Stapleton, Ruth Carter. *The Experience of Inner Healing*, New York: Bantam 1977.

Starfield, B. Is US health really the best in the world? *J the American Medical Association* 2000, 284(4), 483-485.

Stark, EH/ Tilley, RM. *Clinical Review Series: Ostteopathic Medicine*, Acton: Publishing Sciences Group 1975

Starke, Linda (ed). *Vital Signs: The Environmental Trends that are Shaping OurPlanet*, Washington, DC: Earthscan 1999.

Starr, Paul. *The Social Transformation of American Medicine: The Rise of a Sovereign Profession and the Mking of a Vast Industry*, New York: Basic 1982.

Stauber, John/ Rampton, Sheldon. Trust Us We're Experts: How Industry Manipulates Science and Gambles with Your Future, JP Tarcher 2002

Staudacher, C. *Beyond Grief: A Guide for Recovering from the Death of a Loved One*, USA: New Harbinger 1987 London: Condor/ Souvenir 1988.

Steadman, Alice. *Who's the Matter With Me?*, Marina del Rey; CA: De Vorss 1969.

Stearn, Jess. *Edgar Cayce: The Sleeping Prophet*, New York: Bantam 1967.

Steel, Rosemary. Personal communication 1988.

Steele, Judy. Personal communication 2002 www.schoolforliving.org .

Steere; David A. *Spiritual Presence in Psychotherapy; A Guide for Caregivers*, Brunner/ Mazel 1997.

Stein, Diane. *Essential Reiki*, Freedom, CA: Crossing 1996.

Steiner, Rudolph. The lost temple and how it is to be restored, *Caduceus* 1989, No. 7, 26.

Stelter, Alfred. *Psi-HealinG*, New York: Bantam 1976.

Stemberg, J. *The Writer on Her Work: Contemporary Women Writers Reflect on Their Art and*

Stephenson, James. A review of investigations into action of substances in dilutions greater than 1 x 10 (to minus 24th power), i.e. microdilutions, *J the American Institute of Homeopathy 1955*, 48, 327-355.

Sternfield, M. et al. The role of acupuncture in asthma: changes in airway dynamics and LTC4 induced LAI, *American J Clinical Medicine* 1989 17 129-134.

650 References

Stevens, B et al. Charge build-up on the body as basis for the 'human aura' and certain PK events (Summary), In W. 0. Roll, R. L. Morris, & J. D. Morris (eds), *Research in Parapsychology 1974,* Metuchen, NJ: Scarecrow Press 1975, 77-80.

Stevens, Christopher. The development of the Alexander Technique and evidence for its, *British Journal of Therapy and Rehabilitation* 1997, 2(11), 621-626. http://www.stat.org.uk/research/earlier.html

Stevens, L. *An intervention study of imagery with diabetes mellitus,* Doctoral dissertation, University of North Texas. 1983.

Stevensen, CJ. The psychophysiological effects of aromatherapy massage following cardiac surgery, *Complementary Therapies in Medicine* 1994, 2, 27-35

Stevensen, C. Aromatherapy, In: Micozzi 1996 137-148.

Stevenson, C et al. Garlic for treating hypercholesterolemia, *Annals of Internal Medicine* 2000, 133(6), 420-429.

Stevenson, Ian. *20 Cases Suggestive of Reincarnation,* Charlottesville, VA: University Press of Virginia 1974a.

Stevenson, Ian. *Xenoglossy: A Review and Report of a Case,* Charlottesville, VA: University Press of Virginia 1974b.

Stevenson, Ian. *Children Who Remember Previous Lives: A Question of Reincarnation,* Charlottesville, VA: Univ. of Virginia 1987.

Stevenson, Ian. *Reincarnation and Biology: A Contribution to the Etiology of Birthmarks and Birth Defrects, Vols. I and II*, Westport, CT: Greenwood 1995.

Stevinson, C/ Honan, W/ Cooke, B/ Ernst, E. Neurological complications of cervical spine manipulation, *J Royal Society of Medicine 2001,* 94, 107-110.

Stewart, D. *Please Don't Stand on My Catheter* (Sponsored by Orange Co. Chapter of American Heart Assn.) Fullerton, CA: Sultana 1982.

Stewart, Ian/ Joines, Vann TA. Today, Chapel Hill, NC: Lifespace 1991

Stiles, W. *How Hypnotherapy Can Help You: The Complementary & Alternative Method for Wellness*, New York: Kendall, Hunt 1994.

Still, Andrew Taylor. *Osteopathy: Research and Practice*, Seattle, WA: Eastland 1992.

Stillings, Dennis. The phantom leaf revisited: An interview with Allan Detrich, *Archaeus* 1983, 1(l), 41-51.

Stillings, Dennis. Observations on fire-walk-ing, *Psi Research 1985,4(2),* 46-50.

Stoddard, Sandor. *The Hospice Movement*, New York: Vintage/ Random House 1992.

Stoff, Jesse A/ Pellegrino, Charles R. *Chronic Fatigue Syndrome: The Hidden Epidemic*, New York: HarperPerennial 1992 (14 p. of refs).

Stokes, G/ Whiteside, D. *One Brain: Dyslexia Learning Connection and Brain Integration*, Burbank, CA: Three in One Concepts 1984.

Stoll, Andrew L. *Omega-3 Connection: The Groundbreaking Antidepression Diet and Brain Program*. New York: Simon & Schuster 2002

Stone, H/ Winkelman, S. *Embracing Ourselves: The Voice Dialogue Method*, San Rafael, CA: New World 1989.

Stone, Julie. Ethical issues in complementary and alternative medicine, *Complementary Therapies in Medicine* 2000, 8, 207-213.

Stone, J/ Matthews, J. *Complementary Med-icine and the Law*, Oxford, UK: Oxford University 1996.

Stone, Randolph. *Polarity Therapy: The Complete Collected Works*, Sebastopol, CA: CRCS 1986.

Stone, Randolph. *Health Building: The Conscious Art of Living Well*, Sebastopol, CA: CRCS 1999.

Strain, JJ. Psychotherapy and medical conditions, in: Golman, D/ Gurin, J. (eds), *Mind-Body Medicines*, New York: Consumer Reports 1993.

Strand, Clark. *The Wooden Bowl: Simple Meditations for Everyday Life*, Newleaf 1988.

Stratton, KR et al (eds). Adverse events associated with childhood vaccines; evidence bearing on causality, Washington

DC: Institute of Medicine, National Academy Press 1994, 211-236.

Strickland, Donna. Is humor healing?, *Bridges* (ISSSEEM Magazine) 1995, 6(3) 11-14.

Studdert, David M/ Eisenberg, David M et al. Medical malpractice implications of alternative medicine, *J the American Medical Association* 1998, 280(18), 1610-1615.

Study of Magico-Religious Practitioners. *Unpublished doctoral dissertation,* Univ. California Irvine 1984.

Stuff.co.nz. NZ has 'disturbing' rate of medical error – study, May 8, 2003 http://www.stuff.co.nz/stuff/0,2106,24587 78a10,00.html

Stux, G/ Pomeranz, B. *Acupuncture textbook and atlas*, Berlin: Springer-Verlag 1987.

Styles, JL. The use of aromatherapy in hospitalized children with HIV, *Complementary Therapies in Nursing* 1997, 3, 16-20.

Sucher, BM. Myofascial release of carpal tunnel syndrome, *J American Osteopathic Association* 1993a, 93(1), 92-101.

Sucher, BM. Myofascial manipulation release of carpal tunnel syndrome documentation with magnetic resonance imaging, *J the American Osteopathic Association* 1993b, 93(12), 1273-1278.

Sucher, BM. Palpatory diagnosis and manipulative management of carpal tunnel syndrome, *J the American Osteopathic Association* 1994, 94(8), 647-663.

Sucher, BM/ Hinrichs, RN. Manipulative treatment of carpal tunnel syndrome: biomechanical and osteopathic intervention to increase the length of the transverse carpal ligament, *J the American Osteopathic Association* 1998, 98(12), 679-686.

Sugano, H/ Uchida, S/ Kuramoto, I. A new approach to the study of subtle energies, *Subtle Energies* 1994, 5(2), 143-165.

Sugrue, Thomas. *There is a River,* New York: Dell 1970.

Sui, Choa Kok. *Pranic Healing,* York Beach, ME: Samuel Weiser 1980.

Sullivan, A. *A Path to Healing*, New York: Coubleday 1998.

Sullivan, HS. *The Interpersonal Theory of Psychiatry*, New York: Norton 1953.

Sullivan, S. Evoked electrical conductivity on the lung acupuncture points in healthy individuals and confirmed lung cancer patients, *American J Acupuncture* 1985, 13, 261-266.

Sumrall, Joe. *Lighten Up*, Santa Fe, NM: Bear & Co. 1992.

Sun, Y. The realm of traditional Chinese medicine in suggestive care of cancer patients, *Recent Results in Cancer Research* 1988 108, 327-334.

Sundblom, D. Markus, Haikonen, Sari et al. The effect of spiritual healing on chronic idiopathic pain - A medical and biological study, *Clinical J Pain* 1994 10, 286-302.

Sung, YF/ Kutner, MH/ Cerine, FC/ and Frederickson, EL. (1977) Comparison of the effects of acupuncture and codeine on postoperative dental pain, *Anestb Analg ... Cu n- Res* 56: 473-478.

Surawicz, FG et al. Cancer, emotions and mental illness: The present state of understanding, *American J Psychiatry* 1976, 133, 1306-4309.

Surman, OS et al. Hypnosis in the treatment of warts, *Archives of General Psychiatry* 1973, 28, 439-441.

Sutherland, WG. *Teachings in the Science of Osteopathy*, Wales, A. (ed), Cambridge, MA: Rudra 1990 .

Svoboda, Robert. *Prakruti: Your Ayurvedic Constitution*, Albuquerque, NM: Geocom 1988.

Svoboda, Robert E. *Ayurveda: Life, Health and Longevity*, New York: Viking Penguin 1993.

Swan, Ingo. *Everybody's Guide to Natural ESP: Unlocking the Extrasensory Power of Your Mind* (out of print)

Sweeney, BM. *Rhythmic Phenomena in Plants,* London: Academic 1969,

Sweeney, T. *Unending Dialogue: Voices from an AIDS Poetry Workshop*, London: Faber & Faber 1992.

Swift, Gayle. A contextual model for holistic nursing practice, *J Holistic Nursing* 1994 12(3), 265-281.

Swift, Jonathan. *Polite Conversation,* 1738 (from Ornish 1996).

Sykes, Pat. *You Don't Know John Cain?* Gerrard's Cross, Bucks, England: Van Duren 1979.

Sylvia, Claire with Novak, William. *A Change of Heart, a Memoir,* New York: Warner 1997.

Sys, SU et al. Personality as independent predictor of long-term mortality in patients with coronary artery disease, *Lancet* 1996, 347, 417-421.

Szasz, Thomas. *The Myth of Mental Illness,* New York: Quill 1984.

Szymanski, Jan A. Application of electric field measurements in research of bio-energotherapeutic phenomena, *Proc. 6th International Conference on Psychotronics 1986,* pp 68-71.

T

Tabori, Paul/ Raphael, Phyllis (eds). *Beyond the Senses,* London: Souvenir 1971.

Taimni, IK. *The Science of Yoga,* Wheaton, IL: Theosophical 1967.

Takahashi, Masaru/ Brown, Stephen. *Qigong for Health: Chinese Traditional Exercise for Cure and Prevention,* New York: Japan 1986.

Takata, M. Zur Ermittlung des Ovulationstages bei der Frau, *Archiv fur Gynakologie* 1938.

Takata, M. Uber eine neue biologisch wirksame Komponente dec Sonnenstrahlung (Heliobiologie). A.M.G.B. Series B, No. *5,* 1951.

Talbot, Michael.*The Holographic Universe,* New York: Harper Collins 1991.

Tandon, MK. Acupuncture for bronchial asthma? A double-blind crossover study, *Medical J Australia* 1991 154(6), 409-412.

Tang, JL/ Zhan, SY/ Ernst, E. Review of randomised controlled trials of traditional Chinese medicine, *British Medical J* 1999, 319, 160-161.

Tansley, David V/ Rae, Malcolm/ Westlake, Aubrey T.*Dimensions of Radionics: A Manual of Rodionic Theory and Practice for the Health Care Professional,* Hengiscote, England: Health Science Press 1977.

Targ, Russell/ Harary, Keith.*Mind Race,* New York: Villard Books 1984

Targ, Russell/ Katra, Jane.*Miracles of Mind: Exploring Non-Local Consciousness and Spiritual Healing,* New World Library 1999.

Targ, Russell/ Puthoff, Hal.*Mind-Reach,* New York: Delta/ Delacorte 1977

Tart, Charles.*Altered States of Consciousness,* NY: John Wiley & Sons, 1969.

Tart, Charles. States of consciousness and state-specific sciences, *Science* 1972a, 176, 1203-1210.

Tart, CT. Concerning the scientific study of the human aura, *J Society for Psychical Research,* 1972b, 46, 1-21.

Tart, Charles T. *Transpersonal Psychologies,* New York: Harper & Row 1975a.

Tart, Charles T. *States of Consciousness,* New York: E.P. Dutton 1975b.

Tart, Charles. cknowledging and dealing with the fear of psi, *J the American Society for Psychical Research* 1984, 78(2), 133-143.

Tart, Charles. Psychics' fears of psychic powers, *J the American Society for Psychical Research* 1986a, 80(3), 279-292.

Tart, Charles. *Waking Up,* Boston: New Science/ Shambhala 1986b.

Tart, Charles T. Geomagnetic effects on GESP: Two studies, *J the Society for Psychical Research* 1988, 82, 193-216.

Tashkin, DP et al. Comparison of real and simulated acupuncture and isoproterenol in methacholine-induced asthma, *Annals Allergy* 1977, 39:379-387.

Tashkin DP et al. A controlled trial of real and simulated acupuncture in the management of chronic asthma, *J Allergy and Clinical Immunology* 1985, 76, 855-864.

Tasso, Jodi/ Miller, Elizabeth. The effects of the full moon on human behavior, *J Psychology* 1976, 93(l), 81-43.

Tatum, John. Clinical intuition and energy field resonance, in: Leskowitz 2000, 39-53.

Taub-Bynum, E. Bruce. *The Family Unconscious: An Invisible Bond,* Wheaton, IL: Quest/ Theosophical 1984.

Taubes, Gary. An electrifying possibility, *Discover* 1986 (April), 23-37.

Taubes, Gary. What if it's all been a big fat lie? *New York Times Magazine Desk* July 21, 2002, Sunday Available at http://www.nytimes.com .

Tausig, M. Measuring life events, *J Health and Social Behavior* 1982,23,52-64. (From CG Ellison 1994)

Taylor, MA/ Reilly, D/ Llewellyn-Jones, RH/ McSharry, C/ Aitchison, TC. Randomised controlled trial of homoeopathy versus placebo in perennial allergic rhinitis with overview of four trial series, *BMJ* 2000; 321: 471-476 http:/ / bmj.com/ cgi/ content/ abstract/ 321/ 7259/ 471

Taylor, J. Lionel. Quote from *The Stages of Human Life;* p 157, (From Montague 1921)

Taylor, JG/ Balanovski, E. Is there any scientific explanation for the paranormal? *Nature* 1979, 279, 631-633.

Taylor, Kylea. The Breathwork Experience; Exploration and Healing, in: *Nonordinary States of Consciousness*, Hanford Mead Publishers 1994.

Taylor, Roger. Torsion fields, *Network: The Scientific and Medical Network Review* 2000, 72, 27.

Taylor, SE. *Positive Illusions: Creative Self-Deception and the Healthy Mind,* New York: Basic Books 1989.

Taylor, Thomas KF. The Laying on of Hands (editorial), *Australia and New Zealand J Medicine* 1978, 8(6), 587-588.

Taylor-Reilly, David. The difficulty with homeopathy: A brief review of principles, methods and research, *Complementary Medical Research* 1988, 3(1), 70-78. (57 refs)

Taylor-Reilly, David/ Taylor, Morag Anne. Potent placebo or potency, *British Homeopathic J* 1985, 74(3),

Taylor-Reilly, David/ Taylor, Morag. *The Difficulty with Homeopathy,* Paper Presented at the British Pharmaceutical Conference, Manchester 1987.

Taylor-Reilly, David et al. Is homeopathy a placebo response: Controlled trial of homeopathic potency, with pollen in hayfever as model, *Lancet* 1986 (October), 881-886. 65-74.

Taylor-Smith, A. Poliomyelitis and pro-

phy-laxis, *British Homoeopathic J* 1950, 40, 65-77.

Teeguarden, Iona. *Acupressure Way of Health: Jin Shin Do*, Tokyo: Japan Publications 1978.

Teilhard de Chardin, Pierre. Attirbuted

Temoshok, L. Biopsychosocial studies on cutaenous malignant melonama: psychosocial factors associated with prognostic indicators, progression, psychophysiology, and tumor-host response, *Social Science and Medicine* 1985, 20, 833-840.

Temoshok, L. Personality, coping style, emotion, and cancer: towards and integrative *model, Cancer* Surveys 1987, 6, 545-567.

Templer, DI/ Veleber, DM. The moon and madness: a comprehensive perspective, *J Clinical Psychology* 1980, 36, 865-868.

Tenforde, TW/ Kaune, WT. Interaction of extremely low frequency electric and magnetic fields with humans, *Health Phys 1987*, 53, 585-606.

Ter Riet, G et al. Acupunctuur en nekpijn/ rugpijn: de effectiviteit van acupunctuur, *Huisarts en Wetenschap* 1989a, 32(6), 223-227 (Dutch)

Ter Riet, G et al. Acupunctuur bij migraine en spanningshoofdpijn: de effectiviteit van acupunctuur, *Huisarts en Wetenschap* 1989b, 32(7), 263-272 (Dutch)

Ter Riet, G et al. Acupuncture and chronic pain: a criteria-based meta-analysis, *J Clinical Epidemiology* 1990a, 43(11) 1191-1199.

Ter Tiet, G et al. A meta-analysis of studies into the effect of acupuncture on addiction, *British J General Practice* 1990b, 40(338), 379-382.

Terman, M. Light therapy, In: Micozzi, 1996 149-159.

Terman, M et al. Light therapy for seasonal affective disorder: a review of efficacy, *Neurophsychopahrmacology* 1989, 2 1.

Terman, M et al. The visual input stage of the mammalian circadian pacemanking system: II The effect of light and drugs on retinal function, *J Biological Rhythms* 1991, 6, 31.

Terman, M et al. Light treatment for sleep disorders: consensus report IV. Sleep phase and duration disturbances, *J Biological Rhythms* 1995 10 135.

Terpstra, Ok et al. Comparison of vaccination of mice and rats with Hemophilus influenza and Bordetella pertussis as models, Clin Exp Pharmacol Physiol, March-April, 1979; 6(2):139-149.

Terrell, SJ. *This Other Kind of Doctors: Traditional Medical Systems in Black Neighborhoods in Austin, Texas,* New York: AMD Press 1990.

Terrett, ACJ/ Vernon, H. A controlled study of the effect of spinal manipulation on paraspinal cutaenous pain tolerance levels, *American J Physical Medicine and Rehabilitation* 1984, 63, 217-225.

Teschler, Wilfried. *The Polarity Healing Handbook: A Practical Introduction to the Healing Therapy of Energy Balancing,* San Leandro, CA: Interbook 1986.

Thase, M.E. When are psychotherapy and pharmacotherapy combinations the treatment of choice for major depressive disorders? *Psychiatric Quarterly* 1999, 70(4), 333-346.

Thakkur, Chandrashekhar. *Introduction to Ayurveda, the Science of Life,* New York: ASI 1974.

Thie, John F. Touch for Health, Marina del Rey, CA: DeVorss 1979.

Thigpen, Corbett H/ Cleckley/ Harvey, M. *The Three Faces of Eve*, Popular Library 1983.

Thomas, KJ/ Fitter, MJ. Evaluating complementary therapies for use in the National Health Service: 'Horses for courses'. Part 2: Alternative research strategies, *Complementary Therapies in Medicine* 1997, 5, 94-98.

Thomas, M/ Eriksson, SV/ Lundeberg, T. A comparative study of diazepam and acupuncture in patients with osteoarthritis pain: a placebo controlled study, *Anierican J Clinical Medicine* 1991 19:95-100.

Thomas, Alexander/ Chess, Stella/ Birch, Herbert G. *Temperament and Behavior Disorders of Children,* New York: New York University 1968.

Thomas, CB/ Greenstreet, RL. Psychobiological characteristics in youth as predictors of five disease states: Suicide, mental illness, hypertension, coronary heart disease, and tumor, *Johns Hopkins Medical J* 1973, 132. 16-43.

Thomas, Kate. *The Kundalini Phenomenon,* New Media 2000.

Thomas, KJ et al. Use of non-orthodox and conventional health care in Great Britain, *British Medical J* 1991, 302, 207-210.

Thomas, Lewis. *The Lives of a Cell: Notes of a Biology Watcher,* New York: Viking 1974.

Thomasen, PR et al. Effectiveness of spinal manipulative therapy in treatment of primary dysmenorrhea: a pilot study, *J Manipulative Physiology and Therapy* 1979, 2 140-145.

Thommen, George S. *Is This Your Day?* New York: Crown 1973.

Thompson, CJS. *Magic and Healing,* London: Rider 1946.

Thompson, William Irwin. *Evil and World Order*, New York: Harper and Row 1976.

Thoreau, Henry David. "Economy" in *Walden* 1854.

Thrash, Agatha/ Thrash, Calvin L Jr. *Home Remedies: hydrotherapy, massage, char-coal, and other simple treatments*, Groveland, CA: New Life 1981.

Thurston, H. *Physical Phenomena of Mysticism,* London: Burns Oates 1952.

Tierra, Michael. *The Way of Herbs*, New York: Washington Square 1983.

Tierra, Michael (ed). *American Herbalism: Essays on Herbs and Herbalism by Members of the American Herbalist Guild,* Freedom, CA: Crossing 1992.

Tiller, William A. *Radionics, radiesthesia and physics, In: Varieties of Healing Experience: Exploring Psychic Phenomena in Healing, an Interdisciplinary Symposium, Los Altos, CA,* Academy of Parapsychology and Medicine 1971 (October30), pp 55-78.

Tiller, William. Some energy field observations of man and nature, In: Krippner, Stanley/ Rubin, Daniel (eds). *The Kirlian Aura*, Garden City, NY: Anchor/ Doubleday 1974.

Tiller, William A. Kirlian photography as an electrotherapeutics research tool, *Acupuncture and Electrotherapeutic Res. International J* 1976, 2, 33-42.

Tiller, William. Homeopathy: A laboratory for etheric science? *J Holistic Medicine* 1983, 5(1), 25.

Tiller, William A. Towards a scientific rationale of homeopathy, *J Holistic Medicine* 1984, 6(2), 130-147.

Tiller, William A. *Science and Human Transformation: Subtle Energies, Intentionality and Consciousness* 1997.

Tiller, William A. Conscious Acts of Creation: The Emergence of a New Physics, *International Journal of Healing and Caring – On line* 2003a, 3(1).

Tiller, William A. Towards a quantitative model of both local and non-local energetic/ informa-tion healing, *Journal of Healing and Caring – On line* 2003b, 3(2).

Tiller, William A. Intention Imprinted Electrical Devices: Their effects upon both materials and space, *Keynote at Fifth Annual Energy Psychology Conference, Toronto* 2003c.

Tillotson, Alan K. Personal communications 1982.

Tinterow, M. (ed). *Foundations of Hypnosis*, Springfield, IL: Charles Thomas 1970.

Tipping, Colin. *Radical Forgiveness*, Atlanta: GOLDENeight Publishers 1997.

Tisserand, Maggie. *Aromatherapy for Women*, New York: Thorson 1985.

Tisserand, Robert. *The Art of Aromatherapy: The Healing and Beautifying Properties of the Essential Oils of Flowers and Herbs*, New York: Inner Traditions International 1977

Tisserand, Robert. *Aromatherapy, to Heal and Tend the Body*, Santa Fe, NM: Lotus Light 1988.

Tisserand, Robert / Balacs, Tony. *Essential Oil Safety, A Guide for Health Care Professionals*, Edinburgh, UK: Churchill Livingstone 1995.

Tolstoy, Leo. Quoted in Borysenko 1993, p.62.

Tomatis, Alfred A. *The Conscious Ear: My Life of Transformation Through Listening*, Barrytown, NY: Station Hill 1991.

Tomatis, Alfred A. *The Ear and Language*, Stoddart 1997.

Tomatis, Alfred A et al. *The Conscious Ear: My Life Transformed Through Listening*, Station Hill Press 1992.

Tomlinson, Henry. *The Divination of Disease: A Study in Radiesthesia*, Sussex, England: Health Science 1953.

Tomlinson, H. Divination of disease, *J the British Society of Dowsers* 1964, 28, 213-215.

Tompkins, Peter/ Bird, Christopher. *The Secret Life of Plants*, New York: Harper & Row 1973.

Topper, MD. The traditional Navajo medicine rnan: therapist, counselor, and community leader, *J Psychoanalytic Anthropology* 1987 10, 217-250.

Torri, S et al. Contingent negative variation (CNV) and the psychological effects of odour, In: Van Toller, S/ Dodd, GH. (eds). *Perfumery: The Psychology and Biology of Fragrance*, London: Chapman and Hall 1988 107-121

Touitou, Y/ Haus, E (eds). *Biologic Rhythms in Cliniali and Laboratory Medicine*, Berlin/ New York: Springer-Verlag 1994 (many p. refs).

Trager, Milton / Guadagno-Hammond, Cathy. *Trager Mentastics: Movement as a Way to Agelessness*, Barrytown, NY: Station Hill 1987.

Tresidder, Andrew. *Lazy Person's Guide to Emotional Healing*, Newleaf 2000.

Trinder, WH. *Dowsing*, Guildford, England: Billing 1962. (Orig. 1939)

Trock, DH. The effect of pulsed electromagnetic fields in the treatment of osteoarthritis of the knee and cervical spine. Report of randomized, double-blind, placebo-controlled trials, *J Rheumatol* 1994; 21(10): 1903-1922.

Trock, DH et al. A double-blind trial of the clinical effects of pulsed electromagnetic fields in osteoarthritis, *J Rheumatology* 1993, 20, 456-460.

Trock, D et al. The effect of pulsed electromagnetic fields in the treatment of OA of the knee and cervical spine, *J Rheumatology* 1994, 21, 1903

Tromp, Sol W. *Psychical Physics: A Scientific Analysis of Dowsing, Radiesthesia and Kindred Divining Phenomena*, New York: Elsevier 1949.

Trotter, RT. Folk medicine in the Southwest: myths and medical facts, *Postgraduate Medicine* 1985. 78 167-179.

Trousdall, P. Reflexology meets emotional needs, *International J Alternative and Complementary Medicine* 1997 (Nov), 9-12.

Trowbridge, John Parks/ Walker, Morton. *The Yeast Syndrome: How to Help Your Doctor Identify and Treat the Real Cause of Your Yeast-Related Illness*, New York/London: Bantam 1986 (well referenced, with an appendix of medical doctors who treat this).

Trungpa, C. *Shambhala: The Sacred Path of the Warrior*, San Francisco: Shambhala 1995.

Tsu, Lao. *Tao Te Ching*

Tsutani, K. Evaluation of herbal medicine: an East Asian perspective, in: Lewith, T.T/ Aldridge, D (eds). *Clinical Research Methodology of Complementary Therapy*, London: Hodder and Stoughton 1993.

Tulder MWv, Cherkin DC, Berman B, Lao L, Koes BW. Acupuncture for low back pain (Cochrane Review), The Cochrane Library Issue 1. Oxford: Update Software, 2000.

Tunnell, Gilbert B. Three dimensions of naturalness: An expanded definition of field research, *Psychological Bulletin* 1977, 84(3), 426-437.

Tunyi, I et al. The influence of geomagnetic activity upon the psychotronical diagnosis and therapy, *Proceedings of the 6th International Conference on Psychotronic Research 1986*, 118-119.

Turner, Gordon. *An Outline of Spiritual Healing*, London, Psychic Press 1970. (Orig. 1963)

Tweedie, Irina. *The Chasm of Fire: A Woman's Experience of Liberation through the Teachings of a Sufi Master*, Longmead, England: Element 1988.

Nitch, Grandmother Twylah. In McFadden, p. 109

U

US News Books. *The Brain: Mystery of Mailer and Mind*, Washington, DC: US News Books 1982, 7(14), 4.

Udupa, KN. *Disorders of Stress and Their Management by Yoga*, Benares, India: Benares Hindu University 1978.

Udupa, KN et al. Studies in physiologica, endocrine, and metabolic response to the practice of yoga in young, normal volunteers, *J Research in Indian Medicine* 1971, 6, 345-355

Ueland, B. *If You Want to Write: A Book About Art, Independence, and Spirit*, St. Paul, MN: Graywolf 1987.

Uhlenhuth, EH et al. Drug doctor's verbal attitude and clinical setting in the symptomatic response to pharmacotherapy, *Psychopharmacologia* 1966, 9, 392-418.

Uhlenhuth, EH et al. The symptomatic relief of anxiety with meprobamate, phenobarbital and placebo, *American J Psychiatry* 1959, 115, 905-910.

Ullman, Dana. *Homeopathy: Medicine for the 21st Cnetury*, Berkeley: North Atlantic 1988.

Ullman, Dana. *Homeopathic Medicine for Children and Infants*, Los Angeles: Tarcher 1992.

Ullman, Montague. Herpes simplex and second degree burn induced under hypnosis, *American J Psychiatry* 1947, 3, 828-830.

Ullman. Montague. The Dream, Schizophrenia, and Psi Phenomena, *Paper read at* 1st International Conf. of Parapsychology, Utrecht 1953.

Ullman, Montague. On the psyche and warts. 1. Suggestion and warts: A review and comment, *Psychosomatic Medicine* 1959, 21(6), 474-488.

Ullman, Montague. Parapsychology and psychiatry Chapter 52.2a. In: Freedman, A/ Kaplan, H/ Saddock, B (eds). *Comprehensive Textbook of Psychiatry*, Baltimore: Williams and Wilkins 1974 (2nd ed), 2552-2561.

Ullman, Montague. Psychopathology and psi phenomena, In: Wolman, Benjamin B (ed). *Handbook of Parapsychology Chapter VI, 3*, New York: Van Nostrand Reinhold 1977, p 557-574.

Ullman, M/ Dudek, S. On the psyche and warts: II. hypnotic suggstion and warts, *Psychosomatic Medicine* 1960, 22, 68-76.

Underhill, Evelyn. *Mysticism; A Study in the Nature and Development of Man's Spiritual Consciousness*, London: University/ Methuen 1960. (Orig. 1911)

Underwood, Peter. *Complete Book of Dowsing*, London: Rider 1980.

Unschuld, PU. *Medicine in China: History of Ideas*, Berkeley, CA: University of California 1985.

Uphoff, Walter/ Uphoff, Mary Jo. *New Psychic Frontiers: Your Key to New Worlds,*. Gerards Cross, Bucks, England: Colin Smythe 1980.

Upledger, John E. *Craniosacril Therapy II: Beyond the Dura,* Seattle, WA: Eastland 1986.

Upledger, John E. *Your Inner Physician and You: CranioSacral Therapy, Somato-Emotional Release*, Berkeley, CA: North Atlantic 1992.

Upledger, John E. CranioSacral Therapy part II: as it is today, *Subtle Energies* 1995a, 6(2), 135-166.

Upledger, John E. CranioSacral Therapy part III: in the future, *Subtle Energies* 1995b, 6(3), 201-216.

Upledger, John E/ Vrederoogd, Jon D. *Craniosacral Therapy,* Seattle, WA: Eastland 1983.

US Pychotronics Association http://www.psychotronics.org

Utt, R. *Applied Physiology Acupressure Formatting for Brain Physiolgoy*, Tucson, AZ: Applied Physiology Publishing 1991a.

Utt, RI. *The Law of Five Elements*, Tucson, AZ: International Institute of Applied Physiology 1991b.

Utts, Jessica: Replication and meta-analysis in parapsychology, *Statistical Science* 1991, 6(4) 363-403.

V

Vallbona, C/ Hazlewood, CF/ Jurida, G. Response of pain to static magnetic fields in postpolio patients: a double-blind pilot study, *Arch Phys Med Rehabil* 1997; 78(11): 1200-1203.

Vallbona, C et al. Response of pain to static magnetic fields in postpolio patients: a double-blind pilot study, *Archives of Physical Medicine and Rehabilitation* 1997.

Valnet, Jean. *Practice of Aromatherapy*, Rochester, VT: Inner Traditions 1990.

Valnet, Jean/ Tisserand, Robert (ed). *The Practice of Aromatherapy*, Rochester, VT: Inner Traditions Intl 1990.

Van Buchen, FL et al. Therapy of acute otitits media: myringotomy, antibiotics, or neither? A double-blind study in children, *Lancet* 1981, 2(8252), 883-887.

van de Castle, RL. The facilitation of ESP through hypnosis, *American J Clinical Hypnosis* 1969, 12(1), 37-56.

van Campen, Crétien (Editor) et al. Bibliography: Synesthesia in Art and Science, http://mitpress2.mit.edu/e-journals/Leonardo/isast/spec.projects/synesthesiabib.html

van de Hasselt, P/ van Immerssel, W/ Klijn, JAJ. Kirlian photography: The myth of bioplasma, *Medikon* 1974 (April).

van der Lugt, Bart/ Firth, Shirley. *The Hospital as a Temple*, Davidhuis, Slotlaan 31, 3062 PL Rotterdam, Netherlands, davidhuis@hetnet.nl

van der Post, Laurens. *Jung and the Story of Out Time,* New York/ London: Penguin 1974

van der Post, Laurens. *The Voice of the Thunder*, New York/ London: Penguin 1994.

van Gelder, Dora (Kunz), *The Real World of Fairies*, Wheaton, IL: Quest/Theosophical 1978.

Van Rij, AM et al. Chelation therapy for intermittent claudication: a double-blind, randomized, controlled trial, *Circulation* 1994, 90, 1194-1199.

Van Wijk, R et al. A molecular basis for understanding the benefits from subharmful doses of toxicants: an experimental approach to the concept of hormesis and the homeopathic similia law, *Biomedical Therapies* 1997, 15, 4-13 (cited in Eskinazi 1999).

658 References

Vandenbroucke, JP/ de Craen, AJ. Alternative medicine: a "mirror image" for scientific reasoning in conventional medicine, *Ann Intern Med* 2001; 135: 507-513 www.ncbi.nlm.nih.gov/ entrez/ query.fcgi?cmd=retrieve&db=pubmed&list_uids=11578154&dopt=Abstract

Vargas, Luis A et al. Exploring the multidimensional aspects of grief reactions, *American J Psychiatry* 1989, 146(11), 1484-89.

Vasiliev, Leonid L. *Mysterious Phenomena of the Human Psyche, Trans*lated by Volochova, Sonia from Russian). New Hyde Park, NY: University Books 1965.

Vasquez, Steven. *Brief Strobic Photostimul-ation*, Hurst, TX: Health Institute of North Texas 1995 (1225 Precinct Line Road, Hurst, TX 76053)

Vaughan, Allan. Investigation of Silva Mind Control claims, In: *Research in Parapsychology 1973*, Metuchen, NJ: Scarecrow 1974, 51.

Vaughan, Frances.Transpersonal dimensions of psychotherapy, *ReVision* 1979 (Winter/ Spring), 26-30.

Vaughan, Frances. *The Inward Arc*, Nevada City, CA: Blue Dolphin 1995.

Vaz, A.L. Double-blind clinical evaluation of the relative efficacy of glucosamine sulphate in the management of osteoarthritis of the knee in outpatients, *Current Medical Research Opinion* 1982, 8, 145-149.

Verhoef, MJ/ Casebeer, AL/ Hilsden, RJ. Assessing efficacy of complementary medicine: adding qualitative research methods to the "Gold Standard", *J Altern Complement Med.* 2002, 8(3),275-81.

Vernon, H. Manipulative therapy in the chiropractic treatment of headaches: a retrospective and prospective study*, J Manipulative Physiology and Therapy* 1982, 5 105-112.

Vernon, M. *The Psychology of Perception,* Baltimore, MD: Penguin 1962.

Verny, Thomas/ Kelly, John. *The Secret Life of the Unborn Child.* New York: Dell 1986.

Vickers AJ. *Massage arid Aromatherapy: A Guide for Health Care Professionals*, London: Chapman and Hall 1996a.

Vickers, AJ. Can acupuncture have specific effects on health? A systematic review of acupuncture antiemesis trials, J R Soc Med 1996b; 89: 303- 311.

Vickers, Andrew. Evidence-Based Medicine and Complementary Medicine," ACP *J Club* 1999, 130(1), A13-14.

Vickers, Andrew, et al. How should we research unconventional therapies? *Interna-tional J Technology Assessment in Health Care* 1997, 13(1), 111-121.

Vilenskaya, Larissa V. Optimal period for biofield activity, *International J Paraphysics* 1976a, 19(1 & 2), 9-12.

Vilenskaya, Larissa. A scientific approach to some aspects of psychic healing, *International J Paraphysics* 1976b, 10(3), 74-79.

Vilenskaya, Larissa. Psychoregulation and psychic healing, *Parapsychology in the USSR, Part I,* San Francisco: Washington Research Center 1981, 26-33.

Vilenskaya, Larissa. Bioelectronics in Leningrad and Alma-Ata, *Psi Research* 1982, 1(4), 27-35.

Vilenskaya, Larissa. An eyewitness reports firewalking in Portland, Oregon, *Psi Research* 1983, 2(4), Vilenskaya, Larissa. Psi and Qigong in China: Interview with Paul Dong, *Psi Research* 1985a, 4(1), 8 1-95.

Vilenskaya, Larissa (ed). Soviet 'accumulators' of healing energies, *Psi Research* 1985b, 4(1), 68-78.

Vilenskaya, Larissa. Qigong. psi, healing and human potential in the People's Republic of China, *Psi Research* 1985c, 4(314), 124-133.

Vilenskaya, Larissa. *Firewalking,* Falls Village, CT: Bramble 1991.

Villoldo, Alberto/ Jendresen, Erik. *Dance of the Four Wind: Secrets of the Inca Medicine Wheel*, Rochester, VT: Destiny 1995.

Villoldo, Alberto/ Krippner, Stanley. *Healing States: A Journey into the World of Spiritual Healing and Shamanism,* New York: Fireside/ Simon & Schuster 1987.

Vincent, CA. The treatment of tension headache by acupuncture: A controlled single case design with time series analysis, *J Psycbosomatic Research* 1990, 34: 553-561.

Vincent, C.A/ Richardson, P.H. Acupuncture for some common disorders: a review of evaluative research, *J the Royal College of General Practitioners* 1987, 37, 77-81.

Vinokurava, Svetlana. Life in a magnetic web, *J Paraphysics* 1971, 5(4), 131-136.

Virsik, et al. The effect of acupuncture on bronchial asthma, *Progress in Respiratory Research 1980* 14, 271-275.

Vishnu-devananda, S. *Hatha Yoga Pradipika*, New York: Om Lotus 1987.

Vishnudevananda, Swami. *The Complete Illustrated Book of Yoga*, New York: Harmony 1980.

Vitale, Barbara Meister. *Unicorns are Real: A Right-Brained Approach to Learning*, New York: Warner 1986.

Vital-Ionisation bei der Bestrablung den Menschen, *Helvetica Media Acta* 1950.

Vithoulkas, George. *The Science of Homeo-pathy*, New Delhi: B. Jain 1980.

Vithoulkas, George. Homeopathic experimentation: The problem of double-blind trials and some suggestions, *J Complementary Medicine* 1985, 1(1), 10-15.

Vivikananda, Swami. *Raja Yoga,* Calcutta, India: Advaita Ashram 1982.

Vlamis, Gregory. *Flowers to the Rescue: The Healing Vision of Dr. Edward Bach*, Rochester, VT: Healing Arts 1988.

Vodovnik, L/ R. Karba. Treatment of chronic wounds by means of electric and electromagnetic fields, Part 1, literature review. Med. Biol. Eng. and Comput. 1992.(May),257-266.

Vogel, R.I. et al. The effect of topical application of folic acid on gingival health, Vogel, V.J. *American Indian Medicine*, Norman, OK: University of Oklahoma 1970.

Vogel, R.I. et al. The effect of folic acid on gingival health, *J Periodontology* 1976, 47, 667-668.

Vogel, Virgil J. *American Indian Medicine*, University of Oklahoma 1971.

Voll, R. Twenty years of electroacupuncture diagnosis in Germany, a progress report, *American J Acupuncture*, 1975, 3(Special EAV issue), 7-17.

Voll, R. Special EAV Issue, *American J Acupuncture* 1978.

Voll, R. The phenomenon of medicine testing in electroacupuncture according to Voll, *American J Acupuncture* 1980, 8, 97-104.

Vollmar, Klausbernd. *Journey through the Chakras: Exercises for Healing and Internal Balancing*, Bath, England: Gateway 1987.

von Bertalanffy L. General systems theory and psychiatry, In: Arieti, S (ed). *American Handbook of Psychiatry,* New York: Basic Books 1966, 705-710.

von Franz, Marie-Louise. *On Divination and Synchronicity: The Psychology of Meaningful Chance,* Toronto: Inner City 1980.

von Franz, Marie-Louise. *On Dreams and Death: A Jungian Interpretation, Trans.* by Emmanuel X. Kennedy and Vernon Brooks) Boston/ London: Shambhala 1987.

von Franz, Marie-Louise/ Hillman, James. *Jung's Typology*, Zurich: Spring 1971.

von Hauff, M/ Praetorius, R. The performance structure of alternative medical practices - a public health structure analysis - a pilot study, University of Stuttgart (Published by Soziale Hygiene, Verein Für ein Erweiteres Heilwesen, Bad Liebenzell 1991; Trans. Jurgens, H. Anthroposophical Therapy and Hygiene Association 1993.

von Pohl, Gustav Freiherr. *Earth Currents: Causative Factor of Cancer and Other Diseases*, Diessen nr Munich: Jos C. Hubers Verlag 1932; Frech-Verlag GmbH 1987 (English, ISBN 3-7724-9402-1).

Vorbach, E.U. et al. Efficacy and tolerability of St John's Wort extract L1160 versus imipramine in patients with severe depressive episodes according to ICD-10, *Pharmacopsychiatry* 1997, 30 (Supp 2), 81-85.

Vuckovic, N. Integrating qualitative methods in randomized controlled trials: the experience of the Oregon Center for Complementary and Alternative Medicine, *J Altern Complement Med.* 2002, (3), 225-7.

Vuksan, V. et al. American ginseng (*Panax quinquefolius L*) reduces postprandial glycemia in nondiabetic subjects and subjects with type 2 diabetes mellitus, *Archives of Internal Medicine* 2000, 160(7), 1009-10013.

W

W.F. On the so-called divining rod, or virgula divine, *Proceedings of the Society for Psychical Research* 1897-1898, 13, 2-282.

Waagen, GN et al. Short-term trial of chiropractic adjustments for the relief of chronic low back pain, *Manual Medicine* 1986, 2, 63-67.

Waddell, E. Quality touching to communicate caring, *Nursing Forum* 1979, 18, 288-292.

Wadden, T.A/ Anderson, C.H. The clinical use of hypnosis, *Psychology Bulletin* 1982, 91, 215-243.

Wade, Carlson. *Healing and Revitalizing Your Vital Organs,* New York: Parker Publishing Inc. 1978.

Wade, JF. *The effects of the Callahan phobia treatment technique on self concept*, Doctoral Dissertation, Professional School of Psychological Studies, California.

Wadeson, H. The active muse, *The Arts in Psychotherapy* 1993, 20, 173-185.

Wagner, Glenn N. Osteopathy, In: Micozzi, 1996, 79-90.

Wakefield, AJ / Montgomery, S. Measles, mumps, rubella vaccine: through a glass darkly, Adv Drug React Toxicol Rev, 2001, 19(3), 1-19.

Wakefield, D. *The Story of Your Life: Writing a Spiritual Autobiography*, Boston: Beacon 1990.

Walach, Harald. Methodology Beyond Clinical Trials," in: Ernst, Edzard and Eckhart G. Hahn (eds), *Homeopathy, A Critical Appraisal*, Butterworth – Heinemann Oxford 1998).

Walleczek, Jan. *Self-Organized Biological Dynamics and Nonlinear Control,* Cambridge 2000.

Walker, M. The healing powers of Qigong

(Chi Kung) in 4 parts, 1994, January-May Issues.

Walker, L.G. et al. Hypnotherapy for chemotherapy side effects, *British J Experimental Clincial Hypnosis* 1988, 5(2), 79-82.

Walker, L.G. et al. Psychological, clinical and pathological effects of relaxation training and guided imagery during primary chemotherapy, *British J. of Cancer* 1999, 80(12), 262-268.

Walker, Martin. *Dirty Medicine: Science, Big Business and the Assault on National Health Care*, London: Slingshot 1995.

Walker, Morton. *The Chelation Way: The Completer Book of Chelation Therapy*, Garden City Park, NY: Avery 1990.

Walker, Norman W. *You Can Regain the Vitality of Your Youth: Colon Health, the Key to a Vibrant Life*, Prescott, AZ: Norwalk 1979.

Wall, V.J/ Womack, W. Hypnotic versus active cognitive strategies for alleviation of procedural distress in pediatric oncology patients, *american J Clinical Hypnosis* 1989, 31(3), 181-189.

Wallace, Robert Keith. *The Neurophysiology of Enlightenment*, Fairfield, IA: Maharishi International Univ. Neuroscience 1986.

Wallas, L. *Stories for the Third Ear: Using Hypnotic Fables in Psychotherapy*, New York: WW Norton 1988.

Wallas, L. *Stories that Heal: Reparenting Adult Children of Dysfunctional Families using Hypnotic Stories in Psychotherapy*, New York: WW Norton 1991.

Walsh, R/ Rauche, L. Precipitation of acute psychotic episodes by intensive meditation in individuals with a history of schizophrenia, *American J Psychiatry* 1979, 136, 1085-1086.

Walsh, Roger N/ Vaughan, Frances. *Beyond Ego: Transpersonal Dimensions in Psychology*, Los Angeles: Tarcher 1980.

Walter, Katya, *Tao of Chaos: DNA & the I Ching - Unlocking the Code of the Universe*, Rockport, MA/ Shaftesbury, England: Element 1994.

Walther, S. *Applied Kinesiology, Vol. I. Basic Procedure and Muscle Testing*, Pueblo, CO: Systems DC 1981.

Walther, S. *Applied Kinesiology: Synopsis*, Pueblo, CO: Systems DC 1988.

Wambach, Helen. *Reliving Past Lives; The Evidence Under Hypnosis,* New York: Harper & Row 1978.

Wambach, Helen. *Life Before Life,* New York: Bantam Books 1979.

Wampold, Bruce E. *The Great Psychotherapy Debate: Models, Methods, and Findings,* Lawrence Erlbaum Assoc. 2001

Wang, HH et al. A study in the effectiveness of acupuncture analgesia for colonoscopic examination compared with conventional premedication, *American J Acupuncture* 1992, 20:217-221.

Wang, Shouhang et al. Clinical study of the routine treatment of cancer coordinated by Qigong, *Proceedings of the Second World Conference for Academic Exchange of Medical Qigong, Beijing 1993 129.*

Wangchen, Geshe. *Awakening the Mind of Enlightenment: Meditations on the Buddhist Path,* London: Wisdom 1986.

Wangyal, T. *Wonders of the Natural Mind: The Essence of Dzogchen in the Native Bon Tradition of Tibet,* Barrytown, NY: Station Hill 1993.

Ward, R. (ed) *Foundations for Osteopathic Medicine,* Baltimore, MD: Williams & Wilkins 1997.

Ware, JE et al. *SF-36 Health Survey Manual and Interpretation Guide,* Boston, MA: New England Medical Center, The Health Institute 1993.

Warnecke, G. Psychosomatic disorders in the female climacteric: clinical efficacy and tolerance of kava extract WS-1490, *Fortsch Medicine* 1991, 109, 119-122.

Washburn, M. Observations relevant to a unified theory of meditation, *J Transpersonal Psychology* 1978 10(1).

Wastebusters, Ltd. *The Green Office Manual,* Washington, DC: Earthscan 1998.

Watkins, AD. The role of alternative therapies in the treatment of allergic disease, *Clinical and Experimental Allergy* 1994, 24, 813-825. (137 refs)

Watkins, Alfred. *The Old Straight Track,* London: Methuen 1925.

Watkins, John G/ Watkins, Helen H. Hypnosis, multiple personality and ego states as altered states of consciousness, In: Wolman, Benjamin B/ Ullman, Montague (eds). *Handbook of States of Consciousness,* New York: Van Nostrand Reinhold 1986, 133-158.

Watkins, Mary M. *Waking Dreams,* New York: Harper & Row 1977.

Watson, Lyall. *Neophilia: The Tradition of the New.* Sceptre/ Hoder & Stoughton 1989.

Watson, Andrew/ Drury, Neville. *Healing Music,* Chatswood, Australia: Nature and Health 1987.

Watson, David. *Fear No Evil: A Personal Struggle with Cancer,* London: Hodder & Stoughton 1984.

Watson, F. *Aromatherapy Blends and Remedies: Over 800 Recipes for Everyday Use,* HarperSanFrancisco 1996.

Watson, J. *Postmodern Nursing: The Emergence of Transpersonal Caring-Healing,* Edinburgh, Scotland: Churchill Livingstone (Harcourt-Brace) 1999.

Watson, Lyall. *The Romeo Error: A Matter of Life and Death,* New York: Anchor/ Doubleday 1974.

Watts, Alan. *Psychotherapy East and West,* New York: Ballantine 1961.

Watzlawick, P/ Weakiand, J.H/ Fisch, R. *Change,* New York: Norton 1974.

Weber, Renée. The enfolding-unfolding universe: A conversation with David Bohm, *ReVision* 1978 (Summer/ Fall), 24-51.

Weber, Renée. Philosophical foundations and frameworks fur healing, *ReVision* 1979 (Fall).

Weber, Renée. Compassion, motedness and detachment: Their role in healing, A conversation with Dora Kunz, *Newsletter of the American Holistic Nurses 'Association* 1984, 3(8), 1-6.

Webster, H. *Taboo, A Sociological Study,* Stanford, CA: Stanford University 1942.

Weed, JJ. *Wisdom of the Mystic Masters* (8th ed.), West Nyack, NY: Parker 1970.

Weeks, Nora. *The Medical Discoveries of Edward Bach Physician,* Saffron Walden, UK: CW Daniel 1973.

662 References

Weil, Andrew. *Health and Healing: Understanding Conventional and Alterna-tive Medicine,* Boston, MA: Houghton Mifflin 1983.

Weil, Andrew. *Spontaneous Healing,* New York: Fawcett 1995.

Weiler PC, et al. *A measure of malpractice: medical injury, malpractice litigation, and patient compensation,* Cambridge, MA: Harvard University 1993.

Weininger O. Mortality of albino rats under stress as a function of early handling, *Canadian J Psychology* 1953, 7, 111-114.

Weininger, O. Physiological damage under emotional stress as a function of early experience, *Science* 1954, 119, 285-286.

Weintraub, M. Alternative medical care: Shiatsu, Swedish muscle massage, and trigger point suppression in spinal pain syndrome, *American J Pain Management* 1992a, 2(2), 74-78.

Weintraub, M. Shiatsu, Swedish muscle massage, and trigger point suppression in spinal pain syndrome, *American Massage Therapy J* 1992b, 31(3), 99 109.

Weintraub, M. Magnetic bio-stimulation in painful diabetic peripheral neuropathy: a novel intervention - a randomized, double-blind placebo crossover study, *American J Pain Management* 1999.

Weiskott, G.N. Moon phases and telephone counseling calls, *Psychological Reports* 1974, 25, 752-754.

Weiskott, Gerald N/ Tipton, George B. Moon phases and state hospital admissions, *Psychological Reports* 1975, 37, 486.

Weiss, Brian. *Through Time into Healing,* London: Piatkus 1995.

Weiss, Brian. *Only Love is Real,* New York: Warner/ London: Piatkus 1996.

Weiss, Brian. *Many Lives, Many Masters,* New York: Simon & Schuster 1988/ London: Piatkus 1994.

Weiss, Jordan. *Psychoenergetics: A Method of Self-Discovery and Healing,* Oceanview Publishing, (10900 Warner Ave, Suite 117, Fountain Valley, CA 92708) 1994.

Weiss, Rudolph Fritz. *Herbal Medicine,* Beaconsfield, UK: Beaconsfield 1988.

Weiss, S.J. The language of touch: A resource to body image, *Issues in Mental Health Nursing* 1978, 1, 17-29.

Weiss, S.J. The language of touch, *Nursing Research* 1979, 28, 76-80.

Weissman, G. reviewer. JAMA. 1998;280:2128. Review of: Belli A, Coulehan

Wellisch, David K. A family systems approach to coping with cancer, In: Mikesell, Richard H. et al. (eds) *Integrating Family Therapy: Handbook of Family Psychology And Systems Theory,* Washington, DC American Psychological Association 1995

Welwood, John. *Journey of the Heart: Intimate Relationship and the Path of Love,* London: Mandala/ Grafton/ HarperCollins 1991.

Wenz, K/ McWhirter, J.J. Enhancing the group experience: creative writing exercises, *J for Specialists in Group Work* 1990, 15, 37-42.

Werbach, Melvyn R. *Nutritional Influences On Illness: A Sourcebook of Clinical Research,* Tarzana, CA: Third Line Press 1988.

Werbach, M.R. *Healing through Nutrition,* New York: HarperCollins 1994.

Werbach, Melvyn R/ Murray, Michael T. *Botanical Influences on Illness: A sourcebook of Clinical Research,* Tarzana, CA: Third Line 1994.

Werntz, DA. Cerebral hemispheric activity and autonomic nervous function, *Dissertation Abstracts International* 1981, 42, 06B, University Microfilms DDJ81-25444.

Werntz, DA et al. Alternating cerebral hemispheric activity and the lateralization of autonomic nervous function, *Human Neurobiology* 1983, 4, 225-229.

Werntz, DA et al. Selective hemispheric stimulation by unilateral forced nostril breathing, *Human Neurobiology* 1987, 6, 165-171.

Wertheimer, N/ Leeper, E. Electrical wiring and childhood cancer, *International J Epidemiology* 1982, 11, 345-355.

West, C. Samuel. *The Golden Seven Plus One, Conquer Disease with Eight Keys to Health, Beauty, and Peace*, Orem, UT: Samuel 1981.

West, John Anthony/ Toonder, Jan Gerhard. *The Case for Astrology*, New York: Coward-McCann 1970.

West, William. Integrated counselling, psychotherapy and healing: an inquiry into counselors and psychotherapists whose work includes healing, *British J Guidance and Counseling* 1997, 25(3), 291-311.

Westfeldt, LF. *Matthias Alexander: The Man and His Work*, Long Bech, CA: Centerline 1984.

Westlake, Aubrey. *The Pattern of Health: A Search for a Greater Understanding of the Life Force in Health and Disease*, Berkeley, CA: Shambala 1973.

Wethered, Vernon D. *The Practice of Medical Radiesthesia,* London: L.N. Fowler 1967.

Wethington, E/ Kessler, RC. Perceived support, received support and adjustment to stressful life events, *J Health and Social Behavior* 1986,27, 78-89, (From CG

Wetzel, MS/ Eisenberg, DM/ Kaptchuk, TJ. Courses involving complementary and alternative medicine at US Medical Schools, *J the American Medical Association* 1998, 280, 784-787.

Wever R. Einfluss Schwacher Elektro-mag-netischer Felder auf die Circadiane Periodik des Menschen. Naturwissen-schaften 1968 55:29-32

Wever, R. ELF-effects on human circadian rhythms, In: Persinger M A (ed) *ELF and VLF Electromagnetic Field Effects*, Plenum Press, New York, 1974 pp 101-144)

Wharton, Richard/ Lewith, George. Complementary medicine and the general practitioner, *British Medical J* 1986, 292, 1498-1500.

Wheatley, D. LI-160 , and extract of St John's Wort, vs amitriptyline in mildly to moderately depressed outpatients: a controlled 6-week clinical trial, *Pharmacopsychiatry* 1997, 30 (Supp), 77-80.

Whisenant, William F. *Psychologtical Kinesiology: Canging the Bdy's Beliefs*,

HI: Monarch Butterfly Productions 1994.

Whitaker, Carl. The Roots of Psychotherapy, New York: Bruner, Mazel 1981.

Whitaker, Julian/ Adderly, Brenda. *The Pain Relief Breakthrough: The Power of Magnets to Relieve Backaches, Arthritis, Menstrual Cramps, Carpal Tunnel Syndrome, Sports Injuries and More*, New York: Dutton 1998.

Whitaker, Kay Cordell. *The Reluctant Shaman: A Woman's First Encounters with the Unseen Spirits of the Earth*, HarperSanFrancisco 1991.

Whitaker, L. Healing the mother/ daughter relationship through the therapeutic use of fairy tales, poetry, and story, *J Poetry Therapy* 1992, 6, 35-44.

White AR. Neurophysiology or acupuncture analgesia, In: Ernst, E. White, A eds, Acupuncture: a Scientific Appraisal, Oxford: Butterworth-Heinemann, 1999:60-92.

White, AR. Ernst, E. A systematic review of randomized controlled trials of acupunct-urc for neck pain. Br J Rheumatol 1999; 38: 143- 147.

White, AR/ Ernst, E. Economic analysis of complementary medicine: a systematic review, *Complementary Therapies in Medicine* 2000, 8(2), 111-118.

White, AR/ Ernst, E. The case for uncontrolled clinical trials: a starting point for the evidence base for CAM, *Complementary Therapies in Medicine* 2001, 9, 111-115.

White, A et al. Acupuncture for smoking cessation (Cochrane Review), In: Update Software, Ed. The Cochrane Library. Oxford: 1999.

White, AR et al. A blinded investigation into the accuracy of reflexology charts, *Complementary Therapies in Medicine* (UK) 2000, 8, 166-172.

White, AR et al. Clinical trials of acupuncture: consensus recommendations for optimal treatment, sham controls and blinding, *Complementary Therapies in Medicine* 2001, 9, 237-245

White, Ian. *Australian Bush Flower Essences*, Forres, Moray, Scotland: Findhorn Foundation 1994.

White, John. *The Highest State of Consciousness*, NY: Anchor/ Doubleday 1972.

White, John. *Kundalini: Evolution and Enlightenment*, New York: Paragon 1990; Anchor 1979.

White, John/ Krippner, Stanley (eds). *Future Science*, Garden City; NY: Anchor/ Doubleday 1977.

White, Leonard/ Tursky, Bernard/ Schwartz, Gary (eds). *Placebo*, New York: Guilford 1985.

White, P. Complementary medicine in cancer care: legal issues of medical negligence and redress, *J Radiotherapy in Practice* 1999, 1, 135 – 142.

White, M.E/ Epston, D. *Narrative Means to Therapeutic ends*, New York: WW Norton 1990.

White, RA. *Kirlian Photography Bibliography* (3rd ed.), Dix Hills, NY: Parapsychology Sources of Information Center 1988.

Whitman, Walt. *I Sing the Body Electric* 1855.

Whitmont, Edward C. *Psyche and Substance: Essays on Homeopathy in the Light of Jungian Psychology*, Berkeley, CA: Homeopathic Education Services and North Atlantic Books 1980

Whitmont, Edward C. *The Alchemy of Healing: Psyche and Soma*, Berkeley, CA: Homeopathic Education Services and North Atlantic Books 1993

Whitmont, Edward C. The role of mind in health, disease and the practice of homeopathy, *Frontier Perspectives* 1996, 5(2), 24-30.

Whitton, J.L/ Cook, S.A. Can humans detect weak magnetic fields? *New Horizons* 1978, 2(4), 1-6.

Whorwell, PJ et al. Controlled trial of hypnotherapy in the treatment of severe refractory irritable bowel syndrome, *Lancet* 1984, 2, 132-1234.

Whorwell, PJ Hypnotherapy in irritable bowel syndrome, *Lancet* 1989, 1, 622.

Whorwell, P.J. et al. Physiological effects of emotion: assessment via hypnosis, *Lancet* 1992, 340, 69-72.

Whyte, George Starr. Cosmo-electric culture. (Reviewed in: Mann, W. Edward:

Orgone, Reich and Eros. New York: Touchstone/ Simon & Schuster 1973.)

Wichtl, M. *Herbal Drugs and Phytopharmaceuticals*, in: Bisset, Norman (ed), Stuttgart: Medpharm Scientific 1994.

Wickramasesekera, I. *Clinical Behavioral Medicine: some Concepts and Procedures*, New York: Plenum 1988.

Wicks, R. *Self-ministry through Self-understanding*, Chicago: Loyola University 1983.

Wilber, Ken. Eye to eye - science and transpersonal psychology, *ReVision* 1979, 2(1).

Wilber, Ken. *The Atman Project: A Transpersonal View of Human Development*, Wheaton, IL: Quest 1980.

Wilber, Ken. *No Boundary: Eastern and Western Approaches to Personal Growth*, Boulder, CO: Shambala 1981.

Wilber, Ken. Are the Chakras real? In: White, John. *Kundalini: Evolution and Enlightenment*, 1990, 120-137.

Wilber, Ken. *Grace and Grit: Spirituality and Healing in the Life and Death of Treya Killam Wilber*, Boston, MA: Gill and Macmillan 1991.

Wilber, Ken. *One Taste*, Boston: Shambhala 1999.

Wilber, Ken/ Engler Jack/ Brown, Daniel P. *Transformations of Consciousness: Conven-tional and Contemplative Perspectives on Development*, Boston: New Science Library/ Shambala 1986.

Wilcock, GK. Lilienfeld, S. Gaens, E. on behalf of the Galantamine International-1 Study Group, Efficacy and safety of galantamine in patients with mild to moderate Alzheimer's disease: a multicenter, randomized, controlled trial, *Br Med J* 2000;321:1-7 (Abstract at http://www.galantamine.cc/research/galantamine-research-4.htm).

Wiles, M.R. Reproducibility and inter-exam-iner correlation of motion palpation findings of the sacroiliac joint, *J the Canadian Chiropractic Association* 1980, 24, 59-66.

Wilk, CA et al. vs. AMA et al. Complaint 76C3777 filed October 12 in the United States District Court for the Northern District of Illinois, Eastern Division.

Wilkinson, H. P/ Gauld, A. Geomagnetism and anomalous experiences 1868-1980, *Proceedings of the Society for Psychical Research* 1993, 57, 275-310.

Wilkinson, S. Aromatherapy and massage in palliative care, *International J palliative Nursing* 1995, 1(1), 21-30.

Willard, Richard D. Breast enlargement through visual imagery and hypnosis, *American J Clinical Hypnosis* 1977, 19(4), 195-200.

Williams, J.E. Stimulation of breast growth by hypnosis, *J Sexual Research* 1973 10, 316-326.

Williams, M.B. Verbalizing silent screams: the use of poetry to identify the belief systems of adult survivors of childhood sexual abuse, *J Poetry Therapy* 1991, 5, 5-20.

Williams, Redford. *The Trusting Heart*, New York: Times 1989.

Williamson, SA et al. Differential effects of –endorphin fragments on human natural killing, *Brain Behavioral Immunology* 1987, 1, 329-335 (cited in Eskinazi 1999).

Williamson, T. Dowsing achieves new credence, *New Scientist* 1979 (Feb.). (From Krippner: *Human Possibilities*)

Wills, P. *The Reflexology Manual*, New York: Inner Traditions 1995.

Wilson, Annie/ Bek, Lilla. *What Colour are You? The Way to Health Through Colour,* Wellingborough, England: Turnstone 1981.

Wilson, B. Chronic exposure to ELF fields may induce depression, *Bioelectromagnetics* 1988, 9: 195-205.

Wilson, CWM. Human allergic disease and medical dowsing, *J the British Society of Dowsers* 1986, 31, 256-268.

Wilson, DF. Therapeutic touch: Foundations and current knowledge, *Alternative Health Practitioner* 1995 1(1), 55-66.

Wilson, DH et al. The effects of pulsed electromagnetic energy on peripheral nerve regeneration, *Annals of New York Academy of Science* 1974, 238, 575-585 (Workshop on Alternative Medicine).

Wilson, Greg. *Vaccination and Behavioral Disorders, a Review of the Controversy,* Tuntable Creek Publishing, PO Box 1448, Lismore NSW 2480, Australia, 2000, pages 48-49.

Wilson, John Rowan (ed). *The Mind,* Alexandria, VA: Time-Life 1981.

Wilson, Sheryl C/ Barber, Theodore X. The fantasy-prone personality: Implications for understanding imagery, hypnosis and parapsychological phenomena, *Psi Research* 1982,1(3), 94-116; also in: Sheikh, Anees A (ed). *Imagery: Current Theory REsearch and Application*, New York: John Wiley 1983.

Wingerson, Lois. Training the mind to heal, *Discovery* 1982 (May). 80-85.

Winkelman, Michael James. A Cross-Cultural

Wirth, Daniel P/ Cram, Jeffrey R. The psychophysiology of nontraditional prayer, *International J Psychosomatics* 1994, 41(1-4), 68-75.

Wise, Anna. *The High Performance Mind: Mastering Brainwaves for Insight, Healing, and Creativity*, New York: Tarcher/ Putnam 1995.

Wisechild, L. *She Who Was Lost Is Remembered: Healing from Incest Through Creativity*, Seal Press 1991.

Wiseman, A. Soviets link magnetic body fields to health, *Times* 1987 (23 March).

Witt, JR. Relieving chronic pain, *Nurse Practitioner* 1984, 9(1), 36-38

Witt, P/ Parr, C. Effectiveness of Trager psychosocial integration in promoting trunk mobility in a child with cerebral palsy: a case report, *Physical and Occupational Therapy in Pediatrics* 1986, 8, 75-93.

Wittlinger, H/ Wittlinger, G. *Textbook of Dr. Vodder's Manual Lymph Drainage*, 3rd ed. Heidelberg, Germany: Haug 1990.

Woelk, H et al. Treatment of patients suffering from anxiety: double-blind study: kava special extract versus benzodiazepines, *Ztschr Allegemeinmedicine* 1993, 69, 271-277.

Wohlfarth, H. Psychological evaluation of experiments to assert the effects of color-stimuli upon the autonomous nervous system, *Exerpta Medica, Neurology and Psychiatry* 1958, 2(4).

666 References

Wohlfarrh, H. The effects of color - psychodynamic environmental modification on disciplinary incidences in elementary schools over one school year: a controlled study, *International J Biosocial Research* 1984a, 6(l), 44-53.

Wohlfarth, H. The effects of color - psychodynamic environmental modification on absences due to illness in elementary schools: a controlled study, *International J Biosocial Research* 1984b, 6(1), 54-51.

Wohlfarth, H. The effects of color - psychodynamic environmental color & lighting modification of elementary schools on blood pressure and mood: a controlled study, *International J Biosocial Research* 1985, 7(l), 9-16.

Wohlfarth, H/ Wohlfarth, Sam C. The effect of color psychodynamic environmental modification upon psychophysiological and behavioral reactions of severely handicapped children, *International J Biosocial Research* 1982, 3(1), l0-38.

Wolf, F.A.: *Taking the Quantum Leap: The New Physics for Nonscientists*, San Francisco: Harper & Row 1981.

Wolf, Harri. *Applied Iridology,* San Diego, CA: National Iridology Research 1979.

Wolf, S. Effects of suggestion and conditioning on the action of chemical agents in human subjects - the pharmacology of placebos, *J Clinical Investigations* 1950,29, 100-109.

Wolfe, LS/ Millet, J. Bradford: Control of postoperative pain by suggestion under general anesthesia, *American J Clinical Hypnosis* 1960, 3, 109-112.

Wolfe, Sidney M. *Worst Pills, Best Pills: A Consumer's Guide to Avoiding Drug-Induced Death or Illness,* New York: Pocket 1999.

Wolfe, Tom. An overview of green tea as a therapeutic agent, *Integrative Medicine Consult* 2000, 2(4), 42-43.

Wolinski, Steven. Ericksonian hypnosis and meditation, In: Leskowitz 2000, 95-104.

Wolman, Benjamin/ Dale, Laura/

Schmeidler, Gertrude/ Ullman, Montagu. *Handbook of Parapsychology*, New York: Van Nostrand Reinhold 1977.

Wolman, Benjamin B/ Ullman, Montague. *Handbook of Stales of Consciousness,* New York: Van Nostrand Reinhold 1986.

Wolpe, J. *Psychotherapy by Reciprocal Inhibition,* Palo Alto, CA: Stanford Univ. 1958.

Wong, ND et al. A comparison of Chinese traditional and Western medical approaches for the treatment of mild hypertension, *Yale J Billogical Medicine* 1991, 64(1), 79-87.

Wood, C. Is hope a treatment for cancer? *Advances* 1996, 12, 67-71.

Wood, Ernest. *Yoga,* Harmonsworth, England 1950.

Wood, Matthew. *Seven Herbs: Plants as Teachers*, Berkeley, CA: North Atlantic 1986.

Wood, Matthew. *The Book of Herbal Wisdom: Using Plants as Medicines*, Berkeley, CA: North Atlantic 1997.

Wood, Matthew/ Dr. Edward Bach. The flower essences, in: *The Magical Staff: The Vitalist Tradition in Western Medicine*, Berkeley, CA: North Atlantic 1992, 185-194.

Woodham, Anne/ Peters, David. *Encyclopedia of Healing Therapies: The Definitive guide to More than 90 Alternative therapies & the Best Complementary Treatment Options for Over 200 Health Problems*, London/ New York: Dorling Kindersley 1997.

Wooding, Valerie. *John Cain Healing Guide,* England: Van Duren 1920.

Woody, EZ et al. A conceptual analysis of hypnotic responsiveness: experience, individual differences, and context, In: Fromm, E/ Nash, MR (eds).*Contemporary Hypnosis Research*, New York: Guilford 1992, 3-33.

Woolfson, A/ Hewitt, D. Intensive aromacare, *International J Aromatherapy* 1992, 4(2), 12-14.

Workshop on Alternative Medicine. *Alternative Medicine: Expanding Medical Horizons, A Report to the National Institutes of Health on Alternative Medical*

Systems and Practices in the United States, NIH Publication No. 94-066, December 1994, US Govt. Printing Office, Mail Stop SSOP, Washington, DC 20402-9328 (Outstanding resource with many pages of refs on each subject, popularly called 'The Chantilly Report').

Worrall, Olga. Personal communication 1982.

Worwood, Valerie. *The Fragrant Mind*, Novato, CA: New World 1996.

Worwood, Valerie Ann. *The Fragrant Heavens: the Spiritual Dimensions of Fragrance in Aromatherapy*, Novato, CA: New World 1999.

Wozniac, Jerzy. Physics of radiesthesic phenomena, In: *Proceedings of 6th International Conference on Psychotronics Research 1986*. 34-36.

Wren, Kathleen R. and Norred, Carol L. *Real World Nursing Survival Guide: Complementary & Alternative Therapies*, Saunders/Elsevier 2003.

Wright, Jonathan V. *Guide to Healing and Nutrition*, Emmaus, PA: Rodale 1984.

Wright, JV. Interview with Abraham Hoffer, *Nutrition and Healing*, September 1994.

Wright, Machaelle Small. *Flower Essences: Reordering Our Understanding and Approach to Illness and Health*, Jeffersonton, VA: Perelandra 1988.

Wright, Stephen C/ Sayre-Adams, Jean. *Sacred Space: Right Relationship and Spirituality in Health Care*, Edinburgh, UK: Churchill Livingstone 2000.

Wright, Susan Marie. *Development and Construct Validity of the Energy Field Assessment Form* (Dissertation), Rush University College of Nursing 1988.

Wullimier, Ferdinand. *Psychology & Its Role in Spirituality*, Shri Ram Chandra Mission 1996.

www.brughjoy.com

www.mcn.org/b/aletheia

www.ninegates.com

Wydra, N. *Feng Shui: The Book of Cures*, Chicago, IL: Contemporary 1996.

Wyon, Y et al. Effects of acupuncture on climacteric vasomotor symptoms, quality of life, and urinary excretion of neuropeptides among postmenopausal women, *Menopause* 1995, 2:3-12.

Wyschgrod, E. Empathy and sympathy as tactile encounter, *The J Medicine and Philosophy* 1981, 6, 25-43.

Y

Yagodinsky, Victor. The magnetic memory of the virus, *J Paraphysics* 1972, 6(4), 141.

Yamashita, H. et al. Systamatic review of adverse events following acuppuncture: the japanese literature, *Complementary Therapies in Medicine* 2001, 9, 98-104.

Yan, Naihau. Sensational Qigong feats, *China Reconstructs* 1985, 34(7), 60-61. (From *Psi Research* 1985,4(3/ 4), 139)

Yang, X et al. Clinical observation on needling extrachannel points in treating mental depression, *J Traditional Chinese Medicine* 1994 14:14-18.

Yang, Sihuan. et al. The influence of qigong training on coherence of EEG during one year period, *Proceedings of the Second World Conference for Academic Exchange of Medical Qigong, Beijing 1993*, 72.

Yeats, William Butler. Among School Children, St. 8, in *The Tower, Fragments, 1.*

Yellowtail, T/ M, Fitzgerald. *Yellowtail, Crow Medicine Man and Sun Dance Chief: An Autobiography*, Norman, OK: University of Oklahorna 1991.

Yeshi, Donden. *Health Through Balance: An Introduction to Tibetan Medicine*, Ithaca, NY: Snow Lion 1986.

Yochim, K. the collaborative poem and inpatient group psychotherapy, *J Poetry Therapy* 1994, 7, 145-150.

Yoga J, 2054 University Ave. Berkeley, CA 94704 (510) 841-9200.

Yogananda, P. *Autobiography of a Yogi*, Los Angeles: Self-Realization Fellowship 1946.

Yogananda, P. *Scientific Healing Affirmations: Theory and Practice of Concentration*, Los Angeles, CA: Self-Realization Fellowship 1962.

Yongje, Zhao et al. Biodetector experiments on human body radiation physics. *Psi Research,* 1982, 1(1), 77-84.

Young, Alan. Some implications of medical beliefs and practices for social anthropology, *American Anthropologist* 1976,78(1), 5-24.

Young, DE/ Aung, SKH. An experimental test of psychic diagnosis of disease, *J Alternative and Complementary Medicine* (UK) 1997, 3, 39-53.

Young, JC. *Medical Choice in a Mexican Village,* New Brunswick, NJ: Rutgers University 1981.

Young, M. *Cry of the Eagle: Encounters with a Cree Healer,* Buffalo, NY: University of Toronto 1989.

Young, TM. Nuclear magnetic resonance studies of succussed solutions, *J the American Institute of Homeopathy* 1975,68, 8-16.

Younus, Jawaid/ Collins, Alison. A survey estimating the prevalence and factors affecting the use of complementary therapy by adult cancer patients and their physicians perspectives, in: Newfoundland, Canada. *International J Healing and Caring, On line* 2002, 2(3).

Yuan, Zhifu. Family Acupuncture Center, San Clemente, CA 92672, USA - Survey of 100 doctors using simulated qigong In the USA (2nd World Conference for Academic Exchange of Medical Qigong, Beijing 1993 – from Qigong Database of Sancier).

Z

Zahourek, R ed. *Relaxation and Imagery*, Philadelphia: W.B. Saunders. 1988.

Zand, J et al. *Smart Medicine for a Healthier Child,* New York: Avery 1998.

Zang, J. Immediate antiasthmatic effect of acupuncture in 192 cases of bronchial asthma, *J Traditional Chinese Medicine* 1990 10, 89-93.

Zeng, Qingnan. Qigong - ancient way to good health, *China Reconstructs* 1985, 34(7), 56-57. (From *Psi Research* 1985,4(3/ 4), 139)

Zert, Vlastimil. Psychotronic research as an active assistance in modern bioengineering, *Proceedings of 4th International Conference on Psychotronic Research. Seo Paulo 1979,* 123-130.

Zhang, W et al. Acupuncture treatment of

apoplectic hemiplegia, *J Traditional Chinese Medicine* 1987, 7:157-160.

Zhu, V et al. Paraspinal muscle cerebral-evoked potentials in patients with unilateral low back pain, *Spine* 1993 18 1096-1101.

Zhvirblis, VE. Asymmetry versus chaos, or 'What is the biofield?', Translated by Larissa Vilenskaya), *Psi Research* 1982, 1(1),85-95.

Zimmer, C. The healing power of maggots, *Discover.* 1993; 14(8):17.

Zimmerman, B. et al. *is Marijuana the Right Medicine for You?* New Canaan, CT: Keats 1998.

Zimmerman, J. New technologies detect effects in healing hands, *Brain/Mind Bulletin* 1985, 10(2), 20-23.

Zimmerman, J. Laying-on-of-hands healing and therapeutic touch: a testable theory, *BEMI Currents: J the Bioelectro-mag-netics Institute* 1990, 2, 8-17.

Zimmerman, Katherine. *Breakthrough: The Emotional Freedom Techniques,* 1999 (order at www.trancetime.com)

Zimmerman, L et al. Effects of music in patients who had chronic cancer pain, *Western J Nursing Research* 1989 11, 29~309.

Zlokazov, VP, et al. Bioenergetic aspects of the relationship between the image of perception and the perceived object, Translated from Russian by Vilenskaya, Larissa, *Psi Research* 1982, 1(3), 11-21.

Zucker, Martin. *The Veterinarian's Guide to Natural Remedies for Dogs*, New York: Three Rivers/ Crown 1999.

Zuckerman, Diana M. The Need to Improve Informed Consent for Breast Cancer Patients, *J the American Medical Women's Association* 2000, 55, 285-289

Zukav, Gary. *The Dancing Wu Li Masters,* New York William Morrow 1979

Zukav, Gary. *The Seat of the Soul,* New York: Simon & Schuster/ London: Fireside 1990.

Zunin, Ira D. PC-SPES for prostate cancer, *Integrative Medicine Consult* 2001, 3(1), 1, 5.

Glossary

Ablating - removing tissues.

Absent healing - See *Distant healing.*

AC – Alternating current.

Acupuncture - A complete system of treatment for physical and psychological problems developed in China thousands of years ago. Acupuncture points are stimulated along bioenergy lines (*meridians*) that run from toes and fingers to head. Each meridian corresponds to a bioenergy organ, roughly correlated with physical organs.

Allobiofeedback – Physiological measurements are taken from a subject and shown to a healer who is asked to alter the subject's physiological state based on the readings from the instruments.

Alternative (Altered) State of Consciousness (ASC) – State in which consciousness differs from our everyday experience of awareness, as in dreams or mystical states, often characterized by unusual changes in time perception, distortions of everyday reality experiences, perceptions of transcendent realities, etc. *Alternative* appears to be a term that is more accepting of the normality of these states than *Altered*.

AMA – American Medical Association.

Anthroposophic medicine – System of natural therapies devised by Rudolph Steiner.

Appplied kinesiology – Muscle strength testing that reveals the activity of acupuncture meridians and is thereby correlated with states of health and illness of various parts of the body. Used also for accessing unconscious awareness.

Aromatherapy – Use of aromatic oils via olfactory sensing, massage and/or oral ingestion.

Armoring – Term developed by Wilhelm Reich to describe muscle tensions that served defensive purposes, protecting people from conscious awareness of their problems

ASC – See Altered State of Consciousness.

Aspirate - Remove fluid, as from a cyst; *Alt:* Breathe foreign matter into the lungs.

Astral body – Energy body that can separate from the physical body in Out of Body Experiences (OBE's, discussed in Volume III of Healing Research)

Astrology – Correlations between the positions of heavenly bodies, astrological signs, and aspects of people's lives such as compatibilities in their relationships with others, propitious and unpropitious days for various activities, and predictions of the future.

Aura - The bioenergy field around the body may be seen by sensitive people as constantly shifting colors that reflect the states of body, emotions, mind, relationships and spirit.

Ayurveda – System of medicine from the Indian continent involving diets, pulse diagnosis and other approaches specific to particular body types.

Bagua – Patterns of energetic factors that relate to various locations in a room or house, correlating with aspects of a person's life (e.g. prosperity, relationships, health).

Barbara Brennan healing - 4 year course of healing with strong emphasis on psychological and bioenergy approaches.

Bigu – Specialized practice of qigong in which people learn to live with minimal or no food intake for long periods of time.

Bioenergy - Healers and healees often report sensations of heat, tingling, vibration, or electrical sensations during healing treatments. This suggests an exchange of some sort of energy occurring during healing treatments. So far, no consistent findings of energies have been identified across different healing modalities.

Bioenergy Medicine - Therapies that address bioenergies. These include acupuncture, applied kinesiology, craniosacral osteopathy, homeopathy, flower essences, spiritual healing and others.

Blinds - Conditions established in a randomized controlled research study where the subjects and/or the experimenters (including therapists and evaluators) do not know who is receiving the treatment and who is not.

Bodhisattva - In Mahayana Buddhism, " 'one whose essence (*sattva*) is perfected wisdom (*bodhi*),' a being who, having brought himself to the brink of Nirvana, voluntarily renounces his prize that he may return to the world to make it accessible to others. He deliberately sentences himself to age-long servitude that others, drawing on his acts of supererogation, may enter Nirvana before him." Huston Smith, *The Religions of Man* p.121

Bodymind – The combined entity that is the body and the mind, acting in synchrony with each other. (alt. *Mind-body*)

Candidiasis – Infection with a yeast, *candida albicans*, that can produce all the symptoms of chronic fatigue syndrome.

Centering – Finding a balanced state of being in which distractions do not intrude to mar the focus on healing. This facilitates maximal effects of intent for healing.

Chakra - Bioenergy center along the midline of the body, identified in Chinese medicine and spiritual healing as a "transformer" for bioenergies entering the body. Healing may be given at chakras that provide energies to particular parts of the body.

Chakra Reference Chart http://www.healer.ch/Chakras-e.html

Chelation – Treatment with intravenous EDTA that is alleged to clear atherosclerosis, toxic chemicals from the blood.

Chronic fatigue syndrome (cfs) – Syndrome of unexplained cause (after ruling out Candidiasis) that includes muscle and joint pains, weakness, fatigue, food and other allergies and "brain fog." Very similar to Chronic Fatigue Syndrome.

Clairsentience – Psychic ability to know about physical objects without information from our ordinary senses (sight, sound, smell, taste, or touch) about these objects.

Clairvoyance – Psychic perception (clairsentience) that is perceived as mental imagery. (*Clairvoyance* is often used as a generic term for abilities to perceive directly from an object without the ordinary five senses of sight, sound, taste, smell and touch. I prefer the term *clairsentience* for this general ability, which can include also *clairaudience* – the hearing of psychic perceptions; *telesomatic reactions* – the mirroring in the body of the intuitive person of the sensations being experienced in the subject; smelling and tasting being less common but also possible as translations of psychic information into conscious awareness in the psychic person.)

Clairvoyant – A person who has clairvoyance.

Complementary/Alternative Medicine (CAM) - Therapies that are not generally offered within conventional medical care (such as acupuncture, homeopathy, spiritual healing, and many more) are grouped under the term CAM.

Control group ("Controls") – Comparison group of subjects, with similar characteristics to a second group that is given an experimental treatment. The differences in responses of the two groups over a period of time are taken to be a measure of the effect of treatment. This controls for the effects of suggestion, which may bring about changes that could mistakenly be attributed to the experimental treatment.

Conversion reaction – Paralysis or sensory deficits that are produced unconsciously as defenses against feelings that are unacceptable to the person. (Alt. □*hysterical symptoms*)

Cosmobiology – Correlations between the positions of heavenly bodies as related to limited, discretely observable phenomena such birth, surgical bleeding, personality characteristics, and death by murder or suicide;.

Craniosacral manipulation - sensations of energy pulsations around the head and spine (and by more sensitive practitioners, anywhere around the body) guide practitioners for assessment and treatment

Craniotomy - Operation on the contents of the skull

Cult - Group in which the leader cannot be questioned, which uses coercion to discourage members from leaving.

Curanderismo – Healing within Latin American traditions.

Debulk - remove part of a tumor mass

DC – Direct current.

Dermal vision (alt. *dermal optics; skin vision*) – The ability to perceive colors (and sometimes forms) through skin perception rather than vision through the eyes.

Deva – Nature spirit.

Dissociativve disorder - A "split" in the personality, usually from severe emotional trauma early in life, leading to multiple personalities.

Distal – In the direction that is away from the center of the body.

Distant (absent) healing - Spiritual healing can be sent from any distance apparently with equal effects. This is done as mental focus/intent, meditation or prayer.

Distant Mental Influence on Living Systems (DMILS).- *See* Psi healing.

Divine healing - Many healers feel that healing is brought about by a Divine intervention.

Dowsing – Using a device such as a dowsing rod or pendulum to serve as an indicator of intuitive awarenesses.

Dysmenorrhea – Pain during menstruation.

Effectiveness - How well a treatment works when used by the average therapist with the average client in the usual treatment setting.

Efficacy - How well does a treatment work in a randomized controlled trial (RCT) or other assessment setting compared to a placebo or to another treatment of known efficacy.

Efficiency - The level of efforts needed to produce an effect.

Electrodermal response – Skin electrical resistance measurements that are associated with physical and mental states of tensions. (This is the basis of the lie detector test.)

Electroencephalogram (EEG) – Brain wave test, providing very rough pictures of the electrical activity of the brain., measured with electrodes on the scalp.

Electromyogram (EMG) – Measure of electrical activity in muscles.

EM – Electromagnetic.

Emic - Explanation that acknowledges that peoples from cultures other than our own, behaving in manners that are different from ours, usually have their own legitimate cultural explanations for their beliefs and behaviors. (Contrasted with *etic*)

Enuresis – Lack of control over urination.

Etic - Explanations based on Western convictions that modern science can provide "objective" explanations for every phenomenon - within the frameworks of Western scientific paradigms. (Contrasted with *emic*)

Faith healing - This is a term, particularly in the media, commonly used synonymously with any type of spiritual healing. Within religious settings, it may connote a belief that faith in religious tenets is required for healing to occur. While faith may facilitate healing for believers, a lack of response to healing is sometimes interpreted as indicating lack of faith. This could add guilt to distress already present from whatever brought a person for healing. The responses of non-human organisms to healing suggests that faith on the part of the recipient of healing is not always necessary.

Faraday cage – Cage built of conducting wire that blocks EM radiations from entering the space within the cage, used for studying EM effects in isolation from environmental EM "noise."

Feng Shui (alt. *Geomancy***)** – Oriental intuitive system of identifying environmental energies that can influence health and illness.

Fibromyalgia (FM) – Syndrome of unexplained cause that includes muscle and joint pains, weakness, fatigue, food and other allergies and "brain fog." Very similar to Chronic Fatigue Syndrome.

Flower Essences - Very dilute solutions of bionergetic essence of flowers, used in a manner similar to homeopathy to stimulate natural defenses. Originally developed by Edward Bach, there are now many other varieties, including Alaskan, Australian, Desert Alchemy, Green Hope Farm, Pacific, Perelandra, and others.

Galvanci Skin Response (GSR) – *See* Electrodermal response.

Gastroscopy – Insertion of a long, flexible tube with fiber optics or a camera into the stomach to examine the stomach wall.

Gauss – A measure of the strength of magnetic field. Technically: the centimeter-gram-second unit of magnetic flux density, equivalent to 10^{-4} tesla.

Geobiological – Earth energies that influence biological systems.

Geomancy – See Feng Shui.

Geopathic – Negative earth energies that can cause pathology in biological systems.

Gestalt – A broad, overall picture, encompassing many details rather than focusing in on a narrow aspect of an item.

Healing Touch (HT) - Developed out of Therapeutic Touch, Healing Touch extends the focus of healers to include chakra diagnosis and treatment, the use of pendulums to augment intuitive awareness, and spiritual awareness. Healing energy is perceived as being channeled through the healer from a universal source.

Hertz – Cycles of electromagnetic pulses per second.

Holistic - Often used to indicate use of CAM therapies or partial aspects of these therapies.

Holographic – In a holographic image, any portion of the picture can be cut away and each portion will contain the whole picture. This is used as a metaphor for the fact that everything in the universe appears to be interconnected, so that each of us is a part of the "All."

Homeopathy - Treatment with extremely dilute substances to stimulate the body's natural defenses.

Homeostasis - The state of healthy balance maintained by the body's automatic regulating systems. For instance, temperature, blood chemicals, hormones, and blood pressure are all kept within specific ranges so that the body can function at optimal biological levels.

Hypnoanalgesia – Pain relief through hypnosis.

Hysterical symptoms – *See: Conversion reaction.*

Ideomotor responses – Automatic responses of the body that occur under hypnosis, conveying information about the unconscious mind.

Imagery - Mentally picturing a state of being (such as being healthy) or an action (such as a sports activity) can bring the mind and body into that state. Imagery exercises are used to relieve pain, deal with cancers and AIDS, and enhance sports performance.

Integrative care - the blending of complementary/ alternative medicine (CAM) with conventional medical practice. On the one hand this is motivated by patients' demands for services that complement conventional medical care, and on the other hand by health care providers' awareness of economic opportunities and to a lesser extent by their awareness of the benefits of complementary therapies.

Knowing that there is an alternative to the Western medical model, particularly as it is practiced under managed care, may alert you to new, productive, more satisfying options through integrative care. There are many such models and practices.

Intuition - Inner awarenesses that may provide information and guidance, not based on sensory inputs or logical deductions. Many healers have strong intuitive gifts.

Kirlian photography – Photographic images created by passing high voltage and low amperage electrical pulses through objects that are in contact with the photographic film.

Kundalini – Bioenergies said (in Eastern traditions) to lie dormant at the base of the spine until advanced states of spiritual development, when the energies rise up the spine and bring about further dramatic spiritual transformations.

Laying-on of hands healing - Healing is often given with the healer's hands near to or lightly touching the body of the healee. This is a generic, descriptive term.

LeShan healing - Distant ("Type I") healing. Developed by Lawrence LeShan, PhD, taught by Joyce Goodrich, PhD.

Lymphedema – Swelling due to blockage of the lymph vessels.

m – Meter.

Mantra – Word or phrase that is repeated many times as a focus for meditation.

Medical dowsing - Dowsers are able to locate underground water or other resources, using their intuitive gifts. Some dowsers are also able to intuitively identify physical and psychological problems and to give healing. Some of the other healing modalities (e.g. Healing Touch) also teach the use of pendulums and other ways of accessing intuitive awareness.

Mental healing - Used in *Index Medicus* to identify spiritual healing as defined on this site.

Meridian Based Therapies – Therapies derived from acupressure. You press or tap on various acupressure points, usually while reciting an affirmation that focuses your mind on your problem. Excellent for anxieties, fears, phobias, eliminating old hurts, installying positive beliefs, sports performance enhancement, reducing/eliminating physical pais an dallergies, and more.
See: MBTs at http://www.wholistichealingresearch.com/Refcrences/MBTs.htm
WHEE (Wholistic Hybrid of Eye Movement Desensitization and Reprocessing (EMDR) and Emotional Freedom Technique (EFT)
www.wholistichealingresearch.com/Articles/Selfheal.htm

MHerz – Megahertz; millions of cycles per second.

Mind-body - See *bodymind*

Mitogenetic Radiation – Apparent energies emitted by plant roots that promote cell division in nearby roots of other plants.

Moxa – Herbs that are burned slowly at one end, as the other end is applied to an acupuncture point (the procedure is called *moxibustion*).

Myopathy – Muscle disease.

Namaste - Hindu greeting, "may the divine in you resonate with the divine in me."

Neoplasm - Cancer

Neurolinguistic Programming (NLP) - A treatment method derived from hypnotherapy, utilizing *anchoring* of positive and negative feelings by touching the body while focusing on positive and negative memories and images. This is called *anchoring* feelings. The positive anchors cancel the negative ones.

Neuropeptide – A protein found in brain cells, providing a chemical means of communication between nerve cells; also found in white cells, and speculated to enable communication between brain cells and white cells.

Nirvana – A blissful transcendent state, the ultimate state of meditation and enlightenment.

Nocebo – Negative placebo reaction, as when a doctor says, "I don't know how well this is likely to work, but we might as well try it because there is nothing else left to do." With such programming, a person is likely to expect no benefit from the medicine, so self-healing is not activated. The mechanism is similar, but the effects are opposite to those of the placebo reaction.

Nocturia – Bed-wetting.

Noetic – Spiritual, beyond description.

Non-Local Consciousness - The mind can reach across space and time to obtain and share information with other people, with the collective consciousness of groups of people or of all of mankind, and with transpersonal consciousnesses (spirits, spiritual luminaries, and God). This is possible through telepathy (mind-to-mind communication), clairsentience (knowing directly from the physical world), precognition and retrocognition (knowing the past or future). *Non-local consciousness* and *non-local mind* are terms coined by Larry Dossey, MD.

Orgone – Energies identified by Wilhelm Reich, produced by various static devices with layered organic and inorganic materials, said to influence states of health and illness.

Osteoarthritis – Arthritis due to degeneration (not due to inflammation or infection).

Paranormal healing - Term used in some European literature for spiritual healing as defined on this website.

PEMF - Pulsed Electromagnetic Fields; electromagnetic fields produced in rapid pulsations.

Placebo - A treatment that has no intrinsic healing benefits but is perceived by the recipient to be a potent intervention and therefore influences the recipient to improve. This is a form of suggstion. It is acknowledged in research as the *experimenter effect*. A negative suggestion can also produce a negative, or *nocebo*, effect.

Polarity Therapy - Energy balancing between various points on the body. Developed by Randolph Stone, an osteopath, naturopath, and chiropractor.

Positron emission tomography - Diagnostic imaging technique that uses radioactive materials absorbed in tissues

Potentize – Create a homeopathic remedy.

Prana – Eastern word for bioenergy.

Probability - See *Statistics*.

Prospective studies – Studies in which the research protocol is planned in advance of the experiment and the subjects are then treated and studied. (Contrasted with *retrospective* studies, in which the research is designed and people are studied after they have had treatments.)

Prayer healing - Healing may be offered as formal prayer in a house of worship or may be sent as personal prayer for the healing of someone in need. Within some religious settings the laying-on of hands is also practiced, by clergy and also by lay congregants.

Precognition – Knowing the future through psychic awareness.

Probiotics – Using bacteria for positive effects in the body.

Psi - Psi (taken from the Greek letter, Ψ) is a term from parapsychology, encompassing the psychic modalities of telepathy, clairsentience, pre- and retro-cognition, and psychokinesis (PK, or "mind over matter"). Parapsychologists have viewed healing as biological PK, or Distant Mental Influence on Living Systems (DMILS). Many healers have psychic gifts.

Psychic healing - See ##*Spiritual healing*

Psychoneurocardiology – Combination of relaxation, meditation, diet, physical exercises and group support for treating heart disease (particularly atherosclerotic problems).

Psychoneuroimmunology (PNI) - .Relaxation, meditation, and imagery exercises that can enhance immune system activity.

Psychosynthesis – A combination of approaches involving imagery, relaxation, meditation and more.

Qigong healing – Chinese healing, including self-healing through gentle physical movements and meditation, along with external *qi* healing given by the Master.

Quantum healing – Spiritual healing may overlap with quantum physics.

Radiesthesia and Radionics – In Britain there are practitioners of radiesthesia and radionics, dowsers who use instruments with dials for dowsing (radiesthesia) and distant healing (radionics). These have been outlawed in America by the Food and Drug Administration.

Randomized controlled trial (RCT) – Study in which subjects are randomly assigned to treatment and comparison (control) groups, where assessments are made on both groups prior to and following treatment.

Reductionistic – Explanations which assume that the whole is composed of separate, distinct parts. (Contrasted with *holographic* or *wholistic* explanations, which assume that each part is interconnected with everything else.)

Reichian therapy – Therapy based on Reich's *orgone energy* theories and methods.

Reiki – Japanese system of laying-on of hands and distant healing taught world-wide. Training in Levels I, II, and Master.

Respant – "Responsible participant," a term suggested by Bernie Siegel, to replace the word "patient."

Retrocognition - A psychic ability in which one knows information about the past without personal experience or sensory inputs that would account for this information.

Rolfing – Massage with very strong, even painful pressure.

Samadhi – Enlightenment; union with God

Secondary gain – Psychological benefits derived from primary physical or emotional symptoms. For instance, pain may bring sympathy or may be used as a convenient excuse to avoid something that is unwanted.

Seer – A person with psychic abilities, who can see beyond our everyday reality – perceiving past and future events that are relevant to those who consult them.

Self (spelled with capital "S" – The part of ourself that is aware of a transpersonal, spiritual dimension, of which we are an integral part.

Self healing - Dealing with your own problems through relaxation, meditation, imagery, prayer, giving yourself spiritual healing, and the like.

Shadow - Those aspects of ourselves that we are uncomfortable acknowledging (perceived weaknesses, traumatizing experiences, socially unacceptable thoughts and desires, etc.) and often bury in our unconscious mind.

Shamanic/shamanistic healing - Shamans in traditional cultures mediate between the worlds of matter/ flesh and those of spirit. They are gifted individuals who have undergone extensive apprenticeships in herbal, bioenergy, and spirit healings. They heal through herbs, bioenergy treatments, chants, drumming, other rituals, and prayer.

Shen Tao - A variant of acupressure, that attributes its efficacy to visualizations of energy flows from the acupuncturist to the patient when the acupuncture points are touched with the therapist's finger.

SHEN Therapy - Touch healing method taught internationally. Developed by Richard Pavek, an American scientist.

Skin vision – *See dermal vision.*

Somatoemotional – Body connections with the emotions.

Soul – That part of a person which survives death integrates aspects of the person's most recent personality with their eternal Self. (Some prefer to call this part the spirit. See also spirit for my explanation of my preference for soul here and spirit there.)

Spirit – That part of a person which survives death and still retains aspects of the person's personality. (Some prefer to call this part the soul. I prefer spirit because of the popular use of this term to denote those who have passed on but return to communicate through channeled messages or as apparitions. See also soul.)

SQUID - Superconducting quantum interference device, used in innovative studies for measuring electromagnetic fields around the body.

Spiritual healing - is a systematic, purposeful intervention by one or more persons aiming to help another living being (person, animal, plant, or other living system) by means of focused intention, hand contact, or *passes* to improve their condition. Spiritual healing is brought about without the use of conventional energetic, mechanical, or chemical interventions. Some healers attribute spiritual healing occurrences to God, Christ, other "higher powers," spirits, universal or cosmic forces or energies, biological healing energies or forces residing in the healer, psychokinesis (mind over matter), or self-healing powers or energies latent in the healee. Psychological interventions are inevitably part of healing, but spiritual healing adds many dimensions to interpersonal factors.

Statistics - Mathematical analyses that provide a measure of the likelihood that research findings could have occurred by chance. These are often expressed as a probability ("p") with a number indicating the degree of possible random occurrence of the observed results. For instance, a probability of less than one time in a hundred is abbreviated as $p < 0.01$. The minimum limit generally acccepted as a valid demonstration of significance is 5 times in a hundred, or $p < 0.05$.

Subtle energy - See *Bioenergy*.

Succussion – Shaking a homeopathic remedy to activate it during or following dilutions.

SUDS score - Subjective Units of Distress Score. On a scale of 0 - 10, with "10" being the worst you could possibly feel when focused on your problem, and "0" for not feeling bad at all. Used as a sequential assessment for stress reduction treatments. Can also be used to assess building of positive feelings.

Synesthesia – A crossed-sensory perception. A sense organ (eye, ear, etc.) can sometimes convey information obtained by unusual stimulation, not ordinary to that particular sense, such as hearing colors or skin vision.

Temporo-Mandibular Joind (TMJ) – The joint where the jaw hinges onto the skull.

Thanatology – Study of how we deal with death.

Therapeutic Touch - Bioenergy healing, developed by Dolores Krieger, Ph.D., RN, professor of nursing at New York University and Dora van Gelder Kunz, a gifted clairsentient and healer. Taught and used worldwide, especially by nurses, with certification courses. Taught also to laypersons.

Thoughtography – Projection of mental images onto photographic film.

Unconventional healing - Used sometimes to distinguish spiritual healing from conventional, allopathic treatments.

Tinnitus – Ringing in the ears.

Traditional Chinese Medicine (TCM) - Acupuncture combined with herbal therapies and other Eastern techniques.

Transcendent Realities – Realms in which we encounter our "higher self," spirits, angels, "The Being of Light," Christ, Buddha, God (in his many descriptions and manifestations) and have other spiritual experiences – such as a clear awareness of being one with everything. It is often difficult to describe these experiences in words. They may be accompanied by feelings of bliss.

Transpersonal – Relating to consciousness that extends beyond our personal boundaries, including psychic and spirit dimensions, alternative states of consciousness, mystical experiences, collective consciousness and spiritual awarenesses.

V – Volt.

Vibrational healing - Bioenergies are difficult to describe and define in words. One of the sensations reported by healers and healees during healing is that of vibration.

Waiqi – External qi, emitted by the qigong master for healing or other physical effects on material objects.

Wholistic healing - addresses body, emotions, mind, relationships (with others and with Gaia, our planet), and spirit

I include the "W" to indicate that I am addressing *whole person care*, helping the person who has the disease and not just treating the symptoms or the disease the person has. This is different from the commonly-used *holistic*, which in many instances represents the inclusion of a few pieces of CAM modalities in a conventional medical setting (e.g. using acupuncture for symptoms of pain, without utilizing the broader spectrum of acupuncture potential to address the entire energetic balance of the person being treated).

Witness – Physical object belonging to the person who is being analyzed from a distance by a dowser .

Yang - The sunny side of the slope, and may be associated with the sun, masculinity, strength, brightness, assertiveness, movement, extroversion, growth and excitation.

Yin - the shady side of the slope, and may be associated with qualities of femininity, openness, passivity, receptivity, introversion, diminution, repose, weakness, and coolness.. *Yin* and *yang* are polar opposites that must be balanced in order for life to proceed in harmony.

Names Index

Subject Index

About the Author

Daniel J. Benor, M.D. is a wholistic psychiatrist who includes bodymind approaches, spiritual awareness and healing in his practice. Dr. Benor is the author of Healing Research, Volumes I-IV and many articles on wholistic, spiritual healing. He appears internationally on radio and TV. He is a Founding Diplomate of the American Board of Holistic Medicine, Coordinator for the Council for Healing, a non-profit organization that promotes awareness of spiritual healing, and on the advisory boards of the journals, *Alternative Therapies in Health and Medicine*, *Subtle Energies* (ISSSEEM), *Frontier Sciences*, and the Advisory Council of the Association for Comprehensive Energy Psychotherapy (ACEP). He is editor and producer of the International Journal of Healing and Caring – On Line www.ijhc.org. See more by and about Dr. Benor at: www.WholisticHealingResearch.com